Pacific Salmon:
Ecology and Management of Western Alaska's Populations

Pacific Salmon: Ecology and Management of Western Alaska's Populations

Edited by

Charles C. Krueger

Great Lakes Fishery Commission
2100 Commonwealth Blvd., Suite 100, Ann Arbor, Michigan 48105, USA

Christian E. Zimmerman

U.S. Geological Survey, Alaska Science Center
4210 University Drive, Anchorage, Alaska 99508, USA

AMERICAN FISHERIES SOCIETY SYMPOSIUM 70

Proceedings of the symposium

Sustainability of the Arctic-Yukon-Kuskokwim Salmon Fisheries

Held in Anchorage, Alaska, USA
6–9 February 2007

American Fisheries Society
Bethesda, Maryland
2009

A suggested citation format for this book follows.

Entire Book

Krueger, C. C., and C. E. Zimmerman, editors. 2009. Pacific salmon: ecology and management of western Alaska's populations. American Fisheries Society, Symposium 70, Bethesda, Maryland.

Chapter within the Book

Utter, F. M., M. V. McPhee, and F. W. Allendorf. 2009. Population genetics and the management of Arctic-Yukon-Kuskokwim salmon populations. Pages 97–123 *in* C. C. Krueger and C. E. Zimmerman, editors. Pacific salmon: ecology and management of western Alaska's populations. American Fisheries Society, Symposium 70, Bethesda, Maryland.

Front cover photo: Drift gillnetting in the Kuskokwim River upstream of Aniak, Alaska for Chinook salmon in late June 2008 (photo by David Cannon).

Back cover photo (top) of two fishermen drift gillnetting for Chinook salmon in the Kuskokwim River near Chuathbaluk in late June 2008, courtesy of David Cannon; back cover photo (bottom) of split salmon drying on a rack, courtesy of Kevin G. Smith/AlaskaStock.com ©2009

Cover design courtesy of Paul Vecsei, 2009
Ten color plates provided by Joseph R. Tomelleri

Printed in South Korea.

Library of Congress Control Number 2009909349
ISBN 978-1-934874-11-0
ISSN 0892-2284

American Fisheries Society Web site address: *www.fisheries.org*

American Fisheries Society
5410 Grosvenor Lane, Suite 100
Bethesda, Maryland 20814
USA

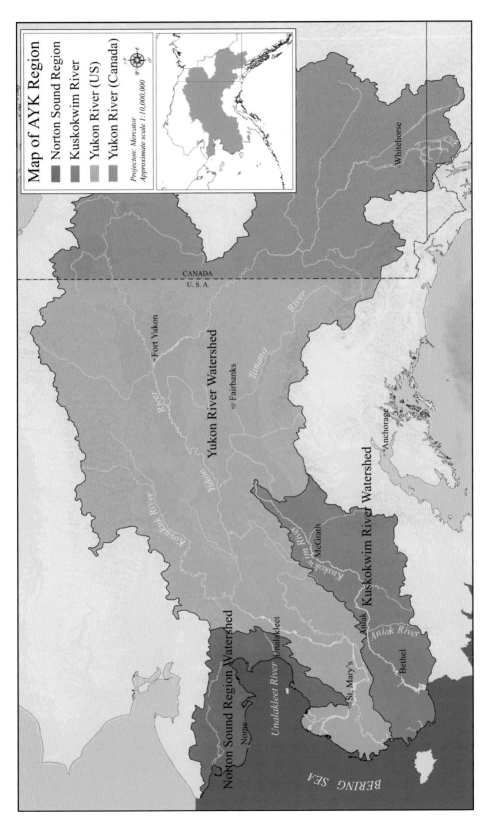

Map of AYK Region

Norton Sound Region
Kuskokwim River
Yukon River (US)
Yukon River (Canada)

Projection: Mercator
Approximate scale 1:10,000,000

Table of Contents

Introduction

Section I: Ecology of AYK Salmon

Freshwater Ecology of AYK Salmon

Estuarine and Marine Ecology of Salmon in the Bering Sea and North Pacific

Section II: Human Dimensions of AYK Salmon

Section III: Management of AYK Salmon

Freshwater Salmon Management

Governance

Management

Section V: New Challenges, New Approaches

Section VI: Peer Reviewer Acknowledgments

Chinook Salmon (ocean life stage)
Oncorhynchus tshawytscha

Chinook Salmon (spawning life stage)
Oncorhynchus tshawytscha

Chum Salmon (ocean life stage)
Oncorhynchus keta

Chum Salmon (spawning life stage)
Oncorhynchus keta

Coho Salmon (ocean life stage)
Oncorhynchus kisutch

Coho Salmon (spawning life stage)
Oncorhynchus kisutch

Pink Salmon (ocean life stage)
Oncorhynchus gorbuscha

Pink Salmon (spawning life stage)
Oncorhynchus gorbuscha

Sockeye Salmon (ocean life stage)
Oncorhynchus nerka

Sockeye Salmon (spawning life stage)
Oncorhynchus nerka

Arctic-Yukon-Kuskokwim
Sustainable Salmon Initiative

SIGNATORY ORGANIZATIONS

Alaska Department of Fish & Game
> Commissioner Denby Lloyd
> (Former contributing Commissioners: Frank Rue & McKie Campbell)

Association of Village Council Presidents
> President Myron Naneng
> (Former contributing President: Arthur Lake)

Bering Sea Fishermen's Association
> Executive Director Karen Gillis
> (Former contributing Executive Directors: Adelheid Herrmann & Henry Mitchell)

Kawerak, Incorporated
> President Loretta Bullard

NOAA Fisheries
> Alaska Regional Administrator James Balsiger

Tanana Chiefs Conference
> President Jerry Issacs
> (Former contributing Presidents: Steve Ginnis & Buddy Brown)

U.S. Fish and Wildlife Service
> Alaska Regional Director Geoff Haskett
> (Former contributing Directors: David Allen, Rowan Gould & Tom Melius)

STEERING COMMITTEE

John White
> Bering Sea Fishermen's Association

John Linderman
> Alaska Department of Fish and Game, Commercial Fisheries Division
> (Former contributing members: Daniel Bergstrom & Gene Sandone)

Jim Simon
Alaska Department of Fish and Game, Subsistence Division
(Former contributing member: Jim Magdanz)

Jennifer Hooper
Association of Village Council Presidents
(Former contributing members: Tim Andrew & Allen Joseph)

Mike Smith
Tanana Chiefs Conference
(Former contributing member: George Yaska)

Rod Simmons
United States Fish & Wildlife Service

Weaver Ivanoff
Kawerak, Incorporated
(Former contributing member: William "Middy" Johnson)

Pete Hagen
National Marine Fisheries Service
(Former contributing member: Jack Helle)

SCIENTIFIC AND TECHNICAL COMMITTEE

Christian E. Zimmerman
U.S. Geological Survey, Alaska Science Center

Charles Krueger
Great Lakes Fishery Commission

Eric Volk
Alaska Department of Fish and Game, Commercial Fisheries Division
(Former contributing members: John Hilsinger, Linda Brannian, and John Clark)

Caroline Brown
Alaska Department of Fish and Game, Subsistence Division
(Former contributing member: Marianne See)

Katherine W. Myers
University of Washington, School of Aquatic and Fisheries Sciences
(Former contributing members: Phil Mundy, Exxon Valdez Oil Spill Trustee
Council; Gordon Kruse, University of Alaska)

Greg Ruggerone
    Natural Resources Consultants, Inc.
    (Former contributing member: Jack Stanford, University of Montana)

STAFF

Karen Gillis, Program Director
Joseph Spaeder, Research Coordinator
Katie Williams, Program Administrator

Preface

On behalf of the Arctic-Yukon-Kuskokwim Sustainable Salmon Initiative (AYK SSI), I am pleased to present *Pacific Salmon: Ecology and Management of Western Alaska's Populations*, the proceedings from our 2007 symposium held in Anchorage, Alaska.

Within this volume are 56 chapters that explore the causes for change in salmon populations and the effects of these changes on rural Alaskan communities. The text covers the entire life cycle of salmon from juvenile rearing, to estuarine and marine life phases to upstream migration and spawning. The effects of subsistence, commercial, and sport fisheries on AYK salmon populations and on rural communities are also explored.

Indeed, this volume is a capstone to the AYK SSI's program and serves to achieve the purpose of the program which is to:

> *...assemble existing information, gain new information and improve techniques for understanding the trends and causes of variation in salmon abundance and human use of salmon that support sustainable use and restoration through a collaborative and inclusive process.*

The text further demonstrates the Initiative's continued efforts to support sustainable salmon management upon which so many people depend throughout the Arctic-Yukon-Kuskokwim region.

Our success in this publication depended greatly on the consistent hard work of our seven AYK SSI member organizations and their representatives to our Steering Committee (listed previously), whom I thank for their leadership and commitment. In addition, the efforts of Senators Stevens and Murkowski and Congressman Young in supporting the Initiative demonstrate their intense passion for Alaska. It is through the cooperative efforts of this highly diverse partnership that this publication was possible.

A special thanks goes to the AYK SSI staff, especially to Karen Gillis, program director, and Joseph Spaeder, research coordinator. Each quietly and effectively worked in the background to make the symposium a success, and to conduct the arduous work of preparing this publication. Thanks!

I hope you find this volume a fascinating story of salmon and people of the AYK region!

Dr. John White
Chairman, Steering Committee
Arctic-Yukon-Kuskokwim
Sustainable Salmon Initiative

May 15, 2009

Symbols and Abbreviations

The following symbols and abbreviations may be found in this book without definition. Also undefined are standard mathematical and statistical symbols given in most dictionaries.

A	ampere		G	giga (10^9, as a prefix)
AC	alternating current		gal	gallon (3.79 L)
Bq	becquerel		Gy	gray
C	coulomb		h	hour
°C	degrees Celsius		ha	hectare (2.47 acres)
cal	calorie		hp	horsepower (746 W)
cd	candela		Hz	hertz
cm	centimeter		in	inch (2.54 cm)
Co.	Company		Inc.	Incorporated
Corp.	Corporation		i.e.	(id est) that is
cov	covariance		IU	international unit
DC	direct current; District of Columbia		J	joule
			K	Kelvin (degrees above absolute zero)
D	dextro (as a prefix)			
d	day		k	kilo (10^3, as a prefix)
d	dextrorotatory		kg	kilogram
df	degrees of freedom		km	kilometer
dL	deciliter		*l*	levorotatory
E	east		L	levo (as a prefix)
E	expected value		L	liter (0.264 gal, 1.06 qt)
e	base of natural logarithm (2.71828…)		lb	pound (0.454 kg, 454g)
			lm	lumen
e.g.	(exempli gratia) for example		log	logarithm
eq	equivalent		Ltd.	Limited
et al.	(et alii) and others		M	mega (10^6, as a prefix); molar (as a suffix or by itself)
etc.	et cetera			
eV	electron volt		m	meter (as a suffix or by itself); milli (10^{-3}, as a prefix)
F	filial generation; Farad			
°F	degrees Fahrenheit		mi	mile (1.61 km)
fc	footcandle (0.0929 lx)		min	minute
ft	foot (30.5 cm)		mol	mole
ft³/s	cubic feet per second (0.0283 m³/s)		N	normal (for chemistry); north (for geography); newton
g	gram		*N*	sample size

NS	not significant	tris	tris(hydroxymethyl)-aminomethane (a buffer)
n	ploidy; nanno (10^{-9}, as a prefix)		
o	ortho (as a chemical prefix)	UK	United Kingdom
oz	ounce (28.4 g)	U.S.	United States (adjective)
P	probability	USA	United States of America (noun)
p	para (as a chemical prefix)	V	volt
p	pico (10^{-12}, as a prefix)	V, Var	variance (population)
Pa	pascal	var	variance (sample)
pH	negative log of hydrogen ion activity	W	watt (for power); west (for geography)
ppm	parts per million	Wb	weber
qt	quart (0.946 L)	yd	yard (0.914 m, 91.4 cm)
R	multiple correlation or regression coefficient	α	probability of type I error (false rejection of null hypothesis)
r	simple correlation or regression coefficient	β	probability of type II error (false acceptance of null hypothesis)
rad	radian	Ω	ohm
S	siemens (for electrical conductance); south (for geography)	μ	micro (10^{-6}, as a prefix)
		′	minute (angular)
		″	second (angular)
SD	standard deviation	°	degree (temperature as a prefix, angular as a suffix)
SE	standard error		
s	second	%	per cent (per hundred)
T	tesla	‰	(per thousand)

Introduction

American Fisheries Society Symposium 70:3–10, 2009
© 2009 by the American Fisheries Society

Ecology and Management of Western Alaska Pacific Salmon:
Introduction to the Proceedings

CHARLES C. KRUEGER*
*Great Lakes Fishery Commission
2100 Commonwealth Boulevard, Suite 100, Ann Arbor, Michigan 48105, USA*

CHRISTIAN E. ZIMMERMAN
*U. S. Geological Survey, Alaska Science Center
4210 University Drive, Anchorage, Alaska 99508, USA*

JOSEPH J. SPAEDER
*Arctic-Yukon-Kuskokwim Sustainable Salmon Initiative
Bering Sea Fishermen's Association
Post Office Box 2087, Homer, Alaska 99603, USA*

Abstract.—The Arctic-Yukon-Kuskokwim region encompasses over 40% of the State of Alaska. The region includes the watersheds of Norton Sound up to and including the village of Shishmaref, the Yukon River watershed within Alaska and Canada, and the Kuskokwim River watershed (including the coastal watersheds north of Cape Newenham), plus the Bering Sea and North Pacific Ocean marine ecosystems (see frontispiece map). Dramatic declines in salmon runs to the AYK region from 1997 to 2001 created havoc within the subsistence culture of rural Alaskan communities and left fishery managers and scientists puzzled over the causes for the declines, unsure of best management measures for the future. Since 2003, salmon stocks across the region have fluctuated widely. The Arctic-Yukon-Kuskokwim Sustainable Salmon Initiative (AYK SSI) is an innovative partnership between public and private institutions which provides a forum for regional organizations and state and federal agencies to cooperatively identify and address salmon research and restoration needs. The AYK SSI provided the means to interconnect state, federal, and Alaska Native organizations to collaboratively participate in the symposium, and to fund the symposium and this book. The symposium and this text seeks to describe the management of salmon fisheries in the AYK region, to communicate what is known and what needs to be known about ecological processes that cause change in salmon populations; and to discuss the effects on rural communities caused by variability in abundance of salmon. This book provides a single reference text for the region that serves as an access point to information that formerly resided in a variety of storage media—from file drawers to web sites to the primary literature—and one that links information across the freshwater and marine ecosystems of the region. Our hope is that the availability of this information would encourage future students, managers, and researchers to focus their interests on AYK salmon, and promote the long-term sustainability of Alaska's salmon producing ecosystems.

*Corresponding author: ckrueger@glfc.org

Introduction

Western Alaska salmon and freshwater fishes of the Arctic-Yukon-Kuskokwim (AYK) region have been critical to the survival of the people and wildlife for thousands of years. Recent fluctuations (natural or human-induced) in the abundance of salmon populations have resulted in enormous stress and strain on the people and communities that depend so heavily on them. Dramatic declines in salmon *Oncorhynchus* runs across the AYK region from 1997 to 2001 created havoc within the subsistence culture of rural Alaskan communities and left fishery managers and scientists puzzled over the causes for the declines and unsure of best management measures for the future. These weak runs were the product of brood years (year classes) when escapement of adults to spawning streams was often considered more than adequate (e.g., Bue et al. 2009; this volume). These very steep declines in abundance occurred across much of the region suggesting that one common variable, possibly unfavorable ocean conditions for salmon survival, could have been the cause (e.g., Grebmeier et al. 2006; Ruggerone and Nielsen 2009, this volume).

Since 2003, salmon stocks across the region have fluctuated widely. Some stocks have returned to former levels such as fall chum salmon *O. keta* in the Tanana and Chandalar rivers (Bue et al. 2009, this volume). A sharp increase in abundance has occurred during individual years within the period 2004–2006 for some species such as sockeye salmon *O. nerka* in the Kuskokwim River drainage (Linderman and Bergstrom 2009, this volume), and coho salmon *O. kisutch* in the Norton Sound region (Menard et al. 2009, this volume). Unfortunately, some stocks increased briefly only to decline again, such as fall chum salmon in the Sheenjek River, (Bue et al. 2009, this volume) and the large, multi-stock Canadian main-stem Chinook salmon *O. tshawytscha* (Evenson et al. 2009, this volume). Other stocks have never recovered such as Chinook salmon in the North River, a tributary of the Unalakleet River in the Norton Sound region (Menard et al. 2009, this volume).

What was the cause for these wild fluctuations? Some of the highest recorded runs occurred from brood years when escapement was far less than what managers believed to be necessary for sustainable fisheries. Based on stock–recruitment relationships one would have expected weak runs, not strong ones. Did ocean conditions become favorable? If so, all runs would have been expected to respond with increased abundance. Yet, some runs never recovered while others briefly improved but declined again. The lack of uniform variation suggests that stock-specific variables might have been more important during the current decade than region-wide factors.

Outside of Alaska, such as in Washington and Oregon, depressed salmon runs can easily be attributed, in part, to stream habitat degradation associated with hydroelectric power facilities and other land uses (Williams and Lichatowich 2009, this volume; Lichatowich and Williams 2009, this volume). For the most part, stream habitats in the AYK region are intact, and yet salmon runs fluctuate greatly. The rivers are essentially undammed, the watersheds have few roads, and human population density is low. In spite of the apparent lack of obvious stressors in the freshwater domain, variability in salmon returns underscores the complexity of AYK salmon dynamics, and how much remains to be learned to understand the salmon dynamics of the AYK region.

To advance our understanding of the causes for the declines and recoveries of salmon in this region, the AYK Sustainable Salmon Initiative (AYK SSI) convened a symposium February 6–9, 2007 in Anchorage, Alaska featuring over 65 presentations and attended by over 300 participants. Many of these presentations were converted to the manuscripts which comprise this book (proceedings). Below we describe the region, its salmon species, the AYK SSI, and the purpose and organization of the symposium, and this volume. Last, we offer a section of acknowledgments of special people who contributed to the success of the symposium and this volume.

Arctic-Yukon-Kuskokwim Region

The AYK salmon ecosystem, including oceans and rivers, is a complex set of physical, chemical, and biological environments which support the production of salmon (e.g., Stanford et al. 2005). Encompassing over 40% of the State of Alaska, the AYK region includes the watersheds of Norton Sound up to and including the village of Shishmaref, the Yukon River watershed within Alaska and Canada, and the Kuskokwim River watershed (including the coastal watersheds north of Cape Newenham), plus the Bering Sea and North Pacific Ocean marine ecosystems (see frontispiece map). One portion of the marine environment alone, the eastern Bering Sea, is home to a rich variety of biota, including the world's most extensive eelgrass beds; at least 450 species of fish, crustaceans, and mollusks; fifty species of seabirds; and twenty-five species of marine mammals (PICES 2004). This ecosystem with its myriad of species contains complex sets of biological relationships (e.g., competition, predation) and physical processes (e.g., wind, temperature, ocean currents) which interact to cause salmon populations to vary.

AYK Region's Salmon Species

Five species of salmon use the river drainages of the AYK region for juvenile rearing and adult spawning, and the Bering Sea and North Pacific for growth until maturity. The common names of the salmon species are pink *O. gorbuscha*, chum, coho *O. kisutch*, sockeye, and Chinook (see color plates). A sixth species of *Oncorhynchus*, the rainbow trout *O. mykiss*, also occurs in the Kuskokwim River drainage, but does not use ocean habitats for growth as part of its life cycle and is not considered in this book. Chum salmon are widely distributed in this region, including much of the upper reaches of the Yukon and Kuskokwim river watersheds. Coho (or silver) salmon are distributed throughout the region to Point Hope, north of Kotzebue Sound, but tend to be more abundant farther south in the region. Similarly, northern Kotzebue Sound marks the northern edge of the region for Chinook and sockeye salmon. Chinook salmon reside primarily in the Kuskokwim and Yukon river drainages, and are somewhat less abundant in the Norton Sound drainages. Pink salmon have a wide distribution within the region, with the exception of the upper portion of the Kuskokwim River drainage and the middle and upper reaches of the Yukon River drainage. Mecklenburg et al. (2002) provides taxonomic descriptions and more detail about these species' various ranges in Alaska.

Chinook, chum, and coho salmon support a variety of important fisheries within the region. Pink salmon have become increasingly important in Norton Sound area fisheries in recent years (Menard et al. 2009, this volume). Lacking large, productive lake systems, the AYK region hosts low abundances of sockeye salmon in comparison to drainages farther south, such as in Bristol Bay; however, their abundance seems to be growing in the Kuskokwim River drainages (Linderman and Bergstrom 2009, this volume).

Each species is uniquely organized across space and time into populations which separate during spawning but may co-mingle while in the ocean and during their spawning migrations up rivers. A population is a group of fish of the same species which aggregates during the spawning season and interbreeds. Because of the genetic relationship among members within a population, genetically based traits can accumulate within the population over time (Utter et al. 2009; this volume). The degree of isolation among populations is dependent on population-isolating mechanisms, such as natal homing and the geographic distance among the spawning grounds of populations.

What is the AYK Sustainable Salmon Initiative?

The Arctic-Yukon-Kuskokwim Sustainable Salmon Initiative (AYK SSI) is an innovative partnership between public and private institutions which provides a forum for regional organizations and state and federal agencies to cooperatively identify and address salmon research and restoration needs. The formation of the AYK SSI was in response to disastrously low salmon returns to western Alaska in the late 1990s and early 2000s, which created numerous hardships for the people and rural communities that depend heavily on the salmon fishery. Between 1997 and 2002, the unexpected and dramatic declines of AYK salmon runs prompted a total of 15 disaster declarations in different watersheds within the region by the Governor of Alaska and federal agencies (AYK SSI 2006). Some stocks in the region have been in a decline for more than a decade and a half, leading to severe restrictions on commercial and subsistence fisheries.

Created via a memorandum of understanding in February 21, 2002 (and revised in 2003), the AYK SSI partnership includes the Association of Village Council Presidents (AVCP); the Tanana Chiefs Conference (TCC); Kawerak, Inc.; Bering Sea Fishermen's Association; Alaska Department of Fish and Game (ADF&G); National Marine Fisheries Service; and the U.S. Fish & Wildlife Service (USFWS). In 2001, the partners established the AYK SSI and created a process and structure to ensure the coordinated expenditure of research funds. The AYK SSI is governed by an eight-member Steering Committee (SC) and advised by a six-member Scientific Technical Committee (STC). As of June 2006, U.S. Congress had appropriated $20.5 million to support the AYK SSI.

The first step for the AYK SSI was to collaboratively develop and implement a comprehensive research plan to address the program's core goal:

To understand the trends and causes of variation in salmon abundance and fisheries through the assembly of existing information, gaining new information, and improving management and restoration techniques through a collaborative and inclusive process. (AYK SSI 2006).

This research plan identifies significant knowledge gaps and establishes a set of research priorities that complement other relevant research programs in the region without duplication of effort. In doing so, the plan provides a science-based roadmap to guiding the Initiative's "Invitations to Submit Research Proposals" and to help ensure that available funds target the highest priority research questions and issues.

Goals and Objectives of the Salmon Symposium

The goal of the symposium was to communicate what is known, and needs to be known, about:

• ecological processes that cause change in salmon populations,

• the effects on rural communities caused by the variability in abundance of salmon runs, and

• the management of salmon fisheries in the AYK region.

The symposium sought to accomplish this goal by focusing on six objectives:

1. Summarize and communicate the state of contemporary scientific and traditional ecological knowledge about the marine and freshwater ecosystems that support the salmon fisheries and culture of the Arctic-Yukon-Kuskokwim region.

2. Identify key ecological processes that cause changes in salmon abundance.

3. Describe the current governance by state, federal, and international agencies vested with fishery management authority, and propose organizational mechanisms to enhance collaboration and improve coordination.

4. Review and discuss the AYK Research and Restoration Plan (AYK SSI 2006) and the critical information needed to better understand the key ecological processes and to improve management in the region.

5. Advance the understanding of symposium participants of the ecology, fisheries, and management of AYK salmon.

6. Communicate the results of the symposium through publication.

The symposium featured keynote addresses, paper presentations, and panel discussions organized around four thematic sessions:

• Biology and Ecology of Salmon

• Human Dimensions of Salmon

• Fishery Management Strategies: Lessons from Local, Regional, and International Experiences

• Synthesis and Integration: Intersections among Ecology, Local Knowledge, and Management

In addition to summarizing and communicating the state of contemporary knowledge, the symposium sought to facilitate integration and synthesis through a series of concluding breakout sessions. The purpose of the breakout groups was to generate discussion that would cut across and integrate more than one discipline. Ten integrative themes that bridged traditional disciplinary boundaries and research approaches were developed to help focus breakout group discussions. Each breakout group provided a small group forum (six to ten people) for discussion and exploration of one of the ten themes.

How is the Book Organized?

The structure of this book follows the general organization of the symposium. The first section addresses the ecology of AYK salmon and is broken into freshwater and estuarine-marine ecology. The second section explores the social, economic, and cultural linkages to AYK salmon. The third section focuses on fishery management of AYK salmon which links the preceding ecology and human dimensions sections. The management section includes chapters on freshwater and marine management of salmon, including subsistence, commercial, and sport fisheries management. The fourth section looks outside of the AYK region to learn about ecology, human dimensions, and management elsewhere, and to apply lessons learned elsewhere to AYK salmon fisheries. The last section includes a series of perspectives papers representing some of the keynote presentations from the symposium and products from the breakout sessions. These papers examine the challenges of salmon ecology and management, and explore new approaches to understanding AYK salmon.

Why a Symposium Proceedings?

The proceedings bridges retrospective studies summarizing existing knowledge with new approaches and conceptual frameworks for understanding AYK salmon. In putting this picture together in an integrative way, the editors hope that a better understanding of the past declines will result, and that the volume will help chart future management approaches. The intent of publishing a book was to provide a portal to information about salmon ecology and management of the AYK region, as none currently exists. This book provides a single reference text for the region and serves as an access point to information that formerly resided in a variety of storage media—from the minds of managers and researchers to drawers of historical files to web sites to the primary literature.

We believe the text is unique first, by linking ecological and management information across the freshwater and marine ecosystems embracing the entire life cycle of the salmon, and second, by including human dimensions chapters. The human dimensions chapters range from discussions about the role of traditional ecological knowledge (Brelsford 2009, this volume) to the economics of AYK fisheries (Knapp 2009, this volume). By presenting what is known about AYK salmon and then identifying information gaps, this book will serve as a valuable guide for future research and assessment programs. Our hope is that the availability of this information might inspire students, managers, and researchers to invest their expertise in studying and managing AYK salmon.

Acknowledgments

The idea of a symposium was generated in 1999 out of a need to identify what was known and not known about the ecology and management of subsistence fisheries in the AYK region. At that time, the federal government had assumed responsibility for subsistence fishery management on federal public lands in Alaska (Buklis 2002) and was planning to implement a study program. The U.S. Fish and Wildlife Service desired to establish a program that funded new projects that would yield valuable information and assist management decision making. The question immediately arose, "what were the critical information needs of the region?" The first step in identifying knowledge gaps was to determine what was known, and this need became the motivation and subsequent genesis to hold an interdisciplinary symposium and generate a book. Several discussions of this idea occurred between the senior author (CK) and several employees of the Alaska Department of Fish and Game and with Taylor Brelsford, Tom Boyd, and Peggy Fox, now former employees of the U.S. Fish and Wildlife Service, Office of Subsistence Management. The idea continued to develop into 2000, spurred on by discussion between one of the authors (CK) and a wider cast of characters including David Policansky of the National Research Council and Michael Rearden (formerly refuge manager of the Yukon Delta National Wildlife Refuge). Late in 2000, these discussions eventually and fortunately connected the senior author with Joseph Spaeder (a co-author here) of the Bering Sea Fishermen's Association. In 2002, the AYK Sustainable Salmon Initiative was formed and Christian Zimmerman (a co-author here) of the U.S. Geological Survey was appointed chair of the Scientific and Technical Committee, bringing together the three authors of this chapter. The AYK SSI facilitated the required linkages among the state, federal, and Alaska Native organizations to organize such a symposium and provide funding. Five years of further planning were required before the advent of the symposium in 2007. Two more years were required for final publication. All good things come with time!

Many, many people contributed to make this volume possible. We extend our deep appreciation to all past and present members of the Steering Committee and Scientific and Technical Committee who are identified in the beginning pages of this volume, whose vision and hard work made this project possible. Of special assistance has been Karen Gillis, AYK SSI Program Director, and John White, long-time chair of the AYK SSI Steering Committee, both of whom provided consistent and unwavering support. Many others provided direct assistance with the running of the symposium and include: Rob Bochenek, Taylor Brelsford, Ed Farley, Christopher Goddard, Michele Henzler, John Hilsinger, Steve Klein, Nate Mantua, Megan McPhee, Jamal Moss, Matt Nemeth, Evelyn Pinkerton, Gene Sandone, Marianne See, Jack Stanford, Katie Williams, Mark Wipfli, and Mara Zimmerman. Dave Cannon of Aniak, Alaska provided several of the photos used in the volume. Paul Vecsei voluntarily assisted with the design of the cover. Joseph Tomelleri provided the wonderful paintings of Pacific salmon. The Great Lakes Fishery Commission provided editorial workspace and facilities to senior author. We thank the over 110 anonymous reviewers who generously offered their time and expertise in reviewing the papers in this volume (listed in the back of the volume). Special assistance in editing papers was provided by Caroline Brown, Scott Miehls, Katherine Myers, Holly Patrick, Marianne See, Eric Volk, and American Fisheries Society Publications Director, Aaron Lerner and Books Production Coordinator, Kurt West. Thanks to all!

References

AYK SSI (Arctic-Yukon-Kuskokwim Sustainable Salmon Initiative). 2006. Arctic-Yukon-Kuskokwim salmon research and restoration plan. Bering Sea Fishermen's Association, Anchorage, Alaska.

Brelsford, T. 2009. "We have to learn to work together:" current perspectives on incorporating local and traditional/indigenous knowledge into Alaskan fishery management. Pages 381–394 in C. C. Krueger and C. E. Zimmerman, editors. Pacific salmon: ecology and management of western Alaska's populations. American Fisheries Society, Symposium 70, Bethesda, Maryland.

Bue, F. J., B. M. Borba, R. Cannon, and C. C. Krueger. 2009. Yukon River fall chum salmon fisheries: management, harvest, and stock abundance. Pages 703–742 in C. C. Krueger and C. E. Zimmerman, editors. Pacific salmon: ecology and management of western Alaska's populations. American Fisheries Society, Symposium 70, Bethesda, Maryland.

Evenson, D. F., S. J. Hayes, G. Sandone, and D. J. Bergstrom. 2009. Yukon River Chinook salmon: stock status, harvest, and management. Pages 675–701 in C. C. Krueger and C. E. Zimmerman, editors. Pacific salmon: ecology and management of western Alaska's populations. American Fisheries Society, Symposium 70, Bethesda, Maryland.

Grebmeier, J. M., J. E. Overland, S. E. Moore, E. V. Farley, E. C. Carmack, L. W. Cooper, K. E. Frey, J. H. Helle, F. A. McLaughlin, and S. L. McNutt. 2006. A major ecosystem shift in the northern Bering Sea. Science 311:1461–1464.

Knapp, G. 2009. Commercial salmon fisheries of the Arctic-Yukon-Kuskokwim region: economic challenges and opportunities. Pages 463–486 in C. C. Krueger and C. E. Zimmerman, editors. Pacific salmon: ecology and management of western Alaska's populations. American Fisheries Society, Symposium 70, Bethesda, Maryland.

Lichatowich, J. A., and R. N. Williams. 2009. Failures to incorporate science into fishery management and recovery programs: lessons from the Columbia River. Pages 1005–1019 in C. C. Krueger and C. E. Zimmerman, editors. Pacific salmon: ecology and management of western Alaska's populations. American Fisheries Society, Symposium 70, Bethesda, Maryland.

Linderman, J. C., Jr., and D. J. Bergstrom. 2009. Kuskokwim management area: salmon escapement, harvest, and management. Pages 541–599 in C. C. Krueger and C. E. Zimmerman, editors. Pacific salmon: ecology and management of western Alaska's populations. American Fisheries Society, Symposium 70, Bethesda, Maryland.

Mecklenburg, C. W., T. A. Mecklenburg, and L. K. Thorsteinson, editors. 2002. Fishes of Alaska. American Fisheries Society, Bethesda, Maryland.

Menard, J., C. C. Krueger, and J. R. Hilsinger. 2009. Norton Sound salmon fisheries: history, stock abundance, and management. Pages 621–673 *in* C. C. Krueger and C. E. Zimmerman, editors. Pacific salmon: ecology and management of western Alaska's populations. American Fisheries Society, Symposium 70, Bethesda, Maryland.

PICES (North Pacific Marine Science Organization). 2004. Marine ecosystems of the north Pacific. PICES Special Publication 1.

Ruggerone, G. T., and J. Nielsen. 2009. A review of growth and survival of salmon at sea in response to competition and climate change. Pages 241–265 *in* C. C. Krueger and C. E. Zimmerman, editors. Pacific salmon: ecology and management of western Alaska's populations. American Fisheries Society, Symposium 70, Bethesda, Maryland.

Stanford, J. A., M. S. Lorang, and F. R. Hauer. 2005. The shifting habitat mosaic of river ecosystems. Verhandlungen der Internationalen Vereinigung fur Theoretische und Angewandte Limnologie 29:123–136.

Utter, F. M., M. V. McPhee, and F. W. Allendorf. 2009. Population genetics and the management of Arctic-Yukon-Kuskokwim salmon populations. Pages 97–123 *in* C. C. Krueger and C. E. Zimmerman, editors. Pacific salmon: ecology and management of western Alaska's populations. American Fisheries Society, Symposium 70, Bethesda, Maryland.

Williams, R., and J. Lichatowich. 2009. Science and politics—an uncomfortable alliance: lessons learned from the fish and wildlife program of the Northwest Power and Conservation Council. Pages 1021–1046 *in* C. C. Krueger and C. E. Zimmerman, editors. Pacific salmon: ecology and management of western Alaska's populations. American Fisheries Society, Symposium 70, Bethesda, Maryland.

Section I

Ecology of AYK Salmon

American Fisheries Society Symposium 70:13–15, 2009

Ecology of Pacific Salmon:
Introduction

CHRISTIAN E. ZIMMERMAN

U.S. Geological Survey, Alaska Science Center
4210 University Drive, Anchorage, Alaska 99508, USA

CHARLES C. KRUEGER

Great Lakes Fishery Commission
2100 Commonwealth Boulevard, Suite 100, Ann Arbor, Michigan 48105, USA

A key component of the program goal of the Arctic-Yukon-Kuskokwim Sustainable Salmon Initiative (AYK SSI) is to "..understand the trends and causes of variation in abundance and fisheries..." of Pacific salmon(AYK SSI 2006). To achieve this goal, information concerning population biology, freshwater ecology, marine ecology, and population dynamics is needed to understand the variables controlling population abundance and trends. The papers in this section were selected to address these topics and divided into two broad habitat-based themes: freshwater and marine.

The freshwater ecology theme contains papers that examine habitat, food supply, and energetics of juvenile salmon in streams and rivers, population genetics, conservation of genetic diversity, and the role of environmental variation in controlling salmon productivity. Freshwater ecology and the role of habitat in controlling salmon populations in the AYK region have received little attention in the past by researchers (AYK SSI 2006). A primary goal for this section was to begin to remedy this significant knowledge gap. In organizing this section, we invited papers from those who have worked on these topics both in the region

and from elsewhere. Bradford et al. (2009, this volume) discusses the production of juvenile Chinook salmon *Oncorhynchus tshawytscha* in the upper Yukon River relative to habitat. Wipfli (2009, this volume) then discusses the role of food supply in controlling growth and productivity of juvenile salmonids in streams and the connection to nutrients imported by adult salmon migrating from marine waters. Beauchamp (2009, this volume) links food supply, temperature mediated metabolism, and food capture ability to examine growth potential using bioenergetic modeling. Then, Nemeth et al. (2009, this volume) focuses on the role of habitat in controlling the freshwater productivity of salmon with an examination of habitat/salmon productivity relations in two Norton Sound rivers.

The genetics section begins with Utter et al. (2009, this volume) who review the current state of knowledge concerning population structure of salmon throughout the AYK region. Waples (2009, this volume) discusses the importance of maintaining genetic variability to conserve salmon. Beacham et al. (2009, this volume) present population structure of chum salmon *O. keta* and discuss opportunities of identifying stock of origin in mixed-stock fisheries. Finally, Gilk et al. (2009, this volume) reports on an AYK SSI funded study aimed at describing previously unrecognized ecotypic variation in chum salmon in the Kuskokwim River.

The second theme on ecology shifts the focus to estuarine and marine habitats. Hillgruber and Zimmerman (2009, this volume) review what is known about juvenile salmon as they migrate through estuarine and near-shore habitats in the AYK region. Farley et al. (2009, this volume) and Myers et al. (2009, this volume) discuss salmon data collected in the Bering Sea and North Pacific Ocean. Ruggerone and Nielsen (2009, this volume) discuss marine growth and survival of AYK salmon in response to both climate and competition with hatchery salmon. Continuing this discussion of carrying capacity and growth in the marine environment, Eggers (2009, this volume) reconstructs the possible biomass of salmon in high seas habitats using return and capture data from rivers surrounding the Pacific Ocean. Finally, Royer and Grosch (2009, this volume) presents data concerning variability in marine habitats.

As described throughout this section, knowledge gaps remain concerning the ecology of salmon populations in the AYK region. Continued, multi-disciplinary research is needed to investigate the role of physical habitat, climate induced environmental variability, and biological response in salmon populations if we are to meet the goals of AYK SSI and improve our ability to predict the abundance of salmon returning to the AYK region.

References

AYK SSI (Arctic-Yukon-Kuskokwim Sustainable Salmon Initiative). 2006. Arctic-Yukon-Kuskokwim salmon research and restoration plan. Bering Sea Fishermen's Association, Anchorage, Alaska.

Beacham, T. D., K. D. Le, M. Wetklo, B. McIntosh, T. Ming, and K. M. Miller. 2009. Population structure and stock identification of chum salmon from western Alaska determined with microsatellite DNA and major histocompatibility complex variation. Pages 141–160 in C. C. Krueger and C. E. Zimmerman, editors. Pacific salmon: ecology and management of western Alaska's populations. American Fisheries Society, Symposium 70, Bethesda, Maryland.

Beauchamp, D. A. 2009. Bioenergetic ontogeny: linking climate and mass-specific feeding to life-cycle growth and survival of salmon. Pages 53–71 in C. C. Krueger and C. E. Zimmerman, editors. Pacific salmon: ecology and management of western Alaska's populations. American Fisheries Society, Symposium 70, Bethesda, Maryland.

Bradford, M. J., A. von Finster, and P. A. Milligan. 2009. Freshwater life history, habitat, and the production of Chinook salmon from the upper Yukon Basin. Pages 19–38 in C. C. Krueger and C. E. Zimmerman, editors. Pacific salmon: ecology and management of western Alaska's populations. American Fisheries Society, Symposium 70, Bethesda, Maryland.

Eggers, D. M. 2009. Historical biomass of pink, chum, and sockeye salmon in the North Pacific Ocean. Pages 267–305 in C. C. Krueger and C. E. Zimmerman, editors. Pacific salmon: ecology and management of western Alaska's populations. American Fisheries Society, Symposium 70, Bethesda, Maryland.

Farley, E. V., J. Murphy, J. Moss, A. Feldmann, and L. Eisner. 2009. Marine ecology of western Alaska juvenile salmon. Pages 307–329 in C. C. Krueger and C. E. Zimmerman, editors. Pacific salmon: ecology and management of western Alaska's populations. American Fisheries Society, Symposium 70, Bethesda, Maryland.

Gilk, S. E., D. B. Molyneaux, T. Hamazaki, J. A. Pawluk, and W. D. Templin. 2009. Biological and genetic characteristics of fall and summer chum salmon in the Kuskokwim River. Pages 161–179 in C. C. Krueger and C. E. Zimmerman, editors. Pacific salmon: ecology and management of western Alaska's populations. American Fisheries Society, Symposium 70, Bethesda, Maryland.

Hillgruber, N., and C. E. Zimmerman. 2009. Estuarine ecology of juvenile salmon in western Alaska: a review. Pages 183–199 *in* C. C. Krueger and C. E. Zimmerman, editors. Pacific salmon: ecology and management of western Alaska's populations. American Fisheries Society, Symposium 70, Bethesda, Maryland.

Myers, K. W., R. V. Walker, N. D. Davis, J. L. Armstrong, and M. Kaeriyama. 2009. High seas distribution, biology, and ecology of AYK salmon: direct information from high seas tagging experiments, 1954–2006. Pages 201–239 *in* C. C. Krueger and C. E. Zimmerman, editors. Pacific salmon: ecology and management of western Alaska's populations. American Fisheries Society, Symposium 70, Bethesda, Maryland.

Nemeth, M. J., B. C. Williams, R. C. Bocking, and S. N. Kinneen. 2009. Freshwater habitat quantity and coho salmon production in two rivers: an initial study to support the development of habitat-based escapement goals in Norton Sound, Alaska. Pages 73–96 *in* C. C. Krueger and C. E. Zimmerman, editors. Pacific salmon: ecology and management of western Alaska's populations. American Fisheries Society, Symposium 70, Bethesda, Maryland.

Royer, T. C., and C. E. Grosch. 2009. North Pacific and Bering Sea ecosystems: how might they change? Pages 331–343 *in* C. C. Krueger and C. E. Zimmerman, editors. Pacific salmon: ecology and management of western Alaska's populations. American Fisheries Society, Symposium 70, Bethesda, Maryland.

Ruggerone, G. T., and J. Nielsen. 2009. A review of growth and survival of salmon at sea in response to competition and climate change. Pages 241–265 *in* C. C. Krueger and C. E. Zimmerman, editors. Pacific salmon: ecology and management of western Alaska's populations. American Fisheries Society, Symposium 70, Bethesda, Maryland.

Utter, F. M., M. V. McPhee, and F. W. Allendorf. 2009. Population genetics and the management of Arctic-Yukon-Kuskokwim salmon populations. Pages 97–123 *in* C. C. Krueger and C. E. Zimmerman, editors. Pacific salmon: ecology and management of western Alaska's populations. American Fisheries Society, Symposium 70, Bethesda, Maryland.

Waples, R. S. 2009. Conserving the evolutionary legacy of Arctic-Yukon-Kuskokwim salmon. Pages 125–139 *in* C. C. Krueger and C. E. Zimmerman, editors. Pacific salmon: ecology and management of western Alaska's populations. American Fisheries Society, Symposium 70, Bethesda, Maryland.

Wipfli, M. S. 2009. Food supplies of stream-dwelling salmon. Pages 39–52 *in* C. C. Krueger and C. E. Zimmerman, editors. Pacific salmon: ecology and management of western Alaska's populations. American Fisheries Society, Symposium 70, Bethesda, Maryland.

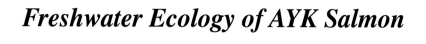

Freshwater Ecology of AYK Salmon

American Fisheries Society Symposium 70:19–38, 2009

Freshwater Life History, Habitat, and the Production of Chinook Salmon from the Upper Yukon Basin

MICHAEL J. BRADFORD[*]

Fisheries and Oceans Canada and Cooperative Resource Management Institute
Simon Fraser University, Burnaby, British Columbia V5A 1S6, Canada

ALAN VON FINSTER AND PATRICK A. MILLIGAN

Fisheries and Oceans Canada
100-419 Range Road, Whitehorse, Yukon Territory Y1A 3V1, Canada

Abstract.—Potential yield and escapement goals for salmon populations are often determined with stock-recruit relations, but for many Chinook salmon *Oncorhynchus tshawytscha* populations, this information is lacking or is uninformative. One alternative is a habitat-based approach, but the complex early life history of Chinook salmon presents challenges to biologists and managers wishing to use this method. Published fry and smolt data from other populations is summarizd, which show that habitat limitation in the freshwater rearing stage is common and may limit production. The freshwater life history of Chinook salmon from the Canadian portion of the Yukon basin is then reviewed to evaluate the potential link between habitat, migration and density-dependent mortality that leads to population regulation. There is a significant downstream redistribution of age-0 fish from spawning areas in June and July that results in juveniles being distributed throughout a variety of habitats, at great distances from natal streams. DNA analysis of the population of origin of migrants showed significant inter-populational variation in dispersal behaviour. Spatially extensive sampling is required to determine the full range of juvenile habitat for the Canadian populations, and to quantify relations between the number of parent spawners and juvenile abundance and distribution. This fuller understanding is needed to determine if freshwater rearing habitat limits the productivity of this population complex.

Introduction

Salmon populations are usually managed on the basis of achieving a desired number of spawners that satisfies a specified management goal such as a sustainable yield. Escapement goals and estimates of potential yield are frequently derived from the analysis of historical stock-recruit (SR) data. Such

[*]Corresponding author: Mike.Bradford@dfo-mpo.gc.ca

analysis requires many years (>20 cohorts in most cases) of accurate data containing sufficient contrast in order to be able to generate unbiased and precise estimates of model parameters and management goals. Shortcomings of SR analysis are well-known and pervasive (Hilborn and Walters 1992; Walters and Martell 2004).

Curvilinear stock-recruit relations (such as the Ricker model) result from compensation, which is defined as density-dependent survival in one or more points in the life cycle that causes productivity to decrease as abundance increases (Hilborn and Walters 1992). Compensation is usually caused by competition for food or space in habitats that are in limited supply; for salmon it is most often observed in the freshwater part of the life cycle. When those habitats are well-defined, relations between salmon abundance and freshwater habitat quantity and quality can be used to predict yields and set escapement goals (Greene and Beechie 2004). Well-known examples include relationship between sockeye salmon *Oncorhynchus nerka* smolt yield and lake size and productivity (Shortreed et al. 2000), and coho salmon *O. kisutch* production, stream size, and stream habitat quality (Bradford et al. 1997; Sharma and Hilborn 2001). Habitat-based methods may be a viable alternative to SR analysis for setting management targets when SR data are unavailable or are deficient (Bodtker et al. 2006).

Development of a habitat-based method for estimating the production of stream-type Chinook salmon *O. tshawytscha,* such as those from the upper Yukon River populations, is more problematic compared to other salmon species because their use of freshwater habitats is not well defined. Juveniles are not restricted to a specific habitat type, and are found in natal streams, the margins of large rivers, small nonnatal tributary streams and lakes (Healey 1991). Stream-type Chinook salmon are large-bodied, fecund (~9,000 eggs in Yukon River fish, Healey and Heard 1984), and often spawn in aggregations in large rivers that provide favorable environments for egg-to-fry survival. This means that potentially large numbers of fry emerge from spawning areas each spring, and must find suitable rearing habitats, preferably with low levels of competition somewhere in the river basin to complete the freshwater stage of the life cycle. Thus the dispersal of juve-

niles to other, sometimes distant, habitats is a common feature of the stream-type life history (Connor et al. 2001).

The effect of this indeterminate or "open" early life history on compensation will depend on the relationship between abundance, dispersal, and survival. We divided the freshwater period into three phases- the initial dispersal of newly emerged fry in the spring, the dispersal of juveniles in the summer and fall, and the survival of juveniles once the main period of dispersal has ceased. For the first phase we consider the effect of population size (in terms of spawners or eggs deposited in spawning areas) on the rate of production and dispersal of newly emerged fry from spawning areas. Three hypotheses are proposed (Figure 1). In the first, the proportion of eggs deposited that emerges as fry and disperses downstream is a decreasing function of density. Here, competition among spawners for prime spawning areas and redd superimposition results in greater egg mortality at high abundance (e.g., West and Mason 1987). In the second case the proportion of migrants is independent of density so that the number of migrants increases linearly with abundance. Here abundance does not affect survival or dispersal; dispersal may be viewed as a strategy employed by families to disperse offspring through a range of habitats as a form of bet hedging (Bradford and Taylor 1997). This pattern has been observed in coho salmon fry, where the number of migrant fry was linearly related to spawner abundance (Bradford et al. 2000). In the final scenario, the proportion migrating is an increasing function of initial abundance. This is the case where the occupation of habitats is by a space-filling process, with juveniles being forced to move further downstream with increasing abundance as habitats become filled. For other salmonid species, competition among juveniles for feeding territories has been proposed as a mechanism for this pattern of dispersal (Crisp 1993; Einum et al. 2006).

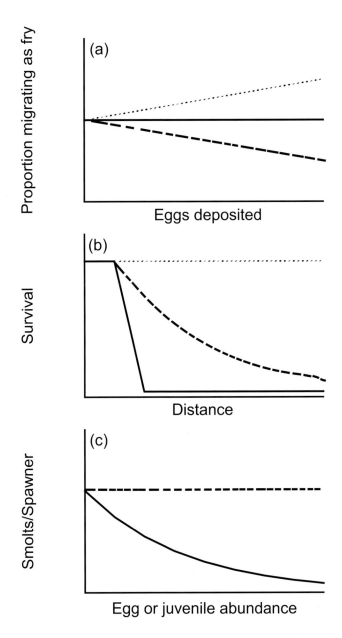

FIGURE 1. (a) Possible relations between the proportion of deposited eggs that migrate as newly emerged fry and egg abundance for that cohort. The dotted line is the case in which the proportion migrating increases with density. The solid line is the constant dispersal rate case and the dashed line represents density-dependent mortality in the egg-fry stage. (b) Hypothetical relations between survival and migration distance for juvenile Chinook salmon *Oncorhynchus tshawytscha* moving from spawning grounds to summer rearing habitats. Dotted line: no cost of migration; dashed line: survival decreases with the distance or time spent traveling; solid line: a survival threshold created by unsuitable downstream habitats. (c) Egg-smolt survival as a function of egg abundance, illustrating the density-independent (dashed line), and density-dependent survival (solid line) cases.

The second phase is a period of redistribution of juveniles (Healey 1991). For this phase, the relation between downstream dispersal and survival is considered. In the simplest case, survival is independent of dispersal, so there is no cost to downstream migration (Figure 1b). For the second scenario, the cost of dispersal is a function of the extent of the dispersal (in terms of either time or distance). Although this functional form is often used when modeling the effects of dispersal on population dynamics (Hanski 1999), the evidence supporting it is lacking for salmonids. In the most extreme case, dispersers experience very low survival in downstream habitats and make little contribution to recruitment. This is an example where the downstream habitats are completely unusable, as has been observed for coho salmon fry in coastal streams that are forced to move to the ocean before they are physiologically capable of living in a saline environment (Crone and Bond 1976). This situation is unlikely for stream-type Chinook salmon in large river ecosystems.

The third component of our conceptual model for the freshwater dynamics of Chinook salmon is the relation between abundance and survival for juveniles once their major migrations within freshwater have been completed. For many stream-dwelling salmonids, density dependent competition for space and food ultimately limits production (Chapman 1966), which is measured as the number of smolts produced by the habitat. Such limitation would result in a negative relation between juvenile survival and abundance (Figure 1c).

The migration and survival components can then be combined to describe the effects of indeterminate habitat use on juvenile population dynamics and the form of density dependence in juvenile mortality. In the case where rate and distance of dispersal from the natal area is unrelated to initial abundance, juvenile density throughout the range will vary with spawner abundance. Density-dependent survival can occur in the larger habitat arena if competition for food or rearing space occurs in the downstream habitats once migration has occurred. The extent of competition will depend on how large an area is available for rearing, the number of migrants, and presence of conspecific competitors from other populations using the same nonnatal rearing areas.

The second model is a space-filling model, where fish occupy successively more distant habitats with increasing abundance as habitats closer to the spawning areas fill up with migrating juveniles. Compensation will occur if there are costs to migration (dashed line, Figure 1b), because in years of high abundance juveniles will be forced to migrate further, and will be subject to greater rates of mortality. In addition, these juveniles will compete with conspecifics of other migrating populations. Compensation will be minimized if the cost of migration is low and if there are abundant habitats downstream of the natal stream. A testable prediction from this hypothesis is that juveniles will be distributed further downstream in years of higher abundance.

At the population level, the combined effects of competition and dispersal on compensation in the freshwater life stages are difficult to predict because it will depend on the density of juveniles produced in the spawning stream, the configuration and suitability of rearing habitats in downstream locations, and the factors that lead to the dispersal of each brood through these habitats. Compensation is likely the strongest (and easiest to estimate) when the population is limited in its dispersal, and weakest when the population has plasticity in habitat use, resulting in each brood being distributed over a large area. As each population will likely differ in dispersal propensity (Bradford and Taylor 1997) and will be situated in a different landscape configuration, inter-populational variation in compensation is also likely.

In this review, these concepts are applied to populations of Chinook salmon that spawn in the Canadian portion of the Yukon River basin (that we call the "upper Yukon") (see Evenson et al. 2009, this volume). There are no long-term data on the dynamics of the early life stages of these populations, nor is there sufficient understanding of the freshwater life history to identify stages and habitats where density-dependent mortality is likely to occur. Consequently, two approaches to addressing this issue are taken. First, demographic data is reviewed from Chinook salmon populations from other areas to provide a species-level overview of their freshwater population dynamics. Second, the existing knowledge of the freshwater life history cycle of upper Yukon River Chinook salmon is summarized from studies conducted and other published works to draw inferences about their population dynamics, and to identify data gaps and research needs to further the goal of determining the limits to productivity of this population complex.

A Review of Empirical Data from Other Chinook Salmon Populations

In instances where population-specific data are lacking, it is often useful to summarize information from similar populations to draw out generalities for the species (Hilborn and Liermann 1998). Time series of egg, fry, parr, and smolt abundance data for Chinook salmon populations were gathered from outside the Yukon River basin. These data were evaluated for the presence of density-dependent survival and dispersal behavior for both newly emerged fry and older migrants (sensu Figure 1a, c). The data sought were estimates of total egg deposition and the abundance of newly emerged fry, older parr (2–3 months postemergence)

or yearling smolts that migrated from the stream. Migration rates (S), indexed by stream, i, and year, t, were calculated as ratio of migrants/eggs, and analyzed with a general linear model of the form:

$$\ln(S_{it}) = \alpha_i + \beta_i Eggs_{it} + \varepsilon_{it}$$

where α_i is the population-specific log-migration rate at low abundance, β_i is the slope of the relation between log-migration and the number of deposited eggs, and ε_{it} is a normally distributed error term. This model was fit using the SAS procedure GLM. The population-specific parameters were averaged (α' and β') using the ESTIMATE option in GLM. A standard error (SE) for each parameter was also calculated.

Five dataseries were found for which the ratio of the number of newly emerged fry migrants per deposited egg could be calculated. The combined parameter estimates for the fry data were $\alpha' = -1.61$ (SE 0.25, $P < 0.001$) and $\beta' = -1.14 \times 10^{-4}$ (SE 1.29×10^{-4}, $P = 0.38$). The nonsignificant value for β' suggests that the overall support density-dependent migration is weak and that the rate fry migration was independent of population size (Figure 2, left column). A significant negative slope would be expected if density effects in the spawning grounds were causing survival to decline at high abundances (i.e., Figure 1a, dashed line).

The analysis also suggests that the fry migration rate is not the result of interactions with conspecifics that would cause the proportion migrating to increase with abundance due to crowding in natal areas (Crisp 1993; Einum et al. 2006). The results are more consistent with Bradford and Taylor's (1997) hypotheses that the population differ in their dispersal propensities and that causes a constant proportion of the population to disperse from the natal areas independent of density.

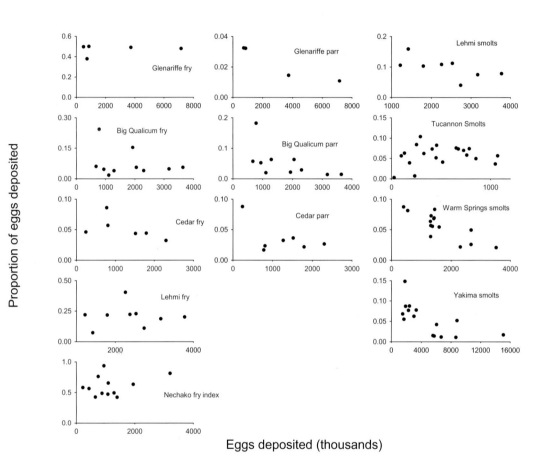

FIGURE 2. Compilation of freshwater life history data for eight Chinook salmon *Oncorhynchus tshaw-ytscha* populations. In each case, the proportion of eggs deposited that result in new emerged fry, parr, or smolt migrants is plotted against the total egg deposition for that cohort. A negative slope indicates decreasing rates of production at higher densities, which may be the result of habitat limitation. For the Nechako River, an index of fry abundance rather than absolute abundance is presented. For the Tucannon River, the point near the origin was considered an outlier and was not used. Data sources are listed in Bradford (1995) with the addition of: Glenariffe, Unwin (1986); Cedar, Volkhardt et al. (2006), Nechako, NFCP (2005) and Tucannon, Gallinat and Ross (2007).

Seven datasets were analyzed for the production of parr or yearling migrants from natal streams. The combined parameter estimates were $\alpha' = -2.59$ (SE 0.16, $P < 0.001$) and $\beta' = -2.54 \times 10^{-4}$ (SE 9.7×10^{-5}, $P = 0.010$). The significant negative estimate for β' suggests that density-dependent mortality is a common feature of this life stage. The proportion of eggs that result in migrating or yearling migrants decreases with increasing egg deposition, confirming that habitat-based limitations to production do occur, similar to that observed for the other freshwater rearing-dependent salmon species. The absence of density-dependent mortality in the egg-to-fry stage in the previous analysis suggests that compensation is occurring in rearing rather than incubation habitats. Density-dependent growth has also been observed in some of the streams (Bjornn 1978; Lindsay et al. 1989) supporting the hypothesis that juvenile rearing habitats may be a limiting factor for productivity.

The impact of density-dependent smolt production in the natal stream on the regulation of the whole population depends on how much of the cohort resides in the natal stream relative to downstream habitats. In the case of stream-type salmon in the Lehmi River, Idaho, nearly 70% of migrants were newly emerged fry, presumably moving to downstream habitats (Bjornn 1978). In the other populations, the proportion of fry migrants is lower. In cases where a large fraction of the population migrates to downstream habitats, the overall implications of compensation in the natal stream may be overwhelmed by the factors affecting the survival of fry migrants in downstream habitats.

The combined effects of density-dependent survival in natal streams, and interactions among migrants from many populations in downstream habitats within a basin are illustrated by the aggregate smolt-spawner data for all stream-type populations of the Snake River basin of Idaho and Oregon (Petrosky et al. 2001; Figure 3). Those data suggest that the smolt production rate decreases gradually as abundance increases so that the curvature in the resulting stock-recruit relation is relatively shallow. Within the available data, smolt production appears to be limited to about 2.5 million yearlings. Relatively weak density dependence for the population aggregate may occur in a situation like the Snake River because there are many different populations and habitats involved, and variation in migratory behavior and habitat utilization among populations within the basin.

Freshwater Life History of Upper Yukon River Chinook Salmon

In the absence of extensive abundance data to evaluate the population dynamics of upper Yukon River Chinook salmon, existing information from research studies, surveys, and other sources is summarized to provide an overview of the freshwater life history of this population complex.

Spawning populations

Maturing Chinook salmon enter the Yukon River in June, cross into Canada in July, and spawn in August and early September (Gilbert 1922). Spawners have been observed at more than 100 locations in the Canadian basin, but only a few populations are regularly monitored. Total escapement to the Canadian basin has been estimated since 1982 using a mark–recapture program conducted near the international border; the series has recently been rescaled based on alternative estimation techniques (Figure 4). The Canadian portion of the basin accounts for approximately half of the total production in the Yukon River (Eiler et al. 2006; Smith et al. 2005; Evenson 2009). Results from radio tagging and DNA analysis indicate that the most significant spawning populations occur

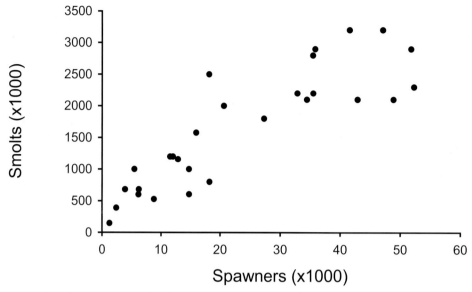

FIGURE 3. Relation between the abundance of spawners and the subsequent production of yearling smolts for the large Snake River watershed in Idaho and Oregon. Data are from Petrosky et al. (2001).

in tributaries draining the eastern side of the basin, with the Stewart, Pelly, Little, and Big Salmon Rivers comprising more than half of the total.

No detailed studies of spawning behaviour or the habitats used for spawning have been conducted in the upper Yukon basin. Observations suggest spawning habitats are similar to those found in other rivers, with large mainstems and large tributaries being the main locations (e.g., Walker 1976). Milligan et al. (1985) noted the importance of areas immediately downstream of lake outlets for spawning, as this likely provides a stable, relatively sediment-free environment for egg and alevin development. A limited number of smaller streams with either surface or groundwater storage support significant spawning populations. In the absence of storage, smaller streams may be vulnerable to freezing solid and will be less suitable as spawning habitat.

The fecundity of Yukon River Chinook salmon ranges from about 6,000 eggs/female in the headwaters (JTC 2006) to nearly 9,000 in lower reaches (Healey and Heard 1984). Estimates of survival from the egg-to-emergent fry stage for Chinook salmon are not available for the Yukon River and are few elsewhere. For larger rivers, estimates appear to be in the 30–40% range (Unwin 1986; Bennett et al. 2003; McMichael et al. 2005).

Early life history

The combination of high fecundity and good egg-fry survival means that very large numbers of fry are produced from Chinook salmon spawning areas. For example, 5600 salmon were estimated to have spawned in the Big Salmon watershed in 2005 (JTC 2006). Assuming a 1:1 sex ratio, 7,000 eggs/female and 35% survival, 6.9 million fry could be produced. Spawning occurs along about 150 km of river (Walker et al. 1974), resulting in a yield of about 46,000 fry/km. These very high densities have likely lead to the evolution of dispersal strategies for stream-type Chinook salmon to reduce within-cohort competition (Healey 1991; Bradford and Taylor 1997).

The emergence of Chinook salmon fry from spawning gravels and the downstream dispersal of fry usually takes place in the spring months (Healey 1991). The migration of newly emerged fry from spawning areas in Tatchun Creek, a short lake-fed tributary in the central Yukon peaks in late May (Walker 1976), which is slightly later than the peak observed for upper Fraser River basin in central British Columbia (Bradford and Taylor 1997). Catches of 35–40 mm fry in late May and early June in various sampling programs in the upper Yukon (e.g., Brown et al. 1976) suggest a similar timing among populations. The spatial extent of the downstream migration of newly emergent fry from spawning grounds cannot be assessed with the available information, although migration distances in excess of 100 km have been observed in the Fraser River basin (Bradford and Taylor 1997), especially in instances where a combination of high stream gradient and spring snowmelt freshets create strong currents at the

time of emergence. Thus, there is the potential for considerable interpopulation variation in downstream dispersal depending on the habitat configuration of each stream, as well as annual flow conditions.

A second downstream migration of age-0 juveniles that takes place in late June and early July has been reported at two locations along the Yukon River mainstem. This migration was first observed at the Whitehorse rapids dam in the headwaters of the basin in 1960 and 1973 (Brown et al. 1976; Figure 5); a migration of similar timing was also observed ~600 km downstream at Dawson City by Bradford et al. (2008).

At the time of the June–July migration these juveniles average 50–55 mm in length and weigh ~2 g. Based on a length at emergence in late May of 38 mm, their length increased at a rate of approximately 0.4 mm/d (Bradford et al. 2001). It is not known whether this growth occurred in natal streams, at a location downstream of the natal stream, or during a saltatory downstream migration.

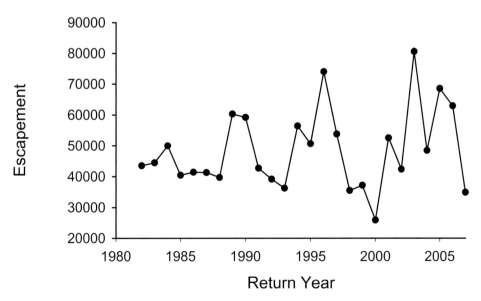

FIGURE 4. Number of adult Chinook salmon *Oncorhynchus tshawytscha* spawning in Canadian waters estimated from a mark–recapture program near the International border (JTC 2006), recalibrated using supplementary telemetry and sonar estimates.

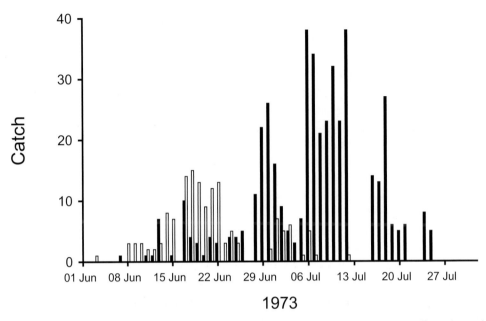

FIGURE 5. Daily catches of juvenile Chinook salmon *Oncorhynchus tshawytscha* yearlings (open bars) and fry (filled bars) migrants captured by a trap located below the Whitehorse rapids dam. Redrawn from Walker et al. (1976). The average length of smolts was 93 mm, and the size of fry at the peak of migration was 55–60 mm.

A migration of underyearlings in late June and July has not often been observed in other stream-type Chinook populations, although it is more common for ocean-type or fall Chinook populations that migrate to estuaries or the ocean after a few months of rearing and growth in freshwater (Lister and Walker 1966; Healey 1991). Prior to dam construction, the downstream migration of underyearlings in the Columbia and Snake Rivers consisted only of newly emerged fish in April (Mains and Smith 1964). This pattern has also been observed in various tributaries of the Fraser River (Bradford and Taylor 1997). One exception is the regulated Nechako River, where there is a prominent June migration of fish into the Fraser River that originated from spawning areas located more than 200 km upstream (Russell et al. 1983). It is possible that the altered hydrograph resulting from dam operations has stimulated a change in the migratory patterns of this population.

A notable feature of the June migration in the Yukon mainstem is that juveniles traveling downstream colonize the many small nonnatal streams that drain into the mainstem. The timing of this colonization has been inferred from minnow trapping and electrofishing in these streams (Perry et al. 2003), and by the operation of a fence on Croucher Creek, near Whitehorse (Bradford et al. 2001). The colonization begins with the aggregation of fish in late June and July in the mixing zones at the confluence of the stream and the mainstem. Synoptic sampling of a large number of nonnatal streams tributary to the Yukon River mainstem suggests that juveniles will colonize any unobstructed stream where the discharge and habitat conditions permit (A. von Finster, unpublished data). While the low-gradient areas within the floodplain of the mainstem river are likely the most densely colonized locations (Mossop and Bradford 2006), juveniles have been captured more than 40 km upstream from the mouths of some nonnatal streams in late summer.

The densities of juvenile Chinook salmon in the lower reaches of these nonnatal streams are relatively high and related to habitat conditions, largely driven by the gradient of the stream channel (Mossop and Bradford 2006). Reach-averaged densities in excess of 1 fish/m² were observed in the best streams, with local densities exceeding 10 fish/m² (Bradford et al. 2001). Interannual variation in the density of juveniles in two nonnatal streams was related to the abundance of parent spawners (Figure 6), suggesting that the colonization of the lower reaches of these streams was partly a function of the supply of juveniles migrating downstream from natal areas.

Tagging studies in Croucher Creek confirmed that fish remained in the stream through the summer months and their mean length increased at a rate of about 0.3 mm/d, reaching a length of 70 mm in September. Croucher Creek is located in the southern Yukon and is relatively warm in July and August (10–15°C, Bradford et al. 2001). In comparison, the streams that were investigated near Dawson City were underlain with extensive permafrost, and temperatures only reach 4–7°C in midsummer and cool rapidly in September (Mossop and Bradford 2006). In these streams the increase in length between July and August was slightly greater than Croucher Creek at 0.5 mm/d; however, growth decreased substantially between August and early October to less than 0.1 mm/d. No relation between the mean size of juveniles in August and summer water temperatures among streams was observed (Figure 7), indicating a remarkable capability of these fish to increase in size at temperatures that are often thought to constrain growth opportunities (Brett 1979).

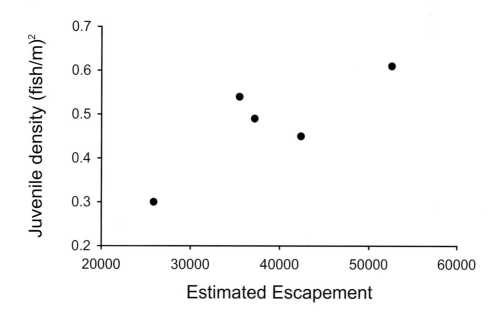

FIGURE 6. The average density of juvenile Chinook salmon *Oncorhynchus tshawytscha* in the lower reaches of two nonnatal streams (Baker and Ensley Creeks) near Dawson City as a function of the estimated Canadian escapement (1998–2001) for those broods.

Limited investigations of juvenile Chinook salmon in mainstem habitats have been conducted in the Yukon Basin. Juveniles have been captured in the Canadian Yukon River mainstem near Minto (Figure 8; Walker 1976) and further downstream in the Dawson City area. Juveniles were found in a variety of habitats near Minto, but were common only at creek mouths (Figure 8) in the Dawson area. The mean size of fish in the mainstem was similar to that observed in nonnatal rearing streams (Figure 7), in spite of the generally warmer temperatures in the larger rivers.

A fall redistribution of juveniles, mainly from tributary streams to mainstem rivers at the onset of winter has been observed for headwater streams in the Columbia basin (Bjornn 1971; Lindsay et al. 1989). No systematic sampling of migrations in the Yukon system at this time of the year has been conducted, and this would be challenging given the sometimes rapid onset of freezing conditions. Survey electrofishing of very small streams in the Dawson area found a sharp decline in abundance in early October (Bradford, unpublished data) relative to that found in midsummer, and a slight increase in the catch of juveniles in the mainstem Yukon River (Figure 7) suggest that downstream migration to overwintering habitats in large rivers may occur. The movement of juvenile Chinook salmon into groundwater-fed off-channel habitats to the Klondike River has also recently been documented (A. von Finster, unpublished data).

The freshwater portion of the life cycle is completed by the seaward migration of smolts after a year (or sometimes two) of rearing. At both the Whitehorse Rapids hydroelectric dam (Figure 5) and nearby Croucher Creek (Bradford et al. 2001,) the seaward migration of yearlings peaked in mid-June. At Dawson City, the peak of migration was slightly earlier (Bradford et al. 2008), which may have been the result of an early timing of out-migration from the large salmon-producing rivers upstream of the trapsite.

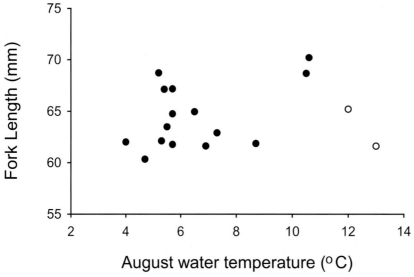

FIGURE 7. The mean fork length of 0+ juvenile Chinook salmon *Oncorhynchus tshawytscha* sampled in August 1999–2001 in small nonnatal streams (solid symbols) and the Yukon River (open symbols) as a function of the water temperature at the time of sampling.

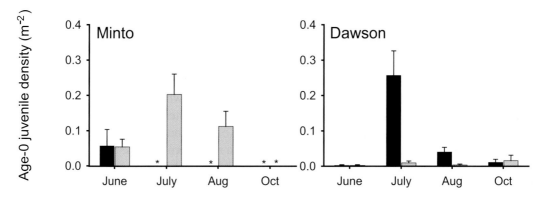

FIGURE 8. Average nearshore densities of age-0 Chinook salmon *Oncorhynchus tshawytscha* captured by single pass electrofishing or single beach seine sets (15 m fine mesh net) in the Yukon River. Data were collected at two locations that differ greatly in suspended sediment loads- Minto, upstream of the White River, and Dawson, 100 km downstream from the inflows of the highly turbid White River. Solid bars are catches at the mouths of small clear creeks, shaded bars are catches at other locations away from creekmouths. Asterisks indicate that no samples were taken. Error bars are 1 SE. Sample sizes vary from 3 to 43.

The timing of the smolt run is later than observed in many southern rivers (Healey 1991), where the migration usually occurs in April or May. A notable exception is the Columbia River, where the yearling migration in 1954 and 1955 peaked in June (Mains and Smith 1964). A later migration may be caused by the need for growth in the spring for juveniles to reach a threshold size before migration. This growth, and consequently the time of migration, may be affected by the environmental conditions, especially the effects of snowmelt on temperature and discharge. At Coucher Creek, the overwintering size of juvenile fish was about 70 mm fork length and 3 g mass, yet at migration, their size had increased to 89 mm and their mass more than doubled to 7.2 g (Bradford et al. 2001). Based on tag recoveries, the date of migration was found to be dependent on the size of the fish at the end of the previous summer, with larger fish being more likely to migrate earlier in the spring than those that were smaller, presumably because the lat-ter group were required to meet the threshold size before migration. In the Salcha River in central Alaska, Loftus and Lenon (1977) noted that most of the stomachs of migrating yearlings were full, with the diet dominated by chironomids, plecoptera, and ephemeroptera. This is consistent with the observation of rapid growth during the spring months in Croucher Creek (Bradford et al. 2001).

The fate of migrating yearlings downstream of the international border is unknown. Based on the fastest migration rates observed for wild stream-type yearlings (50 km/d) in unimpounded segments of the Snake and Columbia Rivers (Raymond 1968), Yukon River Chinook salmon are likely to take more than 40 d to reach the estuary, suggesting a midsummer entry into the ocean. The limited sampling that has been conducted in the estuary yielded only a few juveniles caught mainly in June (Martin et al. 1986). These fish may have come from Alaskan spawning streams located closer to the estuary.

TABLE 1. Estimated composition of juvenile and adult Chinook salmon *Oncorhynchus tshawytscha* migrating past Dawson City as yearling juveniles in 2004 (2002 brood), adult spawners in 2003, and age-0 juveniles in 2004 (2003 brood) based on microsatellite DNA analysis. Sample sizes are indicated in parentheses. NA indicates a stock that was not represented in the baseline at the time of analysis. Locations of stocks are indicated by number in Figure 9.

| | 2002 Brood | 2003 Brood | |
Stock Group	Yearlings (209)	Spawners (558)	Juveniles (271)
Yukon Mainstem	3.2	6.5	0.3
White/Kluane Rivers	1.0	NA	0.1
Headwaters	0.5	5.9	1.3
Teslin River	1.7	6.5	1.8
Stewart River	21.9	17.8	3.8
Pelly River	39.7	18.4	16.7
Carmacks Area	31.2	45.0	75.9

Note: Headwaters stock includes fish spawning upstream of Whitehorse and the Takhini River; Carmacks Area includes the Little Salmon, Big Salmon, Tatchun and Nordenskiold Rivers; Yukon Mainstem is the Chinook population spawning near Minto.

Other stocks are underrepresented in the catch of age-0 fish at Dawson. This includes stocks most distant from Dawson, the upper Yukon and Teslin groups, as well as the Yukon mainstem population, for which juveniles may find sufficient rearing habitat in the mainstem areas adjacent to the spawning grounds (Brown et al. 1976) or in intervening areas. Also underrepresented are juveniles from the nearby Stewart River basins, where most spawning occurs well upstream of the mouth and sufficient habitat may exist immediately downstream of the spawning areas such that juveniles are not forced into migrating downstream as far as the Yukon River. This speculation is supported by the much higher proportions of Pelly, Stewart and Yukon Mainstem origin fish in the sample of yearlings taken at Dawson compared to the fry (Table 1). Although the yearlings were from a different brood year for which we do not have the parental distribution, the more even distribution across stocks indicates that some populations do not migrate as far as underyearlings, and that smolts were produced by habitats nearer to the spawning areas.

Summary

Earlier it was proposed that the presence of compensatory mortality in these populations is likely a complex function of abundance, habitat quantity and quality and annual variation in weather and streamflow. Competition among populations will depend on these factors and the configuration of natal streams in relation to the availability of nonnatal rearing habitas. The DNA analysis of migrating juveniles confirms that there is considerable variability in migrations among populations. Some spawning streams are quite long and the spawning is located in the headwaters resulting in a significant amount of habitat being available to be colonized during emergence and subsequent downstream dispersal. Other river systems are much shorter, leading to a concentration of spawning not far upstream of mainstem rivers. In these cases, it is unlikely that there is enough habitat for a significant portion of the brood within the natal stream; consequently, the occupation of downstream habitats will be more extensive. However, the significance of the migratory component of these populations to overall production is unknown as the proportion of each brood exhibiting the various migratory strategies has not been estimated.

The meta-analysis of abundance data for other populations suggests that limitation in the rearing stage for juvenile fish may be source of compensatory mortality that ultimately leads to population regulation in many Chinook salmon populations. In the Yukon River basin we found that the density of juveniles in two nonnatal streams was related to upstream spawner abundance, suggesting that these habitats were not completely colonized under present-day spawner levels. Spatially extensive sampling, coupled with DNA analysis of population origin is needed to evaluate the extent of juvenile distribution, and the importance of various habitat types to production. The full range of some populations may extend well into the central Yukon Basin in Alaska, though others may be restricted to their natal streams if sufficient habitat exists. Systematic sampling of habitats for both abundance and stock composition over a wide spatial scale and in years of high and low abundance may provide insight into the relationship between habitat type, population size and downstream migration. Similarly, annual sampling for stock composition and abundance at key locations near the periphery of the range of migrants may provide insight into the effects of variation in abundance and environmental conditions on dispersal and survival. Unfortunately, the feasibility of a habitat-based approach to estimating production potential will require these extensive studies to better understand the life histories of these populations.

Acknowledgments

Much of the research carried out by the authors in this paper and the other cited works were funded by the Environmental Strategic Science Research Fund of Fisheries and Oceans Canada with additional support from the Restoration and Enhancement Fund of the Yukon River panel. Jake Duncan and John Candy collected and analyzed the Dawson DNA samples, Jeff Grout, Jean Jang, Brent Mossop, and Russell Perry and many others assisted in the field. Daniel Hirner prepared Figure 9. Lars Jessup and three anonymous reviewers provided comments on a draft manuscript. We thank the AYKSSI program for their interest and support of this work.

References

Beacham, T. D., J. R. Candy, K. L. Jonsen, J. Supernault, M. Wetlo, L. Deng, K. M. Miller, R. E. Withler, and N. Varnavskaya. 2006. Estimation of stock composition and individual identification of Chinook salmon across the Pacific Rim by use of microsatellite variation. Transactions of the American Fisheries Society 135:861–888.

Bennett, D. H., W. P. Connor, and C. A. Eaton. 2003. Substrate composition and emergence success of fall Chinook salmon in the Snake River. Northwest Science 77:93–99.

Bjornn, T. C. 1971. Trout and salmon movements in two Idaho streams as related to temperature, food, stream flow, cover and population density. Transactions of the American Fisheries Society 100:423–438.

Bjornn, T.C. 1978. Survival, production and yield of trout and Chinook salmon in the Lemhi River, Idaho. College of Forestry, Wildlife and Range Sciences Bulletin 27. University of Idaho. Moscow, Idaho.

Bodtker, K. A., R. M. Peterman, and M. J. Bradford. 2006. Accounting for uncertainty in estimates of escapement goals for Fraser River sockeye salmon that are based on productivity of nursery lakes in British Columbia, Canada. North American Journal of Fisheries Management 27:286–302.

Brabets, T. P., B. Wang, and R. H. Meade. 2000. Environmental and hydrologic overview of the Yukon River basin, Alaska and Canada. U.S. Geological Survey Water-Resources Investigations Report 99–4204.

Bradford, M. J. 1995. Comparative review of Pacific salmon survival rates. Canadian Journal of Fisheries and Aquatic Sciences 52:1327–1338.

Bradford, M. J., J. Duncan and J.W. Jang. 2008. Downstream migrations of juvenile salmon and other fishes in the upper Yukon River. Arctic 61(3):255–264.

Bradford, M. J., S. Moodie, J. Grout. 2001. Use of a small non-natal stream of the Yukon River by juvenile Chinook salmon, and the role of ice conditions in their survival. Canadian Journal of Zoology 79:2043–2054.

Bradford, M. J., R. A. Myers, and J. R. Irvine. 2000. Reference points for coho salmon (*Oncorhynchus kisutch*) harvest rates based and escapement goals based on freshwater production. Canadian Journal of Fisheries and Aquatic Sciences 57:677–686.

Bradford, M. J., and G. C. Taylor. 1997. Variation in dispersal behaviour of newly emerged Chinook salmon (*Oncorhynchus tshawytscha*) from the upper Fraser River system, British Columbia. Canadian Journal of Fisheries and Aquatic Sciences 54:1585–1592.

Bradford, M. J., G. C. Taylor, and J. A. Allan. 1997. Empirical review of coho salmon smolt abundance and the prediction of smolt production at the regional level. Transactions of the American Fisheries Society 126:49–64.

Brett, J. R. 1979. Environmental factors and growth. Pages 599–677 *in* W. S. Hoar, D. J. Randall, and J. R. Brett, editors. Fish physiology, Volume VIII, Bioenergetics and growth. Academic Press, New York.

Brown, R. F., M. S. Elson, and L. W. Steigenberger. 1976. Catalogue of aquatic resources of the upper Yukon River drainage (Whitehorse area). Canada Fisheries and Marine Service Technical Report PAC/T 76-4.

Chapman, D. W. 1966. Food and space as regulators of salmonids populations in streams. American Naturalist 100:345–357.

Crisp, D. T. 1993. Population densities of juvenile trout (*Salmo trutta*) in five upland streams and their effects upon growth, survival and dispersal. Journal of Applied Ecology 30:759–771.

Connor, W. P., A. R. Marshall, T.C. Bjornn, and H. L. Burge. 2001. Growth and long-range dispersal by wild subyearling spring and summer Chinook salmon in the Snake River basin. Transactions of the American Fisheries Society 130:1070–1076.

Crone, R. A., and C. E. Bond. 1976. Life history of coho salmon, *Oncorhynchus kisutch*, in Sashin Creek, southeastern Alaska. Fishery Bulletin (U.S.) 74:898–923.

Eiler, J. H., T. R. Spencer, J. J. Pells, and M. M. Masuda. 2006. Stock composition, run timing, and movement patterns of Chinook salmon returning to the Yukon River basin in 2003. U.S. Department of Commerce, National Oceanic and Atmospheric Administration Technical Memorandum NMFS-AFSC-163.

Einum, S., Sundt-Hansen, and K. H. Nislow. 2006. The partitioning of density-dependent dispersal, growth and survival throughout ontogeny in a highly fecund organism. Oikos 113:489–496.

Evenson, D. F., S. J. Hayes, G. Sandone, and D. J. Bergstrom. 2009. Yukon River Chinook salmon: stock status, harvest, and management. Pages 675–701 *in* C. C. Krueger and C. E. Zimmerman, editors. Pacific salmon: ecology and management of western Alaska's populations. American Fisheries Society, Symposium 70, Bethesda, Maryland.

Everest, F. H., and D. W. Chapman. 1972. Habitat selection and spatial interaction by juvenile Chinook salmon and steelhead trout in two Idaho streams. Journal of the Fisheries Research Board of Canada 29:91–100.

Gallinat, M. P. and Ross, L. A. 2007. Tucannon River spring Chinook salmon hatchery evaluation program, 2006 annual report. Washington Department of Fish and Wildlife, Olympia, Washington.

Gilbert, C. H. 1922. The salmon of the Yukon River. U.S. Bureau of Fisheries Bulletin 38:317–349.

Greene, C. M., and T. J. Beechie. 2004. Consequences of potential density-dependent mechanisms on recovery of ocean-type Chinook salmon (*Oncorhynchus tshawytscha*). Canadian Journal of Fisheries and Aquatic Sciences 61:590–602.

Hanski, I. 1999. Metapopulation ecology. Oxford University Press, Oxford, UK.

Healey, M. C. 1991. Life history of Chinook salmon (*Oncorhynchus tshawytscha*). Pages 341–394 *in* C. Groot and L. Margolis, editors. Pacific salmon life histories. UBC Press, Vancouver, B.C.

Healey, M. C., and W. R. Heard. 1984. Inter- and intrapopulation variation in the fecundity of Chinook salmon (*Oncorhynchus tshawytscha*) and its relevance to life history theory. Canadian Journal of Fisheries and Aquatic Sciences 41:476–483.

Hilborn, R., and M. Liermann. 1998. Standing on the shoulders of giants: learning from experience. Reviews in Fish Biology and Fisheries 8:273–283.

Hilborn, R. and C. J. Walters. 1992. Quantitative Fisheries Stock Assessment. Chapman and Hall, New York.

JTC (Joint Technical Committee of the Yukon River US/Canada Panel). 2006. Yukon River salmon 2005 season summary and 2006 season outlook. Alaska Department of Fish and Game, Division of Commercial Fisheries, Regional Information Report No 3A06–03, Anchorage AK.

Lindsay, R. B., B. C. Jonasson, R. K. Schroeder and B. C. Cates. 1989. Spring Chinook salmon in the

Deschutes River, Oregon. Oregon Department of Fish and Wildlife Information Report 89–4.

Lindsey, C. C., and McPhail, J. D. 1986. Zoogeography of fishes of the Yukon and Mackenzie basins. Pages 639–673 in C. H. Hocutt and E. O. Wiley, editors. The zoogeography of North American freshwater fishes. Wiley, New York.

Lister, D. B., and C. E. Walker. 1966. The effect of flow control on freshwater survival of chum, coho and Chinook salmon. Canadian Fish Culturist 37:3–25.

Loftus, W. F., and H. L. Lenon. 1977. Food habits of the salmon smolts, *Oncorhynchus tshawytscha* and *O. keta*, from the Salcha River, Alaska. Transactions of the American Fisheries Society 106:235–240.

Mains, E. M., and J. M. Smith. 1964. The distribution, size, time, and current preferences of seaward migrant Chinook salmon in the Columbia and Snake Rivers. Fisheries Research Papers, Washington Department of Fisheries 2(3):5–43.

Martin, D. J., D. R. Glass, C. J. Whitmus, C. A. Simenstad, D. A. Milward, E. C. Volk, M. L. Stevenson, P. Nunes, M. Savoie, and R. A. Grotefendt. 1986. Distribution, seasonal abundance, and feeding dependencies of juvenile salmon and non-salmonid fishes in the Yukon River Delta. NOAA OCSEAP Final Report, 55(1998):381–770.

McMichael, G. A., C. L. Rakowski, B. B. James, and J. A. Lukas. 2005. Estimated fall Chinook salmon survival to emergence in dewatered redds in a shallow side channel of the Columbia River. North American Journal of Fisheries Management 25:876–884.

Milligan, P. A., W. O. Rublee, D. D. Cornett, and R. A. Johnston. 1985. The distribution and abundance of Chinook salmon (*Oncorhynchus tshawytscha*) in the upper Yukon basin as determined by a radio tagging and spaghetti tagging program: 1982–83. Canadian Technical Report of Fisheries and Aquatic Sciences 1352.

Mossop, B., and M. J. Bradford. 2004. Importance of large woody debris for juvenile Chinook salmon habitat in small boreal forest streams in the upper Yukon River basin, Canada. Canadian Journal of Forest Research 34:1955–1936.

Mossop, B., and M. J. Bradford. 2006. Using thalweg profiling to assess and monitor juvenile salmon (*Oncorhynchus* spp.) habitat in small streams. Canadian Journal of Fisheries and Aquatic Sciences 63:1515–1525.

NFCP (Nechako Fisheries Conservation Program) 2005. Nechako Fisheries Conservation Program technical data review 1988–2002. Vancouver, B.C.

Perry, R. W., M. J. Bradford, and J. A. Grout. 2003.

Effects of disturbance on contribution of energy sources to growth of juvenile Chinook salmon (*Oncorhynchus tshawytscha*) in boreal streams. Canadian Journal of Fisheries and Aquatic Sciences 60:390–400.

Petrosky, C. E., H. A. Schaller, and P. Budy. 2001. Productivity and survival rate trends in the freshwater spawning and rearing stage of Snake River Chinook salmon (*Oncorhynchus tshawtscha*). Canadian Journal of Fisheries and Aquatic Sciences 58:1196–1207.

Raymond, H. L. 1968. Migration rates of yearling Chinook salmon in relation to flows and impoundments in the Columbia and Snake rivers. Transactions of the American Fisheries Society 97:356–359.

Reynolds, J. B. 1997. Ecology of overwintering fishes in Alaskan freshwaters. Pages 281–302 in A. M. Milner and M. W. Oswood, editors. Freshwaters of Alaska: ecological syntheses. Springer-Verlag, New York.

Russell, L. R., K. Conlin, K. Johansen, and U. Orr. 1983. Chinook salmon studies in the Nechako River: 1980, 1981 and 1982. Canadian Manuscript Report of Fisheries and Aquatic Sciences 1728.

Sharma, R., and R. Hilborn. 2001. Empirical relationships between watershed characteristics and coho salmon (*Oncorhynchus kisutch*) smolt abundance in 14 western Washington streams. Canadian Journal of Fisheries and Aquatic Sciences 58:1453–1463.

Shortreed, K. S., J. M. B. Hume, and J. G. Stockner. 2000. Using photosynthetic rates to estimate the juvenile sockeye salmon rearing capacity of British Columbia lakes. Pages 505–521 in E. E. Knudsen, C. R. Steward, D. D. MacDonald, J. E. Williams, and D. W. Reiser, editors. Sustainable fisheries management: Pacific salmon. CRC Press LLC, Boca Raton, New York.

Smith, C. T., W. D. Templin, J. E. Seeb, and L. W. Seeb. 2005. Single nucleotide polymorphisms provide rapid and accurate estimates of the proportions of U.S. and Canadian Chinook salmon caught in Yukon River fisheries. North American Journal of Fisheries Management 25:944–953.

Unwin, M. J. 1986. Stream residence time, size characteristics and migration patterns of juvenile Chinook salmon (*Oncorhynchus tshawtscha*) from a tributary of the Rakaia River, New Zealand. New Zealand Journal of Marine and Freshwater Research 20:231–252.

Volkhardt, G., D. Seiler, L. Fleischer, and K. Kiyohara. 2006. Evaluation of downstream migrant salmon production in 2005 from the Cedar River and Bear Creek. Report to the Washington Department of Fish and Wildlife, Wild Salmon Production/Evaluation Program. Olympia, Washington.

Walker, C. E., R. F. Brown, and D. A. Kato. 1974. Catalogue of fish and stream resources of Carmacks area. Canada Fisheries and Marine Service Technical Report. PAC/T 74–8.

Walker, C. E. 1976. Studies on the freshwater and anadramous fishes of the Yukon River within Canada. Canada Fisheries and Marine Service Technical Report PAC/T 76–7.

Walters, C. J. and S. J. D. Martell. 2004. Fisheries Ecology and Management. Princeton University Press, Princeton, New Jersey.

West, C. J., and J. C. Mason. 1987. Evaluation of sockeye salmon (*Oncorhynchus nerka*) production from the Babine Lake Development Project. Pages 176–190 in H. D. Smith, L. Margolis and C.C. Wood, editors. Sockeye salmon (*Oncorhynchus nerka*) population biology and future management. Canadian Special Publication of Fisheries and Aquatic Sciences 96.

American Fisheries Society Symposium 70:39–52, 2009

Food Supplies of Stream-Dwelling Salmonids

MARK S. WIPFLI[*]

U.S. Geological Survey, Alaska Cooperative Fish and Wildlife Research Unit
School of Fisheries and Ocean Sciences & Department of Biology and Wildlife
Institute of Arctic Biology
University of Alaska Fairbanks, Fairbanks, Alaska 99775, USA

Abstract.—Much is known about the importance of the physical characteristics of salmonid habitat in Alaska and the Pacific Northwest, with far less known about the food sources and trophic processes within these habitats, and the role they play in regulating salmonid productivity. Freshwater food webs supporting salmonids in Alaska rely heavily on nutrient, detritus, and prey subsidies from both marine and terrestrial ecosystems. Adult salmon provide a massive input of marine biomass to riverine ecosystems each year when they spawn, die, and decompose, and are a critical food source for young salmon in late summer and fall; riparian forests provide terrestrial invertebrates to streams, which at times comprise over half of the food ingested by stream-resident salmonids; up-slope, fishless headwater streams are a year-round source of invertebrates and detritus for fish downstream. The quantity of these food resources vary widely depending on source, season, and spatial position within a watershed. Terrestrial invertebrate inputs from riparian habitats are generally the most abundant food source in summer. Juvenile salmonids in streams consume roughly equal amounts of freshwater and terrestrially-derived invertebrates during most of the growing season, but ingest substantial amounts of marine resources (salmon eggs and decomposing salmon tissue) when these food items are present. Quantity, quality, and timing of food resources all appear to be important driving forces in aquatic food web dynamics, community nutrition, and salmonid growth and survival in riverine ecosystems.

Introduction

Salmonid habitat has traditionally been viewed largely from a physical habitat perspective—large wood abundance and distribution, cover, pool size and frequency, water temperature, space, and other attributes associated with physical qualities (Bilby and Bisson 1998; Reeves et al. 1998). Food resources within this habitat, with some exceptions (Chapman 1966; Elliott 1975), have

been given far less consideration. However, because biota require both shelter and nourishment, suitable habitat (space) must also include suitable and reliable food supplies. Food can be a key driver in salmonid populations and productivity in freshwater ecosystems (Chapman 1966; Elliott 1975; Hunt 1975; Dunbrack 1988; Dedual and Collier 1995), and may very likely be the limiting factor in salmonid populations in some streams at certain times of the year. Studies from the Pacific Northwest and southeast

*Corresponding author: mark.wipfli@uaf.edu

Alaska have shown that natural food supplements, carcasses, and eggs from salmon runs for example, increase growth rates, energy stores, and possible survival rates of anadromous and resident salmonids (Bilby et al. 1998; Wipfli et al. 2003; Heintz et al. 2004). In Great Lakes streams, Johnson and Ringler (1979a) noted salmon eggs as being important for rearing salmonids. Prey subsidies entering streams from riparian forests also influenced growth and competition for food among rearing salmonids in Japan (Nakano et al. 1999; Baxter et al. 2005). Food and nutrient supplements to streams have also resulted in increased salmonid growth (Mason 1976; Wipfli et al. 2004), and can have large effects on populations in general, including fishes (Polis et al. 1997). The purpose of this paper is to synthesize what is known about salmonid food supplies, particularly relating to salmonid ecosystems in Alaska, and to provide suggestions for key areas of research.

Nutrient and Food Limitation in Alaska Streams

Prevailing evidence from Alaska stream ecosystems supports the notion that aquatic productivity is nutrient-limited (Peterson et al. 1993; Mitchell and Lamberti 2005). The underlying geology throughout much of Alaska is relatively low in phosphorus (P), compared to other regions like parts of the western U.S. (Grimm and Fisher 1986), leading to low dissolved P concentrations and high nitrogen (N):P ratios in streams, although there are some exceptions in areas with underlying ancient sea beds, such as the southern Kenai peninsula (D. Rinella, Environment and Natural Resources Institute, personal communication). Nutrients in streams stimulate primary producers (algae), that in turn feed stream invertebrates (Stockner and Shortreed 1978; Peterson et al. 1993). These invertebrates are the food base for young salmon

and other fishes in streams and other aquatic habitats (Allen 1951; Chapman 1966; Wipfli 1997; Allan et al. 2003). Subsequently, factors or processes that restrict the production or delivery of food (invertebrates) in streams will most certainly influence the salmonid populations that freshwater ecosystems support.

Sources of Food for Stream-Resident Salmonids in Alaska

It has long been recognized that benthic production in streams is a major source of prey for stream fishes (Allen 1951; Allan et al. 1978; Waters 1988). More recent studies though have highlighted some of the other food sources and trophic pathways that either do or could play a major role in regulating salmonid populations. Nutrients from adult salmon runs stimulate stream periphyton and invertebrate communities (Wipfli et al. 1998, 1999; Claeson et al. 2006; Monaghan and Milner 2008), further enhancing existing benthic production and contributing to the benthic food base (Figure 1). Multiple marine-derived nutrient (MDN) effects on aquatic and riparian ecosystems have been documented throughout the Pacific Northwest and beyond (Mathisen et al. 1988; Bilby et al. 1998; Stockner 2003; Zhang et al. 2003; Johnston et al. 2004; Bartz and Naiman 2005; Yanai and Kochi 2005). Eggs from spawning salmon and fragments of flesh from rotting, postspawning salmon are food for young salmon and other fishes, and augment the growth rates and condition of fishes that feed on these foods (Bilby et al. 1998; Wipfli et al. 2003; Heintz et al. 2004; Hicks et al. 2005; Lang et al. 2006). Salmon carcasses hauled out of streams by scavengers or washed ashore during floods are oviposited upon by adult flesh flies; maggots quickly devour the rotting salmon tissue (Johnson and Ringler 1979b; Hocking and Reimchen 2006) and often get flushed back into streams from

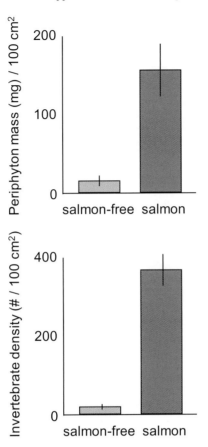

FIGURE 1. Benthic periphyton mass and invertebrate density in salmon and salmon-free reaches of a salmon stream in southeastern Alaska. Redrawn from Wipfli et al. (1998).

rain and consumed by juvenile fishes (M.S. Wipfli, personal observation) (Figure 2). Riparian forests and associated habitats also provide a large amount of food, largely in the form of terrestrial insects, to stream fishes in Alaska (Wipfli 1997) (Figure 3). The same phenomenon in salmonids and other fishes has been observed in other parts of the world, but sometimes to a lesser extent (Loftus and Lenon 1977; Mason and Macdonald 1982; Nielsen 1992; Edwards and Huryn 1995; Cloe and Garman 1996; Kawaguchi and Nakano 2001; Utz and Hartman 2007). Further, streams lined with at least some deciduous plant species may provide more prey than those surrounded by coniferous species (Allan et al. 2003; Romero et al. 2005) (Figure 4). Fishless headwater streams deliver a year-round supply of nutrients, organic detritus, and invertebrates to foodwebs downstream that contain rearing salmonids (Wipfli and Gregovich 2002) (Figure 5). Again, deciduous plants along headwater streams increase the amount of prey provided to fishes and other consumers in downstream habitats (Piccolo and Wipfli 2002) (Figure 6). Nutrients and food from these sources substantiate basal food supplies for stream salmonids (Figure 7).

Variability in Food Supply

Much natural variation exists in the amount and timing of prey and other food inputs into streams, both spatially and tem-

FIGURE 2. Blow fly (Diptera) larvae consuming salmon carcasses along the Kenai River in southcentral Alaska.

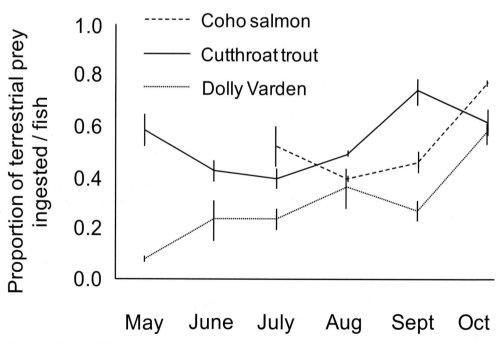

FIGURE 3. Terrestrial invertebrates ingested by stream-resident salmonids as a proportion of total prey (terrestrial and aquatic invertebrates) in southeastern Alaska. Redrawn from Wipfli (1997).

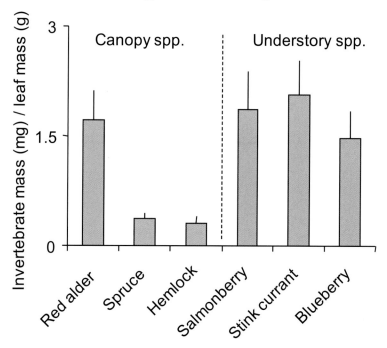

FIGURE 4. Terrestrial invertebrate mass on riparian plant foliage along southeastern Alaska streams. Redrawn from Allan et al. (2003).

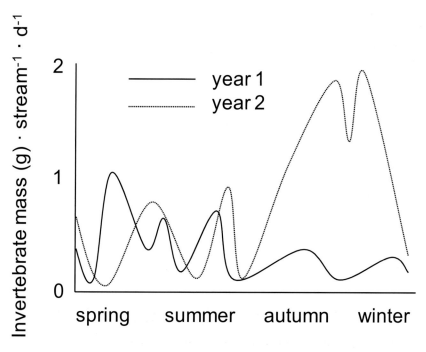

FIGURE 5. Drift of invertebrates from fishless headwater streams to downstream fish-bearing habitats in southeastern Alaska. Redrawn from Wipfli and Gregovich (2002).

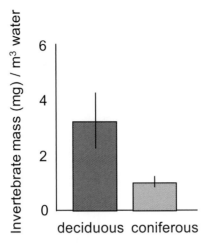

FIGURE 6. Drift of aquatic and terrestrial invertebrates from fishless headwater streams to downstream fish-bearing streams within deciduous (red alder) and coniferous (largely western hemlock and Sitka spruce) riparian cover in southeastern Alaska. Redrawn from Piccolo and Wipfli (2002).

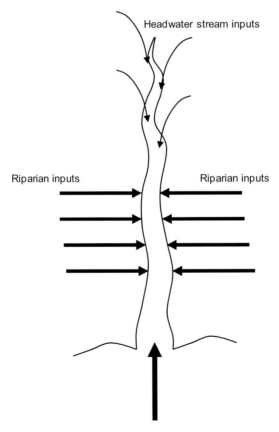

FIGURE 7. Sources of food for stream-dwelling salmonids, originating from marine, terrestrial, and headwater sources, that supplement in-stream, basal food production.

porally. Salmon life histories dictate when, where, and how much marine-derived biomass and nutrients (MDN) get deposited in streams. Sockeye salmon *Oncorhynchus nerka* and Chinook salmon *O. tshawytscha* return to freshwater early in the season (summer), relative to other salmon species, and often distribute themselves more widely throughout stream networks, than do pink *O. gorbuscha* and chum *O. keta* salmon (Groot and Margolis 1991). The latter tend to spawn lower in drainages, closer to salt water, and adults return mid- to late summer, and in some areas, into fall for systems receiving late-run chum salmon. Coho *O. kisutch* salmon, like sockeye and Chinook salmon, distribute themselves more widely in drainages, often penetrating well into headwater reaches, and return to their natal streams in autumn and even early winter (Groot and Margolis 1991). Watersheds that receive largely pink and chum salmon returns, could see a large but short influx of salmon, and therefore a pulse of eggs, decomposing salmon tissue, and MDN, occurring sometime in summer. Conversely, systems receiving returns of other species such as sockeye, Chinook, and coho salmon, may experience a more gradual and moderate MDN influx throughout summer, fall, and into winter, more characteristic of the Copper River Delta of southcentral Alaska, and the Kuskokwim and Yukon rivers of west and central Alaska. Run sizes often vary widely from drainage to drainage, among stream reaches within drainages, and from year to year, and therefore will affect the foodwebs benefiting from this MDN influx. A more gradual and moderate influx spread across a longer stretch of the year, particularly if received during the warmer months of summer and early fall, will likely benefit consumers of this material, as opposed to large, but short lived runs. Salmon harvesting variably reduces escapements, depending upon the system, and can greatly reduce MDN inputs into watersheds.

Inputs of terrestrial invertebrates from streamside plants is also highly variable, with inputs coinciding with growing season (largely summer), and is highly dependant on invertebrate life history, degree-days, and weather, among others (Price 1997). Stream-dwelling fishes see the largest terrestrial inputs in summer, when insects and other invertebrates are generally most active and abundant. Spatial differences within drainages are also likely large. River continuum theory states that small streams receive more allochthonous inputs from their riparian habitats than larger streams, based on stream area, and therefore it follows that smaller streams nearer the headwaters would receive greater inputs of terrestrial insects than larger streams (Vannote et al. 1980), decreasing as the stream margin to stream width ratio decreases. Terrestrial prey inputs were large in several small streams in southeastern Alaska during the summer months, then tapered into autumn (Wipfli 1997; Allan et al. 2003). Outbreaks of forest insect pests, such as alder sawflies or spruce bark beetles, would also be expected to provide sudden and large, but potentially short-lived pulses of prey to stream fishes. As with MDN inputs, more gradual and moderate inputs of terrestrial prey, over a broader window of time, would likely be more beneficial to consumers simply as a consequence of food reliability, compared to more sudden and short-lived pulses of prey. This would simply allow consumers more time to take advantage of the prey resource subsidy.

As with MDN and terrestrial prey inputs, delivery of prey from headwater habitats to fishes is highly variable, both across streams, and among seasons and years (Wipfli and Gregovich 2002). Headwater delivery can be relatively large in spring and summer, probably a function of insect life history and greater activity levels, but can also be large during periods of high rainfall in autumn, where the rain events act to flush invertebrates from the high gradient headwater streams (Wipfli and Gregovich 2002). Relative to the amount of food that originates from terrestrial and marine sources, direct headwater sources appear to be of little consequence for downstream fish at the large watershed scale, but potentially very important locally where fishless headwaters feed immediately into fish-bearing reaches. Many invertebrates drifting from headwaters may not drift far, in some cases just a few meters (E. Green, University of Alaska Fairbanks, personal communicaiton), so they may not benefit consumers further downstream of the immediate zone of subsidy.

Implications for the Arctic-Yukon-Kuskokwim (AYK) Region

Although little published work on food resources important for fishes in the AYK region exists (although see Loftus and Lenon 1977), the patterns seen and lessons learned from other parts of Alaska, the Pacific Northwest, and other places have relevance to AYK systems. The same fundamental trophic processes exist—in headwaters, the flow of prey from fishless to fish-bearing streams; in fish-bearing habitats, terrestrial prey infall into streams; and in streams receiving salmon runs, salmon-derived food (e.g., salmon eggs) and marine nutrient inputs (Figure 7). And because these processes exist, they are also predicted to also influence salmonid food webs and rearing salmonids, as they do in other parts of the state (Wipfli 1997; Wipfli and Gregovich 2002; Wipfli et al. 2003).

There are, however, certain physical, chemical, and biological conditions that could govern the extent to which these trophic processes are expressed, and their effects felt, lesser or greater, by fish communities. For example, underlying geology influences stream water chemistry, including concentrations of nutrients that limit primary production (Grimm and Fisher 1986). Phosphorus, and to a lesser extent nitrogen, are often limiting in streams, and P seems to be the prevailing limiting nutrient in most Alaska streams (Peterson et al. 1993; J. Jones University of Alaska Fairbanks, personal communication), unlike places where salmon carcasses in already nutrient-rich systems have had little effect on producers (Rand et al. 1992). Concentrations and relative proportions of nutrients in AYK systems will influence associated primary production, and subsequent aquatic productivity, influencing the amount of benthic invertebrates available as prey for fishes. Physical disturbance from spawners, although often localized and brief, may also influence how the benthos responds to MDN influx (Moore et al. 2004; Monaghan and Milner 2009). Another example is ecoregional control of both instream and riparian processes. Allochthonous inputs of plant material may differ – quantity, quality, and timing of inputs – depending upon riparian plant cover (e.g., species and density). Further, the studies in Alaska that have shown a strong dependence by stream fishes on terrestrial prey were completed in coastal spruce-hemlock rainforests of southeastern Alaska, which is a far different ecoregion and climate than AYK, which is largely interior lowlands and spruce-hardwood forested lowland and uplands (USGS 1995). Forest and other plant cover types could play a major role in the amount, timing, and type of terrestrial invertebrates that fall prey to fishes from riparian systems (Allan et al. 2003). The dryer climates of interior AYK could be much different than the coastal regions of AYK and throughout Alaska. Also, the timing, magnitude, and duration of salmon runs would influence the effects felt from MDN. Marine inputs from salmon spread across a broader season would likely have different overall effects than the same amount of salmon biomass entering nearly all at once, simply allowing consumers a broader window of time to take advantage of the marine pulse. For example, the strong runs of pink salmon in some southeastern Alaska streams, occurring over a relatively short duration, can be expected to have different food web effects than runs of Chinook and chum salmon that may span a much broader window, even though nearly an equal amount of marine biomass may enter any given systems. Finally, turbidity from glacial melt will alter fish reactive distances for feeding fish, affecting predation rates (Sweka and Hartman 2001). The AYK region is heavily influenced by glaciers, thus turbidity and subsequently the extent to which feeding fishes can take advantage of prey resources is altered (reduced).

Research Needs

Although gains have been made in understanding the factors and processes that control foodweb and fish productivity in riverine ecosystems, much needs to be learned about the role of nutrients and food, and interactions with other habitat features. The topics below are some key areas needing research. This is by no means an exhaustive list, but merely a short-list of immediate needs to fill obvious and large knowledge gaps.

1. Extent to which food controls fish demographics and production

Much effort has gone into understanding effects of habitat on fishes throughout the Pacific Northwest, but relatively little has been studied on food (beyond simply diet analyses), especially the extent to which it plays a role in freshwater salmon productivity and demographics. Missing is a thorough understanding of the role of food, and the fundamental nutrient cycling, flux, and movement that supports basal resources for fishes, not only for AYK and other parts of Alaska, but globally. An understanding is required of the the po-

tential benefits of different food sources and types across different fish species, ages, and life history types. For example, some species likely benefit more from MDN or terrestrial subsidies than others. Knowing how important food resources are in controlling salmonid production in freshwater systems, relative to physical habitat, is needed and would greatly benefit the understanding of salmonid ecology and management in fresh water. Also knowing how much of the food supply translates into actual availability and usage by fishes is crucial, although it can be very difficult to accurately assess (from feeding inefficiencies as a consequence of competition, predator avoidance, food resource saturation, drifting particulates, turbidity, etc.). In a similar vein, understanding how food supplies and temperature interact to influence fish bioenergetics, in both food-limited and food-surplus conditions (Dion and Hughes 2004), would help clarify key environmental controls on salmonids. This information would not only be very useful in the AYK region, but is also needed throughout Alaska and beyond. Also, beginning to understand the nutritional value of the different food sources, and if and how food quality (e.g., lipid-rich salmon eggs versus schleritized adult beetles) (Cummins and Wuycheck 1971) plays a role in salmon demographics and productivity is also an area ripe for research; it would greatly advance the understanding of salmonid ecology, and could benefit management.

2. Key food sources for fishes—watershed scales

Knowing the interplay between physical habitat and food, including how habitat controls food resources would be valuable to understand more thoroughly. Getting a fuller understanding of the relative importance of the various food sources—e.g., headwaters, terrestrial prey infall, marine inputs, hyporheic and benthic production—would aid the-understanding of which trophic processes are most important for fishes, throughout different parts of the drainage and different times of the year, and would be helpful for understanding broader fish ecology and productivity. Is in-stream benthic production enough to support the level of fish production a given unit of habitat is capable of supporting, or do fishes rely on 'external subsidies' from marine (MDN) or terrestrial sources? Does more food mean more fish or fish biomass? What is the relative importance of the various food sources through time (across season and over years) and space (throughout a drainage)? Another very important aspect is the different nature of lake versus stream ecosystems, and the difference in the way they process and their food webs utilize nutrient pulses. Lake systems may reach carrying capacity more quickly, given their relatively more closed nature, compared to streams. Lake food webs are primary production, plankton based; streams are benthic insect dominated and these food webs rely heavily on allochthonous litter for basal resources. The hyporheic zone can be a refuge and source of insects for stream benthic communities, but not the case for plankton in lakes. Streams also have much more nutrient and prey exchange with their riparian zones than lakes. These differences clearly need to be fleshed out and better understood. Lake systems support sockeye salmon, riverine systems mostly support the other salmon species.

3. Under what conditions do marine-derived nutrients affect ecosystem and species productivity

Although much has been learned about effects of MDN throughout the Pacific Northwest and Alaska (Bilby et al. 1998; Wipfli et al. 1998; Gende et al. 2002; Schindler et al. 2003), especially within the past ten years, the surface has barely been scratched. There is a need to move beyond small scale and case studies, and look at the broader (through time and space) implications and effects. What effect does run timing have on the extent of MDN effects (summer versus fall runs)? What are the effects of run duration and magnitude on consumers? What physical (e.g., underlying geology) and chemical (baseline nutrient concentrations) drivers, and across what scales, influence the extent to which MDN effects are felt? Evidence suggests that many environmental variables exist that modulate the extent to which MDN effects are felt, including disturbance from spawning, light levels, stream flow and inherent aquatic productivity, and others (Wipfli et al. 1998; Ambrose et al. 2004; Chaloner et al. 2004; Moore et al. 2004; Wilzbach et al. 2005; Claeson et al. 2006). Also, which species rely on MDN? When? Where?

4. Extent and type of nutrient limitation in freshwater ecosystems

Although work on nutrient limitation is scant, the evidence that does exist suggests that aquatic systems throughout much of Alaska are nutrient limited (Peterson et al. 1993; Mitchell and Lamberti 2005). If systems are P or N limited, then events like salmon runs would be expected to have a greater positive effect on productivity, from the sudden influx of N and P, than systems that are not nutrient limited (c.f. Rand et al. 1992). There are many questions around the topic of stream nutrients and productivity that persist. To what extent are AYK and other Alaska freshwater systems limited by nutrients? Is P the predominant limiting nutrient, or N, or is co-limitation more often the case? Some evidence from southeastern Alaska suggests that carbon (energy) rather than nutrients (N or P) plays a more important role in affecting fishes (Wipfli et al., unpublished data). Salmon eggs are a lipid-rich, high energy food. A dose of this high quality carbon for rearing fishes, when salmon spawn in late summer or fall, just before going into the winter, could quite possibly have very important consequences for juvenile fishes that other food sources don't offer. Or are systems limited by a number of trophic factors—nutrients for bottom-up production, and carbon for upper trophic levels? Further, when, where, and to what extent do consumer species regulate food availability? Predators and competitors can greatly modify to extent to which consumers (e.g., juvenile salmonids) capitalize on food resources, and under certain conditions can largely override food effects and benefits.

5. Resource management implications and consequences

How natural resources are managed—at sea, on land, and in freshwater—will clearly influence riverine trophic processes and subsequent aquatic and fish productivity. Salmon harvests, at sea and in freshwater, will reduce MDN flux to rearing habitats, but how much is acceptable, and without negative consequences? Gresh et al. (2000) pointed out that Pacific Northwest systems are suffering a serious nutrient deficit from chronically low salmon returns. Understanding how many spawners are necessary to keep riverine ecosystems productive (particularly in those with inherently low nutrient concentrations as a function of specific geologies that naturally provide very little nutrients to streams during weathering processes, characteristic of much of Alaska) will aid in determining system-specific, ecologically-based escapement goals. Climate change will also affect MDN influx to streams as marine distributions likely shift north, shrink, or even disappear with warming (Welch et al. 1998; Mantua 2009, this volume), compounding harvesting effects. On land, contaminated runoff and effluents from mining, agriculture, and municipalities, and sedimentation from logging will affect in-stream food sources as aquatic insects are very sensitive to contamination and environ-

mental quality (Naiman and Bilby 1998). Finally, understanding how forest management activities such as clear-cut logging, riparian restoration, and young-growth forest thinning ultimately affect riparian forest conditions and productivity, and in turn affect the flow of food from terrestrial systems to stream salmonids is important (Wipfli 1997; Piccolo and Wipfli 2002; Allan et al. 2003).

Recommendations.—From a research perspective, answering these questions will go a long way towards understanding the broader controls of habitat, and the influence of food and nutrients within these habitats, on the demographics, productivity, and ecology of stream fishes. This information will contribute to a fuller understanding of the environmental drivers that generate population fluctuations and regulate salmonid productivity in freshwater, and will also shed light on how resource management activities in turn feed back to affect food webs and fish productivity. It is recommended that these questions be approached and research programs be planned in concert with resource managers to carefully craft hypotheses that provide not only sound science but also information that will be most useful for aiding resource management. It is also recommended that information on food resources for fishes, including existing (albeit scant) and new as it becomes available, be carefully contemplated and considered, and incorporated into management decisions as much as practical and possible.

References

Allan, J. D. 1978. Trout predation and the size composition of stream drift. Limnology and Oceanography 23:1231–1237.

Allan, J. D., M. S. Wipfli, J. P. Caouette, A. Prussian, and J. Rodgers. 2003. Influence of streamside vegetation on terrestrial invertebrate inputs to salmonid food webs. Canadian Journal of Fisheries and Aquatic Sciences 60:309–320.

Allen, K. R. 1951. The Horowki stream: a study of a trout population. New Zealand Marine Department Fisheries Bulletin 10.

Ambrose, H. E., M. A. Wilzbach, and K. W. Cummins. 2004. Periphyton response to increased light and salmon carcass introduction in northern California streams. Journal of the North American Benthological Society 23:701–712.

Bartz, K. K., and R. J. Naiman. 2005. Effects of salmon-borne nutrients on riparian soils and vegetation in Southwest Alaska. Ecosystems 8:529–545.

Baxter, C. V., K. D. Fausch, and W. C. Saunders. 2005. Tangled webs: reciprocal flows of invertebrate prey link streams and riparian zones. Freshwater Biology 50:201–220.

Bilby, R. E., and P. A. Bisson. 1998. Function and distribution of large woody debris. Pages 324–346 in R. J. Naiman and R. E. Bilby, editors. River ecology and management. Springer, New York.

Bilby, R. E., B. R. Fransen, P. A. Bisson, and J. K. Walter. 1998. Response of juvenile coho salmon (*Oncorhynchus kisutch*) and steelhead (*Oncorhynchus mykiss*) to the addition of salmon carcasses to two streams in southwestern Washington, USA. Canadian Journal of Fisheries and Aquatic Sciences 55:1909–1918.

Chaloner, D. T., G. A. Lamberti, R. W. Merritt, N. L. Mitchell, P. H. Ostrom, and M. S. Wipfli. 2004. Variation in responses to spawning Pacific salmon among three southeastern Alaska streams. Freshwater Biology 49:587–599.

Chapman, D. W. 1966. Food and space as regulators of salmonid populations in streams. American Naturalist 100:345–357.

Claeson, S. M., J. L. Li, J. E. Compton, and P. A. Bisson. 2006. Response of nutrients, biofilm, and benthic insects to salmon carcass addition. Canadian Journal of Fisheries and Aquatic Sciences 63:1230–1241.

Cloe, W. W., and G. C. Garman. 1996. The energetic importance of terrestrial arthropod inputs to three warm-water streams. Freshwater Biology 36:105–114.

Cummins, K. W., and J. C. Wuycheck. 1971. Caloric equivalents for investigations in ecological energetics. Internationale Vereinigung fuer Theoretische und Angewandte Limnologie Verhandlungen 18:1–158.

Dedual, M., and Collier, K. J. 1995. Aspects of juvenile rainbow trout (*Oncorhynchus mykiss*) diet in relation to food supply during summer in the lower Tongariro River, New Zealand. New Zealand Journal of Marine and Freshwater Research 29:381–391.

Dion, C. A., and N. F. Hughes. 2004. Testing the ability of a temperature-based model to predict the growth of age-0 Arctic grayling. Transactions of the American Fisheries Society 133:1047–1050.

Dunbrack, R. L. 1988. Feeding of juvenile coho salmon (*Oncorhynchus kisutch*): maximum appetite, sustained feeding rate, appetite return, and body size. Canadian Journal of Fisheries and Aquatic Sciences 45:1191–1196.

Edwards, E. D., and Huryn, A. D. 1995. Annual contribution of terrestrial invertebrates to a New Zealand trout stream. New Zealand Journal of Marine and Freshwater Research 29:467–477.

Elliott, J. M. 1975. Number of meals in a day, maximum weight of food consumed in a day and maximum rate of feeding for brown trout, *Salmo trutta* L. Freshwater Biology 5:287–303.

Gende, S. M., R. T. Edwards, M. F. Willson, and M. S. Wipfli. 2002. Pacific salmon in aquatic and terrestrial ecosystems. BioScience 52:917–928.

Grimm, N. B., and S. G. Fisher. 1986. Nutrient limitation in a Sonoran Desert stream. Journal of the North American Benthological Society 5:2–15.

Gresh, T., J. Lichatowich, and P. Schoonmaker. 2000. An estimation of historic and current levels of salmon production in the northeast Pacific ecosystem: evidence of a nutrient deficit in the freshwater systems of the Pacific Northwest. Fisheries 25(1):15–21.

Groot, C., and L. Margolis. 1991. Pacific salmon: life histories. University of British Columbia Press, Vancouver.

Heintz, R. A., B. D. Nelson, J. P. Hudson., M. Larsen, L. Holland, and M. S. Wipfli. 2004. Marine subsidies in freshwater: Effects of salmon carcasses on the lipid class and fatty acid composition of juvenile coho salmon. Transactions of the American Fisheries Society 133:559–567.

Hicks, B. J., M. S. Wipfli, D. W. Lang, and M. E. Lang. 2005. Marine-derived nitrogen and carbon in freshwater-riparian food webs of the Copper River Delta, southcentral Alaska. Oecologia 144:558–569.

Hocking, M. D., and T. E. Reimchen. 2006. Consumption and distribution of salmon (*Oncorhynchus* spp.) nutrients and energy by terrestrial flies. Canadian Journal of Fisheries and Aquatic Sciences 63:2076–2086.

Hunt, R. L. 1975. Food relations and behavior of salmonid fishes. 6.1 Use of terrestrial invertebrates as food by salmonids. Pages 137–151 in A. D. Hassler, editor. Coupling of land and water systems. Springer, New York.

Johnson, J. H., and N. H. Ringler. 1979a. Predation on Pacific salmon eggs by salmonids in a tributary of Lake Ontario. Journal of Great Lakes Research 5:177–181.

Johnson, J. H., and N. H. Ringler. 1979b. The occurrence of blow-fly larvae (Diptera: Calliphoridae) on salmon carcasses and their utilization as food by juvenile salmon and trout. Great Lakes Entomologist 12:137–139.

Johnston, N. T., E. A. MacIsaac, P. J. Tschaplinski, and K. J. Hall. 2004. Effects of the abundance of spawning sockeye salmon (*Oncorhynchus nerka*) on nutrients and algal biomass in forested streams. Canadian Journal of Fisheries and Aquatic Sciences 61:384–403.

Kawaguchi, Y., and S. Nakano. 2001. Contribution of terrestrial invertebrates to the annual resource budget for salmonids in forest and grassland reaches of a headwater stream. Freshwater Biology 46:303–316.

Lang, D. W., G. H. Reeves, D. D. Hall, and M. S. Wipfli. 2006. The influence of fall-spawning coho salmon (*Oncorhynchus kisutch*) on growth and production of juvenile coho salmon rearing in beaver ponds on the Copper River Delta, Alaska. Canadian Journal of Fisheries and Aquatic Sciences 63:917–930.

Loftus, W. F., and H. L. Lenon. 1977. Food habits of the salmon smolts, *Oncorhynchus tshawytscha* and *O. keta*, from the Salcha River, Alaska. Transactions of the American Fisheries Society 106:235–240.

Mantua, N. 2009. Patterns of change in climate and Pacific salmon production. Pages 1143–1157 *in* C. C. Krueger and C. E. Zimmerman, editors. Pacific salmon: ecology and management of western Alaska's populations. American Fisheries Society, Symposium 70, Bethesda, Maryland.

Mason, C. F., and S. M. Macdonald. 1982. The input of terrestrial invertebrates from tree canopies to a stream. Freshwater Biology 12:305–311.

Mason, J. C. 1976. Response of underyearling coho salmon to supplemental feeding in a natural stream. Journal of Wildlife Management 40:775–788.

Mathisen, O. A., P. L. Parker, J. J. Goering, T. C. Kline, P. H. Poe, and R. S. Scalan. 1988. Recycling of marine elements transported into freshwater systems by anadromous salmon. Internationale Vereinigung fur Theoretische und Angewandte Limnologie 23:2249–2258.

Mitchell, N. L., and G. A. Lamberti. 2005. Responses in dissolved nutrients and epilithon abundance to spawning salmon in southeast Alaska streams. Limnology and Oceanography 50:217–227.

Monaghan, K. A., and A. M. Milner. 2008. Salmon carcasses as a marine-derived resource for benthic macroinvertebrates in a developing postglacial stream, Alaska Canadian Journal of Fisheries and Aquatic Sciences 65:1342–1351.

Monaghan, K. A., and A. M. Milner 2009. The effect of anadromous salmon redd construction on macroinvertebrate communities in a recently formed stream in coastal Alaska. Journal of the North American Benthological Society 28(1):153–166.

Moore, J. W., D. E. Schindler, and M. D. Scheuerell. 2004. Disturbance of freshwater habitats by anadromous salmon in Alaska. Oecologia 139:298–308.

Naiman, R. J. and R. E. Bilby, editors. 1998. River ecology and management. Springer-Verlag, New York.

Nakano, S., Miyasaka, H., and Kuhara, N. 1999. Terrestrial-aquatic linkages: Riparian arthropod inputs alter trophic cascades in a stream food web. Ecology 80:2435–2441.

Nielsen, J. L. 1992. Microhabitat-specific foraging behavior, diet, and growth of juvenile coho salmon. Transactions of the American Fisheries Society 121:617–634.

Peterson B. J., and 16 co-authors. 1993. Biological responses of a tundra river to fertilization. Ecology 74:653–672.

Piccolo, J. J., and M. S. Wipfli. 2002. Does red alder (*Alnus rubra*) along headwater streams increase the export of invertebrates and detritus from headwaters to fish-bearing habitats in southeastern Alaska? Canadian Journal of Fisheries and Aquatic Sciences 59:503–513.

Polis, G. A., W. B. Anderson, and R. D. Holt. 1997. Toward an integration of landscape and food web ecology: the dynamics of spatially subsidized food webs. Annual Review of Ecology and Systematics 28:289–316.

Price, P. W. editors 1997. Insect ecology. Wiley, New York.

Rand, P. S., C. A. S. Hall, W. H. McDowell, N. H. Ringler, J. G. Kennen. 1992. Factors limiting primary productivity in Lake Ontario tributaries receiving salmon migrations. Canadian Journal of Fisheries and Aquatic Sciences 49:2377–2385.

Reeves, G. H., P. A. Bisson, and J. M. Dambacher. 1998. Fish communities. Pages 200–234 *in* R. J. Naiman and R. E. Bilby, editors. River ecology and management. Springer, New York.

Romero, N., R. E. Gresswell, and J. L. Li. 2005. Changing patterns in coastal cutthroat trout (*Oncorhynchus clarki clarki*) diet and prey in a gradient of deciduous canopies. Canadian Journal of Fisheries and Aquatic Sciences 62:1797–1807.

Schindler, D. E., M. D. Scheuerell, J. W. Moore, S. M. Gende, T. B. Francis, and W. J. Palen. 2003. Pacific salmon and the ecology of coastal ecosystems. Frontiers in Ecology and the Environment 1:31–37.

Stockner, J. G., editor. 2003. Nutrients in salmonid ecosystems: sustaining production and biodiversity. American Fisheries Society, Symposium 34, Bethesda, Maryland.

Stockner, J. G., and K. R. Shortreed. 1978. Enhancement of autotrophic production by nutrient addition in a coastal rainforest stream on Vancouver Island. Journal of the Fisheries Research Board of Canada 35:28–34.

Sweka, J. A., K. J. Hartman. 2001. Influence of turbidity on brook trout reactive distance and foraging success. Transactions of the American Fisheries Society 130: 138–146.

USGS. 1995. Ecoregions of Alaska. U.S. Government Printing Office, Washington, D.C.

Utz, R. M., and K. J. Hartman. 2007. Identification of critical prey items to Appalachian brook trout (*Salvelinus fontinalis*) with emphasis on terrestrial organisms. Hydrobiologia 575:259–270.

Vannote, R. L., Minshall, G. W., Cummins, K. W., Sedell, J. R., and Cushing, C. E. 1980. The river continuum concept. Canadian Journal of Fisheries and Aquatic Sciences 37:130–137.

Waters, T. F. 1988. Fish production-benthos production relationships in trout streams. Polskie Archiwum Hydrobiologii 35:545–561.

Welch, D. W., Y. Ishida, and K. Nagasawa. 1998. Thermal limits and ocean migrations of sockeye salmon (*Oncorhynchus nerka*): long-term consequences of global warming. Canadian Journal of Fisheries and Aquatic Sciences 55:937–948.

Wilzbach, M. A., B. C. Harvey, J. L. White, and R. J. Nakamoto. 2005. Effects of riparian canopy opening and salmon carcass addition on the abundance and growth of resident salmonids. Canadian Journal of Fisheries and Aquatic Sciences 62:58–67.

Wipfli, M. S., J. P. Hudson, and J. P. Caouette. 2004. Restoring productivity of salmon-based food webs: contrasting effects of salmon carcass and salmon analog additions on stream-resident salmonids. Transactions of the American Fisheries Society 133:1440–1454.

Wipfli, M. S., J. P. Hudson, J. P. Caouette, and D. T. Chaloner. 2003. Marine subsidies in freshwater ecosystems: salmon carcasses increase the growth rates of stream-resident salmonids. Transactions of the American Fisheries Society 132:371–381.

Wipfli, M. S., and D. P. Gregovich. 2002. Export of invertebrates and detritus from fishless headwater streams in southeastern Alaska: implications for downstream salmonid production. Freshwater Biology 47:957–969.

Wipfli, M. S., J. P. Hudson, D. T. Chaloner, and J. P. Caouette. 1999. Influence of salmon spawner densities on stream productivity in Southeast Alaska, USA. Canadian Journal of Fisheries and Aquatic Sciences 56:1600–1611.

Wipfli, M. S., J. P. Hudson, and J. P. Caouette. 1998. Influence of salmon carcasses on stream productivity: response of biofilm and benthic macroinvertebrates in southeastern Alaska, USA. Canadian Journal of Fisheries and Aquatic Sciences 55:1503–1511.

Wipfli, M. S. 1997. Terrestrial invertebrates as salmonid prey and nitrogen sources in streams: contrasting old-growth and young-growth riparian forests in southeastern Alaska, USA. Canadian Journal of Fisheries and Aquatic Sciences 54:1259–1269.

Yanai, S., and K. Kochi. 2005. Effects of salmon carcasses on experimental stream ecosystems in Hokkaido, Japan. Ecological Research 20:471–480.

Zhang, Y., J. N. Negishi, J. S. Richardson, and R. Kolodziejczyk. 2003. Impact of marine-derived nutrients on stream ecosystem functioning. Proceedings of the Royal Society of London, B 270:2117–2123.

American Fisheries Society Symposium 70:53–71, 2009

Bioenergetic Ontogeny: Linking Climate and Mass-Specific Feeding to Life-Cycle Growth and Survival of Salmon

DAVID A. BEAUCHAMP[*]

U.S. Geological Survey, Washington Cooperative Fisheries and Wildlife Research Unit
University of Washington School of Aquatic and Fisheries Sciences
Box 355020, Seattle, Washington 98105, USA

Abstract.—Size-selective mortality is a dominant variable regulating the dynamics of salmon populations. Body size, growth rate, and energy state during one life stage influence survival during that and subsequent life stages. Therefore, simultaneously examining allometric processes, foraging, and thermal constraints on growth within and among life stages can provide a powerful analytical framework for identifying critical periods and sizes during the life cycle of salmon, and for understanding the processes that contribute to the specific ecological bottlenecks confronting different species or stocks of salmon. A bioenergetics model was used to simulate generalized growth responses to a factorial combination of body size, daily feeding rate, and prey energy density over a continuous range of temperatures (0–24°C). The results of these simulations indicated that: 1) smaller salmon benefit from higher potential scope for growth or activity than larger salmon, based on the different allometric relationships for maximum consumption, metabolism, and waste; 2) optimal temperatures for growth decline with increasing body size; 3) optimal temperatures for growth also decline as daily rations decline; 4) thermal tolerances (temperature thresholds beyond which weight loss will occur) also shift to cooler temperatures for larger salmon and when ration sizes decline; 5) increasing the composite energy density of the diet can increase both optimal growth temperature, and thermal tolerance, especially at larger body sizes; 6) after spawners enter freshwater, the amount of energy and days available to migrate, and successfully spawn at a given upstream location was very sensitive to ambient river temperature, and the swimming speed required to reach the spawning grounds. When placed in the context of climate variability, seasonal shifts in temperature, and food availability, these simulations suggest that growth will be more frequently limited by feeding rate (prey availability) and prey quality than by temperature, especially for smaller, younger life stages. Larger salmon should be more sensitive to temperature change, but reductions in optimal growth temperature and thermal tolerance would be magnified for all life stages, if either feeding rate or prey quality were to be reduced. Given intense size-selective mortality during one or more early life stages, this simulation framework could be adopted to identify the key factors limiting growth to critical sizes during critical periods in the life cycle of specific salmon stocks.

---

*Corresponding author: davebea@u.washington.edu

Introduction

The fitness of organisms can be strongly influenced by their energetic status across the continuum of their life cycle (Brett 1983; Quinn 2005). All life stages of salmon are affected to some degree by prior energetic performance, with immediate or delayed consequences for growth, survival, or reproductive success. Size-selective mortality, especially during early freshwater and marine life stages, strongly influences the ultimate run size for most species of salmon (Holtby et al. 1990; Mortensen et al. 2000; Beamish and Mahnken 2001; Beamish et al. 2004; Moss et al. 2005; Beauchamp et al. 2007; Farley et al. 2007; Cross et al. 2008); therefore, growth performance can be directly linked to survival.

Growth reflects the integrative responses to physiological, environmental, and ecological processes experienced throughout the history of an organism. Given geographic and climatic variability, plus myriad differences in life history strategies among stocks and species, the challenge becomes how to identify which factors most influence growth rate during specific life stages and seasons, and then determine whether these processes pose a critical limitation to salmon production. Under what conditions are growth limited by seasonal prey availability or temperature, and are different sizes or life stages of salmon more sensitive to changes in the growth environment? Bioenergetics models provide a useful framework for examining the dynamic growth responses of fish while explicitly accounting for changes in body mass, thermal regime, feeding rate, and the energetic quality of prey.

Bioenergetics models are energy balance equations where energy inputs from consumption C must equal energy losses due to metabolism M and waste W, with the remaining energy, surplus or deficit, allocated to growth or weight loss G (including reproductive investment and loss) of the consumer.

$$C = M + W + G$$

The Wisconsin Bioenergetics model (Hanson et al. 1997) is the most widely used form of this type of model (Hansen et al. 1993; Ney 1993) and provides parameters for numerous freshwater and some marine species of fish and several invertebrates. The models contain mass-dependent functions for maximum daily consumption and metabolism, temperature-dependent functions for maximum daily consumption and metabolism (basal respiration and activity), and a temperature- and ration-dependent function for waste. Specific dynamic action (SDA) is treated as a constant proportion of consumption. The model operates on a daily time step, thus enabling simulations to account for changing conditions at fine-scale temporal resolution.

In the most common applications of the model, consumption C is estimated as a proportion (P-value) of a theoretical maximum daily consumption rate Cmax ($g \cdot g^{-1} \cdot d^{-1}$):

$$C = p \cdot C_{max}.$$

The model computes Cmax based on the body mass and temperature experienced by the consumer on each day of the simulation. Based on the initial and final body mass of a consumer, its thermal experience and diet composition over a specific time interval, the model calculates consumption by iteratively fitting the average P-value needed to grow to the final body mass observed on the final day of the simulation interval. So, P-value represents feeding rate, expressed as a unit-less proportion of the maximum daily consumption rate, and $C = p \cdot C_{max}$ represents the consumption rate estimate, expressed as a daily proportion of the body weight of the consumer ($g \cdot g^{-1} \cdot d^{-1}$), or in absolute terms ($g \cdot d^{-1}$).

Fish require less biomass of high-energy food (in terms of energy density: J/g wet weight [WWT]) to achieve a given growth rate than would be needed if lower-energy food were eaten instead. After satisfying losses due to metabolism and waste, the model converts the remaining energy surplus or deficit into positive or negative growth, respectively, by dividing this remaining energy (J) by the energy density (J/g) of the consumer to calculate the incremental change in body mass (g). The model can also be used to simulate growth responses to different feeding rates for different combinations of consumer size, temperature, and food quality, by changing the P-value to imply different levels of food availability.

Based on the basic bioenergetic principles presented above, four factors play a major role in determining the growth performance of salmon: body mass, temperature, feeding rate, and energetic content of consumers and their prey. Because all of these factors vary considerably over the life cycle of salmon, it is important to examine how they affect growth over a reasonable range of conditions that might be encountered seasonally and through the ontogeny of salmon. The objective was to demonstrate how basic bioenergetic processes interact with seasonal changes in environmental conditions, food availability, and the energetic quality of the available food, to create different constraints or opportunities for growth and survival throughout the ontogeny of salmon. Bioenergetics model simulations were used to show how body mass, temperature, feeding rate, and prey quality interact to define growth limits among various life stages of salmon. Energetic trade-offs that arise within or among habitats through time could strongly influence the spatial-temporal distribution, feeding, and growth patterns of juvenile salmon during freshwater, estuarine, and marine life stages. Growth performance during these periods could determine survival during current and subsequent life stages.

Methods

To demonstrate how the basic bioenergetic responses should vary between juvenile and older Pacific salmon, I first simulated how maximum consumption rates versus metabolic and weight losses are expected to change across a range of body masses (0.2-g fry through 5,000-g sub-adults or adults) and temperatures, based on established allometric and thermal relationships. I then used the simulated specific daily growth rates, resulting from maximum consumption at different temperatures and body masses to demonstrate how thermal responses are expected to vary among sizes or life stages of salmon. The effects of temperature, feeding rate, and energy density of prey (J/g wet weight [J/g WWT]) were examined first for a 10-g consumer (e.g., a juvenile salmon during its first growing season in marine waters) to demonstrate the expected thermal responses of growth to changes in availability and energetic quality of food. These factorial combinations of temperature, feeding rate, and prey energy density were applied to simulations for every order-of-magnitude increase in body mass, to examine potential growth responses of Pacific salmon through seasonal variability within and among life stages throughout their anadromous life cycle. Finally, the effects of different temperatures and swimming speeds on energy loss during the nonfeeding upriver spawning migrations were simulated to estimate the relative change in the time and energy available to reach the spawning grounds, with sufficient energy remaining to spawn successfully.

A spreadsheet version of the Wisconsin Fish Bioenergetics model formulation (Hanson et al. 1997) was constructed to facilitate these simulations. All of the salmonid models (with the exception of lake trout *Salvelinus namaycush*) share the same functional forms of equations for the effects of body mass and temperature on maximum consumption, metabolism, and waste, although parameter values differ somewhat among species (Hanson et al. 1997). The model for sockeye salmon *Oncorhynchus nerka* (Beauchamp et al. 1989) was used to emulate the general relationships of the other salmonid species, because bioenergetic responses have been the most thoroughly studied for this species (e.g., Brett 1983). Although the magnitude of responses at different body sizes or temperatures would differ somewhat among species, these simulations were intended to reflect a generalized response, in relative terms, to the four primary sources of bioenergetic variability experienced by salmonids throughout their life cycle. A true comparison of growth performance among species would require careful species-specific parameterization and corroboration of functions for consumption, respiration (e.g., Trudel and Welch 2005), waste, and the growth response (Bajer et al. 2004a, 2004b; Madenjian et al. 2000, 2004).

The Wisconsin Bioenergetics model has been parameterized for sockeye salmon (Beauchamp et al. 1989), coho *O. kisutch* and Chinook salmon *O. tshawytscha* (Stewart and Ibarra 1991), and steelhead *O. mykiss* (Rand et al. 1993). The sockeye salmon model has been used as a surrogate parameter set for pink salmon *O. gorbuscha* (Hanson et al. 1997; Cross et al. 2005) and chum salmon *O. keta* (Orsi et al. 2004); no specific parameter set has been formalized for either pink or chum salmon. Bioenergetics models for many species, including Pacific salmon, have borrowed physiological parameters from other species, calling into question how accurately the specific physiological responses of a species can be simulated (Boisclair and Tang 1993; Ney 1993; Trudel and Welch 2005). Despite these concerns, salmonid models have generally performed well at estimating consumption when compared to independent measures of consumption and growth in controlled laboratory conditions

(Madenjian et al. 2004), or to estimates of *in situ* consumption in both freshwater (Beauchamp et al. 1989; Ruggerone and Rogers 1992; Mazur and Beauchamp 2006) and marine environments (Brodeur et al. 1992). In these cases, the model produced consumption estimates within ± 10% of independently derived, field-generated estimates for the same consumers. These examples were applied to the same life stages or size ranges as that of salmon spending their first growing season in the ocean. Although comparing one estimate to another does not ensure that either one represents the true value, such corroborations encourage confidence in these approaches, and support the applications of these models to compare consumption and growth performance, at least in relative terms at a minimum, with reasonable expectation that the model estimates are considerably better than that. When evaluating these models, the key consideration should be the level of uncertainty associated with simulation results (i.e., estimation of consumption versus estimating growth, respiration, or waste) within the context of the objectives specified for the model applications.

Allometric changes in scope for growth and thermal tolerance

The model generated response curves through the ontogeny of salmonids, to compare maximum consumption C_{max} to the combined losses from metabolism and waste for a range of body masses (0.2–5,000 g) in order to demonstrate how allometric responses changed the proportion of ingested energy that was available for growth. To demonstrate how different components of the energy budget varied in response to temperature, modeled values for C_{max}, C_{max} – waste, and metabolism, were plotted for a 10-g sockeye salmon feeding at temperatures of 0–25°C on an unlimited supply of food containing an average composite energy density of 4,000 J/g wet weight (J/g WWT).

Factorial effects of body mass, feeding rate, prey energy density, and temperature

To examine how scope for growth differed among key life stages of salmon in freshwater, estuarine, and marine habitats, temperature-dependent growth was modeled in response to factorial combinations of body mass, temperature, feeding rate, and prey quality. Daily growth rates ($g \cdot g^{-1} \cdot d^{-1}$) were simulated for 1-, 10-, 100-, and 1000-g sockeye salmon over a range of 0–25°C at 1°C increments and at feeding rates of 100%, 50%, and 25% of C_{max} (P-value = 1.0, 0.5, and 0.25 in the Wisconsin model, respectively) on either low- or high-energy diets. For the low-energy diet, prey energy density was set at 2,800 J/g to emulate the average value for lower energy prey commonly eaten by salmon in most habitats like: immature forms of many (but not all) aquatic insects in streams and lakes; copepods and cladocerans in lakes; many benthic invertebrates in estuaries and nearshore marine habitats; smaller copepods, hyperiid amphipods, larvaceans, pteropods, and coelenterates in coastal and pelagic marine waters (Kaeriyama et al. 2000; Brodeur et al. 2007; and Armstrong et al. 2008). Simulations were repeated using a higher prey energy density of 5,000 J/g to emulate a diet composed primarily of higher quality prey which are at least seasonally available in most habitats like: terrestrial insects and adult forms of aquatic insects in streams, lakes, estuaries and nearshore and pelagic coastal marine waters; larger copepods, gammarid amphipods, euphausiids, juvenile fish, and squid (Davis et al. 1998; Aydin et al. 2005). Subadult and adult salmon frequently exhibit high feeding rates on high-quality prey with energy densities exceeding 7,000 J/g WWT (e.g., Aydin et al. 2005), so the "high-energy" prey scenarios using energy density of 5,000 J/g represents a conservative estimate of growth potential.

Nonfeeding energy expenditures during spawning migration

The effects of flow regime and temperature on the energetics of adults returning to the spawning grounds were simulated by modeling daily temperature-dependent costs of standard and active metabolism, without additional energy inputs from consumption or the associated losses from waste and SDA. Adult salmon generally stop feeding just before entering freshwater and must survive on existing energy stores in order to complete migration and spawning (Gilbert 1922; Quinn 2005). Osmoregulation costs during this stage have not been quantified adequately; however early work by Rao (1968) indicated that costs for juvenile salmonids were minimized in brackish waters (salinities of 7 ppt) and increased in both higher salinities and freshwater. The rate of energy expenditure should be largely determined by water temperature, flow regime, and distance (Hinch and Rand 1998; Hendry and Berg 1999; Crossin et al. 2004; Quinn 2005). Thermal, physical, or velocity barriers to migration reduce energy stores both as a function of time (i.e., days of routine metabolic costs expended without progress toward the spawning grounds) and as additional costs due to heightened activity or effects of elevated temperature (Rand et al. 2006).

Empirical studies have reported that the energy density for spawners at death averaged 45% of the energy density at river entry (Hendry and Berg 1999; Quinn 2005), and generally equated to total body energy density of 4,000–4,100 J/g (Crossin et al. 2004). Spawners expended 15% of their original whole-body energy contained at river entry, at the spawning grounds through gonadal loss and associated spawning activity (Hendry and Berg 1999; Quinn 2005). Therefore, it is assumed that spawners needed to reach the spawning grounds with a minimum of 60% of their original energy content at river entry in order to expend the final 15% on spawning activity and gonadal loss before reaching the presumed lethal threshold of 45% of the original energy content at stream entry.

Model simulations examined the effects of swimming speed (70, 115, 150 cm/s) and river temperature (8°, 12°, 16°C) on the life span (days), and rate of energy depletion (proportion of energy at stream entry) for 3-kg adult sockeye salmon starting their upstream spawning migration. A representative upstream migration was simulated at 12°C, swimming 115 cm/s, representing the sum of the average focal current velocity and average upstream migration rate, assuming active unidirectional migration for 24-h per day (Brett 1983; Hinch et al. 1996; Hinch and Rand 1998; Quinn 2005). The effect of swimming speed was examined by simulating energy loss for 70, 115, and 150 cm/s at 12°C. The effect of temperature was examined by simulating energy losses at 8°, 12°, and 16°C at a swimming speed of 115 cm/s.

Results and Discussion

General Allometric and Thermal Response

The model simulations indicated that as body size increases, the maximum potential daily feeding rate (C_{max}, $g \cdot g^{-1} \cdot d^{-1}$) declines, and energy losses from metabolism and waste also become progressively smaller fractions of the consumer's body weight; however, C_{max} declines at a faster rate than the loss terms (Figure 1a). Metabolic and waste losses become a larger percentage of the energy budget for larger fish than for smaller individuals. Thus, a larger fraction of the energy budget is available for growth or activity in smaller salmon. For example, when eating a composite diet averaging 4,000 J/g at 10°C, metabolic and waste losses would equal 53% of C_{max} for a 1-g salmon versus 67% of C_{max} for a 1,000-g salmon under similar conditions. The ratio of energy losses to total energy consumed increases with both increasing body mass and temperature (Figure 1b). At warmer temperatures (e.g., 18–22°C in Figure 1b), this ratio exceeds 1.0 sooner for larger fish, providing further evidence that larger fish should exhibit lower thermal tolerance than smaller conspecifics.

For any given body mass, the surplus energy available for growth, activity, or scope for coping with other stressors is represented by the difference between a dome-shaped temperature-dependent curve for C_{max} and an exponentially-increasing temperature-dependent curve for metabolic losses (Respiration + SDA). Because waste losses are a relatively constant proportion of consumption, the response for (C_{max} – Waste) will also be a dome shaped curve (Figure 2). The optimal temperature for growth will always be lower than the temperature where C_{max} is highest, because metabolic and waste losses become a larger fraction of the energy budget at higher temperatures (Figure 2).

Under identical feeding and temperature conditions, the interaction between these allometric and thermal relationships result in smaller salmon growing at a much faster percentage of their body weight and exhibiting higher thermal tolerance (the range of temperatures over which positive growth can be maintained) than larger salmon (Figure 3a). The dome-shaped temperature-dependent growth curves for all sizes of salmon exhibit a wide plateau around maximum growth when feeding at C_{max}. This suggests that when food is not limited, growth should be relatively insensitive to a fairly wide range in temperature change, except at the lower and upper thermal extremes. However, salmon often feed well below C_{max} at various times through their life cycle. These lower feeding rates reduce growth, reduce and accentuate the optimal temperatures for growth, and more sharply delineate thermal tolerance limits for maintaining a positive energy balance (Figure

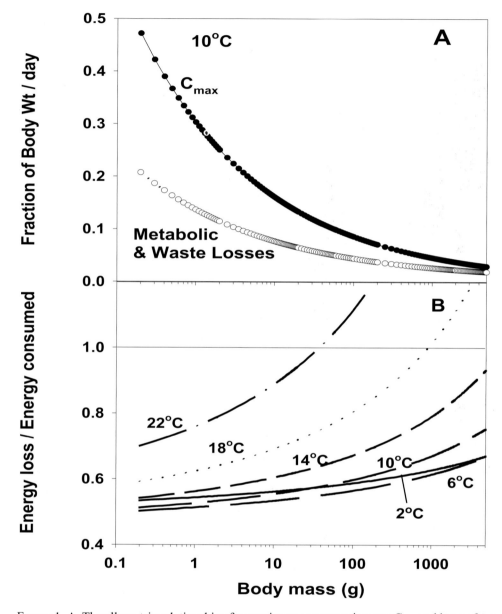

FIGURE 1. **A.** The allometric relationships for maximum consumption rate C_{max} and losses from metabolism plus waste for 0.2-g to 5,000-g sockeye salmon at 10°C. **B.** The ratio of energy losses (metabolism + waste) to energy consumed at C_{max} for temperatures of 2–22°C. Curves above horizontal line at 1.0 indicates that weight loss occurs even when feeding at C_{max}. Note that body mass on the x-axis is plotted on a $\log_{10}$ scale.

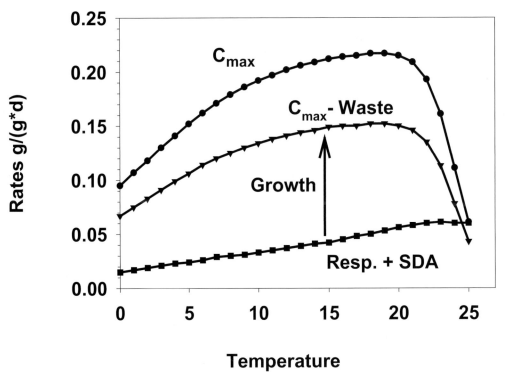

FIGURE 2. Thermal dependence of C_{max}, respiration and waste losses for a 10-g sockeye salmon feeding on prey with average energy density of 4,000 J/g.

3b). Reducing the feeding rate from 100% to 25% of C_{max} reduces growth even lower than 25% of the maximum growth rate, because metabolic losses represent a larger fraction of the energy budget under reduced rations. As feeding rate declines, positive growth is also restricted to a narrower and cooler range of temperatures (Figure 3b). However, shifting to higher-quality prey can ameliorate the effects on growth and thermal tolerance. By shifting from a low-energy diet averaging 2,800 J/g to a higher-energy diet averaging 5,000 J/g, fish that fed at 25% of C_{max} could now achieve nearly the same growth rate and thermal tolerance levels as if they were feeding at 50% C_{max} (Figure 3b). The interacting relationships of temperature, feeding rate, and the energy quality of prey as expressed in Figure 3b will be applied to different life

stages of salmon (represented by 10-fold increases in body mass) to explore their relative influence on growth throughout the life cycle of Pacific salmon species.

Energetics of fry and juvenile stages

Model simulations indicated that juvenile salmon (0.2–10 g) can tolerate relatively wide thermal variation around their optimal growth temperature without significant reduction in growth rate. When feeding at 50% of C_{max} on a diet of "normal" prey averaging 2,800 J/g, juveniles can sustain positive growth rates up to temperatures of 23°C. But they would lose weight above 19–20°C, if ration declined to 25% C_{max} (Figure 4a, c). Improved prey quality (e.g., 5,000 J/g) would dramatically improve both growth and thermal tolerance,

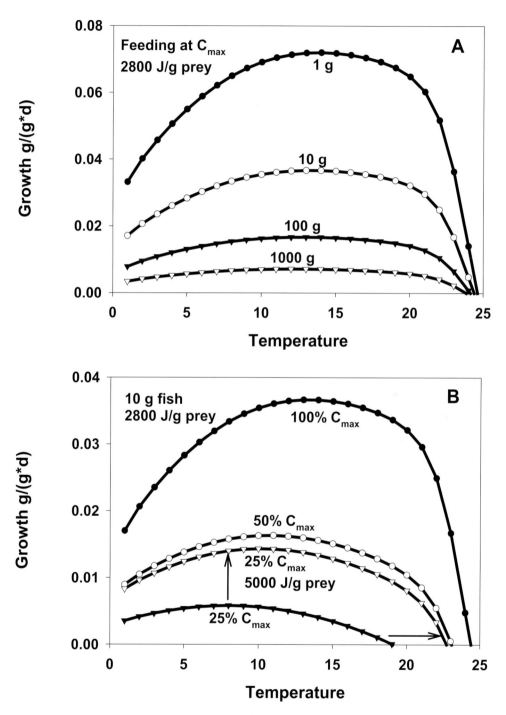

FIGURE 3. **A.** Thermal effects on daily growth rate for sockeye salmon of different body masses feeding at C_{max} on common low-energy prey (2,800 J/g). **B.** Temperature-dependent growth for 10-g sockeye salmon at different feeding rates on 2,800 J/g prey and effect of the shifting to 5,000 J/g prey on growth (vertical arrow) and thermal tolerance (horizontal arrow) for a fish feeding at 25% C_{max}.

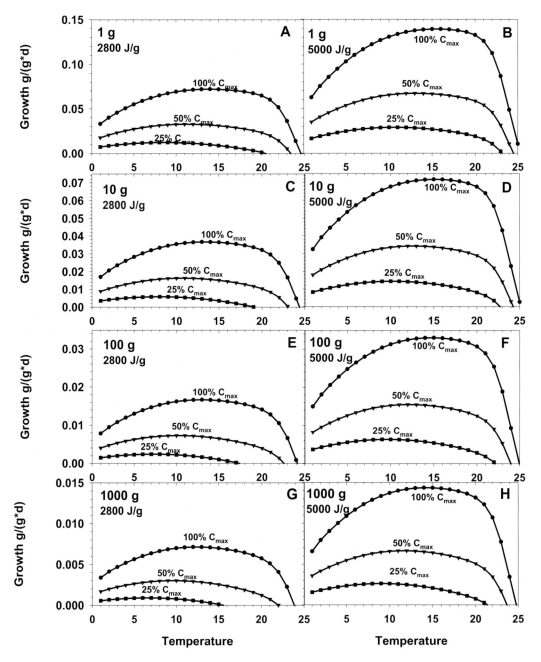

FIGURE 4. The change in daily growth rate in response to temperature and feeding rate for 1–1,000 g sockeye salmon feeding on a composite diet with a mean energy density of 2,800 J/g wet body weight (left panels) and 5,000 J/g (right panels).

particularly at low feeding rates (Figure 4b, d). In the following subsections, these simulation results are discussed within the context of seasonal habitat use by the life stages associated with this size range (1–10 g) for each species of salmon.

Juvenile pink and chum salmon in the estuary and early marine life.—Following emergence from their redds, pink and chum salmon fry typically migrate immediately to the estuary and reside in estuarine or nearshore marine habitats for days or weeks, before moving into epi-pelagic waters of sounds, bays, and coastal regions. Feeding rates can be highly variable (25–100% C_{max}) during this initial stage, and major diet constituents contain low to moderate energy density (2,000–3,600 J/g wet weight [WWt]) like epibenthic and pelagic crustacean zooplankton (small copepods, amphipods), noncrustacean zooplankton (e.g., larvaceans, pteropods, coelenterates), and larval or pupal aquatic insects. Higher-quality prey items (4,000–6000 J/g WWt) available to pink and chum salmon during this stage might include terrestrial or adult aquatic insects, larval crab and shrimp, euphausiids, and large copepods. Juvenile pink and chum salmon typically experience low to moderate temperatures during this life stage (5–12°C, Willette et al. 1999; 7–13°C, Orsi et al. 2000; 9–15°C, Duffy et al. 2005). The widest fluctuations in temperature and prey quality or quantity would likely be experienced during estuarine rearing, wherein diel and tidal cycles differentially affect access, depth, thermal and prey regimes in the main river channel, among different tidal channels and salt marshes, and the outer estuary. If abundant prey supported feeding rates near C_{max} during spring, then growth could be limited by low ambient temperatures; however, if food availability and feeding rates declined (e.g., ≤ 50% C_{max}), growth would be regulated by feeding rate and less by fluctuating or cold temperatures (Figure 4a, c). If predominantly high-energy prey were available, growth would improve considerably, and thermal constraints on growth would become more pronounced at cooler temperatures (Figure 4b, d).

Sockeye salmon fry and fingerlings in lakes.—Most sockeye salmon fry emerge from redds and migrate immediately to a nursery lake to rear for 1–2 years before migrating to sea. Sockeye salmon populations exhibit relatively plastic smoltation responses to growth rate and body size in terms of the percentage of juveniles that migrate to sea as age-1 or age-2 smolts. Factors that affect growth performance during the lake-rearing phase can determine which life history strategy will be adopted, along with all of the associated fitness consequences.

Initially, feeding rates (e.g., 10–40% of C_{max}) and prey quality (larval and pupal chironomids and small-bodied cyclopoid or calanoid copepods averaging 2,000–3,400 J/g) can be low until the spring-summer zooplankton bloom (e.g., Beauchamp et al. 2004). During spring and summer, higher densities of zooplankton support higher feeding and growth rates by juvenile sockeye salmon, and the energy density of cladocerans and larger calanoid copepods can be somewhat higher than during winter (especially ovigerous females). Terrestrial and adult aquatic insects represent some of the limited types of higher-energy prey available to lake-rearing sockeye salmon. Thermal stratification can create a vertical gradient for temperature and prey availability in some lake basins. Predation risk, mediated by light and turbidity, create additional ecological constraints against simply feeding in regions that maximize growth. In response to these physiological, environmental, and ecological constraints, juvenile sockeye salmon often perform diel vertical migrations (DVM) in an attempt to optimize the ratio of predation risk versus growth performance (Eggers 1978; Clark and

Levy 1988; Scheuerell and Schindler 2003; Hardiman et al. 2004). Different populations would conceivably exhibit unique solutions to this puzzle, ranging from no DVM in turbid glacial lakes or predator-free lakes, to strong DVM in relatively clear (e.g., Secchi depths >5 m) lakes with significant predator populations.

Although less common in sub-arctic lakes, seasonal access to exploitable zooplankton for juvenile sockeye salmon can be limited by thermal barriers. For example, warm epilimnetic waters ≥20°C could become a thermal refuge for zooplankton while zooplankton in the metalimnion were depleted by planktivores. However, a 1-g fish feeding at 25% C_{max} in a 12–16°C thermocline would derive a clear growth advantage by feeding on higher densities of zooplankton in a 20°C epilimnion, if prey availability could support a significantly higher feeding rate (e.g., ≥ 50% C_{max}; Figure 4a). A similar growth benefit would accrue if feeding on higher-quality terrestrial or adult aquatic insects (≥5,000 J/g) in the warmer surface film as compared to metalimnetic feeding on zooplankton even at less than 25% C_{max} (Figure 4a–b). A 10-g sockeye salmon in the same lake would experience the same relative energy trade-offs as a 1-g fish, but the specific growth rates would be lower and the upper thermal tolerance limits, and the overall thermal growth dependence pattern would shift to cooler temperatures by 1–2°C (Figure 4c–d). In general, a 1 g sockeye salmon should exhibit higher specific growth rates and tolerate slightly warmer temperatures than a 10 g conspecific.

Coho and Chinook salmon fry and parr during stream residence.—Alaskan populations of juvenile coho and Chinook salmon reside in streams, side-channels, and ponds for approximately a year, whereas coastal populations of ocean-type Chinook salmon at lower latitudes, migrate to sea during their first year and often use estuarine, nearshore marine, and coastal epi-pelagic habitats extensively (Brodeur et al. 2004; Quinn 2005). Stream-rearing salmon feed primarily on insects and other invertebrates in the drift and on the surface, but their food also include benthos in ponds and off-channel habitats. Temperatures should be more spatially uniform within a stream with the largest deviations coming from marginal habitats that are insulated from the main channel or from localized areas of groundwater intrusion. Thermal conditions tend to vary more closely with air temperatures over both diel and seasonal cycles, particularly in smaller streams that lack significant groundwater influence. Temperature-dependent growth limitation would be more likely in flowing than standing waters, because the wider diel and seasonal temperature fluctuations are more prone to cross growth-limiting levels at either the lower or upper ends of the thermal range. Unlike in other habitats, stream-rearing salmonids aggressively defend feeding territories (Quinn 2005), adding an additional energetic cost that is currently not well quantified (but see Yamamoto et al. 1998). Stream-rearing salmon maintain feeding positions in the current, but typically occupy low-velocity regions (e.g., near bottom, shear zones, complex substrate, or other structure) adjacent to the higher currents that delivery drift organisms. Although routine activity costs associated with maintaining position in a stream have been assumed to be similar to the cruising costs expended by juveniles feeding in lakes, ponds, and marine systems, the maneuvering required for drift-feeding requires an average 4.7 times higher activity cost than constant swimming at an average speed (Boisclair and Tang 1993; Hughes and Kelly 1996).

Stream-rearing juvenile coho and Chinook salmon (body mass range of approximately 0.3–10 g) exhibit widely variable feeding rates, experience broad temperature fluctuations, and feed on a mix of prey that vary considerably in energy density from generally lower quality aquatic insect larvae, pupae, and other aquatic invertebrates (1,100–4,500 J/g WWt, midpoint = 2,800 J/g) to higher-energy terrestrial and adult aquatic insects (3,800–12,700 J/g WWt; Hanson et al. 1997; Gray 2004; McCarthy et al. 2009). At low temperatures and low feeding rates during spring, model simulations suggest that growth should be relatively insensitive to wide temperature fluctuations up to about 10°C; however, if food was plentiful, lower temperatures could inhibit growth at higher feeding rates (50–100% C_{max}; Figure 4a–d). Feeding rate and prey quality tend to influence growth rate most during warmer seasons; growth is relatively insensitive to temperature variability during this period, except at extremely warm temperatures or when both food quality and quantity are severely restricted. During the summer, higher temperatures could provide fast growth opportunities if accompanied by higher feeding rates. Conversely, low feeding rates would lead to weight loss at temperatures above 19°C for juveniles feeding at ≤25% C_{max} on lower-energy aquatic insect larvae, pupae or nymphs (Figure 4c). The contribution of high-energy prey like adult aquatic insects and seasonal subsidies from terrestrial insects become particularly important for supporting higher growth rates and improving thermal tolerance during warmer summer conditions (e.g., shift from 2,800 J/g food to 5,000 J/g at 50% C_{max}; Figure 4b, d).

Energetics of salmon in marine waters.— By their first summer in marine waters, most juvenile salmon species (10–100 g) feed in epi-pelagic coastal and shelf waters at high feeding rates (50–100% C_{max}; Brodeur et al. 1992; Duffy 2009; Orsi et al. 2004; Cross et al. 2005; Beauchamp et al. 2007) consisting of a broad range of prey sizes and quality, from low-energy taxa like crustacean and noncrustacean zooplankton (2,000–4,000

J/g) to higher energy prey like euphausiids, fish, and squid (4,000–7,000 J/g; Davis et al. 1998; Kaeriyama et al. 2004; Aydin et al. 2005; Mazur et al. 2007). Over the potential range of temperatures experienced by juvenile salmon during the first summer-fall in the ocean, growth was strongly influenced by feeding rate, but was relatively insensitive to a wide range of temperatures (Figure 4c–f). For juvenile pink salmon in the Gulf of Alaska, a nearly threefold increase in marine survival corresponded to the higher growth exhibited in the years when average summer feeding rates exceeded 85% C_{max} compared to years when feeding rates were lower (Beauchamp et al. 2007; Cross et al. 2008). The years with higher growth and survival corresponded with the coolest and warmest temperature conditions, whereas the low survival years had intermediate temperatures (Cross 2006). Further increases in feeding rate could produce substantial increases in growth rate, but more dramatic changes in growth rate would result by shifting to prey of significantly higher or lower energy density (Figures 4c and 4e versus 4 d and 4f). Prior growth performance could influence this transition to higher quality prey. For instance, faster-growing coho and Chinook salmon could become more piscivorous or shift to piscivory earlier, because larger body size relieves the constraints of gape-limitation, swimming speed, capture success, and their own vulnerability to larger predators (Keeley and Grant 2001).

At low temperatures during winter and spring (2–8°C, Welch et al. 1998; Aydin et al. 2005), growth for juvenile and sub-adult salmon (100–1,000 g) should be limited primarily by feeding rate and prey quality (Figure 4e–h). However, very low feeding rates could also restrict the upper thermal limit, beyond which weight loss will occur. For instance, at 25% C_{max}, a 100-g salmon feeding on low quality prey would lose weight above 17°C (Figure 4e), whereas a 1,000-g salmon would lose weight above 15°C (Figure 4 g).

In these cases, both thermal tolerance and growth rate would increase dramatically by a shift to higher quality prey or a higher feeding rate. Similar responses were suggested by Welch et al. (1998); Figure 4 graphically demonstrates the important interactions among feeding rate, food quality, and temperature as potential compensatory or exacerbating effects on growth for salmon of different sizes.

During summer, subadult and adult salmon ($\geq$1,000 g) feed at a very high rate on high quality prey (e.g., fish and squid) in coastal waters or the open ocean. Some species exploit a much wider depth range as subadults and adults than during juvenile life stages, thus gaining access to a broader suite of prey and experiencing generally cooler temperatures. Again, focusing on higher-energy prey will improve growth rates for any given feeding rate (Figure 4 g–h). Spatial or temporal heterogeneity in temperature, prey availability, or prey quality provides opportunities to optimize growth by selecting times and regions that offer high growth potential (e.g., Goyke and Brandt 1993).

Adult salmon also tend to feed and grow at a very high rate before migrating back to the spawning grounds. When feeding near C_{max} on high energy prey, growth can approach 1.5% body weight per day (Figure 4 h), so body mass could increase by 30–50% in the final month of ocean feeding. This creates an important trade-off between spending additional time foraging versus the costs of migrating later. Although homeward migration in the ocean does not preclude feeding, foraging efficiency likely declines as migration becomes more deliberate, and reduces opportunities for focused foraging in high-energy patches.

Adult migration and spawning

At 8°C and swimming consistently at a speed of 115 cm/s (accounting for both rate of distance traveled and average focal velocity),

a 3-kg adult sockeye salmon would need to spawn within 50 d after river entry, but would only have 24 d at 12°C, or 11 d at 16°C (Figure 5). At 12°C, by reducing the required swimming speed from 115 cm/s to 70 cm/s, the time available until spawning would increase from 24–68 d, whereas increasing swimming speed to 150 cm/s would reduce migration and spawning time to only 5 d. After arriving on the spawning grounds, spawning activity would presumably expend energy more rapidly than indicated by the lines descending below the dashed spawning energy threshold line in Figure 5, but rates would vary among populations and within populations among years due to differences in spawner density, distribution and behavior, predators, and ambient environmental conditions. Recent research has developed more sophisticated simulations of spawner energy allocation and depletion during spawning migrations (e.g., Crossin et al. 2004; Rand et al. 2006) that are beyond the scope of this paper, but they are essentially specific and important refinements of this core bioenergetic approach.

Energy status of adults on spawning grounds can also affect reproductive success in several ways. Higher energy status on the spawning grounds allows more scope for the activity required for mate selection and defense of mates or redds. Higher net energy acquisition during the feeding stages of the life cycle leads to higher fecundity and potentially larger eggs, resulting in higher embryo quality. Female size is positively correlated with depth and substrate size of her redd. Redd site selection and construction confer higher protection from over-spawning, egg predation, and could reduce energy expenditure by eggs and alevins in response to the temperature and discharge regime during incubation. The resulting fry would emerge with higher yolk reserves, and would be more resilient to early environmental stressors or delayed feeding due to a mismatch with the seasonal food supply (e.g., Hampton et al. 2006).

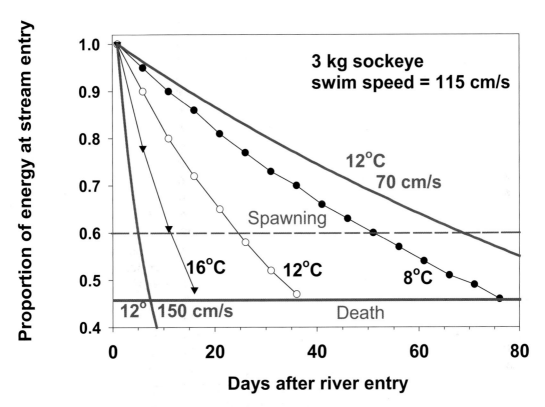

FIGURE 5. Estimated rates of energy depletion after spawners enter the river for three temperatures and an average swimming speed in water of 115 cm/s. Solid lines reflect energy depletion at 12°C with average swimming speeds of 70 cm/s or 150 cm/s as labeled. Death is assumed at energy depletion to 45% of the total energy at river entry (solid horizontal line). Gonadal and activity losses on the spawning grounds expend 15%, so spawners must reach the spawning grounds with at least 60% of total body energy content at river entry (dashed horizontal line).

Conclusions

In this paper, a generalized bioenergetics approach was presented as a conceptual framework for considering how basic allometric and thermal responses of salmon can be used to evaluate how growth rate should respond to the combined effects of body size, temperature, feeding rate (a surrogate measure of food supply), and prey quality. Some general patterns emerged from these analyses: 1) Smaller salmon benefit from higher potential scope for growth or activity than larger salmon, based on the different allometric relationships for maximum consumption, metabolism, and waste; 2) Optimal temperatures for growth decline with increasing body size; 3) Optimal temperatures for growth also decline as daily rations decline; 4) Thermal tolerances (temperature thresholds beyond which weight loss will occur) also shift to cooler temperatures for larger salmon and when ration sizes decline; 5) Increasing the composite energy density of the diet can increase both optimal growth temperature and thermal tolerance, especially with larger body sizes; 6) After spawners enter freshwater, the amount of energy and days available to migrate and successfully spawn at a given upstream location were very sensitive to ambient river temperature and the swimming speed required to reach the spawning grounds.

When placed in the context of climate variability and seasonal shifts in temperature and food availability (e.g., Mantua 2009, this volume), these simulations suggest that growth will be more frequently limited by feeding rate (prey availability) and prey quality than by temperature, especially for smaller, younger life stages. Larger salmon should be more sensitive to temperature change, but reductions in optimal growth temperature and thermal tolerance would be magnified for all life stages, if either feeding rate or prey quality were reduced (see also Myers et al. 2009, this

volume). Even when temperature has minimal direct effect on metabolism and growth, it can exert profound effects on timing, species composition, and productivity for other species in the food web, which can lead to large indirect effects on salmon growth and survival through temporal-spatial match-mismatches with prey or predators (Willette et al. 1999; Hampton et al. 2006; Beauchamp et al. 2007). Each population encounters a somewhat unique combination of environmental and ecological conditions at different life stages and seasons. This simulation framework could be adopted to identify key factors that limit growth during critical periods in the life cycle of specific salmon stocks. Given intense size-selective mortality during one or more early life stages, growth limitations or opportunities could create trade-offs that stimulate shifts in habitat use, diet, behavior, or select for different life history strategies.

Depending on the life stage and seasonal conditions, the ingested energy remaining after metabolic and waste losses can be allocated to somatic growth, lipid storage, gonadal investment, or additional activity. Conversely, energy deficits reduce lipid reserves, somatic mass, gonadal investment, and energy available for additional activity (e.g., for migration, spawning) or tolerance for stressors (extreme temperatures, contaminants, pathogens, migration barriers, etc.). Although minor weight or energy loss might not impose significant consequences for some life stages, severe or persistent energy loss should reduce fitness substantially by direct mortality, mediated mortality, or reduced reproductive investment. Juvenile salmon exhibit strong size-selective mortality (Parker 1968; Holtby et al. 1990; Mortensen et al. 2000; Beamish and Mahnken 2001; Beamish et al. 2004; Moss et al. 2005; Farley et al. 2007; Cross et al. 2008, 2009), so periods of weight loss or even reduced growth rate could translate into higher mortality in subsequent life stages.

References

Armstrong, J. L., J. L. Boldt, A. D. Cross, J. H. Moss, N. D. Davis, K. W. Myers, R. V. Walker, D. A. Beauchamp, and L. J. Haldorson. 2005. Distribution, size and interannual, seasonal and diel food habits of the northern Gulf of Alaska juvenile pink salmon, *Oncorhynchus gorbuscha*. Deep Sea Research II 52:247–265.

Armstrong, J. L., K. W. Myers, D. A. Beauchamp, N. D. Davis, R. V. Walker, J. L. Boldt, J. J. Piccolo, L. J. Haldorson, and J. H. Moss. 2008. Interannual and spatial feeding patterns of hatchery and wild juvenile pink salmon in the Gulf of Alaska in years of low and high survival. Transactions of the American Fisheries Society 137:1299–1316.

Aydin, K. Y., G. A. McFarlane, J.R. King, B.A. Megrey, and K. W. Myers. 2005. Linking oceanic food webs to coastal production and growth rates of Pacific salmon (*Oncorhynchus* spp.), using models on three scales. Deep Sea Research II 52:757–780.

Bajer, P. G., R. S. Hayward, G. W. Whitledge, and R. D. Zweifel. 2004a. Simultaneous identification and correction of systematic error in fish bioenergetics models: demonstration with a white crappie (*Pomoxis annularis*) model. Canadian Journal of Fisheries and Aquatic Sciences 61:2168–2182.

Bajer, P. G., G. W. Whitledge, and R. S. Hayward. 2004b. Widespread consumption-dependent systematic error in fish bioenergetics models and its implications. Canadian Journal of Fisheries and Aquatic Sciences 61:2158–2167.

Beamish, R. J., and C. Mahnken. 2001. A critical size and period hypothesis to explain natural regulation of salmon abundance and the linkage to climate and climate change. Progress in Oceanography 49:423–437.

Beamish, R. J., C. Mahnken, and C. M. Neville. 2004. Evidence that reduced early marine growth is associated with lower marine survival of coho salmon. Transactions of the American Fisheries Society 133:26–33.

Beauchamp, D. A., D. J. Stewart, and G. L. Thomas. 1989. Corroboration of a bioenergetics model for sockeye salmon. Transactions of the American Fisheries Society 118:597–607.

Beauchamp, D. A., and eight coauthors. 2004. Temporal-spatial dynamics of early feeding demand and food supply of sockeye salmon fry in Lake Washington. Transactions of the American Fisheries Society 133:1014–1032.

Beauchamp, D. A., A. D. Cross, J. Armstrong, K. W. Myers, J. H. Moss, J. L. Boldt, and L. J. Haldorson. 2007. Bioenergetic responses by Pacific salmon to climate and ecosystem variation. North

Pacific Anadromous Fish Commission Bulletin 4:257–268.

Boisclair, D., and M. Tang. 1993. Empirical analysis of the influence of swimming pattern on the net energetic cost of swimming in fishes. Journal of Fish Biology 42:169–183.

Brett, J. R. 1983. Life energetics of sockeye salmon, *Oncorhynchus nerka*. Pages 29–63 *in* W. P. Aspey and S. I. Lustick, editors. Behavioral energetics: the cost of survival in vertebrates. Ohio State University Press, Columbus.

Brodeur, R. D., E. A. Daly, M. V. Sturdevant, T. W. Miller, J. H. Moss, M. E. Thiess, M. Trudel, L. A. Weitkamp, J. Armstrong, and E. C. Norton. 2007. Regional comparisons of juvenile salmon feeding in coastal marine waters off the west coast of North America. Pages 183–203 *in* C. B. Grimes, R. D. Brodeur, L. J. Haldorson, and S. M. McKinnell, editors. The ecology of juvenile salmon in the northeast Pacific Ocean: regional comparisons. American Fisheries Society, Symposium 57, Bethesda, Maryland.

Brodeur, R. D., R. C. Francis, and W. G. Pearcy. 1992. Food consumption of juvenile coho (*Oncorhynchus kisutch*) and chinook (*O. tshawytscha*) on the continental shelf off Washington and Oregon. Canadian Journal of Fisheries and Aquatic Sciences 49:1670–1685.

Brodeur, R.D., J.P. Fisher, D.J. Teel, R.L. Emmett, E. Casillas, and T.W. Miller. 2004. Juvenile salmonid distribution, growth, condition, origin, and environmental and species associations in the Northern California Current. Fisheries Bulletin 102:25–46.

Clark, C. W., and D. A. Levy. 1988. Diel vertical migrations by juvenile sockeye salmon and the antipredation window. American Naturalist 131:271–290.

Cross, A. D. 2006. Early marine growth and consumption demand of juvenile pink salmon in Prince William Sound and the northern coastal Gulf of Alaska. Doctoral dissertation, University of Washington, Seattle.

Cross, A. D., and D. A. Beauchamp, J. L. Armstrong, J. L. Boldt, N. D. Davis, L. J. Haldorson, J. H. Moss, K. W. Myers, and R. V. Walker. 2005. Modeling bioenergetics of juvenile pink salmon in Prince William Sound and the coastal Gulf of Alaska. Deep Sea Research II 52:347–370.

Cross, A. D., D. A. Beauchamp, J. H. Moss, K. W. Myers. 2009. Interannual variability in early marine growth, size-selective mortality, and marine survival for Prince William Sound pink salmon. Marine and Coastal Fisheries: Dynamics, Management and Ecosystem Science 1:57–70.

Cross, A. D., D. A. Beauchamp, K. W. Myers, and J. H. Moss. 2008. Early marine growth of pink salmon in Prince William Sound and the coastal Gulf of Alaska during years of low and high survival. Transactions of the American Fisheries Society 137:927–939.

Crossin, G. T. and six coauthors. 2004. Energetics and morphology of sockeye salmon: effects of upriver migratory distance and elevation. Journal of Fish Biology 65:788–810.

Davis, N. D., K. W. Myers, Y. Ishida. 1998. Caloric value of high-seas salmon prey organisms and simulated salmon growth and prey consumption. North Pacific Anadromous Fisheries Commission Bulletin 1:146–162.

Duffy, E. J. 2003. Early marine distribution and trophic interactions of juvenile salmon in Puget Sound. Master's Thesis. University of Washington, Seattle.

Duffy, E. J. 2009. Factors during early marine life that affect smolt-to-adult survival of ocean-type Puget Sound Chinook salmon (*Oncorhynchus tshawytscha*). Doctoral dissertation, University of Washington, Seattle.

Duffy, E. J., D. A. Beauchamp, and R. M. Buckley. 2005. Early marine life history of juvenile Pacific salmon in two regions of Puget Sound. Estuarine Coastal and Shelf Science 64:94–107.

Eggers, D. M. 1978. Limnetic feeding behavior of juvenile sockeye salmon in Lake Washington and predator avoidance. Limnology and Oceanography 23:1114–1125.

Farley, E. V., Jr., J. M. Murphy, M. D. Atkison, L. B. Eisner, J. H. Helle, J. H. Moss, and J. L. Nielsen. 2007. Early marine growth in relation to marine-stage survival rates for Alaska sockeye salmon (*Oncorhynchus nerka*). Fishery Bulletin 105:121–130.

Gilbert, C. H. 1922. Salmon of the Yukon River. U.S. Bureau of Fisheries Bulletin 38:317–332.

Goyke, A. P., and S. B. Brandt. 1993. Spatial models of salmonine growth in Lake Ontario. Transactions of the American Fisheries Society 122:870–883.

Gray, A. 2004. The salmon river estuary: restoring tidal inundation and tracking ecosystem response. Doctoral dissertation. University of Washington, Seattle.

Hardiman, J. M., B. M. Johnson, and P. J. Martinez. 2004. Do predators influence the distribution of age-0 kokanee in a Colorado reservoir? Transactions of the American Fisheries Society 133:1366–1378.

Hampton, S., P. Romare, and D. E. Seiler. 2006. Environmentally controlled *Daphnia* spring increase with implications for sockeye salmon fry in Lake Washington, USA. Journal of Plankton Research 28:399–406.

Hansen, M. J., D. Boisclair, S. B. Brandt, and S. W. Hewett. 1993. Applications of bioenergetics models to fish ecology and management-where do we go from here? Transactions of the American Fisheries Society 122:1019–1030.

Hanson, P. C., T. B. Johnson, D. E. Schindler, and J. F Kitchell. 1997. Fish Bioenergetics 3.0 for Windows. Center for Limnology, University of Wisconsin-Madison and the University of Wisconsin Sea Grant Institute. WISCU-T-97-001.

Hendry, A. P., and O. K. Berg. 1999. Secondary sexual characters, energy use, senescence and the cost of reproduction in sockeye salmon. Canadian Journal of Zoology 77:1663–1675.

Hinch, S. G., M. C. Healey, R. E. Diewert, M. A. Henderson, K. A. Thomson, R. Hourston, and F. Juanes. 1996. Potential effects of climate change on marine growth and survival of Fraser River sockeye salmon. Canadian Journal of Fisheries and Aquatic Sciences 52:2651–2659.

Hinch, S. G., and P. S. Rand. 1998. Swim speeds and energy use of upriver-migrating sockeye salmon (*Oncorhynchus nerka*): role of local environment and fish characteristics. Canadian Journal of Fisheries and Aquatic Sciences 55:1821–1831.

Holtby, L. B., B. C. Anderson, and R. K. Kadowaki. 1990. Importance of smolt size and early ocean growth to inter-annual variability in marine survival of coho salmon (*Oncorhynchus kisutch*). Canadian Journal of Fisheries and Aquatic Sciences 47:2181–2194.

Hughes, N. F., and L. H. Kelly. 1996. A hydrodynamic model for estimating energetic cost of swimming maneuvers from a description of their geometry and dynamics. Canadian Journal of Fisheries and Aquatic Sciences 53:2484–2493.

Kaeriyama, M., M. Nakamura, R. Edpalina, J.R. Bower, H. Yamaguchi, R.V. Walker, and K. W. Myers. 2004. Change in feeding ecology and trophic dynamics of Pacific salmon (*Oncorhynchus* spp.) in the central Gulf of Alaska in relation to climate events. Fisheries Oceanography 13:197–207.

Keeley, E. R., and J. W. A. Grant. 2001. Prey size of salmonid fishes in streams, lakes, and oceans. Canadian Journal of Fisheries and Aquatic Sciences 58:1122–1132.

Mazur, M. M., and D. A. Beauchamp. 2006. Linking piscivory to spatial-temporal distributions of pelagic prey fish with a visual foraging model. Journal of Fish Biology 69:151–175.

Mazur, M. M., M. T. Wilson, A. B. Dougherty, A. Buchheister, and D. A. Beauchamp. 2007. Temperature and prey quality effects on growth of juvenile walleye pollock *Theragra chalcogramma*: a spatially explicit bioenergetics approach. Journal of Fish Biology 70:816–836.

Madenjian, C. P., D. V. O'Connor, S. M. Chernyak, R.

R. Rediske, and J. P. O'Keefe. 2004. Evaluation of a Chinook salmon (*Oncorhynchus tshawytscha*) bioenergetics model. Canadian Journal of Fisheries and Aquatic Sciences 61:627–635.

Madenjian, C. P., D. V. O'Connor, and D. A. Nortrup. 2000. A new approach toward evaluation of fish bioenergetics models. Canadian Journal of Fisheries and Aquatic Sciences 57:1025–1032.

Mantua, N. 2009. Patterns of change in climate and Pacific salmon production. Pages 1143–1157 *in* C. C. Krueger and C. E. Zimmerman, editors. Pacific salmon: ecology and management of western Alaska's populations. American Fisheries Society, Symposium 70, Bethesda, Maryland.

McCarthy, S. G., J. J. Duda, J. M. Emlen, G. R. Hodgson, and D. A. Beauchamp. 2009. Linking habitat quality with trophic performance of steelhead along forest gradients in the South Fork Trinity River watershed, California. Transactions of the American Fisheries Society 138:506–521.

Mortensen, D., A. Wertheimer, S. Taylor, and J. Landingham. 2000. The relation between early marine growth of pink salmon, *Oncorhynchus gorbuscha*, and marine water temperature, secondary production, and survival to adulthood. Fishery Bulletin 98:319–335.

Moss, J. H., and D. A. Beauchamp, A. D. Cross, K. W. Myers, E. V. Farley, J. M. Murphy, J. H. Helle. 2005. Higher marine survival associated with faster growth for pink salmon (*Oncorhynchus gorbuscha*). Transactions of the American Fisheries Society 134:1313–1322.

Myers, K. W., R. V. Walker, N. D. Davis, J. L. Armstrong, and M. Kaeriyama. 2009. High seas distribution, biology, and ecology of Arctic-Yukon-Kuskokwim salmon: direct information from high seas tagging experiments, 1954–2006. Pages 201–239 *in* C. C. Krueger and C. E. Zimmerman, editors. Pacific salmon: ecology and management of western Alaska's populations. American Fisheries Society, Symposium 70, Bethesda, Maryland.

Ney, J. J. 1993. Bioenergetics modeling today—growing pains on the cutting edge. Transactions of the American Fisheries Society 122:736–748.

Orsi, J. A., M. V. Sturdevant, J. M. Murphy, D. G. Mortensen, and B. L. Wing. 2000. Seasonal habitat use and early marine ecology of juvenile Pacific salmon in southeastern Alaska. North Pacific Anadromous Fish Commission Bulletin 2:111–122.

Orsi, J. A., A. C. Wertheimer, M. V. Sturdevant, E. A. Fergusson, D. G. Mortensen, and B. L. Wing. 2004. Juvenile chum salmon consumption of zooplankton in marine waters of southeastern Alaska: a bioenergetics approach to implications of hatch-ery stock interactions. Reviews in Fish Biology and Fisheries 14:335–359.

Parker, R. R. 1968. Marine mortality schedules of pink salmon of the Bella Coola River, central British Columbia. Journal of the Fisheries Research Board of Canada 25:757–794.

Quinn, T. P. 2005. The behavior and ecology of pacific salmon and trout. American Fisheries Society, Bethesda, Maryland and University of Washington Press, Seattle.

Rand, P. S., D. J. Stewart, P. W. Seelback, M. L. Jones, and L. R. Wedge. 1993. Modeling steelhead population energetics in Lakes Michigan and Ontario. Transactions of the American Fisheries Society 122:977–1001.

Rand, P. S., and eight coauthors. 2006. Effects of river discharge, temperature, and future climates on energetics and mortality of adult migrating Fraser River sockeye salmon. Transactions of the American Fisheries Society 135:655–667.

Rao, G. M. M. 1968. Oxygen consumption of rainbow trout (*Salmo gairdneri*) in relation to activity and salinity. Canadian Journal of Zoology 46:781–786.

Ruggerone, G. T., and D. E. Rogers. 1992. Predation on sockeye salmon fry by juvenile coho salmon in Chignik Lakes, Alaska: implications for salmon management. North American Journal of Fisheries Management 12:87–102.

Scheuerell, M. D., and D. E. Schindler. 2003. Diel vertical migration by juvenile sockeye salmon: empirical evidence for the antipredation window. Ecology 84:1713–1720.

Stewart, D. J., and M. Ibarra. 1991. Predation and production by salmonid fishes in Lake Michigan, 1978–88. Canadian Journal of Fisheries and Aquatic Sciences 48:909–922.

Trudel, M., and D. Welch. 2005. Modeling the oxygen consumption rates in Pacific salmon and steelhead: model development. Transactions of the American Fisheries Society 134:1542–1561.

Welch, D. W., Y. Ishida, and K. Nagasawa. 1998. Thermal limits and ocean migrations of sockeye salmon (*Oncorhynchus nerka*): long-term consequences of global warming. Canadian Journal of Fisheries and Aquatic Sciences 55:937–948.

Willette, T. M., R. T. Cooney, and K. Hyer. 1999. Predator foraging mode shifts affecting mortality of juvenile fishes during the subarctic spring bloom. Canadian Journal of Fisheries and Aquatic Sciences 56:364–376.

Yamamoto, T., H. Ueda, and S. Higashi. 1998. Correlation among dominance status, metabolic rate and otolith size in masu salmon. Journal of Fish Biology 52:281–290.

American Fisheries Society Symposium 70:73–96, 2009

Freshwater Habitat Quantity and Coho Salmon Production in Two Rivers: an Initial Study to Support the Development of Habitat-Based Escapement Goals in Norton Sound, Alaska

MATTHEW J. NEMETH* AND BENJAMIN C. WILLIAMS

LGL Alaska Research Associates, Inc.
1101 E. 76th Street, Suite B, Anchorage, Alaska 99518, USA

ROBERT C. BOCKING

LGL Limited environmental research associates
9768 Second Street, Sidney, British Columbia V8L 3Y8, Canada

SIMON N. KINNEEN

Norton Sound Economic Development Corporation
Fisheries Research & Development Program
P.O. Box 358, Nome, Alaska 99762, USA

Abstract.—Data were collected in Norton Sound from 2002 through 2006 to support the development of habitat-based models of coho salmon smolt production and adult escapements. Length of stream rearing habitat available to juvenile coho salmon in the summer was estimated at 83 km on the Nome River and 277 km on the North River, using a combination of *a priori* predictions of fish distribution and subsequent field sampling. The likely range of smolts produced by this habitat was modeled using three different relationships of habitat quantity and smolt production developed elsewhere. The estimated escapement of adult salmon needed to produce this range of smolts resulted in counts from 2,632 to 3,649 fish in the Nome River and from 8,766 to 10,481 fish in the North River, using various literature values of production, survival, and fecundity. A field study conducted in the next two years to estimate actual smolt abundance in the Nome River yielded estimates of 92,820 (95% Cī = 84,615 – 101,026) in 2005 and 122,079 (95% CI = 112,612 – 131,546) coho salmon in 2006; these smolt abundances were within the range estimated by the *a priori* models. Through 2007, average adult coho salmon escapement to both rivers had also been within the 95% confidence interval predicted from two of the three smolt models, within 2% and 18% of the point estimate of one model, and within 27% and 32% of the second. Overall, models based on production estimates and life history variables developed outside of the region were relatively accurate for predicting coho salmon rearing distributions, smolt production per km of total rearing habitat, and adult spawner abundance. Based on this, habitat-based models used to help develop escapement goals in other regions may be similarly useful in the Norton Sound region.

---

*Corresponding author: mnemeth@lgl.com

Introduction

The need to incorporate ecosystem features into escapement goals and harvest management has recently received increased attention (e.g., Bradford et al. 1997; Nickelson 1998; Bradford et al. 2000; Knudsen 2000) and is a fundamental part of the concept of ecosystem-based salmon management. Incorporating freshwater rearing habitat into escapement goals (a target number or range of adult salmon spawners needed to produce the next generation) holds promise for coho *Oncorhynchus kisutch*, Chinook *O. tshawytscha*, and sockeye *O. nerka* salmon because of a consistent, documented relationship between freshwater habitat and abundance (Bradford et al. 1997; Shortreed et al. 1999; Parken et al. 2006). Coho salmon smolt abundance, for example, is most likely a function of freshwater rearing habitat quantity and quality, and can be modeled based on a relatively simple set of habitat characteristics (Figure 1; Bradford et al. 1997). Once production of juvenile salmon is known, it can be incorporated into life cycle models that use relationships between habitat and production, survival under different environmental pressures, or some combination to predict a range of adults that can be supported by the habitat (Nickelson 1998).

In theory, habitat-based approaches should be more useful for species that have relatively long freshwater residences, such as sockeye, coho, and Chinook salmon and steelhead trout *O. mykiss*. In practice, such approaches are currently being used to manage salmon throughout the Pacific northwest, including Chinook and coho salmon in British Columbia (Bocking and Peacock 2005; Parken et al. 2006), Oregon (Sharr et al. 2000; PFMC 2003), and Washington (Volkhardt et al. 2007). A similar approach has been used for decades to estimate the production capacity of sockeye salmon from rearing lakes (Koenings and Burkett 1987; Shortreed et al.

1999). Approaches vary among situations, but all rest on the premise that the production of salmon from freshwater ecosystems should be linked to the quantity and quality of habitat within the ecosystem. The strength of this linkage between habitat and production may vary among populations, of course, or potentially be overridden by other biotic or abiotic factors.

Habitat-based production estimates can be especially useful in Norton Sound, a part of the AYK region for which no biological escapement goals exist for Chinook, coho, or sockeye salmon (Brannian et al. 2006; Menard et al. 2009, this volume). The Alaska Department of Fish and Game (ADF&G) is required to develop escapement goals for salmon as part of their mandate to manage salmon resources for sustained yields (ADF&G 2001). Although it is well-accepted that escapement ranges must be at some minimum level to ensure long-term sustainability of a population, the minimum level appropriate for each population is often uncertain (Knudsen 2000). Historically, escapement goals have been established using methods that require observational data on salmon abundance over many years for each "stock," or population. With at least 12 major watersheds, numerous tributaries per watershed, and five species of salmon, there are potentially hundreds of stocks of salmon in the Norton Sound region. Developing escapement goals for all these using spawner-return methods will take a high, sustained level of data collection covering multiple rivers, species, and years—an effort that may not technically or financially possible. If habitat affects coho salmon production in Norton Sound, there may be some cases in which habitat features can be used to establish an escapement range, thereby providing a cost-effective alternative to counting adult salmon returns to a watershed for many years.

The habitat features that influence production in Norton Sound have not yet been

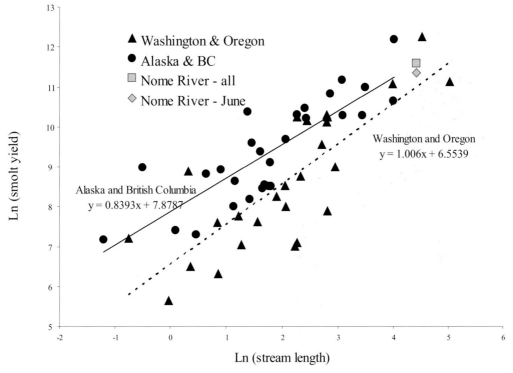

FIGURE 1. Yield of coho salmon *Oncorhynchus kisutch* smolts as a log-linear function of stream length, by geographical group. Dataset from Bocking and Peacock (2005), adapted from Bradford et al. (1997). Mean production of Nome River smolts in 2005 and 2006 have been added to the plot as gray square (estimate for entire summer) and gray diamond (estimate for peak of run in June only). Trendlines do not include Nome River data points.

studied, but can be guided by results from research elsewhere. Large datasets from British Columbia and southeast Alaska show that latitude and length of available stream are useful predictors of smolt abundance at the regional scale (Figure 1; Bradford et al. 1997; Bocking and Peacock 2005). The importance of specific habitat features, however, can change with scale. At the watershed scale, smolt abundance has been associated with stream length, watershed area, valley slope, stream gradient, and the abundance of microhabitat types (Nickelson et al. 1992; Bradford et al. 1997; Sharma and Hilborn 2001). Overall, models that incorporate just a few habitat features are better correlated with salmon production than models that use several or many features. In southeast Alaska,

Shaul et al. (2003) suggested that the mean annual coho salmon smolt production (excluding low escapement years) was the best estimator of a watershed's smolt production capability. This mean annual smolt production can be thought of as carrying capacity, using the definition by Burns (1971) that it is a long-term average around which we should expect fluctuations.

In 2003, we began a study to evaluate whether length of stream rearing habitat could accurately predict a range of coho salmon smolt abundance, which could then be used to develop a habitat-based goal of adult escapement. The main study goal was to determine the range of adult coho salmon to fully seed the amount of rearing habitat available to juvenile coho salmon in two

Norton Sound rivers. The specific objectives of the project were to (1) predict a range of smolts produced based on kilometers of rearing habitat available to juvenile coho salmon; (2) use these smolt estimates in a theoretical life cycle model to predict the number of adult salmon needed to produce this smolt abundance; (3) replace theoretical model inputs with values generated from empirical studies within Norton Sound; and (4) revise the adult production estimates based on empirical results.

Although the premise of the coho salmon production model is that freshwater habitat limits adult production, marine survival is also known to affect adult returns (Bradford 1995). Therefore, we also tagged emigrating smolts to estimate marine survival rates, which will help partition survival into freshwater and marine components. A time series of marine survival estimates also allows researchers to assess associations between variance in adult escapement and marine survival.

Study Area

The study was conducted on the Nome and North rivers in northwestern Alaska (Figure 2). The Nome River empties directly into Norton Sound, 5 km east of the town of Nome. The North River empties into the Unalakleet River approximately 8 km upstream from where the Unalakleet River empties into Norton Sound, at the town of Unalakleet (Figure 2). Both rivers have an annual high water event in June from snowmelt and again in August or September from rainfall. Ice thaws earlier and forms later on the North River compared with the Nome River; ice-out time during the study was generally in the middle of May in the North River and in late May in the Nome River.

The Nome River is a fourth-order watershed (at 1:63,360 scale) approximately 51 km long that drains 420 km^2 and has an estimated mean discharge of 6.5 m^3/s (Selkregg 1976; as reported by Webb and McLean 1991). The

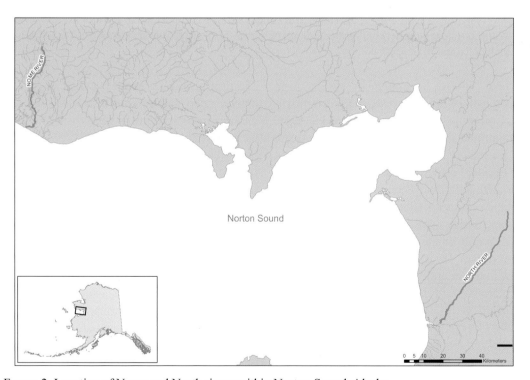

FIGURE 2. Location of Nome and North rivers within Norton Sound, Alaska.

outlet is narrow and subject to tidal influence. The Nome River in its current state is essentially a nonestuarine system emptying directly into Norton Sound, with only sporadic mixing of fresh and marine waters in the lower river (Nemeth et al. 2005).

The Alaska Department of Fish and Game (ADF&G) has operated a weir on the Nome River since 1996. The coho salmon run has been covered from 2001 through 2007 (operation dates through at least September 10), during which years coho salmon counts have ranged from 548 to 8,216, with a mean of 3,595 (Kent 2007; Table 1). The count of 548 fish came in 2003, when coho salmon returns to the Nome subdistrict were classified as "very poor" (Menard 2003). The escapement in 2006 was the highest measured at the weir, and coho salmon returns throughout much of Norton Sound were considered unusually high.

The North River is a fifth-order tributary that empties into the Unalakleet River near the town of Unalakleet, Alaska (Figure 2). The largest tributary is the Little North River, which enters the main stem North river approximately 6.5 km upstream from the confluence of the North and Unalakleet rivers. A counting tower has been operated at approximately river km 5 on the North river since 1996. The tower was been operated late enough in the year to cover the coho salmon run from 2001 through 2007, with the exception of 2002. Coho salmon counts in these six complete-coverage years ranged from 5,837–19,944 fish, with a mean of 12,806 (Table 1). A review of available escapement and harvest data is provided by Menard et al. (2009).

Methods

Components of the model

Coho salmon smolt production (carrying capacity) estimates were developed on the Nome and North rivers by combining the ki-

lometers of assumed rearing habitat with literature values of smolt production per unit of juvenile rearing habitat (e.g., Bradford et al. 1997; Bocking and Peacock 2005). The resulting smolt abundance estimates were then fed into a life history model to back-calculate the number of adults needed to produce this number of smolts (e.g., Nickelson and Lawson 1998). Finally, literature values used in the life history model were replaced with empirical values where possible (Table 2).

The expected distribution of coho salmon rearing habitat within the Nome and North river drainages was estimated from topographical maps and existing reports and information (Scott and Webb 1985; Webb and McLean 1991) following the methods of Bradford et al. (1997). The total kilometers of stream (including mainstem and tributaries) meeting model criteria was calculated for both rivers using digital topographic maps (scale = 1:63,360) and ArcView 3.1 (ESRI, Redlands CA). To be considered potential coho salmon rearing habitat, stream reaches were required to be third order or higher (Strahler 1957), have gradients less than 8%, and be no more than two branches off the mainstem Nome or North rivers. The number of branches off the mainstem is referred to hereafter as the B-value.

Representative stream reaches (first- to fourth-order) were then identified and targeted for field surveys to test assumptions about coho salmon distribution, using presence or absence of rearing fish. Field surveys were conducted in June and August of 2003 and 2004 on each stream. Sampling sites were spread throughout the drainage, targeting a mix of mainstem and tributary reaches, stream orders, and locations low, medium, and high in each drainage. Sites were sampled with minnow traps (both 1/4" and 1/8" mesh), and a backpack electrofisher, using a minimum of six traps per site or 100 m of electrofishing (Nemeth et al. 2004).

Nemeth et al.

TABLE 1. Historical escapement of coho salmon *Oncorhynchus kisutch* to the Nome and North rivers, Norton Sound, Alaska. Nome River data from Kent (2007) and Menard (2007); North River data from Menard (2006, 2007) and Joy and Reed (2007).

| Year | Nome River[1] | | North River[2] | |
	Count	Operation End Date	Count	Operation End Date
1985	-	-	2,045	31-Aug
1993	4,349	28-Aug	-	-
1994	726	15-Aug	-	-
1995	1,650	6-Sep	-	-
1996	66	23-Jul	1,229	25-Jul
1997	321	27-Aug	5,768	26-Aug
1998	96	11-Aug	3,361	12-Aug
1999	417	25-Aug	4,792	31-Aug
2000	696	25-Aug	6,961	12-Aug
2001	2,418	11-Sep	12,383	15-Sep
2002	3,418	11-Sep	3,210	30-Aug
2003	548	10-Sep	5,837	13-Sep
2004	2,283	8-Sep	9,646	14-Sep
2005	5,848	11-Sep	19,189	14-Sep
2006	8,216	7-Sep	9,835	NA
2007	2,437	NA	19,944	NA
Mean, 2001–2007[3]	3,595		12,806	

[1] Tower counts for 1993–1995 and then weir counts from 1996–2007.
[2] Tower counts for all years listed.
[3] Excludes 2002 on the North River.

Habitat-based estimates of coho salmon smolt abundance

Three models were used to predict a range of coho salmon smolt production (as measured by abundance) in each watershed. All of the models used relationships between habitat and observed smolt production from a large dataset (474 estimates of annual smolt abundance on 86 streams) developed over 40 years in southeast Alaska, British Columbia, Oregon, and Washington (Bradford et al. 1997; Bocking and Peacock 2005). For Model 1, the smolt production predicted from the log-linear relationship between stream length and smolt production derived from the Alaska and British Columbia subset of these data, using the equation ln(smolt yield) = 7.87868 + 0.8393 × ln(km stream length), from Bocking and Peacock (2005). For Model 2, smolt production on both rivers was predicted by the median smolt production per km from the 86-stream dataset, which was 1,266 smolts/km; the equation for this calculation was (smolt yield) = 1,266 × km stream length (Bocking and Peacock 2005). Finally, Model 3 was formed as a derivative of Model 2 to simulate the effects of an unusually low coho salmon productivity in Norton Sound (e.g., due to factors such as harsh climate or low nutrient availability). This Model 3 used 660 smolts/km, which was the 25% quartile of smolts/

TABLE 2. Variables, input values, and sources used in models of smolt production and adult abundance.

Variable	Value used	Literature only	Norton Sound studies	Source
Fecundity	5,335 eggs/female		X	Nemeth et al 2004
Egg - fry survival	19.8%	X		Bradford 1995
Fry-smolt survival	7.6%	X		Bradford 1995
Adult sex ratio	1:1	X		Assumed
Smolt production Model 1: log stream length vs log smolt production	1,514 smolts/ km (North); 1,755 smolts/km (Nome)	X		Bocking and Peacock 2005; this study
Smolt production Model 2: median smolts per km stream length	1,266 smolts/ km (both rivers)	X		Bocking and Peacock 2005; this study
Smolt production Model 3: 25% quartile of smolt production per stream length	660 smolts/ km (both rivers)	X		Bocking and Peacock 2005; this study
Nome River observed smolt production	1,295 smolts/km (Nome)		X	This study
Rearing habitat use	2 branches off mainstem; under 6% gradient; barriers under 2 m	X	X	Bocking and Peacock 2005; this study

km from dataset used to create model 2. A point estimate was calculated for all models; for Models 1 and 2, the 95% confidence interval was also calculated.

Calculation of adult spawners needed to produce the predicted ranges of coho salmon smolt production

The number of adult coho salmon needed to produce the range of smolts predicted by each model was then estimated using literature values of fecundity, egg deposition, and the survival rates from egg to fry and from fry to smolt (e.g., Nickelson and Lawson 1998). Survival estimates from egg to fry (7.6%) and fry to smolt (19.8%) were taken from Bradford (1995). Fecundity estimates were initially set at 2,500 eggs per female based on literature values (e.g., Sandercock 1991), but were later adjusted to 5,335 eggs per female based on newly-acquired empirical data from the Unalakleet River population (Nemeth et al. 2004). Egg deposition by spawning females was considered to be 100%; although likely an overestimate, this number forced the direction of any bias.

Empirical estimates of smolt abundance from the Nome River, 2005 and 2006

Actual abundance of coho salmon smolts in the Nome River was estimated in 2005 and 2006 using mark–recapture methods. Juvenile coho salmon were captured in a fyke net located 1.5 km upstream from the ocean. Fish captured in this net (Site 1) were marked with a temporary caudal fin clip, sampled for length and age (by taking a scale sample), and released. Coho salmon were then captured in a second fyke net located 1 km downstream (Site 2). All coho salmon captured at Site 2 were then screened for these clips (to identify recaptures from fish released at Site 1), and a second temporary clip was given (to identify recaptures from fish already released at Site 2). Some coho salmon captured at Site 2 were also tagged with coded wire tags.

Abundance of juvenile coho salmon was calculated with two-site mark–recapture methods. Recaptures from Site 1 were broken into strata based on caudal clip and the proportion of smolts observed in the population. The abundance estimate for each stratum was calculated according to the Peterson estimator with Chapman's correction for bias (Ricker 1975), per notation in Carlson et al. (1998).

Abundance was estimated for all juvenile coho salmon, and for the subcomponent thought to be smolts. Pilot studies in 2004 indicated that most fish greater than 80 mm were age-2, the age that contributes the most to adult returns in the Nome River (Kent 2007). Smolts in 2005 and 2006 were considered to be those fish that had the physical appearance of smolts or were greater than 80 mm. Results were stratified into fish above and below 80 mm; smolt abundance estimates included only the size class greater than 80 mm. Abundance for both smolts and presmolts each year was calculated for the entire sampling season (all strata pooled) and for the weeks of peak emigration (typically June 1 through June 30).

Marine Survival of Nome River coho salmon

Fish capture and marking.—Juvenile coho salmon from Sites 1 and 2 were coded wire tagged and released in the Nome River in 2005 and 2006. Fish selected for tagging were anesthetized with clove oil and adipose fin-clipped for future identification. Full-length sequential coded wire tags were injected into the snout of each fish, using the appropriate head molds (Northwest Marine Technologies Mark IV tag injector; Shaw Island, WA). Tagged fish were checked with a NMT quality control device to confirm presence of the tag and then released at their capture site after recovering from anesthesia. During each tagging event (day) up to 250 coho salmon were kept overnight for evaluation of tag retention and tagging mortality. The greatest number of coded wire tags were implanted in those fish thought to be smolts, based on size (>80 mm) and appearance.

Tag retention rates were calculated using a binomial proportion (Carlon and Hasbrouck 1993). The number of tagged fish used for population estimates was adjusted to reflect the number of fish that survived and retained coded wire tags. Tag retention estimates were pooled to afford overall estimates of retention rates, which were then applied to the total number of juvenile coho salmon tagged to provide the number of viable tags released into the population.

Adult coho salmon returning in 2006 were captured in beach seines downstream from the Nome River weir; they were then examined for adipose fin clips that would indicate presence of a coded wire tag.

Data analysis.—Marine survival was calculated using the proportion of tagged adult coho salmon that returned in 2006 versus the number emigrating with tags the prior year. The total number of tagged fish returning as adults in 2006 was estimated by multiplying the proportion of tagged adults in a subsampled population by the total number of adults returning to the system that year, including counts at the Nome River weir and estimates of harvest. Marine survival (e.g., survival from smolt emigration to adult return) was then calculated by dividing the estimated number of adults returning with tags by the number of smolts originally tagged (Ricker 1975).

Results

Based on stream order, gradient, and known barriers, the length of stream habitat available to rearing coho salmon was estimated at 83 km in the Nome River and 277 km in the North River. This habitat consisted of the mainstem and three sub basins on the Nome River and the mainstem and 12 sub-basins on the North River, all of which were third order or higher. Mainstem habitat accounted for 77% of the available coho salmon rearing in the Nome River drainage and 57% of the available coho salmon rearing habitat in the North River drainage (Table 3).

Nearly all of the rearing habitat included in the model was less than 2% gradient. On the Nome River, 94% of the rearing habitat was less than 2% gradient, 5% of the habitat was between 2% and 4% gradient, and a small amount of habitat (less than 1%) was between 4% and 6% gradient. On the North River, 84% of the rearing habitat was less than 2% gradient, 15% of the habitat was between 2% and 4% gradient, and the remaining 1% was between 4% and 6% (Table 3). Gradients over 6% were never included in the model because they were first excluded by high B or low stream order.

Both rivers were sampled in both June and August of 2003 and 2004 to describe juvenile coho salmon rearing in different locations and habitats. In both years, minnow trap CPUE increased in nearly all sites from June to August. Additionally, juvenile coho salmon were present in more sites, and in greater ranges of age classes, in August than in June.

In the Nome River, juvenile coho salmon were caught as high as 55 km upriver in the mainstem, and in tributaries as far upstream as Rocky Mountain Creek (river km 50). Of the three places in which juvenile coho salmon were predicted but not detected, one was blocked by a perched culvert and the other two locations were sampled only in June and not in August, when coho salmon were more widely dispersed. In the North River, juvenile coho salmon were captured as far as 79 km upriver in the mainstem river, and as far as 68 km upriver in tributaries. Juvenile coho salmon were captured in all ten tributaries sampled, although not in all sites in both years. The majority of third-order and higher streams that were surveyed had juvenile coho salmon; the majority of second-order and lower streams that were surveyed did not.

Overall, sampling in 2003 and 2004 supported the predictions of useable summer rearing habitat by the original model. The model overestimated the upstream range of coho salmon rearing in the Nome River (assuming our failure to capture fish above river km 55 was a true negative), but underestimated rearing in at least some 2nd-order streams because coho salmon were present in a portion of the 2nd-order streams sampled to test the validity of their exclusion from the model. In tributaries of the proper gradient class, coho salmon were usually present in streams two branches off the mainstem (tributary forks). Inclusion of these smaller tributaries would substantially increase the amount of habitat, so these streams should only be included in future models after being filtered with finer-scale attributes such as distance up watershed and valley slope to try to determine which ones are likely to be used as rearing habitat (Sharma and Hilborn 2001).

TABLE 3. Stream lengths (m) predicted to be accessible to coho salmon *Oncorhynchus kisutch* smolts in the North and Nome rivers, stratified by gradient and stream order.

Location	3rd order and higher				4th order and higher			
	<2%	<4%	<6%	<8%	<2%	<4%	<6%	<8%
North River								
1 (Little North R.)	25,229	25,229	25,229	25,229	0	0	0	0
2	0	2,735	2,735	2,735	0	0	0	0
3	4,733	5,679	5,679	5,679	0	0	0	0
4	1,596	1,596	1,596	1,596	0	0	0	0
5	1,571	4,575	4,575	4,575	0	0	0	0
6	3,629	6,482	7,674	7,674	0	0	0	0
7	22,100	34,140	34,140	34,140	13,042	14,395	14,395	14,395
8	6,246	13,414	14,084	14,084	2,287	2,287	2,287	2,287
9	0	4,665	4,665	4,665	0	0	0	0
10	21,813	24,563	24,563	24,563	0	0	0	0
11	5,609	6,587	7,110	7,110	0	0	0	0
12	8,222	10,692	10,692	10,692	0	0	0	0
13 (Mainstem North R.)	131,936	134,474	134,474	134,474	122,301	122,301	122,301	122,301
North River Subtotal	232,684	274,832	277,219	277,219	137,630	138,983	138,983	138,983
Nome River								
Osborn Creek	15,845	17,324	17,975	17,975	0	0	0	0
Elk Creek	302	302	302	302	0	0	0	0
Buster Creek	2,146	2,146	2,146	2,146	0	0	0	0
Mainstem Nome R.	60,206	62,814	62,814	62,814	20,684	20,684	20,684	20,684
Nome River Subtotal	78,499	82,586	83,237	83,237	20,684	20,684	20,684	20,684

TABLE 3. Continued.

Location	5th order and higher				Side Channels (<2%)			
	<2%	<4%	<6%	<8%	<2%	<4%	<6%	<8%
North River								
1 (Little North R.)	0	0	0	0	0	0	0	0
2	0	0	0	0	0	0	0	0
3	0	0	0	0	0	0	0	0
4	0	0	0	0	0	0	0	0
5	0	0	0	0	0	0	0	0
6	0	0	0	0	0	0	0	0
7	0	0	0	0	0	0	0	0
8	0	0	0	0	0	0	0	0
9	0	0	0	0	0	0	0	0
10	0	0	0	0	0	0	0	0
11	0	0	0	0	0	0	0	0
12	0	0	0	0	0	0	0	0
13 (Mainstem North R.)	69,782	69,782	69,782	69,782	23,756	23,756	23,756	23,756
North River Subtotal	69,782	69,782	69,782	69,782	23,756	23,756	23,756	23,756
Nome River								
Osborn Creek	0	0	0	0	0	0	0	0
Elk Creek	0	0	0	0	0	0	0	0
Buster Creek	0	0	0	0	0	0	0	0
Mainstem Nome R.	0	0	0	0	0	0	0	0
Nome River Subtotal	0	0	0	0	0	0	0	0

Juvenile coho salmon were also found upstream of the beaver dams in all seven of the tributaries sampled with beaver dams, including tributaries on the North River with multiple dams or relatively large (~2 m) barriers. The only potential barrier above which juvenile coho salmon were not detected in both rivers and years was the perched culvert on Banner Creek, a tributary to the Nome River.

Model 1, generated from the log-linear relationship between stream length and smolt production for British Columbia and Southeast Alaska (Figure 1), estimated smolt production on the Nome River at 146,098 smolts (95% CI: 110,567–181,629) and smolt production on the North River at 419,593 (95% CI: 307,392–531,794). Model 2, which used the median smolt production per km from the same data set, estimated smolt production on the Nome River at 105,370 (95% CI = 72,179–170–836 smolts) and smolt production on the North River at 350,934 smolts (95%CI = 240,390–568,964 smolts). Model 3, which was the most conservative estimate derived from the 25% quartile of the same 40-year data set, estimated smolt production on the Nome River at 54,917 smolts and smolt production on the North River at 182,899 smolts (Table 4).

The number of adult coho salmon needed to produce the estimated mean number of smolts ranged from 1,372 (Model 3) to 3,649 (Model 1) on the Nome River and 4,568 (Model 3) to 10,481 (Model 1) on the North River (Table 4). These estimates were 2% more (Model 1), 28% less (Model 2), and 62% less (Model 3) than the mean escapement observed from 2001 to 2007 on the Nome River (3,595; Table 4). On the North River, these estimates were 18% less (Model 1), 32% less (Model 2), and 64% less (Model 3) than the mean observed escapement from 2001 and 2003–2007 (12,806 adult coho; Table 4). The standard deviations of observed escapements to the Nome and North rivers from 2001 through 2007 overlapped the 95% confidence intervals predicted by models 1 and 2 (Figure 3).

In both years (and in the pilot year in 2004), CPUE of juvenile coho salmon peaked in early to mid-June; coho salmon caught during this time were larger than those caught after June (Figures 4 and 5). These fish were usually bright silver, had few or faded parr marks, and moved quickly between the sampling sites. After the peak migration each year, the catch was comprised of younger, smaller coho salmon, which then grew throughout the remainder of the season (Figure 4). The first half of the run, captured before mid-July, was composed almost entirely of coho salmon over 90 mm in 2004 and 2005, and 80 mm in 2006. The second half of the run, by contrast, was composed primarily of coho salmon 90 mm and smaller in 2004 and 2005, and 80 mm in 2006 (Figure 4). The highest catches of small fish (70 mm and under) were in late summer (July and later) and were sometimes associated with high water events.

Based on the timing of the run peak each year and the consistency with which older, larger fish were replaced by younger, smaller fish after this peak, we classified all fish that were larger than 80 mm and migrated during the peak of the run as smolts. In June of 2006, fish greater than 80 mm were 42% age-1 and 58% age-2 and -3, based on extrapolations from fish subsampled for age. After the peak of the run each year (July and later), fish larger than 80 mm were nearly all age-1 fish, although small numbers of age-2 fish were still captured. We classified these as smolts as well, not knowing their exact contribution to the smolt run, but calculated the abundance of these fish separately from those migrating in June. The distribution of lengths by age-class had a relatively large overlap during many time periods.

In 2005, smolt abundance was estimated at 92,820 fish, with a 95% confidence interval of 84,615–101,026 (Table 5). This estimate

TABLE 4. Estimate of the required number of coho spawners needed to produce the range of smolts predicted by 3 habitat-based production models.

Watershed	North River			Nome River		
Model	1	2	3	1	2	3
Estimated smolt production[1]	419,593	350,934	82,899	146,098	105,370	54,917
Lower 95% CI	307,392	240,390		110,567	72,179	
Upper 95% CI	531,794	568,964		181,629	170,836	
Required fry production[2]	5,520,957	4,617,553	2,406,565	1,922,345	1,386,454	722,588
Lower 95% CI	4,044,629	3,163,031		1,454,833	949,723	
Upper 95% CI	6,997,285	7,486,368		2,389,857	2,247,836	
Required egg deposition	27,883,621	23,320,977	2,154,368	9,708,812	7,002,291	3,649,436
Lower 95% CI	20,427,419	15,974,906		7,347,639	4,796,581	
Upper 95% CI	35,339,823	37,809,941		12,069,986	11,352,707	
Fecundity[3]	5,335	5,335	5,335	5,335	5,335	5,335
Model required spawners	10,453	8,743	4,556	3,640	2,625	1,368
Lower 95% CI	7,658	5,989		2,755	1,798	
Upper 95% CI	13,248	14,174		4,525	4,256	
Spawners/km	38	32	16	44	32	16
Lower 95% CI	28	22		33	22	
Upper 95% CI	48	51		55	51	

TABLE 4. Continued.

Watershed	North River			Nome River		
Model	1	2	3	1	2	3
Observed escapement 2001–2007[4]	12,806	12,806	12,806	3,595	3,595	3,595
% difference in adults	–18%	–32%	–64%	1%	–27%	–62%
Lower 95% CI	–40%	–53%		–23%	–50%	
Upper 95% CI	3%	11%		26%	18%	

[1] Assumes a 7.6 % survival rate from fry to smolt (Bradford 1995).
[2] Assumes a 19.8 survival rate from egg to fry (Bradford 1995).
[3] Data from Unalakleet River (Nemeth et al. 2004).
[4] Excludes 2002 on North River

was for the entire period sampled, which ranged from May 26 through August 26. During the peak of the run (May 26 through July 2), the estimate was 83,194 smolts, with a 95% confidence interval of 75,813–90,575 (Table 5). Overall, fish size declined after July 2, with a definite influx of young-of-year (age-0) fish. Actual smolt production in 2005 was also within the range predicted by Model 2, but was lower than Model 1 and higher than Model 3.

In 2006, smolt abundance was estimated at 122,079 smolts, with a 95% confidence interval of 112,612–131,546 (Table 5). This estimate was for the entire sampling period, which ranged from June 1 through August 8. During the peak of the run (June 1 through June 26), the estimate was 88,025 smolts, with a 95% confidence interval of 80,030–96,021 fish (Table 5). Coho salmon during this time period were bright silver, had few or faded parr marks, and moved quickly between the sampling sites. As in 2005, there was an influx of younger and smaller fish after the peak of the run, and those fish over 80 mm in length were often younger than smolts of the same size during the run peak.

Actual smolt production in 2006 fell within the ranges predicted by Models 1 and 2, but was higher than Model 3.

If the actual smolt estimate of 92,820 in 2005 was used in the life cycle model, it would have predicted 2,318 spawners, 35% fewer than the mean of 3,590 actually observed from 2001 through 2007. In actuality, the parent year-class of those smolts (2002) was 3,418 spawners. The actual estimate in 2006 was 122,091 smolts; if this were used in the life cycle model, it would have predicted 3,049 spawners, or 15% fewer than the mean observed from 2001 through 2007. In actuality, the parent year-class of these fish (2003) was only 548 spawners.

In 2005, coded wire tags were injected into 9,481 juvenile coho salmon between May 29 and June 17. A total of 3,195 tagged fish were retained overnight, spread over 16 nights. Of these, 60 died (presumably due to tagging-associated handling) and 69 shed their tags. Accounting for unequal weighting among the 16 retention groups, removing the tag mortalities, and correcting for tag loss, the final number released with viable CWTs was 9,255 coho salmon smolts.

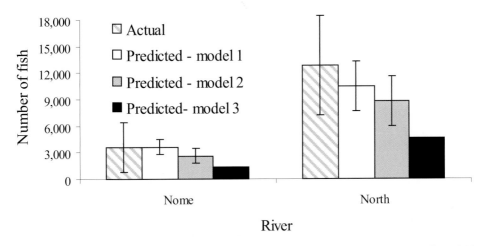

FIGURE 3. Actual escapements of adult coho salmon to the Nome and North rivers from 2001 through 2007, vs. escapements predicted by three habitat-based models, vs. mean actual escapements observed. Data exclude 2002 on the North River because of unreliable escapement data.

88

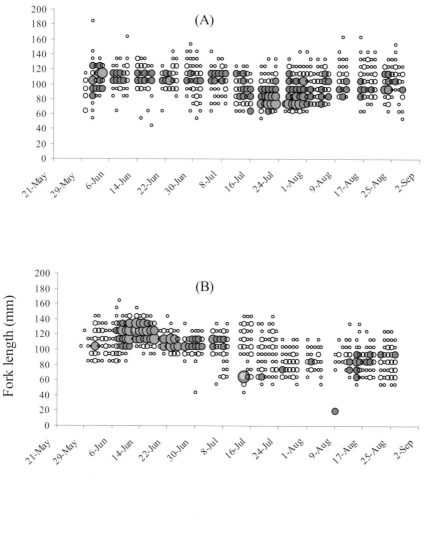

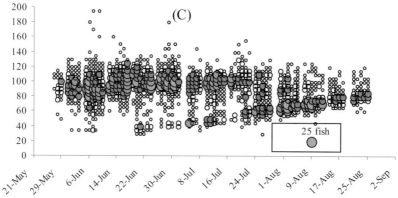

FIGURE 4. Number of juvenile coho salmon by size and date emigrating from the Nome River, Alaska, in 2004 (A), 2005 (B), and 2006 (C).

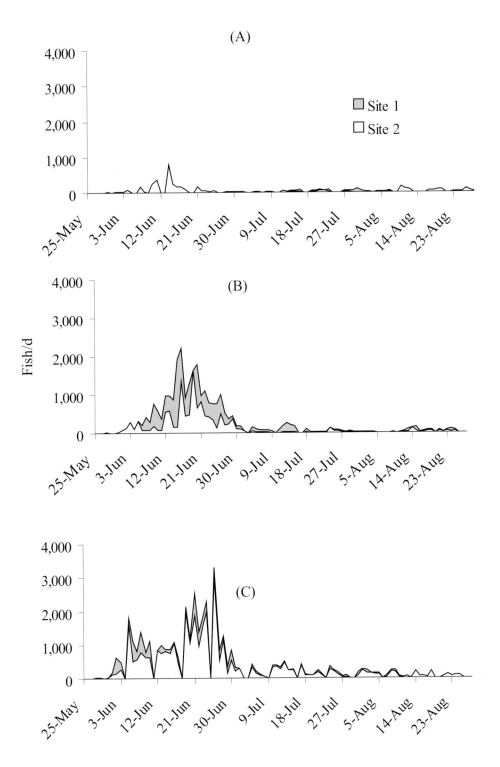

FIGURE 5. Catch per unit effort (fish/day) for juvenile coho salmon in fyke nets at sampling sites 1 & 2 in the Nome River in 2004 (A), 2005 (B), and 2006 (C).

TABLE 5. Abundance estimates by time period for coho salmon smolts in the Nome River, 2005 and 2006. Numbers are for fish that were greater than 80 mm in fork length, and considered smolts.

Year	Release dates	Run portion	(M_h) Releases	(m_h) Marked Recaptures	Captures (u_h) Unmarked	(n_h) Total	$\hat{N}_h$ Abundance Estimate	95% LL CI	95% UL CI
2005									
	May 28–July 2	Run peak	10,947	2,153	14,212	16,364	83,194	75,813	90,575
	July 3–Aug 26	Post peak	692	83	1,387	1,470	12,135	12,135	12,135
	Pooled—all season	Total season	11,639	2,236	15,599	17,834	92,820	84,615	101,026
2006									
	Jun 1–25	Run peak	2,259	376	14,307	14,683	88,025	80,030	96,021
	Jun 26–Aug 25	Post peak	624	135	6,854	6,989	32,122	27,411	36,834
	Pooled—all seasson	Total season	2,883	511	21,161	21,672	122,079	112,612	131,546

When CWT marked smolts returned as adults in 2006, tags were detected in 95 (7.2%) of the 1,311 adult coho salmon screened for CWTs. Expanding this proportion to the entire adult return of 15,123 coho salmon produced an estimated 1,096 tagged adult coho salmon in the population (escapement and harvest data from Kent 2007 and Jennings et al., in press). Survival was estimated as 11.8% for the smolts emigrating from the Nome River in 2005.

Discussion

Field data collected during this study supported the inputs originally taken from the literature to generate the habitat-based production model. Juvenile coho salmon were found in most of the places predicted by our initial habitat classifications, indicating that our estimates of useable rearing habitat were relatively accurate. The smolt production estimates that resulted from our habitat quantity assumptions matched up well with actual smolt production in 2005 and 2006; however, this match could have also resulted if we had under- or overestimated the habitat, as long as we had also over- or underestimated the production per km. Fish were also found upstream of all beaver dams sampled, contrary to some anecdotal concerns that large dams prevent upstream access by either juvenile or adult coho salmon.

We found juvenile coho salmon in the sites they were detected by Scott and Webb (1985) in the 1980s. We also found evidence of juvenile rearing outside of the range of known adult spawning. In three years of spawner distribution surveys using radio telemetry, Joy and Reed (2007) found no coho salmon spawners above approximately river km 68, and none in a major tributary entering from the East known as Sunquist. We found juvenile coho salmon nearly 11 km higher in the mainstem, and nearly 2 km up the Sunquist tributary; both sites were the highest we sampled and not necessarily the uppermost boundary of rearing habitat.

The most needed area of improvement is in determining which second- and third-order streams are used for summer rearing by juvenile coho salmon. We found coho salmon in all 3rd-order tributaries sampled, in keeping with the predictive model. However, we were unable to catch coho salmon in a third-order section of the mainstem of the upper Nome River, indicating that we may have overestimated the amount of mainstem habitat length by 8 km (12%). Conversely, we captured coho salmon in some second-order tributaries that we did not predict, thereby underestimating the length of useable tributary habitat. Future rearing habitat models will need to consider how and when to include these tributaries in estimates of habitat quantity. Adjustment of which stream orders or the number of branches off the mainstem (the B-value) to include may address this issue—for example, including only those second-order streams that are one branch off the mainstem river. Also, we were more likely to find coho salmon using second-order streams low in the watershed than high in the watershed. Bocking and Peacock (2005) found that the addition of second-order streams did not add an appreciable amount to the rearing habitat and subsequent estimate of smolt (and adult) production in British Columbia streams.

Overall, some evidence existed that Nome River production per km was lower than in some other regions included in the regional dataset (Bocking and Peacock), although the Nome River time series is not long enough to test for statistical differences. Mean smolt production in 2005 and 2006 was 1,295 smolts/km, which was lower than the means from southeast Alaska (4,655 smolts/km) and British Columbia (2,199 smolts/km), but similar to the means from Washington (1,174 smolts/km) and Oregon (1,099 smolts/km). One explanation for the rank of the Nome

River may be that the Nome River production is truly closer to Washington and Oregon than it is to southeast Alaska and British Columbia, due to nutrient production, climate, or other factors. An alternative explanation is that the differences were a function of allometric relationships between watershed size and smolt production. Smaller watersheds produce more smolts per km than do larger watersheds (Parken et al. 2006); the Nome River was 50% larger than the largest river in the dataset from southeast Alaska or British Columbia, but only the third largest of the rivers from Washington and Oregon.

The estimates of the actual abundance of coho salmon smolts from the Nome River have two components: one during the peak of the run in June and one afterward in July and August. The run peak in 2005 and again in 2006 was obviously composed of smolts; these fish were primarily age-2, had the appearance of smolts, and did not linger for recapture within the lower river. The abundance estimate of smolts during this time was relatively consistent: 83,194 in 2005 and 88,025 in 2006 (Tables 4 and 5). The second component includes fish that had the size, age, or appearance of smolts, but not all three. These fish were small age-2 fish and large age-1 fish. We included these fish in our estimates of smolts in 2006 because we know that age-1 fish contribute from 5% to 15% of the adult runs each year in Norton Sound streams. Few age-1 juveniles were captured during the peak part of the run (in June), so it seemed plausible that these large, age-1 coho salmon captured in July and August might represent the proportion of age-1 fish seen in returning adults. These coho salmon added about 10% to our smolt estimate in 2005 and 28% in 2006, accounting for most of the overall difference in smolts (92,820 versus 122,079) in the two years.

Several observations support the idea that our combination of age, size, and timing was a feasible way to separate smolts from nonsmolts. First, the 80 mm minimum appeared to include all age-2 and -3 coho salmon that were captured at river mouth (Site 2) during the peak of the run, as well as a few large age-1 fish. Second, fish under 80 mm were captured much more frequently at the upstream site (km 1.5) than at the river mouth (km 0.5). Third, fish under 80 mm that were caught at the upper site were often captured multiple times (as indicated by fin clips), indicating they may have been rearing in this upstream area instead of moving downstream. By contrast, fish captured at the river mouth during the peak of the run were rarely caught multiple times (Williams et al. 2006).

Although the predictions of smolt production appeared accurate, we did not attempt to further identify which life stage or specific habitats are responsible for limiting production. Our model assumed a constant production of juveniles per km of all rearing habitat available to juvenile coho salmon in June and August; in reality, different rearing habitats undoubtedly have different production potential, and only some are used at whatever life stage is most limiting to eventual smolt production (e.g., Reeves et al. 1989; Anderson and Hetrick 2004). Without knowing this, our estimate is simply an observational study indicating that whatever the idiosyncrasies of habitat in Norton Sound may be, the overall production per km is within the range of datasets compiled in other regions.

One of the assumptions in Norton Sound has been that freshwater production is limited by overwintering habitat because much of the habitat used in the summer freezes in winter and is thus not available to rearing coho salmon. Any habitat reduction from summer to winter may not mean that overwintering habitat limits production; it may be that when fish consolidate in winter habitats, they are able to exist in high densities because they have little need for feeding or growth. If the total useable habitat shrinks by half in the winter but coho salmon are able to survive at twice the densities, the contraction of habitat from summer to winter may not have an overly large effect on total freshwater production. Fish grew little during this time from late August to June (based on scale patterns), indicating that they may have little nutritional needs during the winter. If fish only feed and grow during the summer, it may be the availability of seasonally-useable summer habitat that limits production.

Annually, the actual number of returning spawners since 2001 has fallen both below and above the range predicted when the smolt abundance estimates from Model 1 and 2 were placed into a life cycle model. The mean escapement from 2001 through 2007, however, is within the range predicted by both models on each river (Figure 3). This suggests that the recent annual returns of coho salmon to the Nome and North rivers (means of 3,590 and 12,860 adults) should be viewed as a reasonable number of adults needed to produce the number of smolts supportable by the total habitat on each river.

The 12% survival from smolting to adult is slightly higher than the 9.8% average survival noted in a species review by Bradford (1995), but within the range of 2.9% to 19.8% reported by Shaul (1994) for populations from southeast Alaska populations. The relatively high survival rate for Nome River smolts from 2005 may help explain the record returns of coho salmon to Norton Sound in 2006.

Conclusions and Recommendations

The original objectives of the project were able to be addressed in a stepwise way, replacing theoretical components of the model with results from empirical studies. In general, most empirical results from the Nome and North rivers were consistent with predictions from the literature. These include juvenile rearing habitat use, smolt production

per km of stream habitat available to juvenile coho salmon, marine survival of smolts, and the actual returns of adult spawners. However, fecundity of adult coho salmon was much higher than literature values. No empirical studies of survival exist for egg to smolt from Norton Sound populations.

Adult escapement, smolt abundance, and marine survival should continue to be assessed over time to determine interannual variability. This time series will also allow managers to contrast smolt abundance both in years following high and low adult escapements and in years with differing environmental conditions and pink salmon abundance. Continued smolt monitoring in 2007–2009 should be a high priority because the smolt cohorts from 2007 through 2009 will be from increasingly high adult escapements from 2004 through 2006, including the two highest on record. These cohorts will follow the 2003 parent year, when escapements were the lowest on record in many Norton Sound rivers, thereby providing high contrast in the data from a relatively narrow range of years.

The ability to compare juvenile abundance, marine survival, and biological characteristics in consecutive years with such high contrast will be especially useful for helping investigate issues related to density dependence and the carrying capacity of juvenile coho salmon rearing habitat. The time series will also allow freshwater survival to be estimated by matching adult escapements to subsequent smolt production.

Finally, smolt production should be estimated on another Norton Sound river to estimate whether substantial variability exists between the Nome and other rivers. Quantifying such variability would then indicate the confidence with which managers could apply the Nome River results to rivers throughout the Norton Sound region (one of the long-term intentions of the project). Optimally, this second river would be one with habitat that differs from that of the Nome, so that a broad range of habitats are compared. The river should also, preferably, have an adult enumeration project in place so that smolt production estimates can be matched with adult escapement.

Acknowledgments

Primary funding (75%) for this study was provided by the National Oceanic and Atmospheric Administration through Cooperative Agreement NA16FW1272 Research and Prevention Relative to the 1999 Norton Sound Fishery Disaster. Matching funds (25%) were provided by the Norton Sound Economic Development Corporation. We thank the Norton Sound Scientific Technical Committee for useful review comments that improved the design of this study. The manuscript was improved by C. Zimmerman of the USGS and two anonymous reviewers. W. Jones and F. DiCicco of the Alaska Department of Fish and Game also provided substantial help with site reconnaissance, coho salmon information, and field logistics. Special thanks go to C. Lean of NSEDC for assistance with site reconnaissance and regional life history information. R. Ferry, M. Johnson, and F. Charles of Unalakleet assisted with logistical planning and boat preparations on the North River. C. Lidstone of Birkenhead Scale Analysis for the age of all scales. B. Haley and G. Wade provided maps. Finally, B. Baxter, S. Haskell, B. Haley, A. Krenz, R. Lean, J. Mikulski, D. Miller, J. Miller, V. Munn, S. Larson, S. Morgan, N. Polk, M. Reeves, and R. Sparks provided enthusiastic assistance with field work.

References

Alaska Department of Fish and Game (ADF&G) and Alaska Board of Fish. 2001. Sustainable salmon fisheries policy for the State of Alaska. Alaska Department of Fish and Game, Juneau.

Anderson, J. L., and N. J. Hetrick. 2004. Carrying capacity of habitats used seasonally by coho salmon in the Kametolook River, Alaska Peninsula National Wildlife Refuge, 2002–2003. U. S. Fish and Wildlife Service, King Salmon Fish and Wildlife Field Office, Alaska Fisheries Technical Report Number 73, King Salmon, Alaska.

Baxter, B. E., and C. Y. Stephens. 2005. Adult and juvenile coho salmon enumeration and coded-wire tag recovery analysis for Zolzap Creek, BC, 2004. Canadian Manuscript Report of Fisheries and Aquatic Sciences No. 2730. Fisheries and Ocean Canada, Prince Rupert, B.C.

Bocking, R. C., and D. Peacock. 2005. Habitat-based production goals for coho salmon in Fisheries and Oceans statistical area 3. LGL environmental research associates, Sidney, British Columbia. Final report for Pacific Scientific Advisory Review Committee, Department of Fisheries and Oceans, Canada.

Bradford, M. J. 1995. Comparative review of Pacific salmon survival rates. Canadian Journal of Fisheries and Aquatic Sciences 52:1327–1338.

Bradford, M. J., G. C. Taylor, and J. A. Allan. 1997. Empirical review of coho salmon smolt abundance and the prediction of smolt production at the regional level. Transactions of the American Fisheries Society 126:49–64.

Bradford, M. J., R. A. Myers, and J. R. Irvine. 2000. Reference points for coho salmon (Oncorhynchus kisutch) harvest rates and escapement goals based on freshwater production. Canadian Journal of Fisheries and Aquatic Sciences 57:677–686.

Brannian, L. K., M. J. Evenson, and J. R. Hilsinger. 2006. Escapement goal recommendations for select Arctic-Yukon-Kuskokwim region salmon stocks, 2007. Alaska Department of Fish and Game, Fishery Manuscript No. 06–07, Juneau, Alaska.

Burns, J. W. 1971. The carrying capacity for juvenile salmonids in some northern California streams. California Fish and Game 57:44–57.

Carlon, J. A., and J. J. Hasbrouck. 1993. Marking juvenile coho salmon in the Kenai River with coded, microwire tags. Alaska Department of Fish and Game. Anchorage Alaska, Fishery Data Series No. 92–52.

Carlson, S. R., L.G. Coggins Jr., and C O. Swanton. 1998. A simple stratified design for mark–recapture estimation of salmon smolt abundance. Alaska Fishery Research Bulletin 5:88–102.

Jennings, G. B., K. Sundet, and A. E. Bingham. In press. Estimates of participation, catch, and harvest in Alaska sport fisheries during 2006. Alaska Department of Fish and Game, Fishery Data Series, Anchorage.

Joy, P., and D. J. Reed. 2007. Estimation of coho salmon abundance and spawning distribution in the Unalakleet River 2004–2006. Alaska Department of Fish and Game, Fishery Data Series No. 07–48, Anchorage, Alaska.

Kent, S. 2007. Salmonid escapements at Kwiniuk, Niukluk and Nome Rivers, 2006. Alaska Department of Fish and Game, Fishery Data Series No. 07–09, Anchorage, Alaska.

Knudsen, E. E. 2000. Managing Pacific salmon escapements: the gap between theory and reality. Pages 237–272 in E. E. Knudsen, C. R. Steward, D. D. MacDonald, J. E. Williams, and D. W. Reiser, editors. Sustainable fisheries management: Pacific salmon. CRC Press, Boca Raton, Florida.

Koenings, J. P., and R. D. Burkett. 1987. The production patterns of sockeye (Oncorhynchus nerka) smolts relative to temperature, euphotic volume, fry density, and forage base within Alaskan lakes. Pages 216–234 in H. D. Smith, L. Margolis, and C. C. Wood, editors. Sockeye salmon (Oncorhynchus nerka) population biology and future management. Canadian Special Publication of Fish and Aquatic Sciences 96.

Menard, J. 2003. Norton Sound season summary 2003. Memorandum to D. Bergstrom, October 14, 2003. Alaska Department of Fish and Game, Juneau.

Menard, J., C. C. Krueger, and J. R. Hilsinger. 2009. Norton Sound salmon fisheries: history, stock abundance, and management. Pages 621–673 in C. C. Krueger and C. E. Zimmerman, editors. Pacific salmon: ecology and management of western Alaska's populations. American Fisheries Society, Symposium 70, Bethesda, Maryland.

Nemeth, M. J., B. H. Haley, and S. Kinneen. 2003. Fecundity of chum and coho salmon from Norton Sound, Alaska. Unpublished Report for the Norton Sound Disaster Relief Fund by LGL Alaska Research Associates and Norton Sound Economic Development Corporation. LGL Alaska Research Associates, Anchorage, Alaska.

Nemeth, M. J., B. Bocking, and S. Kinneen. 2004. Freshwater habitat as a predictor of coho salmon smolt production in two Norton Sound rivers: an initial study to support the development of habitat-based escapement goals. Annual report prepared for the Norton Sound Fishery Disaster Relief Fund by LGL Alaska Research Associates and Norton Sound Economic Development Corporation, Anchorage, Alaska.

Nemeth, M. J., B. Williams, B. H. Haley, and S. Kinneen. 2005. An ecological comparison of juvenile chum salmon from two watersheds in Norton Sound, Alaska: migration, diet, estuarine habitat, and fish community assemblage. Unpublished report for the Norton Sound Disaster Relief Fund by LGL Alaska Research Associates and Norton

Sound Economic Development Corporation, LGL Alaska Research Associates, Anchorage, Alaska.

Nickelson, T. E. 1998. A habitat-based assessment of coho salmon production potential and spawner escapement needs for Oregon coastal streams. Information Report No. 98–4. Oregon Department Fish and Wildlife, Portland, Oregon.

Nickelson, T. E., and Lawson, P. W. 1998. Population viability of oho salmon, Oncorhynchus kisutch, in Oregon coastal basins: application of a habitat-based life cycle model Canadian Journal of Fisheries and Aquatic Sciences 55:2383–2392.

Nickelson, T. E., J. D. Rodgers, S. L. Johnson, and M. F. Solazzi. 1992. Seasonal changes in habitat use by juvenile coho salmon (Oncorhynchus kisutch) in Oregon coastal streams. Canadian Journal of Fisheries and Aquatic Sciences 49:783–789.

Sharr, S. C. Melcher, T. Nickelson, P. Lawson, R. Kope, and J. Coon. 2000. 2000 review of Amendment 13 to the Pacific Coast Salmon Plan. Final draft by the OCN work group. Pacific Fisheries Management Council, Portland Oregon.

Pacific Fishery Management Council (PFMC). 2003. Pacific coast salmon plan. Pacific Fishery Management Council, Portland, Oregon.

Parken, C. K., R. E. McNichol, and J. R. Irvine. 2006. Habitat-based methods to estimate escapement goals for data limited Chinook salmon stocks in British Columbia, 2004. Fisheries and Oceans Canada, Science Branch, Pacific Biological Station. Nanaimo, British Columbia.

Reeves, G. H., F. H. Everest, and T. E. Nickelson. 1989. Identification of Physical Habitats Limiting the Production of Coho Salmon in Western Oregon and Washington. USDA Forest Service, Pacific Northwest Research Station, General Technical Report, PNW-GTR-245 Portland, Oregon.

Ricker, W. E. 1975. Computation and interpretation of biological statistics of fish populations. Bulletin of Fisheries Research Board of Canada 191.

Sandercock, F. K. 1991. Life history of coho salmon. Pages 395–446 in C. Groot and L. Margolis, editors. Pacific salmon: life histories. UBC Press, Vancouver, B.C.

Scott, M., and Webb, J. 1985. Unalakleet River salmon distribution inventory. Unpublished report. U. S. Bureau of Land Management, Fairbanks, Alaska.

Selkregg, L. L. 1976. Alaska regional profiles, Northwest region. University of Alaska, Arctic Environmental Information and Data Center, Anchorage, Alaska.

Sharma, R., and Hilborn, R. 2001. Empirical relationships between watershed characteristics and coho salmon (Oncorhynchus kisutch) smolt abundance in 14 western Washington streams. Canadian Journal of Fisheries and Aquatic Sciences 58:1453–1463.

Shaul, L. 1994. A summary of 1982–1991 harvest, escapements, migratory patterns, and marine survival rates of coho salmon stocks in Southeast Alaska. Alaska Fishery Research Bulletin 1:10–34.

Shaul, L., S. McPherson, E. Jones, and K. Crabtree. 2003. Stock status and escapement goals for coho salmon stocks in Southeast Alaska. Special Publication Number 03–02. Alaska Department of Fish and Game, Juneau, Alaska.

Shortreed, K. S., J. M. B. Hume, and J. G. Stockner. 1999. Using photosynthetic rates to estimate the juvenile sockeye salmon rearing capacity of British Columbia lakes. Pages 505–521 *in* E. E. Knudsen, C. R. Steward, D. D. MacDonald, J. E. Williams, and D. W. Reiser, editors. Sustainable fisheries management: Pacific salmon. CRC Press LLC, Boca Raton, New York.

Strahler, A. N. 1957. Quantitative analysis of watershed geomorphology. Transactions of the American Geophysical Union 38:913–920.

Volkhardt, G., P. Hanratty, D. Rawding, P. Topping, M. Ackley, C. Kinsel, K. Kiyohara, and L. Kishimoto. 2007. Wild salmon forecasts for Puget Sound and Washington coastal systems. Washington Department of Fish and Wildlife, Science Division. Olympia, Washington.

Webb, J. F., and R. F. McLean. 1991. An investigation of coho salmon rearing habitat in selected tributaries of the Nome River. Unpublished report, Alaska Department of Fish and Game, Fairbanks, Alaska.

Williams, B., M. Nemeth, S. Kinneen, and B. Bocking. 2006. Abundance of juvenile coho salmon in the Nome River. Unpublished report prepared for the Norton Sound Disaster Relief Fund by LGL Alaska Research Associates, Inc. and Norton Sound Economic Development Corporation.

American Fisheries Society Symposium 70:97–123, 2009

Population Genetics and the Management of Arctic-Yukon-Kuskokwim Salmon Populations

Fred M. Utter*

*School of Aquatic and Fishery Sciences, University of Washington
Box 355020, Seattle, Washington 98195, USA*

Megan V. McPhee

*Flathead Lake Biological Station, University of Montana
32125 Bio Station Lane, Polson, Montana 59860, USA*

Fred W. Allendorf

*Division of Biological Sciences, University of Montana
Missoula, Montana 59812, USA*

Abstract.—The genetic population structures of chum *Oncorhynchus keta*, Chinook *O. tshawytscha*, coho *O. kisutch*, sockeye *O. nerka*, and pink *O. gorbuscha* salmon within the AYK region are described based on available published and unpublished information. The most detailed genetic data were for chum salmon where major groups included: (1) summer-run fish returning to coastal rivers and the lower reaches of the Yukon and Kuskokwim Rivers, (2) upper Yukon River, and (3) upper Kuskokwim River fall-run populations. AYK Chinook and coho salmon populations showed similar patterns of differentiation within the Yukon and Kuskokwim Rivers, although each species had quite different spatial separation and timing. Based on unpublished genetic data from AYK sockeye salmon populations, Norton Sound populations were grouped together and were distinct from ten other areas within the Yukon and Kuskokwim drainages which had affinities with Bristol Bay populations. Available pink salmon data were insufficient to estimate population structures. Similarity of AYK and Susitna River chum and Chinook salmon populations suggest a common ancestry that may reflect an historical connection of these drainages. Low species-wide indices of among-population genetic variation (F_{ST}) in chum and pink salmon suggest that regionally based conservation strategies for these species will be effective. In contrast, Chinook, coho, and sockeye salmon had higher F_{ST} values and require population-specific strategies. Genetic stock identification methods (mixed stock analysis) provided valuable estimates of oceanic distributions of AYK chum salmon, and in-season estimates of chum, Chinook, and coho salmon stocks migrating within the Yukon and Kuskokwim Rivers. The genetic information now known about salmon in the AYK region will help the formulation and design of future investigations, and will ultimately promote a better understanding, management, and conservation of AYK salmon.

*Corresponding author: fmutter@u.washington.edu

Introduction

Salmon *Oncorhynchus* populations in the Arctic-Yukon-Kuskokwim (AYK) region came to national attention during 1997–2002, when low salmon returns, coupled with a depressed market for wild salmon, led to economic disaster for the residents of this vast and remote area. The AYK Sustainable Salmon Initiative (SSI) was established in 2001 with the objective of directing and supporting research that would illuminate the causes of salmon population variation in space and time, and thereby would enhance management of AYK salmon populations in the future (AYK SSI 2006).

One of the most important tools in salmon management is the use of genetics to determine which salmon populations are being affected by commercial harvest. The best known example of the use of genetics technology is for management of the Bristol Bay sockeye salmon *O. nerka* fishery, where genetic data are used in real time to determine within-season openings and closures (Habicht et al. 2007). This method has proved to be a useful tool for maximizing fishery productivity while minimizing overexploitation of vulnerable stocks.

Due to the potential role of local, national, and international fisheries in reductions in AYK salmon populations, a keen interest exists in improving managers' ability to use genetic data to identify conservation and management units, and to apply these data to more effective management of fisheries that are intercepting AYK salmon stocks. To this end, the authors summarize studies that describe what is known about the genetic diversity and population structure of salmon stocks from the AYK region. By compiling and synthesizing existing genetic data, gaps can be identified in information that must be filled in order to adequately understand, manage, and conserve in perpetuity the Pacific salmon within the AYK region.

Pacific Salmon Genetic Population Structure

Effective management of salmon species requires an understanding of the biological dynamics of their component populations. In particular, knowledge of the structure of genetic variation is needed to make decisions about how to identify and protect the local reproductive units, and how to guide management strategies. Moulton (1939) and Thompson (1959, 1965) provided the first modern description of the importance of local populations and genetic diversity for the management of Pacific salmon. They stated that each local population was genetically adapted to its own environment ("home-stream colony") and had a characteristic level of abundance around which it varied. In any river system, some colonies are capable of supporting exploitation, and others are not; commercial exploitation is likely to lead to the disappearance of some colonies (i.e., the extinction of local populations).

Distinct local populations (demes) and adaptations arise and are reinforced through the strong tendency of salmon to return to spawn in the stream in which they are born (homing), resulting in the local population being the fundamental unit of recruitment (Rich 1939; Ricker 1972). Homing produces a branching, and commonly hierarchical, system of local reproductive populations that are genetically and demographically isolated. Genetic differences among individuals within a local breeding population are the basis for natural selection and adaptive evolution, and genetic differences among breeding populations reflect random events and local adaptation to past environments. The genetic differences among breeding populations represent the broadest pool of genetic variation and are a valuable component of diversity. The capability to adapt to future environments is dependent on variation within the local breeding population as well as variations between populations (Allendorf and Luikart 2007).

This hierarchical organization of biological diversity from deme to species includes the roles of genetic and phenotypic diversity in influencing the ability of a salmon population to respond to long-term environmental change; it is described in detail in other chapters (McPhee et al. 2009, this volume; Waples 2009, this volume; Hard et al. 2009, this volume). Within this structure there are three primary levels that are relevant for the conservation and management of AYK salmon: the local population (McPhee et al. 2009); the stock (McPhee et al. 2009); and the evolutionary significant unit (ESU; Waples 2009).

Here the authors relate the local population and the stock, and consider the ESU in a subsequent section of this chapter. The demographic independence of local salmon populations make them the fundamental unit for recruitment (Rich 1939; Ricker 1972). An adequate number of spawners returning to each local reproductive population is needed to ensure persistence of the many reproductive units that make up a fished stock of salmon. The demographic dynamics of a fish population are determined by the balance between reproductive potential (i.e., biological and physical limits to production) and losses due to natural death and fishing. Therefore, fishery scientists have focused on setting fishing intensity so that adequate numbers of individuals "escape" fishing to provide sufficient recruitment to replace losses.

The distinction between a local breeding population and a fished stock is critical (Beverton et al. 1984). Whereas a local breeding population has a specific meaning—a local population in which mating occurs—*stock* is essentially an arbitrary term and can refer to any recognizable group of population units that are fished (Larkin 1972; NAS 1996); the literature has often been unclear on this distinction. For instance, Helle (1981) defined a stock as a local breeding population, citing Ricker (1972) as his authority. In practice, it is difficult to regulate losses to fishing on the basis of individual local breeding populations. Thousands of local breeding populations make up the West Coast salmon fishery of North America, and many of these are likely to be intermingled in any particular catch. Nevertheless, the result of regulating fishing on a stock basis (e.g., maximum sustained yield) and ignoring the reproductive units that together constitute a stock is the disappearance or extirpation of some of the local breeding populations (Clark 1984). These problems have made it difficult to establish long-term biological escapement goals in the AYK region, where recent efforts have been criticized as inadequate because of insufficient available data relating to abundances and temporal trends of specific breeding populations (Adkison et al. 2001; Tanasichuk 2002).

In this chapter, the authors review what is known regarding genetic diversity and population structure of AYK salmon populations. The focus is on information that informs two important management goals: 1) distinguishing major evolutionary groups within salmon species, and 2) using genetic data from population mixtures to derive estimates of component populations in the mixture (genetic stock identification).

Genetic Methods For Identifying Population Structure

A species' overall pattern of genetic variation can be measured by F_{ST}, the proportion of the total allelic genetic variance that can be attributed to differences among populations where

$$F_{ST} = 1 - H_S/H_T$$

H_S is the mean average *heterozygosity* (the probability that two alleles drawn

Utter et al.

TABLE 1. Distribution of genetic variation at allozyme loci in Pacific salmon species (Altukhov et al. 2000).

Species	H_T	H_S	F_{ST}
Chum salmon	0.0709	0.0688	0.0290
Chinook salmon	0.0736	0.0688	0.0652
Coho salmon	0.0295	0.0262	0.1130
Sockeye salmon	0.0424	0.0395	0.0688
Pink salmon	0.1044	0.0102	0.0191

at random differ) within all subpopulations, and H_T is the expected heterozygosity of the total population obtained from the average allele frequencies. Pacific salmon species have marked differences in their range-wide pattern of distribution of genetic variation (Table 1). For a more detailed summary, see Appendix 2 in Hendry and Stearns (2004).

Many loci are required to accurately estimate this within- and among-population variation over the entire genome. The patterns of genetic structure are determined primarily by the effects of *gene flow, genetic drift,* and *natural selection.* If the allelic variation is selectively *neutral* (not subject to natural selection), then gene flow and genetic drift are expected to affect all loci uniformly. Nevertheless, substantial differences may exist among loci by chance because genetic drift involves random changes in allele frequencies, and these changes will follow different trajectories at different loci. Therefore, reliance on one or two polymorphic loci diminishes power to describe genetic structure of populations (Slatkin and Maddison 1989).

A variety of markers is available for population genetic studies (see Waples et al. 2008). Sunnucks (2000) has reviewed the principle methods for genetic analysis of populations and their advantages and disadvantages. Nuclear markers where both alleles are detectable (i.e., are *codominant*) are preferred because they permit tests for random mating and provide better statistical estimates of allele frequencies than other markers. *Al-lozymes* (variants of protein-coding loci) and *microsatellites* (short regions of tandemly repeated DNA motifs) have been the prevailing codominant markers used to describe genetic population structure. These markers generally give similar estimates of population structure (Allendorf and Seeb 2000) providing that many polymorphic loci are examined. Some dominant nuclear markers such as AFLPs (amplified fragment length polymorphisms) can be informative because it is often possible to examine many markers. Randomly amplified length polymorphisms (RAPDs), another dominant marker in wide use, have had serious repeatability problems and are no longer generally accepted for applications other than genome exploration and marker development.

Single nucleotide polymorphisms (SNPs), or single base-pair differences in DNA sequence, are the most abundant polymorphism in the genome, with one occurring about every 500–1,000 bp in humans (Brumfield et al. 2003). Because the mutation rate at a single base pair is low (about 1×10^{-8} changes per nucleotide per generation), SNPs usually consist of only two alleles (i.e., are bi-allelic markers). For example, a G and a C might exist in different individuals at a particular nucleotide position within a population (or within a heterozygous individual). SNPs have great potential for many applications in describing genetic variation in natural populations. A particularly useful aspect of SNP markers is that little effort is required to standardize genotypic data among laboratories, which is not true for microsatellites (Moran et al. 2006).

Mitochondrial DNA (mtDNA) has been a popular tool for phylogenetic studies. Although somewhat limited relative to nuclear loci in describing genetic population structure within species, mtDNA can provide valuable additional insight when used in conjunction with nuclear loci. Lack of recombination means that although mtDNA has many coding genes, it acts as a single locus. It also is inherited only through the mother, so if females and males have different dispersal behaviors, genetic structure identified only by mtDNA misses half of the story (e.g., green turtles *Chelonia mydas*; Karl et al. 1992). However, this aspect is less critical in salmon, where both males and females tend to home faithfully to their natal spawning ground, and rates of straying probably do not differ between the sexes strongly enough to have major effects on interpretation of genetic structure (see Hendry et al. 2004). Another contrast with nuclear loci is the smaller *effective population size* (N_e) of mtDNA. Because of its haploid genome and maternal inheritance, the N_e of mtDNA is approximately a quarter that of N_e of a nuclear locus.

Conservation Units

Conservation units have been defined by Waples (2009) as major portions of biodiversity that collectively comprise the evolutionary legacy of a species. He describes a two-step process involving description of the (commonly hierarchical) biodiversity within each species, followed by consideration of the appropriate level and amount of biodiversity requiring conservation. The authors have noted above the inadequacy of conservation based on a harvest of mixtures of populations managed for maximum sustainable yield, where less abundant local populations within

the stock follow a trajectory towards extinction. Indeed, such concerns have motivated the increasing focus to include genetic information in management programs. The importance of the ESU (in the context of Waples 1991) as a major hierarchical level has also been mentioned but requires further elaboration. Clearly, ESUs comprised of local populations united by common genetic, behavioral, and life history attributes warrant distinct conservation considerations within the hierarchy. However, Waples (2009) identifies (in the context of the Skagit River) at least seven hierarchical levels within an ESU worthy of consideration for conservation.

Waples (2009) concludes that effective conservation requires situation-specific discernment of which hierarchical levels have priority within an ESU. A major effort in applying these principles in the management of Bristol Bay sockeye salmon is presented in Habicht et al. (2007). In describing the genetic structure of AYK salmon populations, the authors summarize and discuss similar efforts as a step towards accumulating further insights in identifying appropriate conservation units within this vast region.

Genetic Stock Identification

Genetic stock identification (GSI; also referred to as mixed stock analysis or mixture analysis) involves three steps (Pella and Milner 1987; Waples et al. 1990). First, a genetic baseline is established by characterizing multi-locus allele frequencies of known spawning populations and evaluating temporal stability of these characterizations. Second, individuals from mixed-stock collections (e.g., the catch from a fishery) are genotyped. Finally, these individuals either are assigned back to putative source populations, or stock compositions are estimated for the mixture sample using computational algorithms.

Genetic approaches for identifying stock composition are particularly useful for remote areas, such as the AYK region, comprised solely of wild salmon populations where physical tagging (such as coded-wire tags) is not practical. The initial use of allozyme data for GSI applications (Grant et al. 1980) has recently been displaced by microsatellite (Beacham and Wood 1999) and SNP (Seeb et al. 2005) markers (see Utter 2005). Beyond their intrinsic biological value, GSI estimates have become powerful and unique tools to guide real time (presently within 72 h, J. Seeb, ADF&G, personal communication) and post-season salmon management (Winans et al. 1994; Shaklee et al. 1999, Seeb et al. 2000; Seeb et al. 2004). In addition, the forensic value of mixed stock estimates has demonstrated value in resolving disputed origins of chum salmon from vessels involved in illegal high seas fisheries (Wilmot et al. 1999; Kondzela et al. 2002).

The key to a successful stock identification program is a comprehensive genetic baseline that includes all potential source stocks. Algorithms for GSI attempt to assign all individuals to stocks in the baseline, so if some individuals originate from populations not represented in the baseline, inaccuracies will result. The geographic coverage of the baseline must account for where fisheries are conducted; for example, baselines assessing high-seas Bering Sea fisheries require broad coverage around the Pacific Rim as opposed to fisheries located at the mouth of a large river system. Choosing loci based on information content, such as highly variable markers or loci that reflect adaptive divergence between populations, can increase the power to assign individuals, although care must be taken when estimating assignment power based on such a "high-graded" baseline (Anderson et al. 2008). Therefore, successful genetic stock identification requires investment in marker and genetic baseline development.

Genetic Structure of AYK Salmon Populations

The AYK region encompasses a vast part of Alaska, including the Kuskokwim and Yukon Rivers, as well as the rivers draining into Norton and Kotzebue Sounds and the North Slope drainages entering the Arctic Ocean (see maps in Hilsinger et al. 2009; Waples 2009). All five North American species of Pacific salmon (chum *O. keta*, Chinook *O. tshawytscha*, coho *O. kisutch*, sockeye, and pink *O. gorbuscha* salmon) are found within the AYK region. Kotzebue Sound marks the most northern extent of Chinook, coho, and sockeye salmon, whereas pink and chum salmon extend northward into North Slope drainages (Morrow 1980). Chinook and chum salmon extend far upriver in the Yukon River drainage, entering transboundary waters in the Yukon Territory of Canada. Chum, pink, and Chinook salmon are the most valued fisheries in the region (AYK SSI 2006), but sockeye salmon are becoming increasingly important in the Kuskokwim system (Linderman and Bergstrom 2009, this volume). Below the authors summarize the status of genetic studies in the AYK region to date on a species-by-species basis.

Chum salmon

Population Genetic Structure.—A strong effort has been made to clarify the genetic structure of AYK chum salmon because of its abundance, geographic range, and economic importance in this region. Consequently, genetic relationships of chum salmon are clearer than for other AYK salmon species (Table 2). Region-wide information from allozyme (Figure 1; Seeb and Crane 1999a; b) and microsatellite loci (Figure 2, Beacham et al. 2009, this volume) have distinguished similar population groupings of AYK chum salmon. Most

TABLE 2. Genetic studies to date addressing chum salmon *Oncorhynchus keta* in the AYK region. Marker type: A = allozymes, mt = mitochondrial DNA, M = microsatellites, S = SNPs, O = other.

Source	Marker	AYK Regions	Other Regions
Beacham et al. 1988	A	Yukon River	British Columbia
Wilmot et al. 1992	A	Yukon River	none
Park et al. 1993	mt	Kotzebue Sound, Yukon River, Goodnews	Japan, Russia, Alaska Peninsula, South Central Alaska, SE Alaska, British Columbia, Washington
Taylor et al. 1994	O[1]	Yukon River	NE Russia, SE Alaska, British Columbia
Wilmot et al. 1994	A	Norton Sound, Yukon River, Kuskokwim River, Goodnews	Russia, Bristol Bay, Alaska Peninsula
Spearman and Miller 1997	A	Yukon River	none
Scribner et al. 1998	A, mt, M, O[2]	Yukon River	none
Wilmot et al. 1998	A	Western Alaska, Yukon River	Japan, Russia, Alaska Peninsula, Kodiak Island, SE Alaska, BC, WA
Seeb and Crane 1999a	A	Kotzebue Sound, Norton Sound, Yukon River, Kuskokwim River, Goodnews River	Alaska Peninsula, SE Alaska, British Columbia, Washington, Japan, Russia
Seeb and Crane 1999b	A, mt	Kotzebue Sound, Norton Sound, Yukon River, Kuskokwim River, Goodnews	Alaska Peninsula, SE Alaska, British Columbia, Washington, Japan, Russia
Crane et al. 2001	A	Yukon River	none
Abe et al. 2002	mt	Yukon River, Norton Sound	Korea, Japan, Kamchatka, Siberia, Alaska Peninsula, SE Alaska, British Columbia, Washington
Kondzela et al. 2002	A	Kotzebue Sound, Norton Sound, Yukon River, Kuskokwim River	Alaska Peninsula, SE Alaska, BC Coast, Puget Sound, Columbia River, Japan, Russia, China
ADFG 2003	A	Yukon River	none

[1]Minisatellites, [2]*GH2D*

TABLE 2. Continued.

Source	Marker	AYK Regions	Other Regions
Berger et al. 2003	A	Yukon River	none
Olsen et al. 2004a	mt, M	Yukon River	none
Sato et al. 2004	mt	Yukon River	Japan, Korea, Russia, Bristol Bay, Alaska Peninsula, South Central Alaska, SE Alaska, British Columbia, Washington
Seeb et al. 2004	A	Kotzebue Sound, Norton Sound Yukon River, Kuskokwim River	Bristol Bay, Alaska Peninsula, Kodiak Island, SE Alaska, British Columbia, Washington, Japan, Russia
Candy et al. 2005	M	Yukon River	none
Gilk et al. 2005	S	Kuskokwim River	none
Olsen et al. 2006a	M	Kotzebue and Norton sounds	none
Flannery et al. 2007a	mt	Kotzebue Sound, Yukon River	Alaska Peninsula, SE Alaska
Flannery et al. 2007b	O[3]	Yukon River	SE Alaska (Saltery River)
Flannery et al. 2007c	M	Yukon River	none
Beacham et al. 2009, this volume	M, O[4]	Kotzebue Sound, Norton Sound, Yukon River, Kuskokwim River, Goodnews River	Bristol Bay, Alaska Peninsula, B. C. Central Coast, Fraser River
Flannery et al. 2008 Gilk et al. 2009, this volume	M	Yukon River	none
	S	Kuskokwim River	none
Smith and Seeb 2008	M, S	Kotzebue Sound, Norton Sound, Yukon River, Kuskokwim River	Bristol Bay, Alaska Peninsula

[3]AFLPs, [4]MHC

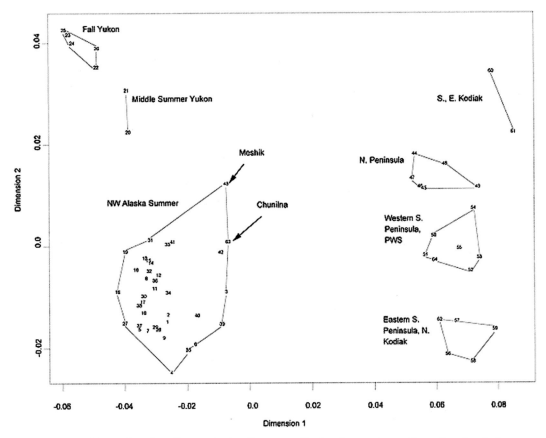

FIGURE 1. Multidimensional scaling analysis of western Alaska chum salmon *Oncorhynchus keta* populations using Cavalli-Sforza and Edwards' (1967; CSE) chord distances for 40 allozyme loci. NW Alaska Summer cluster includes AYK locations from Kotzebue Sound (4), Norton Sound (6), lower Yukon River (9), and Kuskokwim River (10) as well as ten Bristol Bay locations (from Seeb and Crane 1999a).

notable in both data sets is the clear separation of fall-run fish of the interior, upstream portions of the Yukon River from other northwestern Alaska (including AYK) populations. Recent studies (Gilk et al. 2009, this volume; Smith and Seeb 2008) have identified a similar distinction between downstream summer-run fish and upriver fall-run in the Kuskokwim River. The genetic relationships between the upriver Yukon and Kuskokwim Rivers fall-run fish are unknown. However, overlapping groupings among summer-run downstream populations in these and adjacent coastal AYK and other northwestern Alaskan rivers (Seeb et al. 2004; Figures 1 and 2) are consistent with recent or ongoing gene flow throughout these drainages. The genetic similarity of a Susitna River tributary (Chunilna River) to AYK populations (Figure 1) suggests possible post-glacial colonization from an Arctic refuge via a Tanana-Susitna Rivers connection contrasted with other Gulf of Alaska drainages with apparent colonization from eastern Pacific refuges (Seeb and Crane 1999a). The success of nuclear markers for identifying AYK chum populations contrasts with mitochondrial data where a single haplotype predominated throughout the region (Park et al. 1993).

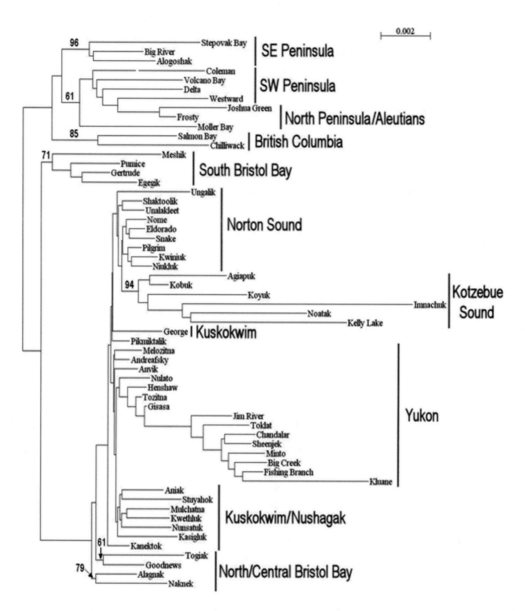

FIGURE 2. Neighbor-joining tree of CSE distances for 59 Alaskan and Canadian chum salmon *Oncorhynchus keta* populations based on 14 microsatellite and one MHC loci (from Beacham et al. 2009).

Management Applications.—The geographical breadth of the allozyme baseline data has resulted in unprecedented analyses of high-seas mixtures of chum salmon. Nineteen genetically-defined regional groups used in mixture analyses (Figure 3; Seeb et al. 2004) have provided a qualitative overview of genetically and geographically discrete chum salmon groupings throughout the species range. Most chum salmon incidentally caught south of the Alaska Peninsula in June sockeye salmon fisheries in 1993, 1994, and in a test fishery in 1996 were destined for AYK and other northwest Alaskan rivers; the proportion of AYK fish in 1996 declined sharply in July. These proportions differed from those estimated off the coast of the Kamchatka Peninsula during the spring and summer of 1998 where AYK fish were estimated to contribute less than 10%. Contributions of AYK chum salmon to the southeastern Bering Sea pollock trawl fishery (see Gisclair 2009, this volume) in the fall of 1994 (38%) and 1995 (48%) (Wilmot et al. 1998) were higher than those of 1996. Immature fish (1994: 84%, 1995: 88%, 1996: 75%) dominated the bycatch of AYK salmon in each of these years; estimated contributions of Yukon River fall-run chum salmon to the AYK totals were 24% in 1994 and 19% in 1995 (Wilmot et al. 1998).

Considerable efforts have been directed towards applying genetic markers to identify subgroups contributing to harvests and test fisheries within the Yukon and Kuskokwim Rivers. The broad stock structure of summer-run down river and fall-run upriver fish within the Yukon River (Figures 1 and 2) has led to precise and accurate estimates of these major groupings throughout their entry into the river (e.g., Flannery et al. 2007c, 2008). However, identification of country-of-origin of fall-run U.S. and Canadian border stocks has been limited by the small genetic differences among populations, and appears to be unresolvable regardless of the marker used

(Flannery et al. 2007b). Similarly, the run-timing and spatial distinctions in the Kuskokwim River have the potential for identifying late-run upriver fish in downstream fisheries (Gilk et al. 2009) based on simulations and preliminary test fishery samplings.

Chinook salmon

Population Genetic Structure.—As with chum salmon, efforts to understand the genetic structure of Chinook salmon populations within the AYK region have been substantial due to declining abundance and the species' importance as a biological, economic, and subsistence resource (Table 3). Initial broad and fine scale insights from an extensive allozyme baseline have been affirmed and extended largely through ongoing microsatellite and SNP markers. Populations of the upper Yukon River were genetically differentiated from those of other northwest Alaska and Bristol Bay rivers, and three Susitna River collections were grouped with AYK rather than grouped with Gulf of Alaska populations (Figure 4). The upper (Canadian) and lower (U.S.) Yukon River populations (Figure 5) were clearly distinguishable based on allozyme, microsatellite, and SNP markers (Figure 6). Within each region, clear substructure consistent with isolation by distance was also apparent from each type of marker. The genetic and geographic subdivision of Chinook salmon within the Kuskokwim River was similar to that observed within lower, middle, or upper regions of the Yukon River (Templin and Seeb 2004). Clear separation of populations at the upper and lower extremes of the river based on allozyme and microsatellite data contrasted with weaker geographic signals from other locations. The picture becomes somewhat clearer with the inclusion of SNP data (W. Templin and L. Seeb, ADF&G, personal communication) which permitted four sub-groups to be resolved (Figure 7).

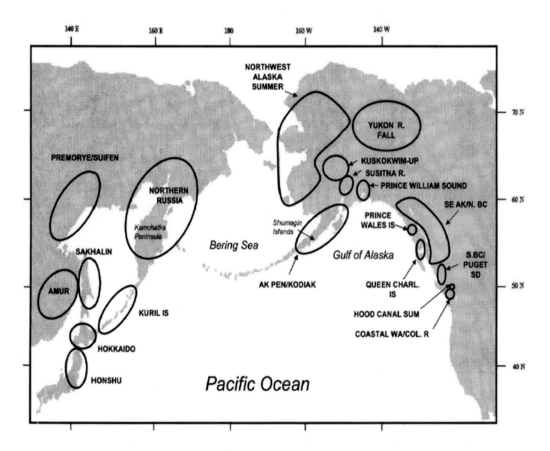

FIGURE 3. Map of the North Pacific Ocean, Gulf of Alaska, and Bering Sea showing 19 genetically-defined regional groups of populations of chum salmon *Oncorhynchus keta* used in mixed stock analyses. Regional groups were identified through gene diversity analyses, multidimensional scaling analyses, and simulations (from Seeb et al. 2004).

TABLE 3. Genetic studies to date addressing Chinook salmon *Oncorhynchus tshawytscha* in the AYK region. See Table 2 for abbreviations of maker types.

Source	Marker	AYK Regions	Other Regions
Gharrett et al. 1987	A	Norton Sound, Yukon River, Kuskokwim River, Goodnews	Bristol Bay, SE Alaska
Beacham et al. 1989	A	Yukon River (Canada only)	none
Wilmot et al. 1992	A	Yukon River	none
Teel et al. 1999	A	Western Alaska, Canadian Yukon	Russia, SE Alaska, Alaska Peninsula, coastal British Columbia, Fraser River, Thompson River, Washington, Oregon, California
Crane et al. 2000	A	Yukon River	SE Alaska
Templin et al. 2004	A, M	Kuskokwim River, Goodnews	none
Moncrieff et al. 2005	A	Yukon River	none
Olsen et al. 2005	M	Yukon River, Kuskokwim River	none
Smith et al. 2005	S	Yukon River	none
Templin et al. 2005	A	Yukon River	none
Beacham et al. 2006	M	Yukon River	Russia, SE Alaska, British Columbia, Columbia River, Thompson River, Fraser River
Flannery et al. 2006a	M	Yukon River	none
Olsen et al. 2006b	O[1]	Kuskokwim River	none
Templin et al. 2006	M	Yukon River	none
Beacham et al. 2008	M	Yukon River	none
Olsen et al. 2009, this volume	M	Yukon River, Kuskokwim River	none
Templin et al. 2008	S	Yukon River	none

[1]*GHp, OtY1*

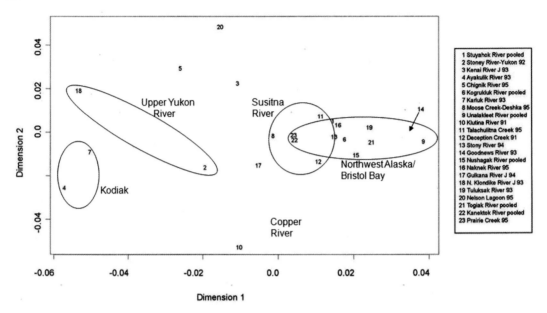

FIGURE 4. Multidimensional scaling groupings of 23 western Alaska Chinook salmon *Oncorhynchus tshawytscha* based on CSE distance measurements from 23 allozyme loci. Modified unpublished figure from ADF&G, courtesy of L. Seeb.

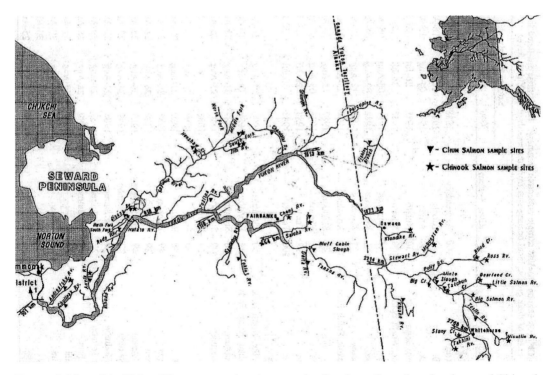

FIGURE 5. Map of the Yukon River system showing samples for chum *Oncorhynchus keta* and Chinook salmon *Oncorhynchus tshawytscha* (from Wilmot et al. 1992).

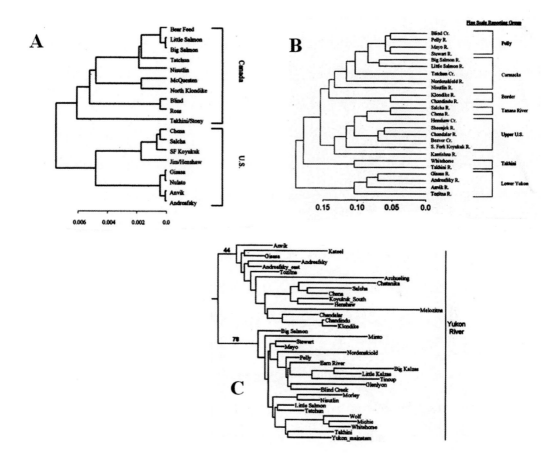

FIGURE 6. Population structures of Yukon River Chinook salmon *Oncorhynchus tshawytscha*. A. Allozymes—UPGMA for Nei's distances (Templin et al. 2005). B SNPs.—UPGMA CSE chord distances (Templin et al. 2008). C. Microsatellites—Neighbor-joining tree CSE chord distances (Beacham et al. 2006).

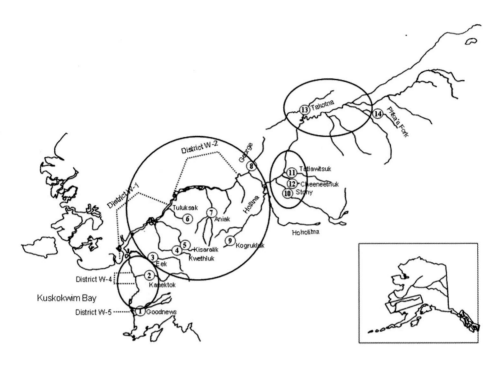

FIGURE 7. Map of Kuskokwim River Chinook salmon *Oncorhynchus tshawytscha* management area (Templin et al. 2004) with encircled groupings based on allozyme, microsatellite, and SNP data (W. Templin and L. Seeb, unpublished data).

Management Applications.—The Chinook salmon genetic data available for the Yukon River have proven useful in estimating contributions of populations from actual or simulated stock mixtures. Unlike chum salmon, estimation within mixtures to country of origin can be achieved with high accuracy using allozyme (Templin et al. 2005), SNP (Smith et al. 2005), or microsatellite (Beacham et al. 2008) nuclear markers. With a current focus on SNP and microsatellite loci, timely and reliable allocations can also be made within regions, frequently to drainage and tributaries (Flannery et al. 2006a; Beacham et al. 2008; Templin et al. 2008). Similarly, simulations within the Kuskokwim River using microsatellite and SNP data for stock mixtures involving the four stock groups (Figure 7) have produced estimates of returns to the respective groups of acceptable accuracy and precision (W. Templin and L. Seeb, ADF&G, personal communication).

Coho salmon

Genetic Population Structure.—Increasing interest by AYK fisheries in this species caused in part by decreasing abundances of chum and Chinook salmon populations has promoted investigation into the population structure of AYK coho salmon (Table 4). A few preliminary geographic surveys using nuclear loci that included AYK rivers indicated their divergence from populations south of the Alaskan Peninsula (Weitkamp et al. 1995; Smith et al. 2001). Subsequent investigations have provided more detailed insights about coho salmon population structure within the AYK region. Based on eight microsatellite loci, the upper Yukon River populations were distinct from downstream and adjacent coastal locations (Figure 8), and were further distinguished by significantly lower genetic diversity (Flannery et al. 2006b). Similar distinctions

TABLE 4. Genetic studies to date addressing coho salmon *Oncorhynchus kisutch* in the AYK region. See Table 2 for abbreviations of maker types.

Source	Marker	AYK Regions	Other Regions
Weitkamp et al. 1995	A	Goodnews River	SE Alaska, British Columbia, Washington, Oregon, California
Carney et al. 1997	mt	Kuskokwim Bay (Eek, Kanektok)	South Central Alaska, SE Alaska
Gharrett et al. 2001	mt	Kuskokwim Bay (Eek, Kanektok), Yukon River	South Central Alaska, SE Alaska, Kamchatka
Smith et al. 2001	mt, M	Yukon River, Kuskokwim River	Alaska Peninsula, SE Alaska, British Columbia, Washington, Oregon, California
Olsen et al. 2003	M	Norton Sound, Yukon River,	Bristol Bay, Alaska Peninsula, SE Alaska
Olsen et al. 2004a	mt, M	Yukon River	none
Olsen et al. 2004b	M	Norton Sound, Yukon River, Kuskokwim River	Bristol Bay, Alaska Peninsula, SE Alaska
Carney et al. 1997	mt	Kuskokwim Bay (Eek, Kanektok)	South Central Alaska, SE Alaska
Flannery et al. 2006b	M	Yukon River, Kuskokwim River	Bristol Bay, Alaska Peninsula, SE Alaska
Crane et al. 2007	M	Kuskokwim River, Kuskowkim Bay, Goodnews	none

characterized mtDNA variation in an upper Yukon River sample (Delta) contrasted with two Kuskokwim Bay collections (Gharrett et al. 2001). Variation among 15 microsatellite loci from nine locations within the Kuskokwim River and three adjacent coastal streams (Figure 9) revealed three geographic and genetic groupings (Crane et al. 2007). The variation was generally consistent with isolation by distance and less distinct than the upper and lower Yukon River populations. Nevertheless, a strong discontinuity existed between the Takotna River and two upstream locations, and as in the Yukon River, the genetic variability (allelic richness, heterozygosity) was lowest in these upstream populations.

Management Applications.—Within both the Yukon and Kuskokwim Rivers, the coho salmon population substructures have been sufficient to simulate accurate regional apportionments from the respective sets of baseline data (Flannery et al. 2006b; Crane et al. 2007) where the extent of inland migration represents the greatest distances (>1000 km) for this species. Within the Kuskokwim River, robust estimates were obtained of upstream fish present in small proportions from a 2001 commercial fishery in the lower Kuskokwim River (Crane et al. 2007).

Sockeye salmon

Population Genetic Structure.—Until recently, the number of genetic studies of AYK sockeye salmon have been fewer than those focused to the south on the prominent Bristol Bay runs (Table 5; Habicht et al. 2007). A species-wide collection of SNP baseline data for 307 populations involving 42 nuclear and 3 mtDNA markers is used by the Alaska Department of Fish and Game (ADF&G; Habicht and J. Seeb, personal communication). AYK representation includes two genetically distinct Norton Sound locations and 10 Yukon River and Kuskokwim River populations aggregated among 27 others in a northwest Bristol Bay grouping. An ongoing study involving genetically diverged lake-type and riverine sockeye salmon populations within the lower Kuskokwim River drainage suggests similar life history and genetic complexities among AYK sockeye salmon (McPhee et al., in press).

Management Applications.—A SNP baseline data set is used to estimate origins of Bering Sea catches of two sockeye salmon groups comprising or including AYK populations and eight other population groupings. Previously, Guthrie et al. (2000) included

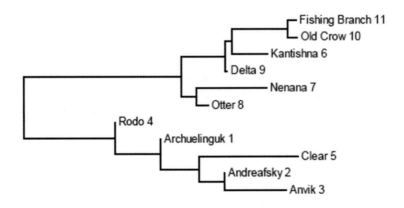

FIGURE 8. Population structure of Yukon River coho salmon *Oncorhynchus kisutch* based on microsatellite data depicted in neighbor joining tree (CSE chord distances, Flannery et al. 2006b).

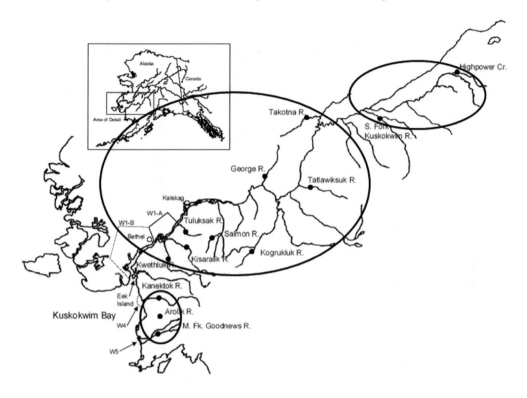

Figure 9. Geographic representation of genetic variation of microsatellite loci of coho salmon *Oncorhynchus kisutch* populations in the Kuskokwim River. (CSE chord distances, Crane et al. 2007).

data from four AYK rivers (Stony, Kanektok, Kagati, Goodnews) among baseline data, including 165 populations (nine stock groups) in mixed stock analyses of immature sockeye salmon captured north (Cape Cheerful, $n = 440$) and south (Cape Prominence, $n = 300$) of Unalaska Island. Comparative genetic data among baseline populations were not presented, although the accuracy in 100% AYK simulations was low (<0.50), presumably reflecting indistinct genetic profiles of these four populations.

Pink salmon

Few genetic data for AYK pink salmon have been collected (Table 6). Two Norton Sound populations were included in surveys involving nuclear loci of even-year (Gharrett et al. 1988) and odd-year (Olsen et al. 1998)

pink salmon. The overall patterns from nuclear and mtDNA data for pink salmon elsewhere throughout the species range (e.g., Gharrett et al. 1988; Hawkins et al. 2002; Noll et al. 2001; Zhivotovsky et al. 1994) point to AYK streams as a fertile area for future investigations. This vast and largely unsampled region promises to yield valuable clues for resolving evolutionary and geological questions stimulated by existing data and their syntheses. Inevitably, better understanding will, in turn, improve the management and conservation of pink salmon.

Synthesis of Genetic Population Structure of AYK Salmon

The low F_{ST} values in chum salmon in the AYK region are consistent with elevated recent gene flow in contrast to those levels like-

TABLE 5. Genetic studies to date addressing sockeye salmon *Oncorhynchus nerka* in the AYK region. See Table 2 for abbreviations of marker types.

Source	Marker	AYK Regions	Other Regions
Varnavskaya et al. 1994	A	Kuskokwim River, Kuskokwim Bay, Goodnews River	Kamchatka, Bristol Bay, Alaska Peninsula, SE Alaska, British Columbia, Washington
Guthrie et al. 2000	A	Kuskokwim River, Kuskokwim Bay, Goodnews River	Bristol Bay, Alaska Peninsula, Kodiak, South Central Alaska, SE Alaska, British Columbia
Elfstrom et al. 2006	S	Norton Sound	Kamchatka, Bristol Bay, South Central Alaska, SE Alaska, Washington
Seeb et al. 2007	S	Norton Sound, Yukon River, Kuskokwim River, Kuskokwim Bay, Goodnews River	Kamchatka, Bristol Bay, Alaska Peninsula, Kodiak, South Central Alaska, SE Alaska, British Columbia, Washington, Idaho
McPhee et al., in press	M	Kwethluk and Holitna rivers (Kuskokwim)	Taku River (British Columbia)

TABLE 6. Genetic studies to date addressing pink salmon *Oncorhynchus gorbuscha* in the AYK region. See Table 2 for abbreviations of marker types.

Source	Marker	AYK Regions	Other Regions
Gharrett et al. 1988	A	Norton Sound	Bristol Bay, Aleutian Islands, Kodiak
Olsen et al. 1998	M	Norton Sound	SE Alaska, British Columbia, Washington

ly experienced by Chinook and coho salmon. Coho (Olsen et al. 2003) and Chinook salmon (e.g., Templin et al. 2008) were more highly differentiated among local populations than chum salmon. Given the high overall F_{ST} values for sockeye salmon (Table 1), management will likely need to focus more on individual stocks than regional groupings.

These generalities may mask run timing distinctions among species within major rivers. Observed divergences between the headwater and downstream populations in the Yukon and Kuskokwim rivers for chum, Chinook, and coho salmon are not surprising given the great distances involved among some spawning populations, but the patterns differ among species. A tendency for early-run Chinook salmon to be destined for upriver locations exists in both rivers (Flannery et al. 2006a; Templin et al. 2004). In coho salmon, upriver fish tend to be early entrants into the Kuskokwim River (Crane et al. 2007); however genetically diverse coho salmon destined for the upper Yukon River appear to have a protracted entry (J. Olsen, U.S. Fish and Wildlife Service, personal communication) beginning in midsummer and coinciding with the entry of the upriver fall run of chum salmon (Flannery et al. 2007c, 2008). The fall runs of chum salmon in both rivers are restricted to upriver areas contrasting with genetically distinct early (summer) runs returning to downstream locations (e.g., Flannery et al. 2007c; Gilk et al. 2005).

The minimal genetic data available for pink and sockeye salmon populations within the AYK preclude general comparisons with species-wide patterns for these species. Beyond the AYK, mosaic patterns of variability and high F_{ST} values of lake-type sockeye salmon contrast with low F_{ST} values and apparent high levels of gene flow among stream-type populations (Wood et al. 2008; Gustafson and Winans 1999). As noted above, these patterns have been observed within the AYK region (McPhee et al., in press), and

provide useful hypotheses for future AYK samplings. Similarly, the contrasting genetic structures noted between even- and odd-year Asian pink salmon provide a useful basis for comparisons of AYK populations.

The Susitna River stands out from adjacent AYK drainages in three of four species where this drainage was sampled. Chum and Chinook salmon from the Susitna River appeared more closely related to Yukon River populations, suggesting colonization from Arctic rather than Pacific refuges (Seeb and Crane 1999a; Crane et al., unpublished data). The absence of samples precludes comparisons of the unique haplotype of all even-year pink salmon sampled in the Susitna River with odd-year fish in the Susitna River (Churikov and Gharrett 2002), or AYK fish of either brood year. Similarly, genetic comparisons of Susitna River coho salmon populations with those of adjacent Cook Inlet and AYK drainages await inclusion of the Susitna River drainage in genetic surveys of this overall region. A survey of allozyme variation among sockeye salmon from upper Cook Inlet (Seeb et al. 2000) that included 14 locations throughout the Susitna River drainage failed to identify notable outlier populations. Although this study included no AYK populations, these findings dampen any tendency to ascribe a generality to the peculiarities suggested for the Susitna River in the more limited samplings of chum, Chinook, and pink salmon. Nevertheless, these preliminary observations point to a need for broader samplings to clarify possible associations of Susitna River populations with those in northern drainages. In addition, sufficient sampling of Yukon River sockeye salmon populations is warranted to exclude or establish an association within the Susitna River drainage.

These temporal, genetic, and geographic complexities of AYK salmon populations reflect the variable and dynamic biological, physical, social, and political interactions that

will determine their persistence, or perhaps
their extinction. Hopefully, the latter alternative can be averted if knowledge and insights
continue to accumulate within a cooperative
and committed research framework.

Acknowledgments

We thank C. Krueger, J. Spaeder, and C.
Zimmerman for giving us the opportunity
to update the 2003 report, C. Krueger and
C. Zimmerman for valuable reviews, and
many individuals for sharing published and
unpublished new information including: T.
Beacham, P. Crane, B. Flannery, S. Gilk, C.
Habicht, J. Olsen, J. Seeb, L. Seeb, C. Smith,
W. Templin, J. Wenburg.

References

Abe, S., S. Sato, H. Kojima, J. Ando, H. Ando, R.
Wilmot, L. Seeb, V. Efremov, L. LeClair, W. Buchholz, D. Jin, S. Urawa, M. Kaeriyama, and A.
Urano. 2002. Genetic differentiation among Pacific Rim populations of chum salmon inferred from
mitochondrial DNA sequence variation. Document 616. North Pacific Anadromous Fish Commission, Vancouver, B.C.

ADF&G (Alaska Department of Fish and Game) 2003.
Yukon River salmon negotiations studies: completion report. ADF&G Regional Information Report
3A03-24. Alaska Department of Fish and Game,
Anchorage.

Adkison, M., E. Knudsen, D. Goodman, R. Hilborn, and
P. R. Mundy. 2001. A preliminary review of Western Alaskan biological escapement goal reports
for the Alaska Board of Fisheries. Independent
Scientific Review Committee, Alaska Department
of Fish and Game, Anchorage.

Allendorf, F. W., and G. Luikart. 2007. Conservation
and the genetics of populations. Blackwell Scientific Publications, Malden, Massachusetts.

Allendorf, F. W., and L. W. Seeb. 2000. Concordance of
genetic divergence among sockeye salmon populations at allozyme, nuclear DNA, and mitochondrial DNA markers. Evolution 54:640–651.

Anderson, E, R. Waples, and S. Kalinowski. 2008. An
improved method for predicting the accuracy of
genetic stock identification. Canadian Journal of
Fisheries and Aquatic Sciences 65:1475–1486.

Altukhov, Y. P., E. Salmenkova, and V. Omelchenko.
2000. Salmonid fishes: population biology, genetics and management. Blackwell Scientific Publications Limited, London.

AYK SSI (Arctic-Yukon-Kuskokwim Sustainable Salm-
on Initiative). 2006. Arctic-Yukon-Kuskokwim
Salmon Research and Restoration Plan. Bering Sea
Fisherman's Association, Anchorage, Alaska.

Beacham, T., K. Jonsen, J. Supernault, M. Wetklo, and
L. Deng. 2006. Pacific Rim population structure of
Chinook salmon as determined from microsatellite analysis. Transactions of the American Fisheries Society 135:1604–1621.

Beacham, T., K. D. Le, M. Wetklo, B. McIntosh, T.
Ming, and K. M. Miller. 2009. Population structure and stock identification of chum salmon
from western Alaska determined with microsatellite DNA and major histocompatibility complex
variation. Pages 141–160 in C. C. Krueger and
C. E. Zimmerman, editors. Pacific salmon: ecology and management of western Alaska's populations. American Fisheries Society, Symposium 70,
Bethesda, Maryland.

Beacham, T., C. Murray, and R. Withler. 1988. Age,
morphology, developmental biology, and biochemical genetic variation of Yukon River fall
chum salmon, and comparisons with British Columbia populations. Fishery Bulletin 86:663–674.

Beacham, T., C. Murray, and R. Withler. 1989. Age,
morphology and biochemical genetic variation of
Yukon River chinook salmon. Transactions of the
American Fishery Society 118:46–63.

Beacham, T., M. Wetklo C. Wallace, J. Olsen, B. Flannery, J. Wenburg, W. Templin, A. Antonovich, and
L. Seeb. 2008. The application of microsatellites
for stock identification of Yukon River Chinook
salmon. North American Journal of Fisheries
Management 28:283–295.

Beacham, T., and C. Wood. 1999. Application of microsatellite DNA variation to estimation of stock composition and escapement of Nass River sockeye
salmon (Oncorhynchus nerka). Canadian Journal
of Fisheries and Aquatic Sciences 56:297–310.

Berger, J., B. Borba, and L. Seeb. 2003. Migration and
run timing of summer vs. fall chum salmon on the
Yukon River, Alaska. Pages 239–240 in V. Keong,
editor. Proceedings of the 21st Northeast Pacific
Pink and Chum Salmon Workshop. Division of
Commercial Fisheries. Alaska Department of Fish
and Game, Anchorage.

Beverton, R. J. H., J. G. Cooke, J. B. Csirke, R. W.
Doyle, G. Hempel, S. J. Holt, A. D. MacCall, D.
Policansky, J. Roughgarden, J. G. Shepherd, M. P.
Sissenwine, and P. H. Wiebe. 1984. Dynamics of
single species: Group report. Pages 13–58 in R. M.
May, editor. Exploitation of marine communities.
Dahlem Konferenzen. Springer-Verlag, Berlin.

Brumfield, R. T., P. Beerli, D. A. Nickerson, and S. V. Edwards. 2003. The utility of single nucleotide polymorphisms in inferences of population history. Trends in Ecology & Evolution 18:249–256.

Cavalli-Sforza, L. L., and A. W. Edwards. 1967. Phylogenetic analysis. Models and estimation procedures. American Journal of Human Genetics 19:233–357.

Candy, J. R., B. G. Flannery, and T. D. Beacham. 2005. Building a collaborative chum salmon microsatellite baseline for the Yukon River genetic stock ID. 22nd Pink and Chum Workshop 2005. Ketchikan, Alaska.

Carney, B., A. Gray, and A. Gharrett. 1997. mtDNA restriction site variation within and among five populations of Alaskan coho salmon. Canadian Journal of Fisheries and Aquatic Sciences 54:940–949.

Churikov, D., and A. J. Gharrett. 2002. Comparative phylogeography of the two pink salmon broodlines: an analysis based on a mitochondrial DNA genealogy. Molecular Ecology 11:1077–1101.

Clark, C. W. 1984. Strategies for multispecies management: objectives and constraints. Pages 303–312 in R. M. May, editor. Exploitation of marine communities. Dahlem Konferenzen. Springer-Verlag, Berlin.

Crane, P., D. Molyneaux, C. Lewis, and J. Wenburg. 2007. Genetic variation among coho salmon populations from the Kuskokwim Region and application to stock-specific harvest estimation. Alaska Fisheries Technical Report 96. U.S. Fish and Wildlife Service, Anchorage.

Crane, P. A., W. J. Spearman, and L. W. Seeb. 2001. Yukon River chum salmon: report for genetic stock identification studies, 1992–1997. Information Report Number 5J01–08. Alaska Department of Fish and Game Regional, Anchorage.

Crane, P. A. W. D. Templin, D. M. Eggers, and L. W. Seeb. 2000. Genetic stock identification of southeast Alaska Chinook salmon fishery catches. Regional Information Report Number 5J00–01. Alaska Department of Fish and Game, Anchorage.

Elfstrom, C. M., C. T. Smith, and J. E. Seeb. 2006. Thirty-two single nucleotide polymorphism markers for high-throughput genotyping of sockeye salmon. Molecular Ecology Notes 6:1255–1259.

Flannery B., T. Beacham, R. Holder, E. Kretschmer, and J. K. Wenburg. 2007c. Stock structure and mixed-stock analysis of Yukon River chum salmon. Alaska Fisheries Technical Report 97. U.S. Fish and Wildlife Service, Anchorage.

Flannery, B., T. Beacham, M. Wetklo, C. Smith, W. Templin, A. Antonovich, L. Seeb, S. Miller, O. Schlei, and J. Wenburg. 2006a. Run timing, migratory patterns, and harvest information of Chinook salmon stocks within the Yukon River. Alaska Fisheries Technical Report 92. U. S. Fish and Wildlife Service, Anchorage, Alaska.

Flannery, B. R. Holder, G. Maschmann,, E, Kretschmer, and J.K. Wenburg. 2008. Application of mixed-stock analysis for Yukon River fall chum salmon, 2006. Alaska Fisheries Technical Report 2008–5. U.S. Fish and Wildlife Service, Anchorage, Alaska.

Flannery, B., L. Luiten, and J. Wenburg. 2006b. Yukon River coho salmon genetics. Alaska Fisheries Technical Report 93. U.S. Fish and Wildlife Service, Anchorage, Alaska.

Flannery, B., J. K. Wenburg, A.J. Gharrett. 2007a. Evolution of mitochondrial DNA variation within and among Yukon River chum salmon populations. Transactions of the American Fisheries Society 136:902–910.

Flannery, B., J. K. Wenburg, and A. J. Gharrett. 2007b. Variation of amplified fragment length polymorphisms in Yukon River chum salmon: population structure and application to mixed-stock analysis. Transactions of the American Fisheries Society 136:911–925.

Gharrett, A. J., A. Gray, and V. Brykov. 2001. Phylogeographic analysis of mitochondrial DNA variation in Alaskan coho salmon. Fishery Bulletin 99:528–544.

Gharrett, A. J., S. Shirley, and G. Tromble. 1987. Genetic relationships among populations of Alaskan Chinook salmon. Canadian Journal of Fisheries and Aquatic Sciences 44:765–774.

Gharrett, A. J., C. Smoot, and A. McGregor. 1988. Genetic relationships of even-year northwestern Alaskan pink salmon. Transactions of the American Fishery Society 117:536–545.

Gilk, S. E., D. B. Molyneaux, T. Hamazaki, J. A. Pawluk, and W. D. Templin. 2009. Biological and genetic characteristics of fall and summer chum salmon in the Kuskokwim River, Alaska. Pages 161–179 in C. C. Krueger and C. E. Zimmerman, editors. Pacific salmon: ecology and management of western Alaska's populations. American Fisheries Society, Symposium 70, Bethesda, Maryland.

Gilk, S., W. Templin, D. Molyneaux, T. Hamazaki, and J. Pawluk. 2005. Characteristics of fall chum salmon Oncorhynchus keta in the Kuskokwim River drainage. Alaska Department of Fish and Game Fishery data Series No. 05–56, Anchorage.

Gisclair, B. R. 2009. Salmon bycatch management in the Bering Sea walleye pollock fishery: threats and opportunities for western Alaska. Pages 799–816 in C. C. Krueger and C. E. Zimmerman, editors. Pacific salmon: ecology and management of western Alaska's populations. American Fisheries Society, Symposium 70, Bethesda, Maryland.

Grant, W. S., G. B. Milner, P. Krasnowski, and F. M. Utter. 1980. Use of biochemical genetic variants for identification of sockeye salmon (*Oncorhynchus nerka*) stocks in Cook Inlet, Alaska. Canadian Journal of Fisheries and Aquatic Sciences 37:1236–1247.

Gustafson, R., and G. Winans. 1999. Distribution and population genetic structure of river- and sea-type sockeye salmon in western North America. Ecology of Freshwater Fish 8:181–193.

Guthrie, C., E. Farley, N. Weemes, and E. Martinson. 2000. Genetic stock identification of sockeye salmon captured in the coastal waters of Unalaska Island during April/May and August 1998. North Pacific Anadromous Fish Commission Bulletin 2:309–315.

Habicht, C. L. Seeb, and J. Seeb. 2007. Genetic and ecological divergence defines population structure of sockeye salmon poulations returning to Bristol Bay, Alaska, and provides a tool for admixture analysis. Transactions of the American Fisheries Society 136:82–94.

Hard, J. J., W. H. Eldridge, and K. A. Naish. 2009. Genetic consequences of size-selective fishing: implications for viability of Chinook salmon in the Arctic-Yukon-Kuskokwim Region of Alaska. Pages 759–780 in C. C. Krueger and C. E. Zimmerman, editors. Pacific salmon: ecology and management of western Alaska's populations. American Fisheries Society, Symposium 70, Bethesda, Maryland.

Hawkins, S., N. Varnavsakaya, E. Matzak, V. Efremov, C. Guthrie, R. Wilmot, H. Mayama, F. Yamazaki, and A. Gharrett. 2002. Population structure of odd-broodline Asian pink salmon and its contrast to the even-broodline structure. Journal of Fish Biology 60:370–388.

Helle, J. H. 1981. Significance of the stock concept in artificial propagation of salmonids in Alaska. Canadian Journal of Fishery and Aquatic Sciences 38:1665–1671.

Hendry, A., V. Castric, M. Kinnison, and T. Quinn. 2004. The evolution of philopatry and dispersal: Homing versus straying in salmonids. Pages 52–91 in Hendry, A. P. and S. C. Stearns, editors. Evolution illuminated: salmon and their relatives. Oxford University Press, New York.

Hendry, A. P., and S. Stearns. 2004. Appendix 2: Genetic differentiation among conspecific salmonid populations at nuclear DNA loci. Pages 384–402 in A. P. Hendry and S. C. Stearns, editors. Evolution Illuminated: Salmon and Their Relatives. Oxford University Press, New York.

Hilsinger, J. R., E. Volk, G. Sandone, and R. Cannon. 2009. Salmon management in the Arctic-Yukon-Kuskokwim region of Alaska: past, present, and future. Pages 495–519 in C. C. Krueger and C.

E. Zimmerman, editors. Pacific salmon: ecology and management of western Alaska's populations. American Fisheries Society, Symposium 70, Bethesda, Maryland.

Karl, S. A., B. W. Bowen, and J. C. Avise. 1992. Global population genetic structure and male-mediated gene flow in the green turtle (*Chelonia mydas*)—RFLP analyses of anonymous nuclear loci. Genetics 131:163–173.

Kondzela, C. M., C. M. Guthrie, S. L. Hawkins, C. D. Russell, J. H. Helle, and A. J. Gharrett. 2002. Genetic relationships among chum salmon populations in southeast Alaska and northern British Columbia. Canadian Journal of Fisheries and Aquatic Sciences 51 (supplement 1):50–64.

Larkin, P. A. 1972. The stock concept and management of Pacific salmon. Pages 11–15 in R. C. Simon and P. A. Larkin, editors. The stock concept in Pacific salmon. University of British Columbia Press, Vancouver, B.C.

Linderman, J. C., and D. Bergstrom 2009. Kuskokwim management area: salmon escapement, harvest, and management. Pages 541–599 in C. C. Krueger and C. E. Zimmerman, editors. Pacific salmon: ecology and management of western Alaska's populations. American Fisheries Society, Symposium 70, Bethesda, Maryland.

McPhee, M. V., T. Tappenbeck, D. Whited, and J. Stanford. In press. Genetic diversity and population structure in the Kuskokwim River drainage support the "recurrent evolution" hypothesis for sockeye salmon life histories. Transactions of the American Fisheries Society.

McPhee, M. V., M. S. Zimmerman, T. D. Beacham, B. R. Beckman, J. B. Olsen, L. W. Seeb, and W. D. Templin. 2009. A hierarchical framework to identify influences on Pacific salmon population abundance and structure in the Arctic-Yukon-Kuskokwim region. Pages 1177–1198 in C. C. Krueger and C. E. Zimmerman, editors. Pacific salmon: ecology and management of western Alaska's populations. American Fisheries Society, Symposium 70, Bethesda, Maryland.

Moncrieff, C. M., D. W. Wiswar, and P. A. Crange. 2005. Phenotypic characterization of Chinook salmon in the subsistence harvest. U. S. Fish and Wildlife Service, Office of Subsistence Management, Fisheries Resource Monitoring Program, 2005 Final Report (Study Number 03–015). Yukon River Drainage Fisheries Association, Anchorage, Alaska.

Moran, P., D. J. Teel, E. S. LaHood, J. Drake, and S. Kalinowski. 2006. Standardizing multi-laboratory microsatellites in Pacific salmon: an historical view of the future. Ecology of Freshwater Fish 15:597–605.

Morrow, J. E. 1980. The freshwater fishes of Alaska. Alaska Northwest Publishing Company, Anchorage.

Moulton, F. R., editor. 1939. The migration and conservation of salmon. Publication of the American Association for the Advancement of Science. Number 8. Washington, D.C.

NAS (National Academy of Sciences). 1996. Upstream: salmon and society in the Pacific Northwest: committee on protection and management of Pacific Northwest anadromous salmonids. National Academy Press, Washington, D.C.

Noll, C., N. Varnavskaya, E. Matzak, S, Hawkins, V. Midanaya, O. Katugin, C. Russell, N. Kinas, C. Guthrie, H. Mayama, F. Yamazaki, B. Finney, and A. Gharrett. 2001. Analysis of contemporary genetic structure of even-brood year populations of Asian and western Alaskan pink salmon. Fishery Bulletin 99:123–138.

Olsen, J. B., T. D. Beacham, K. D. Le, M. Wetklo, L. D. Luiten, E. J. Kretschmer, J. K. Wenburg, C. F. Lean, K. M. Dunmall, and P. A. Crane. 2006a Genetic variation in Norton Sound chum salmon populations. 2005 Arctic Yukon Kuskokwim Sustainable Salmon Initiative Project Final Report. Bering Sea Fishermen's Association, Anchorage.

Olsen, J., S. Miller, W. Spearman, and J. K. Wenburg. 2003. Patterns of intra- and inter-population genetic diversity in Alaskan coho salmon: implications for conservation. Conservation Genetics 4:557–569.

Olsen, J. B., S. J. Miller, K. Harper, J. J. Nagler, and J. K. Wenburg. 2006b. Contrasting sex ratios in juvenile and adult Chinook salmon *Oncorhynchus tshawytscha* (Walbaum) from south-west Alaska: sex reversal or differential survival? Journal of Fish Biology 69A:140–144.

Olsen, J. B., S. J. Miller, W. J. Spearman, and J. K. Wenburg. 2004b. Patterns of genetic diversity in Alaskan coho salmon. Technical Report No. 5. North Pacific Anadromous Fisheries Commission, Vancouver, B.C.

Olsen, J. B., S. J. Miller, K. Harper, and J. K. Wenburg. 2005. Effective population size of Chinook salmon in Yukon and Kuskokwim River tributaries. 2004 Arctic Yukon Kuskokwim Sustainable Salmon Initiative Project Final Report. Bering Sea Fishermen's Association, Anchorage, Alaska.

Olsen, J. B., S. J. Miller, K. Harper, and J. K. Wenburg. 2009. Genetic health and variables influencing the effective number of breeders in western Alaska Chinook salmon. Pages 781–795 *in* C. C. Krueger and C. E. Zimmerman, editors. Pacific salmon: ecology and management of western Alaska's populations. American Fisheries Society, Symposium 70, Bethesda, Maryland.

Olsen, J., L. Seeb, P. Bentzen, and J. Seeb. 1998. Genetic interpretation of broad-scale microsatellite polymorphism in odd-year pink salmon. Transactions of the American Fishery Society 127:353–550.

Olsen, J., W. Spearman, G. Sage, S. Miller, B. Flannery, and J. K. Wenburg. 2004a. Variation in the population structure of Yukon R. chum and coho salmon: evaluating the potential impact of localized habitat degradation. Transactions of the American Fishery Society 133:476–483.

Park, L., M. Brainard, D. Dightman, and G. Winans. 1993. Low levels of intraspecific variation in the mtDNA of chum salmon. Molecular Marine Biology and Biotechnology 2:362–370.

Pella, J. J., and G. B. Milner. 1987. Use of genetic marks in stock composition analysis. Pages 247–276 *in* N. Ryman and F. Utter editors. Population genetics and fishery management University of Washington Press, Seattle.

Rich, W. H. 1939. Local populations and migration in relation to the conservation of Pacific salmon in the Western States and Alaska. American Association for the Advancement of Science Publication 8:45–50.

Ricker, W. E. 1972. Hereditary and environmental factors affecting certain salmonid populations. Pages 19–160 *in* R. C. Simon and P. A. Larkin, editors. The stock concept in Pacific salmon. University of British Columbia, Vancouver.

Sato, S., H. Kojima, J. Ando, R. L. Wilmot, L. W. Seeb, V. Efremov, L. LeClair, W. Buchholz, D.-H. Jin, S. Urawa, M. Kaeriyama, A. Urano, and S. Abe. 2004. Genetic population structure of chum salmon in the Pacific Rim inferred from mitochondrial DNA sequence variation. Environmental Biology of Fishes 69:37–50.

Scribner, K., P. Crane, W. Spearman, and L. Seeb. 1998. DNA and allozyme markers provide concordant estimates of population differentiation: analyses of US and Canadian populations of Yukon River fall-run chum salmon. Canadian Journal of Fishery and Aquatic Sciences 55:1748–1758.

Seeb, L., and P. Crane. 1999a. High genetic heterogeneity in chum salmon in western Alaska, the contact zone between northern and southern lineages. Transactions of the American Fishery Society 128:58–87.

Seeb, L., and P. Crane. 1999b. Allozymes and mtDNA discriminate Asian and North American populations of chum salmon in mixed-stock fisheries along the south coast of the Alaska Peninsula. Transactions of the American Fishery Society 128:88–103.

Seeb, L., P. Crane, C. Kondzela, R. Wilmot, S. Urawa, N. Varnavskaya, and J. Seeb. 2004. Migration of Pacific Rim chum salmon on the high seas: insights from genetic data. Environmental Biology of Fishes 69:21–36.

Seeb, L., C. Habicht, W. Templin, K. Tarbox, R. Davis, L. Brannian, and J. Seeb. 2000. Genetic diversity of sockeye salmon of Cook Inlet, Alaska, and its application to management of populations affected by the *Exxon Valdez* oil spill. Transactions of the American Fisheries Society 129:1223–1249.

Seeb, J. E., C. Habicht, R. Wilmot, C. Guthrie, S. Urawa, and S. Abe. 2007. NPAFC Cooperative Research: The use of genetic stock identification to determine the distribution, migration, early marine survival, and relative stock abundance of sockeye and chum salmon in the Bering Sea. Project 0303 Final Report. North Pacific Research Board, Anchorage.

Seeb, L. W., W. D. Templin, C. T. Smith, C. Elfstrom, S. Urawa, R. L. Wilmot, S. Abe, and J. E. Seeb. 2005. SNPs provide an easily-standardized baseline for NPAFC studies of chum salmon (NPAFC Document 907). Alaska Department of Fish and Game, Anchorage.

Shaklee, J., T. Beacham, L. Seeb, and B. White. 1999. Managing fisheries using genetic data: case studies from four species of Pacific salmon—4. Alaskan chum salmon fisheries. Fisheries Research 43:45–78.

Slatkin, M., and W. P. Maddison. 1989. A cladistic measure of gene flow inferred from the phylogenies of alleles. Genetics 123:603–613.

Smith, C. T., R. J. Nelson, C. C. Wood, and B. F. Koop. 2001. Glacial biogeography of North American coho salmon (*Oncorhynchus kisutch*). Molecular Ecology 10:2775–2785.

Smith, C. T., and L. Seeb. 2008. Number of alleles as a predictor of the relative assignment accuracy of short tandem repeat (STR) and single-nucleotide-polymorphism (SNP) baselines for chum salmon. Transactions of the American Fisheries Society 13:751–762.

Smith, C., W. Templin, J. Seeb, and L. Seeb. 2005. Single nucleotide polymorphisms provide rapid and accurate estimates of the proportions of U.S. and Canadian Chinook salmon caught in Yukon River fisheries. North American Journal of Fisheries Management 25:944–953.

Spearman, W. J., and S. J. Miller. 1997. Genetic stock identification of chum salmon (*Oncorhynchus keta*) from the Yukon River District 5 subsistence fishery. Alaska Fisheries Technical Report Number 40. U.S. Fish and Wildlife Service, Anchorage, Alaska.

Sunnucks, P. 2000. Efficient genetic markers for population biology. Trends in Ecology & Evolution 15:199–203.

Tanasichuk, R. 2002. Proceedings of the Pacific scientific advice review committee salmon subcommittee meeting, May 13–14 2002. Fisheries and Oceans Canada. Pacific Biological Station, Vancouver, B.C.

Taylor, E., T. Beacham, and M. Kaeriyama. 1994. Population structure and identification of North Pacific Ocean chum salmon revealed by an analysis of minisatellite DNA variation. Canadian Journal of Fishery and Aquatic Sciences 51:1430–1442.

Teel, D., P. Crane, C. Guthrie, A. Marshall, D. VanDoornik, and W. Templin. 1999 Comprehensive allozyme database discriminates chinook salmon around the Pacific Rim. Document 440. North Pacific Anadromous Fishery Commission, Vancouver, B.C.

Templin, W., N. A. DeCovich and L. W. Seeb 2006. Genetic stock identification of Chinook salmon harvest on the Yukon River, 2005. Alaska Department of Fish and Game, Division of Commercial Fisheries, Regional Information Report No. 3A06–05, Anchorage.

Templin, W., N. DeCovich, and L. Seeb. 2008. Genetic stock identification of Chinook salmon harvest on the Yukon River 2006. Fishery Data Series 08–15 Alaska Department of Fish and Game, Anchorage.

Templin, W. C. Smith, D. Molyneaux, and L. Seeb. 2004. Genetic diversity of Chinook salmon from the Kuskokwim River. Final Report for Study 01–0070. Alaska Department of Fish and Game, Anchorage.

Templin, W. W. Wilmot, C. Guthrie III, and L. Seeb. 2005. United States and Canadian Chinook salmon population in the Yukon River can be segregated based on genetic characteristics. Alaska Fisheries Research Bulletin 11:44–60.

Thompson, W. F. 1959. An approach to the population dynamics of the Pacific red salmon. Transactions of the American Fisheries Society 88:206–209.

Thompson, W. F. 1965. Fishing treaties and the salmon of the North Pacific. Science 150:1786–1789.

Utter, F. M. 2005. Farewell to allozymes(?). Journal of Irreproducible Results 49:35.

Utter, F. M., and N. Ryman. 1993. Genetic markers and mixed stock fisheries. Fisheries 8(8):11–22.

Varnavskaya, N. V., C. C. Wood, and R. J. Everett. 1994. Genetic variation in sockeye salmon (*Oncorhynchus nerka*) populations of Asia and North America. Canadian Journal of Fisheries and Aquatic Sciences 51S 1:132–146.

Waples, R. S. 1991. Pacific salmon, *Oncorhynchus* spp., and the definition of "Species" under the Endangered Species Act. Marine Fisheries Review 53:11–21.

Waples, R. S. 1995. Evolutionary significant units and the conservation of biological diversity under the

Endangered Species Act. Pages 8–27 *in* J. L. Nielsen and D. A. Powers, editors. American Fisheries Society, Symposium 17, Bethesda, Maryland.

Waples, R. S. 2009. Conserving the evolutionary legacy of Arctic-Yukon-Kuskokwim salmon. Pages 125–139 *in* C. C. Krueger and C. E. Zimmerman, editors. Pacific salmon: ecology and management of western Alaska's populations. American Fisheries Society, Symposium 70, Bethesda, Maryland.

Waples, R., A. Punt, and J. Cope. 2008. Integrating genetic data into management of marine resources: how can we do it better? Fish and Fisheries 4:423–449.

Waples, R. S., G. A. Winans, F. M. Utter, and C. Mahnken. 1990. Genetic approaches to the management of Pacific salmon. Fisheries 15:19–25.

Weitkamp, L., T. Wainwright, G. Bryant, B. Milner, D. Teel, R. Kope, and R. Waples. 1995. Status review of coho salmon from Washington, Oregon, and California. NOAA Technical Memorandum NMFS-NWFSC-24.

Wilmot, R., R. Everett, W. Spearman and R. Baccus. 1992. Genetic stock identification of Yukon River chum and chinook salmon 1987 to 1990. Progress Report US Fish and Wildlife Service, Anchorage, Alaska.

Wilmot, R., R. Everett, W. Spearman, R. Baccus, N. Varnavskaya, and S. Putivkin. 1994. Genetic stock structure of western Alaska chum salmon and a comparison with Russian Far East stocks. Canadian Journal of Fishery and Aquatic Sciences 51(Supplement 1):84–94.

Wilmot, R. L., C. M. Kondzela, C. M. Guthrie, and M. M. Masuda. 1998. Genetic stock identification of chum salmon harvested incidentally in the 1994 and 1995 Bering Sea trawl fishery. North Pacific Anadromous Fishery Commission Bulletin 1:285–294.

Wilmot, R., C. Kondzela, C. Guthrie, A. Moles, E. Martinsons, and J. Helle. 1999. Origins of sockeye and chum salmon seized from the Chinese vessel YING FA. Document 410. North Pacific Anadromous Fisheries Commission, Vancouver.

Winans, G. A.; P. B. Aebersold, S. Urawa, and N. V. Varnavskaya. 1994. Determining continent of origin of chum salmon (*Oncorhynchus keta*) using genetic stock identification techniques: status of allozyme baseline in Asia. Canadian Journal of Fisheries and Aquatic Sciences 51 (Supplement 1):95–113.

Wood, C., J. Bickham, R. J. Nelson, C. Foote, and J. Patton. 2008. Recurrent evolution of life history ecotypes in sockeye salmon: implications for conservation and future evolution. Evolutionary Applications 1:207–221.

Zhivotovsky, L., A. Gharrett, A, McGregor, M. Glubokovsky and M. Feldman. 1994. Gene differentiation in Pacific salmon: facts and models with reference to pink salmon. Canadian Journal of Fishery and Aquatic Sciences 51 (Supplement 1):223–232.

American Fisheries Society Symposium 70:125–139, 2009

Conserving the Evolutionary Legacy of Arctic-Yukon-Kuskokwim Salmon

ROBIN S. WAPLES*

Northwest Fisheries Science Center
2725 Montlake Boulevard East, Seattle, Washington 98112, USA

Abstract.—The legacy of Pacific salmon *Oncorhynchus* spp. can be described as the genetic resources that are the product of past evolutionary events and which represent the future evolutionary potential of the species. A key step in conserving this legacy is identifying conservation units—major chunks of biodiversity that collectively comprise the evolutionary legacy. A variety of methods exist for defining conservation units, but all should follow a two-step process. Step One is describing the (often hierarchical) structure of biodiversity within each species—that is, the evolutionary relationships among populations and metapopulations or larger conservation units. In theory, this is an objective, data-driven exercise. Step Two involves considering questions such as, "Which level in the hierarchy is best for identifying conservation units?" and "How much biodiversity do we need to conserve?" These questions do not have a single 'correct' answer; instead, they must be informed by societal values. In Step Two, therefore, it is important to articulate clear program goals to provide a context for addressing these difficult questions. But defining conservation units is only part of a coherent, long-term conservation strategy; evolution is dynamic, whereas simply conserving certain fixed types promotes stasis. Therefore, equally important is the conservation of evolutionary *processes*, which are the dynamic relationships between salmon and their ecosystems that help shape their evolutionary trajectories. Evolutionary processes include patterns of connectivity, dispersal, and gene flow; sexual selection and natural selection; and interactions with physical and biological features of the habitat. Conserving evolutionary processes requires consideration of the same two steps outlined above. Reflecting on the long-term goals of the Arctic-Yukon-Kuskokwim Sustainable Salmon Initiative will help to focus efforts to identify important units for conservation and vital evolutionary processes for Alaska salmon.

Introduction

Pacific salmon *Oncorhynchus* spp. are abundant, diverse, and widely distributed throughout Alaska, including the Arctic-Yukon-Kuskokwim (AYK) area. Alaskan salmon have provided important cultural and spiritual resources for Native Americans

*Corresponding author: robin.waples@noaa.gov

for millennia, and they play many important roles in modern society as well. This paper is concerned with the evolutionary legacy of AYK salmon: what is it, and how can it be conserved?

A legacy is a bequest, or something handed down from the past. However, the concept of legacy can have important consequences for the future. With respect to conservation of endangered species, Waples (1995) defined evolutionary legacy as "genetic variability that is the product of past evolutionary events and that represents the reservoir upon which future evolutionary potential [of a species] depends." From this perspective, legacy has both backward-looking and forwarding-looking aspects. Recognition of these aspects provides a useful framework for considering the legacy of AYK salmon.

A reasonable first step is to begin by describing the characteristics of the legacy. For AYK salmon, this requires consideration not only of genetic, phenotypic, and life history diversity within each of the species, but also ecological/environmental diversity of the ecosystems the species inhabit, as these conditions shaped the evolution of the biological diversity seen today. A convenient (and common) way to organize this diversity is to aggregate populations or stocks into conservation units that then become the focus of management actions and policy decisions. However, a variety of biologically based methods for defining conservation units can be found in the literature, and these different methods can lead to widely divergent results in the nature and size of the resulting units. Determining which method is most appropriate for a given application requires consideration of normative factors such as societal preferences or legal mandates as well as biological principles. Hence, consideration of management goals and objectives is a crucial component to the process of defining conservation units.

Although defining conservation units is a useful (and sometimes legally required) step, a strictly typological analysis that focuses only on existing genotypes and phenotypes is not sufficient for conserving the legacy of AYK salmon. This insufficiency occurs because evolution is a dynamic process; the array of types that are present today will not be exactly the same as those that occurred at any given time in the past, and conservation of these types will not necessarily ensure long-term persistence into the future. In addition to types, it is important to conserve evolutionary processes that allow populations to respond to future challenges (Moritz 2002). Restoring salmon populations is a complex process that involves both scientific and policy considerations. The rest of this manuscript will consider each of these topics in more detail.

What is the Legacy of AYK Salmon?

Waples et al. (2001) identified three major components of diversity in Pacific salmon: genetic, ecological, and life history.

Genetic diversity

Within the AYK region, much more information is available for population genetic structure than for the other components of diversity (for a recent review see Utter et al. 2009, this volume). Major results for each species are summarized below; see Figure 1 for a map showing the place names. Most of these genetic studies used what are believed to be neutral genetic markers; these markers are useful for providing insights into population histories, but provide no direct information about adaptive differences.

Chum salmon (O. keta).—Chum salmon from northwest Alaska are genetically differentiated from Asian chum, as well as from other Alaskan populations (Seeb and Crane 1999; Seeb et al. 2004), but this genetic group includes populations from Kotzebue Bay and Bristol Bay as well as AYK. Within northwest Alaska, fall-run populations that migrate up to 3,000 km in the Yukon River are particularly distinctive (Bue et al. 2009, this volume; Gilk et al. 2009, this volume).

Chinook salmon (O. tshawytscha).— Western Alaskan Chinook salmon are geneti-

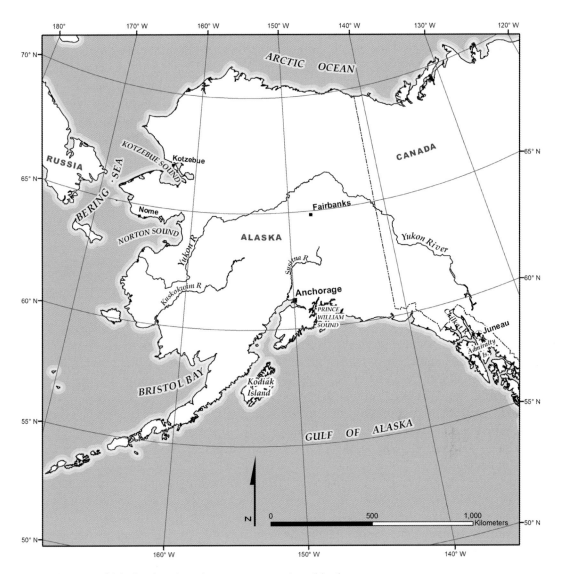

FIGURE 1. Map of Alaska showing place names mentioned in the text.

cally well differentiated from populations in the Chilkat River, the King Salmon River on Admiralty Island, and other areas of southeast Alaska (unpublished data cited in Utter et al. 2009). Within western Alaska, the Copper River, Upper Yukon River, and Kodiak Island form geographically coherent clusters, whereas other populations from Bristol Bay, the Susitna River, and northwest Alaska form a large, geographically heterogeneous genetic group. Within the upper Yukon River, modest but consistent differences are found between U.S. and Canadian populations (Templin et al. 2005; Smith et al. 2005). No clear geographic structuring is evident within the Kuskokwim River basin (unpublished data cited in Utter et al. 2009).

Coho salmon (O. kisutch).—Only limited species-wide genetic data are available for coho salmon (for a broad phylogeographic study that includes some Alaskan populations, see Smith et al. 2005), but within North America levels of population genetic differentiation tend to be fairly low except at the extremes of the range (California and Alaska; Weitkamp et al. 1995). More recent studies focusing on Alaskan populations have found high levels of differentiation (as large or larger than are found for other salmon species) among populations from the Yukon River (Olsen et al. 2004), but the Yukon River samples are not strongly differentiated from samples from other drainages in southwest Alaska (Olsen et al. 2003).

Sockeye salmon (O. nerka).—Little published genetic information exists for AYK sockeye salmon, but populations occur throughout the area and unpublished data referenced by Utter et al. (2009) suggest that a population near Nome is distinctive. Published studies from other areas (Taylor et al. 1996; Winans et al. 1996) consistently show sockeye salmon to have a mosaic pattern of population structure, with large genetic differences among local populations, including many in close proximity to each other.

Pink salmon (O. gorbuscha).—Even- and odd-year pink salmon occur in coastal drainages throughout the AYK region. Although abundant genetic data exist for other geographic areas, information for AYK populations is limited. Published studies from other areas consistently show relatively modest differences among populations within lineages and much larger differences between the even- and odd-year lineages, even for populations in the same stream (Churikov and Gharrett 2002).

Ecological diversity

The AYK covers a large geographic area and encompasses all, or part of, eight different ecosystem provinces in the U.S. portion alone

(accessed at http://www.fs.fed.us/colorimage-map/ecoreg1_akprovinces.html; see also Bailey 1983). These provinces are characterized by different temperature, precipitation, soil, vegetation, and geological regimes, and span a wide range from comparatively mild and wet maritime conditions to extreme continental climates in the interior; for example, the Yukon River is a long, turbid, low-gradient stream that influences environmental conditions throughout much of the AYK.

Life-history diversity

Although a great deal has been written in general about Pacific salmon life histories (Groot and Margolis 1991; Quinn 2005), relatively little published information deals specifically with life history diversity within the AYK region. Nevertheless, some extreme life history types are worth noting. Chum and Chinook salmon both migrate over 3,000 km up the Yukon River to spawn in headwater streams in Canada, and no other salmon in North America (Pacific or Atlantic) make such extensive freshwater migrations (e.g., Evenson et al. 2009, this volume; Bradford et al. 2009, this volume). In some upper Yukon River populations, Chinook salmon do not smolt until age-2 (Beacham et al. 1989), which is rare for the species. More generally, two patterns are evident in data for other North American Pacific salmon populations (Waples et al. 2001) that are probably generally relevant to AYK salmon as well. First, a strong correlation generally exists between the amount of life history diversity expressed within a species and the range of environmental conditions the species experiences. The rich diversity of habitats in the AYK (see above) suggests an *a priori* expectation of considerable life history diversity as well. Second, Chinook and sockeye salmon generally show more life history diversity among populations than is found in pink, chum, and coho salmon.

Identifying conservation units

Identifying conservation units ideally should involve a two-step process (Waples 1995). Step 1 is (at least in theory) an objective exercise and involves characterizing existing patterns of diversity in a systematic way (as discussed above). Watersheds that support Pacific salmon typically have a hierarchical structure that is reflected in the underlying patterns of biodiversity; for example, Puget Sound Chinook salmon have a hierarchical structure (Figure 2; see Figure 3 for map). The highest level of the hierarchy is the biological species, within which two major life history types have been identified (Healey 1991): ocean-type populations, in which juveniles migrate to sea as subyearlings, and stream-type populations, which have yearling smolts. Each of these two juvenile life history types is also associated with a suite of adult behavioral and life history traits (Waples et al. 2004). All Puget Sound populations have the ocean-type life history. Based on evidence for genetic/ecological/ life history differences between Puget Sound populations and those to the north and on the Olympic Peninsula, Puget Sound Chinook are considered to be an Evolutionarily Significant Unit (ESU) within the species (Myers et al. 1998). Nested within the Puget Sound ESU are several Genetic Diversity Units (GDUs) identified by the State of Washington (Busack and Shaklee 1995), one of which includes the Stillaguamish and Skagit Rivers. The Skagit is the largest river in Puget Sound, and its major tributary is the Sauk River, which supports two spawning aggregations of Chinook salmon that are considered to be demographically independent populations (Ruckelshaus et al. 2006). The two populations differ in adult run timing, with Upper Sauk fish generally returning in the spring and Lower Sauk fish returning in the summer.

This example serves to illustrate two key points about conservation units. First, each of these seven hierarchical levels of diversity has potential relevance for conservation. Routine fishery management generally should focus on the lowest hierarchical level (local populations or stocks; Level 7 in this example). Units designated for other purposes (e.g., GDUs or ESUs) might represent amalga-

1 Species (*Oncorhynchus tshawytscha*)

   2 Major life history type (ocean type)

      3 ESU (Puget Sound)

         4 Genetic Diversity Unit (Stillaguamish and Skagit)

            5 Major River Basin (Skagit River)

               6 Major tributary (Sauk River)

                  7a Population (L. Sauk; summer-run)

                  7b Population (U. Sauk; spring-run)

FIGURE 2. Hierarchical levels of biodiversity within Puget Sound Chinook salmon. Level 7 is generally considered a "population" or "stock." Based on Waples' (1991, 1995) framework, NMFS has identified an ESU at Level 3 in this case; this ESU is considered to be a "distinct population segment" (DPS) and is recognized as an ESA "species." It seems likely that application of other published ESU approaches (Dizon et al. 1992; Vogler and DeSalle 1994; Moritz 1994; Bowen 1998; Crandall et al. 2000) would result in recognition of salmon ESUs at either extreme of this continuum of diversity (i.e., either levels 1–2 or 7). After Waples (2006).

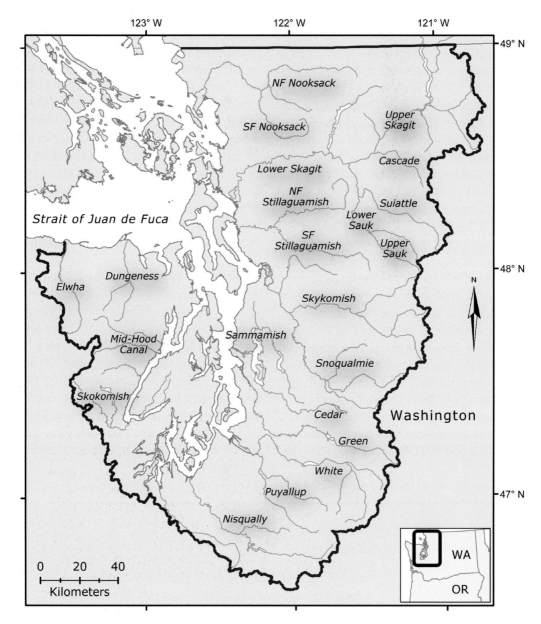

FIGURE 3. Map of Puget Sound showing some of the place names mentioned in the text. Modified from Good et al. (2007).

mations of numerous local populations that share common characteristics; however, the effectiveness of such larger units in promoting conservation depends to a large extent on whether management actions take into consideration the full spectrum of biodiversity, including the lower hierarchical levels.

The second key point is that no single scientifically 'correct' answer exists to the problem of which hierarchical level to focus on for conservation. Recently, the existing ESUs of Pacific salmon was compared with those that would be expected based on criteria for other published ESU concepts (Dizon et al. 1992; Vogler and DeSalle 1994; Moritz 1994; Bowen 1998; Crandall et al. 2000). One clear pattern that emerged from the analysis (Waples 2006) was that these approaches all appeared likely to result in identification of ESUs at one of the extremes of the hierarchy of biodiversity (Figure 2)—that is, at or near the level of local populations, or at or near the level of the biological species. In contrast, the existing ESUs of Pacific salmon identified by the National Marine Fisheries Service (NMFS) generally encompass relatively large geographic areas and include numerous local populations—hence they occupy an intermediate position on the continuum of biodiversity (Figure 2). Thus, different biological approaches for defining conservation units can lead to radically different conclusions about how inclusive the units are. None of these approaches is intrinsically 'correct' or 'best'; any given approach might be the most suitable depending on the circumstances and the goals one is trying to achieve. Therefore, Step 2 in the process of defining conservation units requires consideration of goals and objectives, which should help direct attention to a particular hierarchical level(s) on the continuum of biological diversity. In the next section, this topic is considered with respect to the AYK Sustainable Salmon Initiative (SSI) program.

Most of the differences between the various approaches for identifying ESUs and conservation units concern the relative importance placed on two major factors: isolation and adaptation (Figure 4). For example, the Moritz (1994) approach focuses almost exclusively on units that have experienced long-term isolation, the rationale being that such units are irreplaceable except on extremely long evolutionary time scales. Isolation is typically evaluated using (presumably neutral) molecular markers. In contrast, the framework proposed by Crandall et al. (2000) places more importance on local adaptations because they are the material (and the

product) of contemporary evolutionary processes. Adaptation is more difficult to assess in natural populations, and so it is typically necessary to rely on proxies (e.g., behavioral, phenotypic, or life history traits, or physical features of the habitat) to draw inferences about likely adaptations. The NMFS ESU approach for Pacific salmon (Waples 1991) has always considered both isolation and adaptation to be important.

Several key issues exist that will have to be faced in developing conservation plans for AYK salmon (Figure 4). Most people would agree that Unit A (high scores on both isolation and adaptation axes) should have a higher conservation priority than Unit B (low scores on both axes). But what about Units C (strongly isolated but little evidence for local adaptation) and D (low degree or recent isolation but strong evidence for local adaptation)? Developing priorities for these types of situations requires consideration of policy/management goals as well as biological information and analyses.

Conserving the Legacy of AYK Salmon

Strategies to conserve and restore AYK salmon should be guided by the goals and objectives of the AYK SSI program (accessed at http://www.aykssi.org/). The Mission Statement is "to collaboratively develop and implement a comprehensive research plan to understand the causes of the declines and recoveries of AYK salmon." With respect to guiding principles, the AYK SSI seeks to:

• Address the pressing research needs throughout the salmon life cycle;

• Obtain the greatest good for the fisheries and users in the AYK area and the ecosystems upon which they depend; and

• Develop an AYK Research & Restoration Plan that will provide an ongoing process whereby research activities are guided, selected, reviewed, and modified over time to reflect the outcome and knowledge obtained from research and restoration activities (see AYK SSI 2006).

The goals for the AYK-SSI program are rather broad and would appear to allow considerable latitude for interpretation; they do not appear to direct attention primarily to any particular hierarchical level of diversity. Nevertheless, the title of the program and the references to ongoing processes and ecosystems upon which the resource depends suggest that the concepts of long-term persistence and viability are central to the enterprise. Therefore, the general evolutionary considerations discussed above are relevant, and it will be important to understand the full spectrum of biodiversity within the different salmon species and how these components are interrelated.

Geographic perspective

In thinking about conservation units, the geographic perspective must be broad enough to include all populations that share a common evolutionary lineage. In the example shown in Figure 2, available evidence suggests that all Chinook salmon populations in Puget Sound are more closely related to each other than to other populations outside the sound. In that case, Puget Sound populations are a meaningful group upon which to focus conservation efforts. However, pink and chum salmon populations in Puget Sound are not strongly differentiated from nearby populations in Canada, and as a result ESUs for these species include both Puget Sound and Strait of Georgia populations (Hard et al. 1996; Johnson et al. 1997). For pink and chum salmon, consideration only of the conservation status of Puget Sound populations (or only those in the Strait of Georgia) would not provide a complete picture of a functional biological unit.

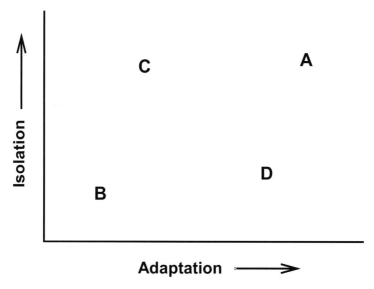

Figure 4. Two axes of population differentiation that are important to consider in identifying conservation units. The isolation axis emphasizes units that have experienced long-term isolation and hence have evolved unique genetic characteristics. The adaptation axis emphasizes units that have strong local adaptations, which reflect different selective regimes in different environments. A–D represent potential conservation units with different degrees of isolation and adaptation. See text for discussion.

Available genetic data suggest that western Alaskan populations of Pacific salmon are, in general, strongly separated from Asian populations, as well as from other populations in Alaska and farther south. However, the AYK salmon populations are not always clearly distinguished from other populations in western Alaska (see genetic summaries for chum, Chinook, and coho salmon above). Some of these affinities might reflect postglacial colonization of more southerly populations from the Arctic rather than Pacific refuges—a scenario that has been proposed to explain the similarity of some Susitna River chum and Chinook populations to those in the AYK (Seeb and Crane 1999; Utter et al. 2009). Some of these apparent affinities may not reflect true evolutionary relationships but could be due to imperfect resolving power of existing samples and genetic markers. Nevertheless, these results emphasize the importance of considering nearby populations to more fully understand ecological and evolutionary relationships of populations within the AYK area.

Level of variation to conserve

How much of the legacy must be conserved? Again, this is a difficult question with no unique answer, and a challenging question for two major reasons. First, evaluating the biological consequences of conservation strategies that might differ in qualitative as well as quantitative ways is extremely complex. Second, even if scientists were able to clearly describe different biological outcomes for alternative recovery/conservation strategies, tough policy decisions would typically be required in choosing which alternative(s) to pursue. In the Pacific Northwest and California, NMFS has undertaken an effort to address both of these challenges for salmon and steelhead that are protected under the U.S. Endangered Species Act (ESA) (Good et al. 2007). The overall process involves regional technical teams charged with identifying a range of biological parameters consistent with ESA recovery, as well as policy/stakeholder groups associated with each technical team that will help determine which recovery scenario(s) are most compatible with other societal goals (for details of the recovery planning process, see http://www.nwfsc.noaa.gov/trt/index.cfm).

To provide a biological framework for the technical aspects of recovery planning, NMFS scientists developed the concept of Viable Salmonid Populations (VSP; McElhany et al. 2000). Within each ESU, the VSP process begins by identifying demographically independent populations or stocks, which are natural units for conducting viability analyses. Next, viability criteria are developed that encompass four aspects of population health: abundance, productivity, spatial structure, and diversity (of ecological/genetic/life history traits). The current status of each population is assessed with respect to the four VSP criteria. Finally, it is necessary to consider how many populations must be at what level of viability before the entire ESU can be considered recovered. This latter step in particular involves both technical and policy challenges. The technical teams must integrate risks across diverse populations into an overall assessment of ESU-level viability. The VSP criteria for spatial structure and diversity are key considerations at this step. To aid in their evaluations, most technical teams have identified strata within each ESU; these strata generally include geographically coherent groups of populations that differ in ecological and/or life history/genetic characteristics. Although every population does not necessarily have to be viable for an entire ESU to be viable, requiring at least some healthy populations in each stratum is the best way to ensure that the entire ESU remains viable into the future.

The technical teams develop a range of whole-ESU viability scenarios that typically

differ with respect to which specific populations are expected to be at particular levels
of viability. These scenarios might differ not
only in the probability of recovery but also in
the time required to achieve recovery. Giv-
en this technical information, along with a
summary of associated uncertainties that are
characterized as accurately as possible by the
technical teams, it is up to the policy/stake-
holder groups to determine which recovery
strategies are most appropriate to pursue. In
this latter step, insofar as permitted under
the legal framework of the ESA, the policy/
stakeholder groups take into consideration
such factors as economic and social variables, risk tolerance, and the importance of
achieving salmon recovery goals that might
extend beyond those mandated by the ESA
(e.g., to provide sustainable harvest or ecosystem services). For an example application
of VSP principles to evaluating population
and ESU-level viability, see http://www.nwf-
sc.noaa.gov/trt/wlc.cfm.

These examples of salmon recovery
planning represent only some of many possible ways of approaching conservation and
recovery of AYK salmon (see Irvine et al.
2005 for discussion of conservation of salmon under Canada's Species at Risk Act), but
they illustrate some important general principles. The legislative and legal framework
of the U.S. Endangered Species Act has led
the NMFS to identify ESUs that cover a
relatively large geographic area (e.g., Puget
Sound; Figure 3), which typically include
20–30 local populations or stocks. ESUs are
the smallest units that can be listed/delisted
under the ESA, and hence consideration of
that hierarchical level is not discretionary in
formal recovery planning. However, as discussed above, the viability analyses and the
process of setting recovery goals explicitly
consider two lower levels in the biological
hierarchy—independent populations and
strata. The goals articulated by the AYK SSI
are rather broad and not limited to any par-

ticular level on the continuum of biodiversity.
The brief summaries in the previous section
describing ecological/life history/genetic diversity among AYK populations are superfi-
cial, and decisions about the most appropriate way to think about conservation units
within the area should be based on a much
more extensive analysis of existing information. If managers and scientists decide it is
important to define formal conservation units
within the AYK, these units might be either
smaller or larger than typical salmon ESUs
that have been identified by NMFS in the Pacific Northwest and California. Regardless of
how large or small the units are, conservation
efforts will be most effective if they consider
the full spectrum of biological diversity and
the relationships among the different hierarchical levels. Previous work on the status of
Alaskan salmon (Wertheimer 1997; Clark et
al. 2006) provides a good basis for more concerted efforts at viability analyses within the
AYK region.

Evolutionary processes

Although some advantages exist to defining conservation units early in the planning
process, preserving existing types will not
necessarily provide for long-term sustainability of the resource. The conservation of evolutionary processes, which are the dynamic
relationships between populations and their
ecosystems that help shape their evolutionary trajectories, is equally important. These
processes include patterns of connectivity,
dispersal, and gene flow; sexual selection and
natural selection; and interactions with physical and biological features of the habitat. The
best way to conserve evolutionary processes
is to conserve functioning natural ecosystems.
If this goal is met, the conservation units that
might be defined today will continue to evolve
and interact with other units, and the species
as a whole will be resilient to the inevitable
environmental changes and challenges in the

future. This in essence is what the VSP criteria for spatial structure and diversity aim to accomplish. Although life history diversity is most likely important to the long-term sustainability of salmon, how to conserve this diversity, except in healthy natural habitats, is unknown. Under the VSP framework, salmon recovery planning focuses on conserving enough high quality habitat, sufficiently well distributed throughout the ESU, so that fundamental evolutionary and ecological processes can continue to play a dynamic role in shaping the ESU in the future.

Restoration strategies under the AYK SSI might vary among the salmon species, not only because the species differ in current conservation status, but also because the variation among species in ecological and life history traits suggests that different geographic scales might be appropriate for conservation efforts. For example, Olsen et al. (2004) found a relatively high degree of genetic differentiation among AYK coho salmon populations and concluded that local populations are relatively small and isolated, and hence susceptible to effects of local habitat degradation. Conservation efforts for this species (and perhaps for Chinook and sockeye salmon as well) might need to begin by focusing on small, local populations. In contrast, pink salmon typically have much lower levels of population differentiation than other salmon species and regularly experience orders of magnitude fluctuations in abundance over generational time periods, which suggests that extinction and recolonization of local populations might be common (Hawkins et al. 2002). In this species local populations in general are not independent, and conservation strategies might take a broader, regional perspective. Most chum salmon population spawn near tidewater and, like pink salmon, tend to be characterized by modest genetic differences among populations within a region. However, chum salmon also make remarkable migrations up the Yukon River, and this provides

considerable opportunity for local differentiation. Therefore, for some Yukon River chum salmon populations it will be important to focus conservation efforts on a smaller scale than elsewhere.

Role of hatcheries

What role might hatcheries play in conserving the legacy of AYK salmon? Hatcheries are responsible for essentially the entire production of chum salmon from Japan (Masuda and Tsukamoto 1998), and many U.S. fisheries for Chinook, coho, and chum salmon are dominated by hatchery fish (Mahnken et al. 1998). A growing interest has developed within the U.S. and Canada in using salmon hatcheries for conservation, and a number of programs have demonstrated the ability to maintain populations over periods of a few decades or several salmon generations. Nevertheless, several factors suggest that it is risky to rely on hatcheries for long-term conservation.

First, salmon hatcheries have been used for over a century in an attempt to compensate for losses to natural populations caused by anthropogenic factors (habitat loss and degradation; blockage of migratory routes; overharvest). However, an historical review indicates that hatchery programs have consistently failed to achieve their stated goals (Lichatowich 1999). Second, no empirical evidence exists that hatcheries can be used to help sustain natural populations indefinitely, or that a temporary supplementation program can result in a viable population once the program is terminated (Waples et al. 2007). Many managers and researchers are concerned that cumulative domestication effects associated with supplementation might reduce the fitness of a depressed natural population to the point at which it cannot survive without permanent hatchery supplementation (Reisenbichler 1997; Lynch and O'Hely 2001; Ford 2002; Araki et al. 2007). The huge Japanese chum salmon hatchery program, which has been successful from a production standpoint, is facing issues related to carrying capacity of the marine environment and effects on wild populations. Some Japanese scientists are now questioning the long-term viability of a system that has completely replaced natural production (Kaeriyama and Edpalina 2004). Finally, hatcheries disrupt natural evolutionary processes and profoundly affect the relationship between salmon and the ecosystems they inhabit. Hatcheries typically substitute for the entire freshwater life cycle of salmon, and adults returning to spawn in hatcheries do not produce carcasses that play such a vital role in providing food and nutrients to terrestrial ecosystems that support natural salmon populations (Bilby et al. 1996; Cederholm et al. 1999).

Conclusion

Scientific panels that have considered salmon recovery issues over the past decade have consistently stressed the importance of conserving a diverse array of natural populations (e.g., National Research Council 1996; Myers et al. 2004; Williams 2006). Alaskan salmon have provided perhaps the best empirical example of the importance of this general principle. Bristol Bay sockeye salmon have supported harvests in the tens of millions of fish for over a century, in spite of substantial changes in marine and freshwater ecosystems. Analysis of a 50+ year time series of abundance data indicates that the relative contribution of different stock complexes to overall harvests has changed dramatically over that time period (Hilborn et al. 2003). Notably, stocks that were minor contributors in the 1950s later came to dominate the fishery. The authors concluded that the rich store of genetic and life history diversity within Bristol Bay sockeye salmon has buffered the resource against environmental fluctuations

and will provide resilience for the resource into the future.

Which components of AYK salmon diversity will play important ecological/evolutionary roles in the future are difficult to predict. However, we can be confident that the existence of this diversity will greatly enhance the sustainability of the resource. In thinking about conserving the legacy of AYK salmon, Aldo Leopold's advice is relevant: "To keep every cog and wheel is the first precaution of intelligent tinkering" (Leopold 1953; p. 147). The scientific challenges are to understand how the cogs and wheels interact, and the biological consequences of losing some of them. The policy/management challenges are to clearly articulate goals and objectives; to decide how to deal with inevitable biological uncertainties; and to weigh society's tolerance to various sources of risk (e.g., risk of losing biodiversity; risk of losing ecosystem services; economic, social, and cultural risks, etc.).

Acknowledgments

I thank Jim and Lisa Seeb and Fred Utter for useful discussions and for sharing unpublished data. Damon Holzer provided the map in Figure 1; Jeremy Davies the map in Figure 3.

References

AYK SSI (Arctic-Yukon-Kuskokwim Sustainable Salmon Initiative). 2006. Arctic-Yukon-Kuskokwim Salmon Research and Restoration Plan. Bering Sea Fishermen's Association, Anchorage, Alaska.

Araki, H., B. Cooper, and M. S. Blouin. 2007. Genetic effects of captive breeding cause a rapid, cumulative fitness decline in the wild. Science 318:100–103.

Bailey, R. G. 1983. Delineation of ecosystem regions. Environmental Management 7:365–373.

Beacham, T., C. Murray, and R. Withler. 1989. Age, morphology and biochemical genetic variation of Yukon River Chinook salmon. Transactions of the American Fishery Society 118:46–63.

Bilby, R. E., B. R. Fransen, and P. A. Bisson. 1996. Incorporation of nitrogen and carbon from spawning coho salmon into the trophic system of small streams: evidence from stable isotopes. Canadian Journal of Fisheries and Aquatic Sciences 53:164–173.

Bowen, B. W. 1998. What is wrong with ESUs? The gap between evolutionary theory and conservation principles. Journal of Shellfish Research 17:1355–1358.

Bradford, M. J., A. von Finster, and P. A. Milligan. 2009. Freshwater life history, habitat, and the production of Chinook salmon from the upper Yukon basin. Pages 19–38 in C. C. Krueger and C. E. Zimmerman, editors. Pacific salmon: ecology and management of western Alaska's populations. American Fisheries Society, Symposium 70, Bethesda, Maryland.

Bue, F. J., B. M. Borba, R. Cannon, and C. C. Krueger. 2009. Yukon River fall chum salmon fisheries: management, harvest, and stock abundance. Pages 703–742 in C. C. Krueger and C. E. Zimmerman, editors. Pacific salmon: ecology and management of western Alaska's populations. American Fisheries Society, Symposium 70, Bethesda, Maryland.

Busack, C., and J. Shaklee, editors. 1995. Genetic Diversity Units and Major Ancestral Lineages of Salmonid Fishes in Washington. Washington Department of Fish and Wildlife Technical Report RAD 95–02.

Cederholm, J. C., M. D. Kunze, T. Murota, and A. Sibatani. 1999. Pacific salmon carcasses: essential contributions of nutrients and energy for aquatic and terrestrial systems. Fisheries 24(10):6–13.

Churikov, D., and A. J. Gharrett. 2002. Comparative phylogeography of the two pink salmon broodlines: an analysis based on a mitochondrial DNA genealogy. Molecular Ecology 11:1077–1101.

Clark, J. H., R. D. Mecum, A. McGregor, P. Krasnowski, and A. Carroll. 2006. The commercial salmon fisheries in Alaska. Alaska Fishery Research Bulletin 12(1):1–146.

Crandall, K. A., O. R. P. Bininda-Emonds, G. M. Mace, and R. K. Wayne. 2000. Considering evolutionary processes in conservation biology. Trends in Ecology and Evolution 15:290–295.

Dizon, A. E., C. Lockyer, W. F. Perrin, D. P. Demaster, and J. Sisson. 1992. Rethinking the stock concept: a phylogeographic approach. Conservation Biology 6:24–36.

Evenson, D. F., S. J. Hayes, G. Sandone, and D. J. Bergstrom. 2009. Yukon River Chinook salmon: stock status, harvest, and management. Pages 675–701 in C. C. Krueger and C. E. Zimmerman, editors. Pacific salmon: ecology and management of west-

ern Alaska's populations. American Fisheries Society, Symposium 70, Bethesda, Maryland.

Ford, M. J. 2002. Selection in captivity during supportive breeding may reduce fitness in the wild. Conservation Biology 16:815–825.

Gilk, S., T. Hamazaki, D. Molyneaux, J. Pawluk, and W. Templin. 2009. Biological and genetic characteristics of fall chum salmon in the Kuskokwim River, Alaska. Pages 161–179 in C. C. Krueger and C. E. Zimmerman, editors. Pacific salmon: ecology and management of western Alaska's populations. American Fisheries Society, Symposium 70, Bethesda, Maryland.

Good, T. P., T. J. Beechie, P. McElhany, M. M. McClure, and M. H. Ruckelshaus. 2007. Recovery planning for Endangered Species Act-listed Pacific salmon: Using science to inform goals and strategies. Fisheries 32:426–440.

Groot, C., and L. Margolis, editors. 1991. Pacific salmon: life histories. University of British Columbia Press, Vancouver.

Hard, J. J., R. G. Kope, W. S. Grant, F. W. Waknitz, L. T. Parker, and R. S. Waples. 1996. Status review of pink salmon from Washington, Oregon, and California. U.S. Dep. Commer., NOAA Tech. Memo. NMFS-NWFSC-25.

Hawkins, S., N. Varnavsakaya, E. Matzak, V. Efremov, C. Guthrie, R. Wilmot, H. Mayama, F. Yamazaki, and A. Gharrett. 2002. Population structure of odd-broodline Asian pink salmon and its contrast to the even-broodline structure. Journal of Fish Biology 60:370–388.

Healey, M. C. 1991. The life history of Chinook salmon (Oncorhynchus tshawytscha). Pages 311–393 in C. Groot and L. Margolis, editors. Pacific salmon: life histories. University of British Columbia Press, Vancouver.

Hilborn, R., T. P. Quinn, D. E. Schindler, and D. E. Rogers. 2003. Biocomplexity and fisheries sustainability. Proceedings of the National Academy of Sciences, USA 100:6564–6568.

Irvine, J. R., M. R. Gross, C. C. Wood, L. B. Holtby, N. D. Schubert, and P. G. Amiro. 2005. Canada's Species at Risk Act: an opportunity to protect "endangered" salmon. Fisheries 30(12):11–19.

Johnson, O. W., W. S. Grant, R. G. Kope, K. Neely, F. W. Waknitz, and R. S. Waples. 1997. Status review of chum salmon from Washington, Oregon, and California. U.S. Department Commer., NOAA Technical Memorandum NMFS-NWFSC-32.

Kaeriyama, M., and R. R. Edpalina. 2004. Evaluation of the biological interaction between wild and hatchery populations for sustainable fisheries management of Pacific salmon. Pages 247–259 in K. M. Leber, S. Kitada, T. Svåsand and H. L. Blankenship, editors. Stock Enhancement and Sea

Ranching: Developments, Pitfalls and Opportunities. 2nd Edition, Blackwell Scientific Publications, Oxford, UK.

Leopold, A. 1953. Round River: from the journals of Aldo Leopold. Oxford University Press, New York.

Lichatowich, J. 1999. Salmon without rivers: a history of the Pacific salmon crisis. Island Press, Washington, D.C.

Lynch, M., and M. O'Hely. 2001. Captive breeding and the genetic fitness of natural populations. Conservation Genetics 2:363–378.

McElhany, P., M. H. Ruckelshaus, M. J. Ford, T. C. Wainwright, and E. P. Bjorkstedt. 2000. Viable salmonid populations and the recovery of evolutionarily significant units. NOAA Technical Memorandum NMFS-NWFSC 42.

Mahnken, C. V., G. Ruggerone, F. W. Waknitz, and T. A. Flagg. 1998. A historical perspective on salmonid production from Pacific Rim hatcheries. North Pacific Anadromous Fish Commission Bulletin 1:38–53.

Masuda, R., and K. Tsukamoto. 1998. Stock enhancement in Japan: review and perspective. Bulletin of Marine Science 62:337–358.

Moritz, C. 1994. Defining 'evolutionarily significant units' for conservation. Trends in Ecology and Evolution 9:373–375.

Moritz, C. 2002. Strategies to protect biological diversity and the evolutionary processes that sustain it. Systematic Biology 51:238–254.

Myers, J. M., R. G. Kope, G. J. Bryant, D. Teel, L. J. Lierheimer, T. C. Wainwright, W. S. Grant, F. W. Waknitz, K. Neely, S. T. Lindley, and R. S. Waples. 1998. Status review of Chinook salmon from Washington, Idaho, Oregon, and California. U.S. Department of Commerce, NOAA Technical Memorandum NMFS-NWFSC-35.

Myers, R. A., S. A. Levin, R. Lande, F.C. James, W.W. Murdoch, and R. T. Paine. 2004. Hatcheries and endangered salmon. Policy Forum. Science 303:1980.

National Research Council. 1996. Upstream: salmon and society in the Pacific Northwest. National Academy Press, Washington, D.C.

Olsen, J. B., S. J. Miller, W. J. Spearman, and J. K. Wenburg. 2003. Patterns of intra- and inter-population genetic diversity in Alaskan coho salmon: implications for conservation. Conservation Genetics 4:557–569.

Olsen, J., W. Spearman, G. Sage, S. Miller, B. Flannery, and J. K. Wenburg. 2004. Variation in the population structure of Yukon River chum and coho salmon: evaluating the potential impact of localized habitat degradation. Transactions of the American Fishery Society 133:476–483.

Quinn, T. P. 2005. The behavior and ecology of Pacific salmon and trout. University of Washington Press, Seattle.

Reisenbichler, R. R. 1997. Genetic factors contributing to declines of anadromous salmonids in the Pacific Northwest. Pages 223–244 in D. J. Strouder, P. A. Bisson, R. J. Naiman, and M. G. Duke, editors. Pacific salmon and their ecosystems: status and future options. Chapman and Hall, New York.

Ruckelshaus, M. H., K. P. Currens, W. H. Graeber, R. R. Fuerstenberg, K. Rawson, N. J. Sands, and J. B. Scott. 2006. Independent populations of Chinook salmon in Puget Sound. U.S. Department of Commerce, NOAA Technical Memorandum, NMFS-NWFSC-78, 125 p.

Seeb, L., and P. Crane. 1999. High genetic heterogeneity in chum salmon in western Alaska, the contact zone between northern and southern lineages. Transactions of the American Fishery Society 128:58–87.

Seeb, L., P. Crane, C. Kondzela, R. Wilmot, S. Urawa, N. Varnavskaya, and J. Seeb. 2004. Migration of Pacific Rim chum salmon on the high seas: insights from genetic data. Environmental Biology of Fishes 69:21–36.

Smith, C., J. Nelson, C. Wood, and B. Koop. 2001. Glacial biogeography of North American coho salmon. Molecular Ecology 10:2775–2785.

Smith, C. T., W. D. Templin, J. E. Seeb, and L. W. Seeb. 2005. Single nucleotide polymorphisms provide rapid and accurate estimates of the proportions of U.S. and Canadian Chinook salmon caught in Yukon River fisheries. North American Journal of Fisheries Management 25:944–953.

Taylor, E. B., C. J. Foote, and C. C. Wood. 1996. Molecular genetic evidence for parallel life-history evolution within a Pacific salmon (sockeye salmon and kokanee, *Oncorhynchus nerka*). Evolution 50:401–416.

Templin, W. D., R. L. Wilmot, C. M. Guthrie III, and L. W. Seeb. 2005. United States and Canadian Chinook salmon populations in the Yukon River can be segregated based on genetic characteristics. North American Journal of Fisheries Management 25:944–953.

Utter, F., M. V. McPhee, and F. W. Allendorf. 2009. Population genetics and the management of Arctic-Yukon-Kuskokwim salmon populations. Pages 97–123 in C. C. Krueger and C. E. Zimmerman, editors. Pacific salmon: ecology and management of western Alaska's populations. American Fisheries Society, Symposium 70, Bethesda, Maryland.

Vogler, A. P., and R. DeSalle. 1994. Diagnosing units of conservation management. Conservation Biology 8:354–363.

Waples, R. S. 1991. Pacific salmon, *Oncorhynchus*

spp., and the definition of "species" under the Endangered Species Act. Marine Fisheries Review 53:11–22.

Waples, R. S. 1995. Evolutionarily significant units and the conservation of biological diversity under the Endangered Species Act. Pages 8–27 *in* J. L. Nielsen, editor. Evolution and the aquatic ecosystem: defining unique units in population conservation. American Fisheries Society, Symposium 17, Bethesda, Maryland.

Waples, R. S. 2006. Distinct population segments. Pages 127–149 *in* J. M. Scott, D. D. Goble, and F. W. Davis, editors. The Endangered Species Act at thirty: conserving biodiversity in human-dominated landscapes. Island Press, Washington, D.C.

Waples, R. S., M. J. Ford, and D. Schmitt. 2007. Empirical results of salmon supplementation in the Northeast Pacific: A preliminary assessment. Pages 383–403 *in* T. M. Bert, editor. Ecological and genetic implications of aquaculture activities. Springer, Dordrecht, Netherlands.

Waples, R. S., R. G. Gustafson, L. A. Weitkamp, J. M. Myers, O. W. Johnson, P. J. Busby, J. J. Hard, G. J. Bryant, F. W. Waknitz, K. Neely, D. Teel, W. S. Grant, G. A. Winans, S. Phelps, A. Marshal,

and B. M. Baker. 2001. Characterizing diversity in salmon from the Pacific Northwest. Journal of Fish Biology 59 (Supplement A):1–41.

Waples, R. S., D. J. Teel, J. Myers, and A. Marshall. 2004. Evolution of life history diversity in Chinook salmon: ancient lineages and parallel evolution. Evolution 58:386–403.

Weitkamp, L., T. Wainwright, G. Bryant, B. Milner, D. Teel, R. Kope, and R. Waples. 1995. Status review of coho salmon from Washington, Oregon, and California. NOAA Technical Memorandum, NMFS-NWFSC-24.

Wertheimer, A. 1997. Status of Alaska salmon. Pages 179–197 *in* D. Stouder, P. Bisson, and R. Naiman, editors. Pacific salmon and their ecosystems: status and future options. Chapman and Hall, New York.

Williams, R. N. 2006. Return to the river: restoring salmon to the Columbia River. Elsevier Academic Press, Burlington, Massachusetts.

Winans, G. A., P. B. Aebersold, and R. S. Waples. 1996. Allozyme variability of *Oncorhynchus nerka* in the Pacific Northwest, with special consideration to populations of Redfish Lake, Idaho. Transactions of the American Fishery Society 125:645–663.

American Fisheries Society Symposium 70:141–160, 2009

Population Structure and Stock Identification of Chum Salmon from Western Alaska Determined with Microsatellite DNA and Major Histocompatibility Complex Variation

Terry D. Beacham[*], Khai D. Le, Michael Wetklo,
Brenda McIntosh, Tobi Ming, and Kristina M. Miller

Fisheries and Oceans Canada, Pacific Biological Station
3190 Hammond Bay Road, Nanaimo, British Columbia V9T 6N7, Canada

Abstract.—Microsatellite and major histocompatibility complex (MHC) variation was surveyed to evaluate population structure and the potential for genetic stock identification in chum salmon *Oncorhynchus keta* populations largely bordering the eastern Bering Sea and northwestern Gulf of Alaska. Variation at 14 microsatellite loci and one MHC locus was surveyed for 59 populations in the study. The genetic differentiation index (F_{st}) over all populations and loci was 0.023, with individual locus values ranging from 0.007 to 0.058. At least 10 regional stocks were observed in the survey area, with populations from Kotzebue Sound (mean F_{st} value usually >0.02 in regional comparisons) and the Alaska Peninsula (F_{st} >0.03) the most distinct of Alaskan populations surveyed. For stock identification applications incorporating DNA variation, chum salmon sampled in rivers' tributaries to the eastern Bering Sea were classified into the following regions: Kotzebue Sound, Norton Sound, lower/middle Yukon River, Tanana River, Kuskokwim River, Nushagak River, north/central Bristol Bay, southwest Bristol Bay, northern Alaska Peninsula/Aleutian Islands, southwest Alaska Peninsula, and southeast Alaska Peninsula. For simulated single-region mixtures, estimated regional stock compositions were generally above 90% for the previously-listed regions except for the Kuskokwim River, Nushagak and north/central Bristol Bay regions. Incomplete characterization of DNA variation for populations in those regions most likely contributed to the lower accuracies of estimated stock compositions in the simulated mixtures. Estimated regional stock compositions of simulated samples comprising fish from several regions were within 1–3% of actual values provided that no contributions from the three under-represented regions were included in the simulated samples. Microsatellite and MHC variation has the potential to provide accurate estimates of regional stock composition for chum salmon fisheries in the Bering Sea and northern Gulf of Alaska.

[*]Corresponding author: Terry.Beacham@dfo-mpo.gc.ca

Introduction

Determination of the origin of salmon in mixed-stock fisheries is key for effective management of the fishery. For chum salmon *Oncorhynchus keta*, scale variation initially provided a technique for determination of origin of individuals to large geographic areas (Tanaka et al. 1969; Ishida et al. 1989), and in some cases reportedly to a specific river drainage (Nikolayeva and Semenets 1983). Variation in trace elements in otoliths have also been reported to be effective in stock identification for Korean populations (Sohn et al. 2005). Annual stability of the characters used to discriminate among stocks is a key requirement of any technique used in stock identification, particularly if the baseline populations cover a wide geographic area. Techniques that rely on environmental variation for stock identification, such as scale pattern analysis or more recently elemental analysis coupled with laser ablation, are prone to annual variation in distinguishing characters such that annual sampling of contributing baseline populations is required. In contrast, genetic characters show a pronounced, well defined stability of allele frequencies relative to population differentiation (Beacham and Wood 1999; Tessier and Bernatchez 1999; Miller et al. 2001). Owing to the relative stability of genetic characters, baseline samples collected in one year can be used to estimate stock compositions of samples collected in following years, or in years previous to collection of the baseline samples. Stock identification applications in chum salmon based upon environmentally-induced variation have generally been replaced by applications based upon genetic variation, owing to the stability of genetic characters used in applications.

Surveys of genetic variation have been demonstrated to be effective in determining salmonid population structure, as well as determining origins of salmon in mixed-stock fisheries (Winther and Beacham 2009, this volume). Initial surveys of population structure of western Alaska and Yukon River chum salmon that incorporated allozyme variation were described by Wilmot et al. (1994). Yukon River fall-run populations were generally distinct from summer-run populations in the same drainage. Northern Alaska Peninsula populations were generally distinct from those in Bristol Bay and more northern areas in Alaska, but some similiarity occurred between Peninsula populations and those in Russia. In a more extensive study of allozyme variation in western Alaska chum salmon, Seeb and Crane (1999a) surveyed a number of populations including some from Kotzebue Sound, Norton Sound, summer-run Yukon River, Kuskokwim River, Kanektok River, Goodnews River, and the Alaska Peninsula. They found that populations from Norton Sound, lower Yukon River summer-run populations, the Kuskokwim River, and Bistol Bay formed a homogenous group with little evidence of geographic differentiation. Populations from Kotzebue Sound populations were reported to display some level of differentiation from those in other areas, but they were still part of a larger cluster of western Alaska populations. In stock identification applications, summer-run populations from Kotzebue Sound, Norton Sound, the Yukon River, the Kuskokwim River, the Kanektok River, and Bristol Bay were all grouped into a single unit, with little ability to provide more refined estimates of stock composition for these groups of populations (Seeb and Crane 1999b). Surveys of direct DNA variation through examination of amplified fragment length polymorphisms have also been conducted for Yukon River chum salmon with respect to population structure and potential stock identification applications (Flannery et al. 2007a). Improvement to existing capability for stock identification of Yukon River chum salmon was limited for this application.

Surveys of microsatellite variation have been effective in determining salmonid population structure in local areas (Small et al. 1998; Banks et al. 2000; Beacham et al. 2004; Utter et al. 2009, this volume), as well as broad-scale differences across the Pacific Rim (Beacham et al. 2005, 2006). Microsatellites have also been of considerable value in estimating stock composition in mixed-stock salmon fisheries, on both a population-specific (Beacham et al. 2003) and regional basis (Beacham et al. 2006). For chum salmon, microsatellite variation provides the potential to examine fine-scale population structure (Chen et al. 2005), as well as fine-scale estimation of stock composition in mixed-stock fisheries (Flannery et al. 2007b). In addition to the microsatellite loci, variation at major histocompatibility complex (MHC) loci has been demonstrated to be very effective in salmonid population differentiation (Miller and Withler 1997; Miller et al. 2001; Beacham et al. 2001). Analysis of variation at microsatellite and MHC loci may provide greater resolution among western Alaska chum salmon populations than had previously been observed with allozymes.

The objectives of the present study were to analyze the variation at 14 microsatellite loci and three major histocompatibility complex (MHC) allele lineages to evaluate population structure of western Alaska chum salmon populations from Kotzebue Sound to the Alaska Peninsula, and then evaluate the utility of the loci surveyed to the practical issue of providing accurate and precise estimates of stock composition in mixed-stock fishery samples. Stock composition analysis was accomplished by the analysis of simulated mixtures, and by estimation of stock composition from known-origin samples.

Methods

Tissue samples were collected from mature chum salmon at a number of rivers in western Alaska during previous analyses of genetic variation (Seeb and Crane 1999a), from other studies in the region, from fall-run Yukon River populations in the Canadian portion of the Yukon River drainage, and from two populations in British Columbia. A total of 59 populations from western Alaska and adjacent regions were surveyed in the study (Table 1; Figure 1). DNA was extracted from the tissue samples using a variety of methods, including a chelex resin protocol outlined by Small et al. (1998), a Qiagen 96-well Dneasy procedure, or a Promega Wizard SV96 Genomic DNA Purification system. Once genomic DNA was available, surveys of variation at 14 microsatellite loci were conducted: *Ots3* (Banks et al. 1999), *Oke3* (Buchholz et al. 2001), *Oki2* (Smith et al. 1998), *Oki100* (primer sequence 5' to 3' F: GGTGTTT-TAATGTTGTTTCCT, R: GTTTCCAGAG-TAGTCATCTCTG), *Ots103* (Nelson and Beacham 1999), *Omm1070* (Rexroad et al. 2001), *Omy 1011* (Spies et al. 2005), *One101*, *One102*, *One104*, *One111*, and *One114* (Olsen et al. 2000), *Ssa419* (Cairney et al. 2000), and *OtsG68* (Williamson et al. 2002).

In general, PCR DNA amplifications for microsatellites were conducted using DNA Engine Cycler Tetrad2 (BioRad, Hercules, CA) using the thermal cycling profile for each locus outlined in Table 2. PCR fragments were initially size fractionated in denaturing polyacrylamide gels using an ABI 377 automated DNA sequencer, and genotypes were scored by Genotyper 2.5 software (Applied Biosystems (ABI), Foster City, CA) using an internal lane sizing standard (GeneScan 500 ROX from ABI). Later in the study, microsatellites were size fractionated in an ABI 3730 capillary DNA sequencer, and genotypes were scored by GeneMapper software 3.0 (Applied Biosystems, Foster City, CA) using an internal lane sizing standard (GeneScan 500 LIZ from ABI).

The MHC locus surveyed was described by Miller et al. (2006) as Exon 3. The three

TABLE 1. Stock identification regional groupings, sampling location, sample collection years, and average number of fish successfully genotyped at each locus (N) for chum salmon surveyed from 59 sites. Allele frequencies for all location samples surveyed in this study are available at http://www-sci.pac. dfo-mpo.gc.ca/mgl/default_e.htm.

Population	Years	N
Kotzebue Sound		
1) Kelly Lake	1991	92
2) Noatak River	1991	45
3) Inmachuk River	2005	194
4) Kobuk River	1991, 2000	374
5) Agiapuk River	2005	180
6) Koyuk River	2005	44
Norton Sound		
7) Niukluk River	2004, 2005	223
8) Pilgrim River	1994, 2004, 2005	474
9) Kwiniuk River	2004, 2005	262
10) Snake River	2004, 2005	394
11) Nome River	2004, 2005	204
12) Eldorado River	2004, 2005	390
13) Unalakleet River	2005	191
14) Shaktoolik River	2005	196
15) Ungalik River	2005	50
Lower Yukon River summer run		
16) Pikmiktalik River	2004, 2005	388
17) Andreafsky River	1987, 1993, 2004	313
18) Anvik River	1988, 1993	182
19) Nulato River	1988, 2003	123
20) Gisasa River	1988, 2003	279
21) Jim River	2002	147
22) Henshaw Creek	2003	193
23) Tozitna River	2002, 2003	347
24) Melozitna River	2003, 2004	161
Tanana River fall run		
25) Toklat River	1990, 1994	241
Upper Alaska fall run		
26) Sheenjek River	1987, 1988, 1989	229
27) Chandalar River	1989, 2001	185
Porcupine River		
28) Fishing Branch	1987, 1989, 1992, 1994, 1997	395
White River		
29) Kluane River	1987, 1992, 2001	453
Mainstem Yukon River		
30) Big Creek	1992, 1995	175
31) Minto Landing	1989, 2002	145

TABLE 1. Continued.

Population	Years	N
Kuskokwim River/Bay		
32) George River	1996	82
33) Kasigluk River	1990	68
34) Kwethluk River	1989	76
35) Nunsatuk River	1994	83
36) Aniak River	1992	86
37) Kanektok River	1989, 1994	171
Nushagak River		
38) Stuyahok River	1992, 1993	74
39) Mulchatna River	1994	82
North/Central Bristol Bay		
40) Goodnews River	1991	92
41) Togiak River	1993	75
42) Alagnak River	1992	77
43) Naknek River	1993	64
South Bristol Bay		
44) Egegik River	1993	86
45) Meshik River	1989	57
46) Gertrude Creek	1987	97
47) Pumice Creek		92
North Peninsula/Aleutians		
48 Moller Bay Creek	1998	93
49) Frosty Creek	1992, 2000	179
50) Joshua Green River	1994	95
Southwest Peninsula		
51) Coleman Creek	1996	70
52) Volcano Bay Creek	1992	104
53) Delta Creek	1996	78
54) Westward Creek	1993	79
Southeast Peninsula		
55) Stepovak Bay	1993	94
56) Big River	1993	87
57) Alogoshak River	1993	91
BC Central Coast		
58) Salmon Bay Creek	2004, 2005	147
Fraser River		
59) Chilliwack River	1992, 2004	177

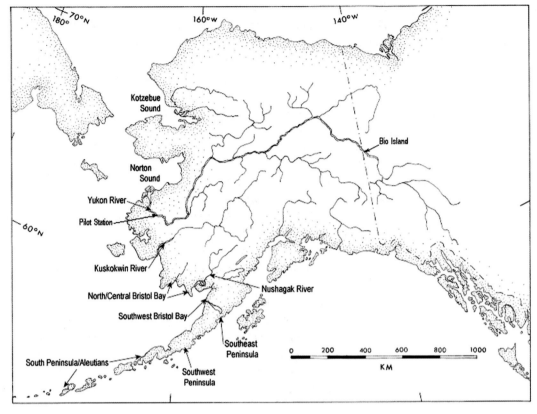

FIGURE 1. Locations of regions defined in the study, as well as the test fishery locations at Pilot Station and Bio Island.

TABLE 2. Microsatellite loci and their associated annealing and extension temperatures and times as well as the number of cycles used in PCR amplifications.

Locus	Annealing	Extension	Cycles
Oke3	48°C/45s	72°C/45s	35
Oki100	50°C/60s	72°C/60s	33
Oki2	47°C/60s	72°C/60s	33
Omm1070	65°C/60s	72°C/60s	40
Omy1011	50°C/30s	72°C/30s	35
One101	52°C/60s	68°C/60s	30
One102	52°C/60s	72°C/60s	35
One104	52°C/30s	70°C/30s	40
One111	52°C/30s	68°C/60s	30
One114	47°C/30s	68°C/60s	30
Ots103	49°C/60s	72°C/60s	30
Ots3	48°C/60s	72°C/60s	40
OtsG68	50°C/60s	72°C/60s	37
Ssa419	57°C/30s	68°C/60s	35

lineages of alleles observed at the locus were the A (L-I of Miller et al. (2006)), UA (L-II), and B (L-III). The A lineage of alleles was amplified with a FAM-labeled sense primer 5'   AAGGGTATGATGGAGAGGATTTC and an antisense primer 5' GATACTTCT-TAAGCCAATCAATGCA. The B lineage of alleles was amplified with a sense primer NED-labeled 5' TCCTAAACAGCAAGCT-GAGA and an antisense primer 5' GATACT-TCTTTAGCCACTCAACGCA. The UA lineage of alleles was amplified with a VIC-labeled sense primer 5' ACTTTCAGTATG-GTTATGATGGAG and an antisense primer 5' CTTCTTTAGCCACTCAACGC. PCRs were conducted in 6μ total volumes, with the UA and B lineage PCRs multiplexed. The thermal cycling profile for the UA/B multi-plex and A lineages involved one cycle of 15 min at 95°C, followed by 33–35 cycles of 60 s at 95°C, 60 s at 50–52°C and 60 s at 72°C , and final maintenance at 4°C . The ampli-fied products were then analyzed with the ABI 3730 sequencer, with the lineage scored as either present or absent in individual fish. With three possible lineages, six genotypes were possible (A/A, A/UA, A/B, UA/B, UA/UA, and B/B), which would be equivalent to a locus with three observed alleles.

Conversion of allele sizes between gel-based and capillary sequencers

Changing automated sequencers dur-ing the course of the study required the ca-pability to convert alleles sizes estimated on the gel-based sequencer (ABI 377) to those estimated on the capillary-based sequencer (ABI 3730). In order to convert allele sizes between the two techniques, we analyzed approximately the same 600 fish using both techniques and determined the distributions of allele frequencies. By inspection of the allele frequencies, we were able to match specific allele sizes obtained from the gel-based sequencer to specific allele sizes from

the capillary sequencer, and then convert the sizing in the gel-based data set to match that obtained from the capillary-based set. Esti-mated allele sizes from both systems were very highly correlated, with over 99.5% con-currence in allele identification for all loci.

Data Analysis

All annual samples available for a loca-tion were combined to estimate population allele frequencies, as was recommended by Waples (1990). F_{ST} estimates for each lo-cus were calculated with FSTAT (Goudet 1995). Each population at each locus was tested for departure from Hardy-Weinberg equilibrium (HWE) using GDA (Lewis and Zaykin 2001). Critical significance levels for simultaneous tests (59 populations, Table 1) were evaluated using sequential Bonferroni adjustment (0.05/59 = 0.0008) (Rice 1989). Cavalli-Sforza and Edwards' (CSE) (1967) chord distance was used to estimate distances among populations. An unrooted neighbor-joining tree based upon CSE was generated using NJPLOT (Perriere and Gouy 1996). Bootstrap support for the major nodes in the tree was evaluated with the CONSENSE pro-gram from PHYLIP based upon 1000 repli-cate trees (Felsenstein 1993). Computation of the number of alleles observed per locus was carried out with GDA (Lewis and Zaykin 2001). Allele frequencies for all location samples surveyed in this study are available at   http://www-sci.pac.dfo-mpo.gc.ca/mgl/Default_e.htm.

Estimation of stock composition

Allele frequencies were determined for each locus in each population and the Statisti-cal Package for the Analysis of Mixtures soft-ware program (SPAM version 3.7) (Debevec et al. 2000) was used to estimate stock compo-sition of simulated mixtures. The Rannala and

Mountain (1997) correction to baseline allele frequencies was used in the analysis in order to avoid the occurrence of fish in the mixed sample from a specific population having an allele not observed in the baseline samples from that population. All microsatellite loci were considered to be in Hardy-Weinberg equilibrium, and expected genotypic frequencies were determined from the observed allele frequencies. Observed genotypic frequencies for the MHC alpha2 locus in each population were used in estimation of stock compositions. Reported stock compositions for simulated fishery samples are the bootstrap mean estimate of each mixture of 150 fish analyzed, with mean and variance estimates derived from 100 bootstrap simulations. Each baseline population and simulated single-population sample was sampled with replacement in order to simulate random variation involved in the collection of the baseline and fishery samples. Analysis of simulated mixtures can be regarded as the initial step in evaluating the power of a set of loci for stock composition estimation. Analysis of single-region mixtures provided some initial evaluation of the capability of the set of genetic markers employed to provide accurate and precise estimates of stock composition, with a target of at least 90% accuracy anticipated for accurate estimation of stock composition for the region. Multi-region mixtures were also simulated, including those regions well estimated in the single region analyses to those inadequately estimated.

Analysis of known-origin samples

A known-origin mixture of 200 fish was constructed by removing five populations from the baseline and randomly selecting 50 fish from the Egegik River population, 40 fish from Frosty Creek, 50 fish from Kelly Lake, 30 fish from Nome River, and 30 fish from Henshaw Creek. The baseline was thus reduced to 54 populations for the analysis. A Bayesian procedure (BAYES) as outlined

by Pella and Masuda (2001) formed the basis of the estimation of stock composition of the known-origin samples. A modified version of the program was developed by the Molecular Genetics Laboratory as a C-based program (cBAYES), which is available from Molecular Genetics Laboratory laboratory website (http://www-sci.pac.dfo-mpo.gc.ca/ mgl/data_e.htm). In the analysis, ten 20,000-iteration Monte Carlo Markov chains of estimated stock compositions were produced, with initial starting values for each chain set at 0.90 for a particular population, which was different for each chain. Estimated stock compositions were considered to have converged when the shrink factor was <1.2 for the ten chains (Pella and Masuda 2001). The last 1,000 iterations from each of the ten chains were then combined, and the mean and standard deviations of estimated stock compositions determined. As only the last 1,000 iterations of each chain were used, and each chain converged to an equivalent answer, the initial starting values for each chain were irrelevant.

Additional samples were obtained from test fisheries at Pilot Station in the lower Yukon River drainage and Bio Island in the upper drainage in the Yukon Territory adjacent to the border between Alaska and the Yukon Territory (Figure 1). Fish sampled in these test fisheries were assumed to be of Yukon River origin. A sample of 498 fish collected between 19 July to 11 August 2004 at Pilot Station was surveyed at 12 microsatellite loci only (*Ots103*, *Omm1070*, MHC not surveyed). A sample of 268 fish collected between 9 August to 4 October 2004 at Bio Island was surveyed for 12 microsatellite loci only, and a sample of 494 fish collected between 30 July to 8 October, 2005 was surveyed for 14 microsatellite loci (no MHC locus). Stock compositions of these samples were estimated with cBAYES incorporating the 59-population baseline.

Results

Loci surveyed

The number of alleles observed at the 14 microsatellite loci surveyed ranged from 20 to 136 (Table 3). F_{st} values for individual loci ranged from 0.01 to 0.06, with larger values typically associated with loci with fewer alleles. The genotypic frequencies observed at the 14 loci generally conformed to those expected under Hardy-Weinberg equilibrium (HWE), with the possible exception of *Oke3*. For this locus, observed heterozygosity was an average of 4% less than that expected (Table 3).

Population structure

Cluster analysis of variation at gene loci generally grouped populations based upon geography (Figure 2). For example, regional structure was observed for populations from the Yukon River, South Bristol Bay and the Alaska Peninsula. Yukon River populations were differentiated from those further south (Kuskokwim River, northern Bristol Bay), and those further north (Norton Sound, Kotzebue Sound). The Pikmiktalik River population was similar to lower Yukon River populations (Figure 2), and was considered to be part of the lower Yukon River complex for stock identification applications. Similarly the Agiapuk River and Koyuk River populations were clustered with other populations from Kotzebue Sound and were considered to be part of the Kotzebue Sound complex of populations (Table 1). The Kanektok River population was considered to be part of the Kuskokwim River complex of populations. The results from the chum salmon populations surveyed to date suggest that unsampled populations contributing to mixed-fishery samples will probably be allocated to sampled populations in the same region.

In pairwise comparisons of over 59 populations, the two populations from British Columbia were the most distinctive group of populations in the survey, with a mean F_{st} value usually >0.03 in regional comparisons (Table 4). Significant genetic differentiation was also observed between Alaska Peninsula populations and those from western Alaska (Table 4). Higher within-region pairwise F_{st} values were observed in some regional groups defined (Yukon River fall run, Alaska Peninsula, British Columbia) as a result of inclusion of genetically distinct groups of populations within each of these three regional groups. Higher observed variation within Kotzebue Sound was due to comparisons including the distinctive Imnachuk River population. The overall level of genetic differentiation among regional groups was indicative of only modest differentiation among groups.

Analysis of simulated single-region mixtures

For Kotzebue Sound, analysis of simulated single-region mixtures (Agiapuk River, Imnachuk River, Kobuk River, and Kelly Lake in equal proportions in the mixtures) indicated that accurate estimates (90% accuracy) of stock composition for this region should be possible (Figure 3). Norton Sound simulated mixtures (Eldorado River, Niukluk River, Nome River, Pilgrim River, Snake River, Unalakleet River in equal proportions) were also estimated with acceptable levels of accuracy. The lower Yukon River summer-run component (Andreafsky River, Anvik River, Gisasa River, Henshaw Creek, Jim River, Tozitna River) was identifiable as a distinct component (Figure 3). The Tanana River fall component (Toklat River) was estimated with an accuracy approaching 95%, as was the Porcupine River component (Fishing Branch).

Simulated samples incorporating only Kuskokwim River populations (Aniak Riv-

TABLE 3. Number of alleles per locus, genetic differentiation index (F_{st}), expected heterozygosity (He), observed heterozygosity (Ho), and number of significant Hardy-Weinberg equilibrium genotypic frequency tests (HWE) for 59 populations listed in Table 1. Standard deviation of F_{st} is in parenthesis.

Locus	Number of alleles	F_{st}	He	Ho	HWE
Oke3	20	0.058 (0.012)	0.69	0.65	5
Ots3	27	0.046 (0.008)	0.75	0.75	3
Oki2	28	0.049 (0.011)	0.86	0.86	2
Ssa419	28	0.016 (0.003)	0.84	0.83	1
Oki100	30	0.023 (0.006)	0.88	0.88	1
One104	34	0.014 (0.003)	0.93	0.93	1
Omy1011	35	0.020 (0.004)	0.92	0.91	0
Omm1070	46	0.007 (0.001)	0.96	0.95	1
Ots103	46	0.015 (0.003)	0.94	0.94	0
One101	47	0.035 (0.006)	0.87	0.86	1
One102	48	0.009 (0.002)	0.91	0.89	1
OtsG68	53	0.013 (0.003)	0.94	0.93	0
One114	54	0.012 (0.003)	0.92	0.91	0
One111	136	0.026 (0.004)	0.93	0.92	1
Average		0.023 (0.004)			

er, Kasigluk River, Kwethluk River, and Nunsatuk River) were poorly resolved, with only about 60% of a sample identifiable as originating from Kuskokwim River drainage populations (Kanektok River included in the Kuskokwim River region) (Figure 3). Similarly, Nushagak River populations of the Bristol Bay region (Stuyahok River, Mulchnata River) were also poorly resolved, with average accuracy of estimated stock compositions for this region being <65%. The North/Central Bristol Bay region (Goodnews River included in the region) was also poorly resolved, with an average accuracy of about 75% for simulated mixtures (Goodnews River, Togiak River) (Figure 3).

Higher accuracies of estimated stock composition for simulated single-region mixtures were observed for Southwest Bristol Bay (Egegik River, Gertrude Creek, Meshik Creek, Pumice Creek,), North Peninsula/Aleutians (Frosty Creek, Joshua Green River, Moller Bay Creek), southwest Alaska Peninsula (Volcano Bay, Delta Creek, Coleman Creek, Westward Creek) and southeast Alaska Peninsula (Alagoshak River, Stepovak Bay, Big River) (Figure 3). Analysis of all simulated mixtures indicated that the genetic markers surveyed provided reliable estimates of stock composition for Kotebue Sound, Norton Sound, the Yukon River, poor resolution of regions from the Kuskokwim River south to central Bristol Bay, and reliable estimation of stock composition from south Bristol Bay to the Alaska Peninsula. These results indicated a mixed success in the completion of the initial step of the evaluation of the microsatellites and MHC loci for stock identification applications. However, if high accuracy of estimated stock compositions of simulated single-region mixtures are obtained, then accurate estimates of stock composition should be possible when multi-region simulated mixtures are evaluated.

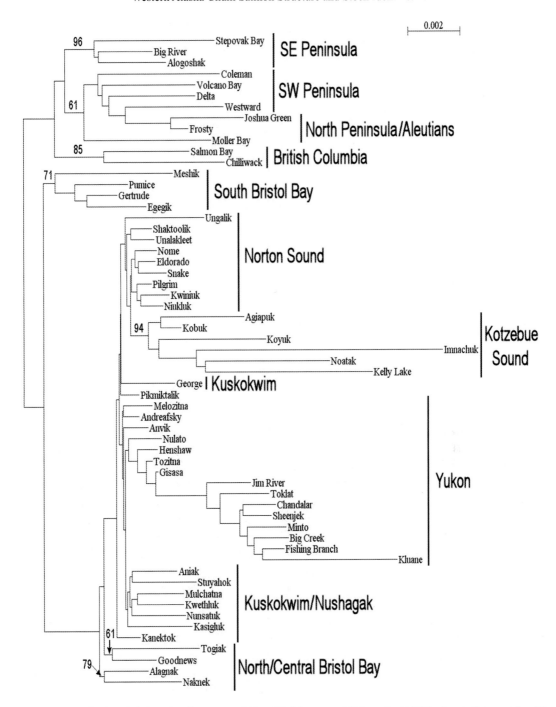

FIGURE 2. Neighbor-joining dendrogram of Cavalli-Sforza and Edwards (1967) chord distance for 59 populations of chum salmon surveyed at 14 microsatellite loci and one MHC locus. Bootstrap values at major tree nodes indicate the percentage of 1,000 trees where populations beyond the node clustered together, and only values > 50% are listed.

TABLE 4. Mean pairwise population F_{st} values observed over 14 microsatellite loci for 59 chum salmon populations from nine regions. Regions were: 1) Kotzebue Sound 2) Norton Sound, 3) Yukon River summer run, 4) Yukon River fall run, 5) Kuskokwim River, 6) Bristol Bay, 7) Nushagak River, 8) Alaska Peninsula, and 9) British Columbia. The Tanana River, Upper Alaska, Porcupine River, White River, and mainstem Yukon River regions were combined into a single Yukon River fall run region. Similarly, the northern/central and southern Bristol Bay regions were combined into a single Bristol Bay region, the North Peninsula, Southwest Peninsula, and Southeast Peninsula regions were combined into a single Alaska Peninsula region, and the British Columbia central coast and Fraser River regions were combined into a single British Columbia region. Boldface font indicates significant difference ($P < 0.05$).

	1	2	3	4	5	6	7	8	9
1	0.029	0.019	0.023	**0.047**	0.021	0.027	0.022	**0.047**	**0.045**
2		0.001	0.004	**0.026**	0.002	0.010	**0.003**	**0.034**	**0.035**
3			0.003	**0.019**	0.003	0.014	0.004	**0.039**	**0.040**
4				0.011	**0.025**	**0.042**	**0.028**	**0.066**	**0.070**
5					0.000	0.009	0.000	**0.035**	**0.036**
6						0.007	0.008	**0.029**	**0.029**
7							0.002	**0.035**	**0.036**
8								**0.015**	**0.029**
9									0.020

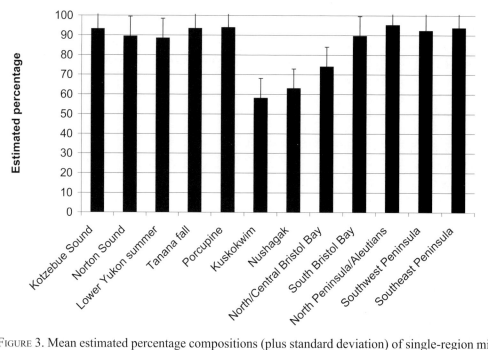

FIGURE 3. Mean estimated percentage compositions (plus standard deviation) of single-region mixtures of chum salmon (correct = 100%). The region designation includes the sum of percentage allocations to all populations in the region. Simulations were conducted with a 59-population baseline, 150 fish in the mixture sample, and 100 resamplings in the mixture sample and baseline samples.

Analysis of simulated multi-region mixtures

Simulated mixtures containing six regional components were evaluated, with the regional contributions of Kotzebue Sound (Agiapuk River 10%, Imnachuk River 10%, Kelly Lake 5% contributions), Norton Sound (Shaktoolik River 10%, Unalakleet River 10%), the Lower Yukon River (Andreafsky River 10%, Anvik River 10%, Tozitna River 10%), Southwest Bristol Bay (Egegik River 10%), North Peninsula/Aleutians (Frosty Creek 10%), and Southwest Alaska Peninsula (Coleman Creek 5%) estimated with a maximum 3% error for a regional contribution (Figure 4a). However, including individuals from a poorly estimated region in the simulated mixtures resulted in higher errors in estimated stock compostions. If the Southwest Bristol Bay, North Peninsula/Aleutians, and Southwest Alaska Peninsula components were replaced with a Kuskokwim River component (Aniak River 10%, Kasigluk River 10%, Kwethluk River 5%), the maximum error for regional estimated stock compositions increased to 9%, with an underestimation of the Kuskokwim River component and overestimation of the Yukon River and Norton Sound components (Figure 4b). Accurate regional estimates of stock composition for multi-region mixtures were dependent upon being able to identify accurately all individual regional components.

Analysis of known-origin samples

Analysis of simulated mixed-stock samples evaluates the effectiveness of the baseline for stock composition analysis under the assumption that the baseline will be representative of all populations contributing to a sample of unknown origin. Mixed-stock samples frequently contain individuals from populations not in the baseline. If regional population structure has been observed, then the contributions of populations in the mixture but not in the baseline should be allocated to other appropriate regional populations in the baseline. This assumption can be directly tested by estimating stock compositions of known-origin samples that are completely independent of the baseline used for analysis, and in which contributing populations have been observed to display a regional structure. Estimated composition of a mixed-stock sample comprising individuals from Kotzebue Sound, Norton Sound, lower Yukon River summer-run, South Bristol Bay, and North Peninsula/Aleutians populations was generally within 3% of the actual regional value (Figure 5a).

Analysis of simulated single-region Yukon River samples suggested that the Yukon River component in mixed-stock samples should be identified with a reasonable degree of accuracy. Analysis of the test fishery samples collected at Pilot Station in the lower river and Bio Island in the Yukon Territory indicated that the samples were estimated to be comprised almost entirely of Yukon River-origin fish as expected (Figure 5b). Summer-run populations were estimated to have comprised only 9.7% of the catch at Pilot Station during a period when fall-run fish were to be expected (19 July–11 August), with fall-run populations estimated at 86.4% of the catch. At Bio Island, 99.5% of the 2004 catch and 99.8% of the 2005 catch were estimated to have been derived from fall-run populations.

Discussion

Reliable, accurate, effective, and practical methods of stock identification are key requirements in the determination of migration pathways for juvenile chum salmon, assessment of the status of juvenile and immature chum salmon in marine feeding areas, and management of fisheries that target chum

A.

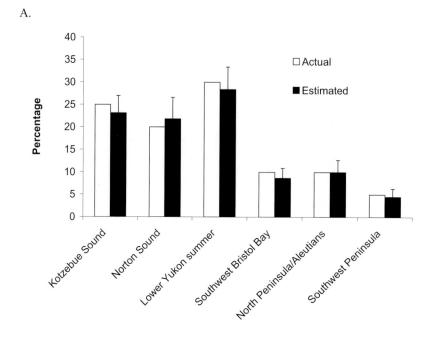

B

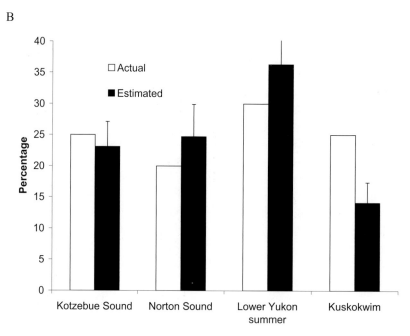

FIGURE 4. (A) Estimated percentage regional stock compositions of simulated mixtures of chum salmon as may be encountered in marine samples. Each mixture of 150 fish was generated 100 times with replacement, and stock compositions of the mixtures were estimated by resampling each of the 59 baseline populations with replacement to obtain a new distribution of allele frequencies. (B) Similar mixtures as in (A) with the 30% Southwest Bristol Bay, North Peninsula/Aleutians, Southwest Alaska Peninsula component replaced with a 30% Kuskokwim River component.

A

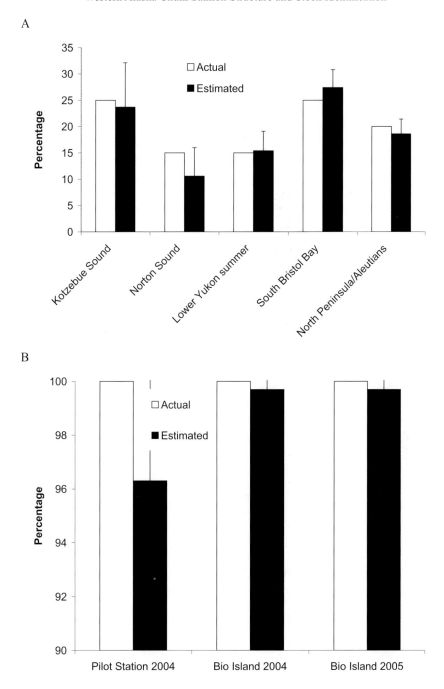

FIGURE 5. (A) Estimated percentage stock composition (plus standard deviation) of a known-origin sample of 200 chum salmon derived from five rivers in western Alaska, Bristol Bay, or the Alaska Peninsula and estimated with a 54-population baseline incorporating variation at 14 microsatellite loci and one MHC locus. Estimated stock composition was derived from cBAYES (see text). (B) Estimated percentage Yukon River origin stock composition of mixed-stock samples taken from test fisheries in the lower river at Pilot Station and in the upper river at Bio Island and estimated with a 59-population baseline incorporating variation at 12–14 microsatellite loci.

salmon during their spawning migration. The most effective stock identification techniques for chum salmon are those that provide reliable discrimination among regional groups of populations. Ideal methods for mixed-stock analysis are those based on biological variation in characters, which differ substantially among populations, show little temporal or annual variation within populations relative to population differences, and can be screened in a rapid, nonlethal, and cost-effective manner for both baseline and mixed-population samples. The survey of microsatellite and MHC loci meet these criteria, and regional population differentiation can be readily used for stock composition analysis.

Regional population structure was generally observed in the chum salmon populations surveyed in this study. A regional population structure is important to the application of genetic variation for stock composition estimation, as a critical assumption in the application is that the portion of the mixed-stock sample derived from unsampled populations is allocated to sampled populations from the same region. This assumption reduces the cost and complexity of developing a baseline for stock composition analysis. However, some grouping of populations outside of traditional designations was required for stock identification applications. For example, the Kotzebue Sound region included two populations outside of Kotzebue Sound proper. The Agiapuk River population, a later-run population (compared with other Norton Sound populations) situated on the southwest coast of the Seward Peninsula northwest of Norton Sound, clustered with Kotzebue Sound populations. Similarly, the Koyuk River population, a later-run population (compared with other Norton Sound populations) in Norton Sound, clustered with Kotzebue Sound populations. Some grouping of populations geographically adjacent to a regional stock was suggested by cluster analysis. For example, chum salmon from the Pikmiktalik River in

Norton Sound, with the Pikmiktalik River being adjacent to the mouth of the Yukon River, were more similar to Yukon River summer-run populations than they were to other populations in Norton Sound. South of the Yukon River, the Kanektok River population was grouped with populations in the adjacent Kuskokwim River drainage, and the Goodnews River population was grouped with the Togiak River population adjacent to Bristol Bay. Although the Goodnews River is not traditionally considered part of the Bristol Bay region, it was included with other Bristol Bay populations in the regional group.

Estimation of stock composition of simulated single-region mixtures provided good levels of accuracy for Kotzebue Sound, Norton Sound, and Yukon River regions: Lower Yukon River summer-run, Tanana River fall-run, and the Porcupine River, which is a fall-run population. Genetic differentiation has been observed previously between summer-run and fall-run populations in the Yukon River based upon variation at allozyme loci (Seeb and Crane 1999a), so accurate discrimination between the two run-time groups is expected. Poor accuracy of estimated stock compositions were observed for the Kuskokwim River, Nushagak River, and North/Central Bristol Bay regions. Although little differentiation among populations in these three regions was observed previously in a survey of allozyme variation (Seeb and Crane 1999a), the population structure observed in the current study suggested that the North Bristol Bay region should be identifiable in mixed-stock analysis.

Accurate estimation of stock composition in mixed-stock samples is dependent upon both the use of genetic markers that display adequate genetic differentiation among regions to be discriminated, as well as sufficient sampling within regions to enable genetic variation present in populations in the region to be characterized adequately. Average population sample size used in regions with accurate estimated stock compositions (Figure 3) from Kotzebue Sound to the North Alaska Peninsula were: Kotzebue Sound 155 fish (5 populations), Norton Sound 265 fish (9 populations), Lower Yukon River summer-run 237 fish (9 populations), Tanana River fall run 241 fish (1 population), South Bristol Bay 83 fish (4 populations), and North Alaska Peninsula 122 fish (3 populations). Regions with lower accuracy in estimated stock compositions were generally characterized by fewer fish surveyed for genetic variation: Kuskokwim River 94 fish (5 populations, Nushagak River 78 fish (2 populations), North/Central Bristol Bay 78 fish (4 populations). Increasing the number of fish surveyed, as well as increasing the number of populations included in the region, would likely increase the accuracy of estimated stock compositions of the North/Central region, perhaps allowing the splitting of the region into a northern component and a central component as suggested by the dendrogram analysis (Figure 3). While an increase in the number of fish surveyed in the Kuskokwim River and Nushagak River regions is necessary to enable genetic variation to be characterized adequately, an increase in sample size alone will likely not be sufficient to enable accurate estimates of stock composition to be obtained for these two regions using the 15 loci surveyed in this study. The addition of markers specifically designed to separate these two regions both from each other and from other regions in western Alaska will be required. These markers could either be additional microsatellites, or perhaps single nucleotide polymorphisms (SNPs) (Smith et al. 2005). It is likely that a combination of microsatellites and SNPs can be employed to provide accurate regional estimates of stock composition of mixed-stock samples.

Evaluating accuracy of stock composition estimates typically initially involves analysis of simulated mixtures to evaluate the accuracy of estimated stock compositions. Should results appear promising, analysis of known-origin samples, independent of the baseline used for estimation of stock compositions is usually conducted. In our study, analysis of simulated mixed-stock fishery samples, as well as analysis of samples of known origin, indicated that reliable estimates of stock composition were obtained. For example, analysis of the 2004 Pilot Station samples was also conducted with a different set of microsatellites by Flannery et al. (2007b). Summer-run populations in that study were estimated at 13% of the seasonal sample, similar to the 10% value estimated in the current study. However, accurate results were only achieved in larger-scale potential applications with no contribution of Kuskokwim River, Nushagak River, or North/Central Bristol Bay populations to the mixed-stock samples. Even if reliable estimates of stock composition have been obtained from both simulated and known-origin samples, a potential still exists for inaccurate estimates of stock composition in real fisheries applications if a significant portion of the mixed-stock sample has been derived from populations or regions inadequately represented in the baseline.

Genetic variation based upon allozymes has been used to estimate stock composition of mixed-stock chum salmon samples obtained from fisheries in the northern Gulf of Alaska (Seeb and Crane 199b) and in the eastern Bering Sea (Wilmot et al. 1998). In these studies, it was not possible to determine fine-scale regional contributions of summer-run chum salmon in western Alaska. The application of DNA-level markers such as microsatellites has substantially improved the resolution that is possible for identifying summer-run chum salmon in western Alaska in mixed-stock fishery samples, such that regional contributions from Kotzebue Sound, Norton Sound, and lower Yukon River populations may be estimated. The increased resolution observed in microsatellite-derived stock composition estimates in chum salmon in the current study has also been observed in sockeye *Oncorhynchus nerka* (Beacham et al. 2005) and Chinook salmon *O. tshawytscha* (Beacham et al. 2006) on a Pacific Rim wide basis. We expect that similar results will also be observed for chum salmon on a Pacific Rim basis, with microsatellite variation perhaps augmented with MHC or other DNA-based variation such as SNPs providing resolution in stock composition estimates not observed previously with other techniques.

Acknowledgments

A very substantial effort was undertaken to obtain samples from chum salmon sampled in this study. S. Johnston and P. Milligan of the DFO Whitehorse office supervised collections of the Canadian portion of the Yukon River drainage. J. Wenburg of the U.S. Fish and Wildlife Service Conservation Genetics Laboratory in Anchorage provided samples from the Alaskan portion of the Yukon River drainage, as well as from many Norton Sound and Kotzebue Sound populations. L. Seeb of the Alaska Department of Fish and Game Gene Conservation Laboratory in Anchorage provided samples from the Kuskokwim River, Bristol Bay, and Alaska Peninsula, as well as other locations. A. J. Gharrett of the University of Alaska Fairbanks provided some additional regional samples. Colin Wallace and John Candy aided in the analysis. Funding for the study was provided by Fisheries and Oceans, Canada.

References

Banks, M. A., M. S. Blouin, B. A. Baldwin, V. K. Rashbrook, H. A. Fitzgerald, S. M. Blankenship, and D. Hedgecock. 1999. Isolation and inheritance of novel microsatellites in chinook salmon (*Oncorhynchus tshawytscha*). Journal of Heredity 90:281–288.

Banks, M. A., V. K. Rashbrook, M. J. Calavetta, C. A. Dean, and D. Hedgecock. 2000. Analysis of microsatellite DNA resolves genetic structure and diversity of chinook salmon (*Oncorhynchus tshawytscha*) in California's Central Valley. Canadian Journal of Fisheries and Aquatic Sciences 57:915–927.

Beacham, T. D., J. R. Candy, K. J. Supernault, T. Ming, B. Deagle, A. Schultz, D. Tuck, K. Kaukinen, J. R. Irvine, K. M. Miller, and R. E. Withler, R. E. 2001. Evaluation and application of microsatellite and major histocompatibility complex variation for stock identification of coho salmon in British Columbia. Transactions of the American Fisheries Society 130:1116–1155.

Beacham, T. D., J. R. Candy, K. J. Supernault, M. Wetklo, B. Deagle, K. Labaree, J. R. Irvine, K. M. Miller, R. J. Nelson, and R. E. Withler. 2003. Evaluation and application of microsatellites for population identification of Fraser River chinook salmon (*Oncorhynchus tshawytscha*). Fishery Bulletin 101:243–259.

Beacham, T. D., J. R. Candy, B. McIntosh, C. MacConnachie, A. Tabata, K. Kaukinen, L. Deng, K. M. Miller, R. E. Withler, and N. V. Varnavskaya. 2005. Estimation of stock composition and individual identification of sockeye salmon on a Pacific Rim basis using microsatellite and major histocompatibility complex variation. Transactions of the American Fisheries Society 134:1124–1146.

Beacham, T. D., J. R. Candy, K. L. Jonsen, J. Supernault, M. Wetklo, L. Deng, K. M. Miller, R. E. Withler, and N. Varnavskaya. 2006. Estimation of stock composition and individual identification of Chinook salmon across the Pacific Rim using microsatellite variation. Transactions of the American Fisheries Society 135:861–888.

Beacham, T. D., M. Lapointe, J. R. Candy, B. McIntosh, C. MacConnachie, A. Tabata, K. Kaukinen, L. Deng, K. M. Miller, and R. E. Withler. 2004. Stock identification of Fraser River sockeye salmon (*Oncorhynchus nerka*) using microsatellites and major histocompatibility complex variation. Transactions of the American Fisheries Society 133:1106–1126.

Beacham, T. D., and C. C. Wood. 1999. Application of microsatellite DNA variation to estimation of stock composition and escapement of Nass River sockeye salmon (*Oncorhynchus nerka*). Canadian Journal of Fisheries and Aquatic Sciences 56:1–14.

Buchholz, W. G., S. J. Miller, and W. J. Spearman. 2001. Isolation and characterization of chum salmon microsatellite loci and use across species. Animal Genetics 32:160–167.

Cairney, M., J. B. Taggart, and B. Hoyheim. 2000. Characterization of microsatellite and minisatellite loci in Atlantic salmon (*Salmo salar* L.) and cross-species amplification in other salmonids. Molecular Ecology 9:2175–2178.

Cavalli-Sforza, L. L., and A. W. F. Edwards. 1967. Phylogenetic analysis: models and estimation procedures. American Journal of Human Genetics 19:233–257.

Chen, J.-P., D.-J. Sun, C.-Z. Dong, B. Liang, W.-H. Wu and S.-Y. Zhang. 2005. Genetic analysis of four wild chum salmon *Oncorhynchus keta* populations in China based on microsatellite markers. Environmental Biology of Fishes 73:181–188.

Debevec, E. M., R. B. Gates, M. Masuda, J. Pella, J.M. Reynolds, and L. W. Seeb. 2000. SPAM (Version 3.2): Statistics program for analyzing mixtures. Journal of Heredity 91:509–510.

Flannery, B. G., T. D. Beacham, R. R. Holder, Kretschmer, and J. K. Wenburg. 2007b. Stock structure and mixed stock analysis of Yukon River chum salmon. U. S. Fish and Wildlife Service, Alaska Fisheries Technical Report Number 97, Anchorage.

Flannery, B. G., J. K. Wenburg, and A. J. Gharrett. 2007a. Variation of amplified fragment length polymorphisms in Yukon River chum salmon: population structure and applications to mixed-stock analysis. Transactions of the American Fisheries Society 136:911–925.

Felsenstein, J. 1993. PHYLIP: Phylogeny Inference Package. University of Washington, Seattle.

Goudet, J. 1995. FSTAT A program for IBM PC compatibles to calculate Weir and Cockerham's (1984) estimators of F-statistics (version 1.2). Journal of Heredity 86:485–486.

Ishida, Y., S. Ito, and K. Takagi. 1989. Stock identification of chum salmon *Oncorhynchus keta* from their maturity and scale characters. Nippon Suisan Gakkaishi 55:651–656.

Lewis, P. O., and D. Zaykin. 2001. Genetic Data Analysis: Computer program for the analysis of allelic data. Version 1.0 (d16c). Free program distributed by the authors over the internet from http://lewis.eeb.uconn.edu/lewishome/software.html (September 2002).

Miller, K. M., and R. E. Withler. 1997. Mhc diversity in Pacific salmon: population structure and trans-species allelism. Hereditas 127:83–95.

Miller, K. M., K. H. Kaukinen, T. D. Beacham, and R. E. Withler. 2001. Geographic heterogeneity in natural selection of an MHC locus in sockeye salmon. Genetica 111:237–257.

Miller, K. M., S. Li, T. J. Ming, K. H. Kaukinen, and A. D. Schulze. 2006. The salmonid MHC class I: more ancient loci uncovered. Immunogenetics 58:571–589.

Nikolayeva, Ye. T., and N. I. Semenets. 1983. A contribution to stock differentiation of chum salmon, *Oncorhynchus keta* (Salmonidae), by scale structure in the first year of growth. Journal of Ichthology 23:18–28.

Nelson, R. J., and T. D. Beacham. 1999. Isolation and cross species amplification of microsatellite loci useful for study of Pacific salmon. Animal Genetics 30:228–229.

Olsen, J. B., S. L. Wilson, E. J. Kretschmer, K. C. Jones, and J. E. Seeb. 2000. Characterization of 14 tetranucleotide microsatellite loci derived from Atlantic salmon. Molecular Ecology 9:2155–2234.

Pella, J., and M. Masuda. 2001. Bayesian methods for analysis of stock mixtures from genetic characters. Fishery Bulletin 99: 151–167.

Perriere, G., and M. Gouy. 1996. WWW-Query: an on-line retrieval system for biological sequence banks. Biochimie 78:364–369.

Rannala, B., and J. L. Mountain. 1997. Detecting immigration by using multilocus genotypes. Proceedings of the National Academy of Sciences USA 94:9197–9201.

Rexroad, C. E., R. L. Coleman, A. M. Martin, W. K. Hershberger, and J. Killefer. 2001. Thirty-five polymorphic microsatellite markers for rainbow trout (*Oncorhynchus mykiss*). Animal Genetics 32:283–319.

Seeb, L. W., and P. A. Crane. 1999a. High genetic heterogeneity in chum salmon in western Alaska, the contact zone between northern and southern lineages. Transactions of the American Fisheries Society 128:58–87.

Seeb, L. W., and P. A. Crane. 1999b. Allozymes and mitochondrial DNA discriminate Asian and North American populations of chum salmon in mixed-stock fisheries along the south coast of the Alaska Peninsula. Transactions of the American Fisheries Society 128:88–103.

Small, M. P., T. D. Beacham, R. E. Withler, and R. J. Nelson. 1998. Discriminating coho salmon (*Oncorhynchus kisutch*) populations within the Fraser River, British Columbia using microsatellite DNA markers. Molecular Ecology 7:141–155.

Smith, C. T., B. F. Koop, and R. J. Nelson. 1998. Isolation and characterization of coho salmon (*Oncorhynchus kisutch*) microsatellites and their use in other salmonids. Molecular Ecology 7:1613–1621.

Smith, C. T., W. D. Templin, J.E. Seeb, and L. W. Seeb. 2005. Single nucleotide polymorphisms provide rapid and accurate estimates of the proportions of U.S. and Canadian chinook salmon caught in Yukon River fisheries. North American Journal of Fisheries Management 25:944–953.

Sohn, D., S. Kang, and S. Kim. 2005. Stock identification of chum salmon (*Oncorhynchus keta*) using trace elements in otoliths. Journal of Oceanography 61:305–312.

Spies, I. B., D. J. Brasier, P. T. L. O'Reilly, T. R. Seamons, and P. Bentzen. 2005. Development and
characterization of novel tetra-, tri-, and dinucle-
otide microsatellite markers in rainbow trout (*Oncorhynchus mykiss*). Molecular Ecology Notes
5:278–281.

Tanaka, S., M. P. Shepard, and H. T. Bilton. 1969. Origin of chum salmon (*Oncorhynchus keta*) in offshore waters of the North Pacific in 1956–1958
as determined from scale studies. International
North Pacific Fisheries Commission Bulletin
26:57–155.

Tessier, N., and L. Bernatchez. 1999. Stability of
population structure and genetic diversity across
generations assessed by microsatellites among
sympatric populations of landlocked Atlantic
salmon (*Salmo salar* L.). Molecular Ecology
8:169–179.

Utter, F. M., M. V. McPhee, and F. W. Allendorf.
2009. Population genetics and the management
of Arctic-Yukon-Kuskokwim salmon populations. Pages 97–123 *in* C. C. Krueger and C. E.
Zimmerman, editors. Pacific salmon: ecology
and management of western Alaska's populations. American Fisheries Society, Symposium
70, Bethesda, Maryland.

Waples, R. S. 1990. Temporal changes of allele frequency in Pacific salmon populations: implications for
mixed-stock fishery analysis. Canadian Journal of
Fisheries and Aquatic Sciences 47:968–976.

Williamson, K. S., J. F. Cordes, and B. P. May. 2002.
Characterization of microsatellite loci in chinook
salmon (*Oncorhynchus tshawytscha*) and cross-
species amplification in other salmonids. Molecular Ecology Notes 2:17–19.

Wilmot, R. L., R. J. Everett, W. J. Spearman, R. Baccus, N. V. Varnavskaya, and S. V. Putivkin. 1994.
Genetic stock structure of Western Alaska chum
salmon and a comparison with Russian Far East
stocks. Canadian Journal of Fisheries and Aquatic
Sciences 51 (Supplement 1):84–94.

Wilmot, R. L., C. M. Kondzela, C. M. Guthrie, and M.
M. Masuda. 1998. Genetic stock identification of
chum salmon harvested incidentally in the 1994 and
1995 Bering Sea trawl fishery. North Pacific Anadromous Fish Commission Bulletin 1:285–299.

Winther, I., and T. C. Beacham. 2009. Application of
Chinook salmon stock composition data for management of the northern British Columbia troll
fishery, 2006. Pages 977–1004 *in* C. C. Krueger
and C. E. Zimmerman, editors. Pacific salmon:
ecology and management of western Alaska's
populations. American Fisheries Socity, Symposium 70, Bethesda, Maryland.

American Fisheries Society Symposium 70:161–179, 2009

Biological and Genetic Characteristics of Fall and Summer Chum Salmon in the Kuskokwim River, Alaska

SARA E. GILK*, DOUGLAS B. MOLYNEAUX, TOSHIHIDE HAMAZAKI,
AND JASON A. PAWLUK

*Alaska Department of Fish and Game, Divison of Commercial Fisheries
333 Raspberry Road, Anchorage, Alaska 99518, USA*

WILLIAM D. TEMPLIN

*Alaska Department of Fish and Game, Gene Conservation Laboratory
333 Raspberry Road, Anchorage, Alaska 99518, USA*

Abstract.—The existence of both fall and summer chum salmon *Oncorhynchus keta* populations in the Kuskokwim River was not recognized by fishery managers until the mid-1990s. Harvest statistics currently do not distinguish between fall and summer chum salmon, and escapement of fall chum salmon is not monitored. Some of the yet undescribed characteristics of fall chum salmon in 2004 are examined by comparing spawning populations of fall and summer chum salmon sampled from four tributaries of the Kuskokwim River. Fall chum salmon ($n = 336$) and summer chum salmon ($n = 1,964$) were examined for mideye-fork length, maximum dorsal-ventral height, maximum width, age, and sex. Fecundity parameters were measured for 15 to 20 females from each of the four sample groups. A baseline of genetic markers was developed for Kuskokwim River chum salmon populations, and its utility for identifying fall chum salmon was evaluated. Multivariate analysis demonstrated a significant difference in size between fall and summer chum salmon, although the differences were not overt to casual observation. The fall chum salmon population had a greater percentage of age-3 fish, but sex ratios were similar. There was no significant difference in fecundity, but fall chum salmon had significantly smaller mean egg weights than summer chum salmon. Analysis of 31 single nucleotide polymorphisms among nine Kuskokwim River spawning populations demonstrated sufficient genetic differences between fall and summer chum populations to distinguish the two runs in mixed stock analyses with a high degree of accuracy (> 92%). Analysis of mixed stock chum salmon catches from fish wheels operated near Kalskag indicated a low occurrence of fall chum salmon in 2004, but no definitive conclusion could be made about run timing past Kalskag. Although fall chum salmon appear to constitute a small proportion of the overall Kuskokwim River chum salmon run, this unique group is an important component of the overall biodiversity and should be maintained to foster long-term sustainable harvest of salmon against changing environmental conditions. This preliminary description of the biology of Kuskokwim River fall chum salmon is the first step in including these distinct populations in sustainable chum salmon management.

---

*Corresponding author: sara.gilk@alaska.gov

Introduction

Throughout their range, chum salmon *Oncorhynchus keta* can be found in two distinct races based on run timing: the earlier running race is often referred to as summer chum salmon, and the later running race is commonly called fall chum salmon (Salo 1991). Fall chum salmon populations have been reported in Asia (Berg 1934), Russia (Lovetskaya 1948; Grigo 1953; Sano 1966), and North America (Gilbert 1922; Helle 1960, Beacham and Murray 1987). Fall and summer populations may use the same migratory pathways and can be found in the same river basin, but typically they use different spawning streams or reaches (e.g., Gilbert 1922; Sano 1966). Fall and summer populations typically have some distinct differences in morphology, fecundity, age composition, and other phenotypic characteristics (e.g., Berg 1934; Lovetskaya 1948, Helle 1960; Sano 1966, Bakkala 1970; Buklis 1981, Beacham 1984), and distinct genetic markers have been identified that can discriminate between many neighboring fall and summer populations (Seeb and Crane 1999).

Fall chum salmon occur in the Kuskokwim River, but their presence has only been recognized by management agencies since the mid-1990s (Seeb et al. 1997a; Seeb et al. 2004, Linderman and Bergstrom 2009, this volume). However, fall chum salmon have long been recognized by residents who harvest the fish for subsistence use in remote regions of the upper Kuskokwim River (e.g., Stickney 1980; Stokes 1985). These fall fish have largely gone unnoticed by Kuskokwim Area fishery managers in part because their abundance and distribution appear to be limited compared to the more plentiful summer chum salmon, and for the lack of any known morphological features that would help differentiate the two races. Harvest monitoring does not distinguish between fall and summer chum salmon in the Kuskokwim Area, and fall chum salmon are not included in the escapement monitoring program.

Kuskokwim River fall chum salmon spawn in late September and October, compared to area summer chum salmon that typically spawn in July or early August (e.g., Costello et al. 2005; Roettiger et al. 2005, Stewart and Molyneaux 2005). Spawning distribution of fall run fish appears to be limited to larger tributaries in the uppermost portion of the Kuskokwim River basin, where visibility is often occluded by glacier flour (Schwanke et al. 2001; Schwanke and Molyneaux 2002; Figure 1), whereas summer chum salmon have a wider spawning distribution with greatest abundance in clear water tributaries of the lower and middle Kuskokwim River basin (Burkey and Salomone 1999). There are no known locations where fall and summer chum salmon co-occur in tributaries of the Kuskokwim River basin.

Genetic evidence distinguishing fall from summer chum salmon in the Kuskokwim River was first reported by Seeb et al. (1997a, 2004) using allozyme markers. This tool was used to analyze two opportunistic collections of chum salmon tissues taken from catches in the lower Kuskokwim River (ADF&G, Gene Conservation Laboratory, unpublished data). One sample collected from the commercial fishery on 17 July 1996 contained 12% ($\pm 4\%$; $n = 207$) fall chum salmon, while a second sample pooled from test fishery catches from 25 July to 1 August 2003 contained 0% ($\pm 3\%$; $n = 118$) fall chum salmon. With seven years lag between these two single event grab samples, conclusions are not definitive, but they do suggest the run timing of fall fish through the lower Kuskokwim River may be concurrent with summer chum salmon. If true, this would put into question the common opinion that fall chum salmon are the small ocean bright "silver bullet" fish seen late in the run each year. It would also be in contrast to the neighboring Yukon River where fall fish enter from mid-July through early September, compared to summer chum salmon that enter

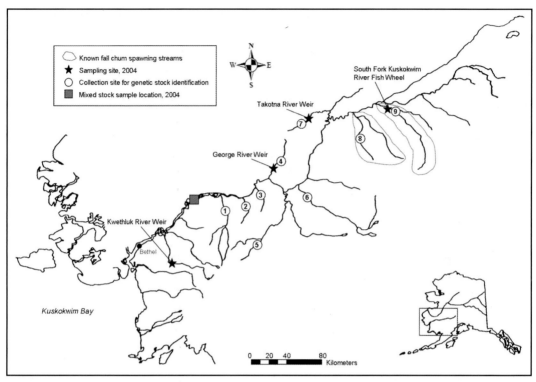

FIGURE 1. The Kuskokwim River drainage, showing known spawning locations of fall chum salmon; sample locations for 2004 age, sex, size, and fecundity studies; sample location for 2004 mixed stock samples; and sample locations of collections analyzed for genetic stock identification of chum salmon using SNP markers: (1) Aniak River, (2) Holokuk River, (3) Oskawalik River, (4) George River, (5) Kogrukluk River, (6) Stony River, (7) Takotna River, (8) Big River, and (9) South Fork Kuskokwim River.

between early June and mid-July (Gilbert 1922; Buklis and Barton 1984; Bue et al. 2009, this volume). The results of the opportunistic collections from the Kuskokwim River raised questions about the migration timing of fall chum salmon, their susceptibility to lower river fisheries, and their contribution to the overall chum salmon run.

Fall chum salmon are generally thought to be a minor component of the annual Kuskokwim River chum salmon run. However, longtime residents assert that fall chum salmon were more abundant in decades past (R. Collins, resident, McGrath, personal communication; N. Mellick, resident, Sleetmute, personal communication). These recollections echo trends reported of sockeye salmon *O. nerka* in Bristol

Bay, where minor producing stocks during one climatic regime had been much more dominant during different climatic regimes (Hilborn et al. 2003). In Bristol Bay, the resilience of sockeye salmon is credited to a sustainable fisheries management plan that emphasizes conservation of the biodiversity within fish stocks (Quinn 2009, this volume). In the Kuskokwim River, fall chum salmon escapement and harvest are not monitored. This lack of recognition of the system's biocomplexity, and of the long-term importance of biodiversity to species resilience and sustainable fisheries management, is a shortfall in the current management program. In contrast, fall chum salmon escapement and harvest are monitored in the neighboring Yukon River (Bue et al. 2009).

This disparity may be addressed in part if there were distinctive characteristics in the morphology, age and sex composition, and run timing to better distinguish between fall and summer chum salmon in the Kuskokwim River, but such features are unknown or undescribed. As a first step in addressing these information gaps, we sought to describe some of the characteristics of Kuskokwim River fall chum salmon in comparison to summer chum salmon. Specific objectives were to: 1) compare biological characteristics of fall and summer chum salmon population in the Kuskokwim River basin, including size, age composition, sex composition, and fecundity; and 2) evaluate the utility of DNA genetic markers to distinguish between summer and fall chum salmon in mixed stocks.

Methods

Study area

The Kuskokwim River is the second largest river in Alaska, draining an area of approximately 130,000 km^2 (Figure 1; Brown 1983). The river arises on the northwestern slope of the Alaska Range, running approximately 1,500 km westward to empty into the Bering Sea in Kuskokwim Bay. Five species of Pacific salmon support subsistence harvests, a fundamental component of local culture, as well as sport and commercial harvests. The subsistence salmon fishery in the Kuskokwim Area is second only to the Yukon River in the annual number of chum salmon harvested; the most recent ten-year average (1995–2004) is 57,981 fish (Coffing 1991, 1997a, 1997b; Coffing et al. 2000; ADF&G 2003; Martz and Dull 2006; Linderman and Bergstrom 2009, this volume).

Age, sex, and size

Fall chum salmon were captured in a live box at a fish wheel located on the South Fork

Kuskokwim River near the village of Nikolai (941 rkm); summer chum salmon were captured with fish traps incorporated into weirs used to monitor escapement on the Kwethluk (190 rkm), George (453 rkm), and Takotna (835 rkm) Rivers (Figure 1; Costello et al. 2005; Roettiger et al. 2005, Stewart and Molyneaux 2005). All locations were proximal to salmon spawning areas. Samples collected at each location consisted of at least three pulses, with each pulse timed to sample a third of the run. The target sample size of each pulse was 170 fish ($\alpha = 0.05$, d = 0.10, $k = 6$; Bromaghin 1993), though this sample size was not always achieved. Sex was recorded for each fish, and three scales were collected for age determination (DuBois and Molyneaux 2001). Using calipers, fish were measured to the nearest millimeter for three morphometric features: 1) maximum width (Katayama 1935), 2) maximum dorsal-ventral height (Finn et al. 1998), and 3) length as mideye to fork-of-tail (DuBois and Molyneaux 2001).

Age, sex, and size compositions of fish from the four sample locations were analyzed to assess differences between fall and summer chum salmon. Sex and age compositions were compared using chi-square tests of independence (Sokal and Rohlf 1995). Variability in size measurements of both males and females over different age groups from summer and fall chum salmon stocks were examined using a multivariate analysis of variance (ANOVA) (MANOVA; Green 1978).

Fecundity

A total of 69 gravid female chum salmon were collected for fecundity measures, with a target of five fish drawn from each pulse sample for a total of 15–20 females for each location. Whole skeins (ovaries) were collected from each fish and individually preserved in labeled vials containing 70% ethyl alcohol until processing. Total number of eggs (absolute fecundity) was estimated for each female by weighing three random subsamples of 100 eggs to the nearest 0.01 g on a digital balance (Mettler Toledo, PG503-S). Fecundity of individual fish was estimated by dividing the total egg skein weight by the subsample weight, then multiplying by the number of eggs in the subsample (100), similar to Nemeth et al. (2003). This was replicated for each subsample, and the number of eggs per female was estimated as the average of the three replicates. Since fecundity is reported to vary with fish length, relative fecundity was also calculated by dividing the fecundity by body length to obtain the number of eggs per cm of body length (Lovetskaya 1948; Nemeth et al. 2003). Hereafter, absolute fecundity refers to the total number of eggs estimated for each fish, and relative fecundity refers to the number of eggs per cm of body length. Mean egg weight was calculated by dividing total skein weight by the absolute fecundity.

Mean and variance in absolute fecundity were reported for both fall and summer salmon populations. These statistics were calculated for both the entire sample and for separate age categories. Females that could not be aged were dropped from further analyses. Fecundity and egg weights of summer and fall chum salmon were compared using ANOVA (Sokal and Rohlf 1995).

Genetic baseline analysis

A single nucleotide polymorphism (SNP) baseline was derived from samples of archived tissues collected as part of previous work involving allozymes (Seeb et al. 1997b). Collections were selected to represent both fall and summer runs of chum salmon from the upper Kuskokwim River drainage, and included Big River (rkm 827) and the South Fork Kuskokwim (rkm 869) for fall chum salmon, and Takotna (rkm 752), Stony (rkm 836), Kogrukluk (rkm 709), George (rkm 446), Oskawalik (rkm 398), Holokuk (rkm 362) and the Aniak

(rkm 307) Rivers for summer chum salmon (Figure 1). Whenever possible, 95 individuals were selected from each population for analysis.

Genomic DNA was extracted and purified using DNAeasy 96 columns (QUIAGEN, Valencia, CA) from individuals from each collection. Thirty-one previously published SNP loci were used in this study (Smith et al. 2005a, 2005b; Elfstrom et al. 2007; Table 1). Loci were genotyped following the methods described in Smith et al. (2005a).

Individual genotypes were recorded for each of the 31 SNP loci. Indeterminate assays (the genotype could not be assigned with certainty) failed polymerase chain reactions, and failed DNA extractions were recorded as failures. Genotype linkage methods (GENEPOP version 3.2, Raymond and Rousset 1995) were used to test for significant association between loci. Four of the SNP loci were located in the mitochondrial DNA, three in the control region (*Oke_CR30, Oke_CR231, and Oke_CR386*) and one in the ND3 region (*Oke_ND3–69*). If genotypes at these loci were not independent of each other (linkage), the locus with the fewest failures was chosen for use in the remaining analyses and the others were excluded. In addition, six of the nuclear SNP loci (three pairs) were located in close proximity: *Oke_GnRH-373/ Oke_GnRH-527, Oke_IL8r-272/Oke_IL8r-406,* and *Oke_GHII-2943/Oke_GHII-3129.* Independence between genotypes at each locus in a pair was investigated by testing for gametic disequilibrium with GENEPOP. Association of genotypes within these pairs of loci was adjusted for in the mixture analysis by combining individual genotypes for both loci in the pair into a composite genotype (incomplete composite genotypes were treated as failures), and the locus pair was treated as a single locus with unique multi-locus genotypes considered as alleles. This treatment assures the independence of loci as required for mixed-stock analysis.

Gilk et al.

TABLE 1. Single nucleotide polymorphisms (SNPs) assayed in Kuskokwim River chum salmon.

Name		DNA Type	Source
Oke_arf-319		nDNA	Smith et al. 2005b
Oke_BAMBI-116		nDNA	Smith et al. 2005b
Oke_CKS-389		nDNA	Smith et al. 2005b
Oke_copa-211		nDNA	Smith et al. 2005b
Oke_Cr231		mtDNA	Smith et al. 2005a
Oke_Cr30	[1]	mtDNA	Smith et al. 2005a
Oke_Cr386	[1]	mtDNA	Smith et al. 2005a
Oke_DM20-548		nDNA	Smith et al. 2005a
Oke_GHII-2943	[2]	nDNA	Elfstrom et al. 2007
Oke_GHII-3129	[2]	nDNA	Elfstrom et al. 2007
Oke_GnRH-373	[3]	nDNA	Smith et al. 2005a
Oke_GnRH-527	[3]	nDNA	Smith et al. 2005a
Oke_GPDH-191		nDNA	Smith et al. 2005b
Oke_hsc71-199		nDNA	Smith et al. 2005b
Oke_il-1racp-67		nDNA	Smith et al. 2005b
Oke_IL8r-272	[4]	nDNA	Smith et al. 2005a
Oke_IL8r-406	[4]	nDNA	Smith et al. 2005a
Oke_Moesin-160		nDNA	Smith et al. 2005b
Oke_ND3-69	[1]	mtDNA	Smith et al. 2005a
Oke_RFC2-618		nDNA	Smith et al. 2005b
Oke_RH1op-245		nDNA	Smith et al. 2005b
Oke_SClkF2R2-239		nDNA	Smith et al. 2005b
Oke_serpin-140		nDNA	Smith et al. 2005b
Oke_Tsha1-196		nDNA	Smith et al. 2005b
Oke_u1-519		nDNA	Smith et al. 2005a
Oke_u200-385		nDNA	Smith et al. 2005b
Oke_u202-131		nDNA	Smith et al. 2005b
Oke_u212-87		nDNA	Smith et al. 2005b
Oke_u216-222		nDNA	Smith et al. 2005b
Oke_u217-172		nDNA	Smith et al. 2005b
Oke_Zp3b-314		nDNA	Smith et al. 2005b

[1] These loci were completely linked.
[2] These loci were linked.
[3] These loci were linked.
[4] These loci were linked.

Population allele frequencies for each SNP locus were computed from individual genotype data for both diploid and haploid loci. When more than one collection was available from a given population the allele frequencies were compared using the log likelihood ratio test of homogeneity, (G-test, Sokal and Rohlf 1995); collections that were not significantly different ($\alpha = 0.05$) were pooled for the remaining analyses. Cavalli-Sforza and Edwards (1967) chord distances were computed from population allele frequencies after adjusting for linked loci. Genetic similarity between populations was visualized using the multidimensional scaling methods in NtSYS (Exeter Software, Setauket, NY).

Genetic mixture analysis

Simulation analyses were conducted to determine the accuracy and precision with which mixture components could be assigned to the fall and summer runs. In these simulations, hypothetical mixtures ($N = 400$) were derived entirely from the run or population under study, and a mixed stock analysis was performed with the baseline being parametrically resampled on each iteration to account for variability due to sampling populations. Average estimates of the proportion of each run (summer and fall) in the mixture were derived from 1,000 simulations. To determine the 90% confidence intervals, the estimates were sorted and the 51st and the 950th estimates indicated the bounds of the confidence interval. Simulations were performed using the Statistical Package for Analyzing Mixtures (SPAM version 3.5, Debevec et al. 2000), and mixture genotypes were randomly generated from the baseline allele frequencies using Hardy-Weinberg expectations. This method was repeated for each population in the baseline as well as for each of the two runs (summer and fall). Mean estimates greater than 90% indicated that populations could readily be identified as summer or fall run, and that the run compo-

nents in mixtures could be identified with a high level of accuracy and precision.

As a first attempt to identify fall chum salmon in mixtures using the SNP baseline, axillary processes were clipped from chum salmon caught in the Kalskag fish wheels (rkm 249) where a tagging project was being conducted independent of our study (Pawluk et al. 2006; Figure 1). Axillary tissues were stored in ethanol using individually labeled 2 mL vials. Corresponding data recorded for each individual fish included date and time of capture, stream bank of capture (i.e., right or left bank), condition of fish, and tag number.

Samples were partitioned into four temporal periods (14 June to 5 July, 6–27 July, 28 July to 17 August, and 18 August to 8 September), and 190 individuals were randomly subsampled for analysis from the pool of samples available in each of the four periods. Given the expected fall chum proportion of approximately 10% during the early period based on the 1996 analysis, and the need to analyze individuals from four periods, a sample size of 190 individuals was chosen to provide acceptable accuracy and precision while efficiently using funds for laboratory analysis. Based on sampling theory and perfect genetic identifiability (Thompson 1992), a sample of 190 would provide an estimate that is approximately $\pm 7\%$ of the true value 90% of the time. Of these subsamples, 125 were chosen from fish caught in the right bank fish wheel, and 65 were chosen from fish caught in the left bank fish wheel. This sampling scheme was designed to compensate for the apparent preference of upriver chum salmon stocks to travel along the right bank (Kerkvliet et al. 2004). The subsamples from each of the four periods were genotyped at each of the 31 SNP loci, and the relative contribution of summer and fall of chum salmon was estimated from the baseline allele frequencies and the multi-locus genotypes for each individual in the sample. All calculations were carried out using the SPAM analysis package.

Results

Age, sex, and size

A total of 336 fall and 1,964 summer chum salmon were sampled for age, sex, and size. Ageable scales with all associated information were available from 280 fall and 1,791 summer chum salmon (Table 2).

There was a significant difference in age compositions between fall and summer chum salmon (chi-square = 224.2, df = 2; $P < 0.0001$), with a higher proportion of younger (age-3) fish in the fall chum salmon population compared to summer chum salmon stocks (54.6% and 15.7%, respectively). There was no significant difference in sex composition between fall and summer chum stocks (chi-square = 0.23, df = 2; $P > 0.05$), with females comprising 45.5% of the fall chum salmon sample and 47.0% of the summer chum salmon samples.

Fall and summer chum salmon had significantly different size measurements among most age and sex classes (MANOVA; Table 2). Fall chum salmon had significantly smaller maximum width than summer chum salmon for all female age classes ($P < 0.001$), but there was no difference in maximum width among male age classes ($P > 0.05$). In addition, fall chum salmon had significantly smaller maximum dorsal-ventral height than summer chum salmon among all sex and age classes ($P < 0.005$). Fall chum salmon had significantly greater mideye-fork lengths than summer chum salmon for all sex and age classes ($P < 0.025$) except age-4 males.

Fecundity

There was no difference in absolute and relative fecundity between fall and summer chum salmon ($P > 0.05$; Table 3); mean absolute fecundity for fall fish was 2,440 eggs (range 1,789–3,453 eggs), while the mean for summer chum salmon was 2,342 eggs (range 1,470–3,270 eggs). However, there was a significant difference in mean weight per egg between fall and summer chum salmon ($F = 28.10$, df = 68, $P < 0.0001$); mean egg weight for fall fish was 140 mg per egg (range 93–213 mg), and the mean egg weight of summer chum salmon was 194 mg per egg (range 120–270 mg).

Genetic baseline analysis

A baseline of allele frequencies for 31 SNPs was developed for nine spawning aggregates of Kuskokwim River chum salmon (Table 4; Figure 1). Sample sizes of at least 95 individuals were available from seven of the nine spawning aggregates; the Holokuk and Oskawalik Rivers had sample sizes of 58 and 48. Genomic DNA was successfully extracted from 827 individuals in the nine baseline collections. All individuals were assayed for genotypes at 31 SNP loci (Table 1). The combined average failure rate for obtaining usable genotypes was 1.4% (range: 0.0% to 5.1%).

Complete linkage was found between mtDNA SNP loci for *Oke_CR30, Oke_CR386,* and *Oke_ND3–69.* Consequently, *Oke_CR386* and *Oke_ND3–69* were dropped from further analyses, but *Oke_CR30* was retained because it had the most complete set of genotypes. *Oke_CR231* showed no allelic variation in the baseline, so it was dropped from the remaining analyses without loss of information.

Of the remaining 27 SNPs located in the nuclear DNA, three pairs were located in close proximity to each other (*Oke_GnRH-373/Oke_GnRH-527, Oke_IL8r-272/Oke_IL8r-406,* and *Oke_GHII-2943/Oke_GHII-3129*), and significant gametic disequilibrium was found in each of the pairs ($P > 0.0001$) indicating that genotypes at one locus of a pair were not independent of the genotypes at the other locus of the pair. Consequently, geno-

TABLE 2. Multivariate analysis results of size characteristics for Kuskokwim River summer and fall chum salmon, 2004.

Sex	Age	Measurement (mm)	Summer chum			Fall chum					Wilks' λ	F Value	P
			N	Mean	CV	N	Mean	CV	F Value	P			
F	3	MEF length	145	511.9	0.054	89	528.3	0.039	22.87	<0.0001	0.539	65.38	<0.0001
		max height		113.1	0.076		106.1	0.075	39.73	<0.0001			
		max width		71.6	0.099		66.8	0.081	30.52	<0.0001			
	4	MEF length	389	535.4	0.056	36	549.7	0.047	7.58	0.0061	0.808	33.92	<0.0001
		max height		119.8	0.093		109.9	0.092	26.14	<0.0001			
		max width		75.1	0.095		68.3	0.157	27.43	<0.0001			
	5	MEF length	307	545.5	0.055	18	562.8	0.045	5.84	0.0162	0.855	18.1	<0.0001
		max height		121.2	0.090		113.0	0.112	9.35	0.0024			
		max width		77.0	0.100		69.6	0.168	14.69	0.0002			
M	3	MEF length	136	535.1	0.051	64	549.3	0.051	11.44	0.0009	0.494	67.03	<0.0001
		max height		135.9	0.083		123.0	0.097	54.84	<0.0001			
		max width		65.9	0.099		65.8	0.127	0.01	0.9247			
	4	MEF length	362	566.0	0.057	39	572.3	0.045	1.37	0.2422	0.916	12.27	<0.0001
		max height		143.2	0.146		128.6	0.097	19.66	<0.0001			
		max width		70.5	0.099		69.7	0.105	0.74	0.3911			
	5	MEF length	443	584.7	0.056	34	599.1	0.056	6.05	0.0142	0.816	35.46	<0.0001
		max height		146.4	0.091		134.5	0.101	25.34	<0.0001			
		max width		72.4	0.094		72.2	0.104	0.03	0.8638			

TABLE 3. Fecundity and egg weight statistics for female Kuskokwim River summer and fall chum salmon, 2004.

Measurement	Summer chum			Fall chum			ANOVA results	
	N	Mean	SE	N	Mean	SE	F Value	P
Absolute Fecundity (no. eggs)	54	2,342	58	13	2,440	109	0.65	0.4222
Relative Fecundity (no. eggs/cm)	54	43.8	1.1	13	45.4	2.1	0.56	0.4556
Egg Weight (mg)	54	194	5	13	140	11	28.10	< 0.0001

TABLE 4. Kuskokwim River collections analyzed for genetic stock identification of chum salmon using SNP markers, 2004.

Collection	Spawn Timing		Population	Sample Size (fish)
Baseline	Summer	1	Aniak River	95
		2	Holokuk River	48
		3	Oskawalik River	58
		4	George River	95
		5	Kogrukluk River	
			1992	45
			1993	50
		6	Stony River	
			Early	95
			Late	56
		7	Takotna River	95
	Fall	8	Big River	95
		9	S Fork Kuskokwim	95
			Subtotal	827
Kalskag mixtures			1: 14 June - 5 July	190
			2: 6 July - 27 July	190
			3: 28 July - 17 Aug	190
			4: 18 Aug - 8 Sept	190
			Subtotal	760
			Total	1,587

types for both loci in a pair were combined into composite genotypes for each locus-pair and treated as a single locus, which left 24 independent SNP loci for comparing spawning aggregates.

Population allele frequencies for each SNP locus were computed from individual genotype data, both diploid and haploid loci. Allele frequencies in collections taken from the same location at different times were compared using the log-likelihood ratio statistic: Kogrukluk River 1992 and 1993 collections (G = 24.7, df = 28, P = 0.64), and Stony River early (1 August 1994) and late (25 September 1994) collections (G = 27.4, df = 28, P = 0.49). Allele frequencies for the temporally separated collections within each location were not significantly different, so they were pooled for the remaining analyses. Computation of Cavalli-Sforza and Edwards (1967) chord distances from population allele frequencies showed evidence of genetic distinction between fall and summer chum salmon; it also showed that genetic diversity between the two fall run populations was greater than diversity seen among seven summer run populations (Figure 2).

Genetic mixture analysis

Simulation analyses conducted to determine the accuracy and precision of assignment to the fall and summer runs indicated that each of the populations in the baseline could be identified to the correct run with a high degree of accuracy (summer ≥95% and fall ≥91%; Table 5). Additional simulations showed that mixtures of chum salmon from the same run could be identified to the correct run with a high degree of accuracy (summer 98% and fall 92%).

Genomic DNA was extracted successfully from 756 chum salmon sampled from the mixed stock catches at the Kalskag fish wheels; these samples were successfully stratified into the four temporal periods with sample sizes of 190, 189, 190, and 187. Stock composition estimates during each of the four periods indicated that fall chum salmon contributed 5% of the chum salmon encountered during the early portion of the analysis from 14 June to 5 July (90% CI: 0.00–0.15; Table 6). In the remaining periods, fall chum salmon were nearly absent (90% CI: 0.00–0.11).

Discussion

Age and sex

Fall chum salmon from the South Fork Kuskokwim River had significantly more age-3 fish than any Kuskokwim River summer chum population. While these differences could have been influenced by differences in gear types used to collect samples, and though there were unusually high numbers of returning age-3 chum salmon reported throughout the Kuskokwim Area in 2004 (Costello et al. 2005; Molyneaux and Folletti 2005; Roettiger et al. 2005; Stewart and Molyneaux 2005), fall chum salmon were reported to have a greater proportion of age-3 fish compared to summer chum salmon in other Asian and North American populations (Helle 1960; Sano 1966; Beacham 1984). Age-4 and -5 fish usually dominate chum salmon populations throughout their range (Bakkala 1970; Helle 1979, Beacham 1984; Clark and Weller 1986). The results of this study are in contrast to the nearby Yukon River, where no significant difference was reported in age composition between fall and summer runs based on samples collected from commercial gillnet catches (Buklis and Barton 1984).

No differences in sex ratios were observed between the South Fork Kuskokwim River fall population and summer chum salmon stocks. No other studies report differences in sex ratios between fall and summer chum populations.

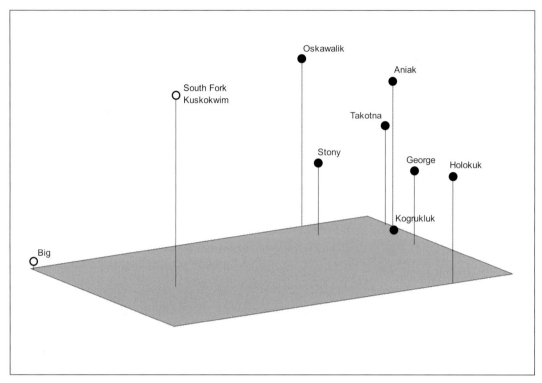

FIGURE 2. Multidimensional scaling plot of pairwise genetic distances (Cavalli-Sforza and Edwards 1967) between chum salmon populations in the Kuskokwim River calculated from allele frequencies at 28 SNP loci. Distances between points in three-dimensional space represent relative genetic distances. Points correspond to summer (solid circles) and fall (open circles) chum salmon collections in Table 3 and Figure 1.

TABLE 5. Percent correct allocation to run time and 90% confidence intervals for mixed stock analysis simulations in which each population comprised 100% of the hypothetical mixtures.

Run	Population	Estimate	90% CI
Summer		0.98	(0.93 - 1.00)
	Aniak River	0.99	(0.96 - 1.00)
	Holokuk River	0.97	(0.91 - 1.00)
	Oskawalik River	0.97	(0.90 - 1.00)
	George River	0.99	(0.95 - 1.00)
	Kogrukluk River	0.98	(0.94 - 1.00)
	Stony River	0.98	(0.95 - 1.00)
	Takotna River	0.95	(0.89 - 1.00)
Fall		0.92	(0.85 - 0.98)
	Big River	0.94	(0.87 - 1.00)
	S Fork Kuskokwim	0.91	(0.83 - 0.98)

TABLE 6. Relative contribution and 90% confidence intervals of Kuskokwim River summer and fall chum salmon encountered at the Kalskag fish wheels during four periods in 2004.

Period	N	Summer		Fall	
		Est	90% CI	Est	90% CI
1: Jun 14 - Jul 5	190	0.95	(0.85 - 1.00)	0.05	(0.00 - 0.15)
2: Jul 6 - 27	189	0.98	(0.91 - 1.00)	0.01	(0.00 - 0.08)
3: Jul 28 - Aug 17	190	1.00	(0.96 - 1.00)	0.00	(0.00 - 0.04)
4: Aug 18 - Sept 8	187	0.99	(0.88 - 1.00)	0.01	(0.00 - 0.11)

Size

Significant differences in overall size indicate that fall chum salmon, as represented by fish from the South Fork Kuskokwim River, tended to have greater mideye-fork length and smaller maximum height and width, when near their spawning area (Table 2). Other studies have reported size differentiation in salmon according to distance of upstream migration, with more interior populations having less robust (i.e., longer and thinner) body shapes (Eniutina 1954; Taylor and McPhail 1985), similar to what was found with the Kuskokwim River fall chum salmon. The less robust body shape is postulated to be an adaptation to longer migrations by helping these fish to minimize energy consumption during upstream migration (Beacham and Murray 1987; Beacham et al. 1988). This was supported by trends seen within Kuskokwim River summer chum salmon populations where mean dorsal-ventral height decreased with increasing distance to the respective spawning grounds of each population (Gilk et al. 2005). Thus, observed differences between summer and fall chum salmon populations seen here may be due to migration distance and not to spawning time because Kuskokwim River fall chum typically spawn in upper basin tributaries.

Other studies have found that fall chum salmon differ in size from summer chum salmon in ways similar to those seen in the Kuskokwim River. Fall chum salmon have greater lengths than summer chum salmon in many river systems, including the Amur River (Berg 1934; Lovetskaya 1948; Grigo 1953), Yukon River (Buklis 1981; Buklis and Barton 1984), and in Prince William Sound (Helle 1960). However, in southern British Columbia, no consistent differences in mean length-at-age were found between early and late spawning populations (Beacham et al. 1983; Beacham 1984). The smaller maximum height and width for Kuskokwim River fall chum salmon relative to summer chum salmon is similar to that seen in the Amur River, Russia (Birman 1951; Grigo 1953).

Differences reported here between Kuskokwim River fall and summer chum salmon reflect the comparative size of fish sampled in close proximity to their respective spawning grounds. These differences in size may not transfer to the same populations if measurements were made when the fish first entered the Kuskokwim River. Because fall chum salmon have greater migration distances, they may initially be larger than summer chum salmon when they first enter the Kuskokwim River, but experience greater weight loss than summer chum salmon by the time they arrive at the spawning grounds. This hypothesis would best be explored by conducting a study of chum salmon near the mouth of the Kuskokwim River coupled with genetic stock identification or tagging that would determine stream of origin.

Fecundity

There was no statistically significant difference in absolute or relative fecundity between Kuskokwim River fall and summer chum salmon. While sample sizes in this study were small, absolute and relative fecundities of Kuskokwim River chum salmon were similar to those reported for chum salmon in other river systems (Salo 1991; Beacham and Murray 1993; Nemeth et al. 2003). In many systems fall chum salmon typically have a greater fecundity than summer chum salmon (Berg 1934; Lovetskaya 1948, Helle 1960; Sano 1966, Bakkala 1970), although this is not the case in the Yukon River (Trasky 1974; Elson 1975; Raymond 1981; Andersen 1983a, 1983b; Beacham et al. 1988).

In contrast to absolute and relative fecundity results, South Fork Kuskokwim River fall chum salmon did consistently have significantly smaller mean egg weights than all summer chum salmon populations, which may explain the smaller maximum width seen in female fall chum salmon (Table 2). This was similar to other studies, which have shown that fall populations and populations spawning in upper portions of drainages tend to have smaller mean egg size than summer populations and populations spawning in lower portions of drainages (Beacham and Murray 1987, 1993). A difference in egg size may be a mechanism to regulate fry emergence timing and may be related to incubation temperature. Beacham and Murray (1993), however, suggest that this is more likely an effect of migration distance, whereby upper river fish allocate more of their energy to migration and less to gonad development. The egg weights reported here are similar to those reported in other river systems, though Kuskokwim River fall chum salmon tend to have smaller egg sizes than those reported for the Amur River, British Columbia rivers, and the Yukon River (Smirnov 1975; Beacham and Murray 1987; Beacham et al. 1988).

Genetic baseline and mixture analyses

Differences in allele frequency at 28 SNP loci were found between fall and summer chum salmon as demonstrated by the multidimensional scaling plot of genetic distances (Figure 2). The similarity between populations within a run in relation to the distinction between the runs was also indicated by the simulations of genetic stock identification (Table 5). These 100% simulations demonstrated that baseline populations can be identified to the correct run with a high degree of accuracy (mean correct allocation ≥91%). In addition, mixtures of chum salmon from the same run could also be correctly allocated to either fall run (92%) or summer run (97%). Disparity in correct allocation between the two runs may be due to the unequal number of populations representing each run in the baseline. Cumulative small misallocations to populations of the wrong run can grow relatively large when a run has many populations to which a small amount can be misallocated. This might explain why the fall run, which is quite distinct but is only represented by two populations, shows a greater amount of misallocation to the summer chum group. Another potential reason might be due to the greater genetic divergence between the fall run populations when compared to summer run populations. Misallocation from a sample taken from any of the summer run populations (which are all very similar) will likely be applied to another summer run population. Conversely, misallocation from a sample taken from either of the fall populations may not be applied to the other fall run population due to the genetic difference between these populations.

No definitive conclusion can be made about run-timing and relative contribution of fall chum salmon from this study. Nonzero proportions of fall run chum salmon were estimated during three of the four periods, but each of the 90% confidence intervals included 0%. The sample size chosen for analysis gave insufficient precision to distinguish low proportions of fall chum salmon in mixed stock analyses in 2004, but it does reinforce the view that the current abundance levels of fall chum are low relative to summer chum salmon. The proportions of fall chum salmon seen in this study (Table 6) were lower than results from an opportunistic mixed-stock sample collected from the lower Kuskokwim River commercial fishery on 17 July 1996. This mixed-stock sample, which was analyzed with the allozyme marker baseline, was composed of 12% (±4%) fall chum salmon (ADF&G, Gene Conservation Laboratory, unpublished data). However, another mixed stock analysis of samples taken in the lower Kuskokwim River between 25 July and 1 August 2003 assigned 99% of the samples as summer run fish (ADF&G, Gene Conservation Laboratory, unpublished data). Although these two opportunistic samples are from different years, they do suggest that fall chum salmon were present earlier in the season, despite the later timing of their spawning. This was unexpected given that in other rivers, such as the neighboring Yukon River, fall chum salmon entered freshwater late in the season. Existing genetic techniques would allow for a better description of the run timing of fall chum salmon in the lower Kuskokwim River by collecting tissue samples from the commercial catch or test fishery. Such analysis would also provide insight into the relative contribution of fall chum salmon to the overall commercial catch. It may also be possible to investigate their historical contribution to the commercial fishery through the genetic analysis of archived fish scales that have been annually collected from the lower Kuskokwim River commercial fishery.

Only two populations of fall chum salmon were available for inclusion in the genetic baseline (Big River and South Fork Kuskokwim River) but anecdotal historical data indicate that these may be two of the main populations of fall chum salmon. It is assumed that unrepresented fall chum salmon populations will be genetically more similar to other fall chum salmon populations than to summer chum salmon populations, but this cannot be tested before more baseline samples of fall populations are collected. Genetic distances indicate that fall chum salmon populations are distinct from each other as well as being distinct from summer chum, and it is possible that an unrepresented component of the fall run is genetically more similar to summer chum salmon than either of the two fall chum salmon populations in the baseline. Unrepresented fall chum salmon in the mixture could be misallocated to the summer run. Improving the representation of additional fall chum salmon populations in the baseline will lead to greater ability to detect fall chum salmon in the mixed stock samples and greater confidence in the estimates. In addition, only about a quarter of the mixed stock samples collected from Kalskag were analyzed, so greater resolution in the proportion of fall chum salmon in the four mixed stock samples collected in 2004 could be achieved by increasing the number of fish analyzed.

Conclusions

While genetic evidence of fall run chum salmon in the Kuskokwim River basin was found in the late 1990s, this project was the first to formally document some biological characteristics in comparison to summer chum salmon within the basin. The results of this study indicate that fall chum salmon are distinct from summer chum salmon by having: a greater proportion of younger (age-3) fish, a greater mideye-fork length and smaller maximum height and width near the spawning grounds, and smaller mean egg weight. While these differences aren't strong enough to readily distinguish Kuskokwim River fall from summer chum salmon in mixed-stock fisheries, genetic analysis shows sufficient differences to distinguish the two runs in mixed-stock analyses. A definitive conclusion about the run timing of fall chum salmon through the lower Kuskokwim River was not achieved in this study. However, more resolution would be possible through genetic analysis of remaining samples collected in 2004 or through samples taken in the commercial or test fisheries near Bethel, and by including unrepresented summer and fall chum salmon populations in the baseline.

Future investigations should incorporate characterization of additional Kuskokwim River fall chum salmon populations, examination of possible interannual variation within populations, more detailed characterization of spawning habitats, determination of run timing through the lower Kuskokwim River, and an investigation of the potential to analyze archived fish scales from the commercial fishery to determine historical run timing and relative contribution of fall chum salmon in the lower Kuskokwim River fishery.

Although fall chum salmon appear to currently constitute a small proportion of the overall Kuskokwim River chum salmon run, this unique group of fish is an important component of the overall biodiversity of the species within the Kuskokwim drainage. A fishery management plan designed for long-term sustainability should incorporate some level of monitoring of fall chum salmon abundance sufficient to ensure maintenance of the natural biocomplexity that facilitates the species resiliency in adapting to environmental change. This preliminary description of the biology of Kuskokwim River fall chum salmon is the first step in including these distinct populations in a sustainable chum salmon management plan.

Acknowledgments

This research would not have been possible without the cooperation of the Kenai Fish and Wildlife Field Office of the U.S. Fish and Wildlife Service, Organized Village of Kwethluk, Kuskokwim Native Association, Takotna Tribal Council, and Nikolai Edzeno' Village Council. Funding was provided by the Arctic-Yukon-Kuskokwim Sustainable Salmon Initiative (project no. 45232) and the State of Alaska.

References

ADF&G (Alaska Department of Fish and Game). 2003. Alaska Subsistence Fisheries, 2002 Annual Report. Alaska Department of Fish and Game, Division of Subsistence, Juneau.

Andersen, F. M. 1983a. Upper Yukon test fishing studies, 1981. Alaska Department of Fish and Game, Division of Commercial Fisheries, Fairbanks, Alaska.

Andersen, F. M. 1983b. Upper Yukon test fishing studies, 1982. Alaska Department of Fish and Game, Division of Commercial Fisheries, Fairbanks, Alaska.

Bakkala, R. G. 1970. Synopsis of biological data on the chum salmon, *Oncorhynchus keta* (Walbaum) 1792. U.S. Department of the Interior, FAO Species Synopsis No. 41, Circular 315, Washington, D.C.

Beacham, T. D. 1984. Age and morphology of chum salmon in southern British Columbia. Transactions of the American Fisheries Society 113:727–736.

Beacham, T. D., A. P. Gould, and A. P. Stefanson. 1983. Size, age, meristics, and morphometrics of chum salmon returning to southern British Columbia during 1981–1982. Canadian Technical Report of Fisheries and Aquatic Sciences 1207.

Beacham, T. D., and C. B. Murray. 1987. Adaptive variation in body size, age, morphology, egg size, and developmental biology of chum salmon (*Oncorhynchus keta*) in British Columbia. Canadian Journal of Fisheries and Aquatic Sciences 44:244–261.

Beacham, T. D., and C. B. Murray. 1993. Fecundity and egg size variation in North American Pacific salmon (*Oncorhynchus*). Journal of Fish Biology 42:485–508.

Beacham, T. D., C. B. Murray, and R. E. Withler. 1988. Age, morphology, developmental biology, and biochemical genetic variation of Yukon River fall chum salmon, *Onchorhynchus keta*, and comparisons with British Columbia populations. Fisheries Bulletin 86: 663–674.

Berg, L. S. 1934. Vernal and hiernal races among anadromous fishes. Izvestya Akademii Nauk SSSR 7: 711–732. Translation from Russian; Fisheries Research Board Canada 16(1959):515–537.

Birman, I. B. 1951. Qualitative characteristics of the stocks and the dynamics of abundance of the autumn chum salmon in the Amur River. Izv. Tickhookean. Nauchno-Issled. Inst. Rybn. Khoz. Okeanogr. 35: 17–31. Translation from Russian; Fisheries Research Board Canada Translation Series 349.

Bromaghin, J. F. 1993. Sample size determination for interval estimation of multinomial probabilities. The American Statistician 47:203–206.

Brown, C. M. 1983. Alaska's Kuskokwim River region: a history. U.S. Bureau of Land Management, Anchorage, Alaska.

Buklis, L. S. 1981. Yukon and Tanana River fall chum salmon tagging studies, 1976–1980. Alaska Department of Fish and Game, Informational Leaflet 194, Juneau, Alaska.

Bue, F. J., B. M. Borba, R. Cannon, and C. C. Krueger. 2009. Yukon River fall chum salmon fisheries: management, harvest, and stock abundance. Pages 703–742 *in* C. C. Krueger and C. E. Zimmerman, editors. Pacific salmon: ecology and management of western Alaska's populations. American Fisheries Society, Symposium 70, Bethesda, Maryland.

Buklis, L. S., and L. H. Barton. 1984. Yukon River fall chum salmon biology and stock status. Alaska Department of Fish and Game, Informational Leaflet No. 239, Juneau, Alaska.

Burkey, C., Jr., and P. Salomone. 1999. Kuskokwim Area salmon escapement observation catalog, 1984–1998. Alaska Department of Fish and Game, Division of Commercial Fisheries, Regional Information Report No. 3A99–11, Anchorage, Alaska.

Cavalli-Sforza, L. L., and A. W. F. Edwards. 1967. Phylogenetic analysis: models and estimation procedures. Evolution 21:550–570.

Clark, J. E. and J. L. Weller. 1986. Age, sex and size of chum salmon (*Oncorhynchus keta* Walbaum) from catches and escapements in Southeastern Alaska, 1984. Alaska Department of Fish and Game, Division of Commercial Fisheries, Technical Data Report 168, Juneau, Alaska.

Coffing, M. 1991. Kwethluk subsistence: contemporary land use patterns, wild resource harvest and use, and the subsistence economy of a lower Kuskokwim River area community. Alaska Department of Fish and Game, Subsistence Division, (Region III unpublished report), Bethel, Alaska.

Coffing, M. 1997a. Kuskokwim area subsistence salmon harvest summary, 1996; prepared for the Alaska Board of Fisheries, Fairbanks, Alaska, December 2, 1997. Alaska Department of Fish and Game, Subsistence Division, (Region III unpublished report), Bethel, Alaska.

Coffing, M. 1997b. Kuskokwim area subsistence salmon fishery; prepared for the Alaska Board of Fisheries, Fairbanks, Alaska, December 2, 1997. Alaska Department of Fish and Game, Subsistence Division, (Region III unpublished report), Bethel.

Coffing, M., L. Brown, G. Jennings, and C. Uttermole. 2000. The subsistence harvest and use of wild resources in Akiachak, Alaska, 1998. Final Project Report to U.S. Fish and Wildlife Service, Office of Subsistence Management, FIS 00–009, Juneau, Alaska.

Costello, D., S. E. Gilk, and D. B. Molyneaux. 2005. Takotna River salmon studies, 2004. Alaska Department of Fish and Game, Commercial Fisheries Division, Fishery Data Series 05–71, Anchorage, Alaska.

Debevec, E. M., R. B. Gates, M. Masuda, J. Pella, J. Reynolds, and L. W. Seeb. 2000. SPAM (Version 3.2): Statistics program for analyzing mixtures. Journal of Heredity 91:509–511.

DuBois, L. and D. B. Molyneaux. 2001. Operational Procedures Manual: 2001 Salmon Age-Sex-Length Sampling Program, Kuskokwim Area. Alaska Department of Fish and Game, Division of Commercial Fisheries, Bethel, Alaska.

Elfstrom, C. M., C. T. Smith, and L. W. Seeb. 2007. Thirty-eight single nucleotide polymorphism markers for high-throughput genotyping of chum salmon. Molecular Ecology Notes 7:1211–1215.

Elson, M. S. 1975. Enumeration of spawning chum salmon in the Fishing Branch River in 1971 and 1972. Canada Department of the Environment, Fisheries and Marine Service, Pacific Region, Technical Report 1973–5, Vancouver, British Columbia.

Eniutina, R. I. 1954. Local stocks of pink salmon in the Amur basin and neighbouring waters. Vopr. Ikhtiol. 2: 139–143. Translated from Russian; Fisheries Research Board Canada Translation 284.

Finn, J. E., E. E. Knudsen, R. Hander, S. Maclean, and A. Gryska. 1998. Estimating freshwater survival and environmental influences on the survival of several Yukon River chum salmon stocks: Progress Report for 1996 and 1997 Brood Years. U.S. Geological Survey Progress Report, Anchorage, Alaska.

Gilbert, C. H. 1922. The salmon of the Yukon River. Bulletin of the U.S. Bureau Fisheries 38:317–332.

Gilk, S. E., W. D. Templin, D. B. Molyneaux, T. Hamazaki, and J. A. Pawluk. 2005. Characteristics of fall chum salmon *Oncorhynchus keta* in the Kuskokwim River drainage. Alaska Department of Fish and Game, Fishery Data Series No. 05–56, Anchorage, Alaska.

Green, P. E. 1978. Analyzing Multivariate Data. Dryden Press, Hinsdale, Illinois.

Grigo, L. D. 1953. Morphological differences between the summer and the autumn chum salmon *Oncorhynchus keta* (Walbuam), *O. keta* (Walbaum) infraspecies autumnalis Berg. Doklady Akademii Nauk SSSR 92(6): 1225–1228. Translation from Russian; Pages 13–17 *in* Pacific salmon: Selected articles from Soviet periodicals. 1961. The Israel Program for Scientific Translations, Jerusalem.

Helle, J. H. 1960. Characteristics and structure of early and late spawning runs of chum salmon, *Oncorhynchus keta* (Walbaum), in streams of Prince William Sound, Alaska. Master's thesis. University of Idaho, Moscow, Idaho.

Helle, J. H. 1979. Influence of marine environment on age and size at maturity, growth, and abundance of chum salmon, *Onchorhynchus keta* (Walbaum), from Olsen Creek, Prince William Sound, Alaska. Doctoral dissertation. Oregon State University, Corvallis, Oregon.

Hilborn, R., T. P. Quinn, D. E. Schindler, and D. E. Rogers. 2003. Biocomplexity and fisheries sustainability. Proceedings of the National Academy of Sciences USA 100(11):6564–6568.

Katayama, M. 1935. Biometric study of dog salmon (*Oncorhynchus keta* Walbaum). Bulletin of the Japanese Society of Scientific Fisheries 4:171–173. Translation from Japanese; U.S. Fish and Wildlife Service, Translation 1, Seattle.

Kerkvliet, C. M, J. Pawluk, T. Hamazaki, K. E. Hyer, and D. Cannon. 2004. A mark-recapture experiment to estimate the abundance of Kuskokwim River sockeye, chum, and coho salmon, 2003. Alaska Department of Fish and Game, Division of Commercial Fisheries, Regional Information Report No. 3A04–14, Anchorage, Alaska.

Linderman, J. C., Jr., and D. J. Bergstrom. 2009. Kuskokwim management area: salmon escapement, harvest, and management. Pages 541–599 *in* C. C. Krueger and C.E. Zimmerman, editors. Pacific salmon: ecology and management of western Alaska's populations. American Fisheries Society, Symposium 70, Bethesda, Maryland.

Lovetskaya, E. A. 1948. Data on the biology of the Amur chum salmon. Izvestiya Tikhookeanskogo nauchno- issledovatel'skogo institute rybnogo khozyaistva okeanografii 27: 115–137. Translation from Russian; Pages 101–126 *in* Pacific salmon: Selected articles from Soviet periodicals. 1961. The Israel Program for Scientific Translations, Jerusalem.

Martz, M., and B. S. Dull. 2006. Lower Kuskokwim River inseason subsistence salmon catch monitoring, 2005. Alaska Department of Fish and Game, Fishery Management Report No. 06–44. Anchorage, Alaska.

Molyneaux, D. B., and D. L. Folletti. 2005. Salmon age, sex, and length catalog for the Kuskokwim Area, 2004 progress report. Alaska Department of Fish and Game, Division of Commercial Fisheries, Regional Information Report No. 3A05–03, Anchorage, Alaska.

Nemeth, M., B. Haley, and S. Kinneen. 2003. Fecundity of chum and coho salmon from Norton Sound, Alaska. Unpublished report for the Norton Sound Disaster Relief Fund by LGL Alaska Research Associates, Inc. and Norton Sound Economic Developmental Corporation.

Pawluk, J., C. M. Kerkvliet, T. Hamazaki, K. E. Hyer, D. Cannon. 2006. A mark-recapture study of Kuskokwim River sockeye, chum, and coho salmon, 2004. Alaska Department of Fish and Game, Fishery Data Series No. 06–52, Anchorage, Alaska.

Quinn, T. P. 2009. Pacific salmon population structure and dynamics: a perspective from Bristol Bay on life history variation across spatial and temporal scales. Pages 857–871 *in* C. C. Krueger and C. E. Zimmerman, editors. Pacific salmon: ecology and management of western Alaska's populations. American Fisheries Society, Symposium 70, Bethesda, Maryland.

Raymond, J. A. 1981. Incubation of fall chum salmon (*Oncorhynchus keta*) at Clear Air Force Station, Alaska. Alaska Department of Fish and Game, Informational Leaflet 189, Juneau, Alaska.

Raymond, M., and F. Rousset. 1995. GENEPOP (version 1.2): population genetics software for exact tests and ecumenicism. Journal of Heredity 86:248–249.

Roettiger, T., F. G. Harris, and K. C. Harper. 2005. Abundance and run timing of adult salmon in the Kwethluk River, Yukon Delta National Wildlife Refuge, Alaska, 2004. USFWS, Alaska Fisheries Data Series Report 2005–7, Kenai, Alaska.

Salo, E.O. 1991. Life history of chum salmon (*Oncorhynchus keta*). Pages 231–310 *in* C. Groot and L. Margolis, editors. Pacific Salmon Life Histories. UBC Press, Vancouver, BC.

Sano, S. 1966. Salmon of the North Pacific Ocean–Part III: A review of the life history of North Pacific Salmon 6. Chum salmon in the Far East. International North Pacific Fisheries Commission 18:41–57.

Schwanke, C. J., D. B. Molyneaux, L. DuBois, and C. Goods. 2001. Takotna River salmon Studies and Upper Kuskokwim River aerial surveys, 2000.

Alaska Department of Fish and Game, Division of Commercial Fisheries, Regional Information Report No. 3A01–02, Anchorage, Alaska.

Schwanke, C. J. and D. B. Molyneaux. 2002. Takotna River salmon Studies and Upper Kuskokwim River aerial surveys, 2001. Alaska Department of Fish and Game, Division of Commercial Fisheries, Regional Information Report No. 3A02–09, Anchorage.

Seeb, L. W., and P. A. Crane. 1999. High genetic heterogeneity in chum salmon in western Alaska, the contact zone between northern and southern lineages. Transactions of the American Fisheries Society 128:58–87.

Seeb, L. W., P. A. Crane, and E. M. Debevec. 1997a. Genetic analysis of chum salmon harvested in the South Unimak and Shumagin Islands June Fisheries, 1993–1996. Alaska Department of Fish and Game, Regional Information Report No. 5J97–17, Anchorage, Alaska.

Seeb, L. W., P. A. Crane, and E. M. Debevec. 1997b. Supplementary appendices: genetic analysis of chum salmon harvested in the South Unimak and Shumagin Islands June Fisheries, 1993–1996. Alaska Department of Fish and Game, Regional Information Report No. 5J97–18, Anchorage, Alaska.

Seeb, L. W., P. A. Crane, C. M. Kondzela, R. L. Wilmot, S. Urawa, N. V. Varnavskaya, and J. E. Seeb. 2004. Migration of Pacific Rim chum salmon on the high seas: insights from genetic data. Environmental Biology of Fishes 69:21–36.

Smirnov, A. I. 1975. The biology, reproduction, and development of the Pacific salmon. Izd. Mosk. Univ. Pl-335. Translated from Russian; Fisheries Marine Service Translation, No. 3861.

Smith, C. T., J. Baker, L. Park, L.W. Seeb, C. Elfstrom, S. Abe, and J. E. Seeb. 2005a. Characterization of 13 single nucleotide polymorphism markers for chum salmon. Molecular Ecology Notes 5:259–262.

Smith, C. T., C. M. Elfstrom, J. E. Seeb, and L. W. Seeb. 2005b. Use of sequence data from rainbow trout and Atlantic salmon for SNP detection in Pacific salmon. Molecular Ecology 14:4193–4203.

Sokal, R. R. and F. J. Rohlf. 1995. Biometry: The principles and practice of statistics in biological research, 3rd edition. Freeman, New York.

Stewart, R., and D. B. Molyneaux. 2005. George River Salmon Studies, 2004. Alaska Department of Fish and Game, Fishery Data Series 05–47, Anchorage, Alaska.

Stickney, A. 1980. Subsistence resource utilization: Nikolai and Telida—Interim Report. Alaska Department of Fish and Game, Technical Paper No. 20, Bethel, Alaska.

Stokes, J. 1985. Natural resource utilization of four upper Kuskokwim communities. Alaska Department of Fish and Game, Division of Subsistence, Technical Paper No. 86, Juneau, Alaska.

Taylor, E. B., and J. D. McPhail. 1985. Variation in body morphology among British Columbia populations of coho salmon, Oncorhynchus kisutch. Canadian Journal of Fisheries and Aquatic Sciences 42:2020–2028.

Thompson, S. K. 1992. Sampling. Wiley, New York.

Trasky, L. T. 1974. Yukon River anadromous fish investigations. Alaska Department of Fish and Game, Division of Commercial Fisheries, Anadromous Fish Conservation Act, Completion Report for period July 1, 1973 to June 30, 1974, Juneau, Alaska.

Estuarine and Marine Ecology of Salmon in the Bering Sea and North Pacific

American Fisheries Society Symposium 70:183–199, 2009

Estuarine Ecology of Juvenile Salmon in Western Alaska: a Review

NICOLA HILLGRUBER[*]

University of Alaska Fairbanks, School of Fisheries and Ocean Sciences
17101 Point Lena Loop Road, Juneau, Alaska 99801, USA

CHRISTIAN E. ZIMMERMAN

U.S. Geological Survey, Alaska Science Center
4210 University Drive, Anchorage, Alaska 99508, USA

Abstract.—In the late 1990s and early 2000s, large declines in numbers of chum salmon *Oncorhynchus keta* and Chinook salmon *O. tshawytscha* returning to the Arctic-Yukon-Kuskokwim (AYK) region (Alaska, USA) illuminated the need for an improved understanding of the variables controlling salmon abundance at all life stages. In addressing questions about salmon abundance, large gaps in our knowledge of basic salmon life history and the critical early marine life stage were revealed. In this paper, results from studies conducted on the estuarine ecology of juvenile salmon in western Alaska are summarized and compared, emphasizing timing and distribution during outmigration, environmental conditions, age and growth, feeding, and energy content of salmon smolts. In western Alaska, water temperature dramatically changes with season, ranging from 0°C after ice melt in late spring/early summer to 19°C in July. Juvenile salmon were found in AYK estuaries from early May until August or September, but to date no information is available on their residence duration or survival probability. Chum salmon were the most abundant juvenile salmon reported, ranging in percent catch from <0.1% to 4.7% and most research effort has focused on this species. Abundances of Chinook salmon, sockeye salmon *O. nerka*, and pink salmon *O. gorbuscha* varied among estuaries, while coho salmon *O. kisutch* juveniles were consistently rare, never amounting to more than 0.8% of the catch. Dietary composition of juvenile salmon was highly variable and a shift was commonly reported from epibenthic and neustonic prey in lower salinity water to pelagic prey in higher salinity water. Gaps in the knowledge of AYK salmon estuarine ecology are still evident. For example, data on outmigration patterns and residence timing and duration, rearing conditions and their effect on diet, growth, and survival are often completely lacking or available only for few selected years and sites. Filling gaps in knowledge concerning salmon use and survival in estuarine and near-shore habitats within the AYK region will aid in assessing the relative roles of all habitats (freshwater to marine) in controlling salmon abundance.

[*]Corresponding author: nhillgruber@alaska.edu

Introduction

In the watersheds of the Arctic-Yukon-Kuskokwim (AYK) region in Alaska (Figure 1), the estuarine residence of Pacific salmon *Oncorhynchus* is a poorly studied life stage. Salmonids typically experience high and variable size-selective mortality during this stage. For example, mortality rates of chum salmon *O. keta*, after ocean entry, may initially range as high as 31–46% per day in Puget Sound (Bax 1983), or 3–25% per day in coastal waters off the coast of Japan (Fukuwaka and Suzuki 2002). In a recent study on hatchery chum salmon in Southeast Alaska, average daily mortality was estimated to be 8.1% for the first 21 d post release (Wertheimer and Thrower 2007). Reasons for these high and variable mortality rates are assumed to be food limitation (Salo 1991) and size-selective predation (Beamish and Mahnken 2001). Only with a better understanding of the role of rearing conditions, such as food resource availability, predator abundance, and physical environmental variability in controlling survival of juvenile salmon will it be possible to evaluate hypotheses of salmon population regulation in western Alaska.

Estuarine and near-shore dependence differ among salmonid species (Healy 1982a; Thorpe 1994). In comparison to most other anadromous salmonids, chum and pink salmon *O. gorbuscha* enter estuaries at a comparatively smaller size and remain longer in brackish water habitats of estuaries or river plumes than other salmon species, such as coho *O. kisutch* and Chinook salmon *O. tshawytscha* (Healey 1982b; Simenstad et al. 1982; Fukuwaka and Suzuki 2002). Consequently, the period of estuarine residency might be of particular importance for these species (chum and pink salmon) because of the intense size-selective predation pressure they may experience in the marine environment (Parker 1971; Simenstad and Salo

1980; Healy 1982b; Simenstad and Wissmar 1984; Moss et al. 2005). In contrast, Healy (1982a) concluded that the degree of estuary dependence of juvenile Pacific salmon may be a function of the existence and use of alternate nursery habitats and the length of estuarine residence. Following this classification system, he considered Chinook and chum salmon as most dependent, followed by coho salmon, while pink and sockeye salmon *O. nerka* were least dependent on estuarine habitat (Healy 1982a).

Early marine survival is affected by both biotic and abiotic conditions either directly through starvation or indirectly through decreased growth rates, which may result in longer periods of vulnerability to predation. Water temperature is a ubiquitous environmental variable that affects ectothermic animals, such as fish, directly through its effects on metabolic processes. Water temperature affects smolting in salmonids, resulting in such diverse responses as shifts in emigration timing, reversal of smolting, premature smolting, or even death (Richter and Kolmes 2005). In addition, temperature, in conjunction with prey availability and abundance, will determine the growth potential and mortality rates of juvenile chum salmon at this stage (Mason 1974; Healey 1982a; Salo 1991). The metabolic costs of migration, smolting, and maintenance are key energetic constraints on the production and survival of juvenile salmon migrating through estuaries and the near-shore environment (Wissmar and Simenstad 1988).

In the last decade, the abundance of chum and Chinook salmon in the AYK region has fluctuated greatly (Adkison and Finney 2003; Linderman and Bergstrom 2009, this volume; Menard et al. 2009, this volume). Declines in numbers of returning chum and Chinook salmon in the late 1990s and early 2000s caused severe social and economic hardship for the people of the AYK region because of lower catches and the associated

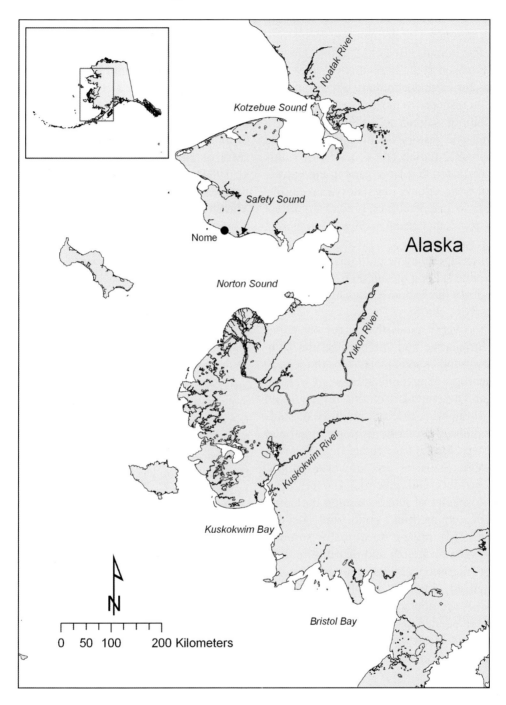

FIGURE 1. Arctic-Yukon-Kuskokwim (AYK) region and estuarine areas that were study sites for juvenile salmon outmigration and rearing habitat use.

regulatory measures directed at reducing fishing pressure (Linderman and Bergstrom 2009, this volume; Bue et al. 2009, this volume; Evenson et al. 2009, this volume). The reasons for these declines are not well understood. In response to the low returns of chum and Chinook salmon to AYK watersheds, a research and restoration plan was designed for the AYK region (AYK SSI 2006); this plan concluded that large gaps in the knowledge of basic salmon life history make it impossible to understand or predict the effect of environmental changes on western Alaska salmon populations. The effects of environmental changes may be particularly dramatic on juvenile salmon during their early marine life, a phase that is poorly studied in the AYK region (NRC 2005).

The overall goal of this review paper is to summarize and compare results from the few studies conducted on the estuarine ecology of juvenile salmon in western Alaska. The emphasis of this review is on chum salmon because the majority of studies examining estuarine ecology of salmon in western Alaska have focused on this species. AYK estuaries are, however, migratory corridors and potential nursery sites for five species of Pacific salmon including Chinook, chum, pink, coho, and sockeye salmon. This review specifically summarizes results on timing and distribution during out-migration, environmental conditions experienced, feeding, growth, and energy content of salmon smolts. In addition, gaps in the knowledge of AYK salmon estuarine ecology are identified with the intention to provide direction for future research.

To encompass the relevant literature for this review, literature searches were conducted with the following electronic search engines: Aquatic Science and Fisheries Abstract ASFA (1971–present) and ISI Web of Science (1980–present). Because most research on estuarine ecology in western Alaska, has not been published in peer-re-

viewed and indexed journals, the search was extended to include interim and final reports of studies conducted in the nearshore area of western Alaska. Only a few studies were found, conducted between 1982 and 2004, including studies by the Alaska Department of Fish & Game, Division of Fisheries Rehabilitation, Enhancement, and Development (Merritt and Raymond 1983; Raymond et al. 1984), the Outer Continental Shelf Environmental Assessment Program (OCSEAP; Martin et al. 1986; Martin et al. 1987), the Norton Sound Disaster Relief Fund (Nemeth et al. 2003; Nemeth et al. 2006), and the North Pacific Research Board (NPRB, Hillgruber et al. 2007).

General Background of Surveys and Study Areas

Studies focusing on the ecology of salmon at this life stage in western Alaska generally represented short-term (1–3 years) efforts disjunctive in time and space (Table 1). Most research on juvenile salmon (including the near-shore ecology of salmon smolts) in the AYK region has focused on chum salmon in the Norton Sound area (Figure 1) because of the continued financial support provided by the Norton Sound Disaster Relief Fund (Nemeth et al. 2003, 2006).

In the Norton Sound area, estuarine research efforts were conducted from 2002 until 2004 in Safety Sound (Figure 1), an oval-shaped bay fed by the Eldorado/Flambeau River. In Safety Sound, salmon juveniles were collected with fyke nets and beach seines (Table 1). On one date in 2003 and two dates in 2004, surface trawls were used to collect juvenile salmon on a station grid in the near-shore habitat of Norton Sound (Nemeth et al. 2006).

In Kotzebue Sound, a one-year study was conducted on chum salmon smolts (Merritt and Raymond 1983). Incidental data on the

TABLE 1. Summary of survey areas, dates, sample gears (GN: gill net, BS: beach seine, PS: purse seine, FN: fyke net, ST: surface tow net), and size and peak emigration period for juvenile chum salmon *O. keta*. Study areas are sorted from north to south.

Study area	Survey year	Survey date	Sample gears	FL [mm]	Peak emigration
Kotzebue Sound[1]	1979–1982	06/01–08/15	BS	n/a	late June
Kotzebue Sound[2]	1980	06/06–08/04	BS	35–50	n/a
Safety Sound[3]	2002	07/02–07/20	FN	55–75	mid July
Safety Sound[4]	2003	06/07–07/21	FN, BS, ST	35–80	mid June and mid July
	2004	06/03–07/31	FN, BS, ST	39–65	mid June
Yukon River delta[5]	1984	12/03–12/13	GN	n/a	n/a
	1985	06/14–09/18	PS, FN, BS, GN	30–109	late June
Yukon River delta[6]	1986	06/06–08/08	BS, ST	29–107	mid/late June
Kuskokwim Bay[7]	2003	06/20–08/26	ST	42–65	mid June
	2004	05/15–06/16	ST	31–66	mid June

[1]Raymond et al. 1984, [2]Merritt and Raymond 1983, [3]Nemeth et al. 2003, [4]Nemeth et al. 2006, [5]Martin et al. 1986, [6]Martin et al. 1987, [7]Hillgruber et al. 2007

timing of occurrence of juvenile chum salmon in Kotzebue Sound were also presented by Raymond et al. (1984). Two studies were carried out in the Yukon River delta as part of an effort directed at examining the effects of a potential oil spill on the estuarine fish community (Martin et al. 1986, 1987); fish were collected with beach seines and surface townets (Table 1). The Yukon River delta studies focused primarily on chum, Chinook, and pink salmon smolts, and yielded only limited data on coho salmon ($N = 4$).

Finally, a two-year pilot study was conducted in Kuskokwim Bay (Hillgruber et al. 2007), a large, shallow, and open estuary fed by the Kuskokwim River in the northeast corner and opening in the west and southwest to the Bering Sea. Sampling of juvenile salmon was conducted using a surface trawl (Table 1). While all species of juvenile salmon were collected, the research was focused on chum salmon feeding success and condition (Burril 2007), and on age and estuarine residence (Hillgruber et al. 2007).

Environmental Conditions

Estuaries are dynamic systems with strong spatial gradients in physical and biological variables, and large seasonal variations in environmental conditions. In AYK estuaries, water temperature is the physical variable expected to most dramatically change with season, because rivers and bays are generally frozen until late spring. Timing of ice break-up is related to Bering Sea climatic and, thus, oceanographic conditions (Stabeno et al. 2007). Based on mean bottom temperature in the eastern Bering Sea, the six warmest years since 1982 were 1996, 1998, and 2002–2005, while 1986, 1992, 1994–1995, 1999, and 2006 were the coldest in the same time frame (Spencer 2008). This environmental variability likely affects timing of ontogenetic events in ectothermic animals, such as juvenile salmonids (Houde 1989).

Following ice break-up, sea surface temperature (SST) in Kuskokwim Bay, the most southerly bay of the AYK region, was homogenously cool (6–8°C) in the middle of May at the onset of juvenile salmon out-migration; it increased to 14°C at the head of the estuary and 10–12°C in the bay towards the middle of June 2004, and the maximum measured SST was 15.6°C (Hillgruber et al. 2007). In 2003, environmental sampling was limited to only few stations later in the sea-son; SST was >14.0°C in late June and late July, slightly decreasing to 13.5°C in late Au-gust. Notably higher temperatures were mea-sured in Safety Sound (northern AYK region), where SST increased from 9.6°C on July 2 to 16.2°C on July 20 at the outlet of Safety Sound into Norton Sound and from 16.6°C to 19.6°C at the head of the bay as measured in 2002 (Nemeth et al. 2003). In addition, interannual differences in the water tempera-ture were apparent, with higher temperatures and an earlier ice break-up in 2004 than in 2003 (Nemeth et al. 2006). Similar seasonal variations in SST were also observed from the Yukon River delta, with temperatures in the delta front areas increasing from 3.9°C in early June to 17.2°C in mid-June (Martin et al. 1987). SST was quite variable, probably a result of tidal and wind (speed, direction) influence on water conditions.

Sea surface salinity (SSS) in estuaries tends to vary horizontally and vertically, but less so seasonally (e.g., Hillgruber et al. 2007). In Kuskokwim Bay, SSS ranged from 0 in the river mouth to values exceeding 30 in the western and northern part of the bay. SSS plots revealed a freshwater plume from the Kuskokwim River extending along the eastern shoreline. In addition, a strong ver-tical stratification was apparent in estuarine waters of the Yukon River delta, with fresher water at the surface and water of higher sa-linity at the bottom (Martin et al. 1987); this stratification was most strongly developed in early June, but weakened in August, probably as the result of increased mixing.

The large watersheds in the AYK region vary dramatically in water clarity as a result of differential loads of glacial silt and sus-pended sediment. While Kuskokwim Bay and the Yukon River delta receive highly tur-bid freshwater, Norton Sound is fed by rela-tively clear rivers. In Kuskokwim Bay, opti-cal backscatter (OBS) was recorded in 2004 as a measure of turbidity. OBS values ranged from 2 to 116 NTU (Nephelometric Turbid-ity Units) in the surface waters, and turbid-ity corresponded to the freshwater plume of the Kuskokwim River. Peak turbidity was observed early in the season and at the head of the estuary, with turbidity levels declining towards the end of the 2004 sampling effort. In the Yukon River delta, water clarity was determined with Secchi disk readings. Water clarity was low throughout the summer sam-pling. Clarity increased with distance from shore, increasing from ≤0.3 m to 1.2 m in offshore waters (Martin et al. 1987).

The interplay of environmental variables needs to be considered to evaluate rearing conditions for juvenile salmon. High temper-atures in the surface waters of the river out-flows might increase metabolic demands to a level not easily balanced by food availability and intake. While juveniles may vertically migrate to avoid the highest temperatures in the surface waters, the equally high turbid-ity levels could severely limit visual prey de-tection at depth and reduce feeding success. Consequently, juvenile fish staging in low sa-linity surface waters of Kuskokwim Bay and the Yukon River Delta likely face a compro-mise between increased metabolic demands and simultaneous decreased feeding success.

Estuarine Fish Communities in Western Alaska

The estuarine fish community in western Alaska was dominated by smelts (Osmeri-dae), whitefishes (Coregoninae), and stickle-backs (Gasterosteidae) (Table 2). In addition, small schooling fishes such as juvenile stages

TABLE 2. Total catch composition of main fish taxa in western Alaska estuarine systems. Blank cells indicate zero catches and j = Juveniles.

Common name	Scientific name	Kuskokwim Bay		Yukon River Delta			Safety Sound		
		2003	2004	1984	1985	1986	2002	2003*	2004*
Chum salmon (j)	*Oncorhynchus keta*	0.4	4.7		2.0	4.7	2.5	1	<0.1
Chinook salmon (j)	*Oncorhynchus tshawytscha*	<0.1	0.2		0.1	0.2	<0.1	<0.1	<0.1
Coho salmon (j)	*Oncorhynchus kisutch*	<0.1	0.8		<0.1		0.1	<0.1	<0.1
Pink salmon (j)	*Oncorhynchus gorbuscha*	<0.1	0.3		0.2		3.5	3	<0.1
Sockeye salmon (j)	*Oncorhynchus nerka*		0.1				0.1		<0.1
Inconnu	*Stenodus leucichthys*			31.8	7.1	0.1		<0.1	
Humpback whitefish	*Coregonus pidschian*			7.1	1.9	<0.1	0.0	4	<0.1
Round whitefish	*Prosopium cylindraceum*							4	<0.1
Least cisco	*Coregonus sardinella*			5.9	1.5	0.4	7.3	23	6
Arctic cisco	*Coregonus autumnalis*				<0.1				
Bering cisco	*Coregonus laurettae*			9.4	0.5	<0.1	11.8	2	<0.1
Broad whitefish	*Coregonus nasus*			2.4	0.2	<0.1		<0.1	
Unidentified whitefishes	*Coregoninae*		<0.1		53.2	4.9			
Northern pike	*Esox lucius*			2.4	0.2				
Rainbow smelt	*Osmerus mordax*	2.8	41.3	29.4[1]	8.2[1]	9.8[1]	6.2	12	1
Pond smelt	*Hypomesus olidus*	61.6	44.3		1.2				
Unidentified smelt	*Osmeridae*				4.2	28.6			
Ninespine stickleback	*Pungitius pungitius*	15.6	5.1		6.6	46.5	4	1	
Threespine stickleback	*Gasterosteus aculeatus*	5.8	0.3		<0.1		5.0	10	68
Pacific herring	*Clupea pallasii*	13.8	<0.1		0.6	2.0	0.2	<0.1	<0.1
Pacific sandlance	*Ammodytes hexapterus*		2.8			<0.1			
Saffron cod	*Eleginus gracilis*	<0.1			3.2	0.6	18.5	13	16
Burbot	*Lota lota*	<0.1		10.6	2.9	0.6		<0.1	<0.1
Arctic flounder	*Pleuronectes glacialis*	<0.1	<0.1		3.4	0.2	36.0	15	5
Starry flounder	*Platichthys stellatus*				1.1	<0.1	1.0	3	1
Arctic lamprey	*Lampetra camtschatica*	<0.1			0.1	1.2			
Fourhorn sculpin	*Myoxocephalus quadricornis*		0.1	1.2	0.3	<0.1	3.4	4	1

*rounded to full number.
[1] identified by Martin et al. (1986, 1987) as Boreal smelt *Osmerus eperlanus*

of Pacific herring *Clupea pallasii* and Pacific sand lance *Ammodytes hexapterus* occurred sporadically in large abundances. Juvenile salmonids were significantly less abundant (Table 2), never making up more than 5% of the total catch. In all AYK estuaries, chum salmon were the most abundant species of Pacific salmon, while sockeye salmon were the least abundant (Table 2).

Timing and Relative Abundance of Juvenile Salmon Out-Migration

Chum salmon.—In AYK estuaries, chum salmon catch ranged from <0.1% to 4.7% (Table 2). Patterns of peak out-migration of chum salmon in western Alaska also appear to be similar among different watersheds. Peak numbers of chum salmon in Kuskokwim Bay were caught in the middle of June in 2004 and in late June in 2003 (Table 1), the latter probably due to the late start of field work that year. Numbers of chum salmon smolts were substantially lower in late July ($N = 3$), and no chum salmon juveniles were caught in late August (Hillgruber et al. 2007). In the Yukon River delta, sampling in 1986 began in early June (Table 1) and chum salmon peak out-migration occurred on June 18, with numbers declining in July and August (Martin et al. 1987). In Safety Sound, peak out-migration differed with the sampling site: juvenile chum salmon catches peaked in mid-June at the head of Safety Sound, while at the outlet site between Safety Sound and Norton Sound, chum salmon out-migration was bimodal, with one group emigrating in June and a second one in mid to late July (Table 1; Nemeth et al. 2003, 2006).

Few data exist on the timing of estuarine residence of chum salmon in western Alaska, but based on results from other estuarine studies, a protracted duration of residence seems likely. For example, in southeastern Alaska, juvenile chum salmon were caught in the lit-

toral habitat of Taku Inlet from the middle of April until late June in 2004 and 2005 (Reese et al. in press). Similarly, in northern Cook Inlet in southcentral Alaska, juvenile chum salmon were caught in June and July (Moulton 1997). In the Yukon and Kuskokwim rivers, juvenile chum salmon probably begin their out-migration in early May prior to ice break-up. This predicted migration timing is supported by Martin et al. (1987), who used emergence timing of chum salmon fry in the upper tributaries to estimate timing of out-migration into the delta. In Kuskokwim Bay, first catches of chum salmon fry in 2004 were recorded on May 15 (Hillgruber et al. 2007); because this date was the first day of field sampling, juvenile chum salmon had likely entered the bay prior to this date. This observation was supported by results from the upper Yukon River, in 2002 to 2004, where chum salmon downstream migration was well underway at the onset of sampling in middle to late May, suggesting an even earlier peak (Bradford et al. 2008). The total duration of the chum salmon out-migration in AYK estuaries may be substantially drawn out over the summer period. Chum salmon juveniles residing in the Yukon River delta have been reported to be present as late as September 13 (Martin et al. 1986). In addition, chum salmon fry in the upper Yukon River tributaries were observed into late July (Bradford et al. 2008) and even August (Gissberg and Benning 1965), suggesting an estuarine arrival well into September. Because environmental conditions such as water temperature and prey availability change dramatically from May through September, it is likely that different cohorts (i.e., temporal groups of juvenile salmon) will experience large differences in estuarine rearing conditions. No information is available on origin, feeding success, growth rates, and survival probability of those juvenile chum salmon that emerge late in the season or rear longer in the upper tributaries and arrive in the estuaries in August and September.

Chinook, coho, pink, and sockeye salmon.—Chinook salmon migration into AYK estuaries appears to occur later in the season than that of chum salmon juveniles. In the Yukon River delta, Chinook salmon juveniles were the second most abundant salmon (Table 2) and were collected from early June until early August, with a peak catch per unit effort (CPUE) occurring in late June (Martin et al. 1987). In the upper Yukon River, downstream migration of Chinook salmon was also later than for chum salmon and differed between age-0 and age-1 juveniles (Bradford et al. 2008); age-0 catches peaked in late June, while age-1 fry downstream migration was in progress at the beginning of sampling in May. Similar observations were made in Kuskokwim Bay, where Chinook salmon represented the fourth most abundant salmon taxon after chum, coho, and pink salmon (Hillgruber et al. 2007). No juvenile Chinook salmon were caught before June, and peak catches were observed in the middle of June.

Coho salmon juveniles were rare in AYK estuaries, and never amounted to more than 0.8% of the catch (Table 2). In the Yukon River delta, only one specimen was collected on July 25, 1985 (Martin et al. 1986), and no coho salmon were caught in the summer of 1986 (Martin et al. 1987). In comparison, coho salmon were abundant in Kuskokwim Bay, where catches peaked in late May in 2004 and CPUE was substantially lower in June. Abundances of coho salmon juveniles were highest at the head of the bay, but estuarine distribution of coho salmon juveniles was widespread, with catches occurring even from the station furthest offshore (Hillgruber et al. 2007).

Sockeye salmon juveniles were only infrequently caught in Kuskokwim Bay, representing no more than 0.1% of the catch (Hillgruber et al. 2007). At the head of Kuskokwim Bay, sockeye salmon juveniles were only collected in May of 2004, with catches peaking at the end of May. Overall catches of sockeye salmon juveniles were very low in 2004 and no sockeye salmon were captured in 2003. The pattern of sockeye salmon distribution and migration appears to indicate only one migration cohort.

Pink salmon amounted to 3% of the total CPUE in 2003 in Safety Sound, but declined to 0% in 2004 (Nemeth et al. 2006). This pattern was consistent with the strong even-year run and weak odd-year pink salmon populations present in Norton Sound area streams. No data on seasonal patterns of out-migration of pink salmon juveniles were presented. Similarly, pink salmon were of low abundance in the Yukon River delta, amounting to only 0.2% of the catch in 1985 (Martin et al. 1986); no pink salmon were caught in 1986 (Martin et al. 1987). In Kuskokwim Bay, pink salmon juveniles represented the third most abundant juvenile salmon taxon in 2004 (Hillgruber et al. 2007). Pink salmon were collected from the middle of May until the middle of June, with peak catches at the end of May. Positive pink salmon catches were also documented for June and July in 2003; no pink salmon were collected in August (Hillgruber et al. 2007). Similar results were obtained from the Yukon River delta, where pink salmon catches peaked in the middle/end of June and declined rapidly thereafter (Martin et al. 1986); few fish were observed in July and no pink salmon were caught in August.

Size, Age, and Duration of Estuarine Residence of Juvenile Salmon

Chum salmon.—Chum salmon length frequency distributions during estuarine residence were similar in Safety Sound, Kuskokwim Bay, and the Yukon River delta (Table 1). Differences between the studies were likely the result of different sampling dates and study durations; for example, the broadest size frequency distribution for chum

TABLE 3. Study area, number of fish examined, capture date, post-emergence otolith increments, and back-calculated date of emergence for juvenile chum salmon collected in the Yukon River delta in June 19–30, 1985, and in Kuskokwim Bay in May 15–June 16, 2004.

Study area	N	Capture dates	Post-emergence age	Emergence dates
Yukon River Delta[1]	30	June 19–June 30	13–29	May 27–June 12
Kuskokwim Bay[2]	192	May 17–June 11	12–44	April 19–May 24

[1]Martin et al. 1986; [2]Hillgruber et al. 2007

salmon juveniles was observed in the Yukon River delta, where sampling began in early June and lasted until September.

Fork length distributions of chum salmon were consistent with a continuing influx of small fry into the estuaries. For example, chum salmon in the 45 mm length class were caught as late as July 16 in Safety Sound (Nemeth et al. 2006). Based on size and catch date, the authors identified four distinct groupings of chum salmon migrating into Safety Sound in 2003 and 2004. In the upper Yukon River, chum salmon juveniles also displayed differences in fork length during the period of downstream migration, i.e., a decrease in mean size of 3 mm FL from May to July (Bradford et al. 2008).

To determine age in days of juvenile chum salmon, Martin et al. (1986) counted the number of otolith increments from the assumed point of emergence to the edge. The emergence check was defined at the point of transition from dark and irregularly spaced to more weakly expressed and regularly spaced increments. Martin et al. (1986) identified this transition point as the hatch check. The small number of increments, however, makes it more likely that this structure corresponds to the emergence from the gravel rather than the hatching of chum salmon eggs, which occurs in fall or winter (J. Finn, U.S. Geological Survey, personal communication). For the purpose of this review, the results will be interpreted from the microstructure analysis as post-emergence increments. The post-emergence age of Yukon River delta chum salmon ranged from 11 to 59 d for fish in the size range of 33–68 mm FL; in Kuskokwim Bay, the age ranged from 12 to 44 d post-emergence for fish in the size range from 45 to 51 mm FL (Table 3). In the Yukon River delta, the number of post-emergence increments was correlated with the fork length of chum salmon ($r^2 = 0.65$, $n = 197$, $P < 0.001$; Martin et al. 1986). The relationship between otolith increments and fork lengths was weaker for fish from Kuskokwim Bay, but was still statistically significant ($r^2 = 0.31$, $n = 192$, $P < 0.001$; Hillgruber et al. 2007).

Only limited information was available on estuarine residence of chum salmon juveniles in western Alaska. In the Yukon River delta, otoliths of 339 chum salmon juveniles in the 33.0–68.4 mm FL size range were examined to determine age and duration of estuarine residence (Martin et al. 1987). Estuarine residence was expected to be recognizable by increased otolith increment width as a result of increased growth rates typically experienced by juvenile salmonids in near-shore waters, but no transition zone in increment width could be identified for Yukon River chum salmon. As a result, duration of estuarine residence could not be estimated (Martin et al. 1987). In Kuskokwim Bay, otolith strontium-to-calcium ratios (Sr/Ca), which are correlated with salinity (Zimmerman 2005), were used as a means of identifying the point of saltwater entry (Hillgruber et al. 2007); preliminary results based on eight otoliths indicate an estuarine residence duration ranging from 8 to 18 d for juvenile chum salmon. Because these fish were captured in the bay, these estimates were minimums and do not represent the total time spent in Kuskokwim Bay.

Chinook, coho, pink, and sockeye salmon.—In the estuarine waters of the Yukon River delta, juvenile Chinook salmon ranged in size from 69 to 128 mm FL with a mean of 96.4 mm FL in 1986 (Martin et al. 1987). Outmigrating Chinook salmon had a bimodal size distribution with the minimum value between the modes located at 102 mm FL. Geographic differences in the size distribution of Chinook salmon size classes were apparent, with fish <102 mm FL more predominant on southerly stations and fish >102 mm FL predominating on northerly stations (Martin et al. 1987). In Kuskokwim Bay, Chinook salmon size distribution ranged from 73 to 113 mm FL with a mean length of 87.1 mm FL. The majority of the fish had a size <100 mm FL, with only 9 fish >100 mm FL. For the Kuskokwim River, based on ages of returning adult Chinook salmon, age-1 (i.e., one winter in freshwater) smolts were dominant but some freshwater age-2 fish were encountered (Molyneaux et al. 2006). Juvenile Chinook salmon from the Yukon River delta or Kuskokwim Bay reached a fork length that in other studies was attributed to a freshwater age-2 (Moulton 1997). These results were in agreement with the observation that these stream-type Chinook salmon were predicted to predominate in populations north of 56°N latitude, with smolt age-2 and age-3 becoming more abundant with increasing latitude and distance from the sea (Taylor 1990). No data concerning age or growth and duration of nearshore residence of coho, pink, or sockeye salmon juveniles in western Alaska were available.

Juvenile Feeding Success, Prey Composition, and Selection

Chum salmon.—In June–September 1985, a total of 82 stomachs from chum salmon caught in the Yukon River delta were examined for diet composition; of these, 69 (84.1%) contained prey items (Martin et al. 1986). In Safety Sound, chum salmon (*n* = 178) feeding incidence (% stomachs containing food) was higher than that observed in the Yukon River delta, ranging from 94.5% in 2002 (Nemeth et al. 2003), to 86.8% in 2003 and to 96.2% in 2004 (Nemeth et al. 2006). Feeding incidence in Kuskokwim Bay also varied among sampling years, with 51% in 2003 and 81% in 2004 (Burril 2007). While the low feeding incidence in 2003 is notable, the result could be due to sampling occurring late in the season (Hillgruber et al. 2007). Nonetheless, juvenile chum salmon in estuaries in western Alaska showed feeding incidences lower than those observed at lower latitudes, e.g., from northern Cook Inlet (98.2%; Moulton 1997) and from Hecate Strait, British Columbia (96.8–100%; Healey 1991).

In Kuskokwim Bay, small calanoid copepods (<2.5 mm), harpacticoid copepods, and adult, winged insects were the primary prey items for juvenile chum salmon. Calanoids and insects combined made up >50% of all prey items by number and >80% of the overall prey biomass (Burril 2007). Prey composition changed with size of smolt, with small smolts relying mostly on insects, while large smolts predominantly fed on calanoid copepods. These results are somewhat different from dietary composition of chum salmon from the Yukon River delta (Martin et al. 1986); diet of chum salmon collected from June to September 1985 contained predominantly insects (Chironomidae: Diptera), most of which were winged adults that were probably consumed on the water surface. In

Safety Sound, the diet of chum salmon varied among years, with a dominance of insects and crustaceans (i.e., mysids) in 2002 and 2003, while chironomid larvae and crustaceans were dominant in 2004 (Nemeth et al. 2006). In addition, the dominant marine crustacean was primarily mysids in 2002, and primarily copepods in 2003. These results on early dietary composition of migrating chum salmon smolts are in agreement with other studies on the early diet of these fish; e.g., prey composition of juvenile chum salmon in Prince William Sound in southcentral Alaska was also dominated by harpacticoid copepods and terrestrial insects (Parker and Massa 1993). Similarly, in Cook Inlet insects were also predominant prey items of early juvenile chum salmon (Moulton 1997). With increasing size and transition from near-shore to more offshore and neritic waters, chum salmon also transition from a diet dominated by epibenthic and terrestrial prey to more planktonic feeding patterns (Pearce et al. 1982; Duffy 2003).

In general, the high proportion of drift insects in the diet of chum salmon during estuarine residence makes an estimate of prey selection difficult, because plankton sampling devices likely under-sample these taxa. In Safety Sound, chum salmon were estimated to consume crustaceans at a ratio similar to their occurrence in the water column (Nemeth et al. 2006). These results differed from dietary patterns of chum salmon in Kuskokwim Bay, where chum salmon were apparently selecting small calanoid copepods (Burril 2007).

Chinook, coho, pink, and sockeye salmon.—Data concerning the diet of other juvenile salmon in the AYK region are few or do not exist. Limited data concerning the diet of Chinook salmon in estuaries of the AYK region exist. In Kuskokwim Bay, the diet of juvenile Chinook salmon was dominated by euphausids, mysids, and amphiphods (Hillgruber, unpublished data). Adult insects, pre-

dominantly dipterans, were also an important part of their diet. These food items were comparable to the diet of juvenile Chinook salmon observed in Cook Inlet, Alaska, which contained notable numbers of insects, particularly later in the season (Moulton 1997). Elsewhere, Chinook salmon juveniles preyed on a wide variety of resources including insects, amphipods, crab larvae, and plankton (Duffy 2003). In Puget Sound, Washington, Chinook salmon shifted to a diet of fishes at a fork length of approximately 150 mm (Duffy 2003). Chinook salmon of that size were not observed in any of the estuarine studies conducted in western Alaska.

In the Yukon River delta, the small sample size ($N = 4$) allowed for only a cursory description of the coho salmon diet; coho salmon juveniles examined had fed on an isopod *Saduria enotmon*, other juvenile salmon, and inorganic debris (Martin et al. 1986). No other data on coho salmon diet in AYK estuaries were available. However, coho salmon in Cook Inlet, Alaska, demonstrated large seasonal variations in prey composition, with insects, calanoid copepods, and fish making up the diet in June, while in July, the diet of five coho salmon was dominated (%N = 96.9%) by insects alone (Moulton 1997).

In the Yukon River delta, pink salmon diet was dominated by chironomid adults and benthic larvae (Martin et al. 1986). In addition, planktonic calanoid and cyclopoid copepods were a frequent but less important component of their diet. No data on the diet of pink salmon were available for any of the other watersheds of western Alaska. Observations from the Yukon River delta were not in agreement with pink salmon diets reported from other areas; for example, pink salmon in the estuary of Porcupine Creek in southeast Alaska fed predominantly on pelagic prey, namely on mollusk larvae, calanoid copepods, and fish larvae (Murphy et al. 1988).

No information on the diet of sockeye salmon smolts was available from the AYK region estuaries; however, juvenile sockeye salmon diet in Bristol Bay was examined by Carlson (1976). Insects were common in the stomachs of sockeye salmon smolts early in the migration (June) and near to freshwater sources. Carlson (1976) presumed that insects were consumed in freshwater and these fish were recent migrants to saltwater. As the season progressed and samples were collected further from freshwater sources, copepods dominated in the diet.

Juvenile Energy Density and Condition

Chum salmon.—Juvenile salmon condition can be estimated by measuring the fish's energy density. Energy density is defined as calories per gram and typically measured using bomb calorimetry. An increase in energy density indicates an increase in lipid storage. In juvenile salmon, the energy density tends to increase with increasing fish size (Trudel et al. 2005), and may vary seasonally or as the result of physiological changes such as smoltification or reproduction (Anthony et al. 2000). In the AYK region, the only data available on the energy density of salmon smolts in estuarine waters were measurements from Kuskokwim Bay (Burril 2007). Chum salmon energy density per gram dry weight significantly decreased with increasing size suggesting that juvenile chum salmon were allocating the majority of their energy to protein synthesis, i.e., growth, and smolting rather than to lipid storage. In addition, energy density decreased with season for fish of any given size-class (Burril 2007), probably as a result of increasing water temperatures and energy demands that were apparently not balanced by an increasing food supply.

Chinook, coho, pink, and sockeye salmon.—No data on energy density and condition of juvenile Chinook, coho, pink, or

sockeye salmon for their estuarine residence in western Alaska were available for this review.

Conclusions

The early marine life stage of Pacific salmon represents a critical period that has been little studied in western Alaskan estuarine systems to date. This review identified several gaps in the understanding of the estuarine ecology of juvenile salmon in western Alaska (Table 4). While some data were available for species such as chum or Chinook salmon, other species were nearly completely neglected. In addition, data on out-migration patterns and residence timing and duration, and rearing conditions and their effect on diet, growth, and survival were often completely lacking or available only for selected years and sites. To answer the many questions related to this important life stage, and to evaluate and predict the potential effects of environmental change, long-term data collection is necessary (Moss et al. 2009).

In our experience, the acquisition of these data through field work in remote western Alaska estuaries is logistically very challenging. Estuaries, such as Kuskokwim Bay are shallow and poorly charted. Shallow-draft vessels capable of towing nets are required to sample juvenile salmon and are not typically available. Fuel, water, and other supplies are expensive and difficult to acquire or transport. Consequently, before launching full-scale field work in these remote sites, pilot studies should be conducted to survey sampling sites and address these and other logistical challenges.

Most of the data available to date were on chum salmon, and were mostly lacking for all other species of salmon. Future studies concerning juvenile salmon in western Alaska estuaries should focus on all species to better describe trophic connections. Of the four coho

TABLE 4. Summary of available data on estuarine rearing conditions and life history parameters of juvenile Pacific salmon in three main watersheds (Kuskokwim Bay, Yukon River delta, Safety Sound) in western Alaska (*indicates that no data are available).

Gaps	Kuskokwim Bay	Yukon River Delta	Safety Sound
Estuarine rearing conditions	5	4	1, 2
Estuarine fish community	5	3, 4	1, 2
Timing of outmigration	A, B, C, D, E[5]	A, B[3,4]	A[1,2]
Estuarine distribution	A, B, C, D, E[5]	A, B[3,4]	*
Estuarine residence	*	*	*
Estuarine prey availability:			
A) Pelagic	5	1, 2	*
B) Epibenthic	*	1	*
C) Neustonic	*	*	*
Estuarine feeding patterns	A[5]	A[3,4]	A[3]
Estuarine diet composition	A[5]	A[3,4]	A[3]
Juvenile condition	A, C[5]	*	*
Estuarine growth	*	A[3,4]	A[1,2]
Juvenile age	A[5]	A[3,4]	*
Estuarine mortality	*	*	*

[1]Nemeth et al. 2003, [2]Nemeth et al. 2006, [3]Martin et al. 1986, [4]Martin et al. 1987, [5]Hillgruber et al. 2007

A: Chum salmon *O. keta*, B: Chinook salmon *O. tshawytscha*, C: Coho salmon *O. kisutch*, D: Pink salmon *O. gorbuscha*, E: Sockeye salmon *O. nerka*

salmon from the Yukon River delta examined for their diet, one was feeding exclusively on unidentified juvenile salmon (Martin et al. 1986). Thus, coho salmon might be an important source of mortality for smaller outmigrating smolts in AYK estuaries. In addition, juvenile salmon other than chum salmon and other estuarine fishes may be important competitors for estuarine habitat and prey. Nemeth et al. (2006) noted a substantial change in the fish catch composition from 2002 and 2003 to 2004, which was demonstrated by a more than 25-fold increase in threespine stickleback *Gasterosteus aculeatus* catches. They suggested that this increase might have resulted in increased competition or even predation pressure for juvenile chum salmon. These findings suggest that future studies focusing on the entire fish community and all prey species are needed to better understand important interconnections that may play an essential role in the population dynamics of juvenile salmon.

No long-term research effort directed at the estuarine residence of juvenile salmonids has occurred in western Alaska. Instead, the only data from the AYK region on this important life stage were derived from a few disjointed studies from different years, different watersheds, and with different sampling regimes. The data currently available were not sufficient to examine interannual differences of the ecology of salmon smolts from western Alaska. Numerous research platforms exist throughout the AYK region to count adult salmon, such as weirs and counting towers, but to date only few studies have attempted to quantify or describe the characteristics of juvenile salmon as they migrate downstream. If we are to better understand the population dynamics of salmon in western Alaska, more effort is needed to determine survival rates of salmon between emergence and saltwater entry because the mortality at this life stage may be a primary determinant of year-class adult abundance.

The Arctic-Yukon-Kuskokwim Sustainable Salmon Initiative has a goal to "..understand the trends and causes of variation in salmon abundance…"; (AYK SSI 2006). To achieve this goal, significantly more work will be needed to determine the processes that control juvenile Pacific salmon survival in freshwater and estuarine habitats of western Alaska.

Acknowledgments

We thank Sean E. Burril and Carl D. Reese for their contributions to our work on Kuskokwim Bay. We thank the organizers of the AYK SSI symposium for inviting our presentation and this manuscript.

References

Adkison, M. D., and B. P. Finney. 2003. The long-term outlook for salmon returns to Alaska. Alaska Fishery Research Bulletin 10(2):83–94.

Anthony, J. A., D. D. Roby, and K. R. Turco. 2000. Lipid content and energy density of forage fishes from the northern Gulf of Alaska. Journal of Experimental Marine Biology and Ecology 248:53–78.

AYK SSI (Arctic-Yukon-Kuskokwim Sustainable Salmon Initiative). 2006. Arctic-Yukon-Kuskokwim salmon research and restoration plan. Available from Bering Sea Fishermen's Association, Anchorage, Alaska.

Bax, N. J. 1983. Early marine mortality of marked juvenile chum salmon (Oncorhynchus keta) released into Hood Canal, Puget Sound, Washington, in 1980. Canadian Journal of Fisheries and Aquatic Sciences 40:426–435.

Beamish, R. J., and C. Mahnken. 2001. A critical size and period hypothesis to explain natural regulation of salmon abundance and the linkage to climate and climate change. Progress in Oceanography 49:423–437.

Bradford, M. J., J. Duncan, and J. W. Jang. 2008. Downstream migration of juvenile salmon and other fishes in the upper Yukon River. Arctic 61:255–264.

Bue, F. J., B. M. Borba, R. Cannon, and C. C. Krueger. 2009. Yukon River fall chum salmon fisheries: management, harvest, and stock abundance. Pages 703–742 in C. C. Krueger and C. E. Zimmerman, editors. Pacific salmon: ecology and management of western Alaska's populations. American Fisheries Society, Symposium 70, Bethesda, Maryland.

Burril, S. E. 2007. Feeding ecology and energy density of juvenile chum salmon, Oncorhynchus keta, from Kuskokwim Bay, western Alaska. Master's thesis. University of Alaska Fairbanks, Fairbanks, Alaska.

Carlson, H. R. 1976. Food of juvenile sockeye salmon, Oncorhynchus nerka, in the inshore coastal waters of Bristol Bay, Alaska, 1966–67. Fishery Bulletin 74:458–462.

Duffy, J. 2003. Early marine distribution and trophic interactions of juvenile salmon in Puget Sound. Master's thesis. University of Washington, Seattle.

Evenson, D. F., S. J. Hayes, G. Sandone, and D. J. Bergstrom. 2009. Yukon River Chinook salmon: stock status, harvest, and management. Pages 675–701 in C. C. Krueger and C. E. Zimmerman, editors. Pacific salmon: ecology and management of western Alaska's populations. American Fisheries Society, Symposium 70, Bethesda, Maryland.

Fukuwaka, M., and T. Suzuki. 2002. Early sea mortality of mark-recaptured juvenile chum salmon in open coastal waters. Journal of Fish Biology 60:3–12.

Gissberg, J. G., and D. S. Benning. 1965. Yukon foundation studies summary report, 1965. U.S. Department of the Interior, U.S. Fish and Wildlife Service, Anchorage, Alaska.

Healey, M. C. 1982a. Juvenile Pacific salmon in estuaries: the life support system. Pages 343–364 in V. S. Kennedy, editor. Estuarine comparisons. Academic Press, New York.

Healey, M. C. 1982b. Timing and relative intensity of size-selective mortality of juvenile chum salmon (Oncorhynchus keta) during early sea life. Canadian Journal of Fisheries and Aquatic Sciences 39:952–957.

Healey, M. C. 1991. Diets and feeding rates of juvenile pink, chum, and sockeye salmon in Hecate Strait, British Columbia. Transactions of the American Fisheries Society 120:303–318.

Hillgruber, N., C. E. Zimmerman, S. E. Burril, and L. J. Haldorson. 2007. Early marine ecology of juvenile chum salmon (Oncorhynchus keta) in Kuskokwim Bay, Alaska. Project R0327, Final Report, North Pacific Research Board, Anchorage, Alaska.

Houde, E. D. 1989. Comparative growth, mortality, and energetics of marine fish larvae: temperature and implied latitudinal effects. Fishery Bulletin 87:471–495.

Linderman, J. C., Jr., and D. J. Bergstrom. 2009. Kuskokwim management area: salmon escapement, harvest, and management. Pages 541–599 in C. C. Krueger and C. E. Zimmerman, editors. Pacific salmon: ecology and management of western Alaska's populations. American Fisheries Society, Symposium 70, Bethesda, Maryland.

Martin D. J., D. R. Glass, C. J. Whitmus, C. A. Simenstad, D. A. Milward, E. C. Volk, M. L. Stevenson, P. Nunes, M. Savoie, and R. A. Grotenfendt. 1986. Distribution, seasonal abundance, and feeding dependencies of juvenile salmon and non-salmonid fishes in the Yukon River Delta. NOAA OCSEAP Final Report 55:381–770.

Martin, D. J., C. J. Whitmus, L. E. Hachmeister, E. C. Volk, and S. L. Schroder. 1987. Distribution and seasonal abundance of juvenile salmon and other fishes in the Yukon Delta. NOAA OCSEAP Final Report 66:123–277.

Mason, J. C. 1974. Behavioral ecology of chum salmon fry (Oncorhynchus keta) in a small estuary. Journal of the Fisheries Research Board of Canada 31:83–92.

Menard, J., C. C. Krueger, and J. R. Hilsinger. 2009. Norton Sound salmon fisheries: history, stock abundance, and management. Pages 621–673 in C. C. Krueger and C. E. Zimmerman, editors. Pacific salmon: ecology and management of western Alaska's populations. American Fisheries Society, Symposium 70, Bethesda, Maryland.

Merritt, M. F., and J. A. Raymond. 1983. Early life history of chum salmon in the Noatak River and Kotzebue Sound. Alaska Department of Fish and Game; Division of Fisheries Rehabilitation, Enhancement, and Development Report #1. Juneau, Alaska.

Molyneaux, D. B., D. L. Folletti, and C. A. Shelden. 2006. Salmon age, sex, and length catalog for the Kuskokwim area, 2005. Alaska Department of Fish and Game, Division of Commercial Fisheries, Regional Information Report N. 3A06–01, Anchorage, Alaska.

Moss, J. H., D. A. Beauchamp, A. D. Cross, K. Myers, E. V. Farley, Jr., J. M. Murphy, and J. H. Helle. 2005. Higher marine survival associated with faster growth for pink salmon (Oncorhynchus gorbuscha). Transactions of the American Fisheries Society 134:1313–1322.

Moss, J. H., N. Hillgruber, C. Lean, J. Mackenzie-Grieve, K. Mull, K. W. Myers, and T. C. Stark. 2009. Conservation of western Alaska salmon stocks by identifying critical linkages between marine and freshwater life stages and long-term monitoring. Pages 1115–1125 in C. C. Krueger

and C. E. Zimmerman, editors. Pacific salmon: ecology and management of western Alaska's populations. American Fisheries Society, Symposium 70, Bethesda, Maryland.

Moulton, L. L. 1997. Early marine residence, growth, and feeding by juvenile salmon in northern Cook Inlet, Alaska. Alaska Fishery Research Bulletin 4(2):154–177.

Murphy, M. L., J. F. Thedinga, and K. V. Koski. 1988. Size and diet of juvenile Pacific salmon during seaward migration through a small estuary in southeastern Alaska. Fishery Bulletin 86:213–222.

Nemeth, M. J., B. Haley, S. Kinneen, and W. Griffiths. 2003. Ecology of juvenile chum salmon from Norton Sound, Alaska. Annual Report to the Norton Sound Disaster Relief Fund by the Norton Sound Economic Development Corporation and LGL Alaska Research Associates, Inc. Anchorage, Alaska.

Nemeth, M. J., B. Williams, B. Haley, and S. Kinneen. 2006. An ecological comparison of juvenile chum salmon from two watersheds in Norton Sound, Alaska: migration, diet estuarine habitat, and fish community assemblage. Final Report for 2003 and 2004 to the Norton Sound Disaster Relief Fund by the Norton Sound Economic Development Corporation and LGL Alaska Research Associates, Inc. Anchorage, Alaska.

NRC (National Research Council). 2005. Developing a research and restoration plan for Arctic-Yukon-Kuskokwim (western Alaska) salmon. National Academies Press, Washington, D.C.

Parker, R. 1971. Size selective predation among juvenile salmonid fishes in a British Columbia inlet. Journal of the Fisheries Research Board of Canada 28:1503–1510.

Parker, D., and J. Massa. 1993. A comparison of diets and apparent growth rates for juvenile pink and chum salmon collected in Prince William Sound, Alaska. Proceedings of the 16th Pink and Chum Salmon Workshop, Juneau, Alaska.

Pearce T. A., J. H. Meyer, and R. S. Boomer. 1982. Distribution and food habits of juvenile salmon in the Nisqually estuary. Washington, 1979–1980. U.S. Fish and Wildlife Service, Olympia, Washington.

Raymond, J. A., M. Merritt, and C. Skaugstad. 1984. Nearshore fishes of Kotzebue Sound in summer. Alaska Department of Fish and Game, Division of Fisheries Rehabilitation, Enhancement, and Development Report 37, Juneau, Alaska.

Reese, C., N. Hillgruber, M. Sturdevant, A. Wertheimer, W. Smoker, and R. Focht. In press. Spatial and temporal distribution and the potential for estuarine interactions between wild and hatchery chum salmon (Oncorhynchus keta) in Taku Inlet, Alaska. Fishery Bulletin.

Richter, A., and S. A. Kolmes. 2005. Maximum temperature limits for Chinook, coho, and chum salmon, and steelhead trout in the Pacific Northwest. Reviews in Fisheries Science 13:23–49.

Salo, E. O. 1991. Life history of chum salmon. Pages 231–310 *in* C. Groot, and L. Margolis, editors. Pacific salmon: life histories. UBC Press, Vancouver, British Columbia.

Simenstad, C. A., and E. O. Salo. 1980. Foraging success as a determination of estuarine and nearshore carrying capacity of juvenile chum salmon (*Oncorhynchus keta*) in Hood Canal. Pages 21–37 *in* B. R. Melteff, and R. A. Neve, editors. Proceeding of the North Pacific Aquaculture Symposium, Alaska Sea Grant, Anchorage, Alaska.

Simenstad, C. A., and R. C. Wissmar. 1984. Variability in estuarine food webs and production supporting juvenile Pacific salmon (*Oncorhynchus*). Pages 273–286 *in* W. G. Pearcy, editor. Workshop on influence of ocean conditions on the production of salmonids. Marine Science Center, Newport, Oregon.

Simenstad, C. A., K. L. Fresh, and E. O. Salo. 1982. The role of Puget Sound and Washington coastal estuaries in the life history of Pacific salmon: an unappreciated function. Pages 343–364 *in* V. S. Kennedy, editor. Estuarine comparisons. Academic Press, New York.

Spencer, P. D. 2008. Density-independent and density-dependent factors affecting temporal changes in spatial distributions of eastern Bering Sea flatfishes. Fisheries Oceanography 17(5):396–410.

Stabeno, P. J., N. A. Bond, and S. A. Salo. 2007. On the recent warming trend of the southeastern Bering Sea. Deep-Sea Research II 54:2599–2618.

Taylor, E. B. 1990. Environmental correlates of life-history variation in juvenile Chinook salmon, *Oncorhynchus tshawytscha* (Walbaum). Journal of Fish Biology 37:1–17.

Thorpe, J. E. 1994. Salmonid fishes and the estuarine environment. Estuaries 17(1A):76–93.

Trudel, M., S. Tucker, J. F. T. Morris, D. A. Higgs, and D. W. Welch. 2005. Indicators of energetic status in juvenile coho salmon and Chinook salmon. North American Journal of Fisheries Management 25:374–390.

Wertheimer, A. C., and F. P. Thrower. 2007. Mortality rates of chum salmon during their early marine residency. Mortality rates of chum salmon during their initial marine residency. Pages 233–247 *in* C. B. Grimes, R. D. Brodeur, L. J. Haldorson, and S. M. McKinnell, editors. The ecology of juvenile salmon in the northeast Pacific Ocean: regional comparisons. American Fisheries Society, Symposium 57, Bethesda, Maryland.

Wissmar, R. C., and C. A. Simenstad. 1988. Energetic constraints of juvenile chum salmon (*Oncorhynchus keta*) migrating in estuaries. Canadian Journal of Fisheries and Aquatic Sciences 45:1555–1560.

Zimmerman, C. E. 2005. Relationship of otolith strontium-to-calcium ratios and salinity: experimental validation for juvenile salmonids. Canadian Journal of Fisheries and Aquatic Sciences 62:88–97.

American Fisheries Society Symposium 70:201–239, 2009

High Seas Distribution, Biology, and Ecology of Arctic-Yukon-Kuskokwim Salmon: Direct Information from High Seas Tagging Experiments, 1954–2006

KATHERINE W. MYERS,* ROBERT V. WALKER, NANCY D. DAVIS,
AND JANET L. ARMSTRONG

*High Seas Salmon Research Program, School of Aquatic & Fishery Sciences
University of Washington, Box 355020, Seattle, Washington 98195, USA*

MASAHIDE KAERIYAMA

*Graduate School of Fisheries Science, Hokkaido University
3-1-1 Minatocho, Hakodate, Hokkaido 041-8611, Japan*

Abstract.—Data from high seas tagging experiments (external tags, coded-wire tags, electronic data storage tags) provide the only direct information on the distribution, biology, and ecology of immature and maturing Arctic-Yukon-Kuskokwim (AYK) salmon (*Oncorhynchus* spp.) migrating in the North Pacific Ocean and Bering Sea. Variation in the spatial and temporal distribution of tagging effort largely reflects changes in international salmon treaty research priorities over the past 52 years (1954–2006). Results of tagging studies indicate that in spring maturing AYK pink *O. gorbuscha* and coho *O. kisutch* salmon and immature and maturing AYK sockeye *O. nerka* and chum *O. keta* salmon are distributed primarily in the northeastern North Pacific Ocean and Gulf of Alaska, and in summer their distribution shifts to the west in the Gulf of Alaska and to the north and west in the Bering Sea. Immature and maturing AYK Chinook salmon *O. tshawytscha* are distributed in the eastern Bering Sea in winter, and immature Chinook salmon are distributed in the central and western Bering Sea in summer. Depth data from electronic tags indicated that Chinook and chum salmon have the deepest vertical distributions among the salmon species. Swimming depths might remain relatively constant across water masses and ocean areas. Bioenergetic simulations indicated that AYK salmon experiencing increased mean summer temperatures in the Bering Sea could suffer reduced growth at all age-maturity stages unless prey availability or prey energy density increased commensurately. Published conceptual models of the high seas distribution and migration patterns of AYK salmon need to be updated with new information from tagging, scale pattern, and genetic studies. New dynamic models would be useful for predicting climate-induced changes in carrying capacity, growth and survival, exploitation by marine fisheries, and timing of adult returns to the AYK region.

---

*Corresponding author: kwmyers@u.washington.edu

Introduction

An issue of concern to Artic-Yukon-Kuskokwim (AYK) salmon fishermen and managers is whether climate-induced changes in ocean conditions or ocean fisheries are contributing to unexpected fluctuations in the abundance of adult Pacific salmon (*Oncorhynchus* spp.) returns to the AYK region (AYK SSI 2006; Mantua 2009, this volume). Climate might affect the marine survival of AYK salmon directly (e.g., lethal sea temperatures) or indirectly by altering their distribution, migration patterns, growth, and trophic interactions. Similarly, fishing might affect salmon survival directly through harvest or indirectly through injury, stress, delayed mortality, and selection changes in growth and run timing (Hard et al. 2009, this volume). Climate and fishing effects might also work in concert to reduce salmon survival. For example, climate-induced ontogenetic effects on population structure and trophic dynamics might be modified through size-selective removals of fish by marine fisheries. If ocean distribution, migration patterns, and trophic interactions of AYK salmon vary by life history stage, then a single climatic or fishery event might have varied effects on different cohorts of salmon from the same population. To better understand how climate and fishing affect the marine survival of salmon, we first need to know when and where they migrate in the ocean. Farley et al. (2009, this volume) provided new information on the distribution, biology, and ecology of juvenile AYK salmon during their first summer and fall at sea. This paper focuses on reviewing information on the distribution, biology, and ecology of older (immature and maturing) marine life history stages of AYK salmon during their extensive high seas feeding migrations.

A number of variables, separately or in combination, have been proposed as causes for the declines of salmon runs in western Alaska during the late 1990s (AYK SSI 2006).

A leading hypothesis is that climate negatively affected the ocean survival of salmon through changes in benthic and pelagic food webs (Kruse 1998). For example, changes in marine nutrients, primary production (cocolithophore blooms), and energy transfer through eastern Bering Sea food webs in 1997–1998 might have resulted in poor feeding conditions that reduced the early ocean growth and survival of juvenile salmon. Late runs and smaller than average body sizes of adult salmon returning to western Alaska in 1997–1998 indicated that immature or maturing salmon were also affected by unusual ocean conditions during their extensive offshore feeding migrations. In addition, high ocean temperatures along coastal migration corridors in the eastern Bering Sea in 1997 or other factors (increased parasitism, predation, competition, and disease) might have caused high mortalities of returning adult salmon.

Although adult returns of many AYK salmon populations have improved since the late 1990s, it is assumed that similar or even more dramatic fluctuations in AYK salmon runs will occur in the near future because of climate change. For example, ongoing transformations in salmon habitats in the Bering Sea ecosystem, including thinning of sea ice and northward movement of subarctic species into the arctic, are associated with global climate change (e.g., Hunt et al. 2002; Overland and Stabeno 2004; Grebmeier et al. 2006). Recent stock identification studies indicate that distribution and abundance of AYK salmon in the northwestern Bering Sea is more extensive than previously known (e.g., Bugaev 2005; Habicht et al. 2005). The cumulative effects of climate change might shift the ocean feeding and overwintering grounds of AYK salmon farther to the north and west into the 200-mi zones (Exclusive Economic Zones, EEZ) of other nations (Russia and Japan). This shift could increase competitive trophic interactions with Asian salmon stocks and alter the risk of interceptions by commercial fisheries in the Russian or U.S. EEZs, e.g., the False Pass salmon fishery (Area M, South Alaska Peninsula; Seeb et al. 2004) or groundfish fisheries in the Bering Sea (e.g., Myers and Rogers 1988; Patton et al. 1998; Wilmot et al. 1998). This underscores the need to improve our ability to predict the effects of climate change and fishing on AYK salmon survival through an improved understanding of the distribution, biology, and ecology of AYK salmon in the ocean.

Numerous studies have contributed to our general knowledge of ocean distribution, biology, and ecology of salmon migrating in the North Pacific Ocean and Bering Sea (e.g., see ocean life history reviews by Burgner 1991; Healey 1991; Heard 1991; Salo 1991; Sandercock 1991). High seas (international waters) research on immature and maturing salmon by the United States, Canada, and Japan began in the mid-1950s, and was coordinated through the cooperative research program of the International North Pacific Fisheries Commission (INPFC). Early INPFC research focused on determining the range limits and migration routes of the different species and stocks of Pacific salmon (Jackson and Royce 1986). Much of the historical INPFC research occurred in the times and areas of operation of the Asian high seas driftnet fisheries for salmon and squid. Salmon distribution and abundance data were collected with a variety of different types of fishing gear (e.g., purse seines, gillnets, longlines). High seas salmon research has continued since 1992 under the auspices of the North Pacific Anadromous Fish Commission (NPAFC).

Accurate methods are needed to identify the natal region or population of origin of salmon in mixed-stock high seas catches. Successful methods have included artificial tags (disk, coded wire), scale pattern analysis, thermal marks on otoliths, natural tags (parasites, otolith trace-elements), and genetics (e.g., Myers et al. 2004). Among these techniques, genetics is now the method of choice. Recent advances in genetic techniques have increased our knowledge of salmon population structure in the Bering Sea. A comprehensive genetic (allozyme) baseline has been developed for chum salmon *O. keta* (Seeb et al. 2004; Beacham et al. 2009, this volume), and new research is contributing to further development and application of comprehensive DNA baselines to stock identification questions about salmon migrating in the high seas (e.g., Seeb et al. 2007).

At present, genetic methods cannot directly identify the population of origin of individual fish caught on the high seas. Genetic methods are "indirect" in that they require the use of statistical procedures to estimate the proportions of baseline populations in mixed-stock samples collected at sea. For most natural populations of Pacific Rim salmon, the historical high seas tagging database (1954–present) is the only direct information available on ocean ranges, seasonal migration patterns, overlaps in distribution, and individual migration and growth rates. Information from high seas tagging is used to validate the results of indirect methods of stock identification. High seas tagging experiments have been designed and implemented primarily through the cooperative research efforts of the INPFC (1955–1992) and the NPAFC (1993–present). Information from high seas tagging experiments have also been used to develop or validate models of the ocean distribution and migration patterns of all major regional stocks of Pacific salmon.

The behaviors and habitats of salmon on the high seas are poorly known. Until recently, the ocean temperatures and depths where salmon swim and the routes of their migrations could only be inferred from fishing, oceanographic sampling, and stock identification studies. Since 1998, high seas salmon researchers have collaborated in the deployment of data storage tags (DSTs) that measure water temperature or water temperature and depth for international cooperative high seas programs. These new tagging technologies have enabled the acquisition of precise detailed data from individual fish as they migrate, and data from a few recoveries have already yielded a wealth of information (Walker et al. 2007).

Increasing evidence shows that the food supply for salmon are limited during their offshore migrations in the North Pacific Ocean and Bering Sea (e.g., Rogers 1980; Rogers and Ruggerone 1993; Aydin 2000; Aydin et al. 2000, 2005; Kaeriyama et al. 2000, 2004; Ruggerone et al. 2003). Since the mid 1970s, an increasing trend has occurred in the commercial catches of Asian and North American salmon. This trend is correlated with climate change (e.g., Beamish and Bouillion 1993), as well as an increase in the production of hatchery salmon and a decrease in the body size of adult salmon returning to both continents, indicating a limit to the carrying capacity of salmon in the ocean (e.g., Kaeriyama 1989; Ishida et al. 1993; Helle and Hoffman 1995; Bigler et al. 1996).

U.S. marine research on salmon carrying capacity in the ocean has focused largely on the early (juvenile) life history phase, when salmon are migrating in waters over the continental shelf during their first summer at sea (Brodeur et al. 2003). Results of international cooperative high seas salmon research, however, suggest that inter- and intra-specific competition for food and density-dependent growth effects occur primarily among older age groups of salmon, when stocks originating from all geographic regions around the Pacific Rim mix and feed in offshore waters (e.g., Ishida et al. 1993, 1995; Tadokoro et al. 1996; Walker et al. 1998; Azumaya and Ishida 2000; Myers et al. 2000; Bugaev et al. 2001; Davis 2003). In addition, time-series analysis of scale pattern and abundance data indicated a substantial decrease in marine survival of western Alaska salmon during years of peak abundance of Asian salmon

(Ruggerone et al. 2003). Effects on marine survival most likely occurred during an overlap period from the winter of the first year at sea, when western Alaska salmon moved off the continental shelf, through at least summer of the second year at sea, when they were distributed across broad regions of the North Pacific Ocean and Bering Sea (Ruggerone et al. 2003).

The most frequently cited conceptual models that pertain to the high seas migrations of AYK salmon are those of Takagi et al. (1981) and Fredin et al. (1977, based on data from Neave et al. 1976). These species- and regional stock-specific models are based largely on coastal recovery data from tagged fish released in the North Pacific Ocean and Bering Sea before 1972. The composite abundance of Pacific Rim salmon species and stocks has been increasing since 1978 (NPAFC 2001). This increase has been attributed to such factors as good fishery management (i.e., near-optimum escapements), the reduction in high seas fishing, more favorable ocean temperatures resulting from a climate regime shift in 1976–1977, and reduced predation in the ocean during winter months (e.g., Rogers 1984). While the mechanisms underlying the causes of major fluctuations in abundance of Pacific salmon largely remain a mystery, models of salmon migrations developed using data collected before the 1977 climate regime shift might not adequately characterize migration patterns during more recent climate regimes.

In this paper, high seas tag data (1954–2006) are analyzed to show the known ocean distribution and migrations patterns of Norton Sound, Yukon River, and Kuskokwim River salmon populations. New information from DSTs on the vertical distribution of salmon is also reviewed. The results are evaluated with respect to indirect information from scale pattern and genetic stock identification analyses, and compared to existing conceptual models of the high seas distribution and migration patterns of salmon. The potential effects of climate change on salmon food habits, bioenergetics, and trophic interactions in the oceanic regions where AYK salmon are distributed are also briefly reviewed. Critical gaps in information and important issues for future high seas research on AYK salmon are identified.

Study Area

The study area encompassed the entire North Pacific Ocean (north of 36°N latitude) and its adjacent seas (Figure 1). To facilitate data analyses and discussion of results, the study area was subdivided into a grid of eight meso-scale regions. For visual and textual reference, this regional grid was placed on all maps showing distribution of releases and recoveries of tagged salmon. Throughout the paper a standard set of acronyms is used to refer to frequently discussed meso-scale regions in Figure 1, as follows: WBS = Western Bering Sea, EBS = Eastern Bering Sea, GOA = Gulf of Alaska, NEP = Northeast Pacific,

NWP = Northwestern North Pacific (north of 46°N), SWP = Southwestern North Pacific (south of 46°N).

Methods

Published and unpublished data from high seas salmon tagging experiments, previously published scientific literature, and processed research reports were analyzed, reviewed and synthesized. The methods used for high seas salmon tagging experiments have been similar throughout the entire period of high seas salmon research (e.g., Davis et al. 1990; Myers et al. 2004). Salmon used in high seas tagging experiments were caught by a variety of types of fishing gear (most frequently floating longlines and purse seines) during research vessel operations at sea. After capture, scales were collected for age determination, fork lengths (FL, tip of snout to fork of tail) were measured, and viable fish were tagged and released. The tags most frequently used have been plastic Petersen disc tags attached to the fish near the dorsal fin. Each disk was labeled with a unique number and

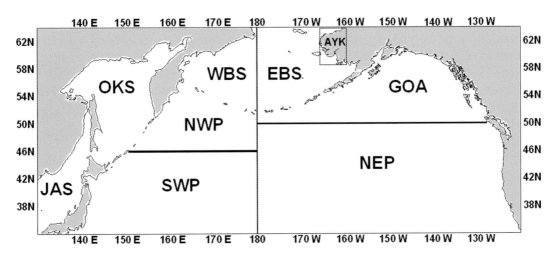

FIGURE 1. Map of study area. AYK = Arctic (Norton Sound), Yukon, and Kuskokwim region of western Alaska; WBS = Western Bering Sea, EBS = Eastern Bering Sea, GOA = Gulf of Alaska, NEP = Northeast Pacific, NWP = Northwestern North Pacific (north of 46°N), SWP = Southwestern North Pacific (south of 46°N), JAS = Japan Sea, OKS = Okhotsk Sea.

additional information identifying the release agency. Release locations, dates, tag numbers, species, and other pertinent information were recorded and were reported in annual documents submitted to INPFC or NPAFC by the release agency. Age was determined by counting the freshwater and ocean annuli on scales.

We used the European method of age designation (Koo 1962), which was the number of freshwater annuli and ocean annuli separated by a dot, e.g., an age 1.2 fish had one freshwater annulus and two ocean annuli on its scale, and was in its fourth year of life. An unknown freshwater or ocean age was designated by the letter "X." If referred only to the ocean age or only to freshwater age, one Arabic numeral was used to indicate the number of annuli on the scale. For example, a freshwater age-0 fish did not have any annuli on the scale, that is, the fish migrated to the ocean in the first year of life.

Because of the immense study area (Figure 1) and the relatively small number of tagged fish released each year, high seas salmon tagging experiments have largely relied on voluntary return of tags by fishermen, processors, and others finding tagged fish in coastal marine or freshwater areas. Recoveries from high seas tagging experiments were reported in annual documents that have been submitted to the INPFC or NPAFC by the release agency. Aro et al. (1971) developed the first INPFC high seas tag recovery computer database by coding all recoveries reported by all nations during 1956–1969. K.V. Aro updated the database every two or three years through 1979. Personnel of the University of Washington, High Seas Salmon Research Program, used the information in INPFC and NPAFC documents, as well as unpublished information provided by Japan, to develop an all-agency high seas tag–release database, and have maintained and updated the high seas tag–release and recovery databases since 1980.

The INPFC and NPAFC tag–release database was analyzed to show spatial and temporal trends in high seas tagging effort. The high seas tag–release database did not include information on the exact latitude and longitude of release. Each database record, defined in this paper as an "operation", summarized the number of releases of each species by date and 2°-latitude by x 5°-longitude area. Spatial distribution of tag–release effort was summarized graphically in several different ways. The number of operations in each 2° x 5° strata over the entire period of high seas tagging experiments (1954–2005) was ranked into four tagging effort categories (low = <25 operations, medium = 25–100 operations, high = 101–271, and highest (only one area with >271 operations). Data on tags released in 2006 were incomplete, and were not included in the analyses. The distribution of releases of tagged fish (% of total releases or numbers) was also summarized by study area subregions, species, month, and year.

All high seas tag recovery data for AYK salmon (1956–2006) were stratified by species, watershed of recovery (Norton Sound, Yukon, Kuskokwim), month of release, and age and maturity group at release; a computer mapping software package was used to plot the high seas release locations (latitude, longitude) of salmon that were later recovered in the AYK region. Quantitative estimates of the stock composition in the high seas tagging area cannot be determined from high seas release and recovery tag data because all stocks were not equally vulnerable to capture for tagging, actual recovery rates in the AYK region were not known (we assumed that many recoveries were not reported), and posttagging mortality and tag loss were time dependent. Results from tagging experiments were compared to published estimates of stock composition using scale pattern and genetic methods. The results were also compared to existing conceptual models of the seasonal ocean migration patterns of AYK salmon (Takagi et al. 1981; Fredin et al. 1977).

Recovery data from two types of DSTs that record depth was used to describe the vertical distribution of salmon. One type (LTD) was a small circuit board potted in a clear urethane, manufactured by Lotek Marine Technologies (model LTD_1100–500 27 × 16 × 8 mm and weighs 5 g). These tags recorded temperature and depth data. Model DST CTD tags were housed in a 27 × 16 × 8 mm ceramic shell and weighed 8 g. These tags, manufactured by Star-Oddi, recorded salinity, temperature, and depth data. LTD tags were attached to fish just anterior to the dorsal fin using two 76 or 64 mm nickel pins, with labeled U.S. and Japanese disk tags placed on the pins on the other side of the fish. DST CTD tags were attached in the same location, but were affixed with stainless steel wire, with a small oval plastic plate on the opposite side of the fish. U.S. and Japanese disk tags were placed on the wires either under the tag or over the plate.

The NOAA Fisheries Groundfish Observer Program data (1997–1999) on fishing depth of trawls was also used to describe the vertical distribution of Chinook salmon *O. tshawytscha* in the eastern Bering Sea (Walker et al. 2007). Myers et al. (2003) described methods used to determine the age composition of Chinook salmon from scale samples collected by the Observer Program.

Results and Discussion

Spatial and temporal variation in high seas salmon tag release and recovery effort

Variation in the spatial and temporal distribution of high seas salmon tagging effort (Figures 2–6) largely reflected changes in IN-PFC and NPAFC research priorities. During the entire period of INPFC, the results of tagging experiments by the United States (1954–1978, 1980, 1982), Canada (1960–1967), and Japan (1954–1991) were used in negotiations regarding the exploitation of North American salmon by Japan's large-scale high seas driftnet fisheries.

The original objective of INPFC research was to delineate the oceanic migrations of Asian and North American salmon with respect to the provisional treaty line at 175°W longitude. U.S. research by the Fisheries Research Institute (FRI), University of Washington, focused on tagging operations in the area south of Adak Island in the central Aleutians (area of highest number of tagging operations; Figure 2). By the mid-1960s this objective had been largely achieved, and INPFC research focused on describing the marine life history of major Asian and North American salmon stocks to provide a basis for more precise management. The high number of tagging operations and percentage of total releases in the central Aleutians and Gulf of Alaska (GOA, Figures 2 and 3) reflects in part the intensive tagging research carried out by FRI and Canada during this period. After the 1960s, the Canadian and U.S. high seas salmon research programs were greatly reduced.

In the late 1960s and 1970s, a major objective of the U.S. research program was to obtain an index of the abundance of the immature sockeye salmon *O. nerka* south of Adak Island in the summer that was used to forecast, one year in advance, the runs of sockeye salmon to Bristol Bay, Alaska. The forecasts were used by the Alaska Department of Fish and Game and the salmon industry in planning the regulation and harvesting of Bristol Bay sockeye salmon. As a part of this work, tagging experiments by FRI continued in the area south of Adak Island (area of highest number of operations, Figure 2).

In 1978–1991, the major objective of the INPFC research program was to identify stocks migrating in the area of the Japanese high seas driftnet fisheries, particularly in

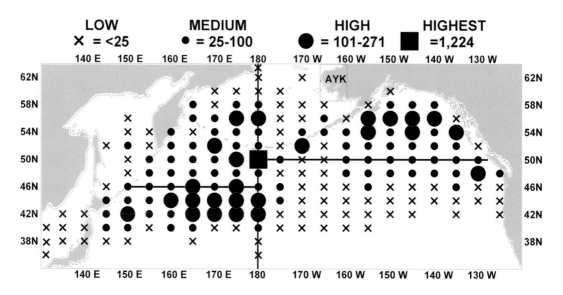

FIGURE 2. Spatial distribution of high seas salmon tagging operations (number of operations in 2° latitude by 5° longitude area strata), 1954–2005.

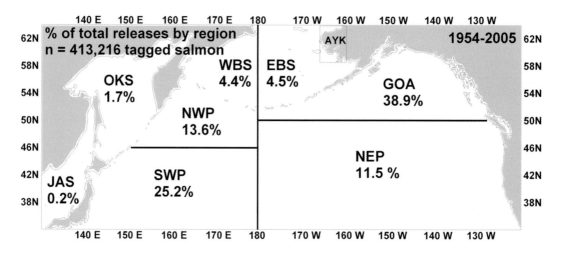

FIGURE 3. Distribution of releases of tagged fish (% of total releases) by region, 1954–2005. WBS = Western Bering Sea, EBS = Eastern Bering Sea, GOA = Gulf of Alaska, NEP = Northeast Pacific, NWP = Northwestern North Pacific (north of 46°N), SWP = Southwestern North Pacific (south of 46°N), JAS = Japan Sea, OKS = Okhotsk Sea.

the southwestern North Pacific (SWP, Figures 1–3). Intensive salmon tagging experiments in the SWP were done largely by Japan (Myers et al. 1993). In addition to the INPFC-related tagging, the U.S.S.R.'s Pacific Research Institute of Fisheries and Oceanography (TINRO) and FRI conducted cooperative high seas salmon tagging operations from 1983 through 1991. Most of the tagging operations during cooperative U.S.S.R.–U.S. research were done in the central North Pacific Ocean and Bering Sea (Davis et al. 1990).

Sockeye, chum, and pink *O. gorbuscha* salmon were the target species of most high seas tagging experiments, primarily because of their high abundance relative to other species. In general, regional differences in species composition of high seas releases of tagged salmon reflect spatial differences in the relative abundance of species (Figure 4). Most fish were tagged in May, June, and July, which were also the primary months of operation of the high seas salmon driftnet fisheries (Figure 5). Therefore, the results of high seas tagging experiments have provided little or no information on salmon distribution and migration patterns in fall, winter, and early spring. With the implementation of the NPAFC research program in 1993, tagging experiments have continued only at a low level (Figure 6, top panel), largely as a part of cooperative Japan–U.S. high seas salmon research aboard Japanese research vessels in the central Bering Sea and North Pacific Ocean (180° survey line) and central GOA and NEP (145°W survey line) in June and July. Cooperative Japan–U.S. tagging research along the 145°W line was terminated in 2002. No U.S. or Canadian high seas salmon research is currently conducted in the GOA or NEP.

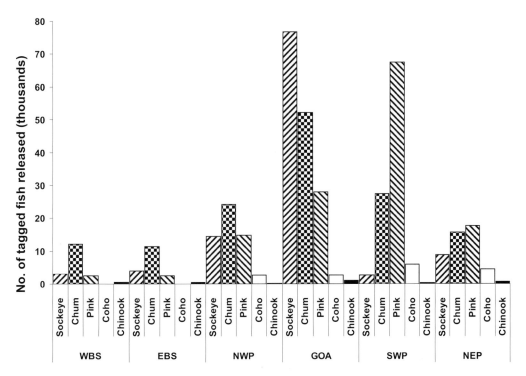

FIGURE 4. Number of tagged fish released by species and ocean region, 1954–2005. WBS = Western Bering Sea, EBS = Eastern Bering Sea, GOA = Gulf of Alaska, NEP = Northeast Pacific, NWP = Northwestern North Pacific (north of 46°N), SWP = Southwestern North Pacific (south of 46°N).

Myers et al.

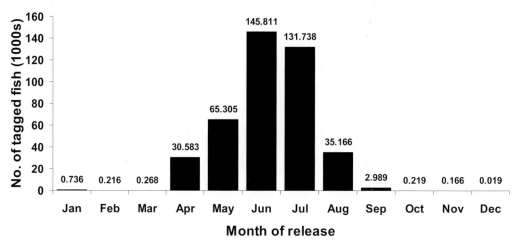

FIGURE 5. Number of releases of tagged salmon (1,000s of fish) by month, 1954–2005.

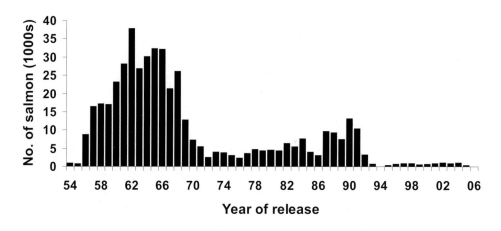

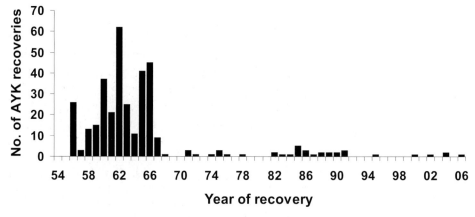

FIGURE 6. Number of salmon released during high seas tagging experiments, 1954–2005 (top panel, total = 413,216 fish); number of reported tagged salmon recoveries in the AYK region (Norton Sound, Yukon, Kuskokwim), 1956–2006 (bottom panel, total = 347 fish).

Throughout the entire period of INPFC and NPAFC research, annual trends in the number of reported recoveries of tagged AYK salmon largely reflected annual trends in the number of salmon released during high seas tagging experiments (Figure 6). The majority of recoveries in the AYK region occurred during the period of intensive tagging from 1956–1966.

Spatial and temporal distribution of AYK salmon

All species of AYK salmon are distributed in epipelagic waters over the eastern Bering Sea shelf during their first summer and fall at sea. Farley et al. (2009, this volume) reviewed information on the distribution, biology, and ecology of AYK juvenile salmon during this life history stage. Except for Chinook salmon, no stock-specific data exist on the distribution and migration patterns of AYK salmon during their first winter at sea. Because the first winter at sea is considered to be a critical period for ocean survival of salmon, this important topic should be a focus of future research on AYK salmon distribution, biology, and ecology.

Pink salmon

Data from tagging experiments provided the only stock-specific information on the high seas distribution, biology, and ecology of maturing AYK pink salmon. No stock identification methods have been used to estimate proportions of AYK pink salmon in mixed-stock high seas catches. AYK pink salmon migrated to the ocean in their first year (freshwater age-0), and spent only one winter at sea, returning to spawn at age 0.1. The few reported recoveries of tagged AYK pink salmon were all from high seas releases of maturing fish ($n = 24$ fish; Figure 7). The sexes of most tagged pink salmon recovered in the AYK region were not reported by fishermen (21 unknown, 2 males, 1 female). The AYK recoveries were dominated by fish that returned to spawn in odd-numbered years (71% of total). The high seas release location of one recovery (Yukon, male, 365 mm FL at release) indicated that by April at least some maturing (age 0.1) AYK pink salmon have migrated far to the southeast in the NEP (Figure 7, top panel). No data exist on the high seas distribution of AYK pink salmon in May. We assumed that in May AYK pink salmon were distributed primarily in the NEP and GOA. Most of the reported recoveries were from fish tagged in June (Figure 7, middle panel), when the distribution of maturing AYK pink salmon has shifted to the west in the NEP and to the north and west in the western GOA, central and eastern Aleutians and EBS. The June recoveries included fish from all three AYK regions (14 Norton Sound, 3 Yukon, 4 Kuskokwim; mean size at release = 450 mm FL), indicating that AYK region populations of pink salmon shared common high seas feeding grounds. One Norton Sound pink salmon tagged in the WBS in June is the westernmost release location for a pink salmon recovered in North America ($n = 3,668$ total recoveries, 1956–2006). One Kuskokwim pink salmon tagged in the NEP in June was located farther to the southwest than any other tagged pink salmon recovered in North America. These two recoveries suggested that the high seas distribution of AYK pink salmon extended farther to the west in the Bering Sea and to the southwest in North Pacific Ocean than any other regional stock of North American pink salmon. By July, many maturing AYK pink salmon returned to coastal areas and spawning streams. However, two recoveries in July indicated that the migration routes of maturing pink salmon returning to the AYK region extended across a broad front in the Bering Sea (Figure 7, bottom panel). On the basis of these few recoveries, it may be speculated that future genetic stock identification studies likely will show a much broader distribution

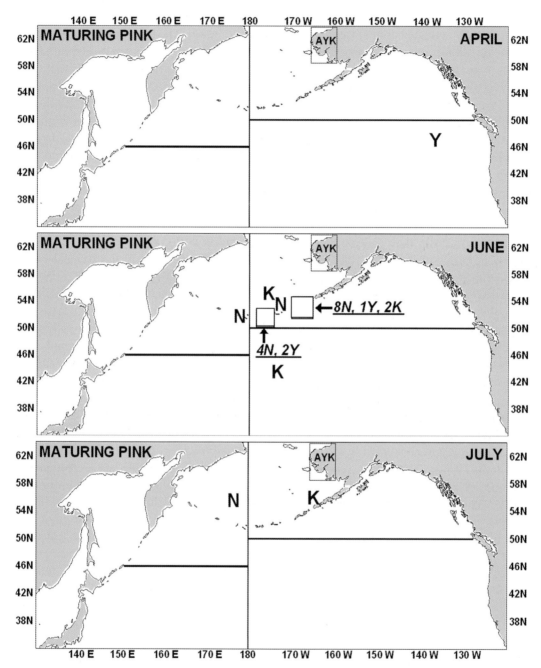

FIGURE 7. The known ocean distribution of maturing AYK pink salmon by month, as indicated by high seas tag experiments, 1954–2006. The letters indicate high seas release location and stock of origin: N = Norton Sound, Y = Yukon, and K = Kuskokwim. All fish were age 0.1 at release. In June (center panel), labeled arrows (underline, italics) pointing at multiple recoveries (inside boxes) show number of recoveries per stock. Number of recoveries by month of release: April = 1 fish, June = 21, July = 2. Reported dates of recovery of adult fish in the AYK region ranged from July 18 to August 6.

of maturing AYK pink salmon, particularly to the west and northwest in the WBS, than indicated by the results of high seas tagging experiments.

Coho salmon

AYK coho salmon *O. kisutch* migrated to the ocean after one, two, or three winters in freshwater, and spent only one winter at sea, returning to spawn at ocean age-1. The few reported recoveries of tagged AYK coho salmon were all from high seas releases of maturing fish (*n* = 18 fish; Figure 8). The sexes of most tagged coho salmon recovered in the AYK region were not reported by fishermen (13 unknown, 3 males, 2 females). Recoveries were made in Norton Sound (2 fish), Yukon (4 fish), Kuskokwim (12 fish). Release locations of tagged fish indicated that in May and June AYK coho salmon (mean size: 481 mm FL, *n* = 5) were distributed in the NEP (Figure 8, top and middle panels). In July, the distribution of maturing AYK coho salmon (mean size: 561 mm FL, *n* = 13) shifted to the west in the NEP and to the north and west in the GOA (Figure 8, bottom panel). By August, maturing AYK coho salmon returned to coastal areas or spawning streams. In general, tag recovery data indicated that the high seas distribution and migration patterns of AYK coho salmon were similar to those of AYK pink salmon, except that the timing of high seas movements and return to coastal areas of coho salmon was about one month later than pink salmon.

Sockeye salmon

AYK sockeye salmon typically migrated to the ocean after one or two winters in freshwater, and spent two, three, or four winters at sea, returning to spawn at ocean age-2, age-3, or age-4. The few reported recoveries of tagged AYK sockeye salmon were from high seas releases of both immature (*n* = 4

fish; Figure 9, left panels) and maturing (*n* = 9 fish; Figure 9, right panels) fish. The sexes of most tagged sockeye salmon recovered in the AYK region were not reported by fishermen (11 unknown, 1 male, 1 female). Recoveries were made in Norton Sound (1 fish), Yukon (2 fish), and Kuskokwim (10 fish). The high seas release locations of four immature AYK sockeye salmon indicated that they were distributed in the GOA in May (*n* = 1,Yukon, age 2.3; 590 mm FL at release), and their distribution shifted westward in late spring and summer (Figure 9, left panels), extending into the western NEP (June, *n* = 1, age 1.2, 428 mm FL at release), central Aleutians (August, *n* = 1, age x.1, 385 mm FL at release), and EBS (July, *n* = 1, age 1.2, 452 mm FL at release). High seas release locations of maturing AYK sockeye salmon (Figure 9, right panels) indicated that they were distributed in the GOA in early spring (April, *n* = 1, age 1.3, 600 mm FL at release), and their distribution shifted westward in May (*n* = 1, age x.3, 580 mm FL) and June into the western GOA, Aleutians, NWP, and EBS (*n* = 6, mean size at release: 555 mm FL). By July most maturing AYK sockeye salmon are probably distributed in the Bering Sea (*n* = 1, age 1.3, 617 mm FL at release) or have already returned to coastal areas and spawning streams.

Chum salmon

AYK chum salmon migrated to the ocean in their first year, and spent two, three, four, or five winters at sea, before returning to spawn at ages 0.2, 0.3, 0.4, or 0.5. The reported recoveries of tagged AYK chum salmon were from high seas releases of both immature (*n* = 22 fish; Figure 10) and maturing (n = 256 fish; Figures 11–13) fish. The sexes of most tagged chum salmon recovered in the AYK region were not reported by fishermen (206 unknown, 30 male, 42 female). Recoveries were reported from Norton Sound (25 fish),

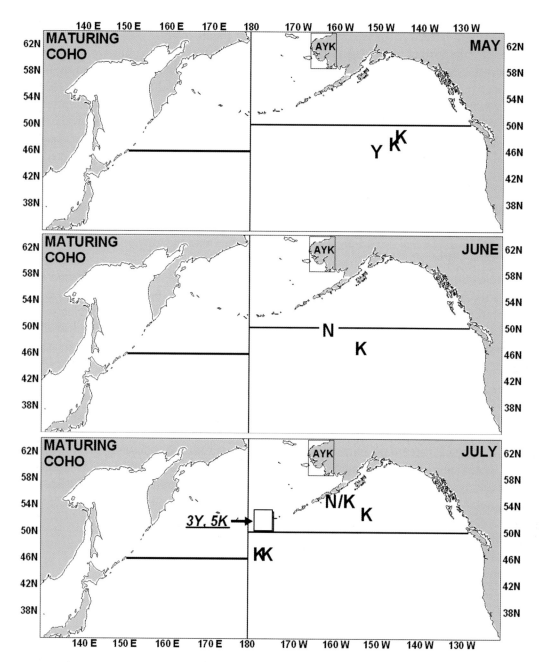

FIGURE 8. The known ocean distribution of maturing AYK coho salmon by month, as indicated by high seas tag experiments, 1954–2006. The letters indicate high seas release location and stock of origin: N = Norton Sound, Y = Yukon, and K = Kuskokwim. All fish were ocean age-1 at release. In July (bottom panel), labeled arrow (underline, italics) pointing at multiple recoveries (inside box) shows number of recoveries per stock. Forward slash between numbers or letters indicates data for two fish released at the same location. Number of recoveries by month of release: May = 3 fish, June = 2, July = 13. Reported dates of recovery of adult fish in the AYK region ranged from August 10 to September 28.

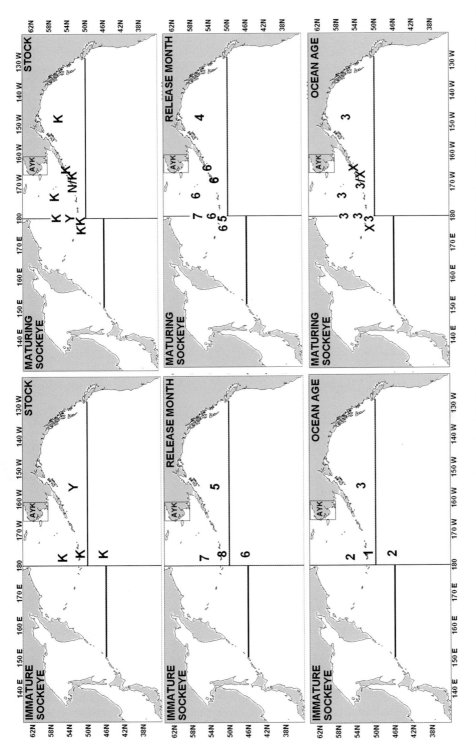

FIGURE 9. The known ocean distribution of immature (left panels, 4 fish) and maturing (right panels, 9 fish) Yukon (Y) and Kuskokwim (K) sockeye salmon by stock (top panels), month of release (center panels), and ocean age-group at release (bottom panels), as indicated by high seas tag experiments, 1954–2006. Forward slash between numbers or letters indicates data for two fish released at the same location. Reported dates of recovery of adult fish in the AYK region ranged from June 17 to September 8.

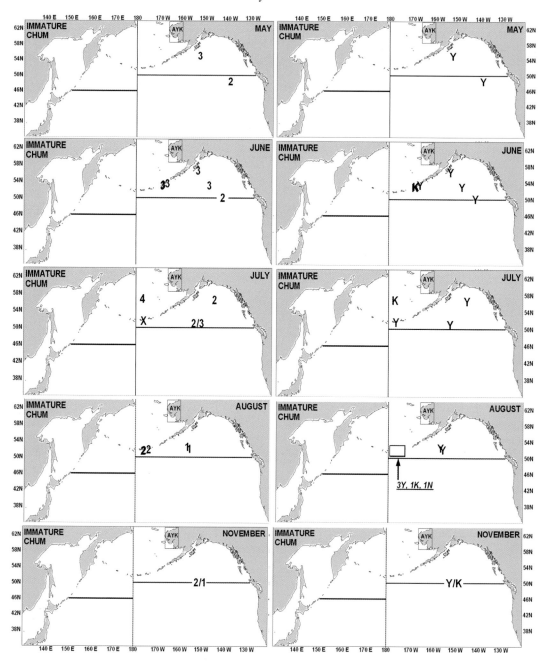

Figure 10. The known ocean distribution of immature Norton Sound (N), Yukon (Y), and Kuskokwim (K) chum salmon by month, ocean age-group (left panels), and stock (right panels), as indicated by high seas tag experiments 1954–2006. Numbers in left panels are ocean age at release; X = ocean age unknown; forward slash between two numbers indicates recoveries from two age groups released at or near the same ocean location. In August (right panel), labeled arrow (underline, italics) pointing at multiple recoveries (inside box) shows number of recoveries per stock. Number of recoveries by month of release: May = 2 fish, June = 6, July = 5, August = 7, November = 2. Reported dates of recovery of adult fish in the AYK region ranged from June 16 to September 24.

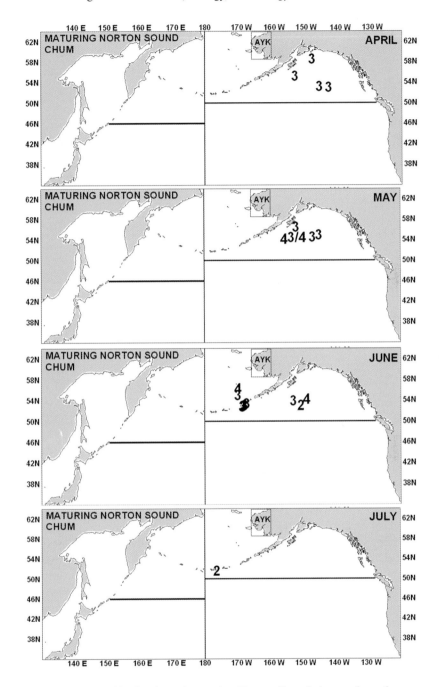

FIGURE 11. The known ocean distribution of maturing Norton Sound chum salmon by ocean age-group and month, as indicated by high seas tag experiments, 1954–2006. Numbers indicate the high seas location and ocean age at release. A forward slash between numbers indicates data for two fish released at the same ocean location. Number of recoveries by month of release: April = 4 fish, May = 6, June = 13, July = 1. Reported dates of recovery of adult fish in the AYK region ranged from June 29 to August 22.

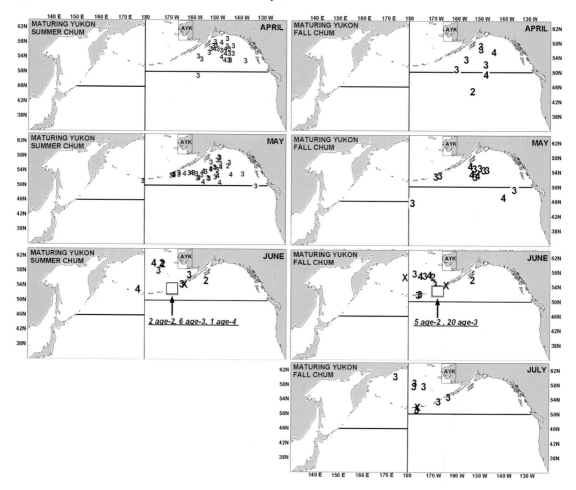

FIGURE 12. The known ocean distribution of maturing Yukon River summer (left panels) and fall (right panels) chum salmon by ocean age-group and month, as indicated by high seas tag experiments 1954–2006. Numbers indicate the high seas location and ocean age at release. X = ocean age unknown. Multiple recoveries from a single age-group of fish released at the same ocean location are not indicated. In June, labeled arrows (underline, italics) pointing at multiple recoveries (inside boxes) show number of recoveries by age-group. Number of recoveries by month of release for summer chum: April = 32 fish, May = 50 fish, June = 18. Number of recoveries by month of release for fall chum: April = 8 fish, May = 13, June = 36, July = 8. Seasonal race was determined by the reported date of recovery of adult fish in the AYK region; summer chum recovery dates ranged from June 5 to July 14; fall chum recovery dates ranged from July 15 to October 1.

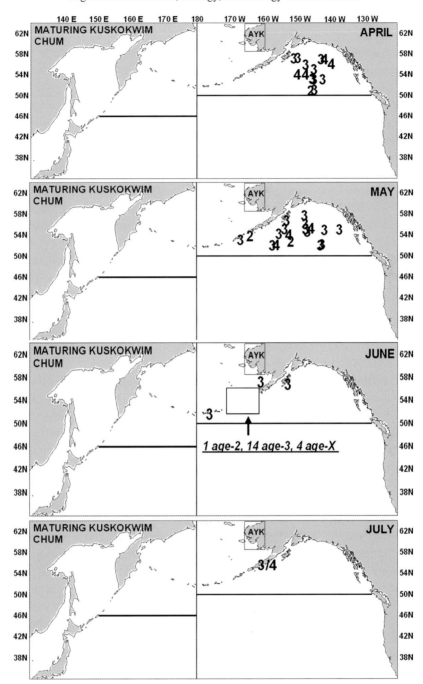

FIGURE 13. The known ocean distribution of maturing Kuskokwim River chum salmon by ocean age-group and month, as indicated by high seas tag experiments, 1954–2006. Numbers indicate the high seas location and ocean age at release. X = ocean age unknown. In June, labeled arrow (underline, italics) pointing at multiple recoveries (inside box) shows number of recoveries per age-group. Forward slash between numbers indicates data for two fish released at the same ocean location. Number of recoveries by month of release: April = 14 fish, May = 19, June = 24, July = 2. Reported dates of recovery of adult fish in the AYK region ranged from June 8 to August 12.

Yukon (189 fish), and Kuskokwim (64 fish). The high seas release locations of immature AYK chum salmon indicated that they were distributed primarily in the GOA, although one older (ocean age 0.4, 622 mm FL at release) immature fish released in the EBS in July 1991 was recovered approximately one year later (June 1992) in the Kuskokwim (Figure 10). From spring to summer, the distribution of immature chum salmon shifts to west or northwest, with older age groups (0.3 and 0.4) moving in advance of younger age groups (0.1 and 0.2). Future genetic stock identification studies likely will show that the NEP is also an important rearing area for immature AYK chum salmon in spring and summer.

Maturing AYK chum salmon were distributed in the NEP and GOA in April (Figures 11–13). In May, their distribution shifts westward in the GOA, and by June distribution has shifted farther to the north and west, extending into the Bering Sea. In July, maturing Yukon summer chum salmon have already returned to coastal areas and spawning streams, and maturing Yukon fall chum salmon were distributed across a broad front in the western GOA, Aleutians, EBS, and WBS (Figure 12).

Few previous analyses of high seas tag data have occurred specific to AYK salmon. In one notable study, Brannian (1984) analyzed high seas tag recovery data (1956–1966) stratified by 10-d period to determine if temporal differences existed in the arrival time of chum salmon stocks in the vicinity of the Alaska Peninsula and eastern Aleutian Islands (172°W–160°W, 52°N–56°N). Her results indicated that Yukon summer chum salmon arrived first (May–early June), Norton Sound and Kuskokwim chum salmon were present throughout June, and Yukon fall chum salmon arrived last in mid to late June. Because of the limited number of reported tag recoveries for all species of AYK salmon (*n* = 347 fish; Figure 6), however, it is concluded

that high seas tag data were insufficient to provide definitive evidence of stock-specific differences in the high seas migration patterns of AYK salmon at temporal scales finer than 1-month periods.

Coastal tagging studies have shown that chum salmon from many populations in Asia and North America, including AYK, were intercepted by the June fisheries along the south side of the Alaska Peninsula in the western GOA (Eggers et al. 1991). Recent genetic studies of chum salmon in the Shumagin Islands fisheries indicate that AYK stocks (Northwest Alaska summer chum salmon) were the largest contributors in early June (as high as 69% in early June test fisheries) and declined through June and July to about 5% (Seeb et al. 2004).

Genetic stock identification (allozyme) estimates of the stock composition of chum salmon in incidental catches by U.S. groundfish trawl fisheries in the EBS in late summer and fall 1994 indicated that 39–55% of the fish originated in Asia, 20–35% in western Alaska, and 21–23% in southeastern Alaska, British Columbia or Washington (Wilmot et al. 1998). In late summer and fall of 1995, 11% of the chum salmon bycatch by the EBS groundfish trawl fishery was sampled, and an estimated 13–51% originated in Asia, 33–53% in western Alaska, and 9–46% in southeastern Alaska, British Columbia or Washington (Wilmot et al. 1998). A substantial portion of the EBS bycatch of western Alaska chum in 1994 and 1995 was composed of immature fish, which invalidated the Fredin et al. (1977) migration model for immature western Alaska chum salmon.

Further study using genetic markers has shown that the Bering Sea was an important rearing area for immature chum salmon from North America, and that their migration patterns were more widespread than previously thought (Seeb et al. 2004). Using genetic baselines from 356 stocks of chum salmon, Seeb et al. (2004) found that Alaskan chum salmon were also using migration corridors along the Kamchatka coast. Hence, Alaskan salmon were vulnerable to fisheries and by-catch from a greater spatial area than previously considered.

Chinook salmon

AYK Chinook salmon typically migrated to the ocean in their second year (freshwater age-1), and spent two, three, four, or five winters at sea, before returning to spawn at ages 1.2, 1.3, 1.4, or 1.5. The reported recoveries of AYK Chinook salmon were from high seas releases of both immature (n = 13 fish) and maturing (n = 1) fish (Figure 14). In addition, there were 19 recoveries of coded-wire-tagged (CWT) fish released from the White-horse Rapids Hatchery in the upper Yukon River (Canadian Yukon Territory; Figure 15). The sexes of many tagged Chinook salmon recovered in the AYK region were not reported by fishermen (8 unknown, 2 male, 4 female). High seas recoveries of CWT Chinook salmon included 9 females, 4 males, and 6 fish of unknown sex. Recoveries of salmon tagged on the high seas were reported from the Yukon (12 fish) and Kuskokwim (2 fish) rivers. The release data for high seas tagged fish showed that immature Yukon and Kuskokwim Chinook salmon were distributed in offshore waters of the EBS and WBS in summer (Figure 14), and that their distribution shifts to the northwest from June to July, extending well into the Russian EEZ.

High seas recoveries of CWT-hatchery fish indicated that juvenile and immature AYK Chinook salmon were distributed in the EBS in fall and winter (October–March, Figure 15). Although freshwater ages differed between hatchery (age-0) and wild (age-1) Yukon River Chinook salmon, it is assumed that immature and maturing hatchery and wild Yukon River salmon have similar ocean distribution and migration patterns. Most of the CWT hatchery fish were recovered by NOAA

fishery observers on U.S. groundfish vessels operating inside of the U.S. EEZ. Hence, recoveries distributed along the eastern Bering Sea shelf break (200-m depth contour) north-westward from Unimak Pass terminate at the international boundary (Figure 15). One recovery of a CWT Chinook salmon on the eastern Bering Sea shelf in June was probably a maturing fish, and suggests that at least some maturing Yukon River fish approach the river mouth from the south (Figure 15, June panel). This observation was substantiated by a recent (2006) recovery of another maturing Yukon River fish that was tagged in June in the southern EBS (Figure 14, top panel).

No reported recoveries of AYK Chinook salmon have occurred from releases of tagged fish in the North Pacific Ocean or from recoveries of coded-wire tagged fish in the North Pacific Ocean (Figures 14 and 15). While it is assumed that at least some AYK Chinook salmon migrated to open ocean areas south of the Aleutian Islands and perhaps to the Gulf of Alaska (e.g., Rogers 1987), the majority of AYK Chinook salmon probably remained in the Bering Sea throughout their ocean life history phase. The overall pattern of recoveries of tagged AYK Chinook salmon suggested seasonal movements of immature fish between summer feeding grounds in the central and northwestern Bering Sea and wintering areas in the southeastern Bering Sea.

Scale pattern analyses have estimated that western Alaska (particularly Yukon River) was the predominant regional stock of Chinook salmon migrating in the Bering Sea (e.g., Major et al. 1978; Myers et al. 1984, 1987; Myers and Rogers 1988; Davis 1990, 1991). In contrast to the results from tagging studies, scale pattern analyses indicated that Asian and North American stocks of Chinook salmon (primarily western and south-central Alaskan) mixed in areas south of the Aleutians to 46°N, with wide variations between years in their estimated proportions. In the SWP (Figure 1), which was the primary fish-

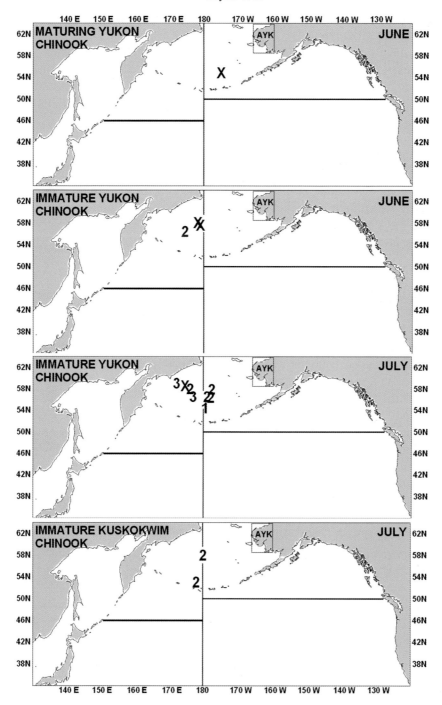

FIGURE 14. The known ocean distribution of maturing (top panel) and immature Yukon and Kuskokwim Chinook salmon by month, as indicated by high seas tag experiments, 1954–2006. The numbers indicate the high seas location and ocean age at release. X = ocean age unknown. Number of recoveries by month of release: June = 4 (1 maturing and 3 immature Yukon fish), July = 10 immature fish (8 Yukon, 2 Kuskokwim). Reported dates of recovery of adult fish in the AYK region ranged from June 2 to July 24.

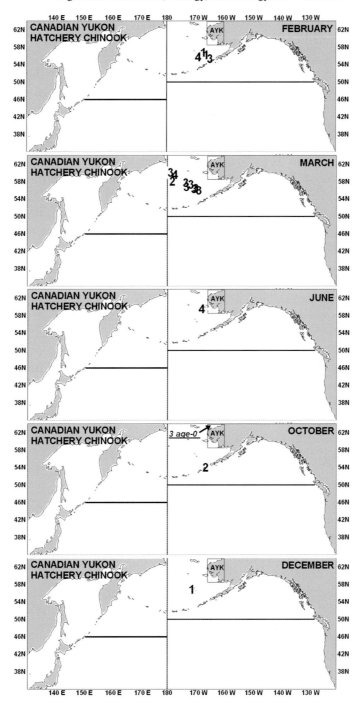

FIGURE 15. The known ocean distribution of Canadian Yukon hatchery Chinook salmon by month, as determined by marine recoveries of coded-wire tagged fish, 1992–2006. Numbers indicate the location and ocean age at recovery. In October, labeled arrow (underline, italics) pointing at AYK region box indicates 3 juveniles (brood year 2001; age 0.0) released from Whitehorse Rapids Fish Hatchery in June 2002 and recovered in Norton Sound in October 2002. Number of ocean recoveries by month: February = 4 fish, March = 9, June = 1, October = 4, and December = 1.

ing area of the Japanese landbased driftnet salmon fishery, scale pattern estimates indicated that most Chinook salmon were from Russian stocks (Myers et al. 1993).

Myers et al. (1987) noted considerable annual variability in scale pattern estimates of the proportions of age 1.2 Yukon River, Kuskokwim River, and Bristol Bay Chinook salmon in the central Bering Sea in July, 1975–1981. In June, Yukon River Chinook salmon were the predominant stock in catches in the central North Pacific Ocean between 170°E and 175°E and in the central Bering Sea between 175°E and 180°. In July 1979–1981, proportions of Yukon River Chinook salmon were higher in catches from the western portion of the fishery area (175°E–180°) than in the eastern portion (180°–175°W). Rogers (1987) used these estimates to calculate interceptions of Yukon River Chinook salmon by the Japanese high seas driftnet fisheries, and found that these interceptions often amounted to over 20% of the domestic catch in the 1970s.

Healey (1991) used high seas disk tag data (1956–1984), coded wire tag recovery data (1980–1986), and the results of scale pattern analyses to describe the distribution and relative abundance of regional stock groups of Chinook salmon in the Bering Sea and North Pacific Ocean. He concluded that in the Bering Sea, western Alaskan Chinook salmon (including Canadian Yukon River fish) were the most abundant stock group, and Russian and central Alaskan stocks were about half as abundant as western Alaskan Chinook salmon. In the western North Pacific Ocean, a broad mixture exists of Russian, western Alaskan, and central Alaskan stocks. Western Alaskan Chinook are probably no more abundant here than Russian stocks (Healey 1991).

Myers and Rogers (1988) estimated that Chinook salmon in the 1979, 1981, and 1982 catches by foreign and joint-venture groundfish fisheries in the EBS were predominant-

ly ages 1.2 (56%) and 1.3 (26%). Regional stock proportion estimates from scale pattern analysis indicated that western Alaska, which included Canadian Yukon fish, was the predominant regional stock of ages 1.2 and 1.3 fish. The proportions of the three western Alaskan subregional stocks (Yukon, Kuskokwim, and Bristol Bay) varied considerably with such variables as brood year, time, and area. Bristol Bay and central Alaska (primarily Cook Inlet) stocks predominated in fall (October–November) catches in the eastern portion of the fishery area (east of 170°W), and Yukon fish predominated in winter (January–February) catches in the western portion (west of 170°W).

Myers et al. (2003) used scale pattern analysis to estimate the age and stock composition of Chinook salmon in the bycatch of U.S. groundfish fisheries in the EBS. They found a strong seasonal difference in the age composition of Chinook salmon in the 1997–1999 bycatch samples, with young (age 1.2) fish dominating fall samples and old (age 1.3 and 1.4) fish dominating winter samples. Myers et al. (2003) concluded that in the EBS in winter, immature (age 1.2 and 1.3) Chinook salmon may be more abundant along the outer shelf break (west of 170°W) and maturing (ages 1.3, 1.4, and 1.5) Chinook salmon may be more abundant along the inner shelf break (east of 170°W). Other factors that may influence the age composition of Chinook salmon in the EBS groundfish fishery bycatch included year-class strength, seasonal- and age-specific changes in the vertical distribution of Chinook salmon, and long-term decreases in body size and increases in age at maturity of western Alaska Chinook salmon.

Despite the decline in abundance of western Alaska Chinook salmon in the late 1990s, Myers et al. (2003) found that western Alaska was the dominant regional stock (average 56%) in bycatch samples from the U.S. domestic trawl fisheries operating in the EBS in 1997–1999. They concluded that: (1) the proportions of western Alaskan regional stocks (Yukon, Kuskokwim, and Bristol Bay) in the EBS varied considerably with such variables as brood year, time, and area; (2) Yukon River Chinook salmon were often the dominant stock in the EBS in winter, particularly among age 1.2 fish in areas west of 170°W and age 1.4 fish in areas east of 170°W; (3) Bristol Bay and Cook Inlet are the dominant stocks of age 1.2 Chinook salmon in the EBS in fall; and (4) age 1.1 Chinook salmon in the EBS in fall were largely Gulf of Alaska stocks (Cook Inlet, southeast Alaska–British Columbia). The combined results of tagging studies and new scale pattern analyses of Chinook salmon catches in the Russian EEZ (Bugaev 2005) suggested that in the summer immature AYK Chinook salmon were distributed farther to the northwest in the WBS than any other North American stocks, which may explain their relatively low percentages in fall 1997–1999 bycatch samples from the EBS.

Vertical distribution

Data from archival tags have yielded precise information about the behavior of salmon and their vertical distribution (Walker et al. 2007). Nine tags with depth data came from recoveries of salmon in western Alaska: seven sockeye salmon (Yukon delta, Kanektok, Nushagak, Egegik, Ugashik, and Bear rivers, and Nelson Lagoon) and two Chinook salmon, both from the Yukon River. Depth data from tags indicated that salmon often remained near the surface at night and moved between the surface and greater depths during the day than at night. Simple descriptors of depth, such as "average depth", did not capture some of the variation in salmon behavior. In summarizing the data, we have taken the maximum depth recorded for each day and averaged all of these daily maxima. This approach gave an overestimate of the usual daily range of the salmon. Depth data from

a limited number of data tags from the Bering Sea and North Pacific ($n = 38$) indicated that Chinook salmon (data from two Yukon River fish) and chum salmon (data from 11 Asian fish) have the deepest vertical distributions (Table 1). Average depths (Chinook salmon: 42 m; chum salmon: 16 m) and average daily maxima (Chinook salmon: 130 m; chum salmon: 58 m) were deeper than those of the other three species. Among sockeye, pink, and coho salmon, sockeye salmon have the shallowest vertical distribution (average 3 m, average daily max 19 m, with occasional excursions to 30–80 m), followed by pink salmon (average 10 m, average daily max 37 m) and coho salmon (average 11 m, average daily max 46 m). The diel pattern was strongest in chum and pink salmon, and was variably expressed, even in a single fish.

Data from all fish but one were from maturing fish in summer and fall. The only tag with overwintering data was from a Chinook salmon, tagged in the Bering Sea in 2002 and recovered two years later in the Yukon River (Figure 16). The behavior of the fish differed markedly between the two winters recorded on the tag. During the first winter, as an immature fish, the Chinook salmon remained below 100 m at temperatures of about 4°C. During the second winter before returning to spawn, the fish was at depths above 50 m at temperatures of 1° to 5°C. The maximum depth this tag model could record was approximately 350 m, which the fish often exceeded.

Eastern Bering Sea trawl bycatch of Chinook salmon included a high percentage of older fish in winter (87% ocean age-3 and older) and younger fish in summer–fall (78% ocean age-1 and -2). Over 90% were caught at depths between 25 m and 175 m below the surface; fewer than 3% were deeper than 300 m (Table 2). Chinook salmon were slightly deeper in autumn (77 m average fishing depth in September–October, versus 65 m January–February), and younger fish tended

TABLE 1. Average ocean swimming depths (meters) of five species of Pacific salmon, as recorded by electronic data storage tags (N = number of tagged fish, Avg = average, Min = minimum depth, Max = maximum depth). The maximum depth that the tags were capable of recording was 344 m. Source: Walker et al. 2007.

	Sockeye	Pink	Coho	Chum	Chinook
N	12	3	10	11	2
Avg depth	3	10	11	16	42
Avg daily min	0	1	0	1	17
Avg night	3	4	8	8	40
Avg day	4	13	12	20	43
Avg night max	9	19	29	33	84
Avg day max	18	36	42	56	125
Avg daily max	19	37	46	58	130
Max	83	74	97	253	344

TD1401-Yukon River Chinook Salmon

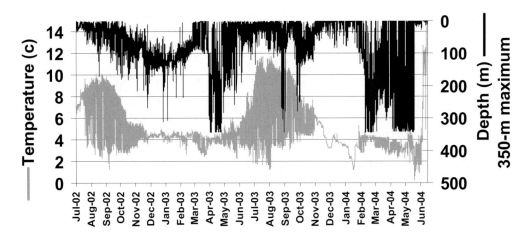

FIGURE 16. A 2-year time series of ocean temperature (left axis, gray line) and depth (right axis, black line) data from a Yukon River Chinook salmon, as recorded by an archival tag (TD1401). The immature (age 1.2) fish was tagged and released in the central Bering Sea (56°30'N latitude, 179°00'W longitude) in July 2002, and was recovered as an adult (age 1.4) in the Yukon River (near Kotlik, Alaska) in June 2004.

TABLE 2. Average depth in meters of bycatch of Chinook salmon in eastern Bering Sea groundfish trawl fisheries (1997–1999), tabulated by ocean age. Percentage of catch within 25-m depth intervals is also presented. Age = ocean age. N = sample size. Source: Walker et al. 2007.

| | January–February | | | | | | September–October | | | | |
Age	1	2	3	4	5	All	1	2	3	4	All
N	39	279	1,317	798	82	2,515	368	1,455	497	20	2,340
Avg. depth (m)	58.1	107.8	65.9	51.2	47.7	65.2	80.8	78.1	69.6	63.0	76.6
Catch (%) within 25-m depth intervals											
0		0.7	1.9	2.5	1.2	1.9	0.0	0.0			
25	79.5	41.6	55.0	62.9	72.0	56.9	33.4	18.6	23.5	30.0	22.1
50	10.3	21.9	29.7	29.6	24.4	28.3	20.4	35.6	45.9	50.0	35.5
75		3.6	2.3	0.9		1.9	15.8	22.5	16.5	15.0	20.1
100		2.2	0.5			0.5	11.4	12.4	7.4		11.1
125	2.6	0.7	0.5	0.3		0.4	9.5	6.9	3.8	5.0	6.6
150			0.3	0.1		0.2	6.8	3.2	2.2		3.5
175			1.3	0.4		1.0	1.9	0.9	0.6		1.0
200	5.1	2.2	1.5	1.5		1.9	0.5				0.1
225		5.0	3.1	0.9	1.2	2.5					
250	2.6	5.4	2.6	0.4		2.6	0.3				0.0
275		9.7	1.3	0.6	1.2	1.7					
300		0.4	0.2			0.1					

to be slightly deeper than older fish. Depth distribution showed a bimodal tendency in winter, with the bulk of fish at 25–75 m and a smaller peak at 200–300 m.

Food habits, bioenergetics, trophic interactions, and climate change

Data from high seas tagging experiments have not yielded direct information on the food habits and trophic interactions of AYK salmon, as tagged salmon were released without sampling for stomach contents. Studies of the food habits and feeding ecology of immature and maturing salmon, however, have taken place concurrently with salmon tagging operations in the Bering Sea and Gulf of Alaska (e.g., Allen and Aron 1958; LeBrasseur 1966; Pearcy et al. 1988; Tadorokoro et al. 1996; Kaeriyama et al. 2004). The results of these and other studies indicated that the distribution of salmon in the open ocean was closely associated with the distribution of their preferred prey. Although salmon are well known to switch their diets depending on the local availability of prey, each species shows rather distinctive food preferences and feeding habits in the open ocean. For example, in the Gulf of Alaska, immature and maturing chum salmon fed almost exclusively on zooplankton; immature and maturing sockeye salmon consumed a more diverse array of prey (zooplankton, fish, squid) than chum salmon; maturing pink salmon were generalists, consuming almost any type of prey; immature and maturing Chinook salmon prefered squid and fish; and maturing coho salmon fed almost exclusively on squid (e.g., Kaeriyama et al. 2000, 2004).

Salmon diets varied by season, age-group, and habitat, as well as in response to inter-specific competition among salmon and changes in climate and ocean conditions. For example, Davis et al. (2004, 2005) examined seasonal differences in the diets of salmon in the Bering Sea. In summer, immature sockeye and chum salmon fed on squid, while in fall,

squid were absent from their diets and more euphausiids were consumed; in contrast, Chinook salmon ate more squid and fewer euphausiids in fall than in summer (Figure 17). Young sockeye and chum salmon contained a higher proportion of hyperiid amphipods than older salmon caught during the summer (Figure 18). However, this trend did not continue through the fall. In summer, the proportion of gelatinous zooplankton consumed by chum salmon increased with ocean age; however, in fall older chum salmon consumed a higher proportion of fish. Fish prey was particularly important to young immature Chinook salmon sampled during summer; however, little variability occurred in Chinook salmon diets with respect to age during the fall. Analysis of diets by ocean age-group incorporates some sized-related shifts in diet; nevertheless, size-related shifts in diet within a single age-group are also important (e.g., Aydin et al. 2005).

A strong biennial cycle occurred in the abundance of maturing pink salmon in the Bering Sea, and (research vessel catches showed a 30- to 50-fold increase in odd-numbered years; Azumaya and Ishida 2000). Data from high seas tagging experiments indicated that these pink salmon were primarily wild populations returning to the Karaginsky region of eastern Kamchatka (Myers et al. 1996). In response to this cycle, density-dependent shifts in prey composition have been observed in the food habits of pink, chum, sockeye, and Chinook salmon in the Bering Sea (e.g., Andrievskaya 1966; Tadokoro et al. 1996; Davis 2003). During even-numbered years when maturing pink salmon were scarce, the total stomach content weight and proportions of energy dense prey (euphausiids, copepods, squid, and fish) increased in the diets of sockeye and pink salmon, proportions of euphausiids and other crustaceans increased in the diets of chum salmon, and the proportion of squid increased in diets of Chinook salmon in summer (Davis 2003; Figure 19). Shifts in the proportion of prey groups

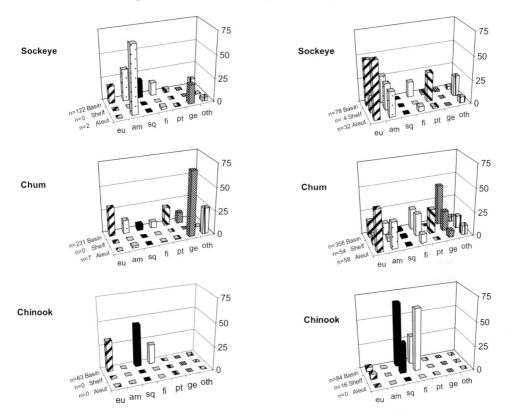

FIGURE 17. Diet composition (mean percent volume) of sockeye, chum, and Chinook salmon collected in the central Bering Sea basin, eastern Bering Sea shelf, and Aleutian Islands during summer (left panels) and fall 2002 (right panels). Prey categories include; eu = euphausiids, am = amphipods, sq = squid, fi = fish, pt = pteropods, ge = gelatinous zooplankton (medusae and ctenophores), and oth = other. Sample size (*n*) shown for each habitat.

reduced diet overlap among salmon, and probably reduced the overall caloric density of the diet consumed. In odd-numbered years when abundance of maturing pink salmon was high, dramatic increases (13% in sockeye, 19% in chum, 72% in pink salmon) occurred in the weight of low energy-density prey (pteropods, amphipods, or gelatinous zooplankton) in salmon stomach contents.

Estimates of daily ration based on field observations of high seas salmon food habits have shown that salmon were feeding at rates close to their physiological maximum, and in relatively short periods, small decreases in daily ration caused by competition, or other causes, could significantly decrease growth

(Davis et al. 1998). Under conditions of reduced growth, salmon may not attain a size large enough to feed on large prey, thereby developing a trophic feedback, such that salmon relinquish the growth potential afforded by a diet of large, more energy-dense prey, and remain competitors for consumption of zooplankton (Aydin et al. 2000).

Kaeriyama et al. (2004) hypothesized that salmon in the open ocean adapted to climate-induced changes in their prey by switching their diets either within or between trophic levels. In the northeastern Pacific, gonatid squids (mainly *Berryteuthis anonychus*) were the dominant prey of all species except chum salmon (e.g., Pearcy et al. 1988; Aydin et al. 2000; Kaeri-

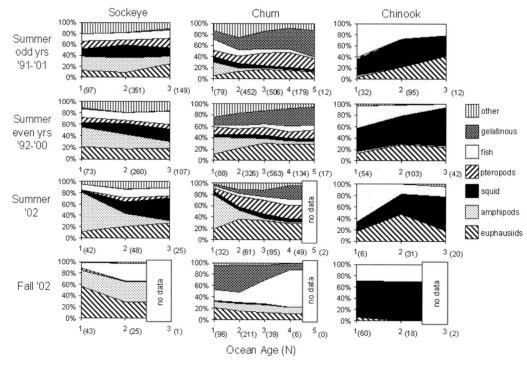

FIGURE 18. Diet composition (mean percent volume) of sockeye, chum, and Chinook salmon collected in the Bering Sea basin stratified by season and ocean age of fish. Sample sources include data for summer in odd-numbered years (1991–2001), summer in even-numbered years (1992–2000), summer 2002, and fall 2002. Ocean age followed by number of salmon stomachs in each age-group containing prey is shown on the x-axis. Age groups labeled with "no data" indicate sample sizes too small to characterize stomach contents ($n \leq 5$). Readers are cautioned that no data are available for fish between age groups.

yama et al. 2000). During the 1997 El Niño and 1999 La Niña events, the amount of squid in the diets of all species except coho salmon was reduced, and chum salmon diets switched from gelatinous zooplankton to a greater diversity of zooplankton prey (Kaeriyama et al. 2004). Climate model projections indicated that by 2050, mean sea surface temperatures (SSTs) in high latitudes could increase 2°C over 1990 values (IPCC 2001). Bioenergetic simulations of sockeye salmon using the Wisconsin bio-energetic model (Hanson et al. 1997), showed conversion efficiencies were lower when modeled conditions included a 2°C increase in sea surface temperatures (scenario 1 versus 2 and 3; Figure 20). This change occurred because as water temperature increases, energy demands

of metabolism and elimination can increase faster than prey consumption. Reduction in conversion efficiency was greater in juvenile and immature fish than maturing fish. Higher energy demands associated with a 2°C increase in SSTs led to an increase in prey consumption of 6–11% (g or kJ) to attain the same weight increment. If higher temperatures accompanied a 10% decrease in prey availability then net production (g) decreased by 26–28% for juvenile and immature fish or 10–18% for maturing sockeye salmon. Sockeye salmon experiencing increased mean summer temperatures could suffer reduced growth at all age-maturity stages unless prey availability or prey energy density increased commensurately (see also Beauchamp 2009, this volume).

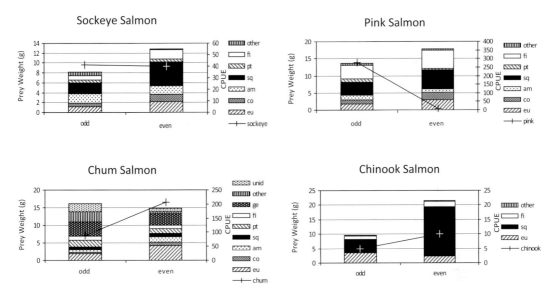

FIGURE 19. Mean weight (g) of each prey category observed in the stomach contents of sockeye, chum, pink, and Chinook salmon and mean catch per unit effort (CPUE = number of fish/50-m tan of research gillnet) observed during odd- and even-numbered years in the central Bering Sea in July 1991–2000. Prey categories include: eu = euphausiids, co = copepods, am = amphipods, sq = squid, pt = pteropods, fi = fish, ge = gelatinous zooplankton, and unid = unidentified.

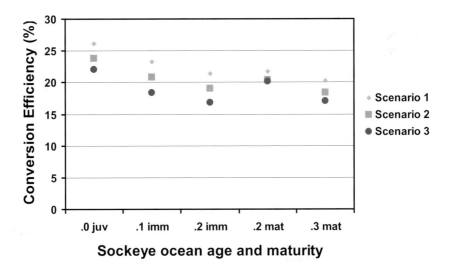

FIGURE 20. Sockeye salmon conversion efficiency (%; growth/consumption) by age and maturity group modeled using a bioenergetics model. Ocean age-0 juveniles modeled for the period from mid-July to mid-September (60 d), ocean age-1 and -2 immature modeled for the period from mid-June to mid-September (90 d), ocean age-2 and -3 maturing modeled for the period from mid-May to mid-July (60 d). Scenario 1 = 2004 SSTs and growth increment based on field observations. Scenario 2 = warmer ocean temperatures (2004 + 2°C SSTs) and the same growth increment as Scenario 1. Scenario 3 = warmer ocean temperatures (2004 + 2°C SSTs) and 10% lower prey availability than Scenarios 1 and 2. Diet compostion and diet energy density identical for all scenarios.

Conceptual models of High Seas Migrations of AYK Salmon

A new conceptual model of the ocean distribution and migration routes of AYK salmon is not provided; however, a clear need exists to update and revise current models. Our results indicated that three major life history patterns of immature and maturing AYK salmon species occur in the open ocean (Figure 21). Pink and coho salmon were similar in that they spend only one winter at sea, and were distributed in the NEP in spring and the NEP and GOA in summer. No published conceptual models exist of the ocean distribution and migration patterns of coho salmon. The current conceptual model for ocean migrations of pink salmon was developed by Takagi et al. (1981). Our results indicated significant extensions in the ocean range of maturing AYK pink salmon to the south in the NEP and to the west in the WBS (Figure 22).

The ocean life history patterns of immature and maturing AYK chum and sockeye salmon were similar in that they spend multiple winters at sea, and were distributed primarily in the GOA in spring and the GOA and Bering Sea in summer (Figure 21). However, the current migration models for chum salmon (Fredin et al. 1977) indicated that immature western Alaska (Bristol Bay and AYK) chum salmon did not migrate to the Bering Sea in summer. Multiple lines of evidence (tags, genetics, scale pattern analysis) indicated that this model is incorrect (e.g., see review by Seeb et al. 2004; Figure 10, July panel). Published conceptual models for western Alaska sockeye salmon pertain largely to Bristol Bay stocks (Fredin et al. 1977; Burgner 1991). No published conceptual models exist for immature and maturing AYK Chinook salmon. More importantly, current models did not account for interannual changes in ocean conditions and climate-related effects on ocean distribution and migration routes of AYK salmon stocks. For example, current conceptual models did not show characteristic differences in open-ocean distribution and migration routes of salmon between "cold" and "warm" ocean years (e.g., Myers et al. 2007; Farley et al. 2009). New dynamic models, incorporating climate change effects on ocean distribution and migration at critical life history stages, would be more useful for predicting changes in carrying capacity, growth and survival, interceptions by marine fisheries, and timing of adult returns to the AYK region.

Information gaps and future research directions

Over the years many leading fishery scientists have acknowledged that critical gaps exist in information on salmon in the open ocean, and have identified future research directions and themes that would contribute to our understanding of the distribution, biology, and ecology of salmon in the North Pacific Ocean and Bering Sea. For example, Larkin (1975) identified three fundamental questions related to high seas salmon research that he considered critical to successful management of Pacific salmon: How do salmon navigate? Do various stocks interact on the high seas? What is the long-term effect of exploitation? Others have considered data on salmon in the open ocean as "nice to know" but not essential to fishery management. After all, they ask: how can we really use that information to better manage our salmon resources? In large part, this skepticism stems from the lack of accurate and precise scientific data on population-specific distribution, biology, and ecology of salmon on the high seas. Recent advances and applications of genetic stock identification techniques to ocean research, which are described in other papers presented at this symposium (e.g., Beacham et al. 2009, this volume), can provide more accurate and precise estimates of the regional

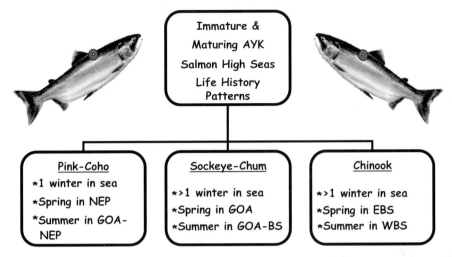

FIGURE 21. Summary of three major high seas life history patterns of immature and maturing Arc-tic-Yukon-Kuskokwim (AYK) salmon, as indicated by the results of high seas tagging experiments, 1954–2006. NEP = northeastern Pacific Ocean, GOA = Gulf of Alaska, BS = Bering Sea, EBS = eastern Bering Sea, WBS = western Bering Sea.

stock composition of salmon migrating in the open ocean. The abundance, body size, and health of maturing salmon returning from the high seas are variables critical to the reproductive success of salmon, provide essential ecosystem services (e.g., nutrient input, food for other species), and determine the success or failure of AYK salmon fisheries and markets. When salmon runs fail, the problem is frequently attributed to mysterious changes in oceanic conditions. Advance information on the status of AYK salmon stocks in the ocean prior to their return to coastal and freshwater habitats would provide input necessary to manage expectations of stakeholders and proactively formulate management actions. Because changes in climate and exploitation by marine fisheries will continue to cause unexpected fluctuations in returns of adult salmon to the AYK region, we cannot continue to rely on limited scientific data from historical research.

New scientific data on AYK salmon distribution and migration patterns, carrying capacity, growth, and stock and fishery interactions in the marine environment are needed. Many important questions should be addressed, as listed below.

1. What is the interannual variation in seasonal distribution and migration patterns of AYK salmon at each ocean life history stage? Where are their critical habitats and foraging areas? What are the boundaries of these areas, the physical, chemical, and biological conditions that define their boundaries (spatial, temporal), and salmon residence times in these areas?

2. What are the primary ocean prey, predators, and competitors of AYK salmon? What is the range of variation in spatial and temporal overlap of salmon and their predators and prey? How do changes in ocean conditions affect predator–prey-competitor relations?

3. What and where are the best habitats for promoting summer growth and winter survival of AYK salmon? How does environment and body condition (e.g., temperature, photoperiod, lipid content) influence their winter survival and size or age at maturity?

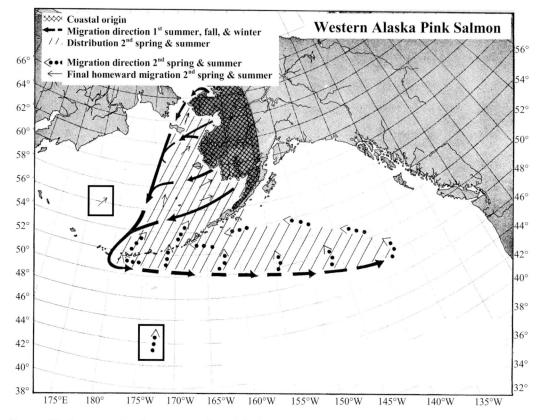

FIGURE 22. An example of a conceptual model of open ocean distribution and seasonal migration patterns of AYK salmon that needs to be updated. This model representing all populations of pink salmon originating in western Alaska was developed using ocean catch, biological, and tag recovery data, 1954–1971. Source: Figure 92, Takagi et al. 1981; Figure 28, Heard 1991). The arrows inside the boxes indicate spring-summer high seas release locations of two maturing pink salmon that were recovered in the AYK region in the 1980s after publication of the Takagi et al. (1981) model.

4. What roles do salmon vertical distribution and migration play in growth, bioenergetics, and survival of AYK salmon in different seasons? How is vertical distribution of salmon affected by stratification of ocean layers and changes in the physical properties of sea surface waters (e.g., temperature, salinity, oxygen)?

5. What is the evidence for competition or density-dependent growth or mortality between AYK salmon and Asian salmon stocks in the Bering Sea (e.g., Russian pink salmon, Hokkaido chum salmon)?

6. How do short-term climate change (e.g., warm winters versus cold winters, El Niño versus La Niña) and long-term climate change (e.g., Arctic Oscillation, Pacific Decadal Oscillation) differ in their effects on distribution, migration, and foraging patterns?

7. How can research trawl data (the current fishing gear of choice for high seas salmon research) be used to accurately estimate salmon abundance? How can remote sensing technologies be used in place of research fishing gear to obtain accurate estimates of salmon abundance?

8. How are environmental conditions and salmon behavior (distribution, migration, and feeding patterns) related to their abundance and survival, and can fishery managers use this information to accurately forecast adult returns?

9. When and where do stock-specific aggregations of AYK salmon form in the ocean? When and where are they most susceptible to interception fisheries? What are the catches and bycatches of AYK salmon in coastal and offshore fisheries both inside and outside the U.S. EEZ?

10. Are large releases of hatchery salmon affecting the health (introduced parasites and diseases) and carrying capacity of AYK salmon in the Bering Sea and Gulf of Alaska?

The best approach to filling these and other information gaps is a long-term, multidisciplinary research and monitoring effort to provide data for ocean assessment, management, and conservation of AYK salmon stocks. Directed research efforts on AYK salmon in the coastal domain are also essential to understanding the causes of short- and long-term variation in ocean survival. Given the low abundance of all species of AYK salmon relative to many other salmon stocks, however, a directed research effort on immature and maturing AYK salmon in the open ocean is not practical. We recommend developing a program of high seas research on AYK salmon in conjunction with other ongoing research programs, as well as making better use of opportunities to collect samples and data from marine commercial and subsistence fisheries. Because AYK salmon migrate in the ocean across international boundaries and in the international waters (high seas) of the Bering Sea and North Pacific Ocean, new research should be closely coordinated with the ongoing international treaty research programs of NPAFC and PICES (North Pacific Marine Sciences Organization).

Acknowledgments

Funding for data analyses and preparation of this manuscript was provided by the Arctic-Yukon-Kuskokwim Sustainable Salmon Initiative. Jerry Berger, Alaska Fisheries Science Center, NOAA Fisheries, provided groundfish trawl fishery data. We thank Charles Krueger and three anonymous reviewers for their helpful editorial comments and suggestions for improving this manuscript. Funding for preparation of this manuscript was provided by the Arctic-Yukon-Kuskokwim Sustainable Salmon Initiative and award NAO4NMF4380162 from the National Oceanic and Atmospheric Administration, U.S. Department of Commerce, administered by the Alaska Department of Fish and Game. The statements, findings, conclusions, and recommendations are those of the authors and do not necessarily reflect the views of the National Oceanic and Atmospheric Administration, the U.S. Department of Commerce, or the Alaska Department of Fish and Game.

References

Allen, G. H., and W. Aron. 1958. Food of salmonid fishes of the western North Pacific Ocean. Special Scientific Report 237. U.S. Fish and Wildlife Service, Washington, D.C.

Andrievskaya, L. D. 1966. Food relationships of the Pacific salmon in the sea. Preliminary translation by United States Joint Publications Research Service, Bureau of Commercial Fisheries.

Aro, K. V., J. A. Thomson, and D. P. Giovando. 1971. Recoveries of salmon tagged offshore in the North Pacific Ocean by Canada, Japan, and the United States, 1956–1969. Fisheries Research Board of Canada, Manuscript Report 1147.

Aydin, K. Y. 2000. Trophic feedback and variation in carrying capacity of Pacific salmon (*Oncorhynchus* spp.) on the high seas of the Gulf of Alaska. Doctoral dissertation, University of Washington, Seattle.

Aydin, K. Y., K. W Myers, and R. V. Walker. 2000. Variation in summer distribution of the prey of Pacific salmon (*Oncorhynchus* spp.) in the offshore

Gulf of Alaska in relation to oceanographic conditions, 1994–98. North Pacific Anadromous Fish Commission Bulletin 2:43–54.

Aydin, K. Y., G. A. McFarlane, J. R. King, B. A. Megrey, and K. W. Myers. 2005. Linking oceanic food webs to coastal production and growth rates of Pacific salmon (*Oncorhynchus* spp.), using models on three scales. Deep-Sea Research II 52:757–780.

AYK SSI (Arctic-Yukon-Kuskokwim Sustainable Salmon Initiative). 2006. Arctic-Yukon-Kuskokwim Salmon Research and Restoration Plan. Bering Sea Fishermen's Association, Anchorage, Alaska.

Azumaya, T., and Y. Ishida. 2000. Density interactions between pink salmon (*Oncorhynchus gorbuscha*) and chum salmon (*O. keta*) and their possible effects on distribution and growth in the North Pacific Ocean and Bering Sea. North Pacific Anadromous Fish Commission Bulletin 2:165–174.

Beacham, T. D., K. D. Le, M. Wetklo, B. McIntosh, T. Ming, and K. M. Miller. 2009. Population structure and stock identification of chum salmon from western Alaska determined with microsatellite DNA and major histocompatibility complex variation. Pages 141–160 *in* C. C. Krueger and C. E. Zimmerman, editors. Pacific salmon: ecology and management of western Alaska's populations. American Fisheries Society, Symposium 70, Bethesda, Maryland.

Beamish, R. J., and D. R. Bouillion. 1993. Pacific salmon production trends in relation to climate. Canadian Journal of Fisheries and Aquatic Sciences 50:1002–1016.

Beauchamp, D. A. 2009. Bioenergetic ontogeny: linking climate and mass-specific feeding to life-cycle growth and survival of salmon. Pages 53–71 *in* C. C. Krueger and C. E. Zimmerman, editors. Pacific salmon: ecology and management of western Alaska's populations. American Fisheries Society, Symposium 70, Bethesda, Maryland.

Bigler, B. S., D. W. Welch, and J. H. Helle. 1996. A review of size trends among North Pacific salmon (*Oncorhynchus* spp.). Canadian Journal of Fisheries and Aquatic Sciences 53:455–465.

Brannian, L. K. 1984. Recovery distribution of chum salmon (*Oncorhynchus keta*) tagged in the North Pacific offshore of the Alaska Peninsula and eastern Aleutian Island chain. Alaska Department of Fish and Game, Informational Leaflet 237.

Brodeur, R. D., K. W. Myers, and J. H. Helle. 2003. Research conducted by the United States on the early ocean life history of Pacific salmon. North Pacific Anadromous Fish Commission Bulletin 3:89–131.

Bugaev, A. V. 2005. Identification local stocks of sockeye and Chinook salmon by scale pattern analysis from trawl catches of R/V "TINRO" worked by program of the Bering-Aleutian Salmon International Survey (BASIS) in September–October 2002. North Pacific Anadromous Fish Commission Technical Report 6:88–90.

Bugaev, V. F., D. W. Welch, M. M. Selifonov, L. E. Grachev, and J. P. Eveson. 2001. Influence of the marine abundance of pink salmon (*Oncorhynchus gorbuscha*) and sockeye salmon (*O. nerka*) on growth of Ozernaya River sockeye. Fisheries Oceanography 10:26–32.

Burgner, R. L. 1991. Life history of sockeye salmon (*Oncorhynchus nerka*). Pages 1–117 *in* C. Groot and L. Margolis, editors. Pacific salmon: life histories. University of British Columbia Press, Vancouver.

Davis, N. D. 1990. Origins of Chinook salmon in the area of the Japanese mothership and landbased driftnet salmon fisheries in 1985 and 1986. International North Pacific Fisheries Commission Document. FRI-UW-9015. Fisheries Research Institute, University of Washington, Seattle.

Davis, N. D. 1991. Origins of Chinook salmon in the Japanese traditional landbased driftnet fishery in 1990 based on scale pattern analysis. International North Pacific Fisheries Commission Document. FRI-UW-9114. Fisheries Research Institute, University of Washington, Seattle.

Davis, N. D. 2003. Feeding ecology of Pacific salmon (*Oncorhynchus* spp.) in the central North Pacific Ocean and central Bering Sea, 1991–2000. Doctoral dissertation. Hokkaido University, Hakodate, Japan.

Davis, N. D., J. L. Armstrong, and K. W. Myers. 2004. Bering Sea salmon diet overlap in fall 2002 and potential for interactions among salmon. North Pacific Anadromous Fish Commission Document 779. School Aquatic & Fishery Sciences, University of Washington, Seattle.

Davis, N. D., M. Fukuwaka, J. L. Armstrong, and K. W. Myers. 2005. Salmon food habits in the Bering Sea, 1960 to present. North Pacific Anadromous Fish Commission Technical Report 6:24–28.

Davis, N. D., K. W. Myers, and Y. Ishida. 1998. Caloric value of high seas salmon prey organisms and simulated ocean growth and prey consumption. North Pacific Anadromous Fish Commission Bulletin 1:146–162.

Davis, N. D., K. W. Myers, R. V. Walker, and C. K. Harris. 1990. The Fisheries Research Institute's high-seas salmonid tagging program and methodology for scale pattern analysis. Pages 863–879 *in* N. C. Parker, A. E. Giorgi, R. C. Heidinger, D. B. Jester, Jr., E. D. Prince, and G. A. Winans, editors. Fish-Marking Techniques. American Fisheries Society, Symposium 7, Bethesda, Maryland.

Eggers, D. M., K. Rowell, and B. Barrett. 1991. Stock composition of sockeye and chum salmon catches in southern Alaska Peninsula fisheries in June. Fishery Research Bulletin No. 91–01, Alaska Department of Fish and Game, Division of Commercial Fisheries, Juneau.

Farley, E.V., J. Murphy, J. H. Moss, A. Feldmann, and L. Eisner. 2009. Marine ecology of western Alaska juvenile salmon. Pages 307–329 in C. C. Krueger and C. E. Zimmerman, editors. Pacific salmon: ecology and management of western Alaska's populations. American Fisheries Society, Symposium 70, Bethesda, Maryland.

Fredin, R. A., R. L. Major, R. G. Bakkala, and G. K. Tanonaka. 1977. Pacific salmon and the high seas salmon fisheries of Japan. Unpublished Processed Report, National Marine Fisheries Service, Northwest and Alaska Fisheries Center, Seattle.

Grebmeier, J. M., J. E. Overland, S. E. Moore, E. V. Farley, E. C. Carmack, L. W. Cooper, K. E. Frey, J. H. Helle, F. A. McLaughlin, and S. L. McNutt. 2006. A major ecosystem shift in the northern Bering Sea. Science 311:1461–1464.

Habicht, C., N. V. Varnavskaya, T. Azumaya, S. Urawa, R. L. Wilmot, C. M. Guthrie III, and J. E. Seeb. 2005. Migration patterns of sockeye salmon in the Bering Sea discerned from stock composition estimates of fish captured during BASIS studies. North Pacific Anadromous Fish Commission Technical Report 6:41–43.

Hanson, P. C., T. B. Johnson, D. E. Schindler, and J. F. Kitchell. 1997. Fish Bioenergetics 3.0. Software published by University of Wisconsin Sea Grant and Center for Limnology, University of Wisconsin-Madison, Madison. WISCU-T-97–001.

Hard, J., W. H. Eldridge, and K. A. Naish. 2009. Genetic consequences of size-selective fishing: implications for viability of Chinook salmon in the Arctic-Yukon-Kuskokwim region of Alaska. Pages 759–780 in C. C. Krueger and C. E. Zimmerman, editors. Pacific salmon: ecology and management of western Alaska's populations. American Fisheries Society, Symposium 70, Bethesda, Maryland.

Healey, M. C. 1991. Life history of Chinook salmon. Pages 311–394 in C. Groot and L. Margolis, editors. Pacific salmon: life histories. University of British Columbia Press, Vancouver.

Heard, W. R. 1991. Life history of pink salmon. Pages 120–230 in K. Groot and L. Margolis, editors. Pacific salmon: life histories. University of British Columbia Press, Vancouver.

Helle, J. H., and M. S. Hoffman. 1995. Size decline and older age at maturity of two chum salmon (Oncorhynchus keta) stocks in western North America, 1972–1992. Pages 245–260 in R. J. Beamish, editor. Climate change and northern fish populations. Canadian Special Publication of Fisheries and Aquatic Sciences 121.

Hunt, G. L., Jr., P. Stabeno, G. Walters, E. Sinclair, R. D. Brodeur, J. M. Napp, and N. A. Bond. 2002. Climate change and control of the southeastern Bering Sea pelagic ecosystem. Deep-Sea Research II 49:5821–5853.

IPCC (Intergovernmental Panel on Climate Change). 2001. Climate Change 2001: Synthesis Report. A Contribution of Working Groups I, II, and III to the Third Assessment Report of the Intergovernmental Panel on Climate Change. [Watson, R.T., and the Core Writing Team, editors] Cambridge University Press, Cambridge, United Kingdom and New York.

Ishida, Y., S. Ito, M. Kaeriyama, S. McKinnell, and K. Nagasawa. 1993. Recent changes in age and size of chum salmon (Oncorhynchus keta) in the North Pacific and possible causes. Canadian Journal of Fisheries and Aquatic Sciences 50:290–295.

Ishida, Y., S. Ito, and K. Murai. 1995. Density dependent growth of pink salmon (Oncorhynchus gorbuscha) in the Bering Sea and western North Pacific. North Pacific Anadromous Fish Commission Document 140. National Research Institute of Far Seas Fisheries, Shimizu, Japan.

Jackson, R. I., and W. F. Royce. 1986. Ocean forum: an interpretative history of the International North Pacific Fisheries Commission. Fishing News Books Ltd., Farnham, Surrey, England.

Kaeriyama, M. 1989. Aspects of salmon ranching in Japan. Physiology and Ecology Japan, Special Publication 1:625–638.

Kaeriyama, M., M. Nakamura, R. Edpalina, J. R. Bower, H. Yamaguchi, R. V. Walker, and K. W. Myers. 2004. Change in feeding ecology and trophic dynamics of Pacific salmon (Oncorhynchus spp.) in the central Gulf of Alaska in relation to climate events. Fisheries Oceanography 13:197–207.

Kaeriyama, M., M. Nakamura, M. Yamaguchi, H. Ueda, G. Anma, S. Takagi, K. Aydin, R.V. Walker, and K.W. Myers. 2000. Feeding ecology of sockeye and pink salmon in the Gulf of Alaska. North Pacific Anadromous Fish Commission Bulletin 2:55–63.

Koo, T. S. Y. 1962. Age designation in salmon. Pages 41–48 in T. S. Y. Koo, editor. Studies of Alaska red salmon. University of Washington Press, Seattle.

Kruse, G. H. 1998. Salmon run failures in 1997–1998: A link to anomalous ocean conditions? Alaska Fishery Research Bulletin 5:55–63.

Larkin, P. A. 1975. Some major problems for further study on Pacific salmon. International North Pacific Fisheries Commission Bulletin 32:3–9.

LeBrasseur, R. J. 1966. Stomach contents of salmon and steelhead trout in the northeastern Pacific Ocean. Journal of the Fisheries Research Board of Canada 23:85–100.

Major, R. L., J. Ito, S. Ito, and H. Godfrey. 1978. Distribution and abundance of Chinook salmon (*Oncorhynchus tshawytscha*) in offshore waters of the North Pacific Ocean. International North Pacific Fisheries Commission Bulletin 38.

Mantua, N. 2009. Patterns of change in climate and Pacific salmon production. Pages 1143–1157 *in* C. C. Krueger and C. E. Zimmerman, editors. Pacific salmon: ecology and management of western Alaska's populations. American Fisheries Society, Symposium 70, Bethesda, Maryland.

Myers, K. W., and D. E. Rogers. 1988. Stock origins of Chinook salmon in incidental catches by groundfish fisheries in the eastern Bering Sea. North American Journal of Fisheries Management 8:162–171.

Myers, K. W., K. Y. Aydin, R. V. Walker, S. Fowler, and M. L. Dahlberg. 1996. Known ocean ranges of stocks of Pacific salmon and steelhead as shown by tagging experiments, 1956–1995. North Pacific Anadromous Fish Commission Document 192. FRI-UW-9614. Fisheries Research Institute, University of Washington, Seattle.

Myers, K. W., C. K. Harris, Y. Ishida, L. Margolis, and M. Ogura. 1993. Review of the Japanese land-based driftnet salmon fishery in the western North Pacific Ocean and the continent of origin of salmonids in this area. International North Pacific Fisheries Commission Bulletin 52.

Myers, K. W., C. K. Harris, C. M. Knudsen, R. V. Walker, N. D. Davis, and D. E. Rogers. 1987. Stock origins of Chinook salmon in the area of the Japanese mothership salmon fishery. North American Journal of Fisheries Management 7:459–474.

Myers, K. W., N. V. Klovach, O. F. Gritsenko, S. Urawa, and T. C. Royer. 2007. Stock-specific distributions of Asian and North American salmon in the open ocean, interannual changes, and oceanographic conditions. North Pacific Anadromous Fish Commission Bulletin 4:159–177.

Myers, K. W., D. E. Rogers, C. K. Harris, C. M. Knudsen, R. V. Walker, and N. D. Davis. 1984. Origins of Chinook salmon in the area of the Japanese mothership and landbased driftnet salmon fisheries in 1975–1981. International North Pacific Fisheries Commission Document, Fisheries Research Institute, University of Washington, Seattle.

Myers, K. W., R. V. Walker, J. L. Armstrong, and N. D. Davis. 2003. Estimates of the bycatch of Yukon River Chinook salmon in U.S. groundfish fisheries in the eastern Bering Sea, 1997–1999. Final Report to the Yukon River Drainage Fisheries Association, Contract Number 04–001. SAFS-UW-0312, School of Aquatic and Fishery Sciences, University of Washington, Seattle.

Myers, K. W., R. V. Walker, H. R. Carlson, and J. H. Helle. 2000. Synthesis and review of US Research on the physical and biological factors affecting ocean production of salmon. North Pacific Anadromous Fish Commission Bulletin 2:1–9.

Myers, K. W., R. V. Walker, N. D. Davis, and R. L. Burgner. 2004. A history of U.S. high seas salmon and steelhead stock identification research. North Pacific Anadromous Fish Commission Technical Report 5:16–17.

Neave, F., T. Yonemori, and R. G. Bakkala. 1976. Distribution and origin of chum salmon in offshore waters of the North Pacific Ocean. International North Pacific Fisheries Commission Bulletin 35.

NPAFC (North Pacific Anadromous Fish Commission). 2001. CD-Rom statistical yearbook 2000–2001 and historical data. Vancouver, B.C.

Overland, J. E., and P. J. Stabeno. 2004. Is the climate of the Bering Sea warming and affecting the ecosystem. Earth and Ocean Sciences 85:309–316.

Patton, W. S., K. W. Myers, and R. V. Walker. 1998. Origins of chum salmon caught incidentally in the Eastern Bering Sea walleye pollock trawl fishery as estimated from scale pattern analysis. North American Journal of Fisheries Management 18:704–712.

Pearcy, W. G., R. D. Brodeur, J. Shenker, W. Smoker, and Y. Endo. 1988. Food habits of Pacific salmon and steelhead trout, midwater trawl catches, and oceanographic conditions in the Gulf of Alaska, 1980–1985. Bulletin of the Ocean Research Institute 26:29–78.

Rogers, D. E. 1980. Density-dependent growth of Bristol Bay sockeye salmon. Pages 267–283 *in* W. McNeil and D. Himsworth, editors. Salmonid ecosystems of the North Pacific. Oregon State University Press, Corvallis.

Rogers, D. E. 1984. Trends in abundance of northeastern Pacific stocks of salmon. Pages 100–127 *in* W. G. Pearcy, editor. Proceedings, the influence of ocean conditions on the production of salmonids in the North Pacific. Oregon State University Press, Corvallis.

Rogers, D. E. 1987. Interceptions of Yukon salmon by high seas fisheries. FRI-UW-8705, Fisheries Research Institute, University of Washington, Seattle.

Rogers, D. E., and G. T. Ruggerone. 1993. Factors affecting marine growth of Bristol Bay sockeye salmon. Fisheries Research 18:89–103.

Ruggerone, G. T., M. Zimmermann, K. W. Myers, J. L. Nielsen, and D. E. Rogers. 2003. Competition between Asian pink salmon (*Oncorhynchus gorbuscha*) and Alaska sockeye salmon (*O. nerka*) in the North Pacific Ocean. Fisheries Oceanography 12:209–219.

Salo, E. O. 1991. Life history of chum salmon (*Oncorhynchus keta*). Pages 231–309 *in* K. Groot and

L. Margolis, editors. Pacific salmon: life histories. University of British Columbia Press, Vancouver.

Sandercock, F. K. 1991. Life history of coho salmon (*Oncorhynchus kisutch*). Pages 397–445 *in* C. Groot and L. Margolis, editors. Pacific salmon: life histories. University of British Columbia Press, Vancouver.

Seeb, L. W., A. Antonovich, M. A. Banks, T. D. Beacham, M. R. Bellinger, S. M. Blankenship, M. R. Campbell, N. A. Decovich, J. C. Garza, C. M. Guthrie III, T. A. Lundrigan, P. Moran, S. R. Narum, J. J. Stephenson, K. J. Supernault, D. J. Teel, W. D. Templin, J. K. Wenburg, S. F. Young, and C. T. Smith. 2007. Development of a standardized DNA database for Chinook salmon. Fisheries 32:540–552.

Seeb, L. W., P. A. Crane, C. M. Kondzela, R. L. Wilmot, S. Urawa, N. V. Varnavskaya, and J. E. Seeb. 2004. Migration of Pacific Rim salmon on the high seas: insights from genetic data. Environmental Biology of Fishes 69:21–36.

Tadokoro, K., Y. Ishida, N. D. Davis, S. Ueyanagi, and T. Sugimoto. 1996. Change in chum salmon (*Oncorhynchus keta*) stomach contents associated with fluctuation of pink salmon (*O. gorbuscha*) abundance in the central subarctic Pacific and Bering Sea. Fisheries Oceanography 5:89–99.

Takagi, K., K. V. Aro, A. C. Hartt, and M. B. Dell. 1981. Distribution and origin of pink salmon (*Oncorhynchus gorbuscha*) in offshore waters of the North Pacific Ocean. International North Pacific Fisheries Commission Bulletin 40.

Walker, R. V., K. W. Myers, and S. Ito. 1998. Growth studies from 1956–1995 collections of pink and chum salmon scales in the central North Pacific Ocean. North Pacific Anadromous Fish Commission Bulletin 1:54–65.

Walker, R. V., V. V. Sviridov, S. Urawa, and T. Azumaya. 2007. Spatio-temporal variation in vertical distributions of Pacific salmon in the ocean. North Pacific Anadromous Fish Commission Bulletin 4:193–201.

Wilmot, R. L., C. M. Kondzela, C. M. Guthrie, and M. S. Masuda. 1998. Genetic stock identification of chum salmon harvested incidentally in the 1994 and 1995 Bering Sea trawl fishery. North Pacific Anadromous Fish Commission Bulletin 1:285–299.

American Fisheries Society Symposium 70:241–265, 2009

A Review of Growth and Survival of Salmon at Sea in Response to Competition and Climate Change

GREGORY T. RUGGERONE[*]

Natural Resources Consultants, Inc.
4039 21st Avenue West, Suite 404, Seattle, Washington 98199, USA

JENNIFER L. NIELSEN

U.S. Geological Survey, Alaska Science Center
4210 University Drive, Anchorage, Alaska 99508, USA

Abstract.—Studies have documented density-dependent growth of salmon in the ocean during early and late marine stages in response to competition between species. However, key questions remain as to whether competition and reduced growth at sea translate to lower survival of salmon, and whether changes in ocean regimes can alter this relationship. Few studies have tested these questions, in part, because the capacity of the ocean to support salmon is dynamic and smaller adult size has been associated with high abundance, which infers high overall survival. In support of salmon management activities in the Arctic-Yukon-Kuskokwim (AYK) region, we review evidence from recent studies suggesting that competition at sea can lead to reduced salmon growth and survival and to potentially lower reproductive potential of survivors. Climate change may, however, also affect prey availability and therefore influence the magnitude of competition. Salmon growth (and survival) responses to competition and climate shifts can vary with season and life stage of salmon. We conclude that growth of salmon is key to their survival and that competition at sea is an important, yet often elusive mechanism affecting salmon population dynamics.

Introduction

Competition has been widely described in terrestrial, freshwater, and some marine communities (e.g., Schoener 1983; Bertness et al. 2001). Some scientists have assumed that interspecific competition may influence abundances and characteristics of offshore marine fish populations (Cushing 1975; National Research Council 1999; Lorenzen and Enberg 2002), whereas others have downplayed its importance in regulating these populations (Sinclair 1988; Shuntov and Temnykh 2005; NPAFC 2005). Quantification of species interactions is important given the growing desire to manage marine fisheries using the concept of ecosystem management (National Research Council 1999).

A number of studies indicate that intraspecific competition at sea can influence body size of adult salmon (e.g., Peterman 1978, 1984; Ishida et al. 1993, 2002; Rogers 1980; Welch and Parsons 1993; Pyper and Peterman 1999; Rogers and Ruggerone 1993; Azumaya and Ishida 2000; Kaeriyama 2005; Martinson et al. 2008). However, few studies

[*]Corresponding author: GRuggerone@nrccorp.com

involve competition between salmon species, even though many studies show considerable spatial and diet overlap and the potential for competition. A primary question is whether intraspecific and/or interspecific competition can influence salmon survival and abundance (Pearcy et al. 1999; Cooney and Brodeur 1998; Heard 1998; Brodeur et al. 2003). This question is difficult to address because high salmon abundance, which may be associated with reduced body size, typically infers high survival. Furthermore, the lack of experimental controls can confound interpretation of studies attempting to test whether competition has influenced salmon survival and abundance. Nevertheless, the importance of competition in regulating salmon growth and population abundance is especially important because up to 5 billion juvenile salmon are released from hatcheries each year (Mahnken et al. 1998), regardless of climate and ocean condition effects on prey availability.

The authors prepared this review of salmon competition at sea in response to a request from the Arctic-Yukon-Kuskokwim (AYK) Sustainable Salmon Initiative. Competition at sea may be important to growth, survival, and age of maturation of AYK salmon because a number of studies have found competition effects among salmon in the Bering Sea and in the North Pacific Ocean where AYK salmon rear and grow. This review is not intended to be an exhaustive review of studies. Rather, the authors supplemented an earlier review of interspecific competition (Ruggerone and Nielsen 2004) with new information, including recent studies within the AYK region. The authors focused this review on competition involving pink salmon *Oncorhynchus gorbuscha*, which are highly abundant, grow rapidly, and often share common prey with other salmon species (e.g., Figure 1). Pink salmon also exhibit an invariable two-year life cycle that can lead to large differences in abundance between odd- versus even-numbered years, a pattern that provides a natural

experimental control for ocean climate conditions that often affect salmon populations in the same manner (Rogers 1984; Beamish and Bouillon 1993; Mantua et al. 1997; Pyper et al. 2005). Additionally, we examined recent studies involving interactions between salmon broods and competition between wild and hatchery salmon in marine waters.

Sockeye and Pink Salmon Interactions

Pink and sockeye salmon *O. nerka* are opportunistic foragers that have similar diets in offshore marine waters (Davis et al. 2000, 2005; Kaeriyama et al. 2000, 2004). Their diet includes prey from several trophic levels, including zooplankton and micronekton such as squid and small fishes. Research in the central North Pacific Ocean demonstrated that zooplankton biomass was lower during June and July of odd-numbered years (Sugimoto and Tadokoro 1997; Shiomoto et al. 1997). These researchers concluded that Asian pink salmon, which are highly abundant during odd-numbered years, had reduced zooplankton abundance over this large region.

Density-dependent shifts in prey composition of pink and sockeye salmon have been observed in response to the bi-ennial cycle of pink salmon and their impact on prey availability (Figure 1; Sano 1963; Ito 1964; Davis 2003; Davis et al. 2005; Myers et al. 2009, this volume). During 1991–2000, stomach contents of pink and sockeye salmon collected in the central Bering Sea declined 24% and 36%, respectively, during even- versus odd-numbered years (high pink salmon abundance) (Davis 2003). However, two key prey of both species (squid and fish) declined more in sockeye salmon (27%) than in pink salmon (7%), suggesting that pink salmon were more efficient at exploiting key prey. During 1991–2000, catch-per-unit-effort (CPUE) of pink salmon in the central Bering Sea was

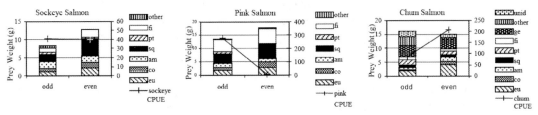

FIGURE 1. Mean weight. (g) of each prey category observed in the stomach contents of sockeye, pink, and chum salmon, and mean CPUE (number of fish/50-m tan of research gillnet) observed during odd- and even-numbered years in the central Bering Sea in July, 1991–2000. eu = euphausiids, co = copepods, am = amphipods, sq = squid, pt = pteropods, fi = fish, ge = gelatinous zooplankton, unid = unidentified. Source: Davis et al. 2005.

approximately 2500% greater in odd- versus even-numbered years (Davis et al. 2005). Pink salmon CPUE was approximately 580% greater than that of sockeye salmon (Figure 1).

Ruggerone et al. (2003) provided evidence that Asian pink salmon, primarily those from the eastern Kamchatka Peninsula, reduced the growth and survival of Bristol Bay sockeye salmon. Annual sockeye salmon scale patterns, 1955–2000, exhibited an alternating-year pattern of growth during the second and third years at sea that was opposite that of Asian pink salmon abundance (Figure 2). Sockeye growth during the first growing season at sea was not reduced because overlap with Asian pink salmon did not begin until the second season at sea, and relatively few pink salmon originate in Bristol Bay. Based on a multiple regression analysis, scale growth of Bristol Bay sockeye during the second year at sea (1966–2000) was negatively correlated with harvests of eastern Kamchatka pink salmon (partial $P < 0.001$), but positively correlated with winter sea surface temperature in the North Pacific Ocean (partial $P < 0.002$; Ruggerone and Nielsen 2004).

Age-specific length of adult sockeye salmon returning to Bristol Bay, 1958–2002, was inversely related to Asian pink salmon abundance during the year prior to homeward migration (Ruggerone et al. 2003,

2007a). This pattern was consistent among all four major age groups and both sexes of sockeye salmon. Pink salmon tended to have the greatest effect on younger age groups (e.g., ages 1.2 and 2.2) and female salmon. The multi-variate analyses indicated that intraspecific competition among sockeye during the homeward migration had a greater effect on sockeye salmon size than did competition with pink salmon during the previous year. However, the effect of pink salmon on growth of sockeye salmon may have been greater than shown in this analysis because slower growing sockeye salmon likely died during the second year at sea, as noted below. This analysis also identified level shifts in sockeye salmon size that were associated with the 1976–1977 and 1989 climate shifts, i.e., sockeye salmon growth increased after the 1976–1977 climate shift but declined after the 1989 shift.

Ruggerone et al. (2005) examined seasonal scale growth patterns of Bristol Bay sockeye salmon in relation to pink salmon abundance during 1955–2000. They reported that the reduction in salmon growth observed during the second and third years at sea began immediately after peak prey availability in spring and continued to the end of the growing season, well after pink salmon had left the high seas (Figure 3). Prey population dynamics that influenced the alternating-year pattern in seasonal sockeye growth

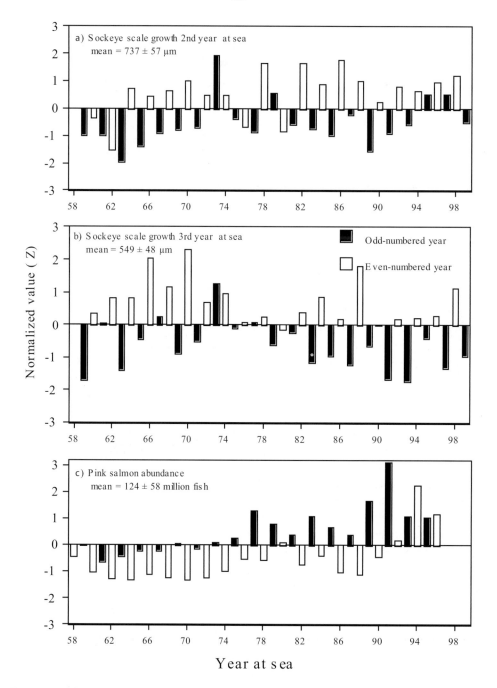

FIGURE 2. Bristol Bay (Egegik stock) sockeye salmon growth during the second (a) and the third grow-ing seasons at sea (b) and the corresponding abundance of maturing Asian pink salmon (c), 1958–1999. Open bars are even years at sea, and closed bars are odd years at sea. Values are normalized, i.e., stan-dard deviations above and below the long-term mean. Source: Ruggerone and Nielsen (2004).

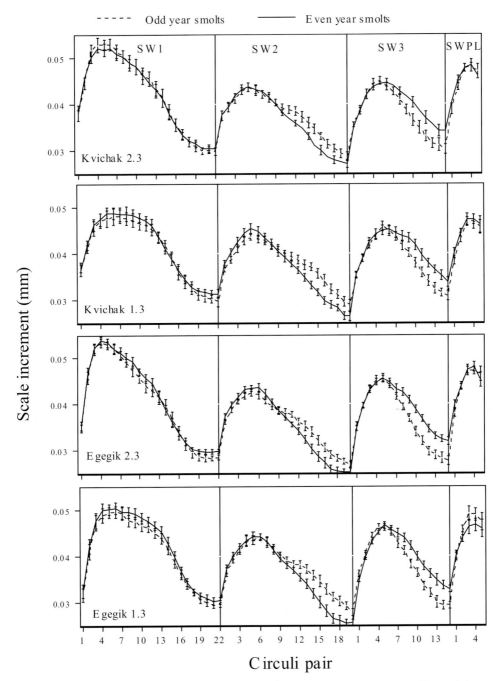

FIGURE 3. Average seasonal scale growth of Bristol Bay (Kvichak and Egegik stocks) ocean age-3 sockeye salmon *Oncorhynchus nerka* that entered the ocean as smolts during odd-(- - - - -) and even-(———) numbered years, 1952–2000. Growth of salmon spending one (age 1.3) and two years (age 2.3) in freshwater are shown separately. Circuli pair ordering restarts at the beginning of each new growing season (SW1, SW2, SW3, SWPL). 95% C.I. are shown at each measurement. Source: Ruggerone et al. (2005).

are poorly understood. They hypothesized that reduced growth of Bristol Bay sockeye salmon during spring through fall of odd-numbered years was caused by high feeding rates of pink salmon, declining zooplankton biomass during summer, and potentially cyclic abundances of key prey that may be maintained by their life history and predation by pink salmon. The contribution of the prey life cycle to the alternating-year patterns of prey abundance and salmon growth at sea is a potentially important factor that needs more investigation. The odd- versus even-year pattern of seasonal growth was consistent before and after the 1976–1977 climate shift. Growth during the first and second years at sea was greater in the recent period during both even- and odd-numbered years.

A key finding of recent pink/sockeye salmon interaction research was that the observed reduction in Bristol Bay sockeye salmon growth during odd-numbered years was associated with a significant reduction in smolt-to-adult survival during 1977–1997 (Figure 4). This analysis was based on annual estimates of salmon smolts that migrated to sea during odd- versus even-numbered years and subsequent age-specific returns of adult salmon. On average, smolt survival declined 35% (from 18.6 ± 3.1% (SE) to 12.1 ± 2.5% survival) when they entered Bristol Bay in even-numbered years and competed with Asian pink salmon during their second year at sea (odd-numbered year; Ruggerone et al. 2003). Sockeye salmon spending the least time in freshwater and the ocean (age-1.2) experienced the greatest reduction in survival (59%), whereas intermediate-age sockeye salmon (age-1.3 and age-2.2) experienced intermediate reduction in survival (30%), and older sockeye salmon (age-2.3) experienced the least reduction in survival (19%) when interacting with Asian pink salmon during their second season at sea. It was hypothesized that reduced growth during the spring through fall of the second growing season at sea led to

greater mortality during winter when demand for prey exceeds prey availability (Nagasawa 2000; Beamish and Mahnken 2001).

The findings of the smolt-to-adult survival analysis were further supported by an analysis of age-specific adult sockeye salmon returns to Bristol Bay. Adult returns were compared based on whether they entered the Bering Sea as smolts during odd- versus even-numbered years. Adult returns declined 22% on average during 1977–1997, when they competed with abundant odd-year pink salmon during their second season at sea (Figure 4; Ruggerone et al. 2003). This effect represented a cumulative loss of 91.8 million adult sockeye salmon, representing an ex-vessel value of $482 million during the 20-year period (Ruggerone and Nielsen 2004). Thus, Asian pink salmon abundance, including the 380% increase in eastern Kamchatka pink salmon abundance between even- and odd-numbered years, was associated with a 35% reduction in sockeye smolt-to-adult survival, and a 22% reduction in adult returns. Although most mortality at sea likely occurs during the first year, these data indicated that measurable mortality can also occur during the second year.

Kvichak sockeye salmon, which historically represented up to 50% of the world's sockeye production during peak cycle years, experienced a sharp decline in adult return per spawner during the 1991–1999 brood years (avg. 0.79 adults per spawner; Ruggerone and Link 2006). This analysis of sockeye salmon population dynamics during the past 45 years indicated the decline was associated with a lower smolt-to-adult survival of Kvichak, Egegik, and Ugashik stocks. The decline in smolt survival was associated with a substantial increase in Kamchatka pink salmon in the early 1990s, including a large increase in even-year pink salmon in Western Kamchatka (see below). The investigators hypothesized that Kvichak, Egegik, and Ugashik stocks experienced a large de-

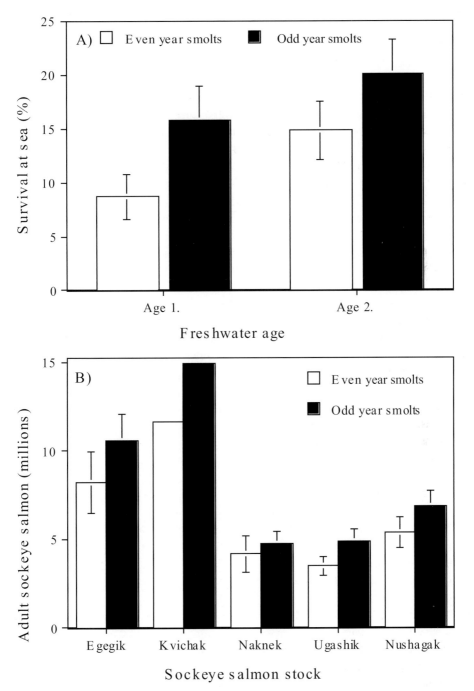

FIGURE 4. Average smolt-to-adult survival of freshwater age-1 and age-2 Bristol Bay sockeye salmon *Oncorhynchus nerka* (A) and corresponding adult returns (B) when smolts entered the ocean during odd- versus even-numbered years (means ± 1 SE), 1977–1997. Sockeye salmon smolts entering the ocean during even-numbered years interacted with odd-year pink salmon during their second year. Sources: Ruggerone et al. (2003), Ruggerone and Nielsen (2004).

cline relative to westside Bristol Bay stocks (e.g., Nushagak District) because they were distributed farther west in the Bering Sea and North Pacific Ocean (Rogers 1987; Myers 1997), and therefore overlapped more with Asian pink salmon. These stocks produce numerous ocean age-2 adults, which tend to be affected more by competition with pink salmon as compared with ocean age-3 sockeye salmon (Ruggerone et al. 2003). The decline in productivity also corresponded with a decline in age-at-length of parent salmon, which was influenced by competition among returning sockeye salmon, competition with Kamchatka pink salmon during the year prior to return, and the 1989 ocean regime shift (Ruggerone et al. 2007a). The investigators hypothesized that the decline in adult size-at-age and less favorable ocean conditions during the homeward migration reduced both fecundity and egg quality of younger parents (ocean age-2) during 1991–1999.

The investigations of Bristol Bay sockeye salmon and Asian pink salmon show that salmon populations originating from distant watersheds can experience interactions that influence growth and survival. McKinnell (1995) examined scale growth trends of British Columbia sockeye salmon and suggested that large numbers of Bristol Bay sockeye salmon reduced the growth of British Columbia salmon when they overlap during late marine life.

Asian pink salmon have been shown to have an adverse effect on the growth of Russian sockeye salmon (Krogius 1964, 1967; Bugaev et al. 2001). Bugaev et al. (2001) examined age and sex-specific mature body weights of Ozernaya River sockeye salmon (eastern Kamchatka Peninsula), 1970–1994, and found that weight of sockeye salmon was inversely related to abundances of local eastern and western Kamchatka pink and sockeye salmon. Although the relationships were weak, Bugaev et al. (2001) suggested that on a per capita basis sockeye salmon had a greater effect on sockeye weight than pink salmon, but

that pink salmon ultimately had a greater effect on sockeye salmon because pink salmon were much more abundant. Krogius (1967) examined annual scale patterns of sockeye salmon collected from the Ozernaya River, 1945–1957, and reported scale growth at sea was inversely related to pink salmon abundance. He hypothesized that competition for food was greatest during midsummer and thereafter when prey availability was less, a finding that is supported by recent analysis of seasonal scale growth trends (Ruggerone et al. 2005). These relationships led Bugaev and Dubynin (2000) and Bugaev (2002) to hypothesize that pink salmon adversely affected the abundance of Kamchatka sockeye salmon.

Chum and Pink Salmon Interactions

Pink and chum salmon *O. keta* have similar life histories during early marine life and both species can be highly abundant. Pink salmon enter marine waters after minimal feeding or rearing in fresh and estuarine waters, whereas chum salmon often feed briefly on freshwater and estuarine prey before entering nearshore marine areas. Juvenile pink and chum salmon are opportunistic foragers, and their diet can be similar in coastal waters (Kaczynski et al. 1973; Beacham and Starr 1982; Duffy 2003).

In the central Bering Sea during 1991–2000, pink salmon abundance was, on average, 200% greater than that of chum salmon (Figure 1; Davis et al. 2005). Chum salmon abundance was greater during even-numbered years apparently in response to a shift in their distribution (Azumaya and Ishida 2000). Bue et al. (2009, this volume) also noted that fall-run chum salmon were typically most abundant during even-numbered years in the Yukon River. Diet of chum salmon changed during odd-numbered years when abundance of pink salmon was relatively great (Figure 1; Sano 1963; Ivankov and Andreyev 1971; Salo

1991; Tadokoro et al. 1996; Davis et al. 2005). Chum salmon may reduce competition with pink and sockeye salmon by consuming gelatinous zooplankton that are seldom consumed by other salmon (Welch and Parsons 1993; Azuma 1995). The shift in the diet of chum salmon in the North Pacific Ocean in response to pink salmon may affect growth of chum salmon during late marine stages (Walker and Myers 1998). Morita et al. (2006a) reported that the growth at sea and maturation rate of age-0.2, age-0.3, and age-0.4 chum salmon in the Bering Sea was negatively related to pink salmon abundance during 1973–2005.

In Puget Sound and the Fraser River, large odd-year runs of adult pink salmon produce large numbers of pink salmon fry that enter marine waters in even-numbered years. In this region, growth of juvenile and adult chum salmon was inversely rated to pink salmon abundance (Phillips and Barraclough 1978; Pratt 1974). Adult abundance, productivity (return per spawner), and survival of chum salmon was lower when juvenile chum salmon entered Puget Sound and the Strait of Georgia in even-numbered years with numerous juvenile pink salmon (Gallagher 1979; Beacham and Starr 1982; Salo 1991; Ruggerone and Nielsen 2004). Beacham and Starr (1982) reported that fry-to-adult survival of Fraser River chum salmon declined 44% (from 1.53% to 0.85% survival) when they entered marine waters in even-numbered years with numerous juvenile pink salmon, 1961–1979. The odd/even-year cycle of chum salmon abundance in the Pacific Northwest is maintained, in part, by a regular alteration in the age-at-maturity that appears to be an evolutionary response to competition with pink salmon (Gallagher 1979; Smoker 1984).

Sinyakov and Ostroumov (1998) evaluated the return per spawner of northeast Kamchatka pink salmon, 1957–1993, as a means to predict adult returns of chum salmon to this region. They suggested that interspecific competition, between pink and chum salmon

was much less important than intraspecific competition and that environmental factors during spawning, downstream migration, and marine periods similarly affected pink and chum salmon. Azumaya and Ishida (2000) reported that age-specific growth of chum and pink salmon in the North Pacific Ocean (change in mean length from year to year) was not related to the density of the other species, but rather that growth was dependent on abundance of conspecifics. The authors suggested that growth of chum salmon was indirectly influenced by pink salmon because pink salmon altered the distribution of chum salmon (Ogura and Ito 1994), leading to high densities of chum salmon in specific ocean regions and density-dependent growth.

Early marine scale growth of Norton Sound chum salmon (Kwiniuk stock) was inversely correlated with an index of pink salmon fry abundance based on spawning escapement of pink salmon during the previous year, 1971–2002 (Figure 5). Approximately 22% of the variability in early marine growth of chum salmon was explained by pink salmon, but the effect of reduced growth on adult return per spawner of chum salmon was not detected.

Chinook and Pink Salmon Interactions

Juvenile and immature Chinook salmon *O. tshawytscha* are opportunistic in their prey selection, but they tend to feed on higher trophic level prey at earlier life stages, as compared with pink salmon, based on diet (Brodeur 1990; Farley et al. 2004; Naydenko et al. 2005) and stable isotope analyses (Welch and Parsons 1993; Kaeriyama et al. 2004). Some diet overlap exists between juvenile pink and Chinook salmon that recently enter marine waters, but it is much less than that between pink and chum salmon (Healey 1980, 1991; Duffy 2003). In the Pacific

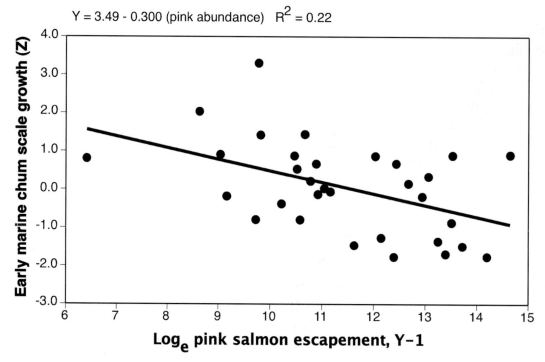

FIGURE 5. Relationship between early marine scale growth of Norton Sound chum salmon *Onco-rhynchus keta* (Kwiniuk stock) and spawning escapement of pink salmon *O. gorbuscha* (Kwiniuk stock) during the previous year, 1971–2002 (Ruggerone and Agler 2008). Early marine chum growth is the differenced value of the normalized (Z) first 10 circuli of age-0.3 and age-0.4 chum salmon during their first year.

Northwest, the size of juvenile pink and sub-yearling Chinook salmon do not differ significantly at the time Chinook salmon enter marine waters because pink salmon fry have been rapidly growing in marine areas for weeks to months.

In the Pacific Northwest, where adult pink salmon are highly abundant in odd-numbered years, the release of 53.5 million coded-wire-tag (CWT) Chinook salmon was used to examine potential competition between subyearling pink and Chinook salmon (Ruggerone and Goetz 2004). Coded-wire-tagged subyearling Chinook salmon released into streams and entering Puget Sound during even-numbered years experienced 62% lower survival than those entering the sea during odd-numbered years, 1984–1997. This pattern was consistent for ten Puget Sound

stocks (range: 36–86% survival reduction depending on stock) and three lower mainland British Columbia stocks near the Fraser River (45–61% survival reduction). Analysis of age-specific recovery rates of Chinook salmon indicated that lower survival from even-year releases was established during the first year at sea. Furthermore, Chinook salmon entering marine waters with numerous juvenile pink salmon in even-numbered years experienced reduced growth during the first year at sea and delayed maturation. In contrast, few pink salmon originate from streams along coastal Washington and lower Vancouver Island. Survival of tagged Chinook salmon released into these streams (9 stocks) did not vary between even- and odd-numbered years ($P > 0.05$). The lack of an alternating-year pattern in coastal stocks and the observation that growth and survival of Chinook salmon were reduced during the first year at sea indicated that survival and growth were primarily influenced in Puget Sound and the lower Strait of Georgia.

The survival pattern of Puget Sound Chinook salmon in relation to pink salmon appeared to be influenced by climate-induced changes in the marine environment. During 1972–1983 and immediately prior to the exceptional 1982/1983 El Niño (Pearcy 1992), the odd/even year survival pattern of Puget Sound Chinook salmon tended to be opposite that during 1984–1997 (Ruggerone and Goetz 2004). Prior to the 1982/1983 El Niño, sea surface temperatures along the coast were relatively cool, upwelling was more frequent, prey availability was greater, peak zooplankton production more closely matched seaward timing of Chinook salmon, and Puget Sound Chinook salmon experienced relatively high survival when they entered Puget Sound with numerous juvenile pink salmon. The researchers provided evidence that salmon predators and prey in the Puget Sound region were much more abundant during 1972–1983. They hypothesized that prior to the 1982/1983 El Niño, growth of juvenile Chinook salmon was relatively high, and pink salmon provided a buffer to abundant predators rather than competition for prey.

The investigation of pink and Chinook salmon interactions in the Puget Sound region provided evidence that climate may alter predator–prey interactions and competition between species (Ruggerone and Goetz 2004). Comparing 1972–1983 to 1984–1997, Chinook survival in Puget Sound declined 50%, juvenile herring (Chinook prey) and piscivorous seabird abundance declined substantially, but pink salmon abundance nearly doubled. A factor contributing to competition and the inverse relationship between pink and Chinook salmon was believed to be warmer temperatures and the observed earlier peak zooplankton production during the recent period. Earlier peak zooplankton production likely favored juvenile pink salmon more than Chinook salmon because juvenile pink salmon enter marine waters months earlier than Chinook salmon. The researchers hypothesized that the primary mortality source for Chinook salmon switched from predators to competitors in response to climate change and associated changes in the marine species in the Puget Sound region. Food web analyses and other studies need to be conducted in order to further evaluate the interaction between Chinook and pink salmon.

Grachev (1967) reported that scale growth of Russia Chinook salmon was influenced by pink salmon (see Ruggerone and Nielsen 2004). Therefore, Ruggerone et al. (2007b) tested the hypothesis that growth of Kuskokwim and Yukon River Chinook salmon was influenced by competition with Asian pink salmon. Competition with western Alaska pink salmon was not expected because pink salmon abundance is low; rather, competition was more likely to occur during the second year and later life stages. Adult length of Yukon Chinook salmon tended to alternate from year-to-year, especially age-1.3 salmon that were larger during odd-numbered years. Annual Chinook salmon scale growth was measured from the 1960s to 2004. Chinook salmon scale growth during the second year at sea (SW2) was consistently greater during odd-numbered years for both age-1.3 and age-1.4 Chinook salmon returning to the Yukon and Kuskokwim Rivers. This finding was opposite of the expected finding that pink salmon, which are less abundant in even years and more abundant in odd years, were directly competing for prey with Chinook salmon. Factors influencing the alternating-year pattern in Chinook salmon growth are unknown, but this pattern suggests that the alternating-year pattern in salmon prey abundance may switch from the lower trophic prey consumed by pink salmon to higher trophic prey and/or older prey consumed by Chinook salmon, i.e., indirect competition.

Coho and Pink Salmon Interactions

Coho salmon *O. kisutch* feed at a higher trophic level (e.g., fishes and squid) than pink salmon during the first season at sea, but diet overlap may increase during the second season as pink salmon switch to larger prey, such as fish and squid (Brodeur 1990; Ogura et al. 1991). Stable isotope ratios suggested some overlap in the trophic level of pink and coho salmon (Welch and Parsons 1993; Kaeriyama et al. 2004). Consistent with the observation of diet overlap during the second growing season, Ogura et al. (1991) reported that final-year growth rates of coho salmon were lower in years of large pink salmon abundance (odd-numbered years) in the western North Pacific Ocean.

Juvenile coho salmon seem to benefit from the presence of pink salmon in the same watershed and/or in nearshore marine areas. Pink salmon can provide important prey for coho salmon. In the Skagit River, Washington, the adult return per spawner of coho salmon was positively correlated with pink salmon spawners co-occurring with sub-yearling coho salmon (Michael 1995). Briscoe (2004) reported that marine survival of Auke Creek coho salmon (Southeast Alaska) was positively correlated with the release of hatchery pink and chum salmon, but this trend may have been caused by common ocean rearing conditions. Abundance of coho harvests in Southeast Alaska was highly correlated with pink salmon harvest (Gaudet and Ruggerone 2007).

In the AYK region, commercial catch of Kuskokwim coho salmon was 49% greater during even- versus odd-numbered years, 1965–2007 (Figure 6). Ruggerone and Agler (2008) examined annual and seasonal scale growth of Kuskokwim coho salmon, 1965–2006. Alternating-year patterns of growth suggested that young-of-the-year coho salmon may have benefited from pink salmon

carcasses, whereas yearling coho may have benefited from predation on pink salmon fry. However, these growth patterns were not correlated with catch trends. Instead, growth of coho salmon during the first year at sea was associated with coho salmon catch during the following year. Marine scale growth of coho salmon during the spring was not associated with pink salmon abundance, whereas growth during the late summer and fall was positively correlated with an index of Asian pink salmon abundance in the Bering Sea. This pattern was opposite that of Bristol Bay sockeye salmon, but similar to that of AYK Chinook salmon.

Interactions Between Salmon Broods

The genetically distinct odd- and even-year lines of pink salmon can lead to significantly different levels of abundance that are maintained, in part, by the invariable two-year life cycle of pink salmon. Ricker (1962) and Heard (1991) reviewed possible mechanisms that might lead to dominance of one line. Potential mechanisms included depensatory mortality where small populations suffer disproportionately greater mortality, depensatory fishing, cannibalism of adults on juvenile pink salmon, fouling of the spawning grounds by dead eggs produced by the dominant line, and food competition. Ultimately, Ricker could find no strong evidence for any single mechanism and suggested that multiple factors likely interact to develop and maintain dominance.

Some evidence suggests that competition between brood lines may help maintain the odd-even cycle pattern in some regions. Considerable attempts to establish or enhance off-year lines of pink salmon through supplementation have failed (Heard 1991). Interestingly, the off-year line in western Kamchatka rebounded following the collapse of the dominant odd-year line in response to sig-

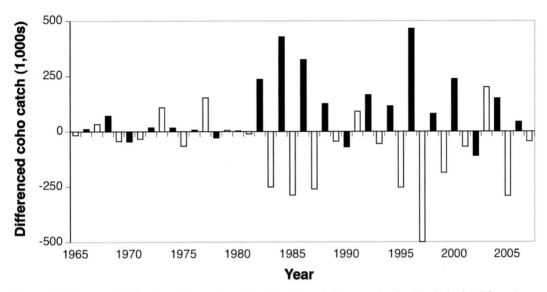

FIGURE 6. Time trend of coho salmon *Oncorhynchus kisutch* harvests in the Kuskokwim River (avg. 279,000 ± 229 fish (SE)). Annual values were differenced $(y_i - y_{i-1})$ in order to highlight the alternating year pattern of catch. Black bars represent even numbered years. Source: Ruggerone and Agler (2008).

nificant over-crowding and mortality on the spawning grounds in 1983 (Figure 7; Bugaev 2002). These findings suggested that the odd-year line was somehow suppressing the even-year line, but not by fouling of the spawning grounds. Intraspecific competition remains a possible mechanism leading to dominant pink salmon cycles, possibly by influencing cyclic patterns in production of prey species in nearshore marine areas. The collapse of the odd-year line of western Kamchatka pink salmon (Figure 7) provides one of the few examples in which a large spawning escapement has led to a major collapse of a salmon population (Walters et al. 2004).

Morita et al. (2006a) offered a new hypothesis for the bi-ennial pattern of pink salmon in the Bering Sea. They reported that body weight of pink salmon captured in the Bering Sea was inversely correlated with chum salmon but not with pink salmon abundance. The relationship between pink salmon growth and chum salmon abundance was consistent for both even- and odd-year pink salmon lines. They suggested that smaller body size of even-year pink salmon was related to greater abundance and competition with chum salmon, and that reduced growth of pink salmon led to fewer even-year pink salmon. An alternative explanation for the relatively small pink salmon size during even-numbered years is that size is related to genetic characteristics of the two genetically-independent lines (Heard 1991).

Interaction between adjacent brood lines is a unique concept, therefore the authors present some relevant findings observed in freshwater lakes that support sockeye salmon. Ricker (1997) concluded that interaction between sockeye brood lines is the likely source of Fraser River cycles. However, Myers et al. (1997) found only weak interactions between brood lines in Fraser River sockeye salmon and suggested that these interactions may not be sufficient to cause the observed cycles.

Eggers and Rogers (1987) reported that peak cycle years of Kvichak sockeye salmon (Bristol Bay) reduced the growth of fry produced by the following brood. Ruggerone and Link (2006) reported that large spawning

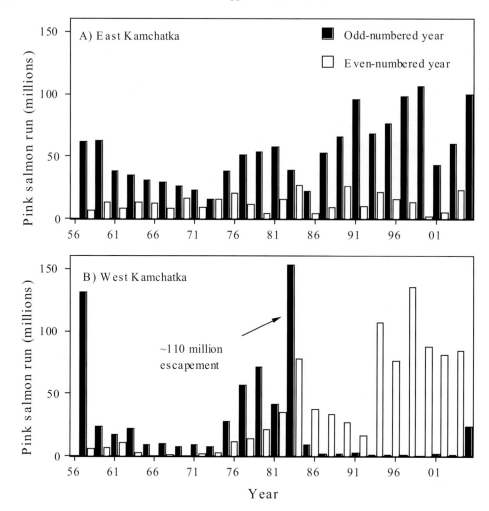

FIGURE 7. Estimated abundance of Eastern (A) and Western (B) Kamchatka pink salmon *Oncorhynchus gorbuscha* during odd versus even-numbered years, 1957–2005. Data sources: Bugaev and Dubynin (2000), Bugaev (2002) and annual reports by Russia to NPAFC.

escapements reduced age-1 smolt weight and total smolt abundance produced by the following brood, in addition to altering the age composition of Kvichak smolts. Brood interaction was a statistically significant factor affecting numbers of Kvichak adults produced per spawner, but only after accounting for interceptions of adult Kvichak salmon in adjacent fishing districts. Suppression of sockeye growth by large previous cohort populations was documented in the Kenai, Ayakulik, and Akalura watersheds in Alaska (Ruggerone

and Rogers 2003). These findings support the concept that growth is a key factor affecting salmon survival. They also provide evidence that management of salmon escapements should consider potential interactions between broods.

Hatchery-Wild Salmon Interactions

Prince William Sound supports the largest releases of hatchery pink salmon in the world. Hatchery production began in the mid-1970s and releases exceeded 222 million juvenile pink salmon by 1985, increasing to average annual releases of 522 million fry during 1985–2003 (Figure 8). The effects of hatchery production on wild pink salmon production in Prince William Sound are controversial. Hilborn and Eggers (2000, 2001) reported that adult run size and return per spawner declined in response to increased hatchery production, and that hatchery salmon replaced rather than augmented wild production. Additionally, they reported that the decline was opposite that of wild pink salmon stocks in Kodiak, Southeast Alaska, and the South Alaska Peninsula, indicating that a factor unique to Prince William Sound was responsible for the decline. The 1989 *Exxon Valdez* oil spill occurred several years after the decline of wild pink salmon, and its contribution to the decline was considered small by Hilborn and Eggers (2000). Spawning escapement reportedly declined in response to smaller wild runs rather than to high harvest rates in the mixed-stock fisher-

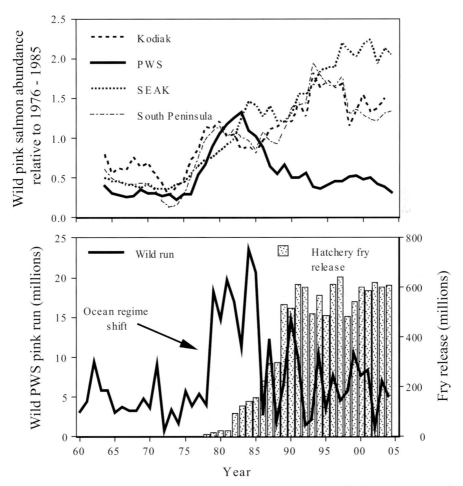

FIGURE 8. Annual abundance of wild pink salmon *Oncorhynchus gorbuscha* (running mean of 5 years) returning to Prince William Sound (PWS), Kodiak, Southeast Alaska (SEAK), and the South Alaska Peninsula relative to 1976–1985 (A), and time series of wild pink salmon returning to Prince William Sound in relation to hatchery pink salmon released into Prince William Sound during the previous year (B). See Hilborn and Eggers (2000).

ies. Willette et al. (1999, 2001) reported that growth and survival of juvenile pink salmon in Prince William Sound was reduced when densities were high. Relatively low production of wild pink salmon in Prince William Sound has continued through 2004, which is opposite that in Kodiak, Southeast Alaska, and the South Alaska Peninsula (Figure 8). If wild pink salmon production had maintained its production level relative to other stocks in the Gulf of Alaska, then approximately 16.4 million additional wild pink salmon would have been produced, on average, during 1986 to 2004. Approximately 23.9 million adult hatchery salmon were produced per year during this period, indicating the net economic benefit of hatchery production may have been minimal.

Wertheimer et al. (2001, 2004) reported that return per spawner of wild pink salmon in Prince William Sound was positively correlated with parent body size, and that ocean temperature during the return year added a small improvement to the model. Return per spawner of wild salmon was negatively correlated with releases of pink salmon fry from hatcheries, as shown by Hilborn and Eggers, but hatchery releases explained less variability in return per spawner than parent body size. Therefore, releases of hatchery pink salmon did not add significant information to the model that included parent body size. Wertheimer et al. (2004) concluded that the effect of hatchery releases on wild adult body size (and subsequent fry production) caused a loss of approximately one million wild pink salmon per year. They did not dismiss the possibility that density-dependent factors affect salmon survival, but they thought its effect was small compared to other factors. This analysis did not explain the great disparity in production of wild pink salmon in Prince William Sound as compared with that of other Alaska stocks.

The authors note that low year-to-year variability in hatchery releases, such as in Prince William Sound, may limit the ability to detect density-dependent relationships between wild and hatchery salmon. Experimental controls are needed and a stronger test would be to evaluate wild pink salmon variability while experimentally varying hatchery releases (Peterman 1978, 1991). Unfortunately, no attempts have been made to experimentally manipulate large-scale production hatcheries in order to test competition hypotheses.

Large-scale hatchery production of Chinook, coho, and steelhead occurs in the Columbia River (Mahnken et al. 1998). Levin et al. (2001) tested the hypothesis that massive releases of hatchery spring Chinook salmon influenced the survival of coded-wire-tagged wild spring Chinook salmon originating in the Snake River, a population that is protected by the Endangered Species Act. They reported that survival of wild Chinook salmon declined in relation to numbers of Chinook released from hatcheries, but only when ocean conditions were unfavorable. They suggested that competition for limited prey resources was a likely mechanism. This finding is consistent with the observation that competition between Puget Sound Chinook and pink salmon occurred during a period of low ocean productivity associated with frequent El Niño events (Ruggerone and Goetz 2004).

Levin and Williams (2002) reported that survival of wild Snake River spring Chinook was inversely correlated with numbers of steelhead released from hatcheries, whereas survival of wild steelhead smolts was not. The effect of ocean conditions was not statistically significant. They concluded that the apparent adverse interaction between Chinook salmon and steelhead trout must occur in freshwater or the estuary because the ocean distribution of the two species is different. The authors did not report the combined influence of hatchery Chinook and hatchery steelhead on survival of wild Chinook salmon.

Japan produces the largest number of hatchery chum salmon, averaging 1.9 billion fry per year in recent years (e.g., Hiroi 1998). A number of studies indicate that large numbers of chum salmon in the ocean may cause density-dependent growth, reduced body condition, and increased age-at-maturation among chum salmon (Ishida et al. 1993; Kaeriyama 1989, 2005; Fukuwaka and Suzuki 2000; Urawa et al. 2000; Klovatch 2000; Zaporozhets and Zaporozhets 2004; Saito 2005). Urawa (2007) noted that juvenile chum salmon experienced severe starvation in the western subarctic gyre during several recent winter surveys. However, Morita et al. (2001) reported that scale growth of chum salmon at sea was more correlated with sea-surface salinity than with catch per effort of chum salmon. Few studies have directly investigated potential interactions between Japanese hatchery chum salmon and wild chum salmon or other salmon species. However, Morita et al. (2006b, 2006c) questioned whether increases in chum and pink salmon catches in Japan were due to increases in hatchery releases or to changes in climate, and whether hatchery production replaced rather than augmented wild salmon production.

Myers et al. (2004) examined food habits of salmon in the Gulf of Alaska and the spatial overlap of western Alaska chum salmon in relation to the distribution of Japanese hatchery chum salmon. Overlap in the diet of different size groups of chum salmon was high, indicating strong potential for intraspecific competition between Japanese hatchery chum and wild chum salmon from western Alaska. Diet overlap between chum and other salmon species tended to be low to moderate in the Gulf of Alaska. Based on their observations, Myers et al. hypothesized that intraspecific and interspecific competition with hatchery chum salmon in the Gulf of Alaska may reduce the growth of immature western Alaska chum salmon, particularly when adverse ocean conditions limit prey availability. A recent analysis of Norton Sound chum salmon indicated adult return per spawner,

adult length-at-age, and scale growth during the second year at sea were inversely correlated with abundance of Asian chum salmon, which are primarily hatchery salmon (Ruggerone and Agler 2008).

Davis et al. (2004, 2005) examined diet overlap among salmon in the Bering Sea. Diet changed with body size and geographic area. However, diet overlap between sockeye and chum salmon in the Aleutian Islands area was very high (>75%). Both Japanese chum salmon (hatchery) and Bristol Bay sockeye salmon (and presumably Kuskokwim sockeye salmon) are highly abundant in this region, indicating high potential for competition for prey, especially during years of lower prey availability.

Orsi et al. (2004) used a bioenergetic approach to estimate prey consumption of hatchery and wild chum salmon in Icy Strait Alaska. They examined zooplankton abundance, and estimated chum salmon abundance to evaluate whether hatchery chum salmon influenced prey availability. They concluded that only a small percentage of the available zooplankton was consumed by juvenile chum salmon. Total daily consumption of zooplankton by all stock groups of juvenile chum salmon was estimated to be between 330 and 1,764 g/km^2 d^{-1} from June to September in the neritic habitat of Icy Strait. They noted that further research was needed to validate assumptions of the approach, including interactions with highly abundant vertically-migrating planktivores.

The authors note that an unknown key when comparing prey consumption with prey availability is whether salmon rely on high density patches of prey in order to forage efficiently. Most field sampling of potential prey tend to average prey over a given surface area or volume of water. If salmon rely on high density patches of prey, then field estimates of prey availability may be misleading. Furthermore, salmon prey abundance in the ocean are difficult to accurately estimate because prey migrate vertically during the diel period and because some prey can avoid sampling gear (Pearcy et al. 1988; Cooney and Brodeur 1998).

Discussion

A variety of studies indicate intraspecific and interspecific competition among salmon in the ocean. Several studies show reduced prey availability and diet shifts in response to large numbers of pink salmon. Some studies indicate that competition affects growth during late marine life when growth-related mortality is likely less (and is more apparent) and consumption rates are high, whereas other studies suggest competition may be greatest when numerous smolts initially enter the ocean (Peterman 1982). Reduced size of returning adults in response to competition may lower salmon reproductive potential and reduce subsequent population abundance, although the magnitude of this effect is unknown. Studies indicate that high numbers of pink salmon may alter the distribution of chum salmon at sea, but their effect on the distribution of sockeye salmon is unknown. A small but growing number of studies indicate that competition can influence both growth and survival of salmon at sea. Effects of competition on survival of Bristol Bay sockeye salmon were most pronounced during the second year at sea, a life stage when little mortality has been previously documented. Studies of Chinook salmon indicate competition was most pronounced when oceanic conditions limit prey availability, whereas studies of sockeye salmon in Alaska indicated competition continued after the 1976–1977 ocean regime shift that led to greater salmon production throughout northern areas.

The influence of competition on growth and survival of salmon is likely small compared with effects of large-scale and regional oceanic conditions that set the stage for prey availability and predator abundance. For example, scale growth of Alaska sockeye salmon during the first two years at sea was consistently greater after the 1977 ocean regime shift that led to greater abundances of Alaska sockeye salmon (Ruggerone et al. 2007a; Martinson et al. 2008). After the regime shift, scale growth declined during late marine life, possibly in response to competition, leading to reduced adult size-at-age.

Competition during late life may affect adult size, which in turn may influence future production. While the effect of salmon body size on fecundity and egg size is generally known, little information is available on changes in the quality of eggs in response to reduced growth and unfavorable oceanic conditions. During the last several months at sea, salmon gain significant weight and transfer much energy into egg production, indicating that competition during the homeward migration may influence future salmon production. The impact of competition may be especially important during periods when wild salmon productivity is low, oceanic productivity that supports prey availability is low, and hatchery production is high.

Some studies suggested that density-dependent growth may occur in the ocean, but concluded that the importance of density-dependent growth and its effect on salmon survival was likely small compared to other factors (Wertheimer et al. 2004; Orsi et al. 2004). Shuntov and Temnykh (2005) presented an inverse relationship between pink salmon biomass in the Okhotsk Sea and average weight of pink salmon, but they found no density-dependence among adult pink salmon returning to eastern Kamchatka where pink salmon runs are exceptionally large in odd-numbered years (Figure 6a). Furthermore, average weight of pink salmon was lower in even-numbered years when abundance was typically low, but this is likely a genetic influence on growth rate (Heard 1991) or possibly a response to competition with chum salmon (Morita et al. 2006a). Some studies indicated that salmon represented a small proportion of nekton in the open ocean, and that salmon consumed less than 10% of all plankton production (Shuntov and Temnykh 2005; NPAFC 2007). The apparently small fraction of total zooplankton consumed by salmon was commonly cited as a reason that density-dependent effects on salmon growth and survival should be minimal. However, as noted above, foraging salmon may depend on high density patches of prey, which may not be adequately measured by scientists.

The discussion provided by Shuntov and Temnykh (2005) and others highlights the need for further research to better explain dynamic interactions between salmon and their prey. For example, after describing the unique seasonal scale-growth patterns of Bristol Bay sockeye salmon (Figure 3), Ruggerone et al. (2005) suggested that the interaction between prey life history (e.g., potential two-year cycle) and intense foraging by pink salmon in odd-numbered years may maintain or amplify the odd-even pattern in prey abundance and salmon growth. Examination of competition using time-series data can be complicated by changing ocean conditions, stock abundances, and the distribution and spatial overlap of salmon at sea. Nevertheless, it is remarkable that the alternating-year pattern of growth exhibited by Bristol Bay sockeye salmon was so strong given their broad distribution in the Bering Sea and North Pacific Ocean, i.e., regions that contain habitats with different prey compositions. This observation, and alternating-year patterns observed among Chinook, coho, and chum salmon in the AYK region, highlights the need to better understand life history and population dynamics of key salmon prey, such as squid, in each of these vast ocean habitats.

Several recent studies indicated that large hatchery production can impact salmon survival at sea, but the degree of impact remains controversial. The controversy stems in part from the fact that large-scale controlled experiments have not been conducted with hatcheries to test density-dependent hypotheses (Peterman 1978, 1991). It is noteworthy that production of chum salmon fry from Japanese hatcheries stabilized after scientists raised concerns that tremendous hatchery production may be limiting growth and survival at sea (e.g., Kaeriyama 1989; Ishida et al. 1993). The lack of controlled experiments to test density-dependent hypotheses is a key reason why some studies have relied upon the alternating-year abundances of wild pink salmon to test such hypotheses.

Another complicating factor when examining density-dependent growth and survival is that scientists do not know how salmon die at sea. Predation is the most obvious source of mortality, and the typical explanation is that smaller fish and/or weaker fish are more vulnerable to predation. However, little quantitative information on predators of salmon at sea is available (Pearcy 1992; Nagasawa 1998; Urawa et al. 2000). Salmon typically represent a small proportion of predator diets in the ocean, therefore quantification of salmon consumed by predators typically has broad bounds. For example, recent field research in the eastern Bering Sea, including the AYK region, indicated that small sockeye salmon in their first year at sea did not survive (Farley et al. 2007). However, exceptionally few predators were captured while sampling with a trawl during daylight, and the source of mortality remains unknown (E. Farley, NOAA Fisheries, personal communication). Alternatively, a key question is whether reduced growth and body condition at sea can lead to greater risk of disease or mortality without being consumed by a predator (e.g., Urawa 2007).

Decades ago there was a general belief that the vast regions of the North Pacific Ocean could readily support growing numbers of hatchery salmon in addition to wild salmon populations (e.g., MacLeod 1977;

American Fisheries Society Symposium 70:267–305, 2009

Historical Biomass of Pink, Chum, and Sockeye Salmon in the North Pacific Ocean

Douglas M. Eggers[*]

Alaska Department of Fish and Game, Division of Commercial Fisheries
P.O. Box 25526, Juneau, Alaska 99802, USA

Abstract.—Limits to the capacity of the North Pacific Ocean to support salmon are suggested based on widespread observations of decreasing size and increasing age of salmon at maturation during time periods where the abundance of salmon has increased throughout the North Pacific rim. The increase in abundance of salmon is partially due to successful establishment of large-scale hatchery runs of chum salmon *Oncorhynchus keta* and pink salmon *O. gorbuscha*. The largest hatchery runs are chum salmon, and because of their long life span relative to the more abundant pink salmon, the increase in hatchery terminal run biomass under-represents the actual increase in salmon biomass. To put the increase in hatchery runs in perspective, the historical (since 1925) terminal runs and biomass of hatchery and wild pink, chum, and sockeye salmon *O. nerka* in the North Pacific Ocean were reconstructed. Various data sets of smolt releases from hatcheries, wild salmon estimates of smolt out-migrants, and subsequent adult returns by age and size were assembled. Age-structured models were fit to these data sets to estimate brood-year specific rates of natural mortality, growth, and maturation. The rates were then used to reconstruct total biomass of the "smolt data" stocks. The estimated ratio of terminal runs to total biomass estimated for the "smolt data" stocks were used to expand the historical time series of terminal run biomass on a species and area basis. The present total biomass (~4 million mt) of sockeye, chum, and pink salmon in the North Pacific Ocean is at historically high levels and is ~3.4 times the low levels observed in the early1970s. At least 38% of the recent ten-year average North Pacific salmon biomass is attributed to hatchery stocks of chum and pink salmon. Recent year terminal run biomass has been greater than the peak levels observed during the mid 1930s.

Introduction

Trends in salmon catch have been used as indicators of climate change (Beamish and Bouillon 1993; Francis and Hare 1994; Hare and Francis 1995). These trends suggest that decadal scale shifts in abundance of salmon have occurred over broad areas of the North Pacific (Beamish and Bouillon 1993; Francis and Hare 1994; Hare and Francis 1995).

Researchers (e.g., Beamish et al. 1999) have hypothesized that the alternates between high and low salmon production regimes are driven by decadal-scale changes. In 1949, a shift occurred from a high to a low production regime (Beamish and Bouillon 1993; Francis and Hare 1994; Hare and Francis 1995). In 1977, conditions shifted back to a high production regime (Beamish and Bouillon 1993; Francis and Hare 1994; Hare and Francis 1995; Hare and Mantua 2000), and

[*]Corresponding author: douglas.eggers@alaska.gov

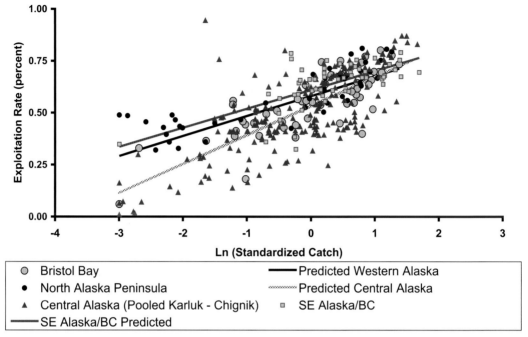

FIGURE 1. Exploitation rate and ln (standardized catch) and fitted standardized catch for sockeye salmon *Oncorhynchus nerka* stocks.

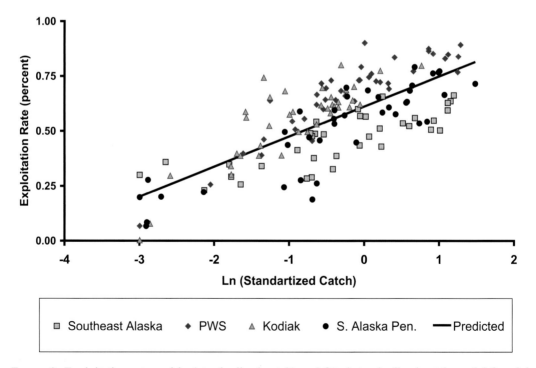

FIGURE 2. Exploitation rate and ln (standardized catch) and fitted standardized catch model for pink salmon *Oncorhynchus gorbuscha* stocks.

ka (coastal waters and rivers from Kotzebue Sound to Unimak Island), central Alaska (from Unimak Island to the Bering River), southeast Alaska-northern British Columbia (Yakutat to about 51°N), and southern British Columbia and Washington.

Commercial catches of pink, chum, and sockeye salmon, in number and weight, for the above regions were from the International North Pacific Fisheries Commission (INPFC 1979), Eggers et al. (2005), Alaska Department of Fish and Game (ADF&G) catch records, and Fisheries and Oceans Canada (DFO) catch records (e.g., Irvine et al. 2006). Escapement of sockeye salmon in Alaska and British Columbia was provided by Eggers and Irvine (2007). Escapements of other species were provided by ADF&G escapement records. Average weights (ratio of reported catch in weight and reported catch in numbers) by species and region were used to estimate total run biomass from total run in numbers for the respective region and species.

Large-scale chum salmon hatcheries were established in the late 1950s in Japan. Releases of chum salmon in the North Pacific increased steadily and releases have been relatively stable since the mid 1980s, averaging 2.9 billion fish (INPFC statistical yearbooks, INPFC 1991; North Pacific Anadromous Fish Commission (NPAFC) statistical yearbooks, NPAFC 2008; ADF&G annual enhancement reports, White 2008; Figure 3). Japan (67.4%) and Alaska (15.8%) released most of the chum salmon (Figure 3). In the reconstructed runs of chum salmon, the Japanese and Alaskan hatchery runs were accounted for and included.

Pink salmon hatcheries were established in the late 1960s in Russia and Japan and in the late 1970s in Alaska. North Pacific releases of pink salmon increased steadily and have been relatively stable since the late 1980s, averaging 1.2 billion fish (Figure 4). Alaska releases most of the pink salmon (64.9%), followed by Russia (29.8%), and Japan (10.3%; Figure 4). In the reconstructed runs of chum

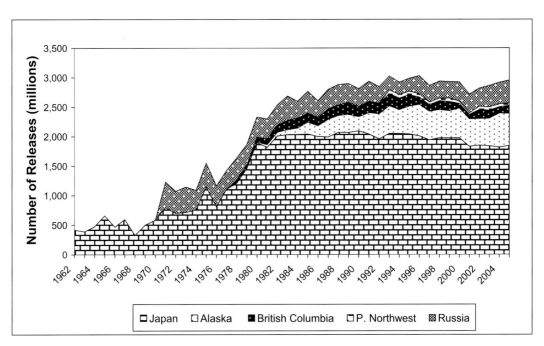

FIGURE 3. Releases of chum salmon *Oncorhynchus keta* smolts from hatcheries in Japan, Russia, Alaska, British Columbia and Pacific Northwest, 1962 to 2005.

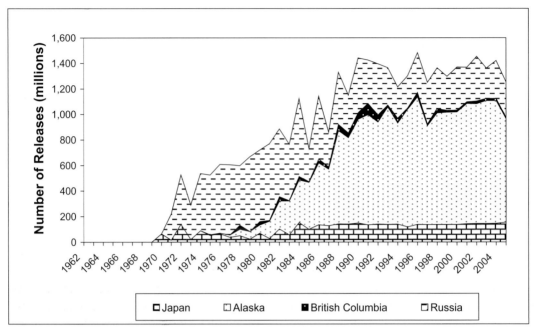

Figure 4. Releases of pink salmon smolts from hatcheries in Japan, Russia, Alaska, British Columbia and Pacific Northwest, 1962 to 2005.

salmon, the Japanese and Alaskan hatchery runs were accounted for, however, hatchery runs in Russia, British Columbia, and the Pacific Northwest, which collectively constitute about 25% of the pink salmon releases since 1990, were not accounted for. Thus, the wild runs of pink salmon in these areas were overestimated to the extent that hatchery runs are not accounted for. Details of terminal run estimation for each region are described below.

Japan.—No appreciable wild runs of salmon exist in Japan, and presently coastal fisheries occur on hatchery fish only. Japanese coastal fisheries, prior to the establishment of hatchery runs, caught pink and chum salmon of Russian origin. Japanese high seas and offshore fisheries exploit maturing and immature salmon that originate from areas throughout Japan, Russia, and western and central Alaska. The catch of pink and chum salmon in Japanese fisheries were considered as a component of the terminal run.

Russia.—Escapement estimates were not available for stocks of pink, chum, and sockeye salmon in Russia. Catches of pink, chum, and sockeye salmon were expanded to total run based on a 60% exploitation rate (Rogers 1999). Hatchery runs were not assessed in Russia, and terminal runs were mixtures of hatchery and wild fish.

Western Alaska.—Western Alaska pink, chum, and sockeye, salmon runs include those of the Arctic-Yukon-Kuskokwim (AYK), Bristol Bay, and north Alaska Peninsula areas. Terminal runs were available for Bristol Bay sockeye salmon, from 1956–2005 and for north Alaska Peninsula sockeye salmon, from 1962–2005. Total runs for Bristol Bay and north Alaska Peninsula sockeye were estimated for years after 1925 prior to escapement monitoring based on the standardized catch model (Figure 1). AYK sockeye salmon runs were small relative to other western Alaska salmon stocks, and fisheries were not fully developed until the 1980s. Runs from

1980 to 2005 were assumed to be twice the catch. These expanded AYK runs averaged 8% of the north Alaska Peninsula sockeye runs over the same period. AYK runs prior to 1979 were estimated by expansion of north Alaska Peninsula sockeye runs for the respective years

Estimates of western Alaska chum salmon runs were problematic. The AYK area has substantial runs of chum salmon, and commercial fisheries were not fully developed until the early 1970s. Further commercial catches of chum salmon in AYK after the mid 1990s do not reflect abundance due to lack of fishing effort. Rogers (1999) provided estimates of western Alaska chum salmon runs from 1952–1998, which were consistent with minimum estimates of western Alaska chum salmon runs from 1980 to 1998 (Witherell et al. 2002). These minimum runs that were based on documented assessments include commercial and subsistence catch, escapements from assessed AYK chum salmon stocks (Clark 2001a, 2001b, 2001c; Clark and Sandone 2001; Eggers 2001; Eggers and Clark 2006), and assessments of Bristol Bay and north Alaska Peninsula chum salmon runs. Estimates of western Alaska chum salmon runs from 1925–1950 and from 1999–2005 were based on expansion of western Alaska chum salmon commercial catch and on average ratios of catch to run from 1951–1961 and 1997–1998, respectively.

Central Alaska.—Central Alaska pink, chum, and sockeye salmon runs include the south Alaska Peninsula, Chignik, Kodiak, Cook Inlet, and Prince William Sound (PWS) areas. Escapement estimates were available for many central Alaska sockeye salmon stocks after the late 1970s when comprehensive escapement monitoring programs were implemented by ADF&G (Eggers and Irvine 2007). Escapement estimates were available for a few Chignik and Kodiak area sockeye salmon stocks before the late 1970s. Total

runs of central Alaska sockeye salmon were estimated using the standardized catch model fit to available catch: exploitation rate time series (Figure 1). Hatchery runs of sockeye salmon occur in the Cook Inlet and PWS areas; however these runs are small relative to the aggregate central Alaska sockeye salmon runs and were not assessed in terminal run reconstructions.

Total runs were available for wild pink salmon stocks in PWS since 1960. Total hatchery runs are available since the initial returns in 1977 (Hilborn and Eggers 1999). Total wild pink salmon runs in PWS for years prior to 1960 were estimated using standardized catch model fit to the PWS time series of catch and exploitation rate (Figure 2). Total Kodiak area pink salmon hatchery runs were available (Hilborn and Eggers 1999) since the initial hatchery returns in 1975. Wild pink salmon runs in central Alaska, outside of PWS, were estimated using the standardized catch model (Figure 2). Total runs for central Alaska chum salmon were estimated by expanding the reported catch by a factor equal to 90% of the respective year pink salmon exploitation rate estimated from the standardized catch model.

Southeast Alaska, British Columbia, Washington.—Total runs of pink salmon from 1925–1960 were estimated using standardized catch model fit to available catch–exploitation rate time series. Escapement estimates for wild chum salmon runs in southeast Alaska were not available. Total runs of wild chum salmon from 1925–1980 were estimated by expanding the reported catch by a factor equal to 90% of the observed pink salmon exploitation rate (for the respective year) estimated based on the standardized catch model. Hatchery runs of chum salmon to southeast Alaska were established with initial returns occurring in 1980. Estimates of hatchery runs of chum salmon in southeast Alaska were available since the onset of production from Southern Southeast Regional Aquaculture Association (SSRAA), Northern Southeast Regional Aquaculture Association (NSRAA), and Douglas Island Pink and Chum (DIPAC). Estimates of wild stock and hatchery chum salmon contributions to common property fisheries in southeast Alaska were based on comprehensive coded wire tagging and otolith marking of the hatchery releases conducted since 1980.

Pink and chum salmon runs to British Columbia and Washington from 1925–2005 were roughly estimated by expansion of commercial catch by 50% exploitation rate (Rogers 1999). Total runs of sockeye salmon were estimated for the combined southeast Alaska, British Columbia, and Washington areas because substantial British Columbia-origin sockeye salmon occur in southeast Alaska and Washington fisheries. Total runs of sockeye salmon were available for southeast Alaska (SEAK) since 1984, northern British Columbia (NBC) since 1952, southern British Columbia (SBC) since 1952, and Washington since 1972 (Eggers and Irvine 2007). Exploitation rates (ratio of SEAK catch to sum of SEAK catch and SEAK escapement) in SEAK fisheries were highly correlated with exploitation rates (ratio of NBC catch to sum of NBC catch and NBC escapement) in NBC fisheries for years where assessments of total runs were available in both areas. Total sockeye salmon runs to southeast Alaska from 1952–1983 were estimated based on regression of exploitation rate in SEAK fisheries to exploitation rates in NBC fisheries. Similar methods were used to estimate escapements of sockeye salmon in Washington (for example, the introduced run to Lake Washington, from 1960–1971). In Washington, exploitation rates (the ratio of Washington catch to sum of Washington catch and escapement) were correlated with SBC exploitation rates. A regression model was used to estimate exploitation rates in Washington for years where Lake Washing-

ton escapements were not assessed. Total sockeye salmon runs to aggregate southeast Alaska, British Columbia, and Washington areas from 1926–1951 were estimated based on the standardized catch model, fit to available combined catch—exploitation rate time series (Figure 1). Hatchery run sizes of sockeye salmon in southeast Alaska were available, but were a minor component of the aggregate sockeye salmon runs.

Assessment of total biomass

A population of salmon at any time of the year (for example, the time of year that maturation occurs) includes the terminal run of mature fish together with the immature age cohorts present in the ocean. For pink salmon, cohorts include age 0.0, for chum salmon cohorts include ages 0.0, 0.1, 0.2, 0.3, and 0.4, and for sockeye salmon cohorts include ages x.0, x.1, and x.2. Abundance of salmon cohorts was estimated at the month of maturation, and was the biomass of terminal runs of mature cohorts together with the immature ocean cohorts present. Biomass of the immature ocean cohorts was estimated by standard cohort analysis (Hilborn and Walters 1992). Expansion factors (ratio of total biomass to terminal run biomass) were specific to species and region, and were assumed to be constant over time. The total biomass to terminal run expansion factor were estimated by fitting age-structured forward projection models to various data sets, where smolt abundance and subsequent returns by age and size were known. The age-structured model enables forward construction of the immature and mature age classes from a cohort of smolts or the backward reconstruction of the immature cohorts from the mature terminal run.

Pink Salmon.—A forward projection model was used to estimate age-specific ocean abundance and biomass of pink salmon. Pink salmon mature at the end of the first year of ocean residence; the stock consists of the aggregate cohorts alive at the month of maturation and include the immature ocean age-0 ($N_{0,0}$) and the mature ocean age-1 ($R_{0,1}$) cohorts. For pink salmon, two ocean life stages were assumed, knife-edged mortality ($1 - z_0$) at entry to the ocean, and a constant mortality rate over the period of ocean residence from entry to maturation.

$$N_{0.0} = S_0 z_0 e^{-\Delta t_0 \mu}$$

$$R_{0.1} = S_0 e^{-\Delta t_1 \mu}$$

Where, S_0 is smolt abundance, Z_0 is initial smolt survival, Δt_0 is ocean age of 0.0 cohort (time of entry to month of maturity), Δt_1 is ocean age of 0.1 cohort (12 months), $N_{0.0}$ is abundance of immature cohort, $R_{0.1}$ is abundance of mature cohort, and μ is natural mortality rate (monthly).

The parameter used to expand terminal run biomass to total biomass is the ratio of terminal run biomass to total biomass. This quantity can be expressed in terms of the cohort (F_c) or in terms of the mature run (F_r), which are the same for pink salmon:

$$F_r = (R_{0.1} w_1) / (R_{0.1} w_1 + N_{0.0} w_0)$$

where w_1 is the mean weight of mature cohort, and w_0 is the mean weight of ocean age-0 cohort.

The model was fit to three pink salmon smolt and adult return data sets: Hokkaido pink salmon hatchery runs (1970–1995 broods; Hiroi 1998), Kodiak pink salmon hatchery (Kitoi Bay hatchery) runs (1972–2003 broods; Hilborn and Eggers 2000), and aggregate Prince William Sound pink salmon hatchery runs (1978–2003 broods; Hilborn and Eggers 2000). The mean weights by age for mature age classes were assessed for each cohort in the data sets. The mean weight for immature pink salmon in the first year of

ocean residence at the month of maturation was assumed to be 0.75 kg for all stocks, and was roughly the average of smolt weight and mature adult weight.

Sockeye Salmon.—A forward projection model was used to estimate freshwater age (a) and ocean age (0) specific ocean abundance and biomass of sockeye salmon. Sockeye salmon may spend one to two years in freshwater and mature at the end of the second or third year of ocean residence. The stock consists of the aggregate cohorts alive at the month of maturation and include the immature age classes ($N_{a.o}$, $a = 1,2$; $o = 0,1,2$) and the mature age classes ($R_{a.o}$ $a = 1,2$; $o = 2,3$) of the cohort. For sockeye salmon, two ocean life stages were assumed, a knife-edged mortality ($1 - z_0$) at entry to the ocean, and a constant mortality rate over the entire period of ocean residence from entry to maturation.

$$N_{a.1} = S_a z_0 e^{-\Delta t_0 \mu_a}$$

$$N_{a.1} = N_{a.o} e^{-\Delta t_1 \mu_a}$$

$$N_{a.2} = (1 - m_{a.2}) N_{a.1} e^{-\Delta t_2 \mu_a}$$

$$R_{a.2} = m_{a.2} N_{a.1} e^{-\Delta t_2 \mu_a}$$

$$R_{a.3} = N_{a.2} e^{-\Delta t_3 \mu_a}$$

where a is freshwater age, o is ocean age, S_a is age a. smolt abundance Z_0 is initial smolt survival, Δt_0 is ocean age of 0.0 cohort (months from time of entry to month of maturation), Δt_o is ocean age of .o cohort (i.e., 12 months for 0.1, 0.2, and 0.3 cohorts), $N_{a.o}$ is abundance of immature ocean age $a.o$ cohort, $R_{a.o}$ is abundance of mature age $a.o$ cohort, $m_{a.o}$ is maturation rate of age $a.o$ cohort, and μ_a is natural mortality rate (monthly).

The parameter used to expand terminal run biomass to total biomass was the ratio of terminal run biomass to total biomass. This quantity can be expressed in terms of the cohort (F_c) or in terms of the mature run (F_r). Fc was calculated by summing over the age classes of a brood year or cohort.

$$R_r = \frac{\sum_{a=1}^{2}\sum_{0=2}^{3} R_{a.o} w_{a.o}}{(\sum_{a=1}^{2}\sum_{0=0}^{3} N_{a.o} w_{a.o} + \sum_{a=1}^{2}\sum_{0=2}^{3} R_{a.o} w_{a.o})}$$

where, $w_{a.o}$ is the mean weight of age $a.o$ mature or immature cohort at the end of the year. R_r was calculated by summing over various age classes across broods that are present at the time of the run.

The model was fit to two sockeye salmon smolt and adult return data sets: Ugashik smolts, (1980–1998 broods, Crawford 2001), Egegik smolts (1979–1998 broods, Crawford 2001).

Chum Salmon.—A forward projection model was used to estimate ocean age (o) specific ocean abundance and biomass of chum salmon. Chum salmon mature between the end of the second through the fifth year of ocean residence, and chum salmon enter the ocean at freshwater age 0. The stock consists of the aggregate cohorts alive at the month of maturation and include the immature age classes ($N_{0.o}$, $o = 0$–5) and the mature age classes ($R_{0.o}$ $o = 2$–5) of the cohort. For chum salmon, three ocean life stages were assumed, a knife-edge mortality ($1 - z_0$) at entry to the ocean, a constant mortality rate over the first year of ocean residence (from the time of entry to the month of maturation the second ocean year), and a constant mortality rate over the remainder of ocean residence (from the month of maturation in the second year of ocean residence to maturation). The following equations were used:

$$N_{0.0} = Sz_0 e^{-\Delta t_0 \mu_o}$$

$$N_{0.1} = N_{0.0} e^{-\Delta t_1 \mu_o}$$

$$N_{0.2} = (1 - m_2) N_{0.1} e^{-\Delta t_2 \mu_{2+}}$$

$$R_{0.2} = m_2 N_{0.1} e^{-\Delta t_2 \mu_{2+}}$$

$$N_{0.3} = (1 - m_3) N_{0.2} e^{-\Delta t_3 \mu}$$

$$R_{0.3} = m_3 N_{0.2} e^{-\Delta t_3 \mu_{1+}}$$

$$N_{0.4} = (1 - m_4) N_{0.4} e^{-\Delta t_4 \mu_{1+}}$$

$$R_{0.4} = m_4 N_{0.3} e^{-\Delta t_4 \mu_{1+}}$$

$$R_{0.5} = m_5 N_{0.4} e^{-\Delta t_5 \mu_{1+}}$$

Where, o is ocean age, S is age a. smolt abundance, z_0 is initial smolt survival, Δt_0 is ocean age of 0.0 cohort (months from time of entry to month of maturation), Δto is ocean age of $.o$ cohort (i.e., 12 months for 0.1 through 0.4), $N_{0.o}$ is abundance of immature ocean age o cohort, $R_{0.o}$ is abundance of mature age 0.o cohort, m_o is maturation rate of age $.o$ cohort, μ_0 is natural mortality rate (monthly, during the first year of ocean residence (entry to month of maturation in ocean year 1), μ_2+ is natural mortality rate (after month of maturation in the second ocean year).

The parameter used to expand terminal run biomass to total biomass was the ratio of terminal run biomass to total biomass. Note this quantity can be expressed in terms of the cohort (F_c) or in terms of the mature run (F_r). R_r was calculated by summing various age classes across broods present at the time of the run.

$$F_r = \frac{\sum_{o=2}^{5} R_{0.o} w_o}{(\sum_{o=1}^{4} N_{0.o} w_o + \sum_{0=2}^{5} R_{0.o} w_o)}$$

The forward projection model was fit to seven chum salmon smolt–adult return data sets: Honshu chum salmon hatchery runs, 1961–1991 broods (M. Kaeriyama, Hokkaido Tokai University, Sapporo, Japan, personal communication); Hokkaido chum salmon hatchery runs, 1961–1991 broods (M.

Kaeriyama, Hokkaido Tokai University, Sapporo, Japan, personal communication), DIPAC chum salmon hatchery runs, 1984–1996 broods (R. Foct, DIPAC Hatchery, Juneau, personal communication); SSRAA summer chum salmon hatchery runs, 1979–1996 broods (Gary Freitag, SSRAA, Ketchikan, personal communication); SRAA fall chum hatchery runs 1979–1996 broods (Gary Freitag, SSRAA, Ketchikan, personal communication); Hidden Falls chum salmon hatchery run, 1977–1996 broods (Chip Blair, NSRAA, Sitka, personal communication); Medvejie chum salmon hatchery run, 1981–1996 broods, (Chip Blair, NSRAA, Sitka, personal communication).

Model Fitting Process.—The mean weights by age for mature age classes were available for each of the above data sets. Annual growth rates for each cohort were estimated by linear regression fit to a sequence of weights (i.e., weights of smolts and mature age classes). Weights of immature cohorts of the same age were assumed to be the same as the mature cohort; and weights of immature age classes (ages 0.0, 0.1, and 0.2) for which mature weights were not available, and were estimated by applying the growth rates to the youngest mature age-class weight available.

The model fit to individual cohorts and included the weight-at-age (of smolts and mature age classes), smolt abundance, and the abundance of the mature age classes. The month-at-maturation and immediate mortality rate (z_0) were fixed for each stock. The maturation rates (m_a) and instantaneous natural mortality rate (μ) were estimated by exact fit of the returning adults for a cohort. Excel solver was used to determine values of maturation and mortality rates where projected returns from a smolt cohort equaled the observed returns from the cohort.

The model fitting procedure was quite robust for all of the data sets examined. Mortality rates were consistent among stocks within a species. Mortality rates were similar for sockeye and chum salmon, and considerably higher for pink salmon (Figure 5). Mortality rates have generally decreased since the 1960s (Figure 5). Age 0.3 maturation rates have consistent trends among stocks. Maturation rates decreased (increased age at maturity) from the 1960s to the early 1990s, and increased after the 1990s (Figure 6). Trends in maturation rates were similar among chum salmon stocks.

It is widely believed that much of ocean mortality for salmon occurs early in the ocean residence period. This interpretation is consistent with the widely observed correlations in the returns of sibling age classes. Natural mortality is not likely to be occuring at a constant rate over the ocean life of salmon. Hence, mortality was modeled as a two-stage process, with an immediate mortality rate ($1 - z_0$) and mortality occurring at constant rate (μ) during the remainder of ocean residence. Insufficient information (i.e., too many model parameters) exists in the smolt data sets to estimate separable immediate survival rate (z_0) from an instantaneous mortality rate (μ). The sensitivity of the estimated expansion factor of total runs and the terminal run to total biomass expansion factor (F_r) was examined by fitting the foreword projection model over a number of immediate survival values (Figure 7). The ratio of terminal run biomass to total biomass was sensitive to the value of z_0, with average (over the broods of available data) F_r decreasing with increasing initial survival rate (Figure 7). The maximum ratios of terminal run biomass to total biomass occurred with natural mortality rate constant over the period of ocean residence (i.e., $z_0 = 1$). To provide a more realistic expansion of total biomass, a subjective value for z_0 of 0.5 was assumed for pink and chum salmon, and 0.6 for sockeye salmon. The larger value assumed for sockeye salmon reflects the higher initial survival expected given the relatively large body size of sockeye salmon smolts.

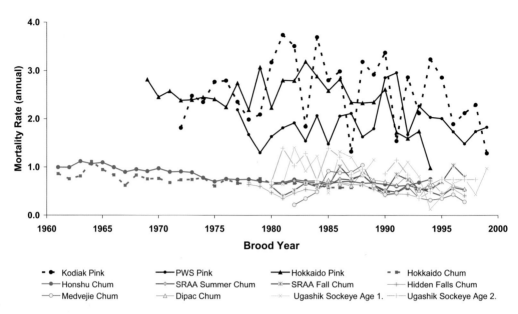

FIGURE 5. Annual mortality rates, by brood year cohort, estimated by forward projection model fit to various smolt–total run data sets.

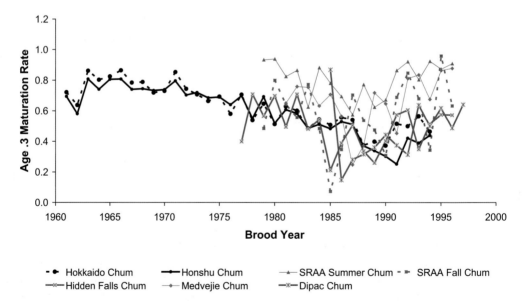

FIGURE 6. Age 0.3 maturation rates estimated for various chum salmon populations by forward projection model fits to various smolt–total run data sets.

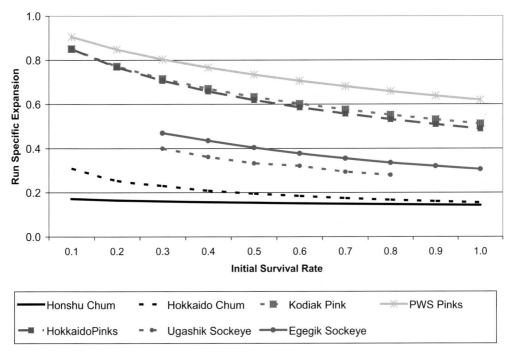

FIGURE 7. Sensitivity of estimated terminal run expansion factor (total biomass/terminal run biomass) to initial survival rate based on forward projection model applied for various to various pink, chum, and sockeye salmon smolt–total run data sets.

The assumption of a constant natural mortality rate over the period of ocean residence is particularly unrealistic for chum salmon. Chum salmon mortality was modeled with rate (μ_0) during the first year of ocean residence from entry to month of maturation in second year of ocean residence) and (μ_{1+}) during ocean residence after the month of maturation in second year of ocean residence. Separate estimates of μ_0 and μ_{1+} were not possible. Mortality rates estimated for pink salmon during ocean residence were used as a surrogate for chum salmon. Pink and chum salmon enter the ocean at similar sizes and would be expected to have similar mortality rates (Parker 1962; Ricker 1964). The monthly mortality rates estimated for pink salmon over their ocean residence averaged 2.5 times the rate estimated for chum salmon integrated over their entire period of ocean

residence. In fitting the model to the chum salmon data sets, the first ocean year mortality rate (μ_0) was 2.5 times the 2+ ocean mortality rate (μ_{2+}).

Terminal run to total biomass expansion factors (F_r) were estimated by run year for each of the pink, chum, and sockeye salmon stocks with smolt data sets (Figure 8). Ratios of terminal runs to total biomass for pink salmon ranged from 0.34 to 0.87, with an average of 0.66, and were consistent among stocks. Terminal run biomass to total biomass ratios for chum salmon ranged from 0.1 to 0.28, averaged 0.19, and were consistent among stocks. Terminal run biomass to total biomass ratios for sockeye salmon ranged from 0.18 to 0.47, averaged 0.33. These ratios were stable over time (Figure 8).

The average ratios of terminal run biomass to total biomass estimated from the

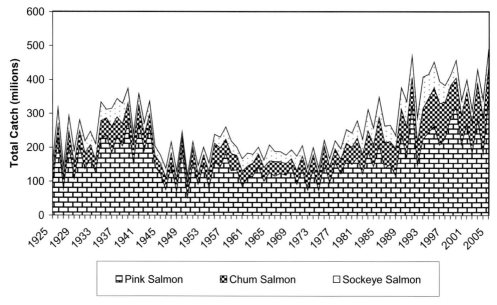

FIGURE 9. Commercial catch of pink, chum, and sockeye salmon (millions of pieces) in the North Pacific Ocean, 1925–2005.

million metric tons since the mid-1990s (Figure 10). Pink salmon comprised the largest component of run biomass averaging 45% of the total. Hatchery runs increased in the North Pacific from nothing in the early 1960s to an average of 0.34 million tons; it constitutes 28% of total runs since the mid 1990s.

The total biomass of the three species increased from 1.3 million metric tons in 1969 to and average of 4 million metric tons since the mid-1990s (Figure 11). Chum salmon were the largest component of salmon biomass averaging 60% of the total since 1990. The biomass of hatchery fish in the North Pacific Ocean increased from zero in the early 1960s to an average of at least 1.5 million tons, and constituted at least 37% total biomass since the mid 1990s.

Discussion

The dramatic increase in abundance of Pacific Salmon in the North Pacific Ocean has been due in large part to an increase in hatchery runs throughout the North Pacific. Increases in abundance of wild runs of salmon coincide with the increase in hatchery runs; however, the rate of increase of wild-run biomass was much lower than the total (hatchery and wild) run biomass. The recent ten-year average of wild-run biomass and total-run biomass increased by 2 and 2.6 fold, respectively, from the low levels of the early 1970s. Similarly, a two-fold increase occurred for wild salmon total biomass and a three-fold increase occurred in total salmon biomass.

Substantial inter-annual variation occurred in the runs and survival of North Pacific salmon stocks (Figure 5; Peterman et al. 1998; Mueter et al. 2002; Eggers and Irvine 2007). The total run and total biomass reconstructions reported here were based on assumptions (e.g., fixed exploitation rates for stocks with incomplete stock assessment) that would mask the inter-annual variation in abundance. The run and total-biomass reconstructions were intended to reflect trends and

TABLE 3. Annual North Pacific total runs of pink salmon in millions of fish.

	North America						Asia					
								Japan					
Year	British Columbia/ Washington	Southeast Alaska[1]	Central Alaska[2]		Western Alaska[3]	N. Amer. Total	Coastal		High Seas and Offshore[4]	Russian Coastal[5]	Asia Total	Pacific Total
			Wild	Hatchery			Wild	Hatchery				
1925	13.8	54.2	12.7		0.0	80.6	8.4		0.0	60.0	68.4	149.0
1926	16.6	60.3	28.2		1.6	106.7	11.5		0.0	244.6	256.1	362.9
1927	13.0	20.8	20.3		0.7	54.8	8.6		0.0	63.8	72.4	127.3
1928	20.8	66.2	16.6		0.1	103.7	8.3		0.0	225.8	234.1	337.9
1929	12.0	44.0	25.2		0.0	81.2	24.4		0.0	48.3	72.7	153.9
1930	11.7	77.4	23.0		0.5	112.6	11.9		0.2	186.1	198.2	310.8
1931	10.0	52.6	20.6		0.0	83.3	27.4		0.1	91.9	119.3	202.6
1932	10.8	45.2	20.5		0.3	76.8	8.6		1.3	195.5	205.5	282.3
1933	7.9	50.3	20.6		0.0	78.9	7.2		1.8	105.5	114.5	193.4
1934	11.9	87.4	31.1		0.1	130.5	7.1		1.3	224.4	232.8	363.3
1935	11.1	57.3	28.1		0.0	96.5	10.6		6.0	257.6	274.2	370.7
1936	13.9	88.0	34.9		1.1	137.9	9.9		1.0	141.1	152.1	290.0
1937	11.5	64.9	40.6		0.0	117.0	9.4		1.2	233.4	244.1	361.1
1938	12.1	57.4	33.0		0.0	102.4	10.7		1.5	216.1	228.3	330.7
1939	6.5	47.0	29.0		0.0	82.6	7.1		2.0	344.3	353.4	436.0
1940	12.2	55.5	40.4		0.5	108.6	3.8		2.5	141.1	147.4	256.0
1941	13.2	101.4	26.1		0.0	140.7	8.4		3.9	286.2	298.5	439.2
1942	13.2	61.7	29.8		0.3	105.1	5.8		4.3	202.8	212.8	318.0
1943	6.4	37.8	38.1		0.0	82.3	2.2		0.0	331.1	333.3	415.6
1944	6.1	39.9	26.0		0.1	72.1	2.3		0.0	162.2	164.5	236.6
1945	6.6	43.7	34.4		0.0	84.7	2.7		0.0	89.6	92.3	177.1
1946	13.0	48.8	30.2		0.1	92.1	1.1		0.0	42.8	43.9	135.9
1947	12.9	31.1	28.5		0.0	72.5	3.0		0.0	147.9	150.9	223.4
1948	12.5	31.6	20.3		0.1	64.5	0.7		0.0	58.3	59.0	123.5
1949	7.1	78.0	20.0		0.0	105.2	6.1		0.0	184.3	190.4	295.6
1950	16.7	23.1	17.4		0.1	57.3	3.1		0.0	40.7	43.8	101.1
1951	15.0	44.6	11.8		0.0	71.4	5.2		0.0	175.3	180.5	252.0
1952	6.8	23.7	16.8		0.1	47.5	1.3		19.5	65.8	86.6	134.1
1953	10.4	15.3	17.5		0.2	43.3	1.6		15.8	163.8	181.1	224.5
1954	13.2	22.2	20.7		1.4	57.4	1.1		19.6	53.2	73.9	131.3
1955	3.9	22.9	23.2		0.1	50.1	2.5		53.4	101.6	157.6	207.7
1956	5.3	30.6	19.7		0.3	55.8	2.1		55.9	83.0	141.0	196.9
1957	5.2	18.5	12.1		0.0	35.9	1.5		79.6	122.5	203.6	239.5
1958	7.5	23.8	21.7		3.6	56.6	18.4		45.9	44.2	108.5	165.1
1959	5.1	20.3	7.8		0.0	33.2	13.0		63.1	54.2	130.3	163.5
1960	4.1	9.3	20.0		1.6	34.9	17.4		28.1	22.6	68.0	102.9
1961	2.8	22.2	16.4		0.3	41.7	7.4		49.2	34.9	91.5	133.2
1962	3.5	23.4	39.4		6.0	72.3	7.7		27.0	18.0	52.7	125.0
1963	3.6	33.6	22.4		0.3	59.9	9.3		55.6	41.0	105.8	165.7
1964	5.1	30.9	34.7		3.5	74.3	5.7		27.3	17.7	50.7	125.0
1965	1.7	22.8	15.8		0.0	40.3	9.6		51.6	57.8	119.0	159.4

[1] Includes Southeast Alaska and Yakatat management areas.
[2] Includes Prince William Sound, Cook Inlet, Kodiak, Chignik, and South Alaska Peninsula management areas.
[3] Includes North Alaska Peninsula, Aleutian Islands, Bristol Bay, and AYK management areas.
[4] Includes mothership, landbased gillnet, landbased longline, and Sea of Japan fisheries.
[5] Includes coastal and freshwater fisheries.

TABLE 3. Continued.

			North America						Asia			
								Japan				
	British Columbia/ Washington	Southeast Alaska[1]	Central Alaska[2]		Western Alaska[3]	N. Amer. Total	Coastal		High Seas and Offshore[4]	Russian Coastal[5]	Asia Total	Pacific Total
Year			Wild	Hatchery			Wild	Hatchery				
1966	3.5	36.0	34.7		5.2	79.4	9.8		30.5	23.4	63.6	143.1
1967	2.8	8.6	15.8		0.1	27.3	14.9		49.2	55.1	119.3	146.6
1968	7.2	38.2	25.5		6.0	76.7	11.7		26.8	16.8	55.3	132.0
1969	3.0	13.9	7.7		0.7	25.3	16.8		48.3	71.3	136.4	161.7
1970	7.9	21.8	24.8		2.5	56.9	9.1		23.5	18.5	51.1	108.0
1971	2.9	22.5	27.9	0.0	0.1	53.4	16.2	1.0	39.8	73.9	130.9	184.3
1972	13.9	25.6	27.4	0.0	0.4	67.2	9.5	0.4	21.4	22.1	53.4	120.7
1973	13.7	18.9	20.6	0.0	0.1	53.3	10.7	2.8	36.2	113.7	163.4	216.7
1974	5.3	16.7	7.9	0.0	2.3	32.3	10.3	0.5	22.2	39.8	72.7	105.1
1975	2.7	17.2	7.9	0.0	0.1	28.0	11.6	2.3	33.7	149.7	197.2	225.2
1976	5.4	20.7	8.9	0.1	2.3	37.5	4.0	1.2	16.5	65.3	87.0	124.5
1977	3.1	42.3	14.8	0.1	0.1	60.4	4.8	1.6	24.1	138.1	168.7	229.1
1978	8.5	44.7	26.1	0.4	12.1	91.8	5.7	1.1	9.7	69.1	85.6	177.4
1979	2.0	37.6	22.1	1.0	1.4	64.1	5.4	0.8	16.8	124.4	147.5	211.6
1980	8.9	37.3	35.3	2.5	11.4	95.4	5.4	0.8	15.1	95.1	116.3	211.7
1981	3.3	43.6	47.7	3.4	1.1	99.1	5.8	0.8	17.8	105.4	129.8	228.9
1982	8.2	47.4	50.4	6.4	6.4	118.7	4.6	0.9	14.7	57.3	77.5	196.2
1983	3.1	67.0	46.3	5.1	0.2	121.7	3.9	1.6	18.1	129.1	152.7	274.4
1984	5.2	57.5	41.2	5.8	11.7	121.4	5.1	0.9	13.5	67.9	87.4	208.8
1985	13.3	103.3	26.2	12.3	0.0	155.2	7.5	1.4	14.7	115.6	139.2	294.3
1986	13.7	91.2	53.8	7.8	1.0	167.5	4.6	1.4	8.0	49.1	63.0	230.6
1987	7.4	36.1	36.1	19.7	0.0	99.3	4.6	2.7	8.5	118.5	134.2	233.5
1988	16.0	29.6	31.9	12.4	2.6	92.6	4.6	1.9	6.6	48.7	61.8	154.4
1989	5.5	93.4	23.7	26.8	0.0	149.4	2.7	3.8	6.9	179.4	192.8	342.2
1990	8.6	60.4	34.7	34.1	2.1	139.9	0.9	3.9	4.8	91.2	100.8	240.6
1991	6.9	93.5	19.5	34.4	0.0	154.3	8.9	4.0	4.3	254.1	271.2	425.4
1992	11.0	66.9	29.2	9.7	2.2	118.9	9.4	2.6	1.3	104.7	118.0	236.9
1993	10.8	91.2	44.0	18.6	0.3	164.9	10.0	8.2	2.7	139.8	160.8	325.7
1994	11.4	96.4	23.6	37.4	4.5	173.2	9.8	9.4	2.9	174.4	196.5	369.7
1995	6.5	87.5	45.0	19.2	0.2	158.4	4.9	7.9	3.2	175.6	191.7	350.1
1996	4.4	120.2	31.9	25.6	1.2	183.2	0.8	17.4	2.8	135.7	156.7	339.9
1997	4.6	68.0	70.3	28.1	0.1	171.1	0.8	9.9	3.1	229.1	242.8	413.9
1998	10.6	76.0	15.3	34.9	1.3	138.1	0.5	19.1	3.7	272.0	295.4	433.5
1999	2.4	126.4	25.4	47.1	0.0	201.4	0.8	11.3	3.9	260.5	276.4	477.8
2000	1.7	41.5	39.6	38.4	1.0	122.2	0.3	17.3	2.0	185.5	205.1	327.3
2001	5.5	111.4	36.2	43.6	0.0	196.8	0.6	6.9	2.4	213.4	223.3	420.0
2002	8.9	80.1	25.8	27.2	0.0	142.0	0.5	13.9	2.4	125.0	141.8	283.8
2003	8.9	90.6	27.8	57.9	0.0	185.2	0.5	13.3	2.8	219.1	235.7	420.9
2004	6.1	80.1	24.6	26.9	0.1	137.9	0.2	6.9	2.3	119.9	129.3	267.2
2005	4.3	100.0	27.7	67.6	0.0	199.6	0.0	10.1	2.2	273.8	286.2	485.8

[1] Includes Southeast Alaska and Yakatat management areas.
[2] Includes Prince William Sound, Cook Inlet, Kodiak, Chignik, and South Alaska Peninsula management areas.
[3] Includes North Alaska Peninsula, Aleutian Islands, Bristol Bay, and AYK management areas.
[4] Includes mothership, landbased gillnet, landbased longline, and Sea of Japan fisheries.
[5] Includes coastal and freshwater fisheries.

TABLE 4. Annual North Pacific total runs of pink salmon in thousands of mt.

	North America						Asia					
			Central Alaska[2]				Japan					
							Coastal		High Seas			
Year	British Columbia/ Washington	Southeast Alaska[1]	Wild	Hatchery	Western Alaska[3]	N. Amer. Total	Wild	Hatchery	and Offshore[4]	Russian Coastal[5]	Asia Total	Pacific Total
1925	68.9	95.4	20.8		0.0	185.1	12.6		0.0	86.7	99.3	284.4
1926	57.6	106.1	46.3		2.5	212.6	17.3		0.0	357.0	374.3	586.9
1927	57.7	36.7	33.3		1.1	128.7	12.9		0.0	91.9	104.8	233.5
1928	58.6	116.5	27.6		0.1	202.9	12.5		0.0	327.8	340.2	543.1
1929	84.0	77.5	41.4		0.0	202.9	36.6		0.0	68.5	105.1	308.0
1930	80.6	136.2	37.7		0.8	255.1	17.9		0.2	273.7	291.8	546.9
1931	78.3	92.6	33.6		0.0	204.5	41.1		0.1	133.1	174.2	378.8
1932	18.5	79.6	33.2		0.5	131.8	12.9		1.6	290.2	304.7	436.6
1933	77.6	88.5	33.4		0.0	199.5	10.8		2.1	152.2	165.1	364.7
1934	36.0	153.9	50.5		0.1	240.5	10.7		1.5	333.0	345.1	585.6
1935	73.6	100.9	45.2		0.0	219.7	15.9		7.2	372.7	395.7	615.4
1936	49.1	154.9	56.8		1.6	262.5	14.9		1.2	209.9	226.0	488.5
1937	74.5	114.2	65.2		0.0	253.9	14.1		1.5	343.0	358.6	612.5
1938	34.3	101.0	53.6		0.0	188.8	16.1		1.8	321.0	338.9	527.7
1939	72.2	82.8	46.5		0.0	201.6	10.7		2.5	506.5	519.6	721.2
1940	16.8	97.7	65.8		0.8	181.1	5.7		3.0	209.6	218.3	399.3
1941	47.8	178.5	42.1		0.0	268.5	12.6		4.7	419.2	436.5	704.9
1942	20.4	108.7	48.4		0.5	178.0	8.7		5.1	302.6	316.4	494.4
1943	47.9	66.5	62.0		0.0	176.5	3.3		0.0	488.0	491.3	667.7
1944	25.5	70.3	42.6		0.2	138.5	3.5		0.0	242.1	245.6	384.1
1945	90.9	76.9	56.3		0.0	224.1	4.1		0.0	133.8	137.8	361.9
1946	9.6	85.9	49.1		0.1	144.7	1.7		0.0	63.8	65.5	210.2
1947	94.9	54.7	46.6		0.0	196.2	4.5		0.0	220.7	225.2	421.4
1948	24.3	55.6	32.7		0.2	112.8	1.1		0.0	87.0	88.1	200.8
1949	90.7	137.3	32.8		0.0	260.8	9.2		0.0	275.0	284.2	545.0
1950	36.6	40.6	28.1		0.1	105.4	4.7		0.0	60.7	65.3	170.7
1951	85.4	78.5	18.9		0.1	182.9	7.8		0.0	258.0	265.8	448.7
1952	50.6	41.8	27.1		0.1	119.6	0.7		23.9	95.3	120.0	239.6
1953	92.2	26.9	28.3		0.3	147.7	0.9		19.4	237.2	257.4	405.1
1954	25.4	39.0	33.1		2.2	99.8	0.6		23.7	77.0	101.3	201.1
1955	91.3	40.3	37.1		0.1	168.8	1.5		71.1	147.2	219.7	388.5
1956	28.6	53.8	32.1		0.4	114.9	1.2		68.6	120.2	190.0	304.9
1957	72.4	32.6	19.4		0.0	124.5	0.9		93.8	177.3	272.0	396.4
1958	33.5	41.9	35.5		5.6	116.5	10.5		65.5	64.0	140.0	256.5
1959	47.0	35.7	12.5		0.1	95.3	7.5		82.8	78.5	168.8	264.1
1960	16.8	14.3	29.3		2.8	63.2	10.0		36.1	32.7	78.7	141.9
1961	53.9	52.5	33.3		0.5	140.2	4.2		65.4	50.5	120.1	260.3
1962	92.5	41.5	53.9		8.3	196.1	4.6		28.9	27.2	60.7	256.8
1963	88.4	47.4	38.1		0.4	174.3	5.3		62.0	59.5	126.8	301.1
1964	36.3	53.2	53.9		4.8	148.3	3.2		30.3	24.3	57.8	206.1
1965	26.8	40.4	24.6		0.0	91.9	5.5		53.3	79.8	138.6	230.5

[1] Includes Southeast Alaska and Yakatat management areas.
[2] Includes Prince William Sound, Cook Inlet, Kodiak, Chignik, and South Alaska Peninsula management areas.
[3] Includes North Alaska Peninsula, Aleutian Islands, Bristol Bay, and AYK management areas.
[4] Includes mothership, landbased gillnet, landbased longline, and Sea of Japan fisheries.
[5] Includes coastal and freshwater fisheries.

TABLE 4. Continued.

Year	British Columbia/ Washington	Southeast Alaska[1]	Central Alaska[2] Wild	Central Alaska[2] Hatchery	Western Alaska[3]	N. Amer. Total	Japan Coastal Wild	Japan Coastal Hatchery	Japan High Seas and Offshore[4]	Russian Coastal[5]	Asia Total	Pacific Total
1966	72.6	72.1	44.0		7.3	196.0	5.6		32.8	34.5	72.9	268.9
1967	70.5	17.6	14.5		0.1	102.7	8.4		50.7	84.5	143.6	246.3
1968	56.5	57.3	37.7		8.8	160.3	6.7		31.1	27.2	65.0	225.2
1969	19.0	27.1	52.7		1.2	100.1	9.4		51.3	105.7	166.3	266.4
1970	52.3	38.5	46.2		4.0	141.1	5.2		25.7	27.0	57.9	199.0
1971	50.0	37.8	34.5	0.0	0.2	122.4	16.4	1.3	42.9	111.4	172.1	294.5
1972	38.9	36.3	15.5	0.0	0.5	91.3	9.7	0.4	25.5	33.9	69.5	160.8
1973	40.5	30.9	14.0	0.0	0.2	85.5	10.9	2.8	40.0	151.5	205.2	290.7
1974	24.4	31.3	17.4	0.0	4.3	77.4	10.4	0.5	24.5	55.0	90.5	167.9
1975	29.8	29.8	28.1	0.1	0.1	87.8	11.8	2.3	34.9	184.0	232.9	320.7
1976	37.2	41.2	48.6	0.1	3.6	130.7	6.3	1.2	21.1	90.8	119.5	250.2
1977	65.8	93.9	41.9	0.2	0.2	201.9	4.5	1.6	28.2	192.0	226.3	428.2
1978	33.4	64.7	58.1	0.7	17.9	174.8	4.5	1.1	11.2	96.1	112.9	287.7
1979	75.0	67.2	79.4	1.7	2.3	225.6	4.4	0.8	18.5	173.0	196.7	422.3
1980	30.6	65.7	75.6	3.8	17.0	192.8	4.7	0.8	14.6	132.2	152.2	345.0
1981	101.4	84.2	83.2	6.3	1.7	276.8	5.9	0.8	18.7	146.6	171.9	448.7
1982	8.7	70.2	64.1	10.2	9.3	162.5	4.3	0.9	15.3	79.6	100.1	262.6
1983	93.8	95.0	40.7	7.6	0.3	237.3	3.9	1.6	19.1	179.5	204.1	441.5
1984	26.3	93.4	89.8	9.7	17.7	236.9	5.2	0.9	12.4	94.4	112.8	349.7
1985	102.2	149.3	59.3	20.0	0.0	330.8	8.8	1.4	16.5	160.7	187.4	518.2
1986	64.3	137.7	50.5	10.9	1.7	265.0	5.4	1.4	8.4	68.3	83.4	348.4
1987	67.4	60.6	37.9	31.2	0.0	197.0	6.5	2.7	9.0	164.7	183.0	380.0
1988	70.2	43.8	57.6	19.7	4.2	195.6	6.4	1.9	6.7	67.8	82.8	278.3
1989	81.3	145.6	29.9	41.4	0.0	298.2	5.1	3.8	7.1	249.4	265.4	563.7
1990	57.1	87.5	40.5	46.1	3.2	234.5	2.4	3.9	4.9	126.9	138.1	372.6
1991	88.7	114.8	58.0	39.8	0.0	301.3	10.0	4.0	4.4	353.2	371.6	672.9
1992	32.5	100.2	37.3	15.0	3.5	188.4	14.9	2.6	1.3	145.6	164.4	352.8
1993	42.3	123.1	64.4	25.9	0.4	256.0	8.0	8.2	2.7	193.4	212.3	468.4
1994	7.4	132.0	49.6	53.3	5.9	248.2	13.8	9.4	3.0	211.3	237.5	485.7
1995	52.3	126.4	112.0	31.0	0.2	321.9	6.6	7.9	3.3	250.2	268.0	589.9
1996	17.2	163.6	23.7	41.4	1.4	247.3	4.3	17.4	2.9	185.8	210.4	457.7
1997	30.9	118.6	38.6	47.5	0.1	235.8	0.7	9.9	3.1	318.9	332.6	568.4
1998	7.8	119.4	65.2	58.0	1.4	251.8	0.7	19.1	3.8	322.6	346.2	598.1
1999	19.1	168.2	49.3	63.6	0.0	300.2	0.6	11.3	3.9	315.0	330.9	631.0
2000	14.4	64.2	37.4	59.0	1.3	176.3	0.7	17.3	2.0	248.6	268.6	444.9
2001	24.8	166.1	43.2	67.5	0.0	301.7	0.4	6.9	2.5	285.7	295.4	597.1
2002	17.2	120.7	40.6	43.4	0.1	222.0	0.5	13.9	2.8	183.7	200.9	423.0
2003	35.5	144.4	45.4	95.5	0.1	320.9	0.6	13.3	2.8	300.5	317.2	638.0
2004	7.2	131.9	64.9	45.1	0.0	249.0	0.5	6.9	2.7	189.5	199.7	448.7
2005	26.2	158.8	74.4	105.5	0.0	364.8	0.2	10.1	2.7	343.0	356.1	720.9

[1] Includes Southeast Alaska and Yakatat management areas.
[2] Includes Prince William Sound, Cook Inlet, Kodiak, Chignik, and South Alaska Peninsula management areas.
[3] Includes North Alaska Peninsula, Aleutian Islands, Bristol Bay, and AYK management areas.
[4] Includes mothership, landbased gillnet, landbased longline, and Sea of Japan fisheries.
[5] Includes coastal and freshwater fisheries.

TABLE 5. Annual North Pacific pink salmon biomass in thousands of mt.

	North America						Asia					
							Japan					
			Central Alaska[2]				Coastal		High Seas			
	British Columbia/	Southeast			Western	N. Amer.			and	Russian	Asia	Pacific
Year	Washington	Alaska[1]	Wild	Hatchery	Alaska[3]	Total	Wild	Hatchery	Offshore[4]	Coastal[5]	Total	Total
1925	104.3	144.5	29.9		0.0	278.7	16.8		0.0	131.4	148.2	426.9
1926	87.3	160.8	66.5		3.8	318.4	23.0		0.0	541.0	564.0	882.4
1927	87.4	55.6	48.1		1.6	192.7	17.2		0.0	139.2	156.4	349.1
1928	88.8	176.6	39.0		0.2	304.5	16.6		0.0	496.6	513.2	817.8
1929	127.3	117.4	59.5		0.0	304.1	48.8		0.0	103.8	152.6	456.8
1930	122.1	206.3	54.6		1.2	384.1	23.8		0.3	414.7	438.8	822.9
1931	118.7	140.3	49.0		0.0	307.9	54.8		0.1	201.6	256.5	564.5
1932	28.1	120.6	48.8		0.8	198.3	17.2		2.2	439.7	459.1	657.4
1933	117.6	134.2	49.2		0.0	301.0	14.4		2.9	230.6	247.8	548.8
1934	54.6	233.1	74.0		0.2	361.9	14.2		2.0	504.5	520.7	882.6
1935	111.5	152.8	67.3		0.0	331.6	21.2		9.5	564.6	595.4	927.0
1936	74.4	234.7	82.8		2.4	394.4	19.8		1.7	318.1	339.5	733.9
1937	112.9	173.0	97.4		0.0	383.3	18.8		2.0	519.7	540.5	923.8
1938	52.0	153.0	78.5		0.0	283.4	21.4		2.4	486.4	510.2	793.6
1939	109.5	125.4	69.5		0.0	304.4	14.2		3.3	767.4	784.9	1,089.
1940	25.5	148.0	95.8		1.2	270.5	7.6		4.0	317.5	329.1	599.6
1941	72.4	270.5	62.2		0.0	405.2	16.8		6.3	635.1	658.2	1,063.
1942	30.9	164.7	70.8		0.8	267.1	11.6		6.8	458.4	476.9	744.0
1943	72.6	100.8	90.3		0.0	263.8	4.4		0.0	739.3	743.7	1,007.
1944	38.7	106.5	61.5		0.3	207.0	4.6		0.0	366.8	371.4	578.4
1945	137.7	116.5	81.5		0.0	335.7	5.4		0.0	202.7	208.1	543.7
1946	14.6	130.1	71.6		0.2	216.4	2.2		0.0	96.7	98.9	315.4
1947	143.8	82.9	67.7		0.0	294.4	6.0		0.0	334.3	340.3	634.8
1948	36.7	84.3	48.5		0.2	169.7	1.4		0.0	131.8	133.2	303.0
1949	137.5	208.0	47.4		0.0	392.9	12.2		0.0	416.7	428.9	821.8
1950	55.4	61.5	41.7		0.1	158.7	6.2		0.0	91.9	98.1	256.8
1951	129.4	119.0	28.2		0.1	276.7	10.4		0.0	390.9	401.3	678.0
1952	76.6	63.3	40.1		0.2	180.2	2.6		31.9	144.4	178.9	359.2
1953	139.8	40.7	7.8		0.4	188.7	3.2		25.8	359.3	388.4	577.1
1954	38.6	59.1	49.9		3.3	150.9	2.3		31.6	116.7	150.6	301.4
1955	138.3	61.1	55.9		0.2	255.4	5.2		94.8	223.0	323.0	578.4
1956	43.4	81.5	46.8		0.6	172.3	4.4		91.5	182.1	277.9	450.2
1957	109.8	49.4	29.1		0.0	188.3	3.1		125.0	268.7	396.8	585.1
1958	50.8	63.5	51.4		8.5	174.2	37.8		87.3	97.0	222.1	396.3
1959	71.3	54.1	18.6		0.1	144.1	26.8		110.4	118.9	256.1	400.2
1960	25.4	21.7	43.6		4.2	94.9	35.7		48.1	49.5	133.3	228.3
1961	81.7	79.5	48.7		0.7	210.7	15.2		87.2	76.5	178.9	389.6
1962	140.1	62.8	79.5		12.5	295.0	16.7		38.5	41.2	96.4	391.3
1963	133.9	71.8	55.3		0.6	261.6	19.1		82.7	90.2	191.9	453.6
1964	55.0	80.6	79.7		7.3	222.7	11.3		40.4	36.9	88.6	311.3
1965	40.6	61.3	36.3		0.0	138.3	19.6		71.1	121.0	211.7	349.9

[1] Includes Southeast Alaska and Yakatat management areas.
[2] Includes Prince William Sound, Cook Inlet, Kodiak, Chignik, and South Alaska Peninsula management areas.
[3] Includes North Alaska Peninsula, Aleutian Islands, Bristol Bay, and AYK management areas.
[4] Includes mothership, landbased gillnet, landbased longline, and Sea of Japan fisheries.
[5] Includes coastal and freshwater fisheries.

TABLE 5. Continued.

			North America					Asia				
								Japan				
	British Columbia/	Southeast	Central Alaska[2]		Western	N. Amer.	Coastal		High Seas and	Russian	Asia	Pacific
Year	Washington	Alaska[1]	Wild	Hatchery	Alaska[3]	Total	Wild	Hatchery	Offshore[4]	Coastal[5]	Total	Total
1966	72.6	109.2	65.3		11.1	258.2	20.1		43.7	52.3	116.1	374.3
1967	70.5	26.6	20.7		0.2	118.0	30.3		67.6	128.0	225.9	343.9
1968	56.5	86.8	56.0		13.3	212.6	23.9		41.5	41.2	106.6	319.2
1969	19.0	41.0	78.3		1.9	140.2	33.6		68.3	160.1	262.1	402.3
1970	52.3	58.4	68.7		6.1	185.6	18.7		34.2	40.9	93.9	279.4
1971	50.0	57.3	49.8	0.0	0.2	157.4	21.9	2.2	57.1	168.8	250.0	407.4
1972	38.9	55.1	23.2	0.0	0.8	118.0	12.9	0.8	34.0	51.4	99.1	217.2
1973	40.5	46.8	20.1	0.0	0.2	107.6	14.5	6.4	53.3	229.5	303.7	411.3
1974	24.4	47.4	25.8	0.1	6.5	104.2	13.9	1.2	32.6	83.4	131.1	235.2
1975	29.8	45.2	40.5	0.1	0.1	115.7	15.7	5.1	46.6	278.8	346.1	461.8
1976	37.2	62.4	72.3	0.2	5.5	177.5	8.4	2.8	28.1	137.6	177.0	354.5
1977	65.8	142.2	61.3	0.2	0.3	269.8	6.0	3.6	37.6	290.9	338.1	607.9
1978	33.4	98.1	86.9	0.7	27.1	246.0	6.0	2.5	14.9	145.6	169.0	415.0
1979	75.0	101.8	116.9	2.4	3.6	299.7	5.8	2.0	24.7	262.1	294.5	594.3
1980	30.6	99.6	108.8	5.2	25.8	270.0	6.3	1.8	19.4	200.3	227.7	497.8
1981	101.4	127.6	111.8	7.8	2.6	351.2	7.8	1.8	25.0	222.1	256.6	607.8
1982	8.7	106.4	89.5	12.8	14.1	231.5	5.7	2.0	20.4	120.7	148.8	380.2
1983	93.8	143.9	58.1	10.0	0.4	306.2	5.3	3.7	25.5	272.0	306.4	612.6
1984	26.3	141.5	128.3	12.8	26.9	335.7	6.9	2.0	16.5	143.1	168.5	504.2
1985	102.2	226.2	80.1	26.3	0.0	434.8	11.7	3.3	22.0	243.5	280.4	715.3
1986	64.3	208.6	75.8	15.6	2.5	366.8	7.2	3.1	11.1	103.4	124.9	491.7
1987	67.4	91.8	50.9	38.4	0.0	248.5	8.7	6.2	12.0	249.6	276.4	524.9
1988	70.2	66.4	86.8	27.3	6.4	257.1	8.5	4.4	9.0	102.7	124.5	381.6
1989	81.3	220.6	44.4	59.3	0.1	405.6	6.9	8.7	9.4	377.8	402.8	808.4
1990	57.1	132.6	57.1	59.4	4.9	311.2	3.3	8.7	6.6	192.2	210.8	521.9
1991	88.7	174.0	86.7	55.7	0.0	405.1	13.4	7.3	5.8	535.2	561.6	966.7
1992	32.5	151.8	57.4	27.0	5.3	273.9	19.9	6.2	1.8	220.6	248.4	522.4
1993	42.3	186.4	99.4	43.9	0.6	372.8	10.7	14.9	3.6	293.0	322.2	695.0
1994	7.4	200.0	72.9	69.2	8.9	358.4	18.4	21.4	4.0	320.2	363.9	722.4
1995	52.3	191.5	169.3	45.3	0.3	458.8	8.8	18.4	4.4	379.1	410.6	869.4
1996	17.2	247.9	34.6	56.2	2.1	358.0	5.8	39.8	3.9	281.5	330.9	688.9
1997	30.9	179.7	57.6	63.5	0.2	331.9	0.9	24.8	4.2	483.2	513.2	845.1
1998	7.8	180.9	96.3	75.8	2.1	363.0	0.9	43.3	5.1	488.8	538.1	901.1
1999	19.1	254.8	71.1	80.8	0.0	425.9	0.8	18.4	5.2	477.3	501.7	927.6
2000	14.4	97.3	53.7	76.5	1.9	243.9	1.0	37.2	2.7	376.6	417.5	661.4
2001	24.8	251.7	62.5	92.5	0.1	431.5	0.5	11.0	3.3	432.8	447.6	879.1
2002	17.2	182.8	61.4	62.9	0.1	324.5	0.7	35.3	3.7	278.3	318.0	642.5
2003	35.5	218.8	64.4	117.2	0.1	436.0	0.8	33.3	3.7	455.3	493.1	929.1
2004	7.2	199.8	96.9	62.2	0.0	366.2	0.7	18.3	3.7	287.1	309.8	676.0
2005	26.2	240.5	106.8	133.3	0.0	506.9	0.3	24.4	3.6	519.7	548.1	1,055.0

[1] Includes Southeast Alaska and Yakatat management areas.
[2] Includes Prince William Sound, Cook Inlet, Kodiak, Chignik, and South Alaska Peninsula management areas.
[3] Includes North Alaska Peninsula, Aleutian Islands, Bristol Bay, and AYK management areas.
[4] Includes mothership, landbased gillnet, landbased longline, and Sea of Japan fisheries.
[5] Includes coastal and freshwater fisheries.

TABLE 6. Annual North Pacific total runs of chum salmon in millions of fish.

Year	North America British Columbia/ Washington	Southeast Alaska[1]	Central Alaska[2] Wild	Central Alaska[2] Hatchery	Western Alaska[3]	N. Amer. Total	Asia Japan Coastal Wild	Asia Japan Coastal Hatchery	High Seas and Offshore[4]	Russian Coastal[5]	Asia Total	Pacific Total
1925	13.8	17.5		4.4	1.5	37.1	4.3		0.0	18.0	22.3	59.4
1926	16.6	12.7		3.7	2.1	35.1	4.7		0.0	27.2	31.9	67.1
1927	13.0	6.3		4.4	1.4	25.2	3.9		0.0	26.8	30.7	55.9
1928	20.8	9.9		6.4	2.4	39.6	2.4		0.0	33.1	35.5	75.1
1929	12.0	5.9		7.9	3.9	29.7	3.8		0.0	43.4	47.2	76.9
1930	11.7	5.4		4.6	1.6	23.3	5.2		0.2	49.7	55.1	78.4
1931	10.0	6.1		3.5	3.5	23.2	5.5		0.4	49.6	55.5	78.7
1932	10.8	12.4		2.7	4.9	30.8	3.3		0.7	37.8	41.8	72.6
1933	7.9	9.9		3.8	1.4	22.9	2.3		1.8	36.1	40.2	63.1
1934	11.9	7.3		4.8	1.8	25.8	4.7		2.6	56.2	63.5	89.3
1935	11.1	10.7		5.1	0.5	27.4	5.6		2.9	48.0	56.5	83.9
1936	13.9	14.7		4.8	1.4	34.8	3.6		3.0	86.0	92.6	127.4
1937	11.5	11.4		3.4	1.9	28.2	3.0		2.8	63.1	68.9	97.2
1938	12.1	9.6		4.0	2.9	28.6	4.4		3.9	71.3	79.6	108.2
1939	6.5	7.5		4.2	5.2	23.4	4.6		3.8	61.0	69.4	92.8
1940	12.2	9.8		5.5	1.8	29.3	3.4		4.6	59.6	67.6	96.9
1941	13.2	5.6		4.8	2.8	26.3	2.8		3.2	56.4	62.4	88.7
1942	13.2	11.3		4.9	0.9	30.2	2.5		2.4	43.8	48.7	78.9
1943	6.4	15.9		3.2	2.2	27.7	2.1		0.0	40.5	42.6	70.3
1944	6.1	15.8		4.8	2.4	29.0	1.6		0.0	29.8	31.4	60.4
1945	6.6	7.4		5.4	4.9	24.4	2.3		0.0	28.6	30.9	55.3
1946	13.0	8.8		4.5	1.4	27.7	2.2		0.0	31.7	33.9	61.5
1947	12.9	8.3		4.0	1.5	26.7	2.7		0.0	32.0	34.7	61.3
1948	12.5	9.8		4.8	3.3	30.4	2.7		0.0	28.8	31.5	61.9
1949	7.1	5.7		4.2	1.6	18.6	3.7		0.0	36.6	40.3	58.9
1950	16.7	13.0		4.2	1.8	35.7	5.4		0.0	28.4	33.8	69.5
1951	15.0	9.2		4.3	3.1	31.6	5.9		0.0	38.5	44.4	76.0
1952	6.8	11.2		6.4	3.2	27.7	2.5		1.5	19.9	23.9	51.5
1953	10.4	12.1		5.8	3.4	31.6	2.4		4.7	15.4	22.4	54.0
1954	13.2	11.7		6.2	3.9	35.0	3.6		13.1	23.8	40.4	75.4
1955	3.9	4.2		3.0	2.9	13.9	2.5		27.5	29.6	59.6	73.6
1956	5.3	6.7		6.9	3.6	22.5	1.9		23.5	34.9	60.3	82.8
1957	5.2	10.2		9.0	3.0	27.5	3.3		18.0	14.4	35.8	63.3
1958	7.5	7.5		5.4	3.2	23.6	3.6		29.4	12.5	45.6	69.2
1959	5.1	3.7		5.4	4.0	18.2	2.2		23.4	17.2	42.9	61.0
1960	4.1	3.5		6.7	5.6	19.9	2.2		20.7	19.6	42.4	62.3
1961	2.8	5.0		4.3	3.8	15.9	3.7		13.5	16.4	33.6	49.5
1962	3.5	4.5		6.0	3.8	17.8	4.3		15.4	15.4	35.1	52.9
1963	3.6	2.9		3.9	3.2	13.6	4.5		15.2	15.7	35.5	49.0
1964	5.1	3.6		6.4	3.7	18.8		4.8	19.3	10.8	34.9	53.7
1965	1.7	3.4		3.0	3.0	11.2		6.1	15.5	14.2	35.8	47.0

[1] Includes Southeast Alaska and Yakatat management areas.
[2] Includes Prince William Sound, Cook Inlet, Kodiak, Chignik, and South Alaska Peninsula management areas.
[3] Includes North Alaska Peninsula, Aleutian Islands, Bristol Bay, and AYK management areas.
[4] Includes mothership, landbased gillnet, landbased longline, and Sea of Japan fisheries.
[5] Includes coastal and freshwater fisheries.

TABLE 6. Continued.

| | | | North America | | | | Asia | | | | |
| | | | | | | | | Japan | | | | |
Year	British Columbia/ Washington	Southeast Alaska[1]	Central Alaska[2] Wild	Central Alaska[2] Hatchery	Western Alaska[3]	N. Amer. Total	Coastal Wild	Coastal Hatchery	High Seas and Offshore[4]	Russian Coastal[5]	Asia Total	Pacific Total
1966	3.5	6.4		4.3	3.0	17.2		5.1	22.3	13.1	40.5	57.7
1967	2.8	5.6		3.0	3.5	14.9		5.9	19.1	8.5	33.5	48.4
1968	7.2	4.5		4.7	3.2	19.5		3.1	17.3	7.4	27.8	47.3
1969	3.0	1.8		2.5	3.3	10.6		5.1	12.9	2.4	20.5	31.1
1970	7.9	5.6		5.7	6.0	25.2		6.6	17.1	5.2	28.8	54.0
1971	2.9	5.2		7.0	4.7	19.8		9.3	16.8	6.1	32.2	52.0
1972	13.9	6.7		7.2	4.7	32.5		7.9	22.4	2.8	33.2	65.6
1973	13.7	6.0		5.7	6.5	31.9		10.5	15.7	3.1	29.4	61.2
1974	5.3	6.4		2.3	6.8	20.8		13.0	21.8	4.0	38.8	59.6
1975	2.7	3.3		2.4	8.4	16.8		20.0	19.3	3.9	43.3	60.1
1976	5.4	4.4		3.6	7.5	21.0		12.4	21.9	6.0	40.3	61.2
1977	3.1	2.5		5.7	9.1	20.4		15.2	12.2	7.5	34.9	55.3
1978	8.5	2.0		3.9	7.3	21.8		18.2	7.3	10.2	35.7	57.5
1979	2.0	3.4		3.2	7.5	16.0		28.0	6.1	12.3	46.4	62.4
1980	8.9	4.7	0.0	5.0	12.0	30.6		25.7	6.3	8.2	40.2	70.8
1981	3.3	2.2	0.0	9.4	11.6	26.5		33.5	5.6	7.9	47.1	73.6
1982	8.2	2.7	0.1	10.1	7.4	28.4		29.9	6.7	7.3	44.0	72.4
1983	3.1	1.8	0.2	8.6	8.0	21.8		37.1	5.7	11.1	53.9	75.7
1984	5.2	6.5	1.6	6.4	11.4	31.1		37.8	5.8	7.1	50.7	81.8
1985	13.3	5.1	1.0	5.8	8.8	34.0		50.9	4.4	13.0	68.3	102.3
1986	13.7	4.8	1.2	9.0	8.9	37.6		46.0	3.0	11.9	60.9	98.5
1987	7.4	5.4	1.3	7.1	8.0	29.2		42.7	2.9	13.9	59.5	88.7
1988	16.0	7.2	1.1	9.7	10.8	44.8		47.2	1.8	13.6	62.6	107.4
1989	5.5	2.3	0.6	3.8	9.0	21.2		54.1	1.5	11.8	67.4	88.6
1990	8.6	2.4	1.1	5.1	6.5	23.6		66.9	1.1	14.1	82.2	105.8
1991	6.9	3.0	1.5	5.1	8.2	24.7		61.4	0.8	10.2	72.5	97.2
1992	11.0	5.2	2.5	4.6	6.4	29.7		44.3	0.0	10.0	54.4	84.1
1993	10.8	5.7	5.1	4.3	4.3	30.2		62.8	0.1	15.4	78.3	108.5
1994	11.4	6.9	7.5	7.0	8.0	40.8		63.3	0.2	20.0	83.5	124.3
1995	6.5	6.7	8.5	6.3	11.0	39.1		75.6	0.2	21.2	97.0	136.0
1996	4.4	8.3	14.0	7.2	7.9	41.7		86.8	0.2	16.4	103.4	145.2
1997	4.6	5.0	10.5	6.1	5.1	31.4		77.9	0.2	14.4	92.5	123.8
1998	10.6	8.1	12.2	3.7	4.9	39.6		59.1	0.2	17.6	76.9	116.4
1999	2.4	6.4	12.0	7.8	6.1	34.8		52.0	0.2	17.2	69.3	104.1
2000	1.7	7.2	13.6	12.7	4.3	39.6		46.4	0.2	20.6	67.1	106.7
2001	5.5	5.7	6.3	8.9	7.6	34.0		64.5	0.1	17.2	81.8	115.8
2002	8.9	3.6	6.1	13.5	3.5	35.6		56.2	0.2	19.8	76.2	111.8
2003	8.9	4.1	9.7	10.0	6.4	39.2		73.5	0.2	15.7	89.4	128.5
2004	6.1	9.0	7.4	6.4	5.4	34.3		74.3	0.2	15.4	89.8	124.1
2005	4.3	3.3	5.2	5.2	9.5	27.5		69.0	0.2	18.1	87.2	114.7

[1] Includes Southeast Alaska and Yakatat management areas.
[2] Includes Prince William Sound, Cook Inlet, Kodiak, Chignik, and South Alaska Peninsula management areas.
[3] Includes North Alaska Peninsula, Aleutian Islands, Bristol Bay, and AYK management areas.
[4] Includes mothership, landbased gillnet, landbased longline, and Sea of Japan fisheries.
[5] Includes coastal and freshwater fisheries.

TABLE 7. Annual North Pacific total runs of chum salmon in thousands of mt.

	North America						Asia					
			Central Alaska[2]				Japan					
							Coastal					
Year	British Columbia/ Washington	Southeast Alaska[1]	Wild	Hatchery	Western Alaska[3]	N. Amer. Total	Wild	Hatchery	High Seas and Offshore[4]	Russian Coastal[5]	Asia Total	Pacific Total
1925	73.0	76.3		15.3	4.6	169.2	13.8		0.0	65.0	78.7	247.9
1926	85.9	55.6		13.1	6.3	160.9	15.0		0.0	98.3	113.3	274.2
1927	66.4	27.5		15.5	4.4	113.9	12.5		0.0	96.9	109.4	223.2
1928	108.3	43.5		22.4	7.5	181.7	7.7		0.0	119.6	127.2	308.9
1929	62.3	25.7		27.8	12.0	127.8	12.2		0.0	156.9	169.1	296.9
1930	60.1	23.4		16.3	5.0	104.8	16.6		0.3	179.5	196.4	301.2
1931	53.1	26.7		12.4	10.8	103.1	17.6		0.8	179.0	197.4	300.5
1932	59.3	54.4		9.3	15.1	138.1	10.6		1.2	136.7	148.5	286.6
1933	42.0	43.1		13.3	4.2	102.6	7.4		3.4	129.3	140.0	242.6
1934	61.0	32.1		16.7	5.4	115.1	15.0		5.0	200.4	220.4	335.6
1935	57.5	46.8		17.9	1.7	123.9	17.9		5.5	169.7	193.1	317.0
1936	72.2	64.1		16.8	4.3	157.4	11.5		5.7	299.9	317.1	474.6
1937	59.6	49.8		12.0	5.8	127.1	9.6		5.3	218.4	233.3	360.4
1938	62.9	41.9		14.0	9.1	127.9	14.1		7.3	246.9	268.2	396.1
1939	34.2	32.6		14.8	15.9	97.4	14.7		7.2	212.1	234.0	331.4
1940	62.5	42.9		19.2	5.6	130.2	10.9		8.7	208.0	227.5	357.7
1941	68.1	24.3		16.7	8.7	117.8	9.0		6.0	197.6	212.6	330.3
1942	58.8	49.3		17.1	2.6	127.9	8.0		4.5	150.4	162.9	290.7
1943	34.0	69.5		11.2	6.7	121.5	6.7		0.0	143.6	150.3	271.8
1944	30.8	69.0		16.7	7.4	123.9	5.1		0.0	106.2	111.3	235.2
1945	35.5	32.5		19.0	15.2	102.3	7.4		0.0	103.2	110.6	212.8
1946	68.7	38.3		15.8	4.3	127.0	7.0		0.0	114.5	121.5	248.6
1947	59.2	36.1		14.0	4.5	113.9	8.6		0.0	115.5	124.1	238.1
1948	64.3	42.8		16.8	10.3	134.3	8.6		0.0	104.2	112.8	247.1
1949	37.3	25.0		14.6	4.8	81.8	11.8		0.0	132.3	144.2	225.9
1950	83.1	56.8		14.6	5.7	160.3	17.3		0.0	102.5	119.8	280.0
1951	70.2	40.2		15.1	9.5	135.0	18.9		0.0	139.0	157.9	292.9
1952	42.1	49.2		22.5	9.8	123.6	8.2		3.1	73.3	84.6	208.2
1953	59.0	52.7		20.2	10.5	142.4	7.8		10.3	56.7	74.8	217.2
1954	81.4	51.3		21.7	12.0	166.3	11.8		29.1	87.7	128.6	294.9
1955	22.0	18.2		10.4	8.9	59.6	8.2		54.4	109.3	172.0	231.5
1956	29.1	29.2		24.3	11.1	93.7	6.2		45.2	128.8	180.2	273.9
1957	35.0	44.8		31.7	9.2	120.7	11.0		33.6	53.3	97.8	218.6
1958	43.2	32.8		19.0	9.8	104.8	12.0		58.2	46.2	116.4	221.1
1959	28.4	16.2		18.9	12.3	75.9	7.3		46.0	63.7	117.0	192.9
1960	22.0	16.1		20.7	15.7	74.5	7.1		42.9	72.2	122.2	196.7
1961	16.2	21.3		15.2	11.9	64.7	12.1		28.9	60.7	101.6	166.2
1962	20.3	19.3		20.8	11.8	72.1	14.2		30.1	56.7	101.0	173.1
1963	18.0	11.5		14.4	9.0	53.0	14.9		31.2	56.0	102.1	155.0
1964	26.5	16.4		24.4	11.8	79.1		15.9	37.1	42.3	95.4	174.5
1965	8.4	15.9		10.5	9.3	44.1		20.0	29.1	52.5	101.6	145.8

[1] Includes Southeast Alaska and Yakatat management areas.
[2] Includes Prince William Sound, Cook Inlet, Kodiak, Chignik, and South Alaska Peninsula management areas.
[3] Includes North Alaska Peninsula, Aleutian Islands, Bristol Bay, and AYK management areas.
[4] Includes mothership, landbased gillnet, landbased longline, and Sea of Japan fisheries.
[5] Includes coastal and freshwater fisheries.

TABLE 7. Continued.

			North America				Asia					
								Japan				
	British Columbia/ Washington	Southeast Alaska[1]	Central Alaska[2]		Western Alaska[3]	N. Amer. Total	Coastal		High Seas and Offshore[4]	Russian Coastal[5]	Asia Total	Pacific Total
Year			Wild	Hatchery			Wild	Hatchery				
1966	19.1	25.0		14.7	10.4	69.2		16.8	42.9	46.0	105.7	174.9
1967	14.7	24.2		10.9	11.1	60.9		19.4	35.2	34.3	88.9	149.8
1968	41.3	22.1		16.9	9.8	90.0		10.2	33.7	22.8	66.7	156.7
1969	15.2	7.4		8.5	9.6	40.7		16.9	25.3	9.8	52.0	92.7
1970	39.2	21.2		17.7	17.5	95.5		21.6	34.7	20.7	76.9	172.5
1971	13.3	19.6		22.0	14.1	68.9		30.7	31.7	18.6	81.0	149.9
1972	73.8	26.9		24.3	15.1	140.1		26.0	40.4	10.5	76.9	217.0
1973	77.3	26.3		21.6	21.6	146.7		34.7	28.5	11.6	74.7	221.4
1974	31.9	25.7		8.7	21.2	87.5		42.7	37.5	15.1	95.3	182.8
1975	13.8	13.6		7.6	26.6	61.5		65.8	33.7	15.5	115.0	176.6
1976	32.1	21.5		13.3	23.4	90.3		40.4	38.0	21.4	99.8	190.0
1977	17.7	11.6		22.1	30.9	82.3		50.3	21.6	26.9	98.8	181.1
1978	47.4	8.6		14.7	23.6	94.3		59.8	14.2	36.6	110.6	204.9
1979	11.4	14.6		11.2	24.2	61.5		90.7	11.3	43.9	145.9	207.3
1980	47.0	21.4	0.1	16.6	36.4	121.6		84.5	12.2	29.3	126.1	247.6
1981	18.8	9.8	0.4	34.0	39.3	102.3		110.3	10.6	28.4	149.2	251.5
1982	43.8	12.3	4.2	37.7	24.9	122.8		98.7	13.1	26.2	138.0	260.8
1983	16.1	7.6	2.2	31.3	25.2	82.3		122.2	11.3	39.8	173.2	255.6
1984	26.8	27.5	3.9	22.9	34.3	115.5		124.5	11.8	25.3	161.6	277.0
1985	62.3	20.9	4.2	20.1	28.3	135.7		167.7	9.0	46.5	223.2	358.9
1986	66.9	19.1	6.3	31.2	27.8	151.4		151.5	6.0	42.7	200.2	351.6
1987	36.5	21.6	4.3	24.3	24.3	111.0		140.4	6.1	49.7	196.3	307.3
1988	82.7	29.5	3.1	36.3	34.8	186.3		155.5	3.7	48.5	207.7	394.0
1989	29.1	10.1	2.7	13.4	28.1	83.4		178.1	2.9	42.3	223.3	306.8
1990	48.3	10.1	5.5	17.5	20.1	101.5		220.6	2.3	50.6	273.5	375.0
1991	31.5	10.9	7.3	15.9	24.3	89.8		196.0	1.6	36.7	234.3	324.1
1992	52.3	18.9	11.2	14.7	19.8	117.0		145.7	0.1	35.9	181.8	298.8
1993	46.4	18.3	16.4	12.2	12.8	106.1		199.9	0.2	61.2	261.3	367.4
1994	56.0	24.0	26.1	23.1	23.5	152.7		208.0	0.3	85.1	293.4	446.1
1995	32.4	24.9	31.7	21.0	34.0	144.1		248.4	0.3	97.2	346.0	490.0
1996	18.9	35.0	59.0	26.8	25.5	165.1		285.3	0.4	80.8	366.4	531.5
1997	21.2	20.5	42.9	22.5	16.2	123.3		255.6	0.4	68.4	324.3	447.6
1998	45.7	32.5	48.9	13.1	14.7	154.9		193.7	0.4	73.9	268.0	423.0
1999	12.4	27.4	51.5	28.0	17.6	136.9		170.4	0.4	73.1	243.9	380.8
2000	8.5	30.8	57.7	46.3	14.4	157.6		152.2	0.3	81.7	234.2	391.8
2001	25.1	23.2	25.2	31.2	25.9	130.5		211.7	0.2	70.4	282.3	412.8
2002	42.5	15.3	25.9	49.7	10.9	144.3		209.6	0.3	77.5	287.5	431.8
2003	41.3	13.4	31.5	30.1	19.1	135.3		277.1	0.3	62.6	340.0	475.4
2004	28.6	33.1	27.3	21.3	15.8	126.2		240.1	0.3	58.9	299.3	425.5
2005	20.8	13.4	21.1	18.0	28.9	102.2		221.9	0.3	63.5	285.7	387.9

[1] Includes Southeast Alaska and Yakatat management areas.
[2] Includes Prince William Sound, Cook Inlet, Kodiak, Chignik, and South Alaska Peninsula management areas.
[3] Includes North Alaska Peninsula, Aleutian Islands, Bristol Bay, and AYK management areas.
[4] Includes mothership, landbased gillnet, landbased longline, and Sea of Japan fisheries.
[5] Includes coastal and freshwater fisheries.

TABLE 8. Annual North Pacific chum salmon biomass in thousands of mt.

	North America						Asia					
			Central Alaska[2]				Japan					
							Coastal		High Seas			
	British Columbia/	Southeast			Western	N. Amer.			and	Russian		Pacific
Year	Washington	Alaska[1]	Wild	Hatchery	Alaska[3]	Total	Wild	Hatchery	Offshore[4]	Coastal[5]	Asia Total	Total
1925	384.3	401.5		80.5	24.3	890.6	72.4		0.0	464.0	536.4	1,427.0
1926	451.9	292.4		68.9	33.4	846.7	79.2		0.0	701.9	781.1	1,627.8
1927	349.7	144.9		81.5	23.3	599.3	65.7		0.0	692.0	757.7	1,356.9
1928	570.0	228.7		118.0	39.5	956.2	40.4		0.0	853.9	894.3	1,850.6
1929	327.9	135.3		146.4	63.1	672.6	64.0		0.0	1,120.9	1,184.9	1,857.6
1930	316.3	123.2		85.6	26.4	551.5	87.6		1.2	1,282.0	1,370.8	1,922.2
1931	279.5	140.7		65.4	56.8	542.5	92.6		3.1	1,278.6	1,374.3	1,916.8
1932	312.3	286.1		48.9	79.4	726.7	55.6		4.7	976.6	1,036.9	1,763.6
1933	220.8	226.8		69.9	22.4	539.9	38.7		12.7	923.6	975.0	1,514.9
1934	320.9	169.0		87.8	28.4	606.0	79.2		18.7	1,431.4	1,529.3	2,135.3
1935	302.7	246.2		94.5	8.7	652.1	94.3		20.6	1,212.1	1,327.0	1,979.1
1936	379.9	337.3		88.5	22.9	828.6	60.6		21.4	2,142.2	2,224.2	3,052.8
1937	313.9	262.0		63.0	30.3	669.1	50.5		19.8	1,560.0	1,630.3	2,299.5
1938	331.2	220.6		73.5	47.7	673.1	74.1		27.3	1,763.4	1,864.8	2,537.9
1939	179.8	171.7		77.6	83.7	512.8	77.5		27.0	1,514.7	1,619.2	2,132.0
1940	329.1	225.6		101.1	29.5	685.3	57.3		32.4	1,485.5	1,575.2	2,260.5
1941	358.4	127.8		88.0	45.6	619.9	47.2		22.4	1,411.7	1,481.2	2,101.1
1942	309.4	259.3		90.0	13.9	672.6	42.1		16.9	1,074.2	1,133.3	1,805.8
1943	179.2	365.9		59.0	35.2	639.3	35.4		0.0	1,025.6	1,061.0	1,700.3
1944	162.1	363.2		88.0	38.9	652.3	26.9		0.0	758.4	785.4	1,437.6
1945	187.0	171.2		100.1	79.9	538.2	38.7		0.0	737.4	776.1	1,314.3
1946	361.7	201.5		83.0	22.4	668.6	37.1		0.0	817.9	854.9	1,523.5
1947	311.8	190.2		73.7	23.9	599.7	45.5		0.0	825.0	870.5	1,470.1
1948	338.4	225.5		88.6	54.2	706.7	45.5		0.0	744.0	789.5	1,496.2
1949	196.4	131.4		77.1	25.5	430.4	62.3		0.0	945.2	1,007.6	1,438.0
1950	437.6	299.1		76.8	30.0	843.5	90.9		0.0	732.1	823.1	1,666.5
1951	369.3	211.6		79.3	50.2	710.5	99.4		0.0	992.9	1,092.2	1,802.8
1952	221.7	258.7		118.2	51.8	650.4	42.9		11.6	523.8	578.3	1,228.8
1953	310.7	277.6		106.2	55.1	749.6	41.2		38.6	404.8	484.6	1,234.2
1954	428.2	269.9		114.3	63.2	875.5	62.0		109.3	626.2	797.4	1,672.9
1955	115.7	95.9		54.9	47.0	313.6	43.2		204.2	781.0	1,028.3	1,341.9
1956	153.3	153.7		127.7	58.3	493.0	32.5		169.6	920.2	1,122.4	1,615.4
1957	184.5	235.6		166.7	48.6	635.4	57.7		125.9	381.0	564.5	1,199.9
1958	227.2	172.4		100.0	51.8	551.4	63.0		218.5	329.8	611.3	1,162.6
1959	149.6	85.3		99.6	64.8	399.3	38.5		172.6	454.8	665.9	1,065.1
1960	115.6	85.0		108.8	82.8	392.2	37.5		161.0	515.5	714.0	1,106.2
1961	85.5	112.2		80.1	62.6	340.3	63.4		108.2	433.3	605.0	945.3
1962	106.6	101.8		109.2	62.1	379.7	74.7		113.0	404.8	592.5	972.1
1963	94.9	60.5		75.6	47.6	278.7	78.5		116.8	400.0	595.3	874.0
1964	139.4	86.3		128.4	62.3	416.5		83.9	139.3	302.4	525.5	942.0
1965	44.2	83.8		55.1	49.1	232.2		105.5	109.1	375.0	589.6	821.8

[1] Includes Southeast Alaska and Yakatat management areas.
[2] Includes Prince William Sound, Cook Inlet, Kodiak, Chignik, and South Alaska Peninsula management areas.
[3] Includes North Alaska Peninsula, Aleutian Islands, Bristol Bay, and AYK management areas.
[4] Includes mothership, landbased gillnet, landbased longline, and Sea of Japan fisheries.
[5] Includes coastal and freshwater fisheries.

Table 8. Continued.

			North America					Asia				
								Japan				
	British Columbia/ Washington	Southeast Alaska[1]	Central Alaska[2]		Western Alaska[3]	N. Amer. Total	Coastal		High Seas and Offshore[4]	Russian Coastal[5]	Asia Total	Pacific Total
Year			Wild	Hatchery			Wild	Hatchery				
1966	100.4	131.7		77.3	55.0	364.3		88.4	160.8	328.6	577.8	942.0
1967	77.2	127.6		57.6	58.2	320.6		101.9	131.9	245.2	479.0	799.6
1968	217.3	116.3		88.8	51.4	473.9		53.6	126.3	163.1	343.0	816.9
1969	79.9	39.0		44.7	50.5	214.1		89.0	94.9	70.2	254.1	468.2
1970	206.1	111.3		93.2	92.3	502.9		113.5	130.1	147.6	391.3	894.2
1971	70.2	103.1		115.6	74.0	362.8		161.4	119.1	132.8	413.2	776.1
1972	388.6	141.3		127.9	79.6	737.4		137.0	151.4	75.0	363.4	1,100.8
1973	406.7	138.3		113.5	113.6	772.1		182.4	106.9	82.6	372.0	1,144.0
1974	167.9	135.1		45.9	111.7	460.5		224.9	140.6	107.9	473.4	934.0
1975	72.6	71.5		40.0	139.8	323.9		346.4	126.5	110.6	583.6	907.5
1976	168.8	113.3		70.1	123.0	475.1		212.6	142.4	152.9	507.9	983.0
1977	93.0	61.0		116.4	162.7	433.1		265.0	80.9	192.0	537.9	971.0
1978	249.3	45.3		77.4	124.4	496.3		314.8	53.4	261.1	629.3	1,125.7
1979	60.1	76.8		59.1	127.5	323.5		477.1	42.3	313.8	833.2	1,156.7
1980	247.5	112.8	4.0	87.5	191.5	643.3		445.0	45.9	209.0	699.9	1,343.3
1981	99.0	51.5	15.0	179.1	206.8	551.4		580.4	39.6	202.7	822.8	1,374.2
1982	230.6	64.5	23.8	198.4	130.8	648.1		519.2	49.3	187.2	755.7	1,403.8
1983	84.5	40.0	31.2	164.6	132.4	452.7		643.0	42.3	284.1	969.4	1,422.2
1984	141.3	144.5	37.7	120.7	180.7	624.9		655.3	44.1	180.8	880.1	1,505.0
1985	327.8	110.0	49.8	105.6	148.9	742.1		882.8	33.6	332.2	1,248.6	1,990.7
1986	352.3	100.4	56.0	164.4	146.4	819.4		797.3	22.7	305.0	1,124.9	1,944.3
1987	192.3	113.9	64.2	127.7	127.8	625.9		739.1	23.0	355.0	1,117.1	1,742.9
1988	435.3	155.1	75.0	191.0	183.0	1,039.		818.4	13.8	346.6	1,178.7	2,218.0
1989	153.4	53.4	86.7	70.6	147.7	511.9		937.4	11.0	302.3	1,250.6	1,762.5
1990	254.0	53.3	98.5	92.3	105.7	603.7		1,161.0	8.6	361.4	1,531.0	2,134.8
1991	165.6	57.2	124.4	83.8	127.8	558.7		1,031.3	6.1	262.0	1,299.5	1,858.2
1992	275.3	99.5	182.6	77.3	104.4	739.1		767.1	0.3	256.8	1,024.2	1,763.3
1993	244.2	96.3	243.4	64.0	67.5	715.4		1,052.1	0.7	437.2	1,490.1	2,205.5
1994	294.8	126.4	306.6	121.4	123.8	973.1		1,094.7	1.2	607.8	1,703.7	2,676.8
1995	170.6	131.2	340.6	110.6	179.1	932.2		1,307.6	1.3	694.1	2,003.0	2,935.2
1996	99.2	184.0	359.6	141.3	134.1	918.2		1,501.5	1.3	576.8	2,079.7	2,997.8
1997	111.5	108.0	335.2	118.4	85.0	758.2		1,345.2	1.3	488.2	1,834.7	2,592.9
1998	240.6	170.9	371.3	69.0	77.2	929.0		1,019.6	1.5	528.0	1,549.1	2,478.2
1999	65.0	144.0	271.2	147.6	92.5	720.3		896.6	1.5	522.5	1,420.6	2,140.9
2000	44.7	162.0	303.8	243.4	75.6	829.5		800.9	1.2	583.5	1,385.5	2,215.0
2001	131.8	121.9	132.8	164.2	136.1	686.9		1,114.0	0.9	502.8	1,617.7	2,304.6
2002	223.7	80.7	136.3	261.3	57.5	759.5		1,103.2	1.3	553.6	1,658.1	2,417.6
2003	217.5	70.4	165.7	158.4	100.4	712.3		1,458.3	1.2	447.2	1,906.8	2,619.1
2004	150.6	174.5	143.6	112.4	83.3	664.2		1,263.8	1.2	420.4	1,685.4	2,349.6
2005	109.6	70.4	110.8	94.7	152.0	537.5		1,168.0	1.2	453.3	1,622.5	2,160.0

[1] Includes Southeast Alaska and Yakatat management areas.
[2] Includes Prince William Sound, Cook Inlet, Kodiak, Chignik, and South Alaska Peninsula management areas.
[3] Includes North Alaska Peninsula, Aleutian Islands, Bristol Bay, and AYK management areas.
[4] Includes mothership, landbased gillnet, landbased longline, and Sea of Japan fisheries.
[5] Includes coastal and freshwater fisheries.

TABLE 9. Annual North Pacific total runs of sockeye salmon in millions of fish.

Year	North America				Asia				Pacific Total
	Southeast Alaska, British Columbia, Washington[1]	Central Alaska[2]	Western Alaska[3]	N. Amer. Total	Japan		Russian Coastal[5]	Asia Total	
					Coastal	High Seas and Offshore[4]			
1925	12.8	9.7	16.8	39.3		0.0	12.1	12.1	51.4
1926	11.2	9.5	37.7	58.4		0.0	24.9	24.9	83.3
1927	10.3	7.3	20.9	38.4		0.0	16.2	16.2	54.7
1928	8.2	8.1	34.2	50.5		0.0	25.3	25.3	75.8
1929	10.6	7.8	24.0	42.4		0.3	21.0	21.3	63.7
1930	17.7	5.7	11.0	34.3		0.6	19.2	19.7	54.0
1931	10.6	6.8	26.5	43.8		1.3	14.9	16.1	59.9
1932	10.9	8.1	32.0	51.0		2.0	12.9	15.0	65.9
1933	9.9	7.4	40.6	57.9		4.9	15.6	20.5	78.4
1934	13.1	10.0	36.5	59.6		2.5	20.9	23.4	83.0
1935	11.3	7.6	9.6	28.5		3.9	11.0	15.0	43.5
1936	12.6	10.9	40.3	63.8		5.8	15.4	21.2	85.0
1937	11.5	9.1	37.4	58.1		4.3	19.4	23.6	81.7
1938	14.1	10.1	40.5	64.7		5.6	23.3	28.9	93.6
1939	10.2	10.5	27.2	47.9		3.2	17.0	20.2	68.2
1940	10.7	7.3	12.8	30.9		4.3	11.4	15.7	46.6
1941	13.6	8.0	16.3	37.9		1.3	12.2	13.5	51.4
1942	17.7	8.0	13.6	39.3		0.0	14.2	14.2	53.5
1943	6.4	9.3	33.4	49.1		0.0	15.4	15.4	64.4
1944	7.9	9.4	21.5	38.8		0.0	9.9	9.9	48.7
1945	9.8	8.9	15.8	34.6		0.0	7.3	7.3	41.9
1946	14.0	7.7	17.4	39.1		0.0	7.5	7.5	46.6
1947	8.4	9.1	32.3	49.8		0.0	5.8	5.8	55.6
1948	7.9	8.3	25.3	41.4		0.0	3.5	3.5	44.9
1949	8.2	8.1	13.7	30.0		0.0	5.0	5.0	35.0
1950	10.4	8.4	17.0	35.8		0.0	5.3	5.3	41.1
1951	10.3	8.1	10.1	28.5		0.6	4.4	4.9	33.4
1952	9.2	7.1	21.8	38.1		1.3	5.4	6.7	44.8
1953	12.7	6.0	14.8	33.4		3.0	3.0	6.0	39.4
1954	16.8	6.4	11.4	34.6		9.9	2.4	12.2	46.8
1955	6.0	5.9	11.4	23.3		7.0	1.8	8.8	32.1
1956	7.4	6.6	26.6	40.6		13.6	3.4	17.0	57.6
1957	9.7	6.2	19.3	35.1		12.5	2.1	14.6	49.7
1958	23.3	12.8	7.3	43.4		9.3	0.6	9.8	53.2
1959	9.1	7.1	14.8	31.0		10.6	2.4	12.9	43.9
1960	6.2	6.9	42.4	55.5		8.3	2.4	10.6	66.1
1961	9.7	6.9	25.6	42.2		9.9	4.6	14.5	56.7
1962	8.6	7.2	9.9	25.8		7.9	2.4	10.3	36.0
1963	8.4	6.7	6.9	22.1		6.1	2.1	8.2	30.3
1964	7.9	7.1	10.3	25.2		5.7	1.6	7.3	32.5
1965	7.8	7.2	60.1	75.1		6.4	2.5	8.9	84.0

[1] Includes Southeast Alaska and Yakatat management areas, British Columbia, and Washington.
[2] Includes Prince William Sound, Cook Inlet, Kodiak, Chignik, and South Alaska Peninsula management areas.
[3] Includes North Alaska Peninsula, Aleutian Islands, Bristol Bay, and AYK management areas.
[4] Includes mothership, landbased gillnet, landbased longline, and Sea of Japan fisheries.
[5] Includes coastal and freshwater fisheries.

TABLE 9. Continued.

Year	North America Southeast Alaska, British Columbia, Washington[1]	Central Alaska[2]	Western Alaska[3]	N. Amer. Total	Asia Japan Coastal	Asia Japan High Seas and Offshore[4]	Russian Coastal[5]	Asia Total	Pacific Total
1966	10.6	7.8	18.9	37.4		6.4	1.9	8.3	45.7
1967	13.7	6.9	12.4	33.0		9.8	1.6	11.4	44.4
1968	11.1	7.6	9.4	28.1		7.5	1.4	8.9	37.0
1969	10.0	6.2	24.5	40.7		6.6	1.0	7.6	48.4
1970	9.9	7.9	44.5	62.4		5.2	2.7	7.9	70.3
1971	13.3	7.0	17.8	38.2		5.2	1.3	6.5	44.7
1972	8.6	6.3	6.9	21.8		5.7	0.6	6.4	28.2
1973	16.1	6.5	2.9	25.5		4.9	1.2	6.1	31.6
1974	14.7	7.2	10.9	32.7		4.5	0.7	5.2	37.9
1975	7.4	6.7	24.4	38.5		4.4	0.9	5.3	43.9
1976	9.4	9.0	12.0	30.4		4.8	0.7	5.5	35.9
1977	13.4	10.4	10.0	33.8		1.9	1.1	3.1	36.9
1978	13.8	10.6	20.3	44.8		2.6	2.0	4.7	49.5
1979	12.8	6.9	45.7	65.5		2.3	1.7	4.1	69.6
1980	8.3	6.5	68.1	82.9		2.3	2.4	4.7	87.5
1981	16.2	9.9	38.1	64.1		2.4	2.3	4.7	68.8
1982	22.6	13.2	25.8	61.6		1.9	1.8	3.7	65.4
1983	12.3	14.5	46.3	73.1		2.0	2.6	4.6	77.7
1984	12.1	14.1	43.2	69.4		1.3	3.8	5.1	74.5
1985	24.1	13.6	41.1	78.9		0.9	5.7	6.6	85.5
1986	21.7	17.6	26.3	65.6		0.6	4.6	5.2	70.8
1987	14.4	21.9	27.4	63.8		0.6	7.2	7.8	71.6
1988	12.3	17.8	24.1	54.2		0.3	5.1	5.3	59.6
1989	24.0	14.7	48.5	87.2		0.3	5.9	6.1	93.3
1990	27.4	18.8	52.6	98.8		0.2	10.0	10.2	108.9
1991	21.5	18.1	49.4	89.0		0.2	8.7	8.9	98.0
1992	17.1	23.4	49.8	90.3		0.0	9.3	9.3	99.6
1993	34.5	18.9	58.5	112.0		0.0	11.5	11.5	123.5
1994	21.4	15.5	55.5	92.4		0.0	7.8	7.8	100.2
1995	11.4	17.1	68.0	96.5		0.0	10.8	10.8	107.4
1996	15.1	20.8	38.5	74.4		0.0	12.3	12.3	86.7
1997	21.6	18.0	20.1	59.7		0.0	8.4	8.4	68.1
1998	10.4	13.7	18.8	42.9		0.0	8.6	8.6	51.5
1999	5.4	20.5	42.0	67.8		0.0	10.0	10.0	77.8
2000	10.2	13.3	30.6	54.1		0.0	10.9	10.9	65.0
2001	12.7	14.3	21.7	48.7		0.0	11.1	11.1	59.8
2002	15.2	13.8	15.9	44.9		0.0	16.0	16.0	60.9
2003	9.1	18.5	23.8	51.3		0.0	11.8	11.8	63.1
2004	6.4	18.3	41.9	66.6		0.0	10.1	10.1	76.7
2005	5.2	18.7	42.7	66.6		0.0	12.7	12.7	79.3

[1] Includes Southeast Alaska and Yakatat management areas, British Columbia, and Washington.
[2] Includes Prince William Sound, Cook Inlet, Kodiak, Chignik, and South Alaska Peninsula management areas.
[3] Includes North Alaska Peninsula, Aleutian Islands, Bristol Bay, and AYK management areas.
[4] Includes mothership, landbased gillnet, landbased longline, and Sea of Japan fisheries.
[5] Includes coastal and freshwater fisheries.

TABLE 10. Annual North Pacific total runs of sockeye salmon in thousands of mt.

Year	North America				Asia				Pacific Total
	Southeast Alaska, British Columbia, Washington[1]	Central Alaska[2]	Western Alaska[3]	N. Amer. Total	Japan		Russian Coastal[5]	Asia Total	
					Coastal	High Seas and Offshore[4]			
1925	40.9	25.3	45.2	111.4		0.0	26.0	26.0	137.4
1926	35.8	24.8	101.0	161.6		0.0	36.8	36.8	198.4
1927	32.9	19.0	56.4	108.3		0.0	39.0	39.0	147.3
1928	26.3	21.1	92.4	139.7		0.0	64.3	64.3	204.0
1929	36.3	20.4	64.5	121.1		0.0	54.5	54.5	175.7
1930	57.6	14.7	29.3	101.6		0.5	54.8	55.3	156.9
1931	35.3	17.6	70.9	123.8		0.9	42.5	43.4	167.2
1932	35.3	21.1	85.4	141.7		1.9	39.0	40.9	182.6
1933	29.7	19.3	109.6	158.5		3.0	29.7	32.8	191.3
1934	44.8	26.1	98.5	169.4		7.2	54.0	61.3	230.7
1935	35.8	19.7	25.4	80.9		3.7	22.4	26.1	107.0
1936	40.3	28.3	107.9	176.5		5.9	45.2	51.1	227.6
1937	36.7	23.7	100.8	161.3		8.6	56.8	65.4	226.7
1938	45.4	26.1	109.7	181.1		6.4	68.4	74.7	255.9
1939	33.7	27.2	73.0	133.9		8.3	49.9	58.3	192.1
1940	32.9	19.1	34.2	86.2		4.8	33.4	38.2	124.4
1941	41.4	20.7	43.7	105.8		6.4	35.7	42.1	147.9
1942	55.7	20.9	36.6	113.2		2.0	41.7	43.7	156.9
1943	20.6	24.0	89.7	134.3		0.0	45.1	45.1	179.4
1944	25.6	24.4	58.1	108.2		0.0	29.1	29.1	137.3
1945	31.0	23.2	42.6	96.8		0.0	21.5	21.5	118.3
1946	41.9	20.0	46.6	108.5		0.0	22.0	22.0	130.5
1947	22.6	23.7	87.3	133.5		0.0	17.0	17.0	150.5
1948	24.1	21.5	68.5	114.2		0.0	10.3	10.3	124.5
1949	23.6	21.1	37.0	81.8		0.0	14.7	14.7	96.4
1950	31.2	21.9	45.4	98.6		0.0	15.5	15.5	114.1
1951	32.7	21.0	27.2	81.0		0.0	12.8	12.8	93.8
1952	30.7	18.4	58.7	107.8		1.5	15.3	16.9	124.6
1953	40.3	15.5	39.5	95.3		3.8	8.5	12.3	107.6
1954	61.8	16.6	30.5	108.8		9.2	6.7	15.9	124.7
1955	18.9	15.3	30.6	64.8		25.8	5.2	30.9	95.7
1956	26.0	17.2	64.7	107.9		20.1	9.5	29.6	137.5
1957	28.4	16.0	54.9	99.4		42.6	5.8	48.4	147.8
1958	72.5	33.4	18.9	124.7		25.6	1.7	27.3	152.0
1959	26.1	18.5	35.5	80.1		19.7	6.7	26.4	106.5
1960	17.5	17.3	95.9	130.6		30.5	6.7	37.2	167.8
1961	29.9	18.7	70.5	119.1		36.7	13.0	49.7	168.8
1962	27.0	18.8	31.1	76.9		24.8	7.8	32.6	109.5
1963	25.7	17.5	23.2	66.4		19.1	5.7	24.8	91.2
1964	26.2	18.3	29.2	73.7		14.3	4.5	18.8	92.5
1965	23.3	19.1	147.0	189.4		25.0	7.0	32.0	221.4

[1] Includes Southeast Alaska and Yakatat management areas, British Columbia, and Washington.
[2] Includes Prince William Sound, Cook Inlet, Kodiak, Chignik, and South Alaska Peninsula management areas.
[3] Includes North Alaska Peninsula, Aleutian Islands, Bristol Bay, and AYK management areas.
[4] Includes mothership, landbased gillnet, landbased longline, and Sea of Japan fisheries.
[5] Includes coastal and freshwater fisheries.

TABLE 10. Continued.

Year	North America				Asia				
	Southeast Alaska, British Columbia, Washington[1]	Central Alaska[2]	Western Alaska[3]	N. Amer. Total	Japan		Russian Coastal[5]	Asia Total	Pacific Total
					Coastal	High Seas and Offshore[4]			
1966	35.8	21.9	58.6	116.2		16.6	6.2	22.8	139.0
1967	38.6	19.4	30.8	88.7		20.5	5.0	25.5	114.2
1968	37.1	22.1	25.1	84.3		16.8	3.7	20.4	104.7
1969	28.9	17.8	55.7	102.4		15.5	2.7	18.2	120.5
1970	31.0	22.5	103.4	156.9		17.8	7.5	25.3	182.3
1971	39.1	21.4	53.1	113.5		11.0	3.9	15.0	128.5
1972	25.8	18.5	20.6	64.9		11.0	1.8	12.8	77.7
1973	49.8	23.1	12.9	85.7		9.4	3.2	12.5	98.3
1974	47.7	21.8	31.3	100.8		8.2	1.8	9.9	110.7
1975	20.2	19.9	66.2	106.3		7.7	2.3	10.1	116.4
1976	27.5	28.1	39.3	94.9		8.8	2.0	10.8	105.7
1977	41.7	37.3	36.1	115.2		4.5	3.1	7.6	122.8
1978	47.0	35.7	62.7	145.4		5.2	5.6	10.8	156.2
1979	37.2	21.2	125.5	183.9		5.0	4.8	9.8	193.7
1980	24.9	18.0	174.9	217.8		5.7	6.5	12.2	230.0
1981	45.7	29.4	114.8	189.9		5.1	6.4	11.5	201.4
1982	75.1	41.5	82.0	198.6		4.1	4.9	9.1	207.6
1983	37.0	41.5	130.1	208.6		4.4	7.1	11.5	220.1
1984	35.3	39.9	115.2	190.5		3.4	10.5	13.9	204.3
1985	69.8	34.1	108.2	212.0		2.6	15.6	18.1	230.1
1986	69.0	47.6	75.7	192.3		1.8	12.6	14.4	206.7
1987	44.9	66.9	76.4	188.3		1.6	19.8	21.5	209.7
1988	37.4	51.5	71.9	160.8		0.7	13.9	14.6	175.4
1989	68.1	43.0	117.1	228.2		0.7	16.1	16.8	245.0
1990	80.4	49.9	131.8	262.1		0.5	27.3	27.9	290.0
1991	59.8	45.9	119.4	225.1		0.4	24.0	24.4	249.6
1992	54.2	66.7	126.5	247.4		0.0	25.6	25.6	273.0
1993	91.0	48.1	158.1	297.2		0.0	31.0	31.0	328.2
1994	63.9	39.2	130.7	233.8		0.0	21.5	21.5	255.3
1995	33.7	43.4	162.9	239.9		0.0	29.8	29.8	269.7
1996	48.4	58.8	117.4	224.5		0.0	33.6	33.6	258.2
1997	57.4	50.2	61.7	169.3		0.0	24.1	24.1	193.3
1998	31.4	33.3	55.4	120.1		0.0	19.5	19.5	139.6
1999	15.4	53.7	93.2	162.3		0.0	22.5	22.5	184.9
2000	29.0	38.8	93.5	161.3		0.0	27.3	27.3	188.5
2001	39.2	39.7	76.0	154.9		0.0	32.9	32.9	187.8
2002	44.5	39.3	50.8	134.6		0.0	44.5	44.5	179.1
2003	27.7	48.4	92.1	168.2		0.0	31.5	31.5	199.8
2004	20.3	47.7	125.5	193.5		0.0	29.9	29.9	223.4
2005	12.1	49.9	121.9	183.8		0.0	35.2	35.2	219.1

[1] Includes Southeast Alaska and Yakatat management areas, British Columbia, and Washington.
[2] Includes Prince William Sound, Cook Inlet, Kodiak, Chignik, and South Alaska Peninsula management areas.
[3] Includes North Alaska Peninsula, Aleutian Islands, Bristol Bay, and AYK management areas.
[4] Includes mothership, landbased gillnet, landbased longline, and Sea of Japan fisheries.
[5] Includes coastal and freshwater fisheries.

TABLE 11. Annual North Pacific sockeye salmon biomass in thousands of mt.

| | North America | | | | Asia | | | | |
| | Southeast Alaska, British Columbia, Washington[1] | Central Alaska[2] | Western Alaska[3] | N. Amer. Total | Coastal | Japan High Seas and Offshore[4] | Russian Coastal[5] | Asia Total | Pacific Total |
Year									
1925	124.0	76.6	137.0	337.6		0.0	78.8	78.8	416.4
1926	108.5	75.0	306.2	489.7		0.0	111.6	111.6	601.3
1927	99.8	57.5	170.9	328.2		0.0	118.2	118.2	446.4
1928	79.6	63.8	279.9	423.3		0.0	194.9	194.9	618.2
1929	110.0	61.7	195.4	367.1		0.0	165.2	165.2	532.3
1930	174.5	44.5	88.9	307.9		0.7	166.2	166.9	474.8
1931	106.9	53.3	214.9	375.2		1.3	128.8	130.1	505.3
1932	106.9	63.8	258.8	429.5		2.9	118.2	121.1	550.6
1933	89.9	58.4	332.0	480.3		4.6	90.1	94.7	575.0
1934	135.9	79.1	298.4	513.4		11.0	163.7	174.7	688.1
1935	108.4	59.7	77.1	245.1		5.7	67.9	73.6	318.7
1936	122.1	85.7	327.1	534.9		8.9	137.1	146.0	680.9
1937	111.3	72.0	305.6	488.9		13.1	172.2	185.3	674.1
1938	137.4	79.2	332.3	548.9		9.7	207.2	216.8	765.7
1939	102.0	82.4	221.2	405.6		12.7	151.3	164.0	569.6
1940	99.8	57.8	103.5	261.2		7.3	101.3	108.6	369.8
1941	125.4	62.7	132.5	320.6		9.7	108.1	117.8	438.4
1942	168.8	63.3	110.8	342.9		3.0	126.5	129.5	472.4
1943	62.3	72.9	271.8	406.9		0.0	136.6	136.6	543.5
1944	77.6	74.0	176.1	327.7		0.0	88.2	88.2	416.0
1945	94.0	70.3	129.2	293.4		0.0	65.1	65.1	358.5
1946	127.0	60.5	141.4	328.8		0.0	66.7	66.7	395.5
1947	68.4	71.9	264.4	404.7		0.0	51.5	51.5	456.2
1948	73.1	65.3	207.5	345.9		0.0	31.3	31.3	377.3
1949	71.6	64.0	112.2	247.8		0.0	44.4	44.4	292.2
1950	94.6	66.5	137.6	298.7		0.0	47.0	47.0	345.6
1951	99.1	63.8	82.5	245.4		0.0	38.9	38.9	284.3
1952	93.0	55.6	178.0	326.6		2.3	46.5	48.8	375.4
1953	122.2	46.9	119.6	288.7		5.8	25.8	31.6	320.3
1954	187.2	50.2	92.3	329.8		14.0	20.2	34.2	364.0
1955	57.2	46.4	92.8	196.4		39.2	15.7	54.8	251.2
1956	78.7	52.3	194.5	325.5		30.5	28.8	59.3	384.9
1957	86.2	48.6	111.2	246.0		64.7	17.7	82.4	328.4
1958	219.6	101.1	156.1	476.8		38.9	5.1	44.0	520.8
1959	79.1	56.0	334.4	469.5		30.0	20.2	50.2	519.8
1960	52.9	52.4	250.5	355.8		46.4	20.2	66.6	422.4
1961	90.6	56.7	144.7	292.0		55.8	39.4	95.2	387.2
1962	81.9	56.9	98.6	237.4		37.7	23.7	61.4	298.8
1963	77.9	53.1	155.2	286.1		29.0	17.2	46.2	332.3
1964	79.5	55.4	311.7	446.7		21.7	13.6	35.4	482.0
1965	70.6	57.8	272.2	400.7		38.0	21.2	59.2	459.9

[1] Includes Southeast Alaska and Yakatat management areas, British Columbia, and Washington.
[2] Includes Prince William Sound, Cook Inlet, Kodiak, Chignik, and South Alaska Peninsula management areas.
[3] Includes North Alaska Peninsula, Aleutian Islands, Bristol Bay, and AYK management areas.
[4] Includes mothership, landbased gillnet, landbased longline, and Sea of Japan fisheries.
[5] Includes coastal and freshwater fisheries.

Table 11. Continued.

| | North America | | | | Asia | | | | |
| | Southeast Alaska, British Columbia, Washington[1] | Central Alaska[2] | Western Alaska[3] | N. Amer. Total | Coastal | Japan High Seas and Offshore[4] | Russian Coastal[5] | Asia Total | Pacific Total |
Year									
1966	108.3	66.3	136.3	310.9		25.2	18.7	43.9	354.8
1967	116.9	58.7	116.5	292.1		31.2	15.2	46.3	338.4
1968	112.4	66.9	181.4	360.8		25.5	11.1	36.6	397.4
1969	87.7	53.8	296.4	437.9		23.6	8.1	31.6	469.5
1970	93.8	68.2	221.8	383.9		27.1	22.7	49.9	433.7
1971	118.3	64.8	112.0	295.2		16.8	11.9	28.7	323.9
1972	78.2	56.1	73.6	207.9		16.7	5.3	22.1	230.0
1973	150.8	69.9	105.9	326.5		14.5	9.5	24.1	350.6
1974	144.7	65.9	169.2	379.8		12.6	5.3	17.9	397.7
1975	61.3	60.3	174.3	295.9		11.9	7.1	19.0	314.9
1976	83.2	85.3	177.6	346.1		13.7	5.9	19.6	365.7
1977	126.4	113.1	244.2	483.7		6.9	9.4	16.4	500.1
1978	142.4	108.1	415.8	666.2		8.0	17.1	25.0	691.3
1979	112.8	64.3	596.2	773.3		7.7	14.5	22.3	795.6
1980	75.6	54.5	525.9	655.9		8.8	19.6	28.5	684.4
1981	138.5	89.0	398.3	625.8		7.9	19.4	27.2	653.0
1982	227.6	125.7	420.4	773.7		6.4	15.0	21.4	795.0
1983	112.1	125.9	466.7	704.6		6.8	21.5	28.3	732.9
1984	107.0	121.0	413.5	641.5		5.2	31.8	37.0	678.5
1985	211.4	103.3	351.2	665.9		3.9	47.2	51.1	717.0
1986	209.1	144.3	338.9	692.3		2.8	38.1	40.9	733.2
1987	136.1	202.8	323.0	662.0		2.5	60.1	62.6	724.6
1988	113.3	156.0	443.6	712.9		1.1	42.2	43.3	756.2
1989	206.5	130.2	573.4	910.1		1.0	48.8	49.9	960.0
1990	243.7	151.2	543.4	938.2		0.8	82.8	83.7	1021.9
1991	181.1	139.2	510.4	830.7		0.6	72.8	73.4	904.1
1992	164.2	202.1	483.7	850.0		0.0	77.6	77.6	927.6
1993	275.7	145.7	536.8	958.3		0.0	94.0	94.0	1052.3
1994	193.7	118.8	580.1	892.6		0.0	65.0	65.0	957.6
1995	102.1	131.4	452.3	685.8		0.0	90.3	90.3	776.1
1996	146.6	178.2	309.4	634.2		0.0	102.0	102.0	736.1
1997	173.9	152.2	297.1	623.2		0.0	72.9	72.9	696.2
1998	95.1	101.0	431.7	627.9		0.0	59.2	59.2	687.1
1999	46.8	162.7	439.6	649.0		0.0	68.3	68.3	717.3
2000	88.0	117.4	390.1	595.5		0.0	82.6	82.6	678.1
2001	118.8	120.2	333.3	572.3		0.0	99.8	99.8	672.0
2002	135.0	119.1	358.2	612.2		0.0	134.9	134.9	747.2
2003	84.0	146.7	540.9	771.6		0.0	95.5	95.5	867.1
2004	61.6	144.6	437.0	643.3		0.0	90.5	90.5	733.7
2005	36.6	151.1	369.3	557.1		0.0	106.8	106.8	663.9

[1] Includes Southeast Alaska and Yakatat management areas, British Columbia, and Washington.
[2] Includes Prince William Sound, Cook Inlet, Kodiak, Chignik, and South Alaska Peninsula management areas.
[3] Includes North Alaska Peninsula, Aleutian Islands, Bristol Bay, and AYK management areas.
[4] Includes mothership, landbased gillnet, landbased longline, and Sea of Japan fisheries.
[5] Includes coastal and freshwater fisheries.

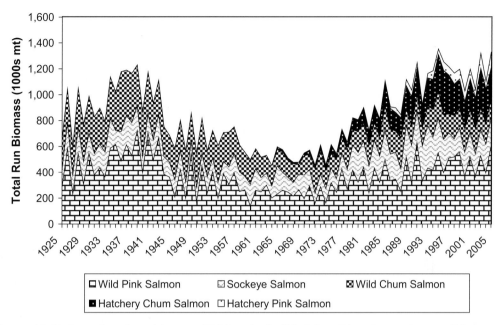

FIGURE 10. Estimated total run biomass (1000s mt) of wild pink, wild sockeye salmon, wild chum, and hatchery pink salmon (includes Alaskan stocks), and hatchery chum salmon (includes Japanese and Alaskan stocks) in the North Pacific Ocean, 1926–2005.

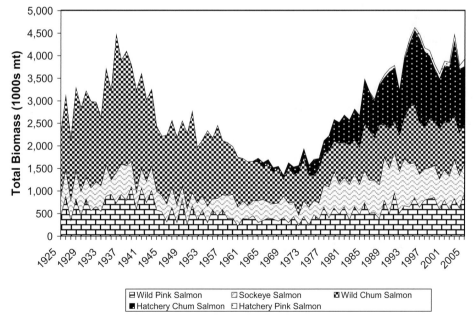

FIGURE 11. Estimated biomass (1000s mt) of wild pink, wild sockeye, wild chum, and hatchery pink salmon (includes Alaskan stocks), and hatchery chum salmon (includes Japanese and Alaskan stocks) in the North Pacific Ocean, 1926–2005.

provide a relative magnitude of minimum hatchery and wild stock abundances. Three methods of total-run reconstruction were used that considered annual variation to different degrees: high, medium, and low level. The first (high level) used cohort reconstructions based on annual stock assessments and brood year specific mortality rates, and reflects the annual variation in abundance. High-level reconstructions were done for Japanese and Alaskan pink and chum salmon hatchery stocks, as well as Bristol Bay sockeye salmon stocks (Table 1). These stocks collectively averaged 36% and 47% of the estimated North Pacific total run and total biomass during the last ten years. Medium-level run reconstructions were based on annual stock assessments of the standardized catch model and reflected some level of inter-annual variation in abundance. These stocks included the high seas catch, central Alaska pink salmon, southeast Alaska pink salmon, western Alaska sockeye salmon, central Alaska sockeye salmon, and southeast Alaska/B.C./Washington sockeye salmon. These stocks collectively comprised 23% and 14% of the estimated North Pacific total run and total biomass during the last ten years. Low-level run reconstructions were based on the application of a constant exploitation rate applied to catch, and reflect inter-annual variation abundance. These stocks included Russian stocks of pink, chum, and sockeye salmon, western Alaska pink and chum salmon, central Alaska chum salmon, southeast Alaska wild chum salmon, and B.C./Washington pink and chum salmon. These stocks collectively comprised 41% and 39% estimated North Pacific total run and total biomass during the last ten years.

The reconstruction of the immature ocean cohort abundance was sensitive to assumptions of how mortality varies over the period of ocean residence. Mortality is widely believed to be much greater during the initial phases of ocean residence (Parker 1962; Ricker 1964, 1976); it is believed that mor-

tality rates decrease with increasing body size (McGurk 1995). Insufficient data (smolts and resultant terminal returns) exists to explicitly fit a biologically realistic model with age-specific maturation and time varying mortality. Somewhat arbitrary assumptions were used in the cohort reconstructions (i.e., the knife-edged mortality at entry and the separable first ocean- and second ocean- year mortality in chum salmon) to capture the higher first ocean-year mortality and to provide a model that was estimable given the data available.

The mortality rates estimated for pink and chum salmon from the various hatchery data sets were generally consistent with the limited early published estimates of mortality rates for pink and chum salmon during the pelagic phase of ocean residence (e.g., Parker 1962; Ricker 1964). Uncertainty exists in the early estimates of marine mortality rates for pink and chum salmon because of unknown mortality that would be associated with the use of fin-clip marking of wild pink salmon smolt cohorts to assess returns and survivals. The mortality rates estimated for sockeye salmon from the Bristol Bay smolt data sets were quite consistent with early published estimates of marine mortality rates for sockeye salmon during the 0.1+ phase of ocean residence (Ricker 1976). These studies used stock-specific relative abundance of mature and immature salmon to derive ocean age-specific mortality rates for sockeye salmon (Fredin 1965; Mathews 1968).

The total run biomass and total biomass reconstructions underestimated the hatchery runs of Pacific salmon. Assessments of chum salmon hatchery runs in Russia, British Columbia, and the Pacific Northwest, which collectively constituted about 17% of the chum salmon releases since 1990, were lacking. Thus, the wild runs of chum salmon in these areas were over estimated to the extent that hatchery runs were not accounted. Assessments of pink salmon hatchery runs in Russia, British Columbia, and the Pacific

Northwest which collectively constituted about 25% of the pink salmon releases since 1990, were similarly lacking. Thus, the wild runs of pink salmon in these areas were over estimated.

Widespread changes in biological characteristics of Pacific salmon that corresponded to increasing abundance have been observed. Decreases in salmon body size coincident with increases in salmon abundance since the early to mid 1970s have been widely observed (Bigler et al. 1994; Helle and Hoffman 1998; Walker et al. 1998; Helle et al. 2007; Eggers and Irvine 2007; Kaeriyama 1998; West and Fair 2006). Increases in age-at-maturity of chum salmon has also been widely observed (Kaeriyama 1998; Helle and Hoffman 1998). Stocks of western and central Alaska sockeye salmon, Asian and central Alaska pink salmon; and Asian and North American chum salmon stocks occur together in the subarctic North Pacific and Bering Sea during ocean residence (Hartt and Dell 1986; French et al. 1976; Fredin et al. 1977; Burgner 1991; Salo 1991; Heard 1992; Urawa et al. 2005; Habicht et al. 2005). These widespread observations of density dependent growth and maturation suggest limits to the capacity of the North Pacific Ocean to support salmon.

References

Beamish, R. J., and D. R. Bouillon. 1993. Pacific salmon production trends in relation to climate. Canadian Journal of Fisheries and Aquatic Sciences 50:1002–1016.

Beamish, R. J., D. J. Noakes, G. A. McFarlane, L. Klyashtorin, V. V. Ivanov, and V. Kurashov. 1999. The regime concept and natural trends in production of Pacific salmon. Canadian Journal of Fisheries and Aquatic Sciences 56:516–526.

Bigler, B. S., D. W. Welch, and J. H. Helle. 1995. A review of size trends among North Pacific salmon (*Oncorhynchus* spp.). Canadian Journal of Fisheries and Aquatic Sciences 53:455–465.

Burgner, R.L. 1991. Life history of sockeye salmon (*Onchorhynchus nerka*). Pages 1–118 *in* Groot, C.

and L. Margolis, editors. Pacific salmon: life histories. UBC Press, Vancouver, British Columbia.

Clark, J. H. 2001a. Biological escapement goal for chum salmon in District One of Norton Sound. Regional Information Report No. 3A01–09. Alaska Department of Fish and Game, Division of Commercial Fisheries, Anchorage.

Clark, J. H. 2001b. Biological escapement goals for Kwiniuk and Tubutulik chum salmon. Regional Information Report No. 3A01–08. Alaska Department of Fish and Game, Division of Commercial Fisheries, Anchorage.

Clark, J. H. 2001c. Biological escapement goal for Andreafsky River chum salmon. Regional Information Report No. 3A01–07. Alaska Department of Fish and Game, Division of Commercial Fisheries, Anchorage.

Clark, J. H., and G. J. Sandone. 2001. Biological escapement goal for Anvik River chum Salmon. Regional Information Report No. 3A01–06. Alaska Department of Fish and Game, Division of Commercial Fisheries, Anchorage.

Crawford, D. L. 2001. Bristol Bay sockeye salmon smolt studies for 2001. Regional Information Report No. 2A01–27. Alaska Department of Fish and Game, Division of Commercial Fisheries, Anchorage.

Eggers, D. M. 2001. Biological escapement goals for Yukon River fall chum salmon. Regional Information Report No. 3A01–10. Alaska Department of Fish and Game, Division of Commercial Fisheries, Anchorage.

Eggers, D. M., and J. H. Clark. 2006. Assessment of historical runs and escapement goals for Kotzebue area chum salmon. Fishery Manuscript No. 06–01. Alaska Department of Fish and Game, Division of Sport Fish and Commercial Fisheries, Anchorage.

Eggers, D. M., J. R. Irvine, M. Fukuwaka, and V. I. Karpenko. 2005. Catch trends and status of North Pacific Salmon. North Pacific Anadromous Fish Commission Document 723, Revision 3. NPAFC, Vancouver, British Columbia.

Eggers, D. M., and J. R. Irvine. 2007. Trends in abundance and biological characteristics for North Pacific sockeye salmon. North Pacific Anadromous Fish Commission Bulletin 4:53–75.

Francis, R. C., and S. R. Hare. 1994. Decadal scale regime shifts in the large marine ecosystems of the North-east Pacific: a case for historical science. Fisheries Oceanography 7:1–21.

Fredin, R. A. 1965. Some methods for estimating ocean mortality of Pacific salmon and applications. Journal of the Fisheries Research Board of Canada 22:33–51.

Fredin, R. A., R.L. Major, R. G. Bakkala, and G. K. Tanonaka. 1977. Pacific salmon and the high seas salmon fisheries of Japan. Unpubl. Processed Rep.,U.S. National Marine Fisheries Service, Northwest and Alaska Fisheries Center, Seattle.

French, R. R., H. Bilton, M. Osako, and A. Hartt. 1976. Distribution and origin of sockeye salmon (*Oncorhynchus nerka*) in offshore waters of the North Pacific Ocean. North Pacific Fisheries Commission Bulletin 34:1–113.

Habicht, C., N. V. Varnavskaya, T. Azumaya, S. Urawa, W. L. Wilmon, C. H. Guthrie III, and J. E. Seeb. 2005. Migration patterns of sockeye salmon in the Bering Sea discerned from stock composition estimates of fish captured during BASIS studies. North Pacific Anadromous Fish Commission Technical Report No. 6. 2004 International Workshop "BASIS-2004: Salmon and Marine Ecosystems in the Bering Sea and Adjacent Waters" October 30–31, 2004 Sapporo, Japan.

Hare, S. R., and R.C. Francis. 1995. Climate change and salmon production in the northeast Pacific Ocean. Pages 357–372 in R. H. Beamish, editor. Ocean climate and northern fish populations. Canadian Special Publication of Fisheries and Aquatic Sciences 121.

Hare, S. R., and N. J. Mantua. 2000. Empirical evidence for the North Pacific regime shifts in 1977 and 1989. Progress in Oceanography 47:103–145.

Hare, S. R., N. J. Mantua, and R. C. Francis. 1999. Inverse production regimes: Alaska and west coast Pacific salmon. Fisheries 24:6–14.

Hartt, A. C., and M. B. Dell. 1986. Early oceanic migrations and growth of juvenile Pacific salmon and steelhead trout. International North Pacific Fisheries Commission Bulletin 46:1–105.

Heard, W. R. 1991. Life history of pink salmon (*Onchorhynchus gorbuscha*). Pages 119–231 in C. Groot and L. Margolis, editors. Pacific salmon: life histories. UBC Press, Vancouver, British Columbia.

Helle, J. S., and M. S. Hoffman. 1998. Changes in size and age at maturity of two North American stocks of chum salmon (*Oncorhynchus keta*) before and after a major regime shift in the North Pacific Ocean. North Pacific Anadromous Fish Commission Bulletin 1:81–89.

Helle, J. S., E. C. Martinson, D. M. Eggers, and O. Gritsenko. 2007. Influence of salmon abundance and ocean conditions on body size of Pacific salmon. North Pacific Anadromous Fish Commission Bulletin 4:289–298.

Hilborn, R., and D. M. Eggers. 2000. A review of the hatchery programs for pink salmon in Prince William Sound and Kodiak Island, Alaska. Transactions of the American Fisheries Society 129:333–350.

Hilborn. R., and C. J. Walters. 1992. Quantitative fisheries stock assessment: choice, dynamics and uncertainty. Chapman and Hall, London, U.K.

Hiroi, O. 1998. Historical trends of salmon fisheries and stock conditions in Japan. North Pacific Anadromous Fish Commission Bulletin 1:23–27.

International North Pacific Fisheries Commission. 1979. Historical catch statistics for salmon of the North Pacific Ocean. North Pacific Anadromous Fish Commission Bulletin 39.

International North Pacific Fisheries Commission. 1991. Statistical yearbook, 1991. International North Pacific Fisheries Commission, Vancouver, British Columbia.

Irvine, J. R., R. Houtman, L. Biagini, and M. Poon. 2006. An update on catch trends for Pacific salmon in British Columbia Canada. North Pacific Anadromous Fish Commission Document 979.

Kaeriyama, M. 1998. Dynamics of chum salmon, *Oncorhynchus keta*, populations released from Hokkaido in Japan. North Pacific Anadromous Fish Commission Bulletin No 1:81–89.

Mathews, S. B. 1968. An estimate of ocean mortality of Bristol Bay sockeye salmon three years at sea. Journal of the Fisheries Research Board of Canada 25:1219–1227.

McGurk, M. D. 1996. Allometry of marine mortality of Pacific salmon. Fishery Bulletin 94:77–88.

Mueter, F. J., D. M. Ware, and R. M. Peterman. 2002. Spatial correlation patterns in coastal environmental variables and survival rates of Pacific salmon in the northeast Pacific Ocean. Fisheries Oceanography 11:205–218.

North Pacific Anadromous Fisheries Commission. 2008. Statistical year book, 2006. North Pacific Anadromous Fisheries Commission, Vancouver.

Parker, R. R. 1962. Estimates of ocean mortality rates for Pacific Salmon (*Oncorhynchus*). Journal of the Fisheries Research Board of Canada 19:561–589.

Peterman, R. M., B. J. Pyper, M. F. Lapointe, M. D. Adkison, and C. J. Walters. 1998. Patterns of covariation survival rates of British Columbia and Alaskan sockeye salmon (*Oncorhynchus nerka*) stocks. Canadian Journal of Fisheries and Aquatic Sciences 55:2503–2517.

Ricker, W. E. 1964. Ocean growth and mortality of pink and chum salmon. Journal of the Fisheries Research Board of Canada 21:905–930.

Ricker, W. E. 1976. Review of the rate of growth and mortality of Pacific salmon in salt water, and noncatch mortality caused by fishing. Journal of the Fisheries Research Board of Canada 33:1483–1523.

Rogers, D.E. 1987. Pacific salmon. Pages 464–475 in D.W. Hood and S.T. Zimmerman, editors. The Gulf of Alaska: physical environment and biological resources. U.S. Government Printing Office, Washington, D.C.

Rogers, D. E. 1999. Estimates of annual salmon runs from the North Pacific, 1951–1998. Unpublished

Manuscript, Fisheries Research Institute, University of Washington, Seattle.

Salo, E. K. 1991. Life history of chum salmon (*Oncorhynchus keta*). Pages 231–310 *in* Groot, C., and L. Margolis, editors. Pacific salmon: life histories. UBC Press, Vancouver, British Columbia.

Urawa, S., T. Ozumaya, P. A. Crane, and L. W. Seeb. 2005. Origins and distribution of chum salmon in the central Bering Sea. NPAFC Technical Report No. 6. 2004 International Workshop "BASIS-2004: Salmon and Marine Ecosystems in the Bering Sea and Adjacent Waters" October 30–31, 2004, Sapporo, Japan.

Walker, R.V., K.M. Myers, and S. Ito. 1998. Growth studies from 1956–95 collections of pink and chum salmon scales in the central North Pacific Ocean. North Pacific Anadromous Fish Commission Bulletin No 1:54–65.

West, F. W., and L. F. Fair. 2006. Abundance, age, sex and size statistics for Pacific salmon in Bristol Bay, 2003. Fishery Data Series No. 06–07. Alaska Department of Fish and Game, Anchorage.

Witherell, D., D. Ackley, and C. Coon. 2002. An overview of salmon bycatch in Alaska groundfish fisheries. Alaska Fishery Research Bulletin 9:53–64.

White, B. 2008. Alaska salmon enhancement program 2007 annual report. Fishery Management Report No. 08–03. Alaska Department of Fish and Game, Divisions of Sport Fish and Commercial Fisheries, Anchorage.

American Fisheries Society Symposium 70:307–329, 2009

Marine Ecology of Western Alaska Juvenile Salmon

EDWARD V. FARLEY, JR.[*], JAMES MURPHY, JAMAL MOSS, ANGELA FELDMANN,
AND LISA EISNER

National Marine Fisheries Service, Alaska Fisheries Science Center
Auke Bay Laboratories
17109 Point Lena Loop Road, Juneau, Alaska 99801, USA

Abstract.—During the past five years (2002–2006), the Auke Bay Laboratory's Ocean Carrying Capacity program conducted surveys of western Alaska juvenile salmon *Oncorhynchus* spp. along the eastern Bering Sea shelf. The goal of our juvenile salmon research is to understand mechanisms underlying the effects of the environment on the distribution, migration, and growth of juvenile salmon in the eastern Bering Sea. The primary findings indicated that there were spatial variations in distribution among species; juvenile coho *O. kisutch* and Chinook *O. tshawytscha* salmon tended to be distributed nearshore and juvenile sockeye *O. nerka*, chum *O. keta*, and pink *O. gorbuscha* salmon tended to be distributed further offshore. In general, juvenile salmon were largest during 2002 and 2003 and smallest during 2006, particularly in the northeastern Bering Sea (NEBS) region. Fish, including age-0 pollock *Theragra chalcogramma* and Pacific sand lance *Ammodytes hexapterus* were important components of the diets for all species of juvenile salmon in some years. However, annual comparisons of juvenile salmon diet indicated a shift in primary prey for many of the salmon species during 2006 in both the NEBS and southeastern Bering Sea (SEBS) regions. In addition, the average CPUE of juvenile salmon fell sharply during 2006 in the SEBS region. It is speculated that spring sea surface temperatures (SST's) on the eastern Bering Sea shelf impact the growth and marine survival rates of juvenile western Alaska salmon through bottom-up control in the ecosystem. Cold spring SST's lead to lower growth and marine survival rates for juvenile western Alaska salmon; warm spring SST's have the opposite effect.

Introduction

Pacific salmon *Oncorhynchus* spp. returns (catch + escapement) to western Alaska have been inconsistent, and at times very weak. During 1998, low returns of Chinook salmon *O. tshawytscha* and chum salmon *O. keta* to western Alaska prompted the State of Alaska to restrict commercial and subsistence fisheries and declare a fisheries disaster for the region (Kruse 1998). Low returns of sockeye

salmon *O. nerka* to Bristol Bay, Alaska also occurred during 1997 and 1998. The regional scale of the decline of these salmon stocks indicates that the marine environment may play a critical role in regulating survival of Pacific salmon.

Ocean conditions are known to significantly affect salmon survival, particularly during the first few months after leaving freshwater (Holtby et al. 1990; Friedland et al. 1996; Beamish et al. 2004). Growth rates of juvenile salmon in the estuarine and near-

[*]Corresponding author: ed.farley@noaa.gov

shore marine environments are thought to be directly linked to their marine survival with larger fish having higher survival rates than small fish (Parker 1968; Pearcy 1992). Size-dependent mortality is believed to occur during two critical periods. The first period is dominated by predation-based mortality occurring shortly after juvenile salmon leave freshwater. During the first critical period, small individuals are vulnerable to a broad spectrum of predators and experience higher size-selective predation than larger fish (Parker 1968; Willette et al. 1999). The second period is controlled by energetic-based mortality occurring after the first summer at sea. During the second critical period, reduced storage capability of smaller individuals make them more vulnerable to overwinter mortality (Beamish and Mahnken 2001). Thus, years with favorable environmental conditions and increased growth rates of juvenile salmon may reduce susceptibility of the salmon to size-selective predation or improve survival during their first winter at sea.

Ecological processes affecting marine survival of eastern Bering Sea salmon stocks are poorly understood due to the lack of basic biological information about the early marine life history of salmon in this region. Until recently, studies of juvenile salmon migration in the eastern Bering Sea were generally focused within Bristol Bay (Hartt and Dell 1986; Isakson et al. 1986; Straty 1974). Information on juvenile salmon in the Arctic, Yukon, and Kuskokwim region was limited to a few studies of juvenile salmon within near-shore locations of Kotzebue Sound (Merritt and Raymond 1983; Raymond et al. 1984), Norton Sound (Nemeth et al. 2003), the Yukon River delta (Martin et al. 1986), and Kuskokwim Bay (Burril 2007; Hillgruber et al. 2007; Hillgruber and Zimmerman 2009, this volume). However, during 2002, scientists from Canada, Russia, Japan, South Korea, and the United States—member nations of the North Pacific Anadromous Fish Commission—cooperated in the design and execution of a field survey of salmon across the entire Bering Sea. The research, designated as Bering-Aleutian Salmon International Survey (BASIS), was developed to clarify the mechanisms of biological response by salmon to climate change.

In this paper, information on juvenile salmon ecology is summarized from the U.S. BASIS research cruises along the eastern Bering Sea shelf from August to October 2002–2006. New information is reported on juvenile salmon distribution, size, and diet, and relative abundance indices (catch per unit effort) for all five species of salmon are provided. The ecological processes that may affect marine survival of western Alaska juvenile salmon during this critical life history period are also discussed.

Methods

Survey

The Auke Bay Laboratory's Ocean Carrying Capacity (OCC) survey of the eastern Bering Sea was generally conducted from mid-August to early October during 2002 to 2006 aboard the chartered fishing vessel *Sea Storm* (38 m in length) and *Northwest Explorer* (49 m in length, 2006 only). The area surveyed was along the eastern Bering Sea shelf (Figures 1a and b). During 2002 and 2003, survey stations were spaced every 15 degrees along latitudinal (60°N to 65°N) and longitudinal (161°W to 168°W) lines (Figure 1a). From 2004 to 2006, stations were spaced every 30 degrees, forming a grid along the eastern Bering Sea shelf (Figure 1b). The eastern Bering Sea was separated into two regions based on distribution and probable stock- and species-specific migration routes for juvenile salmon (Farley et al. 2005). The southeastern Bering Sea (SEBS) region was defined as the area south of lat 60°N (does

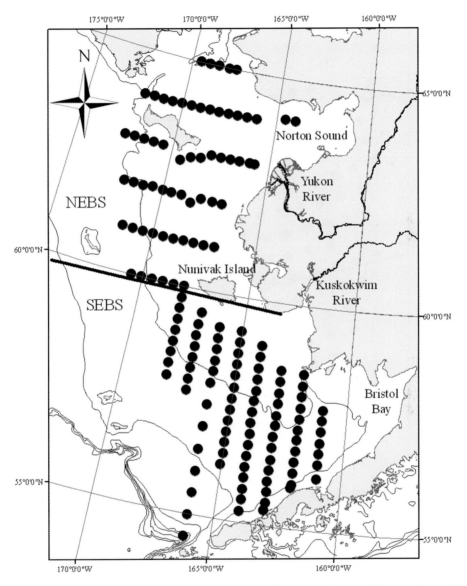

FIGURE 1. Station locations for the U.S. Bering Aleutian Salmon International Survey during 2002 and 2003 (a) and 2004–2006 (b).

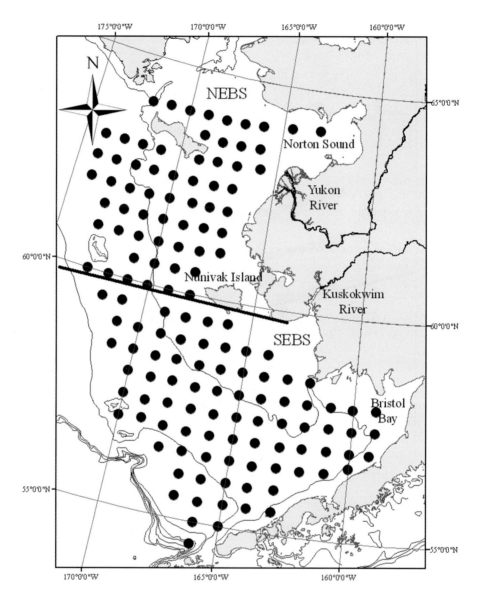

Figure 1. **B.**

not include catches made along 60°N) to the Alaska Peninsula, and the area west of long 161°W to 168°W. The northeastern Bering Sea (NEBS) region was defined as the area between lat 60°N (includes catches made along lat 60°N) and lat 65°N, and from the eastern shoreline of Alaska to long 173°W or the U.S.–Russian border.

Fish were collected using midwater rope trawls, model 400/580 and 300/450, made by Cantrawl Pacific Limited[1] of Richmond, British Columbia. Trawls were 198 m long, had hexagonal mesh in wings and body, and included a 1.2-cm mesh liner in the cod end. Trawls were towed at the surface from 3.5 to 5 knots, with typical horizontal and vertical mouth dimensions of 50 m and 14 m, respectively. The trawls were fished with Noreastern Trawl Systems 5-m alloy doors, 60-m bridles, and 330–366 m of warp line behind the boat. Buoys were secured to the wing tips (2-A5 and 4-A4 buoys) and two buoys were attached to the net sounder to help maintain the headrope near the surface. Wing-tip buoys could be seen floating near the surface when trawling and were used to ensure the headrope was at the surface. A Simrad FS900 net sounder was used to determine dimensions of the trawl mouth opening during each trawl set.

Stations were generally sampled during daylight hours (0730–2100, Alaska Daylight Savings Time); tows before 0800 in September and October were in the dark. All tows lasted 30 min and covered approximately 2.8–4.6 km. Salmon and other fishes captured during the tow were sorted by species and counted. A correlation between catch per unit effort (CPUE; number of salmon caught during a 30 min tow) and time of day was tested and no relationship was found ($r = 0.00$; $P = 0.36$). Standard biological measurements including fork length (nearest 1.0 mm) and body weight (nearest 1.0 g) were taken

[1]Reference to trade names does not imply endorsement by the National Marine Fisheries Service, NOAA.

on board. Diet analyses differed between years. During 2002 and 2003, subsamples of all juvenile salmon species were wrapped in a labeled plastic bag, frozen (–80°C), and shipped to the laboratory for further processing. In the laboratory, stomachs were removed from a random sample of approximately ten juvenile salmon from each trawl station. Individual stomachs were preserved in 10% formalin and placed in an individually labeled vial. During 2004 through 2006, stomachs were removed from a random sample of approximately ten juvenile salmon from each trawl station and analyzed on board.

Distribution of juvenile salmon

Cumulative frequency distributions of the percent total catch of juvenile salmon in relation to distance offshore (latitudinal meridians in decimal degrees for the SEBS region and longitudinal meridians in decimal degrees for the NEBS region) of the Alaska coastline were created to help in the discussion on the interannual variation in distribution of juvenile salmon.

Size of juvenile salmon

Adjusted mean fish lengths were calculated to standardize size across years and regions. Mean length was standardized to September 10 assuming three different daily growth rates: (1) 0 mm/d, representing no daily growth at sea, (2) 0.3 mm/d, the lower end of published ranges for juvenile Pacific salmon, and (3) 1.7 mm/d, representing the upper end of the range (see Fisher and Pearcy 1988; Fukuwaka and Kaeriyama 1994; Orsi et al. 2000 for daily growth rate ranges for juvenile Pacific salmon).

Analysis of variance (ANOVA) tests (ANOVA, fixed effect) were used to examine interannual and regional differences in length for each daily growth rate (i.e., 0 mm, 0.3 mm, or 0.7 mm). The dependent variable in the ANOVA was fork length and the independent variables were year (2002 to 2006), region (SEBS and NEBS), and the interaction among year and region. Data were analyzed using S-Plus statistical software. If a significant difference ($P < 0.05$) occurred, a Sidak multiple comparison test was used to calculate the 95% (α = 0.05, 0.01, 0.001) confidence intervals for all pairwise differences between the dependent variable means (Insightful 2001). The level of significance between the pairwise differences was determined by examining those confidence intervals that excluded zero for the three values of α.

Diets of juvenile salmon

Diet composition, expressed as percent wet weight of stomach contents (%WT), was used as the primary metric in the annual diet analyses and was calculated as

$$\%WT_{i,f,s} = WT_{i,f,s} * (\sum_i WT_{i,f,s})^{-1} * 100$$

where $WT_{i,f}$ is the total weight of prey category i in the fth salmon stomach for each species (s = pink *O. gorbuscha*, chum, sockeye, coho *O. kisutch*, and Chinook) sampled for diet analysis. Stomach content weight was estimated by subtracting the empty stomach weight from the stomach weight with contents. Stomachs were blotted dry prior to weighing. Stomach contents were divided into major taxonomic groups including fish species such as Pacific sand lance *Ammodytes hexapterus*, age-0 walleye pollock *Theragra chalcogramma*, capelin *Mallotus villosus*, and invertebrate taxonomic groups such as amphipods, copepods, euphausiids, megalopa, and tunicates Oikopleura. Two "other" categories were included and described by "other fish," composed of unidentified fish, and fish species that were less than 5% wet weight of the diet within each year (including cottids, clupeids, *Sebastes*, and pleuronectids) and "other zooplankton," composed of

zooplankton species that were less than 5% wet weight of the diet (including arthropods, chaetognaths, *Limacina* spp., and mysids) for each year.

Information was also included on average CPUE of age-0 walleye pollock (SEBS and NEBS regions) and sand lance (SEBS region only; very few sand lance were captured in the NEBS region) during 2002–2006 from our survey as well as an index of spring sea surface temperatures (SSTs) during May 2000 to 2006 in the southeastern Bering Sea (courtesy of http://www.beringclimate.noaa. gov) as references for discussion points on ecological processes affecting juvenile salmon survival. The May temperatures characterizes SST during May in the southeastern Bering Sea that were calculated as mean monthly SSTs averaged over the area 54.3°N to 60°N, 161.2°W to 172.5°W. The data were from the NCEP/NCAR Reanalysis project (Kalnay et al. 1996). The index values are the deviations from the mean value (2.33°C) for the 1970–2000 period normalized by the standard deviation (0.76°C).

Results

Distribution and relative abundance (CPUE)

Offshore distribution and CPUE of juvenile salmon varied among species in the SEBS and NEBS regions (Figures 2a and b; 3a–e).

Juvenile sockeye salmon were mainly distributed offshore with nearly 65% captured between 56.5°N and 58°N in the SEBS region. Within the SEBS region, the average CPUE of juvenile sockeye salmon that varied between 40 and 65 during 2002 to 2004 more than doubled to 140 during 2005, then fell to 20 during 2006 (Figure 3a). Juvenile sockeye salmon were also distributed offshore in the NEBS region with nearly 90% of the catch

a.

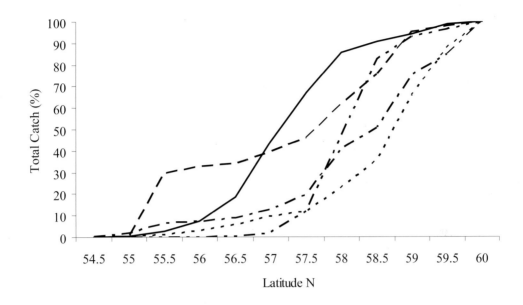

b.

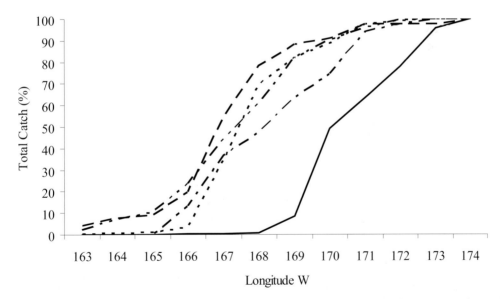

FIGURE 2. Percentage of total catch in relation to (a) latitudinal meridians in the SEBS region and (b) longitudinal meridians in the NEBS region for juvenile pink (– - –), chum (---), sockeye (—), coho (– – –), and Chinook (– - - –) salmon.

Farley et al.

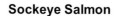

Sockeye Salmon

a

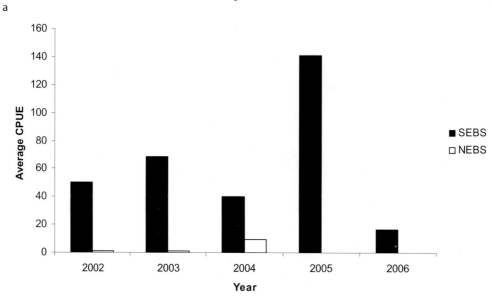

Chum Salmon

b

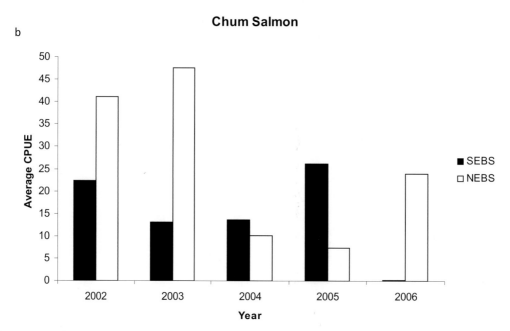

FIGURE 3. Relative abundance (catch per unit effort during a 30-minute trawl haul) of (a) sockeye, (b) chum, (c) Chinook, (d) coho, and (e) pink salmon in the SEBS and NEBS regions during August–October 2002–2006.

c

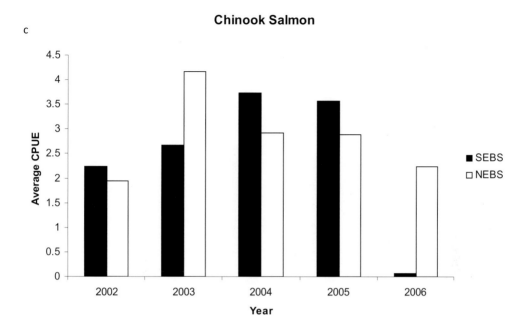

d

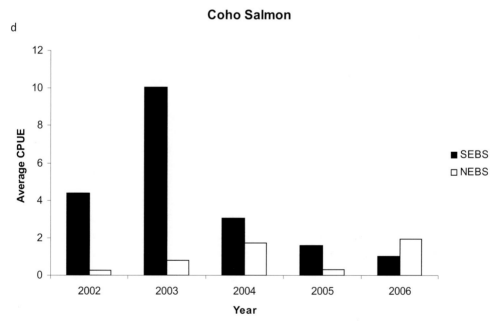

FIGURE 3. Continued.

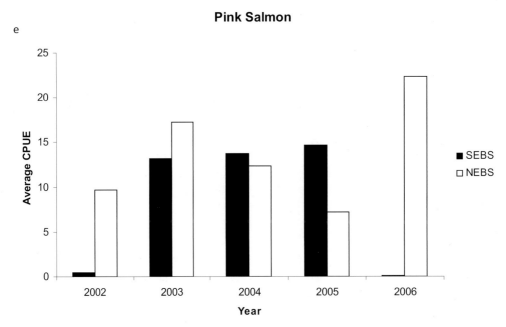

Figure 3. Continued.

occurring west of 169°W. In general, catches of juvenile sockeye salmon in the NEBS region were low in all years (Figure 3a).

Nearly 80% of juvenile chum salmon in the SEBS region were distributed north of lat 58°N directly west of the Kuskokwim River. Within the NEBS region, 75% of the juvenile chum salmon were distributed from 166°W to 169°W. Most of the juvenile chum salmon were captured south and west of the Yukon River, although catches did occur north of the Yukon River (Farley et al. 2005). Average CPUE for juvenile chum salmon was generally higher in the NEBS region than the SEBS region, especially during 2002, 2003 and 2006 (Figure 3b).

In contrast to the offshore distribution of sockeye salmon, juvenile Chinook salmon were mainly distributed nearshore. In the SEBS region, 80% of the juvenile Chinook salmon were distributed north of lat 57.5°N. Nearly 80% of the juvenile Chinook salmon were caught east of 169°W in the NEBS region; roughly 10% of the catch that oc-

curred between 163°W and 165°W transects with stations located within Norton Sound. There were three coded-wire tag recoveries of juvenile Chinook salmon during 2002 that were from the Yukon Territory, Whitehorse Rapids Salmon Hatchery, two within Norton Sound at lat 64.06°N, long 164.31°W station, and one offshore of the Yukon River at lat 63.00°N, long 165.58°W. In addition, the average CPUE of juvenile Chinook salmon was similar for both regions for all years except 2006, where catches of juvenile Chinook in the SEBS region were near zero (Figure 3c).

Juvenile coho salmon in the SEBS region had a bimodal distribution with nearly 30% of the catch occurring south of 55.5°N and 60% captured north of 57.5°N. The average CPUE for coho salmon was higher in the SEBS region for all years except 2006 (Figure 3d). Most of the juvenile coho salmon (60%) were distributed east of 169°W in the NEBS region, with roughly 10% distributed within Norton Sound (163°W to 165°W).

Juvenile pink salmon in the NEBS and SEBS regions had similar distributions to Chinook and chum salmon. The highest catches of juvenile pink salmon within the SEBS region occurred during 2003 to 2005; very few pinks were caught in this region during 2002 and 2006 (Figure 3e). In contrast, average CPUE for juvenile pinks in the NEBS region were high during all years with the highest average CPUE occurring in 2006 (Figure 3e).

Juvenile salmon size

Mean fork lengths at each daily growth rate for all five juvenile salmon species (see Tables 1 and 2) were significantly different among years ($P < 0.001$), between regions ($P < 0.001$; except coho salmon where $P = 0.006$), and between the interaction of regions and years ($P < 0.01$).

SEBS region

Juvenile sockeye salmon in the SEBS region were largest during 2003 and smallest during 2004 and 2005 (Table 1). The multiple comparison test indicated that juvenile sockeye salmon were significantly larger ($P < 0.001$) during 2003 than all other years for the three daily growth rates. Juvenile sockeye salmon were significantly larger ($P < 0.001$) during 2002 than 2004 and 2005 for all three daily growth rates. In addition, juvenile sockeye salmon were significantly larger during 2006 than 2004 ($P < 0.001$) and 2005 ($P < 0.001$ for 0 mm and 0.3 mm; $P < 0.01$ for 1.7 mm) for all three daily growth rates.

The smallest juvenile chum salmon were found during 2005 for all daily growth rates (Table 1). The largest juvenile chum salmon were found during 2003 for daily growth rates of 0 mm and 0.3 mm, and during 2004 for daily growth rates of 1.7 mm. Juvenile chum salmon were significantly larger ($P < 0.001$) in 2004 than 2002, 2003, and 2005,

and significantly smaller ($P < 0.001$) in 2005 than 2002 and 2003 for daily growth rates of 1.7 mm. Juvenile chum salmon were significantly smaller ($P < 0.001$) in 2005 than 2002, 2003, and 2004 for daily growth rates of 0.3 mm, and were significantly larger in 2003 than 2002 ($P < 0.05$), 2004 ($P < 0.001$), and 2005 ($P < 0.001$), significantly larger ($P < 0.001$) in 2002 than 2004 and 2005, and significantly larger ($P < 0.001$) in 2004 than 2005 for daily growth rates of 0.0 mm.

The largest juvenile Chinook salmon were found during 2006 for all three daily growth rates, however, the small sample size ($n = 6$) limits inferences to the size of Chinook salmon in the region (Table 1). If data from 2006 are ignored, the largest average size of Chinook salmon occurred in 2003, significantly larger ($P < 0.001$) than 2002, 2004, and 2005 for daily growth rates of 0.0 and 0.3 mm, and significantly larger ($P < 0.001$) than 2004 for daily growth rates of 1.7 mm. The smallest juvenile Chinook salmon were found during 2004 and were significantly smaller than fish sampled during all other years for each of the daily growth rates ($P < 0.001$ for growth rates of 0.0 and 0.3 mm; $P < 0.001$ for 2003 and 2005, and $P < 0.05$ for 2002 and 2006 for daily growth rates of 1.7 mm).

Juvenile coho salmon were largest during 2003 and smallest during 2005 for all three daily growth rates (Table 1). Juvenile coho salmon lengths in this region were significantly larger ($P < 0.001$) during 2003 than all other years for all three daily growth rates. Juvenile coho salmon collected during 2002 were significantly larger than those captured during 2004 ($P < 0.001$) for daily growth rates of 0 mm, and 2005 ($P < 0.01$) for daily growth rates of 0.3 mm.

The largest juvenile pink salmon occurred during 2002 and the smallest during 2006 for each of the three daily growth rates (Table 1). Juvenile pink salmon were significantly larger during 2002 than those captured during 2004 ($P < 0.01$), for daily growth rates

Farley et al.

TABLE 1. Annual mean ± (SE) fork lengths for daily growth adjusted by 0.0, 0.3, and 1.7 (mm day^{-1}) for juvenile salmon collected in the SEBS region. Statistics include sample size (n).

Species	Year	n	Daily Growth (mm day^{-1})		
			0.0	0.3	1.7
Pink	2002	46	188.8 (4.6)	188.0 (4.4)	186.9 (4.1)
Salmon	2003	790	182.7 (0.5)	180.2 (0.5)	177.0 (0.5)
	2004	653	177.8 (0.7)	179.7 (0.7)	182.3 (0.6)
	2005	876	161.7 (1.0)	164.5 (0.9)	168.1 (0.8)
	2006	14	154.8 (5.0)	157.7 (4.3)	161.6 (3.6)
Chum	2002	1069	184.3 (0.7)	184.6 (0.6)	184.9 (0.6)
Salmon	2003	949	187.1 (0.8)	185.9 (0.7)	184.4 (0.7)
	2004	885	179.7 (0.8)	183.5 (0.7)	188.6 (0.6)
	2005	687	172.0 (0.9)	175.6 (0.7)	180.3 (0.6)
	2006	30	179.9 (3.0)	182.3 (3.0)	185.4 (3.2)
Sockeye	2002	2070	195.7 (0.8)	198.5 (0.7)	202.2 (0.7)
Salmon	2003	2168	208.1 (0.8)	208.0 (0.7)	207.9 (0.7)
	2004	1845	182.9 (0.7)	187.4 (0.7)	193.3 (0.6)
	2005	2265	185.9 (0.7)	189.9 (0.7)	195.2 (0.6)
	2006	614	192.8 (1.2)	195.9 (1.1)	200.1 (1.1)
Coho	2002	228	291.5 (1.7)	292.5 (1.6)	293.9 (1.5)
Salmon	2003	498	309.4 (1.1)	309.3 (1.1)	309.1 (1.1)
	2004	87	277.5 (2.9)	284.0 (2.8)	292.7 (2.8)
	2005	116	276.4 (2.4)	282.1 (2.4)	289.8 (2.4)
	2006	40	285.1 (5.4)	287.2 (5.4)	290.0 (5.5)
Chinook	2002	191	205.6 (1.5)	208.9 (1.4)	213.3 (1.3)
Salmon	2003	190	220.0 (1.4)	219.8 (1.4)	219.6 (1.4)
	2004	258	190.1 (1.3)	196.9 (1.2)	205.9 (1.2)
	2005	291	203.0 (1.2)	208.7 (1.1)	216.4 (0.9)
	2006	6	240.8 (15.6)	240.0 (16.9)	239.0 (18.8)

TABLE 2. Annual mean ± (SE) fork lengths for daily growth adjusted by 0.0, 0.3, and 1.7 (mm day⁻¹) for juvenile salmon collected in the NEBS region. Statistics include sample size (*n*).

Species	Year	*n*	Daily Growth (mm day⁻¹)		
			0.0	0.3	1.7
Pink	2002	392	215.8 (0.8)	212.4 (0.8)	207.9 (0.8)
Salmon	2003	361	188.7 (0.8)	181.4 (0.8)	171.5 (0.8)
	2004	621	192.7 (0.9)	189.8 (0.9)	185.9 (0.9)
	2005	287	188.6 (1.2)	183.3 (1.2)	176.3 (1.2)
	2006	353	150.8 (0.6)	151.0 (0.6)	151.2 (0.6)
Chum	2002	1097	205.3 (0.5)	201.0 (0.4)	195.3 (0.4)
Salmon	2003	714	202.1 (0.7)	195.1 (0.7)	185.8 (0.7)
	2004	482	205.4 (0.9)	202.0 (0.9)	197.4 (0.9)
	2005	258	199.6 (1.1)	194.3 (1.1)	187.2 (1.1)
	2006	645	156.1 (0.5)	156.7 (0.5)	157.6 (0.6)
Sockeye	2002	56	241.7 (3.4)	238.4 (3.4)	234.0 (3.5)
Salmon	2003	29	238.0 (2.8)	230.4 (2.9)	220.2 (2.9)
	2004	352	216.7 (1.0)	212.9 (1.0)	207.8 (1.1)
	2005	12	239.9 (5.6)	233.6 (5.6)	225.1 (5.6)
	2006	2	178.5 (45.5)	180.1 (45.3)	182.4 (45.1)
Coho	2002	16	297.2 (4.4)	293.7 (4.4)	289.1 (4.5)
Salmon	2003	24	289.8 (4.8)	284.5 (4.7)	277.4 (4.7)
	2004	105	311.5 (2.0)	308.5 (1.9)	304.5 (1.8)
	2005	13	286.9 (6.0)	284.6 (5.9)	281.4 (5.7)
	2006	94	263.8 (2.6)	267.1 (2.9)	271.5 (3.5)
Chinook	2002	112	227.6 (3.1)	222.8 (3.2)	216.5 (3.3)
Salmon	2003	129	214.9 (2.7)	207.8 (2.7)	198.4 (2.7)
	2004	175	220.7 (2.0)	219.0 (2.0)	216.7 (2.0)
	2005	129	229.9 (2.7)	225.8 (2.6)	220.2 (2.5)
	2006	106	189.5 (2.2)	190.1 (2.2)	190.8 (2.2)

of 0 mm, 2005 ($P < 0.001$) and 2006 ($P < 0.001$) for daily growth rates of 0.3 mm, and 2003 ($P < 0.05$), 2005 ($P < 0.001$), and 2006 ($P < 0.001$) for daily growth rates of 1.7 mm. Juvenile pink salmon were also significantly larger ($P < 0.001$) during 2003 and 2004 than 2005 and 2006 for daily growth rates of 0 mm and 0.3 mm, and significantly larger during 2003 than 2005 ($P < 0.001$) and 2004 than 2005 ($P < 0.001$) and 2006 ($P < 0.01$) for daily growth rates of 1.7 mm. Juvenile pink salmon were significantly larger ($P < 0.001$) during 2003 than 2004 for daily growth rates of 0 mm, but switched for daily growth rates of 1.7 mm where size of juvenile pink salmon was significantly larger ($P < 0.001$) during 2004 than 2003.

NEBS region

The largest and smallest juvenile chum salmon for all daily growth rates were found during 2004 and 2006, respectively (Table 2). The multiple comparison test indicated that juvenile chum salmon were significantly smaller ($P < 0.001$) during 2006 than the previous four years for each daily growth rate. Juvenile chum salmon during 2002 were significantly larger than 2003 ($P < 0.05$ for 0 mm, $P < 0.01$ for 0.3 mm, $P < 0.001$ for 1.7 mm) and 2005 ($P < 0.001$) for each daily growth rate. Juvenile chum salmon were significantly larger ($P < 0.001$) during 2004 than 2003, 2005, and 2006 for each daily growth rate except 0.0 mm, where juvenile chum salmon during 2004 were significantly larger than 2005 ($P < 0.01$) and 2006 ($P < 0.001$) only.

The smallest juvenile Chinook salmon occurred during 2006 and these fish were significantly smaller ($P < 0.001$) than all other years for daily growth rates of 0.0 mm and 0.3 mm and for all years except 2003 for daily growth rate of 1.7 mm (Table 2). Juvenile Chinook salmon were significantly smaller during 2003 than 2002 ($P < 0.01$ for 0 mm, $P < 0.001$ for 0.3 mm and 1.7 mm), 2004 ($P < 0.001$) for daily growth rates of 0.3 mm and 1.7 mm, 2005 ($P < 0.001$) for all three daily growth rates. In addition, juvenile Chinook salmon were significantly larger during 2005 than 2004 ($P < 0.05$) for daily growth rates of 0 mm.

Juvenile coho salmon captured during 2006 were also significantly smaller than coho salmon captured during 2002–2004 ($P < 0.001$) and 2005 ($P < 0.05$) for daily growth rates of 0 mm, 2002 ($P < 0.001$), 2003 ($P < 0.05$), and 2004 ($P < 0.001$) for daily growth rates of 0.3 mm, and 2004 ($P < 0.001$) for daily growth rates of 1.7 mm (Table 2). Juvenile coho salmon were significantly larger during 2004 than 2003 ($P < 0.01$ for 0 mm; $P < 0.001$ for 0.3 mm and 1.7 mm) and 2005 ($P < 0.05$) for all three daily growth rates.

The largest juvenile pink salmon were found during 2002 and the smallest juvenile pink salmon were found during 2006 for all three daily growth rates (Table 2). Juvenile pink salmon were significantly larger ($P < 0.001$) during 2002 than all other years for each daily growth rate and significantly smaller ($P < 0.001$) during 2006 than all other years for each daily growth rate. In addition, juvenile pink salmon were significantly larger ($P < 0.001$) during 2004 than 2003 and 2005 for all three daily growth rates, and significantly larger ($P < 0.05$) during 2005 than 2003 for a daily growth rate of 1.7 mm.

Size between regions

Fork lengths of juvenile salmon varied between regions and among years (Tables 1 and 2). Lengths of juvenile chum salmon in the NEBS region were significantly larger ($P < 0.001$) during all years and daily growth rates than juvenile chum salmon captured in the SEBS region, except for daily growth of 1.7 mm during 2003. Juvenile Chinook salmon in the SEBS region were significantly larger ($P < 0.001$) than those captured in the

NEBS region during 2003 and 2006 for daily growth rates of 0.3 mm and 1.7 mm. Juvenile coho salmon captured in the SEBS region were significantly larger than those caught in the NEBS region during 2003 ($P < 0.01$ for 0 mm; $P < 0.001$ for 0.3 mm and 1.7 mm) and 2006 ($P < 0.001$), and significantly smaller than those in the NEBS region during 2004 ($P < 0.001$ for 0 mm and 0.3 mm; $P < 0.01$ for 1.7 mm). Juvenile pink salmon were significantly larger ($P < 0.001$) in the NEBS region during 2002–2005 for a daily growth rate of 0.0 mm, significantly larger ($P < 0.001$) in the NEBS region during 2002, 2004, and 2005 for a daily growth rate of 0.3 mm, and significantly larger in the NEBS region during 2002 ($P < 0.001$), 2004 ($P < 0.01$), and 2005 ($P < 0.001$) for a daily growth rate of 1.7 mm. Juvenile pink salmon were significantly larger ($P < 0.001$) in the SEBS region than the NEBS region during 2003 for daily growth rate of 1.7 mm.

Diet—SEBS Region

The prey items in juvenile salmon diets varied between years, but the most notable change in percent wet weight of diet items occurred during 2006 (Figures 4a–d). Age-0 pollock were the dominate prey item in sockeye salmon diets during 2002 through 2005 followed by other fish and sand lance (Figure 4a). However, during 2006 sand lance and euphausiids dominated the diet items followed by megalopa and other fish (Figure 4a). Fish consisting of age-0 pollock, other fish, and sand lance were prey items in the diet of juvenile chum salmon during all years except 2006 (Figure 4b). During 2006, euphausiids composed nearly 95% of the wet weight for the stomach contents of juvenile chum salmon. Juvenile Chinook salmon diets consisted mainly of fish including sand lance, age-0 pollock, and other fish (Figure 4c). Too few juvenile Chinook salmon were captured during 2006 for diet analyses in the SEBS region. The percent wet weight of diet items in juvenile coho salmon diets was similar during 2004 and 2005, consisting mainly of age-0 pollock and sand lance (Figure 4d). However, the percent wet weight of juvenile coho salmon diets changed dramatically during 2006, consisting mainly of euphausiids (Figure 4d). Fish consisting of age-0 pollock and sand lance were important components of the diet items in juvenile pink salmon stomachs during 2004 and 2005, and zooplankton including amphipods, euphausiids, and other zooplankton were important components for the diet during 2006 (Figure 4e).

Diet—NEBS Region

The most notable change in percent wet weight of prey items of juvenile fish in the NEBS region occurred during 2006, where the percent wet weight of sand lance in the diets increased for all five species of salmon (Figures 5a–d). The percent wet weight of fish in the diet of juvenile chum salmon increased during the five-year study (Figure 5a). For instance, amphipods and tunicates dominated the percent wet weight of prey of juvenile chum salmon during 2002; whereas, during 2004 and 2005, juvenile chum salmon diets where composed of approximately 50% fish and 50% zooplankton, increasing to nearly 70% wet weight of fish (50% wet weight of sand lance) by 2006 (Figure 5a). Fish were also important components of the juvenile Chinook salmon diet including sand lance, capelin, age-0 pollock, and other fish (Figure 5b). Juvenile coho salmon prey items consisted mainly of age-0 pollock, other fish, sand lance, and megalopa during 2004 (Figure 5c). However, during 2006, juvenile coho salmon diets consisted mainly of sand lance (nearly 60%), age-0 pollock, and other fish (Figure 5c). For juvenile pink salmon, fish and zooplankton were important components of the diet items during 2004 and 2005; whereas, fish consisting mainly of sand lance

Farley et al.

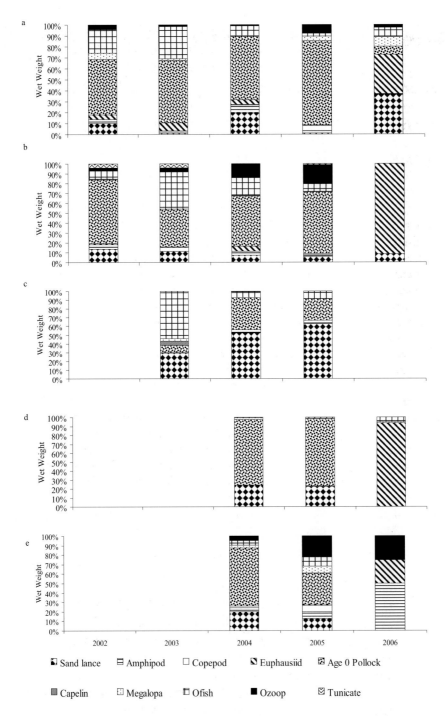

FIGURE 4. Interannual comparison of juvenile salmon diets in the SEBS region expressed as percent by prey weight for (a) sockeye, (b) chum, (c) Chinook, (d) coho, and (e) pink salmon collected along the eastern Bering Sea shelf during August–September 2002–2006. Other zooplankton (Ozoop) include arthropods, chaetognaths, *Limacina* spp., and mysids. Other fish (Ofish) include cottids, clupeids, *Sebastes*, and pleuronectids.

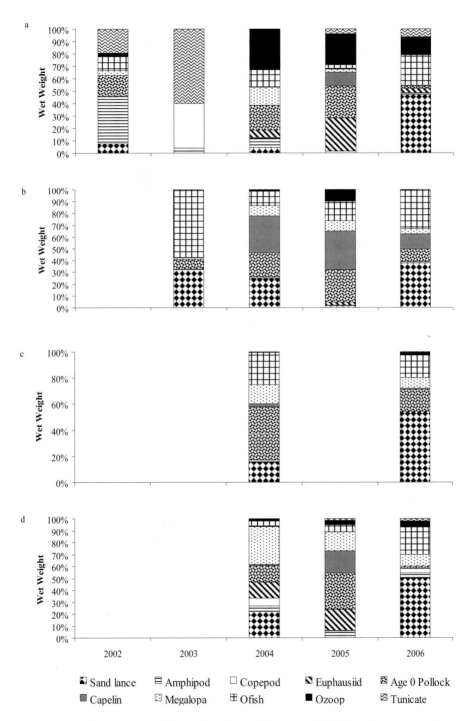

FIGURE 5. Interannual comparison of juvenile salmon diets in the NEBS region expressed as percent by prey weight for (a) chum, (b) Chinook, (c) coho, and (d) pink salmon collected along the eastern Bering Sea shelf during August–September 2002–2006. Other zooplankton (Ozoop) include arthropods, chaetognaths, *Limacina* spp., and mysids. Other fish (Ofish) include cottids, clupeids, *Sebastes*, and pleuronectids.

(50%) were the main component of the diet items in juvenile pink salmon stomachs in this region during 2006 (Figure 5d).

The average CPUE of important fish prey (age-0 pollock and sand lance) in salmon diets is shown in Figures 6a–b. Age-0 pollock increased from 2002 to 2005, then declined during 2006 in both regions (Figure 6a). The average CPUE of sand lance varied among years in the SEBS regions with the highest average CPUE's occurring during 2000 and 2004 (Figure 6b). Sand lance were not captured during 2003 in either region, and the large CPUE during 2002 in the NEBS region comes from a single trawl haul.

Discussion

The first step toward understanding mechanisms associated with highly variable marine survival rates of Pacific salmon is to provide basic biological information during their most critical life history stages. This study presents an examination of the temporal and spatial variation in distribution, size, diet, and average CPUE of five species of juvenile salmon from a systematic survey along the eastern Bering Sea shelf during fall (August–October) 2002–2006. In general, there were spatial variations in distribution among species; juvenile chum, coho, and Chinook salmon tended to be distributed nearshore and juvenile sockeye salmon tended to be distributed further offshore. Juvenile salmon were largest during 2002 and 2003 and smallest during 2004 and 2005 in the SEBS region and 2006 in the NEBS region. Annual comparisons of juvenile salmon diet indicated a shift in primary prey for many of the salmon species during 2006 in both the NEBS and SEBS regions. In addition, the average CPUE of juvenile salmon fell sharply during 2006 in the SEBS region.

Can these data provide insight into ecological processes that affect marine survival of western Alaska juvenile salmon during this critical life history period? A recent critical-size and critical-period hypothesis for Pacific salmon that links climate to ecosystem productivity and marine survival of fish was proposed by Beamish and Mahnken (1999). For this hypothesis, Pacific salmon must achieve a sufficient size by the end of the first marine summer in order to survive the metabolic demands during a period of energy deficit in late fall and winter. The critical-size and critical-period hypothesis links natural mortality of salmon to the productivity of the ocean ecosystem via the availability of nutrients regulating the food supply and hence competition for food (i.e., bottom-up processes; Beamish and Mahnken 1999).

There are several relationships that appear to be important in governing production on the eastern Bering Sea shelf (Hunt et al. 2002). First, the onset of spring net primary production on the eastern Bering Sea shelf is linked to the timing and duration of ice cover and winter winds. Second, mesozooplankton production is higher when the spring bloom occurs in warm water than during years when the bloom occurs in cold water at the ice edge. From these relationships, higher marine survival of juvenile western Alaska salmon would be expected during years with warm water spring blooms as there would be more food available to salmon, possibly leading to high early marine growth rates and reduced size-selective mortality during summer and late fall/winter. Years with cold-water spring blooms should have the opposite effect; food limitation would lead to slower growth during the first year at sea and a higher percentage of fish from a particular brood year not reaching the critical size to survive fall and winter.

The climate record for the Bering Sea indicates the coldest spring sea surface temperatures in the last seven years occurred during 2000, 2001, and 2006; warmer spring temperatures occurred during 2002–2005 (Figure 7). Data presented in this paper rep-a

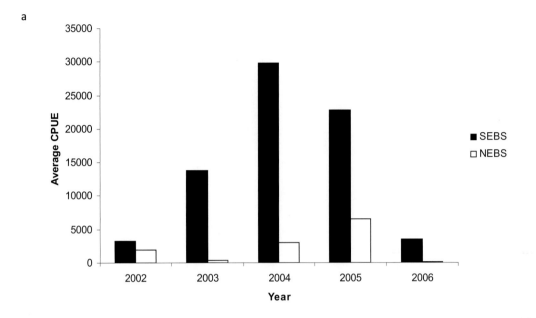

b

SEBS

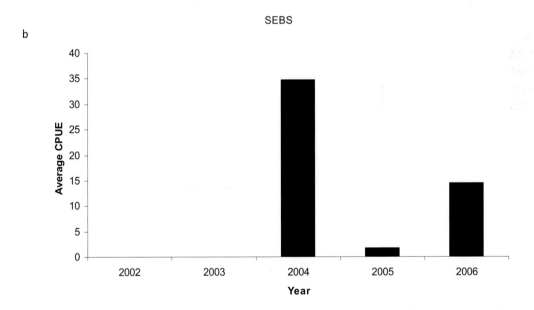

FIGURE 6. Relative abundance (catch per unit effort during a 30-minute trawl haul) of (a) age-0 pollock in the SEBS and NEBS regions and (b) sand lance in the SEBS region during August–October 2002 –2006.

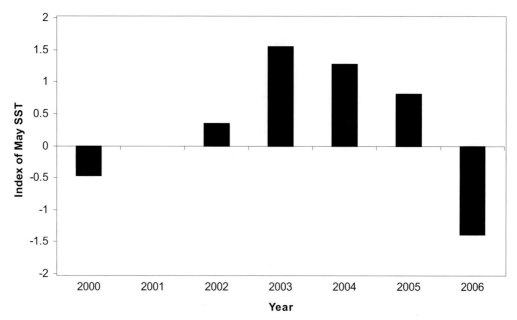

FIGURE 7. Index of May sea surface temperatures (SSTs) calculated as mean monthly SSTs averaged over the area 54.3°N to 60°N, 161.2°W to 172.5°W. The index values are the deviations from the mean value (2.33°C) for the 1970–2000 period normalized by the standard deviation (0.76°C). Data courtesy of http://www.berginclimate.noaa.gov.

resent fish captured during four warm years (2002–2005) and one cold year (2006). However, there are survey data on juvenile Bristol Bay sockeye salmon collected during 2000 and 2001 on the eastern Bering Sea shelf, and recent analyses of these data (2000 to 2002) found that relative marine survival rates were lower for these salmon during 2000 and 2001 (cool), and higher during 2002 (warm; Farley et al. 2007a). Farley et al. (2007a) suggested that the lower relative marine survival rates of Bristol Bay sockeye salmon were attributed to the significantly smaller size of juvenile Bristol Bay sockeye salmon during 2000 and 2001, as these fish would have a higher probability of marine mortality after their first summer at sea due to size-selective mortality. The recent increase in adult returns (2004–2006; Bue et al. 2009, this volume; Linderman and Bergstrom 2009, this volume; Menard

et al. 2009, this volume) to western Alaska rivers also provides evidence that juvenile salmon may have higher marine survival rates during years with warm spring SSTs (2002–2004).

If there is a relationship between spring sea surface temperatures and ocean productivity on the eastern Bering Sea shelf, then lower growth rates and increased marine mortality rates for juvenile salmon would be predicted during 2006, a year with cool spring sea temperatures. Our data indicated that CPUE of all juvenile salmon species declined dramatically in the SEBS region during 2006. The average CPUE of many juvenile salmon species remained high in the NEBS region, however, the fork length for all juvenile salmon species in the NEBS region was significantly lower than the previous years. It is likely that juvenile salmon in the SEBS region experienced lower growth rates after leaving freshwater, and thus higher size-selective mortality due to predation during summer (Parker 1968; Willette et al. 1999). Although average CPUE of juvenile salmon was high in the NEBS region, it would be expected that the significantly lower size of these fish would negatively impact marine survival during late fall and winter as it is likely that smaller fish have lower energy reserves and may have higher overwinter mortality due to starvation (Oliver et al. 1979; Henderson et al. 1988).

Also, if spring sea temperatures are driving pelagic production on the eastern Bering Sea shelf, then it should be expected to see changes in relative abundance of pelagic forage fish species as well. With the exception of 2002, age-0 pollock were abundant during years with warm spring temperatures. In addition to being more abundant, age-0 pollock were important prey items for all juvenile salmon species in the SEBS region. A decline in their abundance during 2006 was reflected in a switch from age-0 pollock to zooplankton as dominant prey for juvenile salmon in that region. Our survey unfortunately does not provide good estimates of pelagic forage fish abundance in the NEBS region. It is noted that a mixture of age-0 pollock, capelin, and sand lance were important components of the juvenile salmon diets during 2002 to 2005, whereas sand lance were the dominant prey item of juvenile chum, coho, and pink salmon in the NEBS region during 2006.

In conclusion, the authors believe that our research on juvenile salmon ecology along the eastern Bering Sea shelf has added insight to our understanding of ecological processes that affect their early marine growth and survival rate. A recent study suggested that regional averages of summer sea surface temperature may be a useful predictor of marine survival rates for Pacific salmon; (i.e., warmer summer SSTs were positively correlated with higher marine survival rates for salmon (Mueter et al. 2002)). Data presented here and prior publications on juvenile Bristol Bay sockeye salmon

suggest that spring SSTs on the eastern Bering Sea shelf likely impact growth rate of juvenile western Alaska salmon through bottom-up control in the ecosystem (Straty 1974; Farley et al. 2007a; Farley et al. 2007b). Cold spring SSTs lead to lower growth and marine survival rates for juvenile western Alaska salmon; warm spring SSTs have the opposite effect.

Acknowledgments

We gratefully appreciate the help of the captains (M. Cavanaugh and S. Brandstitter) and the crew of the FV *Sea Storm,* and captain S. O'Brien and the crew of the FV *Northwest Explorer* for their fine efforts and technical assistance in all aspects of the field surveys. We thank the Yukon River Drainage Fisheries Association for funding technician (T. Hamilton, G. Yaska, and H. George) support during the 2002 to 2005 research cruises. We also thank the two anonymous reviewers, whose comments and suggestions greatly improved the manuscript.

References

Beamish, R. J., and C. Mahnken. 1999. Taking the next step in fisheries management. *In* Ecosystem approaches for fisheries management. Proceedings of the 16th Lowell Wakefield Fisheries Symposium. Alaska Sea Grant College Program AK-SG-99–01.

Beamish, R. J., and C. Mahnken. 2001. A critical size and period hypothesis to explain natural regulation of salmon abundance and the linkage to climate and climate change. Progress in Oceanography 49:423–437.

Beamish, R. J., C. Mahnken, and C. M. Neville. 2004. Evidence that reduced early marine growth is associated with lower marine survival of coho salmon. Transactions of the American Fisheries Society 133(1):26–33.

Bue, F. J., B. M. Borba, R. Cannon, and C. C. Krueger. 2009. Yukon River fall chum salmon fisheries: management, harvest, and stock abundance. Pages 703–742 *in* C. C. Krueger and C. E. Zimmerman, editors. Pacific salmon: ecology and management of western Alaska's populations. American Fisheries Society, Symposium 70, Bethesda, Maryland.

American Fisheries Society Symposium 70:331–343, 2009
© 2009 by the American Fisheries Society

North Pacific and Bering Sea Ecosystems: How Might They Change?

THOMAS C. ROYER* AND CHESTER E. GROSCH

Center for Coastal Physical Oceanography
Department of Ocean, Earth, and Atmospheric Sciences
Old Dominion University, Norfolk, Virginia 23529, USA

Abstract.—The Bering Sea ecosystem can be considered an extension of the North Pacific Ocean ecosystem, especially with respect to coastal and upper ocean conditions. Because marine measurements are more numerous in the North Pacific, it is possible to deduce clear, historical changes in this large-scale marine ecosystem, and to apply them to the Bering Sea and Arctic-Yukon-Kuskokwim fisheries. To address recent changes in the marine conditions in the Northeast Pacific, we place them into centennial and millennial contexts. Ocean monitoring of temperature and salinity versus depth profiles at the mouth of Resurrection Bay near Seward, Alaska (station GAK1) since 1970 reveals significant linear temperature increases of about 1°C throughout the 250 m water column. Concurrent with this warming, the salinity of the upper layer (0–100 m) is decreasing while the lower layer (100–250 m) salinity is increasing. In the recent decade, storminess over the Gulf of Alaska has also increased. All of these changes are consistent with a conceptual model that includes ocean circulation, precipitation, glacial melting, and wind forcing. The model has positive feedbacks, suggesting that changes in the salinity are transporting more heat pole-ward, leading to increased storminess, precipitation, glacial melting, and decreased upper layer salinity and more heating. Superimposed on these linear trends are briefer fluctuations (months to years) that might influence the marine ecosystem. Similar trends in hydrography were reported for briefer records in the Bering Sea and Bering Straits. Sitka air temperatures since 1828 and Gulf of Alaska tree ring data since 700 A.D. suggest that periodic "regime shifts" have occurred at 25–30 year intervals since 1700. The last regime shift (warming) took place in 1977. These changes are likely to impact both marine and freshwater ecosystems used by salmon from the Arctic-Yukon-Kuskokwim region and they may play a role in controlling the growth and abundance of these populations.

Introduction

Low frequency (inter-annual to inter-decadal) climate changes in the ocean and atmosphere have been linked to changes in subarctic North Pacific zooplankton populations (Brodeur and Ware 1992) and the popu-lations of Pacific salmon *Oncorhynchus* spp. (Beamish and Bouillon 1993). As Mantua (2009, this volume) and Schindler and Rodgers (2009, this volume) describe, climate and environmental variability play an important role in controlling salmon productivity in both marine and freshwater habitats. Within the subarctic-arctic North Pacific marine eco-

*Corresponding author: tcroyer@gmail.com

system, linkages have been suggested from the subarctic convergence (located roughly at the latitude of the U.S.-Canadian border) northward within the Gulf of Alaska, westward to the Aleutian Island chain, and through that chain into the Bering Sea (Figure 1; Royer and Stabeno 1998). A portion of the waters in the Bering Sea move northward and pass into the Arctic Ocean through the Bering Straits (Woodgate et al. 2005). The important aspect here is that from British Columbia to the Arctic Ocean, the marine ecosystem(s) are linked.

To understand the low frequency changes taking place in the Arctic-Yukon-Kuskokwim (AYK) region, it is necessary to understand the "upsteam" fluctuations in marine ecosystem. In this paper, the authors start by addressing the interannual changes in the southern portion of the "extended" AYK marine ecosystem. They assume that these changes will eventually appear in the immediate AYK region or will influence the biological production in this region. Because the marine systems of the AYK region are so data-poor (especially with regard to long-time series), the authors used data from the Northeast Pacific Ocean to draw inferences about the Bering Sea.

Sitka Air Temperatures

The air temperature in the vicinity of Sitka, Alaska has been recorded since 1828, making it one of the longest temperature records in the Americas (Royer 1993). Unfortunately the record is intermittent, with gaps ranging from months to decades (Figure 2). For this study, the analysis was limited to the air temperature record that was continuous, 1900–1996. The monthly mean air temperatures were adjusted for numerous station moves using concurrent measurements from old and new locations. A gap of 26 months exists from January 1997 to February 1999. Though observations were made, the records

were not retained or forwarded to NOAA archives. Unfortunately, this gap took place during the 1997–1998 El Nino–Southern Oscillation (ENSO) event.

Over the length of the record, both the entire record and the abbreviated record (1900–1996), no significant trends occurred in the anomalies. The lack of trends was surprising because it is often assumed that global climate warming will occur first and largest at high latitudes. Possibly significant was the relatively low temperatures in the early 1970s and the extreme value of $-8.2°C$ in January 1969. Spectra analyses were used to identify temporal patterns in a time series. The spectra of the abbreviated record (Figure 3), normalized with the variance, containsed a low frequency peak in the power associated with a periodicity of about 17–18 years, similar to that of the lunar nodal tide oscillation of 18.6 years. A lesser peak also occurred at 0.02 cycles per year (50-year period). Drawing attention to the higher frequencies (shorter periods), significant energies existed at 9, 6, 4, 3, and 2 years. These are periods similar to those associated with ENSO events. Wavelet analysis allowed the determination of the strength of the contribution of each period's signal over time. In a record that was not stationary, the contributions of the various periods that vary over time was indicated (Figure 4). The Sitka monthly mean air temperature anomalies (annual signal removed) from 1900 to 1996 were not stationary as displayed with wavelet analysis (Figure 4). This temperature record was composed of many temperature fluctuations with various periods. The variance of the amplitude of the 50-year period component increases to greater than 14 times the mean variance in 1930 and continues throughout the record. From about 1940 to 1970, the 18–20 year period wave energy was significant, declining to less than ten times the variance since about 1980. This means that the contributions of the major components in this temperature signal varied

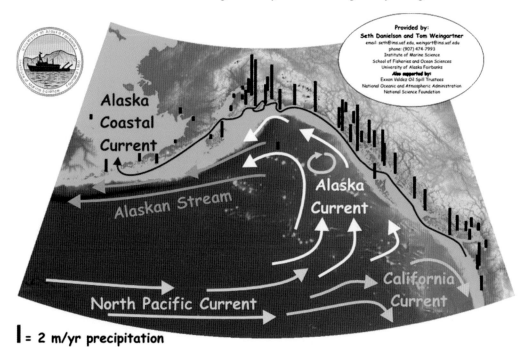

FIGURE 1. Northeast Pacific Ocean circulation schematic diagram (after Weingartner et al. 2002).

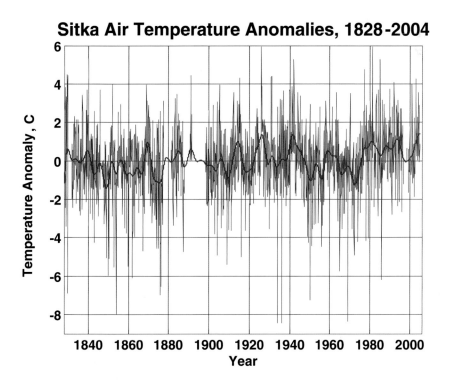

FIGURE 2. Sitka, Alaska air temperature anomalies with five-year average (solid red line).

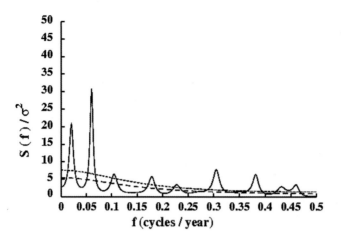

FIGURE 3. Sitka, Alaska air temperature spectra normalized with the variance. The solid line is the spectral amplitude of the Sitka air temperature, the variance associated with each frequency, f (or period, 1/f). The dashed lines are the 99 (upper one) and 95 (lower one) percent confidence levels.

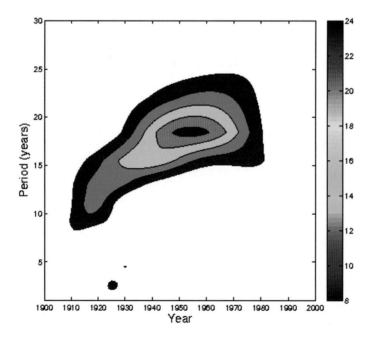

FIGURE 4. Wavelet analysis of the Sitka, Alaska air temperature (1900–1996).

over time, for unknown reasons. Actually it is expected that the lunar nodal tide (18.63 years) contribution should be constant.

Inter-annual changes in the seasonal amplitudes of the Sitka air temperatures indicated that changes in the amplitude of the seasonal signal of this air temperature were most evident in the low (winter) temperatures. (This seasonal trend analysis curve fitting contains 92% of the total record variance.) From about 1936 through the early 1970s, three oscillations in the winter temperature amplitude occurred that deceased from about –7°C, to –7.5°C, to –8°C. The early 1970s were a very unusual period for these air temperatures with the lowest 60-month averaged temperatures since 1828. A question is whether these very cold conditions in the early 1970s or the sustained relatively warm conditions throughout the 1980s were more important to the "regime shifts" reported for the Gulf of Alaska and Bering Sea at that time (Hare and Francis 1995). Analyses for the air temperature at St. Paul Island in the Bering Sea yielded similar seasonal and inter-annual results, supporting the connectivity between the Gulf of Alaska and Bering Sea ecosystems.

Water Temperatures and Salinities near Seward, Alaska

A potential connection between the Sitka air temperatures and the water temperature and salinity near Seward, Alaska is through the Alaska Coastal Current and other shelf circulations (Figure 1). The Alaska Coastal Current is influenced by the freshwater discharges along the coastal Gulf of Alaska (Royer 2005). Increases in this discharge will cause both barotropic and baroclinic geostrophic increases in the coastal current as a result of the increased sea level and the increased cross shelf salinity gradients. These accelerations will increase the transport of relatively warm water from the south (Fig-

ure 5). Increased temperatures will increase the cyclogenesis (storminess) that will also enhance the pole-ward flow in the coastal current. This positive feedback system will enhance the melting of the coastal mountain glaciers in the eastern and northern Gulf of Alaska.

Inter-decadal changes of temperatures and salinities near Seward (Figure 6) reflect the positive feedback processes illustrated (Figure 5) (Royer and Grosch 2006). The upper layer (0–100 m) temperatures contain a linear increase of about 0.03°C per year from 1970 through 2004 (Figure 6a). The lower layer (100–250 m) temperature increases for the same period (Figure 6b) is slightly less (0.024°C per year). The upper layer salinities have decreased (Figure 6c) in accord with increased glacial melting and cyclogenesis. The increase in the lower layer salinity anomalies (Figure 6d) is consistent with enhanced estuarine-like shelf circulation where a shoreward flow of surface deep water compensates for the offshore flow of low salinity surface water.

The acceleration of the coastal flow in the Gulf of Alaska will affect the marine ecosystem in several ways. First, the water column temperatures will increase, possibly shifting species, such as salmon, northward and ultimately westward around the gulf (Welch et al. 1998). The enhanced vertical stratification will decrease the mixed layer depth, helping to retain organisms in the upper layer. This shoaling of the mixed layer depth might be countered by enhanced wind stress (cyclogenesis) that is part of the conceptual feedback system outlined previously (Figure 5). An enhanced mixed layer strength associated with the increased stratification might also reduce upward transfer of the deep nutrients into the euphotic zone, inhibiting the upper layer biological productivity. The increased Alaska Coastal Current will also increase the transport of relatively warm, lower salinity water into the Bering Sea and the AYK region.

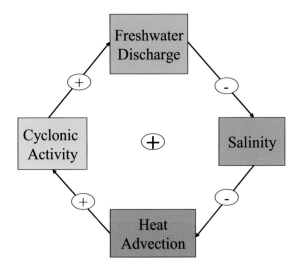

Hydrologic Cycle for Gulf of Alaska

FIGURE 5. Schematic of a potential hydrological cycle for the Gulf of Alaska (from Royer et al. 2001).

Bering Sea Temperatures and Salinities

Biophysical moorings have been deployed on the southeastern Bering Sea shelf since 1995 (Stabeno et al. 2007). While a few of these moorings only lasted a couple of years, one site (M2) has been occupied nearly continuously since 1995 (Figure 7). The M2 site was selected as a location where sea ice occurred every year. A second long-term mooring (M4) was established in 1999 farther north where weak cross shelf flow was suspected. These data have been used to describe the long-term changes in the physical environment of southeastern Bering Sea shelf.

The maximum sea ice extent in the Bering Sea is influenced by the water temperatures, air-sea temperature differences, currents, and winds. At maximum extent, sea ice covers most of the Bering Sea Shelf. To illustrate the extremes in ice coverage, years of maximum extent (1975, 1976, 1995 and 2002), when compared with periods of minimum extent (1979, 2001 and 2005), show that sea ice extent can vary by more than 300 kilometers. Over the last five years (2001–2005), there have been low concentrations of ice within the dark blue box in Figure 8 and significant ice concentrations (>25%) have been limited in duration. The year-to-year variability has also increased in recent years. These decadal shifts in sea ice were accompanied by decadal shifts in the Pacific Decadal Oscillation (PDO) and the Arctic Oscillation (AO). There was also a shift in the AO in 1976, coinciding with the North Pacific temperature "regime" shift. It has been suggested by Stabeno et al. (2007) that a mode shift occurred in the PDO with the first mode weakening and the second mode strengthening since 1989.

Changes in the sea ice amount and timing will affect the salinity and temperature of the water column. These changes will also in turn affect primary production in the water column. As the ice advances, the freezing process injects salt brine into the upper water column, increasing the upper layer density and causing vertical mixing. This tends to distribute seawater with freezing temperatures throughout the mixed layer depth. Later, as the ice

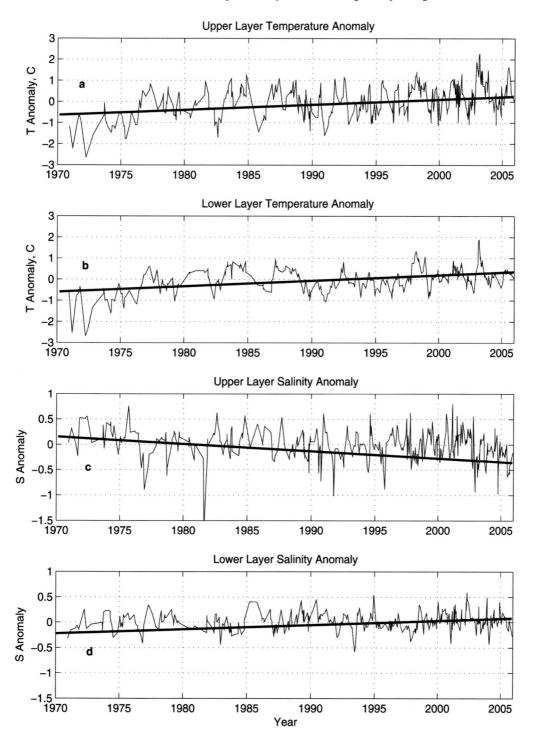

FIGURE 6. Interdecadal upper layer (0–100 m) sea temperature anomalies (panel a), lower layer (100–250 m) temperature anomalies (panel b), upper layer salinity anomalies (panel c) and lower layer salinity anomalies (panel d) measured near the mouth of Resurrection Bay in the Gulf of Alaska (station GAK1) (after Royer and Grosch 2006).

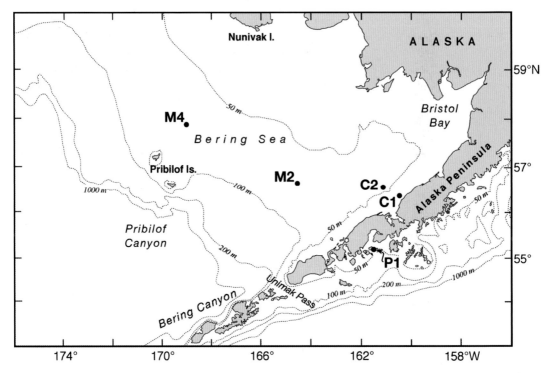

FIGURE 7. Locations of M2 and M4 biophysical moorings on the southeastern Bering Sea shelf (from Stabeno et al. 2007).

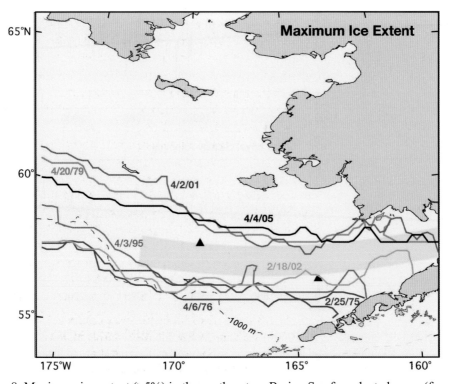

FIGURE 8. Maximum ice extent (>5%) in the southeastern Bering Sea for selected years (from Stabeno et al. 2007).

melts during the retreat, relatively freshwater is released in the surface layers, increasing the stratification. If this takes place in concert with increased solar radiation in the spring, then the upper layers become highly stratified unless spring storms occur to enhance the mixing. Thus, the bottom layers on the shelf may or may not be isolated from the upper layers, depending on the intensity and timing of spring and summer storms.

Sea ice determines the timing and nature of the spring phytoplankton bloom (Stabeno 1998; Stabeno et al. 2001, 2007; Hunt et al. 2002). If ice is present over the shelf after mid-March, the phytoplankton bloom will usually be in the marginal ice zone whereas if the ice retreats prior to mid-March or is absent throughout the year, the spring bloom will not take place until sufficient stratification occurs due to surface heating. The composition of the biological community through much of the remainder of the season depends on how and when the sea ice melts and whether subsequent strong storms occur.

The ocean temperatures recorded at the M2 and M4 moorings in the Bering Sea (Figure 7) showed a seasonal cycle that has been found elsewhere on this shelf (Stabeno et al. 2007). The lowest temperatures occurred when ice was over the moorings. The water column was well mixed in winter (January) and continued until the water column became stratified due to the melting of sea ice or the seasonal solar heating. A two-layer stratification was commonly found in the middle shelf (water depths 50–100 m) in summer with the upper layer (15–35 m) mixed by the wind and the lower layer (35–40 m). A cold pool of water with temperatures below 2°C was often found in this lower layer. In recent years, higher water column temperatures caused a failure of the formation of this cold pool.

The lowest sea surface temperature (SST) at M2 occurred in 1999 and the highest in 2004 when the upper layer temperatures were greater than 12°C (Stabeno et al.

2007). It should be noted that both the upper layer and lower layer temperatures increased in the summer of 2000. The briefer record of temperature at M4 makes the results less definitive (see Stabeno et al. 2007 for further discussion).

The depth integrated temperatures from the M2 and M4 moorings indicated a shift in the temperatures at M2 in about 2000 with above normal temperatures (positive anomalies) (Stabeno et al. 2007). The record also recorded the very cold conditions in 1999, especially in summer. No water with ice concentrations greater than 10% has covered the M2 mooring since 2000. It is believed that this lack of sea ice contributed to the warming observed since 2000 (Stabeno et al. 2007). Continued data acquisition at these mooring sites will allow us to understand the processes that affect the water temperatures on this Bering Sea shelf. Possible mechanisms for the warming over the southeastern Bering Sea shelf include: (1) changes in the direction and magnitude of winter winds over this shelf, (2) shortening of the "ice" season, (3) warmer water in summer leading to delays in ice advection though melting in the following winter, and (4) changes in the flow through Unimak Pass in winter.

Comparing 1975 and 2002, the sea ice extent was greater in 1975 and one additional outbreak of cold air occurred over the Bering Sea in 1975 that resulted in a substantial heat loss from the ocean. In 1975, the eastern extent of the sea ice was much greater, along with the maximum sea ice extent. A mid-March cooling in 1975 resulted in a longer presence of sea ice that year. The wind direction also influences the ice coverage and water temperature. A lack of cold winds out of the north in December and January has occurred since 2000 with less sea ice and higher water temperatures being recorded at M2 (Stabeno et al. 2007).

Three processes can cool the water column in the southeastern Bering Sea: 1) direct heat loss to the atmosphere, 2) horizontal advection of cold water, and 3) cooling of the water column via ice melting. First, the differences in the water column temperatures between 1975 and 2000 could be attributed to an additional period of cooling after mid-March in 1975. Second, even though there is usually a northward transport of relatively warm water, there can be episodes of southward cold water transport. Generally, the northward transport of warm water occurs after the ice retreats from the mooring site, as was observed in January 2000 when the M2 water temperatures increased by more than 2°C (Stabeno et al. 2007). Third, latent heat flux due to melting sea ice is an effective way to reduce the water column temperature. The melting of the sea ice will also retard the advancement of the ice edge, though the advance is also highly controlled by the wind (Stabeno et al. 2007).

The southeastern Bering Sea shelf water column temperatures have increased over the past decade along with a reduction in the concentration, duration, and maximum extent of sea ice. Higher ocean temperatures will add to the sea ice reduction while northerly winds will increase the presence of sea ice at moorings M2 and M4 (Stabeno et al. 2007). It appears that in this conflict between northerly winds and increased heat advection from the south, the latter process is winning. The result is a warmer, less ice-covered Bering Sea, and possibly a less ice covered Arctic Ocean as a consequence of the changes in the marine conditions in the Bering Straits. The trends in the Bering Sea are similar to those in the Gulf of Alaska as discussed earlier in this paper.

Bering Straits Temperatures and Salinities

Woodgate et al. (2006) have used year-round moorings from 1990 to 2004 to describe the inter-annual variability of current flow through the Bering Strait and the changes in the freshwater and heat fluxes into the Arctic Ocean. The data from the moorings span a majority of the strait and were of similar duration as the measurements from the M2 and M4 moorings in the Bering Sea. A general increase in the fluxes occurred from 2001 through 2004 with the heat flux in 2004 being the largest yet recorded (Woodgate et al. 2006). The water temperature has been about 0.5°C higher since 2002. Significant contributions to these heat and freshwater fluxes has been provided by the Alaska Coastal Current, which has a strong freshening and warming since 2002, with an elevated temperature at the eastern channel of the Bering Strait (mooring A2) of about 0.5°C (Woodgate et al. 2006). It is estimated that the Alaska Coastal Current provides about a third of the heat flux and a fourth of the freshwater flux through these straits. These fluxes will contribute to the loss of sea ice in the Arctic Ocean of up to 640,000 km² of 1 m thick ice melted. Woodgate et al. (2006) suggest that weaker northerly winds were the likely cause of most the increased freshwater (up to a 1 million cubic meters per second increase in the volume flux) and heat flux. This increase in freshwater from 2001 to 2004 of about 800 km³ is about 25% of the annual Arctic river runoff. The conclusions of Woodgate et al. (2006) support the general concept that increases of warmer, fresher water exist flowing northward from British Columbia to the Arctic Ocean.

Very Long Temperature Time Series

Proper interpretation of the recently observed increases in the Northeast Pacific Ocean and Bering Sea water temperature requires that the observation be placed in a proper long-term (relative to most) oceanographic time series. Fortunately, a recent paper by Wilson et al. (2007) provides this context. They have analyzed tree-ring data and extracted the annual January–September Gulf of Alaska coastal surface air temperatures. They have interpreted tree-ring width as temperature; that is, wider tree rings imply higher temperatures. Their fossilized tree-ring record begins in 616 AD, providing more that 1,300 years of proxy coastal surface air temperature data for the Gulf of Alaska. In that portion of the record based on living trees (1514–1999), the reconstruction based on tree ring width accounts for 44% of the temperature variance.

To test the validity of this proxy temperature record, Wilson et al. (2006) compared their reconstructed Gulf of Alaska (GOA) temperature time series with the well known indices of Pacific Decadal Oscillation index (PDO) and the North Pacific Index (NPI). The GOA reconstruction correlated significantly (95% C.L.) with both the PDO (0.53) and the NPI (–0.42) (Wilson et al. 2007). Both of these indices are frequently used to describe the present and past climate variability of the North Pacific, so this reconstruction should be useful for investigating past climate patterns (Wilson et al. 2007). These patterns showed that, in general, high coastal sea surface temperatures accompany cooler waters offshore in the central North Pacific Ocean. The reconstructed GOA temperature time series contained not only the North Pacific regime shift of 1976, but also illustrated that there frequently have been other regime shifts.

The entire GOA temperature time series shows numerous regime shifts throughout 1,300 years (Wilson et al. 2007). While the recent decades have been relatively warm, similar earlier warm periods have occurred. Also, an extensive, multi-decadal, very cold period occurred in the middle of the 19th century. More recently, a relatively brief cold period occurred in the early 1970s that preceded the 1977 regime shift.

The spectral analyses using the multi-taper method of this very long time series suggested that the most dominate periodicity is in the range of about 18.7 years. Wilson et al. (2007) also used singular spectrum analysis to determine other dominate periodicities, and they identified the periods (decreasing in importance) of 18.7, 50.4, 38.0, 91.8, 24.4, 15.3, and 14.1 years. A secular period also occurred for more than 150 years. Even though the temperature time series for the Gulf of Alaska is much more complex than a few simple modes of variability, Wilson et al. (2007) followed Minobe's (1999) hypothesis that if the 18.7 and 50.4 year period signals were extracted from the GOA time series, then no regime shifts would occur in the series.

The long-term variability of the GOA temperatures is not well understood; though forcings at various periods are apparent, they are not stationary in time. The forcing mechanisms of these various periods need to be better known. Evidence exists of extra-terrestrial forcing (lunar and solar) at some of these periods such as tidal periods (Royer 1993; McKinnell and Crawford 2007) but further research is required. For example, the combination of the 18.7 year signal due to the lunar nodal tide and a 50.4 year atmospheric signal leads to regime shifts in the GOA sea surface water temperature every 25–30 years, only since 1700 (Wilson et al. 2007). Why only since 1700, and will they continue? None have taken place since 1977, but since spring 2006, the water temperatures at the mouth of Resurrection Bay near Seward, Alaska (station GAK1) in the Gulf of Alaska have been below normal. The spring 2007 temperatures were the lowest since the early 1970s (http://www.ims. uaf.edu/gak1/). The GOA temperatures are highly complex and might be influenced by global ocean and atmospheric processes in addition to solar and lunar.

Discussion

Inter-decadal variations in the temperature and salinity have been observed recently in the Gulf of Alaska, Bering Sea, and Bering Straits. In these regions, the seasonal and shorter variances of the hydrographic properties create a low signal to noise ratio, making the detection of the inter-annual and inter-decadal changes difficult. Fortunately these inter-decadal signals are quite large. The upper layer Gulf of Alaska temperatures are increasing at about 1°C per 30 years as the surface freshens and the deep water salinity increases slightly. The statistical treatments of the hydrographic time series for the Bering Sea and Bering Straits were much less certain due to the brevity of those records. However, the trends seem to be in the same direction as those in the Gulf of Alaska, that is, warming and freshening of the upper layers. The similarity in these trends also supports the hypothesis that these oceanographic regions are linked together dynamically.

In the context of long duration (1,300 years) temperatures for the Gulf of Alaska, the recent thermal changes are not all that unusual with many earlier "regime shifts" found in the historical temperature data. It is also uncertain as to whether global climate changes will have further influences over the 50.4 and 18.7 year cycles previously observed. Possibly the next "regime shift" will negate global warming by an abrupt cooling in this region. Of course, this event would only delay the even larger impact of another regime shift (warming) in approximately in 2032–2037.

Continued systematic ocean observations over many decades are required to assess not only the variations, but also to investigate their causes. Little is known about the specifics of the numerous mechanisms that cause the inter-annual and inter-decadal temperature and salinity changes. The possible candidates include local atmospheric forcing (heat and water budgets and wind forcing), tidal mixing, regional and global ocean circulation, and lunar and solar forcing.

The most recent freshening and warming suggest that the salmon of the Northeast Pacific will be moving pole-ward as the water temperatures increase, as discussed by Welch et al. (1998). The thermal boundaries might eventually move sockeye salmon *O. nerka* out of the northeast Pacific and into the Bering Sea. Similar alongshore poleward movement of salmon populations might occur in the Bering Sea, causing a shift of marine rearing of AYK salmon into the Arctic Ocean.

References

Beamish, R. J., and D. R. Bouillon. 1993. Pacific salmon production trends in relation to climate. Canadian Journal of Fisheries and Aquatic Sciences 50:1002–1016.

Brodeur, R. D., and D. M. Ware. 1992. Interannual and interdecadal changes in zooplankton biomass in the subarctic Pacific Ocean. Fisheries Oceanography 1:32–38.

Hare, S. R., and R. C. Francis. 1995. Climate change and salmon production in the Northeast Pacific Ocean. Pages 357–372 *in* R. J. Beamish, editor. Climate change and northern fish populations. Canadian Special Publication in Fisheries and Aquatic Sciences 121:357–372.

Hunt, G. L., P. Stabeno, G. Walters, E. Sinclair, R. D. Brodeur, J. M. Knapp, and N. A. Bond. 2002. Climate change and control of the southeastern Bering Sea pelagic ecosystem. Deep-Sea Research Part II—Topical Studies in Oceanography 49:5821–5853.

Mantua, N. J. 2009. Patterns of change in climate and Pacific salmon production. Pages 1143–1157 *in* C. C. Krueger and C. E. Zimmerman, editors. Pacific salmon: ecology and management of western Alaska's populations. American Fisheries Society, Symposium 70, Bethesda, Maryland.

McKinnell, S. M., and W. R. Crawford. 2007. The 18.6-year lunar nodal cycle and surface temperature variability in the northeast Pacific. Journal of Geophysical Research 112, C02002, doi:10.1029/2006JC003671.

Minobe, S. 1999. Resonance in bidecadal and penta-decadal climate oscillations over the North Pacific: role in climatic regime shifts. Geophysical Research Letters 26:855–858.

Royer, T. C. 1993. High latitude oceanic variability associated with the 18.6 year nodal tide. Journal of Geophysical Research 98:4639–4644.

Royer, T. C. 2005. Hydrographic responses at a coastal site in the northern Gulf of Alaska to seasonal and interannual forcing. Deep-Sea Research Part II—Topical Studies in Oceanography 52:267–288.

Royer, T. C., and C. E. Grosch. 2006. Ocean warming and freshening in the northern Gulf of Alaska. Geophysical Research Letters 33, L16605, doi:10.1029/2006GL 026767:2006.

Royer, T. C., and P. J. Stabeno. 1998. Polar ocean boundaries, Pages 69–78 in K. H. Brink and A. R. Robinson, editors. The Sea, volume 11. Wiley, New York.

Royer, T. C., C. E. Grosch, and L. A. Mysak. 2001. Interdecadal variability of northeast Pacific coastal freshwater and its implications on biological productivity. Progress in Oceanography 49:95–111.

Schindler, D. E., and L. A. Rodgers. 2009. Responses of Pacific salmon populations to climate variation in freshwater ecosystems. Pages 1127–1142 in C. C. Krueger and C. E. Zimmerman, editors. Pacific salmon: ecology and management of western Alaska's populations. American Fisheries Society, Symposium 70, Bethesda, Maryland.

Stabeno, P. J. 1998. The status of the Bering Sea in the second half of 1997. PICES Press 6(2):8– 9:29.

Stabeno, P. J., N. A. Bond, N. B. Kachel, S. A. Salo, and J. D. Schumacher. 2001. On the temporal variability of the physical environment over the south-eastern Bering Sea. Fisheries Oceanography 10:81–98.

Stabeno, P. J., N. A. Bond, and S. A. Salo. 2007. On recent warming of the southeastern Bering Sea shelf. Deep-Sea Research Part II—Topical Studies in Oceanography 54:2599–2618.

Weingartner, T., B. Finney, L. Haldorson, P. Stabeno, J. Napp, S. Strom, R. Brodeur, M. Dagg, R. Hopcroft, A. Hermann, S. Hinckley, T. Royer, T. Whitledge, K. Coyle, T. Kline, E. Lessard, D. Haidvogel, E. Farley, and C. Lee. 2002. The northeast Pacific GLOBEC Program: coastal Gulf of Alaska. Oceanography Magazine 15:30–35.

Welch, D. W., Y. Ishida, and K. Nagasawa. 1998. Thermal limits and ocean migrations of sockeye salmon (Oncorhychus nerka): long-term consequences of global warming. Canadian Journal of Fisheries and Aquatic Sciences 55:937–948.

Wilson, R., G. Wiles, R. D'Arrigo, and C. Zweck. 2007. Cycles and shifts: 1300 years of multi-decadal temperature variability in the Gulf of Alaska. Climate Dynamics 28:425–440.

Woodgate, R. A., K. Aagaard, and T. J. Weingartner. 2005. Monthly temperature, salinity, and transport variability of the Bering Strait through flow. Geophysical Research Letters 32, L04601, doi:10.1029/2004GL021880.

Woodgate, R. A., K Aagaard, and T. J. Weingartner. 2006. Interannual changes in the Bering Strait fluxes of volume, heat and freshwater between 1991 and 2004. Geophysical Research Letters 33, L15609, doi:10.1029/2006GL026931.

Section II

Human Dimensions of AYK Salmon

American Fisheries Society Symposium 70:347–348, 2009
© 2009 by the American Fisheries Society

Human Dimensions of Arctic Yukon Kuskokwim Salmon: Introduction

JOSEPH J. SPAEDER

Arctic-Yukon-Kuskokwim Sustainable Salmon Initiative
Bering Sea Fishermen's Association
P.O. Box 2087, Homer, Alaska 99603, USA

Since the inception of the Arctic-Yukon-Kuskokwim Sustainable Salmon Initiative (AYK SSI), the program has maintained an interdisciplinary focus by explicitly addressing human dimensions, as well as the biological dimensions, of salmon populations across their full life cycle. The AYK SSI Research and Restoration Plan (2006) includes a research framework entitled: Human Systems and Sustainable Salmon: Social, Economic, and Political Linkages. This framework prioritized studies to contribute to our understanding of how various human activities, institutions, and management structures may affect salmon populations and habitats. A number of research projects have been funded by the AYK SSI over the past seven years to address aspects of these social, cultural, economic, and institutional linkages. Consistent with the research and restoration plan, the 2007 AYK SSI Symposium included a session devoted to the "Human Dimensions of Salmon" which featured presentations addressing human-salmon issues in Alaska, Canada, and the Pacific Northwest.

The five human dimension papers addressing AYK salmon presented in this section, as well as a number of papers in other sections in this volume, attest to this research program's strong interdisciplinary emphasis. In the lead chapter, Wolfe and Spaeder (2009, this volume) present an overview of the patterns and trends in subsistence salmon harvests across the AYK, coupled with a review of social organization and demographic trends which influence the dynamics of subsistence harvests. They include a review of case studies documenting the contributions of traditional ecological knowledge to fishery research and offer reflections on how social and cultural systems might adapt to changing salmon populations. Drawing on a set of Alaska case studies, Brelsford (2009, this volume) provides an overview of the contribution of local and traditional/indigenous ecological knowledge to our shared scientific understanding of salmon. The paper concludes with a discussion of how the lessons learned from these local and traditional/indigenous ecological knowledge studies might benefit the on-going research agenda of the AYK SSI program.

The next two chapters analyze specific case studies from within the AYK region. Magdanz et al. (2009, this volume) present a detailed analysis of the patterns and trends in subsistence harvest of salmon in ten small communities in the Norton Sound region. Using retrospective data, the paper presents and tests a variety of hypotheses about how salmon population trends, community size, and household types influences the resulting salmon harvests in this region. Howe and Martin (2009, this volume) examine a set of demographic and economic characteristics of the AYK region of Alaska. Based on data from a set of lower Kuskokwim River communities, they test a set of hypotheses about the relationships among subsistence harvests, population growth, and commercial fishing.

The last chapter by Knapp (2009, this volume) provides an overview of the AYK region commercial salmon fisheries and discusses the regional and international economic factors affecting the fisheries and their markets. He offers observations on barriers and opportunities to reduce costs, and to increase value and access new markets for these commercial fisheries.

Salmon are influenced by numerous ecological and human variables acting at multiple spatial and temporal scales. These papers highlight the importance of understanding the influence of socio-cultural and economic variables on salmon harvesters and on harvests at the village level (Magdanz et al. 2009; Howe and Martin 2009), the regional scale (Wolfe and Spaeder 2009; Knapp 2009), and well as at the national/international scale (Knapp 2009). These papers also remind us of the need to consider the ways that changing salmon populations, especially sharp declines, can alter social and cultural systems in the AYK region. Lastly, these papers underscore the important contributions of local and traditional knowledge, and the potential alternative management approaches to improve collaboration and coordination between fishery management and resource dependent communities.

References

AYK SSI (Arctic-Yukon-Kuskokwim Sustainable Salmon Initiative). 2006. Arctic-Yukon-Kuskokwim Salmon Research and Restoration Plan. Bering Sea Fishermen's Association, Anchorage, Alaska.

Brelsford, T. 2009. "We have to learn to work together": current perspectives on incorporating local and traditional/indigenous knowledge into Alaskan fishery management. Pages 381–394 *in* C. C. Krueger and C. E. Zimmerman, editors. Pacific salmon: ecology and management of western Alaska's populations. American Fisheries Society, Symposium 70, Bethesda, Maryland.

Howe, E. L., and S. Martin. 2009. Demographic change, economic conditions, and subsistence salmon harvests in Alaska's Arctic Yukon Kuskokwim region. Pages 433–461 *in* C. C. Krueger and C. E. Zimmerman, editors. Pacific salmon: ecology and management of western Alaska's populations. American Fisheries Society, Symposium 70, Bethesda, Maryland.

Knapp, G. 2009. Commercial salmon fisheries of the Arctic-Yukon-Kuskokwim region: economic challenges and opportunities. Pages 463–486 *in* C. C. Krueger and C. E. Zimmerman, editors. Pacific salmon: ecology and management of western Alaska's populations. American Fisheries Society, Symposium 70, Bethesda, Maryland.

Magdanz, J., E. Trigg, A. Ahmasuk, P. Nanouk, D. Koster, and K. Kamletz. 2009. Patterns and trends in subsistence salmon harvests, Norton Sound—Port Clarence area, Alaska 1994–2003. Pages 395–431 *in* C. C. Krueger and C. E. Zimmerman, editors. Pacific salmon: ecology and management of western Alaska's populations. American Fisheries Society, Symposium 70, Bethesda, Maryland.

Wolfe, R., and J. Spaeder. 2009. People and salmon of the Yukon and Kuskokwim drainages and Norton Sound in Alaska: fishery harvests, culture change, and local knowledge systems. Pages 349–379 *in* C. C. Krueger and C. E. Zimmerman, editors. Pacific salmon: ecology and management of western Alaska's populations. American Fisheries Society, Symposium 70, Bethesda, Maryland.

American Fisheries Society Symposium 70:349–379, 2009

People and Salmon of the Yukon and Kuskokwim Drainages and Norton Sound in Alaska: Fishery Harvests, Culture Change, and Local Knowledge Systems

ROBERT J. WOLFE[*]

Robert J. Wolfe and Associates
1332 Corte Lira, San Marcos, California 92069, USA

JOSEPH SPAEDER

AYK Sustainable Salmon Initiative / Bering Sea Fishermen's Association
P.O. Box 2087, Homer, Alaska 99603, USA

Abstract.—Salmon *Oncorhynchus* spp. is a staple food for the Native villages of the Yukon and Kuskokwim drainages and Norton Sound in Alaska. The economy of the area is characterized by the high production of wild foods for local use and low-per-capita monetary incomes. Traditional subsistence activities form the core of village economies. Subsistence harvests, the priority use of salmon designated by state and federal law, have displayed variable trends, primarily linked to local environmental variables and the food needs of people and sled dogs. Commercial fishing of western Alaska salmon stocks intensified during the early 1970s through 1980s, providing income to small-scale fishers selling to export markets. During the 1990s, commercial salmon harvests collapsed resulting in substantial decreases of income to villages. In the Yukon River drainage, families have culled dog teams in response to lower subsistence salmon harvests for dog food, impacting cultural traditions involving sled dogs. Declines in subsistence salmon harvests for food may lead to increased harvests of other wild-food species or cause human out-migration from villages; however, no programs are currently in place to monitor such effects. A growing number of case studies have documented the important contributions of Traditional Ecological Knowledge to fishery research as well as to the formulation of fisheries regulations.

Introduction

This chapter describes trends in the commercial and subsistence salmon *Oncorhynchus* spp. fisheries in western Alaska from the early 20th century to the present, including the fisheries of the Kuskokwim River, Yukon River, and Norton Sound drainages. Declines in the fisheries in each region and their effects on the economies and culture of local communities are described. In addition, the paper summarizes recent efforts to incorporate traditional ecological knowledge (TEK) into salmon research, fishery management, and stock enhancement programs. The chapter was written in support of the Arctic-Yukon-Kuskokwim (AYK) Sustainable Salmon Initiative, a research and restoration program examining the declines in western

*Corresponding author: wolfeassoc@cox.net

salmon Alaska stocks during the late 1990s and early 2000s (AYK SSI 2006).

Subsistence salmon fisheries have provided major sources of food for Alaska Native groups in western Alaska for centuries. Commercial fishing of western Alaska salmon stocks were developed early in the 20th century and intensified during the 1970s (Hilsinger et al. 2009, this volume). In western Alaska, commercial salmon fisheries offered special benefits to Alaska Native villages. Selling fish was an income source for cash-poor villagers, an income source that potentially was renewable and sustainable. Commercial fishing also drew on traditional fishing skills and required the use of boats, motors, and nets already owned by families for subsistence fishing. For local families, commercial fishing income was used to purchase equipment and supplies used for subsistence fishing and hunting. The industry helped reduce the balance of trade deficits of rural areas, paying for imported manufactured goods with fish exports. From the early 1970s into the 1990s, commercial fishing strengthened the economies and cultures of many western Alaska villages. Fishing labor was supplied by the local communities, the technology used was small scale, and risks were low to the participants. Core village subsistence activities were not eroded or replaced but reinforced with earnings of commercial fishers.

However, by the turn of the 21st century, the socio-economic system combining commercial and subsistence fishing was fraying. Two primary forces were at work causing this change. The first was new competition from the aquaculture industry outside the United States; a glut of farmed salmon and hatchery roe depressed world market prices and strained the economic viability of wild-stock fisheries in western Alaska. The second force was that salmon runs declined in western Alaska during the late 1990s and threatened the very existence of the commercial and subsistence fisheries, resulting in restrictive fishery regulations, including closures. The relationships between salmon and people rapidly changed, globally and locally. The purpose of this chapter is to describe the social, economic, and cultural dimensions of these events in western Alaska.

Regional Socio-economic Patterns

Three large geographic regions comprise the geographic focus of this paper– the Norton Sound drainages, the Yukon River drainage, and the Kuskokwim River drainage (the AYK region; Figure 1). In this area, settlements are small, generally less than 500 people, geographically dispersed, and remote from trade centers. Disastrous epidemics of smallpox, influenza, measles, and tuberculosis devastated Alaska Native populations in this region from the early 19th century into the early 20th century. However, by the mid-20th century Alaska Native populations turned a demographic corner in western Alaska, and began a half-century of rapid growth and socio-economic gains. Village populations in the AYK region have grown substantially during the last half century (1950–2000) (Table 1). In the Kuskokwim River drainage, village populations increased from 3,569 to 11,083 people in 36 villages; Bethel, the regional center, grew from 651 to 5,471 people. In the Yukon River drainage in Alaska, village populations grew from 4,316 to 12,248 people in 42 villages. In the Norton Sound drainage, village populations grew from 2,450 to 4,983 people in 14 villages; Nome, the regional center, grew from 1,876 to 3,505 people. Nome, however, did not grow between 1990 and 2000, while substantial village growth rates were far exceeded by Alaska's two urban centers of Anchorage and Fairbanks. Since 1950, the Anchorage area increased by nine-fold, from 35,021 to 319,240 people, primarily by immigration from outside

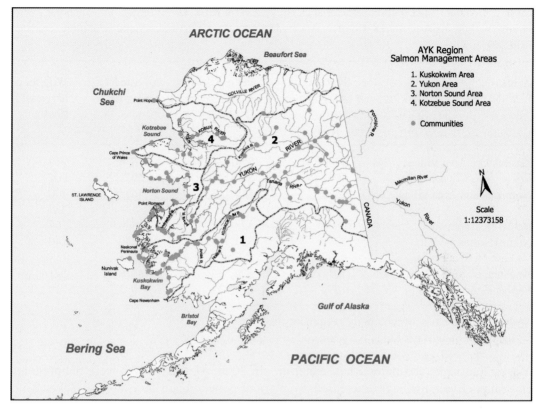

FIGURE 1. Map of the Arctic-Yukon-Kuskokwim region of Alaska.

TABLE 1. Human population trends, 1950–2000 Arctic-Yukon-Kuskokwim region, the Anchorage/Mat-Su area, and the Fairbanks area. (Source: U.S. Census Bureau. 2000)

	Years					
Area	1950	1960	1970	1980	1990	2000
Kuskokwim Area Villages (36)	3,589	5,411	5,965	7,774	9,585	11,083
Bethel (Kuskokwim)	651	1,258	2,416	3,576	4,674	5,471
Yukon Area Villages (42)	4,316	7,010	7,862	9,919	11,204	12,248
Norton Sound Area Villages (14)	2,450	2,775	2,817	3,526	4,202	4,983
Nome (Norton Sound)	1,876	2,316	2,357	2,506	3,500	3,505
AYK Region Total	12,882	18,770	21,417	27,301	33,165	37,290
Anchorage/Mat-Su Area	35,021	88,021	132,894	192,247	266,021	319,240
Fairbanks Area	18,129	42,992	45,864	53,983	77,720	82,840

TABLE 2. Economic and social characteristics Arctic-Yukon-Kuskokwim region, the Anchorage/Mat-Su area, and the Fairbanks area. (Source: Alaska Department of Community and Economic Development 2003).

Area	Percent Alaska Native (2000)	Per capita income (2000)	Adjusted per capita income (2000)*	Wild food harvests** (lbs)
Kuskokwim Area Villages (36)	93%	$9,087	$4,563	739
Yukon Area Villages (42)	89%	$10,403	$5,397	601
Norton Sound Area Villages (14)	93%	$10,382	$4,408	700
Bethel (Kuskokwim)	68%	$20,267	$12,530	261
Nome (Norton Sound)	59%	$23,402	$14,649	240
Anchorage/Mat-Su Area	10%	$20,166	$20,116	21
Fairbanks Area	10%	$24,525	$24,083	19

*Adjusted for the cost of food in the community
** Estimated pounds per capita per year (usable weights) during the 1990s

Alaska. Fairbanks, the major urban center in the Yukon River drainage, increased from 18,129 to 82,840 people. In 2000, the total population of the AYK area (37,290 people) was about half the size of Fairbanks and a tenth of the Anchorage area. Alongside people, dogs comprise another major segment of the area's demographic profile with significance to salmon. Historically, probably as many dogs were consuming salmon as people in the AYK area (discussed below). In 2002, half as many dogs as people were in Yukon River villages (5,345 dogs) (Brase and Hamner 2003), and their proportions in other areas were probably less.

The AYK area is the traditional homeland of several Alaska Native groups. The villages of coastal and lower river areas are primarily occupied by the Yup'ik and Inupiat. Athapaskans live in the upriver villages, including the Deg Hit'an and Upper Kuskokwim in the Kuskokwim River drainage and the Deg Hit'an, Holikachuk, Koyukon, Tanana, Gwich'in, and Han groups in the Yukon River drainage (Langdon 2002).

In 2000, Alaska Natives were the predominate population in the villages—Yukon River villages (89% Alaska Native), Kuskokwim River villages (93%), and Norton Sound villages (93%) (Table 2; Alaska Department of Community and Economic Development 2003). Two regional centers at Nome (59% Alaska Native) and Bethel (68% Alaska Native) showed more cultural mix with significant non-Native populations. By comparison, Fairbanks and Anchorage were predominately non-Native (10% Alaska Native). The patterns of use of salmon as human food and dog food are directly related to the cultural composition of communities. Cultural composition has been found to be the strongest predictor of wild-food harvest levels in Alaskan communities (Wolfe and Walker 1987).

The economies of AYK villages are distinct from those of urban Alaska. Urban areas have comparatively high monetary incomes and low wild-food harvests, while villages have low incomes and high wild-food harvests (Table 2). Based on the 2000 federal census, mean per capita incomes in AYK villages ($9,087–$10,382) were about half the incomes in Fairbanks ($20,166) and Anchorage ($24,525) (Table 2). Low incomes reflect relatively weak cash sectors in local village economies. The high costs of imported goods sold in villages further increases the economic disparity between village and city. When adjusted by the high cost of store food, village per capita incomes ($4,408–$5,397) were a fifth of those in urban areas, with regional centers intermediate (e.g., Bethel; Table 2). Because western Alaska is a cash-poor area, subsistence harvests and income from sustainable industries like commercial salmon fishing take on particular importance for families.

Wild-food harvests comprised the core of village economies in western Alaska in the late 20th century. Based on surveys conducted during the 1980s–1990 s, annual wild-food harvests for human consumption ranged between 601 and 739 lbs per person in AYK villages, or about two lbs per person per day (Table 2; Wolfe and Utermohle 2000). In contrast, annual wild-food harvests were low in Anchorage (19 lbs per person) and Fairbanks (21 lbs per person) where most food is imported from elsewhere. Wild-food harvests at Bethel and Nome are probably intermediate, but are unknown because of a lack of comprehensive household surveys. By adding in the monetary value of wild foods, village per capita incomes rise to about $15,000–$20,000 annually, closer to incomes in urban areas. This calculation assumes a replacement value of $20 per lb for finished subsistence products, an estimate between the market price of traditional Alaska Native cold-smoked salmon in Anchorage ($24 per lb) and $14 per lb of subsistence foods used for the Exxon Valdez settlement in the Gulf of Alaska (Duffield 1997).

General Commercial and Subsistence Relationships

The basic core of the local village economy is subsistence production (Figure 2; see Wolfe 2001; Wolfe et al. 1984; Langdon 1986; Schroeder et al. 1987). Fish runs are harvested by family groups (a domestic mode of production) frequently working from seasonal fish camps. The salmon catch is processed by family members (air dried, cold smoked, frozen, salted, canned, or fermented) into products that are consumed throughout the year. As a rule, a third of village households produce most of the subsistence foods consumed locally (Andrews 1988; Sumida 1986; Sumida and Alexander 1986; Sumida and Andersen 1990). The products are shared with other households, most frequently among extended family networks. Some subsistence products are shared or traded for small amounts of money. In addition, in many communities salmon is processed for dog food, supporting the cultural institutions dependent on sled dogs. Salmon production is part of an annual cycle of subsistence activities in which families participate. Salmon is a staple in most AYK communities, ranked among the top ten resources produced by weight, and is often in the top five resources used. However, the types and proportions of wild subsistence resources used vary substantially among villages.

In communities where commercial fisheries have developed, commercial fishing has become an adjunct to the core subsistence activities (Figure 2; Wolfe 1984). Commercial fishers commonly work within traditional fishing areas with gear used for subsistence fishing. Raw fish or roe are sold to licensed buyers, providing a flow of money to families. Some local jobs also are created in processing fish as frozen, canned, or dried products. Buyer-processors usually are business interests headquartered outside

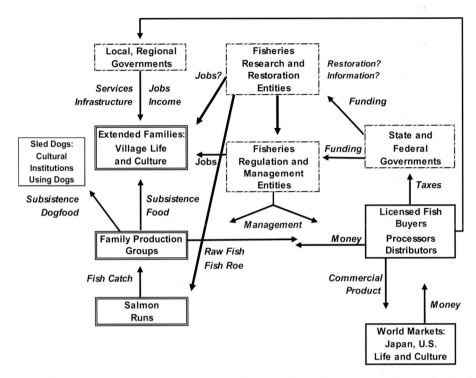

FIGURE 2. People and salmon relationships in the AYK region. Subsistence production is depicted within the four doubled lined boxes.

the region, but also include joint ventures, cooperatives, and businesses linked to Native corporations. The commercial products are distributed to markets in Japan, the United States, and elsewhere. In addition, commercial buyer-processors pay some local taxes.

The declines in commercial salmon fisheries that began in the late 1990s caused major reductions of income for families in western Alaska villages (Knapp 2009, this volume). The total exvessel value of the three fisheries (Yukon, Kuskokwim, and Norton Sound-Port Clarence areas) to commercial fishers fell from about $15.7 million in 1989 to about $2.0 million in 2002 (Table 3).

During the most recent decade, jobs created by local governments have become the primary source of wage income to extended families in villages. In this socio-economic system, commercial fishing and wage em-

ployment are integrated by families into the traditional domestic mode of production of subsistence foods. Salmon have value as both a subsistence product and as a source of monetary income within communities with commercial fisheries.

The fishing power of small-scale gill nets by local fishers is notable. The efficiency of the commercial fishery has increased over time with greater use of drift nets instead of set nets and with greater mobility of fishers using higher horsepower outboards. For example, in the past, Yukon River fishers have met or exceeded commercial harvest guideline ranges set by state management. This fishing power has required state management to shorten fishing periods to provide for escapement of salmon for spawning. Similar increases in efficiency in subsistence fishing methods have also occurred (Wolfe 1982, 1984).

TABLE 3. Income ($ USD) from commercial salmon fisheries by area, 1977–2008 (ex-vessel value). (Source: Alaska Commercial Fisheries Entry Commission).

Year	Yukon Area	Kuskokwim Area	Norton Sound– Port Clarence	Total Areas
1977	$4,267,466	$3,891,950	$546,010	$8,705,426
1978	$5,740,191	$2,337,470	$907,330	$8,984,991
1979	$7,171,515	$3,678,000	$878,792	$11,728,307
1980	$5,789,752	$2,725,134	$572,125	$9,087,011
1981	$10,020,605	$3,766,525	$761,658	$14,548,788
1982	$6,675,742	$4,213,954	$1,069,723	$11,959,419
1983	$6,964,229	$2,670,400	$946,232	$10,580,861
1984	$5,669,624	$5,809,000	$738,064	$12,216,688
1985	$7,019,369	$3,248,089	$818,477	$11,085,935
1986	$6,261,115	$4,746,089	$546,452	$11,553,656
1987	$7,202,358	$6,392,822	$517,894	$14,113,074
1988	$13,379,691	$12,514,489	$760,641	$26,654,821
1989	$10,179,350	$5,171,860	$319,489	$15,670,699
1990	$6,517,794	$4,894,580	$474,064	$11,886,438
1991	$9,552,796	$3,971,423	$413,479	$13,937,698
1992	$11,331,871	$5,295,912	$463,616	$17,091,399
1993	$5,427,795	$3,962,890	$368,723	$9,759,408
1994	$4,786,687	$5,201,611	$863,060	$10,851,358
1995	$7,150,405	$4,209,752	$356,164	$11,716,321
1996	$4,797,993	$2,900,603	$292,264	$7,990,860
1997	$5,889,300	$1,058,808	$326,618	$7,274,726
1998	$1,955,891	$1,634,495	$351,410	$3,941,796
1999	$5,086,539	$551,725	$82,638	$5,720,902
2000	$734,239	$1,197,149	$143,621	$2,075,009
2001	--	--	$56,921	$56,921
2002	$1,722,367	$322,893	$2,941	$2,048,201
2003	$1,997,568	$913,719	$64,859	$2,976,146
2004	$2,971,090	$1,566,933	$139,616	$4,677,639
2005	$2,529,479	$1,192,267	$365,820	$4,087,566
2006	$3,829,613	$1,233,758	$483,163	$5,546,534
2007	$2,623,004	$1,377,484	$696,133	$4,696,621
2008	$1,428,029	$1,485,574	$759,309	$3,672,912

During the 1980s–1990s, a number of community studies were conducted within the Alaska Department of Fish and Game, Division of Subsistence documenting the general pattern of subsistence and employment for villages described above (Fall 1990). For the Kuskokwim area, community studies occurred within the villages of Chuathbaluk and Sleetmute (Charnley 1984); Kwethluk (Coffing 1992); Lime Village (Kari 1983); Nunapitchuk (Andrews 1989); Stony River (Kari 1985); Tuluksak (Andrews and Peterson 1983); central Kuskokwim communities of Aniak, Crooked Creek, and Red Devil (Charnley 1982; Brelsford et al. 1986; Stickney 1981a); and upper Kuskokwim River communities of McGrath, Nikolai, Takotna, and Telida (Stickney 1980; Stickney 1981b; Stokes 1984). For the Yukon River drainage, community studies occurred in Beaver (Sumida and Alexander 1986); Galena (Marcotte 1990); Kaltag (Wheeler 1987); Minto (Andrews 1988); Nenana (Shinkwin and Case 1984); Russian Mission (Pete 1991); Stevens Village (Sumida 1986); Tanana (Case and Halpin 1990); lower Yukon River communities of Alakanuk, Emmonak, Kotlik, Mountain Village, Sheldon Point, and Stebbins (Pete and Wolfe 1991; Wolfe 1981); Yukon River-Koyukuk River communities of Allakaket, Alatna, Bettles, Evansville, and Hughes (Marcotte and Haynes 1984; Marcotte 1986; also Nelson et al. 1982); and upper Yukon River-Porcupine River communities of Arctic Village, Birch Creek, Chalkyitsik, Fort Yukon, and Venetie (Caulfield 1983; Caulfield et al. 1983; Sumida and Andersen 1990). For the Norton Sound area, community studies occurred within the villages of Brevig Mission and Golovin (Conger and Magdanz 1990); Gambell and Savoonga (Ellanna 1983); Nome (Magdanz and Olanna 1984; Magdanz and Olanna 1986); and Shaktoolik (Thomas 1982). For the Yukon River-Kuskokwim River coastal delta and bay areas, studies occurred within Hooper Bay and

Kwigillingok (Stickney 1984) and Goodnews Bay and Quinhagak (Wolfe et al. 1984; Wolfe 1989). In addition to the descriptions in the community studies listed above, several other reports exist describing subsistence salmon fisheries in the AYK area, including for the Kuskokwim River fisheries (Andrews and Coffing 1986; Stokes 1982; Walker and Coffing 1993); for the Yukon River fisheries (Andrews 1986; Caulfield 1981; Huntington 1981; Marcotte 1982; Wolfe 1982); and for the Norton Sound fisheries (Bue and Lean 1999; Magdanz 1992; Magdanz and Punguk 1981; Magdanz et al. 2002; Thomas 1980a,b). Annual subsistence salmon harvest statistics are found in several sources, including for the Kuskokwim River drainage (Alaska Department of Fish and Game 2003a, 2003b; Burkey et al. 2002); and for the Yukon River drainage (Borba and Hamner 2000, 2001; Brase and Hamner 2002, 2003; McNeil 2002).

Trends in Subsistence Fisheries

This section presents and discusses the general trends in subsistence fishing for each of the three sub-regions. Elsewhere in this volume, trends in salmon run sizes and subsistence and commercial fisheries are discussed in detail for the Yukon River drainage (Bue et al. 2009, this volume; Evenson et al. 2009, this volume), the Kuskokwim River drainage and bay (Linderman and Bergstrom 2009, this volume), and the Norton Sound area drainages (Menard et al. 2009, this volume).

Management responses to the declining runs during the 1990s and early 2000s followed state mandates that required management for sustainability, conservation of fish stocks, and subsistence priorities (Hilsinger et al. 2009). Commercial fisheries were restricted first, and if deemed necessary were followed by restrictions of subsistence fisheries. State law requires that fishing regulations provide a reasonable opportunity for subsistence uses when harvestable surpluses are sufficient (AS 16.05.258). To meet this requirement in the AYK area, the Alaska Board of Fisheries have established subsistence harvest thresholds (amounts necessary for subsistence) for eleven western Alaska salmon stock groupings that represent reasonable opportunity standards for subsistence (Table 4).

General trends in subsistence fisheries are presented and discussed below for the Kuskokwim River, Yukon River, and Norton Sound drainages. Commercial fishing trends are also included within selected Figures for each drainage to provide a broader perspective on total salmon harvests. Unlike commercial harvests, no state-imposed guideline harvest caps for subsistence salmon fisheries have occurred, with the exception of one sub-district in the Norton Sound region using Tier II restrictions (Menard et al. 2009). Subsistence production levels have been essentially self-limiting because production is for local use rather than for sale. Until recently, in most communities and for most species, local demand has been substantially below harvestable surplus levels. The trend over the past decade of declining subsistence harvests in each of these three drainages is significant. This trend is discussed in greater detail below.

Subsistence harvests in the Yukon River drainage of all species of salmon grew between the mid-1960s to the early 1990s as a function of increased food needs of growing villages and dog populations (Figure 3). However, with declining salmon runs, subsistence harvests saw a steady decline during the 1990s, primarily representing declines in harvests for dog food (discussed later in this paper).

TABLE 4. Amounts necessary for subsistence by salmon stock and area as determined by the Alaska Board of Fisheries. (Source: Alaska Administrative Codes).

Area	Species/Stock	Amount Necessary	Code
Kuskokwim River Drainage	Chinook salmon	64,500–83,000	5AAC 01.286
	Chum salmon	39,500–75,500	
	Sockeye salmon	27,500–39,500	
	Coho salmon	24,500–35,000	
Kuskokwim Area (bay drainages)	Salmon	7,500–13,500	5AAC 01.286
Yukon-Northern Area	Chinook salmon	45,500–66,704	5AAC 01.236
	Summer chum salmon	83,500–142,192	
	Fall chum salmon	89,500–167,100	
	Coho salmon	20,500–51,980	
Norton Sound District, Subdistrict 1	Chum salmon	3,430–5,716	5AAC 01.186
Norton Sound–Port Clarence Area	Salmon	96,000–160,000	5AAC 01.186

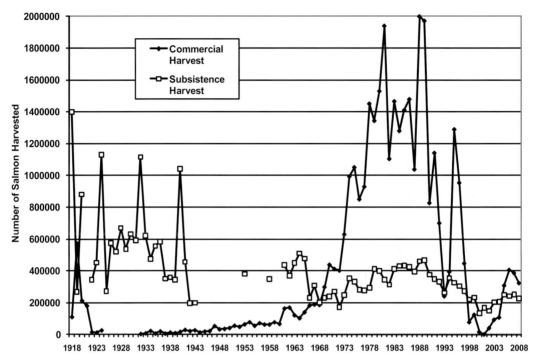

FIGURE 3. Commercial and subsistence salmon catches, Yukon River drainage, Alaska 1918–2008. (Source: Alaska Department of Fish and Game 2007).

Since 1990, total subsistence salmon harvests by Yukon River communities in Alaska decreased about 240,800 fish, from about a total of 375,556 salmon in 1990 to 134,759 salmon in 2000 (a decline of about 64%), with harvests rebounding somewhat to 226,979 salmon by 2008. The largest declines occurred with fall chum *O. keta* and coho *O. kisutch* salmon (Figures 4 and 5). Subsistence fall chum salmon harvests decreased 89% from 167,900 fish (1990) to 19,306 fish (2000), while coho salmon harvests decreased 66% from 43,460 fish (1990) to 14,717 fish (2000). Harvests of fall chum and coho salmon have been near or below the lower subsistence thresholds since 1998. Subsistence summer chum salmon harvests decreased 49% from 115,609 fish (1990) to 58,385 fish (2001), and have also fallen below the lower subsistence threshold during the last ten years (Figure 6). Subsistence Chinook *O. tshawytscha* salmon harvests

decreased 26% from 48,587 fish (1990) to 35,841 fish (2000), falling below the lower subsistence threshold in 2000 and 2002 (Figure 7).

Similar general trends occurred for the subsistence salmon fisheries of the Kuskokwim River drainage as described above for the Yukon River fisheries (Figure 8; also see Howe and Martin 2009, this volume; Linderman and Bergstrom 2009). Since 1989, total subsistence salmon harvests by Kuskokwim River communities decreased about 130,000 fish, from about 309,000 salmon in 1989 to 178,300 salmon in 2007, a decline of about 42.3% (Burkey et al. 2002). Harvest trends before 1989 cannot be assessed with precision because surveys conducted from 1960–1989 used different assessment methods. Subsistence chum salmon harvests fell 63.3% from 139,687 fish (1989) to 51,308 fish (Figure 9), while coho salmon harvests fell 52.6% from 52,918 fish (1989) to 25,107 fish (2007)

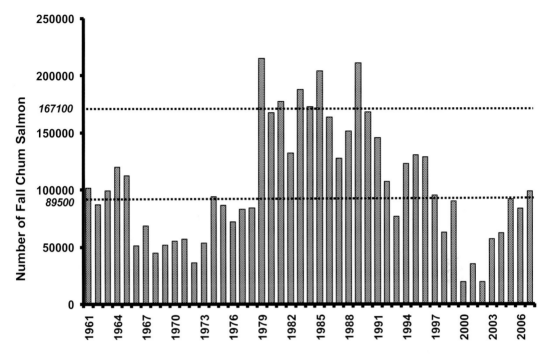

FIGURE 4. Subsistence fall chum salmon harvests, Yukon River, 1961–2007, with upper and lower bounds of subsistence harvest thresholds shown as dashed lines. (Source: Alaska Department of Fish and Game 2007).

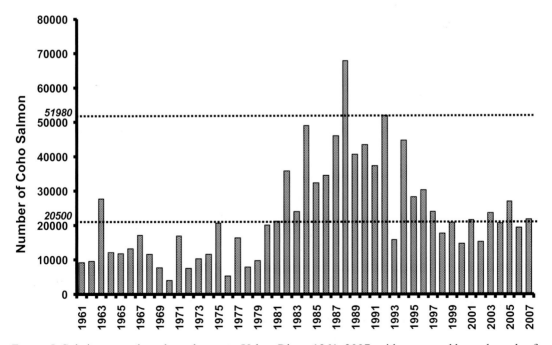

FIGURE 5. Subsistence coho salmon harvests, Yukon River, 1961–2007, with upper and lower bounds of subsistence harvest thresholds shown as dashed lines. (Source: Alaska Department of Fish and Game 2007).

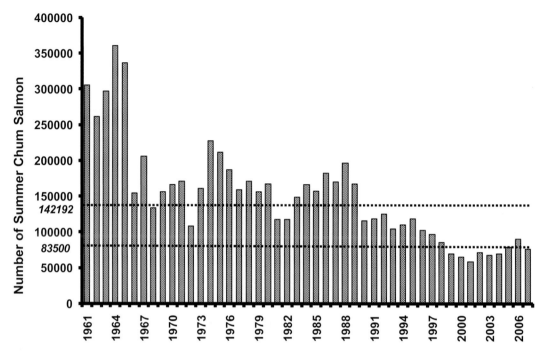

FIGURE 6. Subsistence summer chum salmon harvests, Yukon River, 1961–2007, with upper and lower bounds of subsistence harvest thresholds shown as dashed lines. (Source: Alaska Department of Fish and Game 2007).

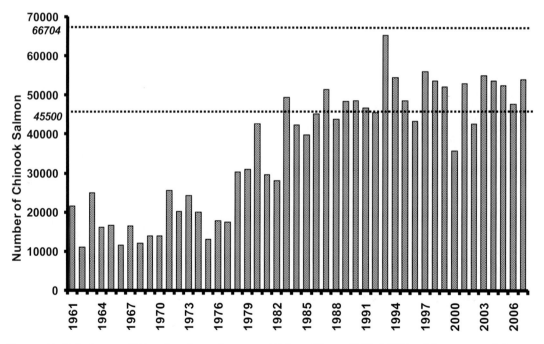

FIGURE 7. Subsistence Chinook salmon harvests, Yukon River, 1961–2007, with upper and lower bounds of subsistence harvest thresholds shown as dashed lines. (Source: Alaska Department of Fish and Game 2007).

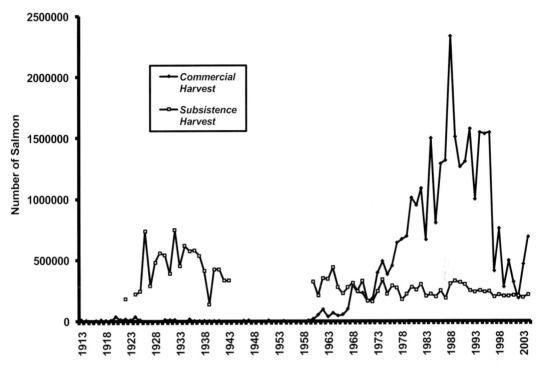

FIGURE 8. Salmon harvests, 1913–2004, Kuskokwim area. (Source: Alaska Department of Fish and Game 2007).

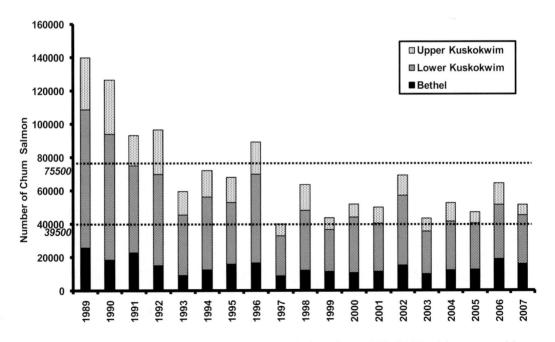

FIGURE 9. Subsistence chum salmon harvests, Kuskokwim River, 1989–2007, with upper and lower bounds of subsistence harvest thresholds shown as dashed lines. (Source: Alaska Department of Fish and Game 2007).

(Figure 10)—each harvests approaching the lower bounds of the amounts necessary for subsistence. Subsistence Chinook and sockeye *O. nerka* salmon harvests (Figures 11–12), while approaching the lower subsistence thresholds, show less definite trends compared with chum and coho salmon. As these trends show, reduced harvests have affected each segment of the river, including lower river communities (Kuskokwim River mouth to the village of Tuluksak), upper river communities (Lower Kalskag to Nikolai), and the regional center, Bethel. The greater harvest potential in the lower river, where most of the human population lives, has posed potential problems for securing adequate harvests for upriver villages. From 2001 to 2006, weekly subsistence fishing closures of three consecutive days in length were implemented during portions of the subsistence harvest season, depending on the in-season estimated abundance of Chinook and chum salmon runs in the Kuskokwim River. The aim of this fishing schedule was to provide fisheries closure - windows for fish passage – that would allow more large fish to reach the spawning grounds than in the past and at the same time provide upriver villages a better opportunity to meet their subsistence needs.

In the lower Kuskokwim Bay (villages of Quinhagak, Goodnews Bay, and Platinum), subsistence salmon harvests declined about 42% from 12,549 salmon (1989) to 7,276 salmon (1996) (Figure 13). Harvests rebounded after 1998 in this area. These estimates did not include harvests within other coastal communities north of the Kuskokwim River mouth (Newtok, Nightmute, Toksook Bay, Tununak, Chefornak, and Mekoryak), where salmon harvests, thought to be comparatively small, were not consistently monitored.

The Norton Sound region as a whole has experienced subsistence harvest declines over the past decade (Figure 14). Subsistence salmon harvest surveys (excluding pink salmon *O. gorbuscha*) in Norton Sound-Port

Clarence Area communities fell from 87,980 to 36,655 salmon (58.3%) from 1995 to 2007 (Magdanz et al. 2009, this volume).

In the Nome area (Norton Sound Subdistrict 1) during the 1990s, subsistence harvests of chum salmon consistently fell below the amount deemed necessary for subsistence uses (Figure 15). This required the Alaska Board of Fisheries in 1999 to establish the first "Tier II" subsistence salmon fishery in Alaska (Menard et al. 2009). Tier II means a subsistence fishery managed to limit participants to those individuals with the greatest dependency and fewest alternatives to fishing salmon. The subsistence restrictions in this area created substantial hardships for the residents of Nome. Local fish camps were idled and traditional fishing areas were closed for a time, forcing shifts of fishing activities away from rivers to marine harvest areas and to more distant fishing locations, and at times, creating competition with neighboring village-based fisheries. In response to these declined stocks, new management plans have focused on better in-season monitoring and ways to restore runs in individual stream systems in the Nome area. Co-management partnerships subsequently developed and cooperatively brought together state, federal, and local entities including Kawerak, the regional Native nonprofit corporation, and the Bering Sea Fishermen's Association, to fund salmon research and restoration projects.

Beginning in 2006, the harvestable surpluses of returning chum salmon to the Nome sub-district streams increased sufficiently that Tier II restrictions were removed. At the same time, increases in runs of pink salmon in the Norton Sound district provided additional fish, although of less quality than chum salmon. Accounts of the Nome fishery history are found in Thomas (1980a,b), Magdanz and Punguk (1981), Magdanz (1992), Magdanz and Olanna (1984, 1986), Bue and Lean (1999), Magdanz et al. (2002), and Menard et al. (2009).

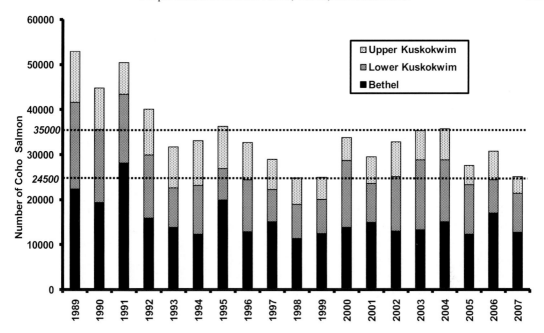

FIGURE 10. Subsistence coho salmon harvests, Kuskokwim River, 1989–2007, with upper and lower bounds of subsistence harvest thresholds shown as dashed lines. (Source: Alaska Department of Fish and Game 2007).

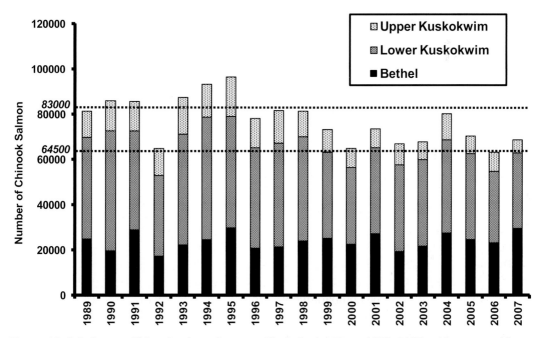

FIGURE 11. Subsistence Chinook salmon harvests, Kuskokwim River, 1989–2007, with upper and lower bounds of subsistence harvest thresholds shown as dashed lines. (Source: Alaska Department of Fish and Game 2007).

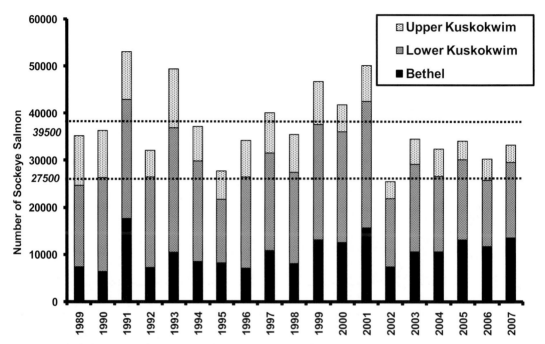

FIGURE 12. Subsistence sockeye salmon harvests, Kuskokwim River, 1989–2007, with upper and lower bounds of subsistence harvest thresholds shown as dashed lines. (Source: Alaska Department of Fish and Game 2007).

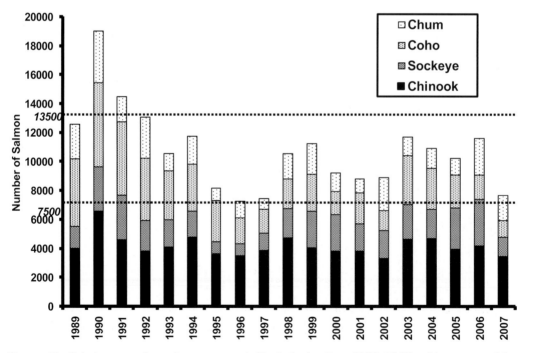

FIGURE 13. Subsistence salmon harvests, south Kuskokwim Bay, 1989–2007, with upper and lower bounds of subsistence harvest thresholds shown as dashed lines. (Source: Alaska Department of Fish and Game 2007).

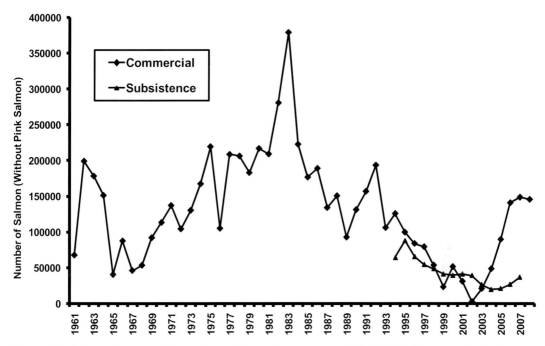

FIGURE 14. Salmon harvests, Norton Sound–Port Clarence area, 1961–2008. (Source: Alaska Department of Fish and Game 2007).

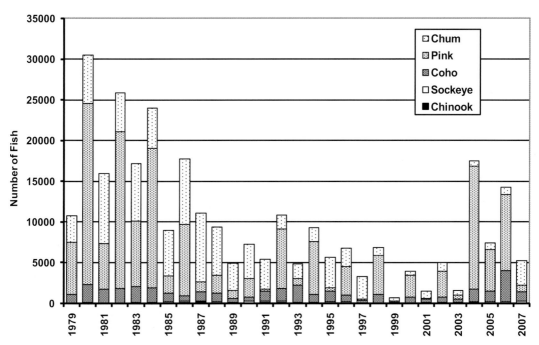

FIGURE 15. Subsistence salmon harvests, Nome Subdistrict, 1979–2007. (Source: Alaska Department of Fish and Game 2007).

Dogs and Salmon

Dogs are major consumers of chum and coho salmon from western Alaskan stocks, especially in the Yukon River drainage, but also to lesser extents in the Kuskokwim River and Bay and Norton Sound areas (Andersen 1992a; b; Gilbert and O'Malley 1921:145; Wolfe 1979:139, 144; Wolfe et al. 2001). For example, during the 1990s the primary use of fall chum (72%) and coho (69%) salmon in Yukon River drainage communities was for feeding dogs based on averages over the time period. The primary use of summer chum salmon (64%) from the Yukon River was for human food. Summer chum salmon harvested by lower river communities were used as human food whereas most summer chum salmon harvested by upriver communities were fed to dogs. Chinook salmon were harvested almost exclusively for human food, although dogs may be fed scraps, diseased fish, and, occasionally, small "jack" salmon.

Throughout the historic period dog teams have been used for winter travel. During the late 20th century, dog teams in Yukon River villages were used for multiple purposes including transportation, hauling goods, subsistence hunting and fishing, subsistence trapping, and racing at winter festivals. Surveys from the early 1990s have indicated that most teams in villages still serve multiple purposes, of which racing is one (Andersen 1992a). Dog mushing has become an educational tool for village youth, who, in the care and maintenance of dog teams, acquire skills, work ethics, and knowledge directly applicable to subsistence activities. "Transportation" is specifically listed as a subsistence use in state and federal statutes. Accordingly, harvesting salmon for dog food is managed under subsistence fishing regulations as a subsistence use.

Salmon harvests for dog food in the AYK region peaked during the early 20th century. During this time period, families commonly kept somewhat less than a dozen sled dogs for general transportation, hauling wood, water, and supplies, trapping, and hunting. In addition, mail carriers were paid under territorial contracts to haul freight on dog sledges between communities. Commercial haulers typically maintained many dogs and ran teams of 10–20 dogs. Dog populations fell during the early-to-mid 20th century as aircraft replaced dogs for transporting freight during winter. Dog population numbers declined again during the 1960s, when their function was replaced by snow machines. The fewest numbers of dogs were maintained in the early 1970s. During the 1970s, dog populations began to increase as part of a revival of dog mushing, especially in interior Alaska. The first Iditarod race was run in 1973 and early rural champions helped revitalize dog mushing as a cultural institution.

In the Yukon River drainage, dog numbers declined from 1966 to 1972 based on information collected by annual state salmon harvest surveys (Figure 16; Brase and Hamner 2003; McNeil 2002; Wolfe et al. 2001). In a seven-year period dog populations increased from about 1,804 dogs (1972) to somewhat over 5,000 dogs (1979). During the 1980s, dog populations in the Yukon River drainage stabilized between about 5,000–6,000 dogs. In the early 1990s, dog populations fed subsistence salmon showed another jump, in part because urban residents in the Fairbanks area were allowed to harvest subsistence salmon (a result of *McDowell v Alaska*). The number of dogs owned by salmon-fishing households peaked at about 8,700 dogs in 1993. From this high point, dog populations decreased during the mid-to-late 1990s to about 5,275 dogs in 2006. Trends in dog populations cannot be tracked in the Kuskokwim River or the Norton Sound area because little historic information exists.

The declining numbers of dogs along the Yukon River during the mid-to-late 1990s were associated with declining harvests of chum and coho salmon for dog food (Figure 16) in a number of Yukon River management districts (Figure 17). Overall, Yukon River salmon harvests for feeding dogs in 2002 were 81% lower than harvests in 1992 (Figure 18). The substantial declines in harvests for dog food have occurred in all Yukon River districts, including declines of 85% in Districts 1–2, 78% in Districts 3–4, 84% in District 5, and 77% in District 6 (Figure 17). However, in terms of numbers of fish, the upriver districts have been most severely affected (Figure 19).

Historically, dogs have been culled, sold, or given away in times of salmon shortages. Trends during the 1990s were consistent with these past practices. In Yukon River drainage villages in Alaska, 39% fewer dogs were present in 2002 than in 1992 (Figure 16). The largest decreases in dog populations were in upriver districts: 29% (District 3–4), 37% (District 5), and 69% (District 6). In lower river villages (Districts 1–2) where salmon were less commonly fed to dogs, dog populations were only 5% lower. Families in upriver areas were more likely to cull dog lots in response to declining chum and coho salmon runs than lower river families.

Relationships between dog numbers and salmon harvests for dog food are complex. In the 1990s, most dogs were fed a mixture of foods, with upper river villages using more salmon than lower river villages, and smaller dog lots using more salmon per dog than larger lots (Andersen 1992). Trends in salmon harvests for human food and for dog food from 1990 to 2002 showed a decline in both, but much more for dog food (Figure 20). Analysis of existing data sets might find statistical relationships between variables such as salmon run size, salmon harvests per dog, district, dog lot size, and commercial dog food use. Information from this type of analysis might be applied in management. Some additional flexibility may be possible in subsistence management regulations, such as identifying reasonable opportunity standards for dog food distinct from salmon harvests for human food, based on customary and traditional practices. Household guideline caps on dog food harvests during low salmon runs might reduce exploitation rates while providing a reasonable opportunity for other subsistence uses. Under such an approach, increased salmon escapements could result from forgone harvests by the largest dog lots specializing in breeding and selling dogs.

Traditional Ecological Knowledge

The term TEK (Traditional Ecological Knowledge) refers to local knowledge gained from long-term experience in a fishery (Berkes et al. 1991; Fehr and Hurst 1996; Miraglia 1998; Moncrieff and Huntington 2002; Moncrieff and Klein 2003; Nakashima 1990; SP Research Associates and Lalande 1991; Wenzel 1999; Yukon River Drainage Fisheries Association 2002; Brelsford 2009, this volume). Local bodies of knowledge exist about salmon, part of the cultural traditions of Alaska Natives and other long-term users of salmon. Local systems of knowledge commonly exist alongside those of academicians, biologists, and government managers. In western Alaska, formal partnerships are being created to bring together salmon experts from these different traditions, such as the Kuskokwim River Salmon Management Working Group (Linderman and Bergstrom 2009). More complete understandings of fish and fisheries result from the collaborations and relationships that develop within such groups. Scientists and managers benefit from access to local knowledge, and local residents gain knowledge from the scientists and managers. The partnerships establish procedures for collecting, sharing, analyzing, interpreting, and using information.

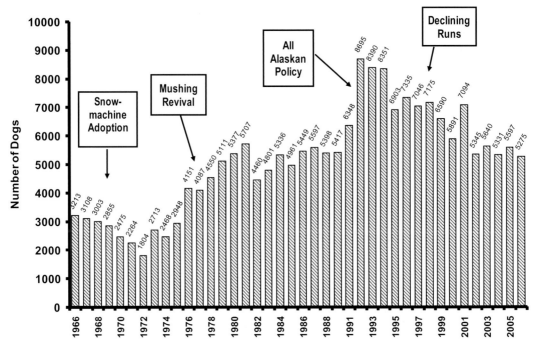

FIGURE 16. Dog population, Yukon River drainage—Alaska, 1966–2006. (Sources: Alaska Department of Fish and Game 2007 and Brase and Hamner 2003; McNeil 2002; Wolfe et al. 2001).

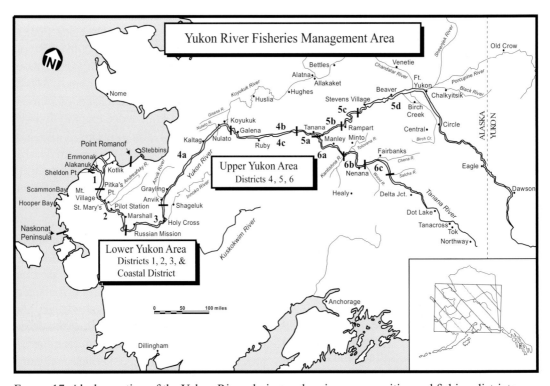

FIGURE 17. Alaska portion of the Yukon River drainage showing communities and fishing districts.

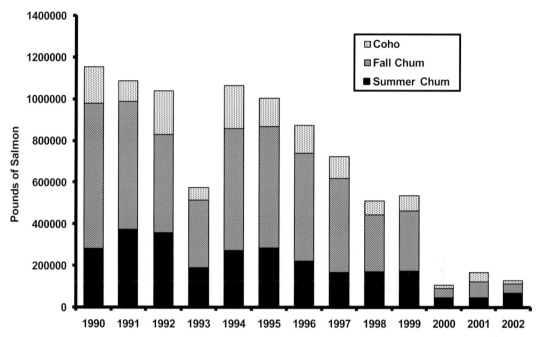

FIGURE 18. Subsistence salmon harvests for dog food, Alaska portion of the Yukon River drainage, 1990–2002. (Source: Alaska Department of Fish and Game 2007).

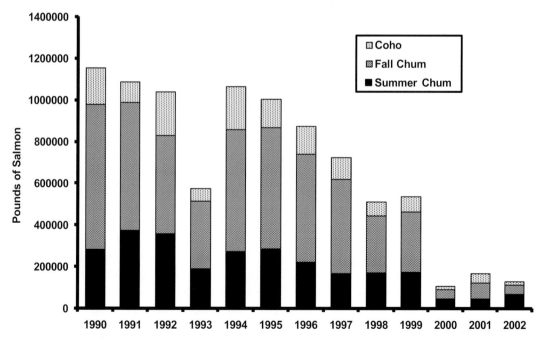

FIGURE 19. Salmon harvested for dog food, all districts in the Alaska portion of the Yukon River drainage, 1990–2002. (Source: Alaska Department of Fish and Game 2007).

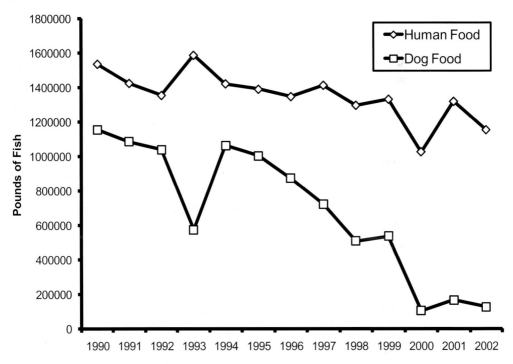

FIGURE 20. Subsistence salmon harvests for human consumption or dog food, Yukon Districts 1–6, 1990–2002 (lbs. of fish). (Source: Alaska Department of Fish and Game 2007).

TEK has entered the salmon regulatory system through the state's fish and game advisory committee system, the federal regional subsistence council system, and *ad hoc* committees formed during Alaska Board of Fisheries meetings. Through such advisory bodies, local experts have formal channels for creating and commenting on proposed fishing regulations (gear, seasons, areas, and so forth), as well as management elements like escapement goals, harvest goals, and in-season monitoring. At advisory meetings, fishery managers typically share information on the previous year's run characteristics, escapements, harvests, and management actions. TEK undoubtedly influences salmon regulations through these reviews. The collaborations necessarily are constrained by the formal meeting formats, the particular areas of expertise of participants, and the regulatory issues on the agenda. The information exchanged within the advisory sessions rare-

ly makes it into a published record. The resulting proceedings may become part of local oral histories, minutes, or written comments filed within a regulatory agency.

TEK may provide input to in-season management decision making of salmon fisheries through co-management entities like YRDFA (Yukon River Drainage Fisheries Association) and the Kuskokwim River Salmon Management Working Group (no similar co-management entity exists in the Norton Sound area). Consultation with co-management entities has been a relatively new component of in-season management on the Kuskokwim and Yukon Rivers, developed during times of low salmon returns. In-season consultations are held between fishery managers and stakeholder entities, such as through weekly teleconferences with Yukon River fishers (Bue et al. 2009). Up-to-date information is exchanged on run strength, catch levels, escapements, water conditions, management options, and other aspects of salmon returns.

Only a few research projects specifically designed to gather and analyze TEK about fish have occurred in the AYK region. Moncrieff and Klein (2003) compiled information on salmon stocks, abundance, and life cycles along the Yukon River, based on interviews with 29 residents of four villages. The project explored several general topics pertaining to salmon. Information provided by local experts on *Ichthyophonus*, a disease that affects salmon, suggests that the disease was historically present in Yukon River Chinook salmon stocks and that numbers of infected fish increased during the 1990s and were exceptionally prevalent. This type of information is pertinent for work on stock-size disease relationships (YRDFA 2002). Information on the number and timing of Chinook salmon runs and traditional indicators of run strength are potentially pertinent for management. The work illustrates that expert knowledge is often localized and derived from long-term observations within traditional-use areas. To describe aspects at large spatial scales, such as salmon life histories within an entire drainage like the Yukon River, combining and synthesizing information from local experts in different places along the river would be required.

Andersen and Fleener (2001) explored beaver-whitefish (*Castor canadensis-Coregonus* spp.) interactions in the Yukon Flats through interviews with fifteen local experts. According to their TEK analysis, during this past century, the Yukon Flats area of the upper Yukon River in Alaska have dried so that some wetlands have transitioned into bottom lands. Concurrently, since the mid-20th century, beaver populations have expanded as fur trapping has declined. Seasonal, high-water flood events have been less frequent. These changes have increased beaver dams and the likelihood that the seasonal movements of fish have been impeded by the dams. Tradi-

tionally, some Alaska Native groups cleared key waterways connecting main-stem and peripheral stream systems to help increase water flow and assist fish migrations. This TEK study focused on declining whitefish populations. How salmon stocks might fit into such ecological processes remains an unexplored research question. A logical next step to this type of research would be to identify affected geographic areas or fish stocks and integrate information on snowfall, rainfall, hydrology, and fish life cycles as well as recent beaver management practices.

The systematic collection of information on climate, habitat, and resource changes as observed at the local level has been an unexplored research area. Information on changes in critical habitats such as near-shore rearing areas or inland spawning areas may be relevant to stock trends. For example, during the early 1980s, residents from the village of Stebbins informed the first author (Wolfe) of earlier springs and later freeze-ups in Norton Sound than in the past. Usually sea ice broke about June 8–10, followed immediately by the first herring *Clupea pallasi* run, but break-up was now occurring in late May with earlier arrivals of herring and salmon. This observation was corroborated down the coast at the village Emmonak, which often did not get fuel oil from St. Michael before June 15–20 because of ice but recently ice has not been a problem. One expert observed that more Chinook salmon were being taken at St. Michael—"they never used to get kings [Chinook salmon]," and that beaver were moving downriver into the coastal flats— "they never used to be there." TEK studies can be designed to collect and analyze this type of trend information. This type of information is possibly relevant to salmon trends, but it remains an untapped research area.

TEK studies are more likely to yield information to help understand salmon stocks if the studies use collaborations of local experts, natural scientists, and social scientists.

The connection of disciplines should occur in the field while collecting data, not afterward with natural scientists reading a social science report and wondering how the data and observations might apply to their research and management problems. Studies with a focus on specific ecological questions will produce better information than general surveys. Small-scale, discrete projects can collect information around specific ecological questions pertaining to salmon. TEK collaborations represent new methodologies that can be applied to difficult ecological and broad-scale questions.

Some results of TEK studies may challenge basic assumptions within scientific traditions. A TEK study of western Alaska salmon fisheries found that in Yup'ik ecological models, fish were assumed to be particularly sensitive to human touch and waste (Wolfe 1989; Gross 1991). Under this ecological model, catch-and-release fishing was thought to entail substantial risks to salmon stocks. This traditional knowledge about salmon-human interactions stirred controversy, because it challenged catch-and-release fishing practices assumed to have acceptable mortality rates by state biologists (see Albertson 2009; this volume; Burr 2009; this volume). The Board of Fisheries considered both the Yup'ik and sport fishing models in deliberating regulations for salmon fishing in the Togiak River and Kanektok River drainages.

A workshop on TEK by YRDFA identified a list of research ideas that might be explored with TEK methods. Topics included documenting local food web, historic fish cycles and fishers responses to them in local areas, and changes in climate on local salmon and salmon habitats (Moncrieff and Huntington 2002).

Information from interviews with local residents that contain TEK are stored in databases for Bristol Bay, Gulf of Alaska, Copper Basin, and for marine mammals, all maintained by the Alaska Department of Fish and Game. The AYK area as yet has no single computerized text database of key respondent materials. As TEK studies are funded, a centralized database for the AYK area would provide a single repository of information. Computerized text databases allow for information to be accessed under key word searches. The primary uses of text databases are for exploring topics of potential interest. Like harvest databases, databases of interview texts are unanalyzed data repositories rather than analyzed materials. In addition to scientific users, text databases are of potential use to school systems as repositories of ecological and cultural information from local experts that are accessible to students.

Discussion

Declining salmon harvests placed stress on the capacity of villages dependent on western Alaska salmon stocks to support themselves. However, the specific details of the cultural effects are unknown because little information has been gathered or published documenting local responses to the recent salmon shortages. The lack of information leaves more questions than answers regarding the extent of economic difficulties of families and villages caused by salmon downturns in abundance.

Village families are accustomed to dynamic natural systems and thus are exceptionally resourceful in dealing with harvest shortfalls of particular wild-food species. In response to the declining abundance of a food species, families may intensify food gathering efforts, such as spending more days harvesting salmon, using more gear, or moving to other locations. Families also may reduce their efforts to harvest a depressed stock. Both types of responses were documented for marine mammals hunters faced with recent declining harbor seal and sea lion populations in the Gulf of Alaska (Wolfe et al. 2002).

Another potential response is for families to increase harvests of other wild resources to make up for shortfalls in subsistence food or monetary income. The details of such food replacement strategies remain to be described. Which species may be substituted, in which villages, and the effects over the short- and long-term periods are unanswered questions. The information from the few community studies in the AYK area is stored in the Community Profile Database of the Alaska Department of Fish and Game. This data set indicates that the mixes of wild resources vary considerably between villages. The abilities of families to replace salmon shortfalls are constrained by the types and abundance of other wild resources available in the areas village residents use for subsistence harvests. In general, coastal villages probably have more wild-food alternatives than inland villages because maritime ecosystems are more diverse and richer. Historically, coastal human populations were larger than inland populations, probably reflecting more secure and abundant food resources. However, from the limited information available, one cannot identify with certainty which villages would be at most risk from reduced salmon runs.

Based on experiences in 1998 and 2000, disaster relief programs that airlift fish to villages cannot hope to replace subsistence salmon shortfalls. Despite considerable effort and cost, a relatively small proportion of the salmon shortfalls were replaced through the airlift programs in 1998 and 2000. By comparison, voucher systems allowing families to purchase subsistence equipment to fish and hunt, or to purchase replacement store foods, appear to be more flexible and efficient emergency relief programs.

If commercial fisheries become marginal economic industries, permit holders are likely to pursue other forms of work. During the last decade, local and regional governments have been major sources of village employment, such as in local school systems, facilities maintenance, and community capital improvement projects. Revenues from Community Development Quota (CDQ) fisheries fund employment in villages having those programs. Commercial fishing might follow the course of trapping in rural villages. With falling fur markets in the mid-20th century, fewer villagers than in the past trapped for sale, fur exports declined, partnerships between trappers and trading companies disappeared, and many trap lines were abandoned. Trapping for local subsistence uses continued while harvests for export sale substantially diminished in importance.

Out-migration by family members is another possible response to downturns of subsistence harvest or changes in employment in villages related to fishing (see Howe and Martin 2009 for additional discussion of demographic trends in the region). In difficult times, families may fragment as individuals move to more promising places. Out-migration from villages may increase regional-center populations (e.g., Bethel, Nome) if more employment is available there. However, Nome's population was stable between 1990 and 2000, suggesting its economy was unable to attract or keep new people. Migration to urban centers, such as Fairbanks and Anchorage, threatens the long-term continuance of local traditions.

Programs to manage, restore, and enhance salmon are potentially new sources of income in villages (see Figure 2). Research, management, and restoration entities based from universities or government agencies generally do not view their primary function as providing jobs in rural villages. Mandates are viewed as "building knowledge bases about salmon," "managing a fishery for sustained yield," or "restoring a salmon stock." However, an equally valid point of view is to view the purpose of such programs as persons making money from salmon through government grants. Grants to enhance a salmon stock on their face resemble capital improvement grants akin to projects to extend a village runway used by the public; it raises the logical question of who receives the income from the grant. This same question was raised when western Alaska salmon stocks were initially eyed for development by commercial or sport fishing interests. In the new enterprise, will the workers be local residents so that income from the new salmon enterprises directly benefit cash-poor villages or go elsewhere? Commercial fisheries were compatible with the cultures and economies of western Alaska villages because they were kept small-scale, employed local people, and brought value to local villages. In a similar fashion, structuring research, management, and restoration programs to involve local workers might provide immediate benefits to villages. Such partnerships may be more likely to receive local support or to be successful in their long-term outcomes. These issues will take on greater importance should the commercial buyer-processor and export market components disappear from the socio-economic system (Figure 2).

Twenty years ago, the Yup'iks of the lower Yukon River were described as a modern hunter-gatherer society successfully adapting within the global economy and integrating commercial salmon fisheries with traditional subsistence patterns (Wolfe 1984). Since that time, the world-wide aquaculture industry has revolutionized the world salmon market, western Alaska salmon runs have crashed, commercial fishing has declined, and unprecedented fishing restrictions have been implemented on commercial and subsistence fisheries. These challenges now threaten the sustainability of AYK villages dependent on salmon. However, alongside these challenges, new enterprises have evolved. Organizations have emerged that bring together the expertise of federal, state, and co-management entities representing stakeholder interests. New stock assessment, management, and restoration programs are being developed and im-

plemented. New research is now exploring emerging ideas about salmon combined with old wisdom from local traditions. Time will tell if these new partnerships will prove fit to meet the new challenges.

Acknowledgments

We are indebted to many people who helped provide materials for this chapter, including the following: Dave Koster, Dan Bergstrom, Bonnie Borba, Caroline Brown, Dave Caylor, Jim Craig, Carmine DiCostanzo, Susan Georgette, John Hilsinger, James Magdanz, Susan McNeil, Susan M. Shirley, James Simon, Robert Walker, and Polly Wheeler. Our thanks especially to the Bering Sea Fishermen's Association for encouraging our participation in the Sustainable Salmon Initiative, and to Karen Gillis for administrative support. Our deep thanks to Chuck Krueger for his careful review and helpful editorial comments. Thanks also to the Alaska Department of Fish and Game, Division of Commercial Fisheries and Division of Subsistence, for the use of their research reports and databases on salmon fisheries.

References

Alaska Department of Community and Economic Development. 2003. Alaska Economic Information System. Alaska Department of Community and Economic Development and the U.S. Department of Commerce, Economic Development Administration. Available: www.dced.state.ak.us/cbd/AEIs_Home.htm (February 2004).

Alaska Department of Fish and Game. 2003a. Alaska subsistence fisheries, 2001 Annual Report. Alaska Department of Fish and Game, Division of Subsistence, Juneau.

Alaska Department of Fish and Game. 2003b. Alaska subsistence fisheries database (ASFDB). Alaska Department of Fish and Game, Division of Subsistence, Juneau.

Alaska Department of Fish and Game. 2007. Alaska subsistence fisheries database 2007 (ASFDB 2007). Alaska Department of Fish and Game, Division of Subsistence, Juneau.

Albertson, L. 2009. Perspectives on angling for salmon on the Kuskokwim River: the catch and release sport fishing controversy. Pages 611–619 in C. C. Krueger and C. E. Zimmerman, editors. Pacific salmon: ecology and management of western Alaska's populations. American Fisheries Society, Symposium 70, Bethesda, Maryland.

Andersen, D. B. 1992a. The use of dog teams and the use of subsistence-caught fish for feeding sled dogs in the Yukon River drainage, Alaska. Technical Paper 210. Alaska Department of Fish and Game, Division of Subsistence, Juneau.

Andersen, D. B. 1992b. Trapping in the Alaska and the proposed European Community import ban on furs taken with leghold traps. Technical Paper 223. Alaska Department of Fish and Game, Division of Subsistence, Juneau.

Andersen, D. B., and C. L. Fleener. 2001. Whitefish and beaver ecology of the Yukon Flats, Alaska. Technical Paper 265. Alaska Department of Fish and Game, Division of Subsistence and Council of Athabascan Tribal Governments, Natural Resources Department, Juneau.

Andrews, E. 1986. Yukon River subsistence fall chum fisheries: an overview. Technical Paper 147. Alaska Department of Fish and Game, Division of Subsistence, Juneau.

Andrews, E. 1988. The harvest of fish and wildlife for subsistence by residents of Minto, Alaska. Technical Paper 137. Alaska Department of Fish and Game, Division of Subsistence, Juneau.

Andrews, E. 1989. The Akulmiut: territorial dimensions of a Yup'ik Eskimo society. Technical Paper 177. Alaska Department of Fish and Game, Division of Subsistence, Juneau.

Andrews, E., and M. W. Coffing. 1986. Kuskokwim River subsistence Chinook fisheries: an overview. Technical Paper 146. Alaska Department of Fish and Game, Division of Subsistence, Juneau.

Andrews, E., and R. Peterson. 1983. Wild resource use of the Tuluksak River drainage by residents of Tuluksak, 1980–1983. Technical Paper 87. Alaska Department of Fish and Game, Division of Subsistence, Juneau.

AYK SSI (Arctic-Yukon-Kuskokwim Sustainable Salmon Initiative). 2006. Arctic-Yukon-Kuskokwim Salmon Research and Restoration Plan. Bering Sea Fishermen's Association, Anchorage, Alaska.

Berkes, F., P. George, and R. J. Preston. 1991. Co-management. The evolution in theory and practice of the joint administration of living resources. Alternatives 18:12–18.

Borba, B. M., and H. H. Hamner. 2000. Subsistence and personal use salmon harvest estimates, Yukon Area, 1999. Regional Information Report 3A00–

23. Alaska Department of Fish and Game, Division of Commercial Fisheries, Anchorage.

Borba, B. M., and H. H. Hamner. 2001. Subsistence and personal use salmon harvest estimates, Yukon Area, 2000. Regional Information Report 3A01–27. Alaska Department of Fish and Game, Division of Commercial Fisheries, Anchorage.

Brase, A. L. J., and H. H. Hamner. 2002. Subsistence and personal use salmon harvests in the Alaska portion of the Yukon River drainage, 2001. Regional Information Report 3A02–32. Alaska Department of Fish and Game, Division of Commercial Fisheries, Anchorage.

Brase, A. L. J., and H. H. Hamner. 2003. Subsistence and personal use salmon harvests in the Alaska portion of the Yukon River drainage, 2002. Regional Information Report 3A03–13. Alaska Department of Fish and Game, Division of Commercial Fisheries, Anchorage.

Brelsford, T. 2009. "We have to learn to work together:" current perspectives on incorporating local and traditional/indigenous knowledge into Alaskan fishery management. Pages 381–394 in C. C. Krueger and C. E. Zimmerman, editors. Pacific salmon: ecology and management of western Alaska's populations. American Fisheries Society, Symposium 70, Bethesda, Maryland.

Brelsford, T., R. Peterson, and T. L. Haynes. 1986. An overview of resource use patterns in the central Kuskokwim: Aniak, Crooked Creek, and Red Devil. Technical Paper 141. Alaska Department of Fish and Game, Division of Subsistence, Juneau.

Bue, F. J., B. M. Borba, R. Cannon, and C. C. Krueger. 2009. Yukon River fall chum salmon fisheries: management, harvest, and stock abundance. Pages 703–742 in C. C. Krueger and C. E. Zimmerman, editors. Pacific salmon: ecology and management of western Alaska's populations. American Fisheries Society, Symposium 70, Bethesda, Maryland.

Bue, F., and C. Lean. 1999. 1999 Norton Sound District salmon report to the Alaska Board of Fisheries. Regional Information Report 3A99–37. Alaska Department of Fish and Game, Division of Commercial Fisheries, Anchorage.

Burr, J. M. 2009. Management of recreational salmon fisheries in the Arctic-Yukon-Kuskokwim Region of Alaska. Pages 521–539 in C. C. Krueger and C. E. Zimmerman, editors. Pacific salmon: ecology and management of western Alaska's populations. American Fisheries Society, Symposium 70, Bethesda, Maryland.

Burkey, C., M. Coffing, J. Estensen, R. L. Fisher, and D. B. Molyneaux. 2002. Annual management report for the subsistence and commercial fisheries of the Kuskokwim Area, 2001. Regional Information Report 3A02–53. Alaska Department of Fish and Game, Division of Commercial Fisheries, Anchorage.

Case, M., and L. Halpin. 1990. Contemporary wild resource use patterns in Tanana, Alaska, 1987. Technical Paper 178. Alaska Department of Fish and Game, Division of Subsistence, Juneau.

Caulfield, R. A. 1981. Final report on the survey of permit holders in the Tanana River subsistence permit fishery, 1981. Technical Paper 14. Alaska Department of Fish and Game, Division of Subsistence, Juneau.

Caulfield, R. A. 1983. Subsistence land use in upper Yukon-Porcupine communities, Alaska. Technical Paper 16. Alaska Department of Fish and Game, Division of Subsistence, Juneau.

Caulfield, R. A., W. J. Peter, and C. L. Alexander. 1983. Gwich'in Athabaskan place names of the Upper Yukon-Porcupine Region, Alaska. Technical Paper 83. Alaska Department of Fish and Game, Division of Subsistence, Juneau.

Charnley, S. 1982. Resource use areas in the Aniak and Oskawalik River drainages. Technical Paper 50. Alaska Department of Fish and Game, Division of Subsistence, Juneau.

Charnley, S. 1984. Human ecology of two central Kuskokwim communities: Chuathbaluk and Sleetmute. Technical Paper 81. Alaska Department of Fish and Game, Division of Subsistence, Juneau.

Coffing, M. W. 1992. Kwethluk subsistence: contemporary land use patterns, wild resource harvest and use, and the subsistence economy of a lower Kuskokwim River area community. Technical Paper 157. Alaska Department of Fish and Game, Division of Subsistence, Juneau.

Conger, A. O., and J. S. Magdanz., 1990. The harvest of fish and wildlife in three Alaska communities: Brevig Mission, Golovin, and Shishmaref. Technical Paper 188. Alaska Department of Fish and Game, Division of Subsistence, Juneau.

Duffield, J. 1997. Nonmarket valuation and the courts: the case of the Exxon Valdez. Contemporary Economic Policy 15:98–110.

Ellanna, L. J. 1983. Bering Strait insular Eskimo: a diachronic study of ecology and Population structure. Technical Paper 77. Alaska Department of Fish and Game, Division of Subsistence, Juneau.

Evenson, D. F., S. J. Hayes, G. Sandone, and D. J. Bergstrom. 2009. Yukon River Chinook salmon: stock status, harvest, and management. Pages 675–701 in C. C. Krueger and C. E. Zimmerman, editors. Pacific salmon: ecology and management of western Alaska's populations. American Fisheries Society, Symposium 70, Bethesda, Maryland.

Fehr, A., and W. Hurst. 1996. A seminar on two ways of knowing: indigenous and scientific knowledge. Inuit Circumpolar Conference and Fisheries Joint Management Council, Aurora Research Institute, Inuvik, Northwest Territories, Canada.

Gilbert, C. H., and H. O'Malley. 1921. Investigation of the salmon fisheries of the Yukon River. Pages 128–154 in W. T. Bower, editor. Alaska fishery and fur-seal industries in 1920. U.S. Bureau of Fisheries, Document 909. U.S. Government Printing Office, Washington, D.C.

Gross, J. 1991. Subsistence fishing patterns on the Togiak River and the impact of sport fishing. Technical Paper 203. Alaska Department of Fish and Game, Division of Subsistence, Juneau.

Hilsinger, J. R., E. Volk, G. Sandone, and R. Cannon. 2009. Salmon management in the Arctic-Yukon-Kuskokwim region of Alaska: past, present, and future. Pages 495–519 in C. C. Krueger and C. E. Zimmerman, editors. Pacific salmon: ecology and management of western Alaska's populations. American Fisheries Society, Symposium 70, Bethesda, Maryland.

Howe, L., and S. Martin. 2009. Demographic change, economic conditions, and subsistence salmon harvests in Alaska's Arctic Yukon Kuskokwim region. Pages 433–461 in C. C. Krueger and C. E. Zimmerman, editors. Pacific salmon: ecology and management of western Alaska's populations. American Fisheries Society, Symposium 70, Bethesda, Maryland.

Huntington, C. C. 1981. Issue paper on subsistence king salmon drift gillnetting, Yukon Area Subdistrict 4-A. Technical Paper 17. Alaska Department of Fish and Game, Division of Subsistence, Juneau.

Kari, P. R. 1983. Land use and economy of Lime Village. Technical Paper 80. Alaska Department of Fish and Game, Division of Subsistence, Juneau.

Kari, P. R. 1985. Wild resource use and economy of Stony River Village. Technical Paper 108. Alaska Department of Fish and Game, Division of Subsistence, Juneau.

Knapp, G. 2009. Commercial salmon fisheries of the Arctic-Yukon-Kuskokwim region: economic challenges and opportunities. Pages 463–486 in C. C. Krueger and C. E. Zimmerman, editors. Pacific salmon: ecology and management of western Alaska's populations. American Fisheries Society, Symposium 70, Bethesda, Maryland.

Linderman, J. C., Jr., and D. J. Bergstrom. 2009. Kuskokwim management area: salmon escapement, harvest, and management. Pages 541–599 in C. C. Krueger and C. E. Zimmerman, editors. Pacific salmon: ecology and management of western Alaska's populations. American Fisheries Society, Symposium 70, Bethesda, Maryland.

Langdon, S. J. 1986. Contemporary Alaska natives economies. University Press of America, New York.

Langdon, S. J. 2002. The Native People of Alaska. Greatland Graphics, Anchorage, Alaska.

Magdanz, J. S. 1992. Subsistence salmon fishing by permit in the Nome Subdistrict and portions of the Port Clarence District. Technical Paper 220. Alaska Department of Fish and Game, Division of Subsistence, Juneau.

Magdanz, J. S., and A. Olanna. 1984. Controls on fishing behavior on the Nome River. Technical Paper 102. Alaska Department of Fish and Game, Division of Subsistence, Juneau.

Magdanz, J. S., and A. Olanna. 1986. Subsistence land use in Nome, a northwest Alaska regional center. Technical Paper 148. Alaska Department of Fish and Game, Division of Subsistence, Juneau.

Magdanz, J. S., and D. E. Punguk. 1981. Nome River Fishery II. Technical Paper 5. Alaska Department of Fish and Game, Division of Subsistence, Juneau.

Magdanz, J. S., S. Tahbone, K. Kamletz, and A. Ahmasuk. 2002. Subsistence salmon fishing by residents of Nome, Alaska, 2001. Technical Paper 274. Alaska Department of Fish and Game, Division of Subsistence, Juneau.

Magdanz, J., E. Trigg, A. Ahmasuk, P. Nanouk, D. Koster, and K. Kamletz. 2009. Patterns and trends in subsistence salmon harvests, Norton Sound–Port Clarence Area, Alaska, 1994–2003. Pages 395–431 in C. C. Krueger and C. E. Zimmerman, editors. Pacific salmon: ecology and management of western Alaska's populations. American Fisheries Society, Symposium 70, Bethesda, Maryland.

Menard, J., C. C. Krueger, and J. R. Hilsinger. 2009. Norton Sound salmon fisheries: history, stock abundance, and management. Pages 621–673 in C. C. Krueger and C. E. Zimmerman, editors. Pacific salmon: ecology and management of western Alaska's populations. American Fisheries Society, Symposium 70, Bethesda, Maryland.

Marcotte, J. A., and T. L. Haynes. 1984. Contemporary resource use patterns in the upper Koyukuk region, Alaska. Technical Paper 93. Alaska Department of Fish and Game, Division of Subsistence, Juneau.

Marcotte, J. R. 1982. The king salmon drift net fishery of the middle Yukon: an overview and study of the 1982 season. Technical Paper 18. Alaska Department of Fish and Game, Division of Subsistence, Juneau.

Marcotte, J. R. 1986. Contemporary resource use patterns in Huslia, Alaska, 1983. Technical Paper 133. Alaska Department of Fish and Game, Division of Subsistence, Juneau.

Marcotte, J. R. 1990. Subsistence harvest of fish and wildlife by residents of Galena, Alaska, 1985–86. Technical Paper 155. Alaska Department of Fish and Game, Division of Subsistence, Juneau.

McNeil, S. L. 2002. Yukon River salmon season review for 2002 and technical committee report. Regional Information Report 3A02–44. Alaska Department of Fish and Game, Division of Commercial Fisheries and the United States and Canada Yukon River Joint Technical Committee, Anchorage, Alaska and Whitehorse, Yukon Territory.

Miraglia, R. 1998. Traditional ecological knowledge handbook: a training manual and reference guide for designing, conducting, and participating in research projects using traditional ecological knowledge. Alaska Department of Fish and Game, Division of Subsistence, Juneau.

Moncrieff, C., and H. Huntington. 2002. YRDFA hosts traditional ecological knowledge workshop. Yukon Fisheries News, Winter: 4–5.

Moncrieff, C. F., and J. Klein. 2003. Traditional ecological knowledge of salmon along the Yukon River. Report 47. Yukon River Drainage Fisheries Association, Anchorage.

Nakashima, D. J. 1990. Application of native knowledge in EIA: Inuit, eiders, and Hudson Bay oil. Canadian Environmental Assessment Research Council, Hull, Quebec.

Nelson, R. K., K. H. Mautner, and G. R. Bane. 1982. Tracks in the wildland. A portrayal of Koyukon and Nunamiut subsistence. Anthropology and Historic Preservation, Cooperative Studies Unit, University of Alaska, Fairbanks.

Pete, M., and R. J. Wolfe. 1991. Subsistence along the lower Yukon River. Alaska Geographic 17:44–59.

Pete, M. C. 1991. Contemporary patterns of wild resource use by residents of Russian Mission, Alaska. Technical Paper No. 127. Alaska Department of Fish and Game, Division of Subsistence, Juneau.

Schroeder, R. F., D. B. Andersen, R. Bosworth, J. M. Morris, and J. M. Wright. 1987. Subsistence in Alaska: Arctic, Interior, Southcentral, Southwest, and Western Regional summaries. Technical Paper 150. Alaska Department of Fish and Game, Division of Subsistence, Juneau.

Shinkwin, A., and M. Case. 1984. Modern foragers: wild resource use in Nenana Village, Alaska. Technical Paper 91. Alaska Department of Fish and Game, Division of Subsistence, Juneau.

SP Research Associates, and A. Lalande. 1991. Integrating indigenous knowledge and western scientific knowledge in community-based resource management. Selected Bibliography. Man and the Biosphere Program. Canadian Commission for UNESCO and the Canadian Environmental Assessment Research Council, Winnipeg, Manitoba, 1991. CEARC, Ottawa.

Stickney, A. A. 1980. Subsistence resource utilization: Nikolai and Telida - Interim Report. Technical

Paper 20. Alaska Department of Fish and Game, Division of Subsistence, Juneau.

Stickney, A. A. 1981a. Middle Kuskokwim food survey II. Technical Paper 53. Alaska Department of Fish and Game, Division of Subsistence, Juneau.

Stickney, A. A. 1981b. Subsistence resource utilization: Nikolai and Telida—Interim Report II. Technical Paper 21. Alaska Department of Fish and Game, Division of Subsistence, Juneau.

Stickney, A. A. 1984. Coastal ecology and wild resource use in the central Bering Sea area: Hooper Bay and Kwigillingok. Technical Paper 85. Alaska Department of Fish and Game, Division of Subsistence, Juneau.

Stokes, J. 1982. Subsistence salmon fishing in the upper Kuskokwim River system, 1981 and 1982. Technical Paper 23. Alaska Department of Fish and Game, Division of Subsistence, Juneau.

Stokes, J. 1984. Natural resource utilization of four upper Kuskokwim communities. Technical Paper 86. Alaska Department of Fish and Game, Division of Subsistence, Juneau.

Sumida, V. 1986. Land and resource use patterns in the Yukon Flats: Stevens Village. Technical Paper 129. Alaska Department of Fish and Game, Division of Subsistence, Juneau.

Sumida, V. A., and C. L. Alexander. 1986. Patterns of land and resource use in Beaver, Alaska. Technical Paper 140. Alaska Department of Fish and Game, Division of Subsistence, Juneau.

Sumida, V. A., and D. B. Andersen. 1990. 1990. Patterns of fish and wildlife use for subsistence in Fort Yukon, Alaska. Technical Paper 179. Alaska Department of Fish and Game, Division of Subsistence.

Thomas, D. C. 1980a. Issue paper on Nome River subsistence salmon fishery. Technical Paper 10. Alaska Department of Fish and Game, Division of Subsistence, Juneau.

Thomas, D. C. 1980b. Nome subsistence salmon research report. Technical Paper 11. Alaska Department of Fish and Game, Division of Subsistence, Juneau.

Thomas, D. C. 1982. The role of local fish and wildlife resources in the community of Shaktoolik, Alaska. Technical Paper 13. Alaska Department of Fish and Game, Division of Subsistence, Juneau.

U.S. Census Bureau. 2000. U.S. Census 2000 Summary. U.S. Department of Commerce, Washington. Available: http://www.census.gov/prod/www/abs/decennial/ (February 2004).

Walker, R. J., and M. W. Coffing. 1993. Subsistence salmon harvest in the Kuskokwim Area during 1989. Technical Paper 189. Alaska Department of Fish and Game, Division of Subsistence, Juneau.

Wenzel, G. W. 1999. Traditional ecological knowledge and Inuit: reflections on TEK research and ethics. Arctic 52:113–124.

Wheeler, P. 1987. Salmon fishing patterns along the middle Yukon River at Kaltag, Alaska. Technical Paper 156. Alaska Department of Fish and Game, Division of Subsistence, Juneau.

Wolfe, R. J. 1979. Food production in a western Eskimo population. University of California, Los Angeles.

Wolfe, R. J. 1981. Norton Sound/Yukon Delta sociocultural systems baseline analysis. Technical Paper 59. Alaska Department of Fish and Game, Division of Subsistence, Juneau.

Wolfe, R. J. 1982. The subsistence salmon fishery of the lower Yukon River. Technical Paper 60. Alaska Department of Fish and Game, Division of Subsistence, Bethel.

Wolfe, R. J. 1984. Commercial fishing in the hunting-gathering economy of a Yukon River Yup'ik society. Etudes/Inuit Studies (Supplementary Issue) 8:159–183.

Wolfe, R. J. 1989. The fish are not to be played with: Yup'ik views of sport fishing and subsistence-recreation conflicts along the Togiak River. Paper presented at the Alaska Anthropological Association Meeting, March 3–4, Anchorage, Alaska.

Wolfe, R. J. 1991. Trapping in Alaska communities with mixed, subsistence-cash economies. Technical Paper 217. Alaska Department of Fish and Game, Division of Subsistence, Juneau.

Wolfe, R. J. 2001. Subsistence food production and distribution in Alaska: social organization, management, and development issues. INUSSUK Arctic Research Journal 1:213–231.

Wolfe, R. J., J. A. Fall, and R. T. Stanek. 2002. The subsistence harvest of harbor seal and sea lion by Alaska Natives in 2001. Technical Paper 273. Alaska Department of Fish and Game, Division of Subsistence and the Alaska Native Harbor Seal Commission, Juneau.

Wolfe, R. J., J. J. Gross, S. J. Langdon, J. M. Wright, G. K. Sherrod, L. J. Ellanna, and V. Sumida. 1984. Subsistence-based economies in coastal communities of southwest Alaska. Technical Paper 89. Alaska Department of Fish and Game, Division of Subsistence, Juneau.

Wolfe, R. J., and C. J. Utermohle. 2000. Wild food consumption rate estimates for rural Alaska populations. Technical Paper 261. Alaska Department of Fish and Game, Division of Subsistence, Juneau.

Wolfe, R. J., C. J. Utermohle, and D. B. Andersen. 2001. Dog populations and salmon harvests for dog food, Yukon River Districts 1–6. Report for the Alaska Board of Fisheries, January 2001, Alaska Department of Fish and Game, Division of Subsistence, Anchorage.

Wolfe, R. J., and R. J. Walker. 1987. Subsistence economies in Alaska: productivity, geography, and development impacts. Arctic Anthropology 24:56–81.

Yukon River Drainage Fisheries Association. 2002.
Traditional ecological knowledge, videotape. Anchorage, Alaska.

American Fisheries Society Symposium 70:381–394, 2009

"We have to Learn to Work Together:"
Current Perspectives on Incorporating Local and Traditional/Indigenous Knowledge into Alaskan Fishery Management

Taylor Brelsford[*]

URS Corporation

560 East 34th Avenue, Suite 100, Anchorage, Alaska 99503, USA

Abstract.—The Arctic-Yukon-Kuskokwim Sustainable Salmon Initiative (AYK SSI) is a research program in Alaska focused on learning from the knowledge and understanding of local indigenous fishing communities. From the mid-1990s, Alaska Natives have urged that local and traditional/indigenous knowledge be recognized as a serious body of ecological insights and stewardship traditions. This paper provides a survey of milestones in Alaska, from the early definitional debates and the rise of systematic methods for documentation, to the growing body of substantive information. The discussion on local and traditional knowledge at the AYK SSI Symposium in February 2007 provided an opportunity to assess achievements and identify obstacles. Participants underscored the continuing challenges of the diverse cultural context for joint research by biologists and local communities, directing attention to foundational questions of trust and respect. Local residents celebrated the great promise for local and traditional/indigenous knowledge to contribute to our shared scientific understanding of salmon and to promote respectful and effective systems of stewardship, but they were also acutely perceptive of the barriers to improved synthesis and mutual learning. The concluding section of this paper explores implications for the on-going research agenda of the AYK SSI, particularly the need for an on-going consultative process to insure that local communities and researchers are mutually aware of methodologies available and the substantive contributions made by local and traditional knowledge research. In this way, the ongoing development of research in this area can draw more fully on the struggles and accomplishments of the preceding decade.

Introduction

The Arctic-Yukon-Kuskokwim Sustainable Salmon Initiative (AYK SSI) has, from its outset, recognized the integral importance of human and cultural dimensions in salmon management. In its organizational structures and research framework, the AYK SSI has embraced local residents as partners in developing knowledge of salmon ecology and generating ideas for improved management of these precious resources (AYK SSI 2006). Local residents of the AYK region possess a multi-generational knowledge and experience in subsistence fisheries (Wolfe and Spaeder 2009, this volume). Discussions on local and tra-

[*]Corresponding author: Taylor_Brelsford@urscorp.com

ditional knowledge at the February 2007 AYK SSI Symposium provided an opportunity to assess a highly productive decade of debate, dialogue, and collaborative field research and documentation. The Synthesis Session Breakout Group on Incorporating Local and Traditional Knowledge at the symposium brought together a diverse group of 22 participants to listen and learn about the state of current work and the prospects for future improvements.

This paper proceeds in three sections. First, the milestones of definitional debate, methods development, and the growing body of substantive information are surveyed, as a way to place in historic context the discussions at the symposium. Second, the perceptive and deeply-felt comments from the discussions at the symposium are summarized. The concluding section then suggests some of the implications of the Synthesis Session Breakout Group for ongoing work within the AYK SSI.

A Review of Alaskan Studies of Local and Traditional/Indigenous Knowledge

The AYK SSI efforts to integrate local and traditional/indigenous knowledge in their research agenda represent one of several explicit efforts by various organizations since the early 1990s. This section surveys selected milestones in developing concepts, methods, and research agendas, in addition to highlighting key substantive contributions from a wide body of recent research.

Milestones

Through the early 1990s, no systematic studies of local and traditional/indigenous ecological knowledge had been conducted, using these terms as we understand them to-

day.[1] At the time, much of the advocacy effort of indigenous organizations, including the Association of Village Council Presidents and the Tanana Chiefs Conference, appears to have been directed towards the institutional reforms of co-management, such as establishment of, and participation in, the Kuskokwim River Salmon Management Working Group (Linderman and Bergstrom 2009, this volume) and comparable to similar approaches used in British Columbia (Gottesfeld et al. 2009, this volume; Pinkerton 2009, this volume). Implicit in this strategy, perhaps, was the expectation that as Alaska Native elders gained a seat at the co-management table, their wisdom and understanding would naturally become part of the management discussion.[2]

Starting in 1994, Alaska Natives initiated a movement towards more systematic attention to local and traditional/indigenous knowledge, and state and federal agencies and researchers began to respond. The first

---

[1] The Inupiat opposition to a moratorium on subsistence bowhead whaling declared in 1979 by the International Whaling Commission was, of course, rooted in the traditional knowledge of the whaling captains. The North Slope Borough studies of the Western Arctic bowhead whale population achieved a significant vindication of this traditional knowledge in conventional, peer-reviewed science, in regard to both population numbers and migration behavior. The whaling captains also inserted their knowledge into management through formation of the Alaska Eskimo Whaling Commission and by establishing cooperative management agreements with the National Oceanic and Atmospheric Administration (Freeman 1989; Huntington 1992; Langdon 1984; U.S. Army Engineer District, Alaska 1999:volume 2, P. 2–7).

[2] In the course of a major interagency, collaborative conference to review and suggest improvement to harvest assessment programs, Alaska Native participants insisted on including a programmatic statement committing the agencies to development of co-management programs (ADF&G and ISER 1996). Among the benefits of co-management in this Statement of Intent was the "incorporation of traditional management and knowledge."

of the breakthrough efforts occurred in 1994, when Rural Alaska Community Action Program (RurAL CAP) and the Indigenous Peoples' Council for Marine Mammals convened a conference examining how traditional ecological knowledge, or traditional knowledge and wisdom, could add to the information base and legitimacy of agency management through the emerging marine mammal co-management regimes. Important issues at this early stage were definitions of traditional ecological knowledge (TEK), contrasting worldviews in western science and Alaska Native communities, and the risk that the holism of traditional knowledge would be ruptured by western scientists seeking fragments to serve agency agendas (Hild 1994).

Shortly after, a pilot project was undertaken by the Inuit Circumpolar Conference (ICC) to explore field methods for documenting the expert knowledge of life-long beluga whale *Delphinapterus leucas* hunters on the U.S. and Chukotkan sides of the Bering Strait. Funded by the U.S. and Canada as part of the Arctic Environmental Protection Strategy, and by the U.S. National Science Foundation, this pilot study was led by Henry Huntington and Nikolai Mymrin. This research demonstrated a rich body of ecological knowledge held by Inupiat and Chukotkan indigenous elders on topics of beluga whale natural history, life cycle, feeding patterns, and impacts of weather on migration timing (Huntington et al. 1999; Mymrin et al. 1999). The ICC pilot project also established several best practice methods, including use of the semi-directed group interview, the use of maps as interview prompts, and community verification of preliminary results (Huntington 1998).

In the mid-1990s, the *Exxon Valdez* Oil Spill Trustees Council responded to local concerns and sponsored the development of a methodological handbook for traditional knowledge research, prepared by the Alaska Department of Fish and Game (ADF&G),

Division of Subsistence (Miraglia 1998). Beginning in 1996, the U.S. Department of the Interior Mineral Management Service (MMS) convened a series of roundtable discussions among subsistence researchers and managers to explore the status of traditional knowledge research among state and federal agencies, with an eye to strengthening the representation of local and traditional/ecological knowledge in environmental review documents for the North Slope area oil and gas leasing programs (MMS 2007).

These foundational efforts laid the groundwork for the basic terms, definitions, and methods that have characterized much work in local and traditional/indigenous knowledge in the years that followed. Many of the concerns examined in these early efforts remain salient today, particularly those focused on incommensurable worldviews and the risk of cooption by nonNative scholars, scientists, and agencies. Nonetheless, it is important to recognize that substantial progress has been made in collaborative research to document local and traditional/indigenous knowledge across Alaska.

The first major Alaskan research program to explicitly focus on "traditional ecological knowledge" came in 1999, when the Federal Subsistence Board established a subsistence fisheries monitoring program. Acting under the direction of the federal courts in October 1999, the Federal Board expanded its jurisdiction to subsistence fisheries (Buklis 2002) and initiated a studies program that included traditional ecological knowledge studies as an integral component. With budgets of approximately $7 million per year in the initial years, approximately $2.5 million per year was allocated for subsistence harvest surveys and traditional ecological knowledge projects. By 2005, over 50 traditional ecological knowledge studies had been funded under this program (Wheeler and Craver 2005).

In 2001, the AYK SSI was established as a consortium of federal, state, and tribal agencies to focus on understanding the recent declines in the abundance of western Alaska salmon runs. Tribal organization representatives exercised a significant role in decisions on the direction and priorities of the program, through membership on the Steering Committee (Krueger et al. 2009; this volume). The conceptual framework for including "local and traditional knowledge" in this research program is articulated both in the National Research Council (NRC) Report contributing to a research and restoration planning effort (NRC 2005), and in the resulting AYK SSI Research and Restoration Plan (AYK SSI 2006.) Importantly, the AYK SSI program has not characterized local and traditional/indigenous knowledge studies as a stand-alone category, but instead seeks to incorporate "local and traditional knowledge" as an integral part of studies in each of the three research framework areas: salmon ecology, human dimensions of salmon use, and ecosystem and fishery management.

By 2007, the completion of dozens of projects focused on local and traditional/indigenous knowledge raised the profile and importance of this information to subsistence management, federal environmental reviews, and fisheries research. Wheeler and Craver (2005) reviewed several important examples of studies funded by the Federal Subsistence Board. Other notable achievements in the federal subsistence monitoring program include highly detailed studies of ecological knowledge and effective subsistence harvest practices for nonsalmon species in the middle Yukon River basin (Anderson et al. 2004; Brown et al. 2005) and Kotzebue Sound (Georgette and Shiedt 2005). These studies and many others with a similar focus have confirmed the contemporary vitality of local and traditional knowledge in subsistence-reliant communities. Many of the natural history observations align with western biological findings, while some observations add localized precision. Where differences in

local and traditional/indigenous knowledge and western science have been identified, the clarification of views through systematic documentation has provided an important basis for further dialogue between managers and local fisheries participants.

The most detailed studies of traditional knowledge of salmon ecology and human uses funded by the Federal Subsistence Board were conducted in the Copper River (Simeone and Kari 2002) and southeast Alaska (Langdon 2006), regions outside the purview of the AYK SSI program. However, these studies broke new ground in Alaska studies of traditional and local knowledge by documenting Ahtna and Tlingit observational knowledge of salmon natural history and harvest practices, and then augmenting this description with richly developed accounts of traditional management and stewardship practices, including underlying beliefs and cosmology. The Ahtna study includes a lengthy narrative (with interlinear Ahtna/English translations) from renowned elder Katie John describing the fish camp at Batzulnetas during her childhood. Of particular interest is the description of selective harvest practices overseen by the fish camp "boss," which ensured that large gravid females were freed from the weir to continue upstream to spawn (Simeone and Kari 2002). The Tlingit study includes a detailed account of stewardship practices based in clans, including the role of "streamscaping" by a clan specialist who was responsible for placing fallen logs and otherwise sculpting pools to provide a "welcoming" habitat for salmon returning to spawn (Langdon 2006). The studies include the great "Salmon Boy" stories of Ahtna and Tlingit societies, which provide what Langdon calls the "mythic charter" for ethical relations between humans and salmon. These beliefs and cosmological perspectives act as the foundations for legitimacy in the traditional stewardship systems. The Ahtna and Tlingit studies, like the others, provide significant information about local understanding of natural history and effective harvest practices. However, by extending recognition and standing to the local self-management and stewardship traditions, the Ahtna and Tlingit studies promote the possibility of new hybrid models for conservation and management, building jointly on these rich and long-standing traditions and values alongside western science and management.

Components of local and traditional/indigenous knowledge

These examples illustrate a coming of age in the topical scope and methods of TEK research in Alaska. A general agreement exists that local and traditional knowledge is observation-based and accumulated by a community through direct experience on the land over generations (Wolfe and Spaeder 2009, this volume). Though based in long-standing traditions, this knowledge is a dynamic body of information, adapting to contemporary conditions.[3] Four core component domains can be identified:

1. Environmental Observations—concerning the weather, the landscape, seasonal availability of animals, life cycles and natural history, and traditional taxonomies.

2. Effective Harvest Practices—including a recurring seasonal sequence for acquiring resources in times of aggregation or primeness (also referred to as the "seasonal round"), harvest techniques, travel routes and intricate systems of place names.

3. Stewardship Traditions—including ethical precepts, such as the prohibition on waste, selective harvest practices, and habitat enhancement.

4. Cosmology and Belief Systems—including the "mythic charters" that articulate the relation of humans and the natural world, giving legitimacy to stewardship practices.[4]

In the Alaska research considered here, the majority of the recent studies of local and traditional/indigenous knowledge have focused on ecological observations as they are connected to successful harvest practices (Wolfe and Spaeder 2009, this volume). However, where the effort has been deployed, it appears that the studies that go on to examine the topics of resource stewardship traditions and underlying cosmologies show enormous promise. Based on the positive reactions from the communities that hosted the Ahtna and Tlingit studies noted above, studies with this breadth in scope likely can help to overcome the concern about fragmenting and excising selected parts from an integrated body of traditional knowledge and belief. However, some evidence suggests that management agencies show hesitancy about funding projects that include the level of stewardship practices and cosmology and beliefs, on the ground that such projects may have less applicability in resource management decisions.

Methods for collecting local and traditional/indigenous knowledge

The completion of many projects focused on local and traditional knowledge

---

[3]Recent discussions with Arctic elders suggest that climate change is diminishing the reliability of traditional understandings of the weather patterns and sea ice, for example (Krupnik and Jolly 2002). For a petition asserting that the severity of climate change related impacts to Inuit communities represent a violation of human rights, see Watt-Cloutier (2005).

[4]These components correspond broadly to the results of a spirited discussion among Canadian researchers. The scheme here corresponds closely with that proposed by Usher (2000), and shares features with the analogous frameworks proposed by Stevenson (1996) and Wenzel (1999). All of these adopt a holistic framing of traditional ecological knowledge which includes self-management practices and belief systems.

documentation since the late 1990s permits a comparison of major methodologies. These methods show a spectrum from projects that maximize use of existing information on one pole to those that expand the range of documentation on local and traditional/indigenous knowledge on the other pole. Similarly, the methods generally range from those than can be achieved in a compressed timeframe with a lower research budget, to those that require greater time, and budget, and/or long-term familiarity and relationships with the participating communities.

Database Compilations of Existing Information.—In the late 1990s, several initiatives emerged to compile existing traditional knowledge from public meeting testimony and other existing published and unpublished interviews. In addition to comparatively low cost, this approach also had the great benefit of treating with respect all of the previous effort by local experts to describe their observations and knowledge. When coded with key words, these databases held the promise of facilitating access to a wide body of information, allowing for searching on particular locations, species, or sociocultural dimensions. In an early example, an environmental review of the Northstar project in the Beaufort Sea west of Prudhoe Bay by the U.S. Army Corps of Engineers identified traditional knowledge quotes from 23 public meetings held on the North Slope between 1979 and 1984 and compiled these into a searchable database with an extensive keyword set (U.S. Army Engineer District Alaska 1999). Shortly after this project was completed, the MMS assembled a comprehensive electronic set of transcripts for 70 public meetings regarding oil and gas leasing on the North Slope from 1975–2001 (Burwell 2001). Although not coded by keywords, this collection of transcripts, amounting to some 4,400 pages, made it feasible for analysts to systematically consult decades

of testimony by North Slope residents. The Northstar traditional knowledge database (U.S. Army Engineer District Alaska 1999) served as a model for a more ambitious effort by NOAA Fisheries staff to compile Alaska Native traditional knowledge regarding fisheries in coastal regions (Sepez et al. 2003). Intended as an ongoing resource for the fisheries agency's environmental reviews, the NOAA Fisheries TEK Database drew information from the ethnographic literature, ADF&G Subsistence Division Technical Papers, films, videos, and unpublished interviews conducted by agency staff. Some 546 entries were coded using geographic, biological and sociocultural key words.

In 2003, the ADF&G Division of Subsistence published an electronic, searchable database "From Neqa to Tepa" (Coiley-Kenner et al. 2003). A highly strategic effort in salvaging and compiling unpublished information from researcher field notes and interviews, this database contained information gathered from 34 communities throughout Bristol Bay and the Alaska Peninsula during the period from 1982–2002. A total of 3,200 records, most less than a page in length, documented local experts' natural history observations and subsistence-use patterns for all species of salmon and 32 non-salmon species. A comprehensive set of geographic, ecological, sociocultural key words allows for targeted retrieval of information. During the first phase, initiated in 2000, the project focused on capturing information from the field notes and supplemental records of Division of Subsistence researchers active over a two-decade period in Bristol Bay. In a second phase initiated in 2002, the database was extended to the Alaska Peninsula communities, and included selected new interviews with knowledgeable residents, in addition to compiling existing field data.

While these databases have significant value, they suffer from limitations of the underlying source data, which was generally collected without a primary focus on local and traditional knowledge as we use that term here. The entries in these databases are often in brief paragraphs rather than fuller narratives, and this may tend towards fragmentation of an integrated body of information. Analysts can search the database by keywords, gathering together many brief excerpts, but it may be challenging to synthesize the holistic perspective of a given community for patterns within the community's traditional use area.

These limitations may be overcome when a database is used as a starting point for establishing a baseline of information and a foundation from which additional interviews are conducted to extend the information in a focused area. For example, in the Northstar environmental review (U.S. Army Engineer District Alaska 1999), the database compilation served as a starting point for supplemental interviewing with Inupiat whaling captains.

Regional Workshops.—The Alaska Native Science Commission (ANSC), drawing on a Board of Directors and staff of recognized Alaska Native cultural leaders, has brought a unique perspective to the collection of traditional knowledge and wisdom. ANSC has drawn particular attention to the contrasting worldviews and epistemologies of indigenous knowledge and western science and has placed great emphasis on respectful relations between those gathering the information and the cultural experts who share their life experiences and understandings for the research. ANSC has participated in projects on environmental contaminants and subsistence foods using the method of convening large regional or national workshops. In the most elaborate of these projects, the Institute of Social and Economic Research (ISER) and ANSC employed a multi-faceted approach to documenting Alaska Native understandings of environmental change related to contami-

nants and subsistence food resources (Kruse et al. 2004). The project also gathered western science information on contaminants and explored the interactions between the two bodies of knowledge. Seven regional workshops were convened and conducted with careful attention to traditional protocols for identification of village expert representatives for the workshops and for conducting the discussions. A wide range of subsistence harvest, nutrition, and contaminant observations were recorded during the workshops and entered into a web-accessible database. Some 1,700 concern comments were identified by the 187 regional meeting participants (Kruse et al. 2004).

As a method, the multi-regional workshop approach had the benefit of broad geography and relative economy of scale. Local and traditional/indigenous knowledge holders from across Alaska were consulted in a relatively compact project schedule, and the regional workshops were conducted in such as way as to allow for speakers to express themselves fully in ways consistent with their cultural practices. A substantial staff effort was required to record the discussions and select and code the comments from the large number of participants. From the comments, it is clear that local observers have a particularly acute awareness of anomalies in animal health and behavior. However, at this broad geographic scale of information gathering, it appears that this method serves to generate hypotheses, which can be addressed through more detailed region-specific contaminants research.

Semi-directive Group Interviews.—The ICC pilot project described above emphasized the value of semi-directive (or semi-structured) group interviews among knowledgeable hunters in a community (Huntington et al. 1999; Mymrin et al. 1999). This method combined the interaction and stimulation of the conversation among the hunters with the comparative high efficiency in cost and time. Huntington noted the exploratory value of the semi-directive interview in which the researcher could follow the lead of local experts, learning of ecological connections, for example, which might have been missed by a rigid questionnaire (Huntington 1998). As with many Canadian projects, the ICC pilot project led by Huntington confirmed the value of maps as a stimulus to conversations about observations of animals throughout the life history and seasonal cycles.

In the Northstar project described above (U.S Army Engineer District Alaska 1999), following the development of the database from previous public testimony, the consultant researchers from Dames and Moore and Steven R. Braund & Associates conducted follow-up group interviews at meetings of whaling captains in the four participating communities. In addition to soliciting information about ice patterns, these interviews went on to ask the whaling captains for advice on project design to withstand pack ice pressures on the artificial island, which served as a drilling platform. These suggestions resulted in design modifications to increase the protection of the artificial island (U.S Army Engineer District Alaska 1999).

The method of semi-directive group interviews has the benefit of considerable economy of financial resources and researcher time, while gathering new and focused information and allowing for exploration of unanticipated ecological relations in the interviews. Because the approach is deployed at the community level, it also promotes a holistic understanding of the community-based body of knowledge, particularly when preliminary results are verified in a subsequent community meeting. Paradoxically, following the success of the demonstration project concerning beluga whales in the Bering Strait, this method has not been widely employed in subsequent research on local and traditional knowledge of fisheries in Alaska.

Intensive Ethnographic Fieldwork.—The majority of projects on fisheries, local and traditional/indigenous knowledge in the past decade, have used well-established methods for ethnographic fieldwork. In the examples noted above, the ADF&G Subsistence Division has supplemented its long-standing method of systematic household surveys regarding harvest practices with interviews of selected local experts concerning their natural history observations associated with this harvest (Wolfe and Spaeder 2009, this volume). With well-established researchers who have worked in their regions for decades, these projects have achieved very high sample sizes. For example, 96% of households participated in the study of the Koyukuk River region (Yukon River drainage) conducted by Brown et al. (2005), which documented uses of, and knowledge about, nonsalmon fishes. In addition, these long-standing working relationships have contributed to very effective interviewing and resulted in extensive information on natural history observations. In the Ahtna and Tlingit projects noted above, the investigators had more than two decades of experience in the regions, which contributed to their success in documenting information about indigenous stewardship practices, environmental ethics, and underlying belief systems (Simeone and Kari 2002; Langdon 2006).

Multi-disciplinary ethnographic field projects that integrate the efforts of fisheries ecologists and social scientists represents another promising approach. As Huntington (2000) has noted, traditional ecological knowledge research typically uses social scientists and methods to collect biological information. A rich example of collaboration is seen in the work of a biologist with significant experience among the indigenous people of the Yukon River (Brown), a Vunta Gwich'in Athabascan wildlife biologist (Fleener), and a long-time Subsistence Division researcher (Anderson). In a series of projects these authors documented local observations and collected new western scientific data concerning the ecological interaction of whitefish and beavers in the Yukon Flats area (Anderson and Fleener 2001; Brown and Fleener 2001).

An integrated interdisciplinary approach is also found in the "natural indicators" project currently being conducted by the Yukon River Drainage Fisheries Association (YRDFA) and an ADF&G Division of Subsistence researcher with funding from the AYK SSI (Mull et al. 2005). Building on YRDFA's previous projects on local and traditional/indigenous knowledge of Yukon River salmon (Moncrieff and Klein 2003), this project systematically explores how Yukon River residents interpret wind and weather, plant conditions, and behavior of birds, wildlife, and nonsalmon fish, as predictive indicators of salmon-run abundance and timing. Quantitative data on weather conditions, water levels, and salmon run parameters will then be compared to the local and traditional knowledge indicators, to develop a conceptual model of interactions. The primary interviews have been completed in the five participating communities. The comparisons with agency data on salmon run abundance and ecological variables are still under development.

While the growing body of documentation on local and traditional/indigenous knowledge in Alaska represents a significant achievement in the past decade, no comprehensive assessment has been made of how this work has improved fisheries management or environmental review in Alaska. However, several inquiries have contributed to such an analysis. Lazrus and Sepez (2005) surveyed NOAA researchers who had prepared a major Alaska groundfish fisheries environmental review. They found that the compilation of Alaska Native traditional environmental knowledge into an electronic database raised the pro-

file and directed researchers to key content of traditional knowledge (what they term "signposting"); however, the database suffered from limitations as to the temporal and spatial scales of the information relative to the topics of analysis. These authors also noted that a database of this sort runs a particular risk of dissociating the content from the context, what they term the "pluck it out and plug it in" model.

Huntington et al. (2002) offered an insightful comparison of the effectiveness of a "technical workshop" as a means for traditional knowledge holders and western scientists to exchange and integrate their diverse systems of knowledge and understanding. The authors highlighted the extensive background work and planning for the highly effective exchange of information in the Barrow Sea Ice Symposium of 2002. They also described 20 years of effective communication and mutual learning in the Alaska Beluga Whale Committee.[5] Agency researchers/managers and Alaska Native experts have jointly examined existing information, identified questions for field research, participated in the field work, and shared in interpreting the results of the projects. The authors attributed the successful communication of this committee to the continuity of the membership and the resulting relationships of respect and trust over two decades.

This small, but promising literature on application and effectiveness suggests that a key step for the developing discipline of local and traditional knowledge would be a broad initiative to identify and systematically evaluate a variety of methods for application in the specific context of Alaska fisheries management.

---

[5]Though not examined in the Huntington et al. 2002 article, the work of the Alaska Eskimo Whaling Commission, the Eskimo Walrus Commission, and the more recently established Alaska Nanuuq Commission would provide comparable cases.

Summary of Symposium Discussions

The symposium discussions in the break-out session focusing on integrating local and traditional knowledge were impassioned, rigorous, and enormously enriched by the spirited participation of several Gwitch'in and Yup'ik elders. However, it was found that the time allotted to this complex topic was a fraction of what might be needed for a full conversation consonant with Alaska Native ways of speaking. Four themes emerged in this discussion.

The cultural context of working together

In the opening comments around the circle of participants, many speakers noted that as scientists, managers, and local residents, we must all continue to strengthen our ways of working together. Several elders elaborated on their cultural perspective as to why it is so important that people learn to work together and to bridge the chasms of discord. In this view, if we continue in conflict, then the animals will become shy and they will not make themselves available. The fates of humans and animals are inextricably tied. For the sake of the salmon and for the future generations of fishing families, we must all make every effort to cooperate.

Foundational questions of trust and respect

Expressed in these discussions were the continuing deep wounds felt by many Alaska Native participants, who perceive most management discussions as cavalier and dismissive of the observations, perspectives, and wisdom of Alaska Native residents. While the speakers recognized and appreciated the effort by the AYK SSI to expand participation, a very strong need remains to develop new skills and formats for listening and learning together in cultur-

ally appropriate ways. Our colleagues challenged us to grow in our sensitivity regarding the language used and the potential for common terms and management concepts to sound disrespectful to Alaska Native participants. As an example, one person explained his concern that the term "traditional knowledge" is comparatively empty, whereas the alternative terms "Yup'ik knowledge" or "Gwitch'in knowledge" would more readily convey the roots and richness of a specific culture's knowledge and wisdom.[6] This summary has used the term "local and traditional/indigenous knowledge" in deference to this concern.

As concrete suggestions, speakers urged that great care be taken in documenting indigenous knowledge to ensure that the "direct voice" of elders comes through, not filtered and distorted by report writers. Similarly, our colleagues noted the great importance of fully acknowledging the contributions of specific elders and particular communities as the sources of important bodies of information and understanding.

Celebrating the potential for a major contribution to knowledge

Throughout the discussion, participants expressed great confidence that local and indigenous knowledge could add to the basic understanding of salmon ecology and potential management reforms. In effect, speakers emphasized that the collective knowledge of their communities was very fine-grained in its geographic scale, representing close ob-

---

[6]In reference to the Central Arctic Inuit, George Wenzel raised the same point in proposing that researchers reconceive traditional knowledge in broader and more culturally specific terms. For that region, he endorsed the term "Inuit Qaujimajatuqangit," defined as "encompass[ing] all aspects of Inuit culture including values, world-view, language, social organization, knowledge, life skills, perceptions, and expectations (Anonymous 1998:1, cited in Wenzel 2004).

servations of local areas. At the same time, this knowledge was very broad in the time scale, in that observations were accumulated over decades and generations.

One speaker noted a particularly valuable example for systematic inquiry. Historically, the small communities of the upper Kuskokwim River basin maintained sustainable subsistence salmon fisheries on small streams with very small runs. But with late 20th century changes in subsistence and commercial fisheries on the Kuskokwim River, fish are not coming back to these upper Kuskokwim River basin streams. Documentation is needed about past and current subsistence fishing patterns, particularly changes in locations, gear types, and mesh sizes. Also, the details of traditional fishery management practices in these communities must be recorded. With careful documentation of these human and cultural dimensions, the incremental contribution of these small streams to overall salmon run dynamics in the upper Kuskokwim River and for the river as a whole would be better understood.

Concerns about barriers

The excitement about the potential contribution of local and indigenous knowledge was tempered by a nuanced set of concerns about barriers to best practices, including conceptual, institutional, and economic obstacles. Participants noted that western science and local and traditional knowledge systems operate with different paradigms and conventions. While western science is largely quantitative and generalizes by extrapolation from small samples, local and traditional/indigenous knowledge is more intensively observational, holistic in appreciation of the many dimensions of ecological relations, and more likely to incorporate spiritual dimensions of inter-

pretation. Finding the language and framework for mutually respectful and mutually informative dialogue about these forms of knowledge and understanding remains a great challenge.

Science and management operate within particular institutional settings, and according to the participants, these often operate to constrain engagement with local and indigenous knowledge. Speakers noted the fragmentation by disciplines, such that fish biologists, habitat biologists, and cultural anthropologists typically operate within separate organizational divisions, with limited or sometimes even strained patterns of interaction. The same point could be made of organizational distinctions between state and federal agencies. These institutional barriers make collaboration difficult in multi-disciplinary inquiry, can inhibit the sharing of results, and prevent holistic synthesis and interpretation of results. The AYK SSI program was recognized as an important effort to bridge these institutional limitations.

Finally, the speakers noted that the promising efforts of recent years now face economic strains such that current levels of studies may not be sustained, and expanded research to fully achieve the potential for this work is unlikely. The AYK SSI, the Federal Subsistence Board, and the ADF&G Division of Subsistence have all contributed to important new work in traditional and indigenous knowledge about salmon fisheries, as well as subsistence fisheries in general. While together these initiatives have resulted in a substantial body of documentation, many other communities and subsistence fisheries could benefit from detailed inquiry. Participants expressed the hope that the AYK SSI would be able to continue to support local and traditional/indigenous knowledge research and its application to management.

Conclusion

The AYK SSI program has created an important forum in which local community representatives, scientists, and managers have been able to engage in robust and probing dialogue on salmon population trends and ecological dynamics, subsistence uses, and improved management practices. Of particular importance has been the effort to integrate local and traditional/indigenous knowledge into fisheries science and management. The discussion during the symposium revealed the extent to which local representatives are appreciative of the initiative but continue to hold very deep concerns about trust and sincerity in agencies' responses to their knowledge and understanding.

Paradoxically, the discussions did not indicate a widespread familiarity on the part of local community representatives with the growing body of traditional/indigenous knowledge research and documentation. Surprisingly, this work is not widely known in the local communities, or alternatively, the people familiar with this work were not active participants in the AYK SSI symposium. Trust and mutual respect likely would improve if the strong, collaborative research designs and the deep respect for traditional ecological understandings and stewardship practices in these studies were better known.

The participants in the discussions on integrating local and traditional/indigenous knowledge clearly have high hopes and aspirations for the AYK SSI program and its projects. Continuing the dialogue on local and traditional/indigenous knowledge begun during the symposium could yield substantial benefits. An on-going discussion forum might provide for more intensive information exchange, so that more participants would be able to look critically at existing work, and to build on this work to highlight specific priorities for new projects to be funded by the AYK SSI.

References

Anonymous. 1998. Towards an *Inuit Qaujimajatuqangit (IQ)* policy for Nunavut: a discussion paper. Mimeo. In possession of G. W. Wenzel, Department of Geography, McGill University, Montreal, Quebec.

Alaska Department of Fish and Game (ADF&G) and Institute of Social and Economic Research (ISER). 1996. Understanding harvest assessment in the north. Synthesis of the Conference on Harvest Assessment April 20–22, 1995. Girdwood, Alaska. Institute of Social and Economic Research, Anchorage.

Anderson, D. B., C. L. Brown, R. J. Walker, and K. Elkin. 2004. Traditional ecological knowledge and contemporary subsistence harvest of non-salmon fish in the Koyukuk River drainage, Alaska. Federal Subsistence Fishery Monitoring Program, Final Report for Study 01–100. U.S. Fish and Wildlife Service, Office of Subsistence Management, Fisheries Resource Monitoring Program, Fishery Information Service, Anchorage.

Anderson, D. B., and C. Fleener. 2001. Whitefish and beaver Ecology of the Yukon Flats, Juneau, Alaska. Final Report No. FIS 00–006, Technical Paper No. 270 Alaska Department of Fish and Game, Division of Subsistence, Anchorage.

AYK SSI (Arctic-Yukon-Kuskokwim Sustainable Salmon Initiative). 2006. Arctic-Yukon-Kuskokwim Sustainable Salmon Research and Restoration Plan. Bering Sea Fishermen's Association. Anchorage, Alaska.

Brown, C., J. Burr, K. Elkin, and R. J. Walker. 2005. Contemporary subsistence uses and population distribution of non-salmon fish in Grayling, Anvik, Shageluk, and Holy Cross. Federal Subsistence Fishery Monitoring Program, Final Project No. 02–037-2. USFWS Office of Subsistence Management, Fisheries Resources Monitoring Program, Fisheries Information Service, Anchorage, Alaska. Technical Paper No. 289.

Brown, R. J., and C. Fleener. 2001. Beaver dam influence on fish in lentic and lotic habitats in the Black River Drainage, Alaska. Final Report No. FIS 00–004. U. S. Fish and Wildlife Service, Fairbanks Fishery Research Office, Fairbanks, Alaska.

Buklis, L. S. 2002. Subsistence fisheries management on federal public lands in Alaska. Fisheries 27(7):10–17.

Burwell, M. 2001. Public hearings related to the proposed activities of the Arctic Continental Shelf and Related Areas. [CD-ROM electronic compilation of transcripts.] Minerals Management Service, Alaska Region, Anchorage.

Coiley-Kenner, P., T. M. Krieg, and D. Holen, compilers. 2003. From Neqa to Tepa. A database with traditional knowledge about fish of Bristol Bay and the northern Alaska Peninsula. Version 2. ADF&G, Juneau.

Freeman, M. M. R. 1989. The Alaska Eskimo Whaling Commission: successful co-management under extreme conditions. Pages 137–153 *in* E. Pinkerton, editor. Cooperative management of local fisheries: New directions for improved management and community development. University of British Columbia Press, Vancouver.

Georgette, S., and A. Shiedt. 2005. Whitefish: traditional ecological knowledge and subsistence fishing in Kotzebue Sound Region, Alaska. Division of Subsistence, Alaska Department of Fish and Game, Technical Paper No. 290. Juneau, Alaska.

Gottesfeld, A., C. Barnes, and C. Soto. 2009. Case history of the Skeena Fisheries Commission: developing aboriginal fishery management capacity in northern British Columbia. Pages 921–939 *in* C. C. Krueger and C. E. Zimmerman, editors. Pacific salmon: ecology and management of western Alaska's populations. American Fisheries Society Symposium 70, Bethesda, Maryland.

Hild, C., editor. 1994. Handbook of the Alaska Native traditional knowledge and ways of knowing workshop. September 13–14, 1994. Anchorage: RurAL CAP and the Indigenous Peoples' Council for Marine Mammals. Rural Alaska Community Action Program, Anchorage.

Huntington, H. P. 1992. Wildlife management and subsistence hunting in Alaska. University of Washington Press, Seattle.

Huntington, H. P. 1998. Observations on the utility of the semi-directive interview for documenting traditional ecological knowledge. Arctic 51:237–242.

Huntington, H. P. 2000. Using traditional ecological knowledge in science: methods and applications. Ecological Applications 10:1270–1274.

Huntington, H. P., P. K. Brown-Schwalenburg, K. Frost, M. E. Fernandez-Gimenez, and D. W. Norton. 2002. Observations on the workshop as a means of improving communication between holders of traditional and scientific knowledge. Environmental Management 30:778–792.

Huntington, H. P., and the Communities of Buckland, Elim, Koyuk, Point Lay, and Shaktoolik. 1999. Traditional Knowledge of the ecology of Beluga Whales (*Delphinapterus leucas*) in the eastern Chukchi and northern Bering seas, Alaska. Arctic 52: 49–61.

Krueger, C. C., C. E. Zimmerman, and J. J. Spaeder. 2009. Ecology and management of western Alaska Pacific salmon: introduction to the proceedings. Pages 3–10 *in* C. C. Krueger and C. E. Zimmer-

man, editors. Pacific salmon: ecology and management of western Alaska's populations. American Fisheries Society Symposium 70, Bethesda, Maryland.

Krupnik, I., and D. Jolly, editors. 2002. The Earth is faster now: indigenous observations of Arctic environmental change. Arctic Research Consortium of the United States, Fairbanks, Alaska.

Kruse, J., P. Cochran, and L. Merculieff. 2004. Traditional knowledge and contaminants project and resource guide project. Final Reports. July 2004. Prepared under EPA Assistance Agreement T-98022601 and T-898077301. Institute of Social and Economic Research and the Alaska Native Science Commission, Anchorage.

Langdon, S. J. 1984. Alaska Native self-regulatory subsistence compacts—Alaska Eskimo Whaling Commission. Pages 42–51 *in* Alaska Native subsistence: current regulatory regimes and issues: Volume XIX. Paper for roundtable discussions of subsistence. October 10–13, 1984. Alaska Native Review Commission, Alaska.

Langdon, S. J. 2006. Traditional ecological knowledge and harvesting of salmon by *Huna* and *Hinyaa* Tlingit. Final Report. Fisheries Information Service Project 02–104. *Lingit* transcription and translation by Kenneth Austin. Research conducted under contract No 43–0109-2–342 between the U.S. Fish and Wildlife Service, Office of Subsistence Management, and Central Council of Tlingit and Haida Indian Tribes of Alaska, Anchorage.

Lazrus, H., and J. Sepez. 2005. The NOAA Fisheries Alaska Native traditional environmental knowledge database. *In* J. Sepez and H. Lazrus, editors, Traditional environmental knowledge in federal natural resource management agencies. Practicing Anthropology 27:33–37.

Linderman, J. C., Jr., and D. J. Bergstrom. 2009. Kuskokwim management area: salmon escapement, harvest, and management. Pages 541–599 *in* C. C. Krueger and C. E. Zimmerman, editors. Pacific salmon: ecology and management of western Alaska's populations. American Fisheries Society Symposium 70, Bethesda, Maryland.

Miraglia, R. A. 1998. Traditional ecological knowledge handbook: a training manual and reference guide for designing, conducting, and participating in research projects using traditional ecological knowledge. Alaska Department of Fish and Game, Division of Subsistence. Anchorage.

Minerals Management Service (MMS). 2007. Traditional knowledge and how MMS uses it in the decision process. Available: http://www.mms.gov/ alaska/native/tradknow/tk_mms2.htm (October 2007).

Moncrieff, C. F., and J. C. Klein. 2003. Traditional ecological knowledge along the Yukon River. U. S. Fish and Wildlife Service, Office of Subsistence Management, Fisheries Resource Monitoring Program, Final Report (Study No. 01–015). Yukon River Drainage Fisheries Association, Anchorage, Alaska.

Mull, K., C. Moncrieff, and C. Brown. 2005. Natural indicators of salmon run abundance and timing. Research Proposal submitted to the AYK SSI for funding 2006–2009. Yukon River Drainage Fisheries Association and Alaska Department of Fish and Game, Division of Subsistence. Anchorage and Fairbanks.

Mymrin, N. I.; the Communities of Novoe Chaplino, Sireniki, Uelen, and Yanrakinnot; and H. P. Huntington. 1999. Traditional knowledge of the ecology of Beluga Whales (*Delphinapterus leucas*) in the northern Bering Sea, Chukotka, Russia. Arctic 52:62–70.

NRC (National Research Council). 2005. Developing a research and restoration plan for Arctic-Yukon-Kuskokwim (Western Alaska) Salmon. Committee on review of Arctic-Yukon-Kuskokwim- (Western Alaska) Research and Restoration Plan for Alaska. The National Academies Press, Washington, D.C.

Pinkerton, E. 2009. The Skeena watershed partnership: learning from success and failure in salmon management. Pages 903–919 in C. C. Krueger and C. E. Zimmerman, editors. Pacific salmon: ecology and management of western Alaska's populations. American Fisheries Society Symposium 70, Bethesda, Maryland.

Sepez, J., C. Package, J. Isaacs, and K. Nixon, editors. 2003. Draft NOAA Fisheries TEK database: a compilation of written source material documenting the traditional ecological knowledge of Alaska Natives, with a focus on marine resources. Alaska Fisheries Science Center, NOAA Fisheries, Seattle.

Simeone, W. E., and J. Kari. 2002. Copper River subsistence evaluation 2000 and traditional knowledge project, part one. In collaboration with the Copper River Native Association, Cheeesh Na' Tribal

Council, and the Chitina Tribal Council. Final Report No. FIS 00–040. Alaska Department of Fish and Game, Division of Subsistence. Anchorage.

Stevenson, M. G. 1996. Indigenous knowledge in environmental assessment. Arctic 49:278–291.

Usher, P. J. 2000. Traditional ecological knowledge in environmental assessment and management. Arctic 53:183–193.

U.S. Army Engineer District Alaska. 1999. Final environmental impact statement Beaufort Sea Oil and Gas Development/Northstar Project. February 1999. Anchorage.

Watt-Cloutier, S. 2005. Petition to the Inter American Commission On Human Rights seeking relief from violations resulting from global warming caused by acts and omissions of the United States. Submitted by Sheila Watt-Cloutier, with the support of the Inuit Circumpolar Conference, on behalf of all Inuit of the Arctic regions of the United States and Canada, Including: [63 Named Co-petitioners]. Available: http://www.ciel.org/Publications/ICC_Petition_7Dec05.pdf (October 2007).

Wenzel, G. W. 1999. Traditional ecological knowledge and Inuit: reflections on TEK research and ethics. Arctic 52:113–124.

Wenzel, G. W. 2004. From TEK to IQ: *Inuit Qaujimajatuqangit* and Inuit cultural ecology. Arctic Anthropology 41:238–250.

Wheeler, P., and A. Craver. 2005. Office of Subsistence Management and issues and challenges of integrating TEK into subsistence fisheries management. *In* J. Sepez and H. Lazrus, editors. Traditional environmental knowledge in federal natural resource management agencies. Practicing Anthropology 27: 15–19.

Wolfe, R. J., and J. J. Spaeder. 2009. People and salmon of the Yukon and Kuskokwim drainages and Norton Sound in Alaska: fishery harvests, culture change, and local knowledge systems. Pages 349–379 in C. C. Krueger and C. E. Zimmerman, editors. Pacific salmon: ecology and management of western Alaska's populations. American Fisheries Society Symposium 70, Bethesda, Maryland.

American Fisheries Society Symposium 70:395–431, 2009
© 2009 by the American Fisheries Society

Patterns and Trends in Subsistence Salmon Harvests, Norton Sound–Port Clarence Area, Alaska 1994–2003

James S. Magdanz[*,1]

Divison of Subsistence, Alaska Department of Fish and Game
1255 W 8th Street, Juneau, Alaska 99802, USA

Eric Trigg and Austin Ahmasuk

Department of Natural Resources, Kawerak, Inc.
P.O. Box 948, Nome, Alaska 99762, USA

Peter Nanouk, David S. Koster, and Kurt Kamletz

Divison of Subsistence, Alaska Department of Fish and Game
1255 W 8th Street, Juneau, Alaska 99802, USA

Abstract.—Using harvest data from 7,838 household surveys from ten small, remote, predominantly Alaska Native communities, this project explored patterns and trends in subsistence harvests of salmon *Oncorhynchus* spp. from 1994–2003. During the study period, estimated subsistence salmon harvests declined by 5.8% annually. Most of the declines occurred during the first five years (1994–1998), when harvests trended lower by about 8% annually. During the latter years (1999–2003), harvests trended lower by about 1% annually across all communities. Seven hypotheses were tested. For six selected salmon stocks as a group, subsistence salmon harvests were not associated with salmon escapements (hypothesis 1). However, for two individual stocks, subsistence harvests were associated with escapements. Community subsistence harvests were associated with community population size (hypothesis 2), while per capita harvests were not associated with community size. About 21% of the households harvested 70% of the salmon, by weight, more concentrated than the 30:70 distributions observed by Wolfe (hypothesis 3) but less concentrated than the widely observed 20:80 Pareto distribution. Household "social type" (age of household heads and household structure) was associated with subsistence harvests (hypothesis 4). Harvests increased with the age of household heads, and households headed by couples reported higher average harvests than households headed by single persons, especially single males. Households that harvested salmon intermittently (i.e., not every year) did *not* account for most of the variation in community salmon harvests (hypothesis 5) and were *not* more likely to fish during years of greater salmon abundance (hypothesis 6). The number of salmon harvested for subsistence was not associated with the number of salmon retained from commercial fishing for personal use (hypothesis 7), although a weak negative association was observed for a small fraction of households with high harvests of Chinook salmon *O. tshawytscha*. Multi-household, extended-family production networks could explain some of the patterns observed in the system, including the power-law distribution of harvests and the stable overall production of households that fished intermittently.

[*]Corresponding author: james.magdanz@alaska.gov
[1]Current address: Alaska Department of Fish and Game, Box 689, Kotzebue, Alaska 99752, USA

Introduction

In rural Alaska, several hundred small, remote, predominantly Native communities harvest millions of fish each year for subsistence, often from stocks targeted by commercial and sport fisheries. When these fish stocks are fully utilized, as is often the case with salmon, conserving the stocks, allocating them among various user groups, and maintaining state and federal priorities for subsistence requires reliable harvest data.

Estimating subsistence harvests in rural Alaska presents many challenges. At least since 1957, managers and researchers have relied extensively on face-to-face household surveys to document rural Alaska subsistence harvests (Raleigh 1957). There is a large and growing body of subsistence fisheries harvest data collected by government agencies like the Alaska Department of Fish and Game and by Native regional nonprofit corporations like Kawerak, Inc. These data sets are of variable quality. In older data sets, sampling rates and strategies often are unknown, few (if any) survey protocols survive, harvest totals usually include participating households only, and expanded estimates for entire communities usually are missing. In newer data sets, survey methods have been more rigorous, quality of the data has improved, and expanded community harvest estimates are the norm.

Agency managers and management boards rely extensively on these subsistence harvest survey estimates. But after the boards adjourn and the annual management reports are written, subsistence survey data are archived and rarely revisited. This study retrieved and compiled ten years of annual subsistence salmon survey data for ten northwest Alaska communities into a panel data set, then explored patterns and trends in subsistence harvests. By "patterns," it means: "a reliable sample of observable characteristics of a person, group, or institution." By "trends," it means: "a statistically detectable change over time." It is, to the authors' knowledge, the first effort to explore an Alaska subsistence fishery using such an extensive panel data set.

The study was conducted in four phases. In the first phase, researchers merged ten separate annual data sets into a single database. In the second phase, researchers revisited each study community, verified household identifiers, and gathered additional data. In the third phase, researchers merged the phase 1 data with phase 2 data. In the fourth phase, researchers explored the aggregated, expanded panel data set, and tested seven hypotheses:

1. Community subsistence salmon harvests were positively associated with salmon escapement.

2. Community subsistence salmon harvests were positively associated with community populations.

3. Approximately 30% of the households harvested approximately 70% of the subsistence salmon (by edible weight).

4. Household social type was associated with the amount of salmon harvested.

5. Households that fished intermittently—that is, they fished in some years and not others—accounted for most of the variation in community salmon harvests.

6. Households that fished intermittently were more likely to fish during years of greater salmon abundance.

7. For households that fished salmon commercially, the number of salmon harvested for subsistence was negatively associated with the number of salmon retained from commercial catches for personal use.

This report begins with a rationale for the analysis. For readers unfamiliar with remote northwest Alaska communities, the report discusses the setting at some length, then describes the methods used to collect, aggregate, and analyze the data. The results of the analyses are presented and then discussed. The discussion concludes with recommendations for collecting, analyzing, and archiving annual subsistence harvest survey data for Alaska.

Rationale for the Analyses

In Alaska, most subsistence harvest surveys can be categorized into two general types. The first type is the occasional, comprehensive survey of the harvests of all species by residents of a single community or small group of communities during a single year, which results in a cross sectional data set. Usually, comprehensive surveys are long, burdensome for respondents, expensive to administer and analyze, and consequently, relatively rare. Nonetheless, most analyses of subsistence systems have been based on the occasional comprehensive survey (c.f. Andrews 1988; Case and Halpin 1990; Davis et al. 2003; Georgette and Loon 1993; Holen et al. 2006; Schroeder and Kookesh 1990; Stanek et al. 2007). A few scholars have gathered comprehensive data from a panel of households for more than one year (c.f. Braund 1993; Burch 1985; Fall and Utermohle 1995, 1999), but collection and analysis of comprehensive panel data sets are not the norm in subsistence research.

A second type of subsistence survey is the recurrent, annual survey of the harvests of a particular species by residents of many communities. Recurrent surveys have been used in Alaska most frequently to estimate subsistence harvests of salmon (Fall et al. 2007a) and migratory birds (Wentworth 2007). More recently, recurrent, annual surveys have been used to estimate subsistence harvests of hali-

but (Fall et al. 2007b), harbor seals, and sea lions (Alaska Department of Fish and Game and Alaska Native Harbor Seal Commission 2008). The annual harvest surveys are short, simple, and less expensive to administer and analyze than the comprehensive surveys. Perhaps because they were conceived primarily as management tools, though, analysis has been limited primarily to annual harvest estimates. As data accumulated, the aggregated annual harvest estimates were analyzed as time series. Like the data from comprehensive surveys, the data from annual surveys have been stored as cross sectional data sets.

One of the confounding factors in both kinds of surveys was widespread cooperation among groups of households in harvesting and processing fish for subsistence. Surveys were administered to a household, and harvests were reported at the household-level. In any analysis based on household level data, one assumption must be that a household is a useful unit of analysis. Some researchers consider households to be the primary unit of subsistence production in northern regions (Usher et al. 2003). That's true when comparing a capital-industrial economy with a domestic-subsistence economy, but it is an exceedingly simple truth about a complex system. Few rural northern households harvest and process wild foods in isolation from other households. Most households produce, process, and distribute wild foods within family-based networks of cooperating households. Magdanz et al. (2002) argue that household production is best understood in the context of extended family networks (see also Wolfe and Spaeder 2009, this volume).

Evidence for the latter perspective was the observation that approximately 30% of the households harvest 70% of the wild foods in most small, rural, subsistence-dependent communities in Alaska (Wolfe 1987; Wolfe et al. 2009). If the analysis was limited to a single type of wild food, such as salmon or seals, specialization in harvests often was even more pronounced. It was not uncommon to find 20% of the households harvesting 80% of a community's total harvest of a particular species while 50% of the households harvested none, as some data in this analysis show.

Regardless of one's perspective about the role of the household in subsistence economies, several things were clear:

• Compared with social networks, households are easy to identify and locate. For practical and logistical reasons, household surveys will continue to be a primary method of gathering wildlife harvest information in the North.

• Households' wild food harvests vary widely and are not normally distributed. This makes it difficult to accurately estimate subsistence harvests with simple random samples.

• Not enough time or money is provided to census every household in the North every year, even for a major species like salmon. Improving the accuracy and precision of harvest estimates will require refinements in sampling and analysis methods.

Given these conditions, the research problem becomes how to compensate for the limitations of the household as a unit of analysis. A better understanding of household harvest patterns is one approach.

Household harvest patterns already have been explored by several researchers. Examining comprehensive survey data from widely dispersed rural Alaska communities, Wolfe found that the ages of household heads and subsistence production were significantly related (Wolfe 1987). In a study of two northwest Alaska communities, researchers identified five different harvesting strata based on household social type (Magdanz et al. 2002). In a study of the economic practices of *Iñuit* in northern Canada, including wild food harvesting, Chabot stratified households based on

the gender and employment status of household heads (Chabot 2003). The northwest salmon survey, which provided the harvest data for this analysis, employed a stratified approach, calculating separate harvest estimates for households that "usually fished" and for households that "usually did not fish" (Georgette et al. 2004). This improved the precision of community harvest estimates.

Given the patterns that researchers have observed, subsistence harvest models incorporating household characteristics should be more reliable. If one wanted to predict future salmon harvests, it would be useful to know, for example, if some households were consistent harvesters in all circumstances, and if so, which ones? Were commercial salmon fishing opportunities associated with subsistence salmon harvests? As a step toward improving harvest models, this study attempted to identify and describe harvest patterns for groups of households in the communities of the northwest salmon survey project.

The Norton Sound–Port Clarence Area of northwestern Alaska provided an unusual opportunity for analyses of subsistence salmon harvest data collected over time. Sampling rates were high, and consistent household identifiers were maintained throughout the decade of surveys.

Setting

As defined in Alaska fisheries regulations, the Norton Sound–Port Clarence Area included all waters draining into Norton Sound and the Bering Sea between Cape Prince of Wales in the north and Point Romanoff in the south (Figure 1). The Norton Sound District included all waters between the westernmost tip of Cape Douglas and Point Romanoff. The Port Clarence District included all waters of Alaska between the westernmost tip of Cape Prince of Wales and the westernmost tip of Cape Douglas.

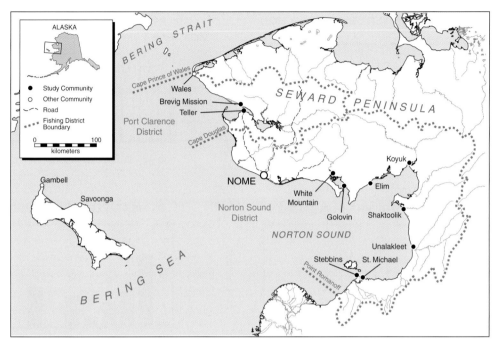

FIGURE 1. Locations of communities within the Norton Sound-Port Clarence Area, Alaska. Annual household subsistence salmon harvest surveys were conducted in 10 communities (solid circles) during 1994–2003.

This section reviews the available salmon species, discusses the study communities populations and economies, and summarizes salmon harvests during the study period. During the study period, similar conditions existed throughout Arctic and Western Alaska (Howe and Martin 2009, this volume; Knapp 2009, this volume).

Five species of Pacific salmon *Oncorhynchus* were found in the Norton Sound–Port Clarence area: Chinook salmon *O. tshawytscha*, sockeye salmon *O. nerka*, coho salmon *O. kisutch*, pink salmon *O. gorbuscha*, and chum salmon *O. keta*. Salmon returns were enumerated at 10 ADF&G and cooperative projects in the area. The Alaska Department of Fish and Game operated two counting towers, one weir, and one test fishery in the area. Other organizations, including Kawerak Inc., the Native Village of Unalakleet, the U.S. Bureau of Land Management, and the Norton Sound Economic Development Corporation

operated two counting towers and four weirs on area streams. ADF&G also conducted in-season aerial surveys to monitor adult salmon escapements (Kent 2007).

Salmon escapement data were not available for all species or for all streams in the Norton Sound–Port Clarence Area. In addition, although most commercial and subsistence harvests occurred in or near terminal streams, migrating Yukon River stocks were present in southern Norton Sound and migrating Kotzebue Sound stocks were present in northern Norton Sound.

Because they do not include all salmon streams, available escapement data should be treated as indices rather than estimates of total salmon abundance. Data from the enumeration projects and aerial surveys showed highly variable, but generally declining escapements of Chinook, chum and coho salmon stocks during the study period (Figure 2) (Kent 2007). In some years, commercial

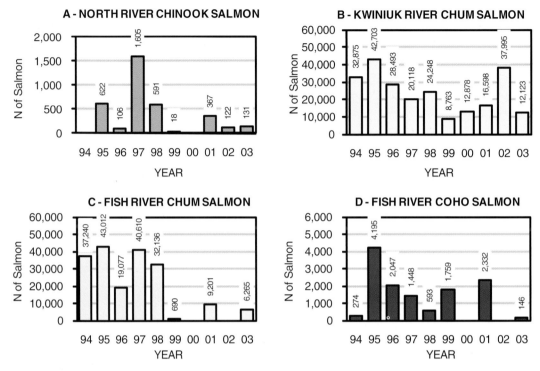

FIGURE 2. Estimates of salmon spawning escapements for four stocks in the Norton Sound-Port Clarence area, Alaska, 1994–2003. Estimates for North River (A) and Kwiniuk River (B) were obtained from counting towers, while estimates for Fish River (C & D) were obtained from aerial surveys.

fishing was closed to protect salmon stocks in northern Norton Sound, in the vicinity of Golovin, White Mountain, and Elim. Sockeye salmon were an exception to the declining trends. Although comparable escapement data were not available, Salmon Lake sockeye stocks began to increase in 1999. Large escapements (>40,000 sockeye) became the norm after 2002 (Burkhart and Dunmall 2006). A complete review of salmon fishery harvests and escapements was provided by Menard et al. (2009, this volume).

During the study period, there were 14 permanent communities in the Norton Sound–Port Clarence Area, beginning with Wales in the northwest and continuing clockwise to the east and south to Stebbins (Figure 1). Ten communities were included in this study; each study community had been surveyed in each year from 1994 through 2003. Except

for White Mountain, the study communities were located on the coast and harvested salmon in both marine and fresh waters. Gambell, Savoonga, and Wales were excluded because they were surveyed only once or twice during the study decade. Nome was excluded because subsistence salmon fishing there was much more strictly regulated, because Nome salmon fishing regulations changed substantially in the middle of the study period, and because Nome subsistence salmon harvest data were gathered using different methods. For these reasons, Nome did not provide a good comparison for the smaller communities for the purposes of these analyses.

In 2003, the study communities ranged in size from 156 people in Golovin to 741 people in Unalakleet. The median community population was 278 people, and the average community population in 2003 was an esti-

Patterns and Trends in Subsistence Salmon Harvests, Norton Sound–Port Clarence Area

mated 337 people (Alaska Department of Labor 2005). Approximately 90% of the communities' residents were Alaska Native (U.S. Census 2001). Native proportions ranged from 86% Native (White Mountain) to 95% Native (Stebbins, Shaktoolik, and Elim). Except in Unalakleet, the largest community, the typical nonNative resident was a school teacher who remained for only a few years.

Between 1994 and 2003, the total population of the ten study communities increased from 3,177 people to 3,555 (Figure 3). Brevig Mission, Elim, Koyuk, St. Michael, and Stebbins increased by more than 20% over the decade, while White Mountain and Shaktoolik increased by about 7%. Golovin declined by 0.6%, while Unalakleet and Teller declined by 3% and 7% respectively, over the ten-year period. There was no geographic pattern to

the growth of community populations; northern communities were as likely to increase as southern communities. Larger communities accounted for most of the growth in the human population.

The cost of living was substantially higher in the study communities than in Anchorage. The University of Alaska estimated that food for a family of four with children ages 6–11 cost 59% more in Nome than in Anchorage. Fuel oil in Nome cost 34% more than in Anchorage (Figure 3). Such comparisons can only be a general guide. The cost of living calculation "ignores the substitution of subsistence-harvested meats, fowl, fish, berries, and other foods for store-bought items" (Fried and Windisch-Cole 2001). The 2000 census estimated the average personal income in the study communities to be $10,841 per

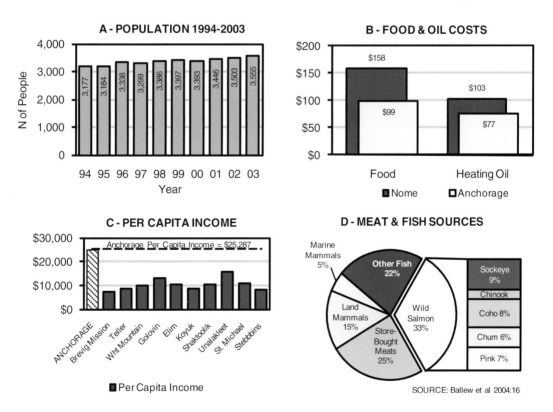

FIGURE 3. Community population sizes, 1994–2004 (A); food and oil costs in 2000 (B); per capita income in 2001 (C); and meat and fish sources in 2002 (D) for communities in the Norton Sound-Port Clarence Area, Alaska.

person per year, ranging from a low of $7,278 in Brevig Mission to a high of $15,845 in Unalakleet (Figure 3). For comparison, the average income in Anchorage was $25,287.

In 2002, the Alaska Native Health Board conducted a statewide diet survey, which included four communities in Norton Sound (Figure 3). In Norton Sound, 151 survey respondents reported consuming an annual total of 17,023 kg of wild foods, including 6,965 kg of salmon, 4,714 kg of other fish, and 3,125 kg of caribou and moose (Ballew et al. 2004:16). Wild fish and meat accounted for 75% of all meat and fish consumed by the respondents. Salmon alone contributed 33% of the total.

Comprehensive survey data were available for only two of the study communities. For 1989, Conger and Magdanz estimated the harvest of all types of wild foods to be 274 edible kg per person per year in Golovin and 263 edible kg per person per year in Brevig Mission. Salmon contributed 73 kg per person in Golovin and 54 kg per person in Brevig Mission. The survey data used in this study reported harvests as numbers of fish. Converted to kilograms of salmon harvested per capita, for comparison, the average estimated salmon harvest was 44 edible kg per person per year in the ten study communities from 1994–2003. The per capita salmon harvest calculated from data in the Alaska Traditional Diet Survey final report was 46 kg. The diet and harvest surveys, using very different methods, produced similar estimates for salmon, land mammals, and other fish, well within confidence intervals.

In addition to fishing for salmon for subsistence, 178 households in the sample (23% of the average number of households surveyed annually) reported that at least one member of the household fished salmon commercially. Commercial fishermen fished primarily to earn money, but they were allowed to retain commercially caught salmon for their personal use. Some did so, and these are included in subsistence harvest totals.

Although an individual may participate in either subsistence or commercial salmon fisheries, the two fisheries operate under very different legal and regulatory frameworks. In Alaska, subsistence uses of salmon have a priority over other consumptive uses of salmon, such as sport and commercial fishing. Under law, when salmon stocks are not sufficient to provide for *all consumptive uses*, as was often the case in Norton Sound during the study period, nonsubsistence uses are restricted or eliminated first. This can be seen clearly in Figure 4B; the decline in commercial harvests was far more substantial than the decline in subsistence harvests from 1994 through 2003.

Commercial salmon fishing occurred in the vicinity of six study communities (White Mountain, Golovin, Elim, Koyuk, Shaktoolik, and Unalakleet), but not in Brevig Mission, Teller, St. Michael, or Stebbins. Commercial harvests declined during the study period, as a result of declining salmon stocks and deteriorating market conditions (Figure 4). Note the highly cyclical nature of the pink salmon commercial fishery, reflecting the cyclical abundance of pink salmon (Menard et al. 2009).

In Norton Sound, on the Yukon River, and on the Kuskokwim River, commercial and subsistence salmon fisheries were similar in many ways (there were no commercial salmon fisheries in Port Clarence). Most commercial salmon fishermen were local Alaska Natives, who used small open skiffs and set gillnets, and who fished close to their home communities (Kohler et al. 2004). Most used some of the income from commercial fishing to support subsistence harvesting and processing activities. Commercial fishing vessels often were used for subsistence activities as well.

Compared with some other Alaska commercial salmon fisheries, the Norton Sound commercial fishery was small. During the ten years, 1994–2003, the Norton Sound commercial salmon catch averaged 311,916

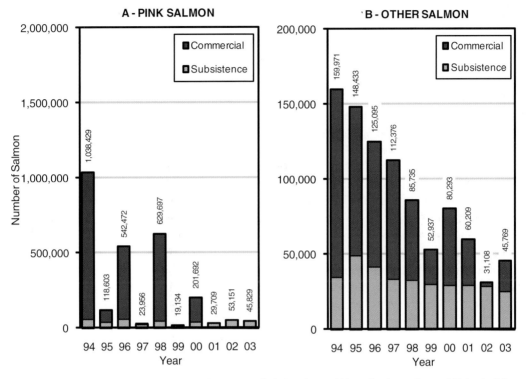

FIGURE 4. Commercial and subsistence harvests of pink salmon (A) and other salmon (B) in the Norton Sound-Port Clarence Area, 1994–2003. Note order of magnitude difference in graph scales.

salmon annually, of which 246,363 were pink salmon (Kohler et al. 2004:105). By comparison, from 1993–2002, the Bristol Bay commercial salmon catch averaged 25,113,484 salmon annually, of which 24,270,531 were sockeye salmon (Weiland et al. 2004).

Pink salmon were less valuable than sockeye salmon. Consequently, the average annual exvessel value of the Norton Sound catch from 1994–2003 was $284,436, while the average annual exvessel value of the Bristol Bay catch from 1993–2002 was almost $101 million (Kohler et al. 2004; Weiland et al. 2004).

Moreover, during the study period, increasing supplies of farmed salmon caused Alaska to fall "from a position of the dominant supplier of salmon to world markets to that of a marginal supplier" and dragged wild salmon prices down (Knapp 2009). Declining salmon abundance resulted in increas-

ing commercial restrictions in some areas of Norton Sound. The number of commercial salmon permit holders with Norton Sound addresses declined from 210 permits in 1994 to 149 permits in 2003. The number of commercial salmon permits fished in Norton Sound declined from 119 permits in 1994 to only 30 permits in 2003 (Kohler et al. 2004).

Commercial fishermen in Norton Sound who stopped fishing commercially did not stop fishing altogether. They fished commercially during years when markets and prices made commercial effort worthwhile. In other years, they fished for subsistence. When engaged in commercial fishing, commercial fishermen were not allowed to subsistence fish (to prevent the sale of subsistence-caught salmon). Commercial fishermen were allowed to retain as many salmon as they wished from their commercial catches, and other members of the commercial fisherman's household were allowed to fish in subsistence fisheries. This created a dynamic relationship between commercial and subsistence fishing, which was explored in this analysis.

During this time, there were no subsistence harvest limits in any of the study communities, subsistence fishing was allowed throughout the salmon runs, and the entire area was open to subsistence salmon fishing, with three exceptions. First, in the mouth of the Unalakleet River, subsistence salmon fishing was closed on Sundays to conserve Chinook salmon. Second, in the Port Clarence District, subsistence salmon fishing was closed two days a week, by regulation. This regulation was not enforced during the study period, and eventually was repealed. Third, in the immediate vicinity of Nome, subsistence salmon fishing was severely limited by fishing periods, harvest limits, closed waters, and other restrictions, including limited access "Tier II" fishing for chum. Nome, however, was not one of the study communities included in this analysis, and the Nome restrictions did not apply to the study communities.

Thus, regulatory changes did not explain changes in subsistence harvest trends or patterns observed in the study communities. Regulatory changes, however, were a factor in declining commercial harvests. During the study period, regulatory responses to declining salmon abundance was focused almost entirely on commercial salmon fisheries.

In sum, the study area included primarily small Alaska Native communities with substantial dependence on wild foods. Per capita incomes, when adjusted for the cost of food, were only about one fourth per capita incomes in Anchorage. While the study communities were of a similar size and ethnic composition, they also differed in important ways. Some had growing populations in the study decade, while others had stable or declining populations. Some had commercial salmon fisheries; others did not. Sockeye and Chinook salmon were more abundant in east-

ern Norton Sound and in Port Clarence than in other portions of the area. Pink salmon were extremely cyclical in some areas, but less cyclical in other areas. Common to all communities was a substantial and long-term reliance upon wild fish as a source of food. Residents of these small communities relied on wild foods for three-fourths of the meat and fish in their diet, and wild salmon were one of the largest contributors to the local diet.

During the study period from 1994–2003, community populations increased about 1% annually. Salmon abundance declined substantially in most areas, resulting in reductions to commercial fishery opportunity and lost income. Subsistence salmon harvests declined as well but, protected in part by subsistence priorities, the declines were not as substantial as commercial harvests.

Methods

The northwest salmon harvest survey project began in 1994 in response to chum salmon declines throughout western Alaska. The purpose was to provide reliable annual estimates of subsistence salmon harvests in Norton Sound, Port Clarence, and Kotzebue Sound for use in fisheries management. The project was modeled on similar efforts in the Yukon River and Kuskokwim River areas of Alaska.

Results of the surveys were published in a series of annual reports (Georgette 1996a 1996b; Georgette and Utermohle 1997, 1998, 1999, 2000, 2001; Georgette et al. 2003a, 2003b, 2004; Magdanz and Utermohle 1994) and summarized in annual management reports (Banducci et al. 2003; Brennan et al. 1999; Bue et al. 1996a 1996b, 1997; Kohler et al. 2004). From each household, the surveys collected the following data:

• Number of people in household.

• Whether household *usually* fished for salmon for subsistence.

• Whether household fished for salmon for subsistence *this year*.

• Number of salmon harvested for subsistence.

• Number of salmon harvested with rods and reels.

• Types of gear used to harvest salmon for subsistence.

• Number of salmon harvested for dog food.

• Number of salmon retained from commercial harvests.

Surveys were kept simple to minimize costs and respondent fatigue, and were consistent to provide comparability from year to year. More detail on survey procedures were described by Magdanz et al. 2005.

Researchers attempted a census in each community each year. For the ten study communities, annual harvest survey samples ranged from 78% of occupied households in 1994, the first year of the project, to 94% in 2002. Over the ten-year duration of the project, the total sample was 88.1% of occupied households.

In analysis, households were divided into two groups: "usually fish" and "usually do not fish," based on their responses to the survey question: "Does your household *usually* subsistence fish for salmon?" Harvest estimates were calculated for each group independently, then summed to estimate total community harvests. After the 2003 season, the Board of Fisheries imposed a permit requirement on five of the study communities, and ADF&G discontinued funding for the northwest salmon surveys. Data analyses for this chapter began the following year, in

2004, and engaged some of the same people who had been working on the surveys. It was conducted in four phases.

In the first phase of the project, researchers retrieved the ten annual harvest survey data files for Norton Sound and Port Clarence, translated them into a common data format, standardized variable names across the years, added a variable to identify the survey year, and then merged the ten separate data sets into a single database. This resulting database included subsistence harvest data from 7,838 annual household surveys representing an 88% sample of occupied households over 10 years.

Researchers were aware that—in a minority of records—a single household might appear in the database under two or more different household IDs. This usually happened when a household was absent from a study community for one or more years, or when one household split into two households. Researchers wanted to correct household IDs in the database so each unique household was identified by a single unique household ID. In addition, researchers were interested in exploring possible relationships between harvest and household characteristics that were not included in the harvest surveys. These household characteristics had to be gathered retrospectively.

So, in the second phase of the project, researchers visited each study community to verify household identifiers and gather additional data about household characteristics. In preparation for each community trip, researchers printed summary tables listing:

• All household IDs used in the community, by year,

• All household heads' names in each study community, by year,

• All people in each community who had commercial fishing permits between 1994 and 2003, and

• Age of every person who received an Alaska Permanent Fund Dividend in 2000.

With these four tables in hand, and working with one or more local key respondents in each study community, researchers reviewed the household ID table line by line. They verified that the same numerical household codes were used for the same household in each year. If a household was surveyed under different codes in different years (as sometimes happened when a household left a community and then returned), the case was flagged for correction. Researchers assigned the commercial fishing permits to the appropriate households. Using the printed table of ages, researchers characterized households as "elder," "mature," "young," or "teacher" in each study year. Finally, researchers identified household heads as "single male," "single female," or "couple."

For each household, verification and characteristics data were recorded on a one-page data verification and collection sheet. At the end of the second phase, researchers had one verification and characteristics form for each household in the sample.

In the third phase, researchers merged the aggregated harvest database from phase 1 with the household characteristics data from phase 2. Household identifier errors affected about 3.2% of the records. Corrected household codes were stored in a new variable, so the original household codes were not lost. A complete list of the variables in the annual databases and in the final aggregated database can be found in Appendix 4 of Magdanz et al. 2005.

In the fourth phase of the project, researchers explored the aggregated, expanded database to identify patterns of subsistence salmon harvesting. For example, some households fished continuously during the 10-year period, while others fished intermittently. Some households' harvests varied little from year to year, other households' harvests varied widely. These patterns were used to further categorize households.

Then researchers tested the following hypotheses:

1. *Subsistence salmon harvests were positively associated with salmon escapement.* Total salmon abundance (escapement plus harvest) was not known for the area as a whole. Although the number of available observations was small, escapement-harvest associations seemed obvious and invited exploration and discussion. For this analysis, researchers selected stocks which had both escapement data and subsistence harvest data for the same year for at least seven of the ten study years. Only six stock-community combinations met this standard. These stocks included Salmon Lake sockeye fished by Brevig Mission and Teller, Fish River chum and coho salmon fished by White Mountain and Golovin, Kwiniuk River chum fished by Elim, and North River Chinook and chum salmon fished by Unalakleet (see Menard et al. 2003). In cases where two communities fished the same stock, the combined community harvest was used in the analysis. Even when sufficient data were available, enumerated stocks usually did not correspond exactly to harvested stocks. For example, the North River escapement data used in this analysis included only about 40% of the Chinook in the Unalakleet River system (Wuttig 1999:14), and did not include any of the Yukon River Chinook that may have been intercepted in marine waters near Unalakleet. As limited as they were, the North River tower counts were some of the best escapement data available for this analysis. Linear regression was used to correlate estimated total subsistence salmon harvests and observed or estimated total escapements; the *f*-test was used for significance.

2. *Community subsistence salmon harvests were positively associated with community populations.* Given general declines in

salmon abundance in the area and the expectation of some association between harvests and escapements, it would be disingenuous to use these data to argue that increasing human populations were associated with decreasing harvests. Nonetheless, the Norton Sound and Port Clarence data provided an opportunity to explore a population-harvest hypothesis, by examining the association between subsistence harvests of salmon and community sizes, without regard for the year. Linear regression was used to correlate estimated total subsistence salmon harvests with estimated community populations; the *f*-test was used for significance.

3. *Approximately 30% of the households harvested approximately 70% of the subsistence salmon (by edible weight).* Annual patterns of individual household harvests in each community and in the region as a whole were explored and illustrated with Pareto cumulative distribution functions. Although the classic Pareto distribution is 20:80, the 30:70 distribution had been observed previously in subsistence harvests (Wolfe 1987), and was found closest to the midpoint of both households and harvests. That is, 30% was 20% *below* 50% of households while 70% was 20% *above* 50% of the harvest. Researchers expected that specialization in harvesting would exist for each community. The goal of this analysis was to illustrate the degree of specialization in salmon harvesting.

4. *Household social type was associated with the amount of salmon harvested (by edible weight).* Researchers categorized surveyed households into two categories that resembled Wolfe (Wolfe 1987; Magdanz et al. 2002) and Chabot (2003). An age-based category followed Wolfe's household social type model. A household-head-type category resembled Chabot's model. Households were categorized year-by-year. A household with a 58-year-old head in 1994 would be catego-

rized as "mature" in 1994 and 1995, and then categorized as "elder" in 1996 when its head reached 60 years of age. It wasn't possible to determine, retroactively, the employment status of heads of households for 800 households in each of 10 years, so the "gender" category only loosely follows Chabot; that is, it used gender but not employment status. The distribution of household harvests (by edible weight) was lognormal, so harvests were transformed from edible weight to log edible weight for multiple regression procedures.

5. *Households that fished intermittently—that is, they fished in some years and not others—accounted for most of the variation in community salmon harvests.* This was tested by comparing the annual salmon harvests of different categories of households over time. Using reported fishing harvests, households were sorted into three categories: "Always Harvested Salmon," "Intermittently Harvested Salmon," and "Never Harvest Salmon." To test the hypothesis that intermittent households accounted for most of the variation in community harvests, harvests (by edible weight) were compared between constantly and intermittently fishing households in each community and in each of the ten study years. The "never harvest" households were not relevant to this hypothesis; they harvested no salmon.

6. *Households that fished intermittently were more likely to fish during years of greater salmon abundance.* For communities with sufficient escapement data, linear regression was used to correlate the number of intermittent fishing households each year with estimated escapements counts or indices; the *f*-test was used for significance.

7. *For households that fished salmon commercially, the number of salmon harvested for subsistence was negatively associated with the number of salmon retained from commercial catches for personal use.* This hypothesis

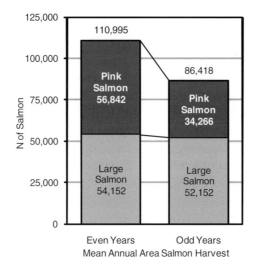

Figure 5. Mean annual subsistence harvests of pink salmon and "large salmon" (Chinook, sockeye, coho, and chum salmon) in even-numbered and in odd-numbered years, Norton Sound-Port Clarence Area, 1994–2003.

was intended to explore the interchangeability of commercial and subsistence fishing in meeting households' economic needs. Specifically, were retained commercially caught salmon a substitute for subsistence-caught salmon? This analysis was limited to the 581 cases in which households reported commercial fishing. For those households, linear regression was used to correlate the number of salmon harvested for subsistence with the number of salmon retained for personal use from commercial fishing.

Analyses were conducted with Microsoft Excel and with the Statistical Program for the Social Sciences (SPSS).

In the harvest trends section, most analyses excluded pink salmon. Pink salmon runs were much stronger in even-numbered years than in odd-numbered years. This was reflected in harvests; pink salmon comprised 52% of the total subsistence salmon harvest in even years, and 39% in odd years (Figure 5). Even-year harvests in the ten study communities averaged 110,995 salmon, while odd-year harvests averaged 86,418 salm-

on—a difference of 24,576 salmon. Of that average annual difference of 24,576 salmon, 22,576 were pink salmon (91.9%). Separating pink salmon harvests from the harvests of other, larger salmon species made it possible to explore trends among the other species.

In the harvest trends section, data were estimated totals. Expanding for unsurveyed households compensates for differences in sample sizes, and makes comparisons among communities more accurate. In the harvest patterns section, data were reported (unexpanded) harvests. In patterns section, groups of households were compared with one another, and the comparisons relied on average (mean) harvests and typical (median) harvests for groups of households. Expanding for unsurveyed households would not affect these comparisons among groups.

Last, the figures used in this paper need to be described. Pareto cumulative distribution function charts were used to show the degree to which salmon harvests were concentrated in a few households. The Pareto cumulative distribution function was particularly useful when comparing salmon harvest patterns among many years or among many communities.

Box plots were used to show the harvesting ranks of individual households and, at the same time, to show the consistency or inconsistency of a particular household's harvests from year to year. To compare households from year-to-year and to control for annual variations in harvest levels, researchers calculated an annual harvest rank for each household in each community. For each year, the highest harvesting household was ranked first for that year. The lowest harvesting household's rank was equal to the number of households surveyed in that year. A household that was surveyed every year from 1994–2003 would have ten rank values ranging between 1 and H, one for each year, where H = the number of households surveyed in the community that year. The rank was a measure of the relative contribution of a particular household to the total community harvest in any single year, regardless of whether the total community harvest was unusually large or unusually small.

The box plots included only households with at least six years of harvest survey data. Each vertical box in the plot included data for a single household, and illustrated the range of ranks for that household over the ten years of the study. The box portion of each box plot included the interquartile range (the middle half of cases in a category) of a single household's harvest rank, bisected by the household's median rank. The whiskers above and below the boxes showed the largest and smallest ranks that were not more than 1.5 times the interquartile range. Outliers were shown as circles and extreme outliers as asterisks.

In the box plots, households were sorted left to right based on their median rank in their community. The households that typically had the highest salmon harvests in the community appeared on the left in each box plot, while the lowest harvesting households appeared on the right. If a household contrib-

uted consistently to the community harvest, that household's rank would be similar from year to year. A consistent community harvest rank that would be indicated by a short vertical box, by short "whiskers" above and below the box, and by no outliers (the circles and asterisks). Inconsistent contributors would be indicated by a tall vertical box, and by long whiskers or outliers.

Results

The authors reviewed subsistence harvest trends for the area as a whole, and for each individual community. The trends review that follows included Chinook, sockeye, coho, and chum salmon (i.e., "large salmon"). In almost every community, subsistence harvests of large salmon were found to have declined during the study period. Subsistence salmon fishing was not restricted in most of the study communities (no limits, no closed periods). The most obvious explanations for changing subsistence harvests were changes in salmon abundance and changes in human populations. The harvest trends section concludes with explorations of associations between salmon escapement and community salmon harvests, and associations between community populations and community harvests.

Building on prior observations by Wolfe (1987), Chabot (2003) and others, the patterns section explores Wolfe's 30:70 hypothesis. It examines associations between salmon harvests and household social type. It compares the annual contributions to the total harvests by households that always harvested salmon with contributions by households that intermittently harvested salmon. Finally, it looks for associations between commercial fishing retention and subsistence harvest.

Harvest trends

In the Norton Sound–Port Clarence Area as a whole, harvests of salmon other than pink salmon declined by about 3,400 salmon annually from 1994–2003. Harvests declined in nine of the ten study communities, with a mean decline of 337 salmon annually per community. The steepest declines occurred in St. Michael, where harvests declined by about 640 salmon annually, and in White Mountain, where large salmon harvests declined by about 570 salmon annually.

Community by community, harvest trends were worse than average in Golovin (trend -11.4% annually), St. Michael (–10.3%), Teller (–8.5%), White Mountain (–7.8%), and Stebbins (–6.0%). Trends were better than average in: Shaktoolik (–5.4%), Elim (–4.7%), Unalakleet (–4.2%), and Koyuk (–2.9%). Brevig Mission was the only community that did not have a decreasing trend over the decade. Brevig Mission harvests were highly variable and the trend was not statistically significant.

While harvests appeared to have stabilized in the latter part of the study period, it would not be correct to characterize the overall situation as improving, at least through 2003. For half of the study communities (White Mountain, Golovin, Koyuk, Unalakleet, and Stebbins), the lowest estimated harvests of the decade occurred in 2003.

In three cases, pairs of communities fished the same stocks and presumably experienced similar levels of salmon abundance. White Mountain and Golovin both relied on Fish River stocks. Brevig Mission and Teller both relied on Kuzitrin River and Salmon Lake stocks. Stebbins and St. Michael both relied on southern Norton Sound stocks. There were some interesting differences in harvest trends between the two communities in each pair.

White Mountain's harvests trended downward at a rate similar to most other Norton Sound communities, losing more than 300 salmon each year. More importantly, harvests in some other communities began to increase after 1999. That was not the case in White Mountain, where residents harvested

a total of only 1,171 large salmon in 2003, compared with 7,368 large salmon in 1995. Golovin, which also saw a large harvest in 1995, fared better than White Mountain. Harvests trended downward, by about 157 salmon annually. If the large 1995 harvest is removed, the trend changes from –157 salmon annual to –39 salmon. Golovin's harvests in 1994 (1,379 large salmon), 2001 (1,538 large salmon), and in 2003 (734 large salmon) were especially low. Golovin depends in part on salmon runs in the Kachavik River, in Golovnin Lagoon, which is not fished by White Mountain.

In St. Michael and Stebbins, chum harvests again were the major factors in the overall decline in harvests of large salmon. In some other communities, declining chum harvests were mitigated in part by stable harvests of other species, but that was not so true in St. Michael and Stebbins. In Stebbins, coho salmon harvests declined with the chum salmon. In St. Michael, pink salmon harvests declined with the chum salmon. In both communities, Chinook salmon harvests declined substantially. Overall, St. Michael's subsistence harvest of large salmon declined by a factor of three, beginning the decade with three years of harvests that averaged 8,316 and ending the decade with four years of harvests that averaged 2,991. Stebbins harvests of large salmon fell by about half, averaging 11,127 during the first three years and 6,009 during the last four years. Unlike other study communities that fished primarily in terminal salmon fisheries, Stebbins and St. Michael harvested both terminal stocks (primarily at the Pikmiktalik River) and migrating Yukon River stocks.

To explore trends in communities of different sizes and in communities with changing human populations, Figure 6 presents the mean annual number of salmon harvested per person for the area as a whole, and for three selected communities. For all ten study communities, the mean number of large salmon harvested annually per person declined by

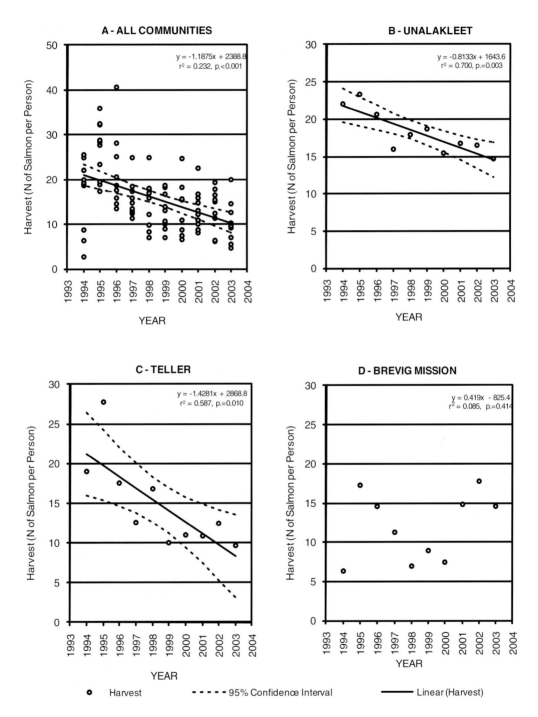

FIGURE 6. Trends in estimated subsistence salmon harvests per person (excluding pink salmon), 1994–2003, for ten Norton Sound-Port Clarence Area communities (A), Unalakleet (B), Teller (C), and Brevig Mission (D).

1.9 salmon annually ($r^2 = 0.232$, $p < 0.001$), from 19.6 salmon per person in 1994 to 10.9 salmon per person in 2003 (Figure 6A). Inter-annual variation in subsistence harvests was less in Unalakleet than in other communities, perhaps because it was the largest study community and thus provided a larger sample of fishing households. For mean annual large salmon harvests per person in Unalakleet (Figure 6B), the trend line was a good fit ($r^2 = 0.700$, $p = 0.003$), decreasing by about 0.8 salmon each year.

In Teller (Figure 6C), per capita harvests decreased by about 1.4 salmon annually ($r^2 = 0.587$, $p = 0.010$), from approximately 20 salmon annually at the beginning of the period to approximately 10 salmon annually at the end of the period. Teller's declines occurred in the first six years. Nearby Brevig Mission was the exception to the rule (Figure 6D). Harvests were highly variable, and the association between years and harvests was not significant ($r^2 = 0.085$, $p = 0.414$). Clearly, though, harvests did not decline during the study period in Brevig Mission, as in every other community.

Worth noting, Brevig Mission's human population increased by 21.3% during the decade, while Teller's population decreased by 7.3%. Yet comparisons of mean harvests per person and per household suggested that the differences between Brevig Mission and Teller were not simply a result of population change. From 1994–2000, Teller's average household harvest ranged from 36.5 to 101.4 large salmon, and was *always greater* than the average household harvest in Brevig Mission. From 2001–2003, Teller's average harvest ranged from 32.5 to 38.4 large salmon per households, and was *always less than* Brevig Mission's average harvest. Brevig Mission's average harvest per household ranged around 50.1 large salmon annually, and showed no significant trend during the study period.

This latter pair of communities, depending upon the same stocks but experiencing different harvest trends, suggested that salmon abundance was not the *only* variable affecting subsistence harvests. Abundance, though, was a logical place to begin hypothesis testing.

Harvests and escapement

Hypothesis 1: *Subsistence salmon harvests were positively associated with salmon escapement.* This association is certain to be true as harvestable surpluses approach zero, but harvestable surpluses in the study area usually were sufficient to meet subsistence needs in the study communities during the study period. As discussed in the methods section, data available to test this hypothesis were exceedingly limited. Most escapement data were incomplete, either aerial survey indexes or counts on one tributary of a larger river system. Consequently, variables other than salmon escapement may have affected the results.

For all eligible escapement-harvest data, subsistence harvests showed little association with escapement ($r^2 = 0.090$, $p = 0.033$). After Removing one outlier harvest that was twice as large as any other estimated harvest, no association was evident ($r^2 = 0.005$, $p = 0.625$) and it was not significant. Thus, for the six various stocks with sufficient data as a group, available escapement data were not a good predictor of subsistence harvests.

For two individual stocks, though, significant associations were observed. The strongest association was for North River Chinook salmon harvested by residents of Unalakleet (Figure 7A). Subsistence harvests of Chinook salmon were strongly and positively associated with Chinook escapements ($r^2 = 0.725$, $p = 0.007$), although harvests and escapements were relatively small. In Figure 7A, note that escapements of several hundred fish were associated with harvests of several thousand fish. North River was only one tributary of the Unalakleet River system, and the North River count served as an index to the status of the full stock.

In a much larger stock, the Kwiniuk River near Elim, where annual escapements ranged between 10,000 and 40,000 chum salmon, a moderately positive association with subsistence harvests was observed ($r^2 = 0.551$, $p = 0.014$) (Figure 7B). For these specific stocks, North River Chinook and Kwiniuk River chum, the hypothesis was supported.

Population and harvest

Hypothesis 2: *Community subsistence salmon harvests were positively associated with community populations.* This, too, would seem to be an obvious relationship for communities dependent upon wild salmon for subsistence; more people require more food. In the ten study communities, the human population increased by about 1% per year from 1994–2003. The total number of households increased from 839 to 903, or about seven households per year. The number of households that "usually fished" increased by only 14 households during the decade, slightly more than one household per year. The number of households that actually *caught* a salmon declined by about two households per year from 1994–2003. During the same period, salmon harvests decreased by about 6% every year. So not only were households catching fewer salmon, fewer households caught even one salmon.

Despite the potentially confounding effects of increasing human populations amid decreasing salmon harvests, the association between community populations and harvests was strong ($r^2 = 0.670$, $p < 0.001$) (Figure 8A). The reason: among the ten communities in this study, larger communities harvested more salmon for subsistence than smaller communities, suggesting that per capita subsistence demands for salmon were quite similar across communities. The hypothesis is supported.

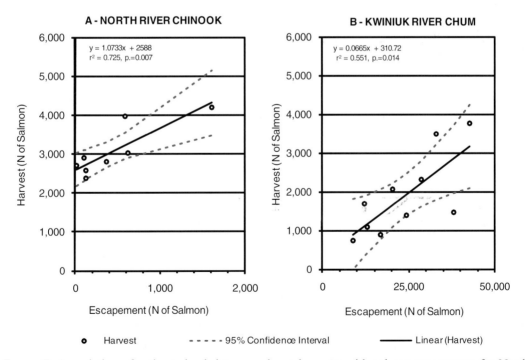

FIGURE 7. Association of estimated subsistence salmon harvests with salmon escapement for North River Chinook stock (A) and Kwiniuk River chum stock (B) in the Norton Sound-Port Clarence Area, 1994–2003.

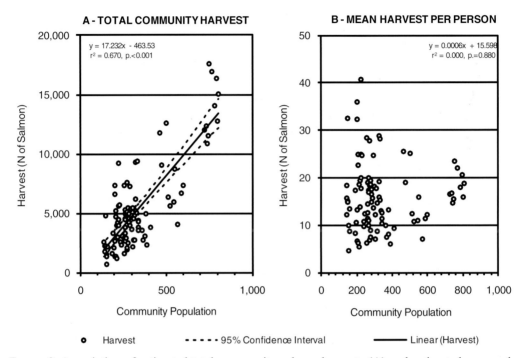

A - TOTAL COMMUNITY HARVEST

y = 17.232x - 463.53
r² = 0.670, p.<0.001

Harvest (N of Salmon)

Community Population

B - MEAN HARVEST PER PERSON

y = 0.0006x + 15.598
r² = 0.000, p.=0.880

Harvest (N of Salmon)

Community Population

○ Harvest   • • • • 95% Confidence Interval   —— Linear (Harvest)

FIGURE 8. Association of estimated total community salmon harvests (A) and estimated mean salmon harvests per person (B) with community populations in ten Norton Sound-Port Clarence Area communities, 1994–2003.

One might expect that in larger communities, more people would rely on the market economy than in smaller communities. If so, mean community per capita salmon harvests would be negatively associated with community size. Mean community per capita harvests were more varied in smaller communities than in larger communities (Figure 8B). However, for the ten study communities, no significant association occurred between community size and estimated harvests per capita ($r^2 = 0.0002$, $p = 0.880$).

Harvest patterns

As noted in the rationale for the analyses, several scholars have observed patterns in the subsistence harvests of wild foods. The basic observations were that some households harvest much more wild food than other households, and that patterns of household harvests

were similar for many different communities, even though they may have utilized quite different species of wild foods. This section first confirms the presence of some previously observed patterns, then examines variables that might explain some of the observed patterns.

The 30:70 Hypothesis

Hypothesis 3: *Approximately 30% of households harvested approximately 70% of subsistence salmon (by edible weight).* The 30:70 hypothesis was first expressed by Wolfe (1987) and further explored by Magdanz (Magdanz et al. 2002). It describes the distribution of all subsistence harvests among households in a particular community. For an individual resource or resource category, like salmon, harvests actually were expected to be *more* concentrated than 30:70. Some households were more successful at fishing and others were more successful at hunting. Consequently, individual resource harvests would be more concentrated than all resource harvests combined.

This analysis showed that, over all communities in all years, 21% of the surveyed households harvested 70% of the salmon (edible weight). The concentration of harvests varied from year to year (Figure 9A). Harvests were *least* concentrated in 1994, when 24% of the households harvested 70% of the salmon, and *most* concentrated in 1999, when only 17% harvested 70% of the salmon. Although the proportion of households that caught 70% of the salmon varied, there was no trend during the decade. However, from 1994 through 2003, the proportion of households that caught at least one salmon declined from 81% to 62%. Harvests tended to be less concentrated in even years when pink salmon were most abundant. In other words, the more salmon were available, the more households fished for salmon, which is what one would expect.

The concentration of harvests varied from community to community (Figure 9B). The concentration of harvests within each community, though, varied considerably. Harvests were *least* concentrated in Elim, where 30% of the households harvested 70% of the salmon, exactly the predicted pattern. Harvests were *most* concentrated in Teller and St. Michael, where only 15% and 12% of the households, respectively, harvested 70% of the salmon.

To further explore the patterns of harvests, household harvests were charted with Pareto cumulative distribution functions, where the x-axis was the cumulative percentage of households in the community, and the y-axis was the cumulative percentage of salmon harvested by those households (Figure 10). Cumulative distribution graphs allowed more detailed comparisons of different harvest patterns, community by community, year by year.

Several aspects of the harvest patterns could be seen in these charts. First, in some

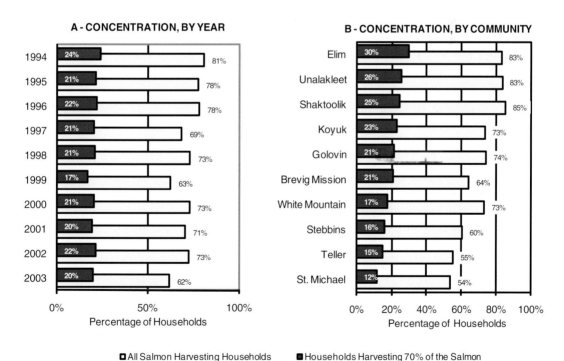

FIGURE 9. Concentration of subsistence salmon harvests by year (A) and by community (B).

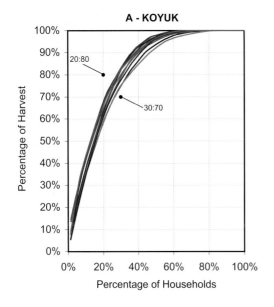
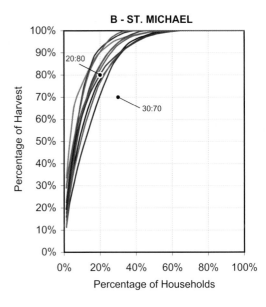

FIGURE 10. Pareto cumulative distribution functions for household subsistence salmon harvests in Koyuk (A) and St. Michael (B), 1994–2003.

communities (Brevig Mission, Unalakleet, Koyuk, and Elim) the concentration of harvests varied little from year to year. The cumulative distribution lines for each year fell quite close to one another, and are of the same general shape (e.g., Koyuk, Figure 10A). This suggested a predictable harvesting system. In other communities (Teller, St. Michael, Stebbins, and Golovin), the concentration of harvests varied considerably from year to year (e.g., St. Michael, Figure 10B). In St. Michael, 23 households (29.7%) took 95.9% of the salmon in 1995, a consequence of unusually high harvests by six households. Those six households alone (8.1% of the population) harvested 72.2% of the salmon that year in St. Michael. That was a high-harvest year, the total harvest of 17,933 kg. was the second highest of the decade.

The analyses showed that a majority of the salmon harvest was concentrated in a minority of the households, more concentrated than the hypothetical 30:70 pattern. The hypothesis was supported. In addition,

in some communities the degree of concentration changed little from year to year. In other communities, the degree of concentration changed considerably from year to year. Given that harvests were concentrated in a minority of households, the next question is: "Which households?"

Household social type

Hypothesis 4: *Household social type was associated with the amount of salmon harvested (by edible weight)*. This hypothesis also follows Wolfe, whose household development model categorizes rural Alaska households into five social types, based on the age of the household heads, on household structure, and on harvests. Chabot, working in Canada, categorized households into four different categories, based on the gender and employment of the household head, and on harvests. Both categorization schemes require advance knowledge of individual household harvests for one of the categories, which limits their utility for predictive modeling. In the categorization scheme in this study, researchers did not use a priori knowledge of harvests to construct any categories. Similar categories could be constructed from census data.

Figure 11 summarizes the results for all communities in all years. Salmon harvests increased with the age of the household heads, as expected, and teacher households harvested less than other households, as predicted by Wolfe's model. Households headed by couples harvested more salmon than households headed by either single men or single women, as predicted by Chabot's model. With the exception of teacher households, these relationships held for the age and head-type categories together. That is, elder couple households harvested more than elder female households, who in turn harvested more than elder male households.

However, these relationships were not consistent in the individual communities.

Among households headed by couples in Brevig Mission, the relationship between head age and harvest was the reverse of the region as a whole. Young and mature households harvested more than their elders. Among households headed by single women or single men, mature households harvested the most. In Teller, households headed by couples and single women followed the expected pattern. But among single men, the mature households were the most productive.

In seven of the eight Norton Sound communities, households headed by elder couples were the highest harvesting category. Otherwise relationships between head-age, head-type, and harvest quantities varied from community to community, in part because of the small number of samples in the single female head, single male head, and teacher categories. In Golovin there were only two cases with single-female heads, an elder household and a mature household. In Unalakleet, where there were at least 30 cases in every category

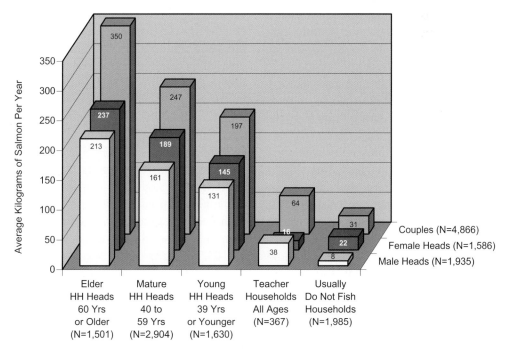

FIGURE 11. Association of estimated household subsistence salmon harvests with household social type (age and gender of household heads) in ten Norton Sound–Port Clarence Area communities, 1994–2003.

except single-female teacher (where $n = 16$), most relationships were as expected.

Consistent and intermittent fishing

Hypothesis 5: *Households that fished intermittently—that is, they fished in some years and not others—accounted for most of the variation in community salmon harvests.*

Hypothesis 6: *Households that fish intermittently were more likely to fish during years of greater salmon abundance.* Like previous hypotheses, these hypotheses explore the contributions of different types of households to communities' harvests.

In each community, some households reported harvesting salmon every year they were surveyed. It was reasonable to expect these households were among the 30% of households that contributed 70% of the harvest, and that the harvests of these "always-harvest-salmon" households would be as consistent as their effort. If these expectations were true, then it was also reasonable to assume that the remainder of the households in the study communities—the "intermittently-harvest-salmon" households—would account for most of the variation in community salmon harvests. It was also reasonable to expect that intermittent households might be more motivated to fish during years of greater salmon abundance.

Across all communities, 33.6% of the surveyed households always harvested salmon, 55.8% intermittently harvested salmon, and 7.7% never harvested salmon. The proportion of households that always harvested salmon varied considerably from community to community. In Shaktoolik, 56% of the households reported harvesting salmon every year, while in St. Michael only 12% of the households reported harvesting salmon every year. The proportion of always-harvest-salmon households tended to increase from Brevig Mission eastward across Norton Sound to Unalakleet, except that Stebbins and St. Michael had fewer always-harvest-salmon households than the other communities.

Households that harvested salmon more frequently ranked among the higher harvesting households in their communities. Households that "Always Harvested Salmon" were typically at the 31st harvest percentile. As the households' harvest frequencies declined, so did their median harvest ranks. However, in every category except "Never Harvest Salmon," there were some households that ranked near the top and the bottom percentiles.

In the area, and in each community, the number of harvest-every-year households was quite stable from year to year. For the region as a whole, the number of always-harvest-salmon households averaged 296 households annually (range 284–318 households), and their numbers were stable during the study period. The intermittently-harvest-salmon households averaged 519 households annually, and increased by about four households annually (0.8%). The never-harvest-salmon households averaged 68 households, and increased by about three households annually (5.1%). Because of increasing populations in the study communities, the survey sample increased by about seven houses annually, from 839 in 1994 to 903 in 2003. Because the number of always-harvest-salmon households remained stable, the proportion of always-harvest-salmon households declined from 36.5% in 1994 to 33.2% in 2003 (Figure 12A).

The proportion of salmon harvested by the two categories of households was remarkably consistent through all regimes of harvest, despite the variation in harvests from a high of 184,578 kg in 1996 to a low of 103,994 kg in 1999. The always-harvest-salmon households harvested 58.6% of the total on average, ranging between 55.4% and 62.0% and trending upwards about 0.3% annually (Figure 12B). Because their numbers changed little, the always-harvested-salmon households were becoming a smaller proportion of the communities over time, yet were taking a larger proportion of the salmon harvest. Compared with the annual variations in the total harvests, however, these trends were small. Harvests by the two categories of households contributed more or less equally to the total harvests.

To test the hypothesis that intermittent households were more likely to fish during years of greater abundance, the number of intermittent fishing households each year was compared with the salmon escapement each year for eight sets of community-escapement data. All but two of the associations were weak or nonexistent, and none of the relationships was significant. Recall, however, that escapement data were very limited.

Although intermittent households were cycling in and out of the fishery, their numbers and their combined contribution to the total harvests were similar from year to year. This was unexpected. These two hypotheses were not supported.

Salmon retained from commercial fishing

Hypothesis 7: *For households that fished commercially, the number of salmon harvested for subsistence was negatively associated with the number of salmon retained from commercial catches for personal use.* This hypothesis was intended to explore a common feature of rural Alaska mixed economies: the interchangeability of commercial and subsistence fishing in meeting some of households' economic needs. Specifically, were retained commercial salmon a substitute for subsistence salmon? The assumption was that if a household retained more commercially-caught salmon for its own use, then that household would need fewer salmon from subsistence fishing, and vice versa. If the hypothesis were true, there should be an inverse relationship between the two variables. As commercial retention decreased, other harvests would increase. If that did happen, then restrictions to commercial salmon fishing might increase demand for subsistence salmon. There were many factors in play, especially markets. Higher salmon prices might discourage fishers from retaining commercial salmon for personal use. This analysis, however, looked only at the relationship between commercial retention and other local sources of salmon for households (i.e., subsistence nets, rods and reels).

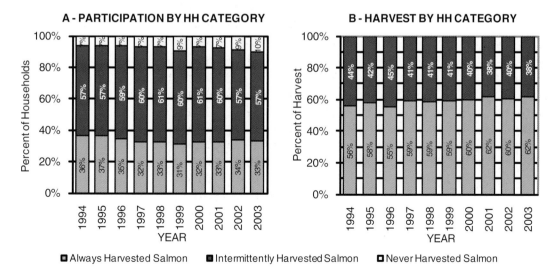

FIGURE 12. Proportion of households participating in subsistence salmon fishing (A) and proportion of total salmon harvests (B) taken by three categories of households.

From 1994 through 2003, 178 surveyed households reported that at least one member of the household fished for salmon commercially. Many households fished commercially in more than one year; 581 surveys in the database reported commercial fishing. This analysis was limited to those 581 cases. Of those, 255 cases (44%) reported retaining salmon from commercial catches. Of a total 101,695 salmon reported in 581 cases, 86,018 came from subsistence nets (85%), 6,766 came from rods and reels (7%), 8,911 were retained from commercial catches (9%). Thus, commercial fishing operations were not a major source of salmon for Norton Sound families, even for those involved in commercial fishing. Commercial fishing households that retained salmon from commercial harvests had higher total salmon harvests (subsistence, sport, and commercial) than commercial fishing households that did not retain salmon.

Among households that retained salmon from commercial fishing, the median amount retained was only ten salmon. The average amount retained was 36 salmon, influenced by 15 households that retained more than 100 salmon. In 58 cases, commercial fishing households relied only on retained commercial salmon for their households' needs. That is, these households harvested no salmon in subsistence and sport fisheries.

Figure 13A compares, for each commercial fishing case, the number of salmon retained from commercial fishing with the number of salmon obtained from subsistence and sport fishing. No association was evident ($r^2 = 0.003, p = 0.181$). When pink salmon were removed from the analysis (Figure 13B), no association was evident either. All cases except for Chinook salmon—the most valuable fish for both commercial and subsistence uses—were removed from the analysis (Figure 13C), and no association was evident ($r^2 = 0.000, p = 0.791$), although the regression line tipped slightly in the expected direction.

When all cases *except* the 73 cases with total harvests of 50 or more Chinook salmon (subsistence harvests plus commercial retentions) were removed (Figure 13D), a very weak negative association was evident ($r^2 = 0.094, p = 0.009$). The 73 commercial fishing households that harvested 50 or more Chinook salmon annually tended to get them from *either* the commercial or subsistence fishery; only 17 of the 73 high harvesting households got Chinook salmon from *both* commercial retention and subsistence. If commercial Chinook salmon fishing were closed, one might expect these high harvesting households to attempt to take Chinook salmon in the subsistence fishery. Except for these 73 high harvesting Chinook salmon cases, the data did not support the hypothesis.

For most species and most households, the number of salmon harvested for subsistence purposes was not significantly associated with the number of salmon retained from commercial harvests for personal use.

Roles of individual households

Given the patterns observed above, it was reasonable to assume that in each community, there existed a stable core of high-harvesting households that took the majority of the salmon year after year. Further, it was reasonable to assume that these were the *same* households year after year. But were they? That is the question explored below.

Figure 14 includes two box plots showing the harvest *ranks* (not harvest amounts) for households in Brevig Mission and Teller. The box plots of ranks allow one to assess the consistency of salmon harvesting by individual households in a particular community (see methodology).

Looking at the Brevig Mission box plot (Figure 14A), the first household on the left had the lowest median rank among all Brevig Mission households. Although its median rank

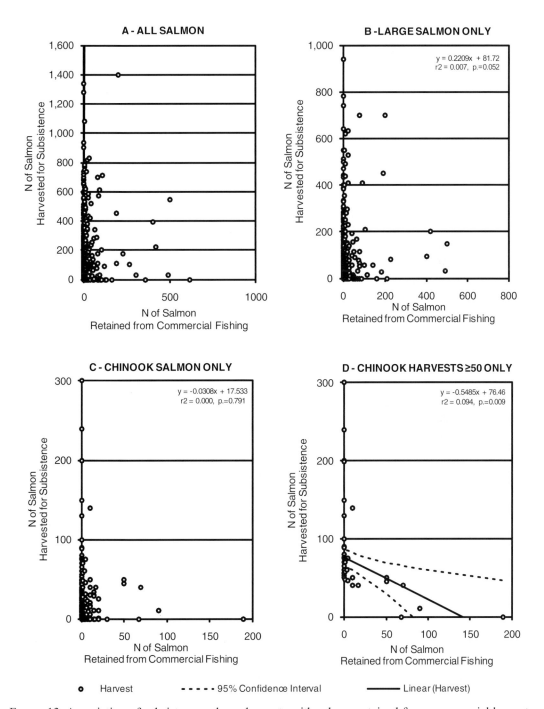

FIGURE 13. Association of subsistence salmon harvests with salmon retained from commercial harvests for all salmon (A), for large salmon only (B), for Chinook salmon only (C), and for Chinook salmon harvested by households whose total harvest was 50 or more Chinook salmon.

was 4.75, in some years it ranked 1st, and in other years it ranked as high as 10th. One year (the circle above the box, an outlier) it was ranked 16th. About half the time, it ranked between 5th and 8th. All in all, it *was* a consistently harvesting household, similar to the "super-households" described by Wolfe (1987). The second household from the left in the Brevig Mission box plot ranked 5th, just below the previous household. But this household's harvests were less consistent and consequently had a much greater range of ranks, from 1st to 53rd. Half the time, it ranked between 1st and 24th. The next ten Brevig Mission households were more consistently high harvesters, similar to the first household, although none was as consistent as the first. From the 12th household on, most household ranks varied considerably until, at the far right, a group of five households consistently ranked at the bottom of the community harvest scale.

Looking at the Teller box plot, the first household on the left was *more* consistent than any other high harvesting household in Teller (Figure 14B). The second and third households also were consistently ranked in the top 20, as was the fifth household. However, there was at least one outlier for the second, third, and fifth households, years in which they ranked about 45th, 36th, and 58th on the community harvest scale, respectively. Other than the very highest and lowest harvesting households, though, consistently ranked households were the exception, not the rule. Even among the very highest harvesting households, there were one or more households that ranked near the top in one or more years and near the bottom in another year. There were two households in Teller and two households in Brevig that ranked first one year and last in another year. The same pattern existed for the lowest harvesting households. Although they typically harvested little; there were several who ranked among the highest harvesting households in one or two years.

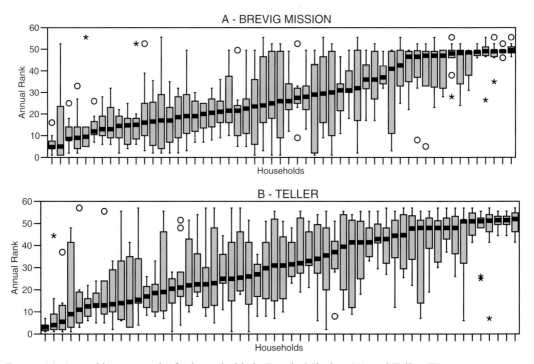

FIGURE 14. Annual harvest ranks for households in Brevig Mission (A) and Teller (B).

Similar box plots were developed for the other eight study communities. In every community, it was rare for any one household to have the highest harvest in more than two years. In Golovin and St. Michael, nine different households were ranked first during the ten years of surveys. In White Mountain, Elim, and Koyuk, eight different households ranked first. The exception was Shaktoolik, were only three households consistently ranked first. Except for Shaktoolik, it would be difficult to predict the high harvesting household in any given year. Variations in ranks were least in Elim and Shaktoolik. Variations in rank were the greatest in St. Michael and Stebbins.

Discussion

Although the ten study communities depended substantially on wild salmon for subsistence and shared a common geography and scale, within those confines each was unique. Growing and shrinking, Iñupiaq and Yu'pik, coastal and inland, with and without commercial fishing, the communities varied in many ways. These similarities and differences among the study communities, the large survey sample (88% of all occupied households), and the long period of data collection (annually from 1994–2003), provided unusual opportunities for analyses of subsistence harvest patterns and trends.

This section first summarizes and discusses subsistence harvest trends, then subsistence harvest patterns. It concludes with comments and recommendations on subsistence fishery data collection and storage.

Harvest trends

For the ten study communities combined, estimated subsistence salmon harvests from 1994 through 2003 declined by 5.8% annu-

ally. Most of the declines occurred during the first five years (1994–1998), when harvests trended lower by about 8% annually. During the latter years (1999–2003), harvests trended lower by about 1% annually across all communities. For the Norton Sound District, it also would be reasonable to characterize harvests as occurring in two regimes. During the first regime, from 1994–1996, harvests clustered around an average of about 115,000 salmon annually. During the second regime, from 1997–2003, harvests on average were a third less, clustered around an average of about 77,000 salmon annually. Either interpretation was evident from the point data.

Salmon escapements also declined during the study period. Declines in abundance were an obvious explanation for declines in subsistence harvests; the association between escapement and subsistence salmon harvests was the first hypothesis to be tested. For the small group of stocks and harvests with sufficient data for analysis, escapement data were not a good predictor of subsistence harvests. For two stocks individually—North River Chinook salmon and Kwiniuk River chum salmon—subsistence harvests were positively associated with escapements.

Why was such an obvious and expected association not evident? There were several explanations.

• Escapement data were available for a minority of stocks.

• Enumerated stocks did not correspond exactly to harvested stocks.

• For some stocks, subsistence harvests were small compared to total salmon abundance.

• Subsistence uses had precedence over non-subsistence uses during resource shortages.

To expand on the last point, under state and federal laws in Alaska, when harvestable surpluses declined, nonsubsistence uses were restricted or eliminated before subsistence uses were restricted. During the study period, it was not uncommon for commercial fishing to be reduced in time or closed altogether while subsistence fishing continued under usual limitations on time and gear. This was evident in the steep decline of commercial salmon harvests from 1994–2003, compared to the more modest decline in subsistence harvests (Figure 4). These laws, by design, mitigate the impacts of declining fish stocks on subsistence harvests.

In sum, associations between escapement and subsistence harvests were confounded by available escapement data, comparable escapement data, fishery scale, and fishery management. While common sense suggests that some association existed, salmon abundance certainly was not the only variable affecting subsistence harvests.

The second hypothesis explored associations between community populations and subsistence salmon harvests. Between 1994 and 2003, the total population of the ten study communities *increased* by 1.0% annually, while subsistence salmon harvests *declined* by 5.8% annually. Subsistence salmon harvests were strongly associated ($r^2 = 0.670$, $p < 0.001$) associated with community size. Although harvests varied from 5–41 salmon per person per year; there was no association between community size and per capita harvest levels. The ability of salmon harvests to scale evenly with community sizes suggests that community sizes may be partly related to the productivity of local salmon streams.

However, the linear positive association between subsistence harvests and community size observed for the study communities did not hold for Nome, the regional center of the Norton Sound–Port Clarence Area. Nome was not included in this study because complete salmon harvests estimates for Nome were available for only one year during the study period. In that year, 2001, Nome's av-erage harvest was 1.6 large salmon per person (Magdanz et al. 2003), compared with an average of 16 large salmon per person per year in the study communities. The implication was that there was a threshold, greater than 800 people (the population of the largest study community) but less than 3,500 people (the population of Nome), at which per capita subsistence salmon harvests began to decline by an order of magnitude.

Harvest patterns

In Norton Sound and Port Clarence, as elsewhere in Alaska, households' subsistence harvests of salmon varied widely, from zero to more than 5,000 salmon a year. Further, for a particular household from one year to the next, subsistence harvests also might vary from zero to thousands of salmon. Despite the variation in subsistence harvests, salmon abundance, and household circumstances, predictable patterns did occur.

• In all communities, a majority of the salmon were harvested by a minority of the households. Specifically, 21% of the households harvested 70% of the salmon (by edible weight). Pareto cumulative distribution functions were useful to illustrate variations in harvest patterns.

• In some communities (e.g., Koyuk and Unalakleet) concentrations of harvests were similar from year to year. In other communities (e.g., Teller and St. Michael) harvests were more concentrated in some years than in other years. As one would expect, in communities where the concentration of harvests varied from year to year, individual household harvests also were more varied.

• Although not true for every community, in general, households with older heads harvested significantly more salmon than households with young heads, and households headed by couples harvested more salmon than households headed by single persons.

• In each community, some households reported harvesting salmon every year. The number of these households was stable over time, even though community populations were slowly growing. Thus the always-harvest-salmon households were becoming a smaller proportion of the communities over time, while gradually contributing a larger proportion of the salmon harvest.

• Although other households were harvesting salmon intermittently, their numbers and their contribution to annual harvests were similar from year to year. Harvests by intermittently harvesting households were not associated with salmon escapements.

Given these patterns, it was reasonable to assume that a stable core of high-harvest households took the majority of the salmon year after year. However, consistently high ranked households were the exception. Even among the very highest harvesting households, there were one or more households that ranked near the top in one or more years and near the bottom in another year (Shaktoolik was the lone exception). There were two households in Teller and two households in Brevig that ranked first one year and last in another year. The same was true of the lowest harvesting households. Although they typically harvested little, in most communities there were several who ranked among the highest harvesting households in one or two years.

The differences between Brevig Mission and Teller were interesting. Located on the northern and southern shores of Port Clarence, respectively, the two communities fished the same salmon runs, and had a similar degree of access. Teller families were more likely to fish protected waters in Grantley Harbor, Tuksuk Channel, and Imuruk Basin, where

they would be less affected by rough weather, which might increase their success. Teller also was more easily accessible (by road) from Nome, increasing competition, which might decrease Teller's success.

There was another possible factor. As demonstrated in the analysis of harvests by household type, elder households (heads 60 years old or older) tended to have the highest harvests, while young households (heads 39 years old or younger) usually harvested about half as much salmon as their elders. Moreover, in most communities, elder and young households were equally numerous. In Brevig Mission, neither condition was true. Not only were young households ($N = 206$) more numerous in Brevig Mission than elder households ($N = 133$), young households harvested more (mean = 356 salmon) than their elders (mean = 326 salmon). The presence of such a larger number of active, young households in Brevig Mission also was, no doubt, a factor in Brevig Mission's substantial population growth.

In the analysis, Pareto cumulative distribution functions were useful for comparing harvest patterns over time or among communities. A consistent pattern of harvest concentration—17% to 24% of households harvested 70% of the salmon each year—meant that Pareto cumulative distribution functions could be used to identify nonrepresentative samples. A Pareto cumulative distribution function for a particular year's harvests that diverged substantially from that population's previous or subsequent patterns would suggest, absent other factors, a biased sample. In 1994, the White Mountain sample was very small, only ten households instead of the usual 60 households. The 1994 sample appeared to have been biased strongly towards high harvesting households, which was evident in the White Mountain cumulative distribution function for 1994. The 1998 sample in White Mountain also was smaller than usual—39 households—but the cumulative distribution for 1998 resembled those for other years, suggesting that the 1998 sample was representative. Pareto cumulative distribution functions also could be used to explore whether household permit data were representative.

The northwest salmon project almost achieved a census in every community in every year, so sampling usually was not an issue. The few exceptions did illustrate the challenges of administering harvest surveys in villages. If a survey is attempting to estimate salmon harvests, untrained community surveyors may try especially hard to contact households known to be high harvesters of salmon. If they are successful in this, their efforts will bias the sample and inflate estimates. Fortunately, this appears to have occurred only once in 100 administrations of the northwest salmon survey (ten communities for ten years).

While there were predictable patterns, there also were paradoxes. In particular: How can households cycle in and out of their communities' fisheries, but have so little effect on their communities' total harvests? One explanation for that phenomenon was introduced in the rationale, namely, that salmon were harvested by cooperative groups of households, typically extended families. Over time, different households in the family group may take primary responsibility for the salmon harvest. If an elder from a high harvesting household becomes ill and the household is unable to fish one summer, a daughter's household steps in, fishes, and distributes the salmon to the elder household. The daughter's typically low-harvesting household suddenly becomes a high harvesting household, and the elder household harvests much less, while the two households' combined harvests of salmon remains constant.

Data about cooperation among fishing households were collected in only one year of the study (1994) and were not analyzed. Nonetheless, multi-household, extended-family production networks could explain some of the patterns observed in the system, including the power-law distribution of harvests and the stable overall production of households that fished intermittently. The power-law distributions of harvests—21% of the households taking 70% of the harvest—were consistent with observations of networked systems (Barabási and Albert 1999). The power-law distributions of the harvests also were similar to Pareto distributions that have been observed most frequently for incomes or property, in which 20% of a population earns 80% of the income or owns 80% of the property. Marquet (2002) observed: "Power laws are ubiquitous within local ecosystems and may hold the clue to understanding large scale patterns in the structure and function of biodiversity."

Conclusion

With the notable exceptions of some MMS studies related to oil development and oil spills (c.f. Braund 1993; Fall and Utermohle 1995, 1999), most analyses in the subsistence literature have relied upon cross-sectional, comprehensive survey data. That is, researchers collected harvest data for many species harvested by residents of a single community in a single year. Comprehensive survey samples often were small. Andrews (1988) interviewed 45 of 48 households in Minto. Holen et al. (2006) surveyed 8 of 10 households in Lake Minchumina and 27 of 32 households in Nikolai. Stanek et al. (2007) surveyed 14 of 15 households in Beluga and 47 of 68 households in Tyonek. The year chosen for a survey may not have been representative and, even if it was, a single year's results provided no information about the many natural variations in subsistence harvesting systems. Comprehensive surveys usually were repeated so infrequently that observations may have lagged changes by a decade or more (see Burch 1985).

Nonetheless, comprehensive surveys

play important roles, providing social, cultural, and economic contexts for understanding subsistence systems and for monitoring long-term change. An excellent example of the applied comprehensive survey was the project that administered surveys to 116 of 175 households in five Bristol Bay communities to establish a baseline in advance of the Pebble Project, a proposed open pit mine in southwest Alaska (Fall et al. 2006).

In comparison, harvest monitoring survey data sets often include thousands of cases from many communities or, in the case of Yukon River salmon, tens of thousands of cases spanning several decades. The number of variables is much smaller than in the comprehensive surveys. Harvest reports for a few species and household size may be the only consistently collected data. But if one is interested in how communities adapted to changing social, economic, or ecological changes over time, then analyses of the harvest monitoring data could be more instructive than analyses of the comprehensive data. The problem is, annual fishery survey data usually are stored as separate cross-sectional datasets for a single year, rather than as panel datasets spanning multiple years.

Fortunately, the data used in this project were collected and stored in ways that allowed for the *ex post facto* creation of a panel data set. This was possible because of an initial decision to use consistent household identification codes across a series of annual harvest surveys, and by the subsequent commitment to that goal by a series of researchers and programmers. When key respondents reviewed household identification codes for this project, they found only 287 cases (3.2%) that needed correction, usually the consequence of a family leaving a community and returning a few years later. The vast majority of codes did indeed track a single household during the study decade. In retrospect, the advantages of such consistency seem self-evident. But it was not easy to do, and is less common than one might

think. Most agency data sets known to these researchers are not so consistent.

Another key to these analyses was a commitment by project leaders to use the same survey form year after year. Although the form design did evolve over time, the core question set remained intact until 2003. The underlying database structure also changed little from year to year, and that made it possible to aggregate ten annual databases into one large database.

Even with consistent household identifiers and survey content, aggregating the annual harvest survey data sets was a substantial undertaking. It is easy to underestimate the time and effort required to join and clean large data files. Errors may not become apparent until analyses are underway, and occasionally require repeating large sections of analyses. There are a number of proposals to join many different kinds of ecological databases in Alaska and the circumpolar Arctic. Such projects are considerable tasks in the best of circumstances.

There is a place for both kinds of surveys: the topically deep but temporally narrow perspective of the comprehensive, cross-sectional surveys, and the temporally broad but topically shallow perspective of the continuing annual surveys. For the most part, though, the potential to explore subsistence harvest patterns and trends through analyses of panel data created from annual harvest survey data has been overlooked. Annual survey projects are viewed as monitoring rather than research. Consequently, they have been primarily the responsibility of fishery managers, who typically work under tight time and budget constraints. That is unfortunate, because the temporal dimension of subsistence is a most interesting perspective, made even more pertinent by rapidly changing climatic conditions. Rich multi-dimensional data that could be used to explore interesting and important research questions remain in the agency archives.

Agencies charged with subsistence harvest monitoring have become much better at collecting and storing data in a consistent manner. The addition of a few questions to categorize households (such as age of household head and household structure) and to identify groups of cooperative households could improve accuracy of estimates and aid in modeling. The first step, though, should be to routinely aggregate annual cross-sectional data into multi-year panel datasets. Such standard practices would make the analyses conducted in this project routine, facilitate the construction of improved subsistence harvest models, and ultimately reduce the costs of estimating Alaska's fishery harvests.

Salmon fishing in Alaska is an inherently unpredictable enterprise. Salmon runs fluctuate; pink salmon runs routinely fluctuate by an order of magnitude. Weather limits effort and frustrates attempts to traditionally dry salmon. Equipment fails; repair parts are difficult to obtain. Perhaps most important, households have varying abilities to harvest salmon and differing needs for salmon, and these change over time, sometimes quite suddenly. Yet the system of subsistence salmon production in northwest Alaska communities exhibited considerable stability. Using long-term subsistence harvest survey data to better understand the mechanisms of that stability would improve estimation of harvests, and may even contribute to the "data-driven understanding of human actions" contemplated by Barabási (2005).

Acknowledgments

The Commercial Fisheries Division of the Alaska Department of Fish and Game and the Bering Sea Fishermen's Association provided most of the funding for the original survey project. Funding for this analysis was provided by the Arctic-Yukon-Kuskokwim Sustainable Salmon Initiative (AYK-SSI), the Bering Sea Fishermen's Association, Kawerak Inc., and the Alaska Department of Fish and Game. We are especially grateful to Karen Gillis, Joseph Spaeder, and members of the AYK-SSI steering committee for their generous support.

Scores of people gathered the data for this project. Eileen Norbert, Rose Atuk-Fosdick, Sandra Tahbone, and Don Stiles supervised the data collection for Kawerak, Inc. The field research team included the following people from 1994–2003. In Brevig Mission: Michael Olanna, Roy Henry, Sarah Henry, Marilyn "Janie" Goodhope, and Matilda Olanna. In Teller: Sam Komok, Lillian Weyanna, Norman Menadelook, Etta Kugzruk, Karla Kugzruk, Tanya Noyakuk, and Carlson Tingook. In White Mountain: Dean Lincoln and Carl "Bones" Brown. In Golovin: Thomas Punguk, Dora Smith, Isaac Larsen, Peter Amaktoolik, Carl "Bones" Brown, and Clarabelle Katchatag. In Elim: Stanton Nakarak, Joel Saccheus, and Amelia Amaktoolik. In Koyuk: Lloyd K. Kimoktoak, Dean Kimoktoak, Leslie Charles, Ruby Nassuk, Fannie Nassuk, Lane Douglas, Becky Anasogak, and Abigail Anasogak. In Shaktoolik: William Takak, Priscilla Savetilik, Carrie Takak, Karen Nashalook, Ralph Takak, and Myron Savetilik. In Unalakleet: Dawn Blankenship, Warren Katchatag, Burkher Ivanoff, Robin Caudill, Gloria Johnson, Nancy Rusin, Louisa Paniptchuk, Teri Paniptchuk, Carla Soxie, Carol Charles, Nixie Nick, Howard Slwooko, Karen Bradley, David Ivanoff, and Jolene Katchatag. In St. Michael: Pius Washington, Dora Lockwood, Harold Cheemuk, Vera Niksik, Steve Otten, Preston Otten, Stephanie Lockwood, and Paul Agibinik. In Stebbins: Cornelius Dan, Ted Katcheak, Joseph Steve, Tania Snowball, Tom Kirk, Rennie Jack, Patrick Katcheak, and George Washington.

Consistent survey instruments and analysis procedures were maintained by ADF&G Division of Subsistence research staff, in particular Susan Georgette, David Caylor, Charles Utermohle, and Robert Walker. ADF&G staff traveled to each community every year, supervising and assisting with the data collection efforts: Betsy Brennan, Carl "Bones" Brown, Erin Lillie, Paul McNeil, Kate Persons, Sandra Prufer, Joel Saccheus, Vicki Vanek, and Cheryl Yamamoto. Charles Lean, Fred Bue, Tracy Lingnau, Tom Kron, Allegra Banducci, Wes Jones, and James Menard provided many helpful suggestions. Bridgette Easley coordinated data for this study, while James Simon supervised our progress and reviewed our results.

James Magdanz would also like to thank Toshihide "Hamachan" Hamazaki with the ADF&G Commercial Fisheries Division, Karen Hyer with the U.S. Fish and Wildlife Service Office of Subsistence Management, and Lawrence Hamilton with the University of New Hampshire for comments and suggestions on statistical analysis, and Charles Lean, James Menard, and Robert Wolfe for comments on the analysis and presentation of results. The authors also appreciate the extensive and insightful comments of the editors and three anonymous reviewers.

References

Alaska Department of Fish and Game and Alaska Native Harbor Seal Commission. 2008. The subsistence harvest of harbor seals and sea lions by Alaska Natives in 2006. Division of Subsistence, Alaska Department of Fish and Game. Technical Paper 339. Juneau.

Andrews, E. F. 1988. The harvest of fish and wildlife for subsistence by residents of Minto, Alaska. Division of Subsistence, Alaska Department of Fish and Game. Technical Paper 137. Juneau.

Ballew, C., A. Ross, R. Wells, V. Hiratsuka, K. J. Hamrick, E. D. Nobmann, and S. Barell. 2004. Final Report on the Alaska Traditional Diet Survey. Alaska Native Epidemiology Center, Anchorage.

Banducci, A., E. L. Brennan, W. Jones, and J. Menard. 2003. Annual Management Report 2002, Norton Sound–Port Clarence—Kotzebue. Division of Commercial Fisheries, Alaska Department of Fish and Game. Regional Information Report No. 3A03–30. Juneau.

Barabási, A.-L. 2005. Network theory—the emergence of the creative enterprise. Science 308:639–641.

Barabási, A.-L., and R. Albert. 1999. Emergence of scaling in random networks. Science 286:509–512.

Braund, S. R. 1993. North Slope Subsistence Study, Wainwright, 1988 and 1989. Minerals Management Service. U.S. Department of the Interior. Technical Report No. 147. Anchorage.

Brennan, E., C. F. Lean, F. J. Bue, and T. Kohler. 1999. Annual Management Report 1998, Norton Sound–Port Clarence—Kotzebue. Division of Commercial Fisheries, Alaska Department of Fish and Game. Regional Information report No. 3A99–32. Juneau.

Bue, F. J., Tracy Lingnau, and Charles F. Lean. 1996a. Annual Management Report 1994, Norton Sound–Port Clarence—Kotzebue. Division of Commercial Fisheries, Alaska Department of Fish and Game. Regional Information Report No. 3A96–02. Juneau.

Bue, F. J., T. Lingnau, C. F. Lean, and E. Brennan. 1996b. Annual management report 1995, Norton Sound–Port Clarence—Kotzebue. Division of Commercial Fisheries, Alaska Department of Fish and Game. Regional Information Report No. 3A96–30. Juneau.

Bue, F. J., T. Lingnau, C. F. Lean, and E. Brennan. 1997. Annual Management Report 1996, Norton Sound–Port Clarence—Kotzebue. Division of Commercial Fisheries, Alaska Department of Fish and Game. Regional Information Report No. 3A97–30. Juneau.

Burch, E. S., Jr. 1985. Subsistence production in Kivalina, Alaska: a twenty-year perspective. Division of Subsistence, Alaska Department of Fish and Game. Technical Paper 128. Juneau.

Burkhart, G., and K. Dunmall. 2006. The Snake River, Eldorado River, and Pilgrim River salmon escapement enumeration and sampling project summary report, 2005. Kawerak Inc. Nome, Alaska.

Case, M., and L. Halpin. 1990. Contemporary wild resource use Patterns in Tanana, Alaska, 1987. Division of Subsistence, Alaska Department of Fish and Game. Technical Paper 178. Juneau.

Chabot, M. 2003. Economic changes, household strategies, and social relations of contemporary Nunavik Inuit. Polar Record 39(208):19–34.

Davis, B., J. A. Fall, and G. Jennings. 2003. Wild resource harvests and uses by residents of Seward and Moose Pass, Alaska, 2000. Division of Subsistence, Alaska Department of Fish and Game. Technical Paper 271. Juneau.

Fall, J. A., D. Caylor, M. Turek, C. Brown, T. Krauthoefer, B. Davis, and D. Koster. Alaska Subsistence

Salmon Fisheries 2004 Annual Report. 2007a. Division of Subsistence, Alaska Department of Fish and Game. Technical Paper 317. Juneau.

Fall, J. A., D. L. Holen, B. Davis, T. Krieg, and D. Koster. 2006. Subsistence harvests and uses of wild resources in Iliamna, Newhalen, Nondalton, Pedro Bay, and Port Alsworth, Alaska, 2004. Division of Subsistence, Alaska Department of Fish and Game. Technical Paper 302. Juneau.

Fall, J. A., D. Koster, and M. Turek. Subsistence harvests of Pacific halibut in Alaska, 2006. 2007b. Division of Subsistence, Alaska Department of Fish and Game. Technical Paper 333. Juneau.

Fall, J. A., and C. J. Utermohle, editors. 1995. An investigation of the sociocultural consequences of outer continental shelf development in Alaska. Minerals Management Service. U.S. Department of the Interior. Technical Report No. 160. Anchorage, Alaska.

Fall, J. A., and C. J. Utermohle, editors. 1999. Subsistence service update: subsistence harvests and uses in eight communities ten years after the Exxon Valdez oil spill. Division of Subsistence, Alaska Department of Fish and Game. Technical Paper 252. Juneau.

Fried, N. and B. Windisch-Cole. 2001. The cost of living in Alaska. Alaska Economic Trends. June 2001. Alaska Department of Labor, Juneau.

Georgette, S. E. 1996a. Norton Sound District subsistence salmon fishery, 1995. Division of Subsistence, Alaska Department of Fish and Game, Juneau.

Georgette, S. E. 1996b. Port Clarence District Subsistence salmon fishery, 1995. Division of Subsistence, Alaska Department of Fish and Game, Juneau.

Georgette, S. E., D. Caylor, and S. Tahbone. 2003a. Subsistence salmon harvest summary northwest Alaska, 2001. Division of Subsistence, Alaska Department of Fish and Game, Juneau.

Georgette, S. E., D. Caylor, and S. Tahbone. 2003b. Subsistence salmon harvest summary northwest Alaska, 2002. Division of Subsistence, Alaska Department of Fish and Game, Juneau.

Georgette, S. E., D. Caylor, and E. Trigg. 2004. Subsistence salmon harvest summary: northwest Alaska, 2003. Division of Subsistence, Alaska Department of Fish and Game, Juneau. Kawerak, Inc., Nome, Alaska.

Georgette, S. E., and H. B. Loon. 1993. Subsistence use of fish and wildlife in Kotzebue, a northwest Alaska regional center. Division of Subsistence, Alaska Department of Fish and Game. Technical Paper 167. Juneau.

Georgette, S. E., and C. J. Utermohle. 1997. Subsistence salmon harvest summary northwest Alaska,

1996. Division of Subsistence, Alaska Department of Fish and Game, Juneau.

Georgette, S. E., and C. J. Utermohle. 1998. Subsistence salmon harvest summary northwest Alaska, 1997. Division of Subsistence, Alaska Department of Fish and Game, Juneau.

Georgette, S. E., and C. J. Utermohle. 1999. Subsistence salmon harvest summary northwest Alaska, 1998. Division of Subsistence, Alaska Department of Fish and Game, Juneau.

Georgette, S. E., and C. J. Utermohle. 2000. Subsistence salmon harvest summary northwest Alaska, 1999. Division of Subsistence, Alaska Department of Fish and Game, Juneau.

Georgette, S. E., and C. J. Utermohle. 2001. Subsistence salmon harvest summary northwest Alaska, 2000. Division of Subsistence, Alaska Department of Fish and Game, Juneau.

Holen, D. L., W. E. Simeone, and L. Williams. 2006. Wild resource harvests and uses by residents of Lake Minchumina and Nikolai, Alaska, 2001–2002. Division of Subsistence, Alaska Department of Fish and Game, Technical Paper 296, Juneau.

Howe, L., and S. Martin. 2009. Demographic change, economic conditions, and subsistence salmon harvests in Alaska's Arctic-Yukon-Kuskowkim Region. Pages 433–461 in C. C. Krueger and C. E. Zimmerman, editors. Pacific salmon: ecology and management of western Alaska's populations. American Fisheries Society, Symposium 70, Bethesda, Maryland.

Kent, S. 2007. Salmonid escapements at Kwiniuk, Niukluk, and Nome Rivers, 2006. Division of Commercial Fisheries, Alaska Department of Fish and Game. Fishery Data Series No. 07–09. Anchorage.

Knapp, G. 2009. Commercial salmon fisheries of the Arctic-Yukon-Kuskokwim: economic challenges and opportunities. Pages 463–486 in C. C. Krueger and C. E. Zimmerman, editors. Pacific salmon: ecology and management of western Alaska's populations. American Fisheries Society, Symposium 70, Bethesda, Maryland.

Kohler, T., A. Banducci, E. Brennan, and J. Menard. 2004. Annual management report 2003, Norton Sound–Port Clarence—Kotzebue. Division of Commercial Fisheries, Alaska Department of Fish and Game. Regional Information Report No. 3A04–19, Juneau.

Magdanz, J. S., S. Tahbone, K. Kamletz, and A. Ahmasuk. 2003. Subsistence salmon fishing by residents of Nome, Alaska, 2001. Division of Subsistence, Alaska Department of Fish and Game. Technical Paper 274, Juneau.

Magdanz, J. S., E. Trigg, A. Ahmasuk, P. Nanouk, D. Koster, and K. Kamletz. 2005. Patterns and trends in subsistence salmon harvests, Norton Sound and Port Clarence, 1994-2003. Division of Subsistence, Alaska Department of Fish and Game. Technical Paper 294, Juneau.

Magdanz, J. S. and C. J. Utermohle. 1994. The subsistence salmon fishery in the Norton Sound, Port Clarence, and Kotzebue Districts, 1994. Division of Subsistence, Alaska Department of Fish and Game, Technical Paper 237, Juneau.

Magdanz, J. S., C. J. Utermohle, and R. J. Wolfe. 2002. The production and distribution of wild food in Wales and Deering, Alaska. Division of Subsistence, Alaska Department of Fish and Game. Technical Paper 259, Juneau.

Marquet, P. A. 2002. Of predators, prey, and power laws. Science 295:2229–2230.

Menard, J., C. C. Krueger, and J. R. Hilsinger. 2009. Norton Sound salmon fisheries: history, stock abundance, and management. Pages 621–673 in C. C. Krueger and C. E. Zimmerman, editors. Pacific salmon: ecology and management of western Alaska's populations. American Fisheries Society Symposium 70, Bethesda, Maryland.

Raleigh, R. F. 1957 Western Alaska salmon investigations, operation report 1957: reconnaissance of salmon fisheries between Cape Newenham and Point Hope, Alaska, 1957. Bureau of Commercial Fisheries, United States Fish and Wildlife Service.

Schroeder, R. F., and M. Kookesh. 1990. Subsistence harvest and use of fish and wildlife resources and the effects of forest management in Hoonah, Alaska. Division of Subsistence, Alaska Department of Fish and Game. Technical Paper 142. Juneau.

Stanek, R. T., D. L. Holen, and C. Wassillie. 2007. Harvest and uses of wild resource in Tyonek and Beluga, Alaska, 2005–2006. Division of Subsistence, Alaska Department of Fish and Game. Technical Paper 321. Juneau.

Usher, P. J., G. Duhaime, and E. Searles. 2003. The household as an economic unit in arctic aboriginal communities, and its measurement by means of a comprehensive survey. Social Indicators Research 61(2).

Weiland, K. A., T. Sands, C. Higgins, L. Fair, D. Crawford, F. West, and L. McKinley. 2004. Annual management report 2003, Bristol Bay Area. Division of Commercial Fisheries, Alaska Department of Fish and Game. Regional Information Report No. 2A04–16. Juneau.

Wentworth, C. 2007. Subsistence migratory bird harvest survey, Yukon-Kuskokwim Delta, comprehensive report 2001–2005. 1998. U.S. Fish and Wildlife Service, Anchorage, Alaska.

Wolfe, R. J. 1987. The super-household: specialization in subsistence economies. Paper presented at the 14th annual meeting of the Alaska Anthropological Association, Anchorage.

Wolfe, R. J., C. L. Scott, W. E. Simeone, C. J. Utermohle, and M. C. Pete. 2009. The "super-household" in Alaska Native subsistence economies. National Science Foundation ARC 0352611.

Wolfe, R. J., and J. Spaeder. 2009. People and salmon of the Yukon and Kuskokwim drainages and Norton Sound in Alaska: fishery harvests, culture change, and local knowledge systems. Pages 349–379 in C. C. Krueger and C. E. Zimmerman, editors. Pacific salmon: ecology and management of western Alaska's populations. American Fisheries Society, Symposium 70, Bethesda, Maryland.

Wuttig, K. G. 1999. Escapement of Chinook salmon in the Unalakleet River in 1998. Division of Sport Fish, Alaska Department of Fish and Game. Fishery Data Series No. 99–10. Juneau.

American Fisheries Society Symposium 70:433–461, 2009
© 2009 by the American Fisheries Society

Demographic Change, Economic Conditions, and Subsistence Salmon Harvests in Alaska's Arctic-Yukon-Kuskokwim Region

E. Lance Howe*and Stephanie Martin

*Department of Economics, University of Alaska Anchorage
Institute of Social and Economic Research
3211 Providence Drive, Anchorage, Alaska 99508, USA*

Abstract.—This paper addresses broad demographic and economic characteristics of the Arctic-Yukon-Kuskokwim region (AYK) of Alaska. AYK human population growth has generally been moderate over time. Because out-migration regularly exceeds in-migration, especially in the villages, population growth is mainly a product of natality. We anticipate future population growth patterns will be similar. In terms of regional characteristics, the linguistically and geographically distinct populations of the AYK region are similar in that they all have active traditional cultures, a strong reliance on subsistence, and relatively high measures of income poverty. While commercial fishing income is not a large contributor to total regional income, it is an important component of income for households in proximity to commercial fish processors. Many commercial fishermen are also subsistence harvesters, and for many, commercial fishing income provides the means to purchase equipment and other inputs to subsistence activities. This paper examines the relationship between subsistence harvests, population growth, and commercial fishing using a simple least squares regression model. We found that earnings from Kuskokwim commercial salmon fisheries are positively correlated with subsistence harvests while earnings from other commercial fisheries reduce subsistence harvests for a set of lower Kuskokwim River communities. Separately, we found that population growth is not positively correlated with subsistence salmon harvests in the same communities.

Introduction

This paper addresses broad demographic and economic characteristics of the Arctic-Yukon–Kuskokwim region (AYK) of Alaska. The AYK region includes vast lands, complex ecosystems, and rich cultures (Krueger et al. 2009; this volume). This paper provides a general overview of the regional characteristics of the people, the economy, and subsistence salmon harvests. Kuskokwim River communities are then examined

to identify specific variables affecting subsistence harvests. In particular, relationships between commercial fishing income, population growth, and subsistence salmon harvests are tested using a simple econometric model. As such general relationships and patterns are identified that can be further explored in more detailed future research. The study uses data from the U.S. Census Bureau, Alaska Department of Labor, Alaska Department of Fish and Game, U.S. Bureau of Economic Analysis, and Alaska Commercial Fisheries Entry Commission.

*Corresponding author: elhowe@uaa.alaska.edu

433

The Region

Four census areas account for the majority of communities in the Arctic-Yukon-Kuskokwim region (Figure 1). The Bethel census area includes most Kuskokwim River communities (up to Stony River). The Wade Hampton census area includes Alaska fishery management areas one and two of the lower Yukon River and all of the coastal district of the Yukon River.[1] To the north is the Nome census area, which includes all communities in the Norton Sound region.[2] To the northeast is the Yukon-Koyukuk census area, stretching from the Canadian Yukon territories to the lower Yukon. The Yukon-Koyukuk census area includes the upper management areas of the Yukon River. As will be discussed later in the paper, rules governing subsistence and commercial fishing vary across management districts of the river systems.

Throughout this paper, the AYK region is defined as the region made up of the Bethel, Wade Hampton, Nome, and Yukon-Koyukuk census areas. This region is a huge geographic area covering 235,000 square miles, nearly as large as the state of Texas. Not unexpectedly, this region is incredibly diverse in language, culture, geography, and ecology. Alaska Native people make up more than 80% of the roughly 40,000 people who live in this region (U.S. Census Bureau 2000). Alaska Natives living in this region include Iñupiat and Yupiit Eskimos, and Athabascan peoples.

Alaska Native people are the largest private landowners of this region. As a product of the Alaska Native Claims Settlement Act, Native village and Native regional corporations have fee simple title to surface and

---

[1]Together the Bethel and Wade Hampton Census areas are equivalent to the Calista Native regional corporation boundary.

[2]The Nome Census area is equivalent to the boundary of the Bering Straits Native regional corporation.

subsurface lands throughout the state. In the interior region of Alaska, the Doyon Alaska Native regional corporation owns and manages roughly 12.5 million acres (Doyon Native regional corporation 2008).[3] In the area encompassed by the Bethel and Wade Hampton census areas, the Calista Native regional corporation owns and manages around 6.5 million acres (Calista Corporation 2008). In the Nome census area, the Bering Straits Native regional corporation owns and manages around 2.1 million acres (Bering Straits Native Corporation 2008). A majority of lands were selected in light of traditional subsistence activities, and the vast majority of lands owned and managed by Native corporations in the AYK region are adjacent to Yukon River and Kuskokwim River watersheds (Figure 1).

The People

In 2000, the AYK region was the residence for about 6% of Alaska's total population and more than 27% of the statewide Alaska Native population (U.S. Census Bureau 2000). In addition to the two regional centers of Bethel and Nome, people in the AYK region live in about 100 small communities ranging in size from 27 people to just over 1,000. Roughly one-third of the AYK communities have populations below 200, another one-third between 200 and 500, and a final third have between 500 and 1,000 people (Figure 2). These data exclude the regional centers of Bethel and Nome with total populations of 5,471 and 3,505, respectively.

The regional centers of Bethel and Nome make up about 23% of the AYK area population (Figure 3). Compared to the villages, a large share of population in the regional centers is non-Native. In 2000, of the roughly 6,300 non-Natives living in the AYK, 50% were from the cities of Bethel or Nome.

---

[3]The vast majority of Doyon Regional Corporation lands are within the Yukon-Koyukuk census area.

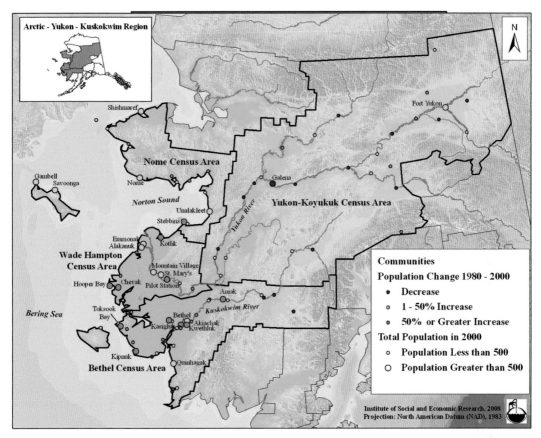

FIGURE 1. Population and population change in Alaska's Arctic-Yukon-Kuskokwim Region. Source: U.S. Decennial Census 1980, 1990, and 2000.

With the exception of the Yukon-Koyukuk census area, the AYK population has increased from 1980–2000 (Figure 3). However, compared to the rest of Alaska, population growth in the AYK region has been relatively slow over time. Average AYK annual growth rates between 1980 and 1990 were about 2% and less than 1% between 1990 and 2000. Statewide annual growth rates of the Alaska Native population were about 3.0% from 1980 to 1990 and 2.3% between 1990 and 2000.[4]

At the same time, patterns of growth differed across places. For example, many villages have nearly doubled in size since 1980. Large population growth also occurred in regional centers during this period. Population growth in the regional centers of Bethel and Nome (2,856 people) accounted for about 27% of the regional AYK population change.[5] A slightly greater share of this growth has occurred in the regional center of Bethel as compared to the regional center of Nome (Figure 3).

Population growth in the AYK region has generally been driven by natural increase (natality), rather than in-migration (Figure 4). Except for in the Bethel census area, between

[4]A small share of this increase can be accounted for by the way that the U.S. Census asked the race question. Prior to 2000 respondents were asked to indicate a "single-race choice" while in 2000 respondents could indicate one or more races. The number we report for 2000 is based on the "Alaska Native race alone or in combination" category. Statewide annual growth rates for the non-Native population were 3.2% from 1980 to1990 and 1.1% from 1990 to 2000.

[5]Between 1990 and 2000 the total change in the AYK population was about 10,500.

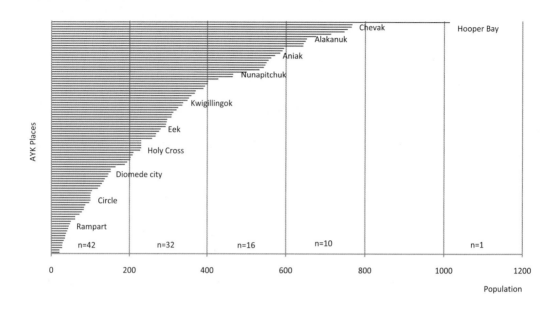

FIGURE 2. Total population of communities in the AYK region, 2000*. Data for the regional centers of Bethel and Nome with total populations of 5,471 and 3,505, respectively, were not included in the figure. Source: US Census 2000, summary file 1.
*Census designated places excluding regional centers of Nome and Bethel.
n=number of places

1990 and 2000, out-migration has exceeded in-migration. In many communities, young adults, and particularly young women, made up a disproportionate share of out-migrants.[6] Overall, births have exceeded deaths and out-migration accounting for the population increase observed in villages. Consequently, in the Bethel, Wade Hampton and Nome census areas children and young adults make up a large share of the population.

---

[6]Hamilton and Seyfrit (1994) note a "gender gap" with a disproportionate share of women leaving rural villages relative to men statewide and specifically in the Bethel census area. Census data from 2000 confirm a similar pattern.

Demographic changes in household composition have likely affected subsistence harvests of salmon. These changes suggest that more people do not necessarily mean increasing harvests. A high birthrate, for example, means there is a high percentage of families with young children. Magdanz et al. (2009, this volume) has shown that families with young children are often less productive subsistence producers. Also, the loss of relatively more women than men may lead to a decrease in subsistence fishing activity, since women have traditionally been the processors of fish in their community. Processing is time and labor intensive and with fewer people to process

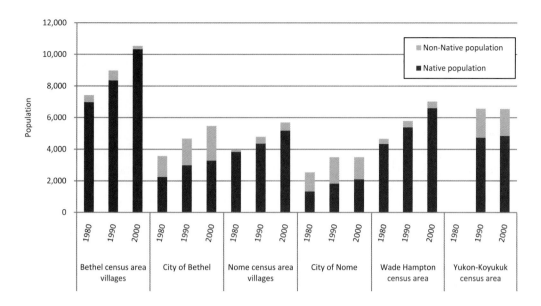

FIGURE 3. Total population and Native share of the total population in the AYK region, 1980–2000.

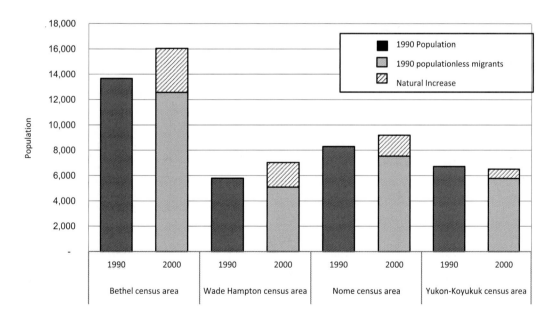

FIGURE 4. Population change in the AYK region, 1990–2000.
Source: Alaska Department of Labor, Administrative Services Division, Research and Analysis, Demographics Unit.

fish, there are incentives to catch fewer fish. Consistent with this feature of the subsistence economy, Magdanz et al. (2009) has also found that single young male heads of household are the lowest subsistence producers.

The Alaska Department of Labor and Workforce Development projects populations in most of the AYK region to grow by about 1% per year through 2020. The exception is the Yukon-Koyokuk census area where the total population is expected to decrease by 0.5% per year. If the Native population grows at the same rate as total population, it will increase by about 5,000 by 2020 (AKDOL 2007).

Finally, the AYK region is rich in traditional culture (Wolfe and Spaeder 2009, this volume). There are a large share of people who actively speak an indigenous language. Indigenous language retention in all AYK regions is greater than averages in other parts of Alaska (Figure 5). In the Bethel Census area a larger share of the population speaks a language other than English compared with any other AYK region. In particular, a much greater share of children in the Bethel census area speak a traditional language relative to children in other AYK regions.

The Economy

This section provides an overview of the AYK regional economy where subsistence activities often interact with the cash economy. The local economies in many parts of the AYK region can be characterized as mixed subsistence and cash economies. This section begins by presenting standard economic data and concludes by discussing the interaction between cash and subsistence in the mixed economy.

In terms of standard economic benchmarks of income and employment, households in the AYK region fall below state averages. In 1999, the median household income of $34,155 in the combined Bethel and

Wade Hampton census area was about 65% of statewide income ($51,571).[7] Median household income in villages outside of the city of Bethel was even lower.[8] In the Nome census area median household income was about $41,250, and median household income in the Yukon-Koyukuk census area was the lowest at $28,666.

For a large share of households in the AYK region, household incomes fall below the federal poverty line. In 1999 just under 10% of the Alaska population lived in households with income less than the poverty line while in the AYK region 21.4% of the population lived in households with income less than the poverty line (Figure 6).[9] In Wade Hampton, about 26% of people live in households with income falling below the poverty line, slightly greater than in the Bethel census area (20%). Residents of the Bethel and Wade Hampton census areas made up just under 4% of the Alaska population yet they accounted for about 9% of the poor. In the Nome and Yukon-Koyukuk census areas respectively, 17% and 24% of the population lived in households with income below the poverty line.

For a large share of poor AYK area households, household income falls significantly below the poverty line (Figure 6.). Of those living in poverty in the AYK region, 32% live in households with income that was less than

---

[7]Unless otherwise noted economic data on income, poverty, and employment is from 2000 U.S. Decennial Census Summary Files Three and Four.

[8]Median household income in the city of Bethel was $57,321 in 1999. Median household income in the entire Bethel census area (including the city of Bethel) was $35,701.

[9]Federal poverty guidelines are based on family size. Although separate guidelines are issued by Congress for Alaska, Hawaii, and the other 48 continguous U.S. states, the U.S. Census applies one set of guidelines when reporting poverty for all 50 U.S. states. The incidence of poverty in Alaska would be higher if Alaska specific poverty guidelines were applied by the U.S. Census. For a family of four, the poverty line used for the 2000 census was around $17,000.

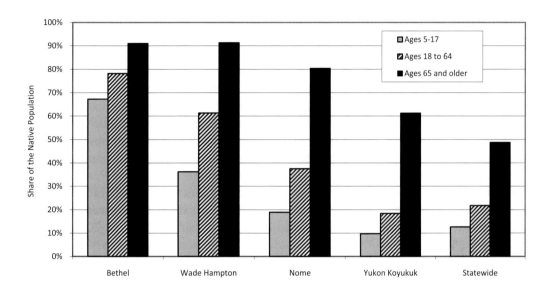

FIGURE 5. Share of Alaska Native population speaking a language other than English, 2000. Source: US Census 2000 Summary File 4.

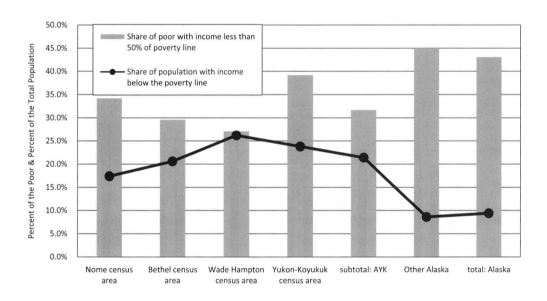

FIGURE 6. Alaska population living in households with income less than the poverty line, 1999. Source: US Census 2000, summary file 3.

21%. About 42% of the working age population villages was not in the labor force. The population "not in the labor force" is particularly high because most people living in villages have good information on available jobs. There are few cash jobs in most villages and many people do not actively "search" or look for employment the same way that someone living in a larger urban area would. Consequently, a large share of the population classified as "out of the labor force" by the U.S. Census Bureau were really unemployed.

Employment patterns also differ by race and gender. The non-Native population has higher employment and labor force participation rates than the Native population (see Appendix Table 1).[10] This difference is largely explained by the fact that many non-Natives with specialized training move to rural Alaska for employment opportunities. In villages of the Bethel and Nome census areas about 66% of the non-Native population worked in the educational services industry as of 2000. In the regional centers of Nome and Bethel about 35% of non-Natives worked in educational or health services industries.[11] Unemployment rates for women were relatively lower than for men. In 2000, unemployment rates for women were around 12% for the region as a whole. In regional centers, unemployment rates among women were less than 8%.

Much of the AYK region is characterized by a mixed subsistence and cash economy. Subsistence harvests of fish, plants, and marine and land mammals play an important role in supporting human food consumption (Wolfe and Spaeder 2009). Frequently, cash earnings from jobs are used as "inputs" to support activities associated with subsistence harvests. Cash is used to pay bills and buy supplies and fuel for subsistence fishing and hunting (Kruse 1982). Few cash jobs and high unemployment rates leads to households relying more on subsistence harvests for food, but also limits their ability to pay for expenses with subsistence activities.

Over time, equipment requiring cash inputs has become a more important part of subsistence harvest activities. Fishing is done in boats with motors, set and drift nets are made of nylon based materials, four-wheelers and snow machines have replaced dog teams. Modern firearms are essential. As a result, cash income has become increasingly important as an input to subsistence harvests in the AYK region.

Subsistence Salmon Harvests

In light of high unemployment, low household incomes, and acute income poverty, subsistence salmon harvests are a critical food source for residents in the AYK region. At the same time, subsistence opportunities are also an important part of the culture.

The link between culture and subsistence was described by Senator Moris Udall (AZ) during debates of what ultimately became the Alaska National Interest Lands Conservation Act (ANILCA). He noted "… it is the intent of this legislation to protect the Alaska Native subsistence way of life, and the Alaska Native culture of which it is a primary and essential element, for generation upon generation, for as long as the Alaska Native people themselves choose to participate in that way of life …."[12] Similarly, Rosita Worl, an Alaska Native anthropologist, noted the multifaceted link between culture and subsistence in her 2002 testimony before a U.S. Senate Committee discussing ANILCA and subsistence hunting and fishing in Alaska. Worl said that "the cultural component includes

---

[10]Non-Natives make up about 30% of the employed population the AYK region. In villages they make up less than 20% of employed workers while in regional centers they make up about 50% of employed workers.

[11]U.S. Census 2000, Summary File Four data.

[12]As quoted on http://www.alaskool.org/projects/subsistence/timeline/ANILCA.htm.

the values and ideologies that govern and direct subsistence behavior or activities. For example, the value of sharing is key to subsistence and the survival of Native societies" (Worl 2002).

Most communities in this region are located on the Yukon and Kuskokwim Rivers, which provide easy access to the subsistence fishery (Figure 1). Salmon harvests occur in the river system as well as in near-shore marine waters for coastal communities. Even the tundra villages (west of Bethel and north of the Kuskokwim River) participate in subsistence salmon harvests. For instance, the majority of families in the village of Nunapitchuk travel up and down the Johnson River to the Kuskokwim River to participate in subsistence salmon harvests.

Subsistence salmon harvests continue to make up a large share of total household consumption in the AYK region. The Alaska Division of Subsistence estimated in 2000 that most households (more than 90%) participated in subsistence fish harvests and that these participation rates were greater than in other Alaska regions (Wolfe 2000). Similarly, a controlled study exploring traditional food use in seven AYK area villages found that on average people derived 22% of their diet from traditional subsistence foods (Bersamin et al. 2007). Elders over 60 years of age derived the most (43%) and youth ages 14–19 derived the least (7%) (Bersamin et al. 2007).

While subsistence harvests remain high, per household subsistence harvests have decreased over time (Figure 9; Wolfe and Spaeder 2009).[13] Prior to 1990, harvests were highest in the Yukon-Koyokuk census area,

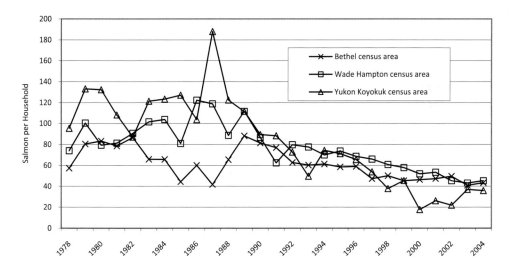

FIGURE 9. Subsistence salmon harvest per household AYK region, 1978–2004.
Source: Hayes et al. 2008; Bue and Hayes 2006; Whitmore, et al. 2005; US Censuses 1970, 1980, 1990, 2000; Calista Corporation 1991.

[13]For our estimates, we combined household counts from the U.S. Census with harvest totals by ADF&G district, considering the Bethel census area to be equivalent to the ADF&G Kuskokwim districts, Wade-Hampton contiguous with the lower Yukon districts, and Yukon-Koyokuk contiguous with the upper Yukon districts.

averaging over 100 fish per household.[14] Since 1990, harvests have declined and there has been less variation among regions. From 1990 through 2004, harvests in the entire AYK region decreased from about 80 fish per household to about 40 per household. From 2000 to 2002, harvests in the Yukon-Koyokuk census area dropped to around 20 fish per household. The Yukon-Koyokuk census area includes most of the upper Yukon River management area (the Yukon River above its confluence with the Koyukuk River, near Galena, in Figure 1). These declines in household harvests over time are consistent with the changes in household composition described earlier in the paper. A similar declining pattern is also described by Magdanz et al. (2009, this volume) for ten communities in the Norton Sound region (1994–2003).

Subsistence harvests vary significantly across households within a community. Wolfe and Walker (1987) found that about 30% of a household's harvest is 70% of traditional foods within a community; this relationship has also been validated in other Western Alaska contexts (Magdanz et al. 2009). The ratio seems to be consistent across communities, but the mix of wages and subsistence change within households as households mature (Wolfe and Walker 1987). Households with young parents are not very productive as hunters or wage earners. As they mature, household adults earn more money, and some use their earnings to buy better equipment and harvest more food. Wolfe and Walker (1987) characterize 'super-households' as those with high incomes and high subsistence productivity. Over time, households age and become less productive; children move out and start their own households and the process begins again.

In terms of formal rules for subsistence harvests, regulations vary among drainages. On the Kuskokwim River, few formal restrictions exist for subsistence salmon harvests (of any species). Subsistence permits or licenses have never been required on the river; no harvest limits for salmon exist, and restrictions on gear and timing are minor (ADF&G 2005).[15] On the Yukon River, generally more regulations govern subsistence salmon harvests (ADF&G 2005). For instance, on the Yukon River, permits and bag limits are enforced in some areas, and gear and timing limitations are more restrictive relative to the Kuskokwim River.[16] In both areas, all local residents (both Native and non-Native) are eligible to participate in subsistence harvests.

Chinook subsistence salmon harvests are important to the Bethel, Yukon-Koyokuk, and Wade Hampton census areas (Figures 10–12). Chinook salmon *Oncorhynchus tshawytscha* are a main subsistence fish for human consumption (Andrews and Coffing 1986). Athough moderate population growth has occurred in the Bethel census area, the relationship between population growth and subsistence Chinook salmon harvests is un-

---

[14]The spike in 1987 for Yukon-Koyokuk is due to a high fall chum salmon harvest.

[15]Some general rules include the gear restrictions that drift nets cannot exceed a total length of fifty fathoms and gill nets can be of any mesh size except nets with six inch or smaller mesh which can only be thirty-five meshes deep (ADF&G, 2005). See footnote 22 in this paper for an exception related to a temporary windows closure. In terms of permits, regulation 5 AAC 01.280 notes that for the entire region "fish may be taken for subsistence purposes without a subsistence fishing permit." In terms of timing, salmon may be taken at any time in Districts 1 and 2. In Districts 4 and 5, salmon may be taken at any time except from June to September 8, twelve hours before, during, and six hours after the opening of the commercial fishery (5 AAC 01.260).

[16]Permits are required in some sub-districts of the Yukon management area, and there are bag limits associated with the permits. In contrast to the Bethel census area, permits are also required in several rivers in the Yukon census area (see regulation 5 AAC 01.230). In terms of timing, a schedule determines when salmon can be harvested on the river and there are varying rules by sub-districts on the closure period following commercial fishing (which are generally more restrictive relative to the Kuskokwim) (see regulation 5 AAC 01.210).

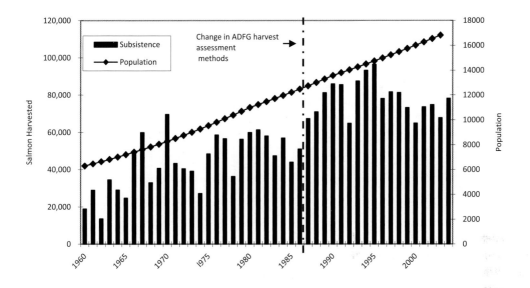

FIGURE 10. Kuskokwim River subsistence Chinook salmon harvest and population of the Bethel census area 1960–2004.
Source: Whitmore et al. 2005; US Censuses 1970, 1980, 1990, 2000; Calista Corporation 1991.

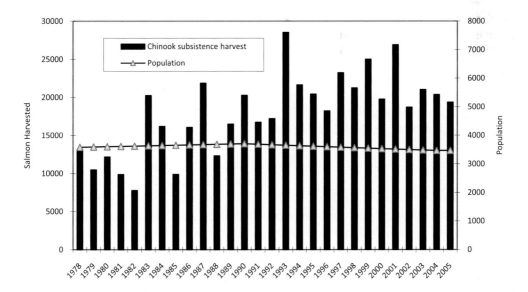

FIGURE 11. Upper Yukon subsistence Chinook salmon harvest and population of the Yukon-Koyokuk census area 1978–2005.
Sources: Bue and Hayes 2006, US Censuses 1970, 1980, 1990, 2000.

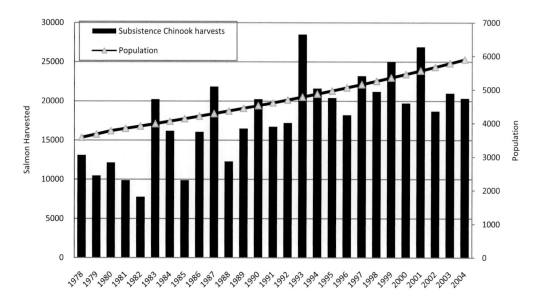

Figure 12. Lower Yukon subsistence Chinook salmon harvest and population of the Wade Hampton census area 1978–2005.
Sources: Bue and Hayes 2006, US Censuses 1970, 1980, 1990, 2000.

clear (Figure 10). From 1970 to about 1985 there appears to be no correlation. In certain periods, such as the period after 1996, population growth is actually negatively related to subsistence salmon harvests. Many other factors influence subsistence harvests, such as the varying abundance of Chinook salmon each year (Linderman and Bergstrom 2009, this volume), but these general data suggest caution in inferring that population growth is always correlated with increased subsistence harvests.

The human population of the Yukon-Koyokuk census area grew very little between 1978 and 2004 (Figure 11). Since population changes were so insignificant, changes in the Chinook salmon harvest are unlikely to be due to human population growth.

Similar to the Yukon-Koyokuk census area, Chinook salmon subsistence harvests have remained relatively constant over time in the Wade Hampton census area (Figure 12). Chinook salmon harvests moderately increased over time, along with population.

Harvests per household averaged four fish in 1978 and 3 fish in 2004.

Increased cash income may have mixed effects on subsistence harvests. Some researchers have hypothesized at the community level that higher income is negatively related to higher subsistence productivity (Wolfe and Walker 1987). Wealthier communities could have relatively lower subsistence harvests; people with higher incomes substitute purchased foods in place of subsistence harvested food. At the same time, cash is an important input to support subsistence activities, and higher incomes may increase subsistence harvests (Kerkvliet and Nebesky 1997).

Commercial Fisheries

AYK regional commercial fishery context

The estimated value of the total gross commercial catch for permit holders residing in the AYK region was $7,894,484 in

2004 (CFEC 2006).[17] Commercial salmon harvests accounted for about 80% of this total. In 2004, chum salmon made up about 10% of total AYK commercial harvests, coho salmon 71%, sockeye salmon 8%, and Chinook salmon 10% (ADF&G 2004). Chinook salmon harvests made up about 70% of value followed by coho salmon at 26% (ADF&G 2004). In more recent years, sockeye *O. nerka* and chum salmon *O. keta* harvests have increased (see Linderman and Bergstrom 2009).[18]

While direct regional earnings from commercial fisheries are not as large as in the Bristol Bay commercial fishery, earnings are an important contributor to income in lower Kuskokwim River and lower Yukon River communities.[19] The vast majority of commercial salmon comes from the lower Yukon River, the lower Kuskokwim River, and nearby coastal marine waters. Hundreds of residents from the AYK region participate in the fishery (Knapp 2009; this volume). Knapp (2009) reports that the average earnings per permit fished was around $4,000. Given median household income of about $30,000 and high rates of income poverty (discussed earlier), earnings from commercial fishing provide an important source of income for AYK area residents participating in the fishery. Permit holders residing in the Bethel census area accounted for about 50% of total estimated AYK commercial salmon earnings in 2004, and permit holders in the Wade Hampton census area accounted for about 45% of the estimated commercial salmon earnings (CFEC 2006).

The Community Development Quota (CDQ) program also plays an important role in the regional commercial fishing industry. In 1992 the North Pacific Fishery Management Council (NPFMC) established the CDQ program "with the goal of creating fisheries related economic development in Western Alaska" (CDQ 2008). A total of six CDQ organizations exist, and three are in the AYK region. The AYK area CDQs include Norton Sound Economic Development Corporation, Yukon Delta Development Fisheries Association, and Coastal Villages Region Fund; these three organizations represent approximately 41 coastal communities. CDQ groups are currently given roughly 7.5% of the Bering Seas/Aleutian Islands quota for pollock *Pollachius virens*, halibut, sable-fish *Anoplopoma fimbria*, and Bering Sea opilio *Chionoecetes opilio*, bairdi *C. bairdi*, and king crab (Northern Economics 2002). In addition to managing quota shares through direct harvests or through the lease of quota, CDQs participate in the development of near-shore commercial fisheries for salmon and herring. For instance, Coastal Villages Region Fund currently operates a salmon processing plant in Quinhagak and will be opening another facility in the Kuskokwim Bay near the city of Platinum.[20] CDQ revenues are invested back into CDQ operations and community devel-

---

[17]The $7,894,484 number (or $6,155,077 for salmon) describes earnings by place of residence. Gross earnings for salmon landed in the AYK area fisheries was approximately $4,741,273 in 2004. The lower Yukon fishery makes up about 61.6% of the total value for salmon and the Kuskokwim/Goodnews Bay fishery about 33% of the value. See regional CFEC fisheries statistics for 2004 at http://www.cfec.state.ak.us/gpbycen/2004/mnu.htm for earnings by place of residence and http://www.cfec.state.ak.us/bit/mnusalm.htm for earnings by regional fishery.

[18]In 2006, sockeye salmon made up about 15% of total AYK commercial harvests, coho salmon 41%, chum salmon 37%, and Chinook salmon 7% (ADF&G 2006).

[19]The Wade Hampton census area includes most districts in the State of Alaska's "lower Yukon salmon management area," and the Bethel census area includes all but one of the districts in Alaska's "Kuskokwim salmon management area." Regional maps are located at http://www.cf.adfg.state.ak.us/region3/finfish/salmon/maps/ayk_all.php.

---

[20]This information is taken from the Coastal Villages Region Fund webpage http://www.coastalvillages.org/projects.html.

opment operations intended to benefit member coastal communities. Because of data limitations it is difficult to identify revenues and employment generated by CDQs in the AYK region.

Commercial fishing income and the Kuskokwim River fishery

Analyses of the Bethel census area were focused to explore the links between commercial fishing, total income, and subsistence salmon harvests more carefully. As indicated in Figure 1, the Bethel census area includes the vast majority of people and places in the Kuskokwim River watershed. The area also includes the lower section of the Kuskokwim River (downstream from the village of Tuluksak), where most commercial fishing occurs. Because of the way economic data have been structured and reported, Bureau of Economic Analysis data for the Bethel census area can be compared to Alaska Commercial Fisheries Entry Commission data. This was an area of focus because corresponding Alaska Department of Fish and Game (ADF&G) subsistence harvest survey data exist for the same lower Kuskokwim communities, allowing us to explore links between commercial and subsistence salmon harvests.

Compared with other Alaska commercial fisheries, the lower Kuskokwim River commercial fishery is relatively small. Yet, as will be described, the commercial fishery plays an important role in this portion of the region and is an important source of income for households using commercial salmon fishing permits.

The commercial fishery directly and indirectly contributes to personal income. Households earn income directly as sole proprietors or as employees of a commercial fishing establishments. Indirectly, various support industries provide employment, and fishing income spent in the region generates additional income, i.e. multiplier effects. Available data limit the focus to only the direct effects of commercial fishing income on total personal income. This is examined overall for the region and then in terms of contribution to incomes of individual permit holders.

Direct earnings from commercial fisheries make up a small share of total personal income for the entire Bethel census area (Figure 13).[21] From 1986 to 2004, earnings from commercial fisheries ranged from as much as 16% to less than 1% of total private earnings. The contribution of fishing income to private earnings has declined since 1995, when fisheries earnings accounted for 3.2% of private earnings. In 2004, fishing income made up about 0.5% of private earnings. To provide some context, income from commercial fishing made up about 10% of private earnings in the Dillingham census area and 3% in the Bristol Bay region in 2004 (Bureau of Economic Analysis 2007). At the same time, if we could exclude the city of Bethel and report data only for lower Kuskokwim River communities, the contribution of commercial fisheries to total earnings would be much greater in the lower Kuskokwim region compared with the regional fishery.

In the Kuskokwim River region, the majority of commercial permit holders reside in the Bethel census area. About 98% of permits fished are owned by people residing in the

[21]The data in this figure are from the U.S. Bureau of Economic Analysis (BEA) Regional Economic Accounts. BEA data provides earnings by place of work. "Earnings" is the sum of wage and salary income disbursed in a year, supplements to wage and salary income, and proprietors' income. Reported "fisheries earnings" includes earnings from all establishments engaged in commercial fishing. As such, BEA data on commercial fishing earnings is a proxy for the income that is generated from commercial fishing. It is not an estimate of total revenue from commercial fishing. Data from the Alaska Commercial Fisheries Entry Commission database (CFEC) provide estimates of total revenue from commercial fishing based on the total catch times the average market price.

Bethel census area. The majority of these permit holders who fished live in lower Kuskokwim River communities because the biggest commercial buyer of salmon is in Quinhagak in Kuskokwim Bay (Figure 1). Since the widespread closures of commercial salmon fisheries in the late 1990's, permit holders living in upriver places do not have access to a major buyer. In 1988 just over 800 permits were fished. The number of permits fished began to decline in 1996 reaching a low of about 400 by 2002 and then increasing to about 500 by 2005.

Prior to 1996, average revenue per permit fished was between $5,000 and $7,000 (see Figure 15)—with an average of about 780 permits fished. In 2004, the average revenue per permit fished was about $3,300 (with 466 permits fished). Considering that median household income in 2000 was around $29,000 for the two census tracts outside of the city of Bethel, commercial fishing in-come is an important component of total income for households using commercial fishing permits in the lower Kuskokwim River communities.

"Economic disaster" and the Kuskokwim River commercial and subsistence fisheries

Total commercial and subsistence salmon harvests for the Kuskokwim River are shown in Figure 14. Chum and coho salmon have historically made up the largest share of total harvests in the Kuskokwim River (Figure 14; see also Linderman and Bergstrom 2009). The 1997 harvest decline corresponded with the precipitous decline in chum and coho salmon runs.

The reduction in total harvests beginning in 1997 was due primarily to a decline in commercial fishing. Commercial fishing harvests began to decline around 1997 as declin-

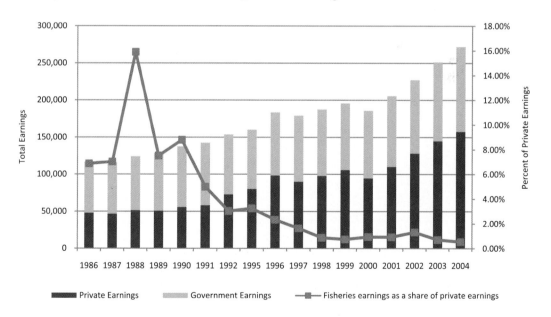

FIGURE 13. Real earnings by place of work, Bethel Census Area*
Source: Regional Economic Information System, Bureau of Economic Analysis, U.S. Department of Commerce.
*Data for 1993 and 1994 not available.

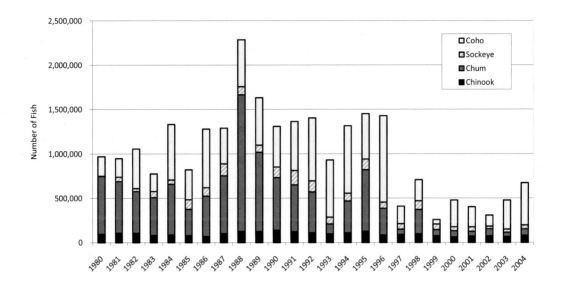

FIGURE 14. Total salmon harvests in the Kuskokwim River, by species, 1980–2004.
Source: Alaska Department of Fish and Game (Whitmore et al. 2005).

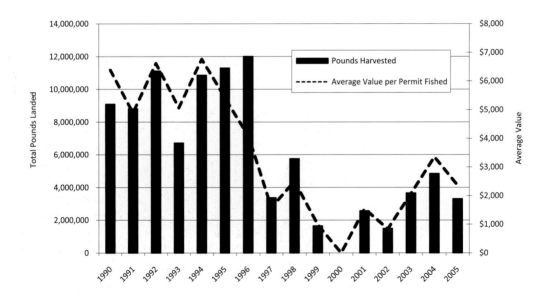

FIGURE 15. Commercial salmon harvests (gill net) and average value per permit fished, Kuskokwim River region, 1990–2005.
Source: AK Commercial Fisheries Entry Commission Database (CFEC).

ing run sizes led to limitations or closures of the commercial fishery (Figure 15). During this period, targeted species changed from predominantly chum salmon prior to 1996 to coho salmon in later years (see Figure 14). Corresponding to this decline in commercial harvests was a price decline—due in part to competition from farmed salmon—which can be seen as early as 1995 (Figure 15; see also Knapp 2009). The average value of each permit fished declined rapidly during this period, dropping from a high of nearly $7,000 in 1994 to about $1,500 in 1997. Because of declining runs and the closure of the commercial fishery, the area was declared a disaster area by the Alaska governor for five of six years.

A major change in the commercial salmon market occurred during this period and contributed to declines in commercial fishing income. Closure of the chum salmon fishery also facilitated the closure of major fish processors/buyers in the city of Bethel. To date, a large buyer of commercial salmon does not exist in the Bethel area. Commercial fisherman in up-river communities were the hardest hit by this change because fisherman in some lower Kuskokwim River communities (e.g., Tuntutuliak and down-river) continued to have access to a major buyer in Quinhagak. In spite of the importance of commercial fishing income for households with commercial permits, the closure of the commercial fishery does not appear to be associated with large out-migration from Bethel or Wade Hampton localities. Between 1995 and 2000, the population only declined about 5% due to out-migration, a smaller population decline relative to almost all other Alaska regions during the same period (U.S. Census 2000).

The subsistence fishery was also affected by the commercial closure, but changes were not as dramatic. In general, subsistence harvests have been relatively constant over time in "bad" years and in "good" years, as compared with the regional commercial fishery (Figure 16). Over the entire period, subsistence harvests averaged around 216,000 fish with a standard deviation of 40,103 fish—the standard deviation of commercial harvests was roughly ten times greater (473,742 fish). Even with the closing of commercial fisheries from 1999 to 2001, subsistence harvests did not increase. Similarly, in 1988, when runs were abundant, subsistence harvests were generally constant.

The stability of subsistence harvests in the Kuskokwim River area is notable because it is not a product of external rules. While the regional commercial fishery is tightly controlled and monitored by the state, the subsistence fishery is largely unregulated, in terms of formal state rules, relative to other Alaska regions. For Kuskokwim River communities, no subsistence bag limits for salmon exist, nor are subsistence permits required. Starting in 2001, some limits to the season and start dates were imposed on the Kuskokwim River, but relative to the lower and upper Yukon River management areas, subsistence salmon harvests remained largely unregulated on the Kuskokwim River.[22]

Mean subsistence harvests have been relatively constant over time compared to commercial harvests; however, an important change in subsistence harvests occurred after the 1997 decline in run sizes. Mean subsistence harvests from 1980 to 1996 were 230,637 fish, while mean harvests after 1997 were 196,913 fish.

---

[22]Starting in 2001, there was a Sunday, Monday, Tuesday closure of the subsistence fishery until the state fisheries managers determined that escapement goals were met. The idea was to create windows for fish passage to allow the earliest part of the runs to escape catch. The schedule has generally been lifted by the end of June. This constraint does not appear to have achieved the State's goal of allowing for greater levels of early escapement (Hamazaki 2008).

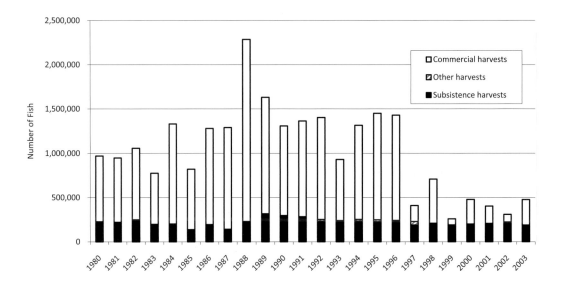

Figure 16. Subsistence as a share of total salmon harvests in the Kuskokwim River, 1980–2003. Source: Alaska Department of Fish and Game (Whitmore et al. 2005).

The harvest change can be observed for lower Kuskokwim communities (down-river of Tuluksak; in Figure 17). Average subsistence harvests in lower Kuskokwim communities (excluding Bethel) were 130,143 fish from 1990 to 1996, but 101,429 from 1997 to 2004. Similarly, the average catch per household prior to 1997 (124 fish) was significantly greater than average catch per household after 1997 (80.5 fish) in lower Kuskokwim communities. The difference between mean harvests is still significant, even including subsistence harvests from the city of Bethel.

Why did subsistence harvests decline during this period? Although salmon escapements declined, it is not clear that these declines were the single factor in reducing subsistence salmon harvests. Competition from commercial fishing actually declined during this period, and subsistence harvests have stayed below their historic average even as run sizes for some species show signs of recovery (Linderman and Bergstrom 2009).

Anecdotal evidence also indicates that subsistence fisherman did not view the period as an absolute disaster. A 2000 ADF&G Kuskokwim fisheries harvest survey asked respondents to rate the "quality" of fishing that year. Sixty-one percent of households indicated chum salmon fishing was good or average and seventy-two percent reported that coho salmon fishing was good or average (Boyd and Coffing 2001). Thus, while a sizeable share of households reported abnormally poor fishing, a majority of households reported average to good fishing.

If reduced salmon escapements were not the single variable behind the decline in harvests on the Kuskokwim River, at least two other factors should be considered. First, self-regulating local institutions may have contributed to the decline in subsistence harvests as local people cut-back on average harvests. As described earlier, the Yup'ik people of the Kuskokwim River region maintain a strong traditional culture. As a people who have been dependent on fluctuating resources for

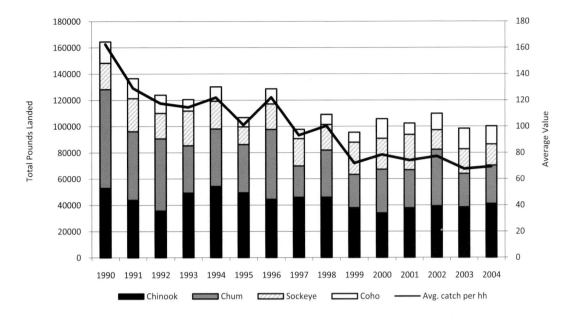

FIGURE 17. Subsistence salmon catch, lower Kuskokwim communities (excluding Bethel), 1990–2004. Source: Alaska Department of Fish and Game Kuskokwim Subsistence Survey.

generations, their informal rules and customs undoubtedly account for such uncertainty (Fienup-Riordan 1986). The extent to which certain informal rules may have affected subsistence harvests after the "economic crisis" period is an important area for future study. Similarly, important future research should describe how informally based local community rules develop in light of resource uncertainty and how these institutions change in light of major disruptions in the normal harvest cycle, such as in the late 1990s economic crisis.

A second explanation involves the relation between subsistence and commercial fishing. Commercial fishing could be an important input to subsistence for households with commercial fishing income. Commercial fishing income, an average of $5,000 to $6,000 per permit holder in the early 1990s, and closer to $3,000 in 2004, could provide important resources to support subsistence

activities for households in the Kuskokwim area. As commercial fishing income declined during this period, households may have reduced the use of certain equipment or could have cut back on the number and distance of fishing trips.

Kuskokwim River commercial fishing income, population growth, and subsistence salmon harvests

We used a simple econometric model to explore relationships among commercial fishing income, population growth, and subsistence salmon harvests for lower Kuskokwim River communities. We formed a panel of subsistence and commercial salmon harvests over time and place, by combining two data sources described below. The use of panel data allowed us to provide a consistent estimate of certain coefficients in spite of omitted variables (Wooldridge 2001). That is, while important explanatory variables may be missing from the data, the use of panel data allowed us to obtain reasonably reliable estimates of the effect of commercial fishing income and population growth on subsistence salmon harvests.

The standard equation we estimate can be written as:

$$y_{it} = x_{it}\beta + c_i + u_{it}$$

where i represents the sixteen lower Kuskokwim places and t corresponds to the period 1990 to 2005. The coefficient c represents a constant term that is group specific (i.e., communities) but does not vary over time, and u is the error term.

The dependent variable in our equation (y) is average household subsistence salmon harvests. This variable was regressed on a small set of independent variables (x) by community (i) over time. Independent variables include three-year average population growth rates, average household income from Kuskokwim River commercial salmon harvests, and average household "other" commercial fishing income. A dummy variable equal to one after 1996 (and zero before) is used to capture the period of the declining chum runs and the associated restrictions on the commercial fishery (i.e., a "shock"). A second dummy variable is used to identify the city of Bethel. Including this dummy variable allows us to control for the fact that household subsistence harvests in Bethel are likely to differ from those in other communities.

Data used in this model were from ADF&G subsistence salmon harvest surveys for lower Kuskokwim River communities and Alaska commercial fisheries data.[23] Since about 1990, ADF&G subsistence

salmon surveys have been conducted annually in several Kuskokwim River communities. These data contain annual subsistence salmon harvests and an annual estimate of the total number of households for each lower Kuskokwim River place. Based on personal correspondence with ADF&G personnel, consistent survey methods and instruments have been used since about 1990. Data from lower river communities (downriver from Tuluksak) including the Tundra Villages was used.[24]

ADF&G data was combined with data from the Alaska Commercial Fisheries Entry Commission (CFEC). CFEC data are also available at a community level for all types of commercial fishing. Commercial salmon fishing income in the Kuskokwim region was separated from other types of commercial fishing income. For residents in the Kuskokwim region, most other types of commercial fishing happen outside of the Kuskokwim River—e.g., earnings from the Bristol Bay salmon fishery. In estimating this equation, both a fixed-effects model and a random-effects model that controls for the fact that the error term (u) does not have constant variance was used.[25] In both cases, similar results occurred.

Results

The analysis offered here should only be considered a small step in a multifaceted approach needed to better understand subsistence harvests in the AYK region. Many

---

[23]Survey methods are outlined in Simon et al. (2007). ADF&G provided these data to us by community over time. We were also given a sample survey instrument and Tracie Krauthoefer (ADF&G Bethel) provided very helpful background information.

[24]Places include Akiachak, Akiak, Atmautluak, Bethel, Eek, Kasigluk, Kipnuk, Kongiganak, Kwethluk, Kwigillingok, Napakiak, Napaskiak, Nunapitchuk, Oscarville, Tuluksak, and Tuntutuliak.

[25]A Hausman test indicates that c_i and x_{it} are correlated, and so we run a fixed effects equation. However, the Hausman test is marginally significant and we also find evidence for heteroskedasticity, consequently we run a random effects model controlling for heteroskedasticity.

complexities of AYK area fisheries exist (e.g., timing, equipment, distribution of permits, fuel costs) that we have not addressed in our analysis. Note also that the results were based on data from the sixteen lower Kuskokwim communities and include the city of Bethel. Futher analysis that yields a better understanding of the links between population growth, the commercial fishery, and the subsistence salmon fishery is warranted.

Earnings from commercial salmon fishery were found to be positively correlated with subsistence salmon harvests. At the community level, income earned from the Kuskokwim River commercial salmon fishery is a significant variable and positively related to subsistence salmon harvests (Appendix Table 2). A similar outcome was observed in both fixed and random effects models, although the relationship was stronger under the random effects model. The model estimates that a $1,000 increase in average household Kuskokwim commercial salmon fishing income would only increase subsistence salmon harvests by about 5–8 fish per household. Given that the average catch per household in this region was about 80 fish, as noted earlier, a $1,000 decrease in income could reduce harvests up to about 10%. The primary finding was that earnings from the commercial salmon fishery are positively related to subsistence salmon harvests.

In contrast to earnings from commercial salmon fishing, the regression results indicated that commercial fishing income from other commercial fisheries is negatively related to subsistence salmon harvests in the Kuskokwim. The negative coefficient on this variable was as strong as the positive effect of earnings from the commercial salmon fishery. One interpretation of this finding is that households holding other commercial fishing permits left the region more frequently to fish in commercial fisheries outside the Bethel census area, and as a result Kuskokwim River subsistence salmon harvests declined.

Regression results indicated that population growth is negatively related to subsistence salmon harvests. Moderate population growth was associated with declining subsistence harvests. This result was based on data from all sixteen communities in thesample, including the city of Bethel. Data used were average annual three-year growth rates; however, similar results occurred for annual growth rates and five-year average annual growth rates. Average annual five-year growth rates is a significant variable and negative for both fixed and random effects models. As discussed earlier, population growth for the region has been moderate over time.

Regression analyses indicated that subsistence salmon harvests declined after 1997. The statistically significant coefficient on the "shock" variable tells us that from 1997 on, households in the sixteen communities harvested fewer fish compared with previous years (i.e., before 1997). As discussed earlier, the harvest decline could be a function of reduced run sizes and/or local informal customs that limited harvests.

Household subsistence salmon harvests were lower for the community of Bethel than for other communities. Bethel households harvested fewer fish, when compared with the households in lower Kuskokwim villages included in our sample—again this result was statistically significant. The result could be due in part to different household composition and a relatively greater share of the population being engaged in the formal cash economy in Bethel (Appendix Table 1).

Discussion

The econometric results provide insight into the links between commercial fishing income, population numbers, and subsistence salmon harvests. Similar to existing studies looking at the general relationship between income and subsistence harvests (e.g., Wolfe and Walker 1987; Kerkvliet and Nebesky 1997), our analyses produced mixed results. It was discovered that income from different sources has different effects on subsistence salmon harvests. Income from commercial salmon fishing is associated with increased subsistence harvests, and therefore the hypothesis that commercial salmon fishing income and subsistence harvests are negatively correlated can be rejected. This evidence was consistent with the notion that households in lower-Kuskokwim River communities use earnings from commercial salmon fishing as an input to support subsistence activities. When income from commercial salmon fishing declined, so did subsistence salmon harvests. In contrast, income from other commercial fishing reduced subsistence salmon harvests. A likely explanation is that households earning income in commercial fisheries elsewhere spend less time subsistence fishing on the Kuskokwim.

Population growth was not associated with greater subsistence salmon harvests. In fact, the econometric results showed a statistically significant and negative relationship between population growth and household subsistence harvests for the sixteen communities (including Bethel) in the sample. While this result may not seem intuitively plausible, the negative relationship observed between population and subsistence harvest is consistent with the economic and demographic changes in the AYK region described earlier. For instance, more households were involved in the cash economy, there were fewer women relative to men living in villages, and families were younger. While households may have greater income for subsistence, the opportunity cost of subsistence harvest also increase. Taking time for subsistence activities may trade off with time available for earning cash income. Also, the number of women living in villages has declined. Because subsistence is a

team effort, men may have harvested fewer fish when women were not there to help in processing. Our earlier observation of an increased number of young families, which are known to harvest fewer fish, is also consistent with our findings. Finally, informal rules and customs, such as avoiding waste, could have mitigated the effects of population increase on subsistence salmon harvests.

These results allow us to reject the hypothesis that subsistence harvests were unchanged after widespread closures of the commercial fishery. Subsistence harvests after 1997 have been consistently below historical average. Lower escapement of salmon undoubtedly accounts for some of this decline, but the role of other factors should also be considered in future research.

Finally, the results provide evidence that Bethel households do not harvest the same amount of salmon as households in other communities. Bethel area households harvest less, when compared with households in the fifteen other villages included in our sample. This result may be explained in part by differences in household composition. Also, these findings are consistent with the hypothesis that greater cash income trades off with subsistence, because incomes are higher in Bethel, and households are more likely to participate in the cash economy.

These econometric results help identify general relationships affecting subsistence salmon harvests and point to variables that can be affected by public policy. Our findings, however, are by no means exhaustive or conclusive. Further investigation that controls for other variables important in the decision to conduct subsistence harvest activities could validate these initial findings and provide more relevant information to policymakers considering regulatory changes of commercial fisheries in different river systems. Many factors influence subsistence salmon harvests, including variability in run sizes, local institutions, and changes in household composition over time. Accounting for these other variables will help refine the relationships identified here. Also, our findings should be considered in light of the relatively small sample of sixteen communities; expanding the analysis to communities in other regions could validate these preliminary findings. Better data at the household level over time, for instance, would allow for better estimates. Also, the analysis could be improved by data that captures more of the complexity of the fishery such as timing, fuel costs, and distance to market. Data allowing exploration of similar relationships on the Yukon River would also provide valuable insight.

Further empirical and analytical modeling of these relationships would also be valuable. For instance, policymakers need to understand how management of the commercial fishery affects subsistence harvests in a region where fishermen often participate in both subsistence and commercial fisheries. Further policy analysis might allow one to better predict changes in subsistence catch given specific levels of commercial catch and income. Such research could also help explain why some households are high subsistence producers in a community and how this changes from year to year.

Summary

This paper addressed broad demographic and economic characteristics of the AYK region. It was noted that regional population growth has been moderate over time, but growth rates have been relatively larger in the regional center of Bethel and in a small number of villages. Out-migration of the human population regularly exceeds in-migration, especially in the villages, and consequently growth is largely a product of natural increase. We anticipate future population growth patterns will be similar.

The linguistically and geographically distinct populations of the AYK region are similar in that they all have active traditional cultures and a strong reliance on subsistence. It was also noted that formal rules governing subsistence and commercial salmon harvests vary across regions, and the effect of these rules on subsistence salmon harvests is an important area for future research.

The AYK region is characterized by high unemployment, low household incomes, and high levels of income poverty. While commercial fishing income is not a large contributor to total regional income, it is an important component of income for communities in proximity to a commercial fish processor and for households using commercial fishing permits. It was discovered that many commercial fishermen were also subsistence harvesters, and that commercial fishing income can provide equipment and other inputs important in supporting subsistence activities.

To explore the relationship between commercial fishing income, population growth, and subsistence salmon harvests we focused on the Kuskokwim River region. A simple econometric regression model provided evidence that subsistence salmon harvests are positively correlated with income from commercial salmon fishing on the Kuskokwim River but negatively related to commercial fishing income from other regions. Subsistence harvests also appear not to have increased with population growth.

Links between subsistence salmon harvests and population growth are complex. Many factors, including local institutions, variability in escapement, and changes in regulations are variables that should receive future attention. Also, the recent sharp rise in fuel prices has made groceries more expensive, causing some households to increase their reliance on subsistence salmon while at the same time increasing the costs of fishing.

There is some anecdotal evidence that high fuel prices are causing people to leave rural Alaska (Martin et al. 2008). The long-term effects of higher fuel prices on salmon harvests remain to be seen.

Acknowledgments

We thank Tracie Krauthoefer, Steve Hayes, and David Koster at the Alaska Department of Fish and Game for helpful correspondence and for providing ADF&G subsistence survey data. We also thank Phillip Mitchell at the Alaska Department of Health and Social Services for providing vital statistics data. We thank Meghan Wilson at the Institute of Social and Economic Research for generating the map used in Figure 1. We also thank Charles Krueger and Linda Leask for valuable editorial input. Finally we thank Joseph Spaeder and two anonymous reviewers for helpful comments on an earlier draft. This research was supported by the University of Alaska special projects fund, Understanding Alaska. Additional support was provided to Howe through National Science Foundation grant #0729063.

References

ADF&G (Alaska Department of Fish and Game). 2004. Alaska commercial salmon harvests and exvessel values. Division of Commercial Fisheries. Available: http://www.cf.adfg.state.ak.us/geninfo/finfish/salmon/catchval/blusheet/04exvesl.php (January 2009).

ADF&G (Alaska Department of Fish and Game). 2005. Alaska subsistence fisheries 2003 Annual Report. Division of Subsistence, Alaska Department of Fish and Game. Juneau.

ADF&G (Alaska Department of Fish and Game). 2006. Alaska commercial salmon harvests and exvessel values. Division of Commercial Fisheries. Available: http://www.cf.adfg.state.ak.us/geninfo/finfish/salmon/catchval/blusheet/06exvesl.php (January 2009).

AKDOL (Alaska Department of Labor and Workforce Development). 2007. Alaska population projections 2007–2030. Juneau, Alaska.

Andrews, E., and Coffing, M. 1986. Kuskokwim River subsistence Chinook fisheries: an overview. Technical Paper No. 146. Division of Subsistence, Alaska Department of Fish and Game, Juneau.

Bering Straits Native Corporation. 2008. Land and natural resources division. Available: http://www.beringstraits.com/lands/lands.html (September 2008).

Bersamin, A., S. Zidenberg-Cherr, J. S. Stern, and B. R. Luick. 2007. Nutrient intakes are associated with adherence to a traditional diet among Yup'ik eskimos living in remote Alaska native communities: the Canhr study. International Journal of Circumpolar Health 66:62–70.

Boyd, T., and M. Coffing. 2001. Bethel post-season subsistence fisheries harvest surveys, 2000. Final Report, Cooperative Agreement No 70181-0-J288. Division of Subsistence, Alaska Department of Fish and Game, Juneau.

Bue, F. J., and S. J. Hayes. 2006. 2006 Yukon area subsistence, personal use and commercial salmon fisheries outlook and management strategies. Fishery Management Report No. 06–32. Divisions of Sport Fish and Commercial Fisheries, Alaska Department of Fish and Game, Anchorage.

Bureau of Economic Analysis (BEA). 2006. U.S. Department of Commerce, Regional Economic Information System. Available: http://www.bea.gov/regional/index.htm (November 2006).

Calista Corporation. 1991. The Calista region: a gentle people—a harsh life. Calista Corporation. Anchorage, Alaska.

Calista Corporation. 2008. Land and natural resources division. Available: http://www.calistacorp.com/landresources/default.asp (September 2008).

CFEC (Commercial Fisheries Entry Commission Data). 2006. State of Alaska, Division of Commercial Fisheries. Available: http://www.cfec.state.ak.us/fishery_statistics/earnings.htm (October 2006).

CDQ (Community Development Quota Program). 2008. State of Alaska, Community Development Quota Program. Available: http://www.commerce.state.ak.us/bsc/CDQ/cdq.htm (September 2008).

Doyon Native Regional Corporation. 2008. Land and natural resources division. Available: http://www.doyonlands.com/lands.html (September 2008).

Fienup-Riordan, A. 1986. When our bad season comes: a cultural account of subsistence harvesting and harvest disruption on the Yukon delta. Alaska Anthropological Association monograph series. Aurora Press, Anchorage.

Hamazaki, H. 2008. Fishery closure "windows" scheduling as a means of changing the Chinook salmon subsistence fishery pattern: is it an effective management tool? Fisheries 33:495–501.

Hamilton, L., and C. Seyfrit. 1994. Coming out of the country: community size and gender balance among Alaskan Natives. Arctic Anthropology 31:16–25.

Hayes, S., F. Bue, B. Borba, K. Boeck, H. Carroll, L. Boeck, E. Newland, K. Clark, and W. Busher. 2008. Annual management report for the Yukon and Northern Areas, 2002–2004. Fishery Management Report No. 08–36. Divisions of Sport Fish and Commercial Fisheries, Alaska Department of Fish and Game, Anchorage.

Kerkvliet, J., and W. Nebesky. 1997. Whaling and wages on Alaska's North Slope: a time allocation approach to natural resource use. Economic Development and Cultural Change 45:651–665.

Knapp, G. 2009. Commercial salmon fisheries of the Arctic-Yukon-Kuskokwim region: economic challenges and opportunities. Pages 463–486 in C. C. Krueger and C. E. Zimmerman, editors. Pacific salmon: ecology and management of western Alaska's populations. American Fisheries Society Symposium 70, Bethesda, Maryland.

Krueger, C. C., C. E. Zimmerman, and J. J. Spaeder. 2009. Ecology and management of western Alaska Pacific salmon: introduction to the proceedings. Pages 3–10 in C. C. Krueger and C. E. Zimmerman, editors. Pacific salmon: ecology and management of western Alaska's populations. American Fisheries Society, Symposium 70, Bethesda, Maryland.

Kruse, J. A. 1982.Subsistence and the North Slope Iñupiat: The effects of energy development. Man in the Arctic Program, Monograph No. 4. University of Alaska, Anchorage.

Linderman, J. C., Jr., and D. J. Bergstrom. 2009. Kuskokwim management area: salmon escapement, harvest, and management. Pages 541–599 in C. C. Krueger and C. E. Zimmerman, editors. Pacific salmon: ecology and management of western Alaska's populations. American Fisheries Society Symposium 70, Bethesda, Maryland.

Magdanz, J., E. Trigg, A. Ahmasuk, P. Nanouk, D. Koster, and K. Kamletz. 2009. Patterns and trends in subsistence salmon harvests, Norton Sound–Port Clarence Area, Alaska, 1994–2003. Pages 395–431 in C. C. Krueger and C. E. Zimmerman, editors. Pacific salmon: ecology and management of western Alaska's populations. American Fisheries Society, Symposium 70, Bethesda, Maryland.

Martin, S., S. Colt, and M. Killorin. 2008. Fuel costs, migration and community viability. Institute of Social and Economic Research. University of Alaska, Anchorage.

Northern Economics. 2002. An assessment of the socioeconomic impacts of the western alaska community development quota program. A report to the Alaska Department of Community and Economic Development Division of Community and Business Development. Available: http://www.commerce.state.ak.us/bsc/CDQ/pub/Final_Report.pdf (September 2008).

Simon, J., T. Krauthoefer, D. Koster, and D. Caylor. 2007. Subsistence salmon harvest monitoring report, Kuskokwim Fisheries Management Area, Alaska, 2004. Technical Paper No. 313. Division of Subsistence, Alaska Department of Fish and Game. Juneau.

U.S. Census Bureau. 1970. U.S. Census 1970 Summary File Data. U.S. Department of Commerce, Washington. Available: http://www.census.gov/prod/www/abs/decennial/1970.htm (March 2009).

U.S. Census Bureau. 1980. U.S. Census 1980 Summary File Data. U.S. Department of Commerce, Washington. Available: http://www.census.gov/prod/www/abs/decennial/1980.htm (March 2009).

U.S. Census Bureau. 1990. U.S. Census 1990 Summary File Data 1–4. U.S. Department of Commerce, Washington. Available: http://www.census.gov/prod/www/abs/decennial/1990.htm (March 2009).

U.S. Census Bureau. 2000. U.S. Census 2000 Summary File Data 1–4. U.S. Department of Commerce, Washington. Available: http://www.census.gov/main/www/cen2000.html (March 2009).

Whitmore, C., M. Martz, D. Bue, J. Linderman, Jr., and R. Fisher. 2005. Annual management report for the subsistence and commercial fisheries of the Kuskokwim area, 2003. Fishery Management Report No. 05–72. Divisions of Sport Fish and Commercial Fisheries, Alaska Department of Fish and Game, Anchorage.

Wolfe, R. 2000. Subsistence in Alaska: a year 2000 update. Alaska Department of Fish and Game, Division of Subsistence, Juneau.

Wolfe, R. J., and J. Spaeder. 2009. People and salmon of the Yukon and Kuskokwim drainages and Norton Sound in Alaska: fishery harvests, culture change, and local knowledge systems. Pages 349–379 in C. C. Krueger and C. E. Zimmerman, editors. Pacific salmon: ecology and management of western Alaska's populations. American Fisheries Society, Symposium 70, Bethesda, Maryland.

Wolfe, R., and R. Walker. 1987. Subsistence economies in Alaska: productivity, geography, and development impacts." Arctic Anthropology 24:56–81.

Wooldridge, J. 2001. Econometric analysis of cross section and panel data. MIT Press, Cambridge, Massachusetts.

Worl, R. 2002. Alaska Native Subsistence Cultures and Economy. Testimony before U.S. Senate, Committee on Indian Affairs, Oversight Hearing on Subsistence Hunting and Fishing In the State of Alaska. Available: http://indian.senate.gov/2002hrgs/041702alaska/worl.PDF (April 2002).

Appendix Table 1. Employment in the AYK region, 2000. Source: US Census 2000, summary file 3 and 4. Unemployment rate refers to the share of civilians in the labor force who are unemployed. Those who are employed or who are actively seeking employment are in the labor force. Working age population is the population 16 and older.

Source	Unemployment Rate	Working age population	Share of the working age population not in the labor force
AYK region: Native	22.0%	19,932	43.7%
AYK region: non-Native	5.5%	5,138	17.8%
Regional Center: Native	16.3%	3,584	39.1%
Regional Center: non-Native	3.4%	2,660	15.5%
Villages: Native	23.3%	16,348	44.8%
Villages: non-Native	7.9%	2,478	20.3%
AYK region: Female	12.0%	11,669	39.5%
Regional Center: Female	7.8%	2,937	31.3%
Villages: Females	13.6%	8,732	42.3%

APPENDIX TABLE 2. Fixed effects (within) and feasible generalized least squares regressions statistics examining associations with the dependent variable (y) of average household subsistence salmon harvests vs. population growth, and earnings. Absolute value of t statistics in parentheses. *significant at 10%; ** significant at 5%; *** significant at 1%.

Source	Fixed effects	FGLS (random effects)
three_year_growth [This variable is the three-year average population growth rate by community.]	−0.451 (1.12)	−1.52 (3.97)***
salmon_earnings [This variable is the average household income from the Kuskokwim commercial salmon fishery by community.]	0.005 (2.02)**	0.008 (3.30)***
other_fisheries_earnings [This variable is the average household income from other commercial salmon fisheries (e.g. Bristol Bay) by community.]	−0.005 (3.37)***	−0.012 (13.86)***
shock [This is a dummy variable equal to one after 1996 and zero otherwise.]	−21.773 (2.87)***	−17.722 (2.82)***
Bethel [This is a dummy variable equal to one for the city of Bethel and zero otherwise.]		−56.235 (11.55)***
constant	106.164 (11.64)***	115.585 (14.89)***
Observations	183	183
Number of places	16	16
R-squared within	0.34	
R-squared between	0.69	
R-squared overall	0.36	
Wald chi²		475.94***

American Fisheries Society Symposium 70:463–486, 2009

Commercial Salmon Fisheries of the Arctic-Yukon-Kuskokwim Region: Economic Challenges and Opportunties

Gunnar Knapp*

Institute of Social and Economic Research
3211 Providence Drive, Anchorage, Alaska 99508, USA

Abstract.—This paper provides an overview of Arctic-Yukon-Kuskokwim (AYK) commercial salmon fisheries, reviews economicvariables affecting the fisheries, and discusses the challenge of increasing the economic benefits from these fisheries. During the years 2004–2006, AYK fisheries accounted for about 1% of total Alaska harvest volume and 2% of total Alaska harvest value. AYK fisheries accounted for 18% of total Alaska permit holdings and 14% of permits fished, but only 1.6% of total earnings. AYK commercial salmon fisheries have faced significant challenges over the past two decades. Harvest volumes fell sharply from the late 1980s to 2002. By 2007, total harvest volume in five of the six AYK fisheries had recovered somewhat from the low levels of the early 2000s, but remained well below the levels of the late 1980s. Prices fell during the 1990s, most importantly because of the growth of salmon farming, which dramatically increased world salmon supply and reduced the market share of Alaska wild salmon. Currently, prices for AYK coho *Onchorhynchus kisutch* and chum salmon *O. keta* remain far below levels of the 1980s, while prices for the Chinook salmon *O. tshawyscha* fisheries are comparable to levels of the late 1980s. Other challenges have included a steep decline in the number of buyers, and a dramatic increase in fuel prices in the late 2000s. AYK wild salmon producers also face new opportunties in world markets to market wild salmon not as a commodity but as a specialty product. Some AYK salmon runs, such as Yukon River Chinook and chum salmon, have unusually high oil content, which have given them reputations as among the best-tasting salmon in the world. To reduce costs and increase value for AYK salmon fisheries, a need exists for (a) implementing improvements in the quality and consistency of salmon products by improvements in how fish are handled at every stage of harvesting, processing, and transportation; (b) sustained investments in marketing; and (c) investments in infrastructure, ranging from ice machines to airport runways, to reduce costs and improve quality.

Introduction

Alaska's Arctic-Yukon-Kuskokwim (AYK) commercial salmon fisheries are economically depressed. Despite increases in catches and prices in recent years, gross earnings remain far below average levels of the 1980s—even before adjusting for the effects of inflation on commercial fishing costs and the purchasing power of commercial fishing income. Participation in AYK commercial salmon harvesting has declined dramatically, as has the number of AYK salmon processors.

*Corresponding author: Gunnar.Knapp@uaa.alaska.edu

Low salmon runs have been a major contributing variable causing the poor economic condition of AYK commercial salmon fisheries. But low salmon runs have not been the only factor. Rapid and dramatic changes in world salmon markets—caused by the development of salmon farming, globalization of the world economy, and many other factors—have lowered prices for some species and created new challenges for AYK salmon to meet the changing world market demands. In 2007 and 2008, soaring fuel costs posed additional challenges for AYK fishermen and processors.

The first section of this paper provides an overview of AYK commercial salmon fisheries and changes in these fisheries over time. The second section reviews economic variables affecting AYK salmon fisheries. The third and final section of the paper discusses the challenge of increasing the economic benefits of AYK commercial salmon fisheries and asks whether changes in fisheries management might help to reduce costs or increase value in AYK commercial salmon fisheries. My purpose is to encourage stakeholders and managers to think broadly—"outside of the box"—about potential management changes that might help to make AYK fisheries more economically successful.

My focus in this paper is solely on AYK *commercial* salmon fisheries. Except where otherwise noted, all references to "salmon fisheries" and all data are for commercial fisheries.

Overview of Arctic-Yukon-Kuskokwim Commercial Salmon Fisheries

Arctic-Yukon-Kuskokwim (AYK) salmon are harvested in subsistence, commercial, and sport fisheries. The relative share of each fishery in total harvests varies widely by area, species, and year. In general, subsistence and commercial harvests account for most of the

catch, while sport fisheries account for only a small share of total harvests (Bue et al. 2009, this volume; Evenson et al. 2009, this volume; Menard et al. 2009, this volume; Linderman and Bergstrom 2009, this volume). Important linkages exist between commercial and subsistence fisheries. Cash income earned in commercial fishing helps to support subsistence activities. Much of the same equipment is used for both commercial and subsistence fishing (Wolfe and Walker 1987).

In general, subsistence fisheries have first priority, and subsistence harvests are relatively more stable than commercial fisheries harvests (Magdanz et al. 2009, this volume). As total runs and harvests declined in the 1990s and early 2000s, subsistence fisheries accounted for an increasing share of total harvests, for example, in the Yukon River fall chum salmon fishery (Figure 1; Bue et al. 2009).

My focus in this paper is on AYK *commercial* salmon fisheries, and in particular on the variables affecting the extent to which commercial fisheries can provide cash income to AYK region residents. Clearly, commercial fisheries represent an important economic activity: they account for a significant share of total harvests and an important part of management effort, and thousands of AYK residents participate in commercial fishing.

From 2004 to 2006, the Kuskokwim and Yukon areas account for most of the harvest volume and value; Norton Sound and Kotzebue Sound catches were much smaller (Table 1). The mix of species harvested varies by area. Between 2004 and 2006, in the Kuskokwim area, coho salmon accounted for the largest share of harvest volume (57%), followed by sockeye *Oncorhynchus nerka* (19%), and Chinook salmon *O. tshawytscha* (10%). In the Yukon area, chum salmon *O. keta* accounted for the largest share of harvest volume (51%), followed by Chinook (36%) and coho salmon *O. kisutch* (13%).

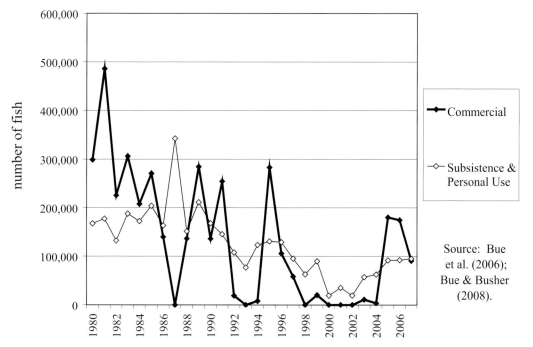

FIGURE 1. Yukon River fall chum salmon *Oncorhynchus keta* harvest.

Ex-vessel prices vary widely by species. Between 2004 and 2006, because Yukon area chinook salmon prices ($3.19/lb) averaged more than ten times higher than chum salmon prices ($0.20/lb), Chinook salmon accounted for 90% of Yukon area exvessel value, while chum salmon accounted for only 8% of exvessel value.

AYK salmon fisheries are relatively small in comparison with other Alaska salmon fisheries. During the years 2004–2006, AYK fisheries accounted for about 1% of total Alaska harvest volume and 2% of total Alaska harvest value (Table 2). AYK fisheries, when compared with those in other regions, accounted for a somewhat larger share of Alaska Chinook salmon fisheries (about 12% of volume and value) and Alaska coho fisheries (about 9% of volume and 3% of value). However, AYK fisheries accounted for an insignificant share of Alaska sockeye and pink salmon harvests—the two species that account for the largest shares of total Alaska salmon harvest volume and value.

In general, AYK salmon ex-vessel prices are significantly lower than those for most other areas of Alaska (Table 3). Yukon Chinook salmon represent an important exception, commanding much higher prices than the statewide average. I discuss reasons for these price differences later in this paper.

Six limited-entry commercial salmon fisheries currently exist in the AYK region (Table 4). Each fishery is defined by area and gear type. Typically each fishery catches multiple species, although one or two species account for most of the catch value. Two fisheries, the Lower Yukon Gillnet (LYG) and Kuskokwim Gillnet (KG) fisheries have much higher total earnings than the other four fisheries and have much larger numbers of permits issued, as well as a higher share of permits fished. In 2003–2005, 81% of LYG permits and 59% of KG permits were fished, compared with only one-fifth or less of the permits in the other four fisheries. However, because so many fewer permits were fished in the four smaller

TABLE 1. Average volume, value, and prices of AYK salmon harvests, by area and species, 2004–2006. Four AYK management areas are summarized: Kuskokwim, Yukon, Norton Sound, and Kotzebue Sound. Volume is measured in thousands of pounds and value is measured in thousands of dollars. Source: ADFG (2008a). Note that in Table 1 and all other tables and figures, prices and values are in nominal dollars (not adjusted for inflation) except where otherwise indicated.

		Area				
	Salmon species	Kuskokwim	Yukon	Norton Sound	Kotzebue	Total
Volume						
	Chinook	390	873	3	1	1267
	Sockeye	732				732
	Coho	2223	307	611		3141
	Pink	4				4
	Chum	540	1219	46	693	2497
	Total	3886	2399	658	693	7636
Ex-Vessel Value						
	Chinook	405	2784	6	3	3198
	Sockeye	357				357
	Coho	713	71	235		1019
	Pink	1				1
	Chum	38	241	7	137	423
	Total	1513	3096	244	138	4991
Share of volume						
	Chinook	10%	36%	0%	0%	17%
	Sockeye	19%	0%	0%	0%	10%
	Coho	57%	13%	93%	0%	41%
	Pink	0%	0%	0%	0%	0%
	Chum	14%	51%	7%	100%	33%
	Total	100%	100%	100%	100%	100%
Share of value						
	Chinook	27%	90%	2%	2%	64%
	Sockeye	24%	0%	0%	0%	7%
	Coho	47%	2%	96%	0%	20%
	Pink	0%	0%	0%	0%	0%
	Chum	2%	8%	3%	99%	8%
	Total	100%	100%	100%	100%	100%

TABLE 2. AYK Fisheries as a percentage of total Alaska harvest volume and value, 2004–2006. Source: ADFG (2008a).

Salmon species	Harvest Volume			Ex-Vessel Value		
	2004	2005	2006	2004	2005	2006
Chinook	11.8%	9.9%	12.3%	15.0%	9.5%	12.9%
Coho	10.4%	8.3%	8.8%	4.9%	3.2%	3.1%
Chum	0.8%	3.0%	2.0%	0.5%	2.2%	1.0%
Sockeye	0.2%	0.3%	0.4%	0.1%	0.2%	0.3%
Pink	0.0%	0.0%	0.0%	0.0%	0.0%	0.0%
All Species	0.9%	0.8%	1.2%	2.0%	1.2%	1.8%

fisheries, average earnings per permit fished were similar: just a few thousand dollars. Average permit prices were also roughly similar among fisheries and were less than $10,000 for all AYK fisheries.

All but four of 19 nonAYK limited entry fisheries had higher total earnings than any of the AYK fisheries (Table 4). However, only five fisheries had more permits than did the LYG and KG fisheries. Average earnings per permit fished were lower for all six AYK fisheries than for any of the other nineteen Alaska fisheries, and average permit prices were lower for all six AYK fisheries than for all but two of the nonAYK fisheries. Thus, in comparison with other Alaska salmon fisheries, the AYK fisheries have relatively large numbers of permit holders (particularly the LYG and KG fisheries), but they have much smaller total and average earnings. Put differently, AYK fisheries accounted for 18% of total Alaska permit holdings and 14% of permits fished, but only 1.6% of total earnings.

AYK commercial salmon fisheries experienced very significant declines in harvest volume between the late 1980s and the 2000–2002 period, reflecting lower salmon runs and resulting restrictions on commercial harvests, as well as lower prices (Figure 2; discussed below). By 2007, total harvest volume in five of the six AYK fisheries had recovered somewhat from the very low levels of the early 2000s, but remained well below the levels of the late 1980s.

The effects of lower AYK salmon harvests were compounded by a steep decline in ex-vessel prices during the 1990s for coho and chum salmon (Figures 3 and 4). Prices have risen since 2002 but remain below prices paid in the 1980s—even without adjusting for the effects of inflation. Ex-vessel prices for Chinook salmon also fell sharply in the early 1990s, but recovered in the late 1990s and rose rapidly after 2003 to record or near-record levels after 2006 (Figure 5). Price trends for each species were similar to those that occurred in most other areas of Alaska, and were driven by similar market forces—which we discuss in the next section of the paper.

Prices for the same AYK fisheries described above were adjusted for inflation based on the only available measure of inflation anywhere in Alaska: the Anchorage Consumer Price Index (CPI) in Figure 6. Adjusted for inflation in this approximate way, prices for the coho and chum salmon fisheries are clearly far below levels of the 1980s, while prices for the Chinook salmon fisheries are comparable to levels of the late 1980s and early 1990s.

A particularly important component of inflation—affecting both the cost of living and the cost of fishing—was the dramatic in-

TABLE 3. AYK and statewide average ex-vessel prices, 2004–2008. Source: ADFG (2008a).

Salmon species	Area	Price/lb					Price/lb as % of statewide average				
		2004	2005	2006	2007	2008	2004	2005	2006	2007	2008
Chinook	Kuskokwim	$2.05	$0.60	$2.95	$0.59	$0.73	106%	26%	97%	14%	17%
	Yukon	$2.58	$3.39	$3.95	$3.68	$4.96	134%	149%	130%	90%	116%
	Statewide Average	$1.93	$2.27	$3.03	$4.07	$4.28	100%	100%	100%	100%	100%
Chum	Kuskokwim	$0.14	$0.05	$0.16	$0.05	$0.05	67%	19%	50%	15%	9%
	Yukon	$0.10	$0.25	$0.20	$0.22	$0.46	48%	93%	63%	65%	87%
	Norton Sound	$0.14	$0.20	$0.14	$0.24	$0.34	67%	74%	44%	71%	64%
	Kotzebue	$0.14	$0.20	$0.22	$0.20	$0.25	67%	74%	69%	59%	47%
	Statewide Average	$0.21	$0.27	$0.32	$0.34	$0.53	100%	100%	100%	100%	100%
Coho	Kuskokwim	$0.33	$0.29	$0.39	$0.38	$0.43	47%	38%	38%	40%	36%
	Yukon	$0.33	$0.23	$0.20	$0.41	$0.91	47%	30%	19%	43%	75%
	Norton Sound	$0.33	$0.34	$0.44	$0.53	$0.77	47%	45%	42%	55%	64%
	Statewide Average	$0.70	$0.76	$1.04	$0.96	$1.21	100%	100%	100%	100%	100%

TABLE 4. Overview of AYK and other Alaska limited entry salmon fisheries: 2003–2005 averages. Data are annual averages of data for the years 2003–2005. Fisheries are sorted by total earnings, which are expressed in thousands of dollars. Averages of share of permits fished, share of permits held by Alaska residents, and average permit price are weighted by total permits issued. Averages of earnings per permit fished are weighted by total permits fished. Source: CFEC (2008).

	Fishery	Total earnings	Total permits issued	Share of permits fished	Share of permits held by Alaska residents	Average earnings per permit fished	Average permit price
AYK fisheries	Lower Yukon Gillnet	$2,428	696	81%	99%	$4,323	$9,267
	Kuskokwim Gillnet	$1,224	782	59%	99%	$2,639	$5,733
	Norton Sound Gillnet	$190	165	21%	98%	$5,062	$4,400
	Kotzebue Gillnet	$72	178	17%	98%	$3,713	$2,167
	Upper Yukon Fish Wheel	$60	143	11%	98%	$3,814	$6,400
	Upper Yukon Gillnet	$11	69	11%	98%	$1,498	$6,567
	Total	$3,985	2,032				
	Average			55%	99%	$3,605	$6,598
Other Alaska Fisheries	Bristol Bay Drift Gillnet	$61,407	1863	77%	49%	$42,965	$39,167
	Southeast Purse Seine	$31,484	415	54%	45%	$140,225	$35,567
	PWS Drift Gillnet	$22,248	539	94%	76%	$43,789	$41,333
	Statewide Power Troll	$22,114	962	71%	81%	$32,225	$19,000
	Kodiak Purse Seine	$16,265	375	37%	75%	$117,209	$11,033
	PWS Purse Seine	$14,003	266	39%	73%	$135,977	$15,567
	Bristol Bay Set Gillnet	$13,160	992	80%	71%	$16,449	$14,133
	Cook Inlet Set Gillnet	$11,538	739	65%	84%	$23,710	$8,733
	Cook Inlet Drift Gillnet	$11,158	571	78%	70%	$24,847	$25,100
	Southeast Drift Gillnet	$11,141	478	76%	74%	$30,738	$24,133
	AK Peninsula Drift Gillnet	$8,217	161	72%	52%	$70,432	$32,833

TABLE 4. Continued.

	Fishery	Total earnings	Total permits issued	Share of permits fished	Share of permits held by Alaska residents	Average earnings per permit fished	Average permit price
Other Alaska Fisheries	Kodiak Set Gillnet	$6,698	188	87%	69%	$40,955	$40,567
	AK Peninsula Purse Seine	$5,733	119	37%	73%	$128,931	$18,633
	Chignik Purse Seine	$5,636	100	57%	82%	$113,632	$173,700
	AK Peninsula Set Gillnet	$4,033	113	78%	83%	$45,516	$46,367
	Statewide Hand Troll	$1,419	1145	27%	89%	$4,434	$4,933
	Yakutat Set Gillnet	$1,232	168	66%	78%	$11,213	$11,067
	Cook Inlet Purse Seine	$1,021	81	32%	92%	$39,008	$10,700
	PWS Set Gillnet	$782	30	90%	82%	$28,646	$61,800
	Total	$249,290	9308				
	Average			66%	71%	$40,837	$24,810

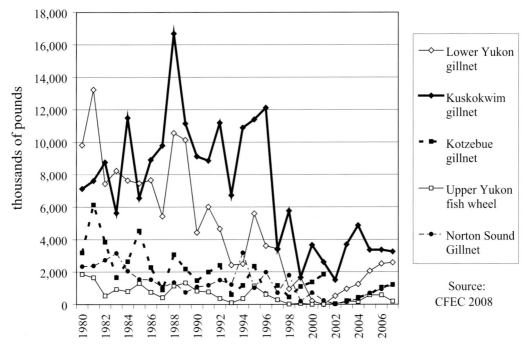

FIGURE 2. Total harvest volume (all species) in selected AYK commercial salmon fisheries.

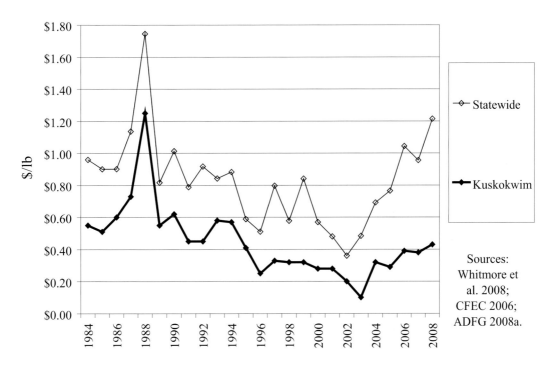

FIGURE 3. Average coho salmon *Oncorhynchus kisutch* exvessel prices, statewide and Kuskokwim area (not adjusted for the effects of inflation).

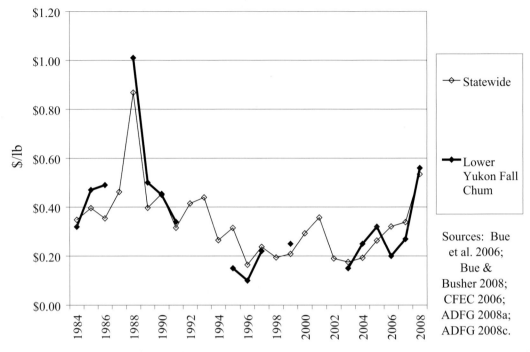

FIGURE 4. Average chum salmon *Oncorhynchus keta* exvessel prices, statewide and Lower Yukon fall chum (not adjusted for the effects of inflation).

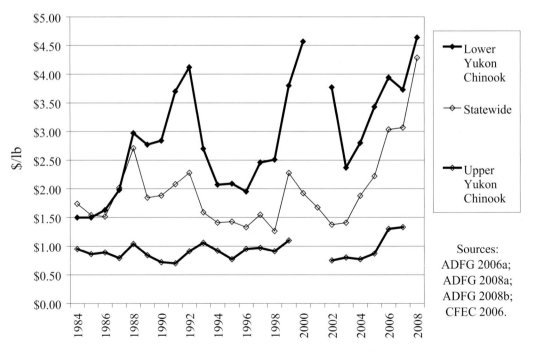

FIGURE 5. Average Chinook salmon *Oncorhynchus tshawyscha* exvessel prices, statewide and Lower and Upper Yukon (not adjusted for the effects of inflation).

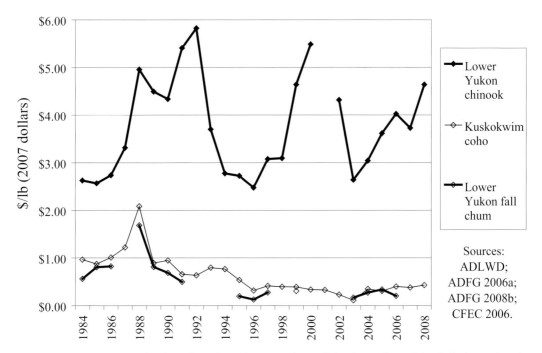

FIGURE 6. Average exvessel prices for selected AYK salmon fisheries, adjusted for inflation using the Anchorage consumer price index.

crease in fuel prices that occurred in the late 2000s. Between July 2003 and July 2008, marine fuel prices in Bristol Bay more than tripled from $1.53/gal to $5.88/gal (PSMFC 2006). Fuel prices possibly increased even more dramatically in more remote areas of western Alaska. The effect of substantially higher fuel costs is to further reduce the real net income from commercial fishing, after subtracting costs from earnings.

The combined effect of declining harvests and prices was a drastic decline in gross earnings (ex-vessel value) of AYK salmon fisheries between the late 1980s and 2000–2002 (Figure 7). Reversal of these trends led to a modest recovery in gross earnings after 2002. However, in the period 2005–2007, nominal gross earnings averaged less than half the level of 1980s, while real gross earnings (adjusted for inflation) averaged less than one-fourth the level of the 1980s (Table 5). As earnings declined, so did the number of permits fished, from an average of 1,926 permits in 1980–

1984 to 1,166 permits in 2005–2007. Even so, average real earnings per permit fished fell to one-third the level of the 1980s.

One of the factors accompanying—and contributing to—the decline in AYK commercial salmon harvests in the late 1990s was a steep decline in the number of buyers (Figure 8). If buyers cannot make a profit buying and processing fish—either because of low volume or low prices—they do not operate. When there are no buyers, commercial fishermen do not fish and salmon are not harvested.

Since 2002, the number of buyers—like harvests, prices and value—has risen, but still remains far below the levels of the 1980s. In recent years, Alaska Department of Fish and Game's preseason capacity surveys have showed that anticipated AYK processing capacity was well below the preseason forecast for the potential commercial harvest—particularly for chum and pink salmon (Table 6). The 2007 report noted that "significant

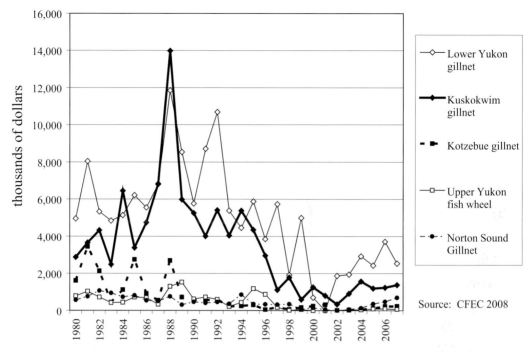

FIGURE 7. Trends in gross earnings in selected AYK commercial salmon fisheries (all species combined).

underutilization of chum salmon appears unavoidable, if the commercial harvest forecast proves accurate" (ADF&G 2006b).

Economic Variables Affecting AYK Commercial Salmon Fisheries

A full review of the causes of changes in AYK commercial fisheries since the 1980s is far beyond the scope of this paper. Clearly changes in fish runs have been a major factor, but economic factors, and particularly changes in salmon markets, have also played an important role. These market changes have been discussed in detail elsewhere (Knapp et al. 2007). Here we briefly review market changes and other economic variables affecting AYK commercial salmon fisheries.

The most obvious variable affecting markets for AYK salmon—and all Alaska wild salmon—has been the rapid growth of salmon farming. Over the past 25 years, salmon farming has dramatically expanded total world salmon supply and changed the sources of supply. Between 1980 and 2006, world farmed salmon and trout supply grew from 13 thousand metric tons to 1,686 thousand metric tons (Figure 9). Growth in farmed salmon production was the major contributing factor to an increase in total world salmon supply from 546 thousand metric tons to 2,605 thousand metric tons. The share of wild salmon in total world supply fell from 98% to 35%, and the share of Alaska wild salmon in total world supply fell from 42% to 13%.

Due primarily to the growth of farmed salmon production (but also the emergence of Russia as an important salmon exporter), Alaska has fallen from a position of the dominant supplier of salmon to world markets to that of a marginal supplier. Salmon buyers can now choose from many potential suppliers other than Alaska.

TABLE 5. Trends in AYK salmon fisheries (averages by period). Units are thousands of pounds for harvests, thousands of dollars for total earnings, and dollars for earnings per permit fished. Real earnings are expressed in 2007 dollars. Source: CFEC (2008).

Period						
	1980–1984	1985–1989	1990–1994	1995–1999	2000–2004	2005–2007
Total pounds harvested	24,817	23,882	17,081	12,660	5,000	8,052
Total nominal gross earnings	$13,041	$18,000	$13,439	$7,636	$2,707	$4,973
Total real gross earnings	$24,813	$30,045	$19,176	$9,665	$3,058	$5,092
Total permits fished	1926	1948	1867	1585	1022	1166
Average nominal earnings per permit fished	$6,772	$9,240	$7,197	$4,818	$2,647	$4,265
Average real earnings per permit fished	$12,885	$15,424	$10,270	$6,098	$2,991	$4,367

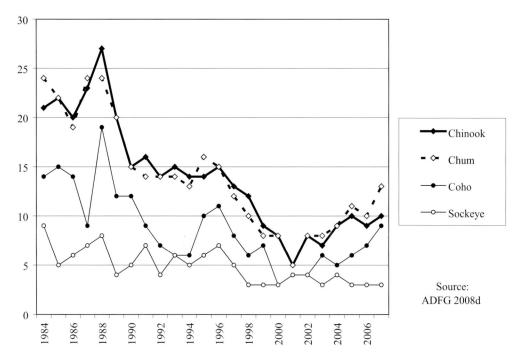

FIGURE 8. Number of salmon buyers in the AYK region, by species.

Just as importantly, salmon farmers have established new market standards for product quality, product form, supply volumes, and consistency of supply. The importance of these factors is growing with globalization of the world economy, which is transforming seafood production, processing, distribution, and retailing. Globalization is contributing to rapid expansion of seafood trade, shifts in labor-intensive seafood processing to countries with low labor costs, restructuring of seafood distribution networks, and increasingly strict international standards for food handling and safety—which are in turn contributing to the rapid growth of aquaculture.

One of the most important changes in the seafood industry associated with globalization is increasing consolidation and market power in the retail and food service industries. In the United States, Europe, and Japan, large retail and food-service buyers are dominating more and more of the seafood market.

These buyers want to buy products that can be supplied consistently, reliably, and in large volumes, that are of consistent quality, that are viewed by consumers as safe, convenient and attractive, which are traceable through the entire chain of production and distribution, and which can be supplied at stable and competitive prices.

These changes in the seafood industry have created new challenges for wild salmon producers. It is more difficult for wild salmon producers than for salmon farmers to meet the demand of large buyers, because they have less control over the volume and timing of production. Unlike salmon farmers, wild salmon producers' ability to supply markets varies widely from year to year—and week to week—and is essentially unpredictable. Closures of some AYK fisheries over the past decade due to disastrously low salmon runs were extreme examples of this inherent challenge facing commercial fisheries for wild salmon.

TABLE 6. ADF&G 2006 and 2007 preseason salmon capacity surveys for the AYK region. Units for forecast and processing capacity are number of fish. Sources: ADFG (2006c, 2007).

Salmon species	Preseason forecast		Estimated processing capacity		Capacity as % of forecast	
	2006	2007	2006	2007	2006	2007
Chinook	92,000	111,000	70,952	81,933	77%	74%
Sockeye	115,000	245,000	72,132	250,472	63%	102%
Coho	410,000	413,000	360,478	793,212	88%	192%
Pink	1,001,000	126,000	14,504	15,000	1%	12%
Chum	1,480,000	1,860,000	507,641	452,863	34%	24%

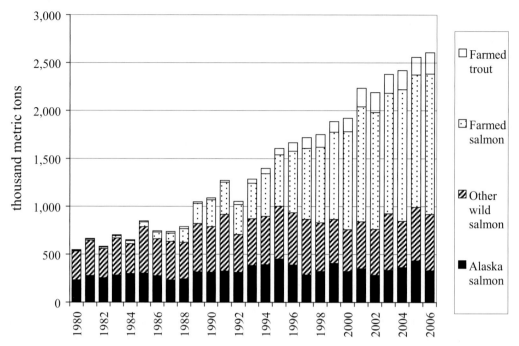

FIGURE 9. World supply of wild and farmed salmon. Data for Alaska are from the Alaska Commercial Fisheries Entry Commission and Alaska Department of Fish and Game. Other data are from the National Marine Fisheries Service and FAO Fishstat+ database. Farmed trout includes rainbow trout *Oncorhynchus mykiss* farmed in saltwater.

Unlike salmon farmers, most wild salmon producers can only supply fresh salmon during relatively short harvest seasons. Variation in production and seasonality add significantly to costs of processing, distribution and marketing—as does wide natural variation in fish species, sizes, and quality. Further challenges for wild salmon in competing with farmed salmon include remoteness from major end markets, undeveloped infrastructure, and high costs of utilities and labor.

Wild salmon producers also face new opportunities in world markets to market wild salmon not as a commodity, but as a specialty product. These derive in part from the dramatic growth in world salmon demand driven by growing year-round availability of farmed salmon in increasing numbers of stores and restaurants, market regions, and product forms, as well as the emergence of new markets in eastern Europe, Russia, and Asia. Increasingly, wild salmon is in relatively limited and fixed supply compared with the total size of the market; herein lies the opportunity for specialty products.

The opportunity for specialty products is strengthened by the growth in specialty stores and restaurants catering to higher-end consumers seeking products superior to those available in mass-market large retail and restaurant chains. These consumers are more likely to perceive wild salmon as better-tasting and more healthy, organic, natural, and environmentally and socially responsible than farmed salmon. These specialty stores and restaurants represent a growing "niche market" opportunity for wild salmon. The challenge for wild salmon in taking advantage of this opportunity is that specialty stores demand consistent high quality, reliable supply, and competitive pricing.

The effects of these challenges and opportunities on Alaska salmon markets is illustrated by the changes in U.S. wholesale prices for fresh troll-caught wild Chinook salmon, fresh farmed Atlantic salmon, and frozen wild chum salmon from 1991 through 2008 (Figure 10). During the 1990s, as world farmed salmon supply expanded more rapidly than demand, farmed salmon wholesale prices trended downwards in the U.S., as they did worldwide. A glut in worldwide supply drove prices particularly low in 2002. Since 2002, prices for farmed salmon have rebounded sharply as growth in farmed salmon production slowed and demand continued to expand.

With farmed salmon production increasingly dominating the USA (and world) supply of fresh and frozen salmon, farmed salmon prices set the overall price level against which wild salmon had to compete. Those wild salmon species perceived as lower-quality than farmed Atlantic salmon, such as chum salmon, were sold at a discount relative to farmed salmon. Those wild salmon species perceived as higher-quality than farmed Atlantic salmon, such as troll-caught Chinook salmon, could command a price premium over farmed Atlantic salmon.

During the 1990s, falling prices of ever more abundant competing farmed salmon dragged wild salmon prices down. Since 2002, increased prices of competing farmed salmon have allowed wild salmon to command higher prices than in the past. Growing niche-market demand for high-quality wild salmon also contributed to an increased price premium for Chinook salmon—perceived to be exceptionally high quality and available only in small volumes. These variables are

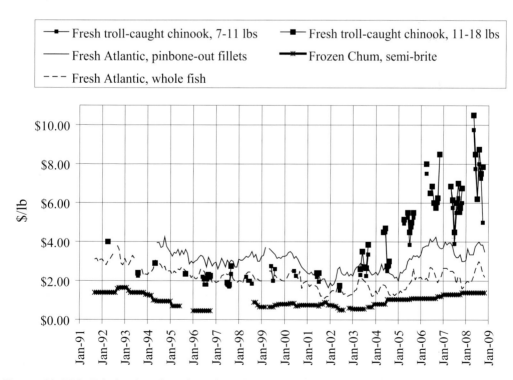

FIGURE 10. U.S. Wholesale prices for selected wild and farmed salmon products. Prices are low list prices for Chilean 2–3 lb fillets, FOB Miami; 6–8 lb Atlantics, FOB Northeast; and 7–11 lb and 11–18 lb troll-caught head-on Chinook salmon *Oncorhynchus tshawyscha*. Source: Urner Barry Publications, Inc., Seafood Price Current.

the fundamental forces driving the ex-vessel price trends for Alaska and AYK salmon (Figures 3–5).

Numerous other variables have also affected world salmon markets, Alaska salmon markets, and AYK salmon markets to varying extents. These factors include a prolonged economic slump in Japan (formerly the most important market for Alaska wild salmon); changing Japanese demand for salmon roe, offset in recent years by growing Russian demand; and changing values of the Japanese yen and other foreign currencies relative to the dollar (USD).

In the future, as farmed salmon production expands, farmed salmon prices may fall again, pulling wild salmon prices back down and reversing the recovery in wild salmon exvessel prices seen since 2002. An important question for all Alaska salmon producers is whether they can offset the potential negative effects of farmed salmon prices on Alaska salmon prices by encouraging the development of niche markets, thus increasing demand and strengthening wild salmon prices relative to farmed salmon (or reducing price discounts for species perceived to be of lower quality). Attention to consistent product quality and aggressive marketing—understanding and meeting buyers' needs—is essential to take full advantage of these opportunities.

AYK commercial salmon fisheries have faced greater challenges than most other Alaska salmon fisheries in competing successfully in the rapidly changing world salmon markets. First among these challenges was the drastic decline in AYK salmon runs during the 1990s. Between 1997 and 2002, the dramatic decline in salmon runs resulted in a total of fifteen disaster declarations in different AYK watersheds by the Governor of Alaska and federal agencies (BSFA 2008). Not being able to harvest or process fish, and the associated uncertainty about the availability of fish in the future, is extremely detrimental to market development (e.g., predictable product availability) and the willingness of fishermen and processors to invest in these fisheries.

A related challenge for AYK commercial salmon fisheries, in comparison with other Alaska commercial salmon fisheries, is the relative importance of AYK subsistence fisheries. Because substantial volumes of fish are harvested in higher-priority subsistence fisheries, a decline in salmon runs causes a relatively greater decline in the availability of fish for commercial harvests than occurs in other areas with lower subsistence demand (Figure 1). This compounds the challenges for processing and marketing imposed by year-to-year variation in salmon runs.

Costs in the AYK region are high for fuel, utilities, labor, and transportation of salmon products by air or water. Relatively small commercial harvest volumes make it difficult to achieve economies of scale in processing and transportation, further adding to costs (Knapp and Reeve 2008). As a result, the AYK region is probably the highest-cost producer of Alaska wild salmon. The region is thus subject to being "last-in and first-out" as a source of supply as markets strengthen or weaken.

AYK chum salmon fisheries have faced competition from large harvests of hatchery chum salmon in other regions of Alaska, which have likely helped to depress buyer interest and prices for AYK chum salmon and its roe. More generally, all AYK chum salmon face competition from other areas of Alaska where salmon runs have generally been stronger than in the AYK region. Competition with these regions has also heightened as some are now beginning to invest in regional brands and marketing (development of niche markets).

Despite these daunting challenges, AYK commercial salmon fisheries have some opportunities compared with other Alaska fisheries. Some AYK salmon runs, such as Yukon River Chinook and chum salmon, have unusually high oil content, which have given them reputations as among the best-tasting salmon in the world (Denn 2008). This difference represents an opportunity to develop new niche markets for AYK salmon—if the challenges of uncertain supply, difficult logistics, and high costs can be overcome.

Another opportunity for the AYK region has been the investments in fisheries development resulting from the western Alaska Community Development Quota (CDQ) program, under which groups of western Alaska communities receive allocations of a share of federally-managed Bering Sea fisheries (DCED). Using earnings derived from these allocations, three of the CDQ groups (Coastal Villages Region Fund, Norton Sound Economic Development Corporation, and Yukon Delta Fisheries Development Association) have made significant investments in salmon processing operations within the AYK region in recent years, expanding markets for salmon fishermen.

Increasing the Economic Benefits of AYK Commercial Salmon Fisheries

How can AYK commercial salmon fisheries overcome the economic challenges they face and take advantage of the economic opportunities they enjoy? What can be done to increase the economic benefits AYK-region residents derive from commercial salmon fisheries? The importance of these questions is magnified by the limited alternative economic opportunities in much of the AYK region (Goldsmith 2007).

Clearly, achieving economically healthy commercial salmon fisheries critically depends on protecting AYK salmon resources. However, the economic benefits of AYK commercial salmon fisheries can also be increased to the extent that it is possible to reduce the costs of catching, processing, and transporting AYK salmon to market, or by increasing the market value of AYK salmon products.

Since the 1990s, an extensive discussion has taken place throughout Alaska about how to reduce costs and increase value for Alaska salmon fisheries. Much of this discussion has focused on the need for (a) improvements in the quality and consistency of salmon products by improvements in how fish are handled at every stage of harvesting, processing and transportation; (b) sustained investments in marketing; and (c) investments in infrastructure, ranging from ice machines to airport runways, to reduce costs and improve quality.

To varying extents, AYK salmon fishermen and processors have been making these kinds of changes and investments. However, the extent to which they have made changes and investments, or are likely to do so in the future, has likely been and will continue to be limited by the extent to which they are profitable for fishermen and processors, given the economic constraints, opportunities, and risks that they face.

Increasing constraints on both federal and state budgets will likely limit the extent to which government can spend more money for marketing, infrastructure investments, or other financial assistance for AYK salmon fisheries. However, it may be possible for government to increase the economic benefits from AYK commercial salmon fisheries without spending more money through changes in how commercial salmon fisheries are managed.

A traditional perspective of fisheries management is that the objectives of management are primarily to achieve biological objectives (such as escapement goals and sustainable harvests; Clark et al. 2009, this volume) and secondarily to achieve allocation objectives (Hilsinger et al. 2009, this volume). But *how* managers achieve biological and allocation objectives also affects costs, prices, risks, and incentives for fishermen and processors. Regulations regarding how fish may be caught affect the quality of fish products that can be delivered to consumers. Regulations regarding where fish may be caught affect the quality of the fish when they are caught and processed, as well as the cost of catching fish and delivering them to processing plants. Regulations regarding when fish are caught affect the timing and consistency of supply and whether fish can be delivered when markets want them; how efficiently fishing boats, tenders and processing plants can be used; and whether supply on any given day matches capacity to produce and ship high-valued products (like fresh fish) or whether fish have to instead be processed into lower-valued products (like frozen and canned fish). Regulations regarding who may fish and under what rules affect how many fishermen operate, their skills, their costs of entering and participating in the fishery, their catches, and their incentives to invest in gear, careful handling of fish, and marketing.

Given the importance of these effects of fishery management regulations, it is important to think carefully about the economic implications of how AYK salmon fisheries are managed, about whether it might be possible to achieve more economically successful fisheries, without more government spending, by implementing changes in how fisheries are managed. Below, I suggest five broad questions for AYK fishermen, processors, and managers to consider in thinking about potential management changes:

1. What are your goals for AYK commercial salmon fisheries? *How important is income from commercial fisheries relative to other goals for AYK fisheries? How willing would stakeholders be to accept changes in commercial fisheries regulations if these changes offered the opportunity to earn more income?*

This is the most important question. If more income from commercial fisheries is not a high priority, or if stakeholders don't want change, little reason exists to explore or pursue change.

2. Are there better ways to harvest AYK salmon commercially? *Could different types of gear lower costs of harvesting? Could different types of gear improve the quality of AYK salmon and earn higher prices for AYK fishermen and processors? Would the benefits of changes in gear outweigh the economic and social costs of changes in how fish are harvested?*

Perhaps the main reason to ask this question is that for decades relatively little change has occurred in how AYK salmon are harvested, despite dramatic technological changes that have occurred in almost every human economic activity. The adoption of the limited entry system in the 1970s specifically defined permits in terms of specific gear types: gillnets and fish wheels. These types of gear were presumably at one time the best suited for these fisheries given available technologies and economic and social circumstances.

Yet clearly gillnets and fish wheels are not the only ways in which it is possible to harvest salmon, nor are they necessarily the best types of gear for AYK fisheries today given available technologies and current economic and social circumstances. For example, tangle nets and fish traps can catch salmon live, increasing the potential for product quality and market value. Many other types of salmon gear beyond those used in Alaska are currently in use in other states and countries.

Could other gear types, potentially in modified form, reduce costs or increase value in AYK salmon fisheries. One way to find out might be to allow small groups of fishermen to test new gear types on an experimental basis. Clearly, introducing new types of gear might require significant changes in fishery regulations or in some cases state law.

3. Could changes to current limited entry regulations allow more economically successful fisheries while also facilitating mangers' ability to meet other goals? What are the potential benefits from management changes that have occurred in other Alaska salmon fisheries, such as the allocation to a cooperative which occurred in the Chignik salmon fishery (Knapp 2008)?

An allocation of most of the salmon harvest to a cooperative in the Chignik salmon fishery during the period 2002–2005 dramatically reduced costs of fuel, insurance, vessel maintenance, and labor in the Chignik salmon fishery. This allocation also enhanced managers' ability to meet escapement goals, because they could work with co-op harvesters as a group to fine-tune fishing to achieve daily escapement goals much more precisely. This approach also encouraged significant innovation and a continuing search for ways to reduce costs and to improve quality and value (Knapp 2008). Allocations to cooperatives possibly could bring similar benefits for AYK salmon fisheries.

The Chignik salmon cooperative was highly controversial and raised numerous issues about the goals of salmon fisheries management and how to restructure fisheries management fairly. The Co-op ended when the Alaska Supreme Court ruled that the Board of Fisheries did not have authority to allocate to a cooperative under Alaska's current Limited Entry Act. But the court also noted that the Alaska legislature has the authority to amend the Limited Entry Act to allow cooperative fisheries (Knapp 2008). Cooperatives for AYK fisheries would likely raise similar issues and also be controversial. But if cooperatives offered sufficient benefits, and enjoyed support, they are clearly possible.

4. Are commercial salmon fisheries happening in the best places and at the best times? Could harvesting AYK salmon in different places or at different times improve the quality of the fish and their value to the market, and/or reduce the costs of harvesting, processing and transporting salmon to market?

AYK fishery managers already work with fishermen and processors to try to schedule fishery openings at times which work best for fishermen and processors, subject to the constraints of run timing and escapement and allocation goals (e.g., Linderman and Bergstrom 2009). But could escapement goals be more successfully met *and* higher value of AYK salmon fisheries be derived if allocation goals were based not on the principle of historical or "fair" shares of fish harvests for different user groups, but rather on historical or "fair" shares of the economic benefits from the fishery? For example, could fishermen and processors in different districts, and/or in Alaska and Canada possibly share in some way the total economic benefits of commercial fisheries between those who had the opportunity to catch and process the fish and those who did not? Could this allow managers more flexibility in where fish are harvested to better optimize for escapement and economic benefit? Devising such a scheme might be a daunting or impossible political task—but it may be worth thinking about and could be facilitated by river-wide fishing cooperatives.

5. Does the current structure of AYK salmon management authority make sense? Do the different local, state, federal, and international agencies and organizations with responsibilities for AYK salmon management work together effectively to achieve biological, social and economic goals? Do they have adequate authority and resources to do so?

Historical and political reasons exist for the current structure of AYK salmon management authority. At any given time, fishermen, processors, and managers have to work with the system as it is. That does not mean, however, that we should not ask whether the system is working as well as it could or should, or whether it could be improved upon (Gaden et al. 2009, this volume).

Clearly, the management of AYK salmon fisheries is an extremely challenging task, given the geographic scale of the region; the length of the river systems; the complexity of their salmon ecology; the needs of multiple and sequential user groups, including international users of Yukon River salmon; interceptions and bycatch of AYK salmon by other fisheries (Gisclair 2009, this volume; Haflinger and Gruver 2009, this volume; Stram and Ianelli 2009, this volume); the division of management responsibilities between multiple agencies; the very high costs which extend to the costs of research and management; and ongoing short-term and longer-term changes in environmental conditions (Hilsinger et al. 2009). Practical challenges include poor understanding of stock-recruit relationships; poor-quality preseason run forecasts; the pulse-character of returns which makes it difficult to develop precise estimates of run strength in advance of allowing fishery openings in lower-river fisheries; and the sequential impact that harvest decisions in lower-river fisheries have on the ability to meet management (harvest and escapement) goals in up-river fisheries and treaty obligations to Canada (e.g., Bue et al. 2009).

Given these inherent challenges, I do not intend to suggest that any significant changes to AYK salmon management are necessarily desirable or feasible in raising these questions. Rather, my goal is to encourage those who know AYK fisheries best to think broadly— "outside of the box"—about possible ways to increase the economic benefits to AYK region residents from commercial salmon fisheries.

Conclusions

Alaska's Arctic-Yukon-Kuskokwim (AYK) commercial salmon fisheries are economically depressed. Both catches and prices are far below average levels of the 1980s—especially adjusting for the effects of inflation and high fuel prices on commercial fishing costs and the purchasing power of commercial fishing income. The number of fishermen and processors remains far below levels of the 1980s.

Low salmon runs have been the most important factor contributing to the decline in value and participation in AYK commercial salmon fisheries. But other factors—including but not limited to competition from salmon farming and globalization of the world economy—have also contributed to lower prices for some species and higher market standards for all species than in the past.

In competing with other Alaska wild salmon fisheries, AYK salmon fisheries face significant challenges including relatively small runs, highly variable and uncertain commercial harvests, very high costs, and logistical challenges in transporting fish to market. AYK salmon fisheries also enjoy opportunities deriving from the inherent high quality of many fish runs and the availability of funding from CDQ groups for investment in AYK salmon fishing and processing.

Given the limited alternative economic opportunities in much of the AYK region, how can AYK commercial salmon fisheries overcome the economic challenges they face and take advantage of the economic opportunities they enjoy? Improvements in quality and investments in marketing and infrastructure have helped and could help more, but they are limited by cost and their profitability for fishermen and processors. Increasing constraints on both federal and state budgets will likely limit the availability of future government funding for investments in, or subsidies to, the fisheries. For this reason, careful thinking is required about whether changes in fisheries management could help to reduce costs or increase value in AYK commercial salmon fisheries. This question can best be answered by the fishermen, processors, and managers who best understand and most depend on AYK commercial salmon fisheries.

References

Alaska Department of Commerce and Economic Development [DCED]. Community Development Quota (CDQ) program website. Available: http://www.dced.state.ak.us/bsc/CDQ/cdq.htm (February 2009).

ADF&G (Alaska Department of Fish and Game). 2006a. 2006 Yukon River Summer Season Summary. Alaska Department of Fish and Game, Anchorage.

ADF&G (Alaska Department of Fish and Game). 2006b. Summary of the 2006 Salmon Capacity Survey. Available: www.cf.adfg.state.ak.us/geninfo/pubs/capacity/06capacity.pdf (April 2006).

ADF&G (Alaska Department of Fish and Game). 2007. Summary of the 2007 Salmon Processing *Capacity Survey*. Available: www.cf.adfg.state.ak.us/geninfo/pubs/capacity/07capacity.pdf (April 2007).

ADF&G (Alaska Department of Fish and Game). 2008a. Alaska Commercial Salmon Harvests and Exvessel Values. Annual data posted on the website of the ADFG Commercial Fisheries Division. Available: www.cf.adfg.state.ak.us/geninfo/finfish/salmon/salmhome.php. (December 2008).

ADF&G (Alaska Department of Fish and Game). 2008b. 2008 Preliminary Yukon River Summer Season Summary. Alaska Department of Fish and Game, Anchorage.

ADF&G (Alaska Department of Fish and Game). 2008c. Data for Yukon River fall fisheries, provided as Excel spreadsheet Yukon Fall Values 2008 – Tab 4. 2008.

ADF&G (Alaska Department of Fish and Game). 2008d. Commercial Operator Annual Report Database. Data provided upon request. Alaska Department of Fish and Game, Anchorage.

ADLWD (Alaska Department of Labor and Workforce Development). Division of Research and Analysis. Anchorage Municipality Annual Average Consumer Price Index, All Items—All Urban Consumers. Available: http://almis.labor.state.ak.us (February 2009).

BSFA (Bering Sea Fishermen's Association). Letter to Carl Artman, Assistant Secretary, Indian Affairs,

U.S. 2008. Department of the Interior, requesting reinstatement of base budget funding of the Bering Sea Fishermen's Assocation, January 21.

Bue, F., B. Borba and D. Bergstrom. 2006. Yukon River Fall Chum Salmon Stock Status and Fall Season Salmon Fisheries: A Report to the Alaska Board of Fisheries. ADF&G Special Publication No. 06–36. Anchorage.

Bue, F., and W. Busher. 2008. 2007 Yukon River Fall Season Summary. Alaska Department of Fish and Game News Release. March 18, 2008.

Bue, F. J., B. M. Borba, R. Cannon, and C. C. Krueger. 2009. Yukon River fall chum salmon fisheries: management, harvest, and stock abundance. Pages 703–742 *in* C. C. Krueger and C. E. Zimmerman, editors. Pacific salmon: ecology and management of western Alaska's populations. American Fisheries Society, Symposium 70, Bethesda, Maryland.

CFEC (Commercial Fisheries Entry Commission). 2006. Data for Alaska statewide salmon harvest volume, value and average prices, provided by request.

CFEC (Commercial Fisheries Entry Commission). 2008. Basic Information Tables for Alaska Salmon Fisheries. Data posed on the CFEC website. Available: http://www.cfec.state.ak.us/fishery_statistics/earnings.htm (February 2009).

Clark, R. A., D. R. Bernard, and S. J. Fleischman. 2009. Stock-recruitment analysis for escapement goal development: a case study of Pacific salmon in Alaska. Pages 743–757 *in* C. C. Krueger and C. E. Zimmerman, editors. Pacific salmon: ecology and management of western Alaska's populations. American Fisheries Society, Symposium 70, Bethesda, Maryland.

Denn, R. 2008. Yukon River chum: Fairy-tale ending for salmon's poor stepsister. Seattle Post-Intelligencer, August 13, 2008.

Evenson, D. F., S. J. Hayes, G. Sandone, and D. J. Bergstrom. 2009. Yukon River Chinook salmon: stock status, harvest, and management. Pages 675–701 *in* C. C. Krueger and C. E. Zimmerman, editors. Pacific salmon: ecology and management of western Alaska's populations. American Fisheries Society, Symposium 70, Bethesda, Maryland.

Gaden, M., C. C. Krueger, and C. Goddard. 2009. Managing across jurisdictional boundaries: fishery governance in the Great Lakes and Arcitc-Yukon-Kuskokwim regions. Pages 941–960 *in* C. C. Krueger and C. E. Zimmerman, editors. Pacific salmon: ecology and management of western Alaska's populations. American Fisheries Society, Symposium 70, Bethesda, Maryland.

Gisclair, B. R. 2009. Salmon bycatch management in the Bering Sea walleye pollock fishery: threats and opportunities for western Alaska. Pages 799–

816 *in* Pacific salmon: ecology and management of Western Alaska's Populations. C.C. Krueger and C.E. Zimmerman, editors. American Fisheries Society, Symposium 70, Bethesda, Maryland.

Goldsmith, S. 2007. The remote rural economy of Alaska. Anchorage, University of Alaska Anchorage, Institute of Social and Economic Research. Available: http://www.iser.uaa.alaska.edu/ Publications/u_ak/uak_remoteruraleconomyak. pdf (February 2009).

Haflinger, K., and J. Gruver. 2009. Rolling hot spot closure areas in the Bering Sea walleye pollock fishery: estimated reduction of salmon Bbycatch during the 2006 season. Pages 817–826 *in* C. C. Krueger and C. E. Zimmerman, editors. Pacific salmon: ecology and management of Western Alaska's Populations. American Fisheries Society, Symposium 70, Bethesda, Maryland.

Hilsinger, J., E. Volk, G. Sandone, and R. Cannon. 2009. Salmon management in the Arctic-Yukon-Kuskokwim Region of Alaska: past, present, and future. Pages 495–519 *in* C. C. Krueger and C. E. Zimmerman, editors. Pacific salmon: ecology and management of Western Alaska's Populations. American Fisheries Society, Symposium 70, Bethesda, Maryland.

Knapp, G., C. Roheim, and J. L. Anderson. 2007. The great salmon run: competition between wild and farmed Salmon. Report prepared for TRAFFIC North America. Available: www.traffic.org (February 2009).

Knapp, G., and T. Reeve. 2008. A village fish processing plant: yes or no? A planning handbook. Available: http://seagrant.uaf.edu/map/pubs/village/villagefishplant.pdf (February 2009).

Knapp, G. 2008. The Chignik salmon cooperative. In R. Townsend, R Shotton, and H. Uchida, H. editors. Case studies in fisheries self-governance. FAO Fisheries Technical Paper. No. 504. FAO, Rome. Available: http://www.fao.org/docrep/010/a1497e/a1497e00.htm (February 2009).

Linderman, J. C., Jr., and D. J. Bergstrom. 2009. Kuskokwim management area: salmon escapement, harvest, and management. Pages 541–599 *in* C. C. Krueger and C. E. Zimmerman, editors. Pacific salmon: ecology and management of western Alaska's populations. American Fisheries Society, Symposium 70, Bethesda, Maryland.

Magdanz, J. S., E. Trigg, A. Ahmasuk, P. Nanouk, D. S. Koster, and K. Kamletz. 2009. Patterns and trends in subsistence salmon harvest, Norton Sound–Port Clarence Area, Alaska 1994–2003. Pages 395–431 *in* C. C. Krueger and C. E. Zimmerman, editors. Pacific salmon: ecology and management of western Alaska's populations. American Fisheries Society, Symposium 70, Bethesda, Maryland

Menard, J., C. C. Krueger, and J. R. Hilsinger. 2009. Norton Sound salmon fisheries: history, stock abundance, and management. Pages 621–673 *in* C. C. Krueger and C. E. Zimmerman, editors. Pacific salmon: ecology and management of western Alaska's populations. American Fisheries Society, Symposium 70, Bethesda, Maryland.

PSMFC (Pacific States Marine Fisheries Commission). 2006. Fisheries economics data program (EFIN), Alaska fuel price data. Available: www.psmfc.org/ efin/data/fuel.html (February 2009).

Stram, D. L., and J. N. Ianelli. 2009. Eastern Bering Sea pollock trawl fisheries: variation in salmon bycatch over time and space. Pages 827–850 *in* C. C. Krueger and C. E. Zimmerman, editors. Pacific salmon: ecology and management of western Alaska's populations. American Fisheries Society, Symposium 70, Bethesda, Maryland.

Whitmore, C., M. Martz, J. C. Linderman, Jr., R. L. Fisher, and D. G. Bue. 2008. Annual management report for the subsistence and commercial fisheries of the Kuskokwim Area, 2004. ADF&G, Fishery Management Report No. 08–25. Anchorage.

Wolfe, R. J., and Walker, R. J. 1987. Subsistence economies in Alaska: productivity, geography, and development impacts. Arctic Anthropology 24:56–81.

Section III

Management of AYK Salmon

American Fisheries Society Symposium 70:489–491, 2009

Introduction to Fishery Management

JOHN R. HILSINGER

Alaska Department of Fish and Game
333 Raspberry Road, Anchorage, Alaska 99518, USA

STEVEN KLEIN

U.S. Fish and Wildlife Service
1011 East Tudor Road, Anchorage, Alaska, 99503, USA

CHARLES C. KRUEGER

Great Lakes Fishery Commission
2100 Commonwealth Boulevard, Suite 100, Ann Arbor, Michigan 48105, USA

This section was organized to examine management strategies in a variety of fisheries in the Arctic-Yukon-Kuskokwim (AYK) region. Current management of Pacific salmon *Oncorhynchus* in the region is based on a mix of local knowledge and Western science used by state, federal, and international organizations to regulate harvests and sustain runs. Management of AYK salmon is characterized by a complex jurisdictional relationship among the State of Alaska, several U.S. federal agencies, and the Canadian federal government. U.S. federal agencies, which managed AYK salmon fisheries until statehood in 1959, continue to play a role in managing marine areas such as through the North Pacific Fishery Management Council, and regulate subsistence fisheries on Federal public lands. International bodies affecting salmon management include the Yukon River Panel organized under the U.S.–Canada Pacific Salmon Treaty and the North Pacific Anadromous Fish Commission, which has a management role in marine areas. The State of Alaska, through the Alaska Department of Fish Game, is the primary manager of the freshwater portions of the salmon life cycle.

The 14 chapters that follow provide descriptions of fisheries management in the AYK region and in marine waters, explain why differences and similarities exist, examine the nature and use of some of the tools used in management, and identify research priorities for the future. Importantly, these papers document the experiences of the fishery managers, often being summarized at the end of the chapters in lessons learned. To more easily allow comparisons among different fisheries, authors were requested to organize their papers around the five questions below:

1) Management Evolution—How did management strategies evolve to solve issues of harvest allocation and escapement?

2) Escapement and Harvest Objectives— What different approaches exist for estimation of escapement and harvest objectives? What are the advantages and disadvantages of each approach?

3) Management Lessons—What lessons can be learned from past management of your fishery? What recommendations do you have to improve management?

4) Information Needs—What are the critical unmet information needs that would improve management?

5) Management Organization—What organizational changes would you suggest to enhance collaboration among jurisdictions while ensuring opportunities for participation by local residents?

The collection of management papers begins with a historical review of the AYK region, detailing salmon management over the past century (Hilsinger et al. 2009, this volume). The historical review sets the context for the next five papers which provide regional descriptions of subsistence, commercial, and sport fishery management within Norton Sound, the Kuskokwim River, and Yukon River watersheds (Burr 2009, this volume; Linderman and Bergstrom 2009, this volume; Menard et al. 2009, this volume; Evenson et al. 2009, this volume; Bue et al. 2009, this volume). Never before have such comprehensive descriptions of these fisheries been provided through such a readily available medium as this volume. The next paper describes the primary conceptual foundation to salmon management (stock-recruitment analysis) currently used in the AYK region (Clark 2009, this volume). The last two papers describe important genetic issues to salmon management (Hard et al. 2009, this volume; Olsen et al. 2009, this volume).

The management section then moves hundreds of miles away from the freshwaters of the AYK region to the vast marine waters of the Bering Sea and Gulf of Alaska. Here rearing and maturing sub-adult salmon ultimately bound for spawning in the AYK region are intercepted in a variety of fisheries, including the Area M (also known as False Pass) salmon fishery, and the Bering Sea-Aleutian Islands trawl fisheries. The latter fishery serves as the focus for three chapters contributed by authors representing the Yukon River Drainage Fisheries Association, the marine fishing industry, National Marine Fisheries Service, and the North Pacific Fishery Management Council. These contributions describe the spatial and temporal complexities of marine regulatory actions and illustrate how collaboration between the fisheries and federal managers is essential if management is to be effective.

Our assessment of AYK salmon management is that these fisheries are sustainable, and managers have done an outstanding job with a paucity of information available. Strengths of AYK salmon management include:

• highly knowledgeable and dedicated managers;

• commercial, sport, and subsistence users that are passionate about sustaining salmon resources;

• multi-disciplinary approaches to management, including use of traditional ecological knowledge and the State of Alaska's Sustainable Salmon Policy; and

• science-based management decision-making with strong local involvement;

Management efforts appear to be working, and expensive restoration and recovery programs have not been necessary. We believe that the lessons and recommendations learned from the local and regional experiences described in these papers will lead to improvements in management and identify strategic research and management priorities.

References

Bue, F. J., B. M. Borba, R. Cannon, and C. C. Krueger. 2009. Yukon River fall chum salmon fisheries: management, harvest, and stock abundance. Pages 703–742 *in* C. C. Krueger and C. E. Zimmerman, editors. Pacific salmon: ecology and management of western Alaska's populations. American Fisheries Society, Symposium 70, Bethesda, Maryland.

Burr, J. M. 2009. Management of recreational salmon fisheries in the Arctic-Yukon-Kuskokwim Region of Alaska. Pages 521–539 *in* C. C. Krueger and C. E. Zimmerman, editors. Pacific salmon: ecology and management of western Alaska's populations. American Fisheries Society, Symposium 70, Bethesda, Maryland.

Clark, R. A., D. R. Bernard, and S. J. Fleischman. 2009. Stock-recruitment analysis in escapement goal development: a case study of Pacific salmon in Alaska. Pages 743–757 *in* C. C. Krueger and C. E. Zimmerman, editors. Pacific salmon: ecology and management of western Alaska's populations. American Fisheries Society, Symposium 70, Bethesda, Maryland.

Evenson, D. F., S. J. Hayes, G. Sandone, and D. J. Bergstrom. 2009. Yukon River Chinook salmon: stock status, harvest, and management. Pages 675–701 *in* C. C. Krueger and C. E. Zimmerman, editors. Pacific salmon: ecology and management of western Alaska's populations. American Fisheries Society, Symposium 70, Bethesda, Maryland.

Hard, J. J., W. Eldridge, and K. Naish. 2009. Genetic consequences of size-selective fishing: implications for viability of Chinook salmon in the Arctic-Yukon-Kuskokwim region of Alaska. Pages 759–780 *in* C. C. Krueger and C. E. Zimmerman, editors. Pacific salmon: ecology and management of western Alaska's populations. American Fisheries Society, Symposium, Bethesda, Maryland.

Hilsinger, J. R., E. Volk, G. Sandone, and R. Cannon. 2009. Salmon management in the Arctic-Yukon-Kuskokwim Region of Alaska: past, present, and future. Pages 495–519 *in* C. C. Krueger and C. E. Zimmerman, editors. Pacific salmon: ecology and management of western Alaska's populations. American Fisheries Society, Symposium 70, Bethesda, Maryland.

Linderman, J. C., and D. J. Bergstrom. 2009. Kuskokwim management area: salmon escapement, harvest, and management. Pages 541–599 *in* C. C. Krueger and C. E. Zimmerman, editors. Pacific salmon: ecology and management of western Alaska's populations. American Fisheries Society, Symposium 70, Bethesda, Maryland.

Menard, J., C. C. Krueger, and J. R. Hilsinger. 2009. Norton Sound salmon fisheries: history, stock abundance, and management. Pages 621–673 *in* C. C. Krueger and C. E. Zimmerman, editors. Pacific salmon: ecology and management of western Alaska's populations. American Fisheries Society, Symposium 70, Bethesda, Maryland.

Olsen, J. B., S. J. Miller, K. Harper, and J. K. Wenburg. 2009. Genetic health and variables influencing the effective number of breeders in western Alaska Chinook salmon. Pages 781–795 *in* C. C. Krueger and C. E. Zimmerman, editors. Pacific salmon: ecology and management of western Alaska's populations. American Fisheries Society, Symposium 70, Bethesda, Maryland.

Freshwater Salmon Management

American Fisheries Society Symposium 70:495–519, 2009
© 2009 by the American Fisheries Society

Salmon Management in the Arctic-Yukon-Kuskokwim Region of Alaska: Past, Present, and Future

JOHN R. HILSINGER*, ERIC VOLK, GENE SANDONE, AND RICHARD CANNON[1]

Alaska Department of Fish and Game
333 Raspberry Road, Anchorage, Alaska 99518, USA

Abstract.—Development and evolution of salmon fisheries management in the Arctic-Yukon-Kuskokwim (AYK) region from the early 1900s to the present is described. Before statehood in 1959, commercial fisheries in the region were managed using a combination of quotas and closures with the aim of protecting the large subsistence fisheries in the region. After statehood, the newly formed Alaska Department of Fish and Game and the Alaska Board of Fish and Game developed a more flexible approach to commercial fisheries management, based more on fishing time than quotas, to allow harvest to vary with run strength. Collection of detailed catch and escapement data as well as biological information such as age, sex, and length laid the foundation for better understanding salmon runs and setting escapement goals. These goals were first established from 1979 to 1984, and were based on average escapements under the principle that maintaining average, or better, escapements should maintain harvests at historical levels. During the late 1980s and early 1990s, management evolved toward more closely regulated fisheries to ensure escapement goals were met. During this time, the department began working cooperatively with resource users in the region through groups such as the Kuskokwim River Salmon Management Working Group and the Yukon River Drainage Fisheries Association. These relationships helped improve public input and use of local knowledge in fishery management as well as developed support for increased research funding. In the late 1990s, run failures throughout the region led to disaster declarations and the designation of many AYK salmon stocks as stocks of concern under the state's Policy for the Management of Sustainable Salmon Fisheries. These run failures contributed to finalization of salmon sharing agreements between the United States and Canada, and signing of the Yukon River Salmon Agreement after 16 years of negotiation. Management of salmon during recent years has focused on refining escapement goals through spawner-recruit analyses, better assessing run strength to help ensure meeting escapement goals, and collecting additional information on population sizes, spawner distribution, and stock identification. The goal of management for the future is to set scientifically defensible escapement goals that provide the greatest likelihood of sustaining salmon runs and to improve run assessment techniques that will ultimately aid in maintaining viable subsistence and commercial fisheries throughout the region.

---

*Corresponding author: john.hilsinger@alaska.gov
[1]Richard Cannon served as the AYK Regional Management Biologist for the Commercial Fisheries Division, ADF&G from 1986–1999. Currently he is employed by the Office of Subsistence Management, U.S. Fish and Wildlife Service 1011 East Tudor Road, Anchorage, Alaska 99503.

Introduction

The Arctic-Yukon-Kuskokwim (AYK) region includes that portion of Alaska north of the Alaska Range, representing roughly 400,000 square miles (an area the size of California, Oregon, Washington, and Idaho combined) or approximately two thirds of Alaska's landmass (Figure 1). The region includes all of the Kuskokwim River drainage, a major portion of the Yukon River drainage (roughly 25% of the Yukon River drainage lies in Yukon Territory and northern British Columbia in Canada), and all rivers that drain into Norton Sound and Kotzebue Sound, and North Slope rivers draining to the Arctic Ocean. For the purposes of this paper, only that portion of the AYK region from the Kuskokwim River to Norton Sound will be discussed here.

Nearly 50,000 rural residents inhabit the area, living in more than 100 different villages and small towns. These rural communities depend heavily on salmon for subsistence and for money necessary to live in a modern economy (ADF&G 2002a; ADF&G 2002b; ADF&G 2003; Brase and Hamner 2002).

Subsistence and commercial fisheries are vitally important to the economy of the region. The cash many residents gain through commercial fishing frequently offsets the increasing costs of fuel, boats, motors, and other gear needed to subsistence hunt and fish. The region supports the largest and most important subsistence fisheries in the state. Some differences exist in the periods for which harvest data are available by area, but in general, average subsistence harvest for the region during the latter part of the 1990s was approximately 650,000 salmon (ADF&G 2002a,b; ADF&G 2003), while commercial harvests during the same period averaged approximately 1.6 million salmon annually. For the period 1999 through 2008, commercial catches have significantly declined.

The AYK region is divided by the State of Alaska into three management areas. The Kuskokwim Management Area includes Kuskokwim Bay and Kuskokwim River, and is managed from an office in Bethel (Linderman and Bergstrom 2009, this volume). The Norton Sound and Kotzebue Districts are managed from an office in Nome (Menard et al. 2009, this volume). The Yukon-Northern Management Area includes the entire Yukon River drainage in Alaska and all the waters draining into the Arctic Ocean and the Chukchi Sea, and is managed from year-around offices in Anchorage and Fairbanks and a seasonal office in Emmonak (Bue et al. 2009, this volume; Evenson et al. 2009, this volume). The area north of Kotzebue Sound and along the Arctic coast has no commercial salmon fisheries and limited subsistence fisheries for salmon and is not a focus in this paper.

Five salmon species return to the region: Chinook *Oncorhynchus tshawytscha*, chum *O. keta*, coho *O. kitsutch*, sockeye *O. nerka*, and pink *O. gorbuscha* salmon (e.g., Gilbert 1922). In addition, two distinct races of chum salmon occur, and are commonly referred to as summer chum and fall chum salmon (Bue et al. 2009). While their occurrence is most obvious in the Yukon River where large runs of both stock groups exist, fall chum salmon also occur in the Kuskokwim River (Gilk et al. 2009, this volume). The major chum salmon runs of the Kotzebue District closely resemble fall chum salmon in run timing, size, and spawning habits.

The importance of each species to the fisheries varies somewhat by area. In the Kuskokwim River area, Chinook and chum salmon are the most important species for subsistence while chum, sockeye, and coho salmon are most important commercially (Linderman and Bergstrom 2009). In the Yukon River area, Chinook, summer chum, and fall chum salmon are important for subsistence as well as for commercial fisheries, though high trans-

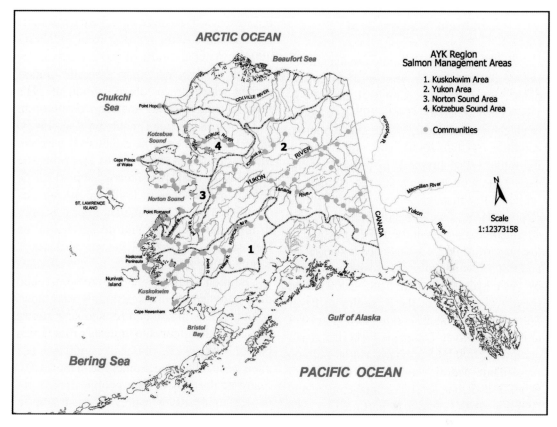

FIGURE 1. Map of the Alaska Department of Fish and Game Arctic-Yukon-Kuskokwim Region showing management areas and communities.

portation costs and limited markets have reduced commercial demand for abundant summer chum salmon in recent years (Bue et al. 2009). In the Norton Sound region, Chinook, chum, and pink salmon are most important for subsistence while Chinook, pink, and coho salmon are sometimes commercially fished (Menard et al. 2009). Much larger runs of sockeye salmon on the Pilgrim River in recent years have attracted subsistence fishers on the road system from Nome. Loss of markets for chum salmon throughout the region since 1994 had a dramatic effect on the economy of the region, especially in years when runs of the other species were also poor.

This paper focuses on the salmon stocks, fisheries, and management of these three areas in the AYK region; the evolution of fisheries management in the AYK region and the efforts by the State of Alaska to improve management, stock assessment, and public interaction is described. This examination will assist in determining the role of fisheries management in the decline and in the rebuilding of salmon stocks in the AYK region; it will also help identify future directions for salmon research and monitoring. Rather than present detailed salmon stock status information, this report chronicles the evolution of management and research in the region and ties together the disparate elements of the overall management system. Detailed descriptions of the stock status and trends within each of the three sub-regions are presented in Bue et al. (2009), Evenson et al. (2009), Linderman and Bergstrom (2009), and Menard et al. (2009).

Chronological Framework for AYK Salmon Management

The history of AYK salmon management can be divided into a number of time segments: 1) pre-statehood Federal era (1900–1959), early statehood (1960–1984), response to changing biological, social, and economic conditions (1985–2000), and preparing for the future (2001-present). Milestones of the early statehood era include: the coming of limited entry management to control fishing effort in 1974; development of chum salmon commercial markets in the 1970s; passage of the State of Alaska's subsistence law in 1978; and full implementation of escapement goals by 1984. Milestones in the 1985–2000 period include: formation of the Kuskokwim River Salmon Management Working Group in 1987 and Yukon River Drainage Fisheries Association in 1990; U.S. Canada Yukon Salmon Agreement negotiations; the evolution toward escapement-based management and adoption of the Alaska Department of Fish and Game escapement goal policy in 1992; loss of markets for chum salmon during the 1990s; fisheries disasters of the late 1990s; and federal involvement in subsistence fisheries starting in 1999. The modern era from 2001 to the present is marked by the adoption of the Policy for the Management of Sustainable Salmon Fisheries in 2001; the revision of the escapement goal policy in 2002; and the rebuilding of salmon stocks throughout the AYK region.

Federal Era: 1900–1959

The history of fisheries management for the Yukon and Kuskokwim rivers before statehood in 1959 was primarily a matter of protecting the large subsistence fisheries for Alaska Natives; this was accomplished by restriction of commercial fishing activity (Pennoyer et al. 1965). Commercial fishing started in the AYK region in the late 1800s, but harvests from these early years were primarily sold locally for dog food (ADF&G 2002b). After the turn of the century, commercial harvest for export from the region started with sales of cured salmon in 1913 from Kuskokwim Bay and canned salmon in 1914 from Kotzebue (Pennoyer et al. 1965). In 1918, a cannery was established near the mouth of the Yukon River. At this time, the fisheries in Alaska were managed by the U.S. Bureau of Fisheries. In 1940, the Bureau was transferred along with the Biological Survey to form the Fish and Wildlife Service in the Department of Interior (Pennoyer et al. 1965; Regnart 1993).

Salmon runs in the region before and during the federal era were highly variable in abundance, with some years showing strong runs and other years having weak runs. Even before 1900, weak runs had significant impacts on local people. Sometime in the 1830s, many of the Koyukukon people moved out of Koyukuk River valley downstream to the Yukon River due to complete failures of the salmon runs (Huntington 1993; p. 132). Similarly in 1897, residents along the Yukon River had to go to Norton Sound to fish due to failures in the salmon runs. Pennoyer et al. (1965) reviewed federal records and noted that in 1917 the salmon run to the Yukon River was very poor and it was necessary to kill many dogs because of lack of food for them. Again in 1919, the run was light, as it was over much of Alaska. Investigators surveying the Yukon River in 1920 determined that the 1919 run had been one of the worst, if not the very worst, on record. The poor run was probably compounded by a burgeoning commercial harvest. In 1920, runs of all species were good; the 1924 run appeared to be the largest since 1912.

The earliest fishery regulations in the region date from 1918. Early regulations on the Yukon River limited commercial harvest to 30,000 cases of canned salmon, 1,000 barrels of pickled salmon, and 200 tierces (a cask larger than a barrel) of mild cured salmon. In 1921, fishing inside the Yukon River for export was prohibited, and fishing outside the river mouth was restricted for the first time.

The White Act 1924–1959

In 1924, Congress passed the White Act in response to increasing reports of depleted runs in Alaska (Cooley 1963; Regnart 1993; Krasnowski 1997). The Act required that not less than fifty percent of any salmon run be allowed to spawn, and that escapement be increased in areas with diminished runs. This fixed harvest rate policy resulted in more stringent regulations and increased federal activity throughout Alaska; in Bristol Bay, federal agents surveyed spawning grounds to determine if spawning escapement equaled or exceeded the catch for the area. The Act also denied the Bureau the power to control the amount of fishing gear by stipulating that no exclusive or individual right to fisheries could be granted.

Implementation of these measures in the AYK region proceeded with little or no actual assessment of escapements or reliable monitoring of harvests. In the same year (1924), all commercial fishing in the Yukon area was prohibited. This closure was extended to Kuskokwim Bay in 1925 and remained in effect until 1930. In 1930, Kuskokwim Bay reopened to commercial harvest, but was limited to 250,000 Chinook and sockeye salmon combined.

By 1931, the use of airplanes to deliver mail reduced the need for large numbers of dried salmon to feed dog teams and reduced demand for salmon. Limited commercial fishing was allowed in Port Clarence District, Yukon District, and additional openings were permitted in Kuskokwim Bay. The combined catch of Chinook and sockeye salmon was limited to 300,000 fish with a maximum of 50,000 fish harvested from the Yukon River and 250,000 fish harvested from the Kuskok-

wim area. Prior to 1935, commercial fishing occurred only in the salt waters off the mouth of the Yukon River and in Kuskokwim Bay. However, in-river fishing resumed in 1935 when commercial fishing was again legalized in the Yukon and Kuskokwim rivers and in Kuskokwim Bay. The quota for the Yukon River was raised to 100,000 Chinook salmon, but no more than 50,000 fish could come from outside the mouth. Fish wheels were made legal for Alaska Natives and for permanent nonnative residents. In 1936, due to concerns about subsistence harvests and escapements, the Yukon River Chinook salmon quota was reduced to 50,000 fish (not more than 25,000 fish could be caught from inside the river). The quota for the Kuskokwim area remained at 250,000 Chinook and sockeye salmon combined.

Throughout the 1930s, the federal government was hampered by lack of funds for fishery monitoring. Funds for biological research on Alaskan salmon fisheries averaged less than $25,000 per year by 1935. By 1939, the entire fishery research staff available to Alaska was four employees stationed in Seattle, and fisheries enforcement and stream guard staffing was approximately half what it was prior to 1933. In the AYK region, little changed in management from 1940 until 1949 when Norton Sound and Kotzebue were opened to commercial fishing. Even for areas opened to commercial fishing, catch records from the era do not indicate that fish were processed.

In 1951, fishing inside the Yukon and Kuskokwim rivers was limited to Alaska Natives and "bonafide" permanent nonnative residents. Chinook salmon nets in the Kuskokwim area were limited to 8½-inch mesh. Quotas were changed to 50,000 Chinook salmon for the Yukon River, though not more than 25,000 fish could be taken inside the mouth of the river. For the Kuskokwim area (both the bay and river), commercial harvests of 250,000 Chinook and sockeye salmon combined were allowed; however, Chinook salmon harvest was not to exceed 15,000 fish inside the river. Subsistence fishery harvests were passively managed with little restriction on harvest.

The Kuskokwim District was closed to commercial fishing from 1952 until 1954 to protect subsistence harvests and escapements. When the fishery reopened, the quotas were set at 3,000 Chinook salmon below the Aniak River (see Figure 1) and 3,000 fish above. The Yukon River quota was set at 50,000 Chinook salmon taken below the mouth of the Anuk River, 10,000 between the Anuk and Anvik rivers, and 5,000 fish taken upstream of the Anvik River (see Figure 2). Commercial harvests of chum salmon occurred in the Yukon River from 1952 to 1954 (ADFG 2002a).

In 1953, portions of Alaska were declared disaster areas by Presidential decree due to poor salmon runs. As a result, more emphasis was placed on conservation and the need for scientific research. Research expenditures by the Bureau of Commercial Fisheries grew dramatically during this time, from less than $100,000 per year in 1948, to $250,000 by 1956, and $900,000 per year in 1959. A permanent U.S. Fish and Wildlife Service biologist, Mr. George Warner, was assigned to the Yukon River part time. During this period, he was the only federal staff member assigned specifically to the AYK region.

From 1954 to 1960, the Yukon River Chinook salmon quota was 65,000 fish. Of this number, 50,000 Chinook salmon could be taken below the mouth of the Anuk River, 10,000 salmon could be taken between the Anuk and Anvik rivers, and 5,000 fish could be taken upstream of the Anvik River.

Assessment of the Federal Era

As this brief history shows, salmon management in the AYK region during the federal era concentrated on use of strict quotas and total closures to limit commercial fishing and protect subsistence. Little data were collected on subsistence catch, escapement, or biology of the fish (Regnart 1993), although estimates of harvest were made for the Yukon River since 1918. Federal agencies had little staff and little money to manage resources in Alaska.

Some key aspects of salmon management after statehood were first established during the federal era; for example, the districts and subdistricts delineated in the federal era are still used to allocate catch along the large inland fisheries of the Yukon and Kuskokwim rivers, as well as to minimize mixed-stock harvests in coastal fisheries. Fixed quotas were also carried forward into statehood for some areas and eventually evolved into guideline harvest ranges (GHR) that are still employed in Kuskokwim River and Yukon River salmon management plans. During these years, the use of strict quotas on the commercial fishery provided protection for subsistence fishing. This protection was carried forward into statehood as a subsistence preference in the AYK region, even before it became state law in 1978.

Several shortcomings of the fishery management and research program in Alaska during the federal era can be noted. A general lack of sufficient biological information existed to effectively manage the fishery. In the Yukon River drainage, with its large subsistence fishery and commercial fisheries dating back to 1918, quantifiable escapement data (numbers of adults escaping fisheries to spawn) dates back only to 1953. From 1953 to 1959, escapement data are available only for a few select summer chum salmon and Chinook salmon runs in lower Yukon River tributaries and for the Tanana River drainage near Fairbanks (Barton 1984). Because the White Act called for a maximum harvest rate of 50%, the development of scientifically based escapement goals to ensure adequate spawning was not a priority. During

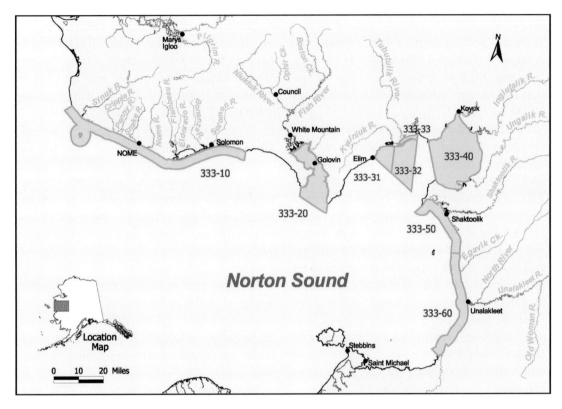

FIGURE 2. Alaska Department of Fish and Game salmon subdistricts in Norton Sound.

this period, fishery management and research staff were stationed in Alaska only during the short fishing season, so timely and accurate documentation of commercial harvest did not occur and little effort was made to document the importance of the subsistence fishery or the impact of commercial harvest on subsistence activities. Inseason management was limited due to the centralized and controlled procedure for adopting and implementing time and area restrictions.

The remoteness of most of the AYK region, the expenses of mounting a comprehensive assessment program in the region, and the relatively low commercial value of the harvest contributed to the development of a program that did not effectively address the sustainability of salmon resources in the region. In contrast, the Bristol Bay area with its large and valuable sockeye salmon fishery south of the Kuskokwim River area developed a large and comprehensive program including data collection and analysis (Baker et al. 2009, this volume). Escapements were tallied as early as 1908 and weirs were established on the Naknek River in 1929 and on the Kvichak River in 1930. Sufficient data were collected to develop brood tables that date back to 1956.

The push for statehood

In 1949, the Territorial Legislature created a Department of Fisheries and Board of Fisheries (board). The Department of Fisheries had no specific regulatory authority, but it provided a mechanism for conducting additional research and enforcement activities. The Territorial Board of Fisheries provided a public forum for Alaska residents to comment on the federal regulatory process. The Territorial Legislature intended that the board and department would assume all powers at statehood then vested in the U.S. Fish and Wildlife Service regarding regulation and conservation of fisheries (Regnart 1993).

Although the board made annual recommendations on changes to fishery management, few recommendations were ever accepted by the U.S. Fish and Wildlife Service. Annual expenditures for the board and department grew and by 1957 were roughly equal to what the federal government was spending on fisheries in Alaska. Over time, several divisions and expanded programs were incorporated into the territorial department including biological research, commercial fisheries, sport fish, watershed management and protection, enforcement, engineering, and game. By 1960, the department had over 60 technical positions involved in fisheries activities.

State of Alaska—Getting Started: 1960–1984

Alaska became a state on January 3, 1959. The State of Alaska assumed management of fisheries on January 1, 1960. This gave the state a year after statehood to organize the Department of Fish and Game, adopt a management system and regulations, and demonstrate to the federal government that the state was ready to assume management of its fish and wildlife.

At this time, many employees of the Territorial Department of Fisheries transferred to the newly formed Alaska Department of Fish and Game. Alaska's desire to assume responsibility for fishery management in the state was one of the driving forces behind the quest for statehood. Depletion of salmon runs, use of fish traps, political influence of processors, and the centralization of decision making

outside of Alaska provided strong motivation for implementing significant changes to the management after statehood. To understand Alaskan fishery management, a brief review of the Alaska Constitution and legislative framework that directed these changes is required.

The Alaska Constitution

Alaska's Constitution laid the framework for fish and wildlife management in Article VIII. Natural Resources. The elements of Article VIII most significant to fisheries management are:

Section 1. Statement of Policy.—It is the policy of the State to encourage the settlement of its land and the development of its resources by making them available for maximum use consistent with the public interest.

Section 2. General Authority.—The legislature shall provide for the utilization, development, and conservation of all natural resources belonging to the State, including land and waters, for the maximum benefit of its people.

Section 3. Common Use.—Wherever occurring in their natural state, fish, wildlife, and waters are reserved to the people for common use.

Section 4. Sustained Yield.—Fish, forests, wildlife, grasslands, and all other replenishable resources belonging to the State shall be utilized, developed, and maintained on the sustained yield principle, subject to preferences among beneficial uses.

Section 15. No Exclusive Right of Fishery.—No exclusive right or special privilege of fishery shall be created or authorized in the natural waters of the State.

Section 15 was amended in 1972 to allow for limited entry, and now reads:

Section 15. No Exclusive Right of Fishery.—No exclusive right or special privilege of fishery shall be created or authorized in the natural waters of the State. This section does not restrict the power of the State to limit entry into any fishery for purposes of resource conservation, to prevent economic distress among fishermen and those dependent upon them for a livelihood and to promote the efficient development of aquaculture in the State.

Legislative direction

According to Article VIII, Section 2, the legislature "shall provide for the utilization, development, and conservation of all natural resources belonging to the State..." Because fish and wildlife were recognized as critically important to the fledgling state, the Department of Fish and Game was created as a cabinet level department run by a Commissioner (Krasnowski 1997) who answered directly to the Governor. To reduce the political influence that dominated fish and wildlife management during the federal era, the Commissioner was selected by the governor from a list of qualified applicants supplied by the eight-member Alaska Board of Fish and Game (which was later split into the Board of Fisheries and the Board of Game (each with seven members) in 1975; Krasnowski 1997). The boards are made up of laymen nominated by the Governor and confirmed by the Legislature to serve a three-year term. To reduce the effects of politics on fish and wildlife management, Commissioners were originally appointed to a five-year term so their tenure would overlap the four-year term of the Governor. This was changed in 1996 so that the Governor can now replace the Commissioner at will.

Alaska Board of Fisheries

The board was established by the legislature (AS 16.05.221) as an independent body with regulatory powers for the purpose of conservation and development of fisheries resources. Board members are appointed by the Governor and must be confirmed by a majority of the legislature. Members are chosen based on "interest in public affairs, good judgment, knowledge, and ability in the field of action of the board, and with a view to providing diversity of interest and points of view in the membership." While the department shares responsibility for conservation and meeting salmon escapements with the board, the sole responsibility for allocating harvest under state statutes and constitutional mandates rests with the board.

To ensure local knowledge enters the regulatory process, 81 local Fish and Game Advisory Committees were established (D. Cote, ADF&G, personal communication), with 29 committees in the AYK region. Each local committee is made up of between five and 15 members, who must represent fish and wildlife uses in the area, maintain a residence in the area, and be an Alaskan resident of voting age. At least three user groups (e.g., subsistence, commercial fishing, recreational fishing, trapping, processing, and photography) should be represented on each committee (Cote and Edens 1999). The state funds Advisory Committee meetings and travel for committee representatives to attend Board of Fisheries meetings.

Regulations for all management areas in the state were originally reviewed on an annual basis. As the complexity of the fisheries increased, this schedule was changed to a three-year cycle. The entire AYK region is reviewed and discussed in a single meeting during the same year as related fisheries such as the Alaska Peninsula/Aleutian Islands. Individuals, groups, Advisory Committees, and the Department of Fish and Game have the opportunity to submit proposals for regulation changes. For example, at the regular AYK region meeting in January 2007, the board considered 58 proposals for changes to regulations for salmon, herring, and freshwater resident species. If management or conservation issues arise between regularly scheduled meetings, the board may be petitioned or a change of agenda may be sought to obtain an out-of-schedule hearing.

Organization of the Department of Fish and Game

Alaska's Department of Fish and Game (ADF&G) was established at statehood with Clarence L. Anderson as Commissioner. The Alaska Board of Fish and Game began promulgating regulations which took effect January 1, 1960, except that any regulations that conflicted with federal control, did not take effect until cessation of such federal control. Regulations adopted in 1960 established salmon management areas that are largely the same as today.

Organization of the department has been modified over time to address the needs of a young and growing state. Up to five divisions within the department have shared the responsibilities of managing and conserving Alaska's salmon resources. At statehood, the importance of commercial fisheries to the state's economy required forming a Commercial Fisheries Division to manage and sustain salmon resources vital to the commercial industry. The commercial fishing industry has always been the largest source of employment and revenue for most of Alaska's coastal communities. The Sport Fish Division which existed before statehood was incorporated into the newly formed ADF&G and addressed the importance of popular and rapidly growing recreational fisheries in Alaska. A Division of Boards was formed to support the work of the Board of Fish and Game, which later became separate Boards of Game and Fisheries. In 1973, the Fisheries Restoration, Enhancement and Development (FRED) Division was formed to oversee the establishment of salmon hatchery programs in Alaska. This Division was later merged with the Commercial Fisheries Division in 1993 and many existing state-run salmon hatcheries were turned over to private nonprofit associations or transferred to the Sport Fish Division. Although management of subsistence fisheries remained the responsibility of the Commercial Fisheries and Sport Fish Divisions, the Subsistence Division was established in 1978 by the legislature to document and study subsistence use of living resources, including salmon. Shortly after statehood, a Habitat Section, which later became a Division, was formed to represent and protect fish and wildlife resources as development of Alaska occurred. However, in 2003, this division was eliminated and vital salmon habitat protection functions transferred to the Alaska Department of Natural Resources by then Governor Murkowski. The Habitat Division was formally returned to the Department of Fish and Game in 2008 by Governor Sarah Palin.

Fisheries divisions within ADF&G have primarily followed a decentralized organizational structure with most management decision-making delegated to area biologists who live and work in the fisheries areas. This approach has worked to help area staff acquire expertise and knowledge about the resources, people, and fisheries within the areas they live and work. One of the primary tools delegated by the Commissioner to state area fishery managers is emergency order authority. This authority allows the local manager to quickly respond to changing conditions within a fishery to implement conservation measures (restriction of harvest) or to allow harvest when data supports the in-season action. Regional and area research and monitoring staff support management by collecting and analyzing an assortment of data on run abundance, run timing, harvest, escapement, and population structure.

Emergency order authority

The authority of the Commissioner to make in-season modifications to fishing seasons, areas, and methods and means of commercial fishing was established immediately after statehood by the Board of Fish and Game, and appeared in the 1960 General Provisions of the regulations as follows:

EMERGENCY REGULATIONS

102.99. Modifications of seasons, fishing periods, areas, methods and means of commercial fishing.

The Commissioner from time to time may shorten, lengthen, close or open any fishing season or period and relax or impose further restrictions on the means, methods or areas of fishing and on the catch of fish permitted to be taken.

In 1963, the statute (AS 16.05.060) was amended to clarify that Chapter 05 did not limit the power of the Commissioner, or his designee, to summarily open or close seasons, areas, or to change weekly periods by emergency order when required by circumstances. The statute further stated that emergency orders had the force and effect of law after field announcement by the commissioner, or an authorized designee, and were not subject to the Administrative Procedures Act.

AYK salmon management and assessment 1960–1984

The State of Alaska through ADF&G assumed management of the fisheries in 1960. What is now known as the Arctic-Yukon-Kuskokwim region was originally established as the Arctic Area and was divided into six districts—Northern, Kotzebue, Port Clar-

ence, Norton Sound, Yukon, and Kuskokwim. Combined subsistence and commercial regulations for the area took up less than three pages in the 1960 regulation book.

Alaska incorporated three elements into its laws and regulations that distinguish Alaskan salmon management from that of many other places. First, the area management concept was established where knowledgeable local staff are responsible for managing fisheries. Second, ADF&G was delegated emergency order authority that allows the area biologist to open and close fisheries based on in-season information. Third, the public regulatory process provided a meaningful role for stakeholders to provide input to the formulation of management plans and regulations.

Fishery management in the AYK region was initiated after statehood; however, due to the absence of federal staff experienced in the area and lack of catch and escapement information, even the most basic information needed to manage fisheries was not available. During this period, the state slowly built staff, a fishery-monitoring program, and began collecting biological information such as age, sex, size, and escapement data on the salmon runs. However, similarities with the earlier federal era continued; because commercial fisheries in this region relative to other regions remained small, state funding for AYK management, monitoring and research continued to be very limited. This period ends with the setting of escapement goals for AYK salmon from 1979 through 1984. During this time, the state established the framework for the regulatory structure, public participation, and allocation of the state's fisheries resources, which continues to the present time.

In 1961, regulations were completely revised from the previous quota system to the flexible fishing time concept. The Arctic Area was renamed the Arctic-Yukon-Kuskokwim Area. The lower Yukon River and lower Kuskokwim River commercial fisheries were put on fishing schedules of four days per week for Chinook salmon in the lower Yukon River, and two days per week in the Kuskokwim River.

Regulations were used to control how many, when, and where fish were caught within each commercial fishery. This type of management was accomplished primarily through restrictions on effort, fishing efficiency by regulating the amount and type of gear, and by scheduling the location, timing, and duration of commercial fishery openings. Subsistence fisheries were passively managed using restrictions to commercial fisheries to ensure harvest opportunities and adequate escapements. Initially designated as an area fishery with one area manager stationed in Anchorage, the AYK Region was officially established in 1972.

An open-to-entry commercial fishery developed until the mid-1970s. During this time market conditions changed and commercial interest in AYK region commercial fisheries increased and expanded. Landings increased from 1.0 million fish in 1970 to over 3.3 million fish in 1980. Ex-vessel values of landed catch of salmon increased from $4.4 million in 1976 to $10.5 million by 1980. During the 1960s and early 1970s, anyone could participate in the fishery, and effort levels grew rapidly in the region (Buklis 1999). In 1972, the Alaska Constitution was amended to allow the state to limit entry into fisheries. The Alaska Legislature adopted statutes creating the Commercial Fisheries Entry Commission in 1973. The statutes AS 16.43.010 were adopted as follows:

(a) It is the purpose of this chapter to promote the conservation and the sustained yield management of Alaska's fishery resource and the economic health and stability of commercial fishing in Alaska by regulating and controlling entry into commercial fisheries in the public interest and without unjust discrimination.

(b) The legislature finds that commercial fishing for fishery resources has reached levels of participation, on both a statewide and an area basis, that have impaired or threaten to impair the economic welfare of the fisheries of the state, the overall efficiency of harvest, and the sustained yield management of the fishery resource.

At the start of the program in 1974, 2341 permits existed for the AYK region including 879 Kuskokwim area permits, 1076 Yukon River permits, 157 Norton Sound permits, and 229 Kotzebue permits. The limited entry program has effectively prevented increases in the numbers of commercial participants throughout the AYK region. In 2008, after 25 years, the numbers of permits declined to 2217, including 841 Kuskokwim permits, 952 Yukon permits, 204 Norton Sound permits, and 220 Kotzebue permits.

Habitat protection

The AYK region has a long history of mining spread across the region. Extensive gold mining activity occurred in the late 1800's and early 1900s throughout the upper Yukon River drainage in Alaska and the Yukon Territories, the Nome Area, and portions of the Kuskokwim River drainage. Destruction of stream habitats occurred in localized areas. Use of stream gravel for site and road development and as transportation corridors contributed to salmon habitat losses. Time and greater public awareness and support for habitat conservation resulted in improvements in habitat quality and quantity.

Soon after statehood, the Alaska Legislature, which at the time desired to ensure the long-term sustainability of the state's abundant and valuable salmon resources, adopted two important salmon habitat protection laws. The Anadromous Stream Act required that any development or construction activity proposed within a water body known to support anadromous fish, including salmon, must seek prior approval. The Migratory Fish Act prohibited any activities in waterways that would disrupt or prevent the passage of fish. In addition, the state's Land Policy Act, administered by the Department of Natural Resources, required preparation of land-use plans for protection and classification of state lands prior to disposal or development. Together, these acts provided the framework for protecting Alaska's salmon habitats including aquatic, riparian, and upland habitats. In addition to state statutes, federal legislation also affects management of salmon habitat in the AYK region.

Under the federal National Coastal Zone Management (CZM) Act of 1972, Alaska adopted a far-reaching CZM Program that allowed local governments and communities to prepare coastal development and habitat conservation programs including protection for anadromous fish habitats on municipal and private lands. Perhaps the most far-reaching U.S. congressional action affecting fish and wildlife habitats in the AYK region is the enactment of the Alaska National Interest Lands Conservation Act of 1980, which placed nearly 50% of the Yukon and Kuskokwim watersheds into federal National Wildlife Refuges or parks.

Under the federal Fish and Wildlife Coordination Act of 1934, consultation with ADF&G was required prior to approval of development activities regarding important salmon habitats being reviewed under the National Environmental Protection Act of 1970 and other federal environmental regulations. Of particular importance to the protection of salmon habitat were provisions of the Clean Water Act of 1948 and its 1972 amendments that required permits for activities in wetland habitats and for point sources of pollution.

This impressive array of local, state, and federal laws and regulations provided the basis for protecting salmon habitats in Alaska; however, their effectiveness depended on providing the responsible resources and funding to implement them. On several occasions, development and mining interests rallied support in the Alaska Legislature to weaken or repeal protection for salmon habitats. Attempts to develop regulations for clarifying the implementation of the Anadromous Waters Act were withdrawn under severe political attack by development interests on several occasions during this period. Attempts by development interests and their legislative supporters to de-fund the department's Habitat Protection Division were annually debated in the Alaska State Legislature. Sufficient public support for salmon and fisheries resources remained in rural and urban districts to thwart these attempts. In time, most development interests learned that by working with resource agencies their projects could move forward provided important habitats were protected. However, loss of localized salmon habitat undoubtedly occurred in some areas where significant development and urbanization occurred. The effects of continued mining activity and new exploration throughout the region remain a concern.

State subsistence law—1978

In 1978, the Alaska Legislature passed the subsistence law (AS 16.05.258) which provided guidance to the management of subsistence fisheries.

1) Subsistence uses were defined as "The noncommercial customary and traditional uses of wild, renewable resources by a resident domiciled in a rural area of the state for direct personal or family consumption as food, shelter, fuel, clothing, tools, or transportation..."

2) Boards of Fisheries and Game were required to provide reasonable opportunity for subsistence uses to occur where a harvestable surplus existed.

3) During times of resource shortage, subsistence uses were given preference over other consumptive uses. That is, when it was necessary to restrict harvest for conservation reasons, other consumptive uses were to be restricted before subsistence.

4) The Subsistence Division was created (Fall 1990).

Throughout the 1960s and early 1970s, salmon management in the AYK region by ADF&G continued protecting subsistence with a subsistence preference by policy. The law has been amended a number of times since 1978, with major revisions in 1986 and 1992. The law now directs the boards to identify stocks, or portions thereof, that are customarily and traditionally taken or used for subsistence. If a portion of that stock can be harvested consistent with sustained yield, the board determines the amount necessary for subsistence uses. If the harvestable surplus exceeds the amounts necessary for subsistence, the board adopts regulations allowing for other uses. If the harvestable surplus is equal to the amount necessary for subsistence, the board adopts regulations to eliminate other uses of the stock. If the harvestable surplus is not sufficient to provide reasonable opportunity for subsistence uses, the board adopts regulations eliminating other uses and may distinguish among subsistence users. The board may implement subsistence limitations based on: 1) customary and direct dependence on the stock, 2) proximity of the domicile of the user to the stock, and 3) the ability of the subsistence user to obtain food if subsistence use is restricted or eliminated. These criteria help to define what is known in the State of Alaska as a Tier II subsistence harvest. Under a Tier II fishery, regulations limit harvest to those users who best meet these criteria. To date, the only Tier II subsistence fishery in the state was implemented in the Nome Subdistrict of Norton Sound in 2000 (Menard et

al. 2009). While this remains a Tier II fishery today, chum salmon harvest restrictions have been unnecessary in recent years due to abundant pink and sockeye salmon, and improved chum salmon runs.

Escapement Goals—1979–1984

Salmon spawning escapement goals were first established for AYK stocks in 1979. By 1984, escapement goals were established for 60 stocks (Buklis 1993) and by 1992, 71 stocks had goals. Because of the mixed-stock nature of most AYK fisheries and the lack of adequate stock identification, spawner-recruit analyses were difficult to perform. According to Buklis (1993), "given the vastness of the area and the limited budget available, low-level fixed-wing aerial surveys of key index systems has typically been the method used to assess spawning escapement abundance." The ADF&G, therefore, was faced with setting escapement goals using limited aerial surveys of key spawning index areas in the absence of stock-specific harvest information.

These early escapement objectives were typically the simple average of historical escapement counts or the trimmed average after removing uncharacteristically high or low counts, or counts made under poor conditions. In a few cases, the escapement counts were from weirs or counting towers, but 55 of the 71 goals were based on aerial surveys of index areas. At the time, these goals were termed "escapement objectives" and they were based on the underlying principle that average or better escapements should provide for sustained yield consistent with historic levels. Under today's Policy for the Management of Sustainable Salmon Fisheries (5 AAC 39.222), these goals would have been termed "sustainable escapement goals." Because spawner-recruit analyses were not possible, the relationship of these goals to maximum sustained yield was unknown.

Assessment of the Early Statehood Era— 1960–1984

At the close of the federal management era, the State of Alaska took over salmon management in 1960 with little of an existing program in place. Management during this era focused on increasing flexibility by shifting toward use of fishing schedules based on time rather than quotas. Quotas evolved toward a guideline harvest level concept where ranges replaced single numbers and harvest became proportional to run strength. Another major development during this time was the beginning of commercial fisheries for chum salmon in most of the management areas. By the close of this period in 1984, escapement goals existed for 60 different salmon runs in the region. The vast majority of these goals were postseason aerial survey goals that were not used for in-season management.

Salmon harvests were often not curtailed to ensure escapement goals would be met. Because of the lack of in-season run and escapement assessment tools in most areas, managers responded to a variety of indicators of low-run strength (i.e., low commercial or test fishing catch rates) by reducing fishing time to limit harvest toward the low end of guideline harvest ranges. Conversely, in times of high-run strength, they increased fishing time to allow harvest to reach the upper end of guideline harvest ranges. Where escapement goals existed in the late 1970s and early 1980s, the goals were used mostly to predict future runs, assuming that average escapements would produce average run sizes and harvests. As more efficient boats, motors, and nets entered the fisheries, these goals were used to assess increased efficiency of the fleet and the need to further reduce fishing time.

Responding to Change: 1984–1999

Commercial salmon fisheries in the AYK region generally provided a cash supplement to the subsistence lifestyle of rural residents who make up the majority of the commercial permit holders. From statehood through 1999, major changes occurred in commercial fishery sales and ex-vessel values. Ex-vessel value grew from $4 million in 1976 to levels ranging from $10–29 million from 1979 through 1995. Declines in run strength and market demand in the mid-1990s resulted in reductions in fisheries values approaching the levels of the mid-1970s when adjusted for inflation. Declines in commercial sales for chum salmon beginning in the early 1990s, due to stock declines and reduced demand, were followed by dramatic reductions in Chinook salmon sales due to poor returns, and coho salmon sales due to loss of market demand (Buklis 1999).

Stock assessment and escapement based management

From 1984 to 1999, salmon management transitioned from fixed harvest ranges to controlling harvest to achieve desired levels of escapement. Meeting escapement goals became the goal of in-season management actions that had profound implications on allocation of harvest. This focus on escapement goals was particularly challenging to managers in the AYK region where escapement monitoring relied primarily on sporadic aerial survey data and a few weirs, towers, or sonar estimates of run abundance.

Given the immense size of the region and the limited budget available, low-level fixed-wing aerial surveys of key index systems was typically the method used to assess salmon spawning escapement. Survey counts were imprecise indices of abundance due to difficulty and inconsistency in observing salmon in spawning areas during a single flight, often when not all spawners were present or when river conditions were turbid.

In 1992, with the adoption of the Department's escapement goal policy, the AYK region re-evaluated its escapement goals (Buklis 1993). A coincident change from largely passive harvest-based management to relatively active escapement-based management caused a major increase in the importance of escapement goals. Commercial and subsistence fisheries could now be restricted or closed to meet escapement goals. Minimum levels of escapement were selected that appeared to support historic harvests of a salmon stock. For most stocks, objectives were typically a simple average of observed escapements for prior years. The underlying principle of this approach was that maintenance of an average or better spawning escapement in the future should provide for sustained yield consistent with historical levels. Biologists acknowledged that a limited time-series of salmon escapement data did not permit spawner-recruit analysis. At that time, escapement objectives based on spawner-recruit analyses were rare (Buklis 1993).

During this period, some needed improvements in run, harvest, and escapement assessment were implemented as funding became available. Management agencies, fisheries and tribal organizations, and other groups pooled limited funds to cooperatively conduct high priority assessment and monitoring projects throughout the region. An infusion of federal dollars to address fisheries disaster declarations, implement treaty obligations on the Yukon River, and bolster commercial fishing opportunities in the region supported the effort to assess spawner-recruit relationships. Sonar, tagging, weirs, towers, and genetic studies generated valuable data for salmon managers in some areas.

An important data requirement for run assessment and management is an accurate assessment of harvest. Commercial harvest reporting regulations in Alaska required fishery participants and processors to record the number and species of all salmon sold on "fish tickets." A similar process has been administered by the Department of Fisheries and Oceans (DFO) for Canadian commercial harvests in the upper Yukon River. Reliable estimates of commercial harvest were available to managers soon after a fishing period ended.

Other types of harvest information were collected during postseason reviews and preseason planning. Personal-use fisheries in Alaska and domestic food fisheries in Canada required reporting of harvest. However, no regulatory requirement existed for reporting subsistence harvests in Alaska. To estimate the subsistence salmon harvest from the villages throughout the region, a voluntary postseason survey program was undertaken. In road accessible portions of the Yukon River drainage and the Nome area, households were required to obtain an annual subsistence-use permit prior to fishing. In these areas, harvest was documented on the permit and returned to ADFG by the end of the fishing season. In Canada, the federal government and First Nations conduct annual studies to estimate the total catch in the Yukon River aboriginal food fishery. Significant uncertainty exists within the estimates of annual subsistence salmon harvests in some areas.

Allocation and conservation—running the gauntlet

During this era, the board adopted or modified regulatory management plans for salmon fisheries throughout the region. Such plans established management goals and conservation and allocation guidelines for the fishery.

While there are many fisheries management issues in the AYK region, two harvest allocation issues have been of special importance. First, subsistence has been the *de facto* priority use of AYK region salmon since the federal era, and is now mandated by law. Virtually all commercial fishermen in the AYK region are local residents who also subsistence fish. Commercial and subsistence fisheries are intimately intertwined, with commercial fishing profits supporting purchase of gear and gasoline necessary for subsistence fishing. In the middle and upper Yukon River, where fish wheels are a common gear type, building or repairing the fish wheel and moving it out to the fishing site may not be economically feasible if no commercial fishery exists.

The second issue is that reliable projections of run size cannot be made until a significant segment of the return has entered the river, and escapement data are unavailable until fisheries have concluded over much of the Yukon or Kuskokwim rivers. While escapement objectives are the foundation of Alaskan salmon management and help ensure long-term conservation of stocks, accurate escapement data are often not available until after the run, too late to provide input to in-season decision making. If estimated run sizes are not sufficient to support necessary escapements and subsistence needs after significant commercial fishing has occurred, subsistence fishing may be restricted to meet escapement goals.

In the gauntlet fisheries on the Yukon and Kuskokwim rivers, commercial fisheries are largest in the lower river and subsistence harvests tend to be larger in the upper river. Errors in assessing the run strength may result in too much lower river harvest and subsistence or commercial fishery closures in the upper river.

ADF&G attempted for years to assess run strength solely by using test fisheries near the mouth of the Yukon River. The first test fisheries started as set net fisheries near Flat Island in the 1960s. In the 1980s, the test fisheries were moved into the three main mouths of the river. While test fisheries can

be useful for estimating run timing and relative run strength if calibrated in-season with more reliable indicators, they do not provide estimates of absolute run strength and their consistency is affected by winds, water levels, and changes in channel morphology. An in-river test fishery is currently conducted near Bethel on the Kuskokwim River. More reliable estimates of run abundance were a critical data need for fisheries managers.

A sonar project was started in the late 1980s at Pilot Station, 123 mi upriver from the mouth of the Yukon River, to provide estimates of the absolute run size of salmon passing upstream. By 1990, the project appeared to work well for chum salmon, but was problematic for Chinook salmon due to uncertainty in species assignment of acoustic targets. With Chinook salmon numbering in the low hundreds of thousands and chum salmon often exceeding one million, small errors in species apportionment of chum salmon resulted in large errors in estimating Chinook salmon abundance. Though improved technology and better net selectivity models have improved accuracy and precision of sonar estimates, the dynamic nature of the lower Yukon River presents on-going challenges for this sonar project.

In the absence of accurate Yukon Chinook salmon run size estimates, managers relied on relative run strength indicators and attempted to spread harvest over the run to avoid impacting any single stock in mixed stock fisheries (Evenson et al. 2009). Run strength estimates for summer and fall chum salmon were more reliable, but as chum salmon run strength began to decline during the 1990s, it was difficult to maintain harvest and achieve escapement goals without taking more restrictive actions later in the runs as fish moved upriver (Bue et al. 2009).

Attempts to develop sonar for the Kuskokwim were unsuccessful. Managers had only test fishery, subsistence, and commercial catches to rely on for run strength assessment (Linderman and Bergstrom 2009). Again, a major component of the management strategy was to distribute harvest more evenly across the run by spreading out commercial fishing periods to prevent over fishing any specific stocks.

These difficulties associated with downriver commercial fisheries and upriver subsistence fisheries created schisms between the upper and lower river users in both the Yukon and Kuskokwim drainages, and between users and department staff. The subsistence fishing priority made it socially and politically sensitive to close subsistence fisheries upriver, especially after commercial fishing had taken place downriver. Fishery managers faced the problem of providing commercial and subsistence harvest opportunity in the lower river without adequate run size information, while providing upper river subsistence opportunity and sufficient fish to meet escapement goals

Cooperative management

By the late 1980s, allocation and conservation issues were widening the gulf between user groups and between the department and the users. Poor Chinook salmon runs to the Kuskokwim River in the mid-1980s led to complaints by upriver fishermen about meeting subsistence needs. As a result, the board and department took steps to reduce Chinook salmon harvests in the lower river by eliminating 8 ½-in mesh nets in 1985 and prohibiting directed Chinook salmon fishing in 1987. These changes to the Chinook salmon fishery, along with efforts to restrict the growing coho salmon commercial fishery, exacerbated already strained relationships among fishing groups and state managers. In response to this growing controversy, the Kuskokwim River Salmon Management Working Group (working group) was formed during the 1987 board meeting (Linderman and Bergstrom 2009).

The working group, composed of representatives of all upriver and downriver stakeholders, provided a forum for fishers to meet together with the department. Prior to the season, the working group met to develop a "management plan" for the coming fishing season. During the fishing season, the working group often met several times a week to review and discuss data, and to make management recommendations regarding fishery openings and the need for adjustments to the preseason management plan. Post season, the working group met with the fisheries managers to discuss issues and proposed regulatory changes and other ways to improve management in the future. Working group meetings started with presentation and discussion of fisheries data, followed by consensus recommendations for management actions in the fishery. Although the ADF&G had the authority to overrule recommendations, most suggestions were implemented. At the time, this collaborative, cooperative approach to fisheries management, though innovative, was viewed as controversial.

Because the working group acted by consensus, various user groups were forced to interact and look at the data together to come to mutually agreeable recommendations. Because the group's decision would be implemented unless vetoed by ADF&G, the process put a large degree of responsibility on the users to make wise decisions. After 20 years, the working group is generally viewed as an essential component of fisheries management for the Kuskokwim River.

The Yukon River experienced some of the same issues pitting up-river and downriver fishermen against each other and against ADF&G. Through the U.S./Canada Treaty negotiation process, which began in 1985, fisheries representatives throughout the river met and got to know each other; this process fostered relationships between the fishermen and the department. Advisors and delegates to these negotiations on both sides of the border became more informed about the status of Yukon River trans-boundary salmon stocks, and they worked together to agree on escapement goals and harvest shares. In the process, delegates reported back to their villages resulting in more-informed resource users who played a prominent role in the development of the Yukon Salmon Agreement, an annex to the U.S./Canada Pacific Salmon Treaty signed in 2001. The escapement objectives and harvest sharing arrangement contained in the Agreement has played an important role in the management of Yukon River Chinook and fall chum salmon. In 1990, U.S. advisors and delegates held a drainage-wide meeting to consider forming a group similar to the working group on the Kuskokwim River. In 1989, the Alaska Legislature provided funds to hold a conference in Bethel to bring Yukon River and Kuskokwim area fishermen together to discuss how a Yukon River working group might be formed. With the support of key legislators, the state administration, and fisheries and tribal organizations, the Yukon River Drainage Fisheries Association was formed in the village of Galena in December of 1990 and much of its structure and operating principles were worked out in the village of St. Mary's in the spring of 1991. This group has functioned for nearly 20 years.

Both of these groups have been effective, because they realized the need to develop a fundamentally different relationship from that of the past—a working relationship based on growing trust and respect for each other and with ADF&G. The organization of these groups has provided a formal setting and process where diverse user groups and managers can listen and talk to each other; these groups also provded a forum to share and discuss technical information and local knowledge for the entire drainage.

Coordination of Yukon River salmon management and conservation between the U.S. and Canada is provided though the Yukon River Salmon Agreement. As an annex to the Pacific Salmon Treaty, the agreement created a bilateral Yukon River Panel, set harvest sharing agreements, and established management plans for Canadian-origin fall chum salmon stocks. The focus of the Panel is on Chinook and fall chum salmon stocks that spawn in the Canadian portion of the Yukon River drainage because these stocks require U.S. protection to ensure adequate numbers of salmon pass upstream for spawning and fisheries in Canada. The Panel makes recommendations to management agencies in both countries. A Joint Technical Committee (JTC) composed of fisheries managers and scientists from both countries advises the Panel.

Assessment of the Period 1984–1999

Substantial changes in fishery management took place in the AYK region from 1984 through 1999. The two most noteworthy were the emergence of more public involvement and responsibility in fisheries management, and the focus of management on escapement goals. Poor salmon runs coupled with the evolution toward managing fisheries specifically to achieve escapement goals resulted in more fisheries restrictions. On the Kuskokwim River, poor salmon escapements in the mid-1980s led to the elimination of large-mesh gillnets in 1985 and the elimination of directed commercial Chinook salmon fishing in 1987. On the Yukon River, large Chinook salmon catches exceeding the guideline harvest ranges and poor escapements in the 1980s led to restrictions in the late 1980s and early 1990s. Fishing periods were shortened and catches were contained within specified harvest levels. As chum salmon runs began to decline from high levels of the 1980s, ADF&G was faced with implementing restrictions and closures of chum salmon fisheries throughout the region.

Management based on harvest and fishing schedule restrictions using escapement goals for postseason evaluation evolved from this period to the 1990s when managers adjusted catches and fishing time specifically for the purposes of meeting escapement goals. Managers were taken to task by the Board of Fisheries and stakeholders when goals were not met. As this period evolved, the ability of management to curtail salmon harvest to meet escapement goals increased. For the first time, subsistence fisheries were closed or restricted.

A key change to the management process during this period was more effective communication among fishery stakeholders. Information was routinely compiled and shared among stakeholders and managers during the fishing season as well as postseason and preseason via the Kuskokwim River Salmon Management Working Group and the Yukon River Drainage Fisheries Association. Changes in the fisheries helped to underscore the need for improved cooperation among user groups and between the public and the department, and the need for more public support for funding to improve research, management, and enforcement.

Current Management

Policy for the management of sustainable salmon fisheries

In March 2000, the Alaska Board of Fisheries adopted 5 AAC 39.222 Policy for the Management of Sustainable Salmon Fisheries (http://www.boards.adfg.state.ak.us/fishinfo/regs/ssfptext.pdf). The goal of this policy was "to ensure conservation of salmon and salmon's required marine and aquatic habitats, protection of customary and traditional subsistence uses and other uses, and the sustained economic health of Alaska's fishing communities." The policy lays out the principles and criteria for management including:

1) Maintaining wild salmon stocks and habitat at levels of resource productivity that assure sustained yields,

2) Salmon fisheries shall be managed to allow escapements within ranges necessary to conserve and sustain potential salmon production and maintain normal ecosystem functioning,

3) Effective management systems should be established and applied to regulate human activities that affect salmon

4) Public support and involvement for sustained use and protection of salmon resources should be sought and encouraged,

5) In the face of uncertainty, salmon stocks, fisheries, artificial propagation, and essential habitats shall be managed conservatively.

The principles and criteria for sustainable salmon fisheries were to be applied by ADF&G and the Board of Fisheries using the best available information. The policy sets out a process for regular review of salmon stock status and identification of specific stocks of concern. Three categories of concern exist: yield concern—stocks that fail to produce expected yields; management concern—stocks that fail to meet established escapement goals; and conservation concern—stocks that are found to be in danger of not being able to rebuild themselves. Stocks are designated as concerns if the stock fails to meet the goal over a period of 4–5 years despite appropriate management measures taken to address the concern. When stocks of concern are identified, department staff members work with the board and public to develop action plans, management plans, and research plans to help return the stock to health.

The policy defined three types of escapement goals: biological, sustainable, and optimal. Biological and sustainable escapement goals are set by the department, while optimal escapement goals (OEG) are set by the board in regulation. Biological escapement goals (BEG) are defined (5AAC 39.222(f) (3)) as "the escapement that provides the greatest potential for maximum sustained yield." Sustainable escapement goals (SEG) are defined (5 AAC 39.222(f)(36) as a level of escapement "…known to provide for sustained yield over a five- to ten-year period, used in situations where a BEG cannot be estimated due to absence of a stock specific catch estimate..." In practice, development of a biological escapement goal can be limited either by lack of stock specific catch data or by lack of total escapement enumeration. Many escapement goals in the AYK region are established as sustainable escapement goals because good escapement information is lacking.

Development of biological escapement goals

In response to the fishery disasters of 1999 through 2000 and the requirement to review escapement goals, the department undertook an extensive review of several AYK region escapement goals. Part of the purpose for this review was to determine if ADF&G was managing for appropriate goals or whether they needed to be revised. Spawner-recruit analyses were performed for Andreafsky and Anvik rivers summer chum salmon stocks (Clark 2001a; Clark and Sandone 2001), Yukon River fall chum salmon (Eggers 2001), Chena and Salcha rivers Chinook salmon (Evenson 2002), Norton Sound Subdistrict 1 chum salmon (Clark 2001b), and Kwiniuk and Tubutulik rivers chum salmon (Clark 2001c).

The spawner-recruit analysis (Clark and Sandone 2001) for Anvik River summer chum salmon is a good example of these analyses. Anvik River is a large tributary to the Yukon River with its confluence 317 mi upstream of the Yukon River mouth. Escape-

ment data has been collected for this stock since 1972, first by tower count, and later by sonar. From 1972 to 1998, escapements ranged from 250,000 spawners in 1973 to almost 1.5 million spawners in 1981. In 1984, an escapement goal was established of 487,000 spawners as counted by the Anvik River sonar project (Buklis 1993). This goal was based on an early spawner-recruit relationship. By 1992, this goal was adjusted to be a minimum of 500,000 spawners counted by Anvik River sonar. Over the 27-year period from 1973 to 1998, summer chum salmon escapement averaged 691,304 fish and showed a six-fold variation over the time period.

Brood tables for the Anvik River were developed using age-composition data from commercial harvests and escapement samples. Analysis of the spawner-recruit relationship resulted in an estimate of 517,827 spawners as the escapement level for the maximum sustained yield (MSY) for the Anvik River summer chum salmon stock. Yield at MSY was estimated at 580,322 fish and the replacement escapement, or the point where the harvestable surplus falls to zero, was estimated at 1.25 million spawners. Based on this analysis, the department established a biological escapement goal range of 400,000–800,000 spawners, which represented the 90% confidence interval of the MSY total escapement (Clark and Sandone 2001). The original goal of more than 500,000 spawners was similar to the estimated MSY escapement of about 518,000 fish. The escapement goal range was revised to 350,000–700,000 fish in 2004 (ADF&G 2004).

Similar analyses for most AYK region salmon stocks were not possible because of a lack of stock-specific harvest information and an inadequate database of total escapement enumeration. Many escapement goals in the region have been based on aerial surveys flown once a season during a time chosen to represent the peak of spawning. These surveys are often hampered by bad weather and results vary depending on the individual flying the survey, run timing for a given year, and water conditions. As a result, the department is generally moving away from aerial survey based goals where possible, replacing them with goals based on more reliable escapement estimators.

Stocks of concern

After continuing near-catastrophic declines in abundance of many AYK region salmon stocks in the late 1990s (e.g., Menard et al. 2009; Bue et al. 2009), the Board of Fisheries in September 2000 designated a number of the salmon stocks as stocks of management or yield concern, based on the definitions provided in the sustainable salmon policy (5 AAC 39.222(f)(21) and (42)). At the time, weak runs of certain chum and Chinook salmon stocks occurred in the Kuskokwim River area, Yukon River drainage, and in Norton Sound drainages. Improved salmon runs recently have resulted in discontinuing some stocks of concern (Yukon summer chum salmon; Kuskokwim chum and Chinook salmon), changing status for Norton Sound sub-district one chum salmon from a management to yield concern, and continuing designations for others (Yukon River and Norton Sound sub-district 5–6 Chinook salmon; Norton Sound sub-district 2–3 chum salmon). Currently, no stocks of management concern occur in the AYK region. Detailed stock status updates for Norton Sound, Yukon and Kuskokwim areas can be found in Bue et al. (2009), Evenson et al. (2009), Linderman et al. (2009), and Menard et al. (2009). In spite of management actions resulting in achievement of most escapement goals, some salmon stocks, including Yukon River Chinook salmon, continue to produce below expected levels.

Federal subsistence program

The State of Alaska manages all fisheries on state and federal lands in Alaska. In 1999, however, the U.S. government assumed responsibility for ensuring that federally qualified rural residents received a priority for subsistence harvest of wild fisheries resources on federal public lands in Alaska, consistent with the mandates of the Alaska National Interest Lands Conservation Act of 1980 and subsequent judicial decisions (Buklis 2002). These lands comprise approximately 50% of the drainages of the Yukon and Kuskokwim rivers in Alaska. This jurisdictional authority also applies to the upper Unalakleet River drainage of Norton Sound. To carry out this responsibility, the Federal Subsistence Program has adopted subsistence fishery regulations for those waters in which the federal Ninth Circuit Court of Appeals found that a Federal Reserve water right exists. These regulations, adopted by the Federal Subsistence Board, generally parallel state regulations but do differ in some significant ways, such as the allowance for the subsistence harvest of fish used in customary trade.

In addition to the federal regulatory program, approximately $3 million per year have been provided to support fisheries monitoring programs for federal waters in the AYK region through a competitive process. Over 90% of these funds have funded salmon stock status and trends, harvest monitoring, and traditional ecological knowledge projects. Approximately 50% of Kuskokwim and 25% of Yukon salmon assessment projects are funded through this program.

Future Challenges and Opportunities

The cornerstone for management of AYK region salmon stocks is the stated goal of Alaska's Policy for the Management of Sustainable Salmon Fisheries, to "ensure conservation of salmon and salmon's required marine and aquatic habitats, protection of customary and traditional subsistence uses and other uses, and the sustained economic health of Alaska's fishing communities" (5 AAC 39.222.). Alaska's system for abundance-based management rooted in achieving escapement goals provides a good framework for assuring adequate spawning numbers to support sustainable subsistence, commercial, and sport harvests. However, the utility of these tools is only as good as the data that support them. While increased state and federal spending in the last decade has greatly improved escapement and harvest monitoring region-wide, major stock and geographic gaps still occur in these assessments. Though a number of escapement monitoring projects funded in the 1990s are beginning to accrue sufficient data to formulate escapement goals, we expect overall spending in the region to decline during the next decade.

On-going research planning efforts generally attempt to prioritize regional salmon research needs by assessing current understanding against specific management or conservation goals. These include the Yukon River Joint Technical Committee (JTC) Research Plan, the Yukon River Panel Restoration and Enhancement Fund prioritization framework, and the Kuskokwim Fisheries Resource Coalition Kuskokwim Watershed Salmon Research Plan. Two recent plans, The Research and Restoration Plan for Norton Sound and the AYK Sustainable Salmon Initiative Research Plan (AYK SSI 2006), are complete. The Yukon River JTC plan identified and prioritized goals, objectives, and issues using the analytical hierarchy process. Goals were identified and prioritized as follows: 1) assess and achieve fishery management objectives, 2) assess, conserve and restore salmon habitats, 3) build and maintain public support of, and meaningful participation in, salmon resource management, and 4)

improve understanding of salmon biology and ecology. Seven objectives under the first goal were identified and prioritized: 1) monitoring or projecting escapements by conservation management unit, 2) assessing abundance inseason, 3) establishing management objectives, 4) improving management and research capability, 5) monitoring harvest by conservation management unit, 6) maintaining and improving harvest management consultation, and 7) investigating and implementing precautionary management. A number of issues under each objective were also identified and prioritized. Other goals were treated similarly, and existing projects that address each issue were identified. Through this process, it will be apparent whether existing projects address highest priority issues, where the greatest information gaps exist, and what projects are needed to fill those gaps.

Similarly, the Kuskokwim Fisheries Resources Coalition was funded to conduct planning for the Kuskokwim River watershed. They proposed a gap analysis and science plan to guide long-term monitoring of the freshwater life history phases of the salmon resources of the Kuskokwim River. Although gap analyses provide a necessary first step towards long-term research planning, strategically implementing projects aimed at stock assessment and escapement monitoring will create tangible long-term benefits addressing the major information gaps that exist for many Kuskokwim River, Yukon River, and Norton Sound stocks. A good example of this success comes from Norton Sound Initiative projects, where gaps identified in the research plan justified funding basic data gathering projects like weirs, towers, and telemetry projects. Our understanding of Norton Sound area salmon stocks has increased greatly, simply because consistent, quality data are being collected in a broad spectrum of places. Maintaining funding for some of these projects is a region-wide challenge going forward.

The vast and remote landscape, the logistical difficulties of collecting timely run assessment and escapement data, and the gauntlet nature of in-river fisheries that characterizes the AYK region create significant challenges for fishery managers. While commercial and subsistence fisheries have occurred in various parts of AYK for over a century, in most areas quality stock assessment and escapement data have only recently been available to manage fisheries in-season and gauge success afterwards. While measures of harvest for commercial fisheries are timely and reliable due to reporting through the fish ticket system, accounting of the substantial subsistence harvests largely depends upon voluntary postseason reporting and may be subject to significant uncertainty. Funding resources from the State of Alaska, the Norton Sound Initiative, Federal Office of Subsistence Management, and AYK Sustainable Salmon Initiative have greatly expanded the use of weirs, towers, and sonar to measure escapement throughout the region and provided somewhat better stock assessment tools for in-season management. Improved genetic techniques and expanded baselines have increased our ability to assess fishery impacts on stock aggregates. With expected declines in federal funding for research and assessment projects, it is important that clear priorities be defined to most effectively meet the goals of the Policy for management of Sustainable Salmon Fisheries.

Alaska's salmon management framework is well-designed to address changing abundance and distribution of salmon species and stocks, because it is based upon in-season assessments of abundance and possesses in-season management flexibility to address fluctuations. Though future effects of climate change on species abundance and distribution are uncertain (Mantua 2009), ocean warming (Myers et al. 2009, this volume; Royer and Grotsch 2009, this volume), changes in flow regimes of rivers (Schindler and Rogers 2009, this volume), and alterations of food webs (Eggers 2009, this volume; Farley et al. 2009, this volume) may have significant, but unknown effects on western Alaska salmon. Critical salmon habitat in AYK is generally undisturbed and nearly pristine, but significant development in the Fairbanks-North Star Borough, and mining activities throughout the region present habitat concerns for some important salmon stocks. Maintaining sustainable harvests, monitoring abundance trends, and ensuring adequate escapement depend upon fundamental data regarding abundance, stock composition, and life history of harvested populations. Collaborative frameworks to fund projects of greatest strategic importance are essential for effective management and conservation of AYK salmon stocks.

References

ADF&G (Alaska Department of Fish and Game). 2002a. Annual management report, Yukon and Northern Areas 2000. Alaska Department of Fish and Game, Division of Commercial Fisheries, Regional Information Report 3A02–29, Anchorage.

ADF&G. 2002b. Annual management report for the subsistence and commercial fisheries of the Kuskokwim Area 2001. Alaska Department of Fish and Game, Division of Commercial Fisheries, Regional Information Report 3A02–53, Anchorage.

ADF&G. 2003. Annual management report 2001 Norton Sound–Port Clarence—Kotzebue. Alaska Department of Fish and Game, Division of Commercial Fisheries, Regional Information Report 3A03–04, Anchorage.

ADF&G. 2004. Escapement goal review of select AYK region salmon stocks. Alaska Department of Fish and Game, Division of Commercial Fisheries, Regional Information Report 3A04–01, Anchorage.

AYK SSI (Arctic-Yukon-Kuskokwim Sustainable Salmon Initiative). 2006. Arctic-Yukon-Kuskokwim Salmon Research and Restoration Plan. Bering Sea Fishermen's Association, Anchorage, Alaska.

Baker, T. T., T. Sands, F. West, C. Westing, and C. Brazil. 2009. Management of the Nushagak District sockeye salmon fishery: how 50 years of data helps. Pages 963–976 in C. C. Krueger and C. E. Zimmerman, editors. Pacific salmon: ecology and management of western Alaska's populations. American Fisheries Society Symposium 70, Bethesda, Maryland.

Barton, L. 1984. A catalog of Yukon River spawning escapement surveys. Alaska Department of Fish and Game, Technical Data Report No. 121, Juneau.

Brase, A., and H. Hamner. 2002. Subsistence and personal use salmon harvests in the Alaska portion of the Yukon River drainage, 2001. Alaska Department of Fish and Game, Division of Commercial Fisheries, Regional Information Report 3A02–32, Anchorage.

Bue, F. J., B. M. Borba, R. Cannon, and C. C. Krueger. 2009. Yukon River fall chum salmon fisheries: management, harvest, and stock abundance. Pages 703–742 in C. C. Krueger and C. E. Zimmerman, editors. Pacific salmon: ecology and management of western Alaska's populations. American Fisheries Society Symposium 70, Bethesda, Maryland.

Buklis, L. 1993. Documentation of Arctic-Yukon-Kuskokwim Region salmon escapement goals in effect as of the 1992 fishing season. Alaska Department of Fish and Game, Division of Commercial Fisheries, Regional Information Report 3A93-03, Anchorage.

Buklis, L. S. 1999. A description of economic changes in commercial salmon fisheries in a region of mixed subsistence and market economies. Arctic 52:40–48.

Buklis, L. S. 2002. Subsistence fisheries management on federal public lands in Alaska. Fisheries 27(7):10–18.

Clark, J. 2001a. Biological escapement goals for Andreafsky River chum salmon. Alaska Department of Fish and Game, Division of Commercial Fisheries, Regional Information Report 3A01–07, Anchorage.

Clark, J. 2001b. Biological escapement goal for chum salmon in Subdistrict One of Norton Sound. Alaska Department of Fish and Game, Division of Commercial Fisheries, Regional Information Report 3A01–09, Anchorage.

Clark, J. 2001c. Biological escapement goals for Kwiniuk and Tubutulik chum salmon. Alaska Department of Fish and Game, Division of Commercial Fisheries, Regional Information Report 3A01–08, Anchorage.

Clark, J., and G. Sandone. 2001. Biological escapement goal for Anvik River chum salmon. Alaska Department of Fish and Game, Division of Commercial Fisheries, Regional Information Report 3A01–06, Anchorage.

Cooley, R. 1963. Politics and conservation: the decline of the Alaska salmon. Harper and Row, New York.

Cote, D., and M. Edens. 1999. Advisory Committee Manual. Alaska Department of Fish and Game, Boards Support Section, Juneau.

Eggers, D. 2001. Biological escapement for Yukon River fall chum salmon. Alaska Department of Fish and Game, Commercial Fisheries Division, Regional Information Report No. 3A01–10, Anchorage.

Evenson, M. 2002. Optimal production of chinook salmon from the Chena and Salcha Rivers. Alaska Department of Fish and Game, Sport Fish Division, Fishery Manuscript Series No. 02–01, Juneau.

Evenson, D. F., S. J. Hayes, G. Sandone, and D. J. Bergstrom. 2009. Yukon River Chinook salmon: stock status, harvest, and management. Pages 675–701 in C. C. Krueger and C. E. Zimmerman, editors. Pacific salmon: ecology and management of western Alaska's populations. American Fisheries Society Symposium 70, Bethesda, Maryland.

Fall, J. 1990. The Division of Subsistence of the Alaska Department of Fish and Game: an overview of its research program and findings: 1980–1990. Arctic Anthropology 27(2):68–92.

Gilbert, C. H. 1922. The salmon of the Yukon River. Bulletin of the Bureau of Fisheries 38:317–332.

Gilk, S. E., D. B. Molyneaux, T. Hmazaki, J. A. Pawluk, and W. D. Templin. 2009. Biolocial and genetic characteristics of fall and summer chum salmon in the Kuskokwim River, Alaska. Pages 161–179 in C. C. Krueger and C. E. Zimmerman, editors. Pacific salmon: ecology and management of western Alaska's populations. American Fisheries Society, Symposium 70, Bethesda, Maryland.

Huntington, S. 1993. Shadows on the Koyukuk: an Alaskan native's life along the river. Alaska Northwest Books, Anchorage.

Krasnowski, P. V. 1997. Alaska's salmon fisheries: management and conservation. Alaska Department of Fish and Game, Juneau.

Linderman, J. C., Jr., and D. J. Bergstrom. 2009. Kuskokwim management area: salmon escapement, harvest, and management. Pages 541–599 in C. C. Krueger and C. E. Zimmerman, editors. Pacific salmon: ecology and management of western Alaska's populations. American Fisheries Society Symposium 70, Bethesda, Maryland.

Menard, J., C. C. Krueger, and J. R. Hilsinger. 2009. Norton Sound salmon fisheries: history, stock abundance, and management. Pages 621–673 in C. C. Krueger and C. E. Zimmerman, editors. Pacific salmon: ecology and management of western Alaska's populations. American Fisheries Society Symposium 70, Bethesda, Maryland.

Pennoyer, S., K. Middleton, and M. Morris, Jr. 1965. Arctic-Yukon-Kuskokwim Area salmon fishing history. Alaska Department of Fish and Game, Informational Leaflet No. 70, Juneau.

Regnart, R. 1993. Comparative history of state management of fisheries in Alaska. Alaska Department of Fish and Game, ANILCA Program, Anchorage.

American Fisheries Society Symposium 70:521–539, 2009

Management of Recreational Salmon Fisheries in the Arctic-Yukon-Kuskokwim Region of Alaska

JOHN M. BURR[*]

Sport Fish Division, Alaska Department Fish and Game,
1300 College Road, Fairbanks, Alaska 99701, USA

Abstract.—The sport fisheries for Chinook *Oncorhynchus tshawytscha* and coho salmon *O. kisutch* are a small but important component of fisheries in the Arctic-Yukon-Kuskokwim region (AYK). In the United States' portion of the Yukon River drainage and in the Kuskokwim River drainage, only 5% of the total harvest (sport, commercial, subsistence) of these species are taken by the sport fisheries. In Norton Sound, sport fisheries harvest is somewhat more important and approximates 10% of the total Chinook and coho salmon harvest. The goal of sport fishery management is to maintain reliable fishing opportunities. In contrast, commercial and subsistence fishery management seeks a maximum sustainable harvest via efficient capture methods to provide for subsistence needs and viable commercial markets. The Alaska Board of Fisheries and Alaska Department of Fish and Game have primary responsibility for managing fisheries. Sport fishery management for salmon in the AYK region has little effect on annual spawning escapements of salmon due to low levels of harvest. Sport fishing gear is inherently inefficient and catch rates are variable. Bag limits are low in number and the focus of many anglers is on catching and releasing salmon, not on harvest. In recent years, catch-and-release fishing has increased and the proportion of salmon harvested from the total sport catch has declined. Catch-and-release fishing has been controversial with some local residents. Sport fisheries often occur upstream of, and after, the subsistence and commercial fisheries have completed their harvests. Maintaining reliable fishing opportunities are particularly critical to the few, small volume, AYK sport fish guide businesses. Clients generally arrange to fish several months before the start of the season. This small industry adds diversity in economic opportunities in rural Alaska. An inseason closure of the sport fishery for salmon can have a devastating economic impact on these small businesses.

Introduction

Most anglers fishing for salmon in the Arctic-Yukon-Kuskokwim (AYK) Region target Chinook salmon *Oncorhynchus tshawytscha* and coho salmon *O. kisutch*; however, some sport fishing also occurs for chum *O. keta* and pink salmon *O. gorbuscha*. In a few exceptional circumstances, chum and pink salmon are specifically targeted by anglers, such as in the pink salmon sport fishery in northwest Alaska near Nome. Sport fisheries for other nonsalmon species such as Arctic grayling *Thymallus arcticus*, Dolly Varden *Salvelinus malma*,

[*]Corresponding author: john.burr@alaska.gov

rainbow trout *O. mykiss*, sheefish *Stenodus leucichthys*, and northern pike *Esox lucius* are more popular within the region. These nonsalmon species provide more than 80% of the region-wide annual sport fishery harvest (Jennings et al. 2004, 2006a, 2006b, 2007, in press). Anglers may catch these species incidentally to salmon fishing or may target these species and incidentally catch salmon.

Salmon angling in the AYK region most often occurs in rivers and only rarely in marine waters along the coastline. The geographic distribution of effort in the AYK region contrasts with the sport fisheries farther south, such as along the Kenai Peninsula and in southeast Alaska where trolling in marine waters for Chinook and coho salmon is popular. The AYK region's streams and rivers are remote and access is typically by boat or airplane. One exception is the area surrounding the community of Nome in the Norton Sound area which has considerable local road access to its streams. Angling is conducted both by boat and from shore using bait casting, spinning, and fly fishing gear.

This paper provides a description of the management, catch and effort, and economic impact of the salmon sport fisheries of the AYK region and discusses the issue of catch-and-release angling. An emphasis on Chinook and coho salmon sport fisheries is provided in this paper.

Description of the Arctic-Yukon-Kuskokwim Regulatory Area

The AYK regulatory area for management of sport fisheries is described in Title 5 of the Alaska Administrative Code (5AAC 70.005, 2004), and includes all drainages of the Bering Sea, Chukchi Sea and the Arctic Ocean, north of a line extending west from Cape Newenham and west of the International boarder near Demarcation Point

(Figure 1). Major drainages within the region include the Kuskokwim, Yukon, Noatak, and Colville rivers. For the purposes of sport fishery regulation, the AYK region is composed of five regulatory areas: Kuskokwim-Goodnews, Yukon River, Tanana River, Northwestern (includes Norton Sound drainages), and North Slope (5AAC 70.006, 2006). Although the upper Copper River/upper Susitna River drainages are also part of this area, these drainages flow to the south into the Gulf of Alaska, and will not be considered in this paper (regulatory area I, Figure 1).

Sport Fishery Management Authority and Policy

The Alaska Board of Fisheries (BOF) and Alaska Department of Fish and Game (ADF&G) have primary responsibility for managing fisheries within the state. The BOF adopts policies, sets escapement goals, establishes fishery management plans, sets fishery regulations, and allocates fishery resources based on consultation with ADF&G and the public. A complete description of the public process by which these tasks are accomplished is available at http://www.boards.adfg.state.us.

The guiding framework for management of all Alaskan salmon fisheries in Alaska is described in detail in the Policy for the Management of Sustainable Salmon Fisheries (5AAC 39.222, 2001). Fundamentally, the policy establishes that salmon populations are to be managed for sustained yield. Sustained yield requires that sufficient adult salmon returning to streams escape fisheries and survive to spawn to complete the life cycle. Establishment of escapement goals and their achievement each year is a primary focus of salmon fishery management. The process by which escapement goals are to be established is referenced in this policy and

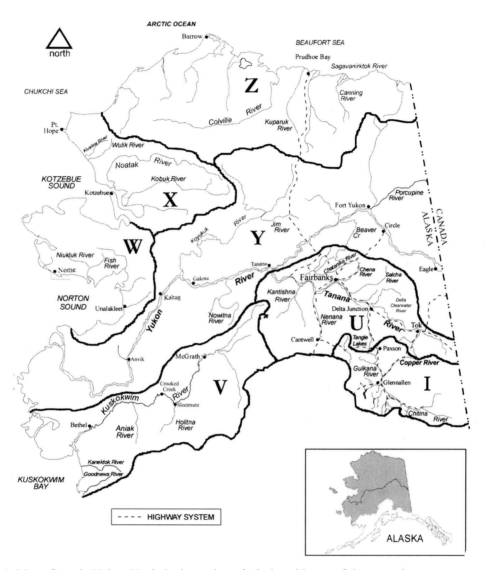

FIGURE 1. Map of Arctic-Yukon-Kuskokwim region of Alaska with sport fishery regulatory areas.

is further articulated in the "Policy for State-wide Salmon Escapement Goals" (5AAC 39.223, 2001). Escapement is achieved by restricting sport, commercial, and subsistence fisheries through regulations such as type of gear and fishery closures by time and area. These regulations must be consistent with the subsistence preference set out in Title 16 of the Alaska Statues (16.05.258, 1992) because regulations affect the allo-

cation of harvestable surpluses among the fisheries.

Management Plans are established by ADF&G through the BOF. A typical management plan for anadromous species outlines allocation of the harvest among beneficial uses, establishes escapement goals which are achieved by opening and closing the various fisheries, and provides guideline harvest ranges by area for fisheries. Management of

were the two most important salmon species in terms of sport catch and harvest in AYK. Together these species comprised more than 60% of the total salmon catch and nearly 70% of the harvest of all salmon species. Chum salmon, and especially pink salmon (during high years), provided locally important sport fisheries particularly in the Norton Sound area of Alaska.

Region-wide, during the last five-year period (2001–2005), the annual average sport catch of Chinook salmon was 18,500 fish of which all but 2,800 fish were released. The annual sport use of coho salmon was higher; approximately 72,000 fish were caught annually of which 11,700 fish were harvested.

Chinook Salmon

Chinook salmon were targeted by both Alaska resident and nonresident anglers.

Approximately two-thirds of the annual total catch of Chinook salmon were caught by nonresidents (Figure 2). In contrast, Alaska resident anglers harvested nearly 60% of all Chinook salmon taken in the AYK region. Alaska residents harvested a greater portion of their catch than nonresidents.

The regulatory areas where most of the sport catch of Chinook salmon occurred were the Kuskokwim and Tanana management areas (Figures 1 and 3). Together these areas accounted for nearly 90% of the total catch. The locations of fisheries for Chinook salmon were different for Alaska resident and nonresident anglers. For residents, more than half of the annual catch came from the road-accessible Tanana area and with about 30% of total catch from the Kuskokwim area. In contrast, for nonresidents nearly 90% of the annual catch of Chinook salmon came from the Kuskokwim area.

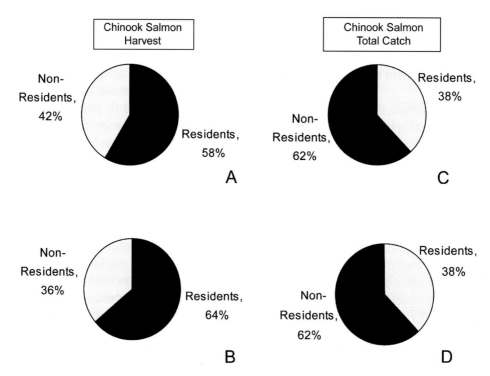

FIGURE 2. AYK Chinook salmon sport harvest and total catch by Alaska resident and non-resident angers. A and C represent average use from 2001–2005; B and D represent average use from 1996–2005.

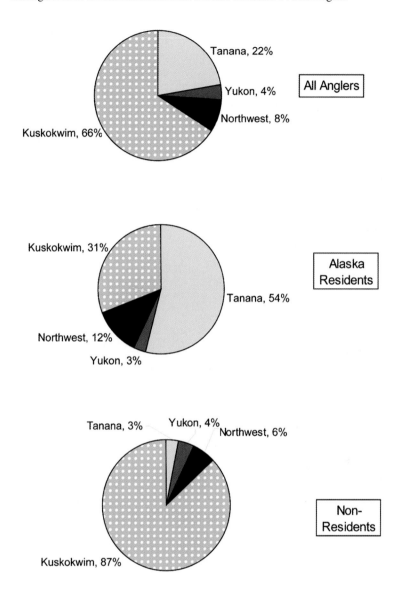

FIGURE 3. Percentage by area and residency of total sport catch of Chinook salmon based on averages from 2001–2005.

The areas in the AYK region where most Chinook salmon were harvested were the Kuskokwim, Tanana (Yukon River drainage) and Northwest (includes Norton Sound drainages) areas (Figures 1 and 4). The Tanana and Northwest areas together provided about 55% of the harvest but only 30% of the total catch, indicating that in these areas anglers kept a slightly greater portion of their catch than in the Kuskokwim area. Most Chinook salmon harvested by resident anglers came from the road accessible Tanana River area (particularly the Chena and Salcha rivers). In contrast, about two-thirds of the Chinook salmon harvested by nonresident anglers came from the Kuskokwim area. Region wide, about 85% of Chinook salmon caught were released (76% for resident, 90% for nonresidents).

Coho Salmon

Nearly three-fourths of the total annual catch of coho salmon was made by nonresident anglers (Figure 5). Though the catch by Alaska resident anglers was only approximately 25% of the total, these anglers harvested more than 50% of all coho salmon taken in AYK region. As with Chinook salmon, Alaska residents harvested a greater portion of their catch of coho salmon than did nonresident anglers.

The regulatory areas in the AYK region where nearly all of the sport catch of coho salmon occurred were the Kuskokwim, Northwest and Tanana management areas (Figures 1 and 6). Approximately two-thirds of the total catch was from the Kuskokwim area. The locations of fisheries for coho salmon were different for Alaska resident and nonresident anglers. For residents, roughly equal portions of the total catch came from these three management areas. In contrast, more than 80% of the annual catch of coho salmon by nonresident anglers

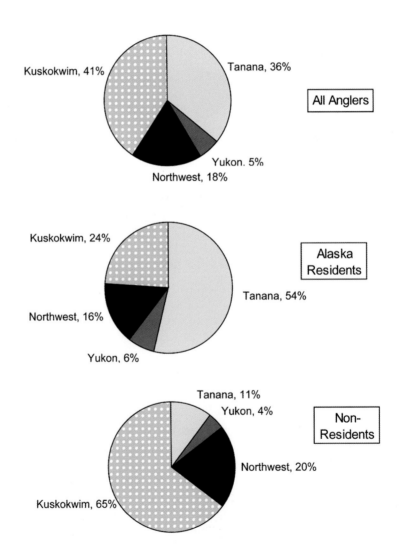

FIGURE 4. Percentage of total sport harvest of Chinook salmon by area and residency, from 2001–2005.

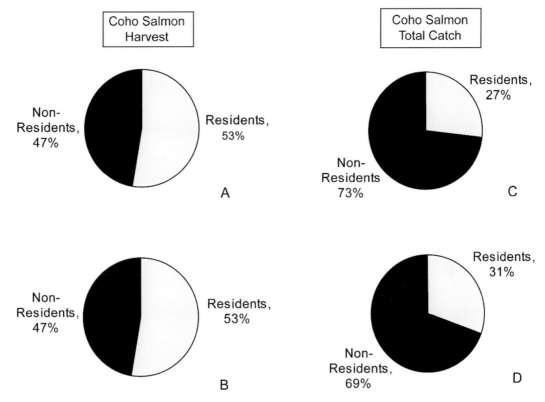

FIGURE 5. Percentage AYK coho salmon sport harvest and total catch by Alaska resident and by non-resident anglers. A and C based on average use from 2001– 2005; B and D are percentage average use from 1996–2005.

came from the Kuskokwim area, with most of the remainder from the Northwest area.

Coho salmon were primarily harvested in the Kuskokwim and Northwest areas. These areas each accounted for about 40% of the annual harvest. The Tanana area provided about 13% of the harvest, primarily from the Delta Clearwater River (Figure 7). Most coho salmon (53%) harvested by resident anglers were from the Northwest area while most of the harvest by nonresidents (59%) was from the Kuskokwim River and Kuskokwim Bay drainages. Region wide, about 82% of coho salmon caught were released (69% for resident, 87% for nonresidents).

Alaska residents harvested a greater portion of their catch of both species than did nonresident anglers. All groups of anglers re-

leased a slightly smaller portion of their catch of coho salmon than of Chinook salmon. Regardless of the species of salmon, anglers chose to release a substantial portion of the fish they caught.

Comparison of Sport Use With Other Uses of Salmon

In AYK, sport fisheries comprise a small but important use of salmon resources. From a survey of sport anglers fishing in AYK, Duffield et al. (2001) reported that a high percentage of both resident (>60%) and nonresident (>50%) anglers specifically fish for salmon. However, the harvest of salmon by sport anglers was low when compared to harvests by other fisheries in AYK (Figures 8 and 9). In

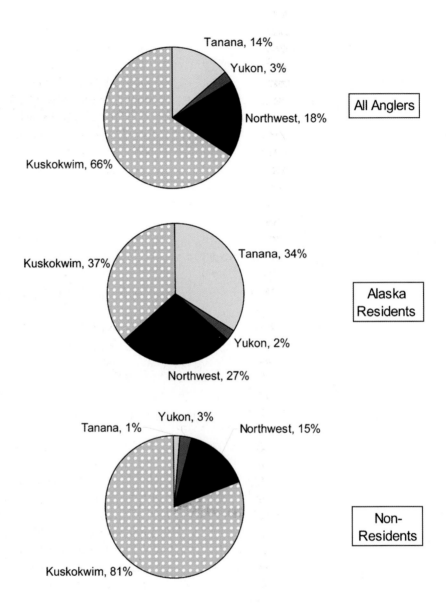

FIGURE 6. Percentage average total sport catch of coho salmon by area and residency from 2001–2005.

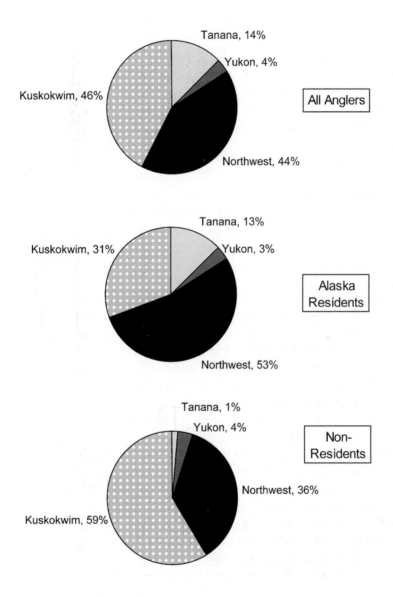

FIGURE 7. Percentage average total sport harvest of coho salmon by area and residency from 2001–2005.

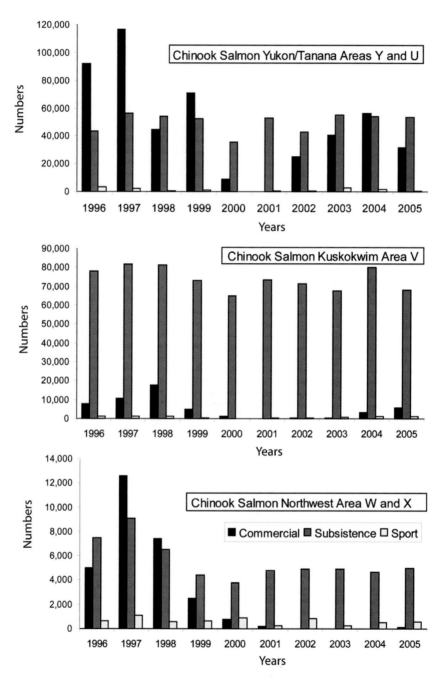

FIGURE 8. Catch (numbers) of Chinook salmon in the AYK region by fishery within major drainage/ management areas. See Figure 1 for locations of Areas.

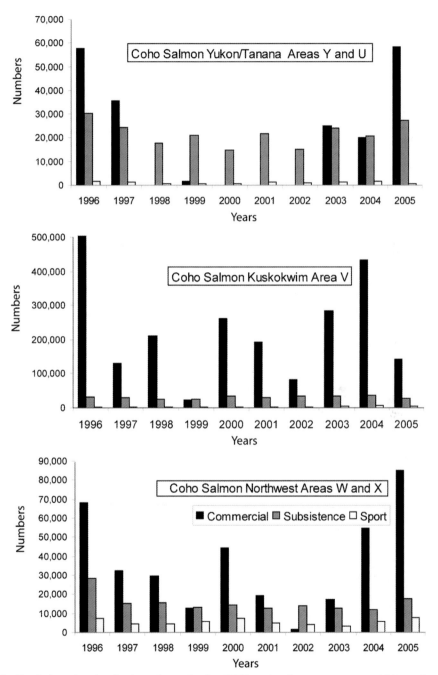

FIGURE 9. Catch (numbers) of coho salmon in the AYK region by user groups within major drainage/ management areas. See Figure 1 for locations of Areas.

the Alaska part of Yukon River drainage and in the Kuskokwim River and Bay drainages, more than 95% of the harvests of all salmon species are taken by the subsistence and commercial fisheries (Evenson et al. 2009; Linderman and Bergstrom 2009). In Norton Sound, commercial and subsistence fisheries harvest approximately 90% of Chinook and coho salmon (Menard et al. 2009, this volume).

Sport fisheries for coho salmon in the AYK region harvest a somewhat higher proportion of the total harvest (all fisheries) than Chinook salmon. During the last five-year period, sport harvests of coho salmon comprised nearly 5% of the total harvest in the Yukon River drainage, 2% of the total harvest in the Kuskokwim area, and 10% of total harvest in Northwest Alaska (Figure 9).

Sport Fishing Guide Services

Currently, several hundred sport fishing guides are licensed to provide services to anglers visiting the AYK region; however, only a small portion of these businesses are geographically located within the region. Also, only a fraction of these services specifically target salmon. Based on interviews with area ADF&G biologists, less than 30 businesses specifically offer guided salmon fishing in the region: 12 operations are in the Kuskokwim River drainage, three guide services are in Kuskokwim Bay, five services are in the Yukon River drainage of which three operate exclusively in the Tanana River portion of the Yukon River drainage, and six operations are in northwest Alaska (two in the Unalakleet River drainage).

Both Alaska resident and nonresident anglers use guide services for salmon fishing. Burr (1999) reported that most (72%) fishing effort for salmon in the Holitna River (Kuskokwim drainage) was by guided, nonresident anglers, and that all nonresident anglers used guide services. These results are typical of remote recreational salmon fish-

ing in the region (Dunaway and Fleischman 1995; Lafferty and Bingham 2002). Although the number of guiding business is small, the impact the industry has on sport fishery is relatively large.

Economic Value of Sport Fisheries

Sport fishing contributes to the Alaskan economy at the statewide and local levels. Sport anglers spend money in the state when they fish (e.g., hotels, restaurants, license fees, gear, air charters, sport lodges, guides). Assessing the magnitude of this activity is difficult and studies that have estimated the contribution by sport fisheries to the economy are few.

Haley et al. (1999) examined the implications of sport fisheries on Alaska's economy. This study estimated the economic impact caused by a hypothetical closure of a sport fishery. The study suggested that the economic impact produced would be different for resident and nonresident anglers. Resident anglers would likely shift their spending to some other area or activity within the state. The likely result would be a net loss to the local economy but not a net loss to state. In contrast, the net loss of such a closure caused by nonresident anglers would occur at both the local/regional and statewide levels. Closure of a sport fishery would cause visitors to shift some spending to other fisheries or other activities in Alaska but would also cause them to shift spending outside of Alaska. Any loss of tourist spending (including visiting anglers) costs jobs and income to the state.

Haley et al. (1999) estimated that $540 million dollars were spent on goods and services attributable to sport fishing statewide; $341 million was spent by resident anglers and $199 million was spent by nonresidents. These estimates were based on surveys conducted in 1993 of expenditures by resident and nonresident households for sport fishing in Alaska.

Guides and charter businesses were also surveyed. The study reports that about 10% of all expenditures statewide were spent for angling within the AYK. The study also reports that in Tanana area of AYK, spending by residents is somewhat more important than spending by nonresidents. However, in the remote portions of the region, the reverse is true.

Duffield et al. (2001) estimated net economic value for salmon *Oncorhychus* spps. sport fisheries in Region III (AYK region including the Copper River drainage—Area I, Figure 1) during 1997. Net economic value (net willingness to pay) is the value anglers place on fishing at the site minus their costs for fishing at the site; the amount of money that a person would be willing to pay to take the trip in addition to what they actually did pay. Overall, the total net economic value for sport fishing in Region III was estimated to be $13,697,500; 67% of this total was attributable to nonresident fishing trips. The estimated net economic value per trip for nonresident anglers was $817 (Table 1). The net value was less for Alaskan residents than it was for nonresidents and varied by location of residence from $122 per trip for Copper River area residents to $192 per trip for residents of southeast Alaska and south-central

Alaska. Estimated average expenditures were highest for nonresidents ($1,893 per trip) in contrast to the average expenditures by Alaska residents ($93 per trip for Seward Peninsula residents and $199 per trip for southeast Alaska and south-central Alaska residents). Salmon fishing trips during which Chinook salmon were specifically targeted were valued much the same as were trips for which coho salmon were the targeted species.

These studies showed that sport fishing provides important benefits to Alaska's economy. In addition to the local areas where fishing occurs, urban areas such as Fairbanks, and transportation centers such as Bethel and Nome benefit from the sale of goods and services. The greatest economic impact is likely to be seen in small rural communities such as Aniak, Crooked Creek, Sleetmute, Anvik, and Unalakleet where established sport fish guiding businesses exist and where a history of sport fishing services exists. The following example illustrates the impact of this industry in remote AYK fisheries.

The Anvik River is one of few locations in the Yukon River drainage outside of the Tanana basin where catch and harvest of salmon by the sport fishery has regularly been reported. One lodge-based sport fish

TABLE 1. Survey results of the salmon sport fishery in the AYK region including the Copper River area during 1997 (from Duffield et al. 2001).

Statistic	Non-Residents	Seward Peninsula	Copper River	Remainder of AYK Region	Remainder of Alaska
Percent of anglers targeting salmon	54.1%	73.1%	62.9%	69.6%	65.2%
Economic Value/trip	$816.50	$136.56	$121.70	$135.90	$191.57
Average Expenditure/ trip	$1,892.90	$ 93.30	$164.07	$162.70	$199.38

guiding business and one or two small volume licensed guides based out of the community provide sport fish guiding services within this and neighboring drainages. The sport fishery targets Chinook and coho salmon primarily for catch-and-release angling. Resident species including northern pike, grayling, and Dolly Varden char are sought by anglers as secondary targets. Most anglers participating in the fishery are guided nonresidents, although local residents do participate in the sport fishery. Current levels of sport use of Chinook salmon are low; the total annual sport catch averages about 200 fish with a harvest of less than 30 fish. An escapement goal of 500 Chinook salmon is in place for an index section of the Anvik River, which is assessed by aerial survey. Escapement counts for the Anvik River have consistently exceeded the escapement goal even in years when the Yukon River drainage as a whole showed generally poor overall returns. In 2000, the Anvik River was one of two Yukon tributaries that exceeded established escapement goals; the index count was 1,394 fish, well exceeding the goal of 500 Chinook salmon. Similarly, the index count in 2001 was 1,430 fish. Though the escapement goals were clearly being met, the Anvik River sport fishery was closed by emergency orders both years (2000 and 2001) because the main-stem Yukon River goals were not being achieved. The closure of the Anvik River salmon fisheries had an immediate negative effect on these local businesses while providing little or no biological benefit. In addition, because sport fishery guides book clients several months prior to the fishing season, business owners reported that anglers were reluctant to book in the seasons after 2001. For example, in 2000 the Anvik River Lodge was under new ownership and business was building up a clientele for whom Chinook salmon was a primary species targeted. Following the closures in 2000 and 2001, bookings declined

by 35% to 40%, representing a loss in gross annual income of approximately $200,000. It took about three years to recover to full bookings and to rebuild the trust of sport anglers.

Catch-and-Release Angling

Catch-and-release angling is generally accepted and widely applied in sport fisheries in North America and Europe. This type of angling focuses on the release of the fish unharmed after capture, and de-emphasizes the harvest or consumptive use of the fish as food. The dominant view of the sport fishing industry and of fishery managers who promote catch-and-release fishing is that such fisheries promotes the conservation of fish populations. This type of fishery allows more fishing opportunities for anglers while reducing fishing mortality to the incidental mortality after release. Alaska statues specifically provide for conservation catch-and-release fishing within the emergency order authority delegated to the commissioner of Fish and Game (5AAC 75.003, 2006). With catch-and-release fishing the opportunity for participation is maintained and the economic value of the fishery is not jeopardized.

Catch-and-release fishing can cause mortality when fish are deeply hooked and injured, or roughly handled. While numerous studies have described catch-and-release mortality for resident fish populations (e.g., Wydoski et al. 1976; Schill et al. 1986), few studies have been conducted of mortality after release of Pacific salmon. Bendock and Alexandersdottir (1990) reported mortality rates of 13% for male and 7% for female Chinook salmon in the Kenai River, Alaska. Vincent-Lang et al. (1993) examined postcapture release mortality of coho salmon in the Little Susitna River, Alaska in both freshwater and in estuary waters. This study reported a 12% mortality rate for coho in freshwater but a 69% mortality rate for coho captured and released in estuary waters. The mortality rates were based on relocation or disappearance of released fish that were radio tagged at the capture location. In another study, specifically designed to investigate differences between catch-and–release mortality in freshwater verses estuary waters, Stuby (2002) did not find differences in mortality for coho salmon related to distance from salt water. This study reported an average mortality for coho salmon of 15% with a range of 7–20%.

Two major sources of catch-and-release mortality have been identified in recreational fisheries: injuries from bleeding and physiological stress stemming from fish being played, landed, and handled (Muoneke and Childress 1994). Severity of bleeding and resulting mortality is primarily related to hook placement such that fish hooked in critical locations such as gills, throat/gullet, and heart showed highest rates of mortality (Bendock and Alexandersdottir 1990; Muoneke and Childress 1994; Wertheimer 1988). Physiological stress, which may contribute to delayed mortality, has been associated with extended retrieval time or from extended exposure to air while the hook is removed or while pictures are taken (Ferguson and Tufts 1992). Using appropriate hook size and type can reduce the number of fish hooked in the critical throat/gullet area and reduce the time needed to remove hooks (Muoneke and Childress 1994; Wertheimer 1988). Because angler behavior can help reduce hooking mortality, the education of anglers in proper handling and careful release of their catch can reduce unintentional mortality in sport fisheries.

The "discovery" of sport fishing opportunities in remote portions of AYK has caused social friction between visiting anglers and local residents, many of whom continue to hold traditional aboriginal values. Although some of the tension is from competition for fishery resources, many of the conflicts between subsistence and sport fishery participants arise from cultural differences concerning the sport fishing practice of catch-and-release fishing (Albertson 2009, this volume).

Concern by rural aboriginal residents about sport fishing practices is based on traditional ethics that are still central to people's beliefs and practices toward their natural world. Some rural residents find catch-and-release fishing incomprehensible; it violates their belief concerning the proper manner in which animals should be treated. The central idea is that living things are aware of the way people treat them. If animals are treated with respect, they will continue to make themselves available for human use. If the animals are abused or disrespected, people are at risk of not being able to catch enough for food (Georgette and Loon 1990; Wolfe 1989). Residents have told researchers that they did not object to visitors fishing as long as the fish were used for food (Georgette and Loon 1990).

Many anglers initially find it strange that catch-and-release can be offensive to local residents. In their view, catch-and-release fishing is the most ethical and conservation-minded form of fishing possible. Sport anglers often value the fishing experience as much or more than harvesting and eating fish. Anglers visiting rural areas often have no means to eat or store all of the fish they catch. When the fish are carefully returned to the water, they believe that the fish will survive to be available to other subsistence or sport fishermen or will subsequently spawn to perpetuate the next generation of fish.

As Alaska's population expands and tourism grows, urban residents and visitors will increasingly seek new, un-crowded areas for sport fishing. It is important that visitors understand and respect traditional values of local residents toward catch-and-release fishing and resource use. Anglers need to practice good handling and release techniques to reduce postrelease mortality of salmon. Minor modifications in behaviors of anglers such as keeping the fish in the water for hook removal and avoiding holding fish up for photographs will help to show respect to the fish and reduce objections to the practice. Education of anglers will become increasingly important to help foster understanding between anglers and local rural Alaska residents. Anglers would do well to adopt an attitude of being guests that have been granted the privilege of fishing the unique waters of Alaska. Some anecdotal evidence does exist that at some locations catch-and-release fishing is becoming more acceptable to local residents (Albertson 2009).

Conclusion

Salmon sport fisheries in the AYK region are small and in nearly all locations, have little impact on salmon runs or on achievement of escapement goals. Although sport fisheries have a minor impact on salmon resources, they are important to the people that participate in these fisheries. Anglers value the fishing experience at least as much as the opportunity to harvest fish. Their participation in the fishery builds strong values for the conservation of the resource and protection of salmon habitat. Salmon sport fisheries provide economic benefits for both urban and rural Alaskans. Unexpected inseason closures of these fisheries have resulted in losses to local businesses serving anglers and to cash strapped local economies. Preserving the opportunity to participate in these sport fisheries through allowing catch-and-and release fishing can greatly reduce the negative economic impact of complete closures while continuing to provide angling opportunities. A primary goal of management of sport fisheries will continue to be to maintain a reliable level of fishing opportunity so that anglers and the businesses that provide services to them can plan to participate in the fisheries.

References

Albertson, L. 2009. Perspectives on angling for salmon on the Kuskokwim River: the catch and release sport fishing controversy. Pages 611–619 *in* C. C. Krueger and C. E. Zimmerman, editors. Pacific salmon: ecology and management of western Alaska's populations. American Fisheries Society, Symposium 70, Bethesda, Maryland.

Bendock, T., and M. Alexandersdottir. 1990. Hook and release mortality of Chinook salmon in the Kenai River recreational fishery. Fishery Data Series Number 90–16. Alaska Department of Fish and Game, Anchorage.

Bue, F. J., B. M. Borba, R. Cannon, and C. C. Krueger. 2009. Yukon River fall chum salmon fisheries: management, harvest, and stock abundance. Pages 703–742 *in* C. C. Krueger and C. E. Zimmerman, editors. Pacific salmon: ecology and management of western Alaska's populations. American Fisheries Society, Symposium 70, Bethesda, Maryland.

Burr, J. M. 1999. Holitna River angler survey, 1998. Fishery Data Series Number 99–39. Alaska Department of Fish and Game, Anchorage.

Duffield, J. W., C. J. Neher, and M. F. Merritt. 2001. Alaska angler survey: use and valuation estimates for 1997 with a focus on salmon fisheries in Region III. Special Publication Number 01–2. Alaska Department of Fish and Game, Anchorage.

Dunaway, D. O., and S. J. Fleischman. 1995. Creel surveys on Chinook and coho salmon sport fisheries on the lower Kanektok River. Fishery Data Series Number 95–22. Alaska Department of Fish and Game, Anchorage.

Evenson, D. F., S. J. Hayes, G. Sandone, and D. J. Bergstrom. 2009. Yukon River Chinook salmon: stock status, harvest, and management. Pages 675–701 *in* C. C. Krueger and C. E. Zimmerman, editors. Pacific salmon: ecology and management of western Alaska's populations. American Fisheries Society, Symposium 70, Bethesda, Maryland.

Ferguson, R. A., and B. L. Tufts. 1992. Physiological effects of brief air exposure in exhaustively exercised rainbow trout (*Oncorhynchus mykiss*): implications for the catch-and-release fisheries. Canadian Journal of Fisheries and Aquatic Sciences 49:1157–1162.

Georgette, S., and H, Loon. 1990. Subsistence and sport fishing of sheefish on the upper Kobuk River, Alaska. Division of Subsistence, Technical Paper 175. Alaska Department of Fish and Game, Anchorage.

Haley, S., M. Berman, S Goldsmith, A. Hill, and H. Kim. 1999. Economics of sport fishing in Alaska. Institute of Social and Economic Research, University of Alaska, Anchorage.

Howe, A. L., G. Fidler, A. E. Bingham, and M. J. Mills. 1996. Harvest, catch, and participation in Alaska sport fisheries during 1995. Fishery Data Series Number 96–32. Alaska Department of Fish and Game, Anchorage.

Howe, A. L., R. J. Walker, C. Olnes, K. Sundet, and A. E. Bingham. 2001a. Revised Edition: Harvest, catch, and participation in Alaska sport fisheries during 1996. Fishery Data Series 97–29 (revised). Alaska Department of Fish and Game, Anchorage.

Howe, A. L., R. J. Walker, C. Olnes, K. Sundet, and A. E. Bingham. 2001b. Revised Edition: Harvest, catch, and participation in Alaska sport fisheries during 1997. Fishery Data Series 98–25 (revised). Alaska Department of Fish and Game, Anchorage.

Howe, A. L., R. J. Walker, C. Olnes, K. Sundet, and A. E. Bingham. 2001c. Revised Edition: Participation, catch, and harvest in Alaska sport fisheries during 1998. Fishery Data Series 99–41 (revised). Alaska Department of Fish and Game, Anchorage.

Howe, A. L., G. Fidler, C. Olnes, A. E. Bingham, and M. J. Mills. 2001d. Participation, catch, and harvest in Alaska sport fisheries during 1999. Fishery Data Series 01–8. Alaska Department of Fish and Game, Anchorage.

Jennings, G. B., K. Sundet, A. E. Bingham, and H. K. Sigurdsson. In press. Participation, catch, and harvest in Alaska sport fisheries during 2005. Fishery Data Series, Number 06–34. Alaska Department of Fish and Game, Anchorage.

Jennings, G. B., K. Sundet, A. E. Bingham, and H. K. Sigurdsson. 2004. Participation, catch, and harvest in Alaska sport fisheries during 2001. Fishery Data Series, Number 04–11. Alaska Department of Fish and Game, Anchorage.

Jennings, G. B., K. Sundet, A. E. Bingham, and H. K. Sigurdsson. 2006a. Participation, catch, and harvest in Alaska sport fisheries during 2002. Fishery Data Series, Number 06–34. Alaska Department of Fish and Game, Anchorage.

Jennings, G. B., K. Sundet, A. E. Bingham, and H. K. Sigurdsson. 2006b. Participation, catch, and harvest in Alaska sport fisheries during 2003. Fishery Data Series, Number 06–44. Alaska Department of Fish and Game, Anchorage.

Jennings, G. B., K. Sundet, and A. E. Bingham. 2007. Participation, catch, and harvest in Alaska sport fisheries during 2004. Fishery Data Series, Number 07–40. Alaska Department of Fish and Game, Anchorage.

Lafferty, R., and A. E. Bingham. 2002. Survey of the rod-reel fisheries in the Aniak River, Alaska, 2001. Fishery Data Series, Number 2–16. Alaska Department of Fish and Game, Anchorage.

Linderman, J. C., Jr., and D. J. Bergstrom. 2009. Kuskokwim Management Area: salmon escapement, harvest, and management. Pages 541–599 in C. C. Krueger and C. E. Zimmerman, editors. Pacific salmon: ecology and management of western Alaska's populations. American Fisheries Society, Symposium 70, Bethesda, Maryland.

Menard, J., C. C. Krueger, and J. R. Hilsinger. 2009. Norton Sound salmon fisheries: history, stock abundance, and management. Pages 621–673 in C. C. Krueger and C. E. Zimmerman, editors. Pacific salmon: ecology and management of western Alaska's populations. American Fisheries Society, Symposium 70, Bethesda, Maryland.

Muoneke, M. I., and W. M. Childress. 1994. Hooking mortality: a review for recreational fisheries. Reviews in Fisheries Science 2:123–156.

Mills, M. J., and A. L. Howe. 1992. An evaluation of estimates of sport fish harvest from the Alaska statewide mail survey. Special Publication Number 92–2. Alaska Department of Fish and Game, Anchorage.

Schill, D. J., J. S. Griffith, and R. E. Gresswell. 1986. Hooking mortality of cutthroat trout in a catch-and-release segment of the Yellowstone River, Yellowstone National Park. North American Journal of Fisheries Management 6:226–232.

Stuby, L. 2002. An investigation of how catch-and-release mortality of coho salmon in the Unalakleet River varies with distance from Norton Sound. Fishery Data Series Number 02–26. Alaska Department of Fish and Game, Anchorage.

Vincent-Lang, D., M. Alexandersdottir, and D. McBride. 1993. Mortality of coho caught and released with sport tackle in the Little Susitna River, Alaska. Fisheries Research 15(44):339–356.

Walker, R. J., C. Olnes, K. Sundet, A. L. Howe, and A. E. Bingham. 2003. Participation, catch, and harvest in Alaska sport fisheries during 2000. Fishery Data Series 03–05. Alaska Department of Fish and Game, Anchorage.

Wertheimer, A. 1988. Hooking mortality of Chinook salmon released by commercial trollers. North American Journal of Fisheries Management 8:346–355.

Wydoski, R. S., G. A. Wedemeyer, and N. O. Nelson. 1976. Physiological response to hooking stressing hatchery and wild rainbow trout (*Salmo gaidneri*). Transactions of the American Fisheries Society 105:601–606.

Wolfe, R. J. 1989. Subsistence—recreational conflicts along the Togiak, Kanektok and Goodnews rivers; a summary. Report to the Alaska Board of Fisheries, Alaska Department of Fish and Game, Division of Subsistence. Anchorage.

American Fisheries Society Symposium 70:541–599, 2009

Kuskokwim Management Area: Salmon Escapement, Harvest, and Management

JOHN C. LINDERMAN, JR.[*] AND DANIEL J. BERGSTROM

Alaska Department of Fish and Game, Division of Commercial Fisheries
333 Raspberry Road, Anchorage, Alaska 99518, USA

Abstract.—The Kuskokwim Management Area supports subsistence, commercial, and sport fisheries for salmon. The area includes the Kuskokwim River, which is the second largest river system in Alaska, and the drainages that flow into Kuskokwim Bay, notably the Kanektok and Goodnews rivers. The salmon fisheries in the region are managed to achieve spawning escapement goals. When salmon abundance is projected to exceed these goals, managers allow harvest by the subsistence, commercial, and sport fisheries. If the harvestable surplus is limited, the subsistence fishery has a priority to access these salmon over the commercial and sport fisheries. This paper describes the status of salmon stocks, fisheries, and management practices used in the Kuskokwim River and Bay. Abundance of Kuskokwim area salmon stocks have been increasing during the 2000s since the poor runs that occurred from 1998 through 2000. Chinook *Oncorhynchus tshawytscha*, chum salmon *O. keta*, and sockeye *O. nerka* salmon stocks have achieved above average to record escapements since 2004. Although abundance of coho salmon *O. kisutch* has decreased in recent years, they achieved a record run in 2003. In most years, escapement goals have been met or exceeded. "Amounts necessary for subsistence" have been achieved for most species each year since 2001, with the exception of sockeye salmon in 2002. Although overall salmon abundance has increased in recent years, commercial fishery harvest has remained below historical averages, primarily because of poor salmon markets, low commercial fishing effort, and limited availability of commercial processing. Expanded escapement monitoring, the development of new escapement goals, estimation of total run sizes, effects of selective fishing, and improvement of commercial markets are all areas for future management and research focus.

Introduction

The Kuskokwim Management Area supports subsistence, commercial, and sport fisheries for salmon and includes the Kuskokwim River and Kuskokwim Bay (Figure 1). Subsistence fisheries in the area harvest more salmon each year than subsistence fisheries in any other region in Alaska (Fall et al. 2007).

Primary species of importance to the fisheries are Chinook salmon *Oncorhynchus tshawytscha*, chum salmon *O. keta*, sockeye salmon *O. nerka*, and coho salmon *O. kisutch*. Two distinct races of chum salmon occur, and are referred to as summer and fall chum salmon (Gilk et al. 2009, this volume). Currently, coho salmon contribute the most to the overall commercial harvest from the Kuskokwim Area. Sport fisheries are small in compari-

*Corresponding author: john.linderman@alaska.gov

son to subsistence and commercial fisheries and can at times target all four species. Pink salmon *O. gorbuscha* are only occasionally a focus of any fishery.

The Kuskokwim River drainage is the second largest river system in Alaska. Historically, Chinook and chum salmon were the focus of the Kuskokwim River fisheries; however, in recent years, coho salmon has increased in importance because of the availability of commercial markets, and chum salmon has declined because of the lack of markets. Chinook salmon is the species of primary interest to the subsistence fisheries of the Kuskokwim River. The timing of the fisheries follows closely the migration of the salmon upriver. Chinook salmon begin entry into the Kuskokwim River in late May, while chum and sockeye salmon begin their entry in mid-June. Chinook and sockeye salmon runs decline rapidly in early- to mid-July. Chum salmon entry to the river declines in late July when coho salmon begin their migration. Coho salmon enter the river during August and into early September.

Kuskokwim Bay includes the important salmon producing streams of the Kanektok and Goodnews Rivers. The fisheries of this portion of the management area focus primarily on sockeye salmon, with secondary commercial fisheries targeting Chinook and coho salmon. The Kanektok and Goodnews Rivers also support a growing sport fishery focused on rainbow trout *O. mykiss*, Dolly Varden trout *Salvelinus malma*, and salmon.

The salmon fisheries of the area are managed to achieve spawning escapement goals, which are typically determined for specific tributary streams rather than by drainages. When salmon abundance is projected to exceed these goals, managers then allow fisheries to harvest the surplus in the subsistence, commercial, and sport fisheries. The subsistence fishery has a priority over other fish-

eries if the harvestable surplus is limited. Escapement is the number of fish allowed to escape the fishery and spawn.

Several types of escapement goals can be used by the State of Alaska depending on the availability and quality of data. A biological escapement goal (BEG) is the number of salmon in a particular stock that the Alaska Department of Fish and Game (ADF&G) has determined should be allowed to escape the fishery in order to spawn to achieve the maximum sustained yield (human use). This determination is based on biological information about the fish stock in question. BEGs for Chinook salmon and sockeye salmon have been proposed for the Goodnews River (Molyneaux and Brannian 2006). A sustainable escapement goal (SEG) is a level of escapement, as indicated by an index or escapement estimate, that is known to provide for sustained yield over a 5–10 year period. SEGs are used when a biological escapement goal cannot be estimated because of the absence of stock-specific catch estimates. Through 2006, SEGs have been the primary management objectives for salmon escapement in the Kuskokwim River and Bay.

In addition to statewide, regional, and district management plans and regulations, the ADF&G's management of Kuskokwim River and Bay salmon stocks is guided by the *Policy for the Management of Sustainable Salmon Fisheries* (SSFP; 5 AAC 39.222, effective 2000, amended 2001). Along with its many guidelines, directives, and definitions, the SSFP also directs ADF&G to provide the Alaska Board of Fisheries (BOF) with reports on the status of salmon stocks and to identify any salmon stocks that present a concern related to yield, management, or conservation during regular BOF meetings. Depending on the information provided, the BOF may respond by officially classifying stocks in terms of their status in accordance with specific designations defined in the SSFP.

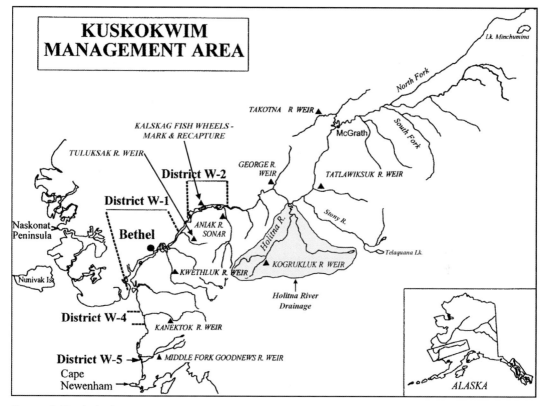

FIGURE 1. Kuskokwim Management Area and salmon monitoring project locations.

In response to the guidelines established in the SSFP, the BOF in 2000 classified Kuskokwim River Chinook and chum salmon as stocks of "yield concern." A stock of "yield concern" is defined as one that has "a concern arising from a chronic inability, despite the use of specific management measures, to maintain expected yields, or harvestable surpluses, above a stock's escapement needs..." (5 AAC 39.22(f)(42). The determination of yield concern was based on low harvest levels for the previous five-year period (1996–2000). Action plans were subsequently developed by ADF&G and approved and implemented by the BOF in 2001 (Burkey et al. 2000a, 2000b). Despite modest improvements in Kuskokwim River Chinook and chum salmon runs from 2001 through 2003, the yield concern classifications were re-affirmed at the January 2004 BOF meeting to maintain the current management approach while allowing for continued stock status and yield evaluation in subsequent years (Bergstrom and Whitmore 2004). The Kuskokwim River Chinook and chum salmon yield concern designations were discontinued by the BOF in 2007 in response to dramatic increases in run abundance since 2002.

This paper reviews the history of the region and describes the status of salmon stocks based on escapement data, fishery harvests, and management practices used in the Kuskokwim River and Bay through the 2006 season. The salmon escapements and harvest for the Kuskokwim River are discussed separately from Kuskokwim Bay because the fisheries differ in their prosecution, the scale of their harvests, and stocks of focus.

Description of the Kuskokwim Management Area

The Kuskokwim Management Area is approximately 50,000 square miles in size, including the Kuskokwim River drainage and all waters that flow into the Bering Sea between Cape Newenham and the Naskonat Peninsula, plus Nunivak and St. Matthew Islands (Figure 1). Two distinct salmon fisheries exist, those within the river and its tributaries, and those targeting stocks returning to streams flowing directly into the Kuskokwim Bay.

The Kuskokwim River is the second largest drainage in the State of Alaska and flows in a southwest direction to the Bering Sea. Commercial fishing has occurred primarily in Districts 1 and 2 (Figure 1), although the District 2 commercial fishery has been inactive for almost a decade. The glacially turbid mainstem is approximately 900 mi long, originating from the interior headwaters of the Kuskokwim Mountains and the Alaska Range. The sparsely populated Kuskokwim River drainage has population centers at Bethel (population 6000+), Aniak (population 572), and McGrath (population 472), plus numerous small villages along its length. No roads exist in the region, except within the cities and villages on the Kuskokwim River.

Several tributaries important for the spawning and rearing of salmon connect to the Kuskokwim River, including the Aniak and Holitna Rivers. For example, the Holitna River is located in the middle Kuskokwim River drainage and comprises one of the largest and most productive tributaries of the Kuskokwim River drainage (Figure 1). The drainage encompasses several sub-basins and tributaries including the Hoholitna River drainage, and the Kogrukluk and Chukowan Rivers. The Holitna River is one of the largest contributors to Kuskokwim River salmon

populations and is believed to account for one-third to one-half of the overall Kuskokwim River salmon production (Molyneaux and Brannian 2006). The drainage provides for a high level of human consumptive use, both locally and throughout the lower half of the Kuskokwim River drainage.

A wide variety of fishing gear is used to catch salmon from the Kuskokwim River. Set nets and drift nets tend to be used most in the lower Kuskokwim River because of the tidal influence and prevalence of sand bars. Upstream from Bethel near Kalskag and Aniak, drift nets, set nets, and a few fish wheels are used; these gears are used throughout the upper Kuskokwim River (Figure 2).

Kuskokwim Bay includes the waters outside the mouth of the Kuskokwim River and mainland coastal streams (Figure 1). Commercial fishing occurs within Districts 4 and 5. Important salmon producing streams include the Goodnews, Kanektok, and Arolik Rivers. Sockeye salmon is the species of greatest interest to the fisheries of these districts. The largest community in this part of the management area is the village of Quinhagak (population 555), located near the mouth of the Kanektok River. Similar to the Kuskokwim River drainage, no roads exist except within villages.

Twenty-three fish species are native to the Kuskokwim Management Area, with most species contributing to the subsistence fishery. In addition to Chinook, chum, coho, and sockeye salmon, pink salmon and rainbow trout (nonanadromous) also occur but are small components of the fisheries. Species also present in the subsistence and sport fisheries include Arctic grayling *Thymallus arcticus*, Dolly Varden char, sheefish *Stenodus leucichthys*, northern pike *Esox lucius*, burbot *Lota lota*, several *Coregonus* species, and Alaska blackfish *Dallia pectoralis*.

FIGURE 2. Drift gillnetting on the Kuskokwim River 12 miles upriver from the village of Aniak (photo by David Cannon).

Data Sources

Kuskokwim River.— Salmon run abundance was initially evaluated inseason using a test fishery operated in the mainstem Kuskokwim River near Bethel (Bue and Martz 2006). The Bethel Test Fishery (BTF) uses catch per unit effort (CPUE) by species to generate in-season indices of salmon run abundance. These indices are compared to historical data for years with similar water level and known levels of escapement and harvest. The BTF can be a useful inseason tool for evaluating current year salmon run abundance, especially early in the run(s) before salmon have moved farther upriver and outside of the primary harvest areas and closer to the spawning grounds. Commercial harvest statistics such as CPUE and total harvest are also used as an index of annual salmon abundance through comparison with historical harvest statistics and trends.

Chinook salmon escapements were evaluated by aerial survey during most years in portions of at least 13 drainages of the Kuskokwim River and by weirs on six tributary streams (Costello et al. 2006a, 2006b; Roettiger et al. 2005; Shelden et al. 2005; Stewart et al. 2006; Zabkar et al. 2005). Weather conditions precluded aerial survey evaluation of Chinook salmon escapements in many streams during 1998 and 1999. A radio-telemetry mark-recapture project to estimate Chinook salmon passage upstream of the Aniak River confluence has been conducted the last five seasons (Pawluk et al. 2006; Stuby 2006). Counts of chum salmon escapements were made at weirs on six tributary streams, by sonar in the Aniak River, and by a mainstem mark-recapture project in 2002 and 2003 (Costello et al. 2006a, 2006b; McEwen 2005; Pawluk et al. 2006; Roettiger et al. 2005; Shelden et al. 2005; Stewart et al. 2006; Zabkar et al. 2005). Sockeye salmon escapements in the Kuskokwim River were monitored by weirs in six tributaries; however, sockeye salmon were not a prominent species in the majority of monitored tributaries (Costello et al. 2006a, 2006b; Roettiger et al. 2005; Shelden et al. 2005; Stewart et al. 2006; Zabkar et al. 2005). Coho salmon escapements were monitored at weirs on six tributaries to the Kuskokwim River, by radio-telemetry on the Holitna River in 2001 and 2002, and by a mark-recapture program on the mainstem Kuskokwim River from 2002 through 2005 (Costello et al. 2006a, 2006b; Pawluk et al. 2006; Roettiger et al. 2005; Shelden et al. 2005; Stewart et al. 2006; Zabkar et al. 2005).

Kuskokwim Bay.— Salmon run abundance was evaluated inseason using commercial harvest statistics such as CPUE and total harvest as an index of annual salmon abundance through comparison with historical harvest statistics and trends. Estimation of escapement of salmon into the Goodnews and Kanektok Rivers used a combination of aerial surveys and weir counts. Aerial surveys of the Kanektok River were conducted from 2004 through 2006 for Chinook and sockeye salmon. A weir was operated on the Kanektok River at River Mile 45 from 2001 through 2005 (Jones and Linderman 2006a). The weir was not operated in 2006 because it was damaged over the winter of 2005–2006. Complete aerial surveys of salmon escapements to the Goodnews River were conducted during 2004 for Chinook and sockeye salmon. Aerial surveys were not conducted in 2005. An aerial survey only of the North Fork Goodnews River was conducted in 2006. Goodnews River drainage escapement was estimated in 2004 and 2005 using the proportion of aerial survey counts between the Middle Fork and North Fork of the Goodnews River, and applying them to the weir escapement counts (Jones and Linderman 2006b).

Harvest Assessment.—Subsistence harvest was assessed both inseason and post season. Inseason harvest assessment is conducted through voluntary interviews of subsistence fishers in the lower Kuskokwim River near Bethel where the majority of subsistence harvest occurs (Dull and Shelden 2007). Additional subsistence fishing information is collected inseason through verbal reports from fishers, community representatives, and through the Kuskokwim River Salmon Management Working Group process (Shelden and Linderman 2007). Inseason subsistence harvest information is qualitative in nature; it is typically used by managers to assess how subsistence harvest is proceeding and to provide indications whether subsistence fishers are meeting their needs.

Subsistence harvest information is also collected post season through evaluation of voluntary harvest calendars and through door-to-door interviews with subsistence fishers in the majority of Kuskokwim Area communities (Fall et al. 2007). This information is used to estimate subsistence salmon harvest by species in each community, and to obtain other information such as gear types used, harvest timing, and subsistence uses (Simon et al. 2007). Subsistence fishing harvest estimates are lagged by approximately one year after harvest occurs. Before 1989, a different methodology was used to estimate subsistence harvest which may have significantly overestimated salmon harvests and underestimated effort (Walker and Coffing 1993). Current methodology used after 1988, relies on the stratification of all households as "usually fish" and "usually do not fish" to provide a sampling of all households (Fall et al. 2007; Walker and Coffing 1993). Previously, only groups with fishing camps were sampled. These camps often involved more than one household; however, often only the primary household returned their calendars. Prior to 1989, subsistence harvest surveys combined sockeye and chum salmon catch; therefore, subsistence harvest of sockeye salmon prior to 1989 is unknown.

Commercial harvest was assessed through the completion of mandatory fish tickets at the time of sale. Information recorded on fish tickets includes the permit holder's information, number of fish harvested by species, total pounds by species, price per pound by species, total price paid, and the total number of fish by species retained for personal use (if any). Fish ticket receipts are delivered to AGF&G staff after each commercial opening and entered into a database that can be queried under multiple parameters (e.g., by species, deliveries, number of fishers, number of fish, pounds). Commercial harvest information is determined and used inseason.

Sport fishing harvest was assessed through analysis of voluntary sport fish harvest surveys (Jennings et al. 2007). Additional fishing guide reporting requirements were implemented in 2006; however, results from this program were not available for this paper. Harvest surveys allow for estimating the number of fish by species that were harvested (retained) and the number of fish by species that were caught and released. Sport fishing harvest estimates are analyzed and produced postseason with results available approximately one year after the fishery occurs.

History of Kuskokwim River Fisheries

Originally, the lower and middle portions of the Kuskokwim River watershed were occupied by groups of Yup'ik Eskimos, part of the many distinct regional groups of Central Yup'ik Eskimos occupying a broad swath along the Bering Sea coast from the south of Norton Sound to the northern portions of the Alaska Peninsula (Oswalt 1980). The Yup'ik regional group *Kusquaqvagmiut* inhabited the lower and middle reaches of the Kuskokwim (Coffing 1991). The low lying tundra region between the lower Kuskokwim and Yukon Rivers was occupied by the *Akulmuit* Yup'ik, who accessed the Kuskokwim River to harvest salmon (Coffing 1991). Groups of Dena'ina (Tanaina) Athabaskan Indians inhabited the upper Kuskokwim region as well as the neighboring watersheds of Cook Inlet,

Iliamna Lake, and the Mulchatna River (Fall et al. 1984). Yup'ik and Athabaskan peoples overlapped and co-existed in mixed settlements along the Kuskokwim River in the region between the present day community of Aniak and the Stony River (Oswalt 1980). Local barter and trade of salmon and salmon products has a long tradition within the local Yup'ik and Athabaskan cultures, and was primarily conducted in the form of food for sled dogs.

Some of the earliest Eurasian exploration of the Kuskokwim area was recorded by Lieutenant L. A. Zagoskin of Russia who explored during the early 1840s portions of the Yukon River and the upper half of the Kuskokwim River (Michael 1967). Within his journal he recorded:

"The Kuskokwim is far poorer than the Yukon in the numbers, variety, and size of its fish." –L.A. Zagoskin (Michael 1967:220)

This interesting contrast between the Kuskokwim and Yukon Rivers by Zagoskin probably did not take into account the large differences in the number of tributaries and drainage sizes of the two rivers. Zagoskin also noted that the basic food of the natives of the Kuskokwim River was fish as opposed to mammals. Fish were used in various forms including boiled, pickled, fried, iced or shredded, and dried. Fences made of poles led fish to traps; the traps were made of spruce slats which would vary in size depending on the type of fish desired to be caught (e.g., burbot, whitefish, salmon). Fish were not only important as food but also were used for clothing.

"Kuskokwim natives made their boots very skillfully of once frozen king [Chinook] salmon skins, with the soles the same … The parka covers worn in snowy weather or in heavy frosts may be made of fishskins, usually burbot or blueback [sockeye] salmon." –L.A. Zagoskin (Michael 1967:212)

Latter descriptions of the Kuskokwim region's fishery resources differed somewhat from Zagoskin's and suggested instead a tremendous abundance of salmon and other fish. For example, Harrison (1905) describes the fishes of the Kuskokwim River as follows:

"The stream teems with fish of many varieties, including king salmon, big fellows, some of them weighing as much as ninety pounds, many varieties of trout, including … dolly varden and rainbow; grayling, and several kinds of whitefish…"

The Klondike gold rush in 1898 brought rapid cultural changes to the Kuskokwim region as well as to the interior of Alaska, and impacted salmon stream habitats. Initially, gold miners came into the area around the Aniak River (Figure 1), but little gold was found. In 1907, the first significant gold discoveries in the Kuskokwim River drainage were made along the Fox and Bear creeks, tributaries of the Tuluksak River. Gold was also found at Crooked Creek and the George River in 1909, approximately 50 mi northeast of Aniak. These areas were subjected to placer mining which undoubtedly damaged stream habitats for salmon. Similarly, gold was discovered at Moore Creek, a tributary of the Takotna River in 1908, and this stream was also subjected to placer mining and later to dragline and bulldozers. The area continued to produce gold into the 1980s. Many of the upriver villages were established as a direct result of gold mining (e.g., McGrath, Medfra, and Takotna), while mining played a large role in the shaping of others (e.g., Georgetown, Sleetmute, and Aniak). The influx of miners to the region brought new technologies for catching fish, most notably the fish wheel. This device was first introduced in 1914 at Georgetown near the mouth of the George River (Figure 1) and during the 1900s was used throughout the mid- and upper Kuskokwim River.

Fisheries management of the Kuskokwim Management Area was originally under the jurisdiction of the U.S. federal government during the years that Alaska was a territory. The Alaska Salmon Fisheries Act was adopted in 1889 and subsequently amended in 1896. The act prohibited the erection of dams, barriers, or other obstructions in Alaska rivers for the purpose of impeding salmon migration, and prohibited commercial fishing above tidewater in streams less than 500 ft in width (Cooley 1963). The first recorded report of commercial fishing operations for export from the Kuskokwim Area date back to 1913 with harvest limited to Kuskokwim Bay. Earliest regulations noted were in 1926 when all commercial fishing was prohibited, although no explanation has been determined for this closure (Pennoyer et al. 1965). The Kuskokwim Bay commercial fishery stayed closed until it was reopened in 1930 for drift nets and set nets.

By 1931, the use of the airplane for carrying mail reduced the use of dog teams, which reduced the demand for dried fish as dog food. As a result, fishery pressure on the salmon stocks declined and more Kuskokwim Bay commercial fisheries were opened. A quota limit of 250,000 Chinook and sockeye salmon combined was established. In 1935, commercial fishing was legalized in the Kuskokwim River, and fish wheels were made legal gear for native aboriginal peoples and permanent white residents. This shift away from the use of chum salmon as dog food caused considerable change in the culture because dried salmon had been used for trading to obtain flour, sugar, and other commodities. This system of trading continued but to a much lesser extent into the 1960s. Over this same period of time, the culture shifted concurrently to a cash economy through increased employment in commercial fishing, canneries and fish processing, construction, and other jobs. The reduction of the use of chum salmon as dog food continued during the 1960s as snow machines became widespread in use.

Various time, season, and quota changes were made during the period from 1936 to 1951. In 1951, considerable local agitation arose over the commercial fishery and, because little interest had been shown in any commercial operation for many years, commercial fishing was closed in 1952. The fishery was reopened in 1954; however, no commercial fishing took place until 1959.

With the advent of statehood, management of the salmon fisheries shifted from the federal government to the State of Alaska in 1960. Commercial harvest in 1961 of Chinook salmon was estimated as 18,918 fish and coho salmon as 5,044 fish, which was considerably smaller than the subsistence harvest of 28,898 Chinook, 130,837 chum, and 54,464 sockeye salmon (Pennoyer et al. 1965). Management of salmon fisheries since statehood has focused on providing adequate opportunity for subsistence fisheries and allowing for commercial fisheries when harvestable surpluses have existed beyond that needed for escapement and subsistence uses. This approach to managing harvest continues today within the context of allowing adequate numbers of salmon to escape the fisheries to spawn and produce the next generation.

Kuskokwim River Salmon Stock Status, Harvest, and Management

Stock status based on escapement

Chinook salmon escapement.—The Chinook salmon escapement index, which is based primarily on aerial surveys of 13 index streams, shows poor escapements from 1998 through 2000, average to above average escapements from 2001 through 2003, and above average to record escapements from 2004 through 2006 (Figure 3; Appendix Table 1). Beginning with the 2001 season, Chinook salmon run sizes have increased and resulted in above average to record escapements in

2004–2006, attaining or exceeding SEGs in nearly all systems (Figure 3). Although the 2006 Chinook salmon run was not as strong as in 2004 and 2005, escapements were still above average, and escapement goals were achieved or exceeded throughout the drainage.

Data from individual rivers shows similar trends as for the entire system based on the index (Figure 3). For example, at the Kogrukluk River weir, Chinook salmon escapements were poor in 1999 and 2000 (Appendix Table 1). The escapement of 5,600 Chinook salmon in 1999 was just above the lower end of the SEG (Sustainable Escapement Goal) range of 5,300–14,000 fish. The escapement of 3,200 fish in 2000 was the lowest since 1976, and below the SEG range. Chinook salmon escapements at the Kogrukluk River weir from 2001 to 2003 were in the middle of the SEG range. Escapements from 2004 through 2006 exceeded the SEG range, with a record escapement of 22,000 fish in 2005.

From 2002 through 2005, Chinook salmon radio-telemetry mark–recapture estimates upstream of the Aniak River were in general agreement (Table 1) with escapement estimates elsewhere in the drainage in these same years (Appendix Table 1). Mark-recapture estimates have also been used in combination with weir escapement estimates to reconstruct the 2002–2005 Chinook salmon runs. Recent radio-telemetry studies both within the Holitna drainage and on the mainstem Kuskokwim River estimated that the Holitna River contributed from 27% to 33% of the overall Kuskokwim River Chinook salmon escapement between 2002 and 2005 (Molyneaux and Brannian 2006).

Variation in parent-year escapement did not explain the poor Chinook salmon runs of 1998–2000, nor the excellent runs of 2004–2006. Parent-year escapements during 1992–1995 that produced the poor runs of 1998 through 2000 were not over harvested. The occurrence of these poor runs were

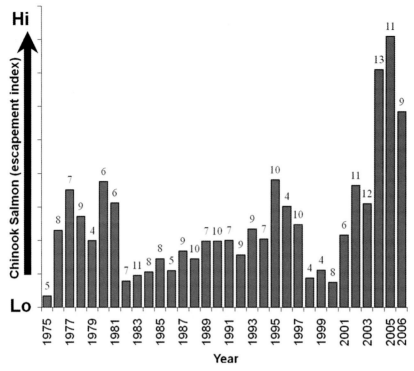

FIGURE 3. The Kuskokwim River Chinook salmon escapement index is a composite of median historical escapements for 13 possible index streams throughout the Kuskokwim River drainage. The number on top of each bar represents the number of index streams surveyed in that year.

surprising because they were the progeny of parent-year escapements of average to above average abundance levels. The poor runs of 1998 to 2000 were possibly the result of poor ocean environments affecting juvenile survival (Farley et al. 2009, this volume; Mantua 2009, this volume; Myers et al. 2009, this volume). Poor salmon runs occurred throughout Western Alaska in 1998–2000 (Hayes et al. 2009, this volume; Menard et al. 2009, this volume). The high escapements documented from 2004 through 2006 were produced from the low parent-year escapements of 1999 through 2001. Hence, recent escapements contradict expected stock-recruitment relationships.

Chum salmon escapement.—Chum salmon escapements from 1999 through 2000 were below SEG levels in the Aniak and Kogrukluk Rivers (Table 2). The 2004

chum salmon run was average to above average in seven rivers surveyed by either weirs or sonar. Increased runs continued in 2005 and 2006, which resulted in two consecutive years of well-above average to record chum salmon escapements (Table 2).

The general trend in chum salmon escapement described above was observed at the individual weir and sonar escapement monitoring projects in the Kuskokwim River drainage (Table 2). For example, Kogrukluk River chum salmon escapements based on weir counts were 13,800 fish in 1999 and 11,500 fish in 2000. Both counts were below the lower end of the SEG range of 15,000–49,000 fish established for the river. Chum salmon escapement counts at the Kogrukluk River weir in 2001, 2003, and 2004 were approximately in the middle of the SEG range. Kogrukluk River weir chum salmon escapement of 197,700 fish in 2005 and 180,510 fish

TABLE 1. Kuskokwim River salmon abundance estimates based on mark-recapture, 2001–2006. Dashes (—) indicate that field operations were incomplete and abundance estimate was not determined. Blanks indicate that no estimates were made for that species in that year.

Year	Chinook	SE	Chum	SE	Sockeye	SE	Coho	SE
Kuskokwim River estimates upstream of Kalskag								
2002			675,659				316,068	
2003			507,772	90,449	90,449		849,494	
2004			—	—	—		386,743	
2005			—	—	—		640,736	
2006			—	—	—		—	
Kuskokwim River estimates upstream of the Aniak River								
2002	100,733	24,267						
2003	103,161	18,720						
2004	146,839	21,980						
2005	145,373	15,528						
2006	n/a	n/a						
Holitna River estimates								
2001	25,405	6,207					63,442	10,063
2002	42,902	6,334	542,172	285,925			157,277	56,624
2003	42,013	4,981	—	—			—	—
2004	81,961	13,150	—	—			—	—
2005	72,690	8,510	—	—			—	—
2006	n/a	n/a	—	—			—	—

TABLE 2. Kuskokwim River chum salmon escapement estimates in number of fish, 1980–2006. Sonar counts considered to be primarily chum salmon. SEG refers to the established Sustainable Escapement Goal (ADF&G 2004). A revised SEG for the Aniak River has been recommended to account for use of new DIDSON sonar methodology (Brannian et al. 2006). Dashes (—) indicate that field operations were incomplete; annual escapement estimate was not determined.

Year	Kwethluk Weir	Tuluksak Weir	Aniak Sonar	Kogrukluk Weir	George Weir	Tatlawiksuk Weir	Takotna Weir
1980			1,600,032				
1981			649,849	57,365			
1982			529,758	64,063			
1983			166,452	9,407			
1984			317,688	41,484			
1985			273,306	15,005			
1986			219,770	14,693			
1987			204,834	—			
1988			485,077	39,540			
1989			295,993	39,549			
1990			246,813	26,765			
1991		7,675	366,687	24,188			
1992	30,595	11,183	87,467	34,105			

TABLE 2. Continued.

Year	Kwethluk Weir	Tuluksak Weir	Aniak Sonar	Kogrukluk Weir	George Weir	Tatlawiksuk Weir	Takotna Weir
1993	—	13,804	15,278	31,899			
1994	—	15,724	474,356	46,635			
1995	—	—	—	31,265			
1996	26,049	—	402,195	48,495	19,393		2,872
1997	10,659	—	289,654	7,958	5,907		1,779
1998	—	—	351,792	36,442	—	—	—
1999	—	—	214,429	13,820	11,552	9,599	—
2000	11,691	—	177,384	11,491	3,492	7,044	1,254
2001	—	19,321	408,830	30,569	11,601	23,718	5,414
2002	35,854	9,958	472,346	51,570	6,543	24,542	4,377
2003	41,812	11,724	477,544	23,413	33,666	—	3,393

Linderman and Bergstrom

TABLE 2. Continued.

Year	Kwethluk Weir	Tuluksak Weir	Aniak Sonar	Kogrukluk Weir	George Weir	Tatlawiksuk Weir	Takotna Weir
2004	38,646	11,796	672,931	24,201	14,409	21,245	1,630
2005	—	35,696	1,151,505	197,723	14,828	55,720	6,467
2006	42,328	23,818	1,042,132	180,510	41,450	32,204	12,608
SEG			220,000—480,000	15,000—49,000			
Average	28,322	11,724	317,688	30,917	11,552	16,658	3,132

in 2006 represented two consecutive record escapements that were approximately three times higher than previous record escapements observed in 1981 and 1982 (Table 2). Escapement in 2005 and 2006 exceeded the upper SEG range by three to four times. Similarly, the Aniak River sonar chum salmon index counts in 1999 and 2000 were below the established SEG range (220,000–480,000 fish), within or above the SEG range from 2001 through 2004, and in 2005 and 2006 were among the highest runs on record. As with Chinook salmon, the high escapements of chum salmon seen in 2005 came from the comparatively low parent year escapements of 2001, contradictory to expected stock-recruitment relationships.

Sockeye salmon escapement.—Among six tributary weir locations, Kogrukluk and Kwethluk rivers had the largest sockeye salmon runs (Table 3). Prior to 2005, Kogrukluk River (Holitna River drainage) sockeye salmon escapements based on weir counts have ranged from 1,176–29,358 fish, with a median escapement of 6,700 fish. Kogrukluk River weir sockeye salmon escapement of 37,960 fish in 2005 and 60,787 fish in 2006 represented two consecutive years of record escapements exceeding the previous two largest escapements (1981 and 1993) by 50–100%. Preliminary results from the 2006 sockeye salmon radio-telemetry program indicated approximately 70% of the 2006 Kuskokwim River sockeye salmon run returned to the Holitna River (S. Gilk, Commercial Fisheries Biologist, ADF&G, Anchorage, personal communication). Kwethluk River sockeye salmon escapement data estimated a record escapement in 2006, similar to the Kogrukluk (Holitna) River. In recent years, small numbers of sockeye salmon have also been returning to other Kuskokwim River tributaries where they had not been observed previously, for example, in the Takotna and Tatlawiksuk Rivers. These data may be the first evidence of newly colonizing populations of sockeye salmon or simply may be the result of straying from the abundant runs elsewhere in the drainage. Besides the Holitna River drainage (Kogrukluk River), other important sockeye salmon spawning tributaries are the Aniak River drainage and the Stony River drainage, which drains Telaquana Lake.

Coho salmon escapement.—Coho salmon have followed a pattern of fluctuating increasing and decreasing escapements over time, with record escapements in 2003 occurring in the five Kuskokwim River tributaries with operating weir programs (Table 4). Since the peak escapements in 2003, coho salmon run abundance decreased from 2004 to 2006. From 2002 to 2005, coho salmon mark-recapture estimates upstream of the Kalskag were in general agreement with escapements estimated elsewhere in the drainage, with the 2003 run being the most abundant (Table 1). The longest weir data series for coho salmon occurs for the Kogrukluk River (Table 4). The coho salmon escapement in 2003 of 74,754 fish in the Kogrukluk River greatly exceeded the upper end of the SEG range (13,000–28,000 fish) and was the highest on record since 1981. Although coho salmon escapements have decreased some since the 2003 record year, the SEG established for the Kogrukluk River has been achieved each year from 2000 to 2006.

Subsistence and commercial fisheries harvest

Subsistence fishery.—The Kuskokwim River subsistence salmon fishery is one of the largest in the state and Chinook salmon is the primary subsistence salmon species (38% of average total harvest 1996–2005) followed by chum salmon (28%), sockeye salmon (19%), and coho salmon (15%; Appendix Tables 2–5). Harvest of salmon for subsistence use can contribute as much as 650 lb per capita in some Kuskokwim River

TABLE 3. Kuskokwim River sockeye escapement estimates in number of fish, 1981–2006. Dashes (—) indicate that field operations were incomplete; annual escapement estimate was not determined.

Year	Kwethluk Weir	Tuluksak Weir	George Weir	Kogrukluk Weir	Tatlawiksuk Weir	Takotna Weir
1981				18,066		
1982				17,297		
1983				1,176		
1984				4,133		
1985				4,359		
1986				4,244		
1987				—		
1988				4,397		
1989				5,811		
1990				8,406		
1991		697		16,455		
1992	1,316	1,083		7,540		
1993	—	2,218		29,358		
1994	—	2,917		14,192		

Table 3. Continued.

Year	Kwethluk Weir	Tuluksak Weir	George Weir	Kogrukluk Weir	Tatlawiksuk Weir	Takotna Weir
1995	—	—		10,996		0
1996	1,801	—		15,385		0
1997	1,374	—	445	13,078		0
1998	—	—	—	16,773		—
1999	—	—	—	5,864	6	—
2000	358	—	22	2,867	0	4
2001	—	997	24	8,773	3	1
2002	272	1,346	17	4,050	1	1
2003	2,928	1,064	11	9,138	—	3
2004	3,302	1,479	174	6,671	10	18
2005	—	2,663	270	37,960	77	35
2006	7,000	992	164	60,787	37	61
Average	1,345	1,083	22	8,406	2	1

Linderman and Bergstrom

TABLE 4. Kuskokwim River coho salmon escapement estimates in number of fish, 1981–2006. SEG refers to the established Sustainable Escapement Goal (ADF&G 2004). Dashes (—) indicate that field operations were incomplete; annual escapement estimate was not determined.

Year	Kwethluk Weir	Tuluksak Weir	George Weir	Kogrukluk Weir	Tatlawiksuk Weir	Takotna Weir
1981				11,455		
1982				37,796		
1983				8,538		
1984				27,595		
1985				16,441		
1986				22,506		
1987				22,821		
1988				13,512		
1989				—		
1990				6,132		
1991		4,651		9,964		
1992	45,605	7,501		26,057		
1993	—	8,328		20,517		
1994	—	7,952		34,695		

TABLE 4. Continued.

Year	Kwethluk Weir	Tuluksak Weir	George Weir	Kogrukluk Weir	Tatlawiksuk Weir	Takotna Weir
1995	—			27,861		
1996	—	—		50,555		
1997	—	—	9,210	12,237		
1998	—	—	—	24,348		
1999	—	—	8,914	12,609	3,455	
2000	25,610	—	11,262	33,135	—	3,957
2001	22,904	23,768	14,398	19,387	10,539	2,606
2002	23,298	11,487	6,759	14,516	11,345	3,984
2003	107,789	39,627	31,925	74,754	—	7,171
2004	64,143	20,336	12,522	26,993	16,408	3,207
2005	—	11,324	8,187	24,113	6,729	2,216
2006	20,188		10,771	17,014	—	5,594
SEG				13,000–28,000		
Average	25,610	8,328	10,236	21,512	10,539	3,971

communities (Coffing et al. 2001). Of an approximately 3,900 households in the drainage, approximately 1,270 households fish for subsistence use (Whitmore et al. 2008). Many other households, though not directly catching salmon, participate by assisting those fishing with cutting, drying, smoking, and other activities and share in the catch. Gillnets, fish wheels, and angling are used to harvest salmon for subsistence. Timing of the subsistence harvests follow closely the migration timing of the salmon as they move upriver (Brelsford et al. 1987). Gillnet mesh size is unrestricted and subsistence fishers primarily use large mesh gillnets when targeting Chinook salmon (~8 in stretch mesh). Age, sex, and length studies indicate a disproportionate number of older and larger than average Chinook salmon are harvested by the subsistence fishery (Molyneaux et al. 2005). Concerns have been expressed about the potential for genetic selection of the salmon stocks because of the fisheries and potential changes in stock-recruitment functions with the loss of large females (see Hard et al. 2009, this volume; Olsen et al. 2009, this volume).

Subsistence harvests since 1988 were only modestly affected by fluctuations in run abundance of salmon (Figure 4; Appendix Tables 2–5). Besides Chinook salmon, chum, sockeye, and coho salmon also provide important contributions to the subsistence harvest. Subsistence harvests have remained within the estimated range needed for subsistence purposes. Subsistence fishing has typically been closed prior to, during, and immediately after a commercial fishing period. However, in recent years, given the lack of commercial fishing in June and July, no subsistence fishing closures occurred. The lack of subsistence closures surrounding commercial fishing periods during the months of June and July in recent years, may have changed historical subsistence fishing patterns.

Commercial fishery.—Coho salmon have been the most abundant species in the commercial harvest over the past five years (85% of harvest) and ten years (54%) (Table 5). Chum salmon have been the next most important species to the commercial harvest in terms of numbers caught. Prior to 1997, chum salmon harvest typically exceeded 200,000 fish; however, over the past five years harvest has averaged only 27,660 fish, primarily attributable to poor market conditions.

With the recent improvement in Chinook salmon runs beginning in 2001, a harvestable surplus in excess of escapement requirements and subsistence needs existed, especially for younger age classes. Additionally, subsistence catch calendars reported that an average of 76% of the harvest was taken from the first half of the run, leaving the second half of the run subject to lower exploitation. A restricted (6 in or smaller) mesh size commercial fishery was allowed for harvest of more abundant sockeye and chum salmon stocks and for an incidental harvest of all ages, sex, and size classes of Chinook salmon. A directed commercial fishery for chum and sockeye salmon was prosecuted from 2004 through 2006 in District 1 (Figure 1), but harvest and duration was limited by poor market conditions for chum salmon, limited processing capacity, and low effort. In District 1, four subdistrict (Figure 5) commercial openings occurred in late June and early July during 2004 and 2005, and two sub-district commercial openings occurred in late June during 2006. No interest from buyers existed to purchase fish in District 2 because of market conditions.

Division of District 1 into two subdistricts and the registration of fishers to a subdistrict (5 AAC 07.370, 2001) allowed for fishing periods to be of shorter length than in the past, which kept harvest within processor capacity (Figure 5). When fish abundance and market interest allowed, a twice weekly subdistrict fishery was implemented in District 1. Many fishers, who had registered in Subdistrict 1-B

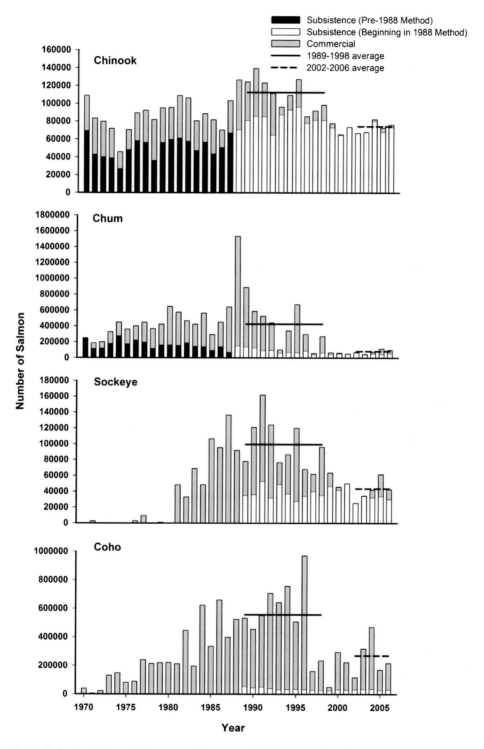

FIGURE 4. Kuskokwim River subsistence and commercial harvests of Chinook, chum, sockeye and coho salmon compared to the 1989–1998 average and the 2002–2006 average. See Data Sources section for a description of the differences in the subsistence harvest estimation procedures.

TABLE 5. Kuskokwim Area commercial salmon harvests by district, 1975–2006.

Year	Districts W-1 and W-2 (Kuskokwim River)				District W-4 (Quinhagak)				District W-5 (Goodnews Bay)			
	Chinook	Chum	Sockeye	Coho	Chinook	Chum	Sockeye	Coho	Chinook	Chum	Sockeye	Coho
1975	22,135	184,171	23	81,945	3,928	35,233	8,584	10,742	2,156	5,904	9,098	17,889
1976	30,735	177,864	2,971	88,501	14,110	43,659	6,090	13,777	4,417	10,354	5,575	9,852
1977	35,830	248,721	9,379	241,364	19,090	43,707	5,519	9,028	3,336	6,531	3,723	13,335
1978	45,641	248,656	733	213,393	12,335	24,798	7,589	20,114	5,218	8,590	5,412	13,764
1979	38,966	261,874	1,054	219,060	11,144	25,995	18,828	47,525	3,204	9,298	19,581	42,098
1980	35,881	483,751	360	222,012	10,387	65,984	13,221	62,610	2,331	11,748	28,632	43,256
1981	47,663	418,677	48,375	211,251	24,524	53,334	17,292	47,551	7,190	13,642	40,273	19,749
1982	48,234	278,306	33,154	447,117	22,106	34,346	25,685	73,652	9,476	13,829	38,877	46,683
1983	33,174	276,698	68,855	196,287	46,385	23,090	10,263	32,442	14,117	6,766	11,716	19,660
1984	31,742	423,718	48,575	623,447	33,633	50,422	17,255	132,151	8,612	14,340	15,474	71,176
1985	37,889	199,478	106,647	335,606	30,401	20,418	7,876	29,992	5,793	4,784	6,698	16,498
1986	19,414	309,213	95,433	659,988	22,835	29,700	21,484	57,544	2,723	10,355	25,112	19,378
1987	36,179	574,336	136,602	399,467	26,022	8,557	6,489	50,070	3,357	20,381	27,758	29,057
1988	55,716	1,381,674	92,025	524,296	13,883	29,220	21,556	68,605	4,964	33,059	36,368	30,832
1989	43,217	749,182	42,747	479,856	20,820	39,395	20,582	44,607	2,966	13,622	19,299	31,849
1990	53,504	461,624	84,870	410,332	27,644	47,717	83,681	26,926	3,303	13,194	35,823	7,804
1991	37,778	431,802	108,946	500,935	9,480	54,493	53,657	42,571	912	15,892	39,838	13,312

TABLE 5. Continued.

Year	Districts W-1 and W-2 (Kuskokwim River)				District W-4 (Quinhagak)				District W-5 (Goodnews Bay)			
	Chinook	Chum	Sockeye	Coho	Chinook	Chum	Sockeye	Coho	Chinook	Chum	Sockeye	Coho
1992	46,872	344,603	92,218	666,170	17,197	73,383	60,929	86,404	3,528	18,520	39,194	19,875
1993	8,735	43,337	27,008	610,739	15,784	40,943	80,934	55,817	2,117	10,657	59,293	20,014
1994	16,211	271,115	49,365	724,689	8,564	61,301	72,314	83,912	2,570	28,477	69,490	47,499
1995	30,846	605,918	92,500	471,461	38,584	81,462	68,194	66,203	2,922	19,832	37,351	17,875
1996	7,419	207,877	33,878	937,299	14,165	83,005	57,665	118,718	1,375	11,093	30,717	43,836
1997	10,441	17,026	21,989	130,803	35,510	38,445	69,562	32,862	2,039	11,729	31,451	2,983
1998	17,359	207,809	60,906	210,481	23,158	45,095	41,382	80,183	3,675	14,155	27,161	21,246
1999	4,705	23,006	16,976	23,593	18,426	38,091	41,315	6,184	1,888	11,562	22,910	2,474
2000	444	11,570	4,130	261,379	21,229	30,553	68,557	30,529	4,442	7,450	37,252	15,531
2001	90	1,272	84	192,998	12,775	17,209	33,807	18,531	1,519	3,412	25,654	9,275
2002	72	1,900	84	83,463	11,480	29,252	17,802	26,695	979	3,799	6,304	3,041
2003	158	2,764	282	284,064	14,444	27,868	33,941	49,833	1,412	5,593	29,423	12,658
2004	2,300	20,429	9,748	433,809	25,465	25,820	34,627	82,398	2,565	6,014	20,922	23,690
2005	4,784	69,139	27,645	142,319	24,195	13,529	68,801	51,708	2,035	2,568	23,933	11,735
2006	2,777	44,070	12,618	185,598	19,184	39,151	106,308	26,831	2,892	11,568	29,857	12,436
Average (2002-2006)	2,018	27,660	10,075	225,851	18,954	27,124	52,296	47,493	1,977	5,908	22,088	12,712

(downstream of Bethel), requested additional fishing time because they believed that Subdistrict 1-B fishers had a harvest disadvantage compared to Subdistrict 1-A (upstream of Bethel) fishers (see Figure 5). Historically, Subdistrict 1-B had higher harvest and effort than in Subdistrict 1-A. However, catch per unit effort (CPUE) in Subdistrict 1-B has been consistently lower than in Subdistrict 1A because of the wider and deeper channel and greater tidal influence in this portion of District 1. Requests for additional time were not granted because: (1) current processor limita-

tions, (2) concerns that fishers would choose to register in Subdistrict 1-B to take advantage of additional fishing time, (3) the potential for allocating a harvest advantage to one group of users over another, and (4) the heightened management complexity of allowing unequal fishing times between subdistricts.

Chinook salmon harvest.—Kuskokwim River Chinook salmon are harvested primarily for subsistence use (Figure 4; Appendix Table 2). Over the period 1988 to 2006, subsistence harvests have ranged from 64,794

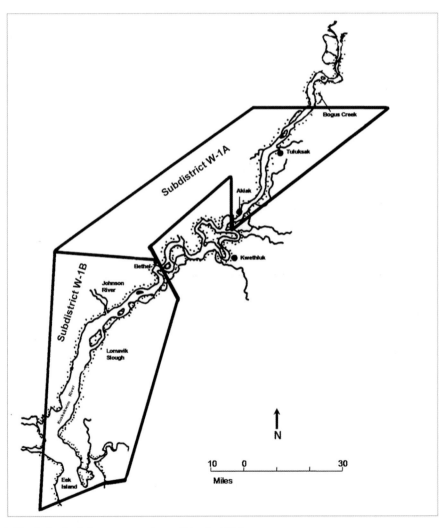

FIGURE 5. Kuskokwim Management Area, District W-1.

fish in 1992 to 96,435 fish in 1995, and have averaged 71,284 fish over the period 2002–2006. Commercial harvest from 1988 to 2006 have ranged from a low of 72 (2002) to high of 55,716 (1988) Chinook salmon. From 1975 through 1992, commercial harvest of Chinook salmon varied less than in recent years and ranged from 19,414–55,716 fish (Table 5). Commercial fishing that targeted Chinook salmon specifically was discontinued in 1987 by regulation, while incidental catches in other fisheries were permitted. From 1993 to 2003 Chinook salmon commercial harvest declined with record low harvests each year 2000 to 2003. Beginning in 2004, Chinook salmon have been harvested incidentally in the commercial chum and sockeye salmon fisheries during late June and July (as described above) with catches ranging between 2,300 and 4,784 fish. Total run estimates indicate low exploitation rates on Chinook salmon in these years ranging from a high of 32% in 2002 to a low of 24% in 2005 (Molyneaux and Brannian 2006).

Chum salmon harvest.—Kuskokwim River chum salmon have been not only an important subsistence species, but also in past years an important salmon species targeted in June and July by commercial fisheries (Figure 4; Appendix Table 3). Record harvests occurred in 1988 when 151,967 salmon were caught in the subsistence fisheries and 1,381,674 fish were caught in the commercial fisheries. Over the past ten years, subsistence harvests have been relatively constant despite fluctuating run sizes (Table 2), ranging from 39,987–63,537 fish. Though record runs have occurred in 2005 and 2006 (~4X average; Table 2), subsistence harvest remained constant (46,036–54,841 fish) and commercial harvests ranged from 44,070–69,139 fish. The lack of increase in commercial harvest in response to the abundance of chum salmon was primarily attributed to the lack of markets and buyers.

The lack of markets, buyers, and processing capacity for chum salmon has been a major impediment in recent years for the commercial fisheries. During 1999 and 2000, low numbers of fish were available for harvest. Only one commercial opening was allowed each year in 1999 and 2000. Although a harvestable surplus existed each year 2001–2006, no market existed for chum salmon in the Kuskokwim River fishery from 2001 through 2003, and only modest commercial fisheries were prosecuted from 2004 through 2006. Chum salmon market and local processing capacity limitations have resulted in few commercial openings which has reduced the fishery effort in June and July when compared to historical levels. Given adequate market interest, processor capacity, and fisher participation, the potential commercial harvests from the 2005 and 2006 chum salmon runs could have been among the highest ever experienced given the record high escapements (Table 2).

Sockeye salmon harvest.—Over the period 1989 to 2006, sockeye salmon have provided a consistent contribution to the subsistence harvest ranging from a low of 25,499 fish in 2002 to a high of 52,982 fish in 1991 (Figure 4; Appendix Table 4). From 1989 to 2006, commercial harvests of sockeye salmon have fluctuated widely from a high of 108,946 fish in 1991 to a low of 84 fish in 2002. The source of the wide variation is attributed to run sizes, number and timing of commercial openings, and the availability of markets, buyers, and processing facilities. Harvest of sockeye salmon was considered incidental to chum salmon harvest from 1987 to 2003; however, management of the sockeye harvest began in 2004 when a harvest guideline of up to 50,000 sockeye salmon was established. An increase in commercial harvest occurred because a directed commercial fishery for chum and sockeye salmon was permitted in District 1 in 2004–2006 during late June and early July (Whitmore et al. 2008). Over these three years, sockeye salmon commercial harvest ranged from 9,748–27,645 fish.

Coho salmon harvest.—Peak total harvest from all fisheries occurred in 1996 when 973,464 coho salmon were caught (Figure 4; Appendix Table 5). This record harvest corresponded with the second highest escapement observed at the Kogrukluk River weir (Table 4). Lowest total catch occurred in 1999, when only 50,808 coho salmon were caught. Similar to sockeye salmon, coho salmon have provided a stable and important component to the subsistence harvest over the time period of 1988 to 2006, ranging from a low 24,864 fish in 1998 to a high of 52,857 fish in 1988. From 2002 to 2006, subsistence harvests have been comparatively stable and have averaged 32,415 fish (range 27,613–35,735 fish). Commercial harvest of coho salmon has fluctuated greatly over the years 1989 to 2006, with peak harvest of 937,299 fish occurring in 1996 and the lowest harvest of 23,593 fish in 1999. Each year since 2004, a coho salmon directed fishery has occurred from late July through about the first week in September (Whitmore et al. 2008). Commercial harvests from 2004 to 2006 ranged from 142,319 fish to 433,809 fish (Table 5). Coho salmon have accounted for the largest number of salmon commercially harvested during this time and have provided the greatest value of all species.

Fishery management

Management of the Kuskokwim Area salmon fishery is complex because of the multiple fisheries, the overlapping multispecies salmon runs, generally high efficiency of existing fisheries, and the large geographic scale of the area with multiple large and important salmon producing tributaries. The ADF&G has primary responsibility for managing fish-

eries within the state. The State of Alaska establishes fisheries regulations at the direction of the Alaska Board of Fisheries. These regulations apply to all lands and waters within the state, including Federal public lands such as the Yukon Delta National Wildlife Refuge, unless superseded by specific Federal regulations related to subsistence fisheries (Buklis 2002). State of Alaska management is guided by the Kuskokwim River Salmon Rebuilding Management Plan (5 AAC 07.365; Bergstrom and Whitmore 2004) adopted in 2001. State and federal management is further advised by discussions held frequently during the summer season with the Kuskokwim River Salmon Management Working Group (Shelden and Linderman 2007). Working Group discussions (sometimes held weekly) includes state and federal fisheries staff, representatives of native organizations, rural residents, and subsistence, commercial, and sport fishing representatives. Information discussed includes subsistence and commercial harvest reports by species, test fish project summaries, and reports from weir, sonar, and aerial survey programs.

Subsistence use requirements.—State and federal management programs provide a harvest priority to subsistence uses. Subsistence use requirements are determined when customary and traditional uses occur in a region. Customary and traditional use, in general, means that the noncommercial, long-term and consistent taking of, use of, and reliance upon fish in a specific area, and the patterns of fish use have been established over a reasonable period of time, taking into consideration their availability. When customary and traditional use has been determined by the state then the subsistence harvest requirements are determined. In 1993, the BOF made a positive finding for customary and traditional use for all salmon in the entire Kuskokwim Management Area (Figure 1). In 2001, the BOF established the amounts necessary for sub-

TABLE 6. Amounts of salmon necessary for subsistence (ANS) for the Kuskokwim Area established by the Alaska Board of Fisheries.

Species	Number of fish
	ANS range for the Kuskokwim River drainage by species
Chinook salmon	64,500–83,000
Chum salmon	39,500–75,500
Sockeye salmon	27,500–39,500
Coho salmon	24,500–35,000
	ANS range for the remainder of Kuskokwim Area
All salmon	7,500–13,500

sistence within the Kuskokwim River drainage by species, and for the remainder of the Kuskokwim Area by all species combined (Burkey et al. 2000a; Table 6).

Kuskokwim River Salmon Rebuilding Management Plan.—The plan addresses Chinook and chum salmon yield concerns that emerged in the late 1990s and 2000. The goal of the Kuskokwim River Salmon Rebuilding Management Plan is to conservatively manage harvests to meet spawning escapement goals, to provide for subsistence levels, and to re-establish harvest by other users within the range of historic levels. This goal was achieved from 2002 to 2006, with all Chinook and chum salmon escapement goals being met or exceeded. Additionally, although harvests the past five years remain below the historical range, the surpluses available for harvest since 2002 were near or above the historical range.

Conservative fisheries management, including the subsistence fishing schedule, adopted by the BOF is the centerpiece of the plan. Important elements of the plan, as amended in 2004, are described below.

1. The primary objectives in June and July will be to provide for escapement and subsistence needs. Salmon fisheries management will be conservative. The commercial fishery will remain closed in June and July unless Chinook and chum salmon run strength is adequate to provide for escapement and subsistence needs, and allow for other uses.

2. A subsistence fishing schedule was established in the Kuskokwim River and all salmon tributaries. During June and July, subsistence fishing will be open for four consecutive days per week and closed for three consecutive days per week. Historically, subsistence fishing was open seven days per week if no commercial fishing periods were allowed. During subsistence fishing closures, all nets greater than four-inch mesh must be removed from the water and fish wheels must be stopped.

3. The subsistence fishing schedule will be implemented in a step-wise manner upriver consistent with run timing. The subsistence schedule will not apply to non-salmon tributaries. Subsistence users will be able to use

gillnets of four-inch or less mesh that target non-salmon species and hook and line (rod and reel) at any time.

4. ADF&G was given the authority to limit gear in the subsistence fishery to gillnets of six-inch or less mesh inseason to conserve Chinook salmon if it becomes necessary.

5. To further conserve Chinook or chum salmon, ADF&G was given the authority to close some areas to subsistence fishing and set daily limits on the number of salmon that can be harvested using subsistence hook and line gear.

6. No directed commercial fishery for Chinook salmon was to occur in the Kuskokwim River. Further, if in-season indicators of run strength suggest sufficient harvest abundance to allow a directed chum salmon commercial fishery, subsistence fishing (schedule) shall revert to the fishing periods as specified in 5 AAC 01.260.

7. The BOF directed ADF&G to manage the commercial coho fishery conservatively to ensure that chum salmon escapement and subsistence needs are met.

8. Explicit instructions were provided by the BOF for relaxing the subsistence fishing schedule when salmon abundance assures that drainage-wide escapement goals and up-river subsistence needs will be met.

9. A commercial guideline harvest level of 0–50,000 sockeye salmon was specified for the Kuskokwim River.

Subsistence fishery management.—The subsistence-fishing schedule as specified in the plan would be implemented by emergency order during the summer fishing season. The schedule established was consistent with the progression of the run upriver becoming

effective downstream of the upper boundary of District 1 at Bogus Creek during the first week, downstream of the upper boundary of District 2 at Chuathbaluk during the second week, and throughout the entire drainage as of the third week. The intent of the fishing schedule of four consecutive days per-week from Wednesday through Saturday was to allow escapement of salmon during closed days, to spread subsistence harvest throughout the run, and to provide a reasonable opportunity for subsistence salmon fishing.

The subsistence fishing schedule was discontinued during the 2002 through 2006 seasons based on the determination that a surplus of Chinook and chum salmon were present above the number needed for escapement and subsistence uses. Since the 2004 season, additional subsistence opportunity was provided through a reduction of the periods closed to subsistence fishing before and after commercial fishing openings. From 2004 through 2006, the period closed to subsistence fishing was established at six hours before, during, and three hours after commercial openings, compared to 12 hours before, during, and six hours after commercial openings during 2001–2003.

Commercial fishery management.—A directed commercial fishery for chum salmon would have been allowed in 2002 and 2003, but no buyers were interested in chum salmon; therefore, no commercial openings occurred. The extremely poor market for chum salmon and local processing limitations were the primary factors that limited the 2004 through 2006 commercial fisheries. Four subdistrict commercial periods occurred in late June of 2004, four periods occurred in late June of 2005, and two periods occurred in late June of 2006. In each of these years, buyers ceased their operations once chum salmon abundance began to overwhelm the commercial harvest. These limitations are not expected to change significantly in the near future. No directed commercial fishery for Chinook salmon was permitted.

Given the scale of record Chinook, chum, and sockeye salmon escapements observed from 2004 through 2006 in the Kuskokwim River, large surpluses of these species were available for commercial harvest. These surpluses were underexploited and contributed, in part, to the record escapements in these years. Given the poor market conditions which have persisted in the Kuskokwim Area for almost a decade, full exploitation of the large harvestable surpluses is unlikely. Along with harvest, the average number of permit holders participating in the fishery has declined significantly to approximately 20% of historical highs. Even if effort had been at, or near, historical highs, market interest in large harvests from the Kuskokwim Area did not exist, especially for chum salmon. Harvest, effort, and value should not be expected to approach historical highs in the Kuskokwim Area in the near future; however, Kuskokwim Area salmon fisheries could grow if the market improved. Kuskokwim River sockeye and Chinook salmon have much higher market interest compared to chum salmon, and their relative abundance is small enough to accommodate current processing capacity.

The Kuskokwim River commercial Chinook salmon fishery has been closed to directed harvest since 1987 with the primary strategy to delay commercial fishing until late June and July to reduce incidental Chinook salmon harvest in other fisheries. This closure was put into effect after a gillnet mesh size restriction of six inches or less went into effect in 1985. These regulations were enacted as conservation measures to improve escapements of Chinook salmon, to provide for subsistence harvest of Chinook salmon, and to allow for a directed commercial fishery on more abundant chum salmon in June and July. The Chinook salmon run has improved since the low run years of 1998–2000,

and harvestable surpluses for uses other than subsistence have been available since 2001.

Sport fishery management.—In general, recreational harvests by sport anglers in the Kuskokwim Area are small when compared to subsistence and commercial harvests (Appendix Tables 2–5). By regulation within the Kuskokwim Area, sport fishing for Chinook salmon begins on May 1 and closes the last week of July. In 2001, a sport fishing emergency order was issued to reduce the possession and bag limit to one Chinook or one chum salmon in the entire Kuskokwim River drainage. In 2002 and 2003, similar sport fishing emergency orders were issued prohibiting the retention of Chinook and chum salmon from May 1 through June 15. After June 15, the possession and bag limits were established at one fish per day for either Chinook or chum salmon. These regulations were subsequently relaxed when salmon abundance increased.

Kuskokwim Bay: Salmon Stock Status and Fishery Management

Quinhagak (District 4)

Salmon Escapement.—Quinhagak (District 4) is located in Kuskokwim Bay approximately 38 mi from the mouth of the Kuskokwim River (Figure 1). The Kanektok River is the principal salmon stream in the area. The Chinook salmon SEG range of 3,500–8,000 fish was achieved or exceeded each year, including a record aerial survey count of 28,375 fish in 2004 (Table 7). The sockeye salmon SEG range of 14,000–34,000 fish was also achieved or exceeded each year (2001 and 2003–2006; no counts made in 2002). Record aerial survey counts of sockeye salmon occurred in 2005 (110,730 fish) and in 2006 (382,800 fish). The record 2006 sockeye salmon aerial survey count was 11 times higher than the upper end of the SEG

TABLE 7. Aerial survey counts from Kuskokwim Bay spawning tributaries, 1961–2006. Estimates are from "peak" aerial surveys conducted under fair, good, or excellent viewing conditions. SEG refers to the established Sustainable Escapement Goal (ADF&G 2004). Dashes (–) indicate aerial survey counts were not conducted.

Year	Kanektok River				Middle Fork Goodnews River				North Fork Goodnews River			
	Chinook	Chum	Sockeye	Coho	Chinook	Chum	Sockeye	Coho	Chinook	Chum	Sockeye	Coho
1970	3,112		11,375									
1971	—		—									
1972	—		—									
1973	814		—									
1974	—		—									
1975	—		6,018									
1976	—	8,697	22,936									
1977	5,787	32,157	7,244									
1978	19,180	229,290	44,215									
1979	—	—	—									
1980	—	—	—	69,325	1,164	3,782	18,926	—	1,228	1,975	75,639	
1981	—	—	—	—	—	—	—	—	—	—	—	
1982	15,900	71,840	49,175	—	1,546	6,300	2,327	—	1,990	9,700	19,160	
1983	8,142		55,940	—	2,500		5,900	—	2,600	—	9,650	
1984	8,890	9,360	2,340	46,830	1,930	9,172	12,897	—	3,245	17,250	9,240	43,925
1985	12,182	53,060	30,840	—	2,050	3,593	5,470	—	3,535	4,415	2,843	—
1986	13,465	14,385	16,270	—	1,249	7,645	16,990	—	1,068	11,850	8,960	—

TABLE 7. Continued.

Year	Kanektok River				Middle Fork Goodnews River				North Fork Goodnews River			
	Chinook	Chum	Sockeye	Coho	Chinook	Chum	Sockeye	Coho	Chinook	Chum	Sockeye	Coho
1987	3,643	16,790	14,940	20,056	2,222	9,696	34,585	—	2,234	12,103	19,786	11,122
1988	4,223	9,420	51,753	—	1,024	5,814	5,831	—	637	3,846	5,820	—
1989	11,180	20,583	30,440	—	1,277	2,922	8,044	—	651	—	3,605	—
1990	7,914	6,270	14,735	—	—	—	—	—	626	—	27,689	—
1991	—	2,475	—	4,330	—	—	—	—	—	—	—	—
1992	2,100	19,052	44,436	—	1,012	3,270	7,200	—	875	1,950	10,397	—
1993	3,856	25,675	14,955	—	—	—	—	—	—	—	—	—
1994	4,670	1,285	23,128	—	—	—	—	—	—	—	—	—
1995	7,386	10,000	30,090	2,900	—	—	—	—	3,314	—	—	—
1996	—	—	—	23,656	—	—	—	—	—	—	—	—
1997	—	—	—	4,892	1,447	—	19,843	—	3,611	—	12,610	—
1998	6,107	7,040	22,020	—	731	3,619	11,632	—	578	2,743	3,497	—
1999	—	—	—	5,192	—	—	—	—	—	—	—	—
2000	1,118	10,000	11,670	10,120	—	—	—	—	—	—	—	—
2001	6,483	11,440	38,610	—	3,561	7,330	29,340	—	2,799	6,945	12,383	—
2002	—	—	—	—	1,470	3,075	3,475	—	1,195	1,208	2,626	—
2003	6,206	2,700	21,335	—	1,210	2,310	21,760	—	2,015	3,370	27,380	—
2004	28,375	—	78,380	—	2,617	—	33,670	—	7,462	—	31,695	—

TABLE 7. Continued.

Year	Kanektok River				Middle Fork Goodnews River				North Fork Goodnews River			
	Chinook	Chum	Sockeye	Coho	Chinook	Chum	Sockeye	Coho	Chinook	Chum	Sockeye	Coho
2005	14,202	—	110,730	—	—	—	—	—	—	—	—	—
2006	8,433	—	382,800	—	—	—	—	—	4,159	—	78,100	—
SEG	3,500 - 8,000	>5,200	14,000 - 34,000	7,700 - 36,000					640 - 3,300		5,500 - 19,500	

range. Complete escapement counts were made at a weir operated at river mile 45 from 2003 through 2005. These counts were 8,231 Chinook, 127,471 sockeye, 40,066 chum, and 72,448 coho salmon in 2003, 19,406 Chinook, 102,443 sockeye, 46,194 chum, and 87,827 coho salmon in 2004, and 12,721 Chinook, 160,702 sockeye, 50,881 chum, and 13,690 coho salmon in 2005 (Table 8; Jones and Linderman 2006a). However, these counts do not include the large number of salmon that spawn downstream of the weir.

Total escapement in the Kanektok River was estimated in 2004 and 2005 using the proportion of aerial survey counts upstream and downstream of the weir and applying them to the weir escapement counts (Jones and Linderman 2006a). In 2004, Chinook salmon total escapement was estimated to be 42,908 fish out of a total run size of 72,561 fish with an exploitation rate of 41%. In 2005, Chinook salmon total escapement was estimated to be 33,110 fish out of a total run size of 61,420 fish with an exploitation rate of 46%. Sockeye salmon total escapement in 2004 was estimated to be 131,873 fish out of a total run size of 168,215 fish with an exploitation rate of 22%. In 2005, sockeye salmon total escapement was estimated to be 278,386 fish out of a total run size of 361,000 with an exploitation rate of 19%. The moderate to low exploitation rates estimated in 2004 and 2005 indicate that these salmon stocks were unlikely to be overexploited under current management.

Harvest.—During the 2005 and 2006 seasons, the processor put fishers on catch limits during several periods in response to the abundance of sockeye salmon to assure all fish caught could be processed. From 2001 through 2006, the commercial salmon harvest ranged from 82,322–191,474 fish (Table 5; Figure 6). Ex-vessel value ranged from $167,615 to $571,965 during these same years. Sockeye salmon comprised the majority of the harvest at 41% followed by coho salmon at 31%, chum salmon at 15%, and Chinook salmon at 13%. Total catch of Chinook salmon in recent years have approximated the average catch 1989–2006 (Figure 6). Subsistence harvests of Chinook salmon have varied little over the past two decades (Figure 6). Low total catches of chum salmon occurred in 1987, 2001, and 2005 (range 9,752–17,999 fish) in contrast to the record total catch of 84,135 fish in 1996 (Figure 6; Appendix Table 7). Sockeye salmon harvests have increased dramatically since 2001 to record levels in 2006. Coho salmon harvests in recent years have attained levels comparable to the early to mid-1990s (Figure 6), attributable to abundant run sizes and favorable commercial markets.

Fishery management.—The objective of the District 4 Management Plan (5 AAC 07.367, 2004; Linderman and Bergstrom 2006) is to maintain a level of sustained yield which will provide for subsistence needs, the economic long-term health of the commercial and sport fishing industries, and recreational fishing opportunities. The management plan further provides direction to open the commercial fishery prior to June 16, to open commercial periods by emergency order, and to provide at least one period per week for fishing unless a severe conservation problem exists. Commercial fishing periods are typically 12 hours in duration. Management of the commercial fishery is based on catch rates compared to prior year catch rates in association with inseason escapement information from the Kanektok River weir and aerial surveys. Typically a fishing schedule of two-12 hour periods per week is established during June targeting Chinook salmon. During July, three 12-hour periods per week typically occur to target sockeye salmon.

During the 2001–2005 seasons, the single registered buyer ceased operation during the last week to 10 days of July when abundance

TABLE 8. Salmon escapements, Middle Fork Goodnews and Kanektok Rivers, 1981–2006. The operational period is inclusive of days when passage was estimated; unless noted otherwise, less than 10% of the total annual escapement is estimated. SEG refers to the established Sustainable Escapement Goal (ADF&G 2004).

Year	Chinook	Chum	Sockeye	Coho	Pink
		Middle Fork Goodnews River			
SEG:	2,000–4,500	>12,000	23,000–50,000	>12,000	
Counting Tower					
1981	3,688	21,827	49,108	356	1,327
1982	1,395	6,767	56,255	91	13,855
1983	6,022	15,548	25,813	0	34
1984	3,260	19,003	32,053	249	13,744
1985	2,831	10,367	24,131	282	144
1986	2,092	14,764	51,069	163	8,133
1987	2,272	17,517	28,871	62	62
1988	2,712	20,799	15,799	6	6,781
1989	1,915	10,380	21,186	1,212	24b
1990	3,636	6,410	31,679	0	3,378
Weir					
1991	1,952	27,525	47,397	1,978	1,694
1992	1,903	22,023	27,268	150	23,030
1993	2,317	14,472	26,044	1,374	253
1994	3,856	34,849	55,751	309	38,705
1995	4,836	33,699	39,009	5,415	330
1996	2,930	40,450	58,264	9,699	14,509
1997	2,937	17,296	35,530	9,619	940
1998	4,584	28,905	47,951	35,441	10,367

Table 8. Continued.

Year	Chinook	Chum	Sockeye	Coho	Pink
			Middle Fork Goodnews River		
SEG:	2,000–4,500	>12,000	23,000–50,000	>12,000	
1999	3,221	19,533	48,205	11,545	914
2000	3,295	14,720	42,197	19,676	2,530
2001	5,398	26,829	22,487	19,630	1,323
2002	3,076	30,233	22,019	27,364	1,328
2003	2,389	21,637	44,390	52,810	1,917
2004	4,266	29,992	52,772	49,611	20,610
2005	4,529	26,428	111,458	13,938	5,925
2006	4,595	54,422	124,256	13,050	18,427
			Kanektok River		
Counting Tower					
1996	6,827	70,617	71,637	—	—
1997	16,731	51,180	96,348	23,172	7,872
1998	—	—	—	—	—
1999	—	—	—	—	—
Weir					
2000	—	—	—	—	—
2001	132	1,058	733	36,440	21
2002	5,343	42,014	58,367	24,883	87,036
2003	8,231	40,066	127,471	72,448	2,443
2004	19,406	46,194	102,443	87,827	98,060
2005	12,721	50,881	160,702	13,690	3,530
2006	—	—	—	—	—

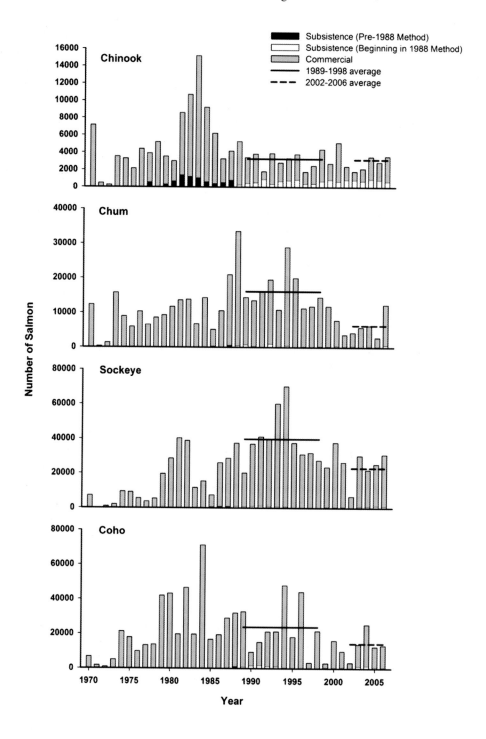

FIGURE 7. Subsistence and commercial harvests of Chinook, chum, sockeye and coho salmon in Kuskokwim Bay, Goodnews Bay (District 5), compared to the 1989–1998 average and the 2002-2006 average. See Data Sources section for a description of the differences in the subsistence harvest estimation procedures.

crease Chinook salmon escapements into the Goodnews River drainage and to assure subsistence harvests will be achieved. The commercial fishery typically opens the last week of June, with fishing periods of 12 hours duration. Management of the commercial fishery is based on in-season catch rates compared to prior year catch rates in association with prior year and in-season escapement levels. Given the current buyer and processing infrastructure available in the Kuskokwim Bay area, District 5 commercial fishing schedules typically mirror those in District 4 given adequate run abundance.

Typically the fishing schedule begins the last week of June with three 12-hour periods scheduled per week. During the 2001–2005 seasons, the single registered buyer ceased operation during the last week to July 10 when sockeye salmon abundance was declining. In early August, the fishery was reopened on a schedule of three-12 hour periods per week targeting coho salmon. In 2006, the local buyer continued purchasing fish throughout July and into the August coho salmon season. Fishing periods were cancelled when catch rates were below average, or when no processor or tender was available. During the 2005 and 2006 seasons, the processor put fishers on catch limits during several periods in response to a high abundance of sockeye salmon to assure those fish harvested could be processed.

Summary

Kuskokwim Area salmon stocks are biologically healthy with runs in recent years resulting in some of the highest escapements observed in the last 30 years. Escapement goals were met or exceeded the majority of time over the past five years, and harvest levels required for subsistence were achieved annually. Significant challenges, however, face the fishery.

Expanded escapement monitoring, the development of new SEGs, estimation of total run sizes, effects of selective fishing, and improvement of commercial markets are all areas for future management and research focus. New information regarding sockeye salmon stocks in the Holitna River system combined with the importance of the Stony and Aniak Rivers suggests the need to expand escapement monitoring on this important species and establish escapement goals for Kuskokwim River sockeye salmon stocks.

Whereas escapement data are useful for understanding harvests, the development of total run estimates (escapement, fishery harvest, natural mortality) would provide the best summary statistic for interpretation of the health of salmon stocks. A Chinook salmon run reconstruction program has been recently initiated based on previous work by Shotwell and Adkinson (2004) using all available data to identify trends in escapement data. This program should prove helpful in understanding the underlying long-term and regional dynamics of salmon abundance.

Selective harvest of Chinook salmon needs to be investigated to determine if management actions should be implemented to address any impacts from differential exploitation of specific age, sex, and size classes by stock. (Hard et al. 2009; Olsen et al. 2009). The potential long-term effect of selection on the genetic health of salmon stocks is an important topic to investigate.

In recent years the harvestable surpluses of Chinook, sockeye, and chum salmon have received low levels of exploitation because of continued poor commercial market conditions, low price, and a lack of adequate local processing capacity. Commercial harvests and value have increased slightly over the lows seen from 1999 through 2003, but harvest, value, and effort remain well below historical highs. Changes in market interest and demand along with mitigating the high costs of processing and transporting harvested fish in such a remote area of the state would be needed to effectively address this issue.

Acknowledgments

The authors would like to acknowledge the many governmental agencies, tribal and non-governmental organizations, and the general public that are involved in Kuskokwim Area fisheries. Fisheries management and assessment programs have long been operated between the ADF&G and many cooperative partners. This has had an overall positive impact on fisheries management and research in the area and has increased effective communication between the department, stakeholders, and other resource management agencies. Doug Molyneaux, Jim Simon, and Mike Coffing of ADF&G provided helpful advice in preparation of this manuscript. Joseph Spaeder assisted with the development of the history section. David Canon of Aniak provided some of the historical mining information. Scott Miehls and Holly Patrick helped develop the tables and Figures. Charles Krueger and three peer reviewers provided helpful comments on earlier drafts of this paper.

References

ADF&G (Alaska Department of Fish and Game). 2004. Escapement goal review of select AYK Region salmon stocks. Division of Commercial Fisheries, Regional Information Report No. 3A04–01. Alaska Department of Fish and Game, Anchorage.

Bergstrom, D. J. and C. Whitmore. 2004. Kuskokwim River Chinook and chum salmon stock status and action plan. Report to the Alaska Board of Fisheries. Division of Commercial Fisheries, Regional Information Report No. 3A04–02. Alaska Department of Fish and Game, Anchorage.

Brannian, L. K., M. J. Evenson, and J. R. Hilsinger. 2006. Escapement goal recommendations for select Arctic-Yukon-Kuskokwim region salmon stocks, 2007. Division of Commercial Fisheries, Fishery Manuscript No. 06–07. Alaska Department of Fish and Game, Anchorage. http://www.sf.adfg.state.ak.us/FedAidPDFs/fm06–07.pdf

Brelsford, T., R. Peterson, and T. L. Haynes. 1987. An overview of resource use patterns in three central Kuskokwim communities: Aniak, Crooked Creek, and Red Devil. Technical Paper Number 141. Alaska Department of Fish and Game, Fairbanks.

Bue, D. G. and M. Martz. 2006. Characterization of the 2004 salmon run in the Kuskokwim River based on test fishing at Bethel. Division of Commercial Fisheries, Fishery Data Series No. 06–37. Alaska Department of Fish and Game, Anchorage.

Buklis, L. S. 2002. Subsistence fisheries management on federal public lands in Alaska. Fisheries 27(7):10–18.

Burkey, C. J., M. Coffing, D. B. Molyneaux, and P. Salomone. 2000a. Kuskokwim River Chinook salmon stock status and development of management/action plan options; report to the Alaska Board of Fisheries. Division of Commercial Fisheries, Regional Information Report No. 3A00–40. Alaska Department of Fish and Game, Anchorage.

Burkey, C. J., M. Coffing, D. B. Molyneaux, and P. Salomone. 2000b. Kuskokwim River chum salmon stock status and development of management/action plan options. Report to the Alaska Board of Fisheries. Division of Commercial Fisheries, Regional Information Report No. 3A00–41. Alaska Department of Fish and Game, Anchorage.

Coffing, M. 1991. Kwethluk subsistence: contemporary land use patterns, wild resource harvest and use, and the subsistence economy of a lower Kuskokwim River area community. Division of Subsistence, Technical Paper Number 157. Alaska Department of Fish and Game, Juneau.

Coffing, M., L. Brown, G. Jennings, and C. J. Utermohle. 2001. The subsistence harvest and use of wild resources in Akiachak, Alaska, 1998. Division of Subsistence, Technical Paper Number 258. Alaska Department of Fish and Game, Juneau.

Cooley, R. A. 1963. Politics and conservation. The decline of the Alaska salmon. Harper and Row, New York.

Costello, D. J., D. B. Molyneaux, and C. Goods. 2006a. Takotna River salmon studies, 2005. Division of Commercial Fisheries, Fishery Data Series No. 06–26, Alaska Department of Fish and Game, Anchorage.

Costello, D. J., R. Stewart, D. B. Molyneaux, and D. E. Orabutt. 2006b. Tatlawiksuk River salmon studies, 2005. Division of Commercial Fisheries, Fishery Data Series No. 06–28. Alaska Department of Fish and Game, Anchorage.

Dull, B. S., and C. A. Shelden. 2007. Lower Kuskokwim River inseason subsistence catch monitoring, 2006. Division of Subsistence, Fishery Management Report No. 07–50. Alaska Department of Fish and Game, Anchorage.

Evenson, D. F., S. J. Hayes, G. Sandone, and D. J. Bergstrom. 2009. Yukon River Chinook salmon: stock status, harvest, and management. Pages 675–701 in C. C. Krueger and C. E. Zimmerman, editors. Pacific salmon: ecology and management of western Alaska's populations. American Fisheries Society, Symposium 70, Bethesda, Maryland.

Fall, J. A., D. Caylor, M. Turek, C. Brown, T. Krauthoefer, B. Davis, and D. Koster. 2007. Alaska subsistence salmon fisheries 2004 annual report. Division of Subsistence, Technical Paper Number 317. Alaska Department of Fish and Game, Juneau.

Fall, J. A., D. J. Foster, and R. T. Stanek. 1984. The use of fish and wildlife resources in Tyonek, Alaska. Division of Subsistence, Technical Paper Number 105. Alaska Department of Fish and Game, Juneau.

Farley, E. V., Jr., J. Murphy, J. Moss, A. Feldmann, and L. Eisner. 2009. Marine ecology of western Alaska juvenile salmon. Pages 307–329 in C. C. Krueger and C. E. Zimmerman, editors. Pacific salmon: ecology and management of western Alaska's populations. American Fisheries Society, Symposium 70, Bethesda, Maryland.

Gilk, S. E., D. B. Molyneaux, T. Hmazaki, J. A. Pawluk, and W. D. Templin. 2009. Biological and genetic characteristics of fall and summer chum salmon in the Kuskokwim River, Alaska. Pages 161–179 in C. C. Krueger and C. E. Zimmerman, editors. Pacific salmon: ecology and management of western Alaska's populations. American Fisheries Society, Symposium 70, Bethesda, Maryland.

Hamazaki, T. 2008. Fishery closure "windows" scheduling as a means of changing the Chinook salmon subsitence fishery pattern: is it an effective management tool? Fisheries 33:495–501.

Hard, J. J., W. Eldridge, and K. Naish. 2009. Genetic consequences of size-selective fishing: implications for viability of Chinook salmon in the Arctic-Yukon-Kuskokwim region of Alaska. Pages 759–780 in C. C. Krueger and C. E. Zimmerman, editors. Pacific salmon: ecology and management of western Alaska's populations. American Fisheries Society, Symposium 70, Bethesda, Maryland.

Harrison, E. S. 1905. Nome and Seward Alaska: history, descriptions, biographies, and stories. The Metropolitan Press, New York.

Jennings, G. B., K. Sundet, and A. E. Bingham. 2007. Participation, catch, and harvest in Alaska sport fisheries during 2004. Division of Sport Fish, Fishery Data Series No. 07–40. Alaska Department of Fish and Game, Anchorage.

Jones, P. W., and J. C. Linderman, Jr. 2006a. Kanektok River salmon monitoring and assessment, 2005. Division of Commercial Fisheries, Fishery Data Series No. 06–48. Alaska Department of Fish and Game, Anchorage.

Jones, P. W., and J. C. Linderman, Jr. 2006b. Goodnews River salmon monitoring and assessment, 2005. Division of Commercial Fisheries, Fishery Data Series No. 06–50. Alaska Department of Fish and Game, Anchorage.

Linderman, J. C., Jr., and D. J. Bergstrom. 2006. Kuskokwim River Chinook and chum salmon stock status and Kuskokwim area fisheries: a report to the Alaska Board of Fisheries. Division of Sport Fish, Special Publication Number 06–35. Alaska Department of Fish and Game, Anchorage.

Mantua, N. 2009. Patterns of change in climate and Pacific salmon production. Pages 1143–1157 in C. C. Krueger and C. E. Zimmerman, editors. Pacific salmon: ecology and management of western Alaska's populations. American Fisheries Society, Symposium 70, Bethesda, Maryland.

Menard, J., C. C. Krueger, and J. R. Hilsinger. 2009. Norton Sound salmon fisheries: history, stock abundance, and management. Pages 621–673 in C. C. Krueger and C. E. Zimmerman, editors. Pacific salmon: ecology and management of western Alaska's populations. American Fisheries Society, Symposium 70, Bethesda, Maryland.

McEwen, M. S. 2005. Sonar estimation of chum salmon passage in the Aniak River, 2004. Division of Commercial Fisheries, Fishery Data Series Number 05–30. Alaska Department of Fish and Game, Anchorage.

Michael, H. N. editors. 1967. Lieutenant Zagoskin's travels in Russian America, 1842–1844. Arctic Institute of North America. Anthropology of the north: translations from Russian sources. Number 7. University of Toronto Press, Toronto, Ontario.

Molyneaux, D. B., D. L. Folletti, L. K. Brannian, and G. Roczicka. 2005. Age, sex, and length composition of Chinook salmon from the 2004 Kuskokwim River subsistence fishery. Division of Commercial Fisheries, Fishery Data Series No. 05–45, Alaska Department of Fish and Game, Anchorage.

Molyneaux, D. B. and L. K. Brannian. 2006. Review of escapement and abundance information for Kuskokwim Area salmon stocks. Division of Commercial Fisheries, Fishery Manuscript Number 06–08. Alaska Department of Fish and Game, Anchorage.

Myers, K. W., R. V. Walker, N. D. Davis, J. L. Armstrong, and M. Kaeriyama. 2009. High seas distribution, biology, and ecology of Arctic-Yukon-Kuskokwim salmon: direct information from high seas tagging experiments, 1954–2006. Pages 201–239 in C. C. Krueger and C. E. Zimmerman, editors. Pacific salmon: ecology and management of western Alaska's populations. American Fisheries Society, Symposium 70, Bethesda, Maryland.

Olsen. J. B., S. J. Miller, K. Harper, and J. K. Wenburg. 2009. Genetic health and variables influencing the effective number of breeders in western Alaska Chinook salmon. Pages 781–795 in C. C. Krueger and C. E. Zimmerman, editors. Pacific salmon: ecology and management of western Alaska's populations. American Fisheries Society, Symposium 70, Bethesda, Maryland.

Oswalt, W. 1980. Historic Settlements along the Kuskokwim River, Alaska. Alaska State Library. Division of State Libraries and Museums, Historical Monograph Number 7. Alaska Department of Education, Juneau.

Pawluk, J., J. Baumer, T. Hamazaki, and D. Orabutt. 2006. A mark-recapture study of Kuskokwim River Chinook, sockeye, chum and coho salmon, 2005. Division of Commercial Fisheries, Fishery Data Series No. 06–54. Alaska Department of Fish and Game, Anchorage.

Pennoyer, S., K. R. Middleton, and M. Morris, Jr. 1965. Arctic-Yukon-Kuskokwim area salmon fishing history. Informational Leaflet 70. Alaska Department of Fish and Game, Juneau.

Roettiger, T., F. G. Harris, and K. C. Harper. 2005. Abundance and run timing of adult Pacific salmon in the Kwethluk River, Yukon Delta National Wildlife Refuge, Alaska, 2004. U.S. Fish and Wildlife Service, Kenai Fish and Wildlife Field Office. Alaska Fisheries Data Series Number 2005-7, Kenai, Alaska.

Shelden, C. A., D. J. Costello, and D. B. Molyneaux. 2005. Kogrukluk River salmon studies, 2004. Division of Commercial Fisheries, Fishery Data Series No. 05–58. Alaska Department of Fish and Game, Anchorage.

Shelden, C. A., and J. C. Linderman, Jr. 2007. Activities of the Kuskokwim River salmon management working group, 2005 through 2006. Division of Commercial Fisheries, Fishery Management Report Number 07–45. Alaska Department of Fish and Game, Anchorage.

Shotwell, S. K., and M. D. Adkinson. 2004. Estimating indices of abundance and escapement of Pacific salmon for data limited situations. Transactions of the American Fisheries Society 133:538–558.

Simon, J., T. Krauthoefer, D. Koster, and D. Caylor. 2007. Subsistence salmon harvest monitoring report, Kuskokwim Fisheries Management Area, Alaska, 2004. Division of Subsistence, Technical Paper Number 313. Alaska Department of Fish and Game, Juneau.

Stewart, R., D. B. Molyneaux, D. J. Costello, and D. Orabutt. 2006. George River salmon studies, 2005. Division of Commercial Fisheries, Fishery Data Series No. 06–29. Alaska Department of Fish and Game, Anchorage.

Stuby, L. 2006. Inriver abundance of Chinook salmon in the Kuskokwim River, 2005. Division of Commercial Fisheries, Fishery Data Series No. 06–45. Alaska Department of Fish and Game, Anchorage.

Walker, R. J., and M. W. Coffing. 1993. Subsistence salmon harvests in the Kuskokwim area during 1989. Division of Subsistence, Technical Paper Number 189. Alaska Department of Fish and Game, Juneau.

Whitmore, C., M. Martz, J. C. Linderman Jr., R. L. Fisher, and D. G. Bue. 2008. Annual management report for the subsistence and commercial fisheries of the Kuskokwim area, 2004. Division of Commercial Fisheries, Fisheries Management Report Number 08–25. Alaska Department of Fish and Game, Anchorage.

Zabkar, L. M., F. G. Harris, and K. C. Harper. 2005. Abundance and run timing of adult Pacific salmon in the Tuluksak River, Yukon Delta National Wildlife Refuge, Alaska, 2004. U.S. Fish and Wildlife Service, Kenai Fish and Wildlife Field Office. Alaska Fisheries Data Series Number 2005–6, Kenai, Alaska.

APPENDIX TABLE 1. Chinook salmon aerial survey (A) and weir escapement (W) counts in Kuskokwim River spawning tributaries, 1980–2006. Estimates are from "peak" aerial surveys conducted between 20 and 31 July with fair or good overall rankings. SEG refers to the formally established Sustainable Escapement Goal (ADF&G 2004). Dashes (—) indicate that field operations were incomplete; aerial and weir escapement surveys were not conducted.

Year	Eek	Kwethluk		Kisaralik	Tuluksak		Aniak	Kipchuk (Aniak)	Salmon (Aniak)	Holokuk	Oskawalik	George	Holitna	Kognukluk	Gagarayah	Cheeneetnuk	Tatlawiksuk	Takotna	Salmon (Pitka)
	(A)	(A)	(W)	(A)	(A)	(W)	(A)	(W)	(A)	(A)	(A)	(W)	(A)	(W)	(A)	(A)	(W)	(W)	(A)
1980	2,378	—	—	1,035	—	—	9,074	—	1,186	—	—	—	—	16,655	—	—	—	—	1,450
1981	—	2,034	—	672	—	—	—	—	—	—	—	—	521	10,993	—	—	—	—	1,439
1982	—	471	—	81	—	—	—	—	—	42	—	—	—	3,009	—	—	—	—	413
1983	188	—	—	—	202	—	1,909	—	231	33	—	—	1,069	4,928	—	—	—	—	572
1984	—	—	—	—	—	—	—	—	—	—	—	—	—	4,619	—	1,177	—	—	545
1985	1,118	51	—	63	142	—	—	—	—	135	—	—	—	5,038	—	1,002	—	—	620
1986	1,739	—	—	—	—	—	424	—	336	100	—	—	650	—	—	317	—	—	—
1987	2,255	—	—	—	—	—	—	193	516	210	193	—	—	8,505	205	—	—	—	473
1988	1,042	610	—	869	188	—	954	—	244	—	80	—	—	11,940	—	—	—	—	452
1989	—	—	—	152	—	—	2,109	994	631	157	113	—	—	10,218	—	—	—	—	—
1990	—	—	—	631	200	—	1,255	537	596	—	—	—	—	7,850	—	—	—	—	—
1991	1,312	—	—	217	358	697	1,564	885	583	—	—	—	—	6,755	—	—	—	—	—
1992	—	—	9,675	—	—	1,083	2,284	670	335	64	91	—	2,022	12,332	328	1,050	—	—	2,536
1993	—	—	—	1,243	—	2,218	2,687	1,248	1,082	114	103	—	1,573	15,227	419	678	—	—	1,010
1994	—	—	—	1,243	—	2,917	—	1,520	1,218	—	—	—	—	20,630	807	1,206	—	—	1,010
1995	—	—	—	—	—	—	3,171	1,215	1,446	181	326	—	1,887	14,199	1,193	1,565	—	—	1,911
1996	—	—	7,415	—	—	—	—	—	985	85	—	7,716	—	13,286	—	—	—	422	—
1997	—	—	10,395	—	—	—	2,187	855	980	165	1,470	7,823	2,093	12,107	—	345	—	1,161	—
1998	522	126	—	457	—	—	1,930	443	557	18	98	—	—	5,570	—	—	1,490	—	—
1999	—	—	—	—	—	—	—	—	—	—	—	3,548	—	3,310	—	—	—	—	—
2000	—	—	3,547	—	—	—	714	182	238	42	186	2,960	301	9,298	143	—	817	345	362
2001	—	—	—	—	—	997	—	—	598	—	—	3,309	1,130	10,104	—	—	2,010	721	1,033
2002	1,236	1,795	8,502	1,727	—	1,346	3,514	1,615	1,236	186	295	2,444	1,578	11,771	452	—	2,237	316	1,255
2003	4,653	2,628	14,474	654	94	1,064	5,569	1,493	1,242	528	844	4,693	4,842	19,503	1,095	810	1,683	378	1,391
2004	5,059	6,801	28,605	6,913	1,196	1,475	—	1,868	2,177	539	293	5,207	2,795	21,993	670	918	2,833	461	1,138
2005	—	5,059	—	4,112	672	2,653	—	1,944	4,097	510	582	3,845	—	19,414	788	1,155	2,918	499	1,809
2006	—	—	14,220	4,734	—	992	5,639	1,618	—	705	386	4,358	3,924	—	531	1,015	1,702	540	928
SEG	580-1,800	—	—	400-1,200	—	—	1,200-2,300	—	330-1,200	—	—	—	970-2,100	5,300-14,000	300-830	340-1,300	—	—	470-1,600
Average	1,312	989	9,089	680	166	1,083	1,909	855	614	107	120	3,548	1,344	10,059	504	810	1,683	400	1,021

APPENDIX TABLE 2. Harvest of Chinook salmon in the Kuskokwim River, 1970–2006. Commercial harvest estimates are for Districts 1 and 2 only. Subsistence harvest estimates after 1988 are not comparable with previous years. See Data Sources section for a description of the differences in the subsistence harvest estimation procedures. Subsistence and sport harvest for 2006 is based on the recent ten-year average. Dashes (—) indicate that field operations were incomplete; harvest estimates were not determined.

Year	Harvest				
	Commercial	Subsistence	Test	Sport	Total
1970	39,290	69,612	857	-	109,759
1971	40,274	43,242	756	-	84,272
1972	39,454	40,396	756	-	80,606
1973	32,838	39,093	577	-	72,508
1974	18,664	27,139	1,236	-	47,039
1975	22,135	48,448	704	-	71,287
1976	30,735	58,606	1,206	-	90,547
1977	35,830	56,580	1,264	33	93,707
1978	45,641	36,270	1,445	116	83,472
1979	38,966	56,283	979	74	96,302
1980	35,881	59,892	1,033	162	96,968
1981	47,663	61,329	1,218	189	110,399
1982	48,234	58,018	542	207	107,001
1983	33,174	47,412	1,139	420	82,145
1984	31,742	56,930	231	273	89,176
1985	37,889	43,874	79	85	81,927
1986	19,414	51,019	130	49	70,612
1987	36,179	67,325	384	355	104,243
1988	55,716	70,943	576	528	127,763

Appendix Table 2. Continued.

	Harvest				
Year	Commercial	Subsistence	Test	Sport	Total
1989	43,217	81,175	543	1,218	126,153
1990	53,504	85,976	512	394	140,386
1991	37,778	85,556	117	401	123,852
1992	46,872	64,794	1,380	367	113,413
1993	8,735	87,513	2,483	587	99,318
1994	16,211	93,243	1,937	1,139	112,530
1995	30,846	96,435	1,421	541	129,243
1996	7,419	78,062	247	1,432	87,160
1997	10,441	81,577	332	1,227	93,577
1998	17,359	81,264	210	1,434	100,267
1999	4,705	73,194	98	252	78,249
2000	444	64,893	64	105	65,506
2001	90	73,610	86	290	74,076
2002	72	66,807	288	319	67,486
2003	158	67,788	409	734	69,089
2004	2,300	80,065	691	1,197	84,253
2005	4,784	68,213	608	1,092	74,697
2006	2,777	73,547	352	808	77,485
Average					
(2002–2006)	2,018	71,284	470	830	74,602

APPENDIX TABLE 3. Harvest of chum salmon in the Kuskokwim River, 1970–2006. Commercial harvest estimates for Districts 1 and 2 only. Subsistence harvest 1970–1984 includes small numbers of Chinook, sockeye, and coho salmon. Test harvest for 1970 includes small numbers of sockeye. Subsistence harvest estimates after 1988 are not comparable with previous years. See Data Sources section for a description of the differences in the subsistence harvest estimation procedures. Subsistence and sport harvest for 2006 is based on the recent ten-year average. Dashes (—) indicate that field operations were incomplete; harvest estimates were not determined.

| Year | Harvest | | | | |
	Commercial	Subsistence	Test	Sport	Total
1970	1,664	246,810	857	-	249,613
1971	68,914	116,391	756	-	185,559
1972	78,619	120,316	756	-	199,421
1973	148,746	179,259	577	-	328,680
1974	171,887	277,170	1,236	-	451,078
1975	184,171	176,389	704	-	361,622
1976	177,864	223,792	1,206	-	403,757
1977	248,721	198,355	1,264	129	447,781
1978	248,656	118,809	1,445	555	370,173
1979	261,874	161,239	979	259	423,784
1980	483,751	165,172	1,033	324	651,305
1981	418,677	157,306	1,218	598	578,374
1982	278,306	190,011	542	1,125	469,946
1983	276,698	146,876	1,139	922	425,565
1984	423,718	142,542	231	520	567,966
1985	199,478	94,750	79	150	294,994
1986	309,213	141,931	130	245	453,082
1987	574,336	70,709	384	566	647,913

APPENDIX TABLE 3. Continued.

| Year | Harvest | | | | |
	Commercial	Subsistence	Test	Sport	Total
1988	1,381,674	151,967	576	764	1,538,784
1989	749,182	139,672	543	2,023	892,959
1990	461,624	126,509	512	533	590,773
1991	431,802	93,077	117	378	526,188
1992	344,603	96,491	1,380	608	457,032
1993	43,337	59,394	2,483	359	111,541
1994	271,115	72,022	1,937	1,280	356,415
1995	605,918	67,861	1,421	226	691,478
1996	207,877	88,966	247	280	299,987
1997	17,026	39,987	332	86	57,889
1998	207,809	63,537	210	291	272,777
1999	23,006	43,601	98	180	67,349
2000	11,570	51,696	64	26	64,330
2001	1,272	49,874	86	112	53,001
2002	1,900	69,019	288	53	73,638
2003	2,764	43,320	409	67	47,864
2004	20,429	52,374	691	117	74,730
2005	69,139	46,036	608	608	120,242
2006	44,070	54,841	352	182	102,640
Average					
(2002–2006)	27,660	53,118	470	205	83,823

APPENDIX TABLE 4. Harvest of sockeye salmon in the Kuskokwim River, 1970–2006. Commercial harvest estimates are for Districts 1 and 2 only. Subsistence harvest estimates after 1988 are not comparable with previous years. See Data Sources section for a description of the differences in the subsistence harvest estimation procedures. Subsistence and sport harvest for 2006 is based on the recent ten-year average. Dashes (—) indicate that field operations were incomplete; harvest estimates were not determined.

| | Harvest | | | | |
Year	Commercial	Subsistence	Test	Sport	Total
1970	117				117
1971	2,606				2,606
1972	102				102
1973	369				369
1974	136				136
1975	23				23
1976	2,971				2,971
1977	9,379				9,379
1978	733				733
1979	1,054				1,054
1980	360				360
1981	48,375				48,375
1982	33,154				33,154
1983	68,855			41	68,896
1984	48,575			-	48,575
1985	106,647			72	106,719
1986	95,433			196	95,629
1987	136,602			217	136,819
1988	92,025			291	92,316

APPENDIX TABLE 4. Continued.

| Year | Harvest | | | | |
	Commercial	Subsistence	Test	Sport	Total
1989	42,747	35,224		33	78,004
1990	84,870	36,274		61	121,205
1991	108,946	52,982		38	161,966
1992	92,218	32,065		131	124,414
1993	27,008	49,347		348	76,703
1994	49,365	37,159		359	86,883
1995	92,500	27,792		95	120,387
1996	33,878	34,214		315	68,407
1997	21,989	40,078		423	62,490
1998	60,906	35,426		178	96,510
1999	16,976	46,677		54	63,707
2000	4,130	41,783		46	45,959
2001	84	50,065	510	231	50,890
2002	84	25,499	228	42	25,853
2003	282	34,452	0	140	34,874
2004	9,748	32,433	742	400	43,323
2005	27,645	34,129	1,062	636	63,472
2006	12,618	30,226	519	231	43,594
Average					
(2002–2006)	7,569	35,316	508	290	43,682

APPENDIX TABLE 5. Harvest of coho salmon in the Kuskokwim River, 1970–2006. Commercial harvest estimates are for Districts 1 and 2 only. Subsistence harvest estimates after 1988 are not comparable with previous years. See Data Sources section for a description of the differences in the subsistence harvest estimation procedures. Subsistence and sport harvest for 2006 is based on the recent ten-year average. Dashes (—) indicate that field operations were incomplete; harvest estimates were not determined.

	Harvest				
Year	Commercial	Subsistence	Test	Sport	Total
1970	38,601				
1971	5,253				
1972	22,579				
1973	130,876				
1974	147,269				
1975	81,945				
1976	88,501				
1977	241,364				
1978	213,393				
1979	219,060				
1980	222,012				
1981	211,251				
1982	447,117				
1983	196,287			1,375	197,662
1984	623,447			1,442	624,889
1985	335,606			136	335,742
1986	659,988			1,222	661,210
1987	399,467			1,767	401,234
1988	524,296			927	525,223

APPENDIX TABLE 5. Continued.

Year	Harvest				
	Commercial	Subsistence	Test	Sport	Total
1989	479,856	52,857		2,459	535,172
1990	410,332	44,786		581	455,699
1991	500,935	50,369		1,003	552,307
1992	666,170	40,167		1,692	708,029
1993	610,739	31,737		980	643,456
1994	724,689	33,050		1,925	759,664
1995	471,461	36,276		1,497	509,234
1996	937,299	32,742		3,423	973,464
1997	130,803	29,035	33,703	2,408	195,949
1998	210,481	24,864	-	2,419	237,764
1999	23,593	25,004	213	1,998	50,808
2000	261,379	33,786	2,828	1,689	299,682
2001	192,998	29,504	1,723	1,204	225,429
2002	83,463	32,780	2,484	2,030	120,757
2003	284,064	35,240	570	3,244	323,118
2004	433,809	35,735	2,259	4,996	476,799
2005	142,319	27,613	1,499	3,539	174,970
2006	185,598	30,706	1,186	1,474	218,964
Average					
(2002–2006)	233,005	32,443	1,894	2,784	270,126

APPENDIX TABLE 6. Annual Chinook salmon harvest for Quinhagak (District 4), Kuskokwim Bay, 1970–2006. Subsistence harvest estimates are for the community of Quinhagak. Subsistence harvest estimates after 1988 are not comparable with previous years. See Data Sources section for a description of the differences in the subsistence harvest estimation procedures.

| Year | Harvest | | | |
	Commercial	Subsistence	Sport	Total
1970	18,269			18,269
1971	4,185			4,185
1972	15,880			15,880
1973	14,993			14,993
1974	8,704			8,704
1975	3,928			3,928
1976	14,110			14,110
1977	19,090	2,012		21,102
1978	12,335	2,328		14,663
1979	11,144	1,420		12,564
1980	10,387	1,940		12,327
1981	24,524	2,562		27,086
1982	22,106	2,402		24,508
1983	46,385	2,542	1,511	50,438
1984	33,633	3,109	922	37,664
1985	30,401	2,341	672	33,414
1986	22,835	2,682	938	26,455
1987	26,022	3,663	508	30,193
1988	13,883	3,690	1,910	19,483
1989	20,820	3,542	884	25,246
1990	27,644	6,013	503	34,160
1991	9,480	3,693	316	13,489
1992	17,197	3,447	656	21,300
1993	15,784	3,368	1,006	20,158
1994	8,564	3,995	751	13,310
1995	38,584	2,746	739	42,069
1996	14,165	3,075	689	17,929
1997	35,510	3,433	1,632	40,575
1998	23,158	4,041	1,475	28,674
1999	18,426	3,167	854	22,447
2000	21,229	3,106	833	25,168
2001	12,775	2,923	947	16,645
2002	11,480	2,475	779	14,734
2003	14,444	3,898	323	18,665
2004	25,465	3,726	228	29,419
2005	24,195	3,083	520	27,798
2006	19,004	3,521	754	23,279
Average (2002–2006)	18,898 3,341	521	22,779	

APPENDIX TABLE 7. Annual chum salmon harvest for Quinhagak (District 4), Kuskokwim Bay, 1970–2006. Subsistence harvest estimates are for the community of Quinhagak. Subsistence harvest estimates after 1988 are not comparable with previous years. See Data Sources section for a description of the differences in the subsistence harvest estimation procedures.

	Harvest			
Year	Commercial	Subsistence	Sport	Total
1970	46,556			46,556
1971	30,208			30,208
1972	17,247			17,247
1973	19,680			19,680
1974	15,298			15,298
1975	35,233			35,233
1976	43,659			43,659
1977	43,707			43,707
1978	24,798			24,798
1979	25,995			25,995
1980	65,984			65,984
1981	53,334			53,334
1982	34,346			34,346
1983	23,090		315	23,405
1984	50,422		376	50,798
1985	20,418	901	149	21,468
1986	29,700	808	777	31,285
1987	8,557	1,084	111	9,752
1988	29,220	1,065	618	30,903
1989	39,395	1,568	537	41,500
1990	47,717	3,234	202	51,153
1991	54,493	1,593	80	56,166
1992	73,383	1,833	251	75,467
1993	40,943	1,008	183	42,134
1994	61,301	1,452	156	62,909
1995	81,462	686	213	82,361
1996	83,005	930	200	84,135
1997	38,445	600	212	39,257
1998	45,095	1,448	213	46,756
1999	38,091	1,810	293	40,194
2000	30,553	912	231	31,696
2001	17,209	747	43	17,999
2002	29,252	1,839	446	31,537
2003	27,868	1,129	14	29,011
2004	25,820	1,112	33	26,965
2005	13,529	915	108	14,552
2006	39,191	1,865	145	41,201
Average (2002–2006)	27,132	1,372	149	28,653

Appendix Table 8. Annual sockeye salmon harvest for Quinhagak (District 4), Kuskokwim Bay, 1970–2006. Subsistence harvest estimates are for the community of Quinhagak. Subsistence harvest estimates after 1988 are not comparable with previous years. See Data Sources section for a description of the differences in the subsistence harvest estimation procedures.

| Year | Harvest | | | |
	Commercial	Subsistence	Sport	Total
1970	5,393			5,393
1971	3,118			3,118
1972	3,286			3,286
1973	2,783			2,783
1974	19,510			19,510
1975	8,584			8,584
1976	6,090			6,090
1977	5,519			5,519
1978	7,589			7,589
1979	18,828			18,828
1980	13,221			13,221
1981	17,292			17,292
1982	25,685			25,685
1983	10,263		0	10,263
1984	17,255		143	17,398
1985	7,876	106	12	7,994
1986	21,484	423	200	22,107
1987	6,489	1,067	153	7,709
1988	21,556	1,261	109	22,926
1989	20,582	633	101	21,316
1990	83,681	1,951	462	86,094
1991	53,657	1,772	88	55,517
1992	60,929	1,264	66	62,259
1993	80,934	1,082	331	82,347
1994	72,314	1,000	313	73,627
1995	68,194	573	148	68,915
1996	57,665	1,467	335	59,467
1997	69,562	1,264	607	71,433
1998	41,382	1,702	942	44,026
1999	41,315	2,021	496	43,832
2000	68,557	1,088	694	70,339
2001	33,807	1,525	83	35,415
2002	17,802	1,099	73	18,974
2003	33,941	1,622	107	35,670
2004	34,627	1,086	112	35,825
2005	68,801	1,633	156	70,590
2006	106,424	2,177	523	109,124
Average (2002-2006)	52,319	1,523	194	54,037

APPENDIX TABLE 9. Annual coho salmon harvest for Quinhagak (District 4), Kuskokwim Bay, 1970–2006. Subsistence harvest estimates are for the community of Quinhagak. Subsistence harvest estimates after 1988 are not comparable with previous years. See Data Sources section for a description of the differences in the subsistence harvest estimation procedures.

| Year | Harvest | | | |
	Commercial	Subsistence	Sport	Total
1970	16,850			16,850
1971	2,982			2,982
1972	376			376
1973	16,515			16,515
1974	10,979			10,979
1975	10,742			10,742
1976	13,777			13,777
1977	9,028			9,028
1978	20,114			20,114
1979	47,525			47,525
1980	62,610			62,610
1981	47,551			47,551
1982	73,652			73,652
1983	32,442		367	32,809
1984	132,151		1,895	134,046
1985	29,992	67	622	30,681
1986	57,544	41	2,010	59,595
1987	50,070	125	2,300	52,495
1988	68,605	4,317	1,837	74,759
1989	44,607	3,787	1,096	49,490
1990	26,926	4,174	644	31,744
1991	42,571	3,232	358	46,161
1992	86,404	2,958	275	89,637
1993	55,817	2,152	734	58,703
1994	83,912	2,739	675	87,326
1995	66,203	2,561	970	69,734
1996	118,718	1,467	875	121,060
1997	32,862	1,264	1,220	35,346
1998	80,183	1,702	751	82,636
1999	6,184	2,021	1,091	9,296
2000	30,529	1,088	799	32,416
2001	18,531	1,525	2,448	22,504
2002	26,695	1,099	1,784	29,578
2003	49,833	2,047	1,076	52,956
2004	82,398	1,209	1,362	84,969
2005	51,708	1,443	1,006	54,157
2006	53,714	1,019	1,742	56,475
Average (2002–2006)	52,870	1,363	1,394	55,627

APPENDIX TABLE 10. Annual Chinook salmon harvest for Goodnews Bay (District 5), Kuskokwim Bay, 1970–2006. Subsistence harvest estimates are for the community of Goodnews Bay. Subsistence harvest estimates after 1988 are not comparable with previous years. See Data Sources section for a description of the differences in the subsistence harvest estimation procedures. Dashes (—) indicate that field operations were incomplete; harvest estimates were not determined.

	Harvest			
Year	Commercial	Subsistence	Sport	Total
1970	7,163			7,163
1971	477			477
1972	264			264
1973	3,543			3,543
1974	3,302			3,302
1975	2,156			2,156
1976	4,417			4,417
1977	3,336	574		3,910
1978	5,218	—		5,218
1979	3,204	338		3,542
1980	2,331	690		3,021
1981	7,190	1,409		8,599
1982	9,476	1,236		10,712
1983	14,117	1,066	31	15,214
1984	8,612	629	—	9,241
1985	5,793	426	323	6,542
1986	2,723	555	—	3,278
1987	3,357	816	—	4,173
1988	4,964	310		5,274
1989	2,966	467	—	3,501
1990	3,303	539	—	3,842
1991	912	917	26	1,855
1992	3,528	374	23	3,925
1993	2,117	708	81	2,906
1994	2,570	784	163	3,517
1995	2,922	883	41	3,846
1996	1,375	415	157	1,947
1997	2,039	449	86	2,574
1998	3,675	718	431	4,824
1999	1,888	871	223	2,982
2000	4,442	703	243	5,388
2001	1,519	895	147	2,561
2002	979	857	224	2,060
2003	1,412	737	10	2,159
2004	2,565	954	100	3,619
2005	2,035	868	0	2,903
2006	2,899	676	79	3,654
Average (2002–2006)	1,978	818	83	2,879

APPENDIX TABLE 11. Annual chum salmon harvest for Goodnews Bay (District 5), Kuskokwim Bay, 1970–2006. Subsistence harvest estimates are for the community of Goodnews Bay. Subsistence harvest estimates after 1988 are not comparable with previous years. See Data Sources section for a description of the differences in the subsistence harvest estimation procedures. Dashes (—) indicate that field operations were incomplete; harvest estimates were not determined.

| Year | Harvest | | | |
	Commercial	Subsistence	Sport	Total
1970	12,346			12,346
1971	301			301
1972	1,331			1,331
1973	15,781			15,781
1974	8,942			8,942
1975	5,904			5,904
1976	10,354			10,354
1977	6,531			6,531
1978	8,590			8,590
1979	9,298			9,298
1980	11,748			11,748
1981	13,642			13,642
1982	13,829			13,829
1983	6,766		10	6,776
1984	14,340		—	14,340
1985	4,784	348	124	5,256
1986	10,355	191	—	10,546
1987	20,381	578	—	20,959
1988	33,059	448	—	33,507
1989	13,622	784	0	14,406
1990	13,194	332	—	13,526
1991	15,892	149	189	16,230
1992	18,520	1,006	0	19,526
1993	10,657	188	156	11,001
1994	28,477	470	15	28,962
1995	19,832	155	0	19,987
1996	11,093	219	0	11,312
1997	11,729	133	24	11,886
1998	14,155	316	50	14,521
1999	11,562	281	47	11,890
2000	7,450	364	12	7,826
2001	3,412	226	21	3,659
2002	3,799	407	99	4,305
2003	5,593	176	0	5,769
2004	6,014	257	0	6,271
2005	2,568	208	0	2,776
2006	11,678	648	0	12,326
Average (2002–2006)	5,930	339	29	6,289

APPENDIX TABLE 12. Annual sockeye salmon harvest for Goodnews Bay (District 5), Kuskokwim Bay, 1970–2006. Subsistence harvest estimates are for the community of Goodnews Bay. Subsistence harvest estimates after 1988 are not comparable with previous years. See Data Sources section for a description of the differences in the subsistence harvest estimation procedures. Dashes (—) indicate that field operations were incomplete; harvest estimates were not determined.

	Harvest			
Year	Commercial	Subsistence	Sport	Total
1970	7,144			7,144
1971	330			330
1972	924			924
1973	2,072			2,072
1974	9,357			9,357
1975	9,098			9,098
1976	5,575			5,575
1977	3,723			3,723
1978	5,412			5,412
1979	19,581			19,581
1980	28,632			28,632
1981	40,273			40,273
1982	38,877			38,877
1983	11,716		14	11,730
1984	15,474		—	15,474
1985	6,698	704	75	7,477
1986	25,112	943	122	26,177
1987	27,758	955	266	28,979
1988	36,368	1,065	—	37,433
1989	19,299	861	146	20,306
1990	35,823	1,123	—	36,946
1991	39,838	1,282	63	41,183
1992	39,194	827	8	40,029
1993	59,293	835	53	60,181
1994	69,490	770	70	70,330
1995	37,351	253	34	37,638
1996	30,717	352	87	31,156
1997	31,451	397	61	31,909
1998	27,161	331	502	27,994
1999	22,910	582	561	24,053
2000	37,252	517	82	37,851
2001	25,654	616	108	26,378
2002	6,304	297	149	6,750
2003	29,423	783	42	30,248
2004	20,922	960	0	21,882
2005	23,933	1,233	0	25,166
2006	29,858	1,007	98	30,963
Average (2002–2006)	22,088	856	58	23,002

APPENDIX TABLE 13. Annual coho salmon harvest for Goodnews Bay (District 5), Kuskokwim Bay, 1970–2006. Subsistence harvest estimates are for the community of Goodnews Bay. Subsistence harvest estimates after 1988 are not comparable with previous years. See Data Sources section for a description of the differences in the subsistence harvest estimation procedures. Dashes (—) indicate that field operations were incomplete; harvest estimates were not determined.

| Year | Harvest | | | |
	Commercial	Subsistence	Sport	Total
1970	6,794			6,794
1971	1,771			1,771
1972	925			925
1973	5,017			5,017
1974	21,340			21,340
1975	17,889			17,889
1976	9,852			9,852
1977	13,335			13,335
1978	13,764			13,764
1979	42,098			42,098
1980	43,256			43,256
1981	19,749			19,749
1982	46,683			46,683
1983	19,660		168	19,828
1984	71,176		—	71,176
1985	16,498	221	386	17,105
1986	19,378	8	—	19,386
1987	29,057	43	—	29,100
1988	30,832	1,162	—	31,994
1989	31,849	907	224	32,980
1990	7,804	1,646	—	9,450
1991	13,312	1,828	297	15,437
1992	19,875	1,353	138	21,366
1993	20,014	1,226	189	21,429
1994	47,499	512	170	48,181
1995	17,875	305	114	18,294
1996	43,836	352	466	44,654
1997	2,983	397	855	4,235
1998	21,246	331	574	22,151
1999	2,474	582	789	3,845
2000	15,531	517	795	16,843
2001	9,275	616	822	10,713
2002	3,041	297	429	3,767
2003	12,658	1,319	681	14,658
2004	23,690	1,617	622	25,929
2005	11,735	839	1,046	13,620
2006	12,561	704	553	13,818
Average (2002–2006)	12,737	955	666	14,358

American Fisheries Society Symposium 70:601–609, 2009

A Perspective on Ecosystem-Based Fishery Management of the Kuskokwim River: a 2015 Vision of the Future

MICHAEL REARDEN* AND DANIEL GILLIKIN

*Yukon Delta National Wildlife Refuge, U.S. Fish and Wildlife Service
P. O. Box 346, Bethel, Alaska 99559, USA*

Abstract.—In this chapter, we discuss our perspective regarding ecosystem approaches to salmon management and the specific types of information required to support these approaches. The development of an ecosystem-based fishery management plan is proposed with a vision of where salmon management could be in the year 2015. Ecosystem management should not be deemed impossible because of incomplete and unavailable information. Instead, research should focus on key drivers, forces, and processes that affect ecosystem resilience and production of ecosystem services (e.g., salmon). Ecosystem management should include a commitment to assessment as an integral part of management so that learning about the systems can occur while they are being managed. Based on our current knowledge, development of a management plan using ecosystem concepts should begin for the Kuskokwim River and its tributaries. Our 2015 vision for the future includes accurate forecasting of salmon runs, fulfillment of subsistence needs both upriver and downriver, strong markets for commercial fisheries, escapement goals being met, and a strong involvement from local residents educated in fishery and ecosystem sciences.

Introduction

Sustainability is a goal that everyone desires—for example, the Arctic Yukon Kuskokwim Sustainable Salmon Initiative, the sponsor of this symposium, uses this concept within its name. One can argue about "how" to achieve the sustainability of salmon populations, but in the end, sustainability of salmon for future generations is what everyone wants. Sustainability is a shared value among subsistence, commercial, and sport users of the salmon resource, and shared among rural residents and state and federal managers. Concerns about, and failures of, current management strategies of salmon fisheries elsewhere (e.g., Ludwig

et al. 1993) have many people thinking that ecosystem management is a better approach that might yield more successes (e.g., Fluharty et al. 1998) and insure sustainability of salmon resources. Ecosystem management is a concept that has been around for a long time but until recently has not been applied well.

This chapter discusses ecosystem approaches to salmon management and the specific types of information required to support these approaches. The development of an ecosystem-based fishery management plan is proposed, followed by a vision of where salmon management could be in the year 2015. A description of the Kuskokwim River fishery is provided by Linderman and Bergstrom (2009, this volume).

*Corresponding author: Michael_Rearden@fws.gov

Fishery Management from an Ecosystem Perspective

The first cry we often hear when the subject of ecosystem management is raised is that, "ecosystems are too complex to understand, much less to use as a concept to manage a fishery," and they throw up their arms and declare "it is impossible." Interestingly in spite of this common belief, some managers just go ahead, make the attempt, and learn as they go; a good example of this approach is the work of the North Pacific Fisheries Management Council. The Council is taking an ecosystems approach to fishery management in the Alaskan Exclusive Economic Zone (NPFMC 2006).

Ecosystem management approaches should not be deemed impossible because of incomplete information. Instead, ecosystem management approaches should include a commitment to assessment as an integral part of management so that learning about the behavior of complex systems can occur (Walters 1986). Certainly, if we must fully understand every detail, interaction, and process to manage ecosystems, then ecosystem management would be impossible. If, however, the focus is on only the major drivers and forces within the ecosystem that directly affect fish populations, then the amount of knowledge required becomes feasible to acquire, and management of fish populations from an ecosystem management perspective becomes conceivable. Research should focus on the key processes that affect ecosystem resilience, and provisions of ecosystem services (e.g., salmon). Ecosystem resilience refers to the ability of a healthy ecosystem to absorb a wide range of disturbances (fire, flood, harvest levels) without fundamentally changing its structure or species composition (Gunderson et al. 2002; Holling 2001). Alternately, a system with little resilience, may be pushed into a new state or regime

by overharvesting, such as in the case of the Newfoundland cod fishery, resulting in a loss of ecological services to human culture (Gunderson and Holling 2002).

Ecosystem management of salmon in the freshwater portion of their habitat seems to be met often with resistance by managers and their agencies, yet the marine fishery agencies managing ocean coastal waters are already implementing such an approach to management. In the Alaskan marine waters, the NOAA—Fisheries (National Oceanic and Atmospheric Administration; formerly National Marine Fisheries Service or NMFS) and the North Pacific Fisheries Management Council have been recognized as being highly successful in the application of ecosystem-based fishery management within highly complex marine systems (USCOP 2004) For example, ecosystem-based management and sustainability are among the core objectives of the North Pacific Fisheries Management Council (NPFMC 2002). Also, NMFS, as directed by the Sustainable Fisheries Act (1996), established an Ecosystem Principles Advisory Panel with guidance from the National Research Council (Fluharty et al. 1998; NRC 2004). If ecosystem-based management can be done in complex marine fisheries, why does it receive such resistance when applied to management of salmon?

If we understand the basic drivers and their effects on the ecosystem, then we should be able manage the harvest of salmon to ensure sustainability of the resource. Our ability to manage using ecosystem concepts will be the result of understanding the various processes that change in time and space that affect salmon populations within rivers, drainages, and regions. Research, the acquisition of new information, focused on the major drivers of the ecosystem that directly affect fish populations, is a critical requirement if this approach to management is to advance. Fortunately, research at the ecosystem level is promoted and being funded by Arctic-Yukon-Kuskokwim Sustainable Salmon Initiative (AYK SSI; Sustainable Salmon Initiative 2006).

As managers of a National Wildlife Refuge, with a mandate to manage for the diversity of many species and their habitats (USFWS 1988), we find the current single species paradigm of salmon management contrary to the management goals of the refuge and other federal conservation units, and out of step with the "best available science" standard that ought to inform management (NRC 2004). Problems exist as a result of the mismatch between managing for single species for maximum sustained yield, and mandates for ecosystem management and conservation. For example, little concern currently exists within salmon management as to whether brown bears on the Kwethluk River (a tributary to the Kuskokwim River) are getting enough salmon to eat. Current salmon management does not consider that populations of resident fish need to receive sufficient marine-derived nutrients from the carcasses of returning salmon. Similarly, we do not ensure that the salmon carcasses will provide critical nutrients to fuel riparian vegetation. Riparian vegetation directly feeds herbivores, such as beavers, and feeds organisms such as aquatic insects indirectly through leaf litter. Beavers actively engineer salmon habitat and significantly influence successional pathways, and increase productivity by creating more productive and complex salmon habitats. Aquatic insects, of course, feed juvenile salmon.

To meet our goals, we must learn more about the ecological relationships within the salmon ecosystem, and discover new ways to conserve biodiversity. We, as managers of critically important sustainable resources, *must* use the best available science to meet our mandates. Success in this endeavor comes with healthy, diverse ecosystems, which are resilient and resistant to change.

Information Needs for Kuskokwim River Salmon Management

Within many subject areas, we lack a basic understanding of processes and relationships among biotic and abiotic components of complex salmon ecosystems. This lack of understanding is especially true for the unstudied (mostly) and remote systems, such as the Kuskokwim River watershed. Progress, however, is being made. The first steps to guide research were made through the Kuskokwim Fisheries Resource Coalition which identified and documented critical research priorities within their publication *Gap Analysis for the Kuskokwim Area Salmon Research Plan* (KFRC 2006). The coalition included a diverse group of subsistence, commercial, and sport fishers, and state and federal managers. Similarly, the goal stated in the AYK SSI Salmon Research and Restoration Plan is: "to understand the trends and causes of variation in salmon abundance..." (Sustainable Salmon Initiative 2006). The AYK SSI program seeks to promote exploration of system-level research hypotheses and questions within not only the Kuskokwim River basin but also in the Yukon River basin and Norton Sound. These two planning efforts have helped to guide the funding of research through the AYK SSI program. As a result, a number of studies have been initiated at the proper scale and scope to address ecosystem-level processes. The development of basin-wide population estimates for salmon, work on juvenile salmon outmigrations, analysis of run reconstructions, studies of the effects of hydrogeomorphological processes on juvenile salmon, and investigations of population genetics of salmon are all contributing to that progress.

These plans (KFRC 2006; Sustainable Salmon Initiative 2006) have the correct focus but the translation of their priorities into funding of projects can be problematic. For example, many of the biological and physical elements of the Kuskokwim River ecosystem have still only been superficially investigated. By our accounting, only 12 of the last 33 AYK SSI funded projects since 2002 could be categorized into this ecosystem-level category. Of course, it might not be quite fair to hold all projects in the past to the standard of plans that were just finalized in 2006. Most of the past projects have focused mainly on the evaluation of current and past salmon abundance, demographics, and harvest. Only a few projects have looked at ecological relationships and processes related to salmon abundance. Research of the latter type is expensive and generally takes years to conduct; however, these types of projects should be given a high priority in the future. If we follow the direction given by the KFRC plan and the AYK SSI Research and Restoration Plan, we can gain a thorough (albeit imperfect) understanding of the forces driving salmon abundance. Once accomplished, it will be time to move on to the next critical step… a plan of management action.

Need for Fishery Ecosystem Management Plan for the Kuskokwim River

The best way to begin to meet the shared vision of sustainability is to develop and implement an ecosystem management plan for the salmon fisheries of the Kuskokwim Basin. The Kuskokwim River fishery ecosystem is an open system with ever-changing boundaries. Ecosystems cannot be understood from a single time, space, or complexity perspective. An ecosystem plan for the Kuskokwim River will have to be adaptive, responsive to changing environmental conditions or human systems, and flexible enough to continually incorporate new knowledge. The plan should specify biological thresholds, or trigger points based on assessment indices that will

mandate management actions to prevent the ecosystem from moving to a condition that it will be unable to recover from and return to its previous state.

A 2015 Vision of the Future

Annually, all of the agencies that participate in salmon management on the Kuskokwim River basin have a meeting after the summer and early fall fisheries. A report is developed and presented that describes how the fishery was regulated in-season combined with details of the fishery that resulted, including the catch per unit effort, total harvest, and escapement numbers in Kuskokwim and its tributaries. At the most recent postseason meeting, and after the 40th bar graph, we started daydreaming and began wondering what that report might be like in 2015. The report, in our vision of the future, went something like this…

Post-season management report in 2015

The past summer was a good year for the Kuskokwim fisheries. Salmon returns in numbers were 12% above the last ten-year average and the 5th highest on record. Commercial harvest was 25% above the last ten-year average and fishermen were pleased. The $1.50/lb paid for chum salmon *Oncorhynchus keta* for the burgeoning fresh-frozen fish market in China brought several million dollars to the local Kuskokwim-basin economy. The coho salmon *O. kisutch* run was, as expected, characterized by a late return of smaller-than-average fish, and was the result of warm-water temperatures and reduced productivity on the Bering Shelf. The return of coho salmon, however, proved to not be of great concern to local residents because the run characteristics were anticipated based on the forecasts made the previous winter. The development of new markets for chum salmon allowed the fishery to target the strong returns of this species and eased the need to fish coho salmon. Nearly 100,000 Chinook salmon *O. tshawytscha* were once again harvested by subsistence users over the length of the river and, from all reports, subsistence needs were met, even those in upriver villages.

The fishery was managed for the third year using ecologically based escapement targets or goals (Piccolo et al. 2009). Whereas, the effects of these new targets will not be known for several years, the participants in the fisheries are willing to support the targets so as to assure future sustainability of the salmon fisheries. The newly developed rapid genetic analysis procedures, paired with chemical analysis of otoliths, allowed accurate detection of the stream-origins of salmon in the fisheries, and thus allowed managers to protect important stocks. Much of this success was a result of the cooperative efforts of the state and federal genetics laboratories. The new escapement targets were combined with new assessment techniques. New stations along the river were established that incorporated sonar, videography, and automated image recognition software, and these stations permitted accurate counts of returning fish. The new approaches to assessment helped to evaluate the effects of in-season management actions and provided information to adjust fishery regulations to protect stocks.

Escapement goals for salmon were not met for every stream. Management continues to have difficulty in estimating total run strength by stock, and to effectively direct harvests of commercial and subsistence fisheries to the most robust and resilient salmon stocks in the system. Several short-term open seasons for commercial fishing in late June took too many George River chum salmon and more Kwethluk River sockeye salmon than expected. More time is needed to refine these new tools and integrate them into our management. Of course, under this new paradigm of ecosystem management, errors are expected.

The management system in place has an explicit approach to assessing and managing uncertainty. As in any ecosystem management strategy, the uncertainty that exists increases the risk of making wrong decisions. Thus, a precautionary, proactive approach is now a key element to management of salmon fisheries in the Kuskokwim River and its tributaries. Once managers were able to distinguish critical stocks in the various fisheries they decided the most effective tool they had to manage for future uncertainty was to end the era of unregulated harvest on stocks of unknown origin. Zone closures, timing windows, gear restrictions and harvest reporting requirements for all user groups were instituted as precautions against overharvesting.

Long-term studies on the Kwethluk River, conducted by the University of Montana through the SaRON (Salmonid Rivers Observatory Network; Stanford 2004) continued this past season. Their work provides us a robust understanding of trophic structure, food web dynamics, nutrient cycling, and habitat use that is critical to juvenile salmon. The SaRON project also continues to demonstrate a clear linkage between the terrestrial and aquatic environments, and how gemorphological and hydrological processes, ultimately, define the productivity of these ecosystems. The concepts, classifications and methods developed through SaRON have begun to be applied to the entire basin. This application will allow the estimation of the intrinsic carrying capacities of individual watersheds and identify watersheds that may be below theoretical capacity. One of the greatest advances in management has been the development of new ecosystem-based salmon escapement targets. These targets were developed through the integration of measures of marine productivity and freshwater habitat carrying capacity.

Because of past research, many of the influences that control salmon abundance are better understood and prediction of salmon returns are improving. This year the predictions came close to the returns of salmon that actually occurred within the Kuskokwim watershed. Currently, the most effective regulatory approach is the manipulation of the fishing effort, selectivity, and the timing of the salmon harvest. This season, with accurate forecasting, processors and buyers were able to allocate their resources more efficiently and deliver new products to new markets. The increase in processor profits provided the fishery higher prices for salmon than in the past.

Reflections on the years prior to 2015

The years prior to this 2015 report were characterized by a lot of dissention and controversy while the ecosystem-based fishery plan was being developed. Ideological and turf conflicts erupted. Fishermen were angry about regulations because the restrictions were based on what they considered a "voodoo science" that incorrectly predicted the strength of future runs. Slowly the salmon-run forecasts became more accurate than in those early years, and as they did, the fishermen became more confident in the new techniques. As time passed, they responded with support for changing the direction of salmon management towards ecosystem management.

Cooperation and collaboration of all stakeholders was a requirement for the successful development and acceptance of ecosystem management in the Kuskokwim basin. The development of our Kuskokwim ecosystem-based management plan was aided significantly by the many Alaska Native people that attained fishery management degrees through the Alaska Native Science and Engineering Program (University of Alaska; http://ansep.uaa.alaska.edu/). In addition, the AYK SSI was the first major organization to step forward with funding for that program in the summer of 2006. This step was a ma-

jor new investment in developing the capacity of local residents to participate in fishery research and assessment studies (Figure 1). By 2012, many of the biologists and managers working on the Kuskokwim plan were Alaska Native people. Culturally, they already had the basis for comprehension of the ecosystem management process and when combined with education in ecosystem, community, and population biology and ecology, they became leaders in the development, and owners of, the plan (Figure 2).

The new plan and its implementation embraces the idea that management occurs in an uncertain world, and therefore, must be adaptable to surprises. This approach promotes learning and expects that flexibility in management is required in a changing environment. For example, this last year an unexpected threat to the Kuskokwim basin from mining arose, which was successfully met.

During the late spring of 2015, a large mining company proposed development of an open pit, cyanide-leach gold mine in the headwaters of the Holitna, the biggest fish producer in the Kuskokwim River drainage. The agencies, fisheries participants, and environmentalists successfully fought back with sound data accumulated from years of research. One of the basic principles of our plan was employed—habitat protection as "insurance" for salmon sustainability. As a result, the State of Alaska declared the Holitna Basin, a conservation reserve, protecting in perpetuity the "fish basket" of the Kuskokwim.

Lastly, the development of an ecosystem-based fishery management plan in 2012 for the Bering Sea allayed many of our concerns about interception fisheries affecting returns to the Kuskokwim River and its tributaries. Meetings between the Kuskokwim fishery managers and the managers of the Bering Sea Ecosystem have occurred regularly for the last three years. As a result, management

FIGURE 1. Capacity building by involving local residents in research and monitoring projects will facilitate collaboration between fishery managers and the various user groups. Left, Adam Fisher of Kwethluk and Darryl Sipary of Saint Mary's assist Jim Finn from U.S. Geological Survey on the Kwethluk River, tributary to the Kuskokwim River. At right, Alaska Native Science and Engineering Program Intern Gunner Oyoumick from Unalakleet maintains the adult salmon counting weir on the Kwethluk River.

FIGURE 2. Educating youth about complex issues and the factors that influence salmon abundance is needed for the next generation of "users" to make informed decisions about their resources. Above, Yukon Delta National Wildlife Refuge fish biologist Dan Gillikin talks to Science Camp Students about watersheds and fluvial geomorphology at the headwaters of the Kwethluk River.

actions are now coordinated consistent with the management plans for both regions. Essentially the entire region (the Kuskokwim River basin, Bering Sea, and North Pacific) where salmon hatch, grow, and return to spawn is now regarded, and managed, as one complete ecosystem.

Conclusion

Hopefully, our ponderings of the future will become reality and the AYK SSI symposium on salmon held in February of 2007 will be remembered as where collaboration really started—when awareness of the potential of ecosystem management began to be realized. We believe that all the symposium participants were at a watershed moment during that symposium—both figuratively and practically. Three key elements, discussed at the symposium, need to be embraced and implemented. First, the current population management approach of salmon should begin now to transition toward adopting an ecosystem perspective. Second, implicit with this transition will be the requirement that managers begin to connect their understanding about freshwater and marine ecosystems as one system. Third, the conceptual transition from population management to an ecosystem perspective should use the elements of adaptive management (Walters 1986) in its implementation and be linked to precautionary decision-making (e.g., Buhl-Mortensen and Toresen 2001). Adaptive management promotes learning and precautionary decision-making acknowledges the risks inherent in uncertainty. The sustainability of our salmon resources require responsible, science-based ecosystem management. By using this management approach, we believe that the salmon in the Kuskokwim River will be secure and sustainable for generations to come.

Acknowledgments

Charles Krueger, Joseph Spaeder, and Christian Zimmerman provided helpful reviews of earlier drafts of this paper.

References

Buhl-Mortensen, L., and R. Toresen. 2001. Fisheries management in a sea of uncertainty: the role and responsibility of scientists in attaining a precautionary approach. International Journal of Sustainable Development 4:245–264.

Fluharty, D., P. Aparicio, C. Blackburn, G. Boehlert, F. Coleman, P. Conkling, R. Costanza, P. Dayton, R. Francis, D. Hanan, K. Hinman, E. Houde, J. Kitchell, R. Langton, J. Lubchenko, M. Mangel, R. Nelson, V. O'Connell, M. Orbach, and M. Sissenwine. 1998. Ecosystem-based fishery management. A report to Congress. U.S. Department of Commerce, National Oceanic and Atmospheric Administration, National Marine Fisheries Service. Washington, D.C. Available: http://www.bio.fsu.edu/mote/Ecosystem_Advisory_Planrpt.pdf (January 2007).

Gunderson, L., and C. S. Holling, editors. 2002. Panarchy: understanding transformations in human and natural systems. Island Press, Washington, D. C., USA.

Holling, C. S. 2001. Understanding the complexity of economic, ecological and social systems. Ecosystems 4:390–405.

KFRC (Kuskokwim Fisheries Resources Coalition). 2006. Gap analysis for the Kuskokwim Area salmon research plan. M. Nemeth, editor. LGL Alaska Research Associates, Inc., Anchorage, Alaska.

Linderman, J. C., Jr., and D. J. Bergstrom. 2009. Kuskokwim management area: salmon escapement, harvest, and management. Pages 541–599 in C. C. Krueger and C. E. Zimmerman, editors. Pacific salmon: ecology and management of western Alaska's populations. American Fisheries Society, Symposium 70, Bethesda, Maryland.

Ludwig, D., R. Hilborn, and C. J. Walters. 1993. Uncertainty, resources exploitation, and conservation: lessons from history. Science 260:17:36.

NPFMC (North Pacific Fisheries Management Council). 2002. Responsible fisheries management into the 21st century. North Pacific Fisheries Management Council, Anchorage, Alaska.

NPFMC (North Pacific Fisheries Management Council). 2006. Aleutian Islands Fishery Ecosystem Plan—Action Plan. North Pacific Fisheries Management Council. Anchorage, Alaska.

NRC (National Research Council). 2004. Improving the use of the "Best scientific information available" standard in fisheries management. National Academy Press, Washington, D.C.

Piccolo, J. J., M. D. Adkison, and F. Rue. 2009. Linking Alaskan salmon fisheries management with ecosystem-based escapement goals: a review and prospectus. Fisheries 34:124-134.

Stanford, J. A. 2004. Salmonid Rivers Observatory Network (SaRON) of the Flathead Lake Biological Station and partners. Flathead Lake Biological Station. The University of Montana, Missoula. Available: http://www.umt.edu/flbs/Research/SaRON.htm (January 2007).

Sustainable Salmon Initiative. 2006. Arctic-Yukon-Kuskokwim salmon research and restoration plan. Bering Sea Fishermen's Association, Anchorage, Alaska.

USCOP (U.S. Commission on Ocean Policy). 2004. An Ocean Blueprint for the 21st Century. Final Report of the U.S. Commission on Ocean Policy. Washington, D.C. Available: http://www.oceancommission.gov. (January 2007).

USFWS (U.S. Fish and Wildlife Service). 1988. Yukon Delta National Wildlife Refuge Comprehensive Conservation Plan, Environmental Impact Statement, Wilderness Review, and Wild River Plan. U.S. Fish and Wildlife Service. Anchorage, Alaska.

Walters, C. 1986. Adaptive management of renewable resources. Macmillan, New York.

American Fisheries Society Symposium 70:611–619, 2009
© 2009 by the American Fisheries Society

Perspectives on Angling for Salmon on the Kuskokwim River: the Catch and Release Sport Fishing Controversy

LaMont E. Albertson[*]

7215 Foxridge Circle, #2, Anchorage 99518, USA

Abstract.—Local resident concern over catch-and-release fishing varies among the residents living within the Kuskokwim River drainage. In the mid-river region near the village of Aniak, a tolerance exists, and sometimes even participation occurs, among the residents regarding the practice. However, in the areas downstream from Aniak, near Kwethluk and Bethel, local residents often express concern over the practice and refer to it as "playing with food." Based on over thirty years as a resident and from my perspective, the concerns by residents over the catch-and-release fishing are changing towards greater acceptance than in the past. This trend will continue if (1) fishery managers recognize that subsistence uses should always be afforded a priority over other fisheries, (2) our local resident advisory group is provided the opportunity to discuss with managers and advise on sport fishing regulations, and (3) an active educational effort is made for all ages regarding ecology, conservation, and fishery management, including how catch-and-release fishing might play a supportive role.

Introduction

Catch-and-release fishing is popular among anglers living in the lower 48 of the United States, especially among those who fish for trout and bass and within the saltwater fly fishing crowd. Anglers exercising this practice are viewed to be consistent with a conservation ethic, and often fishery managers promote the practice through special regulations (e.g., Arlinghaus et al. 2007). Catch-and-release fishing allows fish to withstand much higher levels of fishing pressure than would be possible if all fish caught were harvested. In rural Alaska and especially in the Arctic-Yukon-Kuskokwim region, catch-and-release fishing is often viewed by local residents with disdain (Lyman 2002). However, based on my experience, this local attitude is variable and is changing within the region I am most familiar, the Kuskokwim River watershed (Linderman and Bergstrom 2009).

I have a rich and mixed experience in fishing. I have fished commercially in both Florida and on the Kuskokwim River. I am still an active subsistence fisher on the Kuskowkim River. Also, I currently run a family guiding business on the Aniak River, a tributary of the Kuskokwim River (Figure 1). The Kuskokwim River is the first large river drainage north of Bristol Bay drainages and includes several large tributaries such as the Aniak and Kwethluk rivers. The river and its tributaries support fisheries for a variety of

[*]Corresponding author: lamont@yuut.org

FIGURE 1. Upstream waters of the Aniak River, Alaska. (photo by David Cannon)

salmonids, including Arctic grayling *Thymallus arcticus*, Dolly Varden trout *Salvelinus malma*, rainbow trout *Oncorhynchus mykiss*, chinook salmon *O. tshawytscha*, coho salmon *O. kisutch*, chum salmon *O. keta*, and pink salmon *O. gorbuscha* and also other fish such as northern pike *Esox lucius* (Burr 2009, this volume).

Using my observations over the past 40 years, below I offer my views on catch-and-release fishing, describing how it varies between the lower and mid river communities of the Kuskokwim River, and how I think attitudes towards this practice will change in the future.

The Adventure Begins

Eagles were eating on fish carcasses across the river. A family of tree nesting goldeneyes hustled by, heading downriver. Chum salmon were to my left, to my right,

and directly in front of me. I was knee-deep in water at the confluence of the Aniak and Kuskokwim rivers near the village of Aniak in western Alaska one early morning in the first week of July, 1967, catching and releasing these brightly marked, kype-gifted fish one after the other. They, along with the occasional Chinook, Dolly Varden char, and northern pike were coursing by me in droves reminiscent of schools of bluefish, ladyfish, mackerel and jack crevalle I'd fished for in the Florida waters of the Atlantic a couple months earlier.

This adventure was my introduction to catch-and-release sportfishing in Alaska, and what an impressive introduction it was! The experience was a gift from the fishing gods. I was not too long out of south Florida, which, at that juncture in the United States' history of our fisheries exploitation—notice I didn't say "management"—was the only state in the union more fishy than Alaska. Of course, the truth of that statement had a lot to do with the cold Alaska climate, as this thin-blooded Florida cracker was to soon learn.

The joy of catching and releasing the many salmon was tempered somewhat by my preoccupation with wondering how I was going to honestly use a rod and reel to craft my community, cultural research into the required "village experience journal." This was one of my primary assignments and the reason I had come to Aniak.

The Assignment

Why was I in the village of Aniak anyway? I had been assigned to teach school there by the Alaska State Operated School System, the Ford Foundation, and the University of Alaska. Prior to teaching an eight-week course of study, I was flown out to do a week's research in the village, check out the school, the generators, the classrooms and teaching supplies, get to know the townspeople, and generally just hang out. The trip was to theoretically help me deal with the culture shock of relocating to bush Alaska. In addition, the renowned Jesuit anthropologist, Dr. William Loyens gave me the assignment to keep a journal of my experiences (Loyens 1966). I was to write and do whatever it was that I felt would make me a successful long-term educator in the community of Aniak.

I already knew beyond a shadow of a doubt that Alaska's fishes somehow were going to help me to be a successful educator in Aniak. I had successfully used fishes in elementary, high school, and my undergraduate and graduate college school days in Florida. They had served me well. Clearly, I was going to have to be creative if I was going to convince my stern mentor, Father William Loyens at the University, that catching and releasing scores of salmon was worth the

morning, noon, and evening research effort. Fortunately for me, one of Father Loyens' fellow Jesuits, Father Bob Corrigal, a Yupik priest from the Yukon Kuskokwim Delta, took me under his encouraging wing. Father Corrigal, early in my Alaska adventure, provided a great source of insight into local customs and values. He soon became a first-rate friend and a fellow brother of the outdoors, but I'll come back later to that part of the tale.

I was determined to learn all I could of the region. By using the University of Alaska-Fairbanks library system, it was easy to round up and read most of the contemporary research about the Kuskokwim region. I read U.C.L.A. Professor Wendell Oswalt's studies on the Kuskokwim (e.g., Oswalt 1963), the fishery research of Ken Alt of the Alaska Department of Fish and Game (e.g., Alt 1973), and the early travels of the intrepid Russian explorer, Lt. Zagoskin (Michael 1967). I actually talked to a participant in an Army Signal Corps Survey group who had come up the Nushagak across the divide between the Tikchik Lakes and Aniak Lake not too long after the turn of the century. He told me of the trials of the trip, of having to wear army wools in the summer and at the same time trying to stay cool and avoid mosquitoes. I also read Al McLane, fishing editor for Field and Stream, and carefully noted his report that the Aniak River held the northern-most naturally occurring population of rainbow trout as well as abundant coho salmon (Figure 2). I was also keen on the writing of Frank Dufresne (Dufresne 1966).

None of the literature I read reported that catching and releasing fish was contrary to the spirit of the proper use of fish. That some people did not agree with catch-and-release fishing was information passed on by word of mouth. Back then, such an idea just was not in the literature.

FIGURE 2. School of spawning phase coho salmon in the Aniak River, Alaska.
(photo by David Cannon)

Father Loyens spent time in the Yukon Kuskokwim Delta as an educator and mentioned to our class —"hammered" might be a better choice of words—the importance of honoring local traditions. I knew from personal conversations with Father Corrigal, who was born in the Yukon Kuskokwim Delta, that catching and releasing fish, or "playing with food," as it was called in the steam baths or muqvik was not preferred nor accepted by many local residents. Father Loyens confirmed this as well. Catch-and-release fishing was not the noble thing to do when a person was simply caught up in the sheer joy of angling unrelated to the eating of your catch. This was so different from the Florida of my youth.

The West Palm Beach Fishing Club was as an organization that has a long history since its founding of emphasizing catch-and-release fishing. I had been a member of the club since I was age 10. In 1938, five years prior to my birth, they were operating official catch-and-release sailfish tournaments in the Gulf Stream just a mile or so off of the coast of West Palm Beach. To this day, the club still promotes releasing fish and the club is recognized for their conservation efforts through their foundation. This was my traditional cultural background from Florida. I was steeped in the catch-and-release tradition long before I arrived in Alaska, but now I was in a different culture.

As good fortune would have it, on one of those early anthropological-research fishing forays, I had the company of George Lee, of Athabascan-Chinese extraction, who hailed originally from the middle Yukon. On that particular day of fishing together, I helped him fill his number-three washtub with "dog" (chum) salmon, and then we both caught and released chums and the occasional Chinook salmon until we'd had our fill and the mosquitoes had had theirs too. He enjoyed it as much as I did and was a masterful angler considering the limitations of the gear he was using that day. Whereas some in the region had problems with catch-and-release angling, at least under certain circumstances, local residents could relate to the sheer joy of catching fish unrelated to their harvest.

Middle versus Down-River Fishing Customs

One needs to understand though, the circumstances under which I engaged George that day and in days that followed in conversations regarding local fishing customs. I did not want to offend anyone by my actions. If I did not care, I could have easily slipped around the corner out of sight of anyone because the Aniak River was a long, twisting, oxbow-rich stream (Figure 3). I quickly dis-

covered that at least in the middle Kuskokwim River near the village of Aniak, catch-and-release angling, at least as I was doing it, was not a major problem. Although, I later found out through more conversations and personal time in the steam baths that the local elders did consider the practice somewhat suspect. However, the elders did not mind that I practiced catch and release fishing or that I promoted this practice to my students on our the many, many fishing trips. Today, catch and release fishing by residents is actually a fairly common practice around our village of Aniak. In fact, the Kuskokwim Native Association now operates a silver salmon derby in August of every year and catch-and-release fishing is an element of the derby. This observation, however, is from an area around the middle portion of the Kuskokwim River.

Down river from Aniak, near the villages of Kwethluk and Bethel and even lower in the river, catch-and-release fishing is not uni-

FIGURE 3. Angler fly fishing for salmon in the Aniak River, Alaska. (photo by David Cannon)

versally accepted. The practice of catching and releasing fish can be viewed as "playing with your food." From my perspective, this type of angling may be more tolerated than in the past, but it remains still questionable among many of the local residents. Possibly, our down river residents' attitudes toward the practice have changed just a bit because rod and reel fishing recently became legalized as gear to catch subsistence fish. I'm consistently told by down-river residents that the negative viewpoint of catch-and-release fishing represents a value of the elders. However, in my many conversations with elders, I know of only one elder from the Toksook Bay that has ever owned and espoused that value in a pure sense.

Historically, I gather that the mindset against catch-and-release fishing comes, in part, from remembrance of stories of true hunger or famine from years and generations past. More importantly, my strong sense is that it comes from a very fundamental, soul-deep respect for fish as a personal, immediate or postconsumable resource, but given, in fact, as a gift from God. *Catching a fish is a spiritual thing.*

Does catch-and-release happen in subsistence or commercial fisheries? In our Kuskokwim River Salmon Management Group meetings, I often hear references to releasing fish unharmed from nets when they are not the desired fish, if there is not a market for them, or if all the fish that can possibly be processed for the day have already been caught. I never hear objections to that kind of catch-and-release fishing. I often share my thinking that releasing fish after being caught is a means of protecting the population of fishes for reproductive reasons or as an overall conservation measure. My experience has been that, when framed in this context, there exists an acceptance and understanding of my conservation motives.

Does a Future Exist for Catch-and-Release Fishing?

From my perspective, catch-and-release fishing is being accepted more and more widely along the Kuskokwim River. Note, however, that the idea that our fish are a treasured resource, a birthright, and a gift from God is as strong as ever. The citizens of the Yukon Kuskokwim Delta expect the fish to be managed wisely. State and federal governments are currently helping through educational efforts to inform of the need for conserving and managing our resources wisely. I suspect that catch-and-release fishing will be more and more accepted as people understand the need for conservation.

The involvement of local residents in the management process for all fisheries will only further promote the acceptance of catch-and-release fishing. We, as residents of the region, are more than willing to be participants at all levels of the management process inasmuch as the state and federal governments will allow. In recent years there has been an unprecedented involvement of local residents in advisory roles and in the various research processes *and this needs to continue!*

While, many of our residents still have a concern over playing with food, I believe this concern will continue to change over time. The recognition exists that, as my fellow lover of the fishes in the Aniak River, Calvin Simeon, once said to me, "Once you bonk a fish on the head with a club, that's well beyond playing with your food…" Local attitudes are softening and changing as cultural values mix. However, my strong sense is that regulatory agencies, state or federal, must be vigilant in how they regulate sport fisheries in light of the regulation of subsistence and commercial fisheries. Regulations need to be understood and be fair among the fisheries.

Recommendations

As a resident and a participant in our Yukon-Kuskokwim delta fisheries, I have three recommendations that I think will ensure that attitudes and values adjust as our fisheries change.

First, when subsistence users have a good attitude towards their opportunities to use resources which have almost always been available to them, they can more easily accept sport fishing. Fishery managers must demonstrate through funding and actions that the number one priority for our region's fisheries is subsistence use (Figure 4). The law already recognizes that subsistence use has priority! Does anyone actually think that subsistence management receives the resources they need for state managers to do their jobs? I believe that the region needs an in-region resident subsistence fishery manager to ensure that the appropriate subsistence surveys, research, education, and general development of relationships with subsistence users. Management rules have to be perceived as being applied fairly among all the fisheries. Subsistence is all about feeding families. It is all about connecting with yourself, with your family, with your lifelong community and regional traditions. What can be more important?

Second, the scope of the Kuskokwim River Salmon Management Group should be broadened to provide advice on all issues related to management of fisheries in the region. The group is advisory and not a decision making body, and they accept this role. I believe that state and federal fishery managers, however, would benefit from hearing from local residents concerning regulatory

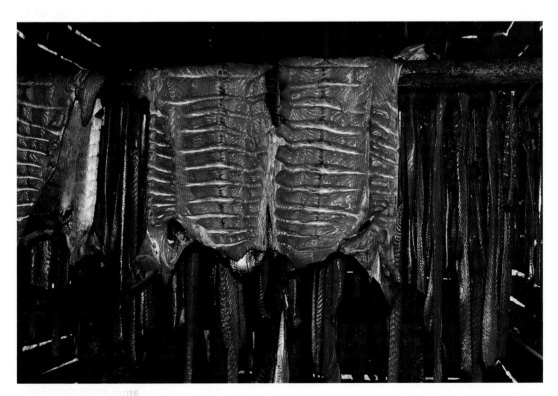

FIGURE 4. Split and drying Chinook salmon from the Kuskokwim River subsistence fishery. (photo by David Cannon).

changes being proposed for all fisheries, including sport fisheries. For an example, the group should discuss and comment upon sport fishing regulations regarding bag limits and catch-and-release fishing. Even more important, we must start discussions about how to manage the environmental impacts of the ever-increasing use of our small rivers by sport anglers and others. Spawning salmon in the upper reaches of our tributaries are being disturbed by large rafting groups and jet boats. Consider, how when salmon are affected, other animals, bears and birds and even vegetation are affected. This use is a new and expanding phenomenon on our small shallow streams and is what I consider to be our most urgent challenge. These areas used to be sanctuaries for large, older grayling, for spawning salmon, for geese, and for nesting harlequin ducks … but no more. Outboard motor size has to be acknowledged as having a significant impact in these areas. Sudden water displacement by passing boats damages shorelines and disturbs the schools of juvenile salmon along the shoreline. Again, these are just a few considerations; there are many others.

Third, and my final recommendation, is that we have to continue educational efforts that will aid in the enlightenment of our young people regarding the conservation of our invaluable fisheries. We need to actively involve the school districts and the university system in creating permanent, usable curriculum for this purpose focused on watershed ecology, conservation, and fishery management. Educational efforts have to be broadened to all ages. For example, when our region's waterfowl populations were threatened twenty years ago, the U.S. Fish and Wildlife Service worked hard with local residents to educate them regarding the reasons for the declines and what actions could be taken to help waterfowl recover.

Conclusion

I went back to the University of Alaska-Fairbanks after my summer work of 1967 and carried my journal, heavy with its emphasis on catch and release fishing research, in fulfillment of my assignment. My Jesuit mentor, Dr. Bill Loyens, fortunately protested not in the least. In fact, over the years when I ran into him while traveling throughout the bush, he would often call my "research" to my attention and gently chide me about my fishing. He did make one comment though, rolling his eyebrows and smiling wryly, "We good Catholics do eat a lot of fish on Fridays, LaMont."

Acknowledgments

Dave Cannon, a resident of the village of Aniak, graciously provided the photos illustrating the beauty of the Aniak and Kuskokwim rivers.

References

Arlinghaus, R., S. J. Cooke, J. Lyman, D. Policansky, A. Schwab, C. Suski, S. G. Sutton, and E. B. Thorstad. 2007. Understanding the complexity of catch-and-release in recreational fishing: an integrative synthesis of global knowledge from historical, ethical, social, and biological perspectives. Reviews in Fisheries Science 15:75–167.

Alt, K. T. 1973. Contributions to the biology of Bering ciso (Coregonus laurettae) in Alaska. Journal of the Fisheries Research Board of Canada 30:1885–1888.

Burr, J. M. 2009. Management of recreational salmon fisheries in the Arctic-Yukon-Kuskokwim Region of Alaska. Pages 521–539 in C. C. Krueger and C. E. Zimmerman, editors. Pacific salmon: ecology and management of western Alaska's populations. American Fisheries Society, Symposium 70, Bethesda, Maryland.

Dufresne, F. 1966. My way was north. An Alaskan autobiography. Holt Rinehart Winston, New York.

Linderman, J. C., Jr., and D. J. Bergstrom. 2009. Kuskokwim management area: salmon escapement, harvest, and management. Pages 541–599 in C. C. Krueger and C. E. Zimmerman, editors. Pacific salmon: ecology and management of western Alaska's populations. American Fisheries Society, Symposium 70, Bethesda, Maryland.

Loyens, W. J. 1966. The changing culture of the Nulato Koyukon Indians. Doctoral dissertation, University of Wisconsin, Madison.

Lyman, J. 2002. Cultural values and change: catch and release in Alaska's sport fisheries. Pages 29–36 *in* J. A. Lucy and A. L. Studholme, editors. Catch and release in marine recreational fisheries. American Fisheries Society Symposium 30, Bethesda, Maryland.

Michael, H. N. 1967. Lieutenant Zagoskin's travels in Russian America 1842–1844. The first ethnographic and geographic investigations in the Yukon and Kuskokwin Valleys of Alaska. Arctic Institute of North American Anthropology of the North: Translations from Russian Sources 7. University of Toronto Press, Toronto, Ontario.

Oswalt, W. 1963. Napaskiak: an Alaskan Eskimo community. University of Arizona Press, Tucson.

American Fisheries Society Symposium 70:621–673, 2009

Norton Sound Salmon Fisheries: History, Stock Abundance, and Management

Jim Menard[*]

Alaska Department of Fish and Game
P.O. Box 1148, Nome, Alaska 99762, USA

Charles C. Krueger

Great Lakes Fishery Commission
2100 Commonwealth Boulevard, Ann Arbor, Michigan 48105, USA

John R. Hilsinger

Alaska Department of Fish and Game
333 Raspberry Road, Anchorage, Alaska 99518, USA

Abstract.—This paper reviews the history of the subsistence, commercial, and sport fisheries, describes variation in salmon runs and harvest over time, and summarizes past management of salmon in the Norton Sound and Port Clarence Management Districts. The drainages of Norton Sound support important subsistence and commercial fisheries for salmon. Sport fisheries are small in comparison. Archeological evidence dating back 2,000 years indicates fishing has been an important part of life for Norton Sound residents for centuries. Since statehood in 1959, salmon abundance and harvest peaked in the late 1970s and early 1980s. The 1998 and 1999 salmon runs were some of the poorest on record. Since 2003, large increases in spawning escapement have been recorded for chum *Oncorhynchus keta*, pink *O. gorbuscha*, coho *O. kisutch*, and sockeye *O. nerka* salmon stocks. Chinook *O. tshawytscha* salmon runs have declined since the late 1990s and not rebounded. Salmon management seeks to allow sufficient escapement to spawning rivers to ensure long-term sustainable yields. Salmon fisheries are managed under three different sets of regulations: subsistence, commercial, and sport. Subsistence harvests are given a priority over commercial and sport harvests. In 1999, due to low salmon returns to spawning streams, the U.S. government declared the Norton Sound region a federal fisheries disaster and the state of Alaska began managing the subsistence fishing in the Nome Subdistrict as a limited entry fishery (Tier II permit). Restoration of salmon is dependent on a wide set of variables including suitable juvenile rearing habitat, favorable ocean conditions for growth and survival, and adequate numbers of returning adults for spawning and producing the next generation of salmon. Regulation of harvest is critical to salmon restoration so that adequate spawning escapements occur and that this critical link within the life cycle of salmon remains unbroken. More restrictive harvest regulations than in the past has allowed more salmon to reach the spawning grounds and helped to restore salmon populations and their fisheries. These harvest

[*]Corresponding author: jim.menard@alaska.gov

restrictions affected not only the fish but also those who fished, and caused changes in fishing patterns in time and space and potentially changed cultural values towards some species.

Introduction

The drainages of Norton Sound represent a hydrogeographically complex region of subarctic streams, rivers, and estuarine lagoons connecting to the northern Bering Sea. These systems support subsistence and commercial fisheries for salmon, which are important to local residents (Magdanz et al. 2009, this volume). Primary species of importance to the subsistence and commercial fisheries are chum salmon *Oncorhynchus keta*, pink salmon *O. gorbuscha*, and coho salmon *O. kisutch*. Small numbers of Chinook salmon *O. tshawytscha* occur throughout the region and also support fisheries. The most important fisheries for Chinook salmon occur in, and adjacent to, the Unalakleet River in the southeastern part of the region. In the western portion of the region, locally important subsistence fisheries also exist for sockeye salmon *O. nerka*, which are available in the Sinuk and Pilgrim rivers in association with their headwater lakes (Glacial and Salmon lakes). Sport fisheries are small in comparison to subsistence and commercial fisheries and can target all five species. A long cultural history of subsistence use of salmon, dating back many centuries, exists among local Norton Sound residents.

Salmon fisheries are managed primarily by the Alaska Department of Fish and Game (ADF&G) to meet spawning escapement goals established for major river systems (e.g., Clark 2001a). Escapement is the number of fish allowed to escape fisheries to provide upstream spawning populations. Three types of escapement goals are used in salmon management. A biological escapement goal (BEG) is the number of salmon in a particular stock that ADF&G has determined should

be allowed to escape the fishery to spawn to achieve the maximum sustained yield (human use). This determination is based on estimates of maximum sustained yield from stock–recruitment relationships (e.g., Clark 2001b). A sustainable escapement goal (SEG) is a level of escapement, as indicated by an index or escapement estimate, which is known to provide for sustained yield over a five to 10-year period. SEGs are used in situations where a biological escapement goal cannot be estimated due to the absence of sufficient stock-specific recruitment data. Optimal escapement goal (OEG) is a specific management objective for salmon escapement that considers both biological and allocative factors, and may differ from the SEG or BEG. When salmon abundance exceeds, or is predicted to exceed, the established escapement goals, ADF&G permits the harvest of salmon by subsistence, commercial, and sport fisheries. When salmon runs are low in abundance, the subsistence fishery has a harvest priority over commercial and sport fisheries. Escapements are estimated by a variety of methods including weirs, counting towers, test fisheries, and aerial surveys. This approach to management in Alaska is summarized in the Policy for the Management of Sustainable Salmon Fisheries (5 AAC 39.222).

Besides escapement management approaches, the Policy for the Management of Sustainable Salmon Fisheries gave authority to the Alaska Board of Fisheries with the ADF&G to designate special management status to specific stocks of salmon. Three categories of concern exist: yield concern—stocks that fail to produce expected yields; management concern—stocks that fail to meet established escapement goals; or conservation concern—stocks that are found to be in danger of not being able to rebuild themselves. Stocks are designated as concerns if the stock fails to meet these criteria over a period of 4–5 years despite appropriate management taken to address the concern. After a stock is designated as a stock of concern, department staff members work with the board and public to develop action plans, management plans, and research plans to help return the stock to its former abundance.

This paper reviews the history of the fisheries in the region, describes the variation in salmon runs over time, and summarizes past management of salmon in the Norton Sound and Port Clarence Management Districts. The review draws upon written resources much of which are not readily available in the primary literature but available from the ADF&G website (www.adfg.state.ak.us). More information can also be located through the references listed in Nemeth (2002).

Norton Sound Salmon and Port Clarence Management Districts

The Norton Sound Salmon Management District includes all Norton Sound drainages to the Bering Sea from Cape Douglas, northwest of the mouth of the Sinuk River, to Point Romanof, south of Stebbins, representing a shoreline distance of approximately 500 mi (Figure 1) plus Saint Lawrence Island. The Port Clarence District includes all drainages from Cape Douglas north to Cape Prince of Wales and includes the villages of Teller and Brevig Mission (Figure 2). Some of the largest drainages in these two districts include (from north to south) the Pilgrim River, Fish-Niukluk rivers, Inglutalik River, Ungalik River, Shaktoolik River, and Unalakleet-North rivers. The Norton Sound District includes six commercial salmon fishing subdistricts and numerous anadromous streams (e.g., subdistrict 333–10; Figure 1).

The sparsely populated Norton Sound region has its largest population center at Nome, on the northwest shore of Norton Sound (population 3,590; census 2005), plus a few small villages scattered through the region, such as Golovin, Shaktoolik, and Unalakleet (Figure 1). Few roads exist in the region (e.g., Nome to Solomon), except within the villages. The region is isolated from the continental road system of North America. Air transportation provides the primary access into the region. The region's isolation and distance from markets affects the demand from commercial processors to purchase fish. The region experiences a sub-arctic climate with extremes of temperatures from –55–85°F. Mean annual air temperatures range from 25–32°F. Soils in the region have discontinuous permafrost and much of the landscape is tundra with few trees.

In addition to Chinook, chum, coho, pink, and sockeye salmon, other species potentially present in the subsistence and/or sport fisheries include Arctic grayling *Thymallus arcticus*, Dolly Varden char *Salvelinus malma*, Arctic char *Salvelinus aplinus*, northern pike *Esox lucius*, burbot *Lota lota*, Arctic lamprey *Lampetra camtschatica*, longnose sucker *Catostomus catostomus*, Alaska blackfish *Dallia pectoralis*, inconnu *Stenodus leucichthys*, and several *Coregonus* species.

Data Sources and Analyses

Escapement Estimation.—Numbers of salmon by species in rivers were estimated by a variety of methods including weirs, counting towers, test fisheries, and aerial surveys. The application of multiple enumeration methods over time to a single river system make it difficult to assess measurement error. Many of the salmon census projects were operated cooperatively between the ADF&G and other local organizations including Norton Sound Economic Development Corporation (NSEDC), the Fisheries Department of Kawerak, Inc.

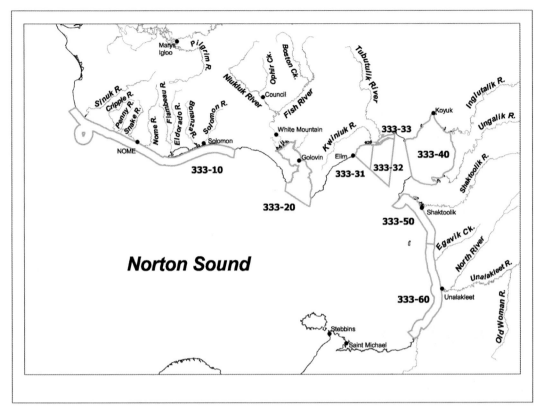

FIGURE 1. Map of Norton Sound Salmon Management District showing rivers, villages, and commercial salmon fishing districts.

(Kawerak; a Native regional nonprofit organization), and the Unalakleet IRA (IRA indicating organized under the 1934 Indian Reorganization Act). NSEDC provided assistance to both ADF&G, Kawerak, and Unalakleet IRA for the operation of escapement counting projects. Grants and contracts from the Norton Sound Research and Restoration initiative (NSSR&R), the Sustainable Salmon Initiative, Bering Sea Fishermen's Association, U.S. Fish and Wildlife Service, and U.S. Bureau of Land Management have provided funding for salmon studies to ADF&G and Kawerak, as well as other organizations.

The escapement data contained within this paper draw from many past projects throughout the region. Counting towers were operated by crews who visually identified and counted salmon passing up and down river within specific time periods. Usually, counts were conducted for a 20-min period each hour and the counts were expanded to the whole hour. The expanded hourly total counts were summed to produce a daily total (Kent 2007). Details of counting tower operations for the Kwiniuk, Niukluk, and Nome rivers (Figure 1) were provided by Kent (2007). Data from the Kwiniuk River counting tower represent the longest continuous escapement data series for Chinook, chum, and pink salmon in Norton Sound. At the Nome River, a counting tower was operated from 1993–1995 and a weir was operated from 1996–2006 by ADF&G. Details of weir construction were provided by Kent (2007). Salmon escapement data for the Eldorado, Pilgrim, and Snake rivers were based on counting tower and weir counts (Figure 3). Methods and data

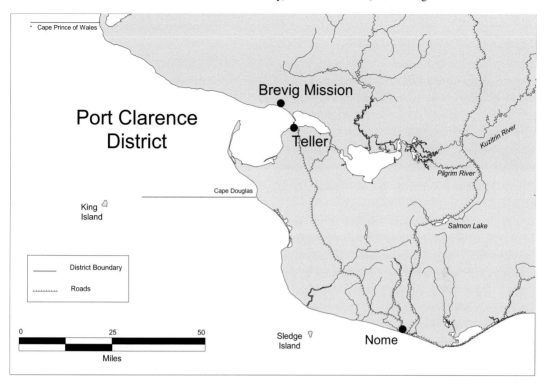

FIGURE 2. Port Clarence Management District on the north of the Norton Sound Management District.

summaries were provided by Burkhart and Dunmall (2005). Sitnasuak Corporation (a for-profit Nome-area Native corporation) established the Eldorado River tower in 1995. During the first two years, operations were not sufficient to obtain an accurate count of salmon. From 1997–2002, Kawerak operated the Eldorado River tower. In midseason 2002, Kawerak stopped using the Eldorado River tower and began making counts using a weir on the river. In 1997, Kawerak established and operated a counting tower at the Pilgrim River. Use of the counting tower was discontinued in 2003 when Kawerak began operations of a weir. Kawerak operated the Snake River tower from 1995–2002 when midseason a weir began to be used to count salmon. In 2000, Bureau of Land Management personnel established a weir on at the outlet of Glacial Lake on Glacial Creek, a tributary to Sinuk River, to count sockeye salmon (Parker 2002). The weir was operational until 2005,

and in 2006 NSEDC and ADF&G operated the weir for two weeks during peak salmon migration. A counting tower was operated at the Pikmiktalik River from 2003–2006 near Stebbins and Saint Michael in southern Norton Sound (Figure 1; Kroeker and Dunmall 2005). In Unalakleet Subdistrict (333–60; Figure 1), a counting tower was operated on the North River, tributary to the Unalakleet River, from 1972–1974, 1984–1986, and 1996–2006 (Jones 2006). In the 2000s, more funding became available for salmon projects in the Norton Sound area in response to the federal salmon disaster declaration in 1999 caused by the poor returns of chum salmon in 1998. With this new funding, operations of weirs and towers were extended into late August and early September to assess the coho salmon run. As a result, time-series data for coho salmon which run rivers in late August and early September were only available for a few years in the 2000s.

FIGURE 3. Snake River, near Nome, Alaska. Photo by Christian Zimmerman.

Harvest Assessment.—Subsistence harvest was assessed by postseason household surveys and through calendars issued with subsistence harvest permits (Magdanz et al. 2009). Household surveys were conducted in Brevig Mission, Teller, Golovin, White Mountain, Elim, Koyk, Shaktoolik, Unalakleet, St. Michael, and Stebbins. Researchers attempted to contact 100% of the households in each of the surveyed communities. Actual sample rates ranged from 83% of households in Golovin to 99% of households in Unalakleet. Overall 93% of the households in the surveyed communities were interviewed (Georgette et al. 2003). Subsistence harvest information was also collected post season through evaluation of voluntary harvest calendars. This information was used to estimate subsistence salmon harvest by species in each community and to capture other information such as gear types used, harvest timing, and subsistence uses. The mix of methods used to estimate harvest requires comparison among years to be cautiously interpreted.

Commercial harvest was assessed through the completion of mandatory fish tickets at the time of sale. Information recorded on fish tickets includes the permit holder's information, number of fish harvested by species, total pounds by species, price per pound by species, total price paid, and the total number of fish by species retained for personal use (if any). Fish tickets receipts were delivered to AGF&G staff after each commercial open-

ing and entered into a database and queried under multiple parameters (e.g., by species, deliveries, number of fishers, number of fish, pounds).

Sport fishing harvest was assessed through analysis of voluntary mail surveys of sport fish harvest. Data collection and calculation procedures are as described in Jennings et al. 2007. Data used in this paper span from 1977–2006, excluding 1979.

History of Norton Sound Salmon Fisheries

Archeological evidence dating back 2,000 years indicates fishing has been a part of life for Norton Sound residents for many centuries (Bockstoce 1979). The largest settlements, precontact with Europeans, were located on the Bering Strait Islands and western Seward Peninsula where marine mammals were the primary subsistence resource. The rest of the region's population lived in small groups scattered along the coast, often moving seasonally to access fish and wildlife resources (Thomas 1982). During summer months, residents would disperse, usually in groups comprised of one or two families, and set up camps near mouths of streams. Harvest levels of fish on any one stream were likely relatively small. The few people in these camps caught enough salmon to feed their families and one or two dogs through the winter (Thomas 1982).

In the late 1890s, gold was discovered on the Seward Peninsula and boomtowns sprang up with thousands of new immigrants flocking to the region. Commerce and the establishment of missions drew the original residents to central year-round communities and reduced traditional seasonal movements. Mining impacted fish populations significantly through alteration of stream habitat. Nearly every stream on the Seward Peninsula had some type of mining operation, which ranged from simple gold panning to sluice boxes to giant bucket line dredges that stood many stories high. One example of extensive effects on a river valley floor occurred within the Solomon River valley. The river, only 30 mi long, had 13 dredges working on it at one time. Most of the stream bed and valley floor was dredged and sifted for gold with devastating effects on salmon juvenile and spawning habitat. Another important effect of the "gold rush" was simply the large number of people who came to live in the region between 1900 and 1930, causing an increased demand on salmon resources (Dufresne 1966). Communities like Nome, which had a population of 30,000 people, and Council, which had a population of 10,000 people, did not exist before gold was discovered (Kohler et al. 2005).

Concurrent with the gold rush in the late 19th century, winter transportation throughout the region consisted of hired dog teams and drivers who carried mail or freight along the coast, and across the state to the ice-free port at Seward. As a consequence of the demand for transportation, the size of the dog teams increased from two or three dogs to as many as ten to twenty dogs (Wolfe and Spaeder 2009, this volume). Dried fish, primarily chum and pink salmon, was used to feed dogs. The increase in numbers of dogs, increased the need to catch more salmon. Dried fish, became a major barter item in response to the increased need for dog food (Thomas 1982). At about the same time, wooden boats began to replace kayaks, (Thomas 1982) which were more efficient to use for catching salmon. All of these changes caused harvests to increase.

The number of people gradually decreased over the 20-year period after the gold rush, as the gold deposits were exhausted. The number of dog teams diminished by the mid 1930s when mail planes and mechanical tractors were introduced. The last mail contract using a dog team ended in 1962 in the village of Savoonga on St. Lawrence Island. Local stores continued to trade and barter in dry fish at Shaktoolik, Saint Michael, Unalakleet, and Golovin (Figure 1). An example of the quantity of dried fish used was the 8x20x40 ft cache at the Shaktoolik store which would be filled to the top with dry fish. One elder reported that the stores would buy the fish for 6 cents a pound, and sell them for 10 cents a pound, or their equivalent in groceries and supplies (Thomas 1982). By the early 1960s, commercial salmon fishing developed into a source of summer cash. During the 1960s, snow machines began replacing the need for dog teams and reduced the need for dried salmon as dog food (ADF&G 2004).

At statehood in 1959, few regulations governed subsistence fishing. Salmon could be taken by gillnet, seines, spear, or fish wheel for subsistence purposes. Restrictions were first implemented for some areas in the 1960s. In Port Clarence District, salmon fishing was restricted to five days a week from July 1 through August 15. In the Unalakleet Subdistrict, no subsistence fishing was allowed near the mouth of the Unalakleet River. In each decade that followed, more subsistence restrictions occurred in the areas surrounding Nome, but few restrictions occurred elsewhere. Spearing was eliminated as a legal method of taking salmon throughout Norton Sound, but few other changes occurred outside the areas where Nome residents fished (Nome Subdistrict; discussed below). In contrast, the commercial fishery was actively managed throughout the same period through regulations.

In 1959 and 1960, ADF&G biologists conducted fishery resource inventories that indicated harvestable surpluses of salmon beyond subsistence needs that were available in several river systems throughout Norton Sound. Commercial fishery regulations were liberalized and processors were encouraged to explore and develop new fishing areas. As a result, commercial salmon fishing activity grew significantly, enabling some local residents to obtain cash income. Most commercial salmon fishers and many workers at salmon buying stations were resident native Alaskans (Yupik, Inupiat, and Siberian Yupik). Commercial fisheries operated set gillnets from outboard skiffs to capture salmon. All commercial salmon fisheries in Norton Sound took place in coastal marine waters.

Commercial salmon fishing in Norton Sound first began in the southern Norton Sound subdistricts of Shaktoolik and Unalakleet in 1961. Over the next several years commercial fishing spread to the remaining subdistricts. Most salmon sold commercially in the 1960s were chum salmon. Chinook salmon catches brought a much higher price, but were only a few thousand fish and only caught in any numbers in the southern Norton Sound subdistricts of Shaktoolik and Unalakleet.

One of the biggest changes in the commercial fishery came with the limited entry program that went into effect in 1977 and restricted those who could fish commercially for salmon. Permits were awarded based on historical participation in the commercial fishery. The trend of decreasing chum and pink salmon catches in mid 1980s and weak chum salmon escapements in the Nome Subdistrict led to commercial, subsistence, and sport restrictions.

In 1999, due to low salmon returns to spawning streams in 1998 and 1999, U.S. government declared the Norton Sound region a federal fisheries disaster. In 2000, U.S. Congress in response to the declaration appropriated five million dollars for the research and restoration of Norton Sound salmon stocks to understand the causes for the depressed salmon runs. The State of Alaska in 2000, 2001, and 2002 also declared the area an economic fish disaster. Catches for almost all salmon continued to be poor in the early 2000s.

In September 2000, based on a review of escapement and harvest data provided by ADF&G, the Board of Fisheries designated the chum salmon stocks in the Nome Subdistrict as a management concern (stocks that fail to meet established escapement goals), and chum salmon stocks in Golovnin Bay Subdistrict and Moses Point Subdistrict as a yield concern (stocks that fail to produce expected yields). Chinook salmon in Shaktoolik Subdistrict and Unalakleet Subdistrict were designated as stocks of yield concern in 2003.

Beginning in the early 2000s, no market interest existed for chum or pink salmon, and the commercial fishery targeted Chinook and coho salmon. Little commercial fishing opportunity occurred in the early 2000s. The 2002 and 2003 seasons had the lowest commercial salmon harvests on record. Few openings for Chinook salmon occurred during this time period as runs continued to be poor. However, the 2006 commercial harvest of coho salmon set a record for the Norton Sound Management Area.

Sport fisheries have been limited in the region with local residents being the primary participants. Few nonresidents typically travel to the region to sport fish in comparison to other Alaska locations. One exception to this general characterization has been sport fishing on the Unalakleet River. The U.S. Air Force operated a recreational fishing camp on the river in the early 1960s. A commercial sport fishing lodge was constructed on the river in the late 1960s (Kent and Bergstrom 2006). This lodge has changed owners, been expanded, and remains in operation.

Changes in Salmon Stock Abundance

Kwiniuk River

Data from the Kwiniuk River counting tower represent the longest continuous escapement data series for Chinook, chum, and pink salmon in Norton Sound. Chum salmon counts in the Kwiniuk River, over the 41-year time period from 1965–2006, averaged 24,897 fish (range 8,508–66,604 fish; Figure 4; Appendix Table 1; Kent 2007). Escapements were smallest in 1976 (8,508 fish), 1985 (9,013 fish), and 1999 (8,763 fish); and largest in 1970 (66,604 fish), 1983 (56,927 fish), and 1984 (54,043 fish). No escapement over 40,000 fish has been observed since 1995. Since 1999, chum salmon escapement ranged between 10,362 and 39,519 fish (average 20,223 fish); and has every year met the BEG range of 10,000–20,000 fish (Clark 2001a; Menard and Bergstrom 2006a). The extensive nature of data for this river allows not only year-to-year analysis but also comparisons over decades. Using simple average escapements, the period from 1965–1984 appears to have produced approximately 30% more returning salmon than the period from 1985–2006. Causes for this shift in production are unknown, but could be related to a Bering Sea physical regime shift in ocean productivity (e.g., Mantua 2009, this volume; Royer and Grosch 2009, this volume) and competition from Asian-origin hatchery salmon (Eggers 2009, this volume). Pink salmon showed three distinct periods of differing variable abundance between odd- and even-year runs (pink salmon have a strict two-year life cycle). From 1965–1972, abundance in even years was greater than in odd years and this pattern also characterized the period from 1984–2006 (Figure 4). However, for 11 years, from 1973–1983, the pattern between even and odd years did not hold, with the largest run occurring in 1981 (odd year)

of 566,417 pink salmon. In general, pink salmon appeared more abundant beginning in 1992 when the first run over a million fish was recorded (1,464,717 pink salmon). Every even-year run after 1992 exceeded 600,000 fish with the largest ever recorded occurring in 2004 (3,054,684 fish). The fewest pink salmon counted in the Kwiniuk River occurred in 1999 (608 fish) when chum salmon escapement was similarly low. Average Chinook salmon escapement for the period from 1979–2006 was 462 fish and ranged from 107 fish in 1979 to 972 fish in 1997. The run in 1999 of 115 Chinook salmon was the second lowest recorded. For coho salmon, only a time series of data from 2001–2006 existed. Escapement during this period ranged from 5,490 fish in 2003 to 22,341 fish in 2006. For most of the 1960s and 1970s, Norton Sound salmon management was based on the catch per unit effort (CPUE) of the commercial catch, aerial surveys, and tower counts made at the Kwiniuk River. Over this time period, the variation in salmon abundance in this river was probably typical for other nearby rivers in the region.

Niukluk River

Chum salmon escapement in the Niukluk River from 1995–2006 varied between 10,770 fish in 2004 to 86,333 fish in 1995 (Appendix Table 2; Menard and Bergstrom 2006a; Kent 2007). Chum salmon showed a consistent pattern of decline over the 12-year period. The average escapement over the past 12 years was 40,476 fish; however, no run since 1998 has exceeded 40,000 fish. The SEG for chum salmon is >30,000 fish and has not been met since 2002 (Menard and Bergstrom 2006a). Pink salmon showed a regular pattern of strong even-year runs and weak odd-year runs, similar to the Kwiniuk River. Over a million pink salmon were counted at the tower in 1996, 1998, and 2006. Chinook salmon varied in abundance from 30 fish in

Menard et al.

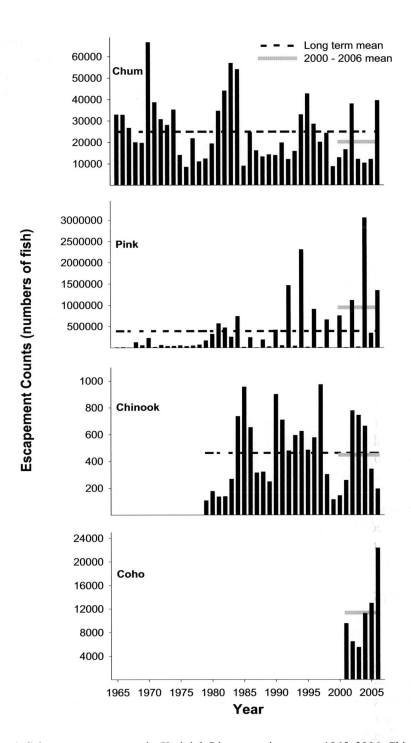

FIGURE 4. Salmon escapement at the Kwiniuk River counting tower, 1965–2006. Chinook counts from 1965–1984 were not expanded but were expanded to cover 24 h periods from 1985 on.

2001 to 621 fish in 2002. ADF&G has operated the Niukluk River counting tower from 1995–2006, and only in 1998 were operations terminated (August 9) before the bulk of the coho salmon run had arrived. Coho salmon escapement ranged from a low of 1,282 fish in 2003 to a high of 12,781 fish in 1996 (excluding data from 1998).

Nome River

Chum salmon counts in the Nome River varied between a low of 1,048 fish in 1999 to a high of 5,677 fish in 2006 (Figure 5; Appendix Table 3; Menard and Bergstrom 2006b; Kent 2007). Chum salmon escapement met the ADF&G escapement goals of 2,900–4,300 fish in each of the last three years, 2004–2006 (Figure 6; SEG; Menard and Bergstrom 2006a). However, poor runs below this level occurred in five of the past 13 years (1994, 1998, 1999, 2002, 2003; 1993 not used because the tower operation did not begin until the last week of July). Pink salmon varied from a low of 2,033 fish in 1999 to a high of 1,051,146 fish in 2004. Here, as in the Kwiniuk and Niukluk rivers, pink salmon showed the pattern of strong even-year runs and weak odd-year runs. Few Chinook salmon were counted in any year and ranged from three fish in 1999 to 69 fish in 2005. Coho salmon counts between 2001 and 2006, averaged 3,789 fish and ranged from 548 fish in 2003 to 8,216 fish in 2006.

Eldorado, Pilgrim (Salmon Lake), Sinuk (Glacial Lake), Snake, and Pikmiktalik Rivers

In 2006, the largest recorded chum salmon escapements occurred in the Eldorado and Pilgrim rivers when numbers counted (>40,000 fish) were about four times the average for these streams (Appendix Tables 4–5). An above average run of chum salmon occurred in the Snake River in 2006 (4,128

fish); however, the two largest chum runs observed in this river occurred in 1997 (6,184 fish) and 1998 (11,067 fish; Appendix Table 6). Similarly during 2006, in the Pikmiktalik River, the chum salmon count was about 50% higher than recorded from 2003–2005 (Appendix Table 7). Weak runs of chum salmon occurred in 1999 in the Eldorado, Pilgrim, and Snake rivers. Optimal escapement goals were met or exceeded three of the five past years in the Eldorado River (OEG = 6,000–9,200 fish) and every year of last five years in the Snake River (OEG = 1,600–2,500 fish; Menard and Bergstrom 2006b). Escapement goals for chum salmon have not been established for the Pilgrim River. Average escapement of Chinook salmon was largest in the Pilgrim River (average 369 fish; range 6–1,016 fish) in comparison to the lower average counts from the Eldorado River (81 fish; range 25–446 fish) and Snake River (average 19 fish; range 0–50 fish). In 2004, large escapements of coho salmon occurred in the Eldorado (1,151 fish; 2nd highest 2001–2005 data series), Pilgrim (1,573 fish; highest escapement recorded 2003–2006), and Pikmiktalik (11,799 fish; 2nd highest in the 2003–2006 period) rivers but not in the Snake River (474 fish; third lowest run in the 2001–2006 data series). The Pilgrim River count of coho salmon may have included as many as 30% misidentified sockeye salmon; however, even with misidentification the count would still be approximately 1,000 fish and highest in the data series. These systems, with the exception of the Pikmiktalik River, had sockeye salmon returns, in addition to chum, pink, Chinook, and coho salmon (Appendix Tables 4–8). No data for other than sockeye salmon were available from the Sinuk River (Glacial Lake) weir. Sockeye salmon were much more abundant in the Pilgrim River (average 36,714 fish; range 3,888–85,417 fish) than in the Sinuk River (Glacial Lake) (average 5,272 fish; range 1,047–11,135 fish). Both the Pilgrim and Sinuk systems had the largest

Figure 5. Nome River near Nome, Alaska. Photo by Christian Zimmerman.

sockeye salmon escapements ever recorded in 2004 and 2005. In the Pilgrim River, from 1999–2002 sockeye salmon run averaged 6,893 fish (range 3,888–12,141 fish) and then increased from 2003–2006 to an average of 59,080 fish, an increase of 860% (range 42,729–85,417 fish); however, the early period counts are biased low because late start dates for operation of the tower (Appendix Table 5). Sockeye salmon escapements were low in the Eldorado and Snake rivers, with typically less than 100 fish counted, and which may represent straying from the larger populations in the Pilgrim and Sinuk rivers.

North River–Unalakleet River

Chum salmon counts in the North River, tributary to the Unalakleet River varied from a low of 1,526 fish in 1998 to a high of 11,984 fish in 2005 (average 5,731 fish; Figure 7; Appendix Table 9). Escapement of chum salmon

from 2003–2005 were high (average 10,626 fish; range 9,859–11,984 fish) in comparison to other years in the data series. Pink salmon showed a pattern of alternating strong even-year runs with weak odd-year runs. Increasing runs of pink salmon have occurred since 2000. The first counts of over a million fish occurred in 2004–2006. Of the Norton Sound rivers with escapement projects, the North River had the largest Chinook salmon counts of any river (average 1,475 fish over 17 years of data; Figure 7; Appendix Table 9). The largest escapements of Chinook salmon occurred over a three-year period, from 1997–1999 when the average was 2,849 fish, about double the long-term average. However, every year since 1999 Chinook salmon escapement counts have been at, or below, the long-term average of about 1,500 fish. From 2001–2006, coho salmon escapement estimates have varied from a low of 3,210 fish in 2002 to a high of 19,189 fish in 2005 (average 10,274 fish; Figure 7). Coho salmon escapement in this system was comparable in numbers to that recorded from the Kwiniuk River (Figure 4).

Fishery Harvest

Nome Subdistrict

Peak catches of salmon combined for all species and fisheries occurred during the period from 1975–1995 (Subdistrict 333–10; Figures 1 and 8; Appendix Table 10). The last commercial harvest was in 1996. Low subsistence harvests occurred from 1996–2002. Chum salmon harvests from 1990 onward have declined greatly and have never exceeded the long-term mean of 6,840 fish (range 28,190 fish (1977) to 337 fish (1999)). Chum salmon subsistence harvests over the past five years have averaged only 805 fish (range 565 fish to 1,114 fish), and did not reflect the increased chum salmon escapement experienced in the same rivers (Figures 4 and 6). The low harvest may indicate a reduced demand for this species within the subsistence fishery. Subsistence harvests of Chinook salmon increased from 2003–2006 in comparison to the immediate years previous (2000–2002) likely in response to increased runs (Figures 4 and 6). Similarly, increased subsistence harvests occurred for pink and coho salmon from 2004–2006, which corresponded to the larger escapements recorded over the same time period (Figures 4 and 6). Pink salmon contributed numerically more than any other species to harvests over the past ten years. Coho salmon subsistence harvest in 2006 (3,808 fish) was the largest estimated over the past 37 years.

Unalakleet Subdistrict

High catches of salmon (>100,000 fish) combined for all species and fisheries oc-

curred during the period from 1978–1984, from 1994–1998, and from 2005–2006 (Figures 1 and 9; Appendix Table 11). Low commercial catch of salmon occurred in 1999 and from 2001–2003. Because of variable methods used to estimate subsistence harvests, comparisons among years should be viewed with caution. Chum salmon harvests (subsistence and commercial) peaked in 1983 (113,621 fish) and were lowest in 1968 (17,847 fish). From 1998–2006, the lowest nine years of chum salmon harvests were estimated. The recent low harvests stands in contrast with the large increase in chum salmon escapement estimated in the North River since 1998 (Figure 7). The largest pink salmon harvest was estimated in 1994 as 511,730 fish. Though pink salmon escapement to the North River increased greatly since 2003 (Figure 7), pink salmon subsistence harvest has remained stable and ranged between 20,883–22,547 fish (2004–2006). Chinook salmon subsistence and commercial harvest combined was estimated to be highest in 1985 (14,018 fish) and in 1997 (15,392 fish) and lowest in 1968 (1,146 fish). Catches of Chinook salmon decreased sharply from 1998–2000 and since has remained stable from 2,000–3,000 fish. Commercial catch since 2000 have been nil due to restrictions placed on the fishery by ADF&G. The variation in Chinook salmon catches generally follows the same pattern of variation observed for escapement in the North River (Figure 7). Coho salmon commercial catch increased every year since 2002 (from 1,079 fish in 2002 to 98,336 fish in 2006) while subsistence harvest appeared stable and varied from 5,978 fish (2004) to 8,301 fish (2002; Figure 9). From 2002–2006, coho salmon escapement estimated in the North River (Figure 7) followed a pattern of increase similar to the commercial fishery harvest increase (Figure 9). The subsistence fishery did not respond to the apparent increased availability of coho salmon.

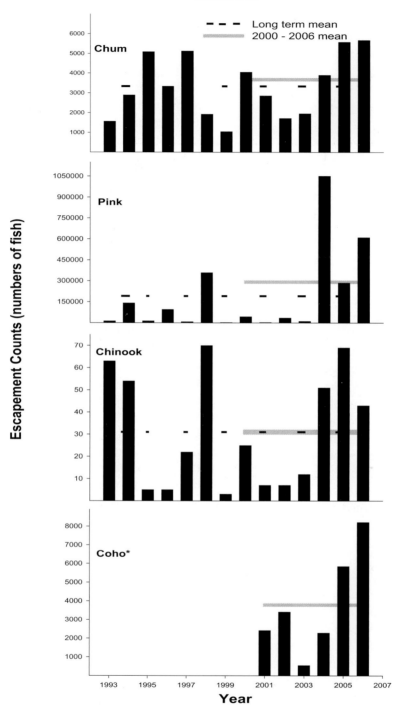

FIGURE 6. Salmon escapement estimated at the Nome River counting tower 1993–1995 and weir 1996–2006. The horizontal dashed line indicates the long term mean. The gray bar indicates the short-term mean 2000–2006. In 1996, the majority of pink salmon escaped through the weir pickets and were not counted. *Coho salmon data for 2001–2006 only; the short term mean reflects this period only. In 2004, an estimated 1,500 coho salmon were not included in the count because of flooding preventing weir operations.

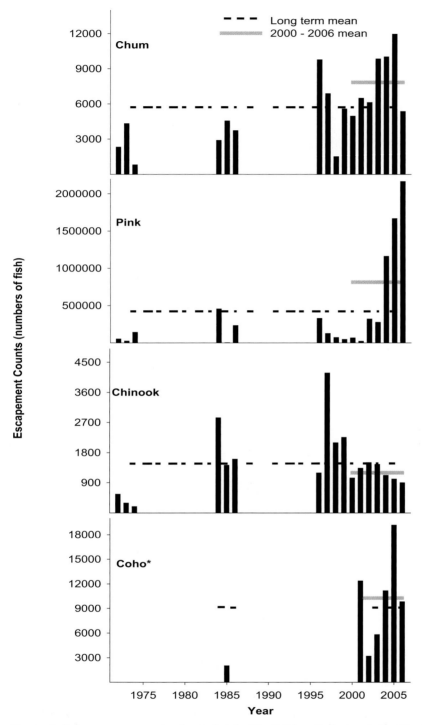

FIGURE 7. Salmon escapement estimated at the North River (tributary to the Unalakleet River) counting tower 1993–1995 and weir 1996–2006. The horizontal dashed line indicates the long term mean. The gray bar indicates the short-term mean 2000–2006. *Coho salmon data for 1985 and 1996–2006 only were used because data were available for at least until August 31 for these years. The long-term coho salmon mean reflects that time period.

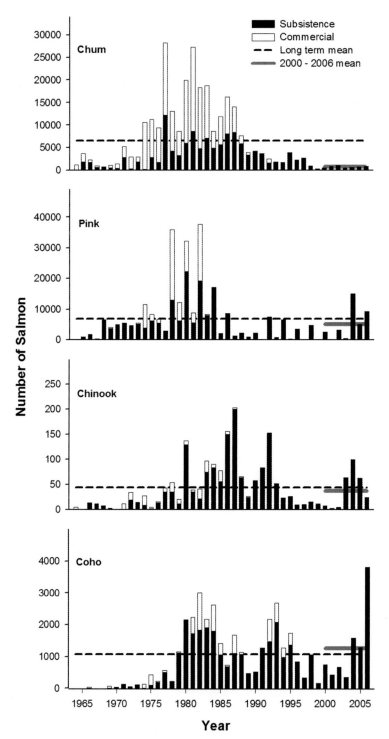

FIGURE 8. Subsistence (black bar) and commercial (white bar) salmon catch by species, by year for Nome Subdistrict, 1964–2006. Subsistence harvest data were incomplete prior to 1975. From 1975–2006 data were from permits returned by fishers. From 1999–2005, permits to subsistence fish chum salmon were restricted in number (Tier II). In 2006, Tier II chum salmon fishing restrictions were suspended.

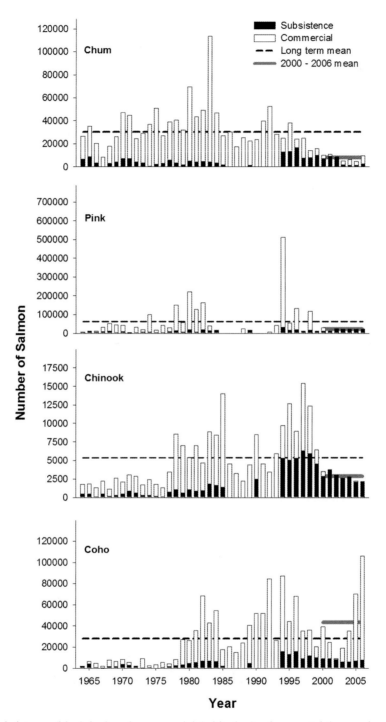

FIGURE 9. Subsistence (black bar) and commercial (white bar) salmon catch by species, by year for Unalakleet Subdistrict, 1964–2006. Subsistence catches from 1966–1972 include fish caught at S. Michael. Subsistence surveys were not conducted from 1986–1988 and from 1991–1993. Subsistence harvest data in 1990 and 2005 included catch from residents of Stebbins and St. Michael. From 1994–2002, subsistence harvest data were estimated by survey and included harvests from Stebbins and St. Michael.

Norton Sound (All Subdistricts)

Catch of salmon (all species) from 1964–2006 combined over all six subdistricts (Figure 1) peaked from 1980–1985 and again peaked from 1994–1997 (Figure 10; Appendix Tables 12–16). Commercial harvest comprised the largest component of total harvest up until 2000 but has sharply declined since then except for the coho salmon harvest. The proportion of the total harvest contributed by the subsistence fishery has increased since 1995. The sport fishery harvest has always been a small component of the total harvest, with most sport-caught salmon being Chinook or coho salmon. Over all subdistricts, a steady decline in catch has occurred since 1986 and has not increased in the 2000s when escapements increased. Pink salmon harvest has been variable reflecting the typical strong even-year and weak odd-year cycle; however, catches did not increase in response to large runs experienced from 2004–2006. Subsistence catch of Chinook salmon markedly increased in 1994, remained stable until 1999, and then declined since. Similar to the Chinook fishery, subsistence catch of coho salmon increased sharply in 1994 and has remained relatively stable at higher levels than previously. Approximately, 75% of the sharp increase in commercial catch of coho salmon after 2002 was attributed to the Unalakleet Subdistrict.

Fishery Management

Authority

In the Norton Sound region, on nonfederal lands, salmon management is the primary responsibility of the ADF&G and a state regulatory Board of Fisheries (BOF), and both are advised by three local advisory committees (Northern Norton Sound, Northern Seward Peninsula, Southern Norton Sound) representing the residents of the different geographic regions of the management area. In 1999, due to several lawsuits, subsistence management on federal lands reverted to the federal government (Buklis 2002). Subsistence fishery regulations in U.S. federal waters generally parallel state management and are under the purview of a regulatory Federal Subsistence Board advised by one regional advisory council (Seward Peninsula). Commercial and sport fisheries on federal lands are managed by ADF&G. Most salmon populations spawn in rivers on nonfederal lands, and thus, freshwater and near-shore marine fisheries are managed solely by ADF&G. Portions of the Kuzitrin and Fish rivers in the Nome area and portions of the Unalakleet River are on federal lands and subject to the dual federal-state management system (Magdanz et al. 2003). State and federal programs provide a priority to subsistence harvest over commercial and sport harvests.

General management approach

Management of salmon in the Norton Sound seeks to allow sufficient escapement of salmon to spawning rivers to ensure long-term sustainable yields. Fishery harvests are controlled through regulations to allow adequate spawning escapements and to permit harvest when salmon abundance exceeds escapement requirements. Salmon fisheries are managed under three different sets of regulations: subsistence, commercial, and sport (Magdanz et al. 2003). Subsistence fisheries are defined as the "noncommercial, customary and traditional uses of wild renewable resources for direct personal or family consumption… and for customary trade, barter, or sharing…" (AS 16.05.940). Any state resident can participate in a state-managed fishery. Commercial fisheries was defined as fishing "with the intent of disposing of [fish] for profit, or by sale, barter, trade, or in commercial channels." (AS 16.05.940). Commercial fisheries since 1977 have required a limited

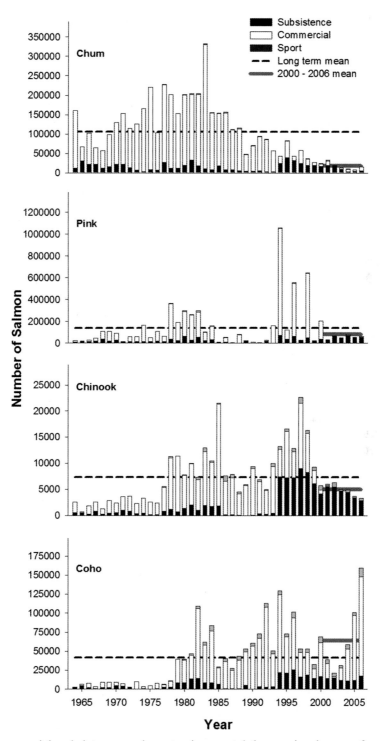

FIGURE 10. Commercial, subsistence, and sport salmon catch by species, by year for all subdistricts in Norton Sound District, 1964–2006. Subsistence harvest 1997–1998 include data from Savoonga and Gamble. Not all subdistricts were surveyed for subsistence harvest from 1983–1993 and from 2004–2006.

-entry permit to participate. Sport fishing was defined as fishing for personal use with a rod and reel (AS 16.05.940) and requires participants to purchase an angling license.

Management in the early 1960s focused primarily on commercial fisheries and relied on catch indices of salmon abundance based on catch per unit of effort (CPUE) statistics and aerial surveys. Comparisons were made between periods to determine when the midpoint of a particular salmon species run occurred, and then were compared between years. Aerial surveys were used to assess escapement of salmon, but as the surveys occurred late in the run, they were not useful for in-season management. The accuracy of aerial survey counts was affected by weather, river conditions, and observer variability in counting the salmon. The surveys were used as an index to escapement and compared between years to determine trends in salmon abundance. Regulations were then formulated in response to changes in salmon abundance.

Current management focuses on using escapement counts for certain species from tower and weir counts, and to a lesser extent on aerial survey data to meet goals for escapement established for subdistricts, and for specific streams. For example, a chum salmon BEG for the Nome Subdistrict was established as 23,000–35,000 fish (Clark 2001b). Managers attempt to ensure sufficient escapement occurs to the spawning grounds, while providing harvest opportunities when returns exceed escapement needs (Menard 2007). If concerns exist over meeting escapement, subsistence fishing may be restricted or closed in season. Commercial fishing is allowed if a market is available and if the commercial fishery will not jeopardize salmon escapement requirements or the reasonable opportunity for subsistence fishing (except in Nome Subdistrict where commercial fishing is closed by regulation). In the sections below, details are provided regarding escape-

ment goal setting, regulatory measures by fishery, and a description of management in the Nome Subdistrict.

Escapement goals

All three types of escapement goals (BEG, SEG, and OEG) are used for salmon management purposes in Norton Sound. Escapement goals have not been established for every species and every river; however, meeting goals for some species in some rivers inadvertently provides protection for other species and protection in adjacent rivers. Escapement goal setting has focused on chum and Chinook salmon in the most important river systems.

Escapement goals have evolved over the years from taking an average of previous years escapement usually determined as an index of escapement from aerial surveys (Buklis 1993) to using time-series data to calculate stock–recruitment relationships and maximum sustained yield. BEGs have the greatest data requirements as they use estimates of maximum sustained yield. BEGs were established using a range of 0.8–1.6 of the escapement required for maximum sustained yield. For example, Clark (2001a) describes the derivation of a BEG for chum salmon in the Kwiniuk and Tubutulik rivers in the Moses Point Subdistrict. SEGs are also used for management of some rivers and are based on historical escapement data averaged over time that have yielded sustainable fisheries. For example, SEGs have been established for Chinook salmon for the Shaktoolik River (400–800 fish; aerial survey goal), Old Woman River (550–1,100 fish; aerial survey goal), and North River (1,200–2,600 fish; fish tower goal; Kent and Bergstrom 2006). OEGs have also been established for some rivers and include considerations of both biological data and harvest needs for the subsistence fishery. OEGs have been established for the Nome, Snake, Eldorado, Kwiniuk, and Tubutulik rivers and these goals are to be used in conjugation with the overall BEG established for the Nome Subdistrict (Clark 2001b; Menard 2007). In 2003 and 2006, ADF&G reviewed escapement goals for various rivers in AYK and provided further recommendations (ADF&G 2004; Brannian et al. 2006).

Subsistence regulation

Few regulations have been used in the management area to control subsistence harvest with the exception of the Nome Subdistrict (discussed in detail below). Typically, subsistence salmon fishing with no harvest limits is allowed seven days a week. Salmon can be taken using gillnet, seine, and fish wheel, and also by angling in northern Norton Sound. Only spearing of salmon is prohibited. Exceptions occur in the Norton Sound Subdistrict and Unakaleet Subdistricts, which are closed to subsistence fishing for several days each week (Magdanz et al. 2003). Also, in the Port Clarence District only the northeastern portion of Salmon Lake can be opened by emergency order for subsistence fishing. In some areas in the Nome and Unalakleet subdistricts, gill nets are limited in length. In 1994, a new regulation banned drift gillnetting in the Unalakleet River. This regulation was adopted to prevent subsistence fishers from using gillnets to drift through deep water holes where Chinook salmon were holding. In the Nome Subdistrict, several upstream areas are closed to salmon fishing to protect spawning salmon. Subsistence fishing is prohibited in the area immediately adjacent to the mouth of the Unalakleet River to encourage escapement of Chinook salmon. Subsistence salmon permits were first required in 1964 for the Pilgrim River drainage, and Salmon Lake in the Port Clarence District, and in 1968 in the Nome Subdistrict. Bag limits were then imposed by permit for species such as chum and coho salmon. Regulation of subsistence fisheries of the Nome Subdistrict is discussed in more detail below. In 2004, the subsistence permit system was expanded outside of the Nome Subdistrict to include most northern Norton Sound villages.

Commercial regulation

Commercial fishing regulations control the time, area, gear, and participation in the fishery. Since the initiation of commercial fishing in the 1960s, only set gillnets have been legal gear. Area boundaries were set for the six subdistricts and only minimal boundary changes have occurred since the 1960s. The commercial fishing schedule initially allowed for two 48-h commercial fishing periods per week except for the Nome Subdistrict, where commercial fishing was allowed seven days a week. The limited entry program went into effect in 1977 and restricted those who could fish commercially for salmon. Permits were awarded based on historical participation in the commercial fishery.

Fishing time was reduced by regulation in the Nome Subdistrict (discussed below), and Moses Point, Shaktoolik, and Unalakleet subdistricts. In the Moses Point Subdistrict, commercial fishing was restricted to two 24-h periods per week in the late 1980s. In the Shaktoolik Subdistrict and Unalakleet Subdistrict, a maximum of two 24-h fishing periods per week are permitted during Chinook salmon runs. All other subdistricts are allowed to commercial fish for up to two 48 h periods per week. Managers have emergency order authority to open and close fishing. In the 2000s, little commercial fishing for Chinook salmon has been allowed because of poor runs.

Gillnet length and mesh size are regulated to control harvest and species caught. Each permit holder is allowed 100 fathoms of gear (600 feet; Figure 11). Restrictions in mesh size allow managers the opportunity to have commercial permit holders target particular salmon species and reduce the harvest of other salmon species. Commercial periods

FIGURE 11. Lifting a gill net for salmon near Grantley Harbor, Norton Sound, Alaska. Photo by Scott Kent.

with mesh size restricted to 4½ inches stretch measure are designed to target pink salmon. Mesh size restrictions of six inches or less stretch measure are used to target chum or coho salmon in commercial fishing periods.

Sport fishery regulation

Sport fishery harvests are regulated by species, daily, and possession bag limits, size limits, and closed areas. General regulations allow the harvest of only one Chinook salmon longer than 20 in and ten salmon of other species with no size limit. In the Nome Subdistrict and Golovnin Bay Subdistrict, chum salmon harvest is limited to three fish; however, chum salmon sport fishing is closed in the waters between the Solomon River to the Sinuk River. Special regulations apply to Chinook fishing in the Unalakleet River where the daily and possession limit is one

fish longer than 20 in and an annual limit of two Chinook salmon longer than 20 in. A harvest record must be filled out immediately upon landing a Chinook salmon. Also on the Unalakleet River, the daily bag and possession limit is ten fish, of which only four fish in combination may be chum, coho, or sockeye salmon.

Nome Subdistrict

The Nome Subdistrict has been subject to the most intensive management regulation of any subdistrict in Norton Sound Management Area (Figure 1). This subdistrict includes the city of Nome, which is home to nearly half of all Norton Sound residents, and hence demands on salmon resources have been higher there than in other subdistricts. High human demand for salmon and environmental damages caused by gold mining to local stream spawning habitats (discussed earlier) when combined with periods of low ocean productivity have generated the need more intensive management to sustain the salmon resources. A chronology of subsistence and commercial regulation is provided below. This section also provides a few comments regarding regulations in the Port Clarence District (Figure 2) because Nome residents travel by road into this district to fish the Pilgrim River for sockeye salmon and can be especially motivated to do so when regulations restrict fishing opportunities in the Nome Subdistrict (Magdanz et al. 2003).

Commercial fishing restrictions in Nome Subdistrict increased each decade since statehood until 1996. In the early 1970s, the commercial fishing schedule in the Nome Subdistrict was restricted to two 48-h periods per week. In 1985, this schedule changed to two 24-h periods per week and the western part of the subdistrict was closed to commercial fishing. The last commercial harvest in the Nome Subdistrict was in 1996.

Subsistence salmon permits were first required in 1964 in freshwaters for the Pilgrim River drainage, and Salmon Lake in the Port Clarence District, and in 1968 required for four rivers, Nome, Sinuk, Snake, and Solomon Rivers in Nome Subdistrict. Also, Grand Central River, a tributary to Salmon Lake was closed to fishing in 1964 to protect spawning sockeye salmon. In the late 1950s, a road was built from Nome to the Salmon Lake area and salmon runs were thought to have decreased as a result of the increased fishing pressure from Nome residents. Catch restrictions were first placed on the Pilgrim River-Salmon Lake area in 1966 and permit holders could harvest no more than 50 fish, of which only 25 fish could be salmon from these waters. In 1968, when permits were required in the four Nome Subdistrict rivers, a 500 salmon limit per permit was established. By regulating salmon harvest by permit, fishery management biologists sought to control

harvest and allow sufficient escapement to meet salmon spawning needs.

In 1972, Salmon Lake in the Port Clarence District was closed to subsistence fishing from July 15 through August 31 to protect sockeye salmon. This closure displaced fishing effort from these waters into Nome Subdistrict waters. In response to this displacement, subsistence fishing in Nome Subdistrict was restricted from five to four days a week in 1973. In 1975, the salmon permit requirement was expanded to include all marine and fresh waters in the Nome Subdistrict. In 1976, permit limits were reduced on the Nome River from 500 to 100 salmon. In 1979, restrictions were placed on beach seining with boundaries set on the Nome, Sinuk, Snake and Solomon rivers, upstream of which no seining could occur. A 1978–1979 Norton Sound stock identification study showed the commercial fishery to be intercepting nonlocal stocks as salmon tagged near Nome were recaptured in fisheries from Golovnin Bay Subdistrict to Kotzebue, north of the Seward Peninsula (Gaudet and Schaefer 1982).

Further restrictions occurred in the mid-1980s in Nome Subdistrict 1 after poor chum salmon escapements occurred in 1982 and 1983. Nome area residents became increasingly concerned about the poor runs of chum salmon (Magdanz and Olanna 1984) and expressed these to ADF&G. During the 1984 fall meeting of the Board of Fisheries, restrictions were placed on the commercial, subsistence, and sport fisheries limiting the number of salmon that could be harvested. Subsistence permit limits in the Nome and Snake rivers were set at 20 chum and 20 coho salmon. Even with these regulations in place, chum salmon escapement goals were difficult to attain. The 1987 returns of chum and pink salmon to Nome streams were poor. In response to the continuing trend of decreasing chum and pink salmon returns, new regulations were adopted by the Board of Fisheries in 1987. The commercial fishery was all but eliminated, bag limits were again lowered on the sport fishery, and the net length used by the subsistence fishery was limited to 50 ft of gillnet in the Nome River. Beach seines were also banned in several streams.

During the next Board of Fisheries meeting, new directives were given to fishery management biologists beginning with the 1991 season. No chum salmon harvests were to be allowed until escapement goals were likely to be met. In 1992, the Board of Fisheries continued to be concerned over the Norton Sound chum salmon fisheries and they considered at that time the declaration of a Tier II subsistence fishery (restricted access fishery). However, this option was rejected by the Board of Fisheries and other restrictions were placed on the fishery (Alaska Board of Fisheries 1992). Unfortunately, the restrictions in harvest and fishing time established during the 1990s failed to halt the

trend of declining salmon runs, particularly chum salmon. Problems were also created by delaying of subsistence harvest until escapement goals were assured. Salmon caught were often split and dried on racks outdoors (Figure 12). Subsistence fishers expressed concern that chum salmon harvests, which were now delayed until later in the run, were difficult to dry properly. The drying weather in late July and August typically tended to be poor due to more rain.

To reverse the decline in runs and to provide for subsistence harvest earlier in the run, the Board of Fisheries in 1999 declared that chum salmon would be managed as a Tier II fishery in the Nome Subdistrict. The Nome Subdistrict chum fishery was the first and has been the only Tier II fishery in the state. Tier I subsistence fisheries, though requiring a permit, were managed as open access fisheries for all state residents. A Tier II fishery was a limited entry fishery with access

FIGURE 12. Split salmon drying near the village of Teller, Port Clarence, Alaska. Photo by Scott Kent.

to the fishery rigidly controlled by allocation of a limited number of permits. Participation was restricted to only those people who demonstrated the greatest dependence on the resource based on a number of factors (5 ACC 01.1.82 and 5 ACC 01.1.84). Each household was allowed one application for a Tier II permit. Households were scored based on the household fishing history and their dependence on chum salmon. For every year a household had fished, one point was scored up to a maximum of 75 points. Ten additional points were available if during the last four years the majority of the harvest was chum salmon. The number of permits awarded was based on the estimated availability of chum salmon and each permit holder was limited in the number of chum salmon that could be harvested.

The Tier II chum salmon fishery allowed managers to open subsistence fishing for a limited number of permit holders early in the summer before confirming that escapement goals would be met. If escapement goals were reached then the fishery would revert to a Tier I fishery and all other subsistence fishers could fish. If escapement goals were not likely to be met, then even Tier II chum salmon fishing could be closed partway through the summer season. In practice Tier II restrictions were lifted usually in late July or early August when coho salmon outnumbered chum salmon to allow Tier I permit holders access to the salmon fishery. During the chum salmon season, periodic beach seine openings have occurred to allow Tier I permit holders to target pink salmon.

In the last several years (2004–2006), salmon runs rebounded to record levels for pink and coho salmon in the Nome Subdistrict. Chum salmon runs have been well above average and record setting in some rivers (Menard and Bergstrom 2006b). With the increase in chum salmon runs, Tier II subsistence fishing was not used in 2006 to control harvest as the numbers of fish above escape-

ment needs exceeded the amount needed for subsistence (Menard 2007).

Management Evolution

Management strategies have evolved dramatically during the nearly five decades of salmon management since statehood (Hilsinger et al. 2009, this volume). In the early years after statehood, management tended to react to changes in salmon harvests by commercial and subsistence fishers. If catches were poor when compared to previous years, fishery managers would take action to reduce harvest by restricting fishing time. Aerial surveys were an important source of data to manage salmon fisheries. The advantage was that a large area could be covered quickly and economically. Aerial surveys did not give the actual escapement of a river or lake, but provided an index of escapement because not all fish were seen during an aerial survey. The number of salmon counted during a survey was compared with other years to determine if run strength was similar, weak, or strong. However, surveys were only flown once over a stream, typically during the peak of the run every year. Weather and water conditions greatly affected survey accuracy. In some years, no acceptable surveys were flown because of poor visibility or weather conditions. Determining species of salmon from the air was difficult. For example, in years of high pink salmon numbers, great difficulties occurred in identifying and counting chum salmon.

A focus on escapement requirements for salmon spawning began in the late 1970s when goals were first established for Norton Sound rivers. These goals gave managers a clear target upon which to base management decisions. In-season decisions to manage on-going fisheries potentially could enhance the possibility of meeting these targets. The adoption of using escapement goals in salmon management drove the need to improve escapement estimates. Prior to the 1990s, most escapement information was collected through aerial surveys. Because aerial surveys most often occurred during the peak of the run to document run strength, the survey method caused in-season management decisions to be made toward the end of the run. In-season management actions when dependent on aerial survey data were, therefore, not as effective as they could have been if management actions had been implemented earlier in the run cycle.

In the 1990s, salmon escapement was monitored more through counting towers and weirs. These data were more accurate and precise, and provided the opportunity to project run strength earlier in the run cycle than with aerial survey data. Fishery management biologists were better able to assess the strength of on-going salmon runs and to implement more effective decisions to ensure escapement goals would be met.

Permit systems in the commercial and subsistence fisheries allowed managers to estimate potential effort that would be exerted each season. The commercial limited entry permit system established in the mid-1970s enabled managers to estimate the number of commercial fishers that would likely participate in a fishery. Similarly, a subsistence permit system was initiated to track effort and for catch reporting. The subsistence permit system (Tier I) also allowed managers to restrict harvest of salmon by having a seasonal catch limits. Further restrictions were implemented by limiting when subsistence fishing could occur. When chum salmon runs were at their lowest abundance in the Nome Subdistrict, a limited entry Tier II subsistence permit system was implemented. This approach gave managers the opportunity to allocate the limited salmon resource to subsistence users with the greatest need.

Information Needs

In the mid-1990s, cooperative partnerships were formed between governmental, nonprofit, and private organizations to improve data collection on salmon runs. In 1999, after a disastrous chum salmon run, a federal grant of $5 million dollars was received to provide increased funding for research and restoration projects. Numerous projects were extended through the summer to early fall, which documented the increase of coho salmon runs that occurred in Norton Sound. The additional projects across northern Norton Sound enabled managers to gain a better understanding of run timing and permitted the careful review of escapement goals for a number of river systems. This funding ended on June 30, 2007 leaving critical escapement monitoring projects unfunded.

Additionally, unmet information needs exist for Chinook salmon in southern Norton Sound. Only one project, North River tower, provides accurate Chinook salmon escapement counts relative to an established escapement goal; however, the proportion of Chinook salmon that use the North River in comparison to the balance of the Unalakleet drainage needs to be reassessed via radio-telemetry mark-recapture estimates. Also, during telemetry studies in 2005 and 2006 in the Unalakleet River, chum and Chinook salmon were obtained by beach seining. Age-sex-length information from Chinook salmon indicated that a large proportion of the fish were jacks (small mature males; Estensen and Evenson 2006). A more rigorous sampling program is needed for Chinook salmon to determine if older age classes than jacks are in decline, similar to the concerns expressed for Yukon River Chinook salmon (Hard 2009, this volume; Evenson et al. 2009, this volume). The sampling program should include carcass surveys in numerous southern Norton Sound rivers to determine if age composition is declining throughout the area or only in major rivers where Chinook salmon are fished.

Last, several rivers nearby to the Unalakleet River have Chinook salmon runs and a few have aerial survey escapement goals. However, information is limited about the contributions of these rivers to the Norton Sound Chinook salmon fishery. Escapement monitoring should be extended to these rivers. Escapement goals for some systems could also be set for some systems based on the quality and quantity of stream habitat (Nemeth et al. 2009, this volume).

Management Lessons

First, management actions such as harvest limits and Tier II permits sometimes can have unintended consequences. Subsistence permits combined with harvest limits first used in the 1960s in the sockeye salmon fishery in the Pilgrim River had unexpected consequences. Permits had little direct effect on the fishery but provided useful information on the numbers of participants and harvest. However, the harvest limits tended to displace fishing effort. For example, the harvest limits associated with the subsistence permits for the Pilgrim River sockeye salmon fishery controlled harvest, but also caused residents to travel to other areas where harvests were not limited. Thus, the limits caused fishing effort to be geographically displaced.

The Tier II permit system in the Nome Subdistrict yielded a similar effect as the original Tier I permit system with harvest limits. The limited fishing allowed in the Nome Subdistrict due to Tier II restrictions caused people to fish in areas adjacent to the Nome Subdistrict such as in the Port Clarence District. Concern was expressed by residents in these adjacent areas about the increase in the number of people fishing (Magdanz

et al. 2003). As a result, the Tier II fishery while protecting chum salmon stocks inside the Nome Subdistrict caused increased harvest pressure on stocks in adjacent areas. In response, ADF&G began restricting fishing time in the adjacent areas.

Second, the reduced use of chum salmon caused by low run sizes and restricted harvest may have changed cultural values toward the species. A shift in values in the subsistence fishery seems to have occurred over the past decade away from chum salmon to coho and pink salmon, and beginning in 2003, to sockeye salmon in response to the record Pilgrim River runs (Figure 13). By 2004, when fishing restrictions began to be liberalized in the Nome Subdistrict, particularly for chum salmon, the managers observed that fewer fishers than expected were interested in fishing for that species. Record numbers of subsistence permits were issued in both the Nome Subdistrict and for the Pilgrim River. Permit holders, instead of fishing for chum salmon, targeted the more abundant pink and coho salmon in the Nome Subdistrict, and sockeye salmon in Port Clarence District, in the Pilgrim River. When Tier II restrictions were suspended in 2006, little interest seemed to exist among fishers in targeting chum salmon. Most people were now targeting other species.

What was the cause for this shift? We speculate that a decade-long limited harvest of chum salmon due to management actions had altered human behavior, fishing practices, and preferences for salmon species. Also, with hook and line becoming legal subsistence gear in the 2000s in northern Norton Sound, a shift was seen in the Nome Subdistrict as the majority of the subsistence catch during large pink salmon runs was caught by hook and line, and not nets.

We believe that harvest regulations allowed many more salmon to reach the spawning grounds and helped to restore salmon populations and their fisheries. However, the

FIGURE 13. Pilgrim River, Alaska. One of a few streams in the Norton Sound region with a substantial run of sockeye salmon. Photo by Christian Zimmerman.

Discussion

restrictions affected not only the fish but also those who fished and caused changes in fishing patterns in time and space and potentially cultural values.

Salmon runs in Norton Sound have fluctuated greatly over the last hundred years. Recently, we went through a period of poor returns for chum and pink salmon that resulted in the disaster declaration of 1999. We have also seen significant ups and down in sockeye salmon abundance. Beginning in 2003 with sockeye salmon, and in 2004 with chum, coho and pink salmon, large increases were seen in salmon runs. Near record to record breaking runs occurred for coho, pink and sockeye salmon during the past three years and chum salmon runs have improved greatly. Unfortunately Chinook salmon runs have continued to decline since the late 1990s and have not shown any rebound. What role has harvest management had in these fluctuations in salmon abundance?

The approach used by ADF&G to restore depressed salmon runs has been to 1) review escapement goals and adjust them as necessary so they accurately reflect the productivity of the stock, 2) reduce harvests to ensure those goals are achieved if at all possible, and 3) implement monitoring programs to ensure that accurate data on escapement number, age, sex, and length are collected and, 4) implement research programs, such as radio telemetry mark-recapture estimates, to ensure that where escapement is counted on tributary rivers, that escapement represents a known and consistent part of the total escapement to the drainage. Besides time and gear restrictions the ADF&G has attempted to reduce harvest by implementing catch limits. If salmon runs were poorer than expected the salmon fishery could be closed by emergency order.

Ensuring escapement goals are met through harvest controls, represents a management action that solves one part of the life cycle required to produce the next generation of salmon. Regulation of harvest ensures that this critical link within the life cycle of salmon remains unbroken. Without adequate escapement to the spawning grounds salmon runs could not have rebounded in recent years. However, restoration of salmon is more complicated and dependent on a wide set of variables including favorable ocean conditions for growth and survival (Mantua 2009), and suitable juvenile rearing and spawning habitats (Hillgruber and Zimmerman 2009, this volume). Ocean conditions likely have large influence on salmon returns each year (Beamish and Sweeting 2009, this volume) and managers have little control over these conditions. On the other hand, managers can affect stream habitats through management of riparian vegetation and in some cases physical reconstruction. Juvenile rearing and spawning habitat have been damaged in some Norton Sound streams due to mining activities and possibilities may exist to restore these habitats. Continued effective harvest management combined with improved stream habitats have the potential to further promote the rebound of salmon runs experienced in recent years in the Norton Sound area.

Acknowledgments

The authors thank the seasonal employees who worked long and irregular hours on field projects and gathered the data so critical to management of Norton Sound salmon fisheries. We also thank Kawerak, Inc., Native Village of Unalakleet, Norton Sound Economic Development Corporation (NSEDC) and U.S. Bureau of Land Management (BLM) for operating escapement counting projects. The Arctic-Yukon-Kuskokwim Sustainable Salmon Initiative, Bering Sea Fishermen's Association, BLM, NSEDC, Norton Sound Salmon Research and Restoration Initiative, and U.S. Fish and Wildlife Service provided funding support for some of the Norton Sound projects. Holly Patrick and Scott Miehls prepared the Figures and appendix tables. Three anonymous peer reviewers provided helpful comments on earlier drafts of this paper.

References

ADF&G (Alaska Department of Fish and Game). 2004. Escapement goal review of select AYK Region salmon stocks. Division of Commercial Fisheries, Regional Information Report Number 3A04–01. Alaska Department of Fish and Game, Anchorage.

Alaska Board of Fisheries. 1992. Norton Sound chum salmon findings. 92–136-FB. Alaska Department of Fish and Game, Anchorage.

Beamish, R. J., and R. M. Sweeting. 2009. The history of surprises associated with Pacific salmon returns signals that critical information is missing from our understanding of their population dynamics. Pages 1159–1168 in C. C. Krueger and C. E. Zimmerman, editors. Pacific salmon: ecology and management of western Alaska's populations. American Fisheries Society, Symposium 70, Bethesda, Maryland.

Bockstoce, J. 1979. The archeology of Cape Nome, Alaska. The University Museum, University of Pennsylvania, Museum of Archaeology and Anthropology, Philadelphia.

Brannian, L. K., M. J. Evenson, and J. R. Hilsinger. 2006. Escapement goal recommendations for select Arctic-Yukon-Kuskokwim region salmon stocks, 2007. Division of Commercial Fisheries, Fishery Manuscript Number 06–07. Alaska Department of Fish and Game, Anchorage.

Buklis, L. S. 1993. Documentation of Arctic-Yukon-Kuskokwim Region salmon escapement goals in effect as of the 1992 fishing season. Division of Commercial Fisheries, Regional Information Report Number 3A93–03. Alaska Department of Fish and Game, Anchorage.

Buklis, L. S. 2002. Subsistence fisheries management on federal public lands in Alaska. Fisheries 27(7):10–18.

Burkhart G., and K. Dunmall. 2005. The Snake River, Eldorado River and Pilgrim River salmon escapement enumeration and sampling project summary report, 2005. Kawerak, Inc., Nome Alaska.

APPENDIX TABLE 10. Continued.

Year	Commercial						Subsistence						Combined					
	Chin	Sock	Coho	Pink	Chum	Total	Chin	Sock	Coho	Pink	Chum	Total	Chin	Sock	Coho	Pink	Chum	Total
1994	0	1	287	0	66	354	23	69	983	6,556	1,673	9,304	23	70	1,270	6,556	1,739	9,658
1995	0	1	369	0	122	492	26	148	1,365	336	3,794	5,669	26	149	1,734	336	3,916	6,161
1996	0	0	9	13	3	25	9	185	828	3,510	2,287	6,819	9	185	837	3,523	2,290	6,844
1997	0	0	0	0	0	0	10	50	325	175	2,696	3,256	10	50	325	175	2,696	3,256
1998	0	0	0	0	0	0	15	14	1,057	4,797	964	6,847	15	14	1,057	4,797	964	6,847
1999	0	0	0	0	0	0	11	85	161	58	337	652	11	85	161	58	337	652
2000	0	0	0	0	0	0	7	26	747	2,657	535	3,972	7	26	747	2,657	535	3,972
2001	0	0	0	0	0	0	2	92	425	113	858	1,490	2	92	425	113	858	1,490
2002	0	0	0	0	0	0	4	79	666	3,161	1,114	5,024	4	79	666	3,161	1,114	5,024
2003	0	0	0	0	0	0	63	76	351	507	565	1,562	63	76	351	507	565	1,562
2004	0	0	0	0	0	0	100	106	1,574	15,047	685	17,512	100	106	1,574	15,047	685	17,512
2005	0	0	0	0	0	0	62	177	1,287	5,075	803	7,404	62	177	1,287	5,075	803	7,404
2006	0	0	0	0	0	0	24	159	3,808	9,329	940	14,260	24	159	3,808	9,329	940	14,260
Short-term average	0	0	0	0	0	0	37	102	1265	5127	786	7318	37	102	1265	5127	786	7318
Long-term average	5	1	189	1,887	3,565	5,430	44	100	951	5,251	3,022	9,213	44	97	1,067	6,840	6,516	14,429

APPENDIX TABLE 11. Commercial and subsistence catch for Chinook (Chin), sockeye (Sock), coho, pink, and chum salmon, by year in Unalakleet Subdistrict, Norton Sound District, with long term mean (1961–2006) and short term mean (2000–2006).

Year	Commercial						Subsistence						Combined					
	Chin	Sock	Coho	Pink	Chum	Total	Chin	Sock	Coho	Pink	Chum	Total	Chin	Sock	Coho	Pink	Chum	Total
1961	5,160	35	13,807	5,162	23,586	47,750	-	-	-	-	-	-	-	-	-	-	-	-
1962	5,089	-	6,739	6,769	30,283	48,880	-	-	-	-	-	-	-	-	-	-	-	-
1963	5,941	18	16,202	1,140	27,003	50,304	-	-	-	-	-	-	-	-	-	-	-	-
1964	1,273	1	79	1	19,611	20,965	488	-	2,227	7,030	6,726	16,471	1,761	-	2,306	7,031	26,337	37,436
1965	1,321	-	2,030	24	26,498	29,873	521	-	4,562	11,488	8,791	25,362	1,842	-	6,592	11,512	35,289	55,235
1966	1,208	-	4,183	5,023	16,840	27,254	90	-	789	6,083	3,387	10,349	1,298	-	4,972	11,106	20,227	37,603
1967	1,751	-	1,544	21,961	8,502	33,758	490	-	484	9,964	-	10,938	2,241	-	2,028	31,925	-	44,696
1968	960	-	6,549	41,474	14,865	63,848	186	-	1,493	11,044	2,982	15,705	1,146	-	8,042	52,518	17,847	79,553
1969	2,276	-	5,273	40,558	22,032	70,139	324	-	1,483	4,230	4,196	10,233	2,600	-	6,756	44,788	26,228	80,372
1970	1,604	-	4,261	30,779	40,029	76,673	495	-	3,907	10,104	7,214	21,720	2,099	-	8,168	40,883	47,243	98,393
1971	2,166	-	2,688	1,196	37,543	43,593	911	-	3,137	2,230	7,073	13,351	3,077	-	5,825	3,426	44,616	56,944
1972	2,235	-	412	28,231	20,440	51,318	643	-	1,818	3,132	4,132	9,725	2,878	-	2,230	31,363	24,572	61,043
1973	1,397	-	8,922	13,335	25,716	49,370	323	-	213	6,233	3,426	10,195	1,720	-	9,135	19,568	29,142	59,565
1974	2,100	-	1,778	93,332	36,170	133,380	313	-	706	7,341	588	8,948	2,413	-	2,484	100,673	36,758	142,328
1975	1,638	-	3,167	12,137	48,740	65,682	163	-	74	4,758	2,038	7,033	1,801	-	3,241	16,895	50,778	72,715
1976	1,211	-	5,141	37,203	24,268	67,824	142	-	694	4,316	2,832	7,984	1,353	-	5,835	41,519	27,100	75,808
1977	2,691	1	2,781	21,001	32,936	59,410	723	-	1,557	8,870	6,085	17,235	3,414	-	4,338	29,871	39,021	76,645
1978	7,525	5	5,737	136,200	37,079	186,546	1,044	-	2,538	13,268	3,442	20,292	8,569	-	8,275	149,468	40,521	206,838
1979	6,354	8	23,696	49,647	30,445	110,150	640	-	3,330	6,960	1,597	12,527	6,994	-	27,026	56,607	32,042	122,677
1980	4,339	3	21,512	203,142	64,198	293,194	1,046	-	4,758	19,071	5,230	30,105	5,385	-	26,270	222,213	69,428	323,299
1981	6,157	47	29,845	123,233	39,186	198,468	869	24	5,808	5,750	4,235	16,686	7,026	71	35,653	128,983	43,421	215,154
1982	3,768	2	61,343	142,856	44,520	252,489	913	2	7,037	20,045	4,694	32,691	4,681	4	68,380	162,901	49,214	285,180
1983	7,022	13	36,098	26,198	109,220	178,551	1,868	33	6,888	13,808	4,401	26,998	8,890	46	42,986	40,006	113,621	205,549
1984	6,804	6	47,904	-	43,317	98,031	1,650	1	6,675	17,418	3,348	29,092	8,454	7	54,579	-	46,665	127,123
1985	12,621	21	15,421	1	25,111	53,175	1,397	3	2,244	55	1,968	5,667	14,018	24	17,665	56	27,079	58,842
1986	4,494	153	20,580	-	30,239	55,466	-	-	-	-	-	-	-	-	-	-	-	-
1987	3,246	141	15,097	97	17,525	36,106	-	-	-	-	-	-	-	-	-	-	-	-
1988	2,218	157	24,232	23,730	25,363	75,700	-	-	-	-	-	-	-	-	-	-	-	-
1989	4,402	222	36,025	-	20,825	61,474	2476	-	4,681	17,500	1,388	-	8,474	-	40,706	17,500	22,213	-
1990	5,998	358	52,015	-	23,659	82,030	-	-	-	-	-	-	-	-	-	-	-	-
1991	4,534	147	52,033	-	39,609	96,323	-	-	-	-	-	-	-	-	-	-	-	-
1992	3,409	229	84,449	6,284	52,547	146,918	-	-	-	-	-	-	-	-	-	-	-	-
1993	5,944	251	26,290	42,061	28,156	102,702	-	-	-	-	-	-	-	-	-	-	-	-
1994	4,400	71	71,019	480,158	12,288	567,936	5,294	819	16,081	31,572	12,732	66,498	9,694	890	87,100	511,730	25,020	634,434
1995	7,617	78	31,280	37,009	24,843	100,827	5,049	807	13,110	17,246	13,460	49,672	12,666	885	44,390	54,255	38,303	150,499
1996	3,644	-	52,200	113,837	7,369	177,050	5,324	608	15,963	19,782	16,481	58,158	8,968	608	68,163	133,619	23,850	235,208
1997	9,067	159	26,079	-	17,139	52,444	6,325	353	9,120	10,804	7,649	34,251	15,392	512	35,199	10,804	24,788	86,695

APPENDIX TABLE 11. Continued.

Year	Commercial						Subsistence						Combined					
	Chin	Sock	Coho	Pink	Chum	Total	Chin	Sock	Coho	Pink	Chum	Total	Chin	Sock	Coho	Pink	Chum	Total
1998	6,413	7	24,534	99,412	6,210	136,576	5,915	639	11,825	17,259	7,962	43,600	12,328	646	36,359	116,671	14,172	180,176
1999	1,927	0	10,264	0	5,700	17,891	4,504	848	10,250	10,791	10,040	36,433	6,431	848	20,514	10,791	15,740	54,324
2000	582	11	29,803	17,278	2,700	50,374	2,887	569	9,487	11,075	7,294	31,312	3,469	580	39,290	28,353	9,994	81,686
2001	116	1	15,102	0	1,512	16,731	3,662	376	9,520	11,710	9,163	34,431	3,778	377	24,622	11,710	10,675	51,162
2002	4	1	1,079	0	339	1,423	3,044	600	8,301	23,599	8,599	44,143	3,048	601	9,380	23,599	8,938	45,566
2003	10	0	13,027	0	3,075	16,112	2,585	283	6,192	21,777	1,785	32,622	2,595	283	19,219	21,777	4,860	48,734
2004	0	40	29,282	0	4,924	34,246	2,801	334	5,978	20,883	1,211	31,207	2,801	374	35,260	20,883	6,135	65,453
2005	101	280	63,437	0	3,192	67,010	2,115	593	6,949	21,836	1,506	32,999	2,216	873	70,386	21,836	4,698	100,009
2006	11	3	98,336	0	6,721	105,071	2,155	326	7,937	22,547	2,712	35,677	2,166	329	106,273	22,547	9,433	140,748
Short-term average	118	48	35,724	2,468	3,209	41,567	2,750	440	7,766	19,061	4,610	34,627	2,868	488	43,490	21,529	7,819	76,194
Long-term average	3,538	75	23,984	46,512	25,697	93,718	1,911	401	5,495	12,544	5,439	25,437	5,214	432	27,490	64,664	30,456	125,648

APPENDIX TABLE 12. Commercial and subsistence catch for Chinook (Chin), sockeye (Sock), coho, pink, and chum salmon, by year in Golovnin Bay Subdistrict, Norton Sound District, with long term mean (1962–2006) and short term mean (2000–2006).

Year	Commercial						Subsistence						Combined					
	Chin	Sock	Coho	Pink	Chum	Total	Chin	Sock	Coho	Pink	Chum	Total	Chin	Sock	Coho	Pink	Chum	Total
1962	45	11	264	10,276	68,720	79,316	-	-	-	-	-	-	45	11	264	10,276	68,720	79,316
1963	40	40	-	19,677	49,850	69,607	-	-	118	5,702	9,319	15,139	40	40	118	25,379	59,169	84,746
1964	27	40	3	7,236	58,301	65,607	-	-	-	-	-	-	27	40	3	7,236	58,301	65,607
1965	-	-	-	-	-	-	2	-	49	1,523	3,847	5,421	2	-	49	1,523	3,847	5,421
1966	17	14	584	4,665	29,791	35,071	4	-	176	1,573	3,520	5,273	21	14	760	6,238	33,311	40,344
1967	10	-	747	5,790	31,193	37,740	3	-	185	2,774	4,803	7,765	13	-	932	8,564	35,996	45,505
1968	12	-	205	18,428	10,011	28,656	4	-	181	4,955	1,744	6,884	16	-	386	23,383	11,755	35,540
1969	28	-	1,224	23,208	20,949	45,409	2	-	190	2,760	2,514	5,466	30	-	1,414	25,968	23,463	50,875
1970	13	-	3	18,721	20,566	39,303	4	-	353	2,046	2,614	5,017	17	-	356	20,767	23,180	44,320
1971	37	-	197	2,735	33,824	36,793	7	-	191	1,544	1,936	3,678	44	-	388	4,279	35,760	40,471
1972	36	-	20	6,562	27,097	33,715	4	-	62	1,735	2,028	3,829	40	-	82	8,297	29,125	37,544
1973	70	-	183	14,145	41,689	56,087	1	-	48	9	74	132	71	-	231	14,154	41,763	56,219
1974	30	-	3	28,340	30,173	58,546	3	-	-	967	205	1,175	33	-	3	29,307	30,378	59,721
1975	17	-	206	10,770	41,761	52,754	-	-	1	2,011	2,025	4,037	17	-	207	12,781	43,786	56,791
1976	12	-	1,311	24,051	30,219	55,593	-	-	-	1,995	1,128	3,123	12	-	1,311	26,046	31,347	58,716
1977	26	-	426	7,928	53,912	62,292	3	-	80	703	2,915	3,701	29	-	506	8,631	56,827	65,993
1978	22	-	94	72,033	41,462	113,611	1	-	-	2,470	1,061	3,532	23	-	94	74,503	42,523	117,143
1979	75	49	1,606	45,948	30,201	77,879	-	-	845	2,546	2,840	6,231	75	49	2,451	48,494	33,041	84,110
1980	36	36	328	10,774	52,609	63,783	12	-	692	10,727	4,057	15,488	48	36	1,020	21,501	56,666	79,271
1981	23	5	13	49,755	58,323	108,119	8	-	1,520	5,158	5,543	12,229	31	5	1,533	54,913	63,866	120,348
1982	78	5	4,281	39,510	51,970	95,844	7	-	1,289	4,752	1,868	7,916	85	5	5,570	44,262	53,838	103,760
1983	52	10	295	17,414	48,283	66,054	-	-	-	-	-	-	-	-	-	-	-	-
1984	31	-	2,462	88,588	54,153	145,234	-	-	-	-	-	-	-	-	-	-	-	-
1985	193	113	1,196	3,019	55,781	60,302	12	2	430	1,904	9,577	11,925	205	115	1,626	4,923	65,358	72,227
1986	81	8	958	25,425	69,725	96,197	-	-	-	-	-	-	-	-	-	-	-	-
1987	166	51	2,203	1,579	44,334	48,333	-	-	-	-	-	-	-	-	-	-	-	-
1988	108	921	2,149	31,559	33,348	68,085	-	-	-	-	-	-	-	-	-	-	-	-
1989	0	0	0	0	0	0	-	-	-	-	-	-	-	-	-	-	-	-

APPENDIX TABLE 12. Contiuned.

Year	Commercial Chin	Sock	Coho	Pink	Chum	Total	Subsistence Chin	Sock	Coho	Pink	Chum	Total	Combined Chin	Sock	Coho	Pink	Chum	Total
1990	52	21	0	0	15,993	16,066	-	-	-	-	-	-	-	-	-	-	-	-
1991	49	1	0	0	14,839	14,889	-	-	-	-	-	-	-	-	-	-	-	-
1992	6	9	2,085	0	1,002	3,102	-	-	-	-	-	-	-	-	-	-	-	-
1993	1	4	2	8,480	2,803	11,290	-	-	-	-	-	-	-	-	-	-	-	-
1994	0	0	3,424	0	111	3,535	253	168	733	8,410	1,337	10,901	253	168	4,157	8,410	1,448	14,436
1995	0	0	1,616	4,296	1,987	7,899	165	34	1,649	7,818	10,373	20,039	165	34	3,265	12,114	12,360	27,938
1996	0	0	638	0	0	638	86	134	3,014	17,399	2,867	23,500	86	134	3,652	17,399	2,867	24,138
1997	19	2	102	20	8,003	8,146	138	427	555	4,570	4,891	10,581	157	429	657	4,590	12,894	18,727
1998	1	0	3	106,761	723	107,488	184	37	1,292	13,340	1,893	16,746	185	37	1,295	120,101	2,616	122,234
1999	0	0	0	0	0	0	60	48	1,234	469	3,656	5,467	60	48	1,234	469	3,656	5,467
2000	0	0	1,645	17,408	164	19,217	169	18	2,335	10,906	1,155	14,583	169	18	3,980	28,314	1,319	33,800
2001	0	43	30	0	7,094	7,167	89	72	880	1,665	3,291	5,997	89	115	910	1,665	10,385	13,164
2002	0	0	0	0	0	0	69	66	1,640	14,430	1,882	18,087	69	66	1,640	14,430	1,882	18,087
2003	0	0	0	0	0	0	166	28	309	5,012	1,477	6,992	166	28	309	5,012	1,477	6,992
2004	0	0	0	0	0	0	164	6	654	19,936	880	21,640	164	6	654	19,936	880	21,640
2005	0	0	0	0	0	0	96	15	686	11,467	1,852	14,116	96	15	686	11,467	1,852	14,116
2006	0	0	0	0	0	0	136	38	1,760	14,670	722	17,326	136	38	1,760	14,670	722	17,326
Short-term average	0	6	239	2,487	1,037	3,769	127	35	1,181	11,155	1,608	14,106	127	41	1,420	13,642	2,645	17,875
Long-term average	32	45	709	16,480	25,931	43,167	64	78	772	5,695	3,027	9,513	78	66	1,243	21,143	27,325	49,830

APPENDIX TABLE 13. Commercial and subsistence catch for Chinook (Chin), sockeye (Sock), coho, pink, and chum salmon, by year in Moses Point Subdistrict, Norton Sound District, with long term mean (1962–2006) and short term mean (2000–2006).

Year	Commercial						Subsistence						Combined					
	Chin	Sock	Coho	Pink	Chum	Total	Chin	Sock	Coho	Pink	Chum	Total	Chin	Sock	Coho	Pink	Chum	Total
1962	27	-	-	11,100	50,683	61,810	-	-	-	-	-	-	-	-	-	-	-	-
1963	15	-	-	2,549	46,274	48,838	5	-	-	5,808	8,316	14,129	20	-	-	8,357	54,590	62,967
1964	32	3	-	3,372	28,568	31,975	-	-	-	63	348	411	32	-	-	3,435	28,916	32,386
1965	-	-	-	-	-	-	16	-	-	1,325	9,857	11,270	-	-	-	-	-	-
1966	17	-	-	2,745	24,741	27,503	14	-	72	2,511	5,409	8,184	31	-	72	5,256	30,150	35,687
1967	-	-	-	-	-	-	39	-	116	1,322	9,913	11,390	-	-	-	-	-	-
1968	12	-	1	9,012	17,908	26,933	2	-	80	6,135	2,527	8,744	14	-	81	15,147	20,435	35,677
1969	29	-	-	11,807	26,594	38,430	9	-	109	1,790	1,303	3,211	38	-	109	13,597	27,897	41,641
1970	39	-	-	13,052	29,726	42,817	16	-	160	4,661	6,960	11,797	55	-	160	17,713	36,686	54,614
1971	95	-	4	922	43,831	44,852	16	-	271	1,046	2,227	3,560	111	-	275	1,968	46,058	48,412
1972	190	-	11	5,866	30,919	36,986	44	-	108	1,579	2,070	3,801	234	-	119	7,445	32,989	40,787
1973	134	-	-	10,603	31,389	42,126	2	-	-	-	298	300	136	-	-	10,603	31,687	42,426
1974	198	-	9	12,821	55,276	68,304	3	-	-	2,382	1,723	4,108	201	-	9	15,203	56,999	72,412
1975	16	-	-	4,407	46,699	51,122	2	-	6	1,280	508	1,796	18	-	6	5,687	47,207	52,918
1976	24	-	232	5,072	10,890	16,218	22	-	-	5,016	1,548	6,586	46	-	232	10,088	12,438	22,804
1977	96	-	6	9,443	47,455	57,000	22	-	225	1,145	1,170	2,562	118	-	231	10,588	48,625	59,562
1978	444	-	244	39,694	44,595	84,977	38	-	407	1,995	1,229	3,669	482	-	651	41,689	45,824	88,646
1979	1,035	-	177	40,811	37,123	79,146	16	-	890	6,078	1,195	8,179	1,051	-	1,067	46,889	38,318	87,325
1980	502	-	-	1,435	14,755	16,692	131	-	229	4,232	1,393	5,985	633	-	229	5,667	16,148	22,677
1981	198	-	5	26,417	29,325	55,945	32	-	2,345	6,530	2,819	11,726	230	-	2,350	32,947	32,144	67,671
1982	253	-	318	9,849	40,030	50,450	1	-	1,835	3,785	3,537	9,158	254	-	2,153	13,634	43,567	59,608
1983	254	-	-	17,027	65,776	83,057	-	-	-	-	-	-	-	-	-	-	-	-
1984	-	-	5,959	28,035	9,477	43,471	-	-	-	-	-	-	-	-	-	-	-	-
1985	816	32	1,803	559	24,466	27,676	67	-	1,389	1,212	947	3,615	883	-	3,192	1,771	25,413	31,291
1986	600	41	5,874	15,795	20,668	42,978	-	-	-	-	-	-	-	-	-	-	-	-
1987	907	15	64	568	17,278	18,832	-	-	-	-	-	-	-	-	-	-	-	-
1988	663	93	3,974	13,703	18,585	37,018	-	-	-	-	-	-	-	-	-	-	-	-
1989	62	0	0	0	167	229	-	-	-	-	-	-	-	-	-	-	-	-
1990	202	0	0	501	3,723	4,426	-	-	-	-	-	-	-	-	-	-	-	-
1991	161	0	0	0	804	965	312	-	2,153	3,555	2,660	8,680	473	-	2,153	3,555	3,464	9,645

APPENDIX TABLE 13. Continued.

Year	Commercial						Subsistence						Combined					
	Chin	Sock	Coho	Pink	Chum	Total	Chin	Sock	Coho	Pink	Chum	Total	Chin	Sock	Coho	Pink	Chum	Total
1992	0	0	3,531	0	6	3,537	100	-	1,281	6,152	1,260	8,793	100	-	4,812	6,152	1,266	12,330
1993	3	0	4,065	0	167	4,235	368	-	1,217	1,726	1,635	4,946	371	-	5,282	1,726	1,802	9,181
1994	0	0	5,345	0	414	5,759	322	104	1,180	9,345	3,476	14,427	322	104	6,525	9,345	3,890	20,186
1995	4	44	3,742	2,962	1,171	7,923	284	17	1,353	2,046	3,774	7,474	288	61	5,095	5,008	4,945	15,397
1996	0	0	1,915	68,609	0	70,524	417	52	1,720	9,442	2,319	13,950	417	52	3,635	78,051	2,319	84,474
1997	844	0	1,409	0	2,683	4,936	619	50	1,213	1,314	2,064	5,260	1,463	50	2,622	1,314	4,747	10,196
1998	105	0	1,462	145,669	2,311	149,547	414	49	1,831	6,891	1,376	10,561	519	49	3,293	152,560	3,687	160,108
1999	0	0	0	0	0	0	424	13	975	1,564	744	3,720	424	13	975	1,564	744	3,720
2000	10	0	5,182	46,369	535	52,096	248	46	1,429	5,983	1,173	8,879	258	46	6,611	52,352	1,708	60,975
2001	7	0	1,696	0	681	2,384	427	70	1,352	1,390	898	4,137	434	70	3,048	1,390	1,579	6,521
2002	0	0	0	0	0	0	565	14	1,801	8,345	1,451	12,176	565	14	1,801	8,345	1,451	12,176
2003	0	0	0	0	0	0	660	39	1,143	2,524	1,687	6,053	660	39	1,143	2,524	1,687	6,053
2004	0	0	0	0	0	0	412	0	704	7,858	683	9,657	412	0	704	7,858	683	9,657
2005	0	0	0	0	0	0	225	9	1,011	3,721	598	5,564	225	9	1,011	3,721	598	5,564
2006	0	0	0	0	0	0	179	13	1,769	5,216	1,267	8,444	179	13	1,769	5,216	1,267	8,444
Short-term average	2	0	983	6,624	174	7,783	388	27	1,316	5,005	1,108	7,844	390	27	2,298	11,629	1,282	15,627
Long-term average	190	10	1,425	13,041	19,202	33,528	180	37	957	3,805	2,496	7,214	343	40	2,424	17,382	20,341	39,833

APPENDIX TABLE 14. Commercial and subsistence catch for Chinook (Chin), sockeye (Sock), coho, pink, and chum salmon, by year in Norton Bay Subdistrict, Norton Sound District, with long term mean (1962–2006) and short term mean (2000–2006).

Year	Commercial						Subsistence						Combined					
	Chin	Sock	Coho	Pink	Chum	Total	Chin	Sock	Coho	Pink	Chum	Total	Chin	Sock	Coho	Pink	Chum	Total
1962	387	7	40	4,402	24,380	29,216	-	-	-	-	-	-	387	7	40	4,402	24,380	29,216
1963	137	2	-	17,676	12,469	30,284	-	-	-	5,097	-	5,097	137	2	-	22,773	12,469	35,381
1964	50	3	-	988	5,916	6,957	-	-	-	-	-	-	50	3	-	988	5,916	6,957
1965	-	-	-	-	-	-	4	-	22	252	3,032	3,310	4	-	22	252	3,032	3,310
1966	-	-	-	-	-	-	7	-	41	929	3,612	4,589	7	-	41	929	3,612	4,589
1967	-	-	-	-	-	-	12	-	14	1,097	2,945	4,068	12	-	14	1,097	2,945	4,068
1968	-	-	-	-	-	-	28	-	71	1,916	1,872	3,887	28	-	71	1,916	1,872	3,887
1969	26	-	-	4,849	3,974	8,849	59	-	189	2,115	3,855	6,218	85	-	189	6,964	7,829	15,067
1970	-	-	-	-	-	-	3	-	10	840	3,500	4,353	3	-	10	840	3,500	4,353
1971	-	-	-	-	-	-	5	-	47	92	2,619	2,763	5	-	47	92	2,619	2,763
1972	43	-	-	1,713	7,799	9,555	30	-	44	2,089	2,022	4,185	73	-	44	3,802	9,821	13,740
1973	28	-	-	1,645	4,672	6,345	1	-	-	10	130	141	29	-	-	1,655	4,802	6,486
1974	21	-	-	654	3,826	4,501	-	-	-	17	900	917	21	-	-	671	4,726	5,418
1975	68	-	89	1,137	17,385	18,679	1	-	-	93	361	455	69	-	89	1,230	17,746	19,134
1976	102	-	95	4,456	7,161	11,814	2	-	-	41	236	279	104	-	95	4,497	7,397	12,093
1977	158	-	1	2,495	13,563	16,217	14	-	-	420	2,055	2,489	172	-	1	2,915	15,618	18,706
1978	470	-	144	8,471	21,973	31,058	12	-	21	1,210	1,060	2,303	482	-	165	9,681	23,033	33,361
1979	856	-	2,547	6,201	15,599	25,203	12	-	697	735	1,400	2,844	868	-	3,244	6,936	16,999	28,047
1980	340	-	-	47	7,855	8,242	22	-	33	4,275	1,132	5,462	362	-	33	4,322	8,987	13,704
1981	63	-	-	177	3,111	3,351	7	-	82	2,314	3,515	5,918	70	-	82	2,491	6,626	9,269
1982	96	-	2,332	2,535	7,128	12,091	1	-	484	2,600	2,485	5,570	97	-	2,816	5,135	9,613	17,661
1983	215	-	204	3,935	17,157	21,511	-	-	-	-	-	-	-	-	-	-	-	-
1984	-	-	-	1,162	3,442	4,604	-	-	-	-	-	-	-	-	-	-	-	-
1985	528	-	384	68	9,948	10,928	-	-	-	-	-	-	-	-	-	-	-	-
1986	139	2	1,512	40	1,994	3,687	-	-	-	-	-	-	-	-	-	-	-	-
1987	544	-	145	16	3,586	4,291	-	-	-	-	-	-	-	-	-	-	-	-
1988	434	2	709	1,749	7,521	10,415	-	-	-	-	-	-	-	-	-	-	-	-
1989	-	-	-	-	-	-	-	-	-	-	-	-	-	-	-	-	-	-
1990	0	0	0	0	0	0	-	-	-	-	-	-	-	-	-	-	-	-

APPENDIX TABLE 14. Continued.

Year	Commercial						Subsistence						Combined					
	Chin	Sock	Coho	Pink	Chum	Total	Chin	Sock	Coho	Pink	Chum	Total	Chin	Sock	Coho	Pink	Chum	Total
1991	0	0	0	0	0	0	-	-	-	-	-	-	-	-	-	-	-	-
1992	27	0	0	0	1,787	1,814	-	-	-	-	-	-	-	-	-	-	-	-
1993	267	0	0	290	1,378	1,935	-	-	-	-	-	-	-	-	-	-	-	-
1994	0	0	0	0	0	0	308	1	370	6,049	4,581	11,309	308	1	370	6,049	4,581	11,309
1995	0	0	0	0	0	0	475	46	985	3,514	5,828	10,848	475	46	985	3,514	5,828	10,848
1996	0	0	0	0	0	0	295	3	676	3,929	4,161	9,064	295	3	676	3,929	4,161	9,064
1997	194	0	0	0	531	725	656	54	322	1,795	4,040	6,867	850	54	322	1,795	4,571	7,592
1998	0	0	0	0	0	0	684	0	388	2,009	6,192	9,273	684	0	388	2,009	6,192	9,273
1999	0	0	0	0	0	0	327	0	167	1,943	4,153	6,590	327	0	167	1,943	4,153	6,590
2000	0	0	0	0	0	0	397	2	267	2,255	4,714	7,635	397	2	267	2,255	4,714	7,635
2001	0	0	0	0	0	0	460	14	276	5,203	4,445	10,398	460	14	276	5,203	4,445	10,398
2002	0	0	0	0	0	0	557	0	509	6,049	3,971	11,086	557	0	509	6,049	3,971	11,086
2003	0	0	0	0	0	0	373	46	510	4,184	3,397	8,510	373	46	510	4,184	3,397	8,510
2004	0	0	0	0	0	0	-	-	-	-	-	-	-	-	-	-	-	-
2005	0	0	0	0	0	0	-	-	-	-	-	-	-	-	-	-	-	-
2006	0	0	0	0	0	0	-	-	-	-	-	-	-	-	-	-	-	-
Short-term average	0	0	0	0	0	0	447	16	391	4,423	4,132	9,407	447	16	391	4,423	4,132	9,407
Long-term average	140	1	283	1,703	5,373	7,428	176	17	271	2,175	2,936	5,394	251	14	425	3,888	7,728	12,242

APPENDIX TABLE 15. Commercial and subsistence catch for Chinook (Chin), Sockeye (Sock), Coho, Pink, and Chum salmon, by year in Shaktoolik Subdistrict, Norton Sound District, with long term mean (1961–2006) and short term mean (2000–2006).

Year	Commercial						Subsistence						Combined					
	Chin	Sock	Coho	Pink	Chum	Total	Chin	Sock	Coho	Pink	Chum	Total	Chin	Sock	Coho	Pink	Chum	Total
1961	140	-	-	29,075	24,746	53,961	-	-	-	-	-	-	140	-	-	29,075	24,746	53,961
1962	1,738	-	2,113	640	8,718	13,209	-	-	-	-	-	-	1,738	-	2,113	640	8,718	13,209
1963	480	11	563	5,138	19,153	25,345	-	-	-	-	-	-	480	11	563	5,138	19,153	25,345
1964	631	79	16	1,969	35,272	37,967	77	-	340	2,132	5,412	7,961	708	79	356	4,101	40,684	45,928
1965	127	30	-	-	8,356	8,516	31	-	107	3,763	3,420	7,321	158	30	107	3,766	11,776	15,837
1966	310	-	956	344	8,292	9,902	142	-	762	1,445	4,183	6,532	452	-	1,718	1,789	12,475	16,434
1967	43	-	88	1,050	1,655	2,836	262	-	387	2,010	4,436	7,095	305	-	475	3,060	6,091	9,931
1968	61	-	130	2,205	2,504	4,900	10	-	458	6,355	1,915	8,738	71	-	588	8,560	4,419	13,638
1969	33	-	276	6,197	8,645	15,151	40	-	193	4,018	3,439	7,690	73	-	469	10,215	12,084	22,841
1970	197	-	155	2,301	15,753	18,406	43	-	210	2,474	2,016	4,743	240	-	365	4,775	17,769	23,149
1971	284	-	238	28	13,399	13,949	87	-	329	494	5,060	5,970	371	-	567	522	18,459	19,919
1972	419	-	11	2,798	12,022	15,250	64	-	235	939	3,399	4,637	483	-	246	3,737	15,421	19,887
1973	289	-	177	6,450	14,500	21,416	51	-	130	3,410	1,397	4,988	340	-	307	9,860	15,897	26,404
1974	583	-	179	5,650	26,391	32,803	93	-	353	1,901	358	2,705	676	-	532	7,551	26,749	35,508
1975	651	2	812	1,774	49,536	52,775	18	-	14	1,394	334	1,760	669	2	826	3,168	49,870	54,535
1976	892	-	129	15,803	15,798	32,622	24	-	121	1,188	269	1,602	916	-	250	16,991	16,067	34,224
1977	1,521	4	418	7,743	36,591	46,277	49	-	170	585	2,190	2,994	1,570	4	588	8,328	38,781	49,271
1978	1,339	7	1,116	46,236	35,388	84,086	81	-	15	3,275	1,170	4,541	1,420	7	1,131	49,511	36,558	88,627
1979	2,377	-	3,383	18,944	22,030	46,734	62	-	1,605	2,575	1,670	5,912	2,439	-	4,988	21,519	23,700	52,646
1980	1,086	-	8,001	1,947	27,453	38,487	57	-	756	3,227	1,827	5,867	1,143	-	8,757	5,174	29,280	44,354
1981	1,484	4	1,191	29,695	21,097	53,471	8	-	525	2,225	3,490	6,248	1,492	4	1,716	31,920	24,587	59,719
1982	1,677	3	22,233	17,019	26,240	67,172	68	-	2,138	3,865	1,165	7,236	1,745	3	24,371	20,884	27,405	74,408
1983	2,742	4	12,877	12,031	67,310	94,964	-	-	-	-	-	-	-	-	-	-	-	-
1984	1,613	-	10,730	1,596	32,309	46,248	-	-	-	-	-	-	-	-	-	-	-	-
1985	5,312	-	2,808	-	13,403	21,523	298	-	1,379	24	298	1,999	5,610	-	4,187	24	13,701	23,522
1986	1,075	29	6,626	-	16,126	23,856	-	-	-	-	-	-	-	-	-	-	-	-
1987	2,214	-	6,193	-	14,088	22,495	-	-	-	-	-	-	-	-	-	-	-	-
1988	671	79	6,096	3,681	21,521	32,048	-	-	-	-	-	-	-	-	-	-	-	-
1989	1,241	43	8,066	0	19,641	28,991	-	-	-	-	-	-	-	-	-	-	-	-

APPENDIX TABLE 15. Continued.

Year	Commercial						Subsistence						Combined					
	Chin	Sock	Coho	Pink	Chum	Total	Chin	Sock	Coho	Pink	Chum	Total	Chin	Sock	Coho	Pink	Chum	Total
1990	2,644	49	4,695	0	21,748	29,136	-	-	-	-	-	-	-	-	-	-	-	-
1991	1,324	55	11,614	0	31,619	44,612	-	-	-	-	-	-	-	-	-	-	-	-
1992	1,098	56	14,660	0	27,867	43,681	-	-	-	-	-	-	-	-	-	-	-	-
1993	2,756	20	11,130	106,743	20,864	141,513	-	-	-	-	-	-	-	-	-	-	-	-
1994	885	8	22,065	502,231	5,411	530,600	1,175	1	2,777	9,133	1,221	14,307	2,060	9	24,842	511,364	6,632	544,907
1995	1,239	5	10,856	37,377	14,775	64,252	1,275	2,480	2,626	7,024	2,480	15,885	2,514	2,485	13,482	44,401	17,255	80,137
1996	1,340	1	13,444	304,982	3,237	323,004	1,114	31	3,615	8,370	4,425	17,555	2,454	32	17,059	313,352	7,662	340,559
1997	2,449	0	4,694	-	5,747	12,890	1,146	62	2,761	5,779	1,612	11,360	3,595	62	7,455	5,779	7,359	24,250
1998	910	0	3,624	236,171	7,080	247,785	982	92	1,872	6,270	1,034	10,250	1,892	92	5,496	242,441	8,114	258,035
1999	581	0	2,398	0	2,181	5,160	818	183	1,556	5,092	467	8,116	1,399	183	3,954	5,092	2,648	13,276
2000	160	3	7,779	85,493	2,751	96,186	440	20	2,799	5,432	2,412	11,103	600	23	10,578	90,925	5,163	107,289
2001	90	0	2,664	0	1,819	4,573	936	143	2,090	10,172	1,553	14,894	1,026	143	4,754	10,172	3,372	19,467
2002	1	0	680	0	261	942	1,230	4	2,169	8,769	800	12,972	1,231	4	2,849	8,769	1,061	13,914
2003	2	0	4,031	0	485	4,518	881	50	2,941	12,332	587	16,791	883	50	6,972	12,332	1,072	21,309
2004	0	0	12,734	0	1,372	14,106	943	12	1,994	7,291	139	10,379	943	12	14,728	7,291	1,511	24,485
2005	50	0	21,818	0	791	22,659	807	0	1,913	12,075	202	14,997	857	0	23,731	12,075	993	37,656
2006	0	0	32,472	0	3,321	35,793	382	36	1,968	4,817	351	7,554	382	36	34,440	4,817	3,672	43,347
Short-term average	43	0	11,740	12,213	1,543	25,540	803	38	2,268	8,698	863	12,670	846	38	14,007	20,912	2,406	38,210
Long-term average	1,017	17	6,294	35,555	16,723	56,234	415	240	1,252	4,541	1,962	8,264	1,197	156	6,445	42,198	15,581	65,331

APPENDIX TABLE 16. Commercial, subsistence, and sportfish catch for Chinook (Chin), sockeye (Sock), coho, pink, and chum salmon, by year for all subdistricts in Norton Sound District, with long term mean (1961–2006) and short term mean (2000–2006).

Year	Commercial						Subsistence						Sport				
	Chin	Sock	Coho	Pink	Chum	Total	Chin	Sock	Coho	Pink	Chum	Total	Chin	Sock	Coho	Pink	Chum
1961	5,300	35	13,807	34,237	48,332	101,711	-	-	-	-	-	-	-	-	-	-	-
1962	7,286	18	9,156	33,187	182,784	232,431	-	-	-	-	-	-	-	-	-	-	-
1963	6,613	71	16,765	46,180	154,749	224,378	5	-	118	16,607	17,635	34,365	-	-	-	-	-
1964	2,018	126	98	13,567	148,862	164,671	565	-	2,567	9,225	12,486	24,843	-	-	-	-	-
1965	128	30	2,030	220	36,795	39,203	574	-	4,812	19,131	30,772	55,289	-	-	-	-	-
1966	1,553	14	5,755	12,778	80,245	100,345	269	-	2,210	14,335	21,873	38,687	-	-	-	-	-
1967	1,804	-	2,379	28,879	41,756	74,818	817	-	1,222	17,516	22,724	42,279	-	-	-	-	-
1968	1,045	-	6,885	71,179	45,300	124,409	237	-	2,391	36,912	11,661	51,201	-	-	-	-	-
1969	2,392	-	6,836	86,949	82,795	178,972	436	-	2,191	18,562	15,615	36,804	-	-	-	-	-
1970	1,853	-	4,423	64,908	107,034	178,218	561	-	4,675	26,127	22,763	54,126	-	-	-	-	-
1971	2,593	-	3,127	4,895	131,362	141,977	1,026	197	4,097	10,863	21,618	37,801	-	-	-	-	-
1972	2,938	-	454	45,182	100,920	149,494	804	93	2,319	14,158	13,873	31,247	-	-	-	-	-
1973	1,918	-	9,282	46,499	119,098	176,797	392	-	520	14,770	7,185	22,867	-	-	-	-	-
1974	2,951	-	2,092	148,519	162,267	315,829	420	-	1,064	16,426	3,958	21,868	-	-	-	-	-
1975	2,393	2	4,593	32,388	212,485	251,861	186	11	192	15,803	8,113	24,305	-	-	-	-	-
1976	2,243	11	6,934	87,919	95,956	193,063	203	-	1,004	18,048	7,718	26,973	-	-	-	-	-
1977	4,500	5	3,690	48,675	200,455	257,325	846	-	2,530	14,296	26,607	44,279	197	0	449	2,402	670
1978	9,819	12	7,335	325,503	189,279	531,948	1,211	-	2,981	35,281	12,257	51,730	303	0	742	7,399	546
1979	10,706	57	31,438	167,411	140,789	350,401	747	-	8,487	25,247	11,975	46,456	-	-	-	-	-
1980	6,311	40	29,842	227,352	180,792	444,337	1,397	-	8,625	63,778	19,622	93,422	52	0	1,455	7,732	1,601
1981	7,929	56	31,562	232,479	169,708	441,734	2,021	38	13,416	28,741	32,866	77,082	70	0	1,504	3,101	1,889
1982	5,892	10	91,690	230,281	183,335	511,208	1,011	8	14,612	54,249	18,580	88,460	409	0	2,986	13,742	2,620
1983	10,308	27	49,735	76,913	319,437	456,420	1,942	86	8,799	21,894	11,492	44,213	687	0	3,823	4,583	2,042

APPENDIX TABLE 16. Continued.

Year	Commercial						Subsistence						Sport				
	Chin	Sock	Coho	Pink	Chum	Total	Chin	Sock	Coho	Pink	Chum	Total	Chin	Sock	Coho	Pink	Chum
1984	8,455	6	67,875	119,381	146,442	342,159	1,733	17	8,470	34,600	8,231	53,051	247	351	7,582	8,322	1,481
1985	19,491	166	21,968	3,647	134,928	180,200	1,830	119	6,496	5,312	18,457	32,214	239	20	1,177	1,138	1,036
1986	6,395	233	35,600	41,260	146,912	230,400	150	107	688	8,720	8,085	17,750	1,077	19	3,926	3,172	1,719
1987	7,080	207	24,279	2,260	102,457	136,283	200	107	1,100	1,251	8,394	11,052	615	924	2,319	1,304	814
1988	4,096	1,252	37,214	74,604	107,966	225,132	63	133	1,076	2,159	5,952	9,383	400	782	5,038	2,912	1,583
1989	5,707	265	44,091	123	42,625	92,811	24	131	5,150	18,424	4,787	4,947	203	165	4,158	3,564	1,497
1990	8,895	434	56,712	501	65,123	131,665	58	234	510	2,233	4,246	7,281	364	198	3,305	7,647	925
1991	6,068	203	63,647	-	86,871	156,789	395	166	3,432	3,749	6,375	14,117	404	237	5,800	1,738	1,415
1992	4,541	296	105,418	6,284	83,394	199,933	252	163	2,762	13,503	2,944	19,624	204	131	4,671	6,403	523
1993	8,972	279	43,283	157,574	53,562	263,670	420	80	3,287	2,599	3,401	9,787	595	10	3,783	2,250	691
1994	5,285	80	102,140	982,389	18,290	1,108,184	7,375	1,162	22,124	71,065	25,020	126,746	600	18	5,547	7,051	536
1995	8,860	128	47,863	81,644	42,898	181,393	7,274	3,532	21,088	37,984	39,709	109,587	438	104	3,705	928	394
1996	4,984	1	68,206	487,441	10,609	571,241	7,245	1,013	25,816	62,432	32,540	129,046	662	100	7,289	5,972	662
1997	12,573	161	32,284	20	34,103	79,141	8,989	1,843	16,267	27,088	24,503	78,690	1,106	30	4,393	1,458	278
1998	7,429	7	29,623	588,013	16,324	641,396	8,295	1,214	19,007	51,933	20,032	100,480	590	16	4,441	6,939	682
1999	2,508	0	12,662	0	7,881	23,051	6,144	1,177	14,343	19,917	19,397	60,978	630	0	5,582	3,039	211
2000	752	14	44,409	166,548	6,150	217,873	4,148	681	17,064	38,308	17,283	77,484	889	45	7,441	2,886	1,097
2001	213	44	19,492	0	11,106	30,855	5,576	767	14,543	30,253	20,208	71,347	271	39	4,802	360	1,709
2002	5	1	1,759	0	600	2,365	5,469	763	15,086	64,353	17,817	103,488	802	0	4,211	4,303	818
2003	12	0	17,058	0	3,560	20,630	4,728	522	11,446	46,336	9,498	72,530	239	572	3,039	2,222	292

APPENDIX TABLE 16. Continued.

Year	Commercial						Subsistence						Sport				
	Chin	Sock	Coho	Pink	Chum	Total	Chin	Sock	Coho	Pink	Chum	Total	Chin	Sock	Coho	Pink	Chum
2003	12	0	17,058	0	3,560	20,630	4,728	522	11,446	46,336	9,498	72,530	239	572	3,039	2,222	292
2004	0	40	42,016	0	6,296	48,352	4,420	458	10,904	71,015	3,598	90,395	535	404	5,806	8,309	498
2005	151	280	85,255	0	3,983	89,669	3,305	794	11,846	54,174	4,961	75,080	216	0	3,959	473	36
2006	11	3	130,808	0	10,042	140,864	2,876	572	17,242	56,579	5,992	83,261	427	22	11,427	5,317	344
Short-term average	163	55	48,685	23,793	5,962	78,658	4,360	651	14,019	51,574	11,337	81,941	483	155	5,812	3,410	685
Long-term average	4,847	121	32,034	106,173	92,971	233,818	2,196	558	7,695	27,635	15,064	52,423	465	144	4,288	4,368	987

APPENDIX TABLE 17. Port Clarence Management District Subsistence harvest, 1963–2006, with long term mean (1963–2006) and short term mean (2000–2006).

Year	Number of Fishing Families Interviewed	Chinook	Sockeye	Coho	Pink	Chum	Total
1963	19	9	4,866	25	1,061	1,279	7,240
1964	22	17	1,475	227	371	1,049	3,139
1965	29	36	1,804	639	1,854	1,602	5,935
1966	26	10	1,000	896	859	2,875	5,640
1967	19	12	2,068	232	767	1,073	4,152
1968	24	40	688	133	1,906	904	3,671
1969	13	2	180	27	548	932	1,689
1970	18	4	588	1,071	1,308	4,231	7,202
1971	22	31	850	959	1,171	3,769	6,780
1972	8	4	68	388	75	2,806	3,341
1973	4	22	46	280	424	1,562	2,334
1974	13	0	28	62	14	2,663	2,767
1975	17	0	244	5	743	1,589	2,581
1976	15	7	291	20	436	6,026	6,780
1977	13	-	-	-	-	-	5,910
1978	26	1	392	0	7,783	705	8,881
1979	26	0	320	35	741	1,658	2,754
1980	22	7	3,195	5	3,170	1,715	8,092
1981	10	8	255	110	765	5,845	6,983
1982	27	23	405	100	4,345	684	5,557
1983	3	17	261	-	615	299	1,192
1989	15	28	535	472	395	410	1,840
1994	127	181	1,979	1,692	3,849	2,042	9,743

APPENDIX TABLE 17. Continued.

Year	Number of Fishing Families Interviewed	Chinook	Sockeye	Coho	Pink	Chum	Total
1995	122	76	4,481	1,739	3,293	6,011	15,600
1996	117	195	4,558	2,079	2,587	1,264	10,684
1997	126	158	3,177	829	755	2,099	7,019
1998	138	287	1,665	1,759	7,812	2,621	14,144
1999	155	89	2,392	1,030	786	1,936	6,233
2000	134	72	2,851	935	1,387	1,275	6,521
2001	160	84	3,692	1,299	1,183	1,910	8,167
2002	159	133	3,732	2,194	3,394	2,699	12,152
2003	204	177	4,495	1,434	4,113	2,430	12,649
2004	376	278	8,688	1,131	5,918	2,505	18,520
2005	335	152	8,492	726	6,615	2,479	18,464
2006	345	102	9,940	1,061	4,939	4,353	20,395
Short-term average	245	143	5,984	1,254	3,936	2,522	13,838
Long-term average	83	67	2,344	715	2,235	2,274	7,564

American Fisheries Society Symposium 70:675–701, 2009

Yukon River Chinook Salmon: Stock Status, Harvest, and Management

Danielle F. Evenson*, Steve J. Hayes, Gene Sandone,
and Daniel J. Bergstrom

Alaska Department of Fish and Game
333 Raspberry Road, Anchorage, Alaska 99518, USA

Abstract.—This paper reviews and describes the status of stocks, fisheries, and management of Chinook salmon *Oncorhynchus tshawytscha* in the Yukon River. The Alaska Department of Fish and Game (ADF&G) manages the Yukon commercial and subsistence fisheries in the Alaskan portion of the drainage and by the Canadian Department of Fisheries and Oceans in the portion in Yukon Territory. The salmon are managed to achieve escapement goals for spawning, to maintain sustained production based upon perceived run strength, and to accomplish approved fishery management plans. The Chinook salmon stocks of the Yukon River have experienced considerable variation in abundance and harvest over the past 50 years. After experiencing poor runs from 1998–2000, Chinook salmon escapement goals have been generally met throughout the Alaska portion of the Yukon River drainage during the past five years, 2004–2008. Typically, about 50% of the Chinook salmon reproduction occurs in Canada. The escapement goal into Canada was not met in 2007 and 2008. The average escapement to the Canadian portion of the Yukon River drainage from 2004 to 2008 was 49,500 Chinook salmon (range 32,500 to 68,500 fish), which was similar to the historical baseline ten-year average (1989–1998) of 50,800 fish. The age-class composition of the Canadian-origin Chinook salmon return from brood-years 1979–1998 indicated a decrease in age-7 salmon from an average of 22% from brood years 1979–1982 to an average of only 8% from brood years 1983–2000. In Alaska, the five-year (2004–2008) average commercial and subsistence combined harvest of 86,573 Chinook salmon was a 55% decrease from 1989 to 1998 average of 156,092 fish. In Canada, total harvest from all sources (domestic, aboriginal, sport, and commercial) from 1980 to 1997 ranged between 10,729 and 22,896 fish. The ten year (1999–2008) average total harvest of 8,739 Chinook salmon was 81% below the lower end of this range. While certainly challenges exist, careful management through the regulation of the fisheries to permit adequate escapements for spawning should ensure the sustainability of the resource for future generations.

Introduction

The Yukon River flows from Yukon Territory and British Columbia westward across the State of Alaska into the Bering Sea. The

*Corresponding author: dani.evenson@alaska.gov

spawning migration of Chinook salmon *Oncorhynchus tshawytscha* into the mouth of the Yukon River begins soon after breakup of the winter ice cover in mid to late May; however, most fish enter the river after mid-June. The migration of Chinook salmon from the Bering Sea into the river is typically finished by mid-July. Yukon River Chinook salmon return as age-2 through age-8 fish, but age-5 and age-6 salmon dominate the run. The spawning grounds for Chinook salmon include many of the drainage's tributaries and the main stem, which can be as far as 1,900 mi upstream in Canada's Yukon Territory. Juvenile salmon emerge from the spawning gravels in the spring and migrate seaward typically after one to two years of rearing (Bradford et al. 2009, this volume). Yukon River Chinook salmon are noted for their high oil content (Gilbert 1922), an adaptation that provides sufficient energy reserves during their long-distance migration.

Based on genetic studies, Chinook salmon in the Yukon River occur in multiple semidiscrete populations organized geographically by main stem and tributary spawning areas. Genetically different populations of Chinook salmon were detectable among tributaries based on variation observed at allozyme loci (e.g., Beacham et al. 1989; Wilmot et al. 1992; Utter et al. 2009, this volume). Other genetic studies based on variation at microsatellite loci have shown that these populations are hierarchically organized into two major groups, which correspond roughly to those populations located in the Yukon Territory and those in the Alaskan portions of the drainage (Beacham et al. 2006). Analyses of harvest samples with single nucleotide polymorphisms demonstrated finer scale resolution of stock aggregates from the lower, middle, and the Canadian Yukon River (Templin et al. 2005). Most Yukon River fisheries harvest a mixture of populations or stocks.

Yukon River salmon stocks have generally remained healthy because of undisturbed spawning, rearing, and migration habitat; but, some habitat issues have adversely affected the salmon production (see discussion in Holder and Senecal-Albrecht 1998). Dams have had minimal impact on salmon habitat

in comparison to drainages elsewhere such as the Columbia River in Washington, Oregon, and Idaho (Lichatowich and Williams 2009, this volume). The only hydroelectric dam exists at Whitehorse, Yukon Territory at river mile 1980 (river km 3,200). A fish ladder and small-scale hatchery are operated at the site to mitigate its effects on salmon. More serious threats to salmon habitat came in early 1900s with mine exploration and development. Mining activity was, and continues to be, an important economic industry within the drainage. Fortunately, most historical mining activity occurred on localized, discrete headwater streams using manual labor, which minimized impacts on spawning habitat. However, in the 1920s mining practices expanded to hydraulic mining and large-scale dredges. Both of these practices disturbed extensive acreage, much of which remains unreclaimed today (Higgs 1995). More rigid enforcement of environmental regulations since the mid-1980s has resulted in mining operations being far less detrimental to fisheries habitat than in the past. Two large hard rock mines are currently permitted in the Tanana River drainage: the Fort Knox mine near Fairbanks (in operation) and the Pogo Creek mine near the Goodpaster River (now in production stage) near Delta.

Fewer than 130,000 people live in the drainage basin. Two small, somewhat urban communities—Fairbanks and Whitehorse—are located on a limited road system and account for about 80% of this population. The remainder of the population resides in over 80 small, remote villages with populations averaging 300 or fewer residents of predominately aboriginal background (Williams 1999; DCED 2002; Statistics Canada 2002). Most village residents depend to varying degrees on fish and wildlife resources for food. Subsistence fishing is thus an important activity for local residents.

In addition to Chinook salmon, chum *O. keta* and coho *O. kisutch* salmon are important contributors to the fisheries (Bue et al. 2009, this volume). Sockeye salmon *O. nerka* and pink salmon *O. gorbuscha* also occur in the Yukon River drainage but are minor in the harvest. Species also present in the subsistence and/or sport fisheries include Arctic grayling *Thymallus arcticus*, Dolly Varden *Salvelinus malma*, inconnu *Stenodus leucichthys*, northern pike *Esox lucius*, burbot *Lota lota*, several *Coregonus* species, and Alaska blackfish *Dallia pectoralis*.

Subsistence, commercial, and sport fisheries occur for Chinook salmon throughout much of the Yukon River drainage. These fisheries occur in the ocean near the mouths of the river, along the entire length of its main stem, and in many tributaries in Alaska and Canada. The subsistence and commercial fisheries use a variety of gear, including gillnets and fish wheels. Based on postseason surveys, harvest by the Alaskan subsistence fishery in recent years has remained stable around 50,000 fish and has recently exceeded the commercial harvest (JTC 2008). Sport fishery harvests have been small relative to subsistence and commercial fishery harvests (500–2,000 fish) in both Alaska and Yukon Territory. Incidental catches of Chinook salmon also occur in fisheries targeting chum salmon. Personal-use fisheries and domestic fisheries allow access to fish for noncommercial purposes to urban residents in Alaska and nonaboriginal residents in Canada. Personal-use and domestic food fisheries are considered a lower priority than subsistence or aboriginal fishing in the allocation of harvest (Borba and Hamner 2001).

Management of the Yukon salmon fishery is difficult because of the complexity of the salmon populations, fisheries, geography, and jurisdiction. Due to the size and complexity of the drainage and the geographic distribution of its fisheries, management for individual stocks or populations is not possible. Chinook salmon occur in multiple populations, each likely with stock-specific growth,

survival, and recruitment functions. The fisheries are very intricate owing to the gauntlet nature of the fishery with harvest of multiple stocks occurring at different times and locations throughout the length of the drainage. Because the Yukon River fisheries are largely mixed stock fisheries, some tributary populations may not be exploited in relation to their actual abundance. Allocation issues exist between lower-river and upper-river fishermen in Alaska. Lower-river fisheries have first access to salmon runs prior to assessment of run strength. If abundance is low and escapement to spawning areas appears inadequate, then it may be necessary to restrict all fisheries inseason, with most impacts absorbed in upper river fisheries. Lastly, important allocation and conservation issues exist between the governments of U.S.-Alaska and Canada-Yukon Territory. Salmon fisheries within the lower Yukon River harvest Canada-bound stocks that are over a thousand miles from their spawning grounds. Discussions between the parties occur within the context of the Yukon River Annex of the Pacific Salmon Treaty (Gaden et al. 2009, this volume).

The salmon fisheries of the Yukon River drainage are managed to achieve escapement goals in specific streams, to ensure passage of salmon from Alaska into the Canadian portion of the drainage, and, when salmon abundance is projected to exceed escapement goals, to provide for consumptive uses. However, due to the long migration distance for many Yukon Chinook salmon stocks, substantial harvest may occur before reliable escapement projections are available. In Alaska, subsistence fishing opportunity has priority over sport and commercial fisheries for the consumptive uses. Management by the state of Alaska is guided by regulations adopted by the Alaska Board of Fisheries (BOF). The *Policy for the Management of Sustainable Salmon Fisheries* (SSFP; 5 AAC 39.222, effective 2000, amended 2001; http://www.adfg.state.ak.us/special/susalpol.pdf) directs the ADF&G to provide the BOF with reports on the status of salmon stocks and to identify any salmon stocks that present a "concern" related to "yield," "management," or "conservation" during regularly scheduled BOF meetings.

Based on recommendations made by ADF&G, the BOF classified the Yukon River Chinook salmon as a yield concern in 2000, based in part on the poor runs of 1998, 1999, and 2000. A stock of yield concern is defined as "a concern arising from a chronic inability, despite the use of specific management measures, to maintain expected yields, or harvestable surpluses, above a stock's escapement needs; a yield concern is less severe than a management concern" (5 AAC 39.222(f)(42)). The SSFP defines chronic inability as "the continuing or anticipated inability to meet expected yields over a four to five year period." The classification of Yukon River Chinook salmon as a yield concern was originally based on low harvest levels for the previous three-year period (1998–2000) and anticipated low harvest in 2001. An action plan was subsequently developed by ADF&G and approved by the BOF in 2001. The BOF continued the classification as a yield concern in 2004 (Lingnau and Bergstrom 2004) and 2007.

Combined subsistence and commercial harvests of Chinook salmon in the Alaska portion of the drainage have decreased, with the most recent five-year average of 86,573 (2004–2008), a harvest approximately 55% below the historic baseline ten-year average, from 1989 to 1998, of 156,092 fish. Harvest by the Alaskan subsistence fishery in recent years has remained stable around 50,000 fish (see Wolf and Spaeder 2009, this volume); however, commercial harvests dropped over 60% during the same time frame.

This paper reviews and describes the status of stocks, fisheries, and management of Chinook salmon in the Yukon River. Much of the focus of this paper is on management

by ADF&G within the Alaskan portion of the drainage; however, information is also provided in regard to Canadian escapement and harvest. An overview of the history of salmon management in Alaska is provided by Hilsinger et al. (2009, this volume).

Yukon River Drainage and Management Area Description

The Yukon River drainage encompasses an area of more than 330,000 square miles (855,000 square kilometers) and represents the fifth largest drainage in North America (Figure 1). The Porcupine River, Tanana River, and Koyukuk River are major tributaries that join the Yukon River as it flows for over 2,300 mi (or approximately 3,700 km) to the Bering Sea. The Yukon River originates from the Llewellyn Glacier, near Atlin Lake, in northwestern British Columbia, within 30 mi (48 km) of the Gulf of Alaska. From this source, the river flows in a northwesterly direction, through the central Yukon Territory of Canada and then westward through central Alaska of the United States to the Bering Sea.

Management in Alaska of the Yukon River drainage occurs within six salmon fishing districts (Figure 1). Districts 1, 2, and 3 are the lower river districts and Districts 4, 5, and 6 are the upper river districts. District 5 represents the Yukon River from near the village of Tanana upstream to the U.S./Canada border. District 6 is wholly comprised of the Tanana River.

Data Sources and Analysis

ADF&G, several U.S. federal agencies, the Canadian Department of Fisheries and Oceans (DFO), native organizations, and various organized groups of fishermen operate salmon stock assessment projects throughout the Yukon River drainage which are used by

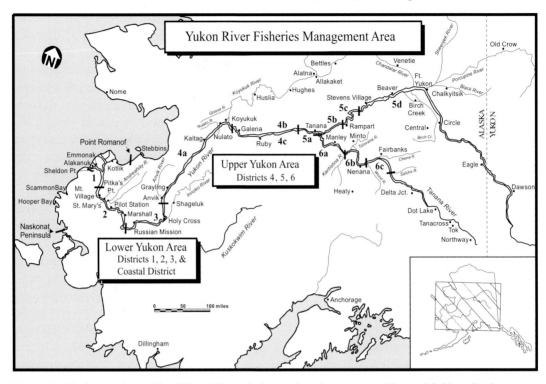

FIGURE 1. Alaska portion of the Yukon River drainage showing communities and fishing districts.

ADF&G and U.S. Fish and Wildlife Service (USFWS) to manage the Chinook salmon fisheries. A set gillnet test fishery near the mouth of the Yukon River and a mainstem sonar project at Pilot Station at river mile 123 (river km 197) are the primary assessment tools to determine the relative run strength and timing of Chinook salmon in the drainage. There are also sonar estimation and a test fishery at Eagle, Alaska (river mile 1,213) to estimate passage into Canadian waters. Subsistence catch reports, discharge, and weather data are also used to estimate relative run strength and timing. Tributaries with established escapement goals have been monitored with counting tower projects in the Chena and Salcha rivers, and with aerial surveys of the Andreafsky, Anvik, Gisasa, and Nulato rivers (Figure 1). Other information has been collected by many of these projects including sex and length composition, scales for age determination, tissue samples for genetic

stock identification, data on resident species, and information from the recovery of tagged fish.

Lower river test fishing.—The lower Yukon River test fishery project located at South, Middle, and North mouths of the river has been conducted since 1980 and uses set gillnets from late May through mid-July to capture Chinook salmon. Four set gillnets of 150 ft (45.7 m) in length with stretch mesh size 8.5 in were used. Catch rates and species composition provided run timing, age composition, and an index of relative abundance for comparisons among years.

Lower river sonar.—The sonar assessment project located near Pilot Station estimated passage of Chinook salmon in the years 1995 and 1997–2008. The sonar data were tabulated in two size classes for Chinook salmon less than or equal to 25.78 in

(655 mm) in length, which corresponds to age-4 and younger fish, and those fish greater than or equal to this length, typically age-5 and older. Test fisheries during June and July use 150 ft (45.7 m) drift gillnets with stretch mesh sizes of 2.75, 4.0, 5.25, 6.5, 7.5, and 8.5 in for species apportionment of sonar data. Species apportionment is an important issue for Pilot Station sonar estimates because large numbers of summer chum salmon co-migrate with Chinook salmon. Errors in species apportionment, range limitations of the sonar, and bank erosion affect the accuracy of the sonar estimates. New technology (DIDSON sonar) and more appropriate net selectivity models (Bromaghin 2005) have improved recent run estimates at Pilot Station.

Border passage estimates.—Because of the marked difference between the Canadian DFO mark-recapture and the ADF&G radio telemetry border passage estimates (Figure 2), ADF&G initiated a sonar project at Eagle, Alaska in 2005 to estimate salmon passage into Canada on the main stem Yukon River, and to determine whether the U.S. has met treaty obligations. Because of favorable river bottom morphology and because Chinook and chum salmon have different run timing with little overlap, this site was a highly favorable location for sonar estimation. In conjunction with the sonar estimates, a test fishery, with gear similar to that used in association with Pilot Station sonar project, is conducted near this site to provide supplemental data for species apportionment. These efforts to assess Chinook salmon passage at Eagle, coupled with genetic stock identification from the various fisheries, provide a means to estimate the annual abundance of the Canada-bound Chinook salmon run. From 2001–2004, a radio telemetry mark–recapture project was implemented to estimate the Chinook salmon passage past Russian Mission (river km 343; Spencer et al. 2006). These estimates were based on the proportion of radio-tagged fish

passing the Canadian border and an independent estimate of the number of Chinook salmon passing into Canada. The goal of this multi-year cooperative study was to describe salmon migratory characteristics, abundance, and spawning distribution. Border passage into Canada was also estimated since 1982 by the Canadian DFO using mark-recapture techniques. The DFO border passage estimates were derived from mark-recapture estimates using two fish wheels near the border at river mile (RM) 1,224 (Figure 3). This border passage estimate by DFO formed the basis for the Chinook salmon escapement goal range in the U.S./Canada Yukon River Salmon Agreement through 2007. In April 2008, the Yukon River panel adopted passage estimates from the Eagle sonar project as the basis for Canadian Chinook salmon escapement goals in the future (Figure 4).

Weirs and counting towers.—Weirs or counting towers are operated by various agencies on the East Fork Andreafsky, Gisasa, Tozitna, Henshaw, Goodpaster, Chena, and Salcha Rivers. These projects provide daily estimates of spawning escapement for Chinook salmon into these important tributaries.

Fish wheels.—Two fish wheel projects have provided additional assessment of Chinook salmon in Alaskan waters. One was located near the mouth of the Tanana River (Fishing District 5-A; Figure 1), and another was located upstream near Nenana (Fishing District 6A). Both of these fish wheels provide indices of Chinook salmon relative abundance (run strength) and run timing through catch per unit effort information.

Harvest estimation.—Commercial harvest information has been obtained through fish tickets, which are completed at the time of each delivery documenting the number and pounds of salmon sold by species, and

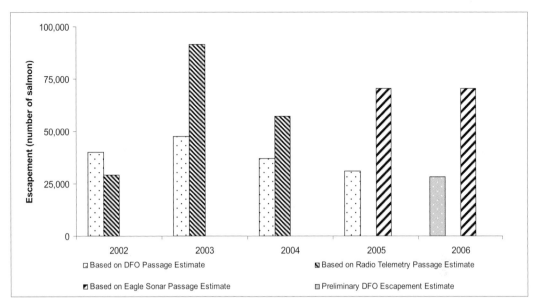

FIGURE 2. Annual Chinook salmon *Oncorhynchus tshawytscha* escapement estimates for the main stem Yukon River in Canada based on the estimated passage into Canada generated by the Canadian DFO mark–recapture estimate, ADF&G radiotelemetry mark–recapture estimate, and the ADF&G sonar passage estimate, 2002–2006.

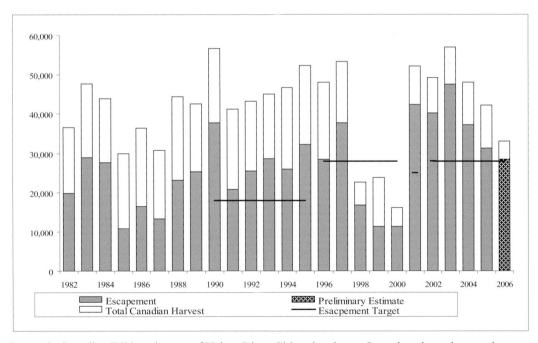

FIGURE 3. Canadian DFO estimates of Yukon River Chinook salmon *Oncorhynchus tshawytscha* passing from Alaska into Canada by harvest and escapement in the main stem of the Yukon River, Canada, 1982–2006 (JTC 2008). Note that in 2008, the Yukon River Panel agreed to use the Eagle Sonar program instead of the DFO fish wheel mark-recapture estimates as the primary tool for estimating border passage. The numbers given in this figure are no longer used.

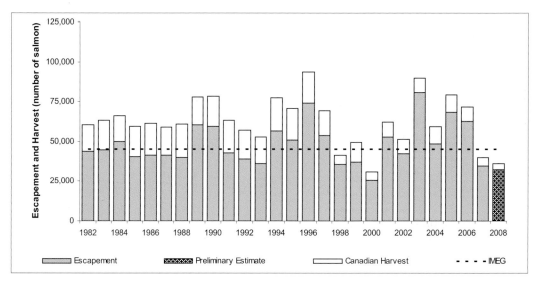

FIGURE 4. Eagle sonar-based estimates of Yukon River Chinook salmon *Oncorhynchus tshawytscha* passing from Alaska into Canada by harvest and escapement in the main stem of the Yukon River, Canada, 1982–2006 (JTC 2009, in press.). In 2008, the Yukon River Panel agreed to a one-year interim management escapement goal (IMEG) of >45,000 Chinook salmon based on Eagle sonar.

date and location caught. Subsistence harvest estimation is obtained through postseason household surveys of most villages in the Alaska portion of the drainage and from subsistence permits required in two areas within District 5 and District 6. Personal-use harvest information is obtained from permits required in the area near Fairbanks, which is designated as a Non Subsistence Area. Sport fish harvests are estimated by a statewide creel survey.

Preseason and inseason forecasts.— Preseason information involves run forecasts based upon historic performance of parent spawning abundance and are generally stated as runs that will be below average, average, or above average. In-season run assessment includes: (1) abundance indices from test fisheries, (2) sonar estimates of passing fish, (3) various escapement assessment efforts in tributaries, (4) commercial and subsistence catch data and (5) catch per unit effort data from monitored fisheries.

Run strength, harvest, and exploitation rates.—The historical baseline for comparison in recent years (since 2000) of run strength and harvests of Yukon River Chinook salmon was the ten-year period, from 1989 through 1998, which was the time series that the Board of Fisheries used to make its determination of Yukon River Chinook salmon as a stock of Yield Concern. Exploitation rate is defined as that portion of the total run that is harvested. Total run estimates, escapement, and stock-specific harvests were used to calculate exploitation rates. Exploitation rates were not estimated for Chinook salmon stocks that spawn in the lower or middle regions of the Yukon River in Alaska because total escapement to these regions were not estimated. However, total run estimates for the upper river component, or the Canadian component, were determined based on border passage estimates (Figure 5).

Exploitation rates on the Canadian stock are estimated using sonar-based estimates at Eagle, Alaska near the U.S.-Canada border in conjuction with U.S. harvest data. Harvest in Alaska had to be apportioned between Alaskan and Canadian origin salmon. From 1982–2003, scale-pattern analysis was used to apportion Alaskan Chinook salmon harvests to the region of origin. This technique was later replaced in 2004 by genetic stock identification (Templin et al. 2005). Apportionment of harvest to stock of origin indicates that the Canadian component comprises approximately 50% of the Alaska harvest, and probably the run. This proportion has remained relatively constant over the years with the exception of 2007 and 2008, whenthe Canadian component of the stock dropped below 40%. Because of the gauntlet nature of Yukon River fisheries and because these spawn the furthest upriver, it is believed that the exploitation exerted on Canadian-origin fish is most likely the highest of any Yukon River Chinook salmon stock.

Age and sex ratio estimation.—Age, sex, and length information were collected from test, commercial, and subsistence fisheries as well as escapement monitoring projects such as weirs and directed carcass collection ef-

forts. The longest term escapement monitoring information was from the annual carcass surveys conducted on the Chena and Salcha rivers in Alaska. Sex and age composition data from both rivers were adjusted to account for biases associated with carcass surveys (Table 1) (Zhou 2002). Estimates are based on data obtained from mark–recapture projects in the Chena River during 1989–1992, 1995, 1996, 1997, 2000, and 2002, and in the Salcha River during 1987–1992, and 1996. Evaluation of the bias associated with carcass surveys was based on recapture rates of fish that were captured and marked with electrofishing gear. A correction factor was developed for each river that adjusts the sex and age compositions in years when only a carcass survey is conducted (i.e., during years abundance it is estimated entirely from tower counts).

Brood year tables were constructed for three Chinook salmon stocks within the Yukon River drainage; the Chena and Salcha Rivers in Alaska and the main stem Yukon River in Canada. The total brood return divided by the parent-year escapement is a measure of the productivity of the stock and

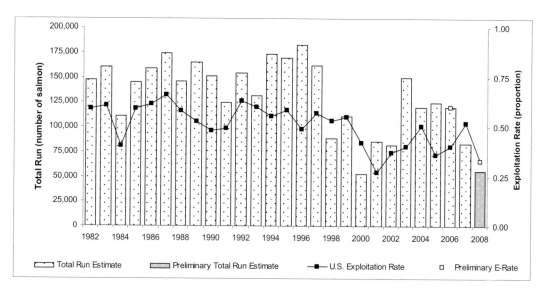

FIGURE 5. Total run and U.S. exploitation rates of Yukon River Canadian-Origin Chinook salmon *Oncorhynchus tshawytscha*, 1982–2008. Border passage estimates are based on Eagle sonar, radio-telemetry, and a three-area escapement index. 2008 data are preliminary.

ing preseason run projections, sonar passage estimates, test fishery indices, age and sex composition, subsistence and commercial harvest reports, and passage estimates from escapement monitoring projects to assess the run size of Chinook salmon inseason for the purpose of implementing this plan. The plan provides specific guidelines to ADF&G for the management of the subsistence, commercial, and sport fisheries for Chinook salmon. Subsistence fishing periods are established based on a schedule to be implemented chronologically, consistent with migratory timing as the Chinook salmon run progresses upstream, by district. Depending on run strength, the schedule is subject to change. Once run size has been determined and a harvestable surplus of salmon exists in excess of subsistence uses, the subsistence fishing schedule may revert to the schedule specified in 5AAC 01.210, (c-h) FISHING SEASONS AND PERIODS. A commercial fishery may be opened when increases in subsistence or test fishery catches of Chinook salmon have occurred over a seven- to ten- day period. A guideline harvest range for Alaskan commercial harvest was established as between 67,350 and 129,150 Chinook salmon with allocation amounts specified by district. Fishing seasons and periods are described in 5 AAC 05.310 and 5 AAC05.320 (http://www.touchngo.com/lglcntr/akstats/aac/title05/chapter005/section310.htm). Definitions of lawful gear such gillnet mesh sizes and fish wheel operations by location are provided in 5 AAC 05.330 (http://www.touchngo.com/lglcntr/akstats/aac/title05/chapter005/section330.htm).

Yukon River Chinook salmon action plan

An action plan was developed in response to the classification of the Yukon River Chinook salmon as a stock of concern under the SSFP and consistent with the Yukon River King Salmon Management Plan (Lingnau and Bergstrom 2004). The goal of the plan is to meet spawning escapement goals, to provide opportunity for subsistence users to harvest levels within the ANS range, and to re-establish the historic range of harvest levels by other users. The plan assesses potential habitat issues affecting the stock, reviews fisheries regulations, identifies information needs, and evaluates escapement goals.

Escapement goals

The salmon fisheries of the Yukon River drainage are managed by time, area, and gear regulations to achieve escapement goals. Escapement is the number of fish allowed to escape the fishery and spawn. A biological escapement goal (BEG) is the number of salmon in a particular stock that ADF&G has determined to escape the fishery to spawn to provide the maximum sustained yield. This determination is based on biological information about the fish stock in question. A sustainable escapement goal (SEG) is an estimate based on historical performance and other variables known to conserve a stock over a five- to ten- year period. SEGs are used in situations where a biological escapement goal cannot be estimated due to the absence of stock-specific catch estimates or a short time series of data. Escapement goals are reviewed on a three-year cycle. Chinook salmon escapement goals include two BEGs and five SEGs established by ADF&G for U.S. tributaries (Table 2; Brannian et al. 2006). Yukon River Chinook salmon escapement goals have generally been met or exceeded in the Alaska portion of the drainage during 2001–2008.

An escapement goal of 33,000–43,000 Chinook salmon for Canadian mainstem passage based on the DFO fish wheel mark-recapture program was agreed to by members of the Yukon River Panel. However, the Panel may recommend annual spawn-

Table 2. Escapement goals established for stocks of Chinook salmon *Oncorhynchus tshawytscha* in the Alaskan waters of the Yukon River drainage. BEG (biological escapement goal) is the number of salmon in a particular stock that ADF&G has determined should be allowed to escape the fishery to spawn to achieve the maximum sustained yield (human use). This determination is based on biological information about the fish stock. A SEG (sustainable escapement goal) is an estimate based on historical performance and other variables known to conserve a stock over a five to ten year period.

Stream/Evaluation Method	Escapement goal (numbers of fish)	Type of goal
East Fork Andreafsky River/Aerial	960–1,900	SEG
West Fork Andreafsky River/Aerial	640–1,600	SEG
Anvik River/Aerial	1,100–1,700	SEG
Nulato River/Aerial (Forks Combined)	940–1,900	SEG
Gisasa River/Aerial	420–1,100	SEG
Chena River/Tower	2,800–5,700	BEG
Salcha River/Tower	3,300–6,500	BEG

ing escapement targets as part of a stock re-building plan for implementation by the Parties through their management entities. They may also revise targets for rebuilt stocks. In April of 1996, the Panel agreed to a six-year rebuilding plan for Canadian main stem Yukon River Chinook salmon stocks with an escapement target of 28,000 Chinook salmon. However, in response to poor runs in 1998–2000, the Panel recommended in 2001 an interim escapement objective of 25,000 Chinook salmon if no commercial fishery occurred and 28,000 Chinook salmon if a commercial fishery occurred in Alaska. Escapements from each year from 2001 to 2006 have met or exceeded this target with a record escapement in 2003 (Appendix Table 2). Consequently, with the understanding that the six consecutive years of good escapements were indicative of a rebuilt run, the Panel returned to its original escapement target of 33,000–43,000 Chinook salmon. The Yukon River Panel has now agreed to estimate border passage and escapements based upon the Eagle sonar program (Figure 4) with an interim management escapement goal (IMEG) of 45,000 fish for 2008.

Management history 2001–2008

Conservative management based on the action plan adopted by the BOF contributed to the successful achievement of escapement goals through 2006. Beginning in 2001, the subsistence salmon fishing schedule adopted by the BOF was implemented upriver consistently with migratory timing. The subsistence fishing schedule is intended to spread subsistence opportunity among users in years of average to below average abundance, especially early in the run. Based on a preseason forecast for a below average run in 2001, no commercial or sport fish fishing occurred in the Alaskan sections of the Yukon River (see Burr 2009, this volume, for discussion of the sport fishing closure). Inseason management actions were taken near the middle of the run to reduce subsistence fishing time to less than the regulatory subsistence fishing schedule. Subsequently, the run was judged to be large enough to provide for escapement and subsistence needs; to conserve summer chum salmon, subsistence gillnets were restricted to eight inch, or larger, mesh size. Post season, managers determined that a foregone surplus of approximately 20,000 Chinook salmon beyond escapement and subsistence needs occurred in the 2001 run.

In 2002–2005, conservative preseason management strategies were developed to not allow commercial fishing until near the midpoint of the Chinook salmon run. Historically, the first commercial opening occurred at the estimated first quarter point of the run. This management strategy provided for passage of a portion of the early run segment through the lower river districts and for more reliable run projections before commercial fishing started. In 2006 and 2007, based on the preseason projections, fishery managers scheduled a short commercial fishing period near the first quarter point (historically June 15) for Chinook salmon. After this fishing period, the harvest was spread out over the middle 50% of the run based on inseason run assessment. Additional harvest after the third quarter point depended on information from assessment projects and available markets. The 2007 run was less than anticipated and the escapement goal for the Canadian mainstem Yukon River was not met. As a result, fishery management in 2008 returned to the more conservative preseason strategy of not allowing commercial fishing until near the midpoint of the Chinook salmon run when inseason run projections can be more accurately estimated. Because the run was below average to poor in 2008, no directed commercial fishing periods for Chinook salmon were allowed. In addition, subsistence fishing periods were reduced by approximately half the time allowed by the management plan during the middle 50% of the run. Further, gillnet mesh size was restricted to six inches or less in Districts 1–3. Even with these harvest reductions, the escapement goal for the Canadian mainstem Yukon River was not met in 2008.

Escapement, Age, and Sex Ratio

Escapement

Chinook salmon escapement goals were generally met throughout the Alaska portion of the Yukon River drainage during 2004–2008, and escapements in monitored systems were generally higher than the low numbers estimated 1998–2001 (Figures 3–4; Appendix Table 1). The Chena and Salcha Rivers are the major Chinook salmon producing tributaries within the Alaska portion of the Yukon River drainage. The BEG for the stock of Chinook salmon that spawns in the Chena River is 2,800–5,700 (Table 2). Between 1986–2008, the Chena River stock of Chinook salmon failed to meet the established escapement goal only in 1989 (Figure 6; JTC 2008). The annual escapement of Chinook salmon in the Chena River in 2005 was not assessed. The Salcha River stock of Chinook salmon has a BEG of 3,300–6,500 (Table 2). The Salcha River Chinook salmon escapement goal has been met in 20 of the past 21 years (JTC 2008); escapements in 1989 failed to meet the goal (JTC 2008).

Escapement observations for those stocks indexed by aerial surveys (1996–2007) with an established SEG are shown in Table 2 (JTC 2008). The East Fork of the Andreafsky River has an SEG of 960–1,700 fish; escapement observations were not obtained in 1996, 1999, and 2003. The West Fork of the Andreafsky Chinook salmon population has an SEG of 640–1,600 fish; escapement observations were not obtained in 1998 and 1999 (Appendix Table 1). In the Anvik River, the SEG is 1,100–1,700 fish; escapement observations were not obtained in 1998, 1999, and 2003. The Chinook salmon SEG in the Nulato River is 940–1,900 fish; escapement observations were not obtained in 1996, 1997, 1999, 2000, 2003, and 2004. The Gisasa River Chinook salmon population has an

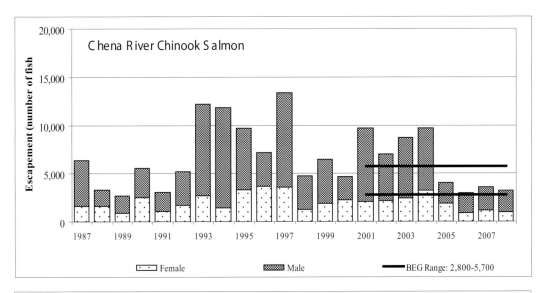

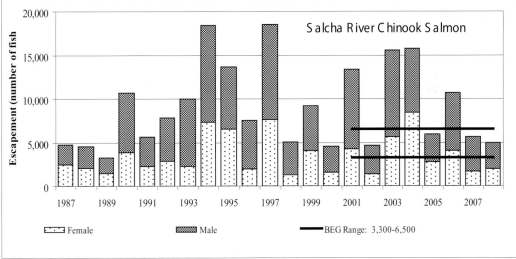

FIGURE 6. Chinook salmon *Oncorhynchus tshawytscha* escapement by year and sex observed in the Chena (above) and Salcha (below) rivers, Alaska, 1987–2008. BEG is the number of salmon in a particular stock that ADF&G has determined should be allowed to escape the fishery to spawn to achieve the maximum sustained yield (human use).

SEG of 420–1,100 fish; escapement observations were not obtained in 1996–2000 and 2003 (Appendix Table 1). Thus, there are 49 escapement observations out of the possible 60 stream by year cells from 1996 to 2007. In 39 of the 49 cases (80%), escapements met or exceeded the escapement goals. A full evaluation of escapement goal performance for these rivers is difficult due to incomplete aerial survey records or incomplete counts due to poor survey conditions.

The average escapement to the Canadian portion of the Yukon River drainage from 2001 to 2008 based on Eagle sonar was 52,900 Chinook salmon (range 33,500–80,600 fish), which was slightly higher than the ten-year average (1989–1998) of 50,800 fish (Appendix Table 2). The rebuilding escapement target of 28,000 Chinook salmon in the Canadian mainstem Yukon River based on the DFO passage estimates was exceeded each year during 2000–2006 (Figure 3). In 2007, Canadian escapement fell well below the rebuilt run escapement target of 33,000–43,000

Chinook salmon (Figure 3). In 2008, Canadian escapement was 27% below the interim management escapement goal of >45,000 Chinook salmon based on Eagle sonar passage estimates (Figure 4).

Age and sex composition

In the Yukon River, Chinook salmon return as age-3 through age-8 fish, though primarily as age-5 and age-6 fish, which are the dominant age classes. Yukon River Chinook salmon life history type is primarily one year in freshwater with only a few two-year freshwater fish contributing to the run (Bales 2008). In the Chena and Salcha Rivers, the largest producers of Chinook salmon in the Alaskan portion of the drainage, age-class and sex composition of Chinook salmon escapements by year were similar during the periods 1989–1998 and 2004–2008 (Table 1; Figure 7). Average percent of age-5 salmon ranged from 35% to 38% for both rivers while average percent of age-6 salmon ranged from 41%

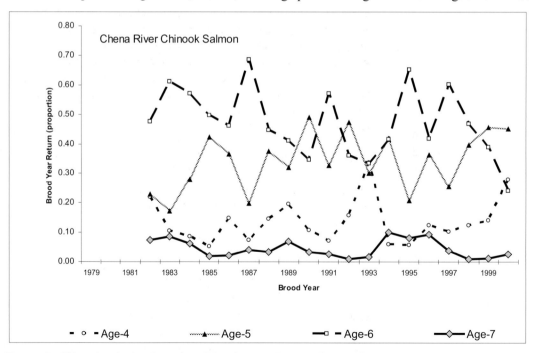

Figure 7. Chinook salmon *Oncorhynchus tshawytscha* age-class composition of Chena River Alaska for the brood years 1982 through 2000.

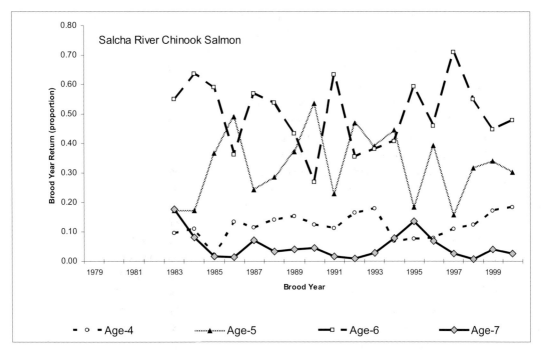

FIGURE 8. Chinook salmon *Oncorhynchus tshawytscha* age-class composition of Salcha River Alaska for the brood years 1983 through 2000.

to 51%. These two age classes accounted for between 77% and 89% of the entire escapement in both rivers. Percent female ranged from 43% in the Chena River during the period 1989–1998–47% in both rivers during the recent period, 2004–2008 (Table 1).

Based on brood year tables, the age-class composition of the Chinook salmon stock in the Chena and Salcha Rivers for the brood years 1982 through 2000 were variable with no discernable pattern of changes (Figures 7–8).

Age-class composition of the Eagle sonar based Canadian-origin Chinook salmon return from brood years 1975–2000 indicated a decrease in age-7 salmon from an average 22% from the brood years 1975 though 1982 to an average of 8% from the ten brood years that followed 1983–1992 (Figure 9). Age-7 salmon have continued to contribute less than 12% to the return for the brood years 1993 through 2000. The large decrease in the age-7

component observed in the Canadian-origin stock between 1982 and 1983 was not readily apparent in the stocks from the Chena or Salcha Rivers (Figures 7–9).

Based on brood year table data using the Eagle sonar program as the basis for escapement estimation, the stock–recruitment relationship was highly variable for Canadian-origin Chinook salmon. Recruit per spawner (R/S) ranged from 1.0 for the 1994 spawning brood year to about 4.6 R/S for fish returning from the 1986 brood year, with an overall average of about 2.9 R/S.

Harvest, Border Passage, and Exploitation Rates

Harvest

In Alaska, the recent five-year (2004–2008) average commercial and subsistence combined harvest of 86,573 Chinook salmon

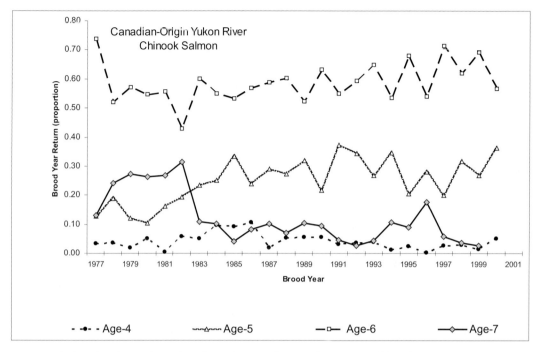

Figure 9. Chinook salmon *Oncorhynchus tshawytscha* age-class composition from Yukon River Canada for the brood years 1978 through 2000.

represented a 55% decrease from the ten-year period, 1989 to 1998 (average harvest of 156,092 fish; Figure 10; Appendix Table 3). Subsistence harvest varied between 11,110 and 42,724 fish between 1961 and 1982 but was generally between 15,000 and 25,000 fish most years. From 1983 onward, subsistence harvest remained above 36,000 fish. Although the subsistence harvest in Alaska has remained stable near 50,000 Chinook salmon most years since 1983, commercial harvests have decreased over 34% from an average of 100,011 annually (1989–1998) to the recent five-year average (2004–2008) of 34,457 fish.

In response to a poor run in 2000, no Alaskan commercial harvest was permitted in 2001 and only 24,128 Chinook salmon were commercially harvested in 2002 (Appendix Table 3). The 2005 and 2006 commercial harvests were within the range of surplus production estimates despite below average run

sizes. In 2007, a small commercial fishery of 33,629 fish was allowed and in 2008, no directed Chinook salmon commercial fisheries were allowed. Recent average sport fishery harvests from 2004 to 2008 (996 fish) were slightly less than historical average harvests (1,502 fish, range 156–2,811 fish) from 1989 to 2008 (Appendix Table 3); most of the sport fishery harvests occurred in terminal areas.

In Canada, total harvest from all sources (domestic, aboriginal, sport, and commercial) from 1980 to 1997 ranged between 10,729 and 22,896 fish. The ten-year (1999–2008) average total harvest of 8,739 Chinook salmon was 81% below the lower end of this range (Figure 4; Appendix Table 2). Since that time, Chinook salmon harvest steeply declined. The lowest harvest period was 1998 through 2000 when the average harvest was 7,761 fish. Catch slightly increased during 2001–2006 and decreased substantially during 2007–2008. Aboriginal harvest typically

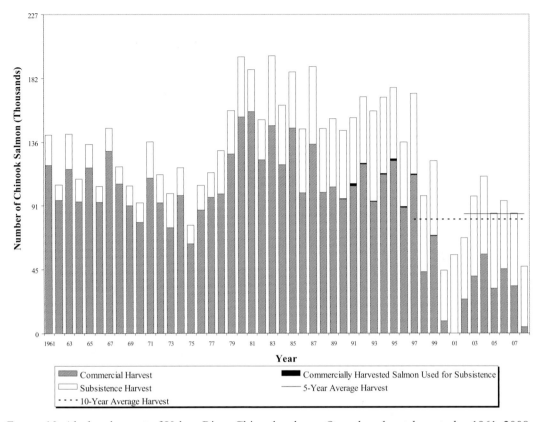

FIGURE 10. Alaskan harvest of Yukon River Chinook salmon *Oncorhynchus tshawytscha*, 1961–2008. Other harvests include personal-use, ADF&G test fish, and Sport Fish harvests. Subsistence, personal-use, and sport fish harvest data were unavailable for 2008. The previous five-year average harvest was substituted.

comprises 70% of the total harvest. Sport fishery harvest has never exceeded 1,230 fish 1980–2008 and has ranged between 0 and 500 fish since 1999. No commercial or domestic fishery occurred in Canada during 2007 or 2008.

Border passage

Border passage into Canada has been estimated since 1982 by the Canadian DFO using mark–recapture techniques, and more recently, by ADF&G using radiotelemetry (2002–2004) and sonar (2004–2008; Figure 2). The Canadian DFO border passage estimates have been derived from mark-recapture estimates using two fish wheels near the border at river

mile (RM) 1,224. This border passage estimate formed the basis for the U.S./Canada Yukon River Salmon Agreement. However, recent analyses indicated that the DFO mark–recapture estimates of border passage did not appear to be consistent through time (JTC 2008). While specific reasons for the discrepancy between these two escapement estimators are not completely understood, Canadian and U.S. scientists have agreed that Eagle sonar represents a technically defensible project that is likely to produce much more accurate and reliable estimates of Canadian Chinook salmon passage than the traditional mark–recapture project. As a result, at their April 2008 meeting, the U.S./Canada Yukon Panel authorized future estimation of Canadian-origin Chinook salmon escapement on the basis the sonar program.

At their fall 2007 meeting, after examining various relationships between aerial survey indices and other independent border passage estimates, the JTC revised the basis for estimating the number of Chinook salmon that spawn in the mainstem Yukon River drainage in Canada (JTC 2008). Using escapement estimates derived from the radio telemetry (2002–2004) and sonar (2005–2007) border passage estimates, in conjunction with the combined aerial survey counts of spawning Chinook salmon within the established index areas in the Big Salmon River, Little Salmon River, and Nisutlin River drainages (3-Area Index), escapements were estimated for the years 1982–2001. These 1982–2007 escapement estimates averaged 48,556 Chinook salmon, ranging from 25,870 in 2000 to 80,594 in 2003 (Figure 4). The JTC also recommended using the Eagle sonar project in the future as the primary assessment of border passage (JTC 2008).

Exploitation rates

Based on stock composition estimates applied to main stem harvests in conjunction with the border passage estimates, the total run size of the Canadian Chinook salmon stock from 1982 to 2007 has been estimated (Figure 5). Based on the newly developed escapement database, total run size of the Canadian Chinook salmon run has ranged from approximately 52,843 fish in 2000 to 182,504 fish in 1996. Accordingly, the exploitation rate that Alaskan fishermen exert on the Canadian stock was calculated. Associated exploitation rates exerted by Alaskan fishermen on this stock ranged from 27% in 2001 to 76% in 1987 (Figure 5). Average U.S. exploitation rates during the recent eight-year period 2000–2007 decreased by 14% from the 1990–1999 average and by 17% from the 1982–1989 average (Figure 5). It is abundantly clear that

recent exploitation rates are low in comparison to historic rates exerted during the 1970s, 1980s, and 1990s, reflecting the conservative fishery management regime in place.

Management Information Needs

The JTC completed a research plan in 2005 and the goals, issues, and needs described in this plan provide a framework for research in the entire Yukon River basin (JTC 2005). This plan identifies key research and conservation needs and is used by each agency internally and to communicate with the public. The plan's comprehensive listing of all research needs for the entire basin also provides a framework for other efforts in the region. Escapement, inseason abundance, harvest monitoring, habitat description, public education, and understanding the connections between salmon biology and ecology are identified as important categories of emphasis.

Long-term stock assessment information is needed to determine changes in abundance, stock-recruitment relationships, and yield of Chinook salmon stocks of the Yukon River drainage. Most stock assessment information collected during the 1960s and 1970s consisted of aerial surveys conducted on a periodic basis, which provided estimates of spawning abundance. Long-term and accurate estimates of abundance and composition of spawning stocks is needed along with harvest estimates from the various fisheries of the Yukon River drainage. Much progress toward these objectives has been made since the late 1980s, and in particular, over the last decade. However, the time series for many data sets are relatively short and obtaining such information is expensive and difficult due to the remoteness of the area.

Summary and Discussion

The Yukon River Chinook salmon stock was designated as a stock of yield concern by the BOF in 2000 after three years of poor runs and reduced yield. Chinook salmon escapement goals were generally met or exceeded throughout the Alaska portion of the Yukon River drainage the past five years (2004–2008), with record escapements in some systems. During the five-year period 2002–2006, escapement goals to the upper drainage portions in Canada have generally been met or exceeded with record escapements from 2001 to 2003. Escapement goals to Canada were not met in 2007 and 2008. Further, combined average commercial and subsistence harvests in Alaskan waters in the recent five-year period (2004–2008) showed a substantial decrease from the ten-year period (1989–1998). Although annual subsistence harvest levels remained stable around 50,000 salmon, commercial harvests have decreased substantially (over 60%) in recent years. Hence, the Yukon River Chinook salmon stock continues to be a yield concern because the average yield since 2000 continues to be well below the average yield during the 1990s. Conservative fishery management actions have included establishment of a subsistence fishing schedule, delaying commercial fishing until the midpoint of the run, and reducing exploitation rate. In 2008, due to a poor run, a complete closure of the Chinook salmon commercial fishery and subsistence fishing reductions were necessary.

An important issue for Yukon Chinook salmon is the apparent decline in size of fish reported by many fishers in recent years. Age-class composition of Canadian-origin Chinook salmon showed a decrease in age-7 salmon from an average 22% (1979–1982 brood years) to an average of 8% (1983–1992 brood years; Figure 9). A reduction in years feeding at sea would reduce the size of the fish. In response to these concerns, the JTC established a Salmon Size Subcommittee to compile relevant literature and existing analyses pertaining to age composition and size of fish trends and potential causes of

these trends (JTC 2006). This informational summary was divided into six sections: history of the Alaskan Yukon River Chinook salmon harvest and fishery sampling, history of the Canadian Yukon River Chinook salmon harvest, summary of prior age, sex and size investigations, summary of Yukon River gillnet selectivity, heritability of traits and potential effects of selective fisheries (Hard et al. 2009, this volume), and oceanic influences on salmon size (Myers et al. 2009, this volume). The JTC report (2006) recognizes several variables that may contribute to trends, including environmental changes in the Bering Sea and Gulf of Alaska, fishery induced selective pressures, and increased competition in the ocean from hatchery fish. The perceived declines in size of Yukon Chinook salmon is hotly debated in regulatory arenas, prompting several proposals before the Federal Subsistence Board and Alaska BOF for reduced gillnet mesh size and depth. Though a number of empirical and modeling studies have attempted to inform this debate, complex biological, economic, social, and regulatory issues make resolution elusive. The difficulties associated with obtaining adequate assessment data throughout the drainage hinders a complete characterization of the problem as well as evaluation of any proposed solutions.

Management of Chinook salmon fisheries in the Yukon River is complex and includes coordinating efforts between the U.S. and Canada for stocks originating in Canada, and between ADF&G and the U.S. federal government for regulation of fisheries in Alaska with two regulatory and advisory group systems, and the involvement of several local and regional organizations. Some type of alternate system might improve the effectiveness and possibly simplify management of salmon fisheries in the Yukon River drainage (see Gaden et al. 2009).

The Chinook salmon stocks of the Yukon River have experienced considerable variation in abundance and harvest over the past 50 years. While certainly challenges exist, careful management through the regulation of the fisheries to permit adequate escapements for spawning should ensure the sustainability of the resource for future generations.

Acknowledgments

The authors thank those employees of the Alaska Department of Fish and Game and all other state and federal government agencies and non-governmental organizations and individuals who worked long and irregular hours at various locations throughout the Yukon River collecting the data used in this report. Two anonymous reviewers and Charles Krueger provided helpful comments on an earlier version of the manuscript.

References

Bales, J. 2008. Salmon Age and Sex Composition and Mean Lengths for the Yukon River Area, 2006. Alaska Department of Fish and Game, Fishery Data Series No. 08–14, Anchorage.

Beacham, T. D., C. B. Murray, and R. E. Withler. 1989. Age, morphology, and biochemical genetic variation of Yukon River Chinook salmon. Transactions of the American Fisheries Society 118:46–63.

Beacham, K., L. Jonsen, J. Supernault, M. Wetklo, L. Deng, and N. Varnavskaya. 2006. Pacific Rim population structure of Chinook salmon as determined from microsatellite variation. Transactions of the American Fisheries Society 135:1604–1621.

Borba, B. M., and H. H. Hamner. 2001. Subsistence and personal use salmon harvest estimates—Yukon Area, 2000. Alaska Department of Fish and Game, Division of Commercial Fisheries, Regional Information Report No. 3A01–27, Anchorage.

Bradford, M. J., A. von Finster, and P. A. Milligan. 2009. Freshwater life history, habitat, and the production of Chinook salmon from the upper Yukon basin. Pages 19–38 in C. C. Krueger and C. E. Zimmerman, editors. Pacific salmon: ecology and management of western Alaska's populations. American Fisheries Society, Symposium 70, Bethesda, Maryland.

Brannian, L. K., M. J. Evenson, and J. R. Hilsinger. 2006. Escapement goal recommendations for select Arctic-Yukon-Kuskokwim region salmon stocks, 2007. Alaska Department of Fish and Game, Fishery Manuscript No. 06–07, Anchorage. Available: http://www.sf.adfg.state.ak.us/FedAidPDFs/fm06–07.pdf (May 2002).

Bromaghin, J. F. 2005. A versatile net selectivity model, with application to Pacific salmon and freshwater species of the Yukon River. Alaska Fisheries Research 74:157–168.

Bue, F. J., B. M. Borba, R. Cannon, and C. C. Krueger. 2009. Yukon River fall chum salmon fisheries: management, harvest, and stock abundance. Pages 703–742 in C. C. Krueger and C. E. Zimmerman, editors. Pacific salmon: ecology and management of western Alaska's populations. American Fisheries Society, Symposium 70, Bethesda, Maryland.

Buklis, L. S. 2002. Subsistence fisheries management on federal public lands in Alaska. Fisheries 27(7):10–18.

Burr, J. M. 2009. Management of recreational salmon fisheries in the Arctic-Yukon-Kuskokwim Region of Alaska. Pages 521–539 in C. C. Krueger and C. E. Zimmerman, editors. Pacific salmon: ecology and management of western Alaska's populations. American Fisheries Society, Symposium 70, Bethesda, Maryland.

DCED (Alaska Department of Community and Economic Development). 2002. Community Database Online, Community Information Summaries. Available: http://dced.state.ak.us/cbd/commdb/CF_COMDB.htm (May 2002).

Gaden, M., C. C. Krueger, and C. Goddard. 2009. Managing across jurisdictional boundaries: fishery governance in the Great Lakes and Arctic-Yukon-Kuskokwim regions. Pages 941–960 in C. C. Krueger and C. E. Zimmerman, editors. Pacific salmon: ecology and management of western Alaska's populations. American Fisheries Society, Symposium 70, Bethesda, Maryland.

Gilbert, C. H. 1922. The salmon of the Yukon River. U.S. Bureau of Fisheries Bulletin 38:317–332.

Hard, J. J., W. Eldridge, and K. Naish. 2009. Genetic consequences of size-selective fishing: implications for viability of Chinook salmon in the Arctic-Yukon-Kuskokwim region of Alaska. Pages 759–780 in C. C. Krueger and C. E. Zimmerman, editors. Pacific salmon: ecology and management of western Alaska's populations. American Fisheries Society, Symposium 70, Bethesda, Maryland.

Higgs, A. S. 1995. A history of mining in the Yukon River basin of Alaska. Northern Land Use Research, Bering Sea Fishermen's Association, Fairbanks.

Hilsinger, J. R., E. Volk, G. Sandone, and R. Cannon. 2009. Salmon management in the Arctic-Yukon-Kuskokwim Region of Alaska: past, present, and future. Pages 495–519 in C. C. Krueger and

C. E. Zimmerman, editors. Pacific salmon: ecology and management of western Alaska's populations. American Fisheries Society, Symposium 70, Bethesda, Maryland.

Holder, R. R., and D. Senecal-Albrecht. 1998. Yukon River comprehensive salmon plan for Alaska. Alaska Department of Fish and Game, Anchorage.

JTC (Joint Technical Committee of the Yukon River US/Canada Panel). 2005. US and Canada Yukon River Salmon Joint Technical Committee strategic plan. The United States/Canada Yukon River Joint Technical Committee, March 2005, Anchorage.

JTC (Joint Technical Committee of the Yukon River US/Canada Panel). 2006. Potential causes of size trends in Yukon River Chinook salmon populations. Alaska Department of Fish and Game, Division of Commercial Fisheries, Regional Information Report No. 3A06–07, Anchorage.

JTC (Joint Technical Committee of the Yukon River US/Canada Panel). 2008. Yukon River salmon 2007 season summary and 2008 season outlook. Alaska Department of Fish and Game, Division of Commercial Fisheries, Regional Information Report No. 3A08–01, Anchorage.

JTC (Joint Technical Committee of the Yukon River US/Canada Panel). 2009 In press. Yukon River salmon 2008 season summary and 2009 season outlook. Alaska Department of Fish and Game, Division of Commercial Fisheries, Anchorage.

Lichatowich, J. A. and R. N. Williams. 2009. Failures to incorporate science into fishery management and recovery programs: Lessons from the Columbia River. Pages 1005–1019 in C. C. Krueger and C. E. Zimmerman, editors. Pacific salmon: ecology and management of western Alaska's populations. American Fisheries Society, Symposium 70, Bethesda, Maryland.

Lingnau, T. L. and D. J. Bergstrom. 2004. Yukon River Chinook salmon stock status and action plan. Alaska Department of Fish and Game, Division of Commercial Fisheries, Regional Information Report No. 3A03–34, Anchorage.

Myers, K. W., R. V. Walker, N. D. Davis, J. L. Armstrong, and M. Kaeriyama. 2009. High seas distribution, biology, and ecology of Arctic-Yukon-Kuskokwim salmon: direct information from high seas tagging experiments, 1954–2005. Pages 201–239 in C. C. Krueger and C. E. Zimmerman, edi-tors. Pacific salmon: ecology and management of western Alaska's populations. American Fisheries Society, Symposium 70, Bethesda, Maryland.

Schultz, K. C., R. R. Holder, L. H. Barton, D. J. Bergstrom, C. Blaney, G. J. Sandone, and D. J. Schneiderhan. 1993. Annual management report for subsistence, personal use, and commercial fisheries of the Yukon Area, 1992. Alaska Department of Fish and Game, Division of Commercial Fisheries, Regional Information Report No. 3A93–10, Anchorage.

Spencer, T. R., T. Hamazaki, and J. H. Eiler. 2006. Mark-recapture abundance estimates for Yukon River Chinook salmon in 2003. Alaska Department of Fish and Game, Fishery Data Series No. 06–31, Anchorage. Available: http://www.sf.adfg.state.ak.us/FedAidPDFs/fds06–31.pdf (May 2002).

Statistics Canada. 2002. Available: http://www.statcan.ca/english/Pgdb/People/Population/demo39a.htm, May 30, 2002 (May 2002).

Templin, W. D., R. L. Wilmot, C. M. Gutherie III, and L. W. Seeb. 2005. United States and Canadian Chinook salmon populations in the Yukon River can be segregated based on genetic characteristics. Alaska Fishery Research Bulletin 11:44–60.

Utter, F. M., M. V. McPhee, and F. W. Allendorf. 2009. Population genetics and the management of Arctic-Yukon-Kuskokwim salmon populations. Pages 97–123 in C. C. Krueger and C. E. Zimmerman, editors. Pacific salmon: ecology and management of western Alaska's populations. American Fisheries Society, Symposium 70, Bethesda, Maryland.

Williams, J. G. 1999. Alaska population overview 1998 estimates. Alaska Department of Labor, Research and Analysis Section, Juneau.

Wilmot, R. L., R. Everett, W. J. Spearman, and R. Baccus. 1992. Genetic stock identification of Yukon River chum and chinook salmon 1987 to 1990. U.S. Fish and Wildlife Service, Anchorage, Alaska.

Wolf, R. J., and J. J. Spaeder. 2009. People and salmon of the Yukon and Kuskokwim drainages and Norton Sound in Alaska: fishery harvests, culture change, and local knowledge systems. Pages 349–379 in C. C. Krueger and C. E. Zimmerman, editors. Pacific salmon: ecology and management of western Alaska's populations. American Fisheries Society, Symposium 70, Bethesda, Maryland.

Zhou, S. 2002. Size-dependent recovery of Chinook salmon in carcass surveys. Transactions of the American Fisheries Society 131:1194–1202.

APPENDIX TABLE 1. Yukon River Chinook salmon *Oncorhynchus tshawytscha* historical escapements from selected tributaries in Alaska, 1961-2008. Only acceptable aerial surveys are included.

| Year | Ground based projects | | Aerial Surveys [a] | | | | |
	Chena River	Salcha River	East Fork Andreafsky	West Fork Andreafsky	Anvik River	Nulato River	Gisasa River
1980				1,500	1,330		951
1981							
1982			1,274	851			421
1983						1,006	572
1984			1,573	1,993			
1985			1,617	2,248	1,051	2,780	735
1986	9,065		1,954	3,158	1,118	2,974	1,346
1987	6,404	4,771	1,608	3,281	1,174	1,638	731
1988	3,346	4,562	1,020	1,448	1,805	1,775	797
1989	2,666	3,294	1,399	1,089			
1990	5,603	10,728	2,503	1,545	2,347		
1991	3,025	5,608	1,938	2,544	875	2,020	1,690
1992	5,230	7,862	1,030	2,002	1,536	579	910
1993	12,241	10,007	5,855	2,765	1,720	3,025	1,573
1994	11,877	18,399				1,795	2,775
1995	9,680	13,643	1,635	1,108	1,996	1,649	410
1996	7,153	7,570		624	839		
1997	13,390	18,514	1,140	1,510	3,979		
1998	4,745	5,027	1,027	1,249	709	1,053	889
1999	6,485	9,198					
2000	4,694	4,595	1,018	427	1,721		
2001	9,696	13,328	1,065	570	1,420	1,884	1,298
2002	6,967	4,644 [a]	1,447	977	1,713	1,584	506
2003	8,739 [b]	15,500 [a,b]		1,578			
2004	9,645 [b]	15,761 [a]	2,879	1,317	3,681	1,321	731
2005	4,075 [b]	5,988	1,492	1,715	2,421	553	950
2006	2,936 [b]	10,679		824	1,876	1,292	843
2007	3,564	5,631	1,758	976	1,529	2,583	593
2008	3,212	5,000 [a]				922	487
10 Yr. Avg.	6,001	9,032	1,610	1,048	2,052	1,448	773
BEGs	2,800-5,700	3,300-6,500	SEGs 960-1,700	640-1,600	1,100-1,700	940-1,900	-1,100

[a] Escapement estimates are conservative because of missed counts due to no or poor visibility.

[b] Expanded counts based on average run timing.

APPENDIX TABLE 2. Total Canadian harvest and Eagle sonar-based escapement of Yukon River Chinook salmon in numbers, 1961–2008 (JTC 2009, in press).

	Mainstem Yukon River Harvest						Total	
Year	Commercial	Domestic	Aboriginal Fishery	Sport [a]	Test Fishery	Combined Non-Commercial	Canadian Harevest	Canadian Escapement
1961	3,446		9,300			9,300	12,746	
1962	4,037		9,300			9,300	13,337	
1963	2,283		7,750			7,750	10,033	
1964	3,208		4,124			4,124	7,332	
1965	2,265		3,021			3,021	5,286	
1966	1,942		2,445			2,445	4,387	
1967	2,187		2,920			2,920	5,107	
1968	2,212		2,800			2,800	5,012	
1969	1,640		957			957	2,597	
1970	2,611		2,044			2,044	4,655	
1971	3,178		3,260			3,260	6,438	
1972	1,769		3,960			3,960	5,729	
1973	2,199		2,319			2,319	4,518	
1974	1,808	406	3,342			3,748	5,556	
1975	3,000	400	2,500			2,900	5,900	
1976	3,500	500	1,000			1,500	5,000	
1977	4,720	531	2,247			2,778	7,498	
1978	2,975	421	2,485			2,906	5,881	
1979	6,175	1,200	3,000			4,200	10,375	
1980	9,500	3,500	7,546	300		11,346	20,846	
1981	8,593	237	8,879	300		9,416	18,009	
1982	8,640	435	7,433	300		8,168	16,808	43,538
1983	13,027	400	5,025	300		5,725	18,752	44,475
1984	9,885	260	5,850	300		6,410	16,295	50,005
1985	12,573	478	5,800	300		6,578	19,151	40,435
1986	10,797	342	8,625	300		9,267	20,064	41,425
1987	10,864	330	6,069	300		6,699	17,563	41,307
1988	13,217	282	7,178	650		8,110	21,327	39,699
1989	9,789	400	6,930	300		7,630	17,419	60,299
1990	11,324	247	7,109	300		7,656	18,980	59,212
1991	10,906	227	9,011	300		9,538	20,444	42,728
1992	10,877	277	6,349	300		6,926	17,803	39,155
1993	10,350	243	5,576	300		6,119	16,469	36,244
1994	12,028	373	8,069	300		8,742	20,770	56,449
1995	11,146	300	7,942	700		8,942	20,088	50,673
1996	10,164	141	8,451	790		9,382	19,546	74,060
1997	5,311	288	8,888	1,230		10,406	15,717	53,821
1998	390	24	4,687		737	5,448	5,838	35,497
1999	3,160	213	8,804	177		9,194	12,354	37,184
2000			4,068		761	4,829	4,829	25,870
2001	1,351	89	7,416	146	767	8,418	9,769	52,564
2002	708	59	7,138	128	1,036	8,361	9,069	42,359
2003	2,672	115	6,121	275	263	6,774	9,446	80,594
2004 [b]	3,785	88	6,483	423	167	7,161	10,946	48,469
2005	4,066	99	6,376	436		6,911	10,977	68,551
2006	2,332	63	5,757	606		6,426	8,758	62,933
2007			4,175	2	617	4,794	4,794	34,903
2008	1	[c]	2,885		513	3,398 [c]	3,399 [c]	34,000
Average								
1961-08	5,709	405	5,488	376 #	608	6,063	11,534	48,017
1999-08	2,259	104	5,922	274 #	589	6,627	8,434	48,743

[a] Includes fish from DFO test fish operations.

[b] Canadian sport fish harvest unknown prior to 1980.

[c] Data are preliminary or unavailable.

Evenson et al.

APPENDIX TABLE 3. Yukon River Chinook salmon harvests (numbers of fish) in Alaska, 1961–2008.

Year	Commercial	Commercial Related [a]	Total Commercial	Subsistence [b]	Personal Use [c]	Test Fish Sales [d]	Sport Fish [e]	Total
1961	119,664	0		21,488				141,152
1962	94,734	0	94,734	11,110				105,844
1963	117,048	0	117,048	24,862				141,910
1964	93,587	0	93,587	16,231				109,818
1965	118,098	0	118,098	16,608				134,706
1966	93,315	0	93,315	11,572				104,887
1967	129,656	0	129,656	16,448				146,104
1968	106,526	0	106,526	12,106				118,632
1969	91,027	0	91,027	14,000				105,027
1970	79,145	0	79,145	13,874				93,019
1971	110,507	0	110,507	25,684				136,191
1972	92,840	0	92,840	20,258				113,098
1973	75,353	0	75,353	24,317				99,670
1974	98,089	0	98,089	19,964				118,053
1975	63,838	0	63,838	13,045				76,883
1976	87,776	0	87,776	17,806				105,582
1977	96,757	0	96,757	17,581			156	114,494
1978	99,168	0	99,168	30,785			523	130,476
1979	127,673	0	127,673	31,005			554	159,232
1980	153,985	0	153,985	42,724			956	197,665
1981	158,018	0	158,018	29,690			769	188,477
1982	123,644	0	123,644	28,158			1,006	152,808
1983	147,910	0	147,910	49,478			1,048	198,436
1984	119,904	0	119,904	42,428			351	162,683
1985	146,188	0	146,188	39,771			1,368	187,327
1986	99,970	0	99,970	45,238			796	146,004
1987	134,760	0	134,760 [f]	55,039	1,706		502	192,007
1988	100,364	0	100,364	45,495	2,125	1,081	944	150,009
1989	104,198	0	104,198	48,462	2,616	1,293	1,053	157,622
1990	95,247	413	95,660	48,587	2,594	2,048	544	149,433
1991	104,878	1,538	106,416	46,773		689	773	154,651
1992	120,245	927	121,172	47,077		962	431	169,642
1993	93,550	560	94,110	63,915	426	1,572	1,695	161,718
1994	113,137	703	113,840	53,902		1,631	2,281	171,654
1995	122,728	1,324	124,052	50,620	399	2,152	2,525	179,748
1996	89,671	521	90,192	45,671	215	1,698	3,151	140,927
1997	112,841	769	113,610	57,117	313	2,811	1,913	175,764
1998	43,618	81	43,699	54,124	357	926	654	99,760
1999	69,275	288	69,563	53,305	331	1,205	1,023	125,427
2000	8,518		8,518	36,404	75	597	276	45,870

Appendix Table 3. Continued.

Year	Commercial	Commercial Related [a]	Total Commercial	Subsistence [b]	Personal Use [c]	Test Fish Sales [d]	Sport Fish [e]	Total
2001				55,819	122		679	56,620
2002	24,128		24,128	43,742	126	528	486	69,010
2003	40,438		40,438	56,959	204	680	2,719	101,000
2004	56,151		56,151	55,713	201	792	1,513	114,370
2005	32,029		32,029	53,409	138	296	483	86,355
2006 [f]	45,829		45,829	48,593	89	817	739	96,067
2007 [f]	33,634		33,634	55,156	136	849	960	90,735
2008 [f]	4,641		4,641	42,933	121	0	1,283 [g]	48,978
Average								
1989-1998	100,011	684	100,695	51,625	989	1,578	1,502	156,092
2004-2008	34,457		34,457	51,161	137	551	996	87,301
1999-2008	34,960		34,992	50,203	154	640	1,016	83,443

[a] Includes salmon harvested for subsistence and an estimate of the number of salmon harvested for the commercial production of salmon roe and the carcasses used for subsistence. These data are only available since 1990. Includes harvest from the Coastal District and test fish harvest that were used for subsistence.

[b] Prior to 1987, and 1990, 1991, and 1994 personal-use harvest was considered part of subsistence.

[c] Includes only test fish that were sold commercially.

[d] Sport fish harvest for the Alaskan portion of the Yukon River drainage. Most of this harvest is believed to have been taken within the Tanana River drainage (see Schultz et al. 1993: 1992 Yukon Area Annual Management Report)·

[e] Includes 653 and 2,136 Chinook salmon illegally sold in Districts 5 (Yukon River) and 6 (Tanana River), respectively.

[f] Subsistence and personal-use data are preliminary.

[g] Data are unavailable at this time. Estimated based on the previous 5-year average.

American Fisheries Society Symposium 70:703–742, 2009

Yukon River Fall Chum Salmon Fisheries: Management, Harvest, and Stock Abundance

Fred J. Bue[*] and Bonnie M. Borba
Alaska Department of Fish and Game, Division of Commercial Fisheries
1300 College Road, Fairbanks, Alaska 99701, USA

Richard Cannon
Office of Subsistence Management, U.S. Fish and Wildlife Service
1011 East Tudor Road, Mail Stop 121, Anchorage, Alaska 99503, USA

Charles C. Krueger
Great Lakes Fishery Commission
2100 Commonwealth Boulevard, Suite 100, Ann Arbor, Michigan 48105, USA

Abstract.—The most abundant salmon of the Yukon River is chum salmon *Oncorhynchus keta,* which make annual spawning runs from the Bering Sea up the Yukon River, traversing more than 1300 river miles across Alaska into Yukon Territory in Canada. Genetically distinct summer and fall runs exist and these runs are differentiated into stocks by timing of migration and by spawning river. The fall-run stocks are harvested from mid-July through early October and most Yukon River fisheries occur on a mixture of populations or stocks. This paper provides descriptions of fall chum salmon life history, the Yukon River fishery and its management, changes in stock abundance over time, and harvest. Six fisheries occur for fall-run chum salmon: subsistence, personal use, aboriginal, domestic, sport, and commercial. Subsistence fisheries in Alaska are comparable to aboriginal fisheries in Canada, as are personal use, sport, and domestic fisheries. The fisheries use a variety of gear including gillnets and fish wheels. Jurisdictionally, management requires cooperation among state, federal, and international organizations during both the ocean and river phases of the salmon life history. The goal of management is to regulate the harvest of commercial and traditional-use fisheries to provide an adequate number of fish for spawning (escapement) to ensure the reproduction of the next generation, and to sustain Alaskan and Canadian fisheries. Subsistence and aboriginal fisheries have priority over other fisheries in allocation of harvest. Regulations are used to control how many fish are caught through restrictions on effort, fishing efficiency, and the scheduling of where, when, and how long fishery openings will be allowed. Over the period 1974–2008, the largest runs of fall chum salmon occurred in 1975, 1995, and 2005 (> 1.47 million fish) and smallest runs occurred in 1999, 2000, and 2001 < 334,000 fish). Odd-year runs tend to be larger than even-year runs. The run failures of 1998–2002 were followed by increased run numbers in 2003–2008. Primary variables that influence the total run of fall chum salmon are the spawning success of previous generations,

*Corresponding author: fred.bue@alaska.gov

natural variability in marine and freshwater survival due to climatic and oceano-graphic processes, and fishery harvests in both marine and freshwater. Salmon escapement numbers typically emulated total run estimates. Every river monitored had low estimated escapements from 1998–2002. From 1974–2008, total harvest of fall chum salmon in Alaska (average 291,982 fish) exceeded Canadian harvests (average 20,314 fish) by an order of magnitude. Some lessons learned from management of this fishery are offered that may be applicable to other fisheries: stakeholder involvement is critical to effective harvest management; rapid, effective information sharing is a requirement for fast-paced, in-season decision-making; limited entry alone did not control harvest; and some things that make management difficult just cannot be changed!

Introduction

The Yukon River originates in British Columbia, Canada and flows over 2,300 mi to its mouth on the Bering Sea coast of western Alaska in the United States. Fewer than 130,000 people live in the drainage basin. Two urban communities, Fairbanks and Whitehorse, are located on a limited road system and account for about 80% of this population in the basin. The remainder of the population resides in over 80 small, remote villages with populations averaging 300 or fewer residents of predominately aboriginal background (Williams 1999; DCED 2002; Statistics Canada 2002).

Most village residents depend to varying degrees on fish and wildlife resources for food. The most abundant salmon is chum salmon *Oncorhynchus keta*, which make annual spawning migrations from the Bering Sea up the Yukon River. Genetically distinct summer and fall runs exist and these runs are organized into populations (or stocks) by spawning site, typically tributary rivers within the sub-drainages (see review Utter et al. 2009, this volume). These stocks are available for harvest from June through early October, and most Yukon River fisheries harvest a mixture of populations or stocks. Three large tributaries of the Yukon River including the Koyukuk, Tanana, and Porcupine rivers all contribute immensely as chum salmon

spawning areas. The fisheries in Alaska and Canada for chum salmon occur in the near-shore coastal areas around the mouths of the Yukon River, along the entire length of its main-stem, and in many tributaries. The fall-run salmon are harvested in Alaskan subsistence and personal-use fisheries in Alaska, and in Canadian aboriginal and domestic food fisheries. Commercial fisheries also exist in both countries depending on run abundance in a particular year. The fisheries use a variety of gear including gill nets and fish wheels.

In addition to chum salmon, Chinook *O. tshawytscha* and coho *O. kisutch* salmon are important contributors to the Yukon River fisheries. The Yukon River drainage also supports sockeye salmon *O. nerka,* which are relatively rare, and pink salmon *O. gorbuscha* that are abundant (in millions) but undesirable in the fisheries. Therefore both species are minor components of the harvest. Other species present in the subsistence and/or sport fisheries include Arctic grayling *Thymallus arcticus*, Dolly Varden char *Salvelinus malma*, inconnu *Stenodus leucichthys*, northern pike *Esox lucius*, burbot *Lota lota*, several *Coregonus* species, and Alaska black-fish *Dallia pectoralis*. Large harvests occur for whitefish and sheefish species for subsistence throughout the drainage while the other species have more localized harvests.

This paper provides descriptions of fall chum salmon life history, the Yukon River fishery and its management, changes in stock abundance over time, and harvest. Harvest is regulated to provide escapement from the fisheries so that spawning will produce the next generation and sustain the fishery. Regulations are also used to allocate harvest among those fishing on the river and were originally based on traditional usage patterns and gear types.

Life History

Summer and fall runs of chum salmon are distinguished from each other by entry date to the river from the ocean, by body morphology (where fall chum salmon are typically more robust and have a higher body fat content than summer chum salmon), and by spawning locations in the Yukon River drainage. Summer-run chum salmon enter the river in June and July, and spawn during July and August in the tributaries of the middle (including the Tanana River 1,000 mi from the sea) and lower Yukon River (below river mile 500) (Buklis 1981). Fall-run chum salmon enter the river in mid-July, August, and early September and spawn in spring-fed tributaries and upwelling areas of the upper Yukon River drainage from the Tanana River in Alaska upstream into Yukon Territory, Canada (Buklis and Barton 1984; Figure 1). Most fall chum salmon stocks of the Yukon River migrate unusually long distances upriver in comparison to other chum salmon stocks in North America (Salo 1991). Impor-

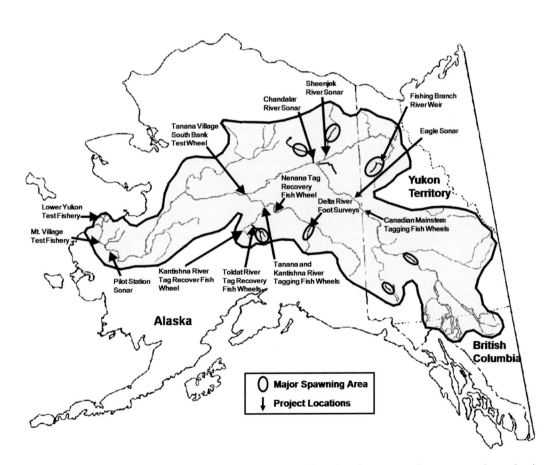

FIGURE 1. Location of major fall chum salmon *Oncorhynchus keta* spawning areas and monitoring projects in the Yukon River drainage.

tant spawning tributaries include the Tanana, Porcupine (tributaries Sheenjek and Fishing Branch rivers), and Chandalar rivers, and the main stem of the Yukon River in Canada. A few fall chum salmon stocks occur downstream of these areas, such as in the Koyukuk River, but these stocks typically comprise less than 5% of the total run (Eggers 2001). Based on genetic data from allozymes, microsatellites, mitochondrial DNA, and amplified fragment length polymorphisms, Yukon River chum salmon populations are structured by seasonal race (summer versus fall) and by geographic region associated with tributary location in the drainage (Wilmot et al. 1994; Scribner et al. 1998; Olsen et al. 2004; Flannery et al. 2007). The level of population differentiation and geographic specificity of stocks, however, is less for chum salmon than observed for some other salmon species such as Chinook salmon (Utter et al. 2009). For management purposes, chum salmon entering the Yukon River after July 15 are considered fall chum salmon; however, late entry of summer chum salmon stocks can occur after this date and have been detected based on genetic analyses (JTC 2008). Egg incubation occurs overwinter, and fry emerge in the spring (April) and immediately migrate downstream with the recession of spring-runoff to the Bering Sea. Based on tagging studies, Yukon River chum salmon feed and grow until maturity in the Gulf of Alaska and eastern Bering Sea (Myers et al. 2009, this volume). Maturity occurs after two to six years of ocean feeding (Bales 2008). Prior to river entry, maturing Yukon fall chum salmon are distributed across a broad area in the western Gulf of Alaska, along the Aleutian Islands, and eastern and western Bering Sea (Myers et al. 2009). Fall chum salmon may be caught in the False Pass salmon fishery in the Aleutians (Seeb and Crane 1999) and as bycatch in the southeastern Bering Sea walleye pollock trawl fishery (Gisclair 2009, this volume; Wilmot et al. 1998).

Description of the Fisheries

Prior to European contact, aboriginal populations living in the drainage developed a well-defined dependence on the abundant salmon resources. The harvest, distribution, and use of locally available, wild fish resources continue to provide essential economic, nutritional, cultural, spiritual, and social benefits to village households (Barker 1993; Berger 1985; McClellan 1987; Fienup-Riordan 1986; Wolfe and Spaeder 2009, this volume). Today, some of the fall chum salmon are frozen, dried, or smoked, and roe from females are preserved for later human consumption. However, a large percentage of salmon caught by the upper Yukon River communities are dried or frozen and fed to sled dogs (Figure 2; Andersen 1992).

Six fisheries for fall chum salmon are identified by U.S and Canadian managers: subsistence, personal use, aboriginal, domestic, sport, and commercial. Subsistence fisheries in Alaska are comparable to aboriginal fisheries in Canada. Both fisheries provide for the traditional and cultural use of fishery resources. In Alaska, the subsistence fisheries are open to all state residents in areas under state management, and to qualified rural residents in areas under federal management (Buklis 2002). The Canadian aboriginal fishery is only open to First Nations people.

Personal-use fisheries in Alaska and Canadian domestic food fisheries allow access to the fish for noncommercial purposes to residents in nonsubsistence areas in Alaska and to nonaboriginal residents in Canada. These fisheries provide Alaskan residents near Fairbanks and nonaboriginal Yukon Territory residents, an opportunity to efficiently harvest fish near their communities. Personal-use and domestic food fisheries are considered by management agencies as a lower priority than subsistence or aboriginal fishing in the allocation of harvest (Borba and Hamner 2001).

FIGURE 2. Fall chum caught from the Yukon River fillets are cut to improve drying and and laid over poles to dry (photos by Mike Parker, ADF&G).

Sport (recreational) fisheries in both Alaska and Canada harvest inconsequential numbers of fall chum salmon (Burr 2008). The sport fishery harvest of chum salmon occurs in areas accessible by roads such as the Tanana River near Fairbanks, but focuses primarily on Chinook and coho salmon (JTC 2008).

Commercial fishing for fall chum salmon in the Yukon River is based on in-season assessment of run size and is managed to allow harvest for surplus fish that exceed those needed for spawning and for subsistence and aboriginal fisheries. Coho salmon are also caught in the fall season fisheries due to the overlap in run timing. In Alaska, commercial fishing may be allowed along the entire 1,200-mi length of the mainstem Yukon River and the lower 225 river mi of the Tanana River. The majority of the commercial harvest, however, occurs in the lower river downstream of the village of Russian Mission (river mile 213) where the flesh quality of the salmon is higher (Figure 1; ADF&G 1993). The fish sold are used for human consumption (fresh, frozen, smoked, and roe) and some are sold as dog food. Fish caught in the upstream districts are typically sold for roe

as its ripeness is prime for the market after adult females have passed upstream of river mile 300. The Canadian commercial fishery is conducted in the main-stem of the upper Yukon River downstream of Dawson City. During recent years, the fall chum salmon commercial fishery is somewhat of a misnomer as virtually all of the catch by the license holders is used to feed their personal sled dog teams (JTC 2008).

Fishery Management

Overview

Management of the Yukon River fall chum salmon fishery is difficult because of biological, geographical, and political complexity. Fisheries for fall chum salmon occur along the entire length of the river and harvest a mixture of stocks that enter the river over a protracted late summer and fall period. Thus, management of individual stocks or populations on the mainstem Yukon River is not possible. Because the Yukon River fisheries are largely mixed-stock fisheries, some tributary populations may not be harvested to the levels they could sustain in relation to their abundance while others, in a particular year, may suffer overexploitation. Harvest issues exist between fishers in the lower-river versus upper-river fishers in Alaska and Canada. Fisheries that occur in the first few hundred miles of river have first access to the salmon runs before assessment of run abundance can be made. If run strength is projected to be low based on assessment in the lower river, then fisheries are restricted in-season. The effects of the regulations can be disproportionately felt by the upriver fisheries because of the sheer length of the river and the protracted time of fish entry. However, if the in-season estimate is below the actual run strength, the salmon will have already passed through the fishery and the result may be a substantial lost opportunity. Lastly, the fisheries in Alaska harvest Canada-bound chum salmon that travel over a thousand miles to their spawning grounds in Yukon Territory. The Yukon River Annex of the Pacific Salmon Treaty between the United States and Canada guides management of these trans-boundary stocks. The salmon fisheries of the Yukon River drainage are managed to achieve escapement goals in specific streams, to ensure passage of salmon from Alaska into the Canadian portion of the drainage, and when salmon abundance is projected to exceed negotiated escapement goals, to provide for consumptive uses. The details of the agreement are described in the Yukon River Salmon Agreement of 2001 (http://www.yukonriverpanel.com/Library/Other/YRS%20Agreement.pdf).

Management authority

Management of salmon during their ocean phase is a complex blend of state, federal, and international authority (Gaden et al. 2009, this volume). In international waters (beyond 200 mi from Alaska's shores, governance occurs through the North Pacific Anadromous Fish Commission (NPAFC).

Members of NPAFC include Canada, Japan, The Republic of Korea, Russia, and the United States. NPAFC representatives are responsible for estimating commercial salmon catch, understanding the variables affecting salmon survival, conducting salmon research (including convening scientific workshops and symposia), sharing information about each party's activities, and coordinating law enforcement. The ocean waters, from three miles to 200 mi offshore of Alaska, is referred to as the Exclusive Economic Zone (EEZ) and is managed through the North Pacific Fishery Management Council established by the *Magnuson-Stevens Fishery Conservation and Management Act* (USGPO 1976). The council has broad representation including the State of Alaska and is coordinated by the U.S. Federal government through the National Marine Fisheries Service. The state of Alaska has sole jurisdictional authority from the coastline out to three miles.

In Alaska freshwaters, a dual management system currently exists between the state of Alaska and the U.S. federal government. The Alaska Department of Fish and Game (ADF&G) and a state regulatory Board of Fisheries (BOF), supported by fourteen local advisory committees representing the different geographic regions of the Alaskan portion of the Yukon River drainage, is the primary management authority for the Yukon River in Alaska. In 1999, the U.S. federal government assumed a management responsibility that may choose to supersede state authority for subsistence fisheries on U.S. federal public lands in Alaska, consistent with the mandates of the Alaska National Interest Lands Conservation Act of 1980, and subsequent judicial decisions (Buklis 2002). These lands comprise approximately 50% of the Yukon River drainage in Alaska. Subsistence fishery regulations in federal waters generally parallel state management and are under the purview of a regulatory Federal Subsistence Board.

In Alaska, subsistence fishing opportunity has priority over personal use, sport, and commercial fisheries for the consumptive uses. Management by the State of Alaska is guided by regulations adopted by the Alaska BOF. The *Policy for the Management of Sustainable Salmon Fisheries* (5 AAC 39.222, effective 2000, amended 2001; http://www.adfg.state.ak.us/special/susalpol.pdf) directs the ADF&G to provide the BOF with reports on the status of salmon stocks and to identify any salmon stocks that present a "concern" related to "yield," "management," or "conservation" during regularly scheduled BOF meetings.

The Department of Fisheries and Oceans (DFO) is responsible for fishery management in the Canadian portion of the Yukon River drainage. DFO works closely with the Yukon Salmon Committee, a regulatory advisory body representing stakeholders, to develop fishery management plans (DFO 2003).

Coordination of management of fall chum salmon between the U.S. and Canada is provided through an agreement appended as an annex to the Pacific Salmon Treaty. In 2001, after sixteen years of negotiation, agreement was reached on the conservation of Yukon salmon between the U.S. and Canada. This agreement revised the annex and created a bilateral Yukon River Panel, and set escapement goals and harvest sharing of the total allowable catch for Canadian-origin fall chum salmon stocks. The Panel's focus on fall chum salmon stocks is on those that spawn in the Canadian portion of the Yukon River drainage because these stocks require U.S. protection to ensure adequate numbers pass upstream across the border (border passage) for spawning and providing for fisheries in Canada. The Panel makes recommendations to management agencies in both countries. A Joint Technical Committee (JTC) composed of fishery managers and scientists from both countries advises the Panel.

Stakeholder involvement

Stakeholders share local knowledge and recent harvest information from their local communities with Alaskan and Canadian agency biologists during weekly teleconferences (sponsored by Yukon River Drainage Fisheries Association (YRDFA)) held during the fishing season. Similarly, the agency biologists report on their fishery stock assessment data and in-season projections. This tradition of information sharing first began in 1993 and provides a real-time exchange of quantitative and qualitative information useful for assessing (in-season) the strength of the ongoing salmon run. In addition, committees of stakeholders representing the Alaska fisheries typically meet during the late fall, winter, and spring months to discuss with state and federal managers the past season, and to plan for the coming season. Fishermen's groups such as YRDFA have worked closely (by consensus) on issues brought before the regulatory body, the Alaska BOF, by working with ADF&G in developing the fall chum salmon management plans along with modifications as needed, based on changes in the fishery and the development of new tools for assessment. Over the past few years, YRDFA has also provided an international educational exchange between the fishermen of Alaska and Canada at the level of the subsistence user.

Fishery management goals

The primary goal of management is to regulate the harvest of commercial and traditional-use fisheries to provide an adequate number of fish for spawning (escapement) thus ensuring the reproduction of the next generation, and to sustain Alaskan and Canadian fisheries. Management plans in Alaska and Canada comprise a suite of guidelines that help both managers and stakeholders to understand the steps necessary to meet the goals for escapement and harvest prior to the fishing season. However, they also have the flexibility to adjust regulations in-season based on on-going assessment. Escapement and harvest objectives are established by the Alaska BOF, ADF&G, and by the Yukon River Panel within the framework of the annex to the Pacific Salmon Treaty. In Alaska, emergency order authority by the ADF&G and special actions by federal managers are used to implement time and area openings or closures and gear restrictions within very short time frames (e.g., within 24 h). Commercial fisheries in Canada are also confined to specific fishing areas where DFO announces openings and closures.

Escapement goals

Escapement goals specify the minimum number, or optimal range, of salmon in the run that should be allowed to spawn to ensure adequate natural reproduction required to sustain the next generation. In Alaska, the current goals are known as biological escapement goals or BEGs. ADF&G establishes BEGs based on stock–recruitment relationships and manages for maximum sustained yields (MSY) (Eggers 2001). ADF&G manages the fall-season fishery as prescribed in the *Yukon River Drainage Fall Chum Salmon Management Plan* (5 AAC 01.249) as amended by the BOF in January 2004 (Table 1). The plan establishes a range for a drainage-wide BEG of 300,000–600,000 fall chum salmon. When the run is projected to be below 300,000 fall chum salmon, all fishing is closed. The only exception is when an individual stock may exceed its own specific escapement goal; then a subsistence fishery may be allowed. When the run size is projected to be between 300,000 and 500,000 fish, the subsistence fishery harvest is managed to achieve an escapement goal of 300,000 fish and personal-use and sport fisheries may be opened when an individual stock exceeds its escapement goal. When the projected run size is more than 600,000 chum

salmon, a drainage-wide commercial fishery may be opened to harvest the surplus of above 600,000 chum salmon. As performance measures, ADF&G monitors run abundance and harvest levels in relation to the established individual tributary BEGs and the drainage-wide BEG to assess whether escapement levels have been met; this includes assessment of harvest levels in the different fisheries. BEGs have been established for specific tributary systems within the upper Yukon River, including the Tanana River (61,000–136,000 spawners), Delta River (6,000–13,000 spawners), Toklat River (15,000–33,000 spawners), Chandalar River (74,000–152,000 spawners), and Sheenjek River (50,000–104,000 spawners) (Eggers 2001). Review of these BEGs is planned for 2009 in preparation for a regular cycle BOF meeting, adding seven more brood years since last evaluation and a more complete evaluation of the Kantishna/Tokat River contribution.

In addition to meeting river-specific BEGs, management in Alaska (state and federal) must also consider the border passage and escapement of Canadian-origin stocks that traverse the Yukon River but are harvested in the Alaskan fishery. Under international agreement, the fall chum salmon fishery in Alaska is managed to deliver to the Canadian border a specific number of fall chum salmon to meet the spawning escapement and fishery needs of the upper river residents. Escapement goals for Canadian waters include greater than 80,000 spawners for the mainstem system, and a range of 50,000–120,000 spawners upstream from the Fishing Branch weir site in the Porcupine River (JTC 2008). The escapement goal for the Fishing Branch River has only been achieved ten times since 1974 and has been under review for the past several years. For the period 2008–2010, the JTC recommended an interim management escapement goal of 22,000–49,000 fall chum spawners and the Yukon Panel approved this recommendation (JTC 2008).

TABLE 1. Yukon River drainage fall chum salmon *O. keta* management plan. Subsistence fishing is managed to achieve a minimum drainage-wide escapement goal of 300,000 salmon. When projected run size is above 600,000 salmon drainage-wide, commercial fisheries may be opened and the harvestable surplus of above 600,000 fish is distributed by district or sub-district in proportion to the guideline harvest levels (5ACC 05.362 (f) and (g) and 5ACC 05.365).

Run size range estimates (numbers of fish)	Recommended management actions				Targeted escapements (numbers of fish)
	Commercial	Personal Use	Sport	Subsistence	
≤300,000	Closure	Closure	Closure	Closure[a]	
300,001 to 500,000	Closure	Closure[a]	Closure[a]	Possible Restrictions[a]	300,000 to 600,000
500,001 to 600,000	Closure Closure	Normal schedule	Retention allowed	Normal Schedule	
>600,000	Commercial fishing considered	Normal schedule	Retention allowed	Normal Schedule	

[a] Less restrictive regulations may be allowed in areas where in-season project data suggest escapements will be achieved.

Information for decision-making

Escapement goals are the foundation for management because they help ensure the long-term conservation of salmon stocks, and thus have a logical priority to be met before harvest objectives are considered. Herein lays the greatest challenge to management! Reliable information on the actual run size in a particular year is not known until the majority of returning fish have entered the river, traversed often more than 1,000 mi of river, and arrived on their spawning grounds. However, the fishery begins in mid-July when the first fall chum salmon enter the river and extends until river freeze-up in late September or October. Fall chum salmon do not enter the river in a bell shaped curve; building and then satiating, they surge in pulses with large orders of magnitude differences over two or three days time and spread throughout the season, making the estimation of total run size a formidable challenge. By the time the run size is known with confidence, the fishery is over in much of the drainage. Thus, management decisions are implemented without having this critical piece of information for comparison to the escapement goals.

Every year a variety of assessment studies are conducted in the open-water period to provide information to help the ongoing prediction of the abundance of the salmon run and to determine whether adequate escapement of spawning-condition adults occurred within specific drainages. In-season predictions of run size are made at least weekly and usually more frequently. Management agencies, aboriginal organizations, and other nongovernmental organizations in Alaska and Canada cooperatively conduct projects throughout the drainage (Figure 1). The first projection of run size is made preseason, based on brood year returns and maturity schedules. The next projection is made after the cessation of the summer chum salmon run based on its relationship with the fall chum salmon run size. After which, during the early portion of the fall chum salmon season, assessment information comes from gillnetting indices and hydro-acoustic estimation near the mouth of the river, combined with fishing reports from down-river villages communicated through the weekly teleconferences. In August, reports from mid-river villages and other assessment projects are added to the in-season accumulation of data that is used to make predictions of the run-size. Fishing periods are adjusted frequently through emergency orders in Alaska as predictions of the run size change over the course of the season. A regulatory management plan adopted by the Alaska BOF provides direction for how managers, during the fishing season, could determine where fishing can occur, the amount of fishing time allowed, and how many fish can be harvested. Key to this entire process is the effective communication of information to the fishery participants. Information is routinely compiled daily and shared among stakeholders and managers via weekly teleconferences, by fax and e-mail during the fishing season, and during postseason meetings in the fall and preseason fisheries planning meetings in late winter and spring. Some of the types of projects that provide information for management decision-making are described below.

Escapement and Run Assessment Projects.—Hydro-acoustic estimates are used to index fall chum salmon runs migrating up the main-stem Yukon River near Pilot Station about 123 mi upstream from the mouth of the river. These sonar passage estimates provide the most complete assessment of the size of the fall chum salmon run moving into the middle and upper portions of the drainage. Daily estimates of fish passage are provided to fishery managers who use these data to evaluate in-season run strength for the Yukon River (Pfisterer 2002).

Test fisheries are conducted to provide data on catch rate, species composition, run timing, age-sex-length composition, and relative abundance of fall chum salmon stocks. The ADF&G conducts test fishing with gillnets in the lower Yukon River about 25 river mis upstream from the ocean (Bales 2008). The Mountain Village Tribal Council also operates a drift gillnet test fishery near Mountain Village (river mile 87) in association with the hydro-acoustic estimation project conducted by the ADF&G near Pilot Station (river mile 123).

Assessment of fall chum salmon abundance occurs in upriver areas as the fish move into spawning tributaries in Alaska and Canada. Historically, aerial surveys were flown to monitor spawning escapements in major index systems throughout the Yukon River drainage. In the Alaskan portion of the drainage, the longest escapement monitoring data set compiled is for the Sheenjek River and includes data from aerial surveys (Barton 1984) and since 1980, hydro-acoustic estimates (e.g., Barton 2000; Dunbar 2008). Similar estimates of fall chum salmon are provided for the Chandalar River (Daum and Osborne 1998; Melegari 2008). With the advent of new technologies and methods of assessment, more precise estimates of abundance have been achieved therefore a shift away from aerial surveys has occurred.

The ADF&G and the U.S. Fish and Wildlife Service have conducted annual mark-recapture projects in the middle portions of the Yukon River drainage. The ADF&G has conducted annual mark-recapture studies in the Tanana River from 1995–2007, upstream of the Kantishna River at river mile 793 and from 1999–2007 on the Kantishna River (Cleary and Hamazaki 2008).

In the Canadian portion of the drainage, DFO has annually estimated the abundance of fall chum salmon crossing the U.S./Canada border of the Yukon River since 1980 (excluding 1981 and 1984) using mark-recapture estimation (Milligan et al. 1984; JTC 2008). The objectives of this program are to provide in-season estimates of the border passage of fall chum salmon, and to provide postseason estimates of the total spawning escapements, harvest rates, migration rates, and run timing. This project is currently transitioning over to hydroacoustic estimates since 2006. The sonar project is a collaborative effort between ADF&G and DFO located on the main-stem of the upper Yukon River near Eagle, Alaska, just downstream from the U.S.-Canadian border (Dunbar and Crane 2007) (Figure 1) and provides estimates of fall chum salmon passage. The latter project assists in evaluating whether the main-stem escapement goal of 80,000 fall chum salmon will be provided for in the Canadian portion of the drainage (Carroll et al. 2007).

The ADF&G conducts weekly spawning ground foot surveys of the major fall chum spawning area in the Delta River of the upper Tanana River, allowing estimates of total spawning abundance to be made annually (JTC 2008). Biologists make visual counts of spawning fish and carcasses on stream walks typically conducted during the peak spawning time. Intensive ground surveys have also been made of the major spawning area in the upper Toklat River at river mile 838 (Barton 1997). In addition, DFO has operated a weir since 1972 and cooperatively with the Vuntut Gwitchin Government since 1991 in the Fishing Branch River to count fall chum salmon escapement to this Porcupine River tributary (JTC 2008).

Harvest Projects.—Commercial harvest reporting regulations in Alaska require fishery participants and processors to record the number and species of all salmon sold on

harvest fish tickets. A similar process is administered by DFO for Canadian commercial harvests. Reliable estimates of commercial harvest are generally available to managers soon after a fishing period has ended. Post season harvests are reported at various fisheries meetings such as the JTC (JTC 2008), as well as summarized in annual season summary documents and annual management reports.

Other types of harvest information are available and are often used while reviewing the outcome of the previous season and planning for the next. Personal-use in Alaska and domestic food fisheries in Canada require reporting of harvest. However, in most areas of the Yukon River drainage no regulatory requirement exists for reporting subsistence harvests. To estimate the subsistence salmon harvest from the majority of the villages, the ADF&G uses a voluntary postseason survey program. Survey data are collected via postseason interviews and follow-up telephone or postal surveys (Busher et al. 2007). In other portions of the Yukon area near the road system, households are required to obtain an annual household subsistence permit prior to fishing. In these areas, harvest is documented on the permit and returned to the ADF&G at the end of the fishing season.

In Canada, the Umbrella Final Agreement committed the federal government and First Nations to conduct annual studies to estimate the total catch in the aboriginal fishery in areas where the levels of need have not been determined. This estimation project, called "The Yukon River Drainage Basin Harvest Study," has been conducted annually since 1996 (DFO 2003).

Actions used to control harvest

Regulations are used to control how many, when, and where fish are caught within the Yukon River drainage for each type of fishery. This type of management is accom-

plished primarily through restrictions on effort, fishing efficiency, and the scheduling
of where, when, and how long commercial
fishery openings will be allowed. Subsistence
fisheries in Alaska and the Aboriginal fishery
in Canada are managed less intensively than
the commercial fisheries. Subsistence fisheries can be restricted or closed to ensure
escapement and when the conservation of
salmon stocks is at stake.

Limited entry.—Fishing effort is controlled by limiting the number of participants
in the Alaskan and Canadian commercial
fisheries. In Alaska, an open entry commercial fishery existed until the mid-1970s. Anyone could participate in the fishery and consequently effort levels grew. In 1976, effort
was capped at approximately 700 commercial
gillnet fishing permits that were issued in the
lower three fishing districts (Figure 3). Additionally, about 70 gillnet and 160 fish wheel
permits were issued in the upper river fishing districts. Permits are considered property,

and can be purchased or sold. In the 1980s
and early 1990s, about 550 of the lower river
permit holders and less than 80 of the upper
river permit holders generally participated in
the fall fishery. In 2008, of a total of 428 commercial permit holders, 251 permits (57%)
were issued for the District 1 in the lowest
portion of the river (Table 2; Figure 3). In
Canada, the fishery is limited to 21 licensed
commercial fishers with an additional eight
licenses guaranteed to, and distributed at the
discretion of First Nations. In the Canadian
portion of the drainage, commercial fisheries
in the main-stem are restricted to portions below Dawson City at river mile 1,319 (DFO
2003). During 2007, 17 of the 21 eligible
commercial fishing licenses were issued
(JTC 2008). Management of the aboriginal
fishery is implemented through the issuance
of communal fishing licenses to First Nations
to conduct fisheries within the traditional
territories of First Nations. Currently, a total of twelve communal licenses are issued
annually to First Nations within the Yukon

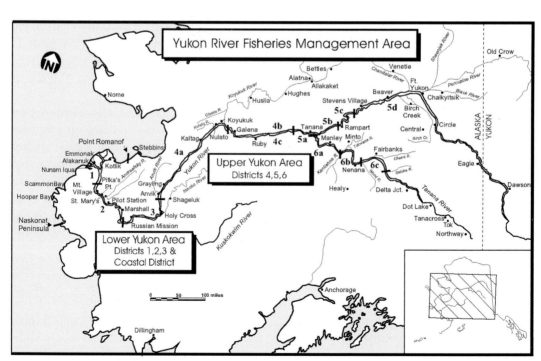

FIGURE 3. State of Alaska's Yukon River fisheries management areas.

TABLE 2. Number of Alaska commercial salmon fishing permit holders who made at least one delivery by district, Yukon River, 1971-2008. Since 1984, the subtotal for the Lower Yukon Area was the "unique" number of permits fished. Consequently, the Districts 1, 2, and 3 totals may add up to be greater than the Lower Yukon Area subtotal. Before 1984, the Districts 1, 2, and 3 totals are summed and the resulting subtotals may reflect that some permit holders operated in more than one district during the year. The sum of Districts 4, 5, and 6 averages may not equal Upper Yukon Area district subtotal due to rounding error.

Fall Chum and Coho Salmon Season Permits

Year	Lower Yukon Area				Upper Yukon Area				Yukon Area
	District 1	District 2	District 3	Subtotal	District 4	District 5	District 6	Subtotal	Total
1971	352	-	-	352	-	-	-	-	352
1972	353	75	3	431	-	-	-	-	431
1973	445	183	0	628	-	-	-	-	628
1974	322	121	6	449	17	23	22	62	511
1975	428	185	12	625	44	33	33	110	735
1976	422	194	28	644	18	36	44	98	742
1977	337	172	37	546	28	34	32	94	640
1978	429	204	28	661	24	43	30	97	758
1979	458	220	32	710	31	44	37	112	822
1980	395	232	23	650	33	43	26	102	752
1981	462	240	21	723	30	50	30	110	833
1982	445	218	15	678	15	24	25	64	742
1983	312	224	18	554	13	29	23	65	619
1984	327	216	12	536	18	39	26	83	619
1985	345	222	13	559	22	39	25	86	645
1986	282	231	14	510	1	21	16	38	548

TABLE 2. Continued.

Fall Chum and Coho Salmon Season Permits

Year	Lower Yukon Area				Upper Yukon Area				Yukon Area
	District 1	District 2	District 3	Subtotal	District 4	District 5	District 6	Subtotal	Total
1987	0	0	0	0	0	0	0	0	0
1988	328	233	13	563	20	20	32	72	635
1989	332	229	22	550	20	24	28	72	622
1990	301	227	19	529	11	11	27	49	578
1991	319	238	19	540	8	21	25	54	594
1992	0	0	0	0	0	0	22	22	22
1993	0	0	0	0	0	0	0	0	0
1994	0	0	0	0	0	1	11	12	12
1995	189	172	0	361	4	12	20	36	397
1996	158	109	0	263	1	17	17	35	298
1997	176	130	0	304	3	8	0	11	315
1998	0	0	0	0	0	0	0	0	0
1999	146	110	0	254	4	0	0	4	258
2000	0	0	0	0	0	0	0	0	0
2001	0	0	0	0	0	0	0	0	0
2002	0	0	0	0	0	0	0	0	0
2003	75	0	0	75	2	0	5	7	82
2004	26	0	0	26	0	0	6	6	32

TABLE 2. Continued.

Fall Chum and Coho Salmon Season Permits

| Year | Lower Yukon Area | | | | Upper Yukon Area | | | | Yukon Area |
	District 1	District 2	District 3	Subtotal	District 4	District 5	District 6	Subtotal	Total
2005	177	0	0	177	0	0	7	7	184
2006	219	71	0	286	0	4	11	15	301
2007	181	122	0	300	0	2	8	10	310
2008	251	177	0	428	0	3	8	11	439
Average									
1971-2007	236	127	9	364	11	17	17	45	406
1998-2007	82	30	0	112	1	1	4	5	117
2003-2007	136	39	0	173	0	1	7	9	182

and Porcupine river systems. Eight domestic fishery licenses are available on the Canadian portion of the Yukon River.

Gear restrictions.—In Alaska, restrictions have been placed on the length and depth of gillnets used in the commercial fishery to limit fishing efficiency. For example, commercial fishers in the lower river districts are restricted to using set gillnets that do not exceed 900 ft in length and drift gillnets not longer than 300 ft. Gillnets with a six-inch or smaller stretch mesh used for chum salmon cannot be more than 50 meshes deep. These gillnet regulations vary somewhat from district to district (5ACC 05.331). Commercial fishing gear was established based on traditional uses such that, fish wheels were most common in up river areas where logs are abundant for construction, drift gillnets were more prominent in the lower river areas, and set gillnets were used in both areas, and these became established as allowable com-

mercial gear types. Subsistence and personal-use fishers can use gillnets, beach seines, angling, and fish wheels but restrictions exist on the length, operation, and number of gillnets fished. For example, a set gillnet cannot exceed 900 ft in length and only one type of gear can be used at the same time. In the Canadian fishery, fishing gear is restricted with each commercial license and is limited to the use of no more than 294 ft of gillnet gear or the operation of no more than three fish wheels (Figure 4).

Quotas.—Allowable quotas for the commercial fisheries vary with predictions of run size (Table 1). The commercial guideline harvest range for fall chum salmon in Alaskan commercial fisheries is from 72,750–320,500 fish, provided that the escapement goal will be met (5 AAC 05.365). This guideline harvest range is further allocated among geographic districts in the Yukon River drainage. Proportional allocations by district were established

FIGURE 4. Fish wheels are a type of gear used to catch fall chum salmon in subsistence and commercial fisheries, and are also used by biologists in mark and recapture studies. (Photo by Stan Zurray).

by the Alaska BOF based on historic harvest records compiled during the development of the fishery. Canadian fishery managers regulate the harvest of fall chum salmon in the main-stem of the Yukon River within a range established by the Yukon River Salmon Agreement. Total allowable catch (TAC) for the Canadian stocks is between zero and 120,000 fall chum salmon; the agreement specifies a Canadian guideline harvest range between 29% and 35% of the TAC. When the TAC is above 120,000 fish, the harvest range in Canada is increased by 50% of the portion of the TAC above 120,000 fish (JTC 2008).

Seasons (fishing periods).—Managers rely on setting the time and area of fishery openings as the primary means to control harvest. Although the number of participants and the types of gear used are controlled, fishing power or capability can still far exceed than that required to catch an allowable harvest. During the 1980s, fishing power further increased because of larger, faster fishing skiffs, increased processing capability, and the use of electronic fish finders. A preseason harvest plan is developed collaboratively with stakeholders by the ADF&G and for the Canadian fisheries, by DFO, using a forecast of the return expected in the coming season based on the past parent-year escapements, and the run abundance and age composition of the previous year.

A subsistence harvest schedule in Alaska specifies the date and hours in which subsistence fishing can occur. During the fall season when the forecast is adequate, the lower river districts are open to subsistence fishing seven days a week. Once commercial fishing begins in lower river districts, subsistence closures are typically scheduled 12 h before, during, and after commercial periods. These measures are taken in attempts to keep subsistence-caught fish from being sold commercially. Subsistence fishing in the upper river district in Alaska is on a weekly fishing schedule with

period length varying between areas based on the efficiency of harvest in those areas and with the intent to spread harvest. Subsistence and commercial fishing in the upper river districts occur concurrently because subsistence dominates the harvest. Adjustments to the subsistence fishing schedule are made in-season to provide more fishing time when subsistence needs are not being met, or to reduce the subsistence harvest to increase spawning escapement when the drainage-wide, run-size estimate is below 300,000 fish. Similarly, DFO fishery managers assess the timing and abundance of fall chum salmon passing the border and announce fishing periods for Canadian fisheries.

The difficulty for fall chum salmon management is that the majority of the commercial harvest is taken in the lower Yukon Area while the majority of the subsistence harvest is taken in the upper Yukon Area. Because subsistence harvest has priority over commercial use, commercial fisheries must be managed conservatively to ensure subsistence harvests are met.

Allocation Priorities.—In Alaska, given the biological escapement goals can be met, the subsistence fishery then has the highest priority for harvest allocation. This aspect of management has become exceedingly complex as fish pass through the patchwork of lands managed by state and federal authorities (Buklis 2002). The subsistence fishery could be closed on state lands but open on federal lands; however, state and federal managers try to develop common regulations. Subsistence-use requirements are determined in Alaska when customary and traditional uses occur in a region. Customary and traditional use, in general, means the noncommercial, long-term and consistent taking of, use of, and reliance upon fish in a specific area, and that the patterns of fish use have been established over a reasonable period of time, taking into consideration the availability of the species. Once the customary and traditional use is determined by the state, then the subsistence harvest requirements are determined. In 1993, the Alaska BOF made a finding for customary and traditional use for all salmon in the Yukon River drainage. This finding was amended in 2001 to include specific amounts reasonably necessary for subsistence (5ACC 01.236) by salmon species. The amount of fall chum salmon considered necessary for subsistence harvests is from 89,500–167,900 fish. In Canada, the aboriginal fishery that provides food for social and ceremonial purposes is constitutionally protected and given priority in management. Only conservation concerns for a stock may supersede this priority. DFO sets a harvest target for the First Nations' fishery and offers suggestions for restricting harvest but allows First Nations to determine their own specific measures to control harvest. Options can include scheduling openings and closures, reducing days of fishing for each fish camp, reducing the number of fish camps, establishing family quotas, or allowing only elders or specific families to fish (DFO 2003).

Role of communication

The regular sharing of information is critical for effective in-season harvest management of Yukon River fall chum salmon and must take place among the biologists and managers representing many federal, state, and territorial agencies, and with stakeholder groups. The weekly teleconferences held during the fishing season to discuss the latest information about the ongoing salmon run are critical to this process.

Stakeholders communicate important information that helps shape in-season decisions that are culturally compatible and guide the overwinter planning for the next fishing season. In Alaska, several stakeholder groups are organized to provide input to state and federal fishery managers. For example, the

Yukon River Drainage Fisheries Association (YRDFA) was formed in 1989 and has a membership of over 200 Yukon River fishers and organizations. Other organizations representing fishery interests, in addition to YRDFA, include the Association of Village Council Presidents, Council of Athabascan Tribal Governments, Tanana Chiefs Conference, and the Bering Sea Fishermen's Association. Many of the members of these groups are also members of federal subsistence regional advisory committees, which provide recommendations to federal managers in Alaska (Buklis 2002) and members of state advisory committees.

In Canada, the main instrument for stakeholder consultation and involvement is the Yukon Salmon Committee, which was established pursuant to the Canadian Yukon Indian Land Claims, Umbrella Final Agreement. The committee develops recommendations for legislation, research, policies, programs, and management plans for Yukon River salmon. The members of the committee come from all parts of the Yukon Territory and represent both First Nations and nonFirst Nations populations to ensure diversity and balance (DFO 2003).

Total Return, Escapement, and Harvest

Total return and basin-wide escapement

Annual variation.—Total run size of fall chum salmon, based on data from escapement projects and harvest estimates, has varied from the low runs of 333,941 fish in 1998, 239,299 fish in 2000, and 382,741 fish in 2001 to high runs of 1,938,275 fish in 1975, 1,470,302 fish in 1995, and a record of 2,286,883 fish in 2005 (Figure 5; Appendix Table 1). The run failures of 1997–2002 were followed by a strong improvement in run sizes between 2003 and 2008. Interestingly, the substantial run and escapement that occurred

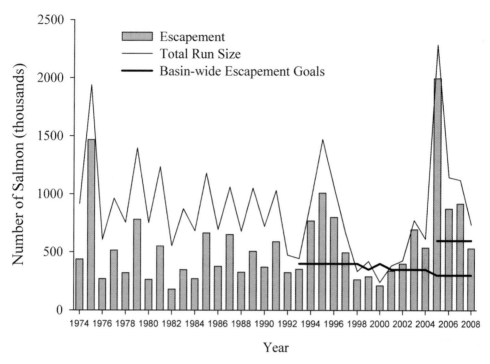

FIGURE 5. Estimated escapement and estimated total return of Yukon River fall chum salmon, with basin-wide escapement goals, 1974–2008.

from 1994–1997 produced of the lowest returns (1998–2002) estimated over the period 1974–2008. The phenomenal return of 2005 was from the reproduction of the lowest escapements of the 2000 and 2001 runs (Figure 5).

Two distinct periods of variation occurred within this time series. The first period from 1974–1991 showed comparatively low variation from year-to-year and ranged from 553,347 (1982) to 1,938,275 (1975) salmon (Figure 5). The second period from 1992 to 2008 showed much greater variation than the first period including both the highest run estimated of 2,286,883 salmon (2005) and the lowest run estimated of 239,299 salmon (2000). Consecutive low runs were experienced over the five-year period from 1998–2002.

Basin-wide escapement of salmon to the spawning grounds generally followed the same variation as total return (Figure 5).

Basin-wide escapement goals varied somewhat since their initial establishment in 1993; but, were not met in 1993 and 1998–2001. Escapement was greater than 350,000 fish every year from 2002–2008, exceeding the current minimum goal of 300,000 fish. The large run and subsequent escapement of 2005 was three times the drainage-wide escapement goal.

Primary variables that influence the total run of fall chum salmon are the spawning success of previous generations, natural variability in marine and freshwater survival due to climatic and oceanographic processes, and ocean fishery harvests. The poor returns and escapement of 1992–1993 can be attributed to poor recruitment from spawning during 1988 and 1989. Extremely cold winter temperatures accompanied by a lack of snow cover may have contributed to poor overwinter survival of eggs and fry. In contrast, the cause of the poor returns and es-

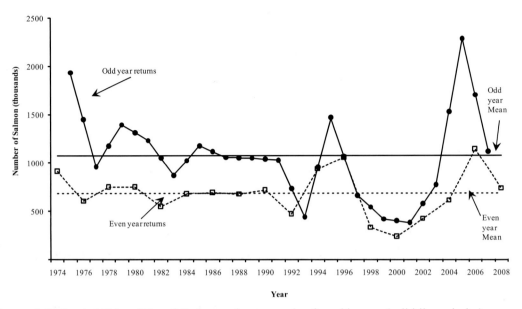

FIGURE 6. Estimated Yukon River fall chum salmon run size for odd years (solid line; circles) versus even years (dashed line; squares), 1974–2008

capement 1998–2002 were not due to poor escapement in earlier years and inadequate egg deposition, as the runs and escapement from 1994–1997 were at, or above average. Returns to individual tributaries were poor throughout the drainage 1998–2002 (see below), and was therefore not due to the collapse of one particularly important contributing stock. The number of returning salmon per spawner by brood year was much less than one and averaged 0.49 from 1994–1997 (range 0.34–0.75) (Appendix Table 2). Salmon returns across the region were also generally poor these same years in Norton Sound drainages (Menard et al. 2009, this volume) and in the Kuskokwim River drainage (Linderman and Bergstrom 2009, this volume) suggesting instead that a common variable among stocks across geographically dispersed drainages caused the poor returns rather than weak or low escapement. Poor returns of fall chum salmon to the Yukon River can be more likely attributed to poor ocean environments (e.g., Kruse 1998; Scheuerell

and Williams 2005; Farley et al. 2009, this volume; Mantua 2009, this volume; Myers et al. 2009). Competition with Asian-origin hatchery chum salmon may have also contributed to the poor returns these years (Myers et al. 2009). Unlike many salmon fisheries throughout the Pacific Northwest in the U.S. (NRC 1996), habitat loss for salmon has been minimal in the Yukon River drainage. Mining has degraded some stream habitats; however, most historical mining activity occurred on localized, discrete, headwater streams using manual labor, which helped to minimize impacts on salmon spawning habitat (Higgs 1995).

Odd versus Even-Year Run Strength.— Regular cycles in Yukon River fall chum salmon were evident in the estimated total returns of fall chum salmon from 1974– 2008 (Figures 5 and 6). Generally, smaller run sizes occurred during even-numbered years than in odd-numbered years; the regularity of this difference was particularly evident over the

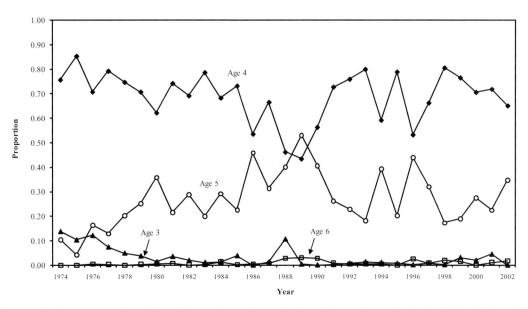

FIGURE 7. Age composition data of returning salmon by brood year (year class) for Yukon River fall chum salmon, 1974–2002.

period from 1974–1991. From 1974 through 2007, estimated total run size in odd-numbered years averaged 1,000,000 fall chum salmon, ranging from approximately 382,000 fish (2001—lowest odd-numbered year run on record) to 2,286,000 fish in 2005. Run size in even-numbered years averages 682,000 fall chum salmon and ranges from approximately 239,000 fish (2000—lowest run on record) to 1,144,000 fish in 2006. The years 1996 and 2006 were the only even-numbered years that total fall chum salmon run size exceeded the average run size for odd-numbered years. The regularly observed low abundance on even-numbered years in fall chum salmon corresponds with the typically abundant pink salmon runs on even-numbered years in the region (e.g., Menard et al. 2009), and possibly the pattern of reduced abundance of even-numbered year fall chum salmon has been caused by the competition with pink salmon (Ruggerone and Nielsen 2009, this volume).

Variation in Age-Class Contribution.—From 1974 to 2003, fall chum salmon runs

have been dominated by returning age-4 and age-5 fish with much smaller contributions from age-3 and age-6 fish (Figure 7; Appendix Table 2; age data from several sources e.g., Menard 1996; Bales 2008). In all years, except 1989, age-4 fish contributed more than age-5 salmon. Estimated annual age composition from 1977 through 2007 has averaged approximately 4% for age-3, 69% for age-4, 27% for age-5, and less than 1% for age-6 fish. From 1974 –1990, age of maturity for Yukon River fall chum salmon increased with declining proportions of age-4 salmon and increasing proportions of age-5 salmon (Figure 7). Since 1990, this trend seems to have reversed showing increased variation over the earlier period. In-season estimates of age prior to 1981 were based on fish sampled at Emmonak from 6-in stretch mesh commercial gillnet catches. Estimates of age from 1981–2000 were based on 6-in set gillnet test fish catches at Big Eddy and Middle Mouth sites. In 2001, fishing gear was changed to 6-in drift gillnets. All test

Bue et al.

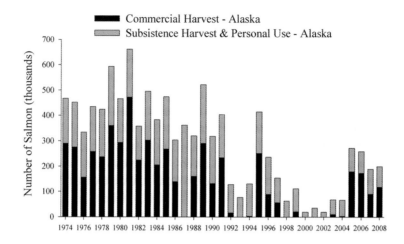

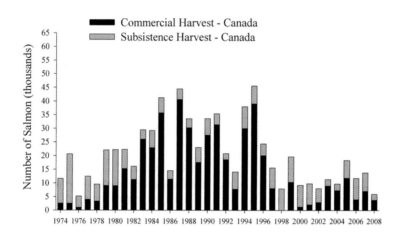

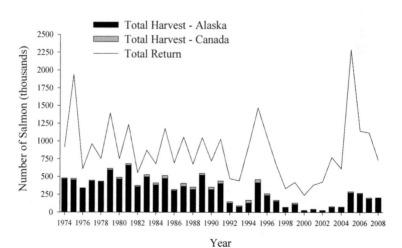

Year

FIGURE 10. Estimated commercial and subsistence harvest of Yukon River fall chum salmon for Alaska and Canada, and total harvest by Alaska and Canada with drainage-wide total return estimate, 1974–2008.

2002 changed the character of the fisheries. Many fishers moved away from using long established fish camps, fishing gear fell into disrepair or was replaced with other types, prices for salmon fell, and market interest shifted to other available fisheries outside the region. With the return of the salmon, fishers and markets are slowly returning and may improve in the future (Figure 11). To encourage market improvement, fishery managers have worked closely with commercial fish buyers to maximize processing capacity and available transportation opportunities (JTC 2008). Frequent short open fishing periods were provided recently and were based on anticipated daily market capacity. Buyers and fishers also worked together to improve the quality of their harvest by more careful fish handling, improved icing techniques, and quicker deliveries.

Canada.—Estimated subsistence harvest (aboriginal, and domestic fisheries harvest combined) averaged 6,443 fish (range 2,068–18,100 fish) over the period 1974–2008 (Figure 10; Appendix Table 1; JTC 2008). Over the time period 1974–2008, the top three harvest years occurred in 1975 (18,100 fish), 1979 (13,000 fish), and 1980 (13,218 fish). The high harvest levels from 1974–2003 (average 8,762 fish; range 3,500–18,100) contrast to the lower levels of the past five years when an average of 5,056 salmon were caught (range 2,068–7,700 fish) (Figure 10). The preliminary harvest in 2007 was 6,721 salmon and was above the five-year average. Participants in the 2007 fall chum salmon fishery described fishing as excellent (JTC 2008). Similar to Alaskan subsistence harvest levels in recent years, the recent low harvests were surprising because the passage of salm-

FIGURE 11. Chum salmon caught by fish wheel on the main-stem of the Yukon River near Rampart, Alaska (Photo by Stan Zuray).

on into Canadian water has been some of the largest ever recorded, especially to the main-stem of the Yukon River (Figure 9). Some of the same variables affecting the Alaskan subsistence fishery in recent years have simi-larly affected the level of subsistence harvest effort in Canadian waters.

Estimated commercial harvest in Cana-dian waters of the Yukon River ranged from 0 in 1998 (fishery was closed) to 40,591 fish in 1987 (average 13,870 fish) over the period 1974–2008 (Figure 10; Appendix Table 1; JTC 2008). The highest commercial harvest levels occurred from 1983–1992 and ranged from 11,464 fish in 1986–40,591 fish in 1987 (average 26,205 fish) (Figure 10). In con-trast, low harvest levels have occurred over the recent period 2003–2008 and ranged from 3,905 fish in 2008–11,931 fish in 2005 (average 6,042 fish) even though passage of salmon over these same five years has been substantial. As mentioned earlier, most of the recent commercial fishery harvest from the Canadian portion of the Yukon River is used to feed personal sled dog teams. During the 1980s and early 1990s, a processing plant ex-isted in Dawson, which provided a market for commercial fishers. The potential exists to re-develop the commercial market by establish-ing a local processing capability and focusing on the sale of value-added products such as smoked salmon and salmon caviar (roe) (JTC 2008).

Conclusion: Lessons Learned

The complexity of the fall chum salmon fisheries of the Yukon River are daunting. Salmon feeding at sea prior to maturity range over thousands of miles of the North Pacific Ocean and Bering Sea, and are subjected to the vagaries of changing ocean conditions, competition from Asian-origin hatchery chum salmon, and bycatch in ocean fisheries. Upon maturity, their spawning run up the Yu-kon River requires for some stocks, a journey of more than a thousand miles past a gauntlet of fisheries and crossing an international bor-der. Jurisdictionally, management requires cooperation among state, federal, and inter-national organizations during both the ocean and river phases of the salmon life history. Some lessons learned from past management of the Yukon River fall chum salmon fishery that may be applicable to fisheries elsewhere are described below.

1. *Stakeholder involvement is critical to effective harvest management.* Effective working relationships among management agencies and stakeholder organizations were critical to forging complex and often controversial rebuilding and harvest alloca-tion agreements, and setting long-term goals that placed the conservation and long-term sustainability of the fall chum salmon re-source as a first priority. Establishing this management strategy also required a multi-disciplinary (biology and social science) ap-proach to fishery management that involved and considered the socio-cultural effects of these decisions.

2. *Rapid, effective information sharing is a re-quirement for fast-paced, in-season decision-making.* Effective tools such as web access to electronic databases and weekly scheduled drainage-wide teleconferences were devel-oped to address the often fast-paced process of in-season management. These tools helped to share data collected from tributary and main-stem monitoring projects throughout the drainage among managers and stakehold-ers throughout the fishing season. Expanded use of the Internet and e-mail in the 1990s greatly enhanced communication between stakeholders and managers, although many villages still require facsimile transmissions to be post locally. This highly interactive process has improved understanding and ac-ceptance of management and challenged all

participants to focus on long-term conservation goals beyond their own local village or agency's interests.

3. *Limited entry alone did not control harvest.* Limited entry was instituted several decades ago to set an upper limit on commercial fishing effort. Initially, this action helped managers control harvest. However, the fishing power of individuals with permits increased as technology improved. In-season management with rapid openings and closings by districts in Alaska became a necessity to control harvest.

4. *Some things that make management difficult just cannot be changed!* The intersection of biology, time, and distance between the fish and fishery makes management of the Yukon River very difficult. Because the commercial fishery is for the most part substantially downstream of the spawning areas, the number of fish reaching the spawning tributaries is not entirely known until after the fisheries are over. In addition, salmon enter the Yukon River from the Bering Sea over a number of weeks, which further complicates the estimation of the run size and timing. Therefore, the escapement required for spawning and reproduction of the next generation cannot be assured before the fishery begins. These biological aspects cannot be changed but require management to adopt a responsive approach to harvest regulations. These aspects, combined with a fishery that harvests many geographically, widely dispersed stocks, along more than 1,000 mi of main-stem river, and a migration that extends over two months, makes for a tough management environment. Critical to effective management of the fishery will be the continued development and refinement of tools to forecast run abundance and provide estimates of uncertainty around the predictions.

Acknowledgments

Helpful information and comments were provided by Dan Bergstrom of ADF&G and Larry Buklis of the U.S. Fish and Wildlife Service on an earlier version of this paper. Scott Miehls and Holly Patrick of the Great Lakes Fishery Commission assisted with preparation of the figures and tables, and provided suggestions on an early draft of the paper.

References

ADF&G (Alaska Department of Fish and Game). 1993. Annual Management Report for Subsistence, Personal Use, and Commercial Fisheries of the Yukon Area, 1992. Alaska Department of Fish and Game. Division of Commercial Fisheries, Regional Information Report. No. 3A-93–10, Anchorage.

ADF&G (Alaska Department of Fish and Game). 2004. Escapement Goal Review of Select AYK Region Salmon Stocks. Alaska Department of Fish and Game, Division of Commercial Fisheries, Regional Information Report No. 3A04–01, Anchorage.

Andersen, D. B. 1992. The use of dog teams and the use of subsistence-caught fish for feeding sled dogs in the Yukon River drainage, Alaska. Alaska Department of Fish and Game, Division of Subsistence, Technical Paper No. 210. Juneau.

Bales, J. 2008. Salmon age and sex composition and mean lengths for the Yukon River area, 2006. Divisions of Sport Fish and Commercial Fisheries, Fishery Data Series 08–14. Alaska Department of Fish and Game, Anchorage.

Barker, J. H. 1993. Always getting ready, Upterrlainarluta: Yup'ik Eskimo subsistence in southwest Alaska. University of Washington Press, Seattle.

Barton, L. H. 1984. Enumeration of fall chum salmon by side-scanning sonar in the Sheenjak River in 1983. Alaska Department of Fish and Game, Division of Commercial Fisheries, AYK Region, Yukon Salmon Escapement Report No. 22, Fairbanks.

Barton, L. H. 1997. Salmon escapement assessment in the Toklat River, 1994. Alaska Department of Fish and Game, Division of Commercial Fisheries, Regional Information Report No. 3A97–35, Anchorage.

Barton, L. H. 2000. Sonar estimation of fall chum salmon abundance in the Sheenjek River, 1999. Alaska Department of Fish and Game, Division of Commercial Fisheries, Regional Information Report No. 3A01–10, Anchorage.

Berger, T. R. 1985. Village journey: the report of the Alaska Native Review Commission. Hill and Wang, New York.

Borba, B. M., and H. H. Hamner. 2001. Subsistence and personal use salmon harvest estimates—Yukon Area, 2000. Alaska Department of Fish and Game, Division of Commercial Fisheries, Regional Information Report No. 3A01–27, Anchorage.

Bue, F. J., B. M. Borba, and D. J. Bergstrom. 2004. Yukon River fall chum salmon stock status and action plan. Alaska Department of Fish and Game, Division of Commercial Fisheries, Regional Information Report No. 3A04–05, Anchorage.

Buklis, L. S. 1981. Yukon and Tanana River fall chum tagging studies, 1976–1980. Alaska Department of Fish and Game, Informational Leaflet 194, Anchorage.

Buklis, L. S. 2002. Subsistence fisheries management on federal public lands in Alaska. Fisheries 27(7):10–18.

Buklis, L. S., and L. H. Barton. 1984. Yukon River fall chum salmon biology and stock status. Alaska Department of Fish and Game, Informational Leaflet 239, Anchorage.

Burr, J. 2008. Fishery management report for sport fisheries in the Yukon Management Area, 2006. Alaska Department of Fish and Game, Divisions of Sport Fish and Commercial Fisheries, Fishery Management Report 08–42, Anchorage.

Busher, W. H., T. Hamazaki, and A. M. Marsh. 2007. Subsistence and personal use salmon harvests in the Alaska portion of the Yukon River drainage, 2005. Alaska Department of Fish and Game, Divisions of Sport Fish and Commercial Fisheries, Fishery Management Report 07–52, Anchorage.

Carroll, H. C., R. D. Dunbar, and C. T. Pfisterer. 2007. Evaluation of hydroacoustic site on the Yukon River near Eagle, Alaska for monitoring passage of salmon across the US/Canada border, 2004. Divisions of Sport Fish and Commercial Fisheries, Fishery Data Series 07–10. Alaska Department of Fish and Game, Anchorage.

Cleary, P. M., and T. Hamazaki. 2008. Fall chum salmon mark-recapture abundance estimation on the Tanana and Kantishna rivers, 2007. Divisions of Sport Fish and Commercial Fisheries, Fishery Data Series 08–35. Alaska Department of Fish and Game, Anchorage.

Daum, D. W., and B. M. Osborne. 1998. Use of fixed-location, split-beam sonar to describe temporal and spatial patterns of adult fall chum salmon migration in the Chandalar River, Alaska. North American Journal of Fisheries Management 18:477–486.

DCED (Alaska Department of Community and Economic Development). 2002. Community Database Online, Community Information Summaries. Available: http://dced.state.ak.us/cbd/commdb/CF_COMDB.htm (May 2002).

DFO (Department of Fisheries and Oceans). 2003. Pacific Region integrated fisheries management plan—Chinook and chum Salmon, Yukon River. Department of Fisheries and Oceans, Whitehorse, Canada.

Dunbar, R. 2008. Sonar estimation of fall chum salmon abundance in the Sheenjek River, 2004. Divisions of Sport Fish and Commercial Fisheries, Fishery Data Series 08–34. Alaska Department of Fish and Game, Anchorage.

Dunbar, R., and A. Crane. 2007. Sonar estimation of Chinook and fall chum salmon in the Yukon River near Eagle, Alaska, 2006. Divisions of Sport Fish and Commercial Fisheries, Fishery Data Series 07–89. Alaska Department of Fish and Game, Anchorage.

Eggers, D. M. 2001. Biological escapement goals for Yukon River fall chum salmon. Division of Commercial Fisheries, Regional Information Report 3A01–10. Alaska Department of Fish and Game, Anchorage.

Farley, E. V., Jr., J. Murphy, J. Moss, A. Feldmann, and L. Eisner. 2009. Marine ecology of western Alaska juvenile salmon. Pages 307–329 in C. C. Krueger and C. E. Zimmerman, editors. Pacific salmon: ecology and management of western Alaska's populations. American Fisheries Society, Symposium 70, Bethesda, Maryland.

Fienup-Riordan, A. 1986. When our bad season comes: a cultural account of subsistence harvesting and harvest disruption on the Yukon Delta. Alaska Anthropological Association Monograph Series No. 1.

Flannery, B., J. K. Wenburg, and A. J. Gharrett. 2007. Evolution of mitochondrial DNA variation within and among Yukon River chum salmon populations. Transactions of the American Fisheries Society 136:902–910.

Gaden, M., C. C. Krueger, and C. Goddard. 2009. Managing across jurisdictional boundaries: fishery governance in the Great Lakes and Arctic-Yukon-Kuskokwim regions. Pages 941–960 in C. C. Krueger and C. E. Zimmerman, editors. Pacific salmon: ecology and management of western Alaska's populations. American Fisheries Society, Symposium 70, Bethesda, Maryland.

Gisclair, B. R. 2009. Salmon bycatch management in the Bering Sea walleye pollock fishery: threats and opportunities for western Alaska. Pages 799–816 in C. C. Krueger and C. E. Zimmerman, editors. Pacific salmon: ecology and management of western Alaska's populations. American Fisheries Society, Symposium 70, Bethesda, Maryland.

Higgs, A. S. 1995. A history of mining in the Yukon River basin of Alaska. Northern Land Use Research, Inc. Fairbanks, Alaska.

JTC (Joint Technical Committee of the Yukon River US/Canada Panel). 2008. Yukon River salmon 2007 season summary and 2008 season outlook. Alaska Department of Fish and Game, Division of Commercial Fisheries, Regional Information Report No. 3A08–01, Anchorage.

Kruse, G. H. 1998. Salmon run failures in 1997–1998: a link to anomalous ocean conditions? Alaska Fishery Research Bulletin 5: 55–63.

Linderman, J. C., Jr., and D. J. Bergstrom. 2009. Kuskokwim management area: salmon escapement, harvest, and management. Pages 541–599 in C. C. Krueger and C. E. Zimmerman, editors. Pacific salmon: ecology and management of western Alaska's populations. American Fisheries Society, Symposium 70, Bethesda, Maryland.

Mantua, N. 2009. Patterns of change in climate and Pacific salmon production. Pages 1143–1157 in C. C. Krueger and C. E. Zimmerman, editors. Pacific salmon: ecology and management of western Alaska's populations. American Fisheries Society, Symposium 70, Bethesda, Maryland.

McClellan, C. 1987. Part of the land, part of the water: a history of the Yukon Indians. Douglas & McIntyre, Ltd. Vancouver, British Columbia.

Melegari, J. L. 2008. Abundance and run timing of adult fall chum salmon in the Chandalar River, Yukon Flats National Wildlife Refuge, Alaska, 2007. Alaska Fisheries Data Series 2008–11. U.S. Fish and Wildlife Service, Fairbanks, Alaska.

Menard, J. 1996. Age, sex, and length of Yukon River salmon catches and escapements, 1994. Alaska Department of Fish and Game, Division of Commercial Fisheries, Regional Information Report 3A96–16, Anchorage.

Menard, J., C. C. Krueger, and J. R. Hilsinger. 2009. Norton Sound salmon fisheries: history, stock abundance, and management. Pages 621–673 in C. C. Krueger and C. E. Zimmerman, editors. Pacific salmon: ecology and management of western Alaska's populations. American Fisheries Society, Symposium 70, Bethesda, Maryland.

Milligan, P. A., W. O. Rublee, D. D. Cornett, and R. A. Johnston. 1984. The distribution and abundance of chum salmon Onchorhynchus keta in the upper Yukon River basin as determined by a radio-tagging and spaghetti tagging program: 1982–1983. Department of Fisheries and Oceans, Yukon River Basin Study, Technical Report No. 35.

Myers, K. W., R. V. Walker, N. D. Davis, J. L. Armstrong, and M. Kaeriyama. 2009. High seas distribution, biology, and ecology of Arctic-Yukon-Kuskokwim salmon: direct information from high seas tagging experiments, 1954–2006. Pages 201–239 in C. C. Krueger and C. E. Zimmerman, editors. Pacific salmon: ecology and management of western Alaska's populations. American Fisheries Society, Symposium 70, Bethesda, Maryland.

NRC (National Research Council). 1996. Upstream: salmon and society in the Pacific Northwest. National Academy Press, Washington, D.C.

Olsen, J., W. Spearman, G. Sage, S. Miller, B. Flannery, and J. K. Wenburg. 2004. Variation in the population structure of Yukon River chum and coho salmon: evaluating the potential impact of localized habitat degradation. Transactions of the American Fisheries Society 133:476–483.

Pfisterer, C. T. 2002. Estimation of Yukon River salmon passage in 2001 using hydroacoustic methodologies. Alaska Department of Fish and Game, Division of Commercial Fisheries, Regional Information Report No. 3A02–24, Anchorage.

Ruggerone, G. T., and J. Nielsen. 2009. A review of growth and survival of salmon at sea in response to competition and climate change. Pages 241–265 in C. C. Krueger and C. E. Zimmerman, editors. Pacific salmon: ecology and management of western Alaska's populations. American Fisheries Society Symposium 70, Bethesda, Maryland.

Salo, E. O. 1991. Life history of chum salmon. Pages 233–309 in C. Groot and L. Margolis, editors. Pacific salmon life histories. UBC Press, Vancouver.

Scheuerell, M. D., and J. G. Williams. 2005. Forecasting climate-induced changes in the survival of Snake River spring/summer Chinook salmon (Oncorhynchus tshawytscha). Fisheries Oceanography 14:448–457.

Scribner, K., P. Crane, W. Spearman, and L. Seeb. 1998. DNA and allozyme markers provide concordant estimates of population differentiation: analyses of US and Canadian populations of Yukon River fall-run chum salmon. Canadian Journal of Fisheries and Aquatic Sciences 55:1748–1758.

Seeb, L., and P. Crane. 1999. Allozymes and mtDNA discriminate Asian and North American populations of chum salmon in mixed-stock fisheries along the south coast of the Alaska Peninsula. Transactions of the American Fisheries Society 128:88–103.

Statistics Canada. 2002. Available: http://www.statcan.ca/english/Pgdb/People/Population/demo39a.htm. (May 2002).

USGPO. 1976. Magnuson-Stevens Fishery Conservation and Management Act, volume 16 U.S.C. 1801–1882. U.S. Government Printing Office.

Utter, F. M., M. V. McPhee, and F. W. Allendorf. 2009. Population genetics and the management of Arctic-Yukon-Kuskokwim salmon populations. Pages 97–123 in C. C. Krueger and C. E. Zimmerman, editors. Pacific salmon: ecology and management of western Alaska's populations. American Fisheries Society, Symposium 70, Bethesda, Maryland.

Williams, J. G. 1999. Alaska population overview 1998 estimates. Alaska Department of Labor, Research and Analysis Section, Juneau.

Wilmot, R., R. Everett, W. Spearman, R. Baccus, N. Varnavskaya, and S. Putivkin. 1994. Genetic stock structure of western Alaska chum salmon and a comparison with Russian Far East stocks. Canadian Journal of Fisheries and Aquatic Sciences 51(Supplement 1): 84–94.

Wilmot, R. L., C. M. Kondzela, C. M. Guthrie, and M. M. Masuda. 1998. Genetic stock identification of chum salmon harvested incidentally in the 1994 and 1995 Bering Sea trawl fishery. North Pacific Anadromous Fish Commission Bulletin 1: 285–294.

Wolfe, R. J., and J. Spaeder. 2009. People and salmon of the Yukon and Kuskokwim drainages and Norton Sound in Alaska: fisher harvests, culture change, and local knowledge systems. Pages 349–379 *in* C. C. Krueger and C. E. Zimmerman, editors. Pacific salmon: ecology and management of western Alaska's populations. American Fisheries Symposia 70, Bethesda, Maryland.

Yukon Internet Site: Map of the Yukon Territory with Links to Information on Yukon Communities. Available: http://www.yukonsite.com/yukon_map.htm. (May 2002).

APPENDIX TABLE 1. Yukon River fall chum salmon estimated harvest and escapement data in numbers of fish, 1974–2008. Alaskan commercial harvest includes only fish sold in the round and test fish where indicated. Alaskan subsistence and personal-use harvest includes commercial-related harvest estimates (chum salmon harvested which provided for roe sales) beginning in 1978. Canadian subsistence harvest includes domestic fisheries and the aboriginal harvests from main-stem Yukon and Porcupine Rivers (JTC 2008).Total escapement estimates through 1994 are based on run reconstruction using monitored tributaries (Eggers 2001). Total escapement estimates from 1995 to 2008 are based on escapements to the Chandalar, Sheenjek, and Fishing Branch rivers, and the Upper Yukon border passage, as well as updates of Kantishna (1995–1998 estimated based on linear regression from 1999 through 2004) and Upper Tanana River population estimates. Harvests were removed from areas that used mark-recapture methods (Upper Tanana River and border passage population estimates). Total exploitation rate equals the sum of the entire river commercial and subsistence harvest divided by the estimated total return. The exploitation rate estimated should be considered a maximum as the annual estimated total escapement figures are thought to be conservative.

Years	Alaska			Canada			Entire River			Estimated Escapement	Estimated Return	Exploitation Rate
	Commercial	Subsistence & Personal Use	Estimated Total Kill	Commercial	Subsistence	Total	Commercial	Subsistence	Total			
1974	289,776	177,453 [a]	467,229	2,544	9,102	11,646	292,320	186,555	478,875	436,485	915,360	0.5232
1975	275,009	177,453 [a]	452,462	2,500	18,100	20,600	277,509	195,553	473,062	1,465,213	1,938,275	0.2441
1976	156,390	177,453 [a]	333,843	1,000	4,200	5,200	157,390	181,653	339,043	268,841	607,884	0.5577
1977	257,986	177,453 [a]	435,439	3,990	8,489	12,479	261,976	185,942	447,918	514,843	962,761	0.4652
1978	236,383	188,081 [a]	424,464	3,356	6,210	9,566	239,739	194,291	434,030	320,487	754,517	0.5752
1979	359,946	233,347	593,293	9,084	13,000	22,084	369,030	246,347	615,377	780,818	1,396,195	0.4408
1980	293,629	172,526	466,155	9,000	13,218	22,218	302,629	185,744	488,373	263,167	751,540	0.6498
1981	472,603	188,507	661,110	15,260	7,021	22,281	487,863	195,528	683,391	551,192	1,234,583	0.5535
1982	224,187	133,241	357,428	11,312	4,779	16,091	235,499	138,020	373,519	179,828	553,347	0.6750
1983	302,598	193,397	495,995	25,990	3,500	29,490	328,588	196,897	525,485	347,157	872,642	0.6022
1984	205,397	177,659	383,056	22,932	6,335	29,267	228,329	183,994	412,323	270,042	682,365	0.6043
1985	267,744	206,472	474,216	35,746	5,519	41,265	303,490	211,991	515,481	664,426	1,179,907	0.4369
1986	139,442	164,043	303,485	11,464	3,079	14,543	150,906	167,122	318,028	376,374	694,402	0.4580
1987	0	361,663 [b,c]	361,663	40,591	3,889	44,480	40,591	365,552 [a]	406,143	651,943	1,058,086	0.3838
1988	161,426 [d]	158,694	320,120	30,263	3,302	33,565	191,689	161,996	353,685	325,137	678,822	0.5210
1989	291,168 [d]	230,978	522,146	17,549	5,471	23,020	308,717	236,449	545,166	506,173	1,051,339	0.5185
1990	133,399 [d]	184,986	318,385	27,537	6,085	33,622	160,936	191,071	352,007	369,654	721,661	0.4878
1991	234,788 [d]	168,890	403,678	31,404	4,014	35,418	266,192	172,904	439,096	591,132	1,030,228	0.4262
1992	17,128	110,903	128,031	18,576	2,239	20,815	35,704	113,142	148,846	324,253	473,099	0.3146

APPENDIX TABLE 1. Continued.

Years	Alaska			Canada			Entire River			Estimated Escapement	Estimated Return	Exploitation Rate
	Commercial	Subsistence & Personal Use	Estimated Total Kill	Commercial	Subsistence	Total	Commercial	Subsistence	Total			
1993	0	76,925	76,925	7,762	6,328	14,090	7,762	83,253	91,015	352,688	443,703	0.2051
1994	3,631	127,586	131,217	30,035	7,973	38,008	33,666	135,559	169,225	769,920	939,145	0.1802
1995	251,854 [d]	163,693	415,547	39,012	6,588	45,600	290,866	170,281	461,147	1,009,155	1,470,302	0.3136
1996	90,059 [d]	146,510	236,569	20,069	4,285	24,354	110,128	150,795	260,923	800,022	1,060,945	0.2459
1997	57,580 [d]	96,899	154,479	8,068	7,512	15,580	65,648	104,411	170,059	494,831	664,890	0.2558
1998	0 [d]	62,869	62,869	0	7,951	7,951	0	70,820	70,820	263,121	333,941	0.2121
1999	21,542 [d]	89,997	111,539	10,402	9,234	19,636	31,944	99,231	131,175	288,962	420,137	0.3122
2000	0	19,307	19,307	1,319	7,917	9,236	1,319	27,224	28,543	210,756	239,299	0.1193
2001	0	35,154	35,154	2,198	7,624	9,822	2,198	42,778	44,976	337,765	382,741	0.1175
2002	0	19,393	19,393	3,065	4,953	8,018	3,065	24,346	27,411	397,977	425,388	0.0644
2003	10,996	57,178	68,174	9,030	2,325	11,355	20,026	59,503	79,529	695,363	774,892	0.1026
2004	4,110	62,436	66,546	7,365	2,385	9,750	11,475	64,821	76,296	537,873	614,169	0.1242
2005	180,249 [d]	91,597	271,846	11,931	6,406	18,337	192,180	98,003	290,183	1,996,700	2,286,883	0.1269
2006	174,542	84,133	258,675	4,096	7,700	11,796	178,638	91,833	270,471	873,987	1,144,458	0.2363
2007 *	90,677	98,886	189,563	7,109	6,721	13,830	97,786	105,607	203,393	916,606	1,119,999	0.1816
2008 *	119,386	80,000	199,386	3,905	2,068	5,973	123,291	82,068	205,359	531,595	736,954	0.2787

APPENDIX TABLE 1. Continued.

Years	Alaska			Canada			Entire River			Estimated Escapement	Estimated Return	Exploitation Rate
	Commercial	Subsistence & Personal Use	Estimated Total Kill	Commercial	Subsistence	Total	Commercial	Subsistence	Total			
5 Yr Averages												
1974-1978	243,109	179,579	422,687	2,678	9,220	11,898	245,787	188,799	434,586	601,174	1,035,759	0.4731
1979-1983	330,593	184,204	514,796	14,129	8,304	22,433	344,722	192,507	537,229	424,432	961,661	0.5843
1984-1988	154,802	213,706	368,508	28,199	4,425	32,624	183,001	218,131	401,132	457,584	858,716	0.4808
1989-1993	135,297	154,536	289,833	20,566	4,827	25,393	155,862	159,364	315,226	428,780	744,006	0.3905
1994-1998	80,625	119,511	200,136	19,437	6,862	26,299	100,062	126,373	226,435	667,410	893,845	0.2415
1999-2003	6,508	44,206	50,713	5,203	6,411	11,613	11,710	50,616	62,327	386,165	448,491	0.1432
2004-2008	113,793	83,410	197,203	6,881	5,056	11,937	120,674	88,466	209,140	971,352	1,180,493	0.1895
All Yr Averages												
1974-2008	152,104	139,879	291,982	13,870	6,443	20,314	165,974	146,322	312,296	562,414	874,710	0.3576
Even yrs 74-08	124,938	124,849	249,787	11,547	5,766	17,312	136,485	130,614	267,099	417,751	684,850	0.3793
Odd yrs 74-08	180,867	155,793	336,661	16,331	7,161	23,492	197,198	162,955	360,153	715,586	1,075,739	0.3345

* Preliminary data.

a Subsistence harvest estimates not available by district until 1978. Subsistence harvests from 1974 to 1978 were estimated as the average subsistence harvest, 1979 to 1986, for the respective districts.

b Although no commercial fall chum salmon fishery occurred in 1987, the harvest includes an estimated 115,829 fall salmon not documented by the ADF&G primarily due to an estimated illegal sales from District 5 and 6 of 42,274 chum salmon, and a documented 110,948 pounds of illegally processed roe. The 115,829 fish were estimated from the roe as follows: an estimated 107,467 pounds of unprocessed fall chum salmon roe times 1.0 lbs/female times 2 (assumes 1:1 sex ratio) minus reported subsistence harvest in Tanana, Ramparts, Fairbanks "Fish Camp", Manley, and Nenana (99,107 fish). Assumes that salmon illegally sold in the round were from these fish that provided roe.

c Included personal use catches beginning in 1987 with the exception of 1991, 1992, and 1994.

d Includes ADF&G commercial test fish sales.

APPENDIX TABLE 2. Yukon River fall chum salmon estimated production (returning salmon) by brood year (year class) and return per spawner estimates 1974–2008. The estimated numbers of salmon which returned were based upon annual age composition observed in lower Yukon River test nets each year, weighted by test fish catch per unit effort.

Year	Number of Salmon				Percent				Total Brood Year Return	Return/ Spawner
	Age 3	Age 4	Age 5	Age 6	Age 3	Age 4	Age 5	Age 6		
1974	91,751	497,755	68,693	0	0.139	0.756	0.104	0.000	658,199	1.51
1975	150,451	1,225,440	61,401	123	0.105	0.853	0.043	0.000	1,437,415	0.98
1976	102,062	587,479	137,039	4,316	0.123	0.707	0.165	0.005	830,895	3.09
1977	102,660	1,075,198	175,688	4,189	0.076	0.792	0.129	0.003	1,357,735	2.64
1978	22,222	332,230	90,580	0	0.050	0.747	0.204	0.000	445,032	1.39
1979	41,114	769,496	274,311	3,894	0.038	0.707	0.252	0.004	1,088,814	1.39
1980	8,377	362,199	208,962	3,125	0.014	0.622	0.359	0.005	582,663	2.21
1981	45,855	955,725	278,386	8,888	0.036	0.742	0.216	0.007	1,288,853	2.34
1982	11,327	400,323	166,754	679	0.020	0.691	0.288	0.001	579,083	3.22
1983	12,569	875,355	223,468	2,313	0.011	0.786	0.201	0.002	1,113,704	3.21
1984	7,089	408,040	174,207	8,516	0.012	0.683	0.291	0.014	597,852	2.21
1985	46,635	874,819	270,984	3,194	0.039	0.732	0.227	0.003	1,195,632	1.80
1986	0	429,749	368,513	4,353	0.000	0.535	0.459	0.005	802,614	2.13
1987	12,413	617,519	290,767	7,720	0.013	0.665	0.313	0.008	928,418	1.42
1988	41,003	175,236	152,368	10,894 [a]	0.108	0.462	0.401	0.029	379,501	1.17
1989	2,744	282,905	345,136 [a]	20,290	0.004	0.435	0.530	0.031	651,075	1.29
1990	710	579,452 [a]	418,448	30,449	0.001	0.563	0.407	0.030	1,029,059	2.78
1991	3,663 [a]	1,024,800	369,103	12,167	0.003	0.727	0.262	0.009	1,409,733	2.38
1992	6,763	653,648	197,073	3,907	0.008	0.759	0.229	0.005	861,392	2.66
1993	7,745	451,327	102,420	3,235	0.014	0.799	0.181	0.006	564,727	1.60
1994	4,322	225,243	149,527	1,603 [a]	0.011	0.592	0.393	0.004	380,695	0.49
1995	2,371	266,955	68,918 [a]	383	0.007	0.788	0.204	0.001	338,627	0.34

APPENDIX TABLE 2. Continued.

Estimated Brood Year Return

Year	Number of Salmon				Percent				Total Brood Year Return	Return/ Spawner
	Age 3	Age 4	Age 5	Age 6	Age 3	Age 4	Age 5	Age 6		
1996	420	165,691 [a]	136,906	8,295	0.001	0.532	0.440	0.027	311,312	0.39
1997	3,087 [a]	244,801	118,343	3,332	0.008	0.662	0.320	0.009	369,563	0.75
1998	651	269,653	57,962	6,694	0.002	0.805	0.173	0.020	334,960	1.27
1999	29,097	705,152	174,424	13,721	0.032	0.764	0.189	0.015	922,394	3.19
2000	8,446	297,012	115,488	0	0.020	0.706	0.274	0.000	420,946	2.00
2001	136,038	2,157,674	675,688	33,600	0.045	0.719	0.225	0.011	3,003,001	8.89
2002	0	444,507	236,656	12,307	0.000	0.651	0.346	0.018	683,312	1.72
2003	24,263	849,743	409,378	16,701	0.019	0.654	0.315	—	1,300,085 [b]	>1.87
2004	0	313,132	173,481	—	—	—	—	—	486,612 [c]	>0.90
2005	2,137	—	—	—	—	—	—	—	—	—
2006	—	—	—	—	—	—	—	—	—	—
2007	—	—	—	—	—	—	—	—	—	—
2008	—	—	—	—	—	—	—	—	—	—
Average All Brood Years (1974-2002)	31,089	598,462	210,628	7,317	0.0324	0.6889	0.2698	0.0094	847,145	2.09
Average Even Brood Years (1974-2002)	20,343	388,548	178,612	6,343	0.0340	0.6540	0.3022	0.0109	593,168	1.88
Average Odd Brood Years (1974-2002)	42,603	823,369	244,931	8,361	0.0307	0.7264	0.2351	0.0077	1,119,264	2.30

[a] Based upon expanded age-composition estimates from fish caught in the test fishery for years 1994 and 2000 when the test fishery terminated early.

[b] Brood year return for age-3, -4, and -5 year fish, indicated that production from brood year 2003 was at least 1.87. Recruits were estimated for brood year where spawner returns were not complete.

[c] Brood year return for age-3 and -4 year fish, indicated that production from brood year 2004 was at least 0.90. Recruits estimated for brood year where spawner returns were not complete.

APPENDIX TABLE 3. Historical escapement of fall chum salmon in the Tanana River and upper Yukon River showing relative contributions of monitored stocks, 1974–2008. Total escapement estimates for Toklat River were calculated using a Delta River migratory time density curve and percentage of live salmon present by survey data in the upper Toklat River (Toklat Springs); based on 1974–1993 Toklat River database (e.g., Barton 1997). Kantishna River population estimates from 1995 to 1998 were based on linear regression of the Kantishra River population estimate and the Toklat River escapement surveys 1999–2004. Kantishna River estimate for 2007 was described by Cleary and Hamazaki 2008). Upper Tanana River estimates from 1974 to 1994 were based on an expansion factor of 8.13 developed from respective year Delta River foot survey escapement counts. Chandalar River estimates from 1974 to 1994 were based on an expansion factor of 1.86 developed from Sheenjek and Fishing Branch River escapement data. Total escapement estimates were calculated using sonar to aerial survey expansion of 2.92 from 1974 to 1980. The assessment project started late in the run from 1981 to 1985; estimated escapements expanded for portion missed using average run timing curves based on bendix sonar counts from the Chandalar (1986–1990) and Sheenjek rivers (1991–1993). Beginning in 1986, estimates were made approximating the run for the period of second week of August through middle of fourth week of September. Estimates of the total Fishing Branch River escapement were calculated using weir counts, unless otherwise indicated. Total main-stem spawning escapement for the Canadian portion of the Yukon River was estimated using border passage minus Canadian harvests (excludes Fishing Branch River escapement); estimates for 1974 to 1979 were based on expansion of the collective Sheenjek River and Fishing Branch River escapements to the Upper Yukon River by a factor of 2.31.

| Year | Tanana River Components | | | Total Tanana River Component | Upper Yukon River Tributaries | | | Canada Main-stem Spawning Escapement | Total Upper Yukon River Component | Total Escapements to Monitored Areas | Relative Contribution of Each Component Stock | | | | | |
	Toklat	Kantishna	Upper Tanana		Chandalar	Sheenjek	Fishing Branch				Toklat/ Kantishna	Upper Tanana	Chandalar	Sheenjek	Fishing Branch	Canadian Main-stem
1974	41,798		48,177	89,975	129,685	117,921	31,525	67,379	346,510	436,485	0.10	0.11	0.30	0.27	0.07	0.15
1975	92,265		30,413	122,678	501,011	227,935	353,282	260,307	1,342,535	1,465,213	0.06	0.02	0.34	0.16	0.24	0.18
1976	52,891		51,411	104,302	61,403	34,649	36,584 [a]	31,903	164,539	268,841	0.20	0.19	0.23	0.13	0.14	0.12
1977	34,887		137,454	172,341	127,816	59,878	88,400 [a]	66,408	342,502	514,843	0.07	0.27	0.25	0.12	0.17	0.13
1978	37,001		90,702	127,703	71,944	42,661	40,800 [a]	37,379	192,784	320,487	0.12	0.28	0.22	0.13	0.13	0.12
1979	158,336		68,051	226,387	206,904	120,129	119,898 [a]	107,500	554,431	780,818	0.20	0.09	0.26	0.15	0.15	0.14
1980	26,346 [b]		41,841	68,187	78,707	38,093	55,268 [c]	22,912	194,980	263,167	0.10	0.16	0.30	0.14	0.21	0.09
1981	15,623		191,471	207,094	137,509	102,137	57,386 [c]	47,066 [d]	344,098	551,192	0.03	0.35	0.25	0.19	0.10	0.09
1982	3,624		34,494	38,118	50,809	43,042	15,901 [a]	31,958	141,710	179,828	0.02	0.19	0.28	0.24	0.09	0.18
1983	21,869		62,757	84,626	79,467	64,989	27,200 [a]	90,875	262,531	347,157	0.06	0.18	0.23	0.19	0.08	0.26
1984	16,758		101,087	117,845	44,241	36,173	15,150 [a]	56,633 [d]	152,197	270,042	0.06	0.37	0.16	0.13	0.06	0.21
1985	22,750		140,712	163,462	203,211	179,727	56,016	62,010	500,964	664,426	0.03	0.21	0.31	0.27	0.08	0.09
1986	17,976		54,596	72,572	99,932	84,207 [e]	31,723	87,940	303,802	376,374	0.05	0.15	0.27	0.22	0.08	0.23

APPENDIX TABLE 3. Continued.

Year	Tanana River Components			Total Tanana River Component	Upper Yukon River Tributaries			Canada Main-stem Spawning Escapement	Total Upper Yukon River Component	Total Escapements to Monitored Areas	Relative Contribution of Each Component Stock					
	Toklat	Kantishna	Upper Tanana		Chandalar	Sheenjek	Fishing Branch				Toklat/ Kantishna	Upper Tanana	Chandalar	Sheenjek	Fishing Branch	Canadian Main-stem
1987	22,117		172,510	194,627	174,317	153,267 [c]	48,956	80,776	457,316	651,943	0.03	0.26	0.27	0.24	0.08	0.12
1988	13,436		146,804	160,240	59,308	45,206 [e]	23,597	36,786	164,897	325,137	0.04	0.45	0.18	0.14	0.07	0.11
1989	30,421		173,829	204,250	123,223	99,116 [c]	43,834	35,750	301,923	506,173	0.06	0.34	0.24	0.20	0.09	0.07
1990	34,739		73,239	107,978	97,191	77,750 [c]	35,000 [f]	51,735	261,676	369,654	0.09	0.20	0.26	0.21	0.09	0.14
1991	13,347		268,009	281,356	107,086	86,496	37,733	78,461	309,776	591,132	0.02	0.45	0.18	0.15	0.06	0.13
1992	14,070		72,433	86,503	87,343	78,808	22,517	49,082	237,750	324,253	0.04	0.22	0.27	0.24	0.07	0.15
1993	27,838		161,734	189,572	61,744	42,922	28,707	29,743	163,116	352,688	0.08	0.46	0.18	0.12	0.08	0.08
1994	76,057		193,662	269,719	186,031	150,565	65,247	98,358	500,201	769,920	0.10	0.25	0.24	0.20	0.08	0.13
1995	54,513 [b]	104,129	268,173	372,302	280,999	241,855 [g]	51,971 [g]	158,092	732,917	1,009,155	0.09	0.24	0.25	0.22	0.05	0.14
1996	18,264	46,919	134,563	181,482	208,170	246,889	77,278	122,429	654,766	800,022	0.06	0.16	0.25	0.30	0.09	0.15
1997	14,511	40,996	71,661	112,657	199,874	80,423 [h]	26,959	85,439	392,695	494,831	0.08	0.14	0.40	0.16	0.05	0.17
1998	15,605	42,723	62,384	105,107	75,811	33,058	13,564	46,305	168,738	263,121	0.16	0.23	0.28	0.12	0.05	0.17
1999	4,551	27,199	97,843	125,042	88,662	14,229	12,904	58,682	174,477	288,962	0.09	0.33	0.30	0.05	0.04	0.20
2000	8,911	21,450	34,844	56,294	65,894	30,084	5,053 [g]	53,742	154,773	210,756	0.10	0.17	0.31	0.14	0.02	0.25
2001	6,007	22,992	96,556	119,548	110,971	53,932	21,669	33,851	220,423	337,765	0.07	0.28	0.33	0.16	0.06	0.10
2002	28,519	56,665	109,961	166,626	89,580	31,642	13,563	98,695	233,480	397,977	0.14	0.27	0.22	0.08	0.03	0.25
2003	21,492	87,359	193,418	280,777	214,416	44,047	29,519	142,683	430,665	695,363	0.12	0.27	0.30	0.06	0.04	0.20
2004	35,480	76,163	123,879	200,042	136,703	37,878	20,274	154,080	348,935	537,873	0.14	0.23	0.25	0.07	0.04	0.28
2005	17,779 [b]	107,719	337,755	445,474	496,484	561,863	121,413	437,920	1,617,680	1,996,700	0.05	0.16	0.24	0.27	0.06	0.21
2006	—	71,135	202,669	273,804	245,090	160,178	30,849	211,193	647,310	873,987	0.08	0.22	0.27	0.17	0.03	0.23
2007	—	81,843	320,811	402,654	228,056	65,435	33,750	214,802	542,043	916,606	0.09	0.34	0.24	0.07	0.04	0.23

APPENDIX TABLE 3. Continued.

Year	Tanana River Components			Total Tanana River Component	Upper Yukon River Tributaries			Canada Main-stem Spawning Escapement	Total Upper Yukon River Component	Total Escapements to Monitored Areas	Relative Contribution of Each Component Stock					
	Toklat	Kantishna	Upper Tanana		Chandalar	Sheenjek	Fishing Branch				Toklat/ Kantishna	Upper Tanana	Chandalar	Sheenjek	Fishing Branch	Canadian Main-stem
2008 *	—	—	—	161,924 [i]	157,843	42,842	20,055	172,402	393,142	531,595	—	0.29	0.28	0.08	0.04	0.31
Avg All Yrs	31,243	60,561	128,527	174,093	151,070	100,858	48,958	97,751	398,637	562,414	0.08	0.24	0.26	0.16	0.08	0.17
Avg 2004-2008	26,630	84,215	246,279	296,780	252,835	173,639	45,268	238,079	709,822	971,352	0.09	0.25	0.26	0.13	0.04	0.25
Biological Escapement Goals	15,000-33,000	—	46,000-103,000	61,000-136,000	74,000-152,000	50,000-104,000	50,000-120,000	>80,000	212,000-441,000	300,000-600,000	0.10	0.23	0.28	0.14	0.05	0.20

* Preliminary data.

[a] Total escapement estimates using weir to aerial survey expansion factor of 2.72, unless otherwise indicated.

[b] Minimal estimate due to late timing of ground survey with respect to peak of spawning.

[c] Initial aerial survey count was doubled before applying the weir/aerial expansion factor of 2.72 because only half of the spawning area was surveyed.

[d] Escapement estimate based on mark-recapture program unavailable. Estimate based upon assumed average exploitation rate.

[e] Expanded sonar replacement estimates for period approximating second week August through middle fourth week September, using Chandalar River run timing data.

[f] Weir was not operated. DFO estimated population of spawners to be approximately 30,000-40,000 fish, based upon a late October 26 aerial survey (7,541 fish actually observed).

[g] Minimal count due to high water events, weir was pulled for nine days in 1995 from August 31 to September 8; in 2000, no counts available for seven days beginning September 24 with slow counts through October 13.

[h] Conservative sonar-estimated escapement due to high water which prevailed during late August through early/mid September. Actual escapement estimated to be 114,000 to 135,000 fish using historic passage estimates for 1986-1996 and 1991-1996.

[i] Tanana River estimate was based on genetic apportionment from samples from the test fishery applied to Pilot Station sonar count and represented all Tanana River fall chum salmon as well as Tanana River summer chum salmon after July 19 to be comparable to the historical mark-recapture estimates.

American Fisheries Society Symposium 70:743–757, 2009

Stock-Recruitment Analysis for Escapement Goal Development: a Case Study of Pacific Salmon in Alaska

ROBERT A. CLARK[*], DAVID R. BERNARD[1], AND STEVE J. FLEISCHMAN

Alaska Department of Fish and Game, Sport Fish Division
Research and Technical Services
333 Raspberry Road, Anchorage, Alaska 99518, USA

Abstract.—The constitutional mandate to sustain yields along with regulatory guidance from the Sustainable Salmon and Escapement Goal policies of the State of Alaska provide the impetus for development and implementation of escapement goals for salmon. When appropriate, a stock-recruitment analysis can provide vital insight on the population dynamics of a salmon stock. This insight can greatly facilitate the development of a scientifically defensible escapement goal to sustain yields from the stock. However, the role of stock-recruitment analysis in escapement goal development is often misunderstood and misapplied. Although many analysts focus on the quantity and quality of the data needed to conduct a stock-recruitment analysis, other factors such as the species of salmon, type and size of fishery, management constraints, social and economic constraints, and information content of the data are also important. Much of the confusion about stock-recruitment analysis arises because, while the analysis is primarily a statistical procedure, the actual development and implementation of an escapement goal is primarily a scientific and practical endeavor. Many see the ultimate goal of a stock-recruitment analysis as the identification of the escapement that produces maximum sustained yield, although in many cases it may identify much more than that, or less. Several case studies are used to illustrate the potential uses of stock-recruitment theory in the development of escapement goals.

Introduction

Article VIII, section 4 of the Alaska Constitution states that (from Harrison 1992):

"Fish, forests, wildlife, grasslands, and all other replenishable resources belonging to the State shall be utilized, developed, and maintained on the sustained yield principle, subject to preferences among beneficial uses."

This mandate for sustainable management of Pacific salmon *Oncorhynchus* spp.

provided the impetus for development of a scientifically defensible escapement goal policy in Alaska. Along with the statutory duties and powers of the Commissioner of the Alaska Department of Fish and Game (ADF&G) and relevant management plans for salmon stocks, the development of escapement goals is regulated by the policy for the management of sustainable salmon fisheries and the policy for statewide salmon escapement goals (Title 5 of the Alaska Administrative Code, Chapter 39).

These two regulatory policies define four

*Corresponding author: bob.clark@alaska.gov
[1]Current email address: drbernardconsulting@gci.net

types of escapement goals, two of which are most important to sustained yield management of salmon stocks. The biological escapement goal (BEG) is defined as: the escapement that provides the greatest potential for maximum sustained yield (MSY). As an alternative to management for MSY, the sustainable escapement goal (SEG) is defined as: the escapement that is known to provide for sustained yield. Both of these escapement goals must be described as ranges that take into account our uncertainty in the data and variation in stock productivity. The two regulatory policies also stipulate that BEGs and SEGs for Pacific salmon be developed from the best available data and be scientifically defensible.

The concept of "scientific defensibility" is embodied in the well-known production models and statistical formulations of stock-recruitment theory. Much of the scientific discourse on salmon production and the maintenance of yields is focused on model selection (e.g., Schmidt et al. 1998), the effect of measurement error on model performance (e.g., Walters and Ludwig 1981), and the incorporation of accumulated knowledge about model parameters into the statistical formulation (e.g., Hilborn and Liermann 1998) or what is herein referred to as stock-recruitment analysis. While these are important considerations in the methodological development of the theory, little of the peer-reviewed literature on stock-recruitment analysis focuses on improvements in data collection and the interpretation of these data in relation to the sustained yield principle in Alaskan law.

It is argued here that current salmon production theory is sufficient to address the question of sustaining yields of Pacific salmon in Alaska via the development of BEGs or SEGs. When used judiciously, stock-recruitment analysis is an important tool in this development. It is also argued that factors such as the species of salmon, type and size of fishery, management constraints, social and economic constraints, and information content of the production data are as important as the availability of data and sophistication of the statistical machinery used for stock-recruitment analyses. Four case histories from fisheries on salmon stocks throughout Alaska are presented to illustrate these often neglected considerations in escapement goal analysis.

Methods

Brood year tables were constructed from escapements (S) and subsequent production (R) from the following stocks that likely represent the range of information content and fishing power typical of salmon fisheries in Alaska (Table 1; Figure 1): early-run Chignik River sockeye salmon *O. nerka* (Ruggerone et al. 1999; Witteveen et al. 2005; Table 2), Chilkat River Chinook salmon *O. tshawytscha* (Ericksen and McPherson 2004; Table 3); Kenai River sockeye salmon, (Hasbrouck and Edmundson 2007; Table 4); and Goodnews River Chinook salmon (Brannian et al. 2006; Table 5).

Simple stock-recruitment analyses were performed on each brood table using the linearized form of the Ricker relationship with multiplicative process error (Hilborn and Walters 1992) to estimate parameters (equation (1) and reference points (equations (2) through (4)). Beginning with the familiar nonlinear form of the stochastic Ricker equation,

$$R = \alpha S \exp(-\beta S)\exp(\varepsilon), \qquad (1a)$$

and then dividing by S and taking natural logs to form the linear regression recipe

$$\ln\left(\frac{R}{S}\right) = \ln\alpha - \beta S + \varepsilon; \; \varepsilon \sim N\left(0, \sigma_\varepsilon^2\right) \text{ (1b)}$$

A linear regression of $\ln(R/S)$ on S will estimate the parameters $\ln\alpha$ (y-intercept),

TABLE 1. Salmon stocks used to illustrate the different techniques for developing an escapement goal based on the number of years of stock-recruit data, information content of these data, and the fishing power of the fisheries on these stocks.

Stock	n (years)	Information Content	Fishing Power
Chignik sockeye	75	high	high
Chilkat Chinook	7	low	very low
Kenai sockeye	28	low	very high
Goodnews Chinook	17	high	low

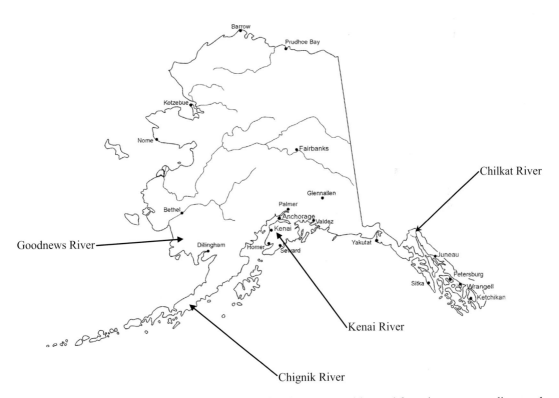

FIGURE 1. The state of Alaska with the location of major communities and four river systems discussed in this paper.

Clark et al.

TABLE 2. Escapements and subsequent production of early-run Chignik River sockeye salmon *Oncorhynchus nerka* for the 1922-1996 brood years (from Ruggerone et al. 1999 and Witteveen et al. 2005).

Brood Year	Escapement	Production	Brood Year	Escapement	Production	Brood Year	Escapement	Production
1922	86,421	963,814	1947	2,386,733	181,112	1972	326,320	995,971
1923	4,642	380,359	1948	384,637	327,295	1973	538,462	1,172,428
1924	121,983	1,322,557	1949	213,269	308,534	1974	364,603	607,596
1925	386,364	117,662	1950	206,270	392,627	1975	319,890	655,827
1926	289,009	530,194	1951	125,126	625,689	1976	548,953	982,361
1927	857,881	2,677,184	1952	34,155	230,820	1977	364,557	2,233,783
1928	507,353	820,981	1953	168,375	357,607	1978	419,732	968,298
1929	995,832	1,054,167	1954	184,953	142,421	1979	491,467	3,612,107
1930	92,955	377,485	1955	256,757	554,495	1980	369,580	1,732,741
1931	96,201	1,128,231	1956	289,096	208,168	1981	570,210	1,833,432
1932	2,151,734	341,298	1957	192,479	350,512	1982	616,117	2,323,643
1933	223,913	621,400	1958	120,862	242,370	1983	426,178	564,174
1934	866,890	1,658,466	1959	112,226	340,946	1984	597,713	636,040
1935	194,636	419,709	1960	251,567	774,756	1985	373,040	772,920
1936	548,039	645,985	1961	140,714	571,645	1986	557,772	2,523,215
1937	205,613	809,550	1962	167,602	693,473	1987	589,299	1,434,036
1938	175,972	1,025,570	1963	332,536	698,703	1988	420,580	1,658,460
1939	1,142,852	489,232	1964	137,073	755,726	1989	384,001	1,706,400
1940	176,307	505,379	1965	307,192	1,948,144	1990	434,550	1,526,844
1941	374,420	1,583,579	1966	383,545	1,303,567	1991	662,660	1,495,503
1942	442,981	3,059,105	1967	328,000	240,712	1992	360,681	929,759
1943	701,859	700,658	1968	342,343	1,210,927	1993	364,261	903,537
1944	291,844	334,093	1969	366,589	476,282	1994	769,465	2,038,909
1945	217,882	245,534	1970	536,257	441,685	1995	366,495	2,117,130
1946	774,130	224,163	1971	671,668	1,383,455	1996	464,748	1,570,375
Average							430,254	983,914
SD							380,963	740,958

TABLE 3. Escapements and subsequent production of Chilkat River Chinook salmon *Oncorhynchus tshawytscha* for the 1991–1997 brood years (from Ericksen and McPherson 2004).

Brood Year	Escapement	Production
1991	5,897	12,932
1992	5,284	5,542
1993	4,472	3,231
1994	6,795	1,645
1995	3,790	4,348
1996	4,920	5,637
1997	8,100	7,081
Average	5,608	5,774
SD	1,465	3,619

TABLE 4. Escapements and subsequent production (in thousands) of Kenai River sockeye salmon *Oncorhynchus nerka* for the 1968–1995 brood years (from Hasbrouck and Edmundson 2007).

Brood year	Escapement	Production
1968	82	916
1969	52	409
1970	72	520
1971	289	863
1972	302	2,186
1973	358	1,995
1974	144	665
1975	129	895
1976	353	1,187
1977	664	2,811
1978	350	3,451
1979	246	1,111
1980	398	2,346
1981	359	2,268
1982	566	8,930
1983	557	8,697
1984	310	3,252
1985	396	2,246
1986	400	1,741
1987	1,333	9,531
1988	839	2,120
1989	1,334	3,898
1990	439	1,334
1991	376	3,926
1992	752	3,469
1993	670	1,287
1994	895	2,511
1995	521	1,421
Average	471	2,714
SD	328	2,455

TABLE 5. Escapements and subsequent production of Goodnews River Chinook salmon *Oncorhynchus tshawytscha* for the 1981–1997 brood years (from Brannian et al. 2006).

Brood year	Escapement	Production
1981	11,454	16,538
1982	4,332	11,870
1983	20,420	9,479
1984	12,003	12,412
1985	10,810	6,030
1986	6,186	11,899
1987	6,762	10,150
1988	8,131	11,255
1989	4,806	18,849
1990	11,292	9,134
1991	6,473	12,069
1992	3,757	7,466
1993	7,076	22,817
1994	11,722	7,006
1995	14,701	24,571
1996	8,907	9,532
1997	10,153	7,187
Average	9,352	12,251
SD	4,211	5,424

β(slope), and σ_ε^2 (residual error). Then $\ln\hat{\alpha}$ is adjusted for lognormal process error (Hilborn 1985),

$$\ln\hat{\alpha}' = \ln\hat{\alpha} + \hat{\sigma}_\varepsilon^2 \big/ 2 \qquad (1c)$$

and to estimate the relevant reference points for salmon management from the regression parameters:

$$\hat{S}_{EQ} = \frac{\ln\hat{\alpha}'}{\hat{\beta}}, \qquad (2)$$

$$\hat{S}_{MSY} \approx \hat{S}_{EQ}\left(0.5 - 0.07\ln\hat{\alpha}'\right), \quad \text{and} \quad (3)$$

$$\hat{\mu}_{MSY} \approx \ln\hat{\alpha}'\left(0.5 - 0.07\ln\hat{\alpha}'\right). \qquad (4)$$

Statistical uncertainty about the parameters and reference points was assessed with a bootstrap technique (Efron and Tibshirani 1993); resampling the residuals of the linear regression with replacement, calculating all parameter estimates and reference points for each bootstrap replicate, and using percentiles of the bootstrap values to obtain interval estimates. Here, for comparison among stocks a nonparametric analog of the coefficient of variation (NPCV) is also calculated for each parameter and reference point (Prager and Mohr 1999):

$$NPCV = \frac{\left(69.15^{th}\ percentile - 30.85^{th}\ percentile\right)}{median}; \qquad (5)$$

where an NPCV of 25% or less was considered precise.

Apart from this analytical recipe for estimating the reference points from the linear regression parameters, it is important to note that $S_{EQ}^{\wedge}$ is an estimate of the carrying capacity of a salmon stock, where carrying capacity is defined as the average escapement of the stock when it is not being fished (Figure 2). Moreover, $\ln^{\wedge}\alpha$ is an estimate of the intrinsic rate of increase of the stock, where intrinsic rate of increase is defined as the natural logarithm of average recruits per spawner as S approaches zero.

These definitions also have relevance to the rate of harvest on a stock while stock-recruitment data are being collected. Walters and Hilborn (1976) showed that in the case of very low harvest rate most of the stock-recruitment data pairs are on the right-hand side of the stock-recruit curve, the carrying capacity of a stock is known, but not the intrinsic rate of increase. Conversely, they also showed that in the case of a very high harvest rate when most of the stock-recruitment data pairs are on the left-hand side of the stock-recruitment curve, the intrinsic rate of increase is known but not the carrying capacity.

Using information from each of the four salmon stocks as examples and the aforementioned principles of stock-recruitment analysis, recommendations for establishing a BEG or SEG were developed for each stock that are scientifically defensible based on information content of the stock-recruit data, the definitions of carrying capacity and intrinsic rate of increase, and the analytical relationship between the two.

Case Studies

Early run Chignik River sockeye salmon.—The Chignik River is located on the Alaska Peninsula near the community of Chignik (Figure 1). Sockeye salmon are primarily harvested in a commercial seine fishery (Bouwens and Poetter 2006). Although a long history of exploitation exists on this

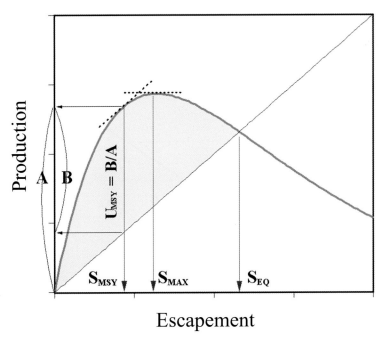

FIGURE 2. Graphical representation of reference points (S_{MSY}, S_{EQ}, μ_{MSY}) on a Ricker stock-recruitment curve. The diagonal line is the replacement line and the shaded region is the area of surplus production.

stock, recent rates of annual exploitation are moderate and range from 51 to 85%, averaging 69% during 1959–2003 (Witteveen et al. 2005). Recent stock assessment consists of escapements estimated by weir and harvests estimated by allocation of age classes to stream of origin based on the relative magnitude of escapements (Witteveen et al. 2005). The brood table consists of 75 years (1922–1996) of escapement and subsequent production estimates (Table 2). Sufficient fishing power occurs in the commercial seine fishery to harvest all available surplus production so that a BEG was desired.

A plot of subsequent production on brood-year escapement indicates that a broad range of escapements have occurred, and that production has not replaced escapement (i.e., data points below the replacement line) in 11 out of 75 years, most notably at the highest levels of escapement (Figure 3). The information content of these data are high because there is information about the intrinsic rate of increase at high exploitation rates and on

carrying capacity at lower exploitation rates. The stock–recruitment analysis indicated that estimates of $\ln\alpha'$ and β were relatively precise with NPCV of 8% and 14%, respectively (Table 6). Estimates of S_{EQ}, S_{MSY}, and μ_{MSY} were also precise (NPCV of 11%, 11% and 5%, respectively), indicating that a BEG based on S_{MSY} could be developed from this analysis (Table 7). A BEG appears to be a good fit to this fishery as there is close correspondence between the observed average exploitation rate (69%) and μ_{MSY} (69%; Table 6).

Chilkat River Chinook salmon.—The Chilkat River is located near the city of Haines in southeast Alaska (Figure 1). Chinook salmon are harvested in commercial and marine sport fisheries located in Lynn Canal as well as in the commercial troll fishery (Ericksen and McPherson 2004). Although a long history of exploitation exists on this stock, recent rates of annual exploitation are low and ranged from 8 to 19%, averaging 12% during 1988–1991. Recent stock assessment

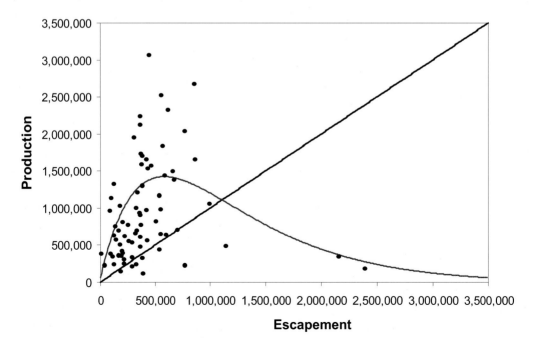

FIGURE 3. Plot of subsequent production on brood year escapement and the estimated Ricker curve from the early-run of Chignik River sockeye salmon *Oncorhynchus nerka*, 1922–1996 brood years.

TABLE 6. Summary of parameter estimates, estimated reference points, and nonparametric CV's (in parentheses) from linear regression and bootstrapping of stock-recruitment data from four salmon stocks in Alaska.

Stock	$\ln\hat{\alpha}'$	$\hat{\beta}$	$\hat{\sigma}_\varepsilon^2$	S_{EQ}	S_{MSY}	μ_{MSY}
Chignik	1.87	1.68×10^{-6}	0.60	1,114,168	410,940	69%
sockeye	(8%)	(14%)	(10%)	(11%)	(11%)	(5%)
Chilkat	0.91	1.38×10^{-4}	0.49	6,590	2,875	40%
Chinook	(67%)	(70%)	(43%)	(19%)	(25%)	(53%)
Kenai	2.11	5.71×10^{-4}	0.29	3,698[a]	1,303[a]	74%
sockeye	(8%)	(51%)	(13%)	(48%)	(50%)	(5%)
Goodnews	1.39	1.08×10^{-4}	0.19	12,843	5,169	56%
Chinook	(19%)	(23%)	(16%)	(10%)	(12%)	(14%)

[a] in thousands.

consists of escapements estimated by mark-recapture and harvests estimated by coded-wire tag recoveries. The brood table consists of seven years (1991–1997) of escapement and subsequent production estimates (Table 3). Prior to this analysis no escapement goal was available for this stock. Although latent fishing power is available that could be brought to bear on this stock, the initial desire was to develop an escapement goal (SEG or BEG) for this stock so existing fisheries could be liberalized when surplus production was realized.

A plot of subsequent production on brood-year escapement indicates that a narrow range of escapements have occurred and that production has not replaced escapement in three out of seven years, indicating that this stock is at or near carrying capacity (Figure 4). Information content of these data are low because there is no information on the intrinsic rate of increase, but there is on carrying capacity. The stock-recruitment analysis indicated that estimates of lnα' and β were imprecise with NPCV of 67% and 70%, respectively (Table

6). Estimates of S_{EQ} and S_{MSY} were notably more precise (NPCV of 19% and 25%, respectively) because there was good information about carrying capacity. The estimate of μ_{MSY} was poor (NPCV of 53%) because of the lack of production data at low escapements and the resulting lack of information about intrinsic rate of increase. The estimate of S_{EQ} is defensible; it differs little from the average of escapements observed while fishing power was low (average $S = 5,608$; Table 3). From the estimate of S_{EQ}, a conservative estimate of S_{MSY} could be developed by assuming lnα' was 0 (assumes return-per-spawner is 1 at low escapements) and solving equation (3) for S_{MSY}. Alternatively, a less conservative estimate of S_{MSY} could be calculated by using an estimate of average lnα' from Chinook salmon stocks in southeast Alaska (average lnα' = 1.92) as was done by Ericksen and McPherson (2004). Although these methods produced an estimate of S_{MSY}, information was still missing on returns at escapements near S_{MSY} for this stock, so that a SEG was recommended instead of a BEG (Table 7).

TABLE 7. Summary of four case studies of salmon escapement goal development.

Stock	n	Information Content	Fishing Power	lnα'	β	Goal type	Basis for goal
Chignik sockeye	75	high	high	known	known	BEG	Ricker regression to estimate SMSY
Chilkat Chinook	7	low	low	unknown	unknown	SEG	Discount from carrying capacity based on average escapement
Kenai sockeye	28	low	high	known	unknown	SEG	Exploitation rate from lnα'
Goodnews Chinook	17	high	low	known	known	BEG or SEG	Ricker regression to estimate SMSY

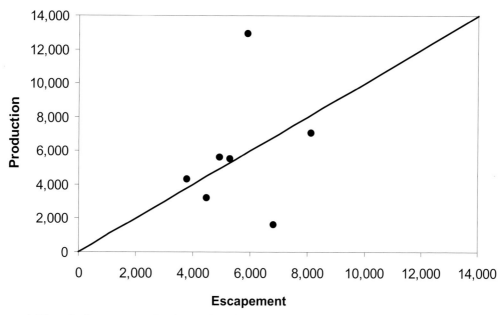

FIGURE 4. Plot of subsequent production on brood year escapement from Chilkat River Chinook salmon *Oncorhynchus tshawytscha*, 1991–1997 brood years.

Kenai River sockeye salmon.—The Kenai River is located on the Kenai Peninsula near the cities of Soldotna and Kenai (Figure 1). Sockeye salmon are harvested in marine commercial, freshwater sport, and personal-use fisheries (Shields 2006). Escapement is estimated with sonar near the mouth of the river, and marine harvests are estimated by allocation of harvests by age-class to stream of origin based on the relative magnitude of escapements (Hasbrouck and Edmundson 2007). Stock assessments have occurred since 1968, with annual exploitation ranging from 48 to 94% and averaging 79%. The brood table consists of 28 years (1968–1995) of escapement and subsequent production estimates (Table 4). The current escapement goal is an SEG of 500–800 thousand (Hasbrouck and Edmundon 2007). There is sufficient fishing power in the currently configured fisheries to harvest all available surplus production so that a BEG was desired.

A plot of subsequent production on brood year escapement indicates that a narrow range of escapements have occurred and that production has always replaced escapement, indicating a lack of information about this stock's carrying capacity (Figure 5). Information content of these data are low because there is information on the intrinsic rate of increase, but little or none on carrying capacity. The stock-recruitment analysis indicated that the estimate of $\ln\alpha'$ was precise (NPCV of 8%) as was the estimate of μ_{MSY} (NPCV of 5%; Table 6). Estimates of β (NPCV of 51%), S_{EQ} (NPCV of 48%), and S_{MSY} (NPCV of 50%) were grossly imprecise (Table 6), which prohibited the development of a defensible BEG. On the other hand, the estimate of μ_{MSY} (74%) is lower than the observed average exploitation rate (81%), indicating that the current SEG should be increased somewhat. Although no defensible BEG could be developed, advice to increase the current SEG is useful to fishery managers (Table 7). While likely not

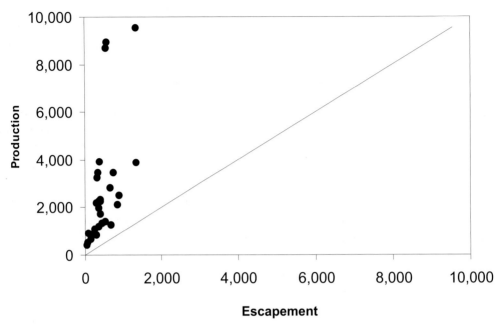

FIGURE 5. Plot of subsequent production on brood year escapement from Kenai River sockeye salmon *Oncorhynchus nerka* (in thousands), 1968–1995 brood years.

optimal in terms of producing MSY, the current SEG has been shown to be defensible and sustainable given that escapements observed since 1968 have always yielded surplus production.

Goodnews River Chinook salmon.—The Goodnews River is located near the community of Goodnews Bay in southwestern Alaska (Figure 1). Chinook salmon are harvested in commercial, sport, and subsistence fisheries (Jones and Linderman 2006) that primarily target sockeye salmon. Escapement is estimated with a weir, and marine harvests are estimated by allocation of harvests by age-class to stream of origin based on the relative magnitude of escapements (Brannian et al. 2006). Recent stock assessments have occurred since 1981, with annual exploitation ranging from 16 to 71% and averaging 33%. The brood table consists of 17 years (1981–1997) of escapement and subsequent production estimates (Table 5). The initial desire was to

replace an SEG range based on escapements indexed with aerial surveys with one (SEG or BEG) developed from a brood table based on weir-based counts of escapement.

A plot of subsequent production on brood-year escapement indicates that a broad range of escapements have occurred, and that production has not replaced escapement (i.e., data points below the replacement line) in 5 out of 17 years, most notably at the highest level of escapement (Figure 6). Information content of these data are high because there is information on the intrinsic rate of increase at high exploitation rates and on carrying capacity at lower exploitation rates. The stock–recruitment analysis indicated that estimates of lnα' and β were relatively precise with NPCV of 19% and 23%, respectively (Table 6). Precise estimates of S_{EQ}, S_{MSY}, and μ_{MSY} were estimated from the parameters (NPCV of 10%, 12% and 14% respectively), indicating that a BEG based on S_{MSY} could be developed from this analysis (Table 7). However, estimated S_{MSY} (5,169 fish) was much lower than the observed average escapement for this stock (9,352 fish), so that the currently configured fishery may be unable to harvest all available surplus production leading to a chronic inability to achieve the BEG. A better option for this fishery might be an SEG constructed around the range of escapements shown to produce sustained yields.

Discussion

As illustrated by the four case studies, the simple stock-recruitment analyses used herein provide vital information regarding population dynamics and information content of the basic adult escapement and production data. This information, when combined with the practical considerations of the fishery such as fishing power and prior knowledge of a particular salmon species can help the ana-lyst and fishery manager develop a scientifi-cally defensible escapement goal that meets the mandates of Alaskan law. As seen in the example of Chignik sockeye salmon, fishery objectives and the information content of the data match and all that is needed is a simple stock–recruitment analysis to develop a BEG that has the potential for producing MSY in the long-term. More sophisticated models and analytical techniques of these stock and recruitment data are available to help refine our analysis, but the basic premise of a de-fensible BEG would remain. Our experience with salmon stocks and fisheries in Alaska is that this situation is the exception rather than the norm.

Situations similar to the Chilkat Chinook salmon and Kenai sockeye salmon case stud-ies are most often seen, where the results of simple stock-recruitment analyses are in-conclusive or partially conclusive, and the

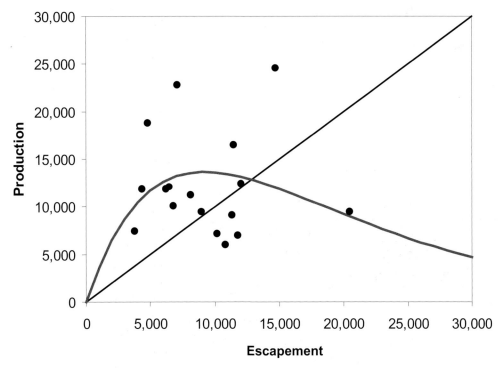

FIGURE 6. Plot of subsequent production on brood year escapement and the estimated Ricker curve from Goodnews River Chinook salmon *Oncorhynchus tshawytscha*, 1981–1997 brood years.

analyst must use theoretical considerations and past knowledge of similar stocks to develop a scientifically defensible escapement goal. In these cases, an SEG is most often recommended to managers because escapement that produces MSY cannot be specified from the available information. In the case of Chilkat Chinook salmon this outcome has little consequence for a fishery that has very low fishing power which likely would not harvest all available surplus production even with generous fishing time. If additional fishing power could be brought to bear on this stock, then information might be gained on production potential at levels of escapements lower than currently observed.

The lack of a BEG is also self perpetuating in the Kenai sockeye salmon fishery because current fishing power is more than sufficient to harvest at rates higher than what might be specified at MSY. This results in production information that is confined to the existing SEG with little potential for gaining information on the carrying capacity of this stock. In this case, it can be argued that the current SEG or one slightly higher has successfully sustained high levels of harvest and is therefore a defensible escapement goal.

Situations similar to Goodnews Chinook salmon are also seen where knowledge of escapement that produces MSY may not be the proper objective for the fishery. In this example, stock assessment data are collected from a fishery that harvests multiple species where fishing power may be adequate to harvest surplus production of one species (sockeye salmon in this example) and not the other species (Chinook salmon). Sufficient information is possessed to develop a BEG from simple stock-recruitment analysis, but may not be elected to set an escapement goal based on this analysis because there is insufficient fishing power to harvest all available surplus production. In this case, the tradeoffs in harvest of two species in a single fishery may best be handled by a BEG for one species and a SEG for the other.

These case studies also illustrate the need for independent corroborative evidence of carrying capacity and intrinsic rate of increase in escapement goal development, especially when one or both pieces of this information are missing or inconclusive in the stock-recruitment analysis. Existing habitat-based and paleolimnological approaches for describing carrying capacity (e.g., Bradford et al. 1997 for coho salmon *O. kisutch*, Parken et al. 2004 for Chinook salmon, Schindler et al. 2005 for lake-rearing sockeye salmon) are valuable tools for the development of escapement goals. The development of these approaches is encouraged for other salmon species such as river-rearing sockeye salmon and chum salmon *O. keta*. Similarly, meta analyses of intrinsic rates of increase for salmon species (e.g., Myers et al. 1999) can provide helpful information on production dynamics and scientific defensibility of an escapement goal, especially when fishing power is low. While the continued statistical development of stock-recruitment analysis is laudable, it is argued that the science of setting escapement goals and understanding of production dynamics of salmon would be better served by an increase in the collection of high quality stock assessment data across a broad range of salmon species, geographic settings, and fishing power.

Acknowledgments

The authors would like to acknowledge the helpful comments and suggestions on the content and presentation of this material from the many Alaska Department of Fish and Game staff that participated in the Escapement Goal Analysis workshops held from March 2006 through February 2007 in Anchorage and Juneau. We also greatly appreciate the helpful external peer reviews provided to us by the AYK SSI Editorial Board.

References

Bouwens, K. A., and A. D. Poetter. 2006. Chignik management area commercial fishery harvest strategy, 2006. Alaska Department of Fish and Game, Fishery Management Report No. 06–23, Anchorage.

Bradford, M. J., G. C. Taylor, and J. A. Allan. 1997. Empirical review of coho salmon smolt abundance and the prediction of smolt production at the regional level. Transactions of the American Fisheries Society 126:49–64.

Brannian, L. K., M. J. Evenson, and J. R. Hilsinger. 2006. Escapement goal recommendations for select Arctic-Yukon-Kuskokwim region salmon stocks, 2007. Alaska Department of Fish and Game, Fishery Manuscript No. 06–07, Anchorage.

Efron, B., and R. J. Tibshirani. 1993. An introduction to the bootstrap. Chapman and Hall, New York.

Ericksen, R. P., and S. A. McPherson. 2004. Optimal production of Chinook salmon from the Chilkat River. Alaska Department of Fish and Game, Fishery Manuscript No. 04–01, Anchorage.

Harrison, G. S. 1992. Alaska's Constitution: a citizen's guide. Alaska Legislative Research Agency, Juneau.

Hasbrouck, J. J., and J. A. Edmundson. 2007. Escapement goals for salmon stocks in Upper Cook Inlet, Alaska: report to the Alaska Board of Fisheries, January 2005. Alaska Department of Fish and Game, Special Publication No. 07-10, Anchorage.

Hilborn, R. 1985. Simplified calculation of optimum spawning stock size from Ricker's stock recruitment curve. Canadian Journal of Fisheries and Aquatic Sciences 42:1833–1834.

Hilborn, R., and M. Liermann. 1998. Standing on the shoulders of giants: learning from experience in fisheries. Reviews in Fish Biology and Fisheries 8:273–283.

Hilborn, R., and C. J. Walters. 1992. Quantitative fisheries stock assessment: choice, dynamics, and uncertainty. Chapman and Hall, New York.

Jones, P. W., and J. C. Linderman, Jr. 2006. Goodnews River salmon monitoring and assessment, 2005. Alaska Department of Fish and Game, Fishery Data Series No. 06–50, Anchorage.

Myers, R. A., K. G. Bowen, and N. J. Barrowman. 1999. Maximum reproductive rate of fish at low population sizes. Canadian Journal of Fisheries and Aquatic Sciences 56:2404–2419.

Parken, C. K., R. E. McNicol, and J. R. Irvine. 2004. Habitat-based methods to estimate escapement goals for data limited Chinook salmon stocks in British Columbia. Fisheries and Oceans Canada, Pacific Scientific Advice Review Committee, Salmon Subcommittee Working Group Paper S2004–05, Nanaimo, British Columbia.

Prager, M. H., and M. S. Mohr. 1999. Population dynamics of Klamath River Chinook salmon: stock-recruitment model and simulation of yield under management. Report to Klamath River Fishery Management Council by the Klamath River Technical Advisory Team. National Marine Fisheries Service, NOAA Southwest Fisheries Science Center Santa Cruz/Tiburon Laboratory, Tiburon, California. Available: http://www.fws.gov/yreka/KFMC-Rpts/KSREPORT.PDF (March 2007).

Ruggerone, G., R. Steen, and R. Hilborn. 1999. Chignik salmon studies: investigations of salmon populations, hydrology, and limnology of the Chignik lakes, Alaska. University of Washington, Fisheries Research Institute, Final Report Anadromous Fish Project FRI-UW-9907, Seattle.

Schindler, D. E., P. R. Leavitt, C. S. Brock, S. P. Johnson, and P. D. Quay. 2005. Marine-derived nutrients, commercial fisheries, and production of salmon and lake algae in Alaska. Ecology 86:3225–3231.

Schmidt, D. C., S. R. Carlson, G. B. Kyle, and B. P. Finney. 1998. Influence of carcass-derived nutrients on sockeye salmon productivity of Karluk Lake, Alaska: importance in the assessment of an escapement goal. North American Journal of Fisheries Management 18:743–763.

Shields, P. 2006. Upper Cook Inlet commercial fisheries annual management report, 2005. Alaska Department of Fish and Game, Fishery Management Report No. 06–42, Anchorage.

Walters, C. J., and R. Hilborn. 1976. Adaptive control of fishing systems. Journal of the Fisheries Research Board of Canada 33:145–159.

Walters, C. J., and D. Ludwig. 1981. Effects of measurement errors on the assessment of stock-recruitment relationships. Canadian Journal of Fisheries and Aquatic Sciences 38:704–710.

Witteveen, M. J., H. Finkle, P. A. Nelson, J. J. Hasbrouck, and I. Vining. 2005. Review of salmon escapement goals in the Chignik Management Area. Alaska Department of Fish and Game, Fishery Manuscript No. 05–06, Anchorage.

American Fisheries Society Symposium 70:759–780, 2009

Genetic Consequences of Size-Selective Fishing: Implications for Viability of Chinook Salmon in the Arctic-Yukon-Kuskokwim Region of Alaska

JEFFREY J. HARD*

*National Marine Fisheries Science, Northwest Fisheries Science Center
Conservation Biology Division
2725 Montlake Boulevard East, Seattle, Washington 98112, USA*

WILLIAM H. ELDRIDGE[1] AND KERRY A. NAISH

*University of Washington, School of Aquatic and Fishery Sciences
Box 355020, Seattle, Washington 98195, USA*

Abstract.—Selective fishing targets potential breeders with particular characteristics, hence, it can change a population in ways that affect its abundance and productivity. Chinook salmon *Oncorhynchus tshawytscha* show a wide range of sizes and ages at adulthood and are exposed to fishing during much of their lives. Size-selective fishing can remove the largest and oldest individuals from a population. What is the role of fishing as a factor affecting size, and what are the genetic consequences of change in size for life history and viability? To address these questions for Chinook salmon in the Arctic-Yukon-Kuskokwim region of Alaska, evolutionary and demographic models of long-lived, large-bodied Chinook salmon are linked to assess the effects of two idealized fishing regimes on age-specific length, spawner abundance, and yield to the fishery. The lengths for fish of each age are treated as distinct but correlated traits. The models showed that a constant exploitation rate above a minimum fish size reduces abundance and yield within 100 years unless genetic variation for, and stabilizing natural selection on, length are sufficient to permit adaptation. Because lengths at age were correlated, fish in all age groups, including those under weak selection, responded to selection by declining in length, and abundance and yield both decreased. When fishing removed fish between a minimum and maximum size limit, fish increased in length during adaptation to fishing, and the population could achieve higher abundance after 100 years than that predicted by a non-genetic model. Under both fishing regimes, the population showed evidence of adaptation to fishing if length was heritable and natural selection on length was evident. Management intervention through aggressive reduction of exploitation rate allowed the population to eventually achieve or exceed pre-fishing abundances and stable catches in both regimes. When sufficiently strong and selective, fishing can cause fish size to evolve rapidly, with potential consequences for viability.

*Corresponding author: Jeff.Hard@noaa.gov
[1]Current address: Stroud Water Research Center, 970 Spencer Road, Avondale, PA 19311, USA

Introduction

Human-induced changes in ecosystems that support fish are receiving increased attention, and there is a growing concern that factors such as habitat degradation or fragmentation, climate change, production of hatchery fish, and fishing may be altering life histories in ways that reduce their ability to cope with future change (Law 2000; Hutchings and Reynolds 2004; Birkeland and Dayton 2005; Hutchings and Fraser 2008; Fenberg and Roy 2008). Human actions like fishing may be altering life histories by selectively restricting breeding to individuals of certain sizes, ages, or maturity status. Within a population, a trait can evolve in response to selection when there is a genetic component to its variability, as indicated by a nonzero heritability. A number of recent studies have attempted to attribute life history changes in both marine and freshwater species to genetic effects of fishing (Olsen et al. 2004; Hutchings 2005; Olsen et al. 2005; Swain et al. 2007). Such changes often appear to involve size and age at maturation, traits with a strong influence on fitness in natural environments (Kuparinen and Merilä 2007). The form of fishing selection, whether directional, disruptive or stabilizing, may also affect trait evolution because it may differ in form and strength from those of natural selection. For example, a study of Windermere pike in the U.K. by Carlson et al. (2007) and Edeline et al. (2007) showed that selection imposed by fishing can drive changes in body size that differ from those imposed by natural selection, increasing the intensity of stabilizing natural selection on the phenotype.

Biologists have recognized for over 100 years that fishing-induced evolutionary change could also affect size and life history in anadromous salmonids (Hard et al. 2008). As is the case for other fishes, direct evidence for evolution in salmon in response to fishing is largely circumstantial; it is restricted to retrospective analyses of phenotypic trends (Hard et al. 2008). In an early study, Vaughan (1947) speculated that fishing might have delayed run timing in southeastern Alaska pink salmon *Oncorhynchus gorbuscha*. Ricker's (1981, 1995) seminal work on Pacific salmon in Canada was, in the end, unable to link changes in mean harvested fish size directly to fishing, but the selective effects of fishing remain as concerns for several populations of these species. Since Ricker's studies, successful attempts to detect genetic effects of fishing on salmon have been rare, in large part because discriminating the effects of selective fishing from environmental causes, such as changes in density-dependent growth, is exceedingly difficult (Hard et al. 2008). Helle and Hoffman (1995, 1998) observed a decrease in body size and an increase in age at maturation for two chum salmon *O. keta* stocks between 1980 and the early 1990s, a trend that showed some association with a major ocean climate regime shift in the North Pacific Ocean in 1976–77. An increase in size at maturity since the mid-1990s may indicate sensitivity to a subsequent change in ocean conditions (Helle and Hoffman 1998). Clearly, density-dependent growth may reflect variable patterns of environmental change, shifts in inter- and intra-specific interactions, or production of hatchery fish. As a result, at least two key issues remain unresolved for salmon populations. First, the impacts of fishing selection on traits correlated with size that affect productivity are not well understood. We are aware of only a handful of studies that have addressed the importance of the architecture of life history on the evolutionary response of salmon to selective fishing (e.g., Healey 1986; Riddell 1986; Hard 2004), and only one of these (Hard 2004) examined the role of correlations among life history traits (see also Walsh et al. 2006). Second, although an evolutionary response to fishing is thought to incur consequences for viability (Policansky 1993a, 1993b; Law 2007), the demographic and ecological consequences of such genetic change have not been evaluated quantitatively. The present study is intended as a start toward addressing these knowledge gaps.

Each approach that has been employed to evaluate the consequences of selective fishing on life history and productivity has its limitations. Model system approaches, such as those employed by Conover and Munch (2002), Munch et al. (2005), and Walsh et al. (2006), have several advantages over simulation but they may have questionable relevance to commercial, recreational, artisanal, or subsistence fishing. The primary value of such approaches is in characterizing responses to selection for fish with simplified life histories in controlled environments. Empirical approaches with species of interest are desirable but are almost always impractical logistically or contentious politically to implement. Modeling or simulation approaches (Law 1991; Hard 2004; Bromaghin et al. 2008) can identify important effects that might be difficult to predict in real populations, but they typically suffer from restrictive, and often unrealistic, assumptions. Nevertheless, such approaches can guide future research and can be valuable in providing a systematic means of identifying the range of potential responses to selection in predictable environments. These models can be useful in evaluating distinctly different scenarios, such as alternative harvest management regimes.

In this paper, we evaluate the potential genetic effects of size-selective fishing on the viability of Chinook salmon *O. tshawytscha* in the Arctic-Yukon-Kuskokwim (AYK) region of Alaska (Evenson et al. 2009, this volume) with a simulation model that focuses on long-lived, large-bodied fish—such as those found in the Yukon River. In recent years, some Yukon River salmon fishermen have expressed concern that adults returning to the river in successive generations have de-

clined in average size. Although evidence for such a trend is mixed (Hyer and Schleusner 2005), such a trend would raise the question whether declining size could reduce viability, possibly by reducing female fecundity or offspring survival. Our approach is one of the first to analyze both evolutionary and demographic aspects of selection and its response for salmon, thereby incorporating evolutionary considerations directly into an analysis of population viability. Our primary objectives were to identify the genetic consequences of size-selective fishing for abundance and yield of Chinook salmon in the AYK region, and to explore the contributions of genetic variability and natural selection on size to mitigate these effects.

Methods

Our assessment of the short-term evolutionary effects of size-selective fishing on Chinook salmon life history involved combining evolutionary and demographic models to determine how selection imposed by fishing alters size and age structure and, consequently, abundance and yield of fish from a population characterized by long life and large size at maturation. By linking these complementary models, we attempted to capture the semelparous reproduction, age and size structure, and inheritance of correlated life history traits for Chinook salmon, based on published estimates and empirically obtained genetic and phenotypic data from this species. Models were used to predict the responses of length at age to selection imposed by two idealized fishing scenarios. More general and sophisticated models, notably those developed by Barton and Turelli (1989) and Kirkpatrick et al. (2002), provide a comprehensive means to evaluate inheritance and evolution of polygenic characters under selection. However, we employed a simple additive genetic model because many of the genetic parameters required for the general models have not been estimated empirically for any population of Chinook salmon.

Selection on length at age.—Potential genetic effects of selection on size was first quantified with a multivariate age-structured model of evolutionary response. This deterministic model integrated nonequilibrium age-structured demography and multivariate response to selection to follow the response of mean age-specific length over time. For our analysis, the changes in z age-specific lengths were tracked for each age, to a maximum age $x = 8$, for $t = 100$ years. (It was assumed that length at each age was normally distributed and that the population's age structure was constant over this period; both assumptions may often be violated in natural populations but we did not explore these effects.) The annual changes in age-specific lengths in the population were determined using the matrix formulas developed by Law (1991):

$$X_{t+1} = (X_t + PP_0^{-1} S_t)T_t C + A_{t+1} C'$$

and

$$A_{t+1} = (A_t + GP_0^{-1} S_t)T_t$$

where X_t and X_{t+1} are matrices of order z by $x + 1$ of age-specific lengths corresponding to years t and $t + 1$, P is the phenotypic covariance matrix for the lengths expressed at different ages, P_0 is a modification of P that has nonzero elements on the diagonal corresponding to traits that are expressed at the same age (P_0^{-1} its inverse), S_t is the matrix of selection differentials on length at age, T_t is a transition matrix that represents the aging of present cohorts through the life history to age x, C and C' are diagonal matrices of order $x + 1$ by $x + 1$ that allow lengths and their breeding values to be updated each year, and A_t and A_{t+1} are the matrices, of order z by $x + 1$, of breeding values for all age-specific

lengths corresponding to years t and $t + 1$ (Law 1991).

These relationships represent a modification of the discrete-generation multivariate breeder's equation, $\Delta z = GP^{-1}s$ (Lande 1979) to accommodate direct and correlated responses to selection in an age-structured population with iteroparous reproduction. In this equation, Δz is a vector of lengths corresponding to matrix X, s is a vector of selection differentials corresponding to the matrix S, and the genetic covariance matrix G is equivalent to matrix A in the equations above. Hard (2004) described this model, its components, and the computation of breeding values, selection differentials, and fitnesses associated with length at age under both directional and disruptive selection scenarios.

To conduct the analysis with realistic estimates of selection and response, we used variance component estimates obtained from a Chinook salmon population at Grovers Creek Hatchery near Suquamish, Washington (Hard 2004; in press) into the model. Table 1 summarizes other values for key parameters that were used to represent Chinook salmon from the AYK region of Alaska. Unlike Grovers Creek Hatchery fish, which is an ocean-type population, AYK Chinook salmon are stream-type populations that generally spend an additional year in freshwater, live longer (up to 8 years) and reach larger sizes (exceeding 1 m in length) at maturation. We recognize this disparity between them but genetic estimates for AYK Chinook salmon life history traits are not available. As Bromaghin et al. (2008) did in a similar study involving stochastic simulation, the genetic estimates from the Grovers Creek population were combined with available phenotypic information from the Yukon River population to represent the key features of AYK Chinook salmon in the life history represented in Figure 1. Two modifications were also made to Law's model to simulate the life history and exploitation of AYK Chinook salmon. First, the model was adapted

TABLE 1. Parameter estimates used for Chinook salmon *Oncorhynchus tshawytscha* in the fishing selection model. Estimates were made from available Chinook salmon data from the Arctic-Yukon-Kuskokwim region of Alaska or were generated in an attempt to produce a life history reflecting a long-lived, large-bodied population, while producing a stable population age structure and growth rate in the absence of fishing. Initial abundances reflect the expected abundances after 100 years in the absence of fishing ($1-\theta = 0$), subject to the empirical age-specific survival, maturation, and fecundity data and the parameters of the stock-recruitment function for the population. Annual growth rates were determined by the breeding values for age-specific length. BV = breeding value; SD = phenotypic standard deviation. Estimates of parameters are for Chinook salmon from several published and unpublished sources (Ratner et al. 1997; Kareiva et al. 2000; Hard 2004; Hyer and Schleusner 2005; Zabel et al. 2006).

Parameter	Value
h^2 of length at ages 1–8	0, 0.34, 0.5
Correlation, r_p, of lengths at age t	0.48 (0.01 in absence of data)
Initial abundance at age 0, N_0	810,642,355
Initial abundance at age 1, N_1	17,834,132
Initial abundance at age 2, N_2	1,599,559
Initial abundance at age 3, N_3	1,266,851
Initial abundance at age 4, N_4	903,011
Initial abundance at age 5, N_5	487,626
Initial abundance at age 6, N_6	87,773
Initial abundance at age 7, N_7	21
Initial abundance at age 8, N_8	0
Initial BV for length at age 0, A_0 (SD)	40 (1.225)
Initial BV for length at age 1, A_1 (SD)	70 (8.062)
Initial BV for length at age 2, A_2 (SD)	230 (50.000)
Initial BV for length at age 3, A_3 (SD)	382 (70.711)
Initial BV for length at age 4, A_4 (SD)	555 (91.191)
Initial BV for length at age 5, A_5 (SD)	704 (126.500)
Initial BV for length at age 6, A_6 (SD)	827 (127.173)
Initial BV for length at age 7, A_7 (SD)	860 (90.373)
Initial BV for length at age 8, A_8 (SD)	900 (94.868)
Proportion female at age 2 (0 at ages < 2)	0.001
Proportion female at age 3	0.001
Proportion female at age 4	0.15
Proportion female at age 5	0.25
Proportion female at age 6	0.75
Proportion female at age 7	0.80
Proportion female at age 8	0.80
Proportion returning to spawn at age 0	0
Proportion returning to spawn at age 1	0
Proportion returning to spawn at age 2	0
Proportion returning to spawn at age 3	0.01
Proportion returning to spawn at age 4	0.10
Proportion returning to spawn at age 5	0.25
Proportion returning to spawn at age 6	0.70
Proportion returning to spawn at age 7	0.99
Proportion returning to spawn at age 8	1.00
Survival to age 1, s_1	0.022
Survival to age 2, s_2	0.136
Annual survival to ages 3–8, s_3–s_8	0.8

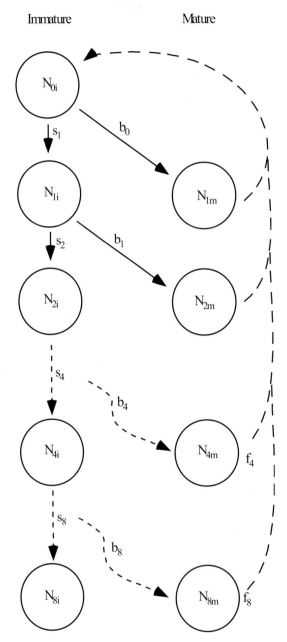

FIGURE 1. Generalized life history of stream-type Chinook salmon *Oncorhynchus tshawytscha* from the Arctic-Yukon-Kuskokwim region of Alaska, depicting the combination of age structure and semelparous reproduction. N_{xi} is the abundance of immature individuals at age x; N_{xm} is the number of individuals maturing and returning to freshwater to spawn at that age. The probability of immature individuals surviving to the next age-class is s_x; the proportion of individuals maturing and returning to spawn the following year is b_x (years range from 0 to 8). Fecundity of mature females at age x is f_x. Harvest occurs on these fish after they initiate maturation and begin upstream riverine migration in their final year of life.

to a semelparous life history by changing the elements of the first column of the transition matrix T_t to 0 except for the last element (which we set to 1). This alteration limits annual updates of breeding values to those contributed by adults maturing at their terminal age. Second, the matrix of breeding values A_t were altered so that these values are updated only for newborn individuals each year; an alteration that better reflects a terminal fishery on returning adults.

It was assumed that all genetic variance for length at age was additive (e.g., no net dominance, epistatic genetic effects, maternal effects). For genetic parameter values, the following was assumed: heritability (h^2) of length at age = 0.34, and correlation among lengths = 0.48 (estimated from empirical data; Hard 2004). The covariance matrices and matrix of selection differentials were considered constant over the 100 years monitored.

Selection imposed by fishing took one of two general, idealized forms (Figure 2). The left panel of Figure 2 depicts directional se-

lection mediated by capture of fish above a fixed length threshold, k (a "minimum size" scenario). The panel on the right depicts disruptive selection mediated by capture of fish between two length thresholds, k_1 and k_2 (a "slot limit" scenario). The mean length at age j is μ_j (Figure 2 depicts the case for a single age). In each case, the fraction of fish longer than k that escape fishing is θ; the fraction removed by fishing is $1-\theta$. Length at age j is normally distributed with phenotypic standard deviation σ_j. The parameter ω defines the width of the fitness function corresponding to length, expressed as the deviation of the inflection point from the optimum in the current generation before fishing. The strength of stabilizing natural selection on size were varied between absent ($\omega = 0$) and weak ($\omega = 3\sigma$) to simulate natural selection countervailing that imposed by fishing (Hard 2004). Selection on size imposed by fishing affects adults maturing at mixed ages, which are represented by overlapping normal distributions of lengths at age. For the minimum size regime, the value of k was set to 600 mm; for

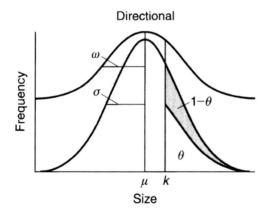 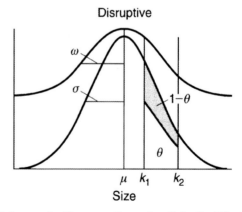

FIGURE 2. Graphical representation of directional ("minimum size") versus disruptive ("slot limit") size selection scenarios resulting from fishing (Hard 2004). These simple idealized cases depict selection on size for a single age-class. The left panel depicts directional selection mediated by harvest of fish larger than fixed threshold, k. The panel on the right depicts disruptive selection mediated by harvest of fish between two size thresholds, k_1 and k_2. The mean size of the population before selection is μ. In each case, the fraction of fish larger than k that escape fishing is θ; and the fraction removed by fishing is $1-\theta$. Size is assumed to be normally distributed with standard deviation σ. ω defines the width of the fitness function for size, corresponding to stabilizing natural selection on size; we assumed relatively weak natural selection on size: $\omega = 3\sigma$ (Hard 2004).

the slot limit regime, k_1 was set to 550 mm and k_2 to 850 mm. We varied h^2 of length at age among three values: 0.0, 0.34, and 0.5, which bracket the range of expected values (see Carlson and Seamons 2008; 0.0 was included to provide a contrast with the other values that represented high environmental variability, and 0.34 is the h^2 estimate measured in Chinook salmon by Hard 2004). The annual proportions of fish removed by fishing $(1-\theta)$ was varie from 0 to 100%, but focused on values of 55% for a minimum size fishing regime and 65% for a slot limit regime for comparison. These values are not equivalent to an annual exploitation rate in a terminal fishery; the exploitation rate is the fraction of maturing fish available and susceptible to fishing annually that are captured rather than survive to spawn, i.e., catch/(catch + escapement), whereas $1-\theta$ is the fraction of all fish susceptible to fishing in a given year (on the basis of length, regardless of maturation state) that are removed by fishing (it therefore also varies with the rate of natural mortality). Actual values of θ are not known for AYK Chinook salmon, but catch estimates of the total Yukon River Chinook salmon run from 1995–2005 averaged 25.5% for the subsistence fishery and 31.7% for the commercial fishery ("2006 Yukon River Salmon Fisheries Outlook," Alaska Department of Fish & Game and U.S. Fish & Wildlife Service, Anchorage, unpublished data). We selected values of θ for the model to be consistent with recent estimates of the annual total exploitation rate for Yukon River Chinook salmon.

Population abundance and fishery yield.—Linking the genetic and demographic models allowed us to explore how size-selective removal might influence abundance and viability. The demographic trajectory of the Chinook salmon population proceeded in the following steps: 1) the freshwater and marine environments were populated with fish aged 0–8 years; 2) a fraction of fish aged 3–8, representative of the length distribution for their age-class, matured and returned to freshwater; 3) size-selective fishing was imposed on the fish returning to freshwater; 4) spawning occurred among the mature fish that survived fishing, and the fecundity of females at each age was determined by the mean length of the age-class after selection (with breeding values of the newborn progeny determined according to the values in Table 1); and 5) simultaneously, immature fish in each age-class aged by one year with the same mean breeding values for length with which they were born—with only those for newborn progeny updating as a result of selection.

To follow the dynamics of the population under fishing through time, we modified the basic approaches used by Ratner et al. (1997), Kareiva et al. (2000) and Zabel et al. (2006) for stream-type Chinook salmon that are based on a Leslie population projection matrix (Leslie 1945; Caswell 2001). The model, a discrete-time model with intervals of one year, accommodates the semelparous reproduction and complex breeding age structure of Chinook salmon (Figure 1). Male and female Chinook salmon from populations like that in the Yukon River may show up to nine age classes ($x = 0$–8 years). The number of individuals at age x in year t, $N_x(t)$, depends on age-specific survival and maturity rates; the probability of surviving from age $x-1$ to x is s_x; the probability of these individuals maturing at age x is b_x (Table 2; Figure 1). Expected female fecundity at age x is f_x, which is estimated as a linear approximation to the relationship between fish length and fecundity estimated by Healey and Heard (1984) for Yukon River Chinook salmon, 450 mm and longer.

The propensity to mature at each age adhered to the following schedule for males and females (corresponding % mature female in parentheses): 0% of fish aged one year and younger mature (<1%), 1% of age-3 fish mature (1%), 10% of age-4 fish mature (15%),

TABLE 2. Population projection matrix for Chinook salmon assuming a maximum age of 8 years. The survival propensities (= 1-natural mortality) from one year (t) to the next ($t+1$), s_t, are given along the off-diagonal of the matrix below the top row. Proportions of fish maturing and returning to spawn (b_t, assumed to be independent of length) are given along the top row, as are female fecundities (f_t). Survival rates and maturation proportions used in the model are given in Table 1. We estimated fecundities from a linear approximation to the function estimated for Yukon River Chinook salmon > 450mm by Healey and Heard (1984). Survival estimates assume no mortality due to upstream adult migration.

$$
\begin{bmatrix}
0 & 0 & 0 & 0 & b_4 f_4 & b_5 f_5 & b_6 f_6 & b_7 f_7 & b_8 f_8 \\
s_1 & 0 & 0 & 0 & 0 & 0 & 0 & 0 & 0 \\
0 & s_2 & 0 & 0 & 0 & 0 & 0 & 0 & 0 \\
0 & 0 & (1-b_2)s_3 & 0 & 0 & 0 & 0 & 0 & 0 \\
0 & 0 & 0 & (1-b_3)s_4 & 0 & 0 & 0 & 0 & 0 \\
0 & 0 & 0 & 0 & (1-b_4)s_5 & 0 & 0 & 0 & 0 \\
0 & 0 & 0 & 0 & 0 & (1-b_5)s_6 & 0 & 0 & 0 \\
0 & 0 & 0 & 0 & 0 & 0 & (1-b_6)s_7 & 0 & 0 \\
0 & 0 & 0 & 0 & 0 & 0 & 0 & (1-b_7)s_8 & 0
\end{bmatrix}
\times
\begin{bmatrix} N_0 \\ N_1 \\ N_2 \\ N_3 \\ N_4 \\ N_5 \\ N_6 \\ N_7 \\ N_8 \end{bmatrix}_t
=
\begin{bmatrix} N_0 \\ N_1 \\ N_2 \\ N_3 \\ N_4 \\ N_5 \\ N_6 \\ N_7 \\ N_8 \end{bmatrix}_{t+1}
$$

25% of age-5 fish mature (25%) 70% of age-6 fish mature (75%), 99% of age-7 fish mature (80%), and 100% of age-8 fish mature (80%). The breeding age distribution was determined by these values and the annual survival rates given in Table 1; these rates were assumed to be independent of fish size for each age-class. Table 2 shows the structure of the population projection matrix corresponding to the age-specific survival rates, fecundities, and maturation propensities. The model employed is deterministic and did not incorporate either demographic or environmental stochasticity into it.

A hockey stick function was used to represent the population's spawner-recruit relationship (Barrowman and Myers 2000). The hockey stick is an alternative to the Ricker and Beverton–Holt functions. It relaxes the assumption of a close linkage between survival to reproduction and spawner density. Use of the hockey stick assumes that recruits increase with spawner abundance in linear fashion to a threshold, above which recruitment is constant at the carrying capacity, regardless of increasing spawner density. A carrying capacity of 11.8 million age-1 recruits was assumed corresponding to a spawner density of 250,000–300,000, then parameterized the model with the initial age-specific abundances shown in Table 1. These values reflect the expected abundances after 100 years in the absence of fishing ($1-\theta = 0$), subject to the empirical age-specific survival, maturation, and fecundity data and the parameters of the stock–recruitment function for the population (Table 1). Estimated population growth rate (λ) in the absence of fishing, given these parameters, was approximately 1.15.

The fitnesses, selection differentials, and responses to selection in the two fishing scenarios were calculated by tracking phenotypes for maturing fish aged 3–7 years under varying levels of heritability and stabilizing natural selection; fish aged 0–2 were not vulnerable to fishing and no fish survived to age 8 in these scenarios (Table 1). Selection differentials, responses to selection, and changes in abundance for 100 years (McElhany et al. 2000) were monitored, with an opportunity for management intervention after 30 years.

Results

Effects of selective fishing on length at age

The complicated age structure of Chinook salmon modeled in these simulations tended to produce complex responses in length at age, because size-selective fishing imposed different selection differentials on lengths of fish of distinct ages. As expected, when length was not heritable, directional selection imposed by size-selective fishing, under a minimum size limit of 600 mm and a fraction of harvestable fish caught ($1-\theta$) of 55%, resulted in negative selection differentials on length but no evolutionary response when length at age was not heritable. When length was heritable ($h^2 = 0.34$) and no stabilizing natural selection on length was present ($\omega = 0$), lengths declined only slightly (Figure 3). When length was heritable and stabilizing natural selection on length was weak but present ($\omega = 3\sigma$), negative selection differentials produced modest phenotypic changes in length (Figure 3). Initial selection differentials were nearly –3.5 mm for 3-year old fish, over –8 mm for 4- and 6-year old fish, and over –10.5 mm for 5-year old fish; these selection differentials showed little trend over time under constant selection. Mature fish of all five ages showed declines in length, ranging from more than –4 mm (age 3) to nearly –8 mm (ages 5 and 6) in 50 years and between –8 and –15 mm in 100 years, with the largest responses expected for 5- and 6-year old fish (–15 mm) (Figure 3). When $h^2 = 0.5$ and $\omega = 3\sigma$, the phenotypic responses in length were about 50% larger than those for $h^2 = 0.34$ (results not shown).

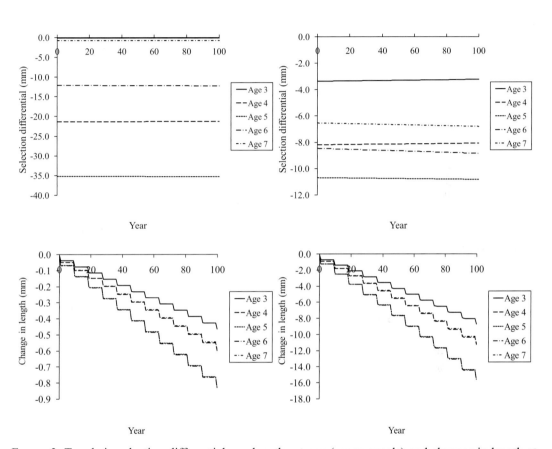

FIGURE 3. Trends in selection differentials on lengths at age (upper panels) and changes in length at age (lower panels) for Chinook salmon *Oncorhynchus tshawytscha* (ages 3–7 years) from the Arctic-Yukon-Kuskokwim region of Alaska under a minimum size limit fishing regime (directional selection) over 100 years of fishing. The minimum size limit is 600 mm, and the fraction of fish removed by fishing $(1-\theta)$ is 55%. The strength of stabilizing natural selection on length is either absent ($\omega = 0$; left panels) or relatively weak ($\omega = 3\sigma$; right panels).

Fishing under a slot limit between 550 and 850 mm with $1-\theta = 65\%$ resulted in both negative and positive selection differentials on length at age. Fishing produced negative selection differentials for 3- and 4-year old fish but positive selection differentials for older fish. When length was heritable ($h^2 = 0.34$) and no stabilizing natural selection on length was present ($\omega = 0$), the selection dif-

ferential increased over time for five-year old fish from about +6 mm to over +25 mm after 100 years (Figure 4). However, when length was heritable and stabilizing natural selection on length was present ($\omega = 3\sigma$), selection differentials were much smaller and phenotypic changes in length correspondly weaker than when $\omega = 0$ (Figure 4). The initial selection differential was approximately –4 mm for 3-

and 4-year old fish, nearly 0 mm for 5-year old fish, and over + 2.5 mm and + 4.3 mm for 6- and 7-year old fish, respectively. Mature fish of all five ages increased in length, ranging from + 6 mm for three-year old fish to over + 11 mm for five- and six-year old fish after 100 years (Figure 4). When $h^2 = 0.5$ and $\omega = 3\sigma$, the phenotypic responses in length were nearly 50% larger than those for $h^2 = 0.34$ (results not shown).

Effects of selective fishing on abundance and yield

Size-selective fishing at high exploitation rates led to rapid reductions in total run abundance and yield to the fishery, especially under a minimum-size limit scenario. Under a minimum length limit of 600 mm and a fraction of harvestable fish caught $(1-\theta)$ of 55%, size-selective fishing caused total run abundance and fishery yield to decline rapidly when stabilizing natural selection on length was absent ($\omega = 0$), regardless of the heritability (Figure 5). The reductions in run abundance and yield were greatest if length was heritable ($h^2 = 0.34$) and $\omega = 3\sigma$; run abundance declined about 30% and yield 35% over 100 years. Mean annual exploitation rate was stable over this period at slightly less than 30%.

Under a length slot limit between 550 and 850 mm and $1-\theta = 65\%$, size-selective fishing caused total run abundance and fishery yield to decline initially when stabilizing natural selection on length was absent ($\omega = 0$) (Figure 5); the rate of change depended on the heritability. If length at age was not heritable, the declines in run size and yield were monotonic, with run size dropping to about 20% of the level before fishing began and catch to about 50% of the initial level. If length at age was heritable ($h^2 = 0.34$), abundance and yield began to recover after 50 years, reaching over 80% of initial levels after 100 years (Figure 5). With $h^2 = 0.5$, re-

covery was complete within 75 years (results not shown). With $h^2 \geq 0.34$ and $\omega = 3\sigma$, total run size and catch increased to the maximum levels within 50 years; the annual exploitation rate rose to a cap of 17% over the period (Figure 5).

The potential to adapt to size-selective fishing conferred a greater demographic benefit when fishing mortality was high. Figure 6 illustrates the effects of fishing on total run size over 100 years when h^2 of length is 0.34 or when h^2 is 0 ($\omega = 0$). Under a minimum size limit of 600 mm, relative run size (abundance$_{h^2 = 0.34}$/abundance$_{h^2 = 0}$) declined initially at all harvest levels but began to increase after 5 years at harvest rates greater than 40%. Relative run size was highest when harvest rates exceeded 70%; at this rate, the relative run size nevertheless began declining gradually after about 35 years, although after 100 years it still exceeded 1.0 (Figure 6). By contrast, under a slot limit of 550–850 mm, relative run size exceeded 1.0 under all harvest rates, reaching maximum values at harvest rates exceeding 50% within 5 years and at harvest rates lower than 50% within 35 years.

Responses to reduced fishing rates

One form of management intervention might correspond to a substantial reduction in harvest rate, such as could occur with elimination of a commercial fishery and leaving subsistence as the only allowable harvest. When represented as a reduction in the proportion of harvestable fish caught $(1-\theta)$ after 30 years, management intervention produced dramatic changes in selection differentials and responses in lengths at age and in abundance under both fishing regimes. Under the minimum size regime, a reduction in $1-\theta$ from 55% to 25% reduced selection differentials by as much as 70% to less than -12 mm for four- and five-year old fish and less than -4 mm for six-year old fish. Declining trends

$\omega = 0$ $\omega = 3\sigma$

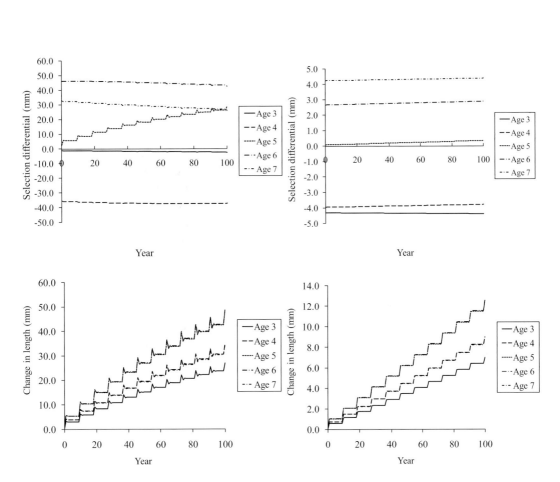

FIGURE 4. Trends in selection differentials on lengths at age (upper panels) and changes in length at age (lower panels) for Chinook salmon *Oncorhynchus tshawytscha* (ages 3–7 years) from the Arctic-Yukon-Kuskokwim region of Alaska under a slot limit fishing regime (disruptive selection) over 100 years of fishing. The minimum length is 550 mm and the maximum length is 850 mm in the slot; the fraction of fish removed by fishing $(1-\theta)$ is 65%. The strength of stabilizing natural selection on length is either absent ($\omega = 0$; left panels) or relatively weak ($\omega = 3\sigma$; right panels).

$\omega = 0$ $\omega = 3\sigma$

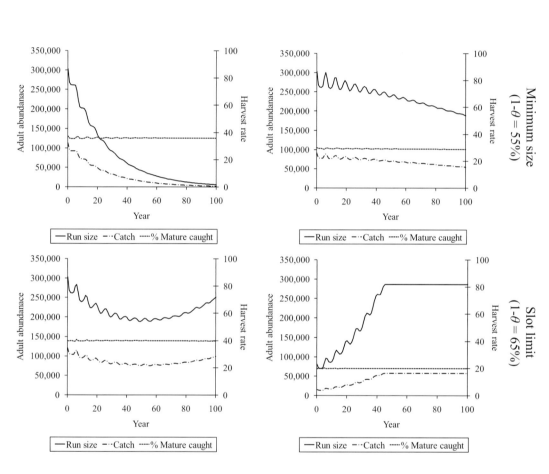

FIGURE 5. Trends in total run size (prespawning abundance), yield of mature adults, and % mature caught, for Chinook salmon *Oncorhynchus tshawytscha* from the Arctic-Yukon-Kuskokwim region of Alaska, under minimum size (upper panels) and slot limit (lower panels) fishing regimes over 100 years of size-selective fishing. The fraction of fish removed by fishing $(1-\theta)$ under the minimum size limit (minimum length 600 mm) is 55%; the fraction of fish removed by fishing under the slot limit (minimum length 550 mm, maximum length 850) is 65%. The strength of stabilizing natural selection on length is either absent ($\omega = 0$; left panels) or relatively weak ($\omega = 3\sigma$; right panels).

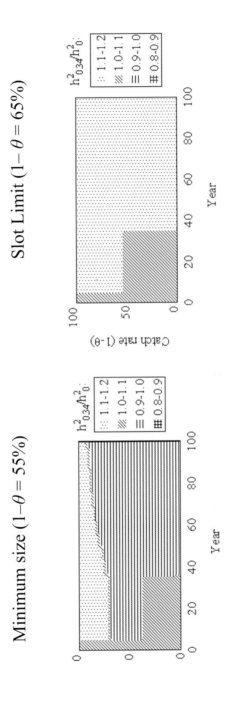

FIGURE 6. Effect of genetic variation for length at age on final abundance, after 100 years, for Chinook salmon *Oncorhynchus tshawytscha* from the Arctic-Yukon-Kuskokwim region of Alaska, under size-selective fishing under minimum size or slot limit fisheries. The graphs depict the ratio of final abundance (total run size) when heritability of length at age is moderate ($h^2 = 0.34$) to final abundance when length is determined entirely by environmental factors ($h^2 = 0$). Directional selection is represented by a minimum size limit of 600 mm (left panel); disruptive selection is represented by a slot limit of 550–850 mm (right panel). The proportion of harvestable fish removed by fishing ($1-\theta$) under each regime varies from 0 to 100%.

in length diminished accordingly when length at age was heritable. Total run size and catch began to increase immediately after the adjustment in harvest rates; run size eventually exceeded prefishing levels and annual catch stabilized at its new level (~35%) within 50 years (Figure 7). These patterns were qualitatively similar when stabilizing natural selection on length was absent (although rates of increase were slower; Figure 7), reflecting the overriding effect of exploitation rate on abundance.

Under the slot limit regime, a reduction in $1-\theta$ from 65% to 25% reduced selection differentials by as much as 65% to less than −11 mm for four-year old fish and + 14 mm for six-year old fish (Figure 7). As in the minimum size scenario, increasing trends in length diminished accordingly under the slot limit scenario when length at age was heritable. Total run size increased sharply after the adjustment in harvest rates; run size exceeded prefishing levels and annual catch stabilized at its new level (~20%) within 10 years. As in the minimum-size fishery, these patterns were qualitatively similar under the slot limit when stabilizing natural selection on length was absent, but changes in run size and catch took longer in that case (Figure 7).

Discussion

A deterministic genetic-demographic model was used to explore how size-selective fishing is likely to affect abundance and yield in an exploited Chinook salmon population, with characteristics like those found in populations from the AYK region of Alaska. An evident decline in the frequency of very large (>900 mm) Chinook salmon from some areas of the Yukon River in recent years (Hyer and Schleusner 2005; Evenson et al. 2009), as well as a more general perception that mean size and age have declined in this population since the 1970s, has precipitated concern that fishing or

another factor is changing the characteristics of AYK Chinook salmon. Subsistence fishing on the run has existed for centuries; exploitation of the population by commercial fisheries, which began in 1918 and has been continuous since 1932, was at peak levels from the early 1960s until the late 1990s (Vania et al. 2002; Evenson et al. 2009). This fishery shares similarities to both regimes simulated here, but probably more closely resembles key features of the minimum-size scenario. In 1998, the exploitation rate was curtailed but since 2001 it has increased again and, although run sizes are not showing consistent trends, fish size has continued to decline. Whether this decline and the disappearance of older fish have resulted from the fishery or from environmental factors that affect growth and maturation is the subject of considerable controversy, and at present neither of these putative factors can be ruled out.

Fishing can impose selection on salmon size, and if sufficient genetic variability underlies variation in size for a population, that population can respond in mean body size (and potentially in other traits) to fishing selection. Whether the population will respond to fishery selection depends on several factors (Law 1991; Hard 2004, in press). First, fishing must be sufficiently strong to impact breeding population size; under constant fishing vulnerability, selectivity, and genetic variability, high harvest rates are more likely than low harvest rates to elicit an evolutionary response. Second, fishing selectivity must be sufficiently high to impose a detectable selection differential. A fishery that removes fish that deviate substantially in size from the population mean, e.g., only the largest fish, is more likely to alter the size and age structure of an exploited population than a fishery that captures a broad range of fish sizes. Removal of the largest fish will have a disproportionate impact because of the contribution of their high fertility to population growth rate (Birkeland and Dayton 2005; Hutchings and Fraser

Minimum size (1-θ = 55→25%)   Slot limit (1-θ = 65→25%)

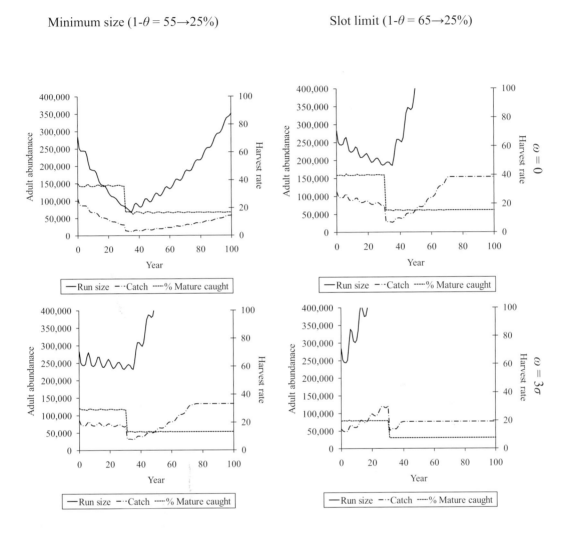

FIGURE 7. Responses of abundance (run size and yield) and catch rate in Chinook salmon *Oncorhynchus tshawytscha* from the Arctic-Yukon-Kuskokwim region of Alaska to a reduction in fishing mortality after 30 years. The left panels depict responses under a minimum size limit (minimum length 600 mm) when 1–θ is initially 55%, then reduced to 25%; the right panels depict responses under a slot limit (minimum length 550 mm, maximum length 850 mm) when 1–θ is initially 65%, then reduced to 25%. The upper panels depict responses when natural selection on length is absent (ω = 0), and the lower panels depict responses in the presence of relatively weak natural selection on length (ω = 3σ). In both cases, h^2 of length at age is 0.34.

2007; Kuparinen and Merilä 2007). Third, in order to detect a response to fishing, the environmental variability that has contributed to observed variation in fish size and size at age must be relatively small. Because of the plasticity of many fish characteristics, single genotypes can produce a range of phenotypes when environmental variation is high.

Like the findings of Law (1991) and Hard (2004), our results indicate that size-selective fishing can produce a detectable evolutionary response in size at age if the harvest rate and selectivity are both sufficiently strong. Bromaghin et al. (2008) found similar responses in their analysis of size-selective exploitation of Yukon River Chinook salmon using a stochastic, individual-based model integrating phenotypic evolution and population dynamics. Under a minimum-size limit for harvestable fish, the lengths of fish of most ages (3–7 years old) declined under selection within 100 years even if the selection differentials on fish of particular ages were small, due to the correlated heritabilities of lengths expressed at different ages. This pattern reflects the genetic and phenotypic covariance structure of length at age; in the unlikely event that lengths at different ages were not under the influence of the same genes, we would expect to see an evolutionary response only in the length of fish belonging to those age groups directly selected upon. Under the minimum size regime, growth is likely to respond to selection as fish become smaller. Adaptation to the regime could take one of two general forms: growth rate increases and fish mature at younger ages, or growth rate declines. Growth rate and length at age in Chinook salmon appear to be positively genetically correlated (Hard 2004); consequently, selection against large size may reduce growth rates. However, for anadromous salmonids, growth rate might accelerate during adaptation to selection on length as a consequence of earlier age at maturity, as these traits also tend to be positively correlated.

Under the slot limit regime, selection differentials on length show different patterns for young versus old fish (selecting for small young fish and large old fish). The responses tend to be toward larger fish at age, especially at older ages. The patterns of change in length suggest that growth would increase under selection on length to avoid the slot. These results are contingent on the specific range of the length thresholds, the selection differentials, and harvest rates (as well as the genetic influences on length at age) evaluated here, but they clearly demonstrate the potential of size selectivity in a fishery to alter the size distribution of a long-lived, large-bodied Chinook salmon population like that in the Yukon River.

The results indicated that, under some circumstances, an evolutionary response to fishing selection could reduce population viability lower than expected due to the immediate demographic reduction caused by harvest. Under a minimum-size limit, both run size and fishery yield of the population can decline detectably within several generations when heritabilities of length at age are greater than zero. If length at age is heritable and stabilizing natural selection on length is weak (through natural or sexual selection on size of breeding adults), these declines tend to be modest; if stabilizing natural selection is absent, these declines are rapid and substantial. Under a slot limit, both run size and yield decline if stabilizing natural selection on length is absent, but show signs of recovery within several decades if length is heritable. If stabilizing natural selection on length is weak, run size and yield increase within 40 years under size-selective fishing at the harvest intensities evaluated here. Therefore, given sufficient genetic variability, a population can adapt to fishing selection to reach a higher abundance, but how a population adapts to fishing depends on its life history characteristics and the type of fishing regime it experiences. In some cases adaptation to a minimum-size fishing regime may reduce future yield (e.g., through a reduction in mean size or age at first spawning).

Aggressive management of harvest to reduce fishing mortality appears to precipitate rapid demographic responses. Management intervention through reduction of exploitation rates after 30 years allowed the population to restore its total run abundance rapidly under both fishing regimes. The responses to reduced fishing mortality allowed the population to achieve or exceed prefishing abundances and catches within several decades under the minimum size regime and in less than a decade under the slot limit regime. As expected, substantial changes in harvest rates are likely to overshadow other management options in effectiveness, including fishing selectivity.

Considerable discussion in the literature has focused on the merits of minimum size limits, slot limits, and other fishing strategies as means to maintain current and preserve future yields. Some researchers have argued that minimum size limits tend to lead to "recruitment overfishing," whereas practices that increase catch of small, young fish tend to lead to "growth overfishing," which is often thought to have less deleterious impacts on productivity and yield (Ricker 1976; Larkin 1978, 1981; Nelson and Soulé 1987). Our results are consistent with these arguments. That said, such arguments often overlook the importance of the level of genetic variation for size and associated life history traits, and the strength of natural selection on them, to the resilience of an exploited population (Allendorf et al. 2008). The results of this study clearly show that a modest genetic influence on size at age can permit adaptation to fishing selection. Such adaptation will take time, however, and during adaptation to fishing selection a population could be highly vulnerable to natural selection affecting growth, size and age at maturation, especially if environmental conditions for survival or growth worsen.

What are the wider implications of these patterns for conservation and management of Arctic-Yukon-Kuskokwim Chinook salmon? Because uncertainty about the condition of these populations may be high, the simplest answer to this question is to permit exploited populations sufficient opportunity to cope evolutionarily with the ecological and evolutionary pressures posed by fishing (see Gerrodette et al. 2002). Because resistance among the public to reducing fishing rates is likely to remain high in most circumstances, it is important to consider reducing fishing selectivity as well as reducing exploitation rates. A timely reduction in exploitation rates in response to declining abundance or productivity is a powerful tool available to management, but reducing selectivity on length can also increase the size or maintain the yield of an exploited population. Our findings indicated that reducing selectivity on size, by allowing a greater proportion of large, old fish to escape harvest, can help to maintain preharvest abundance and yield to the fishery, as well as conserve life history variability. This benefit will be greatest when diminished gear selectivity is combined with substantially reduced exploitation rates (see also Bromaghin et al. 2008). However, the most effective modifications for sustainable fishing are not yet completely clear, and the influence of gear selectivity and the dependence of selectivity on time and area closures or other feasible strategies are two issues that would clearly benefit from additional research.

Management options such as these might not always have the desired effect. The consequences of environmental variation for fish growth, size, and age at maturity might easily—at least in some years—overwhelm the impacts of fishing. Indeed, what cannot be determined yet is whether the selection imposed by fishing, the evolutionary response to it, and any attendant effects on viability will be sufficiently large to detect and therefore require some form of management intervention. Regrettably, our understanding of within-population fishery selection in salmon has not changed appreciably since the commentaries of Larkin (1978, 1981) and the review by Nelson and Soulé (1987). We are not yet able to say with certainty when fishing selection on a particular salmon population, such as those in Alaska's AYK region, will pose a serious problem for long-term management and conservation. Effects of habitat conditions that alter density-dependent growth and maturity may override the selective effects of fishing that reduce abundance or productivity. Nevertheless, fishing selection is likely to compound problems originating from other sources, and the effects of this selection will be cumulative. Some populations which have weakened resilience due to other variables may be especially vulnerable to fishing selection. Such selection could represent a "tipping point" for viability. Cumulative evolutionary changes imposed by fishing along the lines illustrated here could eventually erode a population's capacity to respond to future environmental challenges. Prudent fishery managers should recognize this possibility and attempt to reduce the intensity and selectivity of fishing practices to maintain salmon life history diversity and productivity over the long term.

Acknowledgments

We thank Richard Law and Sue Ratner for helpful discussions of the evolutionary implications of selective fishing and the application of these models. We also thank Jeff Bromaghin, Ryan Nielson, and Danielle Evenson for their insights into the potential genetic effects of fishing on Chinook salmon in the AYK region. We are grateful to Chuck Krueger and two anonymous reviewers for their helpful comments on the manuscript.

References

Allendorf, F. W., P. R. England, G. Luikart, P. A. Ritchie, and N. Ryman. 2008. Genetic effects of harvest on wild animal populations. Trends in Ecology and Evolution 23:327–337.

Barrowman, N. J., and R. A. Myers. 2000. Still more spawner-recruitment curves: the hockey stick and its generalizations. Canadian Journal of Fisheries and Aquatic Sciences 57:665–676.

Barton, N. H., and M. Turelli. 1989. Evolutionary quantitative genetics: how little do we know? Annual Review of Genetics 23:337–370.

Birkeland, C., and P. K. Dayton. 2005. The importance in fishery management of leaving the big ones. Trends in Ecology and Evolution 20:356–358.

Bromaghin, J. F., R. M. Neilson, and J. J. Hard. 2008. An investigation of the effects of selective exploitation on the demography and productivity of Yukon River Chinook salmon. U.S. Fish and Wildlife Service, Alaska Fisheries Technical Report 100, Anchorage, Alaska.

Carlson, S. M., E. Edeline, L. A. Vøllestad, T. O. Haugen, I. J. Winfield, J. M. Fletcher, J. B. James, and N. C. Stenseth. 2007. Four decades of opposing natural and human-induced artificial selection acting on Windermere pike (Esox lucius). Ecology Letters 10:512–521.

Carlson, S. M., and T. R. Seamons. 2008. A review of quantitative genetic components of fitness in salmonids: implications for adaptations to future change. Evolutionary Applications 1:222–238.

Caswell, H. 2001. Matrix population models: construction, analysis, and interpretation, 2nd edition. Sinauer Associates, Sunderland, Massachusetts.

Conover, D. O., and S. B. Munch. 2002. Sustaining fisheries yields over evolutionary time scales. Science 297:94–96.

Edeline, E., S. M. Carlson, L. C. Stige, I. J. Winfield, J. M. Fletcher, J. B. James, T. O. Haugen, L. A. Vøllestad, and N. C. Stenseth. 2007. Trait changes in a harvested population are driven by a dynamic tug-of war between natural and harvest selection. Proceedings of the National Academy of Sciences USA 104:15799–15804.

Evenson, D. F., S. J. Hayes, G. Sandone, and D. J. Bergstrom. 2009. Yukon River Chinook salmon: stock status, harvest, and management. Pages 675–701 in C. C. Krueger and C. E. Zimmerman, editors. Pacific salmon: ecology and management of western Alaska's populations. American Fisheries Society, Symposium 70, Bethesda, Maryland.

Fenberg, P. B., and K. Roy. 2008. Ecological and evolutionary consequences of size-selective harvesting: how much do we know? Molecular Ecology 17:209–220.

Gerrodette, T., P. K. Dayton, S. Macinko, and M. J. Fogarty. 2002. Precautionary management of marine fisheries: moving beyond the burden of proof. Bulletin of Marine Science 70(2):657–668.

Hard, J. J. 2004. Evolution of chinook salmon life history under size-selective harvest. Pages 315–337 in A. Hendry, and S. Stearns, editors. Evolution illuminated: salmon and their relatives. Oxford University Press, New York.

Hard, J. J. In press. Case study of Pacific salmon. U. Dieckmann, O. R. Godø, M. Heino, and J. Mork, editors. Fisheries-induced adaptive change. Cambridge University Press, New York.

Hard, J. J., M. R. Gross, M. Heino, R. Hilborn, R. G. Kope, R. Law, and J. D. Reynolds. 2008. Evolutionary consequences of fishing and their implications for salmon. Evolutionary Applications 1:388–408.

Healey, M. C. 1986. Optimum size and age at maturity in Pacific salmon and effects of size-selective fisheries. Pages 39–52 in D. J. Meerburg, editor. Salmonid age at maturity. Canadian Special Publication in Fisheries and Aquatic Sciences 89.

Healey, M. C., and W. R. Heard. 1984. Inter- and intra-population variation in the fecundity of chinook salmon (Oncorhynchus tshawytscha) and its relevance to life history theory. Canadian Journal of Fisheries and Aquatic Sciences 41:476–483.

Helle, J. H., and M. S. Hoffman. 1995. Size decline and older age at maturity of two chum salmon Oncorhynchus keta stocks in western North America, 1972–92. Pages 245–260 in R. J. Beamish, editor. Climate change and northern fish populations. Canadian Special Publication of Fisheries and Aquatic Sciences 121.

Helle, J. H., and M. S. Hoffman. 1998. Changes in size and age at maturity of two North American stocks of chum salmon (Oncorhynchus keta) before and after a major regime shift in the North Pacific Ocean. North Pacific Anadromous Fisheries Commission Bulletin 1:81–89.

Hutchings, J. A. 2005. Life history consequences of overexploitation to population recovery in Northwest Atlantic cod (Gadus morhua). Canadian Journal of Fisheries and Aquatic Sciences 62:824–832.

Hutchings, J. A., and D. J. Fraser. 2008. The nature of fisheries- and farming-induced evolution. Molecular Ecology 17:294–313.

Hutchings, J. A., and J. D. Reynolds. 2004. Marine fish population collapses: consequences for recovery and extinction risk. Bioscience 54:297–309.

Hyer, K. E., and C. J. Schleusner. 2005. Chinook salmon age, sex, and length analysis from selected escapement projects on the Yukon River. U.S. Fish and Wildlife Service, Alaska Fisheries Technical Report 87, Anchorage, Alaska.

Kareiva, P., M. Marvier, and M. McClure. 2000. Recovery and management options for spring/summer chinook salmon in the Columbia River Basin. Science 290:977–979.

Kirkpatrick, M., T. Johnson, and N. H. Barton. 2002. General models of multilocus evolution. Genetics 161:1727–1750.

Kuparinen, A., and J. Merilä. 2007. Detecting and managing fisheries-induced evolution. Trends in Ecology and Evolution 22:652–659.

Lande, R. 1979. Quantitative genetic analysis of multivariate evolution, applied to brain:body size allometry. Evolution 33:402–416.

Larkin, P. A. 1978. Fisheries management-an essay for ecologists. Annual Review of Ecology and Systematics 9:57–73.

Larkin, P. A. 1981. A perspective on population genetics and salmon management. Canadian Journal of Fisheries and Aquatic Sciences 38:1469–1475.

Law, R. 1991. On the quantitative genetics of correlated characters under directional selection in age-structured populations. Philosophical Transactions of the Royal Society of London B 331:213–223.

Law, R. 2000. Fishing, selection, and phenotypic evolution. ICES Journal of Marine Science 57:659–669.

Law, R. 2007. Fisheries-induced evolution: present status and future directions. Marine Ecology Progress Series 335:271–277.

Leslie, P. H. 1945. On the use of matrices in certain population mathematics. Biometrika 33:183–212.

McElhany, P., M. H. Ruckelshaus, M. J. Ford, T. C. Wainwright, and E. P. Bjorkstedt. 2000. Viable salmonid populations and the recovery of evolutionarily significant units. U.S. Department of Commerce, NOAA Technical Memorandum NMFS-NWFSC-42.

Munch, S. B., M. R. Walsh, and D. O. Conover. 2005. Harvest selection, genetic correlations, and evolutionary changes in recruitment: one less thing to worry about? Canadian Journal of Fisheries and Aquatic Sciences 62:802–810.

Nelson, K., and M. Soulé. 1987. Genetical conservation of exploited fishes. Pages 345–368 in N. Ryman, and F. Utter, editors. Population genetics & fishery management. University of Washington Press, Seattle, Washington.

Olsen, E., G. Lilly, M. Heino, M. Morgan, J. Brattey, and U. Dieckmann. 2005. Assessing changes in age and size at maturation in collapsing populations of Atlantic cod (Gadus morhua). Canadian Journal of Fisheries and Aquatic Sciences 62:811–823.

Olsen, E. M., M. Heino, G. R. Lilly, M. J. Morgan, J.

Brattey, B. Ernande, and U. Dieckmann. 2004. Maturation trends indicative of rapid evolution preceded the collapse of northern cod. Nature (London) 428:932–935.

Policansky, D. 1993a. Evolution and management of exploited fish populations. Pages 651–664 *in* G. Kruse, D. M. Eggers, R. J. Marasco, C. Pautzke, and T. J. Quinn, editors. Management strategies for exploited fish populations. Alaska Sea Grant College Program Report No. 93-02. University of Alaska, Fairbanks, Alaska.

Policansky, D. 1993b. Fishing as a cause of evolution in fishes. Pages 2–18 *in* T. K. Stokes, J. M. McGlade, and R. Law, editors. The exploitation of evolving resources, volume 99. Springer-Verlag, Berlin.

Ratner, S., R. Lande, and B. B. Roper. 1997. Population viability analysis of spring chinook salmon in the south Umpqua River, Oregon. Conservation Biology 11:879–889.

Ricker, W. E. 1976. Review of the rate of growth and mortality of Pacific salmon in salt water, and non-catch mortality caused by fishing. Journal of the Fisheries Research Board of Canada 33:1483–1524.

Ricker, W. E. 1981. Changes in the average size and average age of Pacific salmon. Canadian Journal of Fisheries and Aquatic Sciences 38:1636–1656.

Ricker, W. E. 1995. Trends in the average size of Pacific salmon in Canadian catches. Pages 593–602 *in* R. J. Beamish, editor. Climate change and northern fish populations, volume 121. Canadian Special Publication in Fisheries and Aquatic Sciences 121.

Riddell, B. E. 1986. Assessment of selective fishing on the age at maturity in Atlantic salmon (*Salmo salar*): a genetic perspective. Pages 102–109 *in* D. J. Meerburg, editor. Salmonid age at maturity. Canadian Special Publication in Fisheries and Aquatic Sciences 89.

Swain, D. P., A. F. Sinclair, and J. M. Hanson. 2007. Evolutionary response to size-selective mortality in an exploited fish population. Proceedings of the Royal Society of London Series B 274:1015–1022.

Vania, T., V. Golembeski, B. M. Borba, T. L. Lingau, J. S. Hayes, K. R. Boek, and W. H. Bushner. 2002. Annual Management Report Yukon and Northern Areas 2000. Alaska Department of fish and Game, Division of Commercial Fisheries, Regional Information Report No. 3A02–29, Anchorage, Alaska.

Vaughan, E. 1947. Time of appearance of pink salmon runs in southeastern Alaska. Copeia 1947:40–50.

Walsh, M. R., S. B. Munch, S. Chiba, and D. O. Conover. 2006. Maladaptive changes in multiple traits caused by fishing: impediments to population recovery. Ecology Letters 9:142–148.

Zabel, R. W., M. D. Scheurell, M. M. McClure, and J. G. Williams. 2006. The interplay between climate variability and density dependence in the population viability of chinook salmon. Conservation Biology 20:190–200.

American Fisheries Society Symposium 70:781–795, 2009

Genetic Health and Variables Influencing the Effective Number of Breeders in Western Alaska Chinook Salmon

Jeffrey B. Olsen* **and Steve J. Miller**[1]
Conservation Genetics Laboratory, U.S. Fish and Wildlife Service
1011 East Tudor Road, Anchorage, Alaska 99503, USA

Ken Harper
Kenai Fish and Wildlife Field Office, U.S. Fish and Wildlife Service
P.O. Box 1670, Kenai, Alaska 99611, USA

John K. Wenburg
Conservation Genetics Laboratory, U.S. Fish and Wildlife Service
1011 East Tudor Road, Anchorage, Alaska 99503, USA

Abstract.—In this study, we used genetic and demographic data to estimate and evaluate an indicator of genetic health, the effective number of breeders per year (N_b), in Chinook salmon *Oncorhynchus tshawytscha* populations from western Alaska. Many of these populations show male-biased (70%–85%) sex ratios. Four such populations were examined: two from the Gisasa and Tozitna Rivers in the Yukon River drainage and two from the Tuluksak and Kwethluk Rivers in the Kuskokwim River drainage. Our objectives were to: 1) evaluate the genetic health of each population, and 2) infer the influence of annual fluctuations in census size, male-biased sex ratio, and variance in family size on N_b. Four genetic estimates of N_b were computed for each population to account for possible bias when using low frequency alleles. The lowest N_b estimates ranged from 225 (Tozitna River) to 4,859 fish (Kwethluk River) and were not indicative of a high risk of long-term loss of genetic diversity. Demographic and genetic estimates of the ratio N_b/N, where N is census size, suggested the observed sex ratio bias is unlikely to adversely impact genetic diversity at current population sizes. Variation in family size within each population likely had the largest affect on N_b over the time period examined. However, the time period was relatively short (3–14 years) and the estimates of N_b, could decline if populations show large future fluctuations, including significant decreases, in census size.

*Corresponding author: jeffrey_olsen@fws.gov
[1]Current address: Kenai Fish and Wildlife Field Office, USFWS, P.O. Box 346, Bethel, Alaska 99559, USA

Introduction

Evaluating the health of exploited Pacific salmon *Oncorhynchus* spp. populations that spawn in remote areas is challenging because population-specific census data are sparse or nonexistent. Chinook salmon *O. tshawytscha* in western Alaska are a prime example. This species is the target of multiple mixed-stock fisheries, but adults spawn mostly in remote habitat in tributaries of the Yukon and Kuskokwim Rivers and Norton Sound (ADFG 2004). Recent and unexplained declines in abundance have led to severe restrictions or curtailment of the fisheries, and have heightened interest in evaluating genetic health and variables that may influence it (AYK SSI 2006; Evenson et al. 2009, this volume; Linderman and Bergstrom 2009, this volume). One important variable in this regard is the effective population size (N_e). The effective population size per generation is an indicator of genetic health because it represents the number of breeding adults in an "idealized population" that would lose genetic diversity at the rate observed in the actual population (Wright 1931). This idealized population is assumed to have certain demographic characteristics including a constant size over generations, a sex ratio of 1:1, and variation in family size that is random (follows a Poisson distribution). Violations of these assumptions typically result in a reduction of N_e relative to the census size (N).

In a review of N_e and N in 102 species, Frankham (1995) found that the ratio N_e/N was, on average, about 0.11 and fluctuating population size had the greatest relative influence on N_e in most species. Variance in family size and sex ratio also contributed to the decline in N_e but to a lesser degree. Waples (2002) confirmed that annual fluctuations in population census size can have a large influence on N_e in Pacific salmon. Nevertheless, the influence of the other factors may be as large or larger (e.g., Ardren and Kapuscinski 2003; Shrimpton and Heath 2003). Various studies have shown that Pacific salmon populations can show large (not a Poisson distribution) variation in family size (Geiger et al. 1997; Hedrick et al. 2000; Seamons et al. 2004) and significant sex ratio distortion (e.g., Holtby and Healey 1990; Olsen et al. 2006). With respect to western Alaska Chinook salmon, limited census (escapement) data from weirs, operated intermittently since 1991, have revealed four-fold changes in annual population size, significantly (70–85%) male-biased sex ratios, and in one river, as few as 160 adult females (Wiswar 2001; Gates and Harper 2003). Estimates of the variance in family size are difficult to obtain in wild salmon, and therefore are not available for these populations.

Both demographic and genetic data can be used to estimate N_e. Demographic data (census size, sex ratio, variance in family size) provide a direct estimate of N_e based on the concepts and analytical methods developed by Wright (1931, 1938). Multiple estimates of N_e can be derived from demographic data, accounting for the effects of each of the three factors. Demographic data, however, are often limited in many populations. When data are limited, genetic data can be combined with demographic data to provide insight into the relative influence of the demographic variables affecting N_e (e.g., Ardren and Kapuscinski 2003; Shrimpton and Heath 2003). Genetic data from neutral genetic markers are relatively easy to acquire and provide a single indirect estimate of N_e. This comprehensive estimate reflects all demographic variables and is frequently derived using the temporal method that assumes genetic diversity in a closed finite population decreases over time in inverse proportion to N_e (Caballero 1994). The temporal method for estimating N_e in Pacific salmon is based on the analytical and simulation work of Waples (1990a, 1990b) and Tajima (1992). Waples (1990a, 1990b) showed that annual changes in allele frequencies in Pacific salmon provide an estimate of the effective number of breeders per year (N_b) and N_e is approximately equal to gN_b where g is the mean generation length.

In this study, the authors used both genetic and demographic data to estimate and evaluate N_b in four Chinook salmon populations from western Alaska. The study objectives were to: 1) evaluate the genetic health of each population, and 2) infer the relative influence of the fluctuating population size, male-biased sex ratio and variance in family size on N_b.

Methods

Sample collection, preparation, and genotyping.—Between 2001 and 2003, fin tissue samples were collected from adult Chinook salmon at weirs on the Gisasa and Tozitna Rivers, tributaries of the lower Yukon River, and the Kwethluk and Tuluksak Rivers, tributaries of the lower Kuskokwim River (Figure 1). In 1990 and 2003, respectively, heart and fin tissue samples were collected from juvenile Chinook salmon (Kwethluk River only) using minnow traps. Fin tissue was stored in 2 mL vials and preserved in 100% ethanol. Heart tissue was stored in 2 mL vials and frozen at –70°F. Age-at-return data for each individual was used to stratify adult samples into three consecutive cohorts (individuals of the same age) for computing genetic estimates of N_b (Table 1). Adult age was determined from scale samples analyzed by the Alaska Department of Fish and Game as described by Gates and Harper (2003) and references therein. Only cohorts having a minimum sample size of 50 fish were used (Waples 1990b). The total population sample size censused at the weir ranged from 219 (Tuluksak River) to 516 fish (Kwethluk River). Two to nine years of census data from each weir were available for computing demographic estimates of N_b (Table 2).

Ten microsatellite loci were used to genotype both adult and juvenile samples (*Oke2* and *Oke4*, Buchholz et al. 2001; *Ots3.1*, Banks et al. 1999; *Oki10* and *Oki11*, Smith et al. 1998; *Ots311*, *OtsG3*, *OtsG253b*, *OtsG432*, and *OtsG474*, Williamson et al. 2002). The laboratory methods are described by Flannery et al. (2006). The multi-locus microsatellite genotypes were stored in an Excel (Microsoft) spreadsheet for data analysis. Genotypes and allele frequency data for each locus and cohort are available upon request from the authors.

Genetic diversity within populations.—Estimates of allele frequency, allelic richness (A_r), and observed and expected heterozygosity (H_o, H_e) were computed for each cohort sample. A randomization test was used to test for conformity to Hardy-Weinberg equilibrium for each cohort sample and to test for genotypic equilibrium among all locus pairs across all cohort samples. A G-test of genotypic frequency homogeneity was conducted using permutation to test for genetic differentiation among cohorts within populations. These analyses were performed using the computer program FSTAT version 2.9.3 (Goudet 2001).

Genetic estimates of N_{bi} and N_b.—The computer program SalmonNb (Waples et al. 2007) was used to generate genetic estimates of N_b. SalmonN_b uses the temporal method and assumes a Pacific salmon life history. The genetic data from at least three cohorts were used to estimate the number of effective breeders in year i (N_{bi}) in each population and N_b. Here, N_b is the harmonic mean ($\tilde{N}_b$) of all pairwise estimates of N_b from each cohort pair. Because low frequency alleles may upwardly bias estimates of N_b (e.g., Anderson 2005), the authors first used all alleles and then selected the program's option to compute three additional estimates by excluding alleles with frequencies less than 0.01, 0.02, and 0.05. Genetic estimates of N_{bi} and N_b were denot-

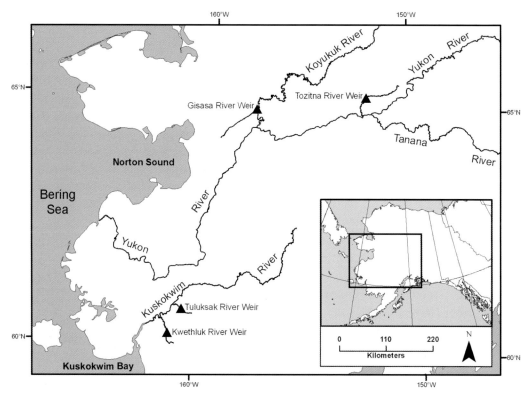

FIGURE 1. Map of western Alaska showing the Kwethluk, Tuluksak, Gisasa, and Tozitna rivers.

ed with a hat (ˆ) and given the subscript G ($\widehat{N}_{bi(G)}$, $\widehat{N}_{b(G)}$).

$N_{b(G)}$ was computed twice for the Kwethluk River population; once using three cohorts (1996–98) and once using five cohorts (1989, 1996–98, 2002). The former allows for inter-population comparison (three-year period for each population) whereas the latter provides intra-population comparison (three-year versus fourteen-year period for Kwethluk River).

Demographic estimates of N_{bi} and N_b.— Census data (annual escapement) from weirs on each river were used to estimate N_{bi} according to the formula

$$\widehat{N}_{bi(SR)} = \frac{4(N_{fi}N_{mi})}{(N_{fi} + N_{mi})}, \tag{1}$$

described by Wright (1931) where $\widehat{N}_{bi(SR)}$ is substituted for N_e, the subscript SR denotes

sex ratio, and N_{fi} and N_{mi} are the number of females and males in year i. This formula assumes that variance in family size follows a Poisson distribution and does not differ between gender.

Two demographic estimates of N_b were computed. The first estimate was computed using the formula

$$\widehat{N}_{b(FPS)} = \tilde{N}_i, \tag{2}$$

where $\tilde{N}_i$ is the harmonic mean of N_i (the total population size in year i) values, and the subscript FPS denotes fluctuating population size. The second estimate adds the sex ratio data and was computed using the formula

$$\widehat{N}_{b(SR)} = (\tilde{N}_{bi(SR)}), \tag{3}$$

where $(\tilde{N}_{bi(SR)})$ is the harmonic mean of $\widehat{N}_{b(SR)}$ values.

TABLE 1. Genetic diversity in Chinook salmon samples from the Yukon and KuskokwimRivers. Abbreviations are: life history stage (LS), adult (A), juvenile (J), sample size (n), allelic richness per locus ($\overline{A}_r$), expected heterozygosity per locus ($\overline{H}_e$), observed heterozygosity per locus ($\overline{H}_o$), index of heterozygote deficit (f). An asterisk (*) denotes the sample did not conform to HWE expectation at the $\alpha = 0.05$ level but did conform when the $\alpha = 0.05$ was adjusted for 14 simultaneous tests.

Drainage/Pop	LS	Sample Year	Cohort	n	$\overline{A}_r$	$\overline{H}_e$	$\overline{H}_o$	f
Yukon R.								
Gisasa R.	A	2001	1995	124	10.3	0.68	0.66	0.023
			1996	72	10.6	0.69	0.68	0.013
			1997	56	10.9	0.68	0.67	0.019
Tozitna R.	A	2002/03	1997	123	9.9	0.69	0.66	0.028*
			1998	190	9.9	0.68	0.67	0.006
			1999	54	9.6	0.68	0.64	0.041*
Kuskokwim R.								
Tuluksak R.	A	2002/03	1996	55	11.1	0.68	0.68	−0.005
			1997	83	11.2	0.69	0.70	−0.015
			1998	81	11.0	0.70	0.69	0.005
Kwethluk R.	J	1990	1989	96	11.1	0.69	0.67	0.023
	A	2002	1996	69	11.4	0.70	0.70	0.000
			1997	116	11.3	0.70	0.70	−0.003
			1998	155	11.2	0.68	0.68	−0.003
	J	2003	2002	80	11.8	0.70	0.70	−0.006
		Avg			10.8	0.70	0.70	

Due to the intermittent nature of the weir samples, the values of $\widehat{N}_{b(FPS)}$ and $\widehat{N}_{b(SR)}$ were computed for two to nine years depending upon the population. Two time periods (1995–1997, 1995–2003) were examined for the Gisasa River population so that a direct comparison could be made with the genetic estimates of $\widehat{N}_{bi(G)}$, and $\widehat{N}_{b(G)}$ from the 1995–1997 cohorts.

Estimates of N_{bi}/N_i and $N_b/\overline{N}$.—Estimates of the ratio N_{bi}/N_i were computed using the $\widehat{N}_{b(SR)}$ and $\widehat{N}_{bi(G)}$ values to evaluate the influence of sex ratio and variance in family size on the effective number of breeders in year i. Three versions of the ratio $N_b/\overline{N}_i$ were com-

puted ($\widehat{N}_{b(FPS)}/\overline{N}_i$, $\widehat{N}_{b(SR)}/\overline{N}_i$, $\widehat{N}_{b(G)}/\overline{N}_i$) to evaluate the decline in the effective number of breeders per year relative to $\overline{N}_i$ (the arithmetic mean annual escapement). These three versions of the ratio represent, in order, the cumulative effect of fluctuating population size, fluctuating population size plus sex ratio, and fluctuating population size plus sex ratio plus variance in family size on N_b. The ratio $\widehat{N}_{bi(G)}/\overline{N}_i$ was only computed for the Gisasa River 1995–1997 and Kwethluk River 2002 cohorts because the estimates of $\widehat{N}_{bi(G)}$ for the other populations did not align temporally with the available census data (see Waples 2005). An estimate of $\widehat{N}_{b(G)}/\overline{N}_i$ was only computed for the Gisasa River.

Olsen et al.

TABLE 2. Estimates of N_{bi} (the effective breeders in year i) from sex ratio ($\widehat{N}_{bi(SR)}$) and genetic ($\widehat{N}_{bi(G)}$) data. Estimates of $\widehat{N}_{bi(G)}$ were computed using all alleles (1), and then excluding alleles with frequencies less than 0.01 (2), 0.02 (3), and 0.05 (4). Two values of $\widehat{N}_{bi(G)}/N_i$ were computed using the smallest and largest estimates of $\widehat{N}_{bi(G)}$. Negative estimates of $\widehat{N}_{bi(G)}$ are denoted with (-). N_i is the total number of adults and N_{mi}, N_{fi} are the total number of males and females, respectively.

Drainage Pop/year	N_i	N_{mi}	N_{fi}	$\widehat{N}_{bi(SR)}$	$\widehat{N}_{bi(SR)}/N_i$	$\widehat{N}_{bi(G)}$				$\widehat{N}_{bi(G)}/N_i$
						1	2	3	4	
Yukon R.										
Gisasa R.										
1995	4023	2174	1849	3997	0.99	1944	1555	380	209	0.05 / 0.48
1996	1952	1571	381	1226	0.63	704	432	5143	200	0.10 / 2.63
1997	3764	2888	876	2689	0.71	1190	402	780	440	0.11 / 0.32
1998	2356	1954	402	1334	0.57					
1999	2631	1876	755	2153	0.82					
2000	2089	1455	634	1766	0.85					
2001	3052	1539	1513	3052	>0.99					
2002	1931	1521	410	1292	0.67					
2003	1852	1158	694	1736	0.94					
Tozitna R.										
1997						424	330	417	352	
1998						(-)	(-)	(-)	(-)	
1999						234	137	114	89	
2002	1596	1392	204	712	0.45					
2003	1819	1492	327	1073	0.59					

TABLE 2. Continued.

Drainage Pop/year	N_i	N_{mi}	N_{fi}	$\hat{N}_{bi(SR)}$	$\hat{N}_{bi(SR)}/N_i$	$\hat{N}_{bi(G)}$ 1	2	3	4	$\hat{N}_{bi(G)}/N_i$
Kuskokwim R.										
Tuluksak R.										
1991	697	496	201	572	0.82					
1992	1083	923	160	545	0.50					
1993	2218	1911	307	1058	0.48					
1994	2917	2226	691	2109	0.72					
1996						349	347	12255	(-)	
1997						(-)	(-)	(-)	1138	
1998						288	249	258	4348	
2002	1346	1028	318	971	0.72					
2003	1064	776	288	840	0.79					
Kwethluk R.										
1989						554	407	446	330	
1992	9675	7275	2400	7219	0.75					
1996						(-)	(-)	(-)	(-)	
1997						1373	1448	2914	3096	
1998						(-)	(-)	(-)	(-)	
2000	3461	2695	766	2386	0.69					
2002	8395	6644	1751	5543	0.66					
2003	14474	11695	2779	8982	0.62	636	2500	11423	1488	0.08 / 1.36

Demographic estimates of N_{bi} and N_b

The estimates of N_{bi} from the sex ratio data ($\widehat{N}_{b(SR)}$) ranged from 545 (Tuluksak River 1992) to 8,982 fish (Kwethluk River 2003) (Table 2). The estimates of N_b that reflect fluctuating population size ($\widehat{N}_{b(FPS)}$) and fluctuating population size plus sex ratio ($\widehat{N}_{b(SR)}$) were both lowest in the Tuluksak River (13 year span) and highest in the Kwethluk River (12 year span) (Table 3). For the Gisasa River, the three-year estimate was greater than the nine-year estimate for both $\widehat{N}_{b(FPS)}$ (2,922 fish and 2,436 fish) and $\widehat{N}_{b(SR)}$ (2,086 fish and 1,838 fish).

Estimates of N_{bi}/N_i and $N_b/\overline{N}$

The ratio $\widehat{N}_{bi(SR)}/N_i$ ranged from 0.45 (Tozitna River 2002) to >0.99 (Gisasa River 2001) and averaged 0.71 overall years and populations (Table 2). Two values of the ratio $\widehat{N}_{bi(G)}/N_i$ were computed for the Gisasa River 1995–1997 and the Kwethluk River 2002 cohorts using the smallest and largest estimates of $\widehat{N}_{bi(G)}$ for each year (Table 2). The low values ranged from 0.05 (Gisasa River 1995) to 0.11 (Gisasa River 1997). The high values ranged from 0.32 (Gisasa River 1997) to 2.63 (Gisasa River 1996). The ratio $\widehat{N}_{b(FPS)}/\overline{N}_i$, that reflects fluctuating population size ranged from 0.77 (Kwethluk River) to >0.99 (Tozitna River) and averaged 0.88 (Table 4). When both fluctuating population size and sex ratio were considered ($\widehat{N}_{b(SR)}/\overline{N}_i$), the values declined, ranging from 0.50 (Tozitna River) to 0.70 (Gisasa River) and averaged 0.58. The ratio $\widehat{N}_{b(G)}/\overline{N}_i$, which accounts for fluctuating population size, sex ratio, and variance in family size, was only computed for the Gisasa River and ranged from 0.08 to 0.33 (Table 4). The ratio $\widehat{N}_{b(SR)}/\widehat{N}_{b(FPS)}$, which isolates the influence of sex ratio on N_b, ranged from 0.50 (Tozitna River) to 0.75 (Gisasa River). The ratio $\widehat{N}_{b(G)}/\widehat{N}_{b(SR)}$, which reflects the proportional decline in N_b due to variance in family size, was only computed for the Gisasa River and ranged from 0.12 to 0.52 (Table 4).

Discussion

Genetic health of western Alaska Chinook salmon

The first study objective was to evaluate the genetic health of each population. Conservation guidelines have been established from theoretical studies that suggest isolated populations with an effective size per generation (N_e) below 500 are at risk of significant long-term loss of genetic diversity (Lande and Barrowclough 1987; Waples 1990a; Allendorf et al. 1997). We used a salmon life history model and derived four estimates of $\widehat{N}_{b(G)}$ for each population by adjusting the threshold for excluding low frequency alleles. Even the lowest estimates of $\widehat{N}_{b(G)}$ translated into estimates of N_e that were well above the threshold of 500. Considering the fact that these populations are not likely isolated, the results did not indicate a high risk of loss of genetic diversity (Wainwright and Waples 1998). However, estimates of N_b (and N_e) often decline as the time period between samples increases because fluctuations in census size are more likely to increase with time (Vucetich et al. 1997). We only examined a three-year period for three of the four populations in this study and it is possible that the estimates of $\widehat{N}_{b(G)}$ for these populations could decline if a longer time period were examined.

Our estimates of N_e (>1,100 fish) appear to be larger than those of Shrimpton and Heath (2003) for five upper Fraser River Chinook salmon populations (<700 fish) with mean annual adult returns and generation times similar to the populations in this study. This difference between west-

TABLE 4. Estimates of the ratio N_b/N. Demographic estimates of N_b (the effective breeders per year) reflect fluctuating population size ($\widehat{N}_{b(FPS)}$), and fluctuating population size plus sex ratio ($\widehat{N}_{b(SR)}$). Two values of $\widehat{N}_{b(G)}/\overline{N}$ and $\widehat{N}_{b(G)}/\widehat{N}_{b(SR)}$ were computed using the largest and smallest estimates of $\widehat{N}_{b(G)}$ (Table 3).

Drainage/ Pop/years	Demographic			Genetic	
	$\dfrac{\widehat{N}_{b(FPS)}}{\overline{N}}$	$\dfrac{\widehat{N}_{b(SR)}}{\overline{N}}$	$\dfrac{\widehat{N}_{b(SR)}}{\widehat{N}_{b(FPS)}}$	$\dfrac{\widehat{N}_{b(G)}}{\overline{N}}$	$\dfrac{\widehat{N}_{b(G)}}{\widehat{N}_{b(SR)}}$
Yukon R.					
Gisasa R.					
95–97	0.90	0.64	0.71	0.08 / 0.33	0.12 / 0.52
95–03	0.93	0.70	0.75		
Tozitna R.					
97–99					
02–03	>0.99	0.50	0.50		
Kuskokwim R.					
Tuluksak R.					
96–98					
91–94/02–03	0.80	0.53	0.67		
Kwethluk R.					
89/96–98/02					
92/00/02–03	0.77	0.52	0.68		

ern Alaska and upper Fraser River Chinook salmon populations may be explained by at least two factors: 1) availability of spawning habitat, and 2) the study period. First, Shrimpton and Heath (2003) showed a positive correlation between available spawning habitat and N_e, and they suggest access to appropriate spawning sites is limiting N_e even as the census size increases. In contrast, no evidence exists that spawning habitat is limiting abundance of the western Alaska Chinook salmon populations in this study (ADFG 2004). Nevertheless, more effort is needed to better document spawning habitat and evaluate its relationship to Chi-

nook salmon abundance in western Alaska. Second, Shrimpton and Heath (2003) also examined a longer time period (5–20 years), which, as mentioned above, may result in lower N_e due to fluctuating population size and the increased likelihood of capturing a period of very low abundance. Shrimpton and Heath (2003) suggest that evidence of population bottlenecks in the 1980s may explain the low N_e estimates of some upper Fraser River Chinook salmon populations. Census data were limited for western Alaska Chinook salmon; however, no evidence exists that these populations have recently experienced a bottleneck.

Factors influencing N_b in western Alaska Chinook salmon

The second study objective was to infer the relative influence of fluctuating population size, male-biased sex ratio and variance in family size on N_b. The demographic data indicated that fluctuating population size had relatively little influence on N_b as indicated by the ratio $\widehat{N}_{b(FPS)}/\overline{N}$ which was no lower than 0.77 (Kwethluk River). However, some differences among the populations are worth noting. For example, the Kwethluk River population showed the lowest $\widehat{N}_{b(FPS)}/\overline{N}$ value due to large differences in escapement in 2000 and 2003 (Table 2). The other population for which escapement data exists for the same two years (Gisasa River) showed little difference. In fact, the value of $\widehat{N}_{b(FPS)}/\overline{N}$ for the Gisasa River population (1995–2003) was relatively high despite having the longest (nine years) data set. These results suggested that variations in population size may be largely population specific, at least for short time periods. Indeed, Shrimpton and Heath (2003) reported estimates of $\widehat{N}_h/\overline{N}$ (analogous to our $\widehat{N}_{b(FPS)}/\overline{N}$) ranging from 0.31 to 0.86 over a 20-year period in five populations of Chinook salmon from the upper Fraser River. Finally, N_e estimates that account for variation in recruitment among cohorts are often smaller than estimates based on the harmonic mean of N (Waples 2002). Recruitment data were not available for these populations.

The estimates of $\widehat{N}_{b(SR)}/\widehat{N}_{b(FPS)}$ depict the proportional decline in N_b due to unbalanced sex ratio. These values were smaller than the corresponding estimates of $\widehat{N}_{b(FPS)}/\overline{N}$, indicating that the male-biased sex ratio affected N_b to a much greater degree than fluctuating population size, at least for the time period examined here. Nevertheless, the influence of sex ratio, like fluctuating population size, appeared to vary substantially depending upon the year and population examined. For exam-

ple, estimates of the single year ratio $\widehat{N}_{bi(SR)}/N_i$ from the Gisasa River population ranged from 0.57 to >0.99 over nine years. The estimates of $\widehat{N}_{bi(SR)}/N_i$ for each population in 2003 ranged from 0.59 to 0.94 (Table 2). This variation both within and among populations suggests that in the short-term the impact of sex ratio on N_b, while typically greater than fluctuating population size, is ephemeral.

Without actual data on variance in family size, we inferred the influence of this variable on N_b by computing the ratio $\widehat{N}_{b(G)}/\widehat{N}_{b(SR)}$ to represent the proportional decline in N_b due to variance in family size. Because this ratio requires genetic and demographic data for the same cohort, it was only possible to estimate for the Gisasa River population. Nevertheless, the largest estimate (0.52) was less than both $\widehat{N}_{b(FPS)}/\overline{N}$ (0.90) and $\widehat{N}_{b(SR)}/\widehat{N}_{b(FPS)}$ (0.71), suggesting variance in family size has a greater influence on N_b than fluctuating population size and sex ratio for this time period. It is also worth noting that the estimates of $\widehat{N}_{bi(G)}/N_i$ for each Gisasa River cohort were generally less than half of the estimates of $\widehat{N}_{bi(SR)}/N_i$, suggesting that variance in family size has a greater influence annually on N_{bi} than sex ratio. Collectively, these results are consistent with studies of reproductive success in Pacific salmon. For example, Geiger et al. (1997) estimated that variance in family size alone could cause the ratio N_e/N to decline below 0.40 in pink salmon (*O. gorbuscha*). The magnitude of the decline varied among pink salmon cohorts and, based on a regression model, ranged from less than 0.40 to greater than 0.60 (Geiger et al. 1997). Thus, variance in family size will vary but will likely have as great, if not greater, influence on N_b than sex ratio. It is also possible that variance in family size differs between males and females (e.g., Hedrick et al. 2000), however evaluating reproductive success in the wild is difficult and no reliable estimates exist.

Implications for management and conservation

In summary, three conclusions can be drawn from the results that are relevant to management and conservation of these populations. First, the genetic estimates of N_b do not suggest these populations are at risk of significant loss of genetic diversity. Current escapement levels appear to be adequate for retaining genetic variation. However, the time period examined was relatively short (3–14 years) and the estimates of N_b could decline if populations show future fluctuations, including significant decreases, in census size. The results suggested that the extent of these census size fluctuations, and consequently their affect on genetic health, could vary significantly among populations. Second, the fact that the two Yukon River populations (Gisasa and Tozitna rivers) showed lower heterozygosity and genetic estimates of N_b suggested these two populations may be more sensitive (than the two Kuskokwim River populations) to fluctuations in census size, sex ratio distortion, and variance in family size. In a broader sense, the vulnerability to loss of genetic diversity may vary regionally and generally be greater in tributaries of the lower Yukon River than the lower Kuskokwim River. Finally, the observed male-biased sex ratio is not likely to adversely impact the genetic diversity at the current annual census size. Rather, the combination of demographic and genetic data suggested variation in family size has the largest affect on N_b over relatively short time periods (<20 years). It must be emphasized, however, that we were only able to evaluate variance in family size for the Gisasa River. Further analysis of the other populations is needed to fully assess this conclusion.

Acknowledgments

Funding for this study was provided by the Arctic Yukon Kuskokwim Sustainable Salmon Initiative through project number 45240. This study benefited from tissue samples collected for projects funded by the Federal Office of Subsistence Management (OSM) Federal Subsistence Fisheries Resource Monitoring Program. Bob Karlen of the Bureau of Land Management, Fairbanks District Office, and Jeff Adams of the USFWS, Fairbanks Field Office organized sample collections from the Yukon River tributaries. Ora Schlei, Eric Kretschmer, and Lynsey Luiten of the USFWS Conservation Genetics Laboratory conducted the laboratory analysis. The findings and conclusions in this article are those of the authors and do not necessarily represent those of the U.S. Fish and Wildlife Service.

References

ADFG (Alaska Department of Fish and Game). 2004. Escapement goal review of select AYK region salmon stocks. Regional Information Report Number 3A04–01. Available: http://www.cf.adfg.state.ak.us/region3/pubs/pubshom3.php?a=y (December 2008).

Allendorf, F. W., D. Bayles, D. L. Bottom, K. P. Currens, C. A. Frissell, D. Hankin, J. A. Lichatowich, W. Nehlsen, P. Trotter, and T. H. Williams. 1997. Prioritizing Pacific salmon stocks for conservation. Conservation Biology 11:140–152.

Anderson, E. C. 2005. An efficient Monte Carlo method for estimating Ne from temporally spaced samples using a coalescent-based likelihood. Genetics 170:955–967.

Ardren, W. R., and A. R. Kapuscinski. 2003. Demographic and genetic estimates of effective population size (Ne) reveals genetic compensation in steelhead trout. Molecular Ecology 12:35–49.

AYK SSI (Arctic-Yukon-Kuskokwim sustainable salmon initiative). 2006. Arctic-Yukon-Kuskokwim salmon research and restoration plan. Bering Sea Fisherman's Association, Anchorage, Alaska. Available: (http://www.aykssi.org/Documents/RRP.pdf (December 2008).

Banks, M. A., M. S. Blouin, B. A. Baldwin, V. K. Rashbrook, H. A. Fitzgerald, S. M. Blankenship, and D. Hedgecock. 1999. Isolation and inheritance of novel microsatellites in Chinook salmon (*Oncorhynchus tshawytscha*). Journal of Heredity 90:281–288.

Buchholz, W. G., S. J. Miller, and W. J. Spearman. 2001. Isolation and characterization of chum salmon microsatellite loci and use across species. Animal Genetics 32:162–165.

Caballero, A. 1994. Developments in the prediction of effective population size. Heredity 73:657–679.

Evenson, D. F., S. J. Hayes, G. Sandone, and D. J. Bergstrom. 2009. Yukon River Chinook salmon: stock status, harvest, and management. Pages 675–701 *in* C. C. Krueger and C. E. Zimmerman, editors. Pacific salmon: ecology and management of western Alaska's populations. American Fisheries Society, Symposium 70, Bethesda, Maryland.

Flannery, B., T. Beacham, M. Wetklo, C. Smith, B. Templin, A. Antonovich, L. Seeb, S. Miller, O. Schlei, and J. Wenburg. 2006. Run timing, migratory patterns, and harvest information of Chinook salmon stocks within the Yukon River. U.S. Fish and Wildlife Service, Conservation Genetics Laboratory, Alaska Fisheries Technical Report Number 92, Anchorage. Available: http://alaska. fws.gov/fisheries/genetics/reports.htm (December 2008).

Frankham, R. 1995. Effective population size/adult population ratios in wildlife: a review. Genetical Research 66:95–107.

Gates, K. S., and K. C. Harper. 2003. Abundance and run timing of adult Pacific salmon in the Tuluksak River, Yukon Delta National Wildlife Refuge, Alaska, 2002. U.S. Fish and Wildlife Service, Kenai Fisheries Resource Office, Alaska Fisheries Data Series Number 2003–1. Available: http:// alaska.fws.gov/fisheries/fieldoffice/kenai/reports. htm (December 2008).

Geiger, H. J., W. W. Z. L. A. Smoker, and A. J. Gharrett. 1997. Variability in family size and marine survival in pink salmon (*Oncorhynchus gorbuscha*) has implications for conservation biology and human use. Canadian Journal of Fisheries and Aquatic Sciences 54:2684–2690.

Goudet J. 2001. FSTAT, a program to estimate and test gene diversities and fixation indices, version 2.9.3. Available: http://www2.unil.ch/popgen/softwares/ (December 2008).

Hedrick, P. W., V. K. Rashbrook, and D. Hedgecock. 2000. Effective population size of winter-run Chinook salmon based on microsatellite analysis of returning spawners. Canadian Journal of Fisheries and Aquatic Sciences 57:2368–2373.

Holtby, B. L., and M. C. Healey. 1990. Sex-specific life history tactics and risk-taking in coho salmon. Ecology 7:678–690.

Kalinowski, S. T., and R. S. Waples. 2002. Relationship of effective to census size in fluctuating populations. Conservation Biology 16:129–136.

Lande, R., and G. F. Barrowclough. 1987. Effective population size, genetic variation, and their use in population management. Pages 87–123 *in* M. E. Soulé, editor. Viable populations for conservation. Cambridge University Press, New York.

Linderman, J. C., Jr., and D. J. Bergstrom. 2009. Kuskokwim management area: salmon escapement, harvest, and management. Pages 541–599 *in* C. C. Krueger and C. E. Zimmerman, editors. Pacific salmon: ecology and management of western Alaska's populations. American Fisheries Society, Symposium 70, Bethesda, Maryland.

Olsen, J. B., S. J. Miller, K. Harper, J. J. Nagler, and J. K. Wenburg. 2006. Contrasting sex ratios in juvenile and adult Chinook salmon (*Oncorhynchus tshawytscha*) from southwest Alaska: sex reversal or differential survival? Journal of Fish Biology 69 (Supplement A):140–144.

Rice, W. R. 1989. Analyzing tables of statistical tests. Evolution 43:223–225.

Seamons, T. R., P. Bentzen, and T. P. Quinn. 2004. The effects of adult length and arrival date on individual reproductive success in wild steelhead trout (*Oncorhynchus mykiss*). Canadian Journal of Fisheries and Aquatic Sciences 61:193–204.

Shrimpton, J. M., and D. D. Heath. 2003. Census vs. effective population size in Chinook salmon: large- and small-scale environmental perturbation effects. Molecular Ecology 12:2571–2583.

Smith, C. T., B. F. Koop, and R. J. Nelson. 1998. Isolation and characterization of coho salmon (*Oncorhynchus kisutch*) microsatellites and their use in other salmonids. Molecular Ecology 7:1614–1616.

Tajima, F. 1992. Statistical method for estimating the effective population size in salmon. Journal of Heredity 83:309–311.

Vucetich, J. A., T. A. Waite, and L. Nunney. 1997. Fluctuating population size and the ratio of effective to census population size. Evolution 51:2017–2021.

Wainwright T. C., and R. S. Waples. 1998. Prioritizing Pacific salmon stocks for conservation: response to Allendorf et al. Conservation Biology 12:1144–1147.

Waples, R. S. 1990a. Conservation genetics of pacific salmon. II. Effective population size and the rate of loss of genetic variability. Journal of Heredity 81:267–276.

Waples, R. S. 1990b. Conservation genetics of pacific salmon. III. Estimating the effective population size. Journal of Heredity 81:277–289.

Waples, R. 2002. Effective size of fluctuating salmon populations. Genetics 161:783–791.

Waples, R. 2005. Genetic estimates of contemporary effective population size: to what time periods do the estimates apply? Molecular Ecology 14:3335–3352.

Waples, R. S., M. Masuda, and J. Pella. 2007. SalmonNb: A program for computing cohort-specific effective population sizes (Nb) in Pacific salmon and other semelparous species using the temporal method. Molecular Ecology Notes 7:21–24.

Weir, B. S., and C. C. Cockerham. 1984. Estimating F-statistics for the analysis of population structure. Evolution 38:1358–1370.

Williamson, K. S., J. F. Cordes, and B. May. 2002. Characterization of microsatellite loci in Chinook salmon (*Oncorhynchus tshawytscha*) and cross-species amplification in other salmonids. Molecular Ecology Notes 2:17–19.

Wiswar, D. W. 2001. Abundance and run timing of adult salmon in the Gisasa River, Koyukuk National Wildlife Refuge, Alaska, 2000. U.S. Fish and Wildlife Service, Fairbanks Fisheries Resource Office, Alaska Fisheries Data Series Number 2001–1.

Wright, S. 1931. Evolution of Mendelian populations. Genetics 16:97–159.

Wright, S. 1938. Size of populations and breeding structure in relation to evolution. Science 87:430–431.

Marine Salmon Management

American Fisheries Society Symposium 70:799–816, 2009

Salmon Bycatch Management in the Bering Sea Walleye Pollock Fishery: Threats and Opportunities for Western Alaska

BECCA ROBBINS GISCLAIR*

Yukon River Drainage Fisheries Association
725 Christenson Drive, Suite 3-B, Anchorage, Alaska 99501, USA

Abstract.—Chinook *Oncorhynchus tshawytscha* and chum *O. keta* salmon bycatch in the Bering Sea Aleutian Islands (BSAI) walleye pollock *Theragra chalcogramma* fishery has increased dramatically in recent years, reaching near record highs for both salmon species. This bycatch must either be thrown back into the water or saved for donation to food banks. Many of these salmon were bound for spawning streams in the Arctic-Yukon-Kuskokwim (AYK) region of western Alaska, where the people of the AYK region await the salmon's return to provide for subsistence and commercial fisheries, and to fulfil a vital cultural role. To examine the interplay between the pollock fishery and western Alaska salmon stocks, this paper reviews important characteristics of the pollock fishery, western Alaska salmon stock status and origins of salmon bycatch in the pollock fishery, legal requirements to reduce bycatch, past and present bycatch management measures, and discusses possibilities for change and improvement to ensure that salmon bycatch and the impacts to western Alaska salmon are reduced. Current management under the voluntary rolling hot spot system provides an adaptive approach to bycatch management, but has not reduced salmon bycatch overall. To be effective, this system needs to be combined with a total cap on salmon bycatch. Technical approaches to reduce salmon bycatch, such as salmon excluder devices, should be developed and implemented. Social devices such as labelling regimes for sustainably caught fish could also play a role in reducing salmon bycatch.

Introduction

The region of western Alaska—from Kotzebue Sound to Chignik—including Bristol Bay and the Arctic-Yukon-Kuskokwim (AYK) region, covers a vast and varied geography. Inhabited by the Inupiat, Yupi'k, and Athabascan peoples, as well as non-aboriginal settlers, the cultures and histories of this area are as varied as the ecosystem. The peo-

ple of these diverse cultures, languages and traditions, however, share a reliance on one vital resource: salmon *Oncorhynchus*. Both commercial and subsistence fisheries provide important sources of sustenance and income. Using set and drift gillnets, angling, and fishwheels, these fisheries target Chinook *O. tshawytscha*, sockeye *O. nerka*, and chum *O. keta salmon* (e.g., Linderman and Bergstrom 2009, this volume). Actual gear used and primary fisheries vary considerably by region.

*Corresponding author: becca@yukonsalmon.org

Fishwheels, for instance are used primarily in the upper Yukon River.

The Chinook and chum salmon of western Alaska are an unintended target of the Bering Sea Aleutian Islands (BSAI) walleye pollock *Theragra chalcogramma* fishery (Haflinger and Gruver this volume; Stram and Ianelli 2009, this volume). In 2006, the pollock fishery caught over 84,000 Chinook and 325,000 chum salmon as bycatch, many of which were been bound for western Alaska streams (NMFS 2008a, 2008c; Myers et al. 2004). In 2007, 121,909 Chinook salmon were caught as bycatch by the pollock fleet, and 94,072 chum salmon were caught by the BSAI pollock fleet according to the National Marine Fisheries Service (NMFS) estimates of salmon bycatch based on observer samples (NMFS 2008a, 2008c). These salmon cannot be retained by the pollock fishery because they are a designated "prohibited species" under the North Pacific Fishery Management Council's groundfish Fishery Management Plan (FMP) and therefore must be discarded or donated to food banks through the Pacific Salmon Donation Program (NPFMC 2008). These salmon, had they returned to their natal river, could have fulfilled vital subsistence needs for people throughout western Alaska, contributed to the local commercial salmon harvest which provides one of the few sources of income for rural communities, or ensured that escapement goals for spawning were met.

This paper reviews important characteristics of the pollock fishery, status of western Alaska salmon, the origins of salmon bycatch in the pollock fishery, the legal requirements for bycatch management, and the past and present bycatch management measures to meet these requirements. The measures used to manage bycatch are described and evaluated in terms of their effectiveness to reduce bycatch. Finally, future possibilities for change and improvement in management of the fishery to reduce bycatch are discussed.

Bering Sea Aleutian Islands Walleye Pollock Fishery: An Overview

The largest fishery in the United States, the BSAI pollock fishery harvests an average of 1.3 million metric tons of pollock a year (NPFMC 2008). The fishery takes place in two distinct seasons throughout the year, the "A" season, which runs from January 20 until the end of March, and the "B" season which runs from June 10 until the end of October or later. The "A" season fishery is primarily a roe fishery, while the "B" season fishery is not. In addition to the roe product, pollock flesh is used for fillets, breaded fish products and surimi, which appears to consumers as imitation crab or lobster in national and international markets. The pollock fleet is a largely Washington and Oregon-based fleet of catcher boats and factory trawlers. In Alaska, groundfish trawlers (which includes pollock boats and others) in 2002, "accounted for 67% of the total fisheries volume landed in Alaska (Gilbertsen 2004). In 2002, the profits from the fishery went primarily out of Alaska, with 196 non-resident fishermen "landing 91% of the 2.7 billion pounds taken in the trawl fishery, earning $220 million of the $241 million total gross value" (Gilbertsen 2004). These Figures include both the Gulf of Alaska and the BSAI groundfish fisheries.

Since 1998 when Congress passed the American Fisheries Act (AFA), the BSAI pollock fishery has been open to set harvesting and processing vessels only (NPFMC 2005). The AFA also established specific quota allocations: "10% to the western Alaska Community Development Quota (CDQ) program and the remainder allocated 50% to the inshore sector, 40% to the offshore sector and 10% to the mothership sector" (NPFMC 2005). The CDQ program is a federal program which allocates a set amount of the BSAI harvest to six CDQ groups.[1] The CDQ groups are regional nonprofit corporations which manage the allocations and other fishery-related projects. The program is intended to include western Alaska communities within 100 mi of the coast in the lucrative fisheries offshore (NPFMC 2008). The inshore sector includes shoreside processors and catcher vessels (Oliver 1999). The offshore sector includes catcher processors, factory trawlers that process pollock on board, and designated catcher vessels which deliver to these catcher processors (Oliver 1999; NPFMC 2005). The mothership sector includes three named motherships and vessels which deliver to those motherships under the AFA (Oliver 1999). The AFA also provided for the formation of fishing cooperatives among pollock boats (NPFMC 2005). Under the co-op provisions, pollock boats are able to distribute their sector's allocation among members.

While the pollock fleet intends to catch pollock only, the midwater trawl nets intercept salmon because salmon and pollock are often intermingled. The amount of salmon caught as bycatch varies throughout the season, and seems largely tied to where the fishery and salmon populations overlap. In 2002–2003, the pollock fishery was responsible for 85% of all the Chinook salmon bycatch caught by the groundfish fishery and 97% of "other salmon" bycatch (on average over 98% of the "other salmon" category is chum salmon) (NPFMC 2005). The fishery is managed by the North Pacific Fishery Management Council (the Council), one of the regional fishery management councils with responsibility for managing fisheries in the U.S. Exclusive Economic Zone (EEZ), which extends from three to 200 nautical miles from shore. The

pollock fishery is not allowed to sell these salmon commercially because salmon are a prohibited species under the Council's FMP (NPFMC 2006a).

Chinook salmon bycatch increased steadily from 2004 to 2007, while chum salmon rose dramatically from 2002 to 2005 (Figures 1 and 2). Chinook salmon bycatch has risen from 34,495 fish in 2002 to more than 121,909 fish in 2007, a number which is almost triple the ten-year average (1997–2006) of 43,328 fish (NMFS 2008a). Chinook salmon bycatch levels decreased substantially in 2008, with only 20,273 fish caught (NMFS 2008a). The difference from the ten year average seems even greater when it is taken into account that the average contains the year of 2000 when many inshore areas were closed to fishing from August to October due to litigation over the Endangered Species Act (ESA)-listed Stellar Sea Lion (Greenpeace v. NMFS, Order No.C98–492Z (W.D. WA, August and December 5, 2008)). The 2007 Chinook salmon bycatch number was the highest on record. The next highest reported bycatch rates of 115,036 fish occurred in 1980 and in 1979 (107,706 fish). These bycatch levels predate the current AFA-designed U.S. pollock fleet (Witherell 1997).

Chum salmon bycatch rates increased similarly from 80,652 fish in 2002 to a record high of 705,963 fish in 2005, with a decrease to 310,545 fish in 2006 and 94,072 fish in 2007 (NMFS 2008b). Chum salmon bycatch was also low in 2008 with only 15,423 chum salmon taken as bycatch (NMFS 2009). The chum bycatch numbers were also higher than historic levels: the 2005 number was more than twice the ten-year average (1997–2006) chum salmon bycatch of 203,070 fish (NMFS 2008b). Prior to 2004, the highest chum salmon bycatch on record was 243,246 fish in 1993. The record high in 2005 almost tripled that previous record (NMFS 2008b).

---

[1]The six CDQ groups are: the Aleutian Pribilof Island Community Development Association (APICDA), the Bristol Bay Economic Development Corporation (BBEDC), the Central Bering Sea Fishermen's Association (CBSFA), the Coastal Villages Region Fund (CVRF), the Norton Sound Economic Development Corporation (NSEDC), and the Yukon Delta Fisheries Development Association (YDFDA).

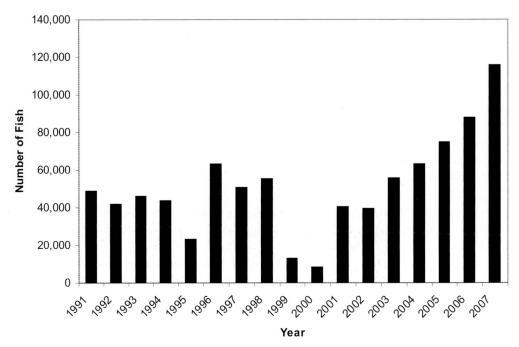

FIGURE 1. Bering Sea/Aleutian Islands Chinook salmon *Oncorhynchus tshawytscha* bycatch in U.S. groundfish fisheries 1996–2007 (NMFS 2008).

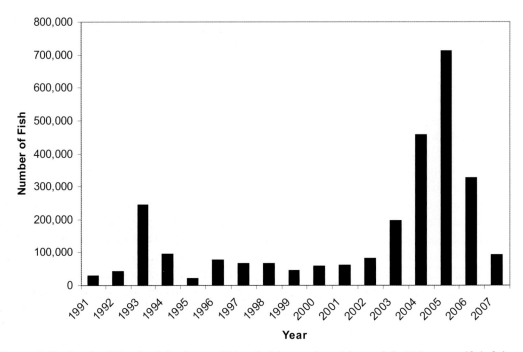

FIGURE 2. Bering Sea/Aleutian Islands non-Chinook (chum salmon) bycatch in U.S. groundfish fisheries 1996–2007 (NMFS 2008).

Status and Origin of Salmon Caught as Bycatch

Many of the salmon caught as bycatch by the BSAI pollock fleet were bound for the rivers of western Alaska, where commercial and subsistence users await their return. While Chinook salmon bycatch numbers in the pollock fishery increased, similar increases were not seen in many in-river salmon runs. Hence, the increased bycatch did not appear to be caused by increases in salmon originating from western Alaska. The stock of origin of these salmon caught as bycatch has not been extensively studied; however, a study of bycatch samples from 1997 to 1999 using scale pattern analysis indicated that on average Chinook salmon stock origins were: 56% western Alaska, 31% Cook Inlet, 8% southeast Alaska-British Columbia, and 5% Kamchatka (Asia) (Myers et al. 2004). Of the western Alaskan portion, 40% of the Chinook salmon were of Yukon River origin, 34% from Bristol Bay, and 26% from the Kuskokwim River (Myers et al. 2004).

A study of chum salmon stock of origin from 1994 and 1995 found that 1994 stock origins were: 38–55% Asian stocks, 20–35% western Alaska stocks, and 21–29% southeasteastern Alaska, British Columbia or Washington stocks. In 1995, stock origins were: 13–51% Asian, 33–53% western Alaska and 9–46% south-eastern Alaska, British Columbia or Washington stocks (Wilmot et al. 1998). The wide ranges reflect differences in stock composition at different times of year, as the authors reported stock composition during varying time periods. Another study of the 1994 samples using scale pattern analysis to determine the stock of origin of age-3 chum salmon found that 50% of the fish were of Asian (Russian or Japanese) origin, 18% from western and central Alaska and 32% from southeastern Alaska, British Columbia or Washington (Patton et al. 1998).

Salmon runs throughout western Alaska experienced run failures in 2000 and 2001. Most runs have recovered from the record low numbers (e.g., Linderman and Bergstrom 2009). In recent years, chum salmon spawning runs have been high throughout western Alaska, with the exception of Norton Sound. Chinook salmon runs, on the other hand, were below average in many rivers in 2007, and have not increased in past years. Yukon River Chinook salmon remain listed as a stock of concern by the Alaska Board of Fisheries (Evenson et al. 2009, this volume). In 2007, Chinook salmon runs in the Yukon, Kuskokwim, and Nushagak rivers were below average in numbers, and well below the run forecasted by the Alaska Department of Fish and Game (ADF&G). The Yukon River Chinook salmon run was 70,000 fish short of the preseason projection by ADF&G. The Kuskokwim and Nushagak rivers were both 100,000 fish short of preseason projections (ADF&G 2007).

In 2007, only 23,000 Chinook salmon in the Yukon River crossed the border into Canada, as measured by the Canadian mark–recapture program (ADF&G 2007). This number fell far short of the border passage target of 45,500 Chinook salmon necessary to meet the Yukon River Panel's established escapement goal (33,000–43,000 fish) and the additional fish required for harvest sharing arrangements of the Yukon River Salmon Agreement (ADF&G 2007; YRSA 2002). While subsistence needs were generally met in the lower Yukon, subsistence fishers in the middle Yukon reported difficulty meeting their needs, and fishers throughout the river reported that additional time and effort was necessary to fulfill subsistence needs. Only a small commercial harvest of 33,600 Chinook salmon was allowed. This commercial harvest was 30% below the ten-year average of 58,254 (ADF&G 2007). Because of the shortfall, no commercial or domestic fisheries were allowed in Canada, although aboriginal (First Nations subsistence) fishing was allowed. In 2008, the run was even weaker than in 2007. In Alaska, no directed commercial fishery was allowed for Chinook salmon, restrictions were placed on subsistence fishing, and the escapement goal agreed to under the Yukon River Salmon Agreement was not met (ADF&G 2008).

Precise estimates of the direct impacts of salmon bycatch in the pollock fleet on specific stocks are not yet available. However, Witherell et al. (2002) used the stock of origin information available at that time in combination with total run size estimates to conclude that bycatch at the level of 30,000 Chinook salmon had a 2.7% impact on western Alaska Chinook runs. A bycatch of 60,000 chum salmon would have a 0.24% impact on western Alaska chum salmon. While these estimates may look small, bycatch numbers have increased dramatically since this paper was published, and the levels of bycatch seen in recent history (in 2007 Chinook salmon bycatch was four times that used by Witherell et al. 2002) would likely have far greater impacts. Current studies are using more recent genetic information along with an adult equivalency model to develop information on the impacts to specific stocks over the years. While precise estimates of the direct impacts to specific stocks are not yet available, as western Alaska Chinook salmon runs struggle to recover, the increasing bycatch numbers in the pollock fishery potentially affect the recovery, on-going fisheries, and long-term sustainability of the resource.

Legal Requirements to Reduce Salmon Bycatch

Reduction of salmon bycatch is required under several domestic and international laws, and various management measures described in the sections below have been implemented under some of these authorities. Perhaps the most relevant legal directive to reduce salmon bycatch is contained in the Magnuson-Stevens Fisheries Conservation Act (MSFCA), the governing law for fisheries management in federal waters of the United States. The Act was originally enacted in 1976, and re-authorized in 1996 and 2006. Under National Standard 9 of the MSFCA (added in 1996), the Council and the NOAA-Fisheries (formerly the National Marine Fisheries Service or NMFS) must "to the extent practicable, (A) minimize bycatch and (B) to the extent bycatch cannot be avoided, minimize the mortality of such bycatch" (MSFCA 2004). While this provides a specific directive to reduce bycatch, the imperative is weakened by the specific language in the act "to the extent practicable," which means outright reductions under any circumstance are *not* required. Rather the "practicability" requirement of National Standard 9, "requires the agency to pursue bycatch minimization in conjunction with other statutory objectives, such as minimizing the economic impact of regulations on fishing communities (National Standard 8, 16 U.S.C. § 1851(a) (8)) and minimizing costs and unnecessary duplication (National Standard 7, 16 U.S.C. § 1851(a)(7), Ocean Conservancy v. Gutierrez, 394 F. Supp. 2 d 147, 158–59 (D.D.C. 2005), Legacy Fishing Co. v. Guttierez, Civil Action 06–0835 (D.D.C.2007)).

Further, in evaluating fishery management actions under National Standard 9, the Councils must consider the "net benefits to the nation." This includes, but is not limited to:

Negative impacts on affected stocks; incomes accruing to participants in directed fisheries in both the short and long term; incomes accruing to participants in fisheries that target the bycatch species; environmental consequences; nonmarket values of bycatch species, which include nonconsumptive uses of bycatch species and existence values, as well as recreational values; and impacts on other marine organisms. (USOFR 2006 § 600.350(d)).

Councils are further required to consider a number of factors in determining whether a management measure "minimizes bycatch or bycatch mortality to the extent practicable, consistent with other national standards and maximization of net benefits to the Nation." (USOFR 2006 § 600.350(d)(3)(i)). These factors include:

A. Population effects for the bycatch species.

B. Ecological effects due to changes in the bycatch of that species (effects on other species in the ecosystem).

C. Changes in the bycatch of other species of fish, and the resulting population and ecosystem effects.

D. Effects on marine mammals and birds.

E. Changes in fishing, processing, disposal, and marketing costs.

F. Changes in fishing practices and behavior of fishermen.

G. Changes in research, administration, and enforcement costs and management effectiveness.

H. Changes in the economic, social, or cultural value of fishing activities, and nonconsumptive uses of fishery resources.

I. Changes in the distribution of benefits and costs.

J. Social effects.

(USOFR 2006 § 600.350(d)(3)(i)).

Finally, in choosing bycatch reduction plans, NMFS and the Councils have an affirmative duty to "give priority to conservation measures." (Natural Resource Defense Council, Inc. v. Daley, 209 F.3 d 747, 753 (D.C. Cir. 2000)). Under this priority, NMFS and Councils can chose management plans with low economic costs only where they "achieve similar conservation measures." (Natural Resource Defense Council, Inc. v. Daley, 209 F.3 d 747, 753 (D.C. Cir. 2000)). The requirements of National Standard 9 are highly fact specific, but overall the standard does provide a legal basis for bycatch reduction.

Another legal basis for reducing salmon bycatch, particularly the bycatch of Yukon River bound salmon, is found in international treaty. The Yukon River Salmon Agreement (YRSA), an annex to the Pacific Salmon Treaty, was agreed to by the United States and Canada in March of 2001 after more than fifteen years of negotiations between the parties (YRDFA 2005). The agreement was formally recognized as an annex to the Pacific Salmon Treaty in 2002. Under the terms of the Yukon River Salmon Agreement, the U.S. agreed to "maintain efforts to increase the in-river run of Yukon River origin salmon by reducing marine catches and by-catches of Yukon River salmon. They shall further identify, quantify and undertake efforts to reduce these catches and by-catches" (YRSA 2002). While the agreement clearly requires reduction in marine bycatch of Yukon River salmon, with no caveats as to practicability, the terms of the agreement call only for "efforts" to reduce bycatch. However, these efforts are designated as "to increase the in-river run of Yukon River origin salmon," so presumably these bycatch efforts must reduce the bycatch of Yukon River salmon to meet the terms of the treaty. The treaty also provides for passage of salmon through the U.S. portion of the Yukon River into Canada. According to the treaty terms a clear obligation exists on the part of the U.S. to pass a set number of Chinook and fall chum salmon across the border to Canada. If a situation were to arise in the future in which no commercial harvest was allowed in Alaska and escapement goals in Canada were not met, the bycatch of Yukon River bound salmon in the pollock fishery could be in direct violation of the YRSA.

Perhaps the most powerful law requiring salmon bycatch reduction in this situation is the Endangered Species Act (ESA). Often referred to as the "pit bull of environmental laws," the ESA prohibits the "taking" or killing of any single member of a species once it is listed under the act (ESA 2000). Any federal action (of which a fishery management plan is one) which may result in a taking requires what is referred to as a §7 consultation. A §7 consultation essentially requires that the relevant agency must certify that the action will not jeopardize the species' existence (ESA 2000). If the action will result in a taking, an Incidental Take Statement (ITS) is required before the action can go forward. Because several listed species of Washington and Oregon Chinook salmon and steelhead *Oncorhynchus mykiss* range in the North Pacific and could be caught as bycatch, the pollock fleet has an ITS (NPFMC 2005). Up to 2006, the ITS was for 55,000 Chinook salmon, a number which has been exceeded—and nearly doubled—in recent years. The exceeding of the ITS has triggered a §7 consultation each time. Thus far the results of the §7 consultation have been "no jeopardy," meaning that the activity can continue. In January 2007, the Northwest Fishery Science Center changed the ITS to a range of 36,000–87,500 fish, recognizing that numbers to date had not "jeopardized" the species and, thus, could be used as the new baseline (NMFS 2007b). While no one has challenged these rulings to date, if salmon bycatch continues at numbers above the ITS, a no-jeopardy determination may be more difficult to uphold, particularly if on-going genetic studies show higher num-

bers of endangered stocks are present in the bycatch than currently known.

Beyond fisheries-specific laws, Executive Order 12898 requires federal agencies to "make achieving environmental justice part of its mission by identifying and addressing, as appropriate, disproportionately high and adverse human health or environmental effects of its programs, policies, and activities on minority populations and low-income populations in the United States and its territories and possessions" (E.O. 12898, 1994). Under this Executive Order, which has been interpreted as evidence of the government's heightened responsibility toward protecting the resources that these communities and cultures have historically depended upon,[2] the National Marine Fisheries Service and the Council are required to address the disparate impacts placed on Alaska's Native communities by increased levels of salmon bycatch in this particular situation. In addition to these specific laws, other nonbinding or less specific international norms and treaties may obligate the reduction of salmon bycatch in the pollock fishery.

Past Measures Used to Limit Salmon Bycatch

Fishery managers have tried many methods of limiting salmon bycatch by the pollock fleet throughout the years. For the period preceding the 1990s, in the so-called "foreign fishing days," when the groundfish harvest was primarily taken by foreign boats, a catch limit of 55,250 Chinook salmon was set in the 1982 Fishery Management Plan (FMP) (Witherell 1997). This limit was allocated among the nations participating in the fishery, and any nation which exceeded their limit was not allowed to fish in much of the Bering Sea for the rest of the season (Witherell 1997). In

---

[2] Campo Band of Mission Indians v. U.S., 2000 U.S. Dist. LEXIS 7269, 7 (Dist. D.C. 2000).

1983, the FMP was amended to provide additional incentives for bycatch reduction by "allocating supplemental groundfish within a fishing season to nations on the basis of their performance" (Witherell 1997).

As groundfish fisheries transitioned to domestic fisheries through joint ventures in the 1980s and then onto fully Americanized fisheries (by 1998), salmon bycatch regulations were reduced (Witherell 1997). In 1990, a new bycatch regulation was introduced, the so-called "penalty box" system. Under this system, individual vessels with high bycatch rates were to be prohibited from fishing for a set period of time. This program was never put into place because of due process issues and observer data concerns, but served as an important precedent for development of the current management measures. A Vessel Incentive Program (VIP) which fined vessels if they exceeded bycatch rates was adopted instead, but this approach was largely not used due to similar due process and data concerns that existed with the "penalty box" system (Witherell 1997). After being unenforced for years, the Council repealed the program in 2006.

Starting in the 1990s, the Council adopted a series of regulations designed to reduce salmon bycatch through time and area closures. A Chum Salmon Savings Area, which was designed based on areas of observed high chum salmon bycatch rates, has been used since 1994 (Figure 3). Under this system, the area is closed to all trawling August 1–31. The area remain closed if 42,000 "other" salmon are caught in the Catcher Vessel Operating Area (CVOA) between August 15 and October 14 (Figure 3; NPFMC 2005). The Chinook Salmon Saving areas have been in place since 1995 (Figure 4). These areas close when 29,000 Chinook salmon are caught. Both of these areas are fixed in their location and do not change over time. Closures occur as follows: "If the limit is triggered before April 15, the areas close im-

mediately through April 15. After April 15, the areas re-open, but are again closed from September 1–December 31.

1. If the limit is reached after April 15, but before September 1, the areas would close on September 1 through the end of the year.

2. If the limit is reached after September 1, the areas close immediately through the end of the year" (NPFMC 2005).

Since implementation, the Chinook Savings Areas have been triggered every year from 2003 to 2006 (NPFMC 2005; NPFMC 2007; NMFS 2007a). Chum Salmon Savings Areas in addition to the August 1–31 closure have been triggered every year from 2002 to 2005, but not in 2006 (NMFS 2006). While the salmon savings areas still exist in regulation, since August of 2006, the entire pollock fleet has been exempt from these closures because they are participating in the Voluntary Rolling Hot Spot system (discussed below).

Voluntary Rolling Hot Spot System for Bycatch Reduction

Salmon bycatch numbers have continued to climb despite the numerous closures of the Chinook and Chum Salmon Savings areas in recent years. Some evidence suggests that the closures inadvertently forced pollock boats to fish in waters with *higher* bycatch rates than those experienced in the savings areas (NPFMC 2005). Given the increasing bycatch, in 2001 the pollock fleet adopted a Voluntary Rolling Hot Spot (VRHS) system. This system, which pollock boats and co-ops voluntarily choose to participate in, was designed to move pollock boats away from areas of high salmon bycatch throughout the season. The areas are not fixed in location, but adjust through time to the changing location of high bycatch areas. Critical to implementation of

FIGURE 3. Chum Salmon Savings Area and Catcher Vessel Operational Area (CVOA) (NPFMC 2005). Shaded area represents savings area. Dotted line indicates CVOA.

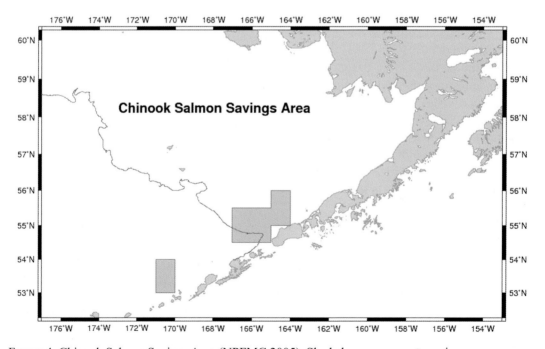

FIGURE 4. Chinook Salmon Savings Area (NPFMC 2005). Shaded area represents savings area.

this voluntary system is catch reporting and analysis. Under the system, boats report their bycatch data and location data via the Vessel Monitoring System (VMS) which tracks to a central administrator, Sea State, a private fisheries firm, within 24 h of their catch. VMS is a satellite-based monitoring system which transmits location data of the vessel on which it is installed and enables Sea State to track the locations of fishing vessels. Sea State then analyzes bycatch rates from the entire fleet and issues orders that close areas with high bycatch rates. If warranted, closures can be made twice a week based on the bycatch data (ICA 2006). The system has been used by the pollock fleet since 2001 for chum salmon and 2003 for Chinook salmon. While the VRHS system was initially used on a voluntary basis in addition to the savings area closure system, in 2005 the Council approved Amendment 84 to the FMP, which adopted the VRHS system as a bycatch reduction measure and granted exemptions to the Chinook and Chum Salmon Savings areas to those boats participating in the VRHS system. Since August of 2006, the pollock fleet has been operating under an Exempted Fishing Permit (EFP) which allowed the provisions of Amendment 84 to go forward while regulations were being adopted (NPFMC 2006b). The final regulations were adopted in October 2007.

The VRHS system operates under established guidelines, agreed upon contractually between the pollock co-ops through an Intercooperative Agreement, or ICA. Because the fishery itself and interactions with salmon are not the same during the two seasons, the VRHS system operates differently in the "A" Season and the "B" Season. The closure system functions around a salmon bycatch base rate, expressed as the number of salmon per metric ton of pollock. In the "A" season, the base rate determines which areas are closed, and to which co-ops the closures apply. For Chinook salmon, the base rate in the "A" Season is initially set at the previous year's

average bycatch rate (but must be between 0.04 and 0.06 Chinook salmon per metric ton of pollock). Prior to 2008, the base rate was adjusted three weeks into the season to the season average for the current year. For the 2008 season, the ICA was modified after a request from western Alaska groups. The A season base rate, after February 14, is now the lower of the one time recalculated rate used in the prior agreement, or a rate calculated on a 3 week rolling average beginning February 14th and on a weekly basis for the remainder of the A season (ICA 2008). Chum salmon bycatch has not historically been present in the "A" season fishery, and therefore, chum salmon closures are not included in the "A" season management regime.

Fishing areas are closed when bycatch rates in those areas exceed the base rate— these areas are designated as "hot spots." Prior to 2008, the total of all "hot spot" areas closed to fishing could not exceed 1,000 square miles. In the 2008 agreement, this area was increased to 1,500 square miles (ICA 2008). If the total amount of area which qualifies based on bycatch rate exceeds 1,500 square miles, not all areas will be closed. In addition, in 2008 a fixed closure area was established by the intercooperative group. The closure begins January 20 and runs for the duration of the A season in an area which historically has had high bycatch rates. This closure area applies to all boats throughout the A season.

In the "A" season, the base rate also determines whether closures apply to a co-op and if so, for how long. Closed "hot spot" areas are not closed to all pollock boats. Closures apply to a specific co-op dependent on their bycatch rate. Closures apply to those with the worst bycatch rates (<125% of the base rate) for seven days at a time and to those with slightly better bycatch rates (75–125% of the base rate) for four days at a time. For those co-ops with the best bycatch rates (>75% of the base rate) the closures do not apply at all. As part of the agreement, along with closures, a "Dirty Dozen" list of the vessels with the worst bycatch rates is published weekly (ICA 2006).

During the "B" Season, the same system of closing areas where bycatch rates exceed a set rate is used. The base rate for Chinook salmon is 0.05 salmon per metric ton of pollock for the 2007 B Season. For the 2008 "B" Season and thereafter, the base rate will be set by Sea State by "dividing the Chinook salmon bycatch during a period of the prior year's Fishery "B" season that Sea State determines in its sole discretion to be representative by the Coops' directed pollock harvest (including CDQ bycatch) for the same period" (ICA 2006). For chum salmon, the base rate is set at 0.19 salmon per metric ton of pollock initially, with an in-season adjustment on September 1 to the average bycatch rate for the three weeks proceeding. In the "B" season, however, Chinook salmon closures apply to all co-ops regardless of their bycatch rate (ICA 2006).

Vessels that violate the agreement are fined $10,000 for the first violation, $15,000 for the second violation in the same year, and $30,000 for the third violation in the same year. Under the agreement, several western Alaska groups are named as third party members of the agreement with the right to enforce violations and payments. Currently the Yukon River Drainage Fisheries Association (YRDFA), Bering Sea Fishermen's Association (BSFA), Association of Village Council Presidents (AVCP), and Tanana Chiefs Conference (TCC) are all named as third party members (ICA 2006).

Problems with the Voluntary Rolling Hot Spot System

While the VRHS system has held great promise in theory as an adaptive approach to bycatch management, in practice the number of salmon caught as bycatch under the system has still been high. The bycatch of salmon has increased over the past five years. VRHS's adaptive feature of using bycatch rates to allow flexibility in the closure system is also its shortcoming. Base levels of bycatch establish the trigger points for management action that when exceeded cause closures and tier assignments. The base levels of bycatch are determined using existing bycatch rates, or those from the previous year. As a result, the VRHS system preserves the bycatch status quo—if high numbers of salmon were caught in the recent past, the pollock fleet can continue to catch many salmon. If not many salmon were caught, fewer salmon can continue to be caught.

The system was designed in this way on the assumption that salmon bycatch would be an indicator of salmon abundance; thus, protections are more necessary in years of low bycatch and hence low abundance. Several notable flaws exist in the relationship between catch and abundance. First, bycatch rates indicate numbers of salmon present in a local area where the pollock fleet is fishing, and thus are not necessarily correlated with overall abundance of salmon returning to western Alaska in the coming years. Second, while some believe that salmon bycatch serves as an indicator of overall salmon abundance, recent experience has not shown that to be true. Though Chinook salmon bycatch in the fishery was high in 2005, 2006, and 2007, western Alaska salmon runs have not shown similar increases, and many have in fact decreased. Finally, even if bycatch was an indicator of overall salmon abundance, a high overall abundance does not mean that every stock is abundant that particular year (Hilborn et al. 2003; Quinn 2009, this volume). Therefore, a salmon bycatch reduction measure based on salmon bycatch rates, and using the existing rates as a determinant of closure areas, does not ensure bycatch reductions commensurate with a particular salmon stock's abundance.

Another potential contributing factor to the failure of the VRHS system to reduce salmon bycatch is that the closure areas cannot exceed 1,500 square miles. Having a maximum in place means that a limit exists on how much area can be closed. While the intent of this maximum is logical—without a limit the pollock fleet could face so many closures that few places would be left to fish. In reality, the limit means an allocative choice that harvesting pollock takes precedence over protecting salmon. While most means of bycatch reduction in any fishery requires choosing one species or user over another, here the failure to effectively reduce salmon bycatch is essentially an allocative decision which favors the pollock fishery over western Alaska's commercial and subsistence salmon fishers and the ecosystem to which the salmon return.

Voluntary Agreements versus Regulation: The Carrot and Stick Approach

While the VRHS system has flaws (discussed above), opportunities exist for improving it. Voluntary agreements have been adopted to deal with environmental problems in many contexts over recent years, particularly in the pollution control context (Kerret and Tal 2005). Voluntary agreements have been posed as an alternative to the traditional "command and control" model of environmental regulation in which the government dictates a limit, or a requirement and industry is required to comply or be penalized. The voluntary agreement approach engages the industry in developing a strategy for achieving the goal; this strategy is embodied in a voluntary agreement between industry members with no oversight role for the government. While these types of agreements have been used primarily in the pollution control context where the gains from command and

control type regulations have already been maximized, the VRHS fits in this same paradigm.

Voluntary environmental agreements have been subject to much criticism: industry negotiations often result in weak requirements and the government and the public have no ability to enforce them. Many of these criticisms hold true for the VRHS system. Notably, voluntary environmental agreements regulating in the area of pollution control and other areas of environmental law have a command and control basis—a floor providing standards to which any voluntary agreement must comply. While the VRHS will have to comply by regulation with the minimum provisions set out for it, no underlying regulation exists that sets a floor for bycatch reduction. Such a regulation should be established., and would provide the necessary backstop.

Management approaches which combine a "carrot and a stick" are oftentimes most effective. For instance, in the well-known case of dolphin bycatch in the tuna *Thunnus* spp. fishery, having a strong stick (in this case a bycatch limit upon attainment of which the entire fishery was shut down) was essential in creating an incentive for reducing bycatch, and for a peer pressure situation between fishers to reduce bycatch (Norris and Hall 2002). Thus, an obvious improvement to the VRHS would be to provide a stick. A bycatch cap which would trigger a regulatory effect that was undesirable to the fishery could provide such a stick. A cap would provide the numerical safeguard to the rate-based VRHS system to ensure that a limit exists on the total number of salmon that can be caught as bycatch. A cap would provide additional incentive to reduce bycatch and, if the consequences of exceeding the cap were drastic enough, peer pressure would increase among pollock boat captains to keep their bycatch low.

A cap, a bycatch level that cannot be exceeded, could be designed in a number of ways: floating or fixed; hard or soft. A float-ing cap indexed to predicted salmon abun-dance would be ideal from a management standpoint in that it could set bycatch lev-els according to current salmon abundance. Unfortunately, preseason or even in-season forecasting of salmon abundance within an acceptable level of accuracy is not possible at this time. A fixed cap set at a negotiated level, however, could provide an interim solution to offer some degree of protection. Another op-tion is hard or soft caps. A hard cap is a set number which when reached would close the fishery. A soft cap, on the other hand, would trigger some lesser degree of time or area clo-sure rather than a full shutdown. While a hard cap which closed the fishery provides the ideal stick, this option is politically difficult. Pulsing, in which a fishery is closed for a set number of days after exceeding a cap could provide a plausible alternative. A soft cap that closes a set area, as the Chinook and Chum Salmon Savings Areas, could be effective as well, but closure areas would need to be rede-signed to ensure they can adapt to changing salmon migration patterns.

A derivative of a fishery-wide cap which has been used successfully in other fisheries is the idea of individual bycatch quotas, by vessel or co-op. Under this type of system, vessels or co-ops are given individual bycatch quotas, or caps. Once they have reached their individual number, they are prohibited from fishing. This creates an obvious economic in-centive to keep bycatch levels low. Boats with low bycatch numbers are rewarded with more opportunity to fish, and this approach "places a direct positive linkage between bycatch reduction and financial reward" (Norris and Hall 2002). Individual bycatch limits when linked to an overall cap for the fishery could provide additional peer pressure to keep by-catch numbers low. This same idea could be adapted into a cap and trade system. Under this system, bycatch would be allocated by vessel or co-op, but could be traded between entities. When a co-op or boat has caught their quota of the salmon bycatch, they could buy more quota from others, if other co-ops or boats had bycatch quota remaining. Many of these bycatch reduction measures are cur-rently being considered by the North Pacific Fishery Management Council through Fish-ery Management Plan Amendment 91. The list of bycatch alternatives currently being considered includes hard caps, and fixed and triggered closures as well as bycatch caps by sector.

Discussion

In general, bycatch reduction measures fall into three categories: regulatory, techni-cal, and social (Hall and Mainprize 2005). While the focus thus far has been on measures that fall under the regulatory category, fixes are also available that fall under the other two categories. Technical solutions are related to the equipment used in the fishery and how it is used. Technical solutions to reducing by-catch are particularly promising because they can provide a win-win for industry and con-servation: fishermen can keep fishing with-out extensive regulation and bycatch can be reduced. In the pollock fishery, efforts have been ongoing to develop a salmon excluder device which capitalizes on the differences between salmon and pollock behavior to re-duce salmon bycatch. While considerable ef-forts have been put into this effort with a fair degree of success, the current excluder "will require further refinements before it would be acceptable for fleet-wide adoption as a device that could be used in day-to-day fishing op-erations" (Gruver, J., United Catcher Boats, Seattle, WA, personal communication).

The social system through economics and politics may provide further opportuni-ties for bycatch reduction. Potential pressure points involve the cost of bycatch to fisher-men that can come through product labeling regimes such as the Marine Stewardship Council (MSC) and public pressure (Hall and Mainprize 2005). Pollock products could be made more attractive to consumers if they can be certified as adhering to specific conservation measures. In this context, labeling regimes have thus far failed as a means of exerting social pressure on the fishery. The pollock fleet was certified by MSC in 2005, despite opposition from ocean conservation groups. The fishery will have to undergo re-certification in 2010, and this could provide an opportunity for increased pressure on the issue, particularly if bycatch numbers continue to climb.

Public pressure can also serve an important role in bycatch reduction by creating political force for the industry and government to act. Bycatch has gained considerable attention in recent years, with the publication of bycatch reports by the marine conservation group, Oceana, and the Marine Fish Conservation Network. This group is an alliance of fishing, seafood, and conservation groups. Salmon bycatch was given considerable attention in the mid- to late 1990s by groups throughout the West Coast, from northern California to Nome. However, as salmon runs improved, the issue has garnered less attention. With the low salmon runs of recent years, interest in the issue seems to be increasing. Public awareness and involvement is a key component particularly in voluntary agreements to ensure that the industry stays focused on the issue (Kerret and Tal 2005).

A greater potential for bycatch reform than the measures discussed above may be available under a new management paradigm: ecosystem-based management (e.g., Reardon and Gillikin 2009, this volume). Traditional fishery management regimes focus on a single species at a time—e.g., the pollock fishery is managed solely for pollock harvest with consideration only given as necessary to some other variables such as salmon bycatch, and protection of marine mammals and seabirds. Ecosystem-based management on the other hand attempts to manage fisheries within the broader framework of the ecosystem, focusing not on a single species at a time, but on the needs of the entire marine ecosystem (Stump et al. 2006).

In recent years as impacts on fish stocks from diverse sources including irrigation, agriculture, and housing development have increased, ecosystem-based management has garnered attention on many fronts. Both the privately-sponsored Pew Oceans Commission and the government-sponsored U.S. Ocean Commission identified a national ocean policy using an ecosystem approach as an important goal for oceans management (Pew Oceans Commission 2003; U.S. Commission on Ocean Policy 2004). While ecosystem-based management would take into account a much broader spectrum of ecosystem needs than salmon bycatch, an ecosystem approach would guarantee that impacts on salmon stocks would be taken into full account in managing the pollock fishery. Looking at the broader ecosystem picture would also ensure that salmon bycatch reduction measures would not have deleterious impacts on other species; for instance, if salmon bycatch management pushed the fleet to an area with high squid bycatch.

Ecosystem-based management could offer protections to an even greater degree for salmon stocks than other approaches. While the North Pacific Fishery Management Council currently takes ecosystem considerations into account in fishery management decisions, a broad-scale shift from single-species management to a broader ecosystem approach would be necessary to adequately address these types of ecosystem concerns. Ecosystem-based management certainly will not be adopted overnight nor will it be simple to implement, but in the long-term, this kind of management shift could prove most valuable for protecting salmon stocks.

Conclusion

Salmon are of vital importance through-out western Alaska for commercial and sub-sistence fisheries, as well as culture. Reducing salmon bycatch in the pollock fishery will help to ensure that these in-river needs are met, and will meet the Council and NMFS's legal ob-ligations to reduce salmon bycatch. Amend-ment 91, currently under consideration by the Council, offers some promising means of reducing salmon bycatch. In particular, a hard cap could place a necessary safeguard over the VRHS system and would allow this promising adaptive management system to go forward while ensuring that salmon bycatch is reduced. The Council process allows participation by ADF&G and for western Alaskan stakehold-ers. western Alaskans should work to ensure that options currently under consideration by the Council, including a hard cap, provide ad-equate limits on salmon bycatch. Beyond the specific alternatives of Amendment 91, many innovative methods are available to further re-duce bycatch. Together these bycatch reduc-tion measures can ensure that salmon bycatch is reduced and that the western Alaska salmon resources are sustained.

Acknowledgments

My sincere thanks to Kristin Mull for her scientific guidance, assistance with graphs, and editing; to Chris Stark for his scientific insight and support, to Chuck Krueger for his patient editing; and to Jill Klein for her support of this project. My thanks to my co-panelists and con-stant sources of information on this subject: Diana Stram, John Gruver, and Karl Hafling-er. This work was supported by grant number NA04NMF4720276 from the National Oceanic and Atmospheric Association (NOAA) award-ed to the Yukon River Drainage Fisheries Asso-ciation. The views expressed do not necessarily reflect the views of NOAA or its sub-agencies.

References

ADF&G (Alaska Department of Fish and Game). 2007. 2007 preliminary Yukon River summer season summary. Alaska Department of Fish and Game. Anchorage.

ADF&G (Alaska Department of Fish and Game). 2008. 2008 Preliminary Yukon River summer season summary. Alaska Department of Fish and Game. Anchorage.

E.O. (Executive Order) 12898. 1994. §§ 1–101.

ESA (Endangered Species Act). 2000. 16 USC §§1531–1544.

Evenson, D. F., S. J. Hayes, G. Sandone, and D. J. Berg-strom. 2009. Yukon River Chinook salmon: stock status, harvest, and management. Pages 675–701 in C. C. Krueger and C. E. Zimmerman, editors. Pacific salmon: ecology and management of west-ern Alaska's populations. American Fisheries So-ciety, Symposium 70, Bethesda, Maryland.

Gilbertsen, N. 2004. Residency and the Alaska fisher-ies. Alaska Economic Trends. December 2004, volume 24, No. 12. Alaska Department of Labor and Workforce Development. Juneau.

Haflinger, K., and J. Gruver. 2009. Rolling hot spot clo-sure areas in the Bering Sea Walleye pollock fish-ery: estimated reduction of salmon bycatch during the 2006 season. Pages 817–826 in C. C. Krueger and C. E. Zimmerman, editors. Pacific salmon: ecology and management of western Alaska's populations. American Fisheries Society, Sympo-sium 70, Bethesda, Maryland.

Hall, S., and B. Mainprize, 2005. Managing by-catch and discards: how much progress are we mak-ing and how can we do better? Fish and Fisheries 6:134–155.

Hilborn, R., T. P. Quinn, D. E. Schindler, and D. E. Rogers. 2003. Biocomplexity and fisheries sus-tainability. Proceedings of the National Academy of Sciences USA 100:6564–6568.

ICA (Inter-coop Agreement). 2006. Salmon bycatch management agreement, 2006–2008 Pollock fish-ery. On file with author, Yukon River Drainage Fisheries Association, Anchorage, Alaska.

ICA (Inter-coop Agreement). 2008. Amended and re-stated Bering Sea pollock fishery rolling hot spot closure salmon bycatch management agreement. On file with author, Yukon River Drainage Fisher-ies Association, Anchorage, Alaska.

Kerret, D., and A. Tal. 2005. Greenwash of green gain? Predicting the success and evaluating the effec-tiveness of environmental voluntary agreements. Pennsylvania State Environmental Law Review 14: 31–84.

Linderman, J. C., Jr., and D. J. Bergstrom. 2009. Kuskokwim management area: salmon escapement, harvest, and management. Pages 541–599 *in* C. C. Krueger and C. E. Zimmerman, editors. Pacific salmon: ecology and management of western Alaska's populations. American Fisheries Society, Symposium 70, Bethesda, Maryland.

MSFCA (Magnuson-Stevens Fishery Management and Conservation Act). 2004. 16 U.S.C. §1851(a)(9).

Myers, K. W., R. V. Walker, J. L. Armstrong, N. D. Davis, and W. S. Patton. 2004. Estimates of the bycatch of Yukon River Chinook salmon in U.S. groundfish fisheries in the eastern Bering Sea, 1997–1999. Report to the Yukon River Drainage Fisheries Association, Anchorage, Alaska.

NMFS (National Marine Fisheries Service). 2006. Fisheries of the Exclusive Economic Zone off Alaska; application for an exempted fishing permit. Federal Register: Nov. 20, 2006 (Volume 71, Number 223).

NMFS (National Marine Fisheries Service). 2007a. Status of fisheries reports. Available: http://www.fakr.noaa.gov/2007/afa2007.pdf. (October 2007).

NMFS (National Marine Fisheries Service). 2007b. Endangered Species Act (ESA) Section 7 consultation – supplemental biological opinion. Consultation F/NWR/2006/06054. National Marine Fisheries Service, Northwest Region, Seattle.

NMFS (National Marine Fisheries Service). 2008a. BSAI Chinook Salmon Mortality Estimates, 1991–2008 . National Marine Fisheries Service, Northwest Region, Seattle, Washington. Available:http://www.fakr.noaa.gov/sustainablefisheries/inseason/chinook_salmon_mortality.pdf. (March 2009).

NMFS (National Marine Fisheries Service). 2008b. BSAI Non-Chinook Salmon Mortality Estimates, 1991–2008. National Marine Fisheries Service, Northwest Region, Seattle, Washington. Available: http://www.fakr.noaa.gov/sustainablefisheries/inseason/chum_salmon_mortality.pdf. (June 2008).

NMFS (National Marine Fisheries Service). 2009. BSAI Non-Chinook Salmon Mortality Estimates, 1991–2009. National Marine Fisheries Service, Northwest Region, Seattle, Washington. Available: http://www.fakr.noaa.gov/sustainablefisheries/inseason/chum_salmon_mortality.pdf. (March 2009).

Norris, S., and M. Hall. 2002. Thinking like an ocean: ecological lessons from marine bycatch. Conservation in Practice 3:6.

NPFMC (North Pacific Fisheries Management Council). 2005. Secretarial Review Draft: Environmental Assessment / Regulatory Impact Review / Initial Regulatory Flexibility Analysis for modifying existing Chinook and chum salmon savings areas. Proposed AMENDMENT 84 to the Fishery Management Plan for Groundfish of the Bering Sea and Aleutian Islands management area. North Pacific Fisheries Management Council, Anchorage, Alaska. Available: http://www.fakr.noaa.gov/npfmc/analyses/BSAI84salmonbycatch505.pdf (December 2008).

NPFMC (North Pacific Fisheries Management Council). 2006a. Fishery Management Plan for groundfish of the Bering Sea Aleutian Islands management area. North Pacific Fisheries Management Council, Anchorage, Alaska.

NPFMC (North Pacific Fisheries Management Council). 2006b. News and notes. volume 5–06, North Pacific Fisheries Management Council, Anchorage, Alaska.

NPFMC (North Pacific Fisheries Management Council). 2007. Bering Sea Aleutian Islands salmon bycatch: February 2007 Staff Discussion Paper. North Pacific Fisheries Management Council, Anchorage, Alaska. Available: http://www.fakr.noaa.gov/npfmc/current_issues/bycatch/Salmonbycatch_discpaper207.pdf (June 2008).

NPFMC (North Pacific Fisheries Management Council). 2008. Initial review draft only NPFMC review: draft Environmental Impact Statement for Bering Sea/Aleutian Islands Chinook salmon bycatch management. North Pacific Fisheries Management Council, Anchorage, Alaska. Available: http://www.fakr.noaa.gov/npfmc/current_issues/bycatch/Salmonbycatch508/EISsalmonbycatch508.pdf (June 2008).

Oliver, C. 1999. Implementing the American Fisheries Act of 1998: current and future actions of the North Pacific Fishery Management Council. North Pacific Fisheries Management Council, Anchorage, Alaska. Available: http://www.fakr.noaa.gov/npfmc/sci_papers/afalaw.pdf (June 2008).

Patton, W., K. W. Myers, and R. V. Walker. 1998. Origins of chum salmon caught incidentally in the eastern Bering Sea walleye pollock trawl fishery as estimated from scale pattern analysis. North American Journal of Fisheries Management 18:704–712.

Pew Oceans Commission. 2003. America's living oceans: charting a course for sea change. A Report to the Nation. Pew Oceans Commission, Arlington, Virginia.

Quinn, T. P. 2009. Pacific salmon population structure and dynamics: a perspective from Bristol Bay on life history variation across spatial and temporal scales. Pages 857–871 *in* C. C. Krueger and C. E. Zimmerman, editors. Pacific salmon: ecology and management of western Alaska's populations. American Fisheries Society, Symposium 70, Bethesda, Maryland.

Rearden, M., and D. Gillikin. 2009. A perspective on ecosystem-based fishery management of the

Kuskokwim River: a 2015 vision of the future. Pages 601–609 *in* C. C. Krueger and C. E. Zimmerman, editors. Pacific salmon: ecology and management of western Alaska's populations. American Fisheries Society, Symposium 70, Bethesda, Maryland.

Stram, D. L., and J. N. Ianelli. 2009. Eastern Bering Sea pollock trawl fisheries: variation in salmon bycatch over time and space. Pages 827–850 *in* C. C. Krueger and C. E. Zimmerman, editors. Pacific salmon: ecology and management of western Alaska's populations. American Fisheries Society, Symposium 70, Bethesda, Maryland.

Stump, K., J. Hocevar, B. Baumann, and S. Marz. 2006. Rethinking sustainability: a new paradigm for fisheries management. Alaska Oceans Program, Center for Biological Diversity, Greenpeace, Trustees for Alaska. Alaska Oceans Program, Anchorage. Available: http://www.greenpeace.org/usa/assets/binaries/rethinking-sustainability (June 2008).

U.S. Commission on Ocean Policy. 2004. An ocean blueprint for the 21st Century. Final Report. Washington, DC.

USOFR (U.S. Office of the Federal Register). 2006. Fishery Conservation and Management, National Oceanic and Atmospheric Administration, Department of Commerce; Magnuson Steven Act Provisions. Code of Federal Regulations, Title 50, Section 350(d). U.S. Government Printing Office, Washington, D.C.

Wilmot, R. L., C. M. Kondzela, C. M. Guthrie, and M. M. Masuda. 1998. Genetic stock identification of chum salmon harvested incidentally in the 1994 and 995 Bering Sea trawl fishery. North Pacific Anadromous Fish Commission Bulletin 1: 285–299.

Witherell, D. 1997. A brief history of bycatch management measures for eastern Bering Sea groundfish fisheries. Marine Fisheries Review 59:15–22.

Witherell, D., D. Ackley, and C. Coon. 2002. An overview of salmon bycatch in Alaska groundfish fisheries. Alaska Fishery Research Bulletin 9:53–64.

YRDFA (Yukon River Drainage Fisheries Association) and Yukon River Panel. 2005. Yukon River salmon agreement handbook, Anchorage, Alaska and Whitehorse, YT. Yukon River Drainage Fisheries Association. Anchorage, Alaska.

YRSA. 2002. Pacific Salmon Treaty, Annex IV Chapter 8 (27)(Yukon River Salmon Agreement)(2002). Yukon River Panel, Whitehorse. Available: http://www.yukonriverpanel.com/Library/Other/YRS%20Agreement.pdf (June 2008).

American Fisheries Society Symposium 70:817–826, 2009
© 2009 by the American Fisheries Society

Rolling Hot Spot Closure Areas in the Bering Sea Walleye Pollock Fishery: Estimated Reduction of Salmon Bycatch During the 2006 Season

KARL HAFLINGER[*]

Sea State Inc.

P. O. Box 74, Vashon, Washington 98070, USA

JOHN GRUVER

United Catcher Boats

4005 20th Ave W., Suite 116, Seattle, Washington 98199, USA

Abstract.—In recent years, salmon bycatch rates have risen significantly in the Bering Sea walleye pollock *Theragra chalcogramma* fishery. Rising numbers of chum *Oncorhynchus keta* and Chinook salmon *O. tshawytscha* bycatch triggered fixed time and area closures, which were designed to reduce salmon bycatch. Vessels forced by these closures to fish in non-traditional areas often found bycatch rates to be higher outside than inside closed areas. This paper describes the fishing industry's development of the hot spot closure area approach and analyzes bycatch during the 2006 "B" season and compares it to predicted catch without the closures. Walleye pollock vessel owners, organized into cooperatives under the American Fisheries Act, designed a plan of rolling hot spot closures that used near-real-time data supplied by observers to identify and close areas of high salmon bycatch. Closed areas changed during the season to match movements of salmon passing through the pollock fishing grounds. Vessels agreed via an inter-cooperative contract to abide by closures determined by a third party (Sea State, Incorporated), with substantial penalties for non-compliance, as determined by data from a satellite vessel monitoring system (VMS) records. This adaptive hot spot closure agreement was accepted by the North Pacific Fisheries Management Council as a replacement for the fixed salmon savings closures. The cooperative agreement was in place and active through an Exempted Fishing Permit during the 2006 "B" season (June 10 to November 1). Results based on data from observers on a sample of vessels indicated that when high bycatch areas were rapidly identified, and closed salmon bycatch was reduced outside of the traditional savings areas. For those boats displaced from closure areas, Chinook bycatch was reduced by 20%, and other salmon bycatch (predominantly chum salmon) by 64%.

[*]Corresponding author: karl@seastateinc.com

Introduction

During the first half of the 1990s, several years of high salmon bycatch levels in the midwater pollock *Theragra chalcogramma* fishery prompted the North Pacific Fishery Management Council (Council) to address the issue (Witherell et al. 2002; Witherell and Pautzke 1997). In 1993, the Council adopted a series of time and area closures that were intended to move the fleet out of areas of highest salmon bycatch when bycatch was expected to be high. The area closures were, with one exception, triggered when the fleet's bycatch of Chinook *Oncorhynchus tshawytscha* and "other salmon" (primarily chum salmon *O. keta*), reached threshold levels. As western Alaska salmon stocks declined in the mid-1990s, these thresholds were never met, a condition that prompted the Council to reduce the thresholds in stages, beginning in 2000. Chinook and chum salmon stocks appeared to rebound with high bycatch numbers being caught in the pollock fishery beginning in 2001 (Stram and Ianelli 2009, this volume). Bycatch over the entire season increased steadily through 2005 for chum salmon, and 2006 for Chinook salmon (Table 1; Stram and Ianelli 2009; Witherell and Pautzke 1997; Witherell et al. 2002).

These increasing salmon bycatch numbers finally led to the triggering of the area closures that had been enacted earlier. Unfortunately, the efficacy of these closures proved questionable (NPFMC 2005). The Council's assumption was that if areas that showed historically high bycatch were closed, the fleet would then be forced to operate in areas where salmon accumulation would be lower than in the closed areas. However, most of those potential harvest areas were not well represented in the analysis because they were not traditional fishing grounds. Upon redirection of pollock fishing effort, it appeared that salmon bycatch rates (numbers of salmon per metric ton of pollock, or N/mt) were actually higher at times outside than inside in the areas that had been closed (NPFMC 2005). At times the salmon savings measures appeared to actually result in an increase in salmon bycatch (NPFMC 2005).

Pollock fishing vessel owners and operators were not surprised by the high salmon bycatch rates found outside of the traditional pollock fishing areas, as experience had shown that salmon could be found in those areas at certain times of the year, and the assumption that closing the traditional fishing grounds in the hopes that salmon bycatch rates were lower elsewhere was untested. In response, fishing industry representatives developed a system of rolling "hot spot" closures designed to restrict fishing in high salmon bycatch areas while still leaving other areas with low salmon bycatch (or "clean areas") open for fishing (Gisclair 209, this volume). This approach required that all participants in the fishery observe closures of selected areas of the ocean. Closures were based on bycatch rates of either Chinook or chum salmon, although closures for Chinook salmon were given priority over chum salmon if high rates of both species were encountered on the fishing grounds. This approach was facilitated by having the fishery organized into fishing cooperatives through the enactment of the American Fisheries Act. The closed "hot spot" areas may change twice weekly, with closures based on bycatch rates reported by federal observers. The actual delineation of the closure areas is based on an initial analysis of spatial patterns in bycatch rates by Sea State Inc., and subsequent consultation with a representative of all pollock cooperatives, the Inter-co-op manager.

Enforcement of the savings closures was accomplished by monitoring each vessel's satellite vessel-monitoring system (VMS), with monetary penalties assessed against vessel operators who fish inside the closure areas. A vessel-level incentive was built into the

Table 1. Pollock catch (mt) and salmon bycatch (*N* = numbers) in the Bering Sea walleye pollock fishery for the years 2000–2006 from August 1 through November 1 and for the entire year. Other salmon are primarily chum salmon.

Year	August 1 to November 1			Entire year		
	Pollock (mt)	Chinook salmon (*N*)	Other salmon (*N*)	Pollock (mt)	Chinook salmon (*N*)	Other salmon (*N*)
2006	546,499	21,244	123,266	1,453,037	80,844	277,996
2005	495,544	42,581	333,401	1,451,268	68,038	638,570
2004	490,934	27,889	380,652	1,437,776	50,714	428,793
2003	526,149	13,083	156,909	1,453,525	44,425	174,070
2002	558,510	12,996	78,407	1,437,789	33,786	83,833
2001	601,151	13,546	47,061	1,351,956	30,163	53,255
2000	562,660	1,618	40,771	1,080,734	5,245	57,541

program in that each week each cooperative was assigned to one of three tiers based on the members' bycatch rates over the preceding two weeks. Cooperatives were assigned to tiers (by Sea State, Inc.) by comparing each cooperative's chum salmon bycatch rate (number of salmon caught per mt of pollock caught for all member vessels, computed over a two-week interval) to a reference "base rate" defined by the intercooperative agreement. The base rate varied throughout the season, and was defined as a three-week running average of chum salmon bycatch rate for all vessels in the fishery. Vessels were then allowed selective access to chum salmon closure areas based on their tier assignment. For all chum salmon closures and Chinook salmon closures in the 'A' season (January–June), vessels may be able to fish inside closed areas based on their tier assignment (Table 2). In the 'B' season (June–October), all vessels were prohibited from fishing inside the Chinook salmon closures regardless of their tier status. Thus, for those closures that allowed selective fishing inside the closure areas (A season), if all the vessels in a cooperative reduce their bycatch rates, significantly more grounds being available to fishing by the cooperative members.

This paper analyzes bycatch during the 2006 "B" season and compares observed bycatch with rolling hot spot closures to predicted bycatch without the closures. The paper represents one of three presentations made at the Arctic-Yukon-Kuskokwim Sustainable Salmon symposium held in 2007 on the topic of salmon bycatch in the walleye pollock fishery (Gisclair 2009; Stram and Ianelli 2009).

Methods

Estimation of the reduction in salmon bycatch due to the rolling "hot spot" closures was based on tracking vessels that fished in an area that subsequently was closed, and then comparing their bycatch afterwards to see if it was lower than expected if the area had not been closed. Observer data obtained from the North Pacific Groundfish Observer Program (NOAA Fisheries) for haul locations was tabulated in each closure area for a 5-d period preceding its closure. For shoreside catcher vessels, bycatch of salmon was determined when vessels delivered their entire catch to a processing plant; thus, although observers estimated the pollock catch in each individual

TABLE 2. Tier assignments and their effect on fishing in the walleye pollock fishery in the Bering Sea. Cooperatives were assigned to tiers (by Sea State, Inc.) by comparing each cooperatives chum salmon bycatch rate (number of salmon caught per mt of pollock caught for all member vessels, computed over a two-week interval) to a reference "base rate" defined by an intercooperative agreement. The base rate varied throughout the season, and was defined as a three week running average of chum salmon bycatch rate for all vessels in the fishery. Vessels were then allowed selective access to chum salmon closure areas based on their tier assignment.

Tier level	Percent of base rate	Effect
1	< 75%	Not subject to closures
2	75%–1.25%	Observe closures for 4 days (Friday to Tuesday)
3	> 1.25%	Observe closures for 7 days (Friday to Friday)

haul of a trip, salmon bycatch was assumed to be spread uniformly among all hauls in a single trip. For these vessels, pollock catch and salmon bycatch were summed across all hauls that had the same "start fishing date" so that hauls with the same bycatch rate were not treated as separate observations. As an example, if two hauls from the same catcher vessel trip occurred in the closed area, they will have the same bycatch rate because the bycatch is pro-rated evenly across all hauls. In the offshore sector, which included catcher processors (vessels that process their own catch) and motherships (vessels that act as a floating processor for a fleet of smaller catcher boats), estimates of pollock weight and salmon numbers were made for each haul. All of these offshore sector hauls, along with combined "trip-level" hauls were considered to be estimates of the bycatch ratio:

$$Ri = \Sigma yi / \Sigma xi$$

where y were counts of Chinook or chum salmon, and x was the walleye pollock catch from individual hauls (offshore sector) or grouped, same-trip hauls (shoreside), and i indicated a separate closure.

The same type of pollock catch and salmon bycatch data for the same vessels for the next five days were then used to compute an expected bycatch by vessel, had those vessels been able to stay and fish inside the now-closed area. The expected bycatch was calculated by summing the pollock catch of all vessels in this category, and multiplying this summed pollock catch by the matching bycatch ratio, Ri above:

$$Bi = (\Sigma Ci) \times Ri,$$

where B is expected bycatch, C is pollock catch per vessel, and R is the bycatch ratio estimator for the ith closure group being tracked, (Snedecor and Cochran 1989).

Actual bycatch for these vessels was estimated by federal observers who sample portions of the vessel's catch to determine catch composition. For vessels delivering to shoreside processors, all salmon are enumerated by vessel observers while the vessel is unloading. Estimation of salmon caught by catcher processors or vessels delivering to motherships was based on sampling some fraction of the catch for all species and expanding the sample fraction to estimate the value of the entire species composition of the haul (see Turnock and Karp 1997). Extrapolations from samples to total catch of all species were supplied by the observer program to Sea State, Inc. Total counts of all salmon delivered to shore plants are provided by the plants to Sea State, Inc. Comparison of the actual salmon bycatch to the expected bycatch was expressed as a percentage reduction in bycatch associated with the displacement of fishing effort from closure areas.

Results

To illustrate the approach used with voluntary hot spot closure, data from September 22, 2006 were graphically displayed on maps (Figures 1–3). This closure went into effect on September 22, 2006, with 23 observed hauls taken in the area to be closed during the five-day period preceding the closure (Figure 1). After the closure, vessels that had been in that closure area (i.e., those whose hauls are shown in Figure 1) either moved a small distance to the southwest (Figure 2), or made large moves to the northwest (Figure 3). Chinook salmon bycatch based on observer data

for the vessels displaced from the closures, for the five-day period after the closure, was 403 Chinook salmon, while expected bycatch if the vessels had not moved, was 903 Chinook salmon, or a 55% reduction in expected bycatch of Chinook salmon.

Salmon bycatch during the 2006 "B" season

Based on observed versus expected bycatch for approximately 40,000 mt of observed groundfish catch associated with boats that fished inside areas before they were closed, and that also had observers after closures, 1,692 Chinook and 62,732 chum salmon were not caught as bycatch or were avoided (Table 3). Salmon closures made on the basis of bycatch rates reduced Chinook salmon bycatch by 22%, and other salmon (mostly chum salmon) bycatch by 66%. Closures made on the basis of other salmon bycatch rates increased Chinook salmon bycatch by 27% while reducing other salmon bycatch by 63% (Table 3). Chinook salmon savings (reduced bycatch)

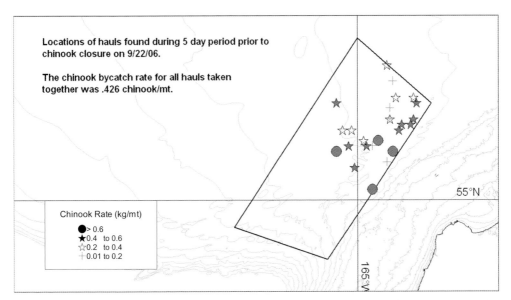

FIGURE 1. Trawl hauls selected for analysis of a voluntary rolling hot spot closure on September 22, 2006 caused by Chinook salmon bycatch in the Bering Sea walleye pollock fishery. Each point symbol on the map represents a haul location, and symbol type indicates bycatch rate according to the legend.

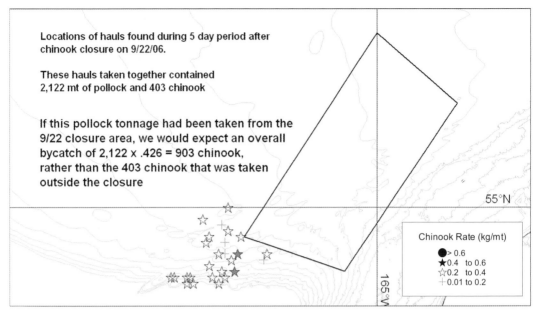

FIGURE 2. Five-day fishing activity for vessels shown in the first map (Figure 1) showing vessel positions and bycatch rate for Chinook salmon that led to a reduction from an expected Chinook salmon bycatch of 903 to 403 fish observed (i.e., counted by observers from the trawl haul positions shown).

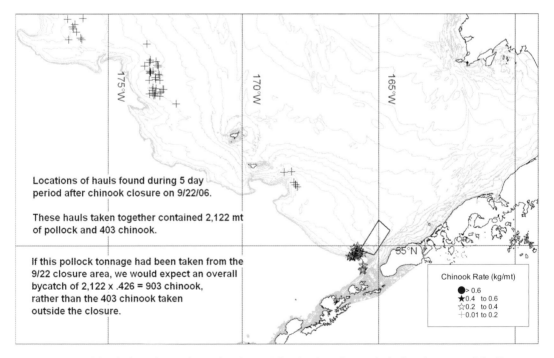

FIGURE 3. Trawl hauls from boats shown in Figure 1 for the five-day period after the start of the September 22, 2006 voluntary rolling hot spot closure (shown as the box) in the Bering Sea walleye pollock fishery.

TABLE 3. Reduction in Chinook and chum salmon bycatch estimated in the Bering Sea walleye pollock fishery due to voluntary rolling hotspot closures during the June to October 2006 period (B season).

	Chinook salmon closures	Chum salmon closures	All closures
Pollock catch after closure (numbers)	24,852	16,839	41,691
Observed chinook salmon bycatch (numbers)	6,270	448	6,718
Expected chinook salmon bycatch (numbers)	8,057	353	8,410
Chinook salmon bycatch reduction (numbers)	1,787	−95	1,692
% reduction	22%	−27%	20%
Observed chum salmon bycatch (numbers)	7,671	27,697	35,368
Expected chum salmon bycatch (numbers)	22,786	75,314	98,100
Chum salmon bycatch reduction (numbers)	15,115	47,617	62,732
% reduction	66%	63%	64%

due to Chinook salmon closures were much higher than bycatch losses due to other salmon closures, with a net Chinook salmon bycatch reduction of 20% due to closures for both Chinook and other salmon. Net chum salmon bycatch reduction or savings due to both type of closures, was 64%. These results were based on evaluation of 20 closures for which observer information was available for five days before and five days after closures were in effect. Closures were sometimes based on deliveries from catcher vessels that did not carry observers, or that dropped off observers after closures were announced; thus, for five of 25 closures made during the season, no evaluation was possible.

All Chinook salmon closures in the 2006 'B' season were located south of the Pribilof Islands (Figure 4). Bycatch rates (N salmon per mt of pollock) for the 2006 "B" season pollock fishery, from September 5, 2006 onward (which was when most Chinook were encountered) were kept to approximately 0.25 Chinook salmon per mt over most of the fishing grounds south of the Pribilof Islands (Figure 5). An exception to this was found in an area of the middle shelf that was characterized by the low bycatch rate of 0.03 salmon per mt (Figure 5). Unfortunately, this area does not usually have fishable concentrations of pollock in the "B" season, and pollock could not be found in this area during most of the period examined. Grounds further to the north were found to have lower bycatch rates than those to the south, but those areas were too far from processing plants for all but the largest shoreside-delivering catcher vessels to fish. This final uniformity in bycatch rates south of the Pribilof Islands was an indication that more extensive closures than those enacted would not have further lowered bycatch; rather, it is apparent that for 2006 no closures short of a complete cessation of pollock fishing south of the Pribilof Islands would have reduced overall bycatch south of the Pribilofs much below a rate of 0.25 salmon per metric ton.

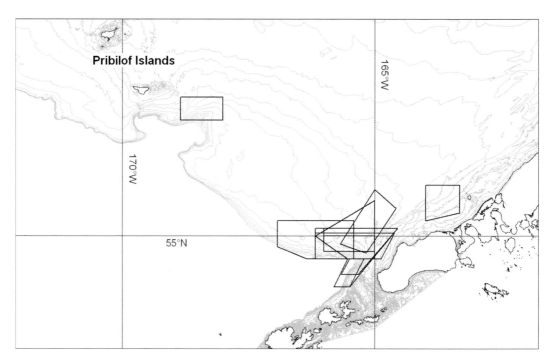

FIGURE 4. All voluntary rolling hot spot closures made south of the Pribilof Islands during the 2006 June–October (B season) in the Bering Sea walleye pollock fishery.

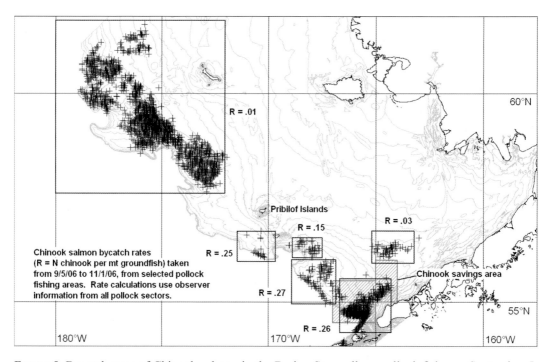

FIGURE 5. Bycatch rates of Chinook salmon in the Bering Sea walleye pollock fishery: September 5, 2006–November 1, 2006.

Discussion

Management of bycatch has clearly become a major challenge to fishery managers. Traditional approaches to bycatch reduction have included time and area closures, and gear modification. While certainly effective in certain instances, often neither will suffice to limit bycatch to acceptable bounds (see Alaska Sea Grant 1995). Time and area closures, in particular, can be placed incorrectly, both on the calendar and in space, as fish often respect neither of these boundaries. Gear modification can be tremendously frustrating to the fishing industry as mechanisms for allowing the release of incidentally caught organisms because changes in gear can reduce the catch rate of the target species.

The rolling hot-spot closures described in this paper were time-area closures and were not based upon historical patterns of abundance. Instead, the closures were based on the overlap of fishing activity and bycatch species distribution, evaluated in near real time via observer reports and enforced via satellite monitoring. This approach is likely to be most useful in addressing bycatch problems in which patterns of overlap between target and incidentally caught species change quickly and unpredictably. Responding to these changes requires the rapid acquisition, transmission, and analysis of data describing both target catch and bycatch. Advances in communication technology over the last decade have made it possible to execute avoidance programs such as described above, and although the approach can require large-scale redistribution of fishing effort (with concomitant cost), the reduction in salmon bycatch can be considerable.

The overall numbers of salmon saved by this program reported here were for those vessels with observers that could be tracked by fishing immediately prior to the closure in the closure area, and then just after the area closed. Other boats, whose activities were also affected by closures but did not have observers or did not fish prior to or after closures, were assumed to have experienced bycatch reductions similar to those boats with observers. Further, some vessels avoided the closure areas entirely and chose instead to fish in the northwest, where salmon were rarely encountered, and to the degree that this decision was influenced by potential closure activity represents another potential but unquantified source of reduced bycatch. For shoreside catcher vessels in particular, the uncertainty over whether or not the grounds they were fishing were to be closed was a significant factor in deciding whether to fish on any given trip. These catcher vessels often typically had only two days in which to fill their vessels with catch and return to port before catch quality degrades. If during the middle of a trip their grounds were taken away by a salmon closure, they could have been forced to return to shore with only a partial load. We cannot quantify the importance of this variable in a captain's decision to fish away from the closure areas, but this concern has been reported and this aspect may be another avenue in which salmon closures reduced bycatch.

Are the voluntary hot spot closures described for this program sufficient to reduce salmon bycatch? The ability to reduce the bycatch rate south of the Pribilof Islands to a nearly-uniform 0.25 Chinook salmon/mt pollock suggests that further efforts to reduce bycatch in the areas that may be fished by small to mid-sized shoreside-delivering catcher vessels, using area closures alone, would likely be ineffective. Current efforts to develop salmon excluders for pelagic trawls may provide some relief, but for the Bering Sea pollock B season, the simplest way to reduce salmon bycatch is to avoid fishing later in the season, and instead concentrate fishing effort earlier in the summer when bycatch is minimal.

References

Alaska Sea Grant. 1995. Solving bycatch, considerations for today and tomorrow. Report Number 96–03. Alaska Sea Grant College Program, Fairbanks.

Gisclair, B. R. 2009. Salmon bycatch management in the Bering Sea Walleye pollock fishery: threats and opportunities for western Alaska. Pages 799–816 *in* C. C. Krueger and C. E. Zimmerman, editors. Pacific salmon: ecology and management of western Alaska's populations. American Fisheries Society, Symposium 70, Bethesda, Maryland.

NPFMC. August 2005. Environmental Assessment / Regulatory Impact Review / Initial Regulatory Flexibility Analysis for modifying existing Chinook and chum salmon savings areas. Proposed AMENDMENT 84 to the Fishery Management Plan for Groundfish of the Bering Sea and Aleutian Islands Management Area.

Snedecor, G. W., and W. G. Cochran. 1989. Statistical methods, 8th edition. Iowa State University Press, Ames, Iowa.

Stram, D. L., and J. N. Ianelli. 2009. Eastern Bering Sea pollock trawl fisheries: variation in salmon bycatch over time and space. Pages 827–850 *in* C. C. Krueger and C. E. Zimmerman, editors. Pacific salmon: ecology and management of western Alaska's populations. American Fisheries Society, Symposium 70, Bethesda, Maryland.

Turnock, J., and W.A. Karp. 1997. Estimation of salmon bycatch in the 1995 pollock fishery in the Bering Sea/Aleutian Islands—a comparison of methods based on observer sampling and counts of salmon retained by fishing vessel and processing plant personnel. Alaska Fisheries Science Center, National Marine Fisheries Service, Seattle.

Witherell, D., D. Ackley, and C. Coon. 2002. An overview of salmon bycatch in Alaska groundfish fisheries. Alaska Fishery Research Bulletin 9:53–64.

Witherell, D., and C. Pautzke. 1997. A brief history of bycatch management measures for Eastern Bering Sea groundfish fisheries. Marine Fisheries Review 59:15–22.

American Fisheries Society Symposium 70:827–850, 2009

Eastern Bering Sea Pollock Trawl Fisheries: Variation in Salmon Bycatch over Time and Space

Diana L. Stram[*]

North Pacific Fishery Management Council
605 West 4th, Suite 306, Anchorage, Alaska 99501, USA

James N. Ianelli

Alaska Fisheries Science Center, National Marine Fisheries Service
7600 Sand Point Way NE Building 4, Seattle, Washington 98115, USA

Abstract.—The Magnuson-Stevens Act emphasizes the importance of minimizing bycatch, to the extent practicable, as part of the goal to achieve sustainable fisheries. Measures to reduce Pacific salmon (*Oncorhynchus* spp.) bycatch for the eastern Bering Sea walleye pollock *Theragra chalcogramma* trawl fisheries have been developed and implemented, resulting in specific closed (no-fishing) areas when established bycatch limits for Pacific salmon are exceeded. These closure areas were designed based on analyses of groundfish observer data collected from 1990–1995, yet in recent years Pacific salmon bycatch in the pollock fishery has consistently exceeded the limits. As a result, large areas were closed to the fishery, and the spatial pattern of fishing by the pollock fleet was altered. An analysis of the effectiveness of the closed-area management system was reviewed by the North Pacific Fishery Management Council (Council) in 2005, and indicated that when areas were closed, salmon bycatch rates were often higher than observed earlier inside the closure areas. Thus, as an interim measure, the Council adopted a program in October 2005 to exempt vessels from the existing closed-area regulations so that near-real time inseason information could be used to establish dynamic closed areas where salmon bycatch levels are high. In this paper, we review information on the previous closed area management system and qualitatively characterize historical bycatch patterns using fishery observer data. Our results show that the spatial and temporal salmon bycatch patterns are highly variable between years. Variability in size and sex composition of the salmon bycatch adds to the complexity of developing effective management options aimed at minimizing the bycatch of the eastern Bering Sea pollock fishery. These results should assist managers in devising alternative approaches for managing salmon bycatch in the pollock trawl fisheries.

[*]Corresponding author: Diana.Stram@noaa.gov

Introduction

The walleye pollock *Theragra chalcogramma* fishery is one of the largest fisheries in the world and represents a major component of all commercial Alaskan fisheries (Hiatt et al. 2006). Compared to most fisheries, the relative bycatch of all other species is low representing only about 1.2% of the total removals by weight due to the pollock fishery, 24% of which is attributed to jellyfish while 63% of the bycatch consisted of other quota-managed target groundfish species (Ianelli et al. 2006). This bycatch compares with nation-wide bycatch estimates of about 22% (Harrington et al. 2005). Harrington et al. (2005) estimated bycatch in all Alaskan fisheries as approximately 11% by weight. However, because the pollock fishery catch is large (average 1.464 million t 2001–2005), the absolute magnitude of bycatch needs to be closely monitored, especially of Pacific salmon *Oncorhynchus* spp. Salmon represent an extremely important resource to Alaska and to the countries surrounding the North Pacific. The stock of origin of salmon species in pollock trawl bycatch in the eastern Bering Sea (EBS) has been shown to have a high proportion originating from western Alaska (Myers et al. 2004; Myers and Rogers 1988; Wilmot et al. 1998; Patton et al. 1998; Myers et al. 2009, this volume). Salmon support large and critically important commercial, recreational, and subsistence fisheries, and are the basis of a cultural tradition in many parts of the state. Witherell et al. (2002) characterized the bycatch from groundfish fisheries in the Bering Sea Aleutian Islands (BSAI) for chum *O. keta* and Chinook *O. tshawytscha* salmon. Their results indicated that while chum salmon bycatch from these fisheries may not have substantial effect on western Alaskan runs, the impact of groundfish fisheries on Chinook salmon stocks may be larger (Witherell et al. 2002). The bycatch of both chum and Chinook salmon in the EBS pollock fishery have reached historic highs since the Witherell et al. (2002) analysis was completed, thus the relative impact of bycatch on those stocks may be greater than previously estimated. Consequently, the bycatch mortality of Pacific salmon stocks due to the fishery requires careful evaluation.

Salmon bycatch in the EBS pollock fishery occurs in both the "A" and "B" seasons. The A-season commences on January 20th and extends until late March or early April, until about 40% of the available pollock quota is reached. This early fishery is focused on the southeast portion of the EBS and targets prespawning pollock. The valuable roe from these fish are the main product form with the flesh used for fillets or surimi. The B-season opens in June and continues generally until mid-October for the remaining 60% of the quota. This fishery is typically spread over the outer shelf edge of the Bering Sea extending to the Russian border. Chinook salmon are commonly taken incidentally by pollock trawl gear during both A- and B-seasons. Chum salmon are primarily taken during the B-season. The pollock fleet is composed of three sectors: catcher-vessels that deliver catches to shore-side processing plants, catcher-vessels that deliver to at-sea processing motherships, and vessels that catch and process their fish on board (catcher-processors). By regulation, catcher-processors are restricted from some near-shore areas because shore-based catcher vessels have more limitations on the locations they can fish.

The inseason salmon bycatch management uses scientific observer data and Chinook salmon bycatch annual limits are currently set at 29,000 fish. If inseason catch estimates exceed this value, a closed area is invoked (Figure 1; top panel; NMFS 1999). The Bering Sea "Chinook Salmon Savings Area" was developed based on an analysis of available observer data from 1990 through 1994 (ADF&G 1995a). The Chinook salmon limit, and the time of year that

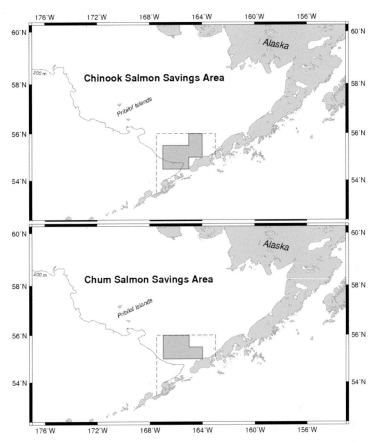

FIGURE 1. NMFS regulatory areas for Chinook salmon (top) and chum salmon (bottom) established in 1996. The dashed outline represents the catcher-vessel operational area (CVOA) management area.

the limit is exceeded, affect how the closure occurs. If the trigger limit is exceeded before April 15, the area closes from that day through the end of the winter-spring fishery (typically late October or early November). In this case, the B-season fishery would be open in all areas from June–September 1st, after which the areas would close for the rest of the year. If the limit is reached after April 15, but before September 1, the areas would close on September 1 through the end of the year. If the limit is reached after September 1, the areas close on that date through the end of the year. Since their establishment, the pollock fishery has been excluded from the Chinook Salmon Savings Areas in each year from 2003–2006 whereas prior to 2003,

the levels of Chinook salmon bycatch were below the limit and closures did not occur. Over this time period, the Chinook salmon bycatch was highest in 2006. During this year, the winter fishery caused the Chinook Salmon Savings Area to close on February 14th. This was the first time the closure occurred during the winter fishery.

For chum salmon, a "Chum Salmon Savings Area" (Figure 1; bottom panel) was established in 1994 by emergency rule, and then formalized in the groundfish Fishery Management Plan in 1995 (ADF&G 1995b). By rule, this area is closed to all trawling from August 1 through August 31. Additionally, if 42,000 "other" salmon (i.e., non-Chinook salmon, 98% of which are chum salmon; NPFMC

2005) are caught in the "catcher vessel operational area" (CVOA) during the period August 14–October 14, an additional closure period will be invoked. This period will begin on September 14 and extend through October 14, unless the limit is reached within this period, in which case it will close on the date the limit is exceeded. Catcher processors are prohibited from fishing in the CVOA during the second half of the year (except for operations associated with community development quotas). Since the establishment of the savings area in 1995, the bycatch levels of "other salmon" have resulted in additional closure periods (beyond the automatic August 1–31 period) from 2002 to 2005, but not in 2006.

In this study, salmon bycatch trends in the walleye pollock fishery were described in terms of annual, seasonal, and daily variation. Also, bycatch was compared between sea-and land-based vessels for differences in catch rates between sexes. Additionally, the relationship between the size of salmon and the level of bycatch was evaluated because understanding this relationship may help explain changes due to salmon behavior and the relative size and sources (Asian or North American origin) of salmon runs.

Methods

The National Marine Fisheries Service (NMFS) trained observers to collect the data used here to evaluate patterns of salmon bycatch. Observers are required to sample all salmon found in the catch. Salmon caught by shore-based "catcher vessels" are sampled at the plant where pollock are delivered. Observers record sex, weight, and total length of salmon by species. Observer sampling protocols are described by NMFS (2007). From the observer collections, two datasets were compiled: haul-specific information and length-frequency information.

The haul-specific dataset included detailed information on pollock catch, total catch of all other groundfish species, haul position, date, time of day, depth of bottom, depth of fishing, vessel type, and numbers of salmon (categorized as either Chinook or non-Chinook salmon). For catch accounting and Pacific Salmon Commission limits, four species of salmon (sockeye, coho, pink, and chum) are aggregated into an 'other salmon' (a non-Chinook salmon species category). Chum salmon comprises over 99.6% of the total catch in this category (NPFMC 2005). Haul-specific data were available from 1990 to 2006 and included only at-sea observations (Table 1). For the purposes of this analysis, the at-sea sampling was considered representative of the salmon bycatch. Fishing operations that were clearly targeting pollock were isolated by including only trawl-haul observations in which pollock catch represented more than 80% (by weight). The actual observed salmon bycatch represents about 82% and 71% of the estimated total catch of Chinook and chum salmon, respectively (during 2003–2006). This estimate suggests that due to the high level of observer coverage, a large fraction of the bycatch was directly observed. The detailed haul information was used to evaluate geographically stratified seasonal and inter-annual bycatch patterns and variability.

The length-frequency dataset included salmon species-specific data from 1998 to 2006. These data included information on large-scale area, date, sex, and length. The salmon sampled for lengths by season and area over years are summarized in Table 2. Fish measured were selected systematically to avoid potential biases. The salmon bycatch length frequency data were examined for seasonal and sex-specific patterns in addition to trends in time. This type of information is important for inferring the age-composition of the bycatch and the potential effects on different spawning groups (i.e., whether the

TABLE 1. Raw observer-data totals of pollock catch (*t*) and salmon (numbers) by seasons. Note that official totals will differ due to expansions to unobserved operations.

Year	A Season (Jan–May)			B Season (Jun–Dec)			Total Pollock	Total Chinook	Total Chum
	Pollock	Chinook	Chum	Pollock	Chinook	Chum			
1990	405,672	3,847	159	583,119	3,039	9,924	988,791	6,886	10,083
1991	328,831	12,078	295	435,318	2,226	12,250	764,149	14,304	12,545
1992	308,989	14,985	645	487,893	7,595	25,762	796,882	22,581	26,407
1993	358,098	12,456	201	474,089	7,898	133,073	832,188	20,354	133,274
1994	392,624	15,179	383	514,568	3,562	67,759	907,192	18,741	68,141
1995	447,995	6,978	377	482,919	2,347	29,912	930,914	9,325	30,289
1996	367,290	24,346	147	421,396	13,328	51,825	788,686	37,673	51,971
1997	343,402	8,100	1,263	398,346	23,192	43,529	741,748	31,292	44,791
1998	384,397	11,527	3,784	413,731	27,492	30,758	798,129	39,019	34,543
1999	331,664	8,441	111	478,312	8,595	30,067	809,976	17,036	30,178
2000	371,911	5,272	238	567,065	4,437	44,617	938,976	9,709	44,855
2001	469,254	17,402	2,291	682,142	13,205	45,621	1,151,396	30,607	47,912
2002	499,437	18,502	1,033	744,601	11,336	64,376	1,244,039	29,838	65,409
2003	519,043	28,721	3,408	755,783	12,940	134,160	1,274,826	41,661	137,568
2004	510,953	21,301	391	732,256	23,994	345,032	1,243,208	45,295	345,423
2005	511,460	27,006	519	747,335	32,423	496,726	1,258,795	59,429	497,245
2006	534,293	54,450	2,308	765,460	23,703	222,115	1,299,753	78,153	224,423

bycatch mortality consists of salmon that are likely to be maturing and returning to rivers within the next several months versus the next couple of years).

Results

Overall, salmon bycatch levels have increased considerably in recent years (Table 3). The catch data for the three species separated by season and latitudinal bands (S = south of 56°N, M = 56° to 58°N, N = north of 58°N) show that inter-annual variability was lowest for pollock, whereas chum salmon was the highest (Table 4). Also, the observed Chinook salmon mean catch level was slightly higher during the A-season than during the B-season, whereas the vast majority of chum salmon were taken during the B-season (Table 4). In addition, the inter-annual variability in the northern region was slightly higher during the B-season than during the A-season for all three species (Table 4).

The catch per hour of fishing for pollock was higher in the A- than the B-season, but has been relatively stable over time, whereas the catch per observed hour fishing has increased dramatically for Chinook salmon during the A-season and for chum salmon during the B-season (Figure 2). Based on cumulative catch over the years, considerable seasonal and inter-annual variability are apparent for Chinook and chum salmon (Figure 3).

The bycatch levels of salmon generally tend to be higher in shore-based catcher vessels than for at-sea catcher processors. The percent of tows with salmon present has increased over time for both shore-based catcher vessels (mean of 42%) and at-sea catcher processors (mean of 17%; Figure 4). Note that the drop in Chinook incidence in tows by the shore-based catcher-vessel fleet in 2000 was due to the closure of the CVOA in the B-season of that year due to conservation concerns over the western stock of Steller sea lion *Eumetopias jubatus*.

TABLE 2. Numbers of Chinook and chum salmon sampled by A (January–May) and B (June–December) seasons and by regions (S = south of 56°, M = 56° - 58°, N = north of 58°).

| Chinook | A season | | | | B season | | | | Annual |
	S	M	N	Total	S	M	N	sub-total	Total
1998	2,008	91	39	2,138	3,550	519	171	4,240	6,378
1999	736	368	16	1,120	394	225	615	1,234	2,354
2000	979	501	2	1,482	5	188	141	334	1,816
2001	2,041	1,776	7	3,824	1,123	2,443	226	3,792	7,616
2002	7,326	2,144		9,470	5,873	403	52	6,328	15,798
2003	11,551	4,405	85	16,041	4,078	2,652	1,007	7,737	23,778
2004	6,996	4,257	13	11,266	8,454	2,577	1,748	12,779	24,045
2005	10,678	3,258	41	13,977	8,901	4,960	2,596	16,457	30,434
2006	14,313	10,440	28	24,781	11,804	1,107	922	13,833	38,614

| Chum | A season | | | | B season | | | | Annual |
	S	M	N	Total	S	M	N	sub-total	Total
1998	471	2	1	474	2,062	524	181	2,767	3,241
1999	15	72		87	160	566	420	1,146	1,233
2000	110	11		121	111	1,727	754	2,592	2,713
2001	529	128		657	2,836	5,553	892	9,281	9,938
2002	152	31	1	184	22,836	2,756	971	26,563	26,747
2003	1,157	430	2	1,589	47,491	9,475	4,291	61,257	62,846
2004	99	104		203	32,369	22,256	10,239	64,864	65,067
2005	76	220	1	297	30,919	18,218	24,534	73,671	73,968
2006	477	196	3	676	26,303	14,584	5,800	46,687	47,363

TABLE 3. Bycatch of salmon (numbers) by Bering Sea Aleutian Islands trawl fisheries 2002–2006 compared to the average bycatch from 1990–2001. Source: NMFS Alaska Regional Office Catch Accounting database.

Year	Chinook	Chum
1990–2001 (average)	37,819	69,332
2002	36,385	81,470
2003	54,911	197,091
2004	62,493	465,650
2005	67,856	703,131
2006	87,524	327,690

Table 4. Summary statistics from observer-data annual catch totals from 1990–2006 by A (Jan–May) and B (June–Dec) seasons and by regions (South = south of 56°, Middle = 56°–58°, North = north of 58°) for walleye pollock *Theragra chalcogramma*, Chinook salmon *Oncorhynchus tshawytscha*, and chum salmon *O. keta*. CV represents the coefficient of variation (over years) computed as the standard deviation divided by the mean. Units are given in the first column.

		A season				B Season				All areas seasons
		South	Middle	North	All areas	South	Middle	North	All areas	
Pollock (t)	Min	152,243	5,170	471	308,989	32,720	31,421	12,420	398,346	741,748
	Max	424,979	306,641	20,968	534,293	366,526	391,267	539,949	765,460	1,299,753
	Median	256,186	151,221	2,302	392,624	233,448	169,122	151,384	514,568	930,914
	Mean	258,791	153,152	4,839	416,783	214,918	165,414	189,335	569,667	986,450
	CV	30%	62%	110%	18%	41%	50%	75%	24%	21%
Chinook (numbers)	Min	2,187	380	74	3,847	163	615	62	2,226	6,886
	Max	31,276	22,757	1,785	54,450	21,879	9,828	5,018	32,423	78,153
	Median	10,926	3,372	238	14,985	5,950	1,854	584	11,336	29,838
	Mean	11,712	4,959	422	17,094	8,055	3,421	1,542	13,018	30,112
	CV	64%	116%	111%	71%	86%	81%	111%	74%	63%
Chum (numbers)	Min	49	1	0	111	5,365	357	27	9,924	10,083
	Max	3,764	1,170	147	3,784	313,119	109,331	100,117	496,726	497,245
	Median	373	24	0	391	28,850	14,520	2,501	45,621	47,912
	Mean	818	202	13	1,033	67,345	25,395	12,407	105,147	106,180
	CV	124%	174%	279%	115%	124%	128%	195%	127%	125%

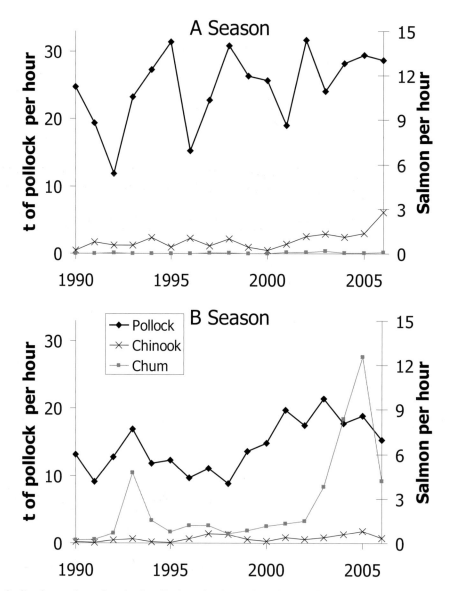

FIGURE 2. Catch rate (t per hour) of pollock and salmon (number per hour) by A (January–April) and B (June–October) seasons, 1990–2006 based on NMFS observer data.

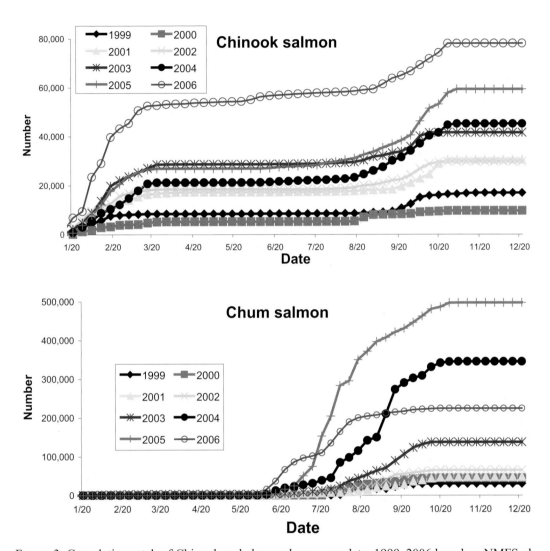

FIGURE 3. Cumulative catch of Chinook and chum salmon over date, 1999–2006 based on NMFS observer data.

Stram and Ianelli

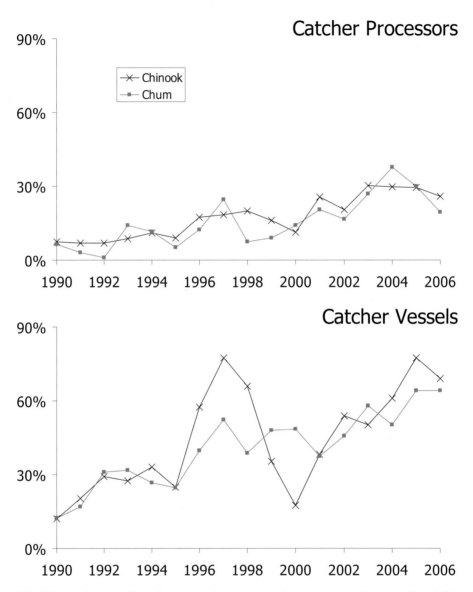

FIGURE 4. Incidents of salmon in pollock tows for at-sea catcher-processors (top panel) and shore-based catcher vessels (bottom panel) based on NMFS observer data, 1990–2006.

Pollock and salmon catch and catch-per-minute were higher during mid-day than during night-time hours (Figure 5). This pattern was consistent with trawl effort, which was highest at mid-day, whereas tows occurring at night represented about 75% of the peak mid-day effort (NMFS unpublished data). While both pollock and salmon have somewhat higher catch rates during mid-day, the catch rate for salmon dropped (relatively speaking) more during night-time hours. The diel changes in catch rate implies that bycatch rates of salmon might be reduced if fishing became more concentrated during night-time hours.

The Chinook salmon bycatch during the A-season came from areas smaller than the area where pollock were caught. This difference indicated that Chinook salmon were not uniformly distributed relative to pollock (Figure 6). During the B-season, bycatch of Chinook salmon tended to occur along the fringes of the areas where pollock catches were concentrated. Chum salmon (for the B-season fishery when the majority of the bycatch occurred) spatial distribution in the pollock fishery was concentrated south of the Pribilof Islands, even though the pollock fishery was concentrated more northerly (Figure 6). Inter-annual spatial variability of these patterns highlight the difficulty in selecting fixed-areas for possible regulatory closures.

The seasonal size composition of Chinook salmon in the pollock fishery during the winter months shows two modes, one at about 52 cm and the other at about 66 cm, with some indication that size increases between June–August (Figure 7). From July–September, the first mode at about 52 cm was not apparent but appeared again in October at about 49 cm, likely representing a new year-class recruiting to the bycatch.

For chum salmon, the seasonal size composition in the pollock fishery was uni-modal, with growth occurring from a mode at about 60 cm length in July to 66 cm length by October (Figure 8). Length frequencies from other times of year are based on relatively fewer samples, and more fish tend to be less than 40 cm. Interestingly, chum salmon caught in June have a modal value of about 68 cm, substantially larger than the mode of ~60 cm observed in July and subsequent months. These large fish may have been maturing AYK chum salmon, as tagging experiments indicated that they were distributed in the EBS fishery area in June (see Figures 11–13 in Myers et al. 2009, this volume).

The pollock fishery caught more female than male Chinook salmon, particularly when total lengths were greater than 55 cm (Figure 9). This pattern may have occurred because more age classes of female Chinook were vulnerable to the fishery as they tend to mature at older ages than male Chinook salmon (Healey 1991). Bycatch of Chinook salmon less than 55 cm total length tended to be males more than females, particularly during the summer and fall (B-season). Chum salmon have an opposite pattern with more males overall and with females being smaller than males (Figure 10). Over time, the trends in these observed sex ratios have remained fairly consistent (Figure 11).

Annually, the bimodality of the Chinook salmon length frequencies in the bycatch was apparent and consistent over time (Figure 12). This consistency suggests that the stock composition of Chinook salmon may not vary much in bycatch from year-to-year. For chum salmon, the inter-annual variability was greater than Chinook salmon, with higher proportions of larger chum salmon in some years than in others (e.g., 2002 and 2006 versus 2005; Figure 13). This variation suggests that different chum salmon stocks may be in the bycatch in different years.

Stram and Ianelli

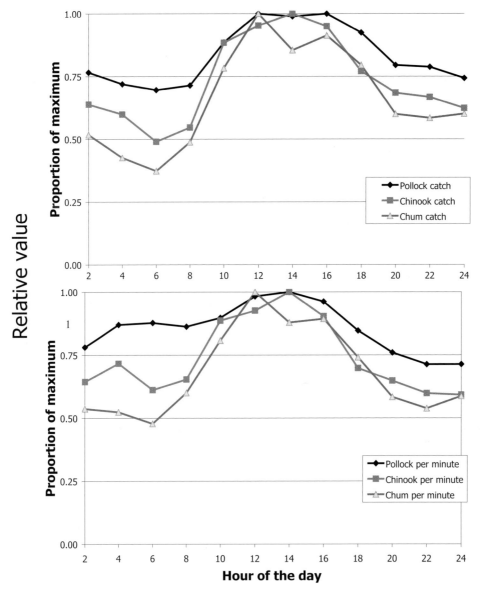

FIGURE 5. The patterns of pollock and salmon catch (top) and catch per minute (bottom) relative to their daily maxima based on NMFS observer data (1990–2006).

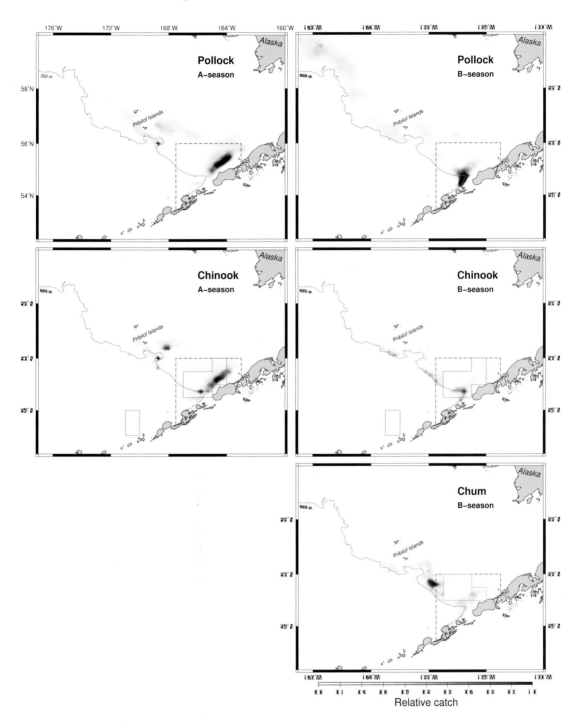

FIGURE 6. The average spatial patterns of pollock, Chinook, and chum salmon catch during the A-season (January–May; left panels), and B-season (June–December) from 2000–2006 NMFS observer data. Note that A-season chum salmon was omitted since catch levels during this period are quite low.

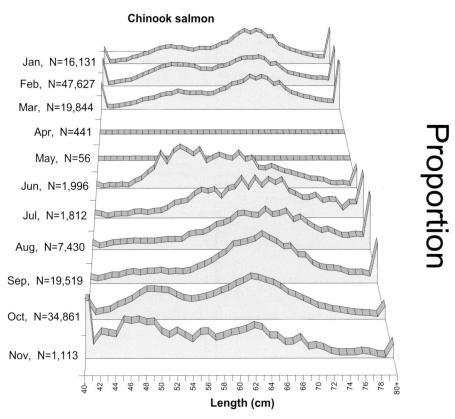

F<small>IGURE</small> 7. Chinook salmon proportions at length by month as taken in the pollock fishery, 1998–2006 combined. Month and sample sizes are shown in the left axis labels.

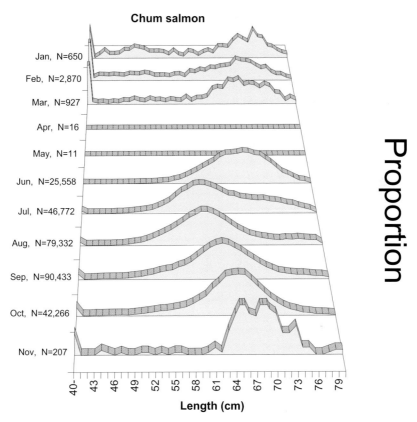

FIGURE 8. Chum salmon proportions at length by month as taken in the pollock fishery, 1998–2006 combined. Month and sample sizes are shown in the left axis labels.

Stram and Ianelli

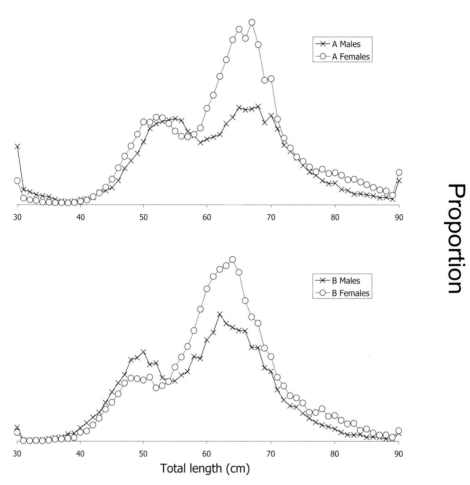

FIGURE 9. Chinook salmon proportions at length by sex for the A-season (January–May, 57% females from 84,099 samples; top panel) and B-season (June–December, 55% females from 66,361 samples; bottom panel) as taken in the pollock fishery, 1998–2006 combined.

Chum salmon

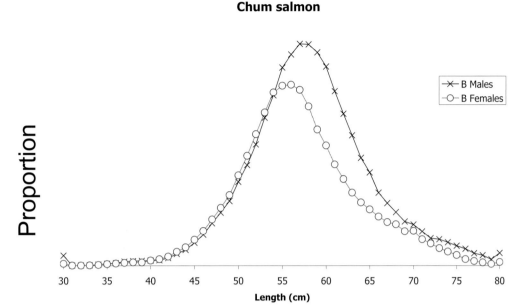

FIGURE 10. Chum salmon proportions at length by sex for the B-season (June–December, 44% females from 287,933 samples) as taken in the pollock fishery, 1998–2006 combined. Chum salmon are much less prevalent (~1% of total chum catch) in A- season hence length frequency samples from those months are omitted.

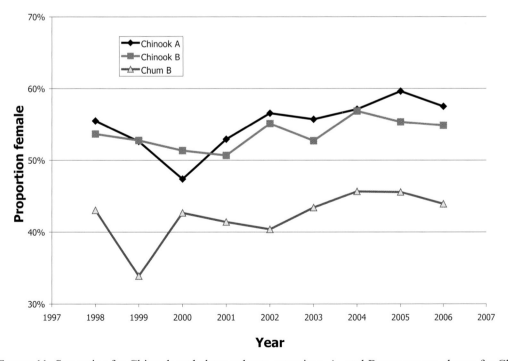

FIGURE 11. Sex ratios for Chinook and chum salmon over time. A- and B-seasons are shown for Chinook since there are significant catches in each of these seasons, chum salmon are primarily taken incidentally during the summer-fall (B) season.

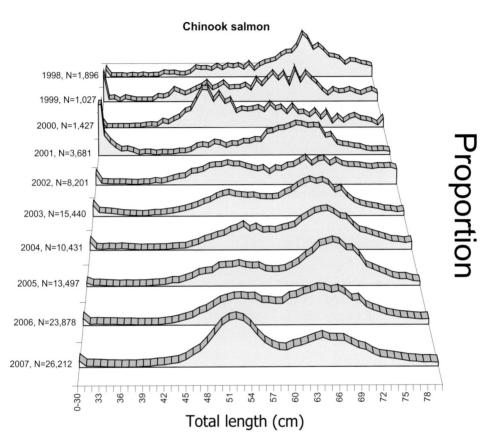

FIGURE 12. Chinook salmon proportions at length by year as taken in the pollock fishery, 1998–2006. Year and sample sizes are shown in the left axis labels.

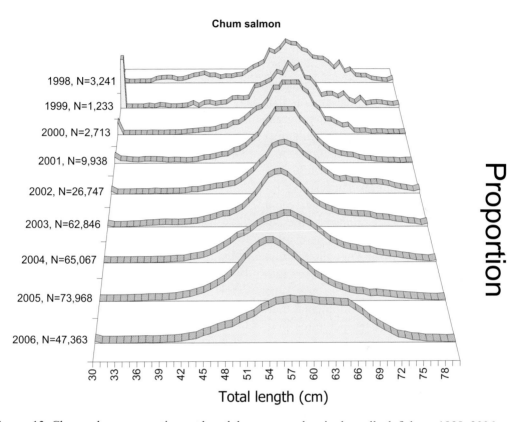

FIGURE 13. Chum salmon proportions at length by year as taken in the pollock fishery, 1998–2006.

Discussion

The patterns of variability in Pacific salmon bycatch in the Bering Sea pollock fishery occurred at spatial and temporal scales that were incompatible with present fixed "Salmon Savings Area" regulations. Hence, in October 2005, the Council adopted an amendment which exempted vessels that participated in an incentive-based program managed by a third-party (non-regulatory) that establishes dynamic in-season area-time closures based on in-season bycatch data (Gisclair 2009, this volume). Thr results confirmed that the variability between years and areas was high and hence supported the development of alternative management measures. The effects of size and age distribution of salmon in the bycatch should be taken into account when establishing these area-time closures. Additionally, if environmental conditions such as sea surface temperatures were shown to affect the distribution of salmon relative to the pollock fishery, then measures to improve environmental monitoring would be warranted and these variables also could be used to define area closures.

Extensive salmon surveys corroborate the relative abundance patterns reported here in our study. Our results suggested that chum salmon catch per unit effort variability was higher than that for Chinook salmon (Figure 2). Observations from inter-annual surveys by the Bering-Aleutian Salmon International Survey (BASIS) program have also shown recent increases in chum salmon in their survey area and similar relative rates when compared to Chinook. Age-specific differences in the distribution between oldest and youngest groups of salmon indicated that the abundance of small immature chum salmon was high in deep-water areas while large immature and maturing chum were distributed in shallow shelf zones and shelf break areas (NPAFC 2004), consistent with our observa-

tions presented here. The overall catch in all areas of the Bering Sea and adjacent North Pacific waters in 2003 showed the highest biomass of salmon since the survey began (2001) and were dominated (75% of total catch) by chum salmon (NPAFC 2004).

Trawl bycatch of chum salmon has continued to increase over this time period (1990–2006; Table 1). While not all of the chum salmon caught were bound for western Alaska, it provides an indicator that ecological conditions favorable to chum salmon survival in the Bering Sea have improved considerably in recent years and that chum salmon productivity might have increased significantly (Bue and Lingnau 2005). Information from the 2002 summer BASIS survey indicated that immature chum salmon in the Bering Sea were of Asian origin (NPAFC 2004). Variation in the observed abundance of Asian-origin chum salmon may be related to variability of migrations of Asian hatchery salmon (Seeb et al. 2004) and related changes in oceanographic temperature patterns affecting chum salmon migration routes (Friedland et al. 2001). Recent BASIS surveys in the eastern and western Bering Sea have provided survey abundance estimates and an overview of the distribution of some size classes of Chinook salmon, and indicated that abundance of juvenile Chinook salmon in 2004 appeared much higher than in either of the previous two years (NPAFC 2004), which was consistent with our findings.

In the 1990s, some studies evaluated the stock composition of the chum salmon bycatch in EBS pollock trawl fisheries (Wilmot et al. 1998; Patton et al. 1998). Wilmot et al. (1998) evaluated bycatch samples of chum salmon from the 1994–1995 pollock trawl fishery in the eastern Bering Sea and employed genetic stock identification (GSI) methodology to evaluate the stock composition of these fish (Wilmot et al. 1998). Results from this study indicated that in 1994 between 39 and 55% of bycatch samples were of Asian origin, 20–35% were western Alaskan stocks, and 21–29% were a combination of southeastern Alaska, British Columbia, and Washington stocks. (Wilmot et al. 1998). The 1995 samples indicated a range of 13–51% Asian, 33–53% western Alaska, and 9–46% southeastern Alaska, British Columbia, or Washington stocks (Wilmot et al. 1998). Estimates of the ratio between immature and maturing fish differed regionally; however, the contribution of maturing fish originating from British Columbia was consistently high both years (Wilmot et al. 1998). Differences in relative stock composition also varied temporally throughout the B-season and by region (Wilmot et al. 1998).

Mixed stock analysis using variation at allozyme loci was used to determine the stock origin of chum salmon caught by a trawl research vessel operating in the central Bering Sea from late August to mid-September 2002 (Urawa et al. 2004). Results indicated that the estimated stock composition for maturing chum salmon was 70% Japanese, 10% Russian, and 20% North American stocks, while immature fish were estimated as 54% Japanese, 33% Russian, and 13% North American (Urawa et al. 2004). The stocks of North American fish were identified as from northwest Alaska, Yukon, Alaskan Peninsula/Kodiak, Susitna River, Prince William Sound, southeast Alaska/northern British Columbia, and southern British Columbia/Washington State. Of these the majority of mature chum salmon for North America stocks came from southern British Columbia/Washington State and Alaska Peninsula/Kodiak (Urawa et al. 2004). For immature chum salmon, the largest contribution for North American stocks came from southeast Alaska/northern British Columbia, followed by Alaska Peninsula/Kodiak and southern British Columbia/Washington State.

A study of Chinook salmon completed in 2003 estimated age and stock composition in the 1997–1999 BSAI groundfish fishery by-

catch samples from the NOAA Fisheries observer program database (Myers et al. 2004). Results indicated that bycatch samples of Chinook salmon were dominated by young (age 1.2) fish in summer and older (age 1.3 and 1.4) fish in winter (Myers et al. 2004). The stock structure was dominated by western Alaskan stocks, with the estimated stock composition of 56% western Alaska, 31% central Alaska, 8% southeast Alaska–British Columbia, and 5% Russia.

As indicated in Myers et al. (2004), the origin of salmon differed by season of catch. In the winter, age 1.4 western Alaskan Chinook salmon caught were primarily from the subregions of the Yukon and Kuskokwim river drainages. In the fall, results indicated that age 1.2 western Alaskan Chinook salmon caught were from subregions of the Kuskokwim River and Bristol Bay with a large component of Cook Inlet Chinook salmon stocks as well. The proportions of western Alaskan subregional stocks (Yukon River, Kuskokwim River, and Bristol Bay) appeared to vary considerably with factors such as brood year, time, and area (Myers et al. 2004). Yukon River Chinook salmon were often the dominant stock in winter while Bristol Bay, Cook Inlet and other Gulf of Alaska stocks were often the dominant stocks in the eastern BSAI in the fall (Myers et al. 2004).

Given information indicating that the closed area system of management was ineffective (NPFMC 2005), the North Pacific Fishery Management Council (Council) exempted vessels from these closures provided they participated in a rolling hot spot (RHS) bycatch management system as an interim measure. This RHS system uses information provided from the fleet to an independent contractor to establish small scale, short-term area closures on a more real-time basis (Gisclair 2009; Haflinger and Gruver 2009, this volume). The Council, however, is continuing to consider alternative measures for managing bycatch. To understand the impact of different management measures for bycatch in the pollock fishery on salmon returns to river systems, spatial and temporal information is required on the origins of salmon taken as bycatch. Additional information on pollock fishery characteristics and patterns in relation to salmon bycatch such as presented here can be used in conjunction with stock of origin information to better inform fishery managers on potential alternative management measures. The Council is currently evaluating an analysis which estimates the relative impact of different levels of bycatch on individual streams, with a particular focus on the river systems in western Alaska. This analysis is designed to assist the Council in comparing the trade-offs of choosing different bycatch cap levels as management measures, and is included as part of an Environmental Impact Statement prepared jointly by the Council and NMFS staff (to be finalized in late 2009).

Two measures of limiting incidental catch are being evaluated in conjunction with revised closure areas. The first measure under consideration is a total limit on the number of salmon allowed in the bycatch. When that limit is exceeded, the pollock fishery would be closed. The second measure under consideration is a "trigger" limit on the number of salmon caught whereby some specified area or series of areas of known high bycatch would close when the limit was reached. These limits would ideally be linked to the abundance levels of salmon stocks so that the bycatch could be managed proportionally to salmon abundance. However, this type of information is unavailable and further complicated by variable conditions of salmon stocks within the same year. Salmon run-size forecasting continues to improve (Hilsinger et al. 2009, this volume), and this information would help understand the magnitude of variability in run size and long-term trends. On-going projects such as surveys from the BASIS program may also eventually allow for some projections to be made of future re-

turns to Alaskan rivers. Additional research projects are combining genetic marker results with in-river abundance estimates to evaluate projected returns to rivers (J. Seeb, University of Washington, personal communication). Scientists continue to improve upon the identification of incidentally caught salmon to stock of origin using a variety of genetic markers (Utter et al. 2009, this volume). However, many current estimates of stock origin are from trawl bycatch samples from the late 1990s, and recent preliminary studies indicated that bycatch patterns and stock of origin results vary by season as well as annually (Myers et al. 2004).

Our results show that the catch rates of salmon and pollock catch varied by the time of day. On average, fewer salmon per ton of pollock were caught at night than during the day. This could be due to different patterns in nocturnal behavior of salmon, combined with the pollock fishing practices. Distinct diurnal patterns in salmon depth preferences were reported by Walker et al. (2007, 2000) and Ishida et al. (2001). For example, Ishida et al. (2001) notes that chum salmon spent 48% of the day and 85% of the night in the upper 10 m of the water column. This observation was consistent with the catch data presented here from trawls operated in waters typically from 40 to 200 m depth in the eastern Bering Sea.

Given run-size information and vulnerability to the pollock fishery, an annually varying cap could be used to more accurately reflect changes in salmon abundance. This type of management would fit well within the current multispecies groundfish management practices that restrict fisheries according to the individual species and species-groups quotas. However, specification of an annual cap would require clear specification of acceptable risks to salmon stocks and clear information on the relative abundance of different salmon stocks occurring in the bycatch (i.e., stock composition). Neither of these requirements is likely to be met in the near future.

In the absence of information on abundance levels, some form of precautionary (low-risk) cap will likely be implemented by the Council. Such a cap would be negotiated among interested parties and could be used as an interim measure which could conceivably be replaced with a biomass-based cap when sufficient information exists. Information from our study provides additional insight on patterns of bycatch by age, region, and season. These results, combined with improved information on stock of origin and predictions of salmon abundance will provide managers with improved scientific advice for developing and evaluating management measures to reduce salmon bycatch in BSAI trawl fisheries.

Acknowledgments

Jim Murphy was helpful in providing advice on interpreting the patterns of salmon bycatch. Chuck Krueger was extremely patient and helpful in providing advice on improving this manuscript. The comments of three anonymous reviewers are also appreciated.

References

Alaska Department of Fish and Game (ADF&G). 1995a. Environmental Assessment/Regulatory Impact Review/Initial Regulatory Flexibility Assessment for Proposed Alternatives to Limit Chinook Salmon Bycatch in the Bering Sea Trawl Fisheries: Amendment 21b. Alaska Department of Fish and Game and the Alaska Commercial Fisheries Entry Commission, Juneau.

Alaska Department of Fish and Game (ADF&G). 1995b. Environmental Assessment/Regulatory Impact Review/Initial Regulatory Flexibility Assessment for Proposed Alternatives to Reduce Chum Salmon Bycatch in the Bering Sea Trawl Fisheries: Amendment 35. Alaska Department of Fish and Game, National Marine Fisheries Service and the North Pacific Fishery Management Council, Juneau.

Bue, F. J., and T. L. Lingnau. 2005. 2005 Yukon area subsistence, personal use, and commercial salmon fisheries outlook and management strategies.

Alaska Department of Fish and Game, Fishery Management Report NO. 05–31, Anchorage.

Friedland, K. D., R. V. Walker, N. D. Davis, K. W. Myers, G. W. Boehlert, S. Urawa, and Y. Ueno. 2001. Open-ocean orientation and return migration routes of chum salmon based on temperature data from data storage tags. Marine Ecology Progress Series 216:235–252.

Gisclair, B. R. 2009. Salmon bycatch management in the Bering Sea walleye pollock fishery: threats and opportunities for western Alaska. Pages 799–816 in C. C. Krueger and C. E. Zimmerman, editors. Pacific salmon: ecology and management of western Alaska's populations. American Fisheries Society, Symposium 70, Bethesda, Maryland.

Haflinger, K., and J. Gruver. 2009. Rolling hot spot closure areas in the Bering Sea walleye pollock fishery: estimated reduction of salmon bycatch during the 2006 season. Pages 817–826 in C. C. Krueger and C. E. Zimmerman, editors. Pacific salmon: ecology and management of western Alaska's populations. American Fisheries Society, Symposium 70, Bethesda, Maryland.

Harrington, J. M., R. A. Myers, and A. A. Rosenberg. 2005. Wasted fishery resources: discarded bycatch in the USA. Fish and Fisheries 6:350–361.

Healey, M.C. 1991. Life history of Chinook salmon. Pages 313–393 in C. Groot, and L. Margolis, editors. Pacific salmon: life histories. University of British Columbia Press, Vancouver.

Hiatt, T. R. Felthoven, H. Geier, A. Haynie, D. Layton, D. Lew, A. Poole, R. Rowe, J. Sepez, C. Seung, E. Springer, and E. Waters. 2006. Stock assessment and fishery evaluation report for the groundfish fisheries of the Gulf of Alaska and Bering Sea/ Aleutian Islands area: economic status of the groundfish fisheries off Alaska, 2005. North Pacific Fishery Management Council, Anchorage.

Hilsinger, J. R., E. Volk, G. Sandone, and R. Cannon. 2009. Salmon management in the Arctic-Yukon-Kuskokwim Region of Alaska: past, present, and future. Pages 495–519 in C. C. Krueger and C. E. Zimmerman, editors. Pacific salmon: ecology and management of western Alaska's populations. American Fisheries Society, Symposium 70, Bethesda, Maryland.

Ianelli, J. N., S. Barbeaux, S. Kotwicki, K. Aydin, T. Honkalehto, and N. Williamson. 2006. Assessment of Alaska Pollock Stock in the Eastern Bering Sea. Pages 35–138 in Stock assessment and fishery evaluation report for the groundfish resources of the Bering Sea/Aleutian Islands regions. North Pacific Fishery Management Council, Anchorage.

Ishida, Y., A. Yano, M. Ban, and M. Ogura. 2001. Vertical movement of a chum salmon *Oncorhynchus keta* in the western North Pacific Ocean as determined by a depth-recording archival tag. Fisheries Science 67:1030–1035.

Myers, K. W., and D. E. Rogers. 1988. Stock Origins of Chinook Salmon in Incidental Catches by Groundfish Fisheries in the Eastern Bering Sea. North American Journal of Fisheries Management 8:162–171.

Myers, K., R. V. Walker, N. D. Davis, and J. L. Armstrong. 2004. High Seas Salmon Research Program, 2003. SAFS-UW-0402, School of Aquatic and Fishery Sciences, University of Washington, Seattle.

Myers, K. D, R. V. Walker, N. D. Davis, J. L. Armstrong, and M. Kaeriyama. 2009. High seas distribution, biology, and ecology of Arctic-Yukon-Kuskokwim salmon: direct information from high seas tagging experiments, 1954–2006. Pages 201–239 in C. C. Krueger and C. E. Zimmerman, editors. Pacific salmon: ecology and management of western Alaska's populations. American Fisheries Society, Symposium 70, Bethesda, Maryland.

National Marine Fisheries Service (NMFS). 1999. Environmental Assessment/Regulatory Impact Review/Initial Regulatory Flexibility Assessment for An Amendment to Further Reduce Chinook Salmon Bycatch in Groundfish Trawl Fisheries of the Bering Sea and Aleutian Islands Area. National Marine Fisheries Service, Juneau, Alaska

National Marine Fisheries Service (NMFS). 2007. 2008 Observer Sampling Manual. North Pacific Groundfish Observer Program, Alaska Fisheries Science Center, NMFS/NOAA. Available: http://www.afsc.noaa.gov/FMA/Manual_pages/MANUAL_pdfs/manual2008.pdf. (November 2007).

North Pacific Anadromous Fish Commission (NPAFC). 2004. Annual Report of the Bering-Aleutian Salmon International Survey, 2003. North Pacific Anadromous Fish Commission, Document 769, Vancouver, B.C.

North Pacific Fishery Management Council (NPFMC). 2005. Environmental Assessment/Regulatory Impact Review/Initial Regulatory Flexibility Assessment for Modifying Existing Chum and Chinook Salmon Savings Areas: Amendment 84, Secretarial Review Draft. North Pacific Fishery Management Council, Anchorage.

Patton, William S., Katherine W. Myers, and Robert V. Walker. 1998. Origins of chum salmon caught incidentally in the eastern Bering Sea walleye pollock trawl fishery as estimated from scale pattern analysis. North American Journal of Fisheries Management 18:704–712.

Seeb, L., P. Crane, C. Kondzela, R. Wilmot, S. Urawa, N. Varnavskaya, J. Seeb. 2004. Migration of Pacific Rim chum salmon on the high seas: insights from genetic data. Environmental Biology of Fishes 69:21–36.

Urawa, S., T. Azumaya, P. Crane, and L. Seeb. 2004. Origin and distribution of chum salmon in the Bering Sea during the early fall of 2002: estimates by allozyme analysis. North Pacific Anadromous Fish Commission Document 794. Toyohira-ku, Sapporo, Japan.

Utter, F. M., M. V. McPhee, and F. W. Allendorf. 2009. Population genetics and the management of Arctic-Yukon-Kuskokwim salmon populations. Pages 97–123 in C. C. Krueger and C. E. Zimmerman, editors. Pacific salmon: ecology and management of western Alaska's populations. American Fisheries Society, Symposium 70, Bethesda, Maryland.

Walker, R. J., V. V. Sviridov, S. Urawa, and T. Azumaya. 2007. Spatio-temporal variation in vertical distributions of Pacific salmon in the ocean. North Pacific Anadromous Fish Commission Bulletin 4:193–201.

Walker, R. V., K. W. Myers, N. D. Davis, K. Y. Aydin, K. D. Friedland, H. R. Carlson, G. W. Boehlert, S. Urawa, Y. Ueno, and G. Anma. 2000. 2000. Diurnal variation in thermal environment experienced by salmonids in the North Pacific as indicated by data storage tags. Fisheries Oceanography 9:2171–186.

Wilmot, R. L., C. Kondzela, M. Guthrie and M. M. Masuda. 1998. Genetic stock identification of chum salmon harvested incidentally in the 1994 and 1995 Bering Sea trawl fishery. North Pacific Anadromous Fish Commission Bulletin 1:285–299.

Witherell, D. W., D. Ackley, and C. Coon. 2002. An overview of salmon bycatch in Alaska groundfish fisheries. Alaska Fishery Research Bulletin 9:53–64.

Section IV

Lessons from Other Fisheries

American Fisheries Society Symposium 70:853, 2009

Introduction to
Lessons from Other Fisheries

CHARLES C. KRUEGER

Great Lakes Fishery Commission
2100 Commonwealth Boulevard, Suite 100, Ann Arbor, Michigan 48105, USA

CHRISTIAN E. ZIMMERMAN

U.S. Geological Survey Alaska Science Center
4210 University Drive, Anchorage, Alaska 99508, USA

Much can be learned from experiences of scientists and managers of fisheries beyond the borders of the Arctic-Yukon-Kuskokwim (AYK) region, in other regions of Alaska, and across North America. By learning from the successes and failures outside Alaska, it is our hope that innovative or improved strategies can be identified to better manage the uncertainties and risks associated with AYK salmon resources. This set of papers examines a broad range of fishery issues outside of the AYK region organized around ecology, governance, and management

The ecology section addresses two important issues. The first issue addresses how one defines the units of management focus. Based on salmon life history traits, varying spatial scales can be used, from a watershed to a specific spawning site. The second issue is the organization of information to assist management decision making. This task can be addressed using various models, including expert opinion, statistical, and simulation models.

The governance section contains three papers which describe non-binding collaborative approaches to management at scales from watersheds to the Laurentian Great Lakes. Such agreements do not have authority to compel action but rely on strong relationships built over time that lead to trust among the participants and their organizations.

The last section on management arose out of the desire to identify and use lessons learned elsewhere to assist in AYK salmon management. This collection of papers includes approaches to fishery management in Bristol Bay, British Columbia, the Columbia River, Oregon, Great Lakes, and Atlantic salmon management in North America and Europe. A common theme within this set of papers is the need to use high quality information interpreted within a proper conceptual model for the system being managed, while at the same time recognizing that the information contains levels of uncertainty that yields risk in management decision making.

Ecology

American Fisheries Society Symposium 70:857–871, 2009

Pacific Salmon Population Structure and Dynamics: A Perspective from Bristol Bay on Life History Variation across Spatial and Temporal Scales

THOMAS P. QUINN*

School of Aquatic and Fishery Sciences, University of Washington
Box 355020, Seattle, Washington 98195, USA

Abstract.—Pioneering scientists pointed out that conservation and management of salmon for human use and as a component of ecosystems depends on understanding their population structure. Many current controversies regarding exploitation rates, interceptions, and resuscitation of depleted populations hinge on issues of population structure. This paper examines the range of spatial scales over which salmon population structure can be defined, using Bristol Bay sockeye salmon *Oncorhynchus nerka* as the example. The region's geology has created similar spawning habitats associated with different lakes, revealing the extent to which evolutionary processes repeat themselves. The life history patterns of the salmon reflect both genetic adaptations to their local environment, facilitated by homing to their natal site for spawning, and also the capability to respond to changing environmental conditions. This combination of variables may explain why similar environmental conditions result in different patterns of population dynamics among the lake systems, giving the Bristol Bay system as a whole more stability than is seen in any single lake. At still finer spatial scales, investigations show that sockeye salmon home not only to specific streams but even to habitat patches within a stream. Nevertheless, records of the presence of other salmon species, notably Chinook *O. tshawytscha*, chum *O. keta*, and pink salmon *O. gorbuscha*, seem to indicate more dynamic population structure, including straying and the possible establishment of new populations in streams where sockeye salmon are numerically dominant. The understanding of these patterns and processes stems largely from a well-conceived and persistent long term program of research and monitoring, and this provides lessons and cautions for research and management in systems where information is less extensive, such as in the Arctic-Yukon-Kuskokwim region.

Introduction

One of the seminal events in the conservation and management of salmon was a symposium, held in Ottawa, Canada in June 1938. The introduction to the volume (Moulton 1939) was written by A. G. Huntsman,

who reviewed the mandate for the meeting in words that would seem all too appropriate today: "… alarm over decreases in the stocks of salmon" and "… the practical problem of getting sufficient salmon for food and for sport." These scientists, working on both Atlantic and Pacific salmon, in Europe and North America, puzzled over many questions

*Corresponding author: tquinn@u.washington.edu

that are still not fully resolved, including open ocean movements and exploitation of mixed populations. Perhaps the most important paper was that by Willis H. Rich, who clearly outlined the requirements for rational management of salmon and other fishery resources (Rich 1939).

"(1) the extent to which the species is broken up into self-sustaining groups; (2) the fluctuations in the birth-death ratio of each independent group and for each life phase... and (3) the causes of these fluctuations, again for each independent group and for each life phase." (p. 45).

Foreshadowing decades of research and hundreds of scientific papers to follow, Rich (1939) went on to point out the three main types of evidence pointing to the existence of independent populations: (1) differences in morphology, including body size, age at maturity, egg size, fat content, and scale patterns, (2) differences is population dynamics, cycles of abundance and other "statistical" differences, and (3) experimental evidence from tagging studies. He went on to describe the importance of understanding ocean migration patterns of salmon, interceptions by fleets in distant areas and along the migration route, and many other issues that are relevant to today's salmon conservation.

The early-middle part of the 20th century also saw many important contributions to the study of population structure and dynamics in Canada (e.g., Clemens et al. 1939; see also reviews in Foerster 1968; Ricker 1972). With respect to salmon in Alaska, the landmark event was the formation of the Fisheries Research Institute (F.R.I.) at the University of Washington (Stickney 1989). W. F. Thompson, first director of F.R.I., reflected on the beginnings of the program and made clear that he and the other pioneers recognized the critical role of the discrete breeding populations in the overall management of the fisheries. He explicitly recognized that variation exists among breeding populations in average

productivity, and also that variation occurs in productivity from year to year (Thompson 1962). The study of salmon population structure was advanced greatly in 1972 with the publication of a symposium volume, The Stock Concept in Pacific Salmon, edited by Raymond Simon and Peter Larkin. The volume was dominated by William Ricker's monograph and this remains the most significant review of the subject (Ricker 1972). Since that time many discoveries have been made, including biochemical and molecular tools for distinguishing populations, and great number of symposia and scientific papers have been published on the subject, including several reviews (McDonald 1981; Scudder 1989; Taylor 1991: Quinn 1999).

Rather than present another such review, the purpose of this paper is to use one geographical region, Bristol Bay in southwestern Alaska, to illustrate a number of salient points in the study of salmon population structure, including areas of continued uncertainty. This geographical area is best known for the large runs of sockeye salmon, *Oncorhynchus nerka*, but lessons can be learned from the other species as well. The premise of this paper is that three key themes pointed out by pioneering scientists working on salmon conservation are still of critical importance today: 1) the importance of geographical scale in organizing the dynamics and structure of salmon populations, and the fisheries that exploit them, 2) the interplay between genetic and environmental factors controlling phenotypic traits, including the role of fisheries, and 3) the nonstatic nature of salmon populations, in abundance and distribution. These three themes are briefly discussed, and then related to the challenges of managing and conserving salmon populations in the vast areas of the Arctic, Yukon, and Kuskokwim regions of Alaska. Finally, conclusions are drawn regarding the establishment and maintenance of long-term data sets, including the blessings and liabilities of such projects.

The Importance of Geography and Spatial Scales for Salmon Populations

The structure of salmon populations depends on three things: 1) the reproductive isolation of breeding populations that results from homing to the natal site, 2) the differences in regimes of natural and sexual selection that result from differences in biotic and abiotic factors among breeding and rearing areas used by a given population, and 3) the genetic basis for traits that affect the fitness of individuals in the environments that they use. The concepts of geography and spatial scale are thus important elements of all three factors contributing to population structure. The first reason for this importance stems from the homing behavior of salmon. In general, the salmon that survive to maturity return to their natal site to breed. The term "natal site" implies some spatial scale. For example, do sockeye salmon home to North America as opposed to Asia, to Bristol Bay as opposed to other regions of North America, to the Nushagak River as opposed to the other major river systems in Bristol Bay, to the Wood River as opposed to the upper Nushagak River itself or its tributaries, to Lake Nerka as opposed to another of the lakes in the Wood River system, to Hidden Lake Creek as opposed to one of the other creeks that flow into this lake, to Hidden Lake Creek itself or to beaches in Hidden Lake, at the headwaters of the creek, and to the specific site in the creek where they were spawned years earlier?

Information on the spatial scale of population structure comes from several sources, primarily studies of variation in selectively neutral genetic traits including polymorphic proteins and DNA microsatellites. In these studies, significant and consistent differences between salmon breeding at two sites can be taken as strong evidence of reproductive isolation but the failure to detect a difference does not mean that none exists. Early work revealed some genetic structure among populations breeding within the Iliamna Lake system, as with other lakes producing sockeye salmon (Varnavskaya et al. 1994), and data from Bristol Bay populations have contributed to the understanding of broad-scale genetic variation in sockeye salmon (Beacham et al. 2006). In many cases, sockeye salmon spawning in adjacent creeks can be distinguished using these selectively neutral traits, and creek spawning sockeye salmon may differ from nearby beach spawning conspecifics (Lin et al. 2008). Genetic divergence seems to result from a combination of variables: geographical distance, temporal isolation, and habitat differences. In general, sockeye salmon (and other species as well) are probably more likely to stray to a location near their natal site than to a distant one, and to a similar habitat (e.g., creek to creek, beach to beach) more than a different one. The likelihood that straying salmon will enter and successfully reproduce is also probably greater if conspecifics are present; thus, populations with distinctly different breeding dates are more isolated than those with more similar breeding dates. In addition, some populations have small effective population sizes (Habicht et al. 2004) and may be more genetically divergent than simple geographical distance, habitat, and timing might suggest (Ramstad et al. 2004), indicating possible past population bottlenecks.

In addition to biochemical and molecular evidence of isolation of populations breeding in nearby areas, variation in phenotypic traits under some degree of genetic control provides further evidence that populations are discrete, and adapted to local conditions. Early stream catalogs (Demory et al. 1964; Marriott 1964) noted differences in the timing of salmon spawning in different habitats that we continue to observe. In general, creeks are occupied early in the season and large rivers (draining lakes) and beaches are occupied late in the season, often for more protracted periods. These differences in timing are, in general, adaptations to the regimes of temperature that the embryos will experience so that they emerge in time to take advantage of feeding opportunities the following spring, though some evidence exists that not all populations emerge synchronously in a lake (Abrey 2005). Experimental evidence from several sources indicates that the date of breeding by salmonids is under strong genetic control (Smoker et al. 1998; Quinn et al. 2000; Sato et al. 2000) so these differences likely reflect genetic adaptations of populations to local conditions. The spawning sockeye salmon in different areas also differ markedly in age at maturity, length at age, body morphology, and egg size (Rogers 1987; Blair et al. 1993; Quinn et al. 1995; Quinn et al. 2001), apparently reflecting the balancing forces of natural and sexual selection. The various lines of evidence indicate that salmon populations are organized into discrete breeding units, with more or less gene flow among them as a function of proximity, habitat similarity, and temporal overlap. In general, phenotypic diversity reflects primarily contemporary selection and so similar habitats in distant locations often give rise to similar phenotypes, whereas genotypic diversity reflects a combination of ancient colonization events that took place long ago, and contemporary gene flow from successful reproduction by strays. For example, male sockeye salmon spawning on lake beaches are typically deep-bodied, and their shape is similar to that of sockeye salmon using similar habitats in a different lake (Quinn et al. 2001). Little gene flow occurs between lakes and it is inferred that the exaggerated male shape evolved independently in each lake.

The question often arises, "What is the spatial unit to which salmon home?" In many cases one might safely conclude that it is the river, and that each female then must select a redd site based on habitat suitability and competition with other females. However, a recent marking experiment indicated that sockeye salmon planted as eyed eggs in the gravel of a small spring-fed pond homed back there as adults rather than to the rest of the small stream below or above the pond (Quinn et al. 2006). The ability of sockeye salmon to home to specific locations within a small stream only partially addresses the question of the spatial scale of homing. In other cases, habitat complexes are used to varying extents among years. Iliamna Lake has many low-lying islands, primarily in the eastern end of the lake, used for spawning by sockeye salmon (Kerns and Donaldson 1968). Sockeye salmon spawn on discrete beach sites on the islands (Leonetti 1997), separated by generally similar but apparently less suitable habitat. Individuals (males as well as females) seldom move between beach sites, even to other sites nearby, once they have begun breeding at a given location (Hendry et al. 1995). The embryos incubate in a matrix of coarse gravel and rocks, in lake water circulated by wind-driven surface currents (Leonetti 1997), and sites not used seem to have finer substrate and poorer water circulation than those used, or are so exposed to storms that the gravel is not stable.

Are the sockeye salmon spawning on all the islands of Iliamna Lake one population, is each island a population, or is each beach on each island a population? The absence of site-specific water sources would seem to present special challenges for homing. Reciprocal transfers of adults from one island to another revealed some tendency to return to the site where the fish were first caught; however, less than what was shown by sockeye from a nearby creek (Blair and Quinn 1991). Aerial surveys of adult salmon revealed that the levels of abundance of sockeye salmon on the beaches are highly correlated among years (Stewart et al. 2003a). This coherence might suggest that they represent one population, but this result might also be explained by the fact that common environmental conditions such as ice cover and lake level would affect all the beaches synchronously, even if they were entirely independent breeding units. Finally, analysis of detailed age composition data provided evidence that the populations were independent, at least to some extent, even though selectively neutral genetic markers could not discriminate them (Stewart et al. 2003b). Thus, the structure of these populations remains ambiguous, and evidence exists for both homing to specific locations and for the exercise of spawning habitat choice by the salmon. These may be examples of metapopulations (Hanski 1999; Schtickzelle and Quinn 2007) that can persist as a whole because there is sufficient asynchrony in the extinction and re-colonization events experienced by the populations using the discrete breeding sites. Alternatively, these may be better termed "messy populations" that expand and contract over habitats of unequal quality, using some regions only when density is greatest, and persisting at the core, high quality areas.

Management of the fisheries takes place at the scale of the district or subdistrict (e.g., Nushagak District and the Wood River), and only limited subsistence and personal use fisheries take place on specific creeks (e.g., Yako Creek in the Wood River system). This conflict between the scale of management and fishing, and the scale of population structure creates the possibility for over-exploitation of certain populations of salmon, or salmon using certain habitat types, especially if they differ in size and timing. Abundant evidence exist that salmon from different populations and habitat types vary in age at maturity, size at age, and morphology, and gillnets are notably size-selective forms of fishing gear, so a high potential for differential exploitation exists (Kendall and Quinn, in press). In general, it seems as though the populations within a system migrate synchronously (Jensen and Mathisen 1987; Rowse 1985), though recent work in the Wood River system indicates that this may not be entirely true (Doctor 2008).

Exploitation can be heavier on late than early-arriving fish, if escapement goals have been met (Quinn et al. 2007), and so there may be selection on run timing as well as size. Larger, older salmon tend to migrate and spawn earlier than smaller ones (Quinn et al. in press), further complicating the possible regimes of selection from fishing. As long as a generous escapement goal to the system as a whole is met, the productivity of populations at low densities may allow them to rebound from a brief period of heavy fishing. However, the possible chronic effects of long-term excessive and selective fishing should not be ignored.

The Genetic and Environmental Effects on Life History Traits

Salmon, like all fish, are a product of both nature and nurture. However, their phenotypic traits are not the result of two independent factors (genetic and environmental) but also the differences among populations in the interaction between these factors. Two examples, the transition from lake-rearing juveniles to seaward migrating smolts, and the transition from ocean-rearing adults to homeward migrating mature adults, illustrate this point. Before delving into this fundamental concept, it is important to note that full documentation of age composition patterns in a given population requires a great deal of data. For several reasons, samples must be collected in a consistent manner over many years to accurately characterize the overall patterns and the variation in age composition and size at age for a population. First, many species have multiple ages at maturity, so at a minimum one entire generation of data would be needed to encompass all possible ages. This aspect is especially important for species with variation in freshwater and marine ages, and sockeye are the most variable species of all Pacific salmon (Healey 1986;

Healey 1987). Second, the environment modulates the proportions of these ages that occur in any given brood year (detailed below), so even complete sampling of an entire brood cycle may not be sufficient. One might be tempted to sample in one year and not worry about these sources of variation but broods vary so much in strength that a highly unrepresentative result might be obtained. Finally, it is difficult to obtain a random sample of fish differing in size (hence age) because the small fish may be systematically underrepresented in the samples from spawning grounds (Zhou 2002). In this kind of work, the temptation is to consider individual salmon sampled for age (based on examination of otoliths or scales) as the unit of replication, or perhaps the numbers of calendar years, but the number of brood cycles may be a more appropriate unit of replication. This fact is sobering for those just beginning to sample a population, especially if it has a long lifespan or complex age structure.

Numerous studies have documented the variation among sockeye salmon populations in average size of smolts (Quinn 2005); thus, the "decision" to initiate seaward migration is not triggered by a species-specific size threshold but rather each population must have evolved its own threshold. In some lakes (e.g., the Wood River system), the vast majority of sockeye salmon smolt after one full year in freshwater whereas in the Ugashik system, the age-1 smolts are similar in size (implying roughly comparable growth rates) but only about half migrate at age-1. In the Egegik River system the age-1 smolts are even larger than those in the other systems but a smaller fraction migrates after one year in the lake than in the Ugashik River system (Quinn 2005). The "decision" to migrate at a young age should be associated with lakes in which mortality risk is high and growth in the second year would be low, or a second year of growth in the lake provides little advantage in marine survival. Despite this general

theory, little if any systematic research has demonstrated the specific costs and benefits of smolt age from system to system. Within a given lake, the proportion of sockeye salmon that leave after a single year, rather than two, depends on growth during the first year; when the fish are large at the end of the first growing season, a larger proportion leave than is observed in years when growth is slower (Koenings and Burkett 1987; Rich et al., in press). Growth variation among years is primarily controlled by temperature and competition, and the relative importance of these two variables varies among lakes. For example, in Lake Aleknagik, the more important factor is competition (Schindler et al. 2005b), whereas in Iliamna Lake, temperature exerts the stronger influence, despite the great variation in number of returning adults (Rich et al., in press).

Mirroring the patterns in smolts, many studies have revealed that size-at-age and age-at-maturity vary among populations, at many spatial scales and for many salmon species, including Chinook salmon *O. tshawytscha* (Roni and Quinn 1995), chum salmon *O. keta* (Beacham and Murray 1987), coho salmon *O. kisutch* (Weitkamp et al. 1995), sockeye salmon (Rogers 1987; Blair et al. 1993; Healey et al. 2000), and steelhead *O. mykiss* (Busby et al. 1996). This variation in age and size is controlled by environmental and genetic processes. Growing conditions at sea are affected by competition and temperature (e.g., Pyper and Peterman 1999; Pyper et al. 1999). Bristol Bay sockeye salmon are so numerous that they have generally been viewed as their own prime competitor but evidence indicates that competition with Asian pink salmon *O. gorbuscha* may also affect them (Ruggerone et al. 2005). In general, the accelerated growing conditions (or large size at seawater entry) are associated with earlier age at maturation (Quinn et al. in press).

The genetic basis for age-at-maturity in salmonids has been shown by experiments on various species, often with the goal of understanding the genetic basis of early male maturity (i.e., jacks) or increasing size at maturity: Chinook salmon (Hard et al. 1985; Hankin et al. 1993; Heath et al. 1994), steelhead (anadromous rainbow trout) (Tipping 1991), and coho salmon (Iwamoto et al. 1984; Appleby et al. 2003). Natural selection from a variety of processes results in variation among populations experiencing common or at least similar growing conditions. For example, sockeye salmon populations that rear in the same lake prior to seaward migration, have access to the same feeding grounds at sea, and return at the same time of year can vary dramatically in age-at-maturity and size-at-age. In the Wood River system, sockeye salmon from large rivers are older, longer for their age, and heavier for their length than those from small streams (Quinn and Buck 2001; Quinn et al. 2001; Rogers 1987). Intense, size-selective predation from bears selects against large, old fish in small streams, sexual selection favors large fish when predation pressure is reduced, and use of large rivers for breeding also seems to favor large fish (Quinn et al. 2001). At a proximate level, it is unclear whether these differences in growth rate at sea result from variation among populations in their feeding distribution (though all have access to the same areas), feeding behavior (e.g., diet, vertical distribution or diel movements), or growth physiology. Perhaps more intriguing than the simple variation in size achieved at sea among populations is the fact that the adults of some populations (e.g., Hansen Creek in Lake Aleknagik) are not only younger and but also smaller for their age than other populations nearby such as Bear Creek (Quinn 2005). This difference implies that it is not merely the growth rate at sea that varies but the relationship between growth and maturity; otherwise, the population with fast-growing fish would compensate by maturing at an earlier age and thus be similar in overall average size at maturity. Thus, at both transition periods (from freshwater to sea, and back again to spawn), population-specific "set-points" or norms of reaction control the relationship between fish size or growth rate and the probability of making the transition. Consequently, different populations may grow at the same rate and yet show different maturation patterns.

The Non-Static Nature of Salmon Populations

The use of the word "population" implies something with a degree of permanence—perhaps not as much as a "species," but not exactly a will o' the wisp either. However, it is important to remember that the great majority of Pacific salmon populations were established since the last glacial period. This period ended ca. 10,000 years ago in some areas but in others, notably Glacier Bay, Alaska, it has been much more recent. Work in Glacier Bay has revealed how rapidly salmon and other fishes can colonize new habitat (Milner and Bailey 1989; Milner et al. 2000), and this is a reminder that salmon populations are not at all static. Thus, each year a small (but ecologically significant) number of maturing salmon do not home but rather stray and spawn in nonnatal waters (Quinn 1993; Hendry et al. 2004). Despite the importance of this phenomenon, neither the prevalence of straying in wild populations nor the underlying mechanisms are known in any detail. In most cases, strays cannot be readily distinguished from conspecifics that homed. In sockeye salmon, natural variation in parasite prevalence among lakes (Quinn et al. 1987) provides evidence of straying but only at this rather coarse spatial scale. Species such as pink and chum salmon that do not acquire extensive and distinct collections of parasites will not be readily distinguished in this manner. Natural variation in thermal regime experienced by the embryos incubating in different sites can induce detectable differences in otolith banding patterns, and these differences can also suggest (but not really demonstrate) straying (Quinn et al. 1999). Natural variation in chemistry among basins can also be used to identify fish (Ingram and Weber 1999; Kennedy et al. 2002; Wells et al. 2003) but this will not be useful in all situations. Thus, the discreteness of existing populations is controlled by balance between isolation and homogenization, though the precise levels are difficult to determine in wild populations and few estimates exist. The homing by the great majority of the salmon and the different regimes of selection tend to isolate the populations but straying and the gene flow that results if the strays reproduce successfully tend to homogenize them. In the case of Bristol Bay sockeye salmon, populations can be phenotypically similar but genotypically different, and vice versa, indicating complex patterns of selection and gene flow. These populations are not static but rather represent the products of ongoing evolutionary processes.

In some cases, a salmon is observed in a river where the species have not been seen before, or where it does not occur regularly. For example, the observation of Chinook salmon in the Mackenzie River was worthy of note (McLeod and O'Neil 1983), as was the observation of a chum salmon much farther up the Fraser River than they normally occur (Welch and Till 1996). Recently, Pacific salmon have been documented in rivers draining into the Arctic Ocean (Babaluk et al. 2000; Stephenson 2006). It is difficult to know whether the incidence of salmon in this region has actually increased, or whether the distributions and behavior of the fish are unchanged but the tendency to observe and report them has increased. Given the recent warming conditions in many areas of Alaska, it is plausible that salmon might stray into new areas but at present the evidence seems to be equivocal.

The overwhelming numerical dominance of sockeye salmon in Bristol Bay presents an interesting opportunity to examine issues of straying and colonization. The staff in the Fisheries Research Institute at the University of Washington have conducted foot surveys of about two dozen creeks in the Wood River system annually to count sockeye salmon since the late 1940s. Beginning in about 1968, the survey forms were changed and records were kept of Pacific salmon species other than sockeye salmon. Coho salmon tend to spawn much later than sockeye salmon in this area, and are rarely observed during the July and August surveys. However, pink, chum, and Chinook salmon have been reported, and their timing overlaps enough with sockeye salmon to yield valuable observations. The sizes of stream gravels and thermal regimes in the streams are apparently suitable for all salmon species, so no obvious reason exists why the species other than sockeye salmon are so scarce. Indeed, the high densities of sockeye salmon and the abundance of suitable gravel (Quinn et al. 1995) suggest that many of the streams are exceptionally good spawning sites. Like sockeye salmon, juvenile pink and chum salmon migrate downstream after emerging from the gravel, so any features of the stream's habitat should affect all juveniles similarly. Despite the apparent suitability of the streams, species of salmon other than sockeye are unusual. Some streams have been surveyed for over 40 years and no salmon other than sockeye salmon have ever been seen, whereas in other streams the annual incidence of nonsockeye ranges up to about 50%. In general, the other species are least often observed in the smallest streams (in terms of width and depth), even though these streams often support high densities of sockeye salmon. The absence of Chinook and chum salmon from small streams is not surprising because they are larger than the sockeye salmon. However, it is less obvious why the pink salmon are in the large and not in the small streams because they are smaller than the sockeye salmon.

Clearly, much remains to be learned about the habitat use and segregation among salmon species in the Bristol Bay area. More fundamentally, the processes determining the distribution patterns of salmon species are poorly known, and it is hard to see how management can succeed without a better understanding of why certain species are in one river but not another, and why their densities and productivities vary so much. The differences in basic habitat requirements (e.g., gravel size, water temperature, dissolved oxygen, stream gradient, habitat complexity, presence or absence of an estuary) of salmon species are not sufficient to explain the vagaries in their distributions. The great number of unsuccessful efforts to transplant salmon and establish new populations within their native range (Withler 1982) suggests that if a stream is suitable for a given species it probably already contains it, and if the species is absent there is probably a good (though often not obvious) reason for its absence. Thus, we are left with a paradox; the distributions of species exhibit elements of rigidity and also elements of plasticity, and the rules underlying these patterns are not clear.

Application of these Concepts to the Conservation of Salmon in the Arctic, Yukon, and Kuskokwim Systems

The importance of long term records

One might well ask, what is the relevance of work on sockeye salmon in the lake-studded Bristol Bay region to those interested in Chinook and chum salmon in the more northerly areas of Alaska? Marked differences exist in the physical attributes of the systems, the nature of the fisheries, the mix of species, the management concerns, and the available data. However, several lessons from the research in Bristol Bay may help those working elsewhere. The first lesson is the value of long-term research and monitoring. Much that we have learned about Bristol Bay sockeye salmon and their ecosystems stems from the long-term data collected by our program and by the Alaska Department of Fish and Game (Baker et al. 2009, this volume). However, most of the methods used to characterize the populations in the Bristol Bay systems are simple, requiring persistence and dedication more than specialized skills. In species with simpler freshwater life history patterns (e.g., pink, chum, and Chinook salmon), it should be possible to obtain important and meaningful data to help define population structure by such phenotypic traits as age composition, size-at-age, fecundity and egg size, and spawning date. I recommend that the mantra for long-term research projects be "*sufficient but sustainable.*" Projects need to collect enough data at enough different spatial scales and levels of ecological organization to be meaningful, yet not so much that they cannot be sustained. Costly projects of short duration are much less desirable (though often more appealing to funding sources) than ones with more modest budgets that are stable over long periods of time.

Importantly, data collected on the fish must be linked to relevant ecological information. The pioneers of the Fisheries Research Institute did not use terms like "global warming" and "climate change" but they measured important physical variables such as the date of ice-out each year, solar radiation, lake level, and water temperature. I had the pleasure of hearing the late Donald Rogers describe how knowledge developed in the Wood River system that he came to know so intimately. He said that initially the staff were unsure what to measure and so they made decisions based on the principles of ecology: physical and biotic factors affecting growth and survival of the target species, and elements of community structure that might also be important. At first, he said, many discoveries were made, as new streams were explored and new things were learned about the biology of the various species, and the ecological processes. This exciting early period was followed by years when it seemed as though they were just putting another "dot on the graph" in terms of annual average fry size, date of ice-out, peak zooplankton density, and so forth. At this point it would have been easy to stop, assuming that everything interesting had already been learned, or to cut back radically on the scope of sampling. However, the biologists were persistent as well as insightful. The records initially showed a lot of variation but later, when viewed over many decades, they slowly revealed the warming trend and shift in salmon productivity that eventually became so obvious and were seen at even broader scales (Beamish and Bouillon 1993; Mantua et al. 1997; Hilborn et al. 2003; Pyper et al. 2005). The early Fisheries Research Institute scientists also did not use the term biodiversity but they had the foresight to monitor not just the sockeye salmon but also the zooplankton and emerging aquatic insects, and they counted and measured the other fish species such as threespine stickleback *Gasterosteus aculeatus*, nine-spine stickleback *Pungitius pungitius*, pond smelt *Hypomesus olidus*, and least cisco *Coregonus sardinella* that were caught in beach seines and tow nets deployed to sample juvenile sockeye salmon. This holistic view of fisheries science can be critical, especially when it is not initially clear which players and processes will be the most important. In summary, *one should first choose the variables to measure wisely, and then sample both consistently and persistently over the long haul.*

On the other hand, it must be acknowledged that long-term research has drawbacks. First, it tends to limit the focus to that site, especially as infrastructure (cabins, boats, etc.) and data build up. The system being studied is well known, but is it representative? One is less likely to notice changes in other places, and indeed the basic ecology (species composition, key biotic and abiotic factors, etc.) of the long-term site may differ from other sites, even ones nearby. Second, maintaining long-term data sets can be a lot of work, both in terms of collecting appropriate data in the field and also the less obvious but absolutely essential task of database management. The Fisheries Research Institute program pre-dated computers, and data entry and storage spanned the eras of pencil and paper, punch cards, magnetic tapes, 5¼ inch and 3½ inch "floppy" disks, zip drives, "flash" drives, and so forth. Third, it can be difficult to maintain financial support for long-term projects. They may seem less innovative than new projects, and the continuous need to demonstrate the timeliness of the long-term project can be tedious. Finally, frustration inevitably occurs when we realize what data we should have been collecting all along but did not. Do we start now, or is it too late? How long will funding continue?

The importance of diversity, and learning from the past

In addition to the importance of long-term data, including a range of biotic and abiotic variables, the research program on sockeye salmon in Bristol Bay has shown that salmon production can come from a range of different habitats, and that patterns of productivity can vary dramatically from one time period to another (Hilborn et al. 2003). Districts (notably the Naknek-Kvichak) that largely supported the fisheries during some periods of the 20th century recently came under stricter regulatory protection from the fishery whereas others (e.g., Egegik and Nushagak) have returned exceptional numbers of adults per spawner. Even within the Naknek-Kvichak district, the production has shifted in recent years as the Kvichak has barely replaced itself while the

Alagnak River system has seen extraordinary levels of sockeye salmon abundance (Clark 2005). Shifts have also occurred within the Iliamna Lake system in terms of the spawning habitats (creeks, rivers, mainland beach and island beaches) that produce most of the salmon. Thus, conservation (and research) should not focus merely on the systems that are presently large or productive, as apparently minor contributors may be dominant in the future. It may seem pointless to sample a stream with few or no salmon, or one dominated by a species that is not presently valued. However, one of the key lessons from Bristol Bay is that things change, and a "snapshot" in any one year may not be representative. Donald Rogers remarked once that after working in Bristol Bay for more than 40 years he was still waiting for an average year. Each year had some unusual features and often unusual combinations of features (migration timing, fish size, temperatures, precipitation, strike by the fishermen, changes in management, etc.).

The variation in production (of salmon and also lower trophic levels) not only spans the recent decades but the prehistoric period was also characterized by large variation, as inferred from several paleolimnological studies (Finney et al. 2002; Finney et al. 2000; Schindler et al. 2005a; Schindler et al. 2006). Perhaps more important than the mere variation in salmon runs inferred from these samples is the conclusion that the total runs of salmon in the past were no larger than those seen during the past century. Optimistic humans tend to view good times as normal and bad times as aberrant but the runs of salmon in parts of Alaska in the late 20th century have been unusually high, when viewed over the longer period of record. Thus, a final lesson from Bristol Bay is that the fishing community and their managers should plan on changes and surprises, some pleasant, and some otherwise. However, the likelihood of surprises in the future does not mean that we should not investigate and plan. Quite the

contrary—future uncertainty makes it all the more important that we initiate and maintain well planned research and monitoring to detect the kinds of changes that will affect our ecosystems and human communities (Beamish and Sweeting 2009, this volume).

Acknowledgments

I thank the pioneers of the Fisheries Research Institute at the University of Washington (notably the late W. F. Thompson, the late O. A. Mathisen, and R. L. Burgner) for their broad vision, and those that followed for their hard work and persistence in collecting the data that we now are privileged to examine. I also thank my colleagues, Ray Hilborn, Daniel Schindler, and the late Donald Rogers, who have given me more insights than can be mentioned here, and the superb staff, graduate and undergraduate students in the program. Funding has come from many sources over the decades but I especially thank the seafood processors for their sustained support. In recent years, the National Science Foundation, the Gordon and Betty Moore Foundation and the Pew Foundation have provided crucial support for infrastructure, database management, and research, for which we are most grateful.

References

Abrey, C. A. 2005. Variation in the early life history of sockeye salmon (*Oncorhynchus nerka*): emergence timing, an ontogenetic shift, and population productivity. Doctoral dissertation. University of Washington, Seattle.

Appleby, A. E., J. M. Tipping, and P. R. Seidel. 2003. The effect of using two-year-old male coho salmon in hatchery broodstock on adult returns. North American Journal of Aquaculture 65:60–62.

Babaluk, J. A., J. D. Reist, J. D. Johnson, and L. Johnson. 2000. First records of sockeye (*Oncorhynchus nerka*) and pink salmon (*O. gorbuscha*) from Banks Island and other records of Pacific salmon in Northwest Territories, Canada. Arctic 53:161–164.

Quinn, T. P. 1999. Revisiting the stock concept in Pacific salmon: insights from Alaska and New Zealand. Northwest Science 73:312–324.

Quinn, T. P. 2005. The behavior and ecology of Pacific salmon and trout. University of Washington Press, Seattle.

Quinn, T. P., and G. B. Buck. 2001. Size and sex selective mortality on adult Pacific salmon: bears, gulls and fish out of water. Transactions of the American Fisheries Society 130:995–1005.

Quinn, T. P., A. P. Hendry, and L. A. Wetzel. 1995. The influence of life history trade-offs and the size of incubation gravels on egg size variation in sockeye salmon (*Oncorhynchus nerka*). Oikos 74:425–438.

Quinn, T. P., S. Hodgson, L. Flynn, R. Hilborn, and D. E. Rogers. 2007. Directional selection by commercial fisheries and the timing of sockeye salmon (*Oncorhynchus nerka*) migrations. Ecological Applications 17:731–739.

Quinn, T. P., I. J. Stewart, and C. P. Boatright. 2006. Experimental evidence of homing to site of incubation by mature sockeye salmon (*Oncorhynchus nerka*). Animal Behaviour 77:941–949.

Quinn, T. P., M. J. Unwin, and M. T. Kinnison. 2000. Evolution of temporal isolation in the wild: genetic divergence in timing of migration and breeding by introduced chinook salmon populations. Evolution 54:1372–1385.

Quinn, T. P., E. C. Volk, and A. P. Hendry. 1999. Natural otolith microstructure patterns reveal precise homing to natal incubation sites by sockeye salmon (*Oncorhynchus nerka*). Canadian Journal of Zoology 77:766–775.

Quinn, T. P., L. Wetzel, S. Bishop, K. Overberg, and D. E. Rogers. 2001. Influence of breeding habitat on bear predation, and age at maturity and sexual dimorphism of sockeye salmon populations. Canadian Journal of Zoology 79:1782–1793.

Quinn, T. P., C. C. Wood, L. Margolis, B. Riddell, and K. D. Hyatt. 1987. Homing in wild sockeye salmon (*Oncorhynchus nerka*) populations as inferred from differences in parasite prevalence and allozyme allele frequencies. Canadian Journal of Fisheries and Aquatic Sciences 44:1963–1971.

Quinn, T. P., K. Doctor, N. Kendall, and H. B. Rich, Jr. 2009. Diadromy and the life history of sockeye salmon: nature, nurture, and the hand of man. Pages 23–42 *in* A. J. Haro, K. L. Smith, R. A. Rulifson, C. M. Moffitt, R. J. Klauda, M. J. Dadswell, R. A. Cunjak, J. E. Cooper, K. L. Beal, and T. S. Avery, editors. Challenges for diadromous fishes in a dynamic global environment. American Fisheries Society, Symposium 69, Bethesda, Maryland.

Ramstad, K. M., C. A. Woody, G. K. Sage, and F. W. Allendorf. 2004. Founding events influence genetic population structure of sockeye salmon (*Oncorhynchus nerka*) in Lake Clark, Alaska. Molecular Ecology 13:277–290.

Rich, H. B., Jr., T. P. Quinn, M. D. Scheuerell, and D. E. Schindler. In press. Climate and intra-specific competition control the growth and life history of juvenile sockeye salmon (*Oncorhynchus nerka*) in Iliamna Lake, Alaska. Canadian Journal of Fisheries and Aquatic Sciences.

Rich, W. H. 1939. Local populations and migration in relation to the conservation of Pacific salmon in the western states and Alaska. Pages 45–50 *in* F. R. Moulton, editor. The Migration and Conservation of Salmon. American Association for the Advancement of Science, Lancaster, PA.

Ricker, W. E. 1972. Hereditary and environmental factors affecting certain salmonid populations. Pages 19–160 *in* R. C. Simon, and P. A. Larkin, editors. The stock concept in Pacific salmon. H. R. MacMillan Lectures in Fisheries, University of British Columbia Press, Vancouver.

Rogers, D. E. 1987. The regulation of age at maturity in Wood River sockeye salmon (*Oncorhynchus nerka*). Canadian Special Publication of Fisheries and Aquatic Sciences 96:78–89.

Roni, P., and T. P. Quinn. 1995. Geographic variation in size and age of North American chinook salmon. North American Journal of Fisheries Management 15:325–345.

Rowse, M. L. 1985. Migration timing of sockeye salmon (*Oncorhynchus nerka*) in the Wood River lake system, Alaska. Master's thesis, University of Washington, Seattle.

Ruggerone, G. T., E. Farley, J. Nielsen, and P. Hagen. 2005. Seasonal marine growth of Bristol Bay sockeye salmon (*Oncorhynchus nerka*) in relation to competition with Asian pink salmon (*O. gorbuscha*) and the 1977 ocean regime shift. Fishery Bulletin 103:355–370.

Sato, H., A. Amagaya, M. Ube, N. Ono, and H. Kudo. 2000. Manipulating the timing of a chum salmon (*Oncorhynchus keta*) run using preserved sperm. North Pacific Anadromous Fish Commission Bulletin 2:353–357.

Schindler, D. E., P. R. Leavitt, C. S. Brock, S. P. Johnson, and P. D. Quay. 2005a. Marine-derived nutrients, commercial fisheries, and production of salmon and lake algae in Alaska. Ecology 86:3225–3231.

Schindler, D. E., D. E. Rogers, M. D. Scheuerell, and C. A. Abrey. 2005b. Effects of changing climate on zooplankton and juvenile sockeye salmon growth in southwestern Alaska. Ecology 86:198–209.

Schindler, D. E., P. R. Leavitt, S. P. Johnson, and B. C. 2006. A five hundred year context for the recent surge in sockeye salmon abundance in the Alagnak River, Alaska. Canadian Journal of Fisheries and Aquatic Sciences 63:1439–1444.

Schtickzelle, N., and T. P. Quinn. 2007. A metapopulation perspective for salmon and other anadromous fish. Fish and Fisheries 8:297–314.

Scudder, G. G. E. 1989. The adaptive significance of marginal populations: a general perspective. Canadian Special Publication of Fisheries and Aquatic Sciences 105:180–185.

Smoker, W. W., A. J. Gharrett, and M. S. Stekoll. 1998. Genetic variation of return date in a population of pink salmon: a consequence of fluctuating environment and dispersive selection? Alaska Fishery Research Bulletin 5:46–54.

Stephenson, S. A. 2006. A review of the occurrence of Pacific salmon (*Oncorhynchus* spp.) in the Canadian western Arctic. Arctic 59:37–46.

Stewart, I. J., R. Hilborn, and T. P. Quinn. 2003a. Coherence of observed adult sockeye salmon abundance within and among spawning habitats in the Kvichak River watershed. Alaska Fishery Research Bulletin 10:28–41.

Stewart, I. J., T. P. Quinn, and P. Bentzen. 2003b. Evidence for fine-scale natal homing among island beach spawning sockeye salmon, Oncorhynchus nerka. Environmental Biology of Fishes 67:77–85.

Stickney, R. R. 1989. Flagship: A history of fisheries at the University of Washington. Kendall Hunt, Dubuque, Iowa.

Taylor, E. B. 1991. A review of local adaptation in Salmonidae, with particular reference to Pacific and Atlantic salmon. Aquaculture 98:185–207.

Thompson, W. F. 1962. The research program of the Fisheries Research Institute in Bristol Bay, 1945–58. Pages 3–36 in T. S. Y. Koo, editor. Studies of Alaska red salmon. University of Washington Press, Seattle.

Tipping, J. M. 1991. Heritability of age at maturity in steelhead. North American Journal of Fisheries Management 11:105–108.

Varnavskaya, N. V., C. C. Wood, R. J. Everett, R. L. Wilmot, V. S. Varnavsky, V. V. Midanaya, and T. P. Quinn. 1994. Genetic differentiation of subpopulations of sockeye salmon (*Oncorhynchus nerka*) within lakes of Alaska, British Columbia and Kamchatka. Canadian Journal of Fisheries and Aquatic Sciences 51 (Supplement 1):147–157.

Weitkamp, L. A., T. C. Wainwright, G. J. Bryant, G. B. Milner, D. J. Teel, R. G. Kope, and R. S. Waples. 1995. Status review of coho salmon from Washington, Oregon, and California. Technical Memorandum NWFSC-24, National Marine Fisheries Service, Seattle.

Welch, D. W., and J. N. Till. 1996. First record of a chum salmon (*Oncorhynchus keta*) from the Thompson River: Adams River spawning grounds, British Columbia. Canadian Field-Naturalist 110:332–334.

Wells, B. K., B. E. Rieman, J. L. Clayton, D. L. Horan, and C. M. Jones. 2003. Relationships between water, otolith, and scale chemistries of westslope cutthroat trout from the Coeur d'Alene River, Idaho: the potential application of hard-part chemistry to describe movements in freshwater. Transactions of the American Fisheries Society 132:409–424.

Withler, F. C. 1982. Transplanting Pacific salmon. Canadian Technical Report of Fisheries and Aquatic Sciences 1079:1–27.

Zhou, S. 2002. Size-dependent recovery of chinook salmon in carcass surveys. Transactions of the American Fisheries Society 131:1194–1202.

American Fisheries Society Symposium 70:873–900, 2009

Data and Modeling Tools for Assessing Landscape Influences on Salmonid Populations: Examples from Western Oregon

KELLY M. BURNETT[*]

USDA Forest Service, Pacific Northwest Research Station
3200 SW Jefferson Way, Corvallis, Oregon 97331, USA

CHRISTIAN E. TORGERSEN

USGS FRESC Cascadia Field Station, University of Washington
College of Forest Resources, Box 352100, Seattle Washington 98195, USA

E. ASHLEY STEEL

Watershed Program, NOAA Fisheries
2725 Montlake Boulevard East, Seattle, Washington 98112, USA

DAVID P. LARSEN

Pacific States Marine Fisheries Commission, c/o U.S. Environmental Protection Agency
200 SW 35th Street, Corvallis, Oregon 97333, USA

JOSEPH L. EBERSOLE

U.S. Environmental Protection Agency, Western Ecology Division
200 SW 35th Street, Corvallis, Oregon 97333

ROBERT E. GRESSWELL

USGS NoROCK 1648 S. 7th Ave., Bozeman, Montana 59717, USA

PETER W. LAWSON

National Marine Fisheries Service, NWFSC/CB
2030 S. Marine Science Drive, Newport, Oregon 97365, USA

DANIEL J. MILLER

Earth Systems Institute, 3040 NW 57th Street, Seattle, Washington 98107, USA

JEFFERY D. RODGERS

Oregon Department of Fish and Wildlife
28655 Highway 34, Corvallis, Oregon 9733, USA

DON L. STEVENS, JR.

Statistics Department, 44 Kidder Hall, Oregon State University, Corvallis, Oregon 97331, USA

[*]Corresponding author: kmburnett@fs.fed.us

Abstract.—Most studies addressing relationships between salmonids, their fresh-water habitats, and natural and anthropogenic influences have focused on relatively small areas and short time periods. The limits of knowledge gained at finer spatiotemporal scales have become obvious in attempts to cope with variable and declining abundances of salmon and trout across entire regions. Aggregating fine-scale information from disparate sources does not offer decision makers the means to solve these problems. The Salmon Research and Restoration Plan for the Arctic-Yukon-Kuskokwim Sustainable Salmon Initiative (AYK-SSI) recognizes the need for approaches to characterize determinants of salmon population performance at broader scales. Here we discuss data and modeling tools that have been applied in western Oregon to understand how landscape features and processes may influence salmonids in freshwater. The modeling tools are intended to characterize landscape features and processes (e.g., delivery and routing of wood, sediment, and water) and relate these to fish habitat or abundance. Models that are contributing to salmon conservation in Oregon include: (1) expert-opinion models characterizing habitat conditions, watershed conditions, and habitat potential; (2) statistical models characterizing spatial patterns in and relationships among fish, habitat, and landscape features; and (3) simulation models that propagate disturbances into and through streams and predict effects on fish and habitat across a channel network. The modeling tools vary in many aspects, including input data (probability samples vs. census, reach vs. watershed, and field vs. remote sensing), analytical sophistication, and empirical foundation, and so can accommodate a range of situations. In areas with a history of salmon-related research and monitoring in freshwater, models in the three classes may be developed simultaneously. In areas with less available information, expert-opinion models may be developed first to organize existing knowledge and to generate hypotheses that can guide data collection for statistical and simulation models.

Introduction

Data and modeling tools that describe multiple spatial and temporal scales are increasingly useful to inform decisions related to salmon sustainability. Most studies addressing relationships between salmonids, their freshwater habitats, and factors that affect these have focused on relatively small areas (10^1–10^2 m^2) and short time periods (<2 years). The limits of knowledge gained at finer spatiotemporal scales have become obvious as society copes with variable and declining salmon populations across entire regions. Other pervasive problems, such as decreasing water quality and quantity (e.g., Carpenter et al. 1998; Postel 2000) and loss of aquatic biodiversity and integrity (e.g., Hughes and

Noss 1992; Stein et al. 2000), have also elicited calls to broaden the extent of freshwater assessment, management, and research (e.g., Fausch et al. 2002; Rabeni and Sowa 2002; Hughes et al 2006). These complexities require integrated landscape research over extended periods. Considering larger extents often does not alleviate the need for fine-grained (high-resolution) information, which is facilitated by geographic information systems (GIS), availability of spatially explicit field and remotely sensed data, and analytical modeling tools (Hughes et al. 2006).

Modeling can be especially useful to the study and management of salmon across spatiotemporal scales, up to and including landscapes or riverscapes (>10^2 km^2 and 10^2–10^3 years). Broad-scale analyses present difficulties in designing replicated, controlled experiments and in obtaining field data on in-channel characteristics over large areas. The Salmon Research and Restoration Plan for the Arctic-Yukon-Kuskokwim Sustainable Salmon Initiative (AYK-SSI) (2006) explicitly recognizes the contribution of modeling in sustaining salmon and salmon fisheries. The Plan highlights models for analyzing and synthesizing information and for identifying and predicting key variables and patterns.

Our goal in this paper is to summarize numerous examples of data collection methods and modeling tools that are contributing to understanding, restoring, and managing salmon and their habitats across western Oregon. A long and productive history of salmon-related data collection and modeling justifies our focus on western Oregon. Given similarities in certain social and ecological characteristics between western Oregon and the AYK region, some data and modeling examples presented may have immediate utility in accomplishing the goals of the AYK-SSI. Other examples may yield opportunities for adaptation and collaboration, while others may stimulate ideas and offer a point of departure. We provide a general overview, rather than specific details, of each example and identify resources beyond this paper to guide the reader interested in further information.

Biophysical and Management Context of Salmon in Western Oregon

Our focus area covers approximately 58,274 km² of western Oregon (Figure 1). It includes the Coast Range, Willamette Valley, and Cascades Level-III Ecoregions (Pater et al. 1998). Elevations extend from sea level along the coast of the Pacific Ocean to 4,390 m in the mountainous inland areas. The terrain is varied, consisting of two mountain ranges, rolling hills, floodplains with productive soils, coastal plains punctuated by headlands, and alluvial and coastal terraces. Rock types are predominately marine sandstones and shales or volcanics that in the Cascade Range are affected by alpine glaciation. The climate is temperate with wet winters and warm dry summers. Mean annual precipitation ranges from 56 cm to 544 cm (Thornton et al. 1997). Precipitation transitions from primarily rain to primarily snow along a west-east gradient. The majority of lowland areas are now managed for agriculture or urban uses but consisted of wetlands, salt marshes, prairies, or oak savannahs before European settlement. The majority of upland areas are managed for timber harvest or recreation. Forested areas are in highly productive pure conifer stands or mixed conifer and hardwood stands; the latter is true particularly along streams. Uplands are characterized by high densities of small, steep streams and lowlands by a few large rivers with historically complex channel patterns.

Streams and rivers support five species of Pacific salmonids: coho salmon *Oncorhynchus kisutch*, Chinook salmon *O. tshawytscha*, chum salmon *O. keta*, rainbow trout/steelhead *O. mykiss*, and coastal cutthroat trout *O. clarkii*. Coho and Chinook salmon are targeted in commercial and recreational fisheries, whereas steelhead and cutthroat trout are primarily taken by sport anglers. Steelhead are listed under the U.S. Endangered Species Act (1973) as a Species of Concern in the Oregon Coastal Evolutionarily Significant Unit (ESU) and as a Threatened Species in the Upper Willamette ESU. Coho salmon are listed as Threatened in the Lower Columbia ESU and in the Oregon Coastal ESU.

Data

Management agencies and research institutions have invested in a wealth of salmon-related biophysical data for western Oregon (Table 1). These data were collected using different designs and methods

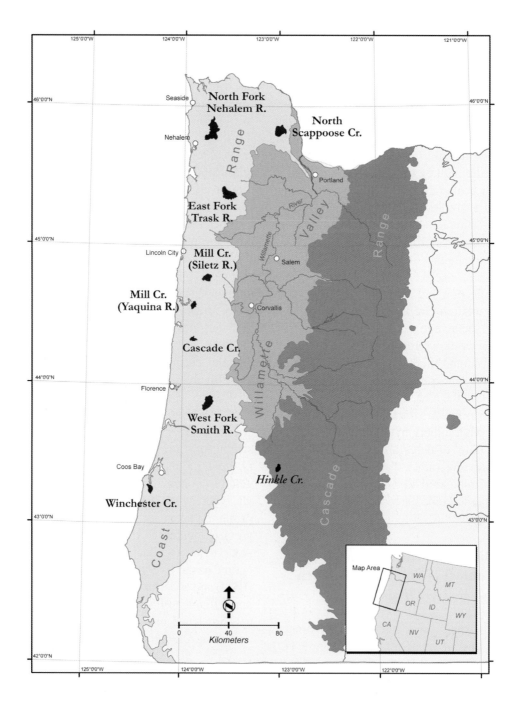

FIGURE 1. Western Oregon as referenced in this paper. Level III Ecoregions (Pater et al. 1998) and intensively monitored basins are highlighted in shades of gray and black, respectively.

TABLE 1. Western Oregon data sets addressed in this paper. Highlighted areas correspond to sub-headings in the text.

Data collection approach	Rationale	Source	Spatial/temporal resolution	Spatial/temporal extent	Types
Probability-based sampling	Monitor and assess condition of wadeable streams	Environmental Monitoring and Assessment Program (EMAP)	Stream reach /annual	Western OR /2000–2004	Fish, aquatic macro-invertebrates, physical habitat, water quality
	Monitor effectiveness of the Northwest Forest Plan	Aquatic and Riparian Effectiveness Monitoring Program (AREMP)	Stream reaches nested in 6th-code Hydrologic Units/ 5 yrs	Federal lands western OR, western WA, northern CA/2002–present	Aquatic macro-invertebrates, physical habitat
	Monitor effectiveness of the Oregon Plan for Salmon and Watersheds	Oregon Plan for Salmon and Watersheds	Stream reach/ annual	Western OR/1997–present	Spawning coho, juvenile salmonids, physical habitat
Intensive Basin Monitoring	Life-cycle monitoring	Oregon Plan for Salmon and Watersheds	8 basins ≤ 75 km²/ annual	Western OR/1997–present	Abundance of migrating adult and juvenile salmonids, physical habitat
	Research juvenile salmonid population dynamics	U.S. EPA Western Ecology Division	Habitat unit–watershed/ seasonal–annual	WF Smith River, 69 km²/ 2002–2005	Fish abundance and movement, physical habitat, water quality, discharge
	Research timber-harvest effects	USGS	Habitat unit–watershed/ seasonal–annual	Hinkle Creek 19 km²/ 2002–2010	Abundance and movement of steelhead and cutthroat trout, physical habitat, water quality, discharge

TABLE 1. Continued.

Data collection approach	Rationale	Source	Spatial/temporal resolution	Spatial/temporal extent	Types
Census	Characterize and monitor	Various agencies and remote sensing technologies	≤25 m/variable	Western OR/variable	Land use/cover
	Monitor and assess	Various agencies with airborne forward looking infrared (FLIR)	1 m/variable	10^1–10^2 m/variable	Water temperature
	Research relationships among watershed, stream habitat, and spatial patterns of cutthroat trout abundance	USGS	Habitat unit/ summer	Western OR/1 yr	Fish and habitat
	Characterize topography	USGS and various remote sensing technologies	≤10 m	Western OR	Digital elevation

to meet a variety of assessment, monitoring, and research objectives. Here we describe in-channel fish and habitat data, as well as landscape data collected using three approaches: (1) probability-based sampling of reaches or watersheds, (2) intensive monitoring of basins, and (3) complete census of an area or stream.

Probability-based sampling to monitor and assess aquatic ecosystems

The ability to assess and monitor trends in aquatic ecosystems over a large area (ESU, ecoregion, or administrative unit such as a National Forest) is of interest to society. Aquatic ecosystems can be characterized using one or more indicators such as a fish species, macroinvertebrate community, or physical habitat feature. A desirable goal might be to describe the abundance and spatial pattern of an indicator. However, conducting a census of these types of indicators across a broad landscape is often impractically expensive. This challenge of characterizing an entirety without a census has been managed in other fields of inquiry by adopting sample surveys (e.g., election polls and health statistics). Textbooks relevant for offering a thorough understanding of the theory and application of sample surveys include Särndal (1978), Cochran (1977), Lohr (1999), and Thompson (1992). The approach relies on selecting and characterizing a statistically representative sample. Unbiased inferences about the entirety are then drawn from measurements on the sample. These survey sampling techniques have been incorporated into a variety of natural resource arenas, including the National Agricultural Statistics Survey, the Forest Inventory and Analysis/Forest Health Monitoring program, and the National Wetlands Inventory. Here we describe three survey sampling programs for monitoring and assessing aquatic ecosystems in western Oregon are described.

Environmental Monitoring and Assessment Program (EMAP).—Responding to a variety of critiques that the nation was able to "assess neither the current status of ecological resources nor the overall progress toward legally mandated goals" at regional and national scales (U.S. House of Representatives 1984), the U.S. Environmental Protection Agency (EPA) initiated the EMAP (Messer et al. 1991). The inland aquatic component (lakes, streams and rivers, and wetlands) began with a survey of the condition of lakes in the northeastern USA. Most recently, a 5-year survey was completed of the condition of streams and rivers in the coterminous western USA, including western Oregon. The national programs, organized and run by EPA's Office of Research and Development (ORD) and Office of Water (OW), are complemented by Regional EMAPs (REMAP). A REMAP is conducted by an EPA regional office along with the states and tribes under their purview, focusing on the condition of inland aquatic ecosystems over smaller areas.

An EMAP or REMAP project consists of two components. The first is a survey design that addresses the need to obtain a statistically representative sample of the targeted resource. The survey design identifies where to sample (e.g., which lakes or which locations in a stream network). The second component is a response design (Stevens and Urquhart 2000; Stevens 2001) consisting of several parts, including which biological, chemical, and physical indicators to measure at each sample location, field protocols for measuring these indicators, and methods to convert the measurements into quantitative indicator scores. The biological condition of aquatic resources is assessed through multi-metric indices of biotic integrity (e.g., Hughes et al. 2004) or through the ratio of taxa at a site to taxa expected if the site were in "reference condition" (e.g., Van Sickle et al. 2005). In combination with the survey design, results are used to infer the frequency distribution of resource conditions and the fraction of the resource that is in various quality classes (e.g., good, fair, poor). Changes over time can be evaluated with repeated sampling.

Statistical foundations supporting the current survey designs are in Stevens (1997), Stevens and Olsen (1999, 2003, 2004). Implementation of the design procedures is available at www.epa.gov/nheerl/arm, as written in a public domain statistical computing language (R Development Core Team 2006). Typical EMAP and REMAP field protocols are documented in Peck et al. (2006). Examples of assessment reports include Herger and Hayslip (2000), Hayslip and Herger (2001), and Stoddard et al. (2005). The survey design component of EMAP was used to select watersheds and stream sites in the following two assessment programs. The response designs are specific to each of those programs.

The Aquatic and Riparian Effectiveness Monitoring Program (AREMP).—As part of the Northwest Forest Plan (NWFP) for federal forestlands in the range of the northern spotted owl *Strix occidentalis caurina* (USDA and USDI 1994), effectiveness monitoring programs were developed for plan components. One of the NWFP components, the Aquatic Conservation Strategy (ACS), is designed to restore and maintain the ecological integrity of watersheds and their aquatic ecosystems on public lands. The AREMP is responsible for monitoring the ACS by evaluating the condition of sixth-code (12-digit) U.S. Geological Survey (USGS) hydrologic units using a combination of upslope, riparian, and in-channel physical and biological indicators (Reeves et al. 2004). Given that 2500–3000 of these hydrologic units comprise the NWFP area, conducting a census is impractical for most of the chosen in-channel indicators. Instead, a statistically representative sample of hydrologic units to be assessed on a five-year cycle was selected using a survey design.

For each year, indicator measurements on each selected hydrologic unit are combined through a knowledge-based logic model to produce a watershed condition score (Gallo et al. 2005; Reeves et al. 2006). The frequency distribution of these scores for sampled hydrologic units in each year is a snapshot of the condition of watersheds across the NWFP area. The expectation is that if the NWFP is working, the frequency distribution of scores will shift over time in a direction indicating watershed conditions are improving. The field phase of monitoring began in 2002; however, landscape-level indicators were estimated from historical remote sensing data (e.g., aerial photography) beginning with implementation of the NWFP in 1994. A 10-year summary of the effectiveness of the ACS is published in Gallo et al. (2005).

Oregon Plan for Salmon and Watersheds.—Dramatic declines in populations of coastal coho salmon led the State of Oregon in 1997 to implement a plan for restoring native populations and the aquatic systems that support them. This plan, called the "Oregon Plan for Salmon and Watersheds," featured an innovative approach to estimate and monitor habitat conditions and total numbers of coho salmon adults and juveniles. These objectives could not be met with census techniques. From the 1950s until implementation of this new approach, fish and habitat monitoring relied on handpicked "index" sites that were not necessarily representative of the larger landscape for which monitoring information was needed. Because the surveys were biased, it was impossible to derive a reliable, statistically rigorous estimate of Oregon coastal coho salmon and their habitats. The new survey design for the Oregon Plan is a spatially balanced, random sample that produces unbiased estimates for which precision can be calculated (Stevens 2002). The surveys feature a rotating panel design, based on the 3-year life cycle of coho salmon, wherein one quarter of the sites are sampled each year, one quarter every 3 years, one quarter every 9 years, and one quarter only once. The rotating panel design is intended to balance the need to estimate status (precision improves with more sites sampled) and the need to detect trends (power improves with more revisits to each site). Although sampling universes of the separate habitat, spawner, juvenile, and water quality surveys that comprise this program vary, the forced coincidence of survey sites where sampling universes overlap enables analyses of habitat and fish relationships across scales (from reach or site to ESU or population).

The information gathered by these surveys, as well as the existence of a monitoring program, was considered by NOAA Fisheries during the listing process for Oregon coastal coho salmon under the Endangered Species Act. The Oregon Department of Fish and Wildlife (ODFW) routinely publishes statistical summaries of the results of these surveys; a published synthesis of results is also available (OWEB 2005a, 2005b). More information on the Oregon Coastal Coho Salmon Assessment and how the Oregon Plan survey information was used in the assessment can be obtained at: http://nrimp.dfw.state.or.us/OregonPlan/.

Intensive basin monitoring

The goal for intensively monitored basins (IMB) is to focus research and monitoring efforts in a particular location. These can be locations for descriptive or experimental research, such as in paired watershed studies. Data may be collected over long periods on many indicators, including water quality and quantity, fish population abundances at different life cycle stages, food-web interactions, and movement of individual fish. Intensively monitored basins are typically selected based on practical rather than statistical consideration. Thus, the scope of inference for results

is not always clear. Landscape classification can help place intensively monitored basins into a broader context and thus help approximate how likely are fine-scale research or monitoring results to represent a larger area.

Life Cycle Monitoring.—In 1998, as part of the Oregon Plan, the ODFW began intensive monitoring in eight basins across western Oregon (Figure 1). The specific objectives of this monitoring are to: (1) estimate abundances of returning adult salmonids and downstream migrating juvenile salmonids, (2) estimate marine and freshwater survival rates for naturally produced coho salmon, and (3) evaluate relationships between freshwater habitat conditions and salmonid production. Although the Life Cycle Monitoring basins were "hand picked" based on the feasibility of trapping upstream migrating adults and downstream migrating juveniles, the basins do represent an array of Oregon coastal landscapes. Work is progressing to identify those that are under- or un-represented by the current Life Cycle Monitoring network and to add new basins. This will allow extrapolation of the findings from the Life Cycle Monitoring basins to most Oregon coastal landscapes. More information about the Life Cycle Monitoring Program can be obtained at: http://nrimp.dfw.state.or.us/crl/default.aspx?pn = SLCMP.

Research on juvenile salmonid population dynamics.—In 2002, the U.S. EPA Western Ecology Division initiated a 4-year study in the West Fork Smith River (W.F. Smith River) to investigate juvenile salmonid population dynamics, specifically focusing on spatial patterns of survival and growth in relation to movement within the basin. The W.F. Smith River is a tributary to the lower Umpqua River draining a 69-km^2 forested basin in the south-central Oregon Coast Range, and is one of the eight Life Cycle Monitoring basins (Figure 1). The study uses a hierarchically organized, spatially nested sampling design. At various spatial scales throughout the basin, environmental characteristics are monitored, including water chemistry and discharge (stream level), temperature and channel morphology (reach level) and channel unit structure (channel unit level). Biological data are collected seasonally and annually at the individual fish (growth, movement) and population (patterns of abundance, survival) levels. Movement, growth and survival parameters are estimated using a mark–recapture approach, and these biological responses are correlated to environmental characteristics at the appropriate spatial and temporal scales.

Key findings from the study include the understanding that habitat configuration and availability can change in response to natural and anthropogenic disturbance. For example, while overwintering habitat may be limiting at most times, summer habitat can be limiting during extreme low summer flows, especially in streams underlain by sandstones. Ebersole et al. (2006) found that summer conditions, including high water temperatures and reduced scope for growth, were associated with reduced overwinter survival of juvenile coho salmon in the W.F. Smith River following a relatively warm, dry summer. Summer habitat could become locally limiting also following restoration of overwintering habitat or improved access to existing winter habitats. In the W.F. Smith River, the potential importance of intermittent tributaries to overwintering juvenile coho salmon was assessed with mark–recapture experiments. Ebersole et al. (2006) found that overwinter growth and survival were enhanced in an intermittent tributary relative to nearby mainstem habitats, and that individual fish moving into the intermittent stream experienced a distinct survival and growth advantage. Intermittent streams in the W.F. Smith River were also important to adult coho salmon, as a disproportionate number of spawners used intermittent streams over several years of study (Wigington et al. 2006).

These findings highlight the importance of considering the dynamic nature of stream habitats for salmon, and the ability of salmon to "track" suitable habitats. Field-derived estimates of movement and survival will be used to parameterize scenarios of dynamic habitat configurations and accessibility that can be compared via simulation models. These scenario-based analyses will allow exploration of the potential implications of habitat changes due to restoration, land use, or stochastic environmental events.

Research on timber-harvest effects.— The response of headwater fish assemblages to contemporary timber harvest practices on private industrial land has not been described at the stream-network scale. Hypothetically, changes in habitat, water quality, or food supply associated with timber harvest affect fish in a dynamic way, but the following questions remain unanswered: (1) How do changes in physical and biological characteristics of tributaries without fish seasonally influence habitat quality in other portions of the stream network? (2) How do seasonal hydrologic changes in headwater streams affect fish behavior and distribution? and (3) Do life history expression, behavior, or diversity of fish fauna vary in response to changed habitat quality, or do organisms redistribute to areas where habitat quality remains unaltered? Sampling, to address these questions, began in Hinkle Creek in 2001 (Figure 1). The Hinkle Creek Study, along with the more recent Alsea Watershed Study and Trask River Watershed Study, comprise the Watershed Research Cooperative (http://watershedsresearch.org/) for examining effects of contemporary forest harvest practices.

Fish abundance has been estimated annually since 2002 in all pools and cascades of Hinkle Creek, with electrofishing as the primary means of fish collection. During each sampling period, all coastal cutthroat trout and steelhead ≥100 mm (fork length) were implanted with a passive integrated transponder (PIT) tag prior to release. Stationary receiver antennae were placed to continuously monitor fish movement at the stream segment scale. Additionally, tagged fish were located with portable sensors during subsequent field visits, typically during winter, spring, and early summer. This information is being used to detect fine-scale shifts in fish distribution and movement patterns (e.g., timing, direction, and distance) that can be compared with reach-scale stream discharge, substrate composition, water temperature, food availability, and geomorphic structure. Fish sampling at a variety of temporal and spatial scales is providing the opportunity to analyze natural variation at multiple scales. Ultimately, terrestrial and aquatic habitat conditions for coastal cutthroat trout demographics will be available for five years before timber harvest (2001–2005) and five years following harvest (2006–2010).

Census

The challenge with census data lies in describing an entirety at a grain size that resolves the desired level of detail without sampling and without overwhelming the ability to collect, process, and store the information. Field and remote sensing techniques have been applied to collect census data on fish, their habitat, and the surrounding landscape. Census data are available for western Oregon describing aquatic and terrestrial characteristics that can change over time and are relatively static.

Land use and land cover.—Land use and land cover are temporally variable characteristics for which census data are commonly collected. Attributes in these layers are monitored directly as indicators of anthropogenic effects on salmon ecosystems (e.g., Gallo et al. 2005) and used as explanatory or predictive variables in salmon-related models (e.g., Steel et al. 2004; Burnett et al. 2006). In addition to describing current conditions, land use and land cover data offer a baseline for projecting landscape attributes into the future under different management scenarios, via models such as those for the Oregon Coast Range (Bettinger et al. 2005; Johnson et al. 2007) or the Willamette River basin (Hulse et al. 2004).

Land use and land cover are typically derived from remotely sensed imagery (e.g., 1.1 km advanced very high resolution radiometer [AVHRR] or 30 m resolution Landsat Thematic Mapper [TM]) in visible or other wavelengths. High-resolution (<1 m) data can now be obtained from airborne laser mapping such as red waveform light detection and ranging (lidar) (Lefsky et al. 2001, 2002). Despite key advantages offered by the high resolution of lidar, the data are relatively expensive to obtain, process, and store for large areas.

The National Land Cover Database (NLCD 1992, 2001) (e.g., Homer et al. 2004; Wickham et al. 2004) provides "current" land cover for western Oregon and is planned for the AYK region. The NLCD is appropriate for generalized characterizations in that it aggregates land cover from TM imagery into about 15 broad classes and classifies forest cover based on only over-story features. An alternative to the NLCD is available for much of western Oregon (e.g., Ohmann and Gregory 2002; Ohmann et al. 2007). It represents forest over- and under-story characteristics as gradients instead of discrete classes and was developed by linking remotely sensed imagery to field-based ground plots (e.g., Forest Inventory and Analysis (FIA); Ohmann and Gregory 2002).

Water temperature.—Stream temperature, a temporally dynamic freshwater characteristic, is one of the most critical environmental determinants of habitat quality for salmon and has been the focus of extensive research and water quality monitoring efforts in the Pacific Northwest (USA) (e.g., Poole and Berman 2001; Poole et al. 2004). Recent technological advances led to widespread deployment in streams of automated monitoring stations, which record water temperature at a fine temporal resolution (~15-min sampling intervals) over multiple months. These data helped to increase awareness of temporal variation in stream temperature and raised new questions about the biological consequences of such thermal heterogeneity. However, this work also highlighted that "temporally continuous" temperature data from in-stream recorders are still spatially limited. The use of airborne forward-looking infrared (FLIR) sensors arose out of the need to map variation in stream temperature at a fine spatial resolution (<1 m) over $10^1 - 10^2$ km.

Thermal infrared remote sensing of stream water temperature, initially explored in Washington and Oregon during the early 1990s, has advanced rapidly. Airborne applications of FLIR from a helicopter were first used to identify groundwater inputs and thermal refugia for salmon (Belknap and Naiman 1998; Torgersen et al. 1999). After the approach was validated for accuracy (Torgersen et al. 2001), applications in water quality management and fisheries increased dramatically. Thermal infrared imagery has been used extensively by management agencies to characterize longitudinal thermal profiles for streams and rivers and to examine sources of cold- and warm- water inputs (ORDEQ 2006). Quantitative models of stream temperature and stream-aquifer interactions use thermal infrared imagery to identify thermal anomalies and to increase the spatial accuracy of stream temperature predictions (Boyd 1996; Loheide and Gorelick 2006; ORDEQ 2006).

Researchers have also investigated the utility of high-altitude air- and space-borne thermal sensors for mapping surface water temperature in rivers of the Pacific Northwest (Cherkauer et al. 2005; Handcock et al. 2006). These approaches hold promise for mapping water temperature synoptically throughout large, remote watersheds. However, the coarse spatial resolution (>5 m) of high-altitude and satellite-based imagery confines its use to larger rivers.

Fish and habitat.—An integrated research program was initiated by the USGS to explore relationships among upslope watershed characteristics, physical stream habitat, and spatial patterns of coastal cutthroat trout abundance during summer low-flow conditions (Gresswell et al. 2006). Variation was evaluated at two spatial scales: (1) across western Oregon (spatial extent) using watersheds as sample units (resolution), and (2) within watersheds using as sample units, the individual elements in the stream habitat hierarchy (channel units, geomorphic reaches, and stream segments). Watersheds were selected at the coarser spatial scale with probability-based sampling, and data were collected on fish and habitat characteristics at the finer scale using a census approach.

Data from the fine-scale censuses were summarized for each watershed to examine variation in cutthroat trout abundance across western Oregon. Because data were collected in a spatially contiguous manner in each watershed, it was possible to evaluate spatial structuring in cutthroat trout abundance (see discussion in Modeling Tools—Spatial Models). It appears that cutthroat trout move frequently among accessible portions of small streams (Gresswell and Hendricks 2007). Individuals congregate in areas of suitable habitat and may form local populations with unique genetic attributes (Wofford et al. 2005). Those that move into larger downstream portions of the network may contribute to the genetic structure of anadromous or local potamodromous assemblages. Viewing habitats as matrices of physical sites that are linked by movement is providing new insights into the study of the fitness and persistence of cutthroat trout populations.

Digital elevation data and its processing.—Census data are available for western Oregon on many characteristics that may be considered temporally invariant, particularly over short periods in salmon-related studies. Depending on the temporal extent, these characteristics can include topography, rock type, and climate. Although relatively static, such characteristics may affect spatial and temporal variability in salmon distribution and their habitats. Spatial layers for some of these data types have been, or could be produced, for the AYK region. Predictions of long-term mean annual surface temperature and precipitation are available for Alaska from two sources: the Spatial Climate Analysis Service (SCAS) and the Alaska Geospatial Data Clearinghouse (AGDC) (Simpson et al. 2005). Digital elevation data have been some of the most important for western Oregon and so are highlighted here. These data have been essential in delineating and describing streams and watersheds (Benda et al. 2007); developing and implementing landscape models, such as those of salmon habitat potential (Burnett et al. 2007) and of processes affecting sediment and wood delivery to streams (e.g., Miller and Burnett 2007); and for landscape classification and inference.

The western Oregon digital elevation data are available as gridded 10-m digital elevation models (DEMs). These were created (Underwood and Crystal 2002) by interpolating elevations at DEM grid points from the digital line graph (DLG) contours on standard 7.5-min topographic quadrangles (USGS 1998) and by drainage enforcing to hydrography on the DLG data. The relatively high resolution is essential for representing streams and hillslopes in the complex and heavily dissected, mountainous terrain of western Oregon. However,

inaccuracies in the 10-m DEMs, arising from the base DLG data, can affect landscape characterization and modeling results (e.g., Clarke and Burnett 2003).

Very high-resolution DEMs can be obtained from lidar data. Such DEMs can be derived by classifying the "last return" or "bare earth" from multiple-return red waveform lidar data. Hydrography can be mapped directly from this lidar. The red laser pulses are absorbed by water, rather than reflected and returned to the sensor; thus water is identified by "no data." Green waveform lidar, which penetrates water and reflects back to the sensor, is commonly used for bathymetric mapping in coastal areas (e.g., Wozencraft and Millar 2005). The Experimental Advanced Airbone Research lidar (EAARL) is a full waveform lidar that can simultaneously map surface topography, in-channel morphology, and vegetation (McKean et al. 2006) and holds great promise for characterizing river networks in both western Oregon and the AYK region.

Digital data on hydrography (1:63,000-scale National Hydrography Dataset [NHD]) and elevation (e.g., 1:63,000-scale National Elevation Data [NED] and 90-m DEMs below 60 degrees, North Latitude) are available for the AYK region; however, the spatial resolution and extent of these data are questionable for much salmon-related landscape modeling. Higher resolution topographic and hydrographic data can be obtained by processing remotely sensed imagery (e.g., Japanese Earth Resources Satellite [JERS-1] Interferometric Synthetic Aperture Radar [SAR] L-band, and Advanced Land Observing Satellite [ALOS] PRISM and SAR data).

The availability of DEMs, together with powerful and inexpensive computers, has prompted development of tools that facilitate terrain analysis or geomorphometry (Pike 2002). Digital elevation models are processed by specialized computer software such as the Terrain Analysis System (TAS) (Lindsay 2005) or NetMap (Benda et al. 2007) to automate and visualize spatial analyses of hill slopes and stream networks. Numerous outputs are produced at the spatial grain of the DEM, including surface-flow direction, gradient, and aspect. Linkages among DEM pixels allow derivation of outputs such as synthetic stream networks, catchment boundaries, drainage area, topographic convergence, tributary junction angles, and valley widths. Outputs from these types of terrain analysis are highly relevant to studies of geomorphology, hydrology, and salmonid ecology.

Modeling Tools

Although a large amount of high-quality data is available for western Oregon, information about the components of salmon ecosystems and their complex interactions will never be complete. Thus, models have been developed to help fill data gaps as well as to simplify, abstract, and project conditions in salmon ecosystems (Table 2). Accuracy and precision of modeled outputs are important ways to measure the success of these models. Another measure is utility—does the model help explain, predict, or organize understanding about how salmon interact with their biotic and abiotic environments? Here we focus on three classes of models: expert opinion models, statistical and spatial models, and simulation models (Figure 2).

Expert-opinion models

An expert-opinion model is a transparent and repeatable means to organize existing knowledge. Such models can help when assessing current conditions, projecting likely outcomes, and making decisions when empirical data or relationships are incomplete or uncertain. In addition, an expert-opinion model can be a framework to expose and document knowledge gaps and assumptions,

and thus catalyze and generate hypotheses and guide future data collection. Therefore, models of this class can be extremely informative in early phases of study.

Expert-opinion models typically consist of a user interface, a database, and a rule base. The rule base is expressed in the architecture, relationships, and distributions of variables in the model. The rule base may be developed with information from a single expert or small group of experts or may be elicited from a larger group of experts through a systematic process (e.g., Schmoldt and Peterson 2000). Expert-opinion models have been developed for a variety fields, including medicine, business, and natural resources management (e.g., Kitchenham et al. 2003; Marcot 2006a; Razzouk et al. 2006). We present three expert-opinion models that are informing natural resources management in western Oregon and that may have relevance to the AYK region.

Bayesian belief networks.—The first example is a nonspatially explicit set of Bayesian belief networks (BBNs) developed by Marcot (2006b) to help implement the Northwest Forest Plan (USDA and USDI 1994). These BBNs predict habitat quality and potential survey sites for several relatively rare species associated with late-successional or old-growth forests. At its most basic, a BBN rule base is an influence diagram that represents probabilistic relationships (arcs) between variables (nodes). Input variables can be represented in various ways; one common form being discrete states with the prior probability of each state based on empirical evidence, expert judgment, or a combination. Expert opinion played a large role in developing influence diagrams and prior probabilities for the western Oregon BBNs. These models were built in the software package Netica (Norsys, Inc.; http://www.norsys.com) but several other packages are available (e.g., BNet.BUILDER, OpenBayes, and SamIam). More information on BBNs for

TABLE 2. Western Oregon models addressed in this paper.

Model class	Type	Objective for use in western Oregon
Expert Opinion	Bayesian belief network	Predict habitat quality and potential survey sites for relatively rare late-successional or old-growth forest associated species
	Knowledge-based logic model	Monitor effectiveness of the Northwest Forest Plan
	Habitat potential model	Describe the intrinsic potential of streams to provide high-quality habitat for salmonids
Statistical and spatial	Statistical models of fish and habitat	Explain or predict variation in biotic, physical-habitat, or water-quality characteristics from landscape characteristics
	Spatial interpolation of probability-based sample data	Predict the spatial pattern of coho salmon abundance on the Oregon coast
	Spatial analysis of census data	Quantify and explain the degree of spatial structure within and among headwater basins in cutthroat trout distribution
Simulation	Coho salmon life cycle	Evaluate potential outcomes of management scenarios and climate change on coho salmon in freshwater and marine environments.
	Disturbance and stream habitat	Evaluate potential outcomes for fish habitat of management scenarios and climate change that affect sediment and wood delivery from fires, storms, and debris flows.

western Oregon and on other BBN applications is available at http://www.spiritone.com/~brucem/bbns.htm.

Knowledge-based logic models.—The second example is a knowledge-based logic model (Gallo et al. 2005) that uses the survey data collected by the Aquatic and Riparian Effectiveness Monitoring Program (AREMP). The logic model was designed to assess and monitor watershed conditions in the area managed under the Northwest Forest Plan (USDA and USDI 1994). This model was constructed with Ecosystem Management Decision Support (EMDS) software (Reynolds et al. 2003) and is linked to a GIS. It was designed to evaluate the proposition that conditions in a watershed are "suitable to support strong populations of fish and other aquatic and riparian-dependent organisms" (Gallo et al. 2005). Truth of this general proposition is evaluated for a watershed by aggregating evaluation scores for model attributes (e.g., road density, channel gradient, percent pool area) according to the hierarchical architecture of the logic model. Each evaluation score is derived by comparing data for the attribute against a curve that expresses the contribution to overall watershed condition. As with any knowledge-based logic model, the shape of the curves may vary by attribute. However, the curves share a common scale (−1.0 to +1.0) that expresses the strength of evidence for a proposition (Zadeh et al. 1996). This scale describes uncertainty about the definition of events rather than uncertainty about

Data   Models

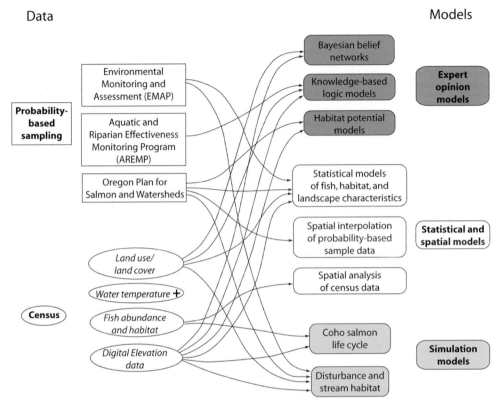

+ These data are available, but are not currently used in the models shown.

FIGURE 2. Relationships between collected data and developed models for western Oregon.

the likelihood of events as with BBNs. In the AREMP knowledge-based logic models, the overall model structure and the attribute curves were based on expert opinion.

Habitat potential models.—The third example focuses on models describing the potential of streams to provide high-quality habitat for salmonids (Steel and Sheer 2002; Burnett et al. 2007). Steel and Sheer (2002) modeled spawning habitat potential for chinook salmon and for steelhead from channel gradient. Burnett et al. (2007) modeled habitat potential for juvenile coho salmon and juvenile steelhead from mean annual stream flow, valley constraint, and channel gradient. In both studies, stream attributes were calculated from climate data and terrain analysis of DEMs, during automated production of

a digital stream network (Miller 2003), and habitat potential was interpreted from these stream attributes based on empirical evidence in published studies. Outputs were data layers and GIS maps depicting species-specific habitat potential for modeled stream networks across 36,000 km in the Willamette and Lower Columbia River basins (Steel and Sheer 2002) and 96,000 km in the Oregon Coast Range (Burnett et al. 2007). Once habitat potential was estimated, these studies answered a variety of questions relevant to conservation, including required spawner densities to meet population viability thresholds (Steel and Sheer 2002), what land covers are adjacent to reaches with high habitat potential (Burnett et al. 2007) and how much high-quality habitat has been lost above anthropogenic barriers (Sheer and Steel 2006).

Outputs of the habitat potential models for the Oregon Coast Range have also been used to estimate fish production potential assuming relatively little human disturbance (Lawson et al. 2004), and to evaluate fish passage and restoration projects (Dent et al. 2005). The model for the Oregon Coast Range was adapted and applied to other areas and to other salmonid species with established relationships to topographic characteristics (e.g., Agrawal et al. 2005; Lindley et al. 2006).

Statistical models

A large amount of high-quality data has allowed western Oregon to become a laboratory for exploring statistical relationships of relevance to understand and manage salmon.

Statistical models of fish, habitat, and landscape characteristics.—Numerous statistical models have been developed recently for western Oregon to examine relationships among salmonids, their habitats, and landscape characteristics. These models are designed so their users can take advantage of census data on landscape characteristics to predict in-channel characteristics that are otherwise difficult or expensive to collect. Analytical techniques applied in these models include classification and regression trees (Wing and Skaugset 2002), discriminant analysis (Burnett 2001), and linear mixed models (Steel et al. 2004). Model objectives were to explain or predict variation in in-channel characteristics such as the amount of large wood in streams (Wing and Skaugset 2002; May and Gresswell 2003), an index of fish biotic integrity (Hughes et al. 2004), densities of juvenile salmonids (Hicks and Hall 2003), deposition of fine sediment (Sable and Wohl 2006), and nitrogen export (Compton et al. 2003). In-channel responses were found to be related to static characteristics (e.g., geology or stream size) as well as those reflecting natural and anthropogenic disturbance (e.g., percent area in large trees or

percent area in red alder *Alnus rubra*). Some of the studies explored mulit-scale relationships by summarizing landscape characteristics across different spatial extents (e.g., buffer and catchment) (e.g., Compton et al. 2003; Van Sickle et al. 2004; Flitcroft 2007). Here the focus is on two of the several studies from western Oregon.

In the first study, Steel et al. (2004) used mixed linear models to identify associations between landscape condition and winter steelhead spawner abundance in multiple watersheds of the Willamette River basin. Their approach identified relationships between landscape conditions and relative redd densities that were consistent over time despite year-to-year fluctuations in fish population size. This general approach has been successful for Chinook and coho salmon in other basins (Pess et al. 2002; Feist et al. 2003). These models explained up to 72% of the spatial variation in year-to-year distribution of spawners. Landscape predictors of redd density included alluvial deposits, forest age, and land use. Predictions of potential redd density from these landscape models were examined along with inventories of known and potential barriers to fish passage. Using this information, barrier removal projects and mitigation for in-stream barriers, common approaches for restoring salmon habitat and populations, were prioritized. The prioritization scheme evaluated the potential quantity and suitability of spawning habitat that would be made accessible by restoration.

The second study explored relationships between landscape characteristics and stream habitat features in the forested, montane Elk River basin (Burnett et al. 2006). The modeled habitat features (mean maximum depth of pools, mean volume of pools, and mean density of large wood in pools) were those found to distinguish between sampled stream segments that were highly used by juvenile Chinook salmon and those that were not (Burnett 2001). Landscape characteristics were summarized at five spatial extents, which varied in the area encompassed upstream and upslope of sampled stream segments. In regressions with landscape characteristics, catchment area explained more variation in the mean maximum depth and volume of pools than any other landscape characteristic, including all those reflecting land management. In contrast, the mean density of large wood in pools was positively related to percent area in older forests and negatively related to percent area in sedimentary rock types. The regression model containing these two variables had the greatest explanatory power at an intermediate spatial extent. Finer spatial extents may have omitted important source areas and processes for wood delivery, but coarser spatial extents likely incorporated source areas and processes less tightly coupled to large wood dynamics. Thus, the multi-scale design of this study suggested the scale at which landscape features are likely to influence stream attributes as well as testable hypotheses for examining influence mechanisms.

Spatial models

These models address the challenges and opportunities presented by spatial autocorrelation among observations. Spatial autocorrelation is a measure of the tendency for points that are close to one another to share more characteristics than points that are farther apart. A high degree of spatial autocorrelation reflects a lack of statistical independence in a dataset, violating the assumptions of standard parametric statistical methods, such as analysis of variance (ANOVA) and least squares regression (Legendre and Fortin 1989). Techniques are available to account for this spatial autocorrelation in standard parametric tests (e.g., mixed models). The fact that most ecological data, and particularly census data, are spatially autocorrelated is viewed simply as a nuisance unless one recognizes that such spatial structure contains information essential to describing and understanding underlying ecological processes (Legendre 1993).

Geostatistical methods provide the means to explicitly identify the presence of spatial structure and to describe these patterns in a quantitative manner (Rossi et al. 1992). Geospatial techniques were developed for, and are typically applied in, settings such as lakes and landscapes that are described by points in two or three dimensions. In these settings, the distance between sample locations can be measured as a straight line between two points, and the effective distance is the same in both directions. However, the effective distance between two points in a stream network may be as the fish swims, not as the crow flies, and may be greater in one direction than the other, depending upon the process of interest. Such issues pertaining to aquatic habitat and organisms within the context of a network topology are increasingly being raised in aquatic monitoring and resource modeling efforts.

Understanding the factors that influence the spatial scale of variation in fish distribution in stream networks is necessary for developing aquatic sampling designs and is widely recognized as a new frontier in studies of river systems (Fagan 2002; Campbell et al. 2007; Flitcroft 2007). Investigation of stream network processes and biological responses may often require census data and models that explicitly consider the configuration of drainage patterns and the juxtaposition of tributary junctions, which play key roles in structuring aquatic habitat and biota in riverine systems (Benda et al. 2004; Kiffney et al. 2006; Rice et al. 2008).

Spatial interpolation of probability-based sample data.—Random process models are important for analyzing environmental data that varies through space and time, especially to predict the value of some environmental variable at an arbitrary point. Kyriakidis and Journel (1999) provide a recent overview and bibliography. In the last ten years, use of hi-erarchical models to analyze dependencies among variables has increased. Hierarchical models have been widely applied to environ-mental data, especially data with space/time components. The basic idea of hierarchical models is that the observed data are modeled as a function depending on unknown param-eters and unobserved random errors. The ran-dom errors in turn are modeled as dependant on unknown parameters. In the Bayesian version, the unknown parameters are given a prior distribution, and the posterior distri-bution is calculated from the observed data. These techniques have been used to develop statistical models that accommodate missing data, temporal and spatial dependencies, la-tent variables, multiple response variables, and nonlinear functional forms. Several years ago, such models were not feasible, because the parameter estimation was too computa-tionally intensive. Several recent theoretical developments have substantially reduced the computational burden, most notably the so-called Gibbs sampler (Geman and Geman 1984; Gelfand and Smith 1990), Markov Chain Monte Carlo (MCMC) techniques (Gilks et al. 1996), and the Metropolis-Hastings algorithm (Metropolis et al. 1953; Hastings 1970). For more details on these algorithms and MCMC, see Robert and Ca-sella (2004), Gelman et al. (1995), and Gel-fand (2000). Smith et al. (2005) have applied these techniques to predict the spatial pattern of coho salmon abundance on the Oregon coast.

Spatial analysis of census data on coastal cutthroat trout.—Data from a census of aquat-ic habitat and coastal cutthroat trout in head-water basins of western Oregon have made it possible to evaluate spatial patterns in fish distribution across multiple scales (Gresswell et al. 2006; Torgersen et al. 2004) as opposed to a single scale predetermined by the sam-pling design (Schneider 1994; Torgersen et

al. 2006). Results of this census for approxi-mately 200 km of stream were mapped in a spatially referenced database (Torgersen et al. 2004). Spatial patterns in the relative abun-dance of coastal cutthroat trout (Bateman et al. 2005) were examined relative to fine- and coarse-scale habitat features, ranging from substrate characteristics within channel units to landscape patterns in topography and land use (Gresswell et al. 2006). Because the cen-sus data could be summarized by different geomorphically defined units (e.g., channel unit, reach, or segment) or by different fixed-length units (e.g., 10 m, 100 m, or 1000 m), investigations into the spatial structure of fish distribution could be addressed in an explor-atory manner. Such analyses of census data have revealed unexpected results in which the distribution of an organism was associated with a predictor variable at one spatial scale but not at another (Schneider and Piatt 1986; Torgersen and Close 2004). Moreover, flex-ibility in the size of the analysis window al-leviates concerns associated with calculations of population density, which is highly scale dependent and can be a misleading indicator of the habitat preferences of an organism (Van Horne 1983; Grant et al. 1998).

The technical hurdles of applying geo-statistical tools to the study of spatial patterns of fish distribution were examined by Ganio et al. (2005), using the census data on coastal cutthroat trout in western Oregon. Their work revealed that cutthroat trout distribution ex-hibited a high degree of spatial structure, that the spatial structure varied among headwater basins, and that this variation could be ex-plained by geology and watershed character-istics, such as elevation, slope, and drainage density.

Simulation models

Simulation models have been developed for western Oregon to assess changes in salm-on abundance and habitat characteristics over time. Simulation models attempt to integrate the many component processes that drive complex dynamic systems. The models may explicitly represent the mechanics of, and relationships between, component processes or derive more from empirical understanding about these. Outputs from one component are typically inputs for the next, and feedback can be incorporated between components. Running a simulation model with different input values can identify components of a system that may be most sensitive to change. Simulation models provide a means to evaluate potential outcomes of management scenarios or climate change on salmonids and their habitats. Such models have been developed for the Willamette Valley in western Oregon (e.g., Bolte et al. 2007; Guzy et al. 2008), and we focus on two examples from the Oregon Coast Range.

Coho salmon life cycle.—A stochastic habitat-based life cycle simulation model for coho salmon on the Oregon Coast was developed from relationships between freshwater habitat characteristics, the capacity of those habitats to support coho salmon at various life stages, and survival rates in those habitats (Nickelson 1998; Nickelson and Lawson 1998). Monte Carlo runs of the model produce likely patterns of coho salmon abundance (and variability in abundance) under a variety of circumstances including variable marine survival. A similar model was developed for coho and chum salmon in Carnation Creek, British Columbia (Holtby and Scrivener 1989). The Oregon Coast model has been used to estimate coastal carrying capacity, to identify under-performing basins, to compare proposed fishery management strategies, and to perform population viability analysis.

The model is based on freshwater reaches of about 1 km, with smolt carrying capacity and parr-to-smolt survival rates estimated from measured habitat characteristics. For each reach, females deposit eggs that hatch into fry. Fry survive to summer parr based on a density-dependent function. Summer parr survive to smolts based on reach-specific survival rates and a maximum capacity. Smolts migrate to the ocean and survive at a variable rate. Most return to their natal reach to spawn, but some migrate to other reaches allowing recolonization of depleted areas. Although the original model did not incorporate a spatially explicit representation of the stream network, newer versions of the model will. These are under development in separate efforts by scientists at the U.S. EPA Western Ecology Division (Leibowitz and White, in press) and at the NOAA NW Fisheries Science Center/Earth Systems Institute.

Landscape disturbance and stream habitat.—Wildfires, landslides, floods, and other natural disturbances are integral to the functioning of aquatic ecosystems (Reeves et al. 1995), but our ability to understand and predict the consequences of altered disturbance regimes is hindered by the large spatial and temporal extents involved. Computer simulations of natural processes can be run over entire regions for millennia, propagating disturbances into and through stream networks and estimating in-channel effects. Integrated simulation models provide baseline outputs for characterizing disturbance regimes unaltered by human activities, and for evaluating future conditions under various management scenarios. A prototype simulation model that integrates multiple processes to estimate stream habitat conditions (USDA Forest Service 2003) has been adapted for western Oregon.

Several component models were necessary to build the integrated habitat simulation model for western Oregon. Regional wildfire models, for example, provide estimates of spatial and temporal variability in stand ages and types under a natural fire regime (Wimberly 2002). An empirical model that relates forest attributes to landslide susceptibility (Miller and Burnett 2007) is used to predict landsliding associated with changes in forest cover. By relating storm characteristics to landslide rates (Benda and Dunne 1997a), climate variability is incorporated into the modeling. Fires, storms, and landslides affect processes of wood recruitment to streams (Benda and Sias 2003), leading to temporal and spatial variability in simulated wood loading (Benda et al. 2003). In the simulation model, the spatial overlap and temporal sequence of interacting events that deliver and transport sediment and wood create a mosaic of channel and related habitat conditions (e.g., number of pools and amount of large wood) that changes over time (USDA Forest Service 2003). Such predictions reveal potential patterns and relationships that can be difficult to discern empirically. This is due to the fact that cause and effect may be separated in time and space (e.g., fires in the headwaters 100 years ago and an aggraded mainstem channel now [Benda and Dunne 1997a]). The integrated habitat simulation model is now being coupled with a habitat-based coho salmon life cycle model (Nickelson 1998; Nickelson and Lawson 1998). The model will produce possible trajectories of salmon abundance as the landscape changes through processes related to climate or management.

Conclusions

Over the past 50 years, western Oregon has been an active locus for collecting data and developing models (Tables 1 and 2; Figure 2) to help understand and manage salmon. Though these efforts have not always proceeded logically and systematically, we have attempted in this paper to organize this experience through hindsight. The AYK-SSI Salmon Research and Restoration Plan (2006) is a strategic framework to guide research and monitoring in collecting the right data the first time around. The authors hope to contribute to these endeavors by offering

managers and scientists working in the AYK region the opportunity to evaluate examples of data and models that have been particularly useful in western Oregon.

Of the many possible lessons to take from the western Oregon experience, some may be readily transferable for meeting objectives of the AYK-SSI Salmon Research and Restoration Plan (2006) and some may not. There are three lessons for designing and initiating data collection that may have particular value for the AYK region. The first is that data are more valuable when their scope of inference is known. Although the scope of inference is determined objectively in the design of a probability-based sampling strategy, it can be approximated through landscape classifications for data collected in intensively monitored basins or case studies. The second lesson relates to striking the right balance between answering the questions of how many and why. Data collected for monitoring and assessment are essential, but may be insufficient, for effectively managing salmon and their habitats. Data collected specifically for research may be necessary to provide critical understanding—to answer the "why" questions about salmon ecosystems. This may be particularly true as populations in the AYK region face new levels or combinations of stressors that are outside the range of recent experience. The third lesson is that upfront integration between interested parties can yield efficiencies in where and what types of data are collected and can increase the utility of any collected data. Meta-analysis of existing data collection efforts and databases can help prioritize information gaps that are critical for meeting regional goals (e.g., Holl et al. 2003). Establishing regular communications among monitoring and research participants will clarify assumptions and expectations and improve opportunities for collaboration, thereby enhancing the likelihood that collected data can contribute to accomplishing multiple objectives.

A key lesson regarding modeling that may prove useful in the AYK region is that all models are "expert opinion" to one degree or another. Consequently, correct predictions should be viewed with a healthy degree of skepticism. Understanding of model precision, which is the potential range of model outputs given known uncertainties in the input data, can aid in the appropriate use of modeled data in a decision-making context (Jones and Bence 2009, this volume. The landscape models we addressed here likely compromise some degree of local accuracy for broad-scale coverage or synthesis. Even so, these models have proven useful. A good model is one that can help explain, predict, or understand salmon and their ecosystems, and the best models are likely to derive from an iterative and adaptive process. Such a process involves organizing existing knowledge and data, collecting data to fill essential gaps, building and running a model, evaluating model outputs against newly collected data or traditional knowledge, and then repeating the entire process.

References

Agrawal, A., R. S. Schick, E. P. Bjorkstedt, R. G. Szerlong, M. N. Goslin, B. C. Spence, T. H. Williams, and K. M. Burnett. 2005. Predicting the potential for historical coho, Chinook, and steelhead habitat in northern CA. NOAA Technical Memorandum, NOAA-TM-NMFS-SWFSC-379.

AYK-SSI (Arctic-Yukon-Kuskokwim Sustainable Salmon Initiative). 2006. Arctic-Yukon-Kuskokwim Salmon Research and Restoration Plan. Bering Sea Fishermen's Association, Anchorage, Alaska.

Bateman, D. S., R. E. Gresswell, and C. E. Torgersen. 2005. Evaluating single-pass catch as a tool for identifying spatial pattern in fish distribution. Journal of Freshwater Ecology 20:335–345.

Belknap, W., and R. J. Naiman. 1998. A GIS and TIR procedure to detect and map wall base channels in western Washington. Journal of Environmental Management 52:147–160.

Benda, L. E., and T. Dunne. 1997a. Stochastic forcing of sediment supply to channel networks from landsliding and debris flow. Water Resources Research 33:2849–2863.

Benda, L. E., and T. Dunne. 1997b. Stochastic forcing of sediment routing and storage in channel networks. Water Resources Research 33:2865–2880.

Benda, L. E., and J. C. Sias. 2003. A quantitative framework for evaluating the mass balance of in-stream organic debris. Forest Ecology and Management 172:1–16.

Benda, L., D. J. Miller, K. Andras, P. Bigelow, G. H. Reeves, and D. Michael. 2007. NetMap: a new tool in support of watershed science and resource management. Forest Science 53:206–219. See also http://www.earthsystems.net.

Benda, L., D. J. Miller, J. Sias, D. Martin, R. E. Bilby, C. Veldhuisen, and T. Dunne. 2003. Wood recruitment processes and wood budgeting. Pages 49–73 in S. V. Gregory, K. L. Boyer, and A. M. Gurnell, editors. The ecology and management of wood in world rivers. American Fisheries Society, Bethesda, Maryland.

Benda, L., N. L. Poff, D. Miller, T. Dunne, G. Reeves, G. Pess, and M. Pollock. 2004. The network dynamics hypothesis: how channel networks structure riverine habitats. BioScience 54:413–427.

Bettinger, P., M. Lennette, K. N. Johnson, T. A. Spies. 2005. A hierarchical spatial framework for forest landscape planning. Ecological Modelling 182:25–48.

Bolte, J. P., D. W. Hulse, S. V. Gregory, and C. Smith. 2007. Modeling biocomplexity actors, landscapes and alternative futures. Environmental Modelling and Software 22(5):570–579.

Boyd, M. 1996. Heat source: stream, river and open channel temperature prediction. Master's thesis. Oregon State University, Corvallis, Oregon.

Burnett, K. M. 2001. Relationships among juvenile anadromous salmonids, their freshwater habitat, and landscape characteristics over multiple years and spatial scales in the Elk River, Oregon. Doctoral dissertation., Oregon State University, Corvallis, Oregon.

Burnett, K. M., G. H. Reeves, S. E. Clarke, and K. R. Christiansen. 2006. Comparing riparian and catchment-wide influences on salmonid habitat in Elk River, Oregon. Pages 175–196 in R. M. Hughes and L. Wang, editors. Influences of landscapes on stream habitat and biological communities. American Fisheries Society, Symposium 48, Bethesda, Maryland.

Burnett, K. M., G. H. Reeves, D. J. Miller, S. Clarke, K. Vance-Borland, and K. Christiansen. 2007. Distribution of salmon-habitat potential relative to landscape characteristics and implications for conservation. Ecological Applications 17:66–80.

Campbell, G. E., W. Lowe, and W. F. Fagan. 2007. Living in the branches: population dynamics and ecological processes in dendritic networks. Ecology Letters 10:165–175.

Carpenter, S. R., N. F. Caraco, D. L. Correll, R.W. Howarth, A. N. Sharpley, and V. H. Smith. 1998. Nonpoint pollution of surface waters with phosphorus and nitrogen. Ecological Applications 8(3):559–568.

Cherkauer, K. A., S. J. Burges, R. N. Handcock, J. E. Kay, S. K. Kampf, and A. R. Gillespie. 2005. Assessing satellite-based and aircraft-based thermal infrared remote sensing for monitoring Pacific Northwest river temperature. Journal of the American Water Resources Association 41:1149–1159.

Clarke, S. E., and K. M. Burnett. 2003. Comparison of digital elevation models for aquatic data development. Photogrammetric Engineering and Remote Sensing 69(12):1367–1375.

Cochran, W. G. 1977. Sampling techniques. 3rd edition. Wiley, New York.

Compton, J. E., M. R. Church, S. T. Larned, and W. E. Hoggsett. 2003. Nitrogen export from forested watersheds in the Oregon Coast Range: the role of N_2-fixing red alder. Ecosystems 6:773–785.

Dent L., A. Herstrom, and E. Gilbert, 2005. A spatial evaluation of habitat access conditions and Oregon Plan Fish Passage Improvement Projects in the coastal Coho ESU. Oregon Plan Technical Report 2. 24 pp. Available: http://nrimp.dfw.state.or.us/OregonPlan/ (March 2007).

Ebersole, J. L., P. J. Wigington, J. P. Baker, M. A. Cairns, M. R. Church, B. P. Hansen, B. A. Miller, H. R. LaVigne, J. E. Compton, , and S. Leibowitz. 2006. Juvenile coho salmon growth and survival across stream network seasonal habitats. Transactions of the American Fisheries Society 135:1681–1697.

Endangered Species Act of 1973 (as amended Pub. L. 93–205, 16 USC 1531 et seq.).

Fagan, W. F. 2002. Connectivity, fragmentation, and extinction risk in dendritic metapopulations. Ecology 83:3243–3249.

Fausch, K. D., C. E. Torgersen, C. V. Baxter, and H. W. Li. 2002. Landscapes to riverscapes: bridging the gap between research and conservation of stream fishes. BioScience 52:483–498.

Feist, B. E., E. A. Steel, G. R. Pess, and R. E. Bilby. 2003. The influence of scale on salmon habitat restoration priorities. Animal Conservation 6:271–282.

Flitcroft, R. L. 2007. Regions to streams: spatial and temporal variation in stream occupancy patterns of coho salmon (*Oncorhynchus kisutch*) on the Oregon Coast. Doctoral dissertation, Oregon State University, Corvallis.

Gallo, K., S. H. Lanigan, P. Eldred, S. N. Gordon, and C. Moyer. 2005. Northwest Forest Plan—the first 10 years (1994–2003): preliminary assessment of the condition of watersheds. U.S. Forest Service General Technical Report PNW-GTR-647, Portland, Oregon.

Ganio, L. M., C. E. Torgersen, and R. E. Gresswell. 2005. A geostatistical approach for describing spatial pattern in stream networks. Frontiers in Ecology and the Environment 3:138–144.

Gelfand, A. E. 2000. Gibbs sampling. Journal of the American Statistical Association 95:1300–1304.

Gelfand, A. E., and A. F. M. Smith. 1990. Sampling-based approaches to calculating marginal densities. Journal of the American Statistical Association 85:398–409.

Gelman, A., J. B. Carlin, H. S. Stern, and D. B. Rubin. 1995. Bayesian Data Analysis. Chapman and Hall, London.

Geman, S., and D. Geman, D. 1984. Stochastic relaxation, Gibbs distributions, and the Bayesian restoration of images. IEEE transactions on pattern analysis and machine intelligence 6:721–741.

Gilks, W. R., W. Clayton, and D. Spiegelhalter, editors. 1996. Practical Markov Chain Monte Carlo. Chapman and Hall, London.

Grant, J. W. A., S. O. Steingrimsson, E. R. Keeley, and R. A. Cunjak. 1998. Implications of territory size for the measurement and prediction of salmonid abundance in streams. Canadian Journal of Fisheries and Aquatic Sciences 55 (Supplement 1):181–190.

Gresswell, R. E., and S. R. Hendricks. 2007. Population-scale movement of coastal cutthroat trout in a naturally isolated stream network. Transactions of the American Fisheries Society. 136:238–253.

Gresswell, R. E., C. E. Torgersen, D. S. Bateman, T. J. Guy, S. R. Hendricks, and J. E. B. Wofford. 2006. A spatially explicit approach for evaluating relationships among coastal cutthroat trout, habitat, and disturbance in small Oregon streams. Pages 457–471 in R. M. Hughes, L. Wang, and P. W. Seelbach, editors. Landscape influences on stream habitats and biological assemblages. American Fisheries Society, Symposium 48, Bethesda, Maryland.

Guzy, M. R., C. L. Smith, J. P. Bolte, D. W. Hulse and S. V. Gregory. 2008. Policy research using agent-based modeling to assess future impacts of urban expansion into farmlands and forests. Ecology and Society 13(1):37.

Handcock, R. N., A. R. Gillespie, K. A. Cherkauer, J. E. Kay, S. J. Burges, and S. K. Kampf. 2006. Accuracy and uncertainty of thermal-infrared remote sensing of stream temperatures at multiple spatial scales. Remote Sensing of Environment 100:457–473.

Hastings, W. K. 1970. Monte Carlo sampling methods using Markov chains and their applications. Biometrika 57:97–109.

Hayslip, G. A., and L. G. Herger. 2001. Ecological condition of Upper Chehalis basin streams. U.S. Environmental Protection Agency, Region 10, Report EPA-910-R-01-005. Seattle.

Herger, L. G., and G. A. Hayslip. 2000. Ecological condition of streams in the Coast Range ecoregion of Oregon and Washington. U.S. Environmental Protection Agency, Region 10, Report EPA-910-R-00-002, Seattle.

Hicks, B. J., and J. D. Hall. 2003. Rock type and channel gradient structure salmonid populations in the Oregon Coast Range. Transactions of the American Fisheries Society 132:468–482.

Holl, K. D., E. E. Crone, and C. B. Schultz. 2003. Landscape restoration: moving from generalities to methodologies. BioScience 53:491–5.

Holtby, L. B., and J. C. Scrivener. 1989. Observed and simulated effects of climatic variability, clear-cut logging and fishing on the numbers of chum salmon (*Oncorhynchus keta*) and coho salmon (*O. kisutch*) returning to Carnation Creek, British Columbia. Pages 62–81 in C. D. Levings, L. B. Holtby, and M. A. Henderson, editors. Proceedings of the national workshop on the effects of habitat alteration on salmonid stocks. Canadian Special Publication of Fisheries and Aquatic Sciences 105.

Homer, C., C. Huang, L. Yang, B. Wylie, and M. Coan. 2004. Development of a 2001 National Landcover Database for the United States. Photogrammetric Engineering and Remote Sensing 70:829–840.

Hughes, R. M., and R. F. Noss. 1992. Biological diversity and biological integrity: current concerns for lakes and streams. Fisheries 17(3):11–19.

Hughes, R. M., S. Howlin, and P. R. Kaufmann. 2004. A biointegrity index (IBI) for coldwater streams of western Oregon and Washington. Transactions of the American Fisheries Society 133:1497–1515.

Hughes, R. M., L. Wang, and P. W. Seelbach, editors. 2006. Landscape influences on stream habitats and biological assemblages. American Fisheries Society Symposium 48. Bethesda, Maryland.

Hulse, D. W., A. Branscomb, and S. G. Payne. 2004. Envisioning alternatives: using citizen guidance to map future land and water use. Ecological Applications 14:325–341. See also http://oregonstate.edu/dept/pnw-erc (March 2007).

Johnson, K. N., P. Bettinger, J. D. Kline, T. A. Spies, M. Lennette, G. Lettman, B. Garber-Yonts, and T. Larsen. 2007. Simulating forest structure, timber production, and socioeconomic effects in a multi-owner province. Ecological Applications 17:34–47. See also http://www.fsl.orst.edu/CLAMS (March 2007).

Jones, M. L., and J. R. Bence. 2009. Uncertainty and fishery management in the North American Great Lakes: lessons from applications of decision analysis. Pages 1059–1081 in C. C. Krueger and C. E. Zimmerman, editors. Pacific salmon: ecology and management of western Alaska's populations. American Fisheries Society, Symposium 70, Bethesda, Maryland.

Kiffney, P. M., C. M. Greene, J. E. Hall, and J. R. Davies. 2006. Tributary streams create spatial discontinuities in habitat, biological productivity, and diversity in mainstem rivers. Canadian Journal of Fisheries and Aquatic Sciences 63:2518–2530.

Kitchenham, B. A., L. Pickard, S. Linkman, and P. Jones. 2003. Modelling software bidding risks. Transactions on Software Engineering 29:542–554.

Kyriakidis, P. C., Journel, A.G.. 1999. Geostatistical space-time models: a review. Mathematical Geology 31:651–684.

Lawson, P. W., E. Bjorkstedt, M. Chilcote, C. Huntington, J. Mills, K. Moore, T. E. Nickelson, G. H. Reeves, H. A. Stout, and T. C. Wainwright. 2004. Identification of historical populations of coho salmon (*Oncorhynchus kisutch*) in the Oregon Coast Evolutionarily Significant Unit. Review Draft. Oregon Northern California Coast Technical Recovery Team. NOAA/NMFS/NWFSC.

Lefsky, M., W. Cohen, and T. Spies. 2001. An evaluation of alternate remote sensing products for forest inventory, monitoring, and mapping of Douglas-fir forests in western Oregon. Canadian Journal of Forest Research 31:78–87.

Lefsky, M. A., W. B. Cohen, G. G. Parker, and D. J. Harding. 2002. Lidar remote sensing for ecosystem studies. BioScience 52:19–30.

Legendre, P. 1993. Spatial autocorrelation: trouble or new paradigm? Ecology 74:1659–1673.

Legendre, P., and M.-J. Fortin. 1989. Spatial pattern and ecological analysis. Vegetatio 80:107–138.

Leibowitz, S.G. and White, D. 2009. Modeling the effect of stream network characteristics and juvenile movement on coho salmon. Pages 203–224 in E. E. Knudsen, J. H. Michael, and C. S. Steward, editors. Pacific salmon environment and life history models: advancing science for sustainable fisheries in the future. American Fisheries Society, Symposium 71, Bethesda, Maryland.

Lindley, S. T., R.S. Schick, A. Agrawal, M. Goslin, T.E. Pearsons, E. Mora, J.J. Anderson, B. May, S. Green, C. Hanson, A. Low, D. McEwan, R.B. MacFarlane, C. Swanson, and J.G. Williams. 2006. Historical population structure of Central Valley steelhead and its alteration by dams. San Francisco Estuary and Watershed Science 4(3):1–19.

Lindsay, J. B. 2005. The Terrain Analysis System: a tool for hydro-geomorphic applications. Hydrological Processes 19:1123–1130.

Loheide, S., and S. Gorelick. 2006. Quantifying stream-aquifer interactions through the analysis of remotely sensed thermographic profiles and *in situ* temperature histories. Environmental Science and Technology 40:3336–3341.

Lohr, S. L. 1999. Sampling: design and analysis. Duxbury Press, Pacific Grove, California.

Marcot, B. G. 2006a. Habitat modeling for biodiversity conservation. Northwestern Naturalist 87:56–65.

Marcot, B. G. 2006b. Characterizing species at risk I: Modeling rare species under the Northwest Forest Plan. Ecology and Society 11(2):10 Available: http://www.ecologyandsociety.org/vol11/iss2/art10/ (March 2007).

May, C. L., and R. E. Gresswell. 2003. Processes and rates of sediment and wood accumulation in headwater streams of the Oregon Coast Range, USA. Earth Surface Processes and Landforms 28:409–494.

McKean, J., W. Wright, and D. Isaak. 2006. Mapping channel morphology and stream habitat with a full waveform water-penetrating green lidar. Geophysical Research Abstracts vol 8, 03159 SRef-ID: 1607–7962/gra/EGU06-A-03159.

Messer, J. J., R. A. Linthurst, and W. S. Overton. 1991. An EPA program for monitoring ecological status and trends. Environmental Monitoring and Assessment 17:67–78.

Metropolis, N., A. W. Rosenbluth, M.N. Rosenbluth, A. H. Teller, and E. Teller. 1953. Equation of state calculations by fast computing machines. Journal of Chemical Physics 21:1087–1092.

Miller, D. J. 2003. Programs for DEM Analysis. In Landscape dynamics and forest management (CD-ROM). U.S. Forest Service, General Technical Report RMRS-GTR-101CD, Fort Collins, Colorado.

Miller, D. J., and K. M. Burnett. 2007. Effects of forest cover, topography, and sampling extent on the measured density of shallow, translational landslides. Water Resources Research, 43, W03433, doi:10.1029/2005WR004807.

Nickelson, T. E. 1998. A habitat-based assessment of coho salmon production potential and spawner escapement needs for Oregon coastal streams. Oregon Department of Fish and Wildlife Information Report 98–4.

Nickelson, T. E., and Lawson, P. W. 1998. Population viability of coho salmon, *Oncorhynchus kisutch*, in Oregon coastal basins: application of a habitat-based life cycle model. Canadian Journal of Fisheries and Aquatic Sciences 55:2382–2392.

Ohmann, J. L., and M. J. Gregory. 2002. Predictive mapping of forest composition and structure with direct gradient analysis and nearest neighbor imputation in coastal Oregon, USA. Canadian Journal of Forest Research 32:725–741.

Ohmann, J. L., M. J. Gregory, and T. A. Spies. 2007. Influence of environment, disturbance, and ownership on forest vegetation of coastal Oregon. Ecological Applications 17:18–33.

ORDEQ (Oregon Department of Environmental Quality). 2006. Water quality: total maximum daily load program. Oregon Department of Environmental Quality, Portland, Oregon.

OWEB (Oregon Watershed Enhancement Board). 2005a. 2003–2005 Oregon plan biennial report, Volume 1. Salem, Oregon.

OWEB (Oregon Watershed Enhancement Board). 2005b. 2003–2005 Oregon plan biennial report, Volume 2. Salem, Oregon.

Pater, D. E., S. A. Bryce, T. D. Thorson, J. Kagan, C. Chectaresppell, J. M. Omernik, S. H. Azevedo, and A. J. Woods. 1998. Ecoregions of western Washington and Oregon. U.S. Geological Survey, scale 1:350,000, Reston, Virginia.

Peck, D. V., A. T. Herlihy, B. H. Hill, R. M. Hughes, P. R. Kaufmann, D. J. Klemm, J. M. Lazorchak, F. H. McCormick, S. A. Peterson, P. L. Ringold, T. Magee, and M. R. Cappaert. 2006. Environmental monitoring and assessment program—surface waters western pilot study: field operations manual for wadeable streams. U.S. Environmental Protection Agency, Office of Research and Development, Report EPA 600/R-05/003, Washington, D.C.

Pess, G. R., D. R. Montgomery, R. E. Bilby, E. A. Steel, B. E. Feist, and H. M. Greenberg. 2002. Correlation of landscape characteristics and land use on coho salmon (*Oncorhynchus kisutch*) abundance, Snohomish River, Washington State, USA. Canadian Journal of Aquatic and Fisheries Science 59:613–623.

Pike, R. J. 2002. A bibliography of terrain modeling (geomorphometry), the quantitative representation of topography—Supplement 4.0. USGS OPEN-FILE REPORT 02–465.

Poole, G. C., and C. H. Berman. 2001. An ecological perspective on in-stream temperature: natural heat dynamics and mechanisms of human-caused thermal degradation. Environmental Management 27:787–802.

Poole, G., J. Dunham, D. Keenan, S. Sauter, D. McCullough, C. Mebane, J. Lockwood, D. Essig, M. Hicks, D. Sturdevant, E. Materna, S. Spalding, J. Risley, and M. Deppman. 2004. The case for regime-based water quality standards. BioScience 54:155–161.

Postel, S. L. 2000. Entering and era of water scarcity: the challenges ahead. Ecological Applications 10(4):941–948.

R Development Core Team. 2006. R: a language and environment for statistical computing. R Foundation for Statistical Computing, Vienna, Austria. http://www.r-project.org.

Rabeni C. F., and S. P. Sowa. 2002. A landscape approach to managing the biota of streams and rivers. in J. Liu, W. W. Taylor editors. Integrating landscape ecology into natural resource management. Cambridge University Press, Cambridge, Massachusetts.

Razzouk, D., J. J. Mari, I. Shirakawa, J. Wainer, and D. Sigulem. 2006. Decision support system for the diagnosis of schizophrenia disorders. Brazilian Journal of Medical and Biological Research 39:119–128.

Reeves, G. H., L. E. Benda, K. M. Burnett, P. A. Bisson, and J. R. Sedell. 1995. A disturbance-based ecosystem approach to maintaining and restoring freshwater habitats of evolutionarily significant units of anadromous salmonids in the Pacific Northwest. Pages 334–349 in J. L. Nielson and D. A. Powers, editors. Evolution and the aquatic ecosystem: defining unique units in population conservation. American Fisheries Society, Symposium 17, Bethesda, Maryland.

Reeves, G. H., D. B. Hohler, D. P. Larsen, D. E. Busch, K. Kratz, K. Reynolds, K. F. Stein, T. Atzet, P. Hays, and M. Tehan. 2004. Effectiveness monitoring for the aquatic and riparian component of the Northwest Forest Plan: conceptual framework and options. U.S. Forest Service General Technical Report PNW-GTR-577, Portland, Oregon.

Reeves, G. H., J. E. Williams, K. M. Burnett, and K. Gallo. 2006. The aquatic conservation strategy of the Northwest Forest Plan. Conservation Biology 13:1220–1223.

Reynolds, K. M., S. Rodriguez, and K. Bevans. 2003. EMDS 3.0 user guide. Environmental Systems Research Institute, Redlands, California. Available: http://www.institute.redlands.edu/emds/ (March 2007).

Rice, S. P., A. G. Roy, and B. L. Rhoads, editors. 2008. River confluences, tributaries and the Fluvial Network. Wiley, New York.

Robert, C. P. and G. Casella. 2004. Monte Carlo Statistical Methods. Springer, New York.

Rossi, R. E., D. J. Mulla, A. G. Journel, and E. H. Franz. 1992. Geostatistical tools for modeling and interpreting ecological spatial dependence. Ecological Monographs 62:277–314.

Sable, K. A., and E. Wohl. 2006. The relationship of lithology and watershed characteristics to fine sediment deposition in streams of the Oregon Coast Range. Environmental Management 37:659–670.

Särndal, C. 1978. Design-based and model-based inference for survey sampling. Scandinavian Journal of Statistics 5:27–52.

Schmoldt, D. L., and D. L. Peterson. 2000. Analytical group decision making in natural resources: methodology and application. Forest Science 46:62–75.

Schneider, D. C. 1994. Scale-dependent patterns and species interactions in marine nekton. Pages 441–467 in P. S. Giller, A. G. Hildrew, and D. G. Raffaelli, editors. Aquatic ecology: scale, pattern and process. Blackwell Scientific Publications, Oxford, UK.

Schneider, D. C., and J. F. Piatt. 1986. Scale-dependent correlation of seabirds with schooling fish in a coastal ecosystem. Marine Ecology Progress Series 32:237–246.

Sheer, M. B., and E. A. Steel. 2006. Lost watersheds: barriers, aquatic habitat connectivity, and salmon persistence in the Willamette and Lower Columbia river basins. Transactions of the American Fisheries Society 135:1645–1669.

Simpson, J. J., G. L. Hufford, C. Daly, J. S. Berg, and M. D. Fleming. 2005. Comparing maps of mean monthly surface temperature and precipitation for Alaska and adjacent areas of Canada produced by two different methods. Arctic 58:137–161.

Smith, R. A., D. L. Stevens, Jr., and J. Rodgers. 2005. A hierarchical Bayesian approach to develop predictive maps of coho salmon abundance in Oregon coastal streams. Poster presented at Statistics for Aquatic Resources Monitoring, Modeling, and Management, Oregon State University, Corvallis, Oregon.

Steel, E. A., B. E. Feist, D. Jensen, G. R. Pess, M. Sheer, J. Brauner, and R. E. Bilby. 2004. Landscape models to understand steelhead (Oncorhynchus mykiss) distribution and help prioritize barrier removals in the Willamette basin, OR, U.S.A. Canadian Journal of Fisheries and Aquatic Sciences 61:999–1011.

Steel, E. A., and M. B. Sheer. 2002. Appendix I: Broad-Scale Habitat Analyses to Estimate Fish Densities for Viability Criteria. In Willamette/Lower Columbia Technical Recovery Team, Interim Report on Viability Criteria for Willamette and Lower Columbia Basin Pacific Salmonids. Available through the Northwest Fisheries Science Center, 2725 Montlake Blvd. East, Seattle, Washington 98112.

Stein, B. A., L. S. Kutner, and J. S. Adams. 2000. Precious heritage: the status of biodiversity in the United States. Oxford University Press, New York.

Stevens, D. L., Jr. 1997. Variable density grid-based sampling designs for continuous spatial populations. Environmetrics 8:167–195.

Stevens, D. L., Jr. 2001. Edge effects. Pages 624–629 in A. El-Shaarawi and W. Piegorsch, editors. Encyclopedia of Environmetrics, Vol 2, Wiley, New York.

Stevens, D. L., Jr. 2002. Sampling Design and Statistical Analysis Methods for the Integrated Biological and Physical Monitoring of Oregon Streams, Oregon Department of Fish and Wildlife Report Number OPSW-ODFW-2002–07.

Stevens, Jr., D. L., and A. R. Olsen. 1999. Spatially restricted surveys over time for aquatic resources. Journal of Agricultural, Biological, and Environmental Statistics 4:415–428.

Stevens, D. L., Jr., and A. R. Olsen 2003. Variance estimation for spatially balanced samples of environmental resources. Environmetrics 14:593–610.

Stevens, Jr., D. L., and A. R. Olsen. 2004. Spatially balanced sampling of natural resources. Journal of the American Statistical Association 99:262–278.

Stevens, Jr., D. L., and N. S. Urquhart. 2000. Response designs and support regions in sampling continuous domains. Environmetrics 11:13–41.

Stoddard, J. L., D. V. Peck, S. G. Paulsen, J. Van Sickle, C. P. Hawkins, A. T. Herlihy, R. M. Hughes, P. R. Kaufmann, D. P. Larsen, G. Lomnicky, A. R. Olsen, S. A. Peterson, P. L. Ringold, and T. R. Whittier. 2005. An ecological assessment of western streams and rivers. U.S. Environmental Protection Agency, Report EPA 620/R-05/005, Washington, D.C.

Thompson, S. K. 1992. Sampling. Wiley, New York.

Thornton, P. E., S. W. Running, and M. A. White. 1997. Generating surfaces of daily meteorological variables over large regions of complex terrain. Journal of Hydrology 190:214–251. See also www.daymet.org (March 2007).

Torgersen, C. E., C. V. Baxter, H. W. Li, and B. A. McIntosh. 2006. Landscape influences on longitudinal patterns of river fishes: spatially continuous analysis of fish-habitat relationships. Pages 473–492 in R. M. Hughes, L. Wang, and P. W. Seelbach, editors. Landscape influences on stream habitats and biological assemblages, Symposium 48. American Fisheries Society, Bethesda, Maryland.

Torgersen, C. E., and D. A. Close. 2004. Influence of habitat heterogeneity on the distribution of larval Pacific lamprey (*Lampetra tridentata*) at two spatial scales. Freshwater Biology 49:614–630.

Torgersen, C. E., R. N. Faux, B. A. McIntosh, N. J. Poage, and D. J. Norton. 2001. Airborne thermal remote sensing for water temperature assessment in rivers and streams. Remote Sensing of Environment 76:386–398.

Torgersen, C. E., R. E. Gresswell, and D. S. Bateman. 2004. Pattern detection in stream networks: quantifying spatial variability in fish distribution. Pages 405–420 in T. Nishida, P. J. Kailola, and C. E. Hollingworth, editors. GIS/spatial analyses in fishery

and aquatic sciences, Volume 2. Fishery-Aquatic GIS Research Group, Saitama, Japan.

Torgersen, C. E., D. M. Price, H. W. Li, and B. A. McIntosh. 1999. Multiscale thermal refugia and stream habitat associations of Chinook salmon in northeastern Oregon. Ecological Applications 9:301–319.

Underwood, J. and R. E. Crystal, 2002. Hydrologically enhanced, high-resolution DEMs. Geospatial Solutions 1:8–14. April 1, 2002: 8–14. Available: http://www.geospatial-online.com (April 2007).

USDA and USDI. 1994. Record of decision for amendments to Forest Service and Bureau of Land Management planning documents within the range of the northern spotted owl. [Place of publication unknown]. U.S. Government Printing Office 1994-589-111/00001 Region 10.

USDA Forest Service. 2003. Landscape dynamics and forest management. U.S. Forest Service General Technical Report RMRS-GTR-101CD, Fort Collins, Colorado.

USGS. 1998. National Mapping Program Technical Instructions: Standards for Digital Elevation Models. U.S. Geological Survey, National Mapping Division. Available: http://rockyweb.cr.usgs.gov/public/nmpstds/demstds.html. (March 2007).

U.S. House of Representatives. 1984. Environmental Monitoring and Improvement Act: Hearings Before the Subcommittee on Natural Resources, Agricultural, Research, and the Environment of the Committee on Science and Technology, March 28, 1984. U.S. Govt. Printing Office, Washington, DC.

Van Horne, B. 1983. Density as a misleading indicator of habitat quality. Journal of Wildlife Management 47:893–901.

Van Sickle, J., J. Baker, A. Herlihy, P. Bayley, S. Gregory, P. Haggerty, L. Ashkenas, and J. Li. 2004. Projecting the biological conditions of streams under alternative scenarios of human land use. Ecological Applications 14:368–380.

Van Sickle, J., C. P. Hawkins, D. P. Larsen, and A. T. Herlihy. 2005. A null model for the expected macroinvertebrate assemblage in streams. Journal of the North American Benthological Society 24:178–191.

Wickham, J. D., S. V. Stehman, J. H. Smith, and L. Yang. 2004. Thematic accuracy of the 1992 National Land-Cover Data for the western United States. Remote Sensing of Environment 91:452–468.

Wigington, P. J., J. L. Ebersole, M. E. Colvin, B. Miller, B. Hansen, H. Lavigne, D. White, J. P. Baker, M. R. Church, S. G. Leibowitz, J. R. Brooks, M. A. Cairns, and J. E. Compton. 2006. Coho salmon dependence on intermittent streams. Frontiers in Ecology and the Environment 4:514–519.

Wimberly, M. C. 2002. Spatial simulation of historical landscape patterns in coastal forests of the Pacific Northwest. Canadian Journal of Forest Resources 32:1316–1328.

Wing, M. G., and A. Skaugset. 2002. Relationships of channel characteristics, land ownership, and land use patterns to large woody debris in western Oregon streams. Canadian Journal of Fisheries and Aquatic Sciences 59:796–807.

Wofford, J. E. B., R. E. Gresswell, and M. A. Banks. 2005. Factors influencing within-watershed genetic variation of coastal cutthroat trout. Ecological Applications 15:628–637.

Wozencraft, J., and D. Millar. 2005. Airborne lidar and integrated technologies for coastal mapping and nautical charting. Marine Technology Society Journal 39:27–35.

Zadeh, L. A., G. J. Klir, and B. Yuan. 1996. Fuzzy sets, fuzzy logic, and fuzzy systems: selected papers by Lotfi A. Zadeh. Advances in fuzzy systems, volume 6. World Scientific, New Jersey.

Governance

American Fisheries Society Symposium 70:903–919, 2009

The Skeena Watershed Partnership:
Learning from Success and Failure in Salmon Management

EVELYN PINKERTON[*]

School of Resource and Environmental Management, Simon Fraser University
Burnaby, British Columbia V5A 1S6, Canada

Abstract.—Watersheds in the Pacific Northwest have been the site of conflicts over access to salmon by commercial, aboriginal, and recreational groups, as well as conflicts among salmon users and other users over how to protect or restore salmon habitat, maintain a sustainable harvest rate, and define research priorities. Watershed and salmon users have sometimes chosen to form partnerships to solve common problems, making the conservation or sustainable management of salmon their central objective. Through examining a British Columbia example which illustrates principles of successful collaborative partnerships, as well as some failures to apply these principles, I consider what aspects of the Canadian experience might contain instructive precautionary lessons relevant to the Arctic-Yukon-Kuskokwim area. Five critical key conditions identified from this examination needed for successful partnerships include: (1) clarification of the role of government as a sponsor (funder) but not a convenor of the partnership, (2) a Memorandum of Understanding clearly spelling out the goals, the rights and duties devolved to partnership bodies, and government commitment not to violate them, (3) fishermen involvement in, and oversight of, all aspects of citizen science, including data collection, analysis of data, creation of fishing plans, monitoring and enforcement of adherence to the fishing plans, research, agenda setting, and (5) sufficient time for parties to develop trust in the process and other parties.

Introduction

Fisheries social scientists worldwide believe that there is much to learn from Alaska, because it offers clear-cut examples of rural fishing-dependent communities and because as a state, Alaska has broadly defined rural subsistence fishing rights and applied them to both aboriginal and non-aboriginal residents. Nonetheless, the British Columbia (BC) experience can offer some lessons of value to Alaskans about the watershed partnership aspects of fisheries management.

In the Arctic-Yukon-Kuskokwim (AYK)

region in southwestern Alaska, the specific fishing sectors and parties are not exactly the same as those in British Columbia, where the divisions of commercial, sport, and aboriginal fisheries are mostly comprised of different individuals, each with different access rights to salmon. For example, in British Columbia, aboriginal communities have unique constitutionally-protected access rights to salmon for food, social, and ceremonial purposes, and over the last two decades have increasingly asserted their rights to sell river-caught salmon commercially and to co-manage salmon with senior governments. In British Columbia, little cross-over in participation

*Corresponding author: epinkert@sfu.ca

exists between sport and commercial fishery categories. Some sport anglers primarily take salmon for subsistence purposes while enjoying no subsistence rights. While in the AYK region the same aboriginal individual may take salmon for commercial, subsistence, or even sport purposes at different times. In British Columbia, these three uses of salmon largely imply three different individuals.[1] Furthermore, in the AYK region, the aboriginal population is clearly predominant and ab-original/non-aboriginal identity is a complex and negotiated matter (Hensel 1996).

Despite these differences, many of the dynamics among commercial, sport, and subsistence uses in the two jurisdictions are strikingly similar, and take the form of upriver versus downriver conflicts.[2] Likewise, many of the options for finding common ground and forming upriver/downriver partnerships, and interacting with senior governments are similar. Therefore a comparison with caveats is in order. Below, a noteworthy British Columbia effort is examined as a cautionary tale for the lessons it has to offer the AYK region regarding both which strategies/approaches have the best chances of success and which put partnerships at risk.

---

[1]The exception to this separation is aboriginal fishermen with individual commercial licenses. Canada currently faces the dilemma that aboriginal fishing rights are collective, while commercial licenses are individual. This implies that at some point individual fishing licenses will be converted to collective rights and counted as part of the calculus of treaty settlements. This is what eventually happened in Washington State where treaty tribes' rights to 50% of the total allowable catch counted as tribal catch the number of salmon taken by tribal fishermen with state-allocated commercial licenses.

[2]Wolfe (2006) documents in Alaskan rivers an opposition which also occurs on the Skeena, although it does not figure prominently in this discussion: some aboriginal fishermen condemn catch-and-release sport fishing as immoral on the grounds that it shows disrespect towards the fish to obtain enjoyment from their suffering, while also threatening their willingness to return to the river (see Albertson 2009, this volume).

Problems in Fisheries Policy, Management, and Research in Alaska and BC

Alaska and BC salmon managers face similar generic dilemmas that could be said to reside in four general questions: (1) How can we get *enough* data/knowledge to hope to manage sustainably? (2) How can we know the data/knowledge we do get is *valid and reliable*? (3) How can we analyze and *interpret* the data accurately, taking enough factors into account? (4) How can we *implement* our analysis?

One reason that the study of co-management has gained more credibility among natural scientists in the last decade is that a growing recognition exists of the *implementation feasibility* problem. That is, even if managers could get all the data they need, and produce an analysis making a case for a particular regulatory action, would they be able to implement it? Implementation feasibility has several dimensions: (1) Is the data credible to fishermen? (2) Is the management policy or general goals made on the basis of the data credible? (3) Are the particular regulatory actions, fishing plans, and allocations based on the data credible? It has been widely documented in the social science literature that the level of compliance with regulations is affected significantly by the level of perceived accuracy of the data, as well as by the perceived legitimacy and practicality of regulations (Kearney 1983; Ostrom 1990; Pinkerton and Weinstein 1995; Jentoft 2000; Hatcher et al. 2000; Pinkerton and John 2008). Are they accurate, fair, and likely to achieve their stated goal? Data and regulations which do not meet this test are neither respected nor observed. Difficulties may occur at the level of monitoring, enforcement, or outright civil disobedience, as in the 2004 case when a public declaration was made that "Kuskokwim fishers, both commercial and subsistence, are very respectful of the law if they understand it and it makes sense to them." (report on a 2004 meeting of the Kuskokwim River Management Group in discussing the civil disobedience of Yupik villagers in the lower Kuskokwim River after the Area M False Pass fishery tripled their time on the mixed stock fishery targeting sockeye salmon *Oncorhynchus nerka* which takes Kuskokwim chum salmon *O. keta* as bycatch, while the Kuskokwim River subsistence fisheries had been reduced in their fishing time on chum salmon 2001–2004).

The most straightforward way of getting around the implementation feasibility problem is for fishermen or fishermen's organizations to play a role in data collection (as they do in the AYK region which relies heavily on reported catch in subsistence fisheries), in data analysis, such as in generating hypotheses about the cause of trends in abundance, and in harvest regulations based on the analysis. If fishermen play any role at all in creating the regulations or the harvest plan, then they have a role in creating legitimacy around the regulations, and around enforcement, reporting offenders.[3]

Peter Larkin (1988) reminded us years ago that they don't actually manage fish, but rather people! The question examined here is: how can cooperation be mobilized among users and between users and government to address the problems noted above? The co-management literature suggests that the allocative, stock abundance, and compliance challenges can be addressed far better with strong partnerships among these parties. The more power-sharing among the parties, the stronger and more resilient will be the part-

nerships (Pinkerton 1991, 1992, 1994; Berkes et al. 1991; Leach and Pelkey 2001; Leach et al. 2002; Smith and Gilden 2002; Plummer 2006; Schumann 2007). Co-management is defined as the sharing of power in management decisions between a community or place-based organization and a government agency. In the Skeena River case discussed below, it involves three place-based organizations or sectors (commercial, sport, aboriginal) and two government agencies (one federal, one provincial). A second generation of co-management studies involves multiple parties or sectors which are able to cooperate with multiple government agencies in the management of fisheries in geographic units such as watersheds (Pinkerton and Weinstein 1995; Hanna 2009, this volume).

The Skeena Watershed Committee Story 1992–1997: A Cautionary Tale[4]

The BC experience 1992–1997 with the Skeena Watershed Committee illustrates both successes and instructive mistakes in an attempt to form partnerships among fishing sectors and between these sectors and senior governments. The Canadian federal Department of Fisheries and Oceans (DFO) considers this effort "a near miss" in that a lot of things were done right. Fisheries scientists can learn as much from what went wrong as from what went right about this story, and many things went right before some mistakes were made. This story is used to draw out general lessons and principles for how cooperation can be mobilized among users and between users and government to address problems. The story involves the kind of cooperative research which is of concern in the AYK region, but the conditions for this were imbedded in a much larger effort to do co-

---

[3]A common pool resource such as fish requires managers to deal with the dilemmas of excluding some users and regulating others. It is extremely difficult to prevent non-licensed users from fishing, and it is extremely difficult to enforce fishing regulations unless there is significant cooperation from and participation among fishermen (Feeny et al. 1990).

[4]Parts of this story have been previously published as Pinkerton and Weinstein 1995 and Pinkerton 1996.

management of data collection, data analysis, harvest design, habitat protection, enhancement, and joint enforcement.

To make the general comparison more meaningful to Alaskans, the Skeena watershed and its fishing sectors in northwest BC are briefly compared to its most similar AYK counterpart, the Kuskokwim River watershed. The Skeena River is smaller than the Kuskokwim River, comprising 32,000 square kilometers, and being the home to some 54,000 residents (12,000 of which are aboriginal) living in 15 communities. In contrast, the Kuskokwim River has fewer residents (11,000) and these are spread out into a larger number (37) of smaller communities. A review of the Kuskokwim River fisheries is provided by Linderman and Bergstrom (2009, this volume). But in both cases the fishing residents live mostly on the lower 320 kilometers of river. Important commercial, aboriginal (subsistence and commercial), and sport fisheries existed on the Skeena River in 1992 when the conflict among these three fishing sectors reached a crisis point that precipitated the formation of the Skeena Watershed Committee. A brief characterization of each sector is necessary to understand the crisis.

(1) *The commercial sector* was made up of some 400 gillnet limited entry permit-holders living in Prince Rupert, a city of 17,000 at the mouth of the Skeena River, and adjacent smaller communities participating in a $100 million 100-year old commercial fishery. All four major BC fish processors had plants in Prince Rupert, and they all had fish buying contracts with, or ownership of, gillnetters to fish the salmon runs of the Skeena and Nass watersheds. Almost half of the fishermen were aboriginal in origin, either resident in their traditional territory on the coast or upriver residents who fished the coast commercially. An additional 600 non-local gillnetters fished the mouth of the Skeena River in varying numbers when

abundance levels were high. They targeted mostly sockeye salmon, (secondarily Chinook *O. tshawytscha* and coho *O. kisutch* salmon) but took steelhead *O. mykiss* as by-catch, which they were not allowed to sell commercially, and which was the preferred target of the sport fishery. They belonged chiefly to the United Fishermen and Allied Workers Union (UFAWU) and the Northern Gillnetters Association (NGA).

(2) *The sport sector* was made up mainly of residents of three communities up-river, whose most militant members were part of the Steelhead Society of BC, which considered itself a conservation organization concerned with the conservation of steelhead trout and also coho salmon stocks. Others belonged to the BC Wildlife Federation.

(3) *The aboriginal sector* was made up of members of three distinct groupings: the Tsimshian (residents in Prince Rupert at the mouth and several adjacent coastal communities), the Gitksan and Wet'suwet'en (residents of communities on the middle river), and the Nanoot'en (also called the Lake Babine Band, near the headwaters of the system). Both Tsimshian and Gitksan fishmen participated in the commercial gillnet fishery at the Skeena River mouth, but it had been the stated intention of the Gitksan since 1982 when they participated in the purchase of gillnet licenses from the fish processing company B.C. Packers, that these commercial licenses would be transferred upriver and used to target sockeye salmon in selective commercial fisheries. During the 1980s the Gitksan asserted their right to fish commercially upriver, a right disputed by DFO. Numerous net seizures and court charges were made, but no successful prosecutions of upriver commercial fishing. All aboriginal fishermen also engaged in food, social, and ceremonial fisheries using set gillnets, and were part of the aboriginal organization called the

Skeena Fisheries Commission (Gottesfeld et al. 2009, this volume).

All of these commercial, sport, and aboriginal fishing groups were resident on the Skeena River, and resemble the major sectors on the Kuskokwim River in the following ways: the subsistence and commercial in-river fishery on the Kuskokwim River is roughly equivalent to the aboriginal sector on the Skeena River which prosecutes both a commercial and a food fishery in-river (Linderman and Bergstrom 2009). The Kuskokwim River situation also contains a key dynamic which parallels the Skeena River in that commercial fisheries prosecuted downstream could severely curtail what was available upriver to sport fisheries.[5] The upriver aboriginal commercial fishery on the Skeena River was unique in that the fishery targeted enhanced (stocked) Babine Lake sockeye salmon that were surplus to spawning escapement (called ESSR: escapement surplus to spawning requirements) and could not be taken in commercial fisheries at the mouth anyway.[6] The commercial versus sport fishery on the Skeena River became the focus of the downriver versus upriver conflict as can be expected in such situations.

---

[5]There were 839 commercial permits on the Kuskokwim, only 19 of which were on the middle or upper river: 694 *in* W-1, 90 *in* Kuskokwim Bay, as of 1999. The commercial/subsistence harvest ratio went from 40/60% before formation of KRSMG to 23/77% after this group formed (Ebbin 2002).

[6]The Pinkut and Fulton sockeye salmon stocks had been significantly increased after DFO completed the artificial spawning channels on these tributaries to Babine Lake at the top of the Skeena River mainstem in 1971. These stocks could tolerate a harvest rate of 80%, but could not be taken in mixed stock fisheries at the Skeena mouth because other co-migrating stocks would have been overfished in the process. Throughout the 1980s, the Gitksan proposed a selective upriver fishery targeting the Excess Salmon to Spawning Requirements (ESSR), sockeye salmon which would otherwise be killed at the Babine fence so that they would not overpopulate the spawning areas.

The senior governmental regulatory agencies on the Skeena River were also roughly similar to the Kuskokwim River situation. The federal DFO managed the five salmon species that were taken commercially, while the provincial Ministry of Environment managed the sixth species supported by the Skeena River, steelhead trout, which cannot be sold commercially, and was targeted by sport fishermen. The principal management agency for the Kuskokwim River is the Alaska Department of Fish and Game (Linderman and Bergstrom 2009)

The conservation and allocation dilemmas on the Skeena River in 1992 can be summarized as follows. (1) *Poor data* existed for 16 steelhead stocks, but there were signs of sharp *decline* in eight of the 16 stocks. This engendered militancy in the sport sector to protect the "last great steelhead trout run." (2) A *decline* in coho escapements from 80,000 to 20,000 fish occurred over 20 years. (3) *Poor data* were available on migration timing, location, and abundance of many smaller stocks of all species. (4) A *commercial bycatch* of steelhead and other small stocks occurred in the mixed stock sockeye salmon-targeting fisheries at the river mouth. (5) A fear existed in the commercial sector that any steelhead they conserved by sacrificing sockeye salmon opportunity would simply be harvested in sport fisheries upriver, a fishery they felt was poorly monitored. These dilemmas reached a crisis point in 1992, forcing the three sectors and two governments to take action.

Stage 1. Selective Fishing Strategies: 1992–1993.

Alarmed by three successive years of decline in the monitored steelhead stocks, the Steelhead Society of BC launched an international campaign and brought intense pressure on DFO to reduce the harvest rate on steelhead (bycatch) in the commercial fishery targeting sockeye salmon. This pressure drove the formation of the Skeena Watershed Committee in 1992 through its combination with another new policy of government, the Aboriginal Fisheries Strategy. This latter policy emerged from 1991 constitutional accords and involved a pilot sales program to move toward limited collective rights to a commercial in-river catch in the traditional territories of aboriginal groups. This new program enabled the Gitksan (one of the upriver aboriginal groups) to finally implement their ESSR fishery (see footnote 6), using selective gear: beach seines which enabled the release of all steelhead trout and coho salmon. The sport sector upriver had already implemented a catch-and-release fishery on steelhead trout and coho salmon. Finally DFO, using threats of total closures, attempted to push the commercial gillnet fishery at the river mouth into using selective gear such as weedlines (which lower gillnets several feet below the water's surface) to avoid catching surface-swimming steelhead. (This also entailed sacrificing a portion of the sockeye salmon).

Most important of all, the Skeena Watershed Committee (SWC) was founded on a Memorandum of Understanding among all parties, signed in 1992, affirming that the parties would "strive to devise solutions to conservation problems which minimize any disruptions to longstanding fisheries," and that "made-in-the-north" solutions would focus on local, specific, and flexible problem solving. The implied equality and good will among all parties through this agreement set the SWC on a strong course toward perceived legitimacy. Furthermore, DFO provided funding ($2 million a year to the SWC and $1 million a year to the aboriginal sector for four years from the federal Green Plan) to conduct research to get better data, analysis of stock abundance, and run timing.

This first stage of problem-solving made only minimal progress toward the goal set by DFO and agreed to by the SWC (reduc-

ing the harvest rate on steelhead trout by 50% in three years). The commercial experiments with selective strategies were too limited in scope, and commercial fishermen felt that they were being asked to make all the sacrifices but getting nothing from other parties in return. A breakthrough did not happen until 1994, when a new set of conditions was created.

Stage 2. New Conditions Creating Success: 1994.

Breakthroughs occurred in the 1994 SWC process when new conditions came into effect involving how decisions were made and the proper role of government. New conditions existed that made the SWC qualify as a multi-party co-management arrangement and as a result authentic power-sharing occurred for the first time.

A number of these conditions involved the creation of a principled decision-making process that was perceived as transparent and fair, and therefore legitimate. Several elements were involved in this new process: (1) *Principled facilitation* of meetings was conducted by a highly experienced professional mediator, who controlled the decision-making process according to the rules of dispute resolution which were agreed to by all parties, including the two governments. (2) The five parties (three fishing sectors, two senior governments) agreed to operate as *five equal partners*. (3) The five parties agreed to operate by *consensus* decision-making. (4) A *MOU* among the five partners spelled out how they would plan jointly, analyze data together, and spend enough time on education and data sharing to reach consensus. (5) The MOU *delegated power* to the SWC, promising that if the five partners agreed on a decision, the federal and provincial ministers would not overrule it. Of these five elements, the last was particularly key in assuring respect for both senior governments and fishing sectors. The federal and provincial ministers did not give up any authority, yet the partners were all genuinely empowered.

Two additional conditions were key in that they involved a clearer definition of the role and power of government in the process: (6) the facilitator took over the convening and chairing role from DFO, which had previously both sponsored (paid for) and convened meetings. When DFO had served as chair during Stage 1, it had been clear that the SWC had only advisory power, and could be easily controlled by DFO. If participants perceive that they have no real power and believe that they are merely being used as tools to impose government's agenda, they are unlikely to work very hard to contribute solutions. A *process convened from outside of government* is required for parties to work toward solutions with much conviction and energy.[7] DFO still sponsored, and paid for, the operations of the SWC. Of course, DFO still exercised considerable power in that it had set the fundamental requirement in place that (7) a clear goal be achieved in a set time. *Parties agreed to the goal* and recommitted themselves to work to achieve this goal (50% reduction in steelhead trout harvest rate in three years) in the most practical and flexible way possible. DFO reserved the right to impose draconian closures if the goal was not reached.

Both the sixth and seventh conditions involved a clearer definition of government's proper role in such multi-party co-management agreements, and the nature of the con-

tract it was making with the fishing parties. Understanding in this area could have been made even clearer and the contract more explicit[8] for it was in this area, specifically the proper role of government, that the understanding of the fishing sectors about the nature of the contract was chiefly violated later on. This violation was because the contract created *de facto co-management rights* in which the rules of the game were fundamentally changed. The SWC partners now had rights to jointly conduct (1) stock assessment, (2) production of a fishing plan, (3) monitoring of fishing (sport, commercial, aboriginal), (4) enforcement, (5) coordination of the fishing of different sectors, (6) stock enhancement, (7) habitat restoration, (8) research, and (9) problem definition and objective setting. This constituted a fairly "complete" form of co-management (Pinkerton 2003) in that it involved rights to participate meaningfully in decisions at the policy and planning as well as operational level.

One of the most important co-management rights was *cooperative research*: commercial, sport, or aboriginal fishermen could serve on a technical sub-committee which discussed research priorities, set research agendas, included local knowledge in research questions asked by 30 research projects, allocated research funds to different programs, received reports on research findings and generally played a highly valued policy role in setting the research agenda.

In Stage 1, minimal connection occurred between research and fishing sector participants in the SWC. The inclusion of fishermen in collecting and analyzing data/knowledge, as well as in designing fishing plans which implement the data, is the most direct way to overcome the implementation feasibility problem discussed earlier. Not surprisingly, when the SWC later failed, fishermen ex-

---

[7]In 1987 Labour Canada funded two of its former employees to set up an independent Public Policy Forum in Ottawa to bring government and the private sector together to identify and deal with contentious issues. Since then the Forum has assisted in setting up sectoral councils that take on issues in a more objective fashion than government or any sector can alone. Government usually contributes at least part of the funding to initiate the process, but the successful processes become mostly self-funding in a short time (Public Policy Forum 1993).

[8]I am indebted to Susan Herman for the insight that a more explicit contract could have helped

pressed some of the greatest regret about losing their role in the research process, a role which made them feel like real participants in management more than any other role. Although funding for research had been made available in Stage 1, fishermen had not felt at that point that they had any real role in the research because they were not authentic partners. But, like government partners in the SWC, they really wanted to understand as much as possible about the dynamics of salmon stock abundance, so they leapt eagerly into the research partner role in Stage 2. Likewise, they valued the honesty of the scientists' acknowledgment of areas of uncertainty; they admired the competence of the scientists; and they were able to contribute their own ideas and hypotheses about what might be occurring and what kinds of research would best address what fishermen wanted to know and would contribute to effective regulation.

The 1994 Fishing Plan

The most immediate and publicly crucial role played by the SWC in the 1994 season under the new conditions was the creation of a fishing plan which would meet the objective of reducing the harvest rate on steelhead trout while causing the least disruption to existing fisheries. In this they achieved an impressive success, produced a fishing plan with more commercial opportunity than government's default plan, while significantly reducing the steelhead harvest rate.

This success was achieved through the following activities. (1) *The mediator caucused with each sector*, producing a document *identifying common ground* among the parties. (2) The common ground document was ratified by the SWC and used as a framework for altering the default DFO time and area closures to protect steelhead and coho salmon. (3) Scientists in the two senior governments developed a stock, effort, and area

computer model to generate options. (4) The commercial sector played with the model and proposed *alternative options*: commercial openings before and after the main steelhead and early coho salmon run had passed, which gave more fishing time, and a higher harvest rate on other species than DFO's default plan. (5) All parties understand that further research would enable a *more flexible and fine-tuned plan*. In other words, the 1994 fishing plan was seen as a good demonstration of the kind of cooperative problem-solving that was possible under the new conditions. The sport sector decided that it was a good enough start and that further progress could be expected in subsequent years.[9]

The 1994 Monitoring and Enforcement Plan.

Almost as important and public as the fishing plan in 1994 was the plan for monitoring and enforcing it. Each fishing sector wanted to be assured that the other sectors were keeping their part of the bargain, which was larger than the fishing plan. There were at least three components of monitoring and enforcement.

One key component addressed the assurance desired by non-aboriginal fishermen that the new aboriginal pilot sales program was not going to involve illegal sales of food fish, and that the agreements between DFO and aboriginal groups involved a fixed amount of sockeye salmon that really were surplus to spawning escapement. The SWC was allowed to review the aboriginal harvest agreements with DFO, as well as the enforcement plans. A discussion occurred about sharing helicopter time between DFO and aboriginal groups to monitor all three fisheries, sport,

---

[9]During 1994, the historical estimated average 36% harvest rate on steelhead was reduced to 21–22%. This was considered a tremendous achievement, even though 18% was the target.

commercial, and aboriginal. In addition, aboriginal groups were willing to coordinate their harvest, including their food fishery, with other fisheries so that a pulsed timing of fishing could be effective in getting stocks of concern to their spawning grounds. A discussion also occurred about a strategy for how enforcement of habitat protection can be coordinated watershed-wide.

The Joint Vision of Overlapping Interests.

What mattered most about the joint enforcement activities, as well as the joint fishing plan, was that the parties were implementing a *joint vision* of their mutual gains through the serving of *overlapping interests* in abundant stocks, healthy habitat, well-monitored fisheries, and effective enforcement. At this stage, the joint vision included discussion of an enhancement strategy to rehabilitate weak stocks. In the 1994 season, the commercial sector was willing to "give to get": it could see the larger benefits forthcoming from cooperation, and saw that it also gained the power to influence management by cooperating in the process. Their willingness to cooperate illustrates a phenomenon that has become well understood in co-management. Even if the outcome is exactly the same (e.g., having harvest opportunities cut), an individual's perception of the outcome is entirely different if he participates in, understands the rationale for, and agrees with the outcome (Jentoft 2005). Having power to make these decisions with full information matters, and contributes to an individual's sense of self-efficacy, or ability to make a difference (Bandura 1982).

Another more positive outcome that emerged from aboriginal groups at different locations in the watershed was the benefits of inter-aboriginal cooperation. They were able to agree on an innovative form of risk sharing and benefit sharing. They agreed to discuss where in the watershed to best harvest each groups' share for maximum opportunity or market value, and to contract with one another to balance market and conservation objectives. That is, sometimes groups fishing at the mouth would not have opportunity because of conservation concerns, but could share the surplus sockeye salmon if taken at the top of the system when conservation concerns were few. At other times, a selective fishery at the mouth might deliver a higher quality sockeye salmon which might be the only product acceptable to the market in that year. This discussion eventually evolved into a broader proposal in 1996 that the profits from the sockeye salmon surplus to spawning escapement taken at the entry to Babine Lake in the ESSR fishery would be divided among the Skeena Watershed Committee, the Babine Lake aboriginal groups, and the Skeena Fisheries Commission (the organization of aboriginal fishing groups on the Skeena River; Gottesfeld et al. 2009). Some of the funds would be spent on coho salmon "soft" enhancement (egg boxes in streams to increase egg to fry survival).

Stage 3. What Went Wrong: 1995–1997.

In the 1995 season a number of occurrences started to erode the effectiveness of the partnership. Some of them related to how government understood its role in the SWC, while others related to how the fishing sectors understood and responded to innovations in the fishing plan which did not work as much in their favor in the 1995 season as they had in 1994.

In 1994 the steelhead run had been stronger than usual and the sockeye salmon run had been unusually weak, creating the best conditions for an innovative fishing plan. DFO had begun using a harvest rate model for calculating the Total Allowable Catch, instead of the traditional fixed escapement model. Traditionally, a weak sockeye salmon run would have meant a very small fishery, with most of the run dedicated to escapement. However, the new harvest rate model called for fishing a *fixed percentage* of the run, no matter how small or large it was. This meant that in 1994 the commercial fishery had more fishing opportunity on sockeye salmon, applying the new model, than it would have had under the old fixed escapement system of calculating the allowable catch (which allowed fishing to occur only after the escapement needs of a variety of stocks had been met). The commercial sector's awareness of this undoubtedly was one element in its support of the 1994 fishing plan. The commercial sector had also preferred the harvest rate model because it permitted a more aggressive fishery on early stocks, as well as stability during uncertainty, and because at 42%, the harvest rate in the model was slightly higher than the average historical harvest rate of 40%.

In 1995, an unusually strong sockeye salmon run co-occurred with a weak steelhead run and yielded a nightmare scenario for conservation. The commercial sector was accustomed to paying off debts in the best year out of four or even out of ten. It was the "bonanza" run years which made their fishery possible. But the new harvest rate model only allowed them to fish a fixed percentage of the bonanza run, whether more salmon were needed for escapement or not. To make matters worse, in 1995 the harvest rate model underestimated the sockeye salmon run size, while the in-river test fishery historically had overestimated it. Naturally the commercial fishermen were inclined to believe a familiar method of measuring the run size. The new harvest rate model and the manner in which it estimated run size had not been explained sufficiently to the fleet by DFO, and it was in fact still being refined.

The members of the SWC who did understand the basics of the harvest rate model might have attempted to explain it to the fleet at large, had it not been for a second government action that went awry. Some of the Green Plan federal funding promised to the SWC was unilaterally reallocated to other purposes by senior DFO officials. Of course, this decision was not made by participants in the SWC, but the action was still perceived as a betrayal by DFO. Fishing sectors had seen the funding as providing one of the conditions under which they had agreed to participate. To make matters worse, the province did not deliver the funding it had promised for steelhead trout research.

In this situation of widespread confusion, distrust, and accusations of betrayal, nobody attempted to defend or explain the harvest rate model to the fleet at large. Accustomed to the fixed escapement model which let them fish more days if the sockeye salmon run size was large and fixed escapement goals were met, the commercial sector responded with outrage when the SWC fishing plan for the number of fishing days was not increased in the presence of a very large sockeye salmon run in 1995. Their protest was of course largely fuelled by the 600 non-local gillnetters who fished the Skeena River in large run years, which knew little of, and possibly cared little for, "made-in-the-north solutions." One coastwide fishermen's organization was inevitably drawn into a historic oppositional position, rather than one based on the new watershed-based model, whose support of, or possible rivalry with, their organization was not clear at this early developmental stage.

The sport sector responded with equal outrage at the commercial protest, especially since early steelhead and coho salmon abundance was quite low in 1995. Although the SWC fishing plan survived the protest, and was not varied, the sport sector had expected more progress, and decided in the next year that it was time to increase protective measures. In 1996 a second and even greater bonanza sockeye salmon year caused the commercial sector to be even more unhappy with their fixed harvest rate fishing opportunity, especially in the context of a forecast overescapement of two million sockeye salmon which could cause disease and pre-spawning mortality leading to poor survival of the next generation. The Skeena Watershed Committee partnered with the Skeena Fisheries Commission and the Babine First Nations to conduct an upriver commercial fishery at the entry to Babine Lake. The commercial sector feared this development could presage a massive reallocation of fishing rights to upstream groups, and the largest processors claimed that sockeye salmon taken at this location would be of poor quality and unmarketable. Equally dissatisfying to the commercial sector was the failure of enhancement funding to materialize, what they believed to be poor catch reporting in the sport fishery, and research results which they believed showed steelhead and coho salmon to be less endangered than claimed. Their attempts to obtain more fishing opportunity and to change the original objective of 50% reduction in steelhead harvest rate were not successful. By October 1996 the commercial sector, which had been participating with less and less enthusiasm, had provisionally withdrawn from the SWC and by December outlined to DFO their requirements for rejoining. Obviously they still thought the process was valuable, but were bargaining for fairer treatment.

In early 1997 the sport fishery sector, especially through the provincial Ministry of Environment representative posted on the Skeena River, unilaterally pressured DFO to extend the SWC plan to the next watershed north (the Nass River), a separate fishing area that was managed chiefly as a seine (large vessel) rather than a gillnet (small vessel) fishery. The sport sector and DFO and provincial scientists who made this decision saw this as a way of reducing interception of steelhead by the seine fleet, and did not understand the political implications of this move. For example, the gillnet fleet which fished the mouth of the Skeena River had a large component of owner-operated vessels which could make independent decisions. In contrast, the seine fleet that fished the Nass was largely owned or controlled through indebtedness by major processors, and their decisions were dictated by the same. As soon as the major processors heard of the DFO plan to extend the SWC process to the Nass River, they took swift and effective action to stop it. In a matter of days, a meeting of the North Coast Advisory Board (representing all commercial fishing and fish processing interests in the north) was called, and a processor representative asked for and got the withdrawal of the commercial sector from the SWC. Commercial sector members of the SWC complied with mixed feeling, withdrawing from the SWC in early 1997, since they were already unhappy and distrustful of government unilateral actions, they perceived this latest action as yet another. Privately, several of them apologized to the DFO members of the SWC. After last minute attempts by DFO and the SWC to revise the new fishing plan to keep the commercial sector involved, the commercial sector announced that its withdrawal from the SWC in March 1997 effectively ended the SWC, according to the terms of the original 1992 MOU. In a March 1997 press release, a nonprocessor member of the commercial sector summarized the dominant feeling as "We were not at the table as a full partner" (Prince Rupert Daily News, March 17, 1997).

Although consideration of events after 1997 is beyond the scope of this paper, it is likely that the commercial sector is far worse off today because of their withdrawal from the SWC, and because they could be more powerful inside the committee than outside it. They exemplify the tragedy of the expectation that older forms of power will continue unchanged after new conditions have been created by new rights (aboriginal), new conservation concerns (bycatch and weak stocks in mixed stock fisheries), and competing lobbies which become more organized and powerful (sport sector). Arguably, fisheries planning on the Skeena River is also less effective without the active cooperation and participation of the commercial sector.

The Key Aspects of Failure

With the benefit of hindsight, it is possible to distinguish key aspects of what went wrong. These consist partly in confusion over what role government was playing inside the process versus what role government could play outside the process without violating trust, i.e., which hat the government could wear appropriately at which times. A more explicit elaboration of the nature of the bargain, the contract, and the mutual obligations of the partners was needed to clarify what each considered essential to maintaining trust and honoring all aspects of the contract. This specification could have been done through a more detailed MOU spelling out expectations, which would have enabled the facilitator to cry foul if it were violated.

A second key aspect of failure was the weakness of "citizen science" (Westley 2002), i.e., a lack of understanding by government of the importance of explaining the new model to fishermen at large. The fishermen believed that as partners they had or could have a reasonable understanding of the management model. An investment in the removal of confusion about the science could have made a large difference.

A third aspect of failure was the lack of understanding of the fragility of the trust and communication, and the need for sufficient time to develop it more fully. Commercial fishermen stated that they gave up on the SWC when they got the impression that sport anglers really wanted to eliminate them entirely. There is a need to be keenly aware of the fact that institutional arrangements such as rules and committee structures merely enable the formation of co-management, but are not the essence of it. The essence lies rather in the human relationships and attitudes that are formed, namely the willingness to work together (see Brelsford 2009, this volume), the belief that together people can learn how to solve problems more effectively than they can apart, and that they each have a valuable contribution to make to the solution. Clearly trust is not built quickly in situations characterized in the past by extreme conflict. Both policy analysts (Leach and Pelkey 2001; Leach et al. 2002) and anthropologists (Smith and Gilden 2002) give "trust" a high priority in the list of conditions or assets required to make watershed partnerships work. (Other conditions identified are funding, education, leadership, clear problem definition, and vision, conditions consistent with the findings of this paper). Theorists in organizational behavior and organizational learning (Argyris and Schon 1978; Gray 1991; Kofinas and Griggs 1996) identify additional conditions which facilitate the building of trust: (1) undertaking joint tasks such as information searches and assigning tasks to subgroups, (2) articulating the values that guide each party's interest in the process, (3) inventorying all technical, financial, and human resources accessible to the collaborators (such that it is recognized all parties have something to offer toward solutions), (4) deciding how to implement and monitor the agreement, and (5) creating a local constituency to support implementation. The last four conditions serve to emphasize the fact that trust building takes considerable time.

Relevance to Problems Identified in the AYK Region

All three key aspects of failure discussed in the preceding section apply to the Kuskokwim River fisheries, or more broadly to the AYK region: the role of government, citizen science, and the slow building of trust. These issues are intertwined in a complex way on the Kuskokwim River because the watershed parties have identified interception and bycatch issues in the False Pass fishery as a concern, implying that they expect government to deal transparently with them about the data and analysis of a fishery outside of their watershed which they believe affects them. The Skeena River story suggests to managers of the Kuskokwim River that an investment by government in sharing and explaining what is known and not known about the impact of this fishery on AYK watersheds would pay off in increased respect for government, and in greater willingness to contribute to monitoring and enforcement in AYK watersheds. If clear data exists demonstrating a significant impact by interception fisheries, addressing this issue by involving the interceptors in some joint decision-making process could be beneficial. If a significant part of the stock abundance of the interceptors' fishery depends on the effective management of watersheds, they have something to lose by not cooperating with those who protect habitat and conduct stock management. If they do not depend significantly on AYK stocks, government can still require them to participate in a joint process as a condition of continuing their fishery. Perhaps they can be offered something for their sacrifice in giving up fishing opportunity to reduce bycatch, such as increased opportunity in abundant years. As the Skeena River situation demonstrated, in an upriver versus downriver or interception versus terminal fishery, asymmetrical costs and benefits exist (Ebbin 2002). It is important to acknowledge that some parties are asked to give more than they get in the short term (as occurred for the commercial sector on the Skeena River), and to seek ways to balance the sacrifices of these parties so that they remain cooperative contributors and identify with the public good and long-term outcomes. Government can act as a leader to get sectors beyond the negotiation of individual interests to reflect broader interests in the health of stocks, ecosystems, and communities.

If such an effort were made, it would be important to spell out the expectations which make explicit the role of government through an MOU which delegates power and responsibilities to fishing sectors, and clarifies the consequences of not abiding by the MOU. If the MOU identifies consensus as the decision mechanism, it is important to be clear that lobbying of government by any one sector will be seen as a violation of the MOU.

Furthermore, sectors outside the watershed are unlikely to see cooperation with watershed partnerships as advantageous unless these partnerships have already worked out a high level of cooperation themselves in data sharing, data analysis, agreement of fishing regulations, monitoring of compliance with regulations, and enforcement of compliance. Key to this is that citizen science within the watershed be at a high level, as demonstrated by (1) a high level of trust in the data/knowledge, (2) fishermen involvement in collecting and analyzing data, (3) fishermen involvement in designing fishing plans based on this data, and (4) fishermen involvement in monitoring and enforcement of all uses. The SWC story shows us the need for social learning, the building of human relationships, and visionary leadership that focuses on the long term. That leadership may have to come from government.

Conclusions: What Have We Learned?

In the beginning of this discussion, four persistent problems in salmon management at the watershed level were considered: (1) How can we get *enough* data/knowledge? (2) How can we know the data we do get is *valid and reliable*? (3) How can we analyze and interpret the data accurately, taking enough factors into account? (4) How can we implement our analysis in an effective fishing plan and other planning for habitat, enforcement, and other functions?

In the SWC case study presented, I considered how these four problems can be addressed through partnerships among fishing sectors and between these sectors and senior levels of government. The SWC experience allowed us to identify the following conditions as facilitators of successful watershed partnerships.

The first four conditions involve the role of government and the first three are primary:

(1) Government can threaten to impose draconian regulations to achieve conservation goals if sectors cannot agree on more flexible regulations to achieve the desired goal. Many cooperative agreements have arisen in the shadow of the threat of less desirable and flexible regulations.

(2) Government can distinguish its role outside the process as a general policy maker (as in setting general conservation goals) from its role inside the process as a partner and stakeholder which does not make unilateral decisions. This role is clearly spelled out in an MOU.

(3) Government can share real power with fishing sectors when they can agree on a harvest plan, through an MOU spelling out the powers and responsibilities of each sec-

tor, and formal rules for making decisions and conducting themselves.

(4) Government can produce funding to allow research to fill key data gaps which will clarify differences of opinion among sectors in the longer term.

The next four conditions involve how an effective decision-making process is conceptualized and executed:

(5) The problem and a goal in addressing it are clearly defined.

(6) Common overlapping interests in the long-term productivity of the watershed can be incorporated into agreements among sectoral interests in such a way that their differing interests can be temporarily set aside.

(7) Asymmetrical costs and benefits are identified, and it is acknowledged that some parties are asked to give more than they get. Government seeks ways to balance the sacrifices of some parties so that they remain cooperative contributors and identify with the public good and long-term outcomes.

(8) The principles of facilitated negotiation are used, even if a facilitator or mediator of appropriate stature, experience, and style cannot be used.

The last four conditions concern the involvement of fishing sectors in the production and sharing of knowledge, and the way in which this motivates them to cooperate with one another and with government:

(9) Citizen science can be practiced: government considers that it is worth the effort to explain new models and levels of uncertainty to the fleet at large, not depending on committee members to carry this difficult burden.

(10) Citizen science can be practiced: government can allow fishing sectors to experiment with selective gear and strategies.

(11) Sufficient time is allowed for enough trust to build so that each sector genuinely accepts the others' right to exist, and even believes that sector has a valuable contribution to make to knowledge about watershed health, and to actions promoting it.

(12) Self-efficacy, or the experience of being powerful enough to accomplish one's goals, is an under-rated tool in fisheries management. When fishing sectors become real partners and trust the data because they participate fully, they feel enough power to become willing to sacrifice if it is part of a negotiated trade-off with conservation justifications.

These conditions are consistent with those identified in the co-management literature about place-based groups and communities, as well as the literature in political science on watershed partnerships. They add new dimensions to both these literatures in identifying the role of MOUs, the necessity for government not to be the convenor of watershed partnerships, and the key importance of fishermen involvement in research. The discussion also addresses the longstanding concern of fisheries managers about getting enough data that is reliable and valid, and thus sufficiently legitimate to allow implementation of fishing plans informed by it. This discussion has also shown that fishermen can be respectful of data limitations and consequent uncertainty, and that including them in a consideration of the state of scientific understanding can reduce the implementation feasibility problem.

A framework for the reconstitution of the Skeena Watershed Committee is now being gradually developed under new conditions including (1) legal action against DFO by an aboriginal group upriver demanding protection of weak sockeye salmon runs from mixed stock fishing by commercial fisheries at the river mouth;[10] (2) renewed pressure from upriver sport organizations for conservation of steelhead trout and coho salmon and for implementation of the new Wild Salmon Policy and the new *Species at Risk Act*; (3) new funding from the Moore Foundation which is focused on the conservation of wild salmon of the Pacific Northwest; (4) the convergent interests of upriver aboriginal fishermen and upriver sport guides to have more fish available for use in-river; and (5) the convergent interests of upriver aboriginal and coastal processors, as well as coastal commercial fishermen, to obtain Marine Stewardship Council certification for all Skeena River caught salmon. These new conditions propel further consideration of the lessons from the past.

Acknowledgments

Many thanks to the people who took the time to explain various aspects of the AYK situation. They helped me focus this discussion on the issues most relevant to the region. These included Joe Spaeder, Taylor Brels-

---

[10]On July 26, 2007 the Gitanyow, claiming an infringement of their aboriginal rights to fish for food on the Kitwanga, launched a suit against DFO demanding that they protect a sockeye salmon run on the Kitwanga River (a tributary of the Skeena), which was alleged to have fallen to less than 10% of its historical abundance because of the mixed-stock commercial fishery at the mouth of the Skeena. At the same time, the upriver sport fishery launched a campaign about new steelhead abundance concerns based on management during the 2006 season when sockeye arrived a month late. Because of these concerns, an Independent Science Review Panel was commissioned to review Skeena Watershed management in light of the Wild Salmon Policy, and the interests of First Nations, commercial and sport fisheries (Walters et al. 2008). Although the Panel did not find evidence that commercial fisheries were overharvesting steelhead, it identified numerous other concerns and recommendations for improved management and policy.

ford, John White, Steve Langdon, Lance Howe, Stephanie Martin, Tracie Krauthoefer, Doug Molyneaux, and Jim Magdanz. Susan Herman and Gary Kofinas gave especially useful feedback on the first draft, presented at the University of Alaska, Fairbanks. The Skeena Watershed Committee participants are thanked as well. I especially thank several dedicated people in Department of Fisheries and Oceans Canada who have shared their perspective on this experience over the last five years.

References

Albertson, L. 2009. Perspectives on angling for salmon on the Kuskokwim River: the catch and release sport fishing controversy. Pages 611–619 in C. C. Krueger and C. E. Zimmerman, editors. Pacific salmon: ecology and management of western Alaska's populations. American Fisheries Society, Symposium 70, Bethesda, Maryland.

Argyris, C., and D. Schon 1978. Organizational learning: a theory of action perspective. Addison-Wesley, Reading, Massachusetts.

Bandura, A. 1982. Self-efficacy mechanism in human agency. American Psychologist 37:122–147.

Berkes, F., P. J. George, and R. J. Preston. 1991. Co-management. Alternatives 18:12–18.

Brelsford, T. 2009. "We have to learn to work together": current perspectives on incorporating local and traditional/indigenous knowledge into Alaskan fishery management. Pages 381–394 in C. C. Krueger and C. E. Zimmerman, editors. Pacific salmon: ecology and management of western Alaska's populations. American Fisheries Society, Symposium 70, Bethesda, Maryland.

Ebbin, S. 2002. What's up: the transformation of upstream-downstream relationships on Alaska's Kuskokwim River. Polar Geography 26:147–166.

Feeny, D., F. Berkes, B. McCay, and J. Acheson. 1990. The tragedy of the commons: 22 years later. Human Ecology 18:1–19.

Gottesfeld, A., C. Barnes, and C. Soto. 2009. Case history of the Skeena Fisheries Commission: developing aboriginal fishery management capacity in northern British Columbia. Pages 921–939 in C. C. Krueger and C. E. Zimmerman, editors. Pacific salmon: ecology and management of western Alaska's populations. American Fisheries Society, Symposium 70, Bethesda, Maryland.

Gray, B. 1991. Collaborating: finding common ground for multi-party problems. Jossey-Bass. San Francisco, California.

Hanna, S. 2009. Sustaining salmon fisheries: the challenge of collaborative management. Pages 1199–1215 in C. C. Krueger and C. E. Zimmerman, editors. Pacific salmon: ecology and management of western Alaska's populations. American Fisheries Society, Symposium 70, Bethesda, Maryland.

Hatcher, A., S. Jaffry, O. Thebaud, and E. Bennett. 2000. Normative and social influences affecting compliance with fishery regulations. Land Economics 76:448–461.

Hensel, C. 1996. Telling our selves: ethnicity and discourse in Southwestern Alaska. Oxford University Press, New York.

Jentoft, S. 2000. Legitimacy and disappointment in fisheries management. Marine Policy 24:141–148.

Jentoft, S. 2005. Fisheries co-management as empowerment. Marine Policy 29:1–7.

Kearney, J. 1983. Common tragedies: a study of resource access in the Bay of Fundy herring fisheries. Master's thesis. Dalhousie University, Nova Scotia.

Kofinas, G., and J. Griggs. 1996. Collaboration and the B.C. Round Table: an early-stage analysis of a "better way" of deciding. Environments 23:17–40.

Larkin, P. 1988. The future of fisheries management: managing the fisherman. Fisheries 13(1):3–9.

Leach, W. D., and N. L. Pelkey. 2001. Making watershed partnerships work: a review of the empirical literature. Journal of Water Resources Planning and Management 127(6):378–385.

Leach, W. D., N. L. Pelkey, and P. Sabatier. 2002. Stakeholder partnerships as collaborative policymaking: evaluation criteria applied to watershed management in California and Washington. Journal of Policy Analysis and Management 21:645–670.

Linderman, J. C., Jr., and D. J. Bergstrom. 2009. Kuskokwim management area: salmon escapement, harvest, and management. Pages 541–599 in C. C. Krueger and C. E. Zimmerman, editors. Pacific salmon: ecology and management of western Alaska's populations. American Fisheries Society, Symposium 70, Bethesda, Maryland.

Ostrom, E. 1990. Governing the commons. The evolution of institutions for collective action. Cambridge University Press. Cambridge, UK.

Pinkerton, E. 1991. Locally based water quality planning: contributions to fish habitat protection. Canadian Journal of Fisheries and Aquatic Sciences 48:1326–1333.

Pinkerton, E. W. 1992. Translating legal rights into management practice: overcoming barriers to the exercise of co-management. Human Organization 51:330–341.

Pinkerton, E. 1994. Local fisheries co-management: a review of international experiences and their implications for salmon management in British Columbia. Canadian Journal of Fisheries and Aquatic Sciences 51:2363–2378.

Pinkerton, E. 1996. The contribution of watershed-based multi-party co-management agreements to dispute resolution: the Skeena Watershed Committee. Environments 23:51–68.

Pinkerton, E. 2003. Toward specificity in complexity: understanding co-management from a social science perspective. Pages 61–77 in D. C. Wilson, J. R. Nielsen and P. Degnbol, editorss. The Fisheries Co-Management Experience: Accomplishments, Challenges and Prospects. Kluwer, Dordrecht, Netherlands.

Pinkerton, E., and L. John. 2008. Creating local management legitimacy. Marine Policy 32:680–691.

Pinkerton, E., and M. Weinstein. 1995. Fisheries that work: sustainability through community-based management. A report to the David Suzuki Foundation, Vancouver, B.C.

Plummer, R. 2006. Sharing the management of a river corridor. A case study of a comanagement process. Society and Natural Resources 19:709–721.

Public Policy Forum. 1993. Making government work. Public Policy Forum, Ottawa, Ontario.

Schumann, S. 2007. Co-management and "consciousness: fishers assimilation of management principles in Chile. Marine Policy 31:101–111.

Smith, C. L., and J. Gilden. 2002. Assets to move watershed councils from assessment to action. Journal of the American Water Resources Association 38:653–662.

Walters, C. J., J. A. Lichatowich, R. M. Peterman, and J. D. Reynolds. 2008. Report of the Skeena Independent Science Review Panel. A Report to the Canadian Department of Fisheries and Oceans and the British Columbia Ministry of the the Environment. Ottawa, Ontario.

Westley, F. 2002. The devil is in the dynamics. Adaptive management on the front lines. Pages 333–360 in L. H. Gunderson and C. S. Holling, editors. Panarchy. Understanding transformation in human and natural systems. Island Press, Washington D.C.

Wolfe, R. J. 2006. Playing with fish and other lessons from the North. University of Arizona Press, Tucson.

American Fisheries Society Symposium 70:921–939, 2009

Case History of the Skeena Fisheries Commission: Developing Aboriginal Fishery Management Capacity in Northern British Columbia

ALLEN GOTTESFELD[*], CHRIS BARNES, AND CRISTINA SOTO

Skeena Fisheries Commission
P. O. Box 166, Hazelton, British Columbia, Columbia V0J 1Y0, Canada

Abstract.—Pacific salmon are important to the First Nations of the Skeena River watershed in British Columbia. The Skeena Fisheries Commission (SFC) was formed in 1985 through a memorandum of understanding between the watershed's five First Nations: Tsimshian, Gitxsan, Gitanyow, Wet'suwet'en, and Lake Babine. SFC focuses on salmon management, research, and conservation through governance and technical committees. This paper describes the development of fishery management capacity of SFC within the context of the cultural importance of salmon, the history of salmon management measures, and land claims. Capacity is analyzed in terms of the ability to perform eight management functions: policy making, negotiation and resource planning; stock assessment; fishery monitoring; enforcement and compliance; research, habitat and enhancement activities; data gathering and analysis for resource planning; creating benefits for fishermen and communities; and training and education. Policy making, negotiating, and planning occur between SFC and the Canadian Department of Fisheries and Oceans (DFO) through formal and informal consultations and monthly technical meetings. SFC also participates in committees at the federal and international levels. Stock assessment activities include spawner enumerations, counting weirs, mark-recapture studies, hydroacoustic surveys, and sampling fish for genetic stock identification. Catch monitoring of the food fishery has been regularly conducted since 1991. First Nation Rangers and federal Fisheries Officers enforce traditional and federal law, respectively. Member First Nations conduct research projects with assistance from SFC staff and infrastructure. Habitat and conservation enhancement projects include road culvert assessments and hatchery rearing of Kitwanga Lake sockeye salmon *Oncorhynchus nerka*. The creation of benefits for communities occurs through two in-river fisheries. Finally, training and education include SFC-run workshops and specialized training by external sources. SFC will conduct most management functions in the future; however, funding remains a constraint to program expansion. Key elements of the success of the SFC include: the cultural imperative to protect fish, the community origin and leadership of the SFC, a favorable political environment, the early recognition of the need for a watershed-wide organization, and the availability of government funding.

---

*Corresponding author: gottesfeld@skeenafisheries.ca

Introduction: Skeena Fisheries Commission Overview

The Skeena River watershed is the second largest in British Columbia, Canada, at 54,432 km². The river mouth is located at approximately 54°N, close to Prince Rupert and just south of the Alaska panhandle (Figure 1). The Skeena River extends from the humid coast through the Coast Mountains into the relatively dry interior plateau. The river supports approximately 300 stocks of salmon of six species adapted to the varying environments of its tributary streams. Most important from a fisheries perspective are the sockeye salmon, *Oncorhynchus nerka*, mostly originating in Babine Lake, and pink salmon, *O. gorbuscha*, originating in the lower portion of the watershed.

The Skeena River drainage is an area of flourishing aboriginal culture based on salmon. The Skeena Fisheries Commission (SFC) is an aboriginal organization focused on fishery management, research, and conservation (Pinkerton 2009, this volume). It was formed through an inter-tribal memorandum of understanding in 1985 and is the only organization in British Columbia to have signed a watershed-level agreement with Canada's Department of Fisheries and Oceans (DFO). This agreement was established in 1991. The SFC signatories are the First Nations with traditional territory in the Skeena River drainage and the adjacent north coast of British Columbia. The SFC includes the Tsimshian, Gitxsan, Gitanyow, Wet'suwet'en, and Lake Babine Nations. The Commission, as directed by signatory First Nations, responds to management and fishing opportunity priorities relating to the broad aboriginal interest in the fishery resource. SFC First Nations seek economic development through fisheries that respect aboriginal rights and maintain the viability of the resource. The SFC has been committed to four principles:

• the obligation to protect, conserve, and catch fish according to traditional law;
• the maintenance of the aboriginal right to fish for food, social, ceremonial, and economic purposes;
• the recognition of the dependence on the fishery resources as a mainstay of economic, social, and cultural well-being; and
• the priority of the right to fish after conservation needs for threatened stocks are met, which supersedes non-aboriginal fishing interests.

The SFC operates through a traditional consensus model, whereby commissioners who form the Governance Committee represent their respective First Nation-level interests. Each commissioner acts as the communication vehicle between the Nation and the Commission. Commissioners direct the SFC's progress by providing governance and accountability for its resources and projects, as well as advocating the Nation's interests at a watershed level. Commissioners set priorities, review plans and reports, and communicate SFC plans and policy back to their Nations. SFC commissioners have typically been the fisheries portfolio managers in their respective Nation's administration. The Commission presents a unified approach to resource management while recognizing that each First Nation in the SFC maintains its own bilateral relationship with the governments of Canada and British Columbia.

The Skeena aboriginal culture, built on thousands of years of effective fishery management, emphasizes the need to conserve salmon. With this perspective, current management challenges of the SFC include:

• maintaining production of the large salmon stocks while increasing attention to less abundant stocks to ensure overall sustainability;
• addressing the biological impacts of resource development;

pled, but statistical analysis is not performed. The numerous food fisheries of coastal Tsimshian are not well monitored because of their diffuse nature and an unwillingness to separate food fisheries from commercial fisheries. In general, the quality of data on Native food fisheries has improved greatly since the involvement of First Nations as managers began in the early 1990s.

SFC member Nations have carried out at least six contracts with the DFO to monitor sport fisheries for salmon in upriver areas. The Provincial fisheries agency is responsible for management of sports fisheries on trout, steelhead, and various nonanadromous fish species. As of 2007, the provincial region staff in the local administrative centre, Smithers, has been unwilling to hire First Nations fishery groups to carry out creel surveys. Poor advertising and a poorly defined contracting procedure facilitates awards to a handful of consultants. The local policy is at variance with Provincial practices and is a holdover from the 1970s.

Enforcement and compliance

Within the territories, traditional law regarding who fishes and where is enforced through political institutions, primarily through the feasting system or "potlatch." SFC member Nations share common elements of law around the use and conservation of fish. These elements of traditional law include:

• an overall context of respect for the fish and its continuance into future generations;
• protection and maintenance of fish habitat;
• strict laws pertaining to the use of fish including the full use and prevention of waste of harvested fish;
• control by the hereditary chiefs of access to all fishing grounds and of all aspects of harvesting, processing, and distribution of

fish and their products (Morrell 1989); and
• high expectations that people will govern themselves according to the traditional law.

Two types of uniformed fisheries compliance officers exist on the Skeena River: (1) Rangers who work for a member Nations' fishery management organization such as the Gitxsan Watershed Authorities and (2) DFO Fisheries Officers. Both groups are primarily aboriginal. The Rangers collect monitoring information on the food and commercial fisheries. A high level of cooperation exists between fishermen and the Rangers in part because they are community members and in part because information collected in the monitoring exercise is never used for enforcement. The Fisheries Officers are local aboriginal people trained by the DFO. They have been working within the DFO system since the early 1990s and are now in or nearing senior positions. Their position within the local communities and their understanding of the requirements of traditional law as well as Canadian law makes them effective.

The practical enforcement of fishing rules occurs in two ways: fishing sites are determined by traditional law, and violations of fish sale are dealt with by the DFO Fisheries officers. By way of an example, in the demonstration fishery that took place in 2006, one fisher illegally retained coho. He was charged by the Fishery Officer and will eventually appear in court. The community of fishermen took immediate action and suspended the miscreant and his house group from further fishing in 2006 or future years pending the legal outcome of the charges. In 2006, in the Excess to Spawning Salmon Requirements (ESSR) fishery, each group fishing in the Babine River developed their own policies (administration and rules) for the season with help from the Gitxsan Watershed Authorities. Disagreements among some fishermen occurred in the Babine River and several individuals were suspended from fishing by the chiefs for not obeying the agreed upon fishing policies.

Research

Each Nation has one or two biologists who, at times, conduct research projects. SFC has a Head Scientist (one of the co-authors) who provides technical assistance and guidance to member Nations for research and other activities. SFC is located in Kispiox, and has a building that includes a laboratory and a Geographic Information Systems (GIS) facility. The Kispiox Biological Laboratory has a range of equipment including various microscopes with cameras, a fume hood, chemicals, weigh scales, a drying oven, and sediment analysis equipment. The facility has been used for scale and otolith reading, sediment analysis, biological sampling of various salmon stages and populations, and plankton analysis for recent sea lice research projects.

Many of the SFC research projects have been able to incorporate traditional ecological knowledge. The Gitxsan have developed a research laboratory on Slamgeesh Lake, a remote fly-in facility in the uppermost Skeena River drainage. It was begun in 1999, at a time when great concern existed about upper Skeena River coho salmon populations. The site was selected because it was an important Gitxsan fishing site and trapping centre, and had received little attention from government managers and biologists. It was certain that the locality was suitable for enumerating salmon since it is known as a former weir and trap site. Fisheries work has been carried out along with work on traditional sites, Gitxsanimukx names, and youth camp involvement.

The Kitwanga Lake Sockeye Restoration project is a reaction to the dismay in Gitanyow about the decline of the sockeye salmon stock that the village depended on. Efforts have been made to restore the sockeye run of the Kitwanga River, which has dropped as

low as several hundred fish some years. The habitat studies described in the next section were informed by aboriginal knowledge of the former spawning sites and population size (which numbered in the tens of thousands).

Most of the research projects that have been carried out in the past eight years have been funded after development of competitive proposals. For the most part, projects have been funded by the DFO and the provincial Ministry of Environment and Ministry of Forests. A few generally small grants have come from environmental organizations and corporate developers in the forestry and energy sectors. In the last few years, funding from the provincial and federal governments for habitat, enhancement, and stock assessment projects has sharply declined. During this period, and to some extent in compensation, the Pacific Salmon Commission Northern Fund has become the largest source for research funding. The SFC is now in a situation where it is often easier to get money for technically demanding projects than simpler labor intensive projects. This makes acquiring and retaining experienced biologists critical, but works against the general need to provide employment opportunity within the native communities.

Habitat and enhancement

In the 1990s, two major programs funded fisheries habitat and enhancement efforts in British Columbia: Habitat Restoration and Salmonid Enhancement Program (HRSEP, 1997–2002) and the Watershed Restoration Program (WRP). The former program, funded by the DFO, supported scores of small enhancement projects—mostly incubation boxes for coho and chum salmon and stream rehabilitation projects (Gottesfeld et al. 2002). Community hatcheries established at Kispiox and Fort Babine produced coho and chinook salmon for enhancement of local stream populations. Coho salmon juvenile density assessments were also popular. The WRP was developed by the Province in 1995 to restore the terrestrial and aquatic productivity of watersheds negatively impacted by logging. Most of the WRP work was conducted by provincial staff and private consultants. The work consisted of fish habitat, riparian, and upslope assessments, and road deactivation. Projects were designed to create or restore off-channel habitat, restore the riparian zone, diversify habitat, and stabilize stream channels. Skeena River projects provided employment to some band members, and projects in Gitanyow and Gitsegukla were run by consultants working from band headquarters.

The effectiveness of the many WRP projects is poorly documented. Few attempts were made to evaluate the response of fish populations to habitat manipulations anywhere in British Columbia. The SFC is currently conducting several projects to evaluate the efficacy of the WRP projects and recommend future restoration efforts.

In the past decade, most of the logging companies pulled out of the Skeena River watershed, as high quality forest stands were harvested. Logging continues in the southern edge of the Skeena River watershed where a mountain pine beetle outbreak has caused timber salvage. The legacy of logging damage to salmon habitat has not been effectively addressed because of a withdrawal of Forest Service staff from the region. Fortunately, many of the streams damaged by logging seem to be recovering on their own.

In the Skeena River watershed, a major impact of logging and development activities such as road and rail construction, is the restriction of fish access to upstream waters, often the result of poorly designed road crossings. Culvert assessments were part of the upslope activities of many WRP projects and some culverts were removed and logging roads deactivated. In the past four years, SFC members mapped and evaluated all of the

paved highway and railroad stream crossings in the Skeena River watershed. Evaluation of impacts to salmon streams is of little value if it does not lead to mitigation. The reports produced by the SFC prioritized the replacement of major structures that isolate salmon habitat. Thus far, planning has occurred and funds secured to restore the highest priority fish access blockage in the Skeena River watershed on the floodplain near Exchamsiks. Additional access restoration projects are planned for the future at one each year.

In 2005–2006, SFC technical staff participated in the Ministry of Forests expert hydrology panel to assess the logging status of all third-order watersheds in the upper Skeena River, to identify the fisheries values, and to examine proposed logging development to determine whether more logging could proceed without hydrological complications.

Overall, efforts to rehabilitate and protect habitat decreased in the past decade as a result of the termination of the WRP and HRSEP. Funding from the Pacific Salmon Commission's Northern Fund now supports some restoration and enhancement efforts. The Northern Fund is especially interested in projects that increase the production of salmon. For example, the Gitanyow Fisheries Authority was recently able to expand productive capacity by about 1,000 coho by opening an extra eight kilometers of prime coho salmon spawning and rearing habitat blocked by beaver dams.

For the past few years, the Gitanyow Nation has developed a program to restore the sockeye salmon production of the Kitwanga River. This program has included environmental monitoring of the lake, assessment of sockeye salmon spawning and rearing habitat, and in the last year, efforts to improve the spawning area by gravel placement and gravel cleaning. In a joint project with the Gitxsan Watershed Authorities, the Kispiox Hatchery is now being used for a conservation enhancement effort to improve the status of Kitwanga Lake sockeye salmon by increasing the smolt output.

Data gathering and analysis for resource planning

The Gitxsan and Wet'suwet'en realized the importance of cartography for resource management in the 1970s. The pursuit of land claims required maps to explain the claim; one of the strong points of the court case was maps of the landscape full of Gitxsan and Wet'suwet'en named features and uses. Initially the maps were prepared by Marvin George, from Hagwilget. Under his leadership the Gitxsan and Wet'suwet'en became one of the earliest adopters of digital mapping and GIS in British Columbia in the late 1980s. Initially, GIS mapping made the numerous modifications of the chief's evolving territorial maps easy to produce. Spatial analysis was soon adopted as the key to the management of cultural resources, forests, fisheries, and mineral deposits. The Sustainable Watershed Assessment Team of the Gitxsan and Wet'suwet'en became one of the leading groups in promoting aboriginal resource management and traveled around Canada giving presentations. The GIS department now has two full-time technicians and produces professional quality maps. The mapping and database capacity is routinely used for recording escapement, mapping spawning beds, mapping environmental impacts, and culvert placement.

Creating benefits for fishermen and communities

From its founding, the SFC strove to expand aboriginal fisheries, to secure the right to fish for sustenance, and to redevelop aboriginal fish sales to provide economic opportunities for First Nations. Beginning in 1992, provisions were negotiated for inland fisheries as ESSR fisheries. High survival of

Lake Babine sockeye salmon in the Pacific Ocean created a series of large returns in the mid 1990s which led to concerns about mixed stock problems at high exploitation rates (over 70%). The large returns also made it easy to allocate part of the catch to more terminal fisheries. The SFC has insisted that ESSR fisheries employ only selective live-capture fishing gear such as dip nets, small beach seines, fish wheels, or fish traps. As fish are removed individually from the gear, nontarget species are released unharmed. So far the ESSR fisheries have only allowed sockeye salmon capture, but a small ESSR fishery occurred at Moricetown for pink salmon in 2004 and 2005. In the years of high harvest, equal or larger numbers of sockeye were taken by the Lake Babine Nation and small numbers by the Tsimshian villages of Kitselas and Kitsumkalum in comparison to the Gitxsan portion of the fishery (Figure 4).

Catching salmon in the Skeena River is far less capital intensive than fishing in competitive fisheries along the coast. It is also much simpler and cheaper to monitor and manage fishing in the river than along the coast. The salmon caught are weighed, iced, and shipped from a few landing stations which are community controlled. The low management costs means that most of the revenue from the ESSR fisheries has gone to the fishing crews, typically more than 80% of the commercial sale price. Part of the remainder, 10% under the terms of the agreement, must be used to pay for salmon stock management and stock assessment expenses. The ESSR fisheries have contributed from tens of thousands of dollars in 1992 to several million dollars in the large fisheries directly to the fishermen. Since participating in the ESSR fishery requires prolonged activity from several weeks to a month, those most likely to benefit from the activity are people in the villages without regular jobs.

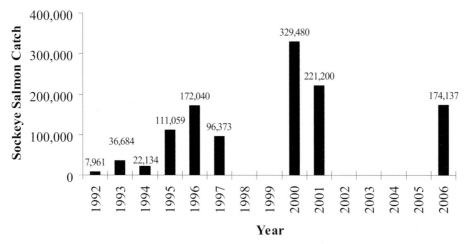

FIGURE 4. Gitxsan Excess to Salmon Spawning Requirements (ESSR) catches. The catch for 2006 is the total of an ESSR fishery at Gisgagaas (92,347) and a commercial demonstration fishery at Kitwanga (81,790).

Although the large proportion of the total catch value that accrues to the fisherman is a positive attribute, the irregularity of annual fisheries openings has prevented capital investment in the fishery and has not created a stable source of income. This is an inevitable feature of an ESSR fishery because upriver fisheries occur only in years of exceptionally large runs.

Starting in 2005, the SFC negotiated an arrangement in which some of the potential salmon catch of coastal gill netters and seine boats is leased and the "fishing rights" exercised in upriver fisheries. In 2005, the first agreement was made, but the sockeye salmon returns were too poor to permit fishing on the coast or upriver. The following year, 2006, was a year of higher sockeye salmon returns, and the first demonstration fishery was held in the Skeena River. The fishery was held simultaneously with a terminal ESSR fishery in the Babine River further upstream. This resulted in a catch of 84,000 fish in the demonstration fishery and 92,000 fish in the ESSR fishery. Together these fisheries caught approximately 8% of the sockeye salmon return.

The demonstration fishery brought in over half a million dollars to the fishers and generated employment in the community; each group of fishers started their own small company, paid off their debts, and made some profit. The fishery took place near Kitwanga and employed only selective gear. This approach avoided bycatch of steelhead trout and chum salmon, which experienced poor returns, as well as coho. A system of fishery openings and closures was used to reduce pressure on wild sockeye stocks. This system appears to have been successful in largely avoiding the early-timed Nanika River run; however, it overlapped the late arrival of Kitwanga Lake sockeye salmon which was sampled at the nearby Kitwanga River fence. The fishing plan was changed with discussion between Gitanyow Fisheries Authority and Gitxsan Watershed Authorities, and a two day closure followed by a week-long closure was instituted to pass many of the Kitwanga River sockeye salmon.

Training and education

The SFC attempts to fill many of the training needs in fisheries biology and management. Training in formal programs was discussed briefly earlier. In-service training needs require that training takes place at several technical levels to meet the needs of our management organizations and employees. We attempt to keep our training sessions local and focused on local problems. We can carry out much of the training using our internal expertise; alternately, we bring in experts to run workshops. Training at the most specialized level sometimes involves sending one or two employees to distant urban centers.

The SFC holds workshops for training technicians of member Nations' staffs in:

• map interpretation, Geographic Position System (GPS) data collection, and introduction to GIS;
    • otolith collection and preservation;
    • scale reading/age interpretation;
    • and data logging.

Technical sessions for tribal biologists and advanced technicians have included:

• a series of sessions to discuss and review Behaviour and Ecology of Pacific Salmon and Trout (Quinn 2005);
    • presentations of special topic lectures at Technical Committee meetings, for example, the dynamics of gravel movement in salmon spawning grounds;
    • and workshops on Chinook salmon, the Core Stock Assessment process, and the Wild Salmon Policy.

Examples of specialized training include hydroacoustic surveys and analysis techniques and advanced GIS topics.

Discussion

Future prospects

The SFC originated at a time when the thrust of efforts was to demonstrate the right to fish. Substantial success has occurred in this effort. At this point, the SFC has become a credible partner with the DFO and at the technical level is involved in ongoing efforts to undertake complementary activities. In the long run, we envision becoming responsible for most if not all technical and management activities now being carried out by the provincial and federal governments.

Real co-management requires comparable levels of expertise and decision making power. For the technical aspects of fishery management, we try not to hire consultants but prefer to train our First Nations members and to hire and retain specialized expertise in the region. Once the technical capacity exists, the SFC can and does compete with consulting companies and government agencies for technical assignments.

The low human population density of the Skeena River watershed means that natural resource exploitation is, and will continue to be, a significant economic sector. The ongoing stream of resource development proposals from corporations such as mining companies, lumber and pulp mills, harbor development, and pipelines raises a series of policy challenges. These challenges could be dealt with in several ways: by taking contracts for environmental assessment, by collecting environmental data to resist the development proposals, or by permitting development with constraints designed to protect First Nations' interests. It is likely that the era of allowing proposals sponsored by developers and governments to proceed on their own is over, to be replaced by new processes acceptable to First Nations empowered by recent Canadian court decisions requiring consultation and accommodation.

At present, SFC funding derives from three sources: two sources are from federal programs (Aboriginal Fisheries Strategy and Aboriginal Aquatic Resources and Ocean Management), the third from research contracts, especially with the Northern Fund of the Pacific Salmon Commission. In the recent past, significant funding came from DFO in support of stock assessment activities and community fisheries programs, from the provincial WRP, and from the provincial Forest Service. In the past decade, a sharp decline in fisheries expenditures has occurred by both levels of government. This situation likely will be exacerbated by ongoing challenges to the DFO such as a response to the LaRoque court decision, which bars using fish sales to offset management costs. At the regional and area management levels of the DFO, the expectation exists that some relief from the budgetary restrictions will come from transferring technical tasks to First Nations. The ability of First Nations to take on these responsibilities is limited mostly by their own small budgets. With the ongoing pattern of reduction in size of government, much more of the research and scientific work is contracted out to consultants. Intercepting these contracts provides a source of funding to technically capable First Nations and enables them to cover other unfunded management biology aspects.

Shaping the research direction of the SFC

Often the perception of the priorities for fisheries projects that can be carried out differs among the provincial and federal governments and the SFC. Differences in decisions about the type of information to be collected, the area where the activity takes place, and the type of research to be conducted arise frequently. In part, these differences are due to differing geographic perspectives. The DFO managers tend to address coast-wide issues and spend much of their time dealing with the coastal commercial fishing industry. First Nations concerns tend to be more local and focused on conservation. Often this involves conservation of smaller units than the DFO has the political

will, capacity, and funding to address. This situation is especially true for many chiefs whose territory includes salmon spawning grounds for stocks that are not large enough to noticeably contribute to coastal catches, but which formerly supported small upriver settlements. Differences with the DFO are discussed in Technical Committee meetings, and in meetings between the Commissioners and area and regional managers. Often these disagreements are resolved in favor of DFO since they control of most of the funding.

In the past few years, minor conflicts have occurred with outside nongovernment conservation groups and academics. These groups tend to represent an urban world view that is insensitive to aboriginal interests. A central part of this view is the assumption by some representatives that they hold a superior understanding of what kinds of conservation activities are needed, a position that makes dialog difficult. In northern British Columbia, a considerable scope for improvement of relationships exists between environmental NGOs and Native groups, including the potential for strong long-term cooperation.

Key elements for success

What factors have contributed to the SFC and its member Nations' successful expansion into fisheries management, and allowed the SFC to develop an effective voice and considerable political influence on federal fisheries policy in British Columbia?

The commitment to protect salmon is a cultural imperative originating in traditional law and an important incentive for involvement in fisheries management. The importance of salmon is universally appreciated in First Nations communities, and this extends to support for fish habitat protection, efforts to enumerate fish, and for restrictions on harvesting weak stocks.

A key aspect of SFC capacity development was that the impetus for training and the development of management capacity came from within the aboriginal community. The understanding of the chiefs and those they selected for training was that fishery management was a critical aspect of the political development of the community. Some of the trainees who started in 1984 gave up well paying jobs to take on the project for their community. The concern and support of the community was clearly communicated to the students during training by one chief, who said, "We'll be watching you."

Leadership in fisheries management was available within SFC member communities, and the potential success of the organization was increased by the presence of key individuals who were technically trained and who assumed leadership roles, such as Neil J. Sterritt, the early Gitxsan and Carrier (now Wet'suwet'en) Tribal Council leader, and Marvin George, a trained forest cartographer. Continuity is important for effecting political change. The success of the SFC and its member nations is in part due to fifteen years of the same people managing the fisheries with a continuity of program and direction.

Increased aboriginal participation in fisheries management emerged within the political context of the 1970s and 1980s, during the push by aboriginal people across North America for autonomy, including control over natural resources. The Sparrow Case in 1990 affirmed communal rights to fish and emphasized the development of co-management models. In the Skeena River region, this push congealed around the partially successful land claims efforts heard in the Delgamuukw case. Other decisions including the Calder[5] case in 1973, which led to the Nisga'a treaty negotiations, the local Gitxsan fisheries cases of 1978 to 1980, and the series of Supreme Court decisions after the Sparrow and Delgamuukw de-

cisions, combined to increase the federal and provincial governments' political will to negotiate and accommodate Native aspirations.

During the Delgamuukw case, the use of outside expertise became familiar to the community and eased the acceptance of outside scientific experts. SFC Nations were thus able to strengthen their proposed policies with scientific studies. For example, Morrell (1985, 1989) contributed to increased awareness and emphasis on "weak-stock management" which has ultimately led to the Wild Salmon Policy. SFC Nations have pushed for a return to more terminal and selective fisheries that would allow for finer tuning of harvest rates and for additional fisheries benefits upriver. These policies were articulated long before the DFO acknowledged conservation problems associated with mixed stock fisheries (Morrell 1985; Wood 2001).

Early on, Skeena First Nations recognized the need for Skeena River-wide management and cooperation between neighboring First Nations, between First Nations and provincial and federal governments, and in a larger realm with broader based organizations such as the Skeena River Watershed Committee (Pinkerton 2009) and panels of the Pacific Salmon Commission.

The convergence of these factors led to the provision of funding from the Federal Government for fishery management efforts as part of fisheries agreements and for technical training of fisheries managers and enforcement staff. The federal HRSEP and the provincial WRP made abundant funding available during the 1990s for simple labor intensive community based programs. Concurrently, funding from the Aboriginal Fisheries Strategy permitted SFC Nations to test various selective methods of capture. SFC Nations also gained legitimacy by choosing to conduct commercial fisheries entirely with selective gear, permitting species which require additional protection to continue their migration unharmed.

---

[5]*Calder v. The Attorney-General of British Columbia* (1973).

Is the SFC a model for other First Nations?

The political success of the SFC is largely dependent on the Canadian and B.C. political milieux and might not be easily transplanted to other jurisdictions. The legal support for aboriginal fisheries is ultimately based on the guarantee of preservation of "existing aboriginal and treaty rights" in the Section 35 of the Constitution Act of 1982 and the uncertainty surrounding the lack of negotiated treaties with most aboriginal groups in B.C. This creates the possibility that litigation may expand aboriginal fishing rights and provides the governments with incentive to investigate co-management.

Extending the SFC experience to other First Nations groups may be difficult even within Canada. A reduction of government funding for relatively simple field tasks such as salmon spawner enumeration, performing herring spawn and Dungeness crab surveys on the coast, and assessing logging damage to streams, makes it difficult for First Nations groups to finance the development of technical expertise and to assume management of their fisheries resources. This situation is unfortunate for Native communities and conservation of the resources. Research funding through the Pacific Salmon Treaty is currently the most significant source of new money. Successful projects under this program require sophisticated scientific input and direction, which is out of reach of most village-based groups. To some extent, funding for technical training and resource data collection is available through the ongoing British Columbia land claims treaty process in the form of Treaty Related Measures. These funds may assist other First Nations in creating or strengthening their natural resource management programs.

References

Gottesfeld, A., K. Rabnett, and P. Hall. 2002. Conserving Skeena fish populations and their habitat. Skeena Fisheries Commission, Hazelton, British Columbia.

Harris, D. C. 2001. Fish, law and colonialism. The legal capture of salmon in British Columbia. University of Toronto Press, Toronto.

Harris, R. C. 2002. Making native space. Colonialism, resistance, and reserves in British Columbia. University of British Columbia Press, Vancouver.

Morrell, M. 1985. The Gitxsan and Wet'suwet'en fishery in the Skeena River system. Gitxsan-Wet'suwet'en Tribal Council, Hazelton, British Columbia.

Morrell, M. 1989. The struggle to integrate traditional Indian systems and state management in the salmon fisheries of the Skeena River, British Columbia. Pages 231–248 in E. Pinkerton, editor. Co-operative management of local fisheries: new directions for improved management and community development. University of British Columbia Press, Vancouver.

Quinn, T. P. 2005. The behavior and ecology of Pacific salmon and trout. American Fisheries Society, Bethesda, Maryland.

Pinkerton, E. 2009. The Skeena watershed partnership: learning from success and failure in salmon management. Pages 903–919 in C. C. Krueger and C. E. Zimmerman, editors. Pacific salmon: ecology and management of western Alaska's populations. American Fisheries Society, Symposium 70, Bethesda, Maryland.

Pinkerton, E., and M. Weinstein. 1995. Fisheries that work. Sustainability through community-based management. The David Suzuki Foundation, Vancouver.

Soto, C. 2006. Socio-cultural barriers to the application of fishers' knowledge in fishery management. Doctoral dissertation. School of Resource and Environmental Management, Simon Fraser University, Burnaby, British Columbia.

Spaeder, J. 2004. Capacity building for tribal-rural fisheries research: initial scoping report and recommendations to the Steering Committee of the Arctic-Yukon-Kuskowim Sustainable Salmon Initiative, AYK Sustainable Salmon Initiative, Bering Sea Fishermen's Association, Anchorage, Alaska.

Wood, C.C. 2001. Managing biodiversity in Pacific salmon: the evolution of the Skeena River sockeye salmon fishery in British Columbia. Pages 4–34 in B. Harvey and D. Duthie, editors. Blue millennium: managing global fisheries for biodiversity. World Fisheries Trust, Victoria, British Columbia.

American Fisheries Society Symposium 70:941–960, 2009

Managing Across Jurisdictional Boundaries: Fishery Governance in the Great Lakes and Arctic-Yukon-Kuskokwim Regions

Marc Gaden*, Charles C. Krueger, and Christopher I. Goddard

Great Lakes Fishery Commission
2100 Commonwealth Boulevard, Suite 100, Ann Arbor, Michigan 48105, USA

Abstract.—Jurisdictional boundaries add a layer of complexity to the already difficult task of managing fisheries. This paper outlines the challenges of cross-border management in the Great Lakes of North America and the Arctic-Yukon-Kuskokwim (AYK) region of Alaska and Yukon Territory and discusses the role of governance regimes established to facilitate fishery management in those regions. Management of the multi-jurisdictional Great Lakes fishery occurs without direct federal oversight. Eight Great Lakes states, the province of Ontario, and several U.S. tribes manage the sport, commercial, and subsistence fisheries within their jurisdiction, though the Canadian and U.S. federal governments make important contributions as well. To help in the development of shared fishery policies, the nonfederal jurisdictions, with the support of the federal agencies and the binational Great Lakes Fishery Commission, signed *A Joint Strategic Plan for Management of Great Lakes Fisheries*, a voluntary, consensus-based agreement. Similar to the Great Lakes, political diffusion is also a characteristic of management of salmon in the AYK region. AYK fishery management must consider state, federal, provincial, territorial, and international treaty jurisdictions. Different from the Great Lakes, federal involvement is much greater in the AYK region because of abundant federal lands combined with federal legislation (e.g., Alaska National Interest Lands Conservation Act of 1980) and the presence of international waters and treaties. Based on lessons from the Great Lakes, a pathway to increasing cooperation and effectiveness of AYK salmon management includes: identification of common interests; adoption of shared goals; information sharing; building of relationships among agencies and individuals; and use of consensus decision-making and accountability mechanisms. Connecting all of the agencies affecting the salmon life cycle and fisheries in the AYK region through an appropriate forum or institution would enhance cooperative and effective AYK salmon management.

Introduction

Great Lakes fishery management occurs in a unique setting as nonfederal governments—the eight Great Lakes states, the province of Ontario, and the U.S. tribes— have primary management authority, despite the international border that runs through four of the five lakes. Federal waters do not exist in the Great Lakes basin because state and provincial boundaries extend to the international border or, in the case of Lake Michigan, to the center of the lake (Piper 1967). The non-

*Corresponding author: marc@glfc.org

federal governments have maintained or attained authority over the fish in their waters.

The Great Lakes ecosystem is biologically complex and fish routinely transcend the basin's many political borders. With so many management agencies present—and with each having independent authority to manage the fishery resources in its waters—some level of cooperation was needed if management policies were to be more consistent with the needs of a lake or the Great Lakes basin as a whole. Multi-jurisdictional cooperation allows fishery managers to leverage each others' resources, better understand all available information, and undertake fishery management on a lake-wide or basin-wide level. Cooperation also prevents agencies from working at cross purposes or undermining each others' initiatives.

With no overarching authority to compel the jurisdictions to institute basin-wide or even harmonized management policies and with a strong interest in protecting their fishery management authority against federal encroachment, the Great Lakes jurisdictions engaged in parochial and uncooperative behavior that lasted from the time of European settlement until the mid-20th century. Parochialism began to fade in the mid-1960s with the establishment of cooperative "lake committees"—committees where the federal, provincial, state, and tribal jurisdictions could share information and understand each others' activities. Cooperation became more strategic with the signing in 1981 of *A Joint Strategic Plan for Management of Great Lakes Fisheries*, a nonbinding agreement that formalized the relationships among the jurisdictions and committed the participants to develop shared management objectives and fishery plans. The Joint Strategic Plan remains the governance institution that the jurisdictions use to coordinate their shared actions. The Joint Strategic Plan reflects a self-organization among the nonfederal jurisdictions, but also allows for

the federal governments and the bi-national Great Lakes Fishery Commission to participate in the process. The commission, being the only bi-national fishery agency on the lakes, facilitates the plan's implementation but does not possess the authority to compel the jurisdictions to behave in any particular way.

Fishery governance over Pacific salmon *Oncorhynchus* spp. in the Arctic-Yukon-Kuskokwim (AYK) region of Alaska and Yukon Territory illustrates similar challenges to those experienced in the Great Lakes region. The AYK region includes the drainages of the Kuskokwim and Yukon rivers, as well as streams and rivers in the Norton Sound area of Alaska, although the salmon of this region move well beyond these borders into international marine waters. The State of Alaska, the United States, and Canada provide a mosaic of management jurisdictions across which salmon must travel. Further, sub-adult salmon in the Bering Sea and the North Pacific likely use international waters or the waters of other countries (e.g., Russia) as ocean feeding grounds. Management authority is complex and includes the State of Alaska, the U.S. federal departments of Interior and Commerce, and the Canadian federal government through the Department of Fisheries and Oceans. Bi-national issues concerning Yukon River salmon are managed by the Yukon River Panel through the Pacific Salmon Treaty between the United States and Canada. Multi-lateral management in international waters is the responsibility of the North Pacific Anadromous Fish Commission. All jurisdictions share a common goal of managing for sustainable salmon fisheries. Different from the Great Lakes, however, is that subsistence fisheries for rural residents uniformly have priority over other fisheries in the State of Alaska and Yukon Territory.

In contrast to the Great Lakes, where the jurisdictions are organized through the Joint Strategic Plan, jurisdictions in the AYK region have not self-organized. Consequently, governance in the AYK region continues largely in an uncoordinated fashion, without the jurisdictions having a forum to seek consensus, develop shared objectives, and exchange information. Some coordination does occur within drainages such as the Yukon River, but formal connections to governance of marine waters does not exist. This paper provides a short overview of jurisdictional authority in the Great Lakes region, presents a brief history of the evolution of cooperation in Great Lakes fishery management, and discusses the regime—the Joint Strategic Plan—under which the jurisdictions cooperate. This paper also compares fishery governance in the Great Lakes region to governance in AYK region, identifies the important lessons from the Great Lakes regime, and suggests some potential applications of these lessons to AYK salmon management.

Fishery Management Authorities of the Great Lakes Basin

Three levels of government are involved in Great Lakes fishery governance: (1) The nonfederal governments (states, the Province of Ontario, and the two U.S. intertribal agencies); (2) the U.S and Canadian federal governments; and (3) the bi-national Great Lakes Fishery Commission. Combined, fourteen jurisdictions—and many more agencies and departments within those jurisdictions—have some role in the Great Lakes fishery, though the nonfederal agencies have primary management authority; the authority to regulate harvest, stock fish, and enforce fishery regulations. Despite the large number of jurisdictions, the role of each type of jurisdiction is defined, accepted, and respected, and the management authorities tend to complement, not contradict or duplicate, each other (Figure 1). Together, the bi-national, federal, and nonfederal management agencies approach

the Great Lakes from the same general perspective and with the same goals in mind:

• Using science-based information as an input to management decisions;

• Sustaining Great Lakes fish stocks; Protecting biological diversity; Promoting balance between predators and prey; and

• Balancing the interests of stakeholders, including those of sport, commercial, and tribal fisheries, the environmental community, and many others.

Provincial, state, and tribal management authority

Primary management authority rests with the states, the Province of Ontario, and two U.S. intertribal agencies. This nonfederal management authority is found in constitutions and common law, and was recognized long ago by courts and tradition. Provinces own the fish in their inland waters, though the British North America Act (the Canadian Constitution) makes management somewhat confusing by suggesting that inland fishery management authority rests with both the provinces and the federal government (Ollivier 1962; Thompson 1974). To work through this awkward situation, Ontario and the federal government have established a working arrangement whereby Ontario develops fishery conservation regulations and then refers these regulations to the federal government for incorporation into the Ontario Fisheries Regulations under the federal Fisheries Act. The province of Ontario then implements the regulations (Dochoda 1999; Gibson 1973; Lamb and Lybecker 1999; Piper 1967; Rideout and Ritter 2002; Thompson 1974). Commercial fishing harvest in the Canadian waters of the Great Lakes is regulated by individual transferable quotas. Such regulations are strictly a property issue and, there-

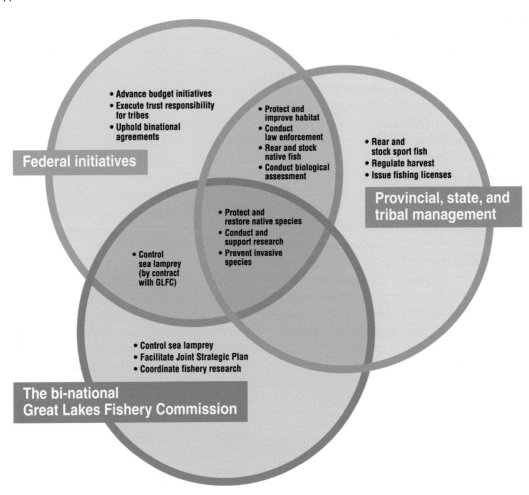

FIGURE 1. Jurisdictional spheres of authority in Great Lakes fishery management (from Gaden 2007).

fore do not require federal approval (Brown et al. 1999).

Canadian First Nations do not have direct management authority in their treaty waters, as courts have ruled provincial and federal regulations do not inherently deny tribal access to fish. In the 1990 case *R. v. Sparrow* (R. v. Sparrow 1990), the court, while explicitly recognizing and affirming Aboriginal treaty rights, nevertheless held that fishing regulations were established to manage fisheries, not to limit Aboriginal rights, and that federal regulatory authorities to manage fisher-

ies were valid. In the Canadian waters of the Great Lakes, Ontario manages on behalf of the First Nations, though the province negotiates fishery management agreements with the First Nations.

In the United States, the states and the tribes have a well-established authority to manage fish and wildlife, particularly the nonmigratory animals that remain entirely within their boundaries (Nielsen 1999; Piper 1967). While resource ownership and enumerated powers define authority in Canada and in the United States, courts first couched, then abandoned authority based on ownership and instead derived authority mostly from enumerated powers. Over time, while states maintained their management authority, the federal government asserted its constitutional powers to play a role in hitherto exclusive state fishery affairs. In the 1920 case *Missouri v. Holland* (Knaebel 1920), for instance, the U.S. Supreme Court upheld a treaty—the *Migratory Bird Treaty Act* (USGPO 1918)—that intruded on state resource management authority; it ruled that because the constitution granted treaty-making authority to the federal government, the federal power could supersede the state authority (Holmes 1920; Killian and Beck 1987; Knaebel 1920; Moore 1965; Willoughby 1979). The *Missouri* case did not deny the fundamental state right to manage resources, but rather it said that times can exist when the national interest is more important than a state interest (Willoughby 1979). Federal involvement in state fishery matters, however, is far from inherent and certainly neither absolute or exclusive. It is important to the nonfederal jurisdictions that the U.S. Constitution does not directly grant Congress the power to manage fisheries. The Tenth Amendment grants authorities not expressly vested in the federal government to the states. Authority over fish, wildlife, and natural resources in state lands and waters is not an express power given to the federal government and, therefore, is retained by the states.

U.S. tribal authority is rooted in the 1832 Supreme Court decision *Worcester v. Georgia* (Peters [1832] 1901), where the court affirmed that an Indian tribe is a political power with authority of self-governance (Cohen 1988). In the 1960s and 1970s, the tribes revisited their still-valid treaties with the federal government and began to assert the fishing rights specified in those treaties; court cases affirmed those rights (Michigan Supreme Court 1971; Michigan Supreme Court 1976; U.S. Court of Appeals 1983; U.S. District Court 1979). After those cases, tribal authority to issue licenses to their members would be protected and tribes would have the ability to block state regulations in the ceded waters, should tribes demonstrate the ability to regulate their members effectively and uphold the state's conservation goals (Busiahn 1985; Schlender (undated); Zorn 1989). Two U.S. intertribal authorities—the Chippewa-Ottawa Resource Authority and the Great Lakes Indian Fish and Wildlife Commission—exist in the Great Lakes basin to coordinate tribal fisheries management. Overall, tribal authority overlaps in many respects with state authority, as both states and tribes regulate harvest, conduct assessment activities, enforce regulations, and undertake many similar day-to-day activities in the same waters.

On a day-to-day basis, the states, the Province of Ontario, and the two U.S. intertribal agencies exercise their fishery management authority by:

•Establishing and enforcing harvest regulations;
•Issuing fishing licenses;
•Stocking fish (primarily states though some tribes as well);
•Undertaking various fishery rehabilitation initiatives;
•Carrying out assessment activities;
•Undertaking measures to protect habitat; and
•Protecting against the introduction of invasive species.

Federal responsibilities

Even though the states, the province, and the two U.S. intertribal agencies retain primary fishery management authority on the Great Lakes, the federal governments are also engaged in the process. Several federal agencies work with the nonfederal agencies to support fishery management. The federal agencies carry out sea lamprey control under contract with the Great Lakes Fishery Commission; work to manage endangered species and restore locally extirpated native species (in consultation with the nonfederal authorities), most notably the lake trout *Salvelinus namaycush* and the lake sturgeon *Acipenser fulvescens*; contribute to the knowledge base by carrying out fish population assessment and other scientific research; negotiate binational agreements; support the common good through budget and other initiatives; protect and rehabilitate habitat; and have the trust responsibility toward tribes. Other federal agencies not directly involved in fishery management are also involved in the overall management effort. For example, Environment Canada, the U.S. Environmental Protection Agency, and the binational International Joint Commission implement laws and agreements to improve water quality in the Great Lakes.

Bi-national responsibilities

The two federal governments maintain a binational fishery agency on the Great Lakes—the Great Lakes Fishery Commission. The commission was established by the 1955 *Convention on Great Lakes Fisheries*—a treaty—though the commission's management mandate is limited, largely because the states were reluctant to cede management authority to a bi-national body (Fetterolf 1980). The destructive sea lamprey *Petromyzon marinus*, which invaded the lakes in the mid-20th century, prompted the state governments to consent to a binational fishery commission to address the basin-wide lamprey problem. The convention granted sea lamprey management authority to the commission. The treaty also charged the commission with coordinating fisheries research on the Great Lakes and making recommendations to governments about fish stocks of common concern (U.S. Department of State 1956). Further, at the request of the nonfederal governments, the commission facilitates the implementation of *A Joint Strategic Plan for Management of Great Lakes Fisheries* (GLFC 1997).

The Evolution of Cooperation and the Great Lakes Joint Strategic Plan

The large number of government authorities in the Great Lakes basin, each with an independent right to manage its fisheries, resulted in incoherent policies. Said historian Margaret Beattie Bogue (2000):

"The divided jurisdiction over the fisheries of the Great Lakes led to almost insurmountable obstacles to conservation efforts. While partition does not always mean stalemate, in this case the division of the waters hamstrung the state or provincial and national efforts to control the exploitation of the fish resource, a constraint recognized as increasingly important beginning in the 1870s as parts of the whole failed effort to find ways to control aggressive overfishing."

Bogue's history of Great Lakes fishing from 1833 to 1933, and data reports from the fishery assessments at the time, describe an era of rapidly depleting fish stocks caused by over-exploitation and a lack of political will to regulate (Bogue 2000; Cobb 1916; Hinrichs 1913; Joslyn 1905; Willoughby 1979). In the late nineteenth and early twentieth centuries, the many jurisdictions had differing philosophies and willingness to conserve the resource. Each jurisdiction dealt with its own political mix of legislators and special interests; these interests usually thwarted fishery regulation (Bogue 2000; Willoughby 1979).

The frustration about political incoherence and the resulting fishery decay prompted repeated attempts to coordinate policies and repeated calls for federal or binational pre-emption over nonfederal authority. Beginning in 1883 and continuing at a regular pace for nearly 60 years, the jurisdictions convened no fewer than 27 international and interstate conferences, and the federal governments signed two binational treaties in an attempt to create a permanent mechanism for cooperative Great Lakes fishery management (Gallagher et al. 1942; Piper 1967). The states and province failed to cooperate primarily because they were unwilling to cede management authority to the federal governments or to a binational institution (Fetterolf 1980); the nonfederal fishery managers were unable or unwilling to persuade their legislatures to implement the recommendations of the many conferences and meetings (Gallagher et al. 1942).

Crisis and the emergence of a coordinating institution helped bring an end to this "era-of-no-cooperation." With the formation of permanent cooperative committees in the late 1940s to deal with the sea lamprey problem and the demise of lake trout, agencies saw a strong need to address the sea lamprey on a basin-wide level and to share information and resources to restore the fishery ravaged by the sea lamprey and other problems. This emergence of cooperation received a boost in 1956 with the formation of the Great Lakes Fishery Commission as an entity the jurisdictions could turn to for help in facilitating ongoing interactions. Cooperation became more regular when the commission formed "lake committees" in 1964 "to strengthen the work of the States and Province in administering the fishery and to further the objectives of the Commission" (GLFC 1964). Federal and nonfederal agencies participated in these committees, though the participants limited their actions primarily to information sharing (as opposed to strategic actions) throughout the rest of the 1960s and 1970s.

Great Lakes fishery management, and the process to facilitate cooperation among many jurisdictions, began to change in the mid- to late-1970s when the jurisdictions were motivated to organize more formally, partially due to a strong interest in strategic planning and partially due to a threat to their authority. "Planning," says Crowe (1983), "is an integrated system for management that includes all activities leading to the development and implementation of goals, programs, objectives, operational strategies, and progress evaluation." Strategic planning is not a particular project or initiative *per se*, rather, it is a "way of doing business . . . a system for decision-making." By the 1970s, Great Lakes fishery managers were beginning to embrace the "ecosystem approach" to management (even though they likely had little shared understanding of that approach), which highlighted their interest in integrating other disciplines into fisheries and working across boundaries in a strategic fashion (Donahue 1988; Grumbine 1994; Krueger and Decker 1999). Strategic fisheries planning on a basin-wide level, many believed, would be beneficial to the Great Lakes community as it would communicate the goals and needs for the fishery; enhance agency, legislative, or public support for an initiative by grounding initiatives in clear plans; and help fishery managers keep pace with the broader environmental movement that was growing more sophisticated in other areas, such as water quality.

Another major force organizing the jurisdictions in the late 1970s was the possibility of U.S. federal intrusion into nonfederal fishery management affairs, particularly through the newly authorized *Magnuson-Stevens Fishery Conservation and Management Act* (USGPO 1976). The act, signed in 1976 by President Gerald Ford, established a formal process for the federal government and the states to govern fishery management activities in U.S. federal waters (i.e., from three miles to 200 mi from the coast). The federal National Oceanic and Atmospheric Administration (NOAA) would lead the regional fishery management councils (Pacific Fishery Management Council 2005; USGPO 1976), but because oceanic states have control over their fisheries to the three-mile limit, the act would provide for state involvement. Under this act, regional councils (made up of federal and state managers, stakeholders, and other interested parties) were established to prepare and present fishery management plans to NOAA, conduct public hearings on the plans, submit periodic reports to NOAA, review fishery harvest policies, and review state and federal actions affecting the fisheries (Furlong 2002; USGPO 1976). The U.S. federal government would implement and enforce the plans through NOAA and the Coast Guard, respectively. Regional councils were set up in the expected places—the Atlantic, Pacific, and Gulf coasts—where federal and state governments needed to cooperate to manage the fishery. About the same time the Magnuson Act went into force, the Comptroller General of the United States concluded in a major report (GAO 1976) that "Congress should consider giving the Secretary of Commerce [the head of NOAA] statutory authority to impose management measures on U.S. fisheries when states fail to do so."

The regional fishery councils (under federal leadership) and the heavy-handed recommendation from the Comptroller General suggested the possibility of a new era of federal dominance over fisheries and environment. Applying the Magnuson Act to the Great Lakes would have been a major change in Great Lakes fisheries governance, as federal waters do not exist in the Great Lakes and federally dominated regional councils would have pervaded state management. The solution, many realized, was to create a regime to coordinate the jurisdictions' activities in the spirit of the Magnuson Act, but in a way that was suited to the Great Lakes region. With a basin-wide strategic plan, the states reasoned, the U.S. federal government would have no pretense to usurp the nonfederal authority in the Great Lakes basin.[1]

A Joint Strategic Plan for Management of Great Lakes Fisheries

The Joint Strategic Plan became the agencies' mechanism for multi-jurisdictional, cooperative strategic planning. The plan calls for agencies to work together to identify their shared goals and objectives, and then to take the steps necessary to achieve them. The plan identifies four broad strategies—consensus, accountability, information sharing, and ecosystem management—to make cooperation occur and succeed.

Consensus

The Joint Strategic Plan is rooted in action by consensus. Consensus is general agreement, the collective opinion, and the judgment reached by most of those concerned. Consensus occurs after all points of view have been heard and when no participant objects to the opinion (GLFC 1997). Joint Strategic Plan participants recognize that consensus does not mean unanimity, or that everyone is completely happy with the outcome, rather, it means everybody agrees or chooses not to disagree. By signing the plan, fishery management agencies pledge to reach consensus on proposed actions before they implement them. Agencies also agree that any change in fishery management practices that affects other jurisdictions must be agreed to by the other jurisdictions. This understanding of consensus was a direct reflection of the jurisdictional realities in Great Lakes fishery

---

[1]At the invitation of the nonfederal jurisdictions and the Great Lakes Fishery Commission, NOAA participated in the development of the Joint Strategic Plan and signed the plan in 1981. By involving NOAA in the process from the earliest stages, the jurisdictions were able to secure acceptance from the U.S. federal government for the Great Lakes fishery management regime under the Joint Strategic Plan instead of under a regional council.

management and, probably more than any other element of the plan, captured the essence of how cooperation occurred. The plan was not designed to force the jurisdictions to do something they do not want to do, rather, it was designed to help produce emergent commonalities and strategic goals. The plan's definition of consensus thus emerged out of the jurisdictions' history of information sharing, coming together as equals, coming together voluntarily, and preserving their autonomy. In the rare instance where consensus cannot be achieved, the Joint Strategic Plan contains provisions for conflict resolution through the Great Lakes Fishery Commission or third parties.

Accountability

The plan's second broad strategy is accountability. Even with the plan, agencies maintain their right to manage their own fisheries and interact with their own stakeholders and legislatures. Some degree of shared accountability serves to encourage agencies to adhere to the shared objectives and plans developed through the plan's process. Because the plan is nonbinding, it relies on "soft" accountability procedures (as opposed to "hard" procedures like law enforcement or sanctions) to encourage implementation. To promote accountability, the plan calls for the production of a decision record—primarily meeting minutes and published documents—to make the decisions and policies clear to the public and to each other. The Joint Strategic Plan also calls upon each agency to submit periodic reports about their activities on each lake and to provide each other with regular reports on progress toward reaching shared objectives. These accountability measures recognize agency independence while still acknowledging that being a part of the plan requires a mutual commitment to implement the management plans. Regular, public reports and a decision record serve to keep

activities transparent. The plan's accountability provisions are "enforced" by the existence of a strong "epistemic community" of peers who generally share the same values, philosophies, and scientific understanding of the resource (Haas 1992) and are able to exert peer pressure or gently coerce colleagues into adhering to the norms of the community (Gaden 2007).

Information sharing

The third broad strategy is information sharing. All agencies rely on sound science and information for their management activities. Information sharing is critical to cooperation because it helps agencies make consistent decisions, it makes the decisions more sound and defensible, and it is economical because agencies can leverage resources. Information sharing also levels the playing field, as it prevents data hoarding, a practice known to happen with valuable products like scientific data. Information sharing is more difficult than might appear. Jurisdictions are often strapped for resources to collect data and even when the data are collected, they are often generated in a variety of formats. The plan calls for agencies to come to consensus on fishery management and assessment data needs, and to implement standards for recording, analyzing, and maintaining the information. The plan also envisions the agencies developing plans to assign who collects the data and seeks ways for agencies to work together to collect data. Agencies and the commission are expected to publish information and make it available through convenient means.

Ecosystem management

The final broad strategy outlined in the plan is ecosystem management. Beginning in the 1970s, officials in the Great Lakes region began to adopt the principle that the lakes must be viewed as systems of interacting biotic and abiotic variables. Fishery managers recognized that they needed to look beyond fish or single species and instead consider and respond to all issues that affect the Great Lakes. Moreover, the officials realized that managing exclusively within their own waters was not an appropriate way to manage. The Joint Strategic Plan calls for fishery agencies to integrate their fish community objectives with environmental objectives and plans developed through other processes. For example, the Canadian/U.S. Great Lakes Water Quality Agreement identifies "Areas of Concern" in the Great Lakes basin that have suffered significant environmental degradation. Each area is to have a "Remedial Action Plan" that defines how the area is to be restored. The plans are intended to take into account "the interrelationships between land,

air, water, and all living things, including humans, and involving all stakeholder groups in comprehensive management" (Hartig 1997). The Joint Strategic Plan calls upon fishery managers to work with environmental officials involved in activities like Remedial Action Plans to integrate fishery needs and objectives with environmental needs and objectives.

Lake committees and technical committees: The Joint Strategic Plan in action

With these four strategies for cooperative fishery management in mind, the jurisdictions use "lake committees" as the primary means to put the Joint Strategic Plan into action (Figure 2). Lake committees comprise high-ranking officials from fishery agencies on each lake who meet to address that lake's

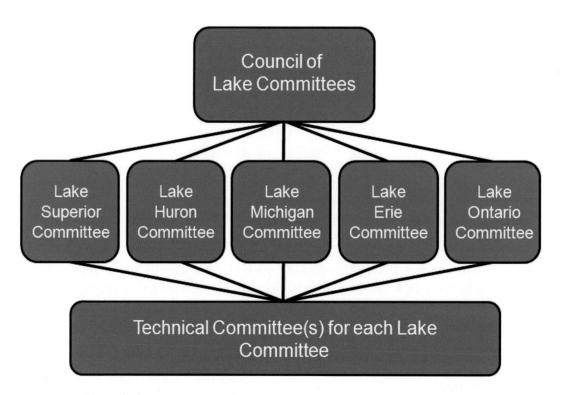

FIGURE 2. Organization of Lake Committees and Lake Technical Committees under the Joint Strategic Plan for Great Lakes Fisheries.

shared needs. For example, fishery managers from jurisdictions on Lake Huron—which include Ontario, Michigan, and the Chippewa-Ottawa Resource Authority—meet as the Lake Huron Committee. A Council of Lake Committees—comprising all members of the lake committees—addresses issues from a basin-wide perspective. The committees are the forum for agencies to work together to identify and achieve their shared goals and objectives. Each lake committee has at least one technical committee;[2] some also have several focused "task groups," that look at specific elements of the fishery such as the coldwater or percid fish communities. Technical committees and task groups consist of field-level professionals from government and academic sectors who undertake such tasks as deciding on data needs, gathering data, interpreting data, and providing advice to the lake committees. Scientists, assessment biologists, and managers who have relevant data to share and who have suitable biological expertise are usually invited to participate in the technical committees. Technical committees and task groups meet regularly and report to the lake committees.

Lake committee members integrate science (developed through the technical committees and other processes) with fishery management policy. This structure allows the field researchers and assessment biologists to develop a shared understanding of the science, as free as possible from political considerations and management biases. A major lake committee product, as called for under the plan, are Fish Community Objectives (e.g., Ryan et al. 2003). Fish Community Objectives are developed together by all of the agencies—federal, nonfederal, and binational—and represent the shared vision for the desired composition of the lake's ecosystem. Objectives often include expected harvest yield and rehabilitation needs. The objectives are based on recommendations from the technical committees and contain both fish and social objectives (such as expected constituent needs and target harvest levels). To fulfill the Fish Community Objectives, the lake committees and technical committees often produce specific restoration plans (e.g., Hansen 1996). Like the Fish Community Objectives, the plans are based on information generated through the lake and technical committees and reflect the deliberations and consensus among the members about what is needed and what is realistic. The agencies—together and individually—use the products of the lake committees to carry out fishery management.

Despite the high level of cooperation under the plan, the Joint Strategic Plan is not able to do several things. Because the plan is nonbinding, shared decisions do not force an agency to act, in any legal sense. The Joint Strategic Plan does not establish an overarching, centralized political authority to compel cooperation, so the Joint Strategic Plan does not impinge upon, reduce, or abrogate the authority of the individual jurisdictions. Finally, the Joint Strategic Plan does not alter federal responsibilities or the duties of the Great Lakes Fishery Commission. The participants, while not bound to the decisions, are expected to adhere to the decisions made through the plan. Nonbinding agreements depend on the goodwill of members for implementation, as they tend to lack the enforcement mechanisms often found in binding agreements (Rabe 1997; Raustiala and Victor 1998; Victor 1997; Weiss 1999; Zimmerman 2002).

In the Great Lakes region, Joint Strategic Plan participants believe multi-jurisdictional governance can be fulfilled with a nonbinding agreement because members must be flexible in their response to fluctuating natural condi-

[2]Lake Ontario's technical committee is less-formal than those on the other lakes because only two jurisdictions—Ontario and New York—manage the lake and because staff at all levels interact across the border on a continual basis.

tions (Gaden 2007). Moreover, participants believe a process that focuses on seeking and advancing shared goals is more valuable than a process that constrains behavior, even though a binding process might enhance compliance. Members are well aware that historical and political realities in the region are such that, with diffuse political authority and guarded independence, a binding agreement would be out of the question. While the members acknowledge that the nonbinding Joint Strategic Plan does not compel action, they believe that it does change their thinking and behavior. Moreover, the Joint Strategic Plan is able to address compliance in a nonbinding fashion by including mechanisms to ensure the participants implement agreed upon fishery management decisions. Such things as reliance on consensus, trust among

the members, ownership in decisions, and accountability—all elements of the Joint Strategic Plan process—help heighten the chances that shared decisions will be implemented (Gaden 2007).

The AYK Governance Regime

In Alaska, currently a four-track management system (Figure 3), whose parts do not automatically converge, exists (Linderman and Bergstrom 2009, this volume). The first track is multi-lateral fisheries management in the ocean beyond the 200-mi limit. Pacific salmon migrate great distances in the ocean and are harvested by several independent nations. In international waters (beyond 200 mi from a nation's shores), governance occurs through the North Pacific Anadromous

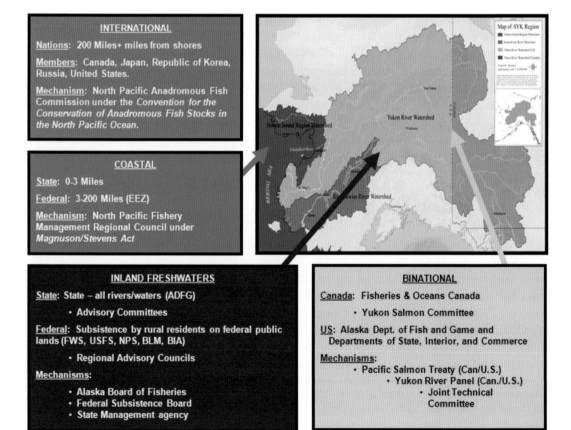

FIGURE 3. The four-track AYK governance regime.

Fish Commission (NPAFC). Members of NPAFC include Canada, Japan, The Republic of Korea, Russia, and the United States. NPAFC representatives are appointed by the respective governments and are responsible for estimating commercial salmon catch, understanding the factors affecting salmon survival, conducting salmon research (including convening scientific workshops and symposia), sharing information about each party's activities, and coordinating law enforcement. A single secretariat, located in Vancouver, British Columbia, supports NPAFC.

The second track, also in the ocean, is exclusively within the domain of the United States. The ocean waters from three miles out to 200 mi is referred to as the Exclusive Economic Zone (EEZ) and is managed through the North Pacific Fishery Management Council established by the *Magnuson-Stevens Fishery Conservation and Management Act* (USGPO 1976; Gisclair 2009, this volume). The council has broad representation, including the State of Alaska, and is coordinated by the U.S. Federal government through the National Marine Fisheries Service. The State of Alaska has sole jurisdictional authority from the coastline out to three miles.

The third governance track occurs in Alaskan freshwaters, where salmon are managed by both the state and the federal governments. Prior to 1999, salmon management in all Alaska waters was the responsibility of the Alaska Department of Fish and Game (ADFG) and a state regulatory Board of Fisheries. The Board is supported by fourteen local advisory committees representing different geographic regions of the AYK, and its membership includes stakeholders. This authority changed in 1999, when the U.S. federal government assumed management responsibility for subsistence fisheries on U.S. federal public lands in Alaska, which was consistent with the Alaska National Interest Lands Conservation Act of 1980 (Bulkis 2002). While salmon management of nonfederal freshwaters remains vested in the ADFG and Board of Fisheries, federal lands comprise large portions of the Yukon and Kuskokwim river drainages; management of federal waters for subsistence fisheries are under the purview of a regulatory Federal Subsistence Board. The Federal Subsistence Board has six members including one each from the federal agencies of Fish and Wildlife Service, Forest Service, National Park Service, Bureau of Land Management, and Bureau of Indian Affairs, plus a chair appointed by the Secretary of Interior. The Federal Subsistence Board is advised by Regional Advisory Councils, which include rural stakeholders who are knowledgeable about, and have experience with the fisheries. Subsistence fishery regulations in federal waters generally parallel state management regulations.

Finally, the fourth track occurs in the Yukon River because the drainage and its salmon cross the international boundary between U.S. (Alaska) and Canada (Yukon Territory) and involves state, territorial, and both federal governments (Bue et al. 2009, this volume). Much of the Canadian portion of the upper drainage of the Yukon River includes important spawning grounds for Chinook salmon *Oncorhynchus tshawytscha* and fall chum salmon *O. keta*. By agreement between the government of Canada and the government of the Yukon Territory, the Department of Fisheries and Oceans (DFO) is responsible for fishery management in the Canadian portion of the Yukon River drainage. DFO works closely with the Yukon Salmon Committee, a regulatory advisory body representing stakeholders, to develop fishery management plans. Coordination of management of salmon between the U.S. and Canada is provided though an agreement appended as an annex to the Pacific Salmon Treaty (Gisclair 2009). In 2002, after years of negotiation, agreement was reached on the conservation of Yukon River salmon between the U.S. and Canada.

This agreement created a bilateral Yukon River Panel, a process to set harvest quotas, and established management plans for Canadian-origin salmon stocks. The focus of the panel is on salmon stocks that pass through the Alaskan portion of the Yukon River and spawn in the Canadian part of the drainage; these stocks require U.S. protection to ensure adequate numbers pass upstream for spawning and to provide for fisheries in Canada. The panel makes recommendations to management agencies in both countries. A Joint Technical Committee composed of fishery managers and scientists from both countries advises the panel.

Though complex jurisdictionally, some common characteristics exist within the AYK salmon management regimes. First, ADFG, the Federal Subsistence Board, the Regional Fishery Management Council, NPAFC, and DFO manage for the conservation of salmon populations and sustainable fisheries. Second, subsistence fisheries have priority for harvest allocation over sport and commercial fisheries by all agencies. This priority for subsistence fisheries, in part, drives a third common characteristic: stakeholder involvement. Solicitation of stakeholder advice within all agencies is well organized through advisory bodies that have regular meetings with the management agencies. Nevertheless, while the governance entities share these common characteristics, cross-cutting mechanisms do not exist to harmonize their activities beyond the reliance on members to share their knowledge about how the other entities operate.

Discussion

Multi-jurisdictional governance is essential in the Great Lakes region and therefore, the governance regime established for the Great Lakes region—the Joint Strategic Plan—is highly tailored to the region. The plan emerged out of several unique conditions including the existence of diffuse authority, nonfederal autonomy, a strong interest in maintaining jurisdictional independence, the threat of federal pre-emption of nonfederal responsibilities, the existence of a neutral third party (the Great Lakes Fishery Commission) to facilitate the Joint Strategic Plan process, and a mutual interest in strategic planning (Gaden 2007). By being a nonbinding agreement that focuses on shared goals and objectives, the plan respects jurisdictional independence. Had the plan not done so, it would either have been a weak agreement or would not have been adhered to. The plan calls for the development of shared fishery management strategies and operational plans, and, thus, focuses on the jurisdictions' mutual interest in seeking and fulfilling mutual goals, instead of constraining behavior. The plan relies on science and the field-level work of the technical committees, thus underpinning shared decisions on sound information and making the policies more defensible. Finally, the plan depends on strong personal relationships among the fishery managers, as personal relationships lead to a strengthened epistemic community, trust, confidence that decisions will be implemented, and caring about future interactions (Axelrod 1984; Gaden 2007; Haas 1992).

The reliance on personal relationships among the fishery managers is probably the plan's most important design principle. People and how they relate to each other are fundamental to the Joint Strategic Plan process. The process encourages members to know one another, as familiarity spawns trust or, at a minimum, an understanding that today's interactions will affect future interactions (Axelrod 1984). The plan is designed to enhance the chances that members will care about the future by helping them benefit professionally from interactions, by creating opportunities for rewarding social interactions, and by helping avoid future opportunity costs. Strong personal relationships help members agree to courses of action with confidence that each will do their best to implement the decisions in the home jurisdiction.

Strong relationships built on trust, moreover, significantly enhance the chances that the shared decisions will be implemented. Fishery managers of the Great Lakes region are like-minded and operate as an epistemic community, a community of individuals who speak the same language and understand each others' perspectives. The lake committee members communicate their philosophies, often have common mentors, and were educated in similar biological programs. The lake committee and technical committee meetings are a place for these like-minded individuals to talk science and management. Members of this fishery management community know when science is not being adhered to, they care about the collegial community, and they are often familiar enough with each other to disagree without jeopardizing future interactions. The social functions and other outings make the meetings more enjoyable, but they also are a place to discuss issues, express new ideas, and help the members get to know one another better. These interactions are based on strong relationships, and such relationships are a key characteristic of the lake committee process.

Perhaps most relevant to relationships in the Joint Strategic Plan process is precisely the fact that human interactions are fragile. Members are generally sensitive to the consequences of diplomatic missteps or acting in a recalcitrant manner. Not only does such behavior make relationships unpleasant, but members jeopardize future relations and opportunities. Because the Joint Strategic Plan process is voluntary, dependent on the goodwill of all for it to succeed, and could lead to substantial rewards for cooperative relationships, members likely pay extra attention to protecting and building relationships by taking great pains to work well with others. The Joint Strategic Plan benefited from the fact that lake committees existed for fifteen years before the plan was produced. This pre-existence of a solid, respected, science-based epistemic community helped the plan from the start, as the members did not have to first establish the relationships needed for them to work together effectively.

Similarities and differences exist between fishery management in the Great Lakes and salmon management in the AYK region. First, the fish of the Great Lakes readily move across political boundaries, circumscribing governance as easily as salmon swim in the North Pacific and between the State of Alaska and Yukon Territory. As a result, management throughout the entire life cycle requires cooperation among multiple jurisdictions. Second, among jurisdictions in the Great Lakes and AYK, interests in conservation, restoration, and the sustainability of the fisheries are shared and held in common among agencies. Third, although common interests occur, differences in management focus also exist among individual jurisdictions within both the Great Lakes and the AYK region. For example, walleye *Sander vitreus* and yellow perch *Perca flavescens* are managed for a commercial fishery by the Province of Ontario in Lake Erie, in contrast to the State of Ohio which manages solely for sport fisheries in Lake Erie for the same species. In Alaskan freshwaters, the federal government is solely concerned with the management of salmon for subsistence fisheries, whereas the State of Alaska, while having a similar priority for subsistence fisheries, must also balance the interests of commercial and sport fisheries.

Three striking differences occur between the management regimes of the Great Lakes and the AYK region. First, the histories that resulted in current agency relationships are different. The Joint Strategic Plan in the Great Lakes arose in the late 1970s in part out of a concern among the states about the possibility for federal intrusion into state management authority with the potential establishment of a federally led fishery management council in the Great Lakes region through the Magnuson Act (or FCMA). In contrast, whereas the state of Alaska did not want federal fisheries management intrusion into freshwaters, these fears were realized with the assumption of authority for subsistence fishery management on federal lands in 1999 (Bulkis 2002). From this assumption of authority arose the management regime in Alaskan waters of the AYK region.

Second, in the Great Lakes, sub-national governments were partly driven to cooperation by a sincere interest to strategically seek and fulfill shared interests. Organization in the Great Lakes basin was voluntary and exists only so long as it fulfills the needs of the fishery management agencies. In the AYK region, however, additional jurisdictions also arose, not through a common interest, but through a court order, federal legislation, and bi- and multi-lateral agreements. For instance, the state and federal jurisdictions managing subsistence fisheries were not a voluntary marriage, but one of force ordered by federal court. The genesis by force of the AYK partnership makes it fragile at best and adversarial at worst.

Third, in the Great Lakes region, the larger fishery research and management community including provincial, state, tribal, federal, and university participants are linked together through an epistemic community of like-minded professionals who interact regularly through ongoing processes—the lake committees and technical committees. In contrast, the management and research community of the AYK region is fragmented. For example, the Yukon River Joint Technical Committee, as part of the Pacific Salmon Treaty between U.S. and Canada, does not meet with the Kuskokwim Salmon Working Group (Linderman and Bergstrom 2009), even though they have common interests concerning salmon bycatch in the Bering Sea

(Gisclair 2009; Haflinger and Gruver 2009; Stram and Ianelli 2009). No overarching forum exists comparable to the Joint Strategic Plan, the lake committees, and the Great Lakes Fishery Commission that connects all those involved in the marine and freshwater regions that support salmon life history and AYK fisheries. The development of such a forum would promote coordinated management of salmon throughout the entire life cycle and be consistent with the ecosystem management approach.

Based on the Great Lakes experience, what might the future hold for management of AYK fisheries? With the passage of time, AYK management can benefit from a deliberate effort to develop relationships among all agencies and individuals involved in the management of salmon throughout their life cycle. An analogous situation occurred in the Great Lakes when aboriginal interests were afforded management authority over treaty ceded waters in the 1980s (Gaden 2007). During the first ten or so years, considerable resentment occurred among state fishery managers over this change in management authority. Nevertheless, over time the presence of tribal authorities was accepted, and now 25 years later tribal representatives are regarded as full peers on the lake committees and lake technical committees, often serving in leadership roles on those committees. In the AYK region, participants should endeavor to establish formal processes to meet regularly and connect the four management tracks. Likely, with time, as federal subsistence and state fishery managers continue their involvement together, participants will come to better trust each other as full partners in cooperative management of salmon.

One possible pathway to improved cooperative management of AYK salmon can be developed based on the Great Lakes experience. Many of the elements are already occurring in the AYK region and likely only need the passage of time to fully mature. First, common or shared interests among the management jurisdictions need to be identified and documented. Some have already been identified in this paper, and others undoubtedly exist. Identifying the shared interests provides the platform for cooperative management to occur. Second, from these shared interests, mutual goals of management can be developed and identified among the management jurisdictions. The development of the Joint Strategic Plan in the Great Lakes served this purpose. In particular, a commitment in the AYK region to an ecosystem approach for salmon management, characterized by working across political boundaries and integrating multiple disciplines into fishery management, could provide the conceptual construct to link different jurisdictions and interests. Third, information sharing has been a critically important step in the Great Lakes management under the Joint Strategic Plan and should be an important element in the AYK region as well. Information is power, and if participants come to consensus on data collection and interpretation, and if the same information is available to everyone, then better, more defensible policies emerge and the playing field is leveled for all participants in the management process. The sharing of honest and high quality biological, social, and political information about management of the salmon fisheries should occur. Full disclosure of information about AYK salmon will engender trust and respect among the management participants. Fourth, when trust and respect are built over time, a commitment to consensus decision making becomes possible. The passage of time is an important element because it allows judgment of the consistency and honesty of behavior. Fifth, consensus decision making, when combined with trust and respect, will permit the development of the requisite accountability mechanisms that will ensure cooperative management.

Conclusion

Management authority over the Great Lakes fishery is spread among several non-federal jurisdictions, with some involvement by the Canadian and U.S. federal governments and the bi-national Great Lakes Fishery Commission. While each jurisdiction's scope of authority is relatively clear and respected, the lack of an overarching mechanism to transcend political boundaries existed for much of the history of the Great Lakes fishery and resulted in parochial or uncooperative behavior. Lake committees were formed in the 1960s to help bridge jurisdictional divides and the interactions became more strategic in 1981 with the adoption of *A Joint Strategic Plan for Management of Great Lakes Fisheries*. Agencies use the Joint Strategic Plan to reach consensus about their shared objectives, to share information, to pool resources, and to approach the fishery management in a more holistic fashion. The plan formalized a culture of cooperation that emerged from the lake committees of the 1960s and 1970s by providing a process for members to work together, reach consensus, pledge accountability to each other, exchange information, and manage the lakes as an ecosystem. Because the plan generated from the jurisdictions and was developed to serve the jurisdictions, members have a sense of ownership in the Joint Strategic Plan which heightens the chances that compliance with shared decisions will occur, even in the absence of provisions that bind.

The Joint Strategic Plan process helps fishery managers in the Great Lakes basin get to know each other and develop durable, working relationships, which builds trust and understanding. Above all, the process is rooted in science, as it relies on the work of the technical committees as the foundation for management decisions. The plan is highly suited to the governance conditions that emerged in the

Great Lakes, particularly the diffuse authority vested in the nonfederal jurisdictions, the fact that the jurisdictions wish to preserve their sovereignty, and the strong interest in seeking mutual objectives. By respecting jurisdictional independence, relying on science, calling for shared objectives and plans, and developing personal relationships, the Joint Strategic Plan contains design principles that help it succeed and make it robust.

The experiences with the Joint Strategic Plan in the Great Lakes might profitably be applied to AYK salmon management. Identification of shared interests, development of common goals, adoption of ecosystem management as an explicit foundation, information sharing, building of relationships among agencies and individuals, adoption of consensus decision making, and the use of accountability mechanisms could all serve to promote cooperative salmon management in the AYK region. We believe that an overarching mechanism or institution is required that would connect the management interests from international waters, the Bering Sea, and North Pacific to the upper Yukon River in Yukon Territory and everything in-between in a common forum. Such a mechanism could be in the form of a nonbinding joint strategic plan for management of AYK salmon fisheries as is used in the Great Lakes. The advantages to such an agreement is its informal and nonbinding nature that does not threaten jurisdictional or constitutional authorities. Regardless of the mechanism used, connecting all of the agencies affecting the salmon life cycle and fisheries should foster cooperative and effective AYK salmon management.

Acknowledgments

We thank the Great Lakes Fishery Commission for supporting this research and the Arctic-Yukon-Kuskokwim Sustainable Salmon Initiative for their invitation to participate in the symposium. We are also grateful to Barry Rabe of the University of Michigan, Elizabeth Brabec of Utah State University, Ann Chih Lin of the University of Michigan, and Denise Scheberle of the University of Wisconsin—Green Bay for their extensive comments on early versions of this manuscript. Finally, comments from John Hilsinger of the Alaska Department of Fish and Game greatly improved this article.

References

Axelrod, R. 1984. The evolution of cooperation. Basic Books, United States of America.

Bogue, M. B. 2000. Fishing the Great Lakes: an environmental history, 1833–1933. University of Wisconsin Press, Madison.

Brown, R. W., M. Ebener, and T. Gorenflo. 1999. Great Lakes commercial fisheries: Historical overview and prognosis for the future. *In* W. W. Taylor, and C. P. Ferreri, editors. Great Lakes fisheries policy and management: A binational perspective. Michigan State University Press, East Lansing.

Bue, F., J., B. M. Borba, R. Cannon, and C. C. Krueger. 2009. Yukon River fall chum salmon fisheries: management, harvest, and stock abundance. Pages 703–742 *in* C. C. Krueger, and C. E. Zimmerman, editors. Pacific salmon: ecology and management of western Alaska's populations. American Fisheries Society, Symposium 70, Bethesda, Maryland.

Bulkis, L. S. 2002. Subsistence fisheries management on federal public lands in Alaska. Fisheries 27(7):10–18.

Busiahn, T. R. 1985. An introduction to native peoples' fisheries issues in North America. Renewable Resources Journal 3(2):23–26.

Cobb, E. W. 1916. Federal control of interstate waters. Transactions of the American Fisheries Society 46:26–29.

Cohen. 1988. Cohen's handbook of federal Indian law. United States Government Printing Office, Washington, D.C.

Crowe, D. M. 1983. Comprehensive planning for wildlife resources. Wyoming Game and Fish Department, Cheyenne.

Dochoda, M. R. 1999. Authorities, responsibilities, and arrangements for managing fish and fisheries in the Great Lakes ecosystem. Pages 93–110 *in* W. W. Taylor, and C. P. Ferreri, editors. Great Lakes fisheries policy and management: a binational perspective. Michigan State University Press, East Lansing.

Donahue, M. 1988. Institutional arrangements for

Great Lakes management. L. K. Caldwell, editor. Perspectives on ecosystem management for the Great Lakes: A reader. State University of New York Press, Albany, New York.

Fetterolf, C. M. 1980. Why a Great Lakes Fishery Commission and why a Sea Lamprey International Symposium? Canadian Journal of Fisheries and Aquatic Sciences 37(11):1588–1593.

Furlong, D. T. 2002. Fishery Management Councils. Improving Regional Ocean Governance in the United States. U.S. Commission on Ocean Policy, Washington, D.C.

Gaden, M. 2007. Bridging jurisdictional divides: Collective action through A Joint Strategic Plan for Management of Great Lakes Fisheries. Doctoral dissertation. University of Michigan, Ann Arbor, Michigan.

Gallagher, H. R., A. G. Huntsman, D. J. Taylor, and J. Van Oosten. 1942. Report and Supplement. U.S. Government Printing Office, Washington, D.C.

GAO. 1976. Action is needed now to protect our fishery resources, GGD-76–34. U.S. General Accounting Office. Available: archive.gao.gov/f0202/093787.pdf (October 2006).

Gibson, D. 1973. Constitutional jurisdiction over environmental management in Canada. University of Toronto Law Journal 23:54–87.

Gisclair, R. R. 2009. Salmon bycatch management in the Bearing Sea walleye pollock fishery: threats and opportunities for western Alaska. Pages 799–816 in C. C. Krueger, and C. E. Zimmerman, editors. Pacific salmon: ecology and management of western Alaska's populations. American Fisheries Society, Symposium 70, Bethesda, Maryland.

GLFC. 1964. Minutes, Great Lakes Fishery Commission Interim Meeting, December 2 and 3, 1964. Great Lakes Fishery Commission, editor. Great Lakes Fishery Commission Annual and Interim Meetings 1964–1965, Ann Arbor, Michigan.

GLFC. 1997. A Joint Strategic Plan for Management of Great Lakes Fisheries. Great Lakes Fishery Commission, Ann Arbor, Michigan.

Grumbine, R. E. 1994. What is ecosystem management? Conservation Biology 8:1–12.

Haas, P. M. 1992. Introduction: Epistemic communities and international policy coordination. International Organization 46(1):1–35.

Haflinger, K., and J. Gruver. 2009. Rolling hot spot closure areas in the Bering Sea walleye pollock fishery: estimated reduction of salmon bycatch during the 2006 season. Pages 817–826 in C. C. Krueger, and C. E. Zimmerman, editors. Pacific salmon: ecology and management of western Alaska's populations. American Fisheries Society, Symposium 70, Bethesda, Maryland.

Hansen, M. J., editor. 1996. A lake trout restoration plan for Lake Superior. Great Lakes Fishery Commission, Ann Arbor, Michigan.

Hartig, J. H. 1997. Great Lakes Remedial Action Plans: Fostering adaptive ecosystem-based management processes. The American Review of Canadian Studies 27(3):437–458.

Hinrichs, H. J. 1913. Federal control over fish in boundary waters. Transactions of the American Fisheries Society 42:129–132.

Holmes, O. W. 1920. State of Missouri v. Holland, United States Game Warden. Pages 255–257 in S. Goldman, editor. Constitutional law: Cases and essays. Harper Collins, New York.

Joslyn, C. D. 1905. The policy of ceding the control of the Great Lakes from state to national supervision. Transactions of the American Fisheries Society 34:217–222.

Killian, J. H., and L. E. Beck, editors. 1987. The Constitution of the United States of America: analysis and interpretation, annotations of cases decided by the Supreme Court of the United States to July 2, 1982. Congressional Research Service, Library of Congress and U.S. Government Printing Office, Washington, D.C.

Knaebel, E. 1920. Missouri v. Holland. 252 United States Reports 416. Banks and Brothers, New York.

Krueger, C. C., and D. J. Decker. 1999. The process of fisheries management. Pages 31–59 in C. C. Kohler, and W. A. Hubert, editors. Inland fisheries management in North America, 2nd edition. American Fisheries Society, Bethesda, Maryland.

Lamb, B. L., and D. Lybecker. 1999. Legal considerations in inland fisheries management. Pages 83–109 in C. C. Kohler, and W. A. Hubert, editors. Inland fisheries management in North America, 2nd edition. American Fisheries Society, Bethesda, Maryland.

Linderman, J. C., Jr., and D. J. Bergstrom. 2009. Kuskokwim management area: salmon escapement, harvest, and management. Pages 541–599 in C. C. Krueger, and C. E. Zimmerman, editors. Pacific salmon: ecology and management of western Alaska's populations. American Fisheries Society, Symposium 70, Bethesda, Maryland.

Michigan Supreme Court. 1971. People v. Jondreau, 384 Mich. 539. Michigan Supreme Court.

Michigan Supreme Court. 1976. People v. LeBlanc, 399 Mich. 31. Michigan Supreme Court.

Moore, J. N. 1965. Federalism and foreign relations. Duke Law Journal 1965(2):248–321.

Nielsen, L. A. 1999. History of inland fisheries management in North America. Pages 3–30 in C. C. Kohler, and W. A. Hubert, editors. Inland fisheries management in North America, 2nd edition.

American Fisheries Society, Bethesda, Maryland.

Ollivier, M. 1962. British North America acts and selected statutes, 1867–1962. Queen's Printer, Ottawa.

Pacific Fishery Management Council. 2005. Information sheet: The Magnuson-Stevens Act. Pacific Fishery Management Council. Available: www.pcouncil.org/facts/msact.pdf (January 2007).

Peters, R. [1832] 1901. Worcester v. Georgia. Pages 515 in S. K. Williams, editor. 31 U.S. Supreme Court Reports 515, volume 31. The Lawyers Cooperative Publishing Company, Rochester, New York.

Piper, D. 1967. The international law of the Great Lakes: a study of Canadian-United States Cooperation. Duke University Press, Durham, North Carolina.

R. v. Sparrow. 1990. 1 S.C.R. 1075, 70 D.L.R. (4th) 385, 46 B.C.L.R. (2d) 1.

Rabe, B. G. 1997. The politics of ecosystem management in the Great Lakes basin. The American Review of Canadian Studies 27(3):411–436.

Raustiala, K., and D. G. Victor. 1998. Conclusions. Pages 659–708 in D. G. Victor, K. Raustiala, and E. B. Skolnikoff, editors. The implementation and effectiveness of international environmental commitments: Theory and practice. The MIT Press, Cambridge, Massachusetts.

Rideout, S. G., and J. A. Ritter. 2002. Canadian and U.S. Atlantic salmon institutions and politics: where are the fish and who cares? Pages 93–116 in K. D. Lynch, M. L. Jones, and W. W. Taylor, editors. Sustaining North American salmon: perspectives across regions and disciplines. American Fisheries Society, Bethesda, Maryland.

Ryan, P. A., R. Knights, R. MacGregor, G. Towns, R. Hoopes, and W. Culligan. 2003. Fish-Community goals and objectives for Lake Erie. Great Lakes Fishery Commission, Ann Arbor.

Schlender, J. H. (undated). The impact of the *Voight* case: On-going and upcoming issues. Great Lakes Indian Fish and Wildlife Commission, Odanah, Wisconsin.

Stram, D. L., and J. N. Ianelli. 2009. Eastern Bering Sea pollock trawl fisheries: variation in salmon bycatch over time and space. Pages 827–850 in C. C. Krueger, and C. E. Zimmerman, editors. Pacific salmon: ecology and management of western Alaska's populations. American Fisheries Society, Symposium 70, Bethesda, Maryland.

Thompson, P. C. 1974. Institutional constraints in fisheries management. Journal of the Fisheries Research Board of Canada 31:1966–1981.

United States Court of Appeals. 1983. LacCourte Oreilles v. Voight, 700 F. 2nd 342. United States Court of Appeals, 7th Circuit.

United States District Court. 1979. U.S. v. Michigan, 623 F2d 448. United States District Court, Western District, Michigan.

USGPO. 1918. Migratory Bird Treaty Act, volume 16 U.S.C. 703–712. U.S. Government Printing Office, Washington, D. C.

USGPO. 1976. Magnuson-Stevens Fishery Conservation and Management Act, volume 16 U.S.C. 1801–1882. U.S. Government Printing Office, Washington, D. C.

Victor, D. G. 1997. The use and effectiveness of nonbinding instruments in the management of complex international environmental problems. Pages 241–250 in M. Gavouneli, editor. American Society of International Law. Proceedings of the 91st Annual Meeting. Compliance with international environmental treaties: the empirical evidence. 11 April, Washington, D. C.

Weiss, E. B. 1999. The emerging structure of international environmental law. Pages 98–115 in N. J. Vig, and R. S. Axelrod, editors. The global environment. Congressional Quarterly Press, Washington, D.C.

Willoughby, W. R. 1979. The joint organizations of Canada and the United States. The University of Toronto Press, Toronto.

Zimmerman, J. F. 2002. Interstate cooperation: Compacts and administrative agreements. Praeger, Westport, Connecticut.

Zorn, J. E. 1989. General principles of Indian law. Great Lakes Indian Fish and Wildlife Commission, Odanah, Wisconsin.

Management

American Fisheries Society Symposium 70:963–976, 2009

Management of the Nushagak District Sockeye Salmon Fishery: How 50 Years of Data Helps

TIMOTHY T. BAKER[*]

Alaska Department of Fish and Game, Division of Commercial Fisheries
333 Raspberry Road, Anchorage, Alaska 99518, USA

TIM SANDS

Alaska Department of Fish and Game, Division of Commercial Fisheries
P.O. Box 230, Dillingham, Alaska 99576, USA

FRED WEST

Alaska Department of Fish and Game, Division of Commercial Fisheries
333 Raspberry Road, Anchorage, Alaska 99518, USA

CHARLOTTE WESTING

Alaska Department of Fish and Game, Division of Wildlife Conservation
P.O. Box 689, Kotzebue, Alaska 99752, USA

CHUCK BRAZIL

Alaska Department of Fish and Game, Division of Sport Fish
333 Raspberry Road, Anchorage, Alaska 99518, USA

Abstract.—The Nushagak Management District includes the drainages of the Wood, Nushagak-Mulchatna and Igushik rivers. Sockeye salmon *Oncorhynchus nerka* have been commercially harvested in the rivers and adjacent marine waters since at least 1893, but it was not until the mid-1950s that consistent escapement data began to be collected for active inseason management. Escapement refers to salmon that have survived (escaped) the fisheries in Bristol Bay and have entered rivers to spawn. Managers now have 50+ years of escapement and harvest data by year class (brood tables) for most systems in Bristol Bay. Brood tables provide excellent information on spawners versus recruits, sibling relationships, and other trends that help with setting escapement goals and forecasting future returns. Catch plus escapement information was used to predict run timing and total run abundance, information useful to inseason management decision making. Comparisons of inseason escapement counts and historical escapement curves are relied on by managers making day-to-day decisions to open and close the commercial fisheries. The managers' primary goal in managing the commercial fisheries is to ensure escapement goals are met in all three river systems while maximizing catch. The long-term catch and escapement datasets for the Nushagak District systems were used to establish stock-specific escapement goals and pre-season run-size forecasting. Daily escapement estimates, aerial surveys, test fishing, and genetic information are essential. Escapement to spawning rivers can exceed 600,000 sockeye salmon in 24 hours.

[*]Corresponding author: tim.baker@alaska.gov

Introduction

Good quality long-term data sets are helpful in the management of large commercial salmon fisheries. One of the largest and most important salmon fisheries in Alaska is the commercial sockeye salmon *Oncorhynchus nerka* fishery that occurs in Bristol Bay (Figure 1). The State of Alaska's Bristol Bay management area includes all coastal and inland waters east of a line from Cape Newenham to Cape Menshikof (Figure 1). The area includes nine major river systems: Ugashik, Egegik, Naknek, Alagnak, Kvichak, Nushagak, Wood, Igushik, and Togiak rivers. Collectively, these rivers are home to the largest commercial sockeye salmon fishery in the world. Sockeye salmon are by far the most abundant salmon species that return to Bristol Bay each year. Chinook *O. tshawytcha*, chum *O. keta*, coho *O. kisutch*, and pink salmon (in even-years) *O. gorbuscha* are also found in smaller numbers than sockeye salmon. The Bristol Bay management area is divided into five management districts (Ugashik, Egegik, Naknek-Kvichak, Nushagak, and Togiak).

Commercial fisheries for sockeye salmon in Bristol Bay were initiated in Nushagak Bay in 1884 after an initial exploratory effort was conducted in 1883 of salting salmon for preservation and transport (Moser 1902). In 1893, salmon catches began to be reported in terms of species and number of fish (Rich and Ball 1928). Since then, gillnets and fish traps have been the preferred methods to capture sockeye salmon. Gillnets were more effective than seines in the strong currents, narrow channels, and soft muddy beaches of the Nushagak Bay. Fish traps and seines were prohibited by law in 1924 (Nelson 1987).

The U.S. federal government was responsible for managing the Bristol Bay fisheries until Alaska Statehood in 1959, when the State of Alaska became responsible for fishery management (Hilsinger et al. 2009, this

volume. With Statehood, local fishery managers were given the authority to open and close fisheries during the summer fishing season (inseason management). The primary goal of management is to ensure that adequate numbers of salmon escape the fisheries to spawn (escapement). The secondary goal is to harvest the surplus of fish in excess of escapement needs, for the maximum benefit of users. The management of fisheries also seeks to have sustainable fisheries, to maintain genetic diversity, to provide for an orderly fishery, and to produce a high-quality product. The Alaska Department of Fish and Game (ADF&G) has the responsibility to manage the fisheries under the regulations and policies set forth by the Alaska Board of Fisheries (BOF) in regulatory management plans. The management plans are designed to promote the conservation of stocks of fish and to specify allocations of fish to the different user groups (commercial fisheries, sport fisheries, subsistence). ADF&G's highest priority is to obtain the escapement goals established for the salmon stocks.

Fishery managers need quality long-term data sets to effectively manage large commercial salmon fisheries like those found in Bristol Bay. Bristol Bay fishery managers are fortunate to have long-term data sets of total production (catch and escapement) for sockeye salmon to inform management decision making. Based on these data sets, escapement goals are established which then become a focus for management to achieve each year.

One of the most important sockeye salmon fisheries in Bristol Bay occurs in the Nushagak District (Figure 2). The Nushagak District is in the northwestern portion of Bristol Bay. Three large river systems flow into the Nushagak District: Wood, Nushagak, and Igushik rivers. The commercial sockeye salmon fishery occurs during the summer season. All salmon may be harvested from June 1 through September 30 during open commercial salmon fishing periods established by emergency order. The majority of sockeye

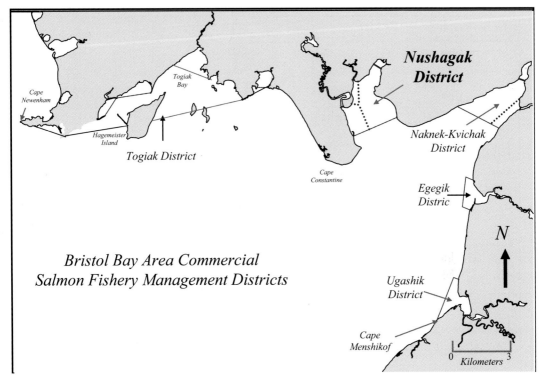

FIGURE 1. Map of Bristol Bay area commercial salmon fishery management districts, Alaska.

salmon are commercially harvested in Nushagak District from June 20 to July 20. Sockeye salmon are taken with both set and drift gillnets. Set gillnets are fished from shore and drift gillnets are fished from boats that cannot exceed 32 ft in length. In this paper, we use the Nushagak District as an example of how long-term data sets are used to help managers make decisions to effectively manage large commercial salmon fisheries.

What Data Are Collected?

The ADF&G estimates salmon escapements in the Wood, Nushagak and Igushik rivers. Counting towers are used to obtain visual counts of sockeye salmon in the Wood and Igushik rivers while hydroacoustics (sonar) is used to enumerate sockeye salmon in the Nushagak River. Daily escapement estimates have been made for sockeye salmon from 1956 to 2006 for the Wood and Igushik rivers and from 1980 to 2006 for the Nushagak River. Daily estimates of harvest in the Nushagak District have been made from 1969 to 2006. Total annual estimates of harvest extend back to 1893.

Age composition of sockeye salmon in the harvest and escapement were estimated each year. The age of salmon was determined by examining patterns of growth observed in scales. Age and growth can be differentiated between freshwater and saltwater life stages. European notation (2.2; Koo 1962) was used to record ages; numerals preceding the decimal refer to the number of freshwater annuli and numerals following the decimal refer to the number of marine annuli. Total age of the fish from the time of egg deposition equals the sum of these numbers plus one. A sampling program exists to collect scales from sockeye salmon from the commercial

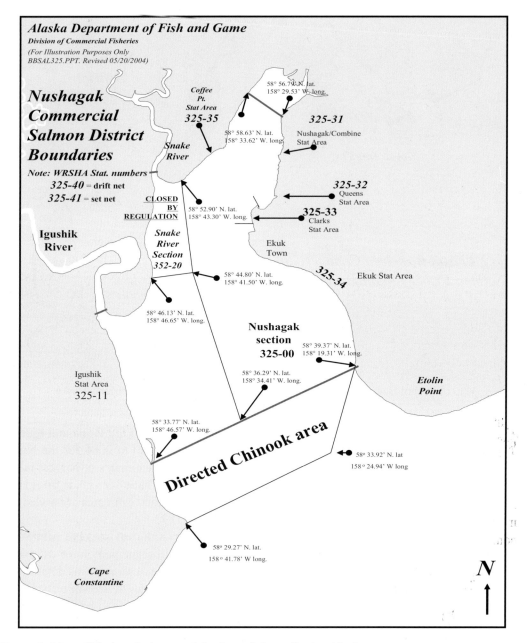

FIGURE 2. Map of Nushagak commercial salmon fishery district, Alaska.

harvest and escapement projects in the rivers. Age-class composition of the harvest and spawning runs were estimated each year. The dominant age classes in the Nushagak District have been age 1.2 and age 1.3 fish and to a lesser extent age 2.2, age 2.3, age 0.3 and age 1.4 fish.

Harvest, escapement, and age composition estimates were combined to estimate the total run size (numbers of fish) for each of the major river systems in the Nushagak District. Total run estimates by age-class have been used to create brood-year tables (abundance by year-class) from 1956—2001 for Wood and Igushik rivers and from 1980–2001 for Nushagak River (Tables 1–3). The sockeye brood-year tables presented here show the number of sockeye salmon that escaped to spawn in that year (escapement) and the number of sockeye salmon by age-class that were produced and returned in subsequent years. For instance in Table 1, the escapement was 1.300 million sockeye salmon in brood year 2000 and the total return was 6.116 million sockeye salmon (Table 1). This total return for brood year 2000 was comprised of 3.184 million age 1.2 fish that returned in 2004; 2.181 million age 1.3 fish that returned in 2005; 120 thousand age 2.2 fish that returned in 2005; and 564 thousand age 2.3 fish that returned in 2006 (Table 1). The return per spawner (R/S) in brood year 2000 was 4.70 sockeye salmon per spawner.

The total run estimates for each of the river systems in the Nushagak District requires that the harvest in the district be correctly allocated to each river. Harvest in the Nushagak District to the Wood, Nushagak and Igushik rivers is allocated using a method based on the age composition that was developed by Bernard (1983). This method separates the harvest by age-class based on the proportion of each age-class observed in each of the escapements. One of the assumptions of this method is that each of the stocks present is equally exploited in the commercial fishery. However, this assumption has probably been invalid in some years. The effect of incorrectly allocating the harvest can have large impacts on the total run size estimates in brood tables. In the case of the Nushagak District, the Wood River is not as likely to be affected because the production from the Wood River is much greater than that of the Nushagak and Igushik rivers. Conversely, the impacts of misallocation to the Nushagak and Igushik rivers are probably much larger than to the Wood River due to their smaller relative production. The current catch allocation method also assumes that only fish from the three river systems (Wood, Nushagak and Igushik) are present in the Nushagak District fishery (no contributions from other nearby systems).

Because of concerns about catch allocation by stock within Bristol Bay, the ADF&G has conducted numerous stock identification studies over the years. In the 1980s, scale-pattern analysis was used to identify stocks within Bristol Bay (Cross and Stratton 1989, 1991; Miller 1995; Stratton and Miller 1993, 1994; Stratton at al. 1992; Van Alen 1982). Beginning in the late 1990s, genetic markers began to be used to identify different stocks of sockeye salmon in Bristol Bay (Habicht et al. 2007). The use of genetic markers has made it possible to better identify the origin of the major stocks of sockeye salmon in Bristol Bay and their contributions to harvest than in the past (Habicht et al. 2007). Eventually, this information will be used to adjust the total run and brood tables for all rivers within Bristol Bay.

Brood Tables: Estimates of Total Return by Year Class

The average total return of sockeye salmon to the Nushagak District (Wood, Igushik, and Nushagak rivers) from the brood years 1980–2000 was 6.575 million sockeye

TABLE 1. Wood River sockeye salmon escapement and return by brood year, 1950–2006.

Brood Year	Escapement	Return by Age Class (in thousands of fish)										Total	R/S [a]
		0.2	1.1	0.3	1.2	2.1	0.4	1.3	2.2	1.4	2.3		
1950	0 [b]	0 [c]	0 [c]	0 [c]	0 [c]	0 [c]	0 [c]	0 [c]	0 [c]	1	57	58 [d]	
1951	0 [b]	0 [c]	0 [c]	0 [c]	0 [c]	0 [c]	0	456	290	3	54	803 [d]	
1952	0 [b]	0 [c]	0 [c]	0	690	0	0	558	29	2	34	1,313 [d]	
1953	0 [b]	0	0	0	301	0	0	331	139	2	34	807	
1954	0 [b]	0	0	0	1,237	0	0	140	1,085	1	66	2,529	
1955	0 [b]	0	0	0	2,407	0	0	833	401	5	143	3,789	
1956	773	0	0	48	774	0	0	627	24	0	0	1,473	1.91
1957	289	0	0	21	136	0	0	257	35	0	0	449	1.56
1958	960	0	1	0	2,145	1	0	389	75	0	32	2,643	2.75
1959	2,209	0	0	1	979	10	0	398	359	1	55	1,803	0.82
1960	1,016	0	6	0	1,474	0	0	1,039	106	2	105	2,733	2.69
1961	461	0	0	10	255	0	0	1,183	24	2	20	1,494	3.24
1962	874	1	2	0	992	1	2	340	116	6	43	1,503	1.72
1963	721	0	0	0	536	1	0	769	76	0	46	1,428	1.98
1964	1,076	0	1	6	452	0	0	347	338	0	74	1,218	1.13
1965	675	2	1	8	472	1	0	999	90	0	213	1,785	2.65
1966	1,209	0	7	29	974	0	0	988	46	7	69	2,120	1.75
1967	516	0	3	21	642	0	0	269	75	2	80	1,092	2.12
1968	649	0	1	0	514	0	0	565	5	4	19	1,108	1.71
1969	604	0	0	4	57	0	0	445	201	10	116	833	1.38
1970	1,162	0	2	0	1,539	0	0	1,002	231	0	26	2,800	2.41
1971	851	3	0	18	456	0	0	576	198	1	49	1,301	1.53
1972	431	2	1	22	779	0	0	631	32	20	27	1,514	3.51
1973	330	1	1	0	213	0	0	1,148	74	3	44	1,484	4.50
1974	1,709	0	3	6	2,956	4	0	1,698	421	5	71	5,164	3.02
1975	1,270	13	47	12	1,592	2	0	1,977	406	2	734	4,785	3.77
1976	817	0	3	0	2,278	3	0	2,589	572	10	265	5,720	7.00
1977	562	0	20	0	1,029	0	0	2,173	40	0	26	3,288	5.85
1978	2,267	0	0	0	1,364	3	0	1,029	784	12	96	3,288	1.45
1979	1,706	0	10	0	2,643	0	0	1,491	24	1	13	4,182	2.45
1980	2,969	0	0	0	453	0	0	978	72	1	101	1,605	0.54
1981	1,233	0	0	0	626	0	0	1,137	60	0	86	1,909	1.55
1982	976	0	4	0	522	0	0	765	121	12	14	1,438	1.47
1983	1,361	0	1	5	1,940	0	2	1,154	15	2	75	3,194	2.35
1984	1,003	0	0	0	586	0	2	1,340	32	15	23	1,998	1.99
1985	939	8	3	15	1,127	0	1	1,390	29	2	12	2,587	2.75
1986	819	7	2	25	1,179	0	1	1,970	70	12	64	3,330	4.07
1987	1,337	25	0	30	1,334	0	14	756	98	8	92	2,357	1.76
1988	867	4	1	8	1,613	0	3	1,425	90	15	34	3,193	3.68
1989	1,186	1	4	16	2,293	0	0	1,922	13	2	39	4,290	3.62
1990	1,069	10	1	10	1,104	1	3	1,208	286	2	169	2,794	2.61
1991	1,160	0	12	9	2,633	0	0	2,466	54	65	71	5,310	4.58
1992	1,286	10	1	57	2,398	0	2	1,674	90	0	49	4,281	3.33
1993	1,176	14	0	3	1,715	0	9	1,161	129	3	191	3,225	2.74
1994	1,472	0	10	0	2,747	1	0	1,993	448	2	91	5,292	3.59
1995	1,482	1	5	0	3,524	0	0	2,594	149	61	35	6,369	4.30
1996	1,650	0	0	0	2,705	0	0	3,675	3	58	13	6,454	3.91
1997	1,512	4	0	63	174	0	4	675	164	25	203	1,312	0.87
1998	1,756	0	3	11	2,910	1	0	3,516	176	9	104	6,729 [e]	3.83
1999	1,512	4	2	42	1,778	1	0	2,239	403	10	144	4,623 [d]	3.06
2000	1,300	0	3	5	3,184	0	0	2,181	120	59 [e]	564 [e]	6,116 [d]	4.70
2001	1,459	4	0	42	2,059	0	0 [e]	4,625 [e]	603 [e]	0 [d]	0 [d]	7,333 [d]	5.03
2002	1,284	15	36	0 [e]	5,783 [e]	0 [e]	0 [d]	0 [d]	0 [d]	0 [d]	0 [d]	5,834 [d]	4.54
2003	1,460	0 [e]	5 [e]	0 [d]	0 [d]	0 [d]	0 [d]	0 [d]	0 [d]	0 [d]	0 [d]	5 [d]	
2004	1,543	0 [d]	0 [d]	0 [d]	0 [d]	0 [d]	0 [d]	0 [d]	0 [d]	0 [d]	0 [d]	0 [d]	
2005	1,497	0 [d]	0 [d]	0 [d]	0 [d]	0 [d]	0 [d]	0 [d]	0 [d]	0 [d]	0 [d]	0 [d]	
2006	4,008	0 [d]	0 [d]	0 [d]	0 [d]	0 [d]	0 [d]	0 [d]	0 [d]	0 [d]	0 [d]	0 [d]	
1956-2001 Avg.													2.81

[a] R/S = return per spawner.
[b] Escapement not available.
[c] Younger age groups not available.
[d] Incomplete returns from brood year escapement.
[e] Estimate from 2006 preliminary return numbers.

TABLE 2. Nushagak River sockeye salmon escapement and return by brood year, 1974–2006.

Brood Year	Escapement [a]	Return by Age Class (in thousands of fish)									Total	R/S [b]
		0.2	1.1	0.3	1.2	0.4	1.3	2.2	1.4	2.3		
1974	185	[c]	[c]	[c]	[c]	[c]	[c]	[c]	[c]	[c]		
1975	752	[c]	[c]	[c]	[c]	[c]	[c]	[c]	[c]	[c]	0 [d]	
1976	470	[c]	[c]	[c]	[c]	[c]	[c]	[c]	38	281	319 [d]	
1977	553	[c]	[c]	[c]	[c]	67	1,946	3	134	11	2,161 [d]	
1978	664	[c]	[c]	436	100	149	779	20	1	6	1,490	2.24
1979	499	18	1	466	494	16	854	6	42	5	1,902	3.81
1980	3,317	19	0	447	84	67	344	162	4	156	1,284	0.39
1981	1,012	9	0	137	170	14	1,476	2	86	32	1,926	1.90
1982	601	35	0	351	164	49	894	2	62	7	1,563	2.60
1983	404	100	0	608	114	122	553	6	16	3	1,521	3.77
1984	593	10	0	226	51	32	566	2	20	6	912	1.54
1985	498	68	0	510	64	62	612	6	13	16	1,350	2.71
1986	990	68	0	837	114	58	676	0	182	64	1,999	2.02
1987	388	140	0	933	36	253	535	36	101	10	2,046	5.27
1988	483	68	0	546	214	120	1,426	12	62	8	2,457	5.09
1989	513	68	0	483	124	35	703	1	18	4	1,435	2.80
1990	680	53	0	761	36	104	253	18	11	7	1,243	1.83
1991	493	10	1	137	172	6	1,010	3	131	19	1,491	3.03
1992	695	85	0	496	228	11	650	9	63	11	1,551	2.23
1993	715	43	0	43	63	2	803	1	119	49	1,124	1.57
1994	509	0	0	55	81	2	665	6	9	53	872	1.71
1995	281	5	1	8	143	0	923	34	106	15	1,236	4.39
1996	504	0	0	6	502	5	1,795	3	58	5	2,374	4.71
1997	373	0	0	129	71	6	254	14	19	86	579	1.55
1998	459	2	0	10	312	3	1,633	64	182	80	2,286 [e]	4.98
1999	312	4	0	40	421	5	1,598	25	71	26	2,190 [d]	7.02
2000	404	7	0	89	233	10	2,892	23	402 [e]	43 [e]	3,699 [d]	9.16
2001	811	11	0	240	294	1 [e]	2,018 [e]	9 [e]	0 [d]	0 [d]	2,573 [d]	3.17
2002	316	10	0	66 [e]	185 [e]	0 [d]	0 [d]	0 [d]	0 [d]	0 [d]	261 [d]	0.83
2003	581	6 [e]	0 [e]	0 [d]	0 [d]	0 [d]	0 [d]	0 [d]	0 [d]	0 [d]	6 [d]	
2004	492	0 [d]	0 [d]	0 [d]	0 [d]	0 [d]	0 [d]	0 [d]	0 [d]	0 [d]	0 [d]	
2005	1,049	0 [d]	0 [d]	0 [d]	0 [d]	0 [d]	0 [d]	0 [d]	0 [d]	0 [d]	0 [d]	
2006	548	0 [d]	0 [d]	0 [d]	0 [d]	0 [d]	0 [d]	0 [d]	0 [d]	0 [d]	0 [d]	
1978-2001 Avg.												3.31

[a] Escapement for brood years 1974-1983 and 1985-1986 are based on Nuyakuk tower plus aerial survey estimates.

Escapement for brood years 1987-2006 are based on Nushagak River sonar estimates.

[b] R/S = return per spawner.

[c] Younger age groups not available.

[d] Incomplete returns from brood year escapement.

[e] Estimate from 2006 preliminary return numbers.

TABLE 3. Igushik River sockeye salmon escapement and return by brood year, 1950–2006.

Brood Year	Escapement	Return by Age Class (in thousands of fish) 0.2	1.1	0.3	1.2	2.1	0.4	1.3	2.2	1.4	2.3	Total	R/S [a]
1950	0 [b]	0 [c]	0 [c]	0 [c]	0 [c]	0 [c]	0 [c]	0 [c]	0 [c]	1	78	79 [d]	
1951	0 [b]	0 [c]	0 [c]	0 [c]	0 [c]	0 [c]	0	615	62	1	29	707 [d]	
1952	0 [b]	0 [c]	0 [c]	0	147	0	0	303	9	5	73	537 [d]	
1953	0 [b]	0	0	0	98	0	0	1	20	3	65	187	
1954	0 [b]	0	0	0	175	0	0	269	204	0	113	761	
1955	0 [b]	0	0	0	454	0	0	781	113	0	94	1,442	
1956	400	0	0	0	169	0	0	523	12	3	36	743	1.86
1957	130	0	0	0	2	0	0	35	19	0	20	76	0.58
1958	107	0	0	0	14	0	0	71	20	0	28	133	1.24
1959	644	0	0	0	101	0	0	155	93	0	22	371	0.58
1960	495	0	0	1	61	0	0	310	44	0	57	473	0.96
1961	294	0	0	1	33	0	1	364	20	0	17	436	1.48
1962	16	0	0	8	20	0	0	280	9	0	9	326	20.38
1963	92	0	0	3	254	0	0	190	36	0	25	508	5.52
1964	129	0	0	1	162	0	0	585	133	0	49	930	7.21
1965	181	0	0	0	371	0	0	436	203	0	80	1,090	6.02
1966	206	0	0	0	66	0	0	383	6	0	15	470	2.28
1967	282	0	0	3	57	0	0	90	13	0	12	175	0.62
1968	195	0	0	0	43	0	0	120	0	2	10	175	0.90
1969	512	0	0	0	1	0	0	131	301	2	103	538	1.05
1970	371	0	0	1	26	0	0	170	41	0	71	309	0.83
1971	211	0	0	1	48	0	0	164	60	0	30	303	1.44
1972	60	0	0	4	89	0	0	109	6	8	13	229	3.82
1973	60	0	0	0	19	0	0	650	25	2	29	725	12.08
1974	359	0	0	7	441	1	0	750	346	4	25	1,574	4.39
1975	241	0	0	0	783	0	0	2,556	137	2	503	3,981	16.52
1976	186	0	0	0	551	3	0	1,411	194	20	215	2,394	12.87
1977	96	0	0	6	294	0	0	1,689	9	8	9	2,015	20.99
1978	536	0	0	0	96	0	0	330	84	1	15	526	0.98
1979	860	0	0	0	422	0	0	406	13	0	5	846	0.98
1980	1,988	0	0	0	20	0	0	271	25	0	56	372	0.19
1981	591	0	0	0	188	0	0	779	8	1	49	1,025	1.73
1982	424	0	0	7	57	0	0	434	9	2	10	519	1.22
1983	180	1	0	0	151	0	0	353	8	2	29	544	3.02
1984	185	0	0	0	41	0	0	641	56	5	36	779	4.21
1985	212	0	0	7	515	0	0	938	86	7	79	1,632	7.70
1986	308	3	0	14	236	0	1	2,231	27	15	30	2,557	8.30
1987	169	2	0	11	158	0	0	587	7	12	29	806	4.77
1988	170	0	0	1	189	0	1	1,056	41	3	36	1,327	7.81
1989	462	0	0	15	508	0	0	1,119	59	7	53	1,761	3.81
1990	366	1	0	3	159	0	0	1,429	183	4	146	1,925	5.26
1991	756	0	0	1	318	0	0	1,314	3	5	20	1,661	2.20
1992	305	0	0	3	44	0	0	148	8	0	26	229	0.75
1993	406	0	0	1	132	0	2	316	20	0	35	506	1.25
1994	446	0	0	0	238	0	0	846	92	1	26	1,203	2.70
1995	473	0	0	0	653	0	0	1,599	15	21	13	2,301	4.86
1996	401	0	0	0	171	0	0	1,237	1	4	4	1,417	3.53
1997	128	0	0	19	34	0	0	52	10	5	58	178	1.39
1998	216	0	0	0	143	0	0	732	28	8	30	941 [e]	4.36
1999	446	0	0	7	206	0	0	310	71	0	297	891 [d]	2.00
2000	413	0	0	0	104	0	0	1,656	71	5 [e]	118 [e]	1,954 [d]	4.73
2001	410	0	0	0	64	0	9 [e]	1,432 [e]	12 [e]	0 [d]	0 [d]	1,517 [d]	3.70
2002	123	0	0	0 [e]	322 [e]	0 [e]	0 [d]	0 [d]	0 [d]	0 [d]	0 [d]	322 [d]	2.62
2003	194	0 [e]	0 [e]	0 [d]	0 [d]	0 [d]	0 [d]	0 [d]	0 [d]	0 [d]	0 [d]	0 [d]	
2004	110	0 [d]	0 [d]	0 [d]	0 [d]	0 [d]	0 [d]	0 [d]	0 [d]	0 [d]	0 [d]	0 [d]	
2005	366	0 [d]	0 [d]	0 [d]	0 [d]	0 [d]	0 [d]	0 [d]	0 [d]	0 [d]	0 [d]	0 [d]	
2006	305	0 [d]	0 [d]	0 [d]	0 [d]	0 [d]	0 [d]	0 [d]	0 [d]	0 [d]	0 [d]	0 [d]	
1956-2001 Avg.													4.46

[a] R/S = return per spawner.
[b] Escapement not available.
[c] Younger age groups not available.
[d] Incomplete returns from brood year escapement.
[e] Estimate from 2006 preliminary return numbers.

salmon with a minimum total return of 2.069 million and a maximum of 11.769 million sockeye salmon (Tables 1–3). The annual commercial harvest from the Nushagak District from 1980—2000 has averaged 4.042 million sockeye salmon with a minimum harvest of 1.307 million and maximum harvest of 7.455 million sockeye salmon. The average total escapement during the same time period in the Nushagak District was 2.445 million with a minimum escapement of 1.520 million and a maximum escapement of 8.274 million sockeye salmon.

The average total return to the Wood River was 2.969 million sockeye salmon from the brood years 1956–2000 with a minimum total return of 449 thousand fish and maximum total return of 6.729 million (Table 1). The Wood River has had an average escapement of 1.138 million sockeye salmon from 1956 to 2000 with a minimum escapement of 289 thousand and a maximum escapement of 2.969 million sockeye salmon. The average annual commercial harvest of sockeye salmon from the Wood River stocks was 1.347 million from the brood years 1956–2000 with a minimum harvest of 148 thousand and maximum harvest of 4.417 million sockeye salmon.

The average total return to the Nushagak River was 1.673 million sockeye salmon from the 1980–2000 brood years with a minimum total return of 579 thousand and maximum total return of 3.699 million sockeye salmon (Table 2). The Nushagak River has had an average escapement of 677 thousand sockeye salmon from the 1980–2000 brood years with a minimum escapement of 281 thousand and a maximum escapement of 3.317 million sockeye salmon. The annual commercial harvest from the Nushagak River has averaged 1.103 million sockeye salmon from the 1980–2000 brood years with a minimum harvest of 406 thousand and maximum harvest of 2.484 million sockeye salmon.

The average total return to the Igushik River has averaged 975 thousand sockeye salmon from the 1956–2000 brood years with a minimum total return of 76 thousand and maximum total return of 3.981 million (Table 3). The Igushik River has had an average escapement of 349 thousand sockeye salmon from the 1956–2000 brood years with a minimum escapement of 16 thousand and a maximum escapement of 1.988 million sockeye salmon. The average annual commercial harvest from the Igushik River was 523 thousand sockeye salmon from the 1956–2000 brood years with a minimum harvest of 28 thousand and maximum harvest of 1.667 million sockeye salmon.

How Are the Data Used?

Total return data are used to set escapement goals for the major stocks of salmon in an area. Escapement goals for salmon in Bristol Bay were recently reviewed in December 2006 based on the Policy for the Management of Sustainable Salmon Fisheries (SSFP: 5 AAC 39.222) and the Policy for Statewide Salmon Escapement Goals (EGP: 5 AAC 39.223) (Baker at al. 2006). The Alaska Board of Fisheries (BOF) adopted these policies into regulation in the winter of 2000–2001 to ensure salmon stocks were conserved, managed, and developed using the sustained yield principle. Two important terms defined in the SSFP are: "Biological Escapement Goal (BEG): the escapement that provides the greatest potential for maximum sustained yield (MSY)" and *Sustainable Escapement Goal* (SEG): a level of escapement, indicated by an index or an escapement estimate, that is known to provide for sustained yield over a 5–10 year period, used in situations where a BEG cannot be estimated due to the absence of a stock specific catch estimate.

Escapement goals for sockeye salmon in Bristol Bay have primarily been evaluated using Ricker spawner-return models (Ricker 1954). Escapement goals have been estimated with this method when "good" estimates of total return (escapement and stock-specific harvest) exist for a stock over several years. Additional methods, such as yield analysis, analysis of smolt information, and risk analysis, have been used when concerns existed about the quality of the total return data.

Individual escapement goals for sockeye salmon have been in place for the major river systems in Bristol Bay since the early 1960s. Current escapement goals for the Nushagak District are: 700 thousand to 1.5 million sockeye salmon for the Wood River; 340 thousand to 760 thousand sockeye salmon for the Nushagak River, and 150 thousand to 300 thousand sockeye salmon for the Igushik River (Baker et al. 2006). The escapement goals for the Wood, Nushagak and Igushik rivers are currently defined as SEGs instead of BEGs (Baker at al. 2006). The primary reason for this definition is the concern about the quality of the stock-specific estimates of harvest for each of these rivers.

The first estimates of run strength of adult salmon returns for a summer season come from preseason forecasts made during the previous winter. Preseason forecasts by ADF&G estimates the number of sockeye salmon expected to return to each major river system in Bristol Bay. The forecasts are usually completed by November in the preceding year. Forecasts include estimates for each age-class predicted to return to a river system. Forecasts are made from models based on the relationship between adult returns and spawners or siblings from previous years. Tested models include simple linear regression and 5-year averages. The models chosen are those with statistically significant parameters that have had the greatest reliability (accuracy and precision) in past years. Data used for forecasting can include all the data available or subsets of the data from certain years.

Some of the first inseason information that ADF&G uses each season is from the Port Moller Test Fishery (Helton 1991), located 185 mi southwest of Cape Constantine (Figure 1) along the Alaska Peninsula. The test fishery program began in 1968. A contracted vessel fishes specific locations along a transect line between Port Moller and Cape Newenham (Figure 1), roughly perpendicular to the migration path of sockeye returning to Bristol Bay. Data collected during the test fishery is used as an indicator of sockeye salmon run strength and timing as well as to estimate age and size composition of the Bristol Bay sockeye run. These data are useful for inseason commercial fishery management because it takes approximately one-week for a sockeye salmon to travel from the Port Moller test fishery to the Bristol Bay inshore fishing districts.

The Port Moller test fishery project has become a vital early indicator of Bristol Bay sockeye salmon run strength and stock composition. Helton (1991) identified the Port Moller test fishery as a powerful Bristol Bay sockeye salmon inseason forecast tool. The catch, age, and stock composition data gathered annually in the Port Moller test fishery provide valuable information for managing Bristol Bay commercial salmon fisheries. Loss of these data would significantly compromise fisheries management capabilities in Bristol Bay.

Genetics analysis of sockeye salmon caught in the Port Moller test fishery began in 2004 and continues through the present. Inseason genetic analysis is used to identify the stock components of the run to assist inseason management decisions to achieve stock-specific escapement goals. Stock composition estimates typically are provided within three to four days after capture by the test fishery. The ability to provide genetic stock composition estimates in such a short period of time has improved the usefulness of the Port Moller test fishery by providing managers with estimates for a group of fish prior to their arrival at the fisheries. The ADF&G conducts other test fishing projects besides Port Moller to provide relative abundance of near shore fish as needed in the Egegik, Naknek-Kvichak, and Nushagak districts.

The ADF&G also conducts inriver test fishing projects within the lower reaches of some rivers. These projects sample fish that have passed the commercial fishery areas, but are downstream of where the counting towers or sonar sites are located. Sockeye salmon require one or more days to travel from where the commercial fishery takes place to where the escapement is estimated. Inriver test fishing is conducted on each tide at set locations during the season. Inriver test fish indices provide a timely indicator of run strength for each river while fish are in transit between the commercial fishery and where fish are counted inriver. Currently, ADF&G conducts inriver test fishing on only the eastside of Bristol Bay in the Ugashik, Egegik, and Kvichak rivers.

ADF&G research biologists also provide managers with numerous inseason predictions of sockeye salmon run strength and escapements for all the major river systems. These predictions include estimates of run timing based on the catch, escapement, and total run. The current year's catch, escapement, and total run information are compared to historical information. This comparison provides measures of the run timing of the current year's run. One of the most difficult tasks is determining if a run is arriving "early" or "late," or if a run is "large" or "small" in abundance. A run may appear to be "large;" however, the run may be arriving "early" and is actually "small." These run attributes are especially important in the Bristol Bay sockeye salmon fishery where the majority of the fish return in a two- to three-week period and a one- or two-day difference in the run timing can mean a projected difference in millions of fish to the total run.

Managers also use catch measures from the fishery to provide additional estimates of the relative run strength of sockeye salmon within a district. Catch per unit effort (CPUE) information often provides indications of the abundance of fish within a district. The use of CPUE as a run strength indicator is dependent upon the accurate and timely inseason reporting of catch by the commercial salmon processors. The ADF&G has developed an inseason catch and escapement database (called "Mariner"). Processors are required to report daily catches that occurred in Bristol Bay. In addition, the ADF&G enters daily escapement for all the major river systems in Bristol Bay. Managers have access to all the information in the Mariner database during the season. The information is also made available to the public in the form of the "Bristol Bay Daily Run Summary" that provides the daily and cumulative catch and escapement to date for all districts within Bristol Bay.

Aerial surveys of the fishing districts and of the spawning streams are conducted inseason to provide additional information about the sockeye salmon that may be present within a district and information about the distribution of the escapement within river systems. Aerial surveys flown within a district often provide advance estimates of escapement similar to inriver test fishing.

Discussion

Managers in Bristol Bay are fortunate to have good inseason information that includes: daily catch and escapement estimates, test fishing (Port Moller, district and inriver), aerial surveys, age composition, and genetic stock identification. These types of inseason information are necessary for the effective management of Bristol Bay fisheries. These fisheries would be managed much more conservatively if this inseason information were not available. This is especially true in a district, like the Nushagak, where the escapement in the Wood River can exceed 600,000 sockeye salmon in 24 hours.

One of the biggest benefits of the long-term Bristol Bay data sets is having the ability to analyze our data for trends or changes in stock-specific production, abundance, age, sex, and size, and their relation to various factors. For example, analyses of sockeye salmon trends in Bristol Bay suggest that shifts or changes in abundance are a result of decadal-scale shifts in climate (Beamish and Bouillon 1993; Francis and Hare 1994; Hare and Francis 1995; Hare and Mantua 2000; Eggers and Irvine 2007). There was an increase in salmon production for most of the rivers within Bristol Bay after 1977. The change in climate or regime shift in 1977 appears to be brought about by warmer sea-surface temperatures and a sharp reduction in sea ice in the Bering Sea (NRC 1996; BESIS 1997).

Having long-term data sets also allow us to select only a portion of the data set for some analyses. For instance, we are currently only using the most recent total return data from the late 1970s to early 2000s in our preseason forecasts for the Wood, Nushagak and Igushik rivers. We anticipate that additional changes in sockeye salmon production will occur in Bristol Bay in the future. When these changes occur, we will have the option of continuing to use the most recent data, using the entire data set, or selecting a different set of the data that has similar salmon production.

Having long-term data sets are not the answer to all our questions. If the return in a year is outside the range of previous observations, then having more stock-recruit data will not necessarily help interpretation of what happened. The total run of sockeye salmon to the Nushagak District in 2006 was over 15 million fish. The 2006 run was over 2 million fish larger than the next largest run of 12.7 million sockeye salmon that occurred in 1980. However, the chances of current data being within the range of previous or historical observations usually increases with the length of the data set being collected.

Long-term data sets like the ones in Bristol Bay are very valuable. One of the biggest mistakes any agency can make is to discontinue or to sporadically fund the efforts to collect abundance data by age, sex, and size. The funding for the Bristol Bay salmon program (for both management and research) has varied dramatically since 1980 (Clark 2005; Clark et al. 2006). Funding declined dramatically during the 1990s and 2000s. Some funding was restored in 2006. However, some projects were discontinued and subsequent data have been lost forever. If data sets are deemed to be important, then every effort needs to be made to keep project funding at necessary levels.

Many areas within Alaska and throughout the North Pacific have not been as fortunate as Bristol Bay with regards to the collection of long-term data sets on salmon. However, it is important that efforts be put in place to start the collection of these long-term data sets. At a minimum, good catch and escapement information should be collected along with basic biological information such as age, sex, length and weight. As part of this process, fishery researchers and managers need to identify and prioritize the data that is collected each year.

Acknowledgments

We would like to acknowledge the effort of all the people who have worked in the Bristol Bay salmon fisheries over the last 50 years. We are benefiting daily from their tireless efforts and we would not have what is considered to be one the best long-term datasets on sockeye salmon in the world had it not been for these efforts.

References

Baker, T. T., L. F. Fair., R. A. Clark, and J. J. Hasbrouck. 2006. Review of salmon escapement goals in Bristol Bay, Alaska, 2006. Alaska Department of Fish and Game, Fishery Manuscript No. 06–05, Anchorage.

Bernard, D. R. 1983. Variance and bias of catch allocations that use the age compositions of escapements. Alaska Department of Fish and Game, Division of Commercial Fisheries. Informational Leaflet 227, Anchorage.

Beamish, R. J., and D. R. Bouillon. 1993. Pacific salmon production trends in relation to climate. Canadian Journal of Fisheries and Aquatic Sciences 50:1002–1016.

BESIS. 1997. The impacts of global climate change in the Bering Sea region, an assessment conducted by the International Arctic Science Committee under its Bering Seas Impacts Group (BESIS), International Arctic Science Committee, Oslo, Norway.

Clark, J. H., A. McGregor, R. D. Mecum, P. Krasnowski, and A. M. Carroll. 2006. The commercial salmon fishery in Alaska. Alaska Fishery Research Bulletin 12(1):1–146.

Clark, J. H. 2005. Bristol Bay salmon, a program review. Alaska Department of Fish and Game, Special Publication No. 05–02, Juneau.

Cross, B. A., and B. L. Stratton. 1989. Origins of sockeye salmon in east side Bristol Bay fisheries in 1987 based on linear discriminant function analysis of scale patterns. Alaska Department of Fish and Game, Division of Commercial Fisheries, Technical Fishery Report 88–13, Juneau.

Cross, B. A., and B. L. Stratton. 1991. Origins of sockeye salmon in east side Bristol Bay fisheries in 1988 based on linear discriminant function analysis of scale patterns. Alaska Department of Fish and Game, Division of Commercial Fisheries, Technical Fishery Report 91–09, Juneau.

Eggers, D. M., and J. R. Irvine. 2007. Trends in abundance and biological characteristics for North Pacific sockeye salmon. North Pacific Anadromous Fish Commission Bulletin 4:53–75.

Francis, R. C., and S. R. Hare. 1994. Decadal scale regime shifts in the large marine ecosystems of the North-east Pacific: a case of historical science. Fisheries Oceanography 7:1–21.

Habicht, C., L. W. Seeb, and J. E. Seeb. 2007. Genetic and ecological divergence defines population structure of sockeye salmon populations to Bristol Bay, Alaska, and provides a tool for admixture analysis. Transactions of the American Fisheries Society 136:82–94.

Hare, S. R., and R. C. Francis. 1995. Climate change and salmon production in the northeast Pacific Ocean. In Ocean climate and northern fish populations. Edited by R. J. Beamish. Canadian Special Publication Fishery and Aquatic Sciences 121:357–372.

Hare, S. R., and N. J. Mantua. 2000. Empirical evidence for north Pacific regime shifts in 1977 and 1989. Progressive Oceanography 47:103–145.

Helton, D. R. 1991. An analysis of the Port Moller offshore test fishing forecast of sockeye and chum salmon runs to Bristol Bay, Alaska. Master's thesis. University of Washington, Seattle.

Hilsinger, J. R., E. Volk, G. Sandone, and R. Cannon. 2009. Salmon management in the Arctic-Yukon-Kuskokwim region of Alaska. Pages 495–519 in C. C. Krueger and C. E. Zimmerman, editors. Pacific salmon: ecology and management of western Alaska's populations. American Fisheries Society, Symposium 70, Bethesda, Maryland.

Koo, T. S. Y. 1962. Age designation in salmon. Pages 37–48 in T. S. Y. Koo, editor. Studies of Alaska red salmon. University of Washington Publications in Fisheries, New Series, Volume I, University of Washington Press, Seattle.

Miller, J. D. 1995. Origins of sockeye salmon in eastside Bristol Bay fisheries in 1993 based on linear discriminant function analysis of scale patterns. Alaska Department of Fish and Game, Division of Commercial Fisheries, Regional Information Report No. 2A95–24, Anchorage.

Moser, J. F. 1902. Salmon investigations of the Steamer Albatross in the summer of 1900. U.S. Fish Commission Bulletin 21:175–217.

Nelson, M. L. 1987. History and management of the Nushagak Chinook salmon fishery. Alaska Department of Fish and Game, Division of Commercial Fisheries, Bristol Bay Data Report No. 87–1, Dillingham.

NRC (National Research Council), 1996. The Bering Sea Ecosystem, Committee on the Bering Sea Ecosystem, Polar Research Board. National Academy Press, Washington, D.C.

Rich, W. H., and E. M. Ball. 1928. Statistical review of the Alaska salmon fisheries-Part I: Bristol Bay and the Alaska Peninsula. U.S. Department of Commerce, Bureau of Fisheries, Document No 1041:41–95.

Ricker, W. E. 1954. Stock and recruitment. Journal of the Fisheries Research Board of Canada 11:559–623.

Stratton, B. L., and Miller, J. D. 1993. Origins of sockeye salmon in eastside Bristol Bay fisheries in 1991 based on linear discriminant function analysis of scale patterns. Alaska Department of Fish and Game, Division of Commercial Fisheries, Technical Fishery Report 93–09, Juneau.

Stratton, B. L., and Miller, J. D. 1994. Origins of sockeye salmon in eastside Bristol Bay fisheries in 1992 based on linear discriminant function analysis of scale patterns. Alaska Department of Fish and Game, Division of Commercial Fisheries, Technical Fishery Report 94–10, Juneau.

Stratton, B. L., J. D. Miller, and B. A. Cross. 1992. Origins of sockeye salmon in eastside Bristol Bay fisheries in 1990 based on linear discriminant function analysis of scale patterns. Alaska Department of Fish and Game, Division of Commercial Fisheries, Technical Fishery Report 92–16, Juneau.

Van Alen, B. W. 1982. Use of scale patterns to identify the origins of sockeye salmon (*Oncorhynchus nerka*) in the fishery of Nushagak Bay, Alaska. Alaska Department of Fish and Game, Division of Commercial Fisheries, Informational Leaflet No. 202, Juneau.

American Fisheries Society Symposium 70:977–1004, 2009

Application of Chinook Salmon Stock Composition Data for Management of the Northern British Columbia Troll Fishery, 2006

Ivan Winther[*]

Fisheries and Oceans Canada, Science Branch, Pacific Region
417-2nd Avenue West, Prince Rupert, British Columbia V8J-1G8, Canada

Terry D. Beacham

Fisheries and Oceans Canada, Science Branch, Pacific Region
Pacific Biological Station
3190 Hammond Bay Road, Nanaimo, British Columbia V9T-6N7, Canada

Abstract.—Fisheries and Oceans Canada has managed the northern British Columbia troll fishery since 1995 to reduce fishing mortality on Chinook salmon *Oncorhynchus tshawytscha* stocks from the West Coast of Vancouver Island (WCVI). This paper describes the fishery and the use of genetic data in mixed-stock analyses for in-season management of Chinook salmon. Microsatellite DNA based stock identification was used in 2006 to regulate the mixed-stock fishery to address WCVI stock specific harvest. Chinook salmon stock compositions were estimated in-season for the 2006 troll fishery harvest and the fishery was managed based on this information to meet catch targets for WCVI Chinook salmon. The best opportunities for the troll fishery to avoid WCVI Chinook salmon stocks were defined spatially (in northern portions of the fishing area) and temporally (in late June and July). The application of stock-specific management allowed the internationally negotiated catch allocation between Canada and the U.S. (Pacific Salmon Treaty) to be reached while reducing the exploitation of WCVI Chinook salmon stocks.

Introduction

In northern British Columbia, the commercial troll fishery is the largest fishery for Chinook salmon *Oncorhynchus tshawytscha,* and is one of two fisheries defined within the management regime implemented by the Pacific Salmon Treaty (Canada and U.S.; Pacific Salmon Commission 2000) for the north coast. Under the revised international agree-ment for the period 1999 to 2008, the northern British Columbia troll and Queen Charlotte Islands sport fisheries were managed in aggregate within the same regime. Canada's domestic allocation policy specifies that harvest allocation to the sport fishery takes precedence over the troll fishery, and that management actions to protect weak stocks are to be implemented first within troll fisheries (Winther and Beacham 2006).

The North Coast troll fishery has been defined as Area F consisting of Pacific Fish-

[*] Corresponding author: Ivan.Winther@dfo-mpo.gc.ca

ery Management Areas 1–10, 101–110, 130 and 142 (Figure 1). The portion of the North Coast troll fishery within the aggregate abundance based regime is the north-western portion of Area F; Areas 1–5, 101–105, 130 and 142. Winther and Beacham (2006) have provided a complete review of history of the northern troll fishery. The size of the troll fleet in Area F was relatively stable from 2002 to 2005, varying between 146 and 168 licensed vessels. Prior to the 2006 season, troll vessel operators were permitted to reselect fishing areas coast wide. Area F received an additional 80 vessels, increasing the total number of licences in the area to 246. The influx of vessels was due to reduced fishing opportuni-

ties in southern areas and the introduction of individual transferable quotas in the northern troll fishery for Chinook salmon.

Stock identification is a key component in the management of mixed stock salmon fisheries. The application of DNA markers for stock identification, particularly microsatellites, has provided much greater resolution among Chinook salmon populations than was possible with previous genetic markers (Beacham et al. 1996; Banks et al. 2000; Beacham et al. 2003b). For example, Chinook salmon populations from specific tributaries in the Fraser River drainage in southern British Columbia can be discriminated with a high degree of accuracy (Beacham et al. 2003a).

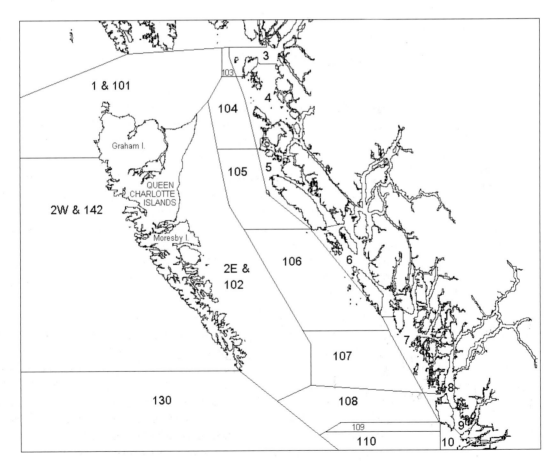

FIGURE 1. The north coast of British Columbia showing Pacific Fishery Management Areas 1 to 10, 101 to 110, 130 and 142.

If the baseline used to estimate stock composition is adequate, microsatellites can be applied successfully on a local basis to provide information on stock composition even when a complex mixture of populations occurs in the catch (Beacham et al. 2006).

The use of DNA markers for stock identification in the northern British Columbia troll fishery began in 2002. Use of this information has helped meet the objectives of allowing the Chinook salmon quota negotiated under the Pacific Salmon Treaty agreement to be harvested while continuing to reduce impacts on stocks of conservation concern from the west coast of Vancouver Island (WCVI; Winther and Beacham 2006). Winther and Beacham (2006) designed a management system for the northern troll fishery that shaped the fishery in time and space to avoid the stocks of conservation concern. The concept was to collect periodic samples using small-scale troll test fisheries to examine in-season trends in stock composition. The trends were used to define when and where full fleet troll fisheries could be conducted. The objectives of the harvest by the full fleet troll fishery were to minimize impact on the stocks of concern while maintaining the greatest likelihood of reaching the total allowable catch defined under the Pacific Salmon Treaty.

The 2006 preseason allocation of Chinook salmon to the northern British Columbia troll fishery was 153,200 fish. The 2006 in-season target for the troll fishery was a maximum harvest rate of 3.2% on Chinook salmon of WCVI origin returning to Canadian waters. This target was estimated at 6,344 fish. A ceiling of 3,000 Chinook salmon was assigned to the troll fishery occurring between October and December of 2005, and the remainder of the allocation was assigned to the summer fishery. Only one vessel participated in the winter fishery and only 25 Chinook salmon were caught so the preseason target for the summer fishery was 153,175 Chinook salmon.

The troll catch target for the summer fishery was reduced slightly to 152,520 Chinook salmon to accommodate the equal division of the allocation among the 246 troll licences. A demonstration fishery to examine the application of individual transferable quotas in the troll fishery, first held in 2005, was continued in 2006. The in-season target for the traditional style or "derby" fishery was 3,720 Chinook salmon and the target for the quota fishery was 148,800 Chinook salmon (620 fish per licence).

The catch ceiling for WCVI Chinook salmon of 6,344 fish represented 4.1% of 153,200 fish of the total allowable catch by the troll fishery. The trigger established for opening the quota fishery was when the proportion of WCVI Chinook in troll test fishery samples dropped below 6%. Similarly, when samples from the commercial catch were above 6% WCVI, a closure of the fishery would occur. Further, decision rules for the quota fishery were to open the fishery as early as 15 May, if the WCVI component of the 1 May sample was less than 6%. Between 15 May and 1 July, the ITQ fishery could open as soon as possible after samples indicated a WCVI component less than 6%. After 1 July, the quota fishery would open regardless of the WCVI component in the samples and closure would occur when the WCVI ceiling (6,344 fish) was met.

The decision rules for the derby fishery were to open as early as 3 June, if the WCVI component of the 15 May sample was less than 6%. Alternatively, the fishery could open as early as 17 June if the results from the samples collected 1 June indicated a WCVI component less than 6%. If all samples were above 6% WCVI the derby fishery would open 1 July regardless of the WCVI component in the samples and would close when the WCVI ceiling was met.

In this paper, the authors describe the use of microsatellite variation in Chinook salmon as a tool for in-season management of stocks of conservation concern encountered by the 2006 northern British Columbia (Area F) troll fishery using the procedures described by Winther and Beacham (2006). The challenge was to provide in-season advice to managers that would allow the troll fishery to maximize catch of Chinook salmon while minimizing the exploitation of Chinook salmon stocks from the West Coast of Vancouver Island. The use of the procedures required the generation of stock trend information for two fishing areas; identification of the stock composition of troll-caught Chinook salmon by time and area in-season; and postseason estimation of catch by stock and age.

Methods

This study followed the sampling regimes and locations defined by Winther and Beacham (2006). Genetic sampling of Chinook salmon consisted of two programs; a troll test fishery designed to provide trends in stock composition through the summer, and a program to define the stock composition of the commercial troll fishery catch.

The primary source of catch data for the commercial troll fishery was from landing validations. A combination of fish slips and harvest logs was used to derive catch estimates for landings of Chinook salmon. Catch and sample data were tabulated for 1 October 2005–30 September 2006 to be consistent with the dates used in presenting Chinook salmon data for the Pacific Salmon Treaty. Catch estimates were weighted by time and area for application to the stock composition data from the genetic samples.

Sample Collection.—A common paper punch was used to collect tissue samples for genetic analysis from the operculum of the Chinook salmon being sampled. One tissue sample was collected from each Chinook salmon. Tissues were preserved in a solu-

tion of 95% nondenatured ethanol in individual vials. Data on the geographic location, date, and sampler accompanied each sample. Samples were forwarded to the Fisheries & Oceans Canada, Molecular Genetics Laboratory at the Pacific Biological Station in Nanaimo. Scale samples were collected on to scale books, five scales per fish, as described by MacLellan (1999).

Test fishery sampling.— Test fishery samples were used to provide trends in stock composition of catch and to manage the commercial troll fishery temporally and spatially. The initial goal was to collect 1400 Chinook salmon tissues from troll test fisheries with 100 tissues collected in each time and area stratum. Test fishing was conducted by an Area F commercial troll fishing vessel designated to catch and sample 100 Chinook salmon at each of two sites during a prescribed period. The test fishery employed seven vessels, one for each time stratum. The sample periods were monthly from April to September with one additional time stratum beginning 15 May to provide additional stock information in advance of the fishery opening proposed for June. The vessels operated standard commercial troll fishing gear rigged with barbless hooks. The sample locations were near La Perouse Reef, south of Langara Island, and near Buck Point, mid way down the west side of the Queen Charlotte Islands (Figure 2).

The total 2006 test fishery catch was 1,237 Chinook salmon and DNA analyses were completed for 1,159 of the fish landed. Complete (100 fish) samples were collected in both locations in April, July, and August. The location of the northern sample in July was modified to test Chinook salmon caught from around Tartu Inlet, an intermediate location between the normal Buck Point site and the La Perouse Reef site. Commercial fishery landings were sampled to make up the La Perouse Reef sample for July. Test

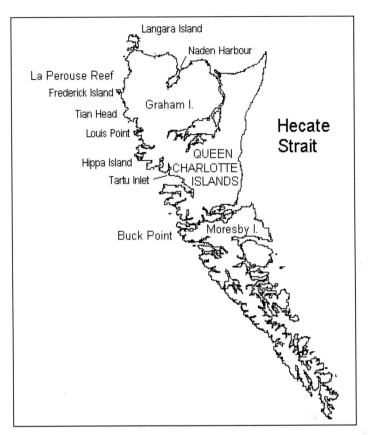

FIGURE 2. 2006 troll test fishery sample sites and locations relevant to the open fishery referred to in the text.

samples beginning 1 May and 15 May were completed for the Buck Point site but fell short by seven and three fish for the La Perouse Reef sample. The June sample from Buck Point was complete but a vessel breakdown left the La Perouse Reef sample with a catch of only 77 Chinook salmon. Only 70 Chinook salmon were collected in the September sample near Buck Point because blue sharks *Prionace glauca* had invaded the area. The September test sample in the La Perouse Reef area was abandoned. The damage inflicted by the sharks to the catch and the gear made it impossible to complete the sample.

Each legal-sized (>67 cm nose-fork length) Chinook salmon encountered by a test fishing vessel was measured for nose-fork length and incised to determine sex. Scales and tissue were collected, and date and location were recorded for each fish.

Commercial troll fishery sampling.—The program to sample the commercial troll fishery landings was designed with the objective of collecting tissues from approximately 1% (~1500 fish) of the Chinook salmon caught in the fishery, and subsampling these collections down to ~1000 fish for genetic analyses. The sampling procedure was a random-stratified approach. Vessel landings were selected at random and a sample of less than 50 fish was collected from each delivery. Within each landing collections were stratified to sample every fifth or tenth fish depending on the size of the delivery. Individual Chinook salmon sampled from commercial fishery landings were sampled for nose-fork length, scales, and tissue. These collections were matched to data on the area fished and date caught.

The sample collection targets were designed larger than the targets for genetic analyses because collection was relatively cheap when compared with genetic analysis. This protocol assured samples across all time and area strata, and allowed for subsampling to best represent the commercial fishery landings. The sample design was approached from the perspective of a binomial problem where Chinook salmon were identified as either from WCVI or not. Available funds dictated the maximum extent of sample analyses. The catch ceiling of WCVI Chinook salmon was ~4% of the total catch (6433 WCVI/153,200). If the actual catch approached the ceiling, the level of precision afforded by the program would provide 95% confidence limits within ~30% of the estimated proportion of WCVI Chinook. Smaller proportions would have respectively broader confidence limits and in-season data representing portions of the 1,000 fish sample target would have respectively broader confidence limits as well.

In addition to the samples of troll fishery landings, Chinook salmon were sampled at sea on the opening day of the troll fishery, 7 June 2006, to provide managers with an early indication of the stock composition of the catch. Samples of the landed catch were not available until a week later. The sampling protocol was to collect a maximum of 25 tissue samples per vessel. No other biological data were collected from the fish sampled at sea.

Commercial fishery sampling objectives were met with a total of 1,750 Chinook salmon sampled from landings and 253 sampled at sea. Genetic analyses were completed for 1,118 of the tissues collected from fishery landings and 245 of the tissues collected at sea. Only one troll test sample of 100 fish collected in August in Area 1/101 occurred in the same time and area as the quota fishery. Consequently, this test sample represented this part of the commercial catch. Analyses were completed for 93 fish in this sample.

Genetic analysis.— Chinook salmon collections were compared against genetic baselines from 250 Chinook salmon populations from southeast Alaska through Canada and the lower United States (Beacham et al. 2006). Samples were analyzed for 13 microsatellite loci using methods of DNA extraction, PCR reaction, electrophoresis, and allele scoring described by Candy et al. (2002) and Beacham et al. (2006). The Molecular Genetics Laboratory at the Pacific Biological Station provided the sample analysis. A new version of the computer program as described by Pella and Masuda (2001) was developed and used for the analyses presented here. This program ,called "c-BAYES," is available from http://www-sci.pac.dfo-mpo. gc.ca/mgl/data_e.htm. The model output presented includes the Bayesian probability estimates for the five most probable populations for each sample.

Age assignment.—Age of fish sampled were determined based on annuli identification from scales. Ages were reported here using the convention of Gilbert and Rich (1927). Ocean-type Chinook salmon were those fish that spent one winter incubating in gravel and migrated to the ocean sometime in the next year after hatch and emergence (designated as X_1 where X = year of life when the fish was caught; e.g., 2_1 is an age-2 salmon with one winter season incubated as an egg). Stream-type Chinook salmon were fish that migrated after one or more summer growing seasons in a stream (designated as X_1+; e.g., 3_2 is an age-3 salmon with one winter in the gravel and one overwinter season as a fry).

Results

The most prevalent stock group in the northern British Columbia troll catch of Chinook salmon was South Thompson (SOTH), followed by North and Central Oregon and Upper Columbia Summer and Fall (Up Col-Su/F) stock groups (Table 1). The WCVI stock group that the fishery was designed to avoid made up the fifth largest component in the catch.

Test fishery samples remained above the trigger point until 15 May when an opportunity to open the fishery was indicated by a sample of 1.7% WCVI in Area 1/101 (Table 2). The Buck Point sample from May 17–18 was 20.7% WCVI (Table 3) so the fishery was opened north of Louis Point on 7 June. Results from the test fishery samples collected in early June were delayed because the test vessel broke down. Consequently the analyses of the fishery samples collected on opening day arrived before the analyses of the test samples. The opening day sample collected below Frederick Island was 15.2% WCVI and the sample collected above Frederick Island was 4.2% WCVI. The test sample collected 3–4 June from Area 1/101 was 11.8% WCVI (Table 2.). Upon receipt of these data on 16 June that the derby fishery likely would exceed its catch limit of WCVI Chinook salmon, the derby fishery was closed on 22 June. Managers kept the quota fishery open to wait for more fishery sample results because most of the fleet had left the area below Frederick Island due to poor catches. On 24 June, the results from the first fishery landings caught between 7 and 19 June indicated a stock composition of 2.5% WCVI. Managers re-opened the derby fishery 29 June and it remained open until 4 July when the fishery met its target catch.

The majority of the troll catch in the quota fishery occurred in late June and July (Figure 3) when low proportions of WCVI Chinook salmon prevailed in Area 101 (Figure 4). The troll derby fishery was also restricted to these times, so most of the troll catches were assigned to the June and July fishery samples (Table 4). A sample collected from Area 101 between 15 and 30 July was comprised of 6.8% WCVI Chinook salmon. Although this sample was above the management trigger and could have initiated a closure, the analysis of this sample occurred postseason and therefore could not be used for in-season management decisions.

Most of the samples collected at the Buck Point site were above the 6% WCVI component necessary to open the fishery (Table 3.). Only the test fish catch was used to assess the Area 2W/142 samples (Table 5). The only Area 2W/142 samples below the 6% trigger were collected at Tartu Inlet from 1 to 3 July and from Buck Point to Tian Head in September. Managers responded to the Tartu Inlet sample by extending the open area from Louis Point down to Hippa Island on 20 July. No management action resulted from the September sample because fishing was poor and the results were received just 10 d before the end of the season. Management decisions for the troll fishery are summarize in Table 6.

The northern British Columbia troll fishery landed a total of 158,363 Chinook salmon in 2006. The summer fishery accounted for a total of 158,338 Chinook salmon, with 153,214 fish caught under the individual transferable quota system and 3,887 fish caught under the regular style or derby fishery. There were 159 licensed vessels that participated in the quota fishery and six vessels that participated in the derby fishery. The test fishery accounted for 1,237 legal-sized Chinook salmon. Daily effort ranged from almost 100 vessels on opening day to zero during bad weather in September. The associated daily catch ranged from ~6000 Chinook salmon on opening day to zero (Figure 3).

TABLE 1. Chinook salmon *Oncorhynchus tshawytscha* catch by stock group and area (see Figure 1) for 2006 northern British Columbia troll fisheries. Total catch in the fishery was estimated to be 158,363 fish from October 1, 2005 to September 30, 2006. The total catch assigned to stock groups represents 158, 338 Chinook salmon, 25 fish less than the total. The missing fish were caught in October 2005 but were not sampled, and therefore no genetic data were available to assign their stock composition. Abbreviations used below are described in Appendix 1. Standard deviations (SD) appear in parentheses.

Stock Group	Area 1 catch	SD	Area 2W catch	SD	Total Catch	SD
Alaska	27	(57.6)	0	(0.4)	27	(57.6)
Alsek	25	(51.3)	1	(1.1)	26	(51.3)
Taku	135	(166.9)	3	(3.1)	138	(167.0)
Stikine	648	(376.9)	2	(2.5)	650	(376.9)
QCI	1,020	(388.1)	0	(0.2)	1,020	(388.1)
NASS	1,325	(466.4)	5	(2.5)	1,330	(466.4)
Skeena	4,539	(1034.5)	11	(4.2)	4,551	(1034.5)
NOMN	5,152	(946.6)	10	(3.8)	5,162	(946.6)
WCVI	6,393	(922.1)	72	(8.4)	6,465	(922.1)
ECVI	2,369	(668.3)	18	(5.0)	2,388	(668.3)
SOMN	115	(152.0)	1	(2.0)	117	(152.0)
UPFR	1,045	(418.1)	7	(2.9)	1,052	(418.1)
MUFR	3,532	(898.3)	10	(3.8)	3,541	(898.4)
NOTH	2,846	(736.8)	4	(2.5)	2,850	(736.8)
SOTH	62,707	(2294.9)	140	(11.1)	62,847	(2295.0)
LWTH	204	(147.2)	0	(0.5)	205	(147.2)
LWFR-Sp	365	(253.1)	1	(1.0)	366	(253.1)
LWFR-Su	133	(131.4)	0	(0.3)	133	(131.4)
LWFR-F	65	(120.4)	1	(1.5)	66	(120.4)
Puget Sound	923	(409.2)	3	(2.7)	927	(409.3)
Juan de Fuca	8	(31.0)	2	(2.2)	11	(31.0)
Coastal Wash	7,790	(1169.2)	49	(7.6)	7,839	(1169.2)
Up Col-Sp	103	(186.3)	0	(0.4)	103	(186.3)
Up Col-Su/F	22,637	(1736.6)	243	(14.5)	22,880	(1736.7)

TABLE 1. Continued.

Stock Group	Area 1 catch	SD	Area 2W catch	SD	Total Catch	SD
Snake-Sp/Su	250	(275.4)	9	(4.3)	260	(275.4)
Snake-F	2,159	(943.9)	26	(8.5)	2,185	(943.9)
Mid Col-Sp	28	(62.6)	1	(0.9)	29	(62.6)
Up Willamette	3,685	(774.4)	16	(5.0)	3,701	(774.4)
Low Col	1,990	(617.3)	14	(4.9)	2,004	(617.4)
North & Central O	23,716	(1697.7)	109	(11.4)	23,825	(1697.7)
South Oregon coas	1,446	(549.3)	8	(4.5)	1,454	(549.3)
Klamath/Trinity	25	(51.8)	1	(1.0)	25	(51.8)
Cent Val-Sp	29	(61.3)	0	(0.4)	29	(61.3)
Cent Val-F	130	(143.1)	0	(0.7)	131	(143.1)

TABLE 2. Chinook salmon *Oncorhynchus tshawytscha* stock composition (%) as estimated in samples from the test fishery conducted prior to the opening of the 2006 troll fishery and later sampled directly from the troll fishery harvest in Area 1/101 (Figure 1). N = number of fish genetically analyzed and used in mixed stock analysis estimates. Abbreviations are described in Appendix 1. Standard deviations appear in parentheses.

Area 1/101 Date Fishery	2006 Apr 4-6 Test	2006 May 11-14 Test	2006 May 15 Test	2006 Jun 3-4 Test	2006 Jun 7 Troll	2006 Jun 7 Troll	2006 Jun 7-19 Troll	2006 Jun 16-26 Troll	2006 Jun 17-26 Troll	2006 Jun 27-Jul 1 Troll
N	84	92	94	76	143	102	183	92	98	87
UPFR	0.1 (0.3)	0.1 (0.3)	1.1 (1.4)	1.5 (1.8)	3.6 (1.7)	2.9 (1.7)	1.7 (1.4)	0.2 (0.5)	2.6 (1.8)	0.1 (0.3)
MUFR	0.1 (0.3)	3.0 (2.1)	3.2 (2.3)	6.1 (3.2)	0.5 (1.1)	0.2 (0.7)	4.5 (2.1)	2.7 (2.5)	3.2 (2.3)	0.2 (0.5)
LWFR-F	0.0 (0.1)	0.0 (0.1)	0.0 (0.1)	1.3 (1.4)	0.1 (0.3)	0.0 (0.2)	0.0 (0.1)	0.0 (0.2)	0.0 (0.1)	0.0 (0.1)
NOTH	1.3 (1.2)	0.1 (0.4)	2.5 (2.1)	0.1 (0.3)	2.5 (1.7)	0.0 (0.2)	0.5 (0.7)	0.0 (0.2)	2.1 (1.8)	4.0 (2.2)
SOTH	11.9 (3.7)	32.6 (5.0)	31.4 (4.9)	33.4 (5.5)	46.2 (4.2)	16.3 (3.6)	33.1 (3.6)	47.1 (5.4)	57.7 (5.3)	49.5 (5.5)
LWTH	0.0 (0.2)	0.8 (1.1)	0.1 (0.3)	0.0 (0.2)	0.0 (0.1)	1.0 (1.0)	0.7 (0.7)	0.0 (0.2)	0.0 (0.2)	0.0 (0.2)
ECVI	2.8 (1.9)	1.6 (1.4)	0.3 (0.7)	0.9 (1.2)	0.9 (0.8)	4.7 (2.2)	0.6 (0.6)	1.8 (1.5)	2.8 (2.1)	1.6 (1.5)
WCVI	8.8 (3.4)	8.5 (3.0)	1.7 (1.6)	11.8 (3.7)	4.2 (1.7)	15.2 (3.6)	2.5 (1.2)	5.5 (2.4)	3.2 (1.9)	0.1 (0.4)
SOMN	0.0 (0.2)	0.0 (0.2)	0.1 (0.5)	0.1 (0.4)	0.0 (0.1)	0.1 (0.4)	0.0 (0.1)	0.0 (0.2)	0.0 (0.2)	0.3 (0.8)
NOMN	9.2 (3.5)	2.6 (2.2)	0.2 (0.6)	1.8 (1.7)	5.4 (2.2)	1.8 (1.5)	5.3 (1.9)	10.1 (3.3)	4.6 (2.5)	0.1 (0.4)
NASS	0.1 (0.3)	2.0 (1.9)	1.6 (1.4)	2.0 (2.4)	4.2 (1.9)	0.9 (1.1)	1.0 (0.9)	0.1 (0.5)	0.1 (0.5)	4.6 (2.4)
LWFR-Sp	0.0 (0.2)	0.0 (0.1)	0.0 (0.1)	0.0 (0.2)	0.0 (0.1)	0.0 (0.1)	0.2 (0.4)	0.0 (0.1)	0.0 (0.2)	0.0 (0.2)
LWFR-Su	0.0 (0.1)	0.0 (0.1)	0.0 (0.1)	0.0 (0.1)	0.0 (0.0)	0.0 (0.0)	0.0 (0.0)	0.0 (0.1)	0.0 (0.1)	0.0 (0.1)
QCI	0.0 (0.1)	0.0 (0.1)	0.0 (0.1)	0.0 (0.1)	0.0 (0.1)	0.0 (0.1)	0.0 (0.0)	1.1 (1.1)	0.0 (0.1)	0.0 (0.1)
Alaska	0.0 (0.1)	0.0 (0.3)	0.0 (0.1)	0.0 (0.1)	0.0 (0.3)	0.0 (0.3)	0.0 (0.1)	0.0 (0.2)	0.0 (0.1)	0.0 (0.1)
Taku	0.1 (0.3)	0.2 (0.7)	2.0 (1.9)	0.3 (1.0)	0.1 (0.5)	0.1 (0.3)	0.1 (0.3)	0.0 (0.2)	0.2 (0.6)	0.0 (0.2)
Stikine	0.1 (0.4)	0.1 (0.4)	1.0 (2.0)	0.1 (0.6)	0.1 (0.4)	2.5 (2.0)	0.0 (0.2)	0.1 (0.3)	0.8 (1.5)	0.0 (0.2)
Skeena	7.3 (5.3)	6.8 (4.3)	4.0 (3.7)	12.5 (4.5)	7.7 (4.6)	1.1 (1.5)	8.1 (2.4)	6.1 (4.9)	1.8 (1.9)	3.3 (2.4)
Alsek	0.0 (0.2)	0.0 (0.2)	0.0 (0.2)	0.0 (0.1)	0.0 (0.2)	0.0 (0.1)	0.0 (0.1)	0.0 (0.1)	0.0 (0.1)	0.0 (0.1)
Puget Sound	0.4 (1.3)	0.5 (1.0)	0.1 (0.3)	0.1 (0.3)	1.3 (1.0)	2.7 (1.8)	0.6 (0.6)	0.0 (0.2)	1.0 (1.3)	0.9 (1.2)
Juan de Fuca	0.0 (0.1)	0.0 (0.1)	0.0 (0.1)	0.0 (0.1)	0.0 (0.0)	0.0 (0.0)	0.0 (0.0)	0.0 (0.0)	0.0 (0.0)	0.0 (0.0)
Coastal Wash	3.0 (2.4)	5.7 (3.1)	3.7 (2.2)	0.6 (1.3)	0.2 (0.5)	3.3 (2.7)	1.4 (1.0)	0.0 (0.2)	7.0 (2.9)	0.3 (0.9)
Low Col	0.0 (0.1)	3.9 (2.4)	0.0 (0.1)	0.2 (0.7)	0.0 (0.1)	2.2 (1.8)	0.4 (0.9)	0.0 (0.2)	0.0 (0.2)	0.0 (0.3)
Up Col-Sp	0.1 (0.4)	0.0 (0.1)	0.0 (0.2)	0.0 (0.2)	0.0 (0.1)	0.0 (0.2)	0.0 (0.1)	0.0 (0.2)	0.0 (0.1)	0.0 (0.2)
Up Col-Su/F	27.1 (6.8)	11.6 (3.5)	16.6 (3.9)	14.6 (4.2)	12.3 (2.8)	22.2 (4.2)	21.7 (3.2)	8.1 (3.3)	6.8 (2.9)	6.9 (2.9)
Snake-Sp/Su	0.3 (1.2)	0.1 (0.3)	0.1 (0.4)	0.1 (0.5)	0.1 (0.2)	0.1 (0.3)	0.0 (0.2)	0.1 (0.3)	0.1 (0.3)	0.1 (0.3)
Snake-F	5.0 (5.1)	0.0 (0.1)	0.0 (0.1)	0.0 (0.1)	1.7 (1.3)	0.0 (0.1)	0.0 (0.1)	4.3 (2.8)	0.0 (0.1)	0.0 (0.1)
North & Central O	15.3 (4.7)	17.5 (4.1)	28.8 (4.7)	10.7 (3.9)	6.8 (2.1)	21.5 (4.6)	11.2 (2.8)	11.1 (3.3)	5.7 (2.9)	20.5 (4.4)
South Oregon coas	0.1 (0.6)	0.0 (0.2)	0.0 (0.1)	0.2 (0.8)	0.1 (0.4)	0.1 (0.4)	3.4 (1.8)	0.0 (0.2)	0.1 (0.5)	0.1 (0.4)
Klamath/Trinity	0.0 (0.2)	0.0 (0.1)	0.0 (0.1)	0.0 (0.1)	0.0 (0.1)	0.0 (0.1)	0.0 (0.1)	0.0 (0.1)	0.0 (0.1)	0.0 (0.2)
Mid Col-Sp	1.0 (1.6)	0.0 (0.1)	0.0 (0.2)	0.0 (0.2)	0.0 (0.1)	0.0 (0.1)	0.0 (0.1)	0.0 (0.1)	0.0 (0.1)	0.0 (0.1)
Up Willamette	5.6 (2.6)	1.1 (1.2)	1.1 (1.1)	1.4 (1.4)	1.8 (1.2)	1.0 (1.8)	2.6 (1.3)	1.2 (1.2)	0.0 (0.1)	6.9 (3.1)
Cent Val-F	0.2 (0.6)	0.8 (1.1)	0.1 (0.3)	0.1 (0.3)	0.0 (0.1)	0.0 (0.2)	0.0 (0.1)	0.1 (0.2)	0.0 (0.2)	0.1 (0.2)
Cent Val-Sp	0.0 (0.1)	0.0 (0.2)	0.0 (0.1)	0.0 (0.2)	0.0 (0.1)	0.0 (0.1)	0.0 (0.1)	0.0 (0.1)	0.0 (0.1)	0.0 (0.1)

TABLE 2. Continued.

Area 1/101 Date Fishery	2006 Jul 1-9 Troll		2006 Jul 6-20 Troll		2006 Jul 14-30 Troll		2006 Jul15-30 Troll		2006 Aug 1-2 Test		2006 Aug 2-13 Troll		2006 Aug 16-Sep 1 Troll		2006 Aug 31-Sep 22 Troll	
N	96		94		93		95		93		94		98		88	
UPFR	0.1	(0.4)	0.3	(0.7)	0.1	(0.3)	0.1	(0.4)	0.2	(0.5)	0.1	(0.4)	0.1	(0.2)	0.1	(0.3)
MUFR	4.8	(2.5)	3.1	(2.1)	0.1	(0.4)	0.6	(1.0)	4.9	(3.3)	0.1	(0.4)	0.1	(0.3)	0.1	(0.3)
LWFR-F	0.1	(0.4)	0.0	(0.2)	0.0	(0.2)	0.1	(0.3)	0.0	(0.2)	0.0	(0.2)	0.1	(0.5)	0.0	(0.1)
NOTH	3.2	(2.2)	2.8	(1.9)	3.5	(2.3)	4.2	(2.3)	0.1	(0.3)	0.3	(0.8)	0.0	(0.2)	0.0	(0.2)
SOTH	49.6	(5.4)	39.9	(5.3)	39.2	(5.3)	34.4	(5.0)	34.9	(5.5)	42.9	(5.4)	11.8	(3.3)	8.2	(3.1)
LWTH	0.0	(0.2)	0.0	(0.2)	0.1	(0.2)	0.0	(0.2)	0.1	(0.3)	0.0	(0.2)	0.1	(0.2)	0.0	(0.2)
ECVI	0.7	(1.3)	1.6	(1.5)	5.2	(2.5)	0.1	(0.3)	0.2	(0.5)	1.8	(1.6)	0.1	(0.3)	0.1	(0.3)
WCVI	2.8	(1.8)	1.3	(1.2)	5.3	(2.5)	6.8	(2.6)	5.8	(2.6)	3.3	(2.2)	6.1	(2.4)	4.5	(2.3)
SOMN	0.1	(0.3)	0.0	(0.2)	0.1	(0.2)	0.0	(0.2)	0.1	(0.4)	0.1	(0.5)	0.1	(0.3)	0.0	(0.2)
NOMN	4.8	(2.4)	5.2	(2.7)	1.4	(1.7)	0.5	(1.0)	0.1	(0.4)	0.1	(0.4)	0.1	(0.4)	0.1	(0.4)
NASS	0.2	(0.7)	0.1	(0.4)	2.0	(1.8)	0.6	(1.2)	0.1	(0.2)	0.1	(0.7)	0.1	(0.2)	0.1	(0.3)
LWFR-Sp	0.9	(1.0)	0.0	(0.1)	0.0	(0.1)	0.0	(0.1)	0.0	(0.2)	1.1	(1.0)	0.0	(0.1)	0.0	(0.1)
LWFR-Su	0.0	(0.1)	0.0	(0.1)	0.0	(0.1)	1.0	(1.0)	0.0	(0.0)	0.0	(0.1)	0.0	(0.1)	0.0	(0.1)
QCI	1.0	(1.0)	0.0	(0.1)	1.1	(1.1)	3.2	(1.8)	0.0	(0.1)	0.0	(0.1)	1.0	(1.0)	0.0	(0.0)
Alaska	0.0	(0.1)	0.0	(0.1)	0.0	(0.2)	0.0	(0.1)	0.0	(0.1)	0.0	(0.1)	0.0	(0.1)	0.0	(0.1)
Taku	0.0	(0.2)	0.6	(1.2)	0.0	(0.1)	0.0	(0.2)	0.0	(0.2)	0.0	(0.1)	0.0	(0.1)	0.0	(0.1)
Stikine	0.1	(0.3)	0.9	(1.4)	0.5	(1.1)	0.1	(0.5)	0.0	(0.2)	2.1	(1.6)	0.0	(0.2)	0.0	(0.2)
Skeena	0.7	(1.4)	6.4	(3.8)	1.7	(2.1)	2.1	(2.2)	0.1	(0.3)	0.1	(0.3)	0.1	(0.3)	0.1	(0.3)
Alsek	0.0	(0.1)	0.0	(0.1)	0.0	(0.1)	0.0	(0.1)	0.0	(0.1)	0.0	(0.1)	0.0	(0.1)	0.0	(0.1)
Puget Sound	1.1	(1.1)	0.5	(1.1)	0.1	(0.5)	0.1	(0.4)	1.4	(1.6)	0.1	(0.5)	0.0	(0.2)	0.0	(0.2)
Juan de Fuca	0.0	(0.1)	0.0	(0.1)	0.0	(0.1)	0.0	(0.1)	0.0	(0.0)	0.0	(0.1)	0.0	(0.1)	0.0	(0.0)
Coastal Wash	5.1	(2.9)	0.2	(0.7)	3.9	(2.2)	10.4	(4.2)	9.7	(3.8)	0.6	(1.3)	20.3	(4.7)	5.4	(2.8)
Low Col	1.3	(1.7)	0.0	(0.2)	4.9	(2.4)	0.2	(0.7)	0.1	(0.5)	4.7	(2.4)	2.8	(2.0)	0.0	(0.3)
Up Col-Sp	0.4	(0.9)	0.0	(0.1)	0.0	(0.1)	0.0	(0.1)	0.0	(0.1)	0.0	(0.1)	0.0	(0.1)	0.0	(0.1)
Up Col-Su/F	6.2	(3.5)	12.6	(3.6)	12.6	(4.1)	13.4	(4.0)	27.7	(5.0)	21.5	(5.2)	27.9	(5.0)	15.4	(4.1)
Snake-Sp/Su	0.5	(1.2)	0.1	(0.5)	0.1	(0.3)	0.3	(0.7)	0.2	(0.6)	0.1	(0.2)	0.2	(0.7)	0.1	(0.3)
Snake-F	1.2	(2.6)	0.1	(0.6)	2.9	(3.1)	3.1	(2.6)	0.2	(1.2)	2.7	(2.9)	0.4	(1.4)	0.0	(0.2)
North & Central O	12.5	(3.7)	23.0	(4.5)	13.0	(3.8)	14.4	(4.2)	10.4	(3.8)	8.6	(3.4)	26.9	(5.3)	65.2	(5.4)
South Oregon coas	0.1	(0.3)	0.0	(0.2)	0.1	(0.3)	0.2	(0.7)	3.3	(2.4)	2.4	(2.4)	1.4	(1.8)	0.1	(0.4)
Klamath/Trinity	0.0	(0.1)	0.0	(0.1)	0.0	(0.1)	0.0	(0.1)	0.0	(0.2)	0.0	(0.1)	0.0	(0.1)	0.0	(0.2)
Mid Col-Sp	0.0	(0.2)	0.0	(0.1)	0.0	(0.1)	0.0	(0.1)	0.0	(0.2)	0.0	(0.1)	0.0	(0.1)	0.0	(0.1)
Up Willamette	2.4	(1.7)	1.1	(1.3)	1.6	(1.8)	3.8	(2.2)	0.3	(0.9)	7.1	(2.9)	0.0	(0.1)	0.0	(0.1)
Cent Val-F	0.1	(0.2)	0.0	(0.2)	0.4	(0.8)	0.1	(0.2)	0.1	(0.2)	0.1	(0.2)	0.1	(0.2)	0.1	(0.4)
Cent Val-Sp	0.0	(0.1)	0.0	(0.2)	0.0	(0.3)	0.0	(0.1)	0.0	(0.1)	0.0	(0.1)	0.0	(0.2)	0.0	(0.1)

TABLE 3. Chinook salmon *Oncorhynchus tshawytscha* stock composition (%) as estimated in samples from the test fishery conducted prior to the opening of the 2006 troll fishery and later sampled directly from the troll fishery harvest in Area 2W/142 (Figure 1). N = number of fish genetically analyzed and used in mixed stock analysis estimates. Abbreviations are described in Appendix 1. Standard deviations appear in parentheses.

Area 2W/142 Date Fishery	2006 Apr 7 Test	2006 May 5-11 Test	2006 May 17-18 Test	2006 Jun 1-2 Test	2006 Jun 3 Test	2006 Jul 1-3 Test	2006 Jul 5-7 Test	2006 Aug 3-4 Test	2006 Sep 1-10 Test
N	96	96	95	79	20	96	85	85	68
UPFR	1.2 (1.1)	0.1 (0.4)	1.4 (1.3)	3.1 (2.3)	2.4 (4.0)	1.1 (1.1)	0.1 (0.4)	0.1 (0.4)	0.1 (0.4)
MUFR	0.1 (0.4)	0.2 (0.5)	0.2 (0.6)	0.6 (1.3)	4.2 (6.1)	0.1 (0.4)	2.8 (1.9)	4.9 (2.6)	0.2 (0.5)
LWFR-F	0.1 (0.6)	0.2 (0.6)	0.0 (0.1)	0.4 (1.0)	0.8 (2.5)	0.0 (0.1)	0.0 (0.2)	0.0 (0.2)	0.3 (1.0)
NOTH	0.0 (0.2)	0.0 (0.2)	0.6 (1.0)	0.1 (0.4)	0.2 (0.9)	0.0 (0.2)	3.1 (2.2)	0.2 (0.6)	0.0 (0.2)
SOTH	4.7 (2.2)	23.9 (4.4)	8.1 (3.0)	17.9 (4.5)	15.9 (8.0)	12.6 (3.5)	40.9 (5.7)	27.6 (5.1)	7.2 (3.2)
LWTH	0.0 (0.2)	0.0 (0.2)	0.0 (0.2)	0.0 (0.2)	0.1 (0.8)	0.0 (0.2)	0.0 (0.2)	0.0 (0.2)	0.1 (0.6)
ECVI	1.2 (1.3)	0.1 (0.5)	7.3 (2.8)	5.2 (2.5)	0.7 (2.2)	1.7 (2.3)	3.6 (2.3)	0.1 (0.3)	0.2 (0.6)
WCVI	9.6 (3.0)	7.0 (2.6)	20.7 (4.3)	10.1 (3.4)	19.3 (8.5)	3.6 (2.0)	7.4 (2.9)	8.0 (3.1)	5.9 (2.9)
SOMN	0.0 (0.2)	0.1 (0.4)	0.1 (0.2)	0.0 (0.2)	0.1 (0.8)	0.8 (1.7)	0.3 (0.8)	0.1 (0.3)	0.0 (0.2)
NOMN	3.4 (2.1)	5.3 (2.7)	0.7 (1.1)	0.2 (0.7)	0.4 (1.4)	0.1 (0.4)	0.1 (0.5)	0.2 (0.5)	0.1 (0.4)
NASS	0.1 (0.3)	0.1 (0.3)	2.5 (1.9)	0.0 (0.3)	9.5 (6.2)	0.1 (0.5)	0.0 (0.1)	0.1 (0.2)	0.0 (0.3)
LWFR-Sp	0.0 (0.1)	0.0 (0.1)	0.7 (1.0)	0.0 (0.1)	0.1 (0.5)	0.0 (0.1)	0.0 (0.2)	0.0 (0.2)	0.0 (0.3)
LWFR-Su	0.0 (0.1)	0.0 (0.1)	0.0 (0.1)	0.0 (0.1)	0.0 (0.3)	0.0 (0.1)	0.0 (0.1)	0.0 (0.1)	0.0 (0.1)
QCI	0.0 (0.1)	0.0 (0.1)	0.0 (0.1)	0.0 (0.1)	0.0 (0.3)	0.0 (0.1)	0.0 (0.1)	0.0 (0.1)	0.0 (0.1)
Alaska	0.0 (0.2)	0.0 (0.1)	0.0 (0.2)	0.0 (0.1)	0.1 (0.6)	0.0 (0.2)	0.0 (0.1)	0.0 (0.1)	0.0 (0.2)
Taku	0.1 (0.4)	0.1 (0.5)	0.1 (0.6)	0.9 (1.9)	0.1 (0.9)	0.0 (0.2)	2.1 (2.5)	0.0 (0.2)	0.4 (1.0)
Stikine	0.2 (0.6)	0.1 (0.3)	0.1 (0.5)	0.1 (0.8)	0.1 (0.7)	0.0 (0.2)	1.7 (2.2)	0.1 (0.3)	0.1 (0.3)
Skeena	0.4 (0.8)	6.6 (3.4)	0.3 (0.9)	3.7 (3.3)	0.3 (1.2)	0.2 (0.6)	0.7 (1.4)	0.1 (0.3)	0.2 (0.5)
Alsek	0.0 (0.1)	0.0 (0.1)	0.4 (1.0)	0.0 (0.1)	0.1 (0.4)	0.0 (0.1)	0.1 (0.3)	0.0 (0.1)	0.0 (0.2)
Puget Sound	0.1 (0.3)	0.1 (0.4)	0.6 (1.1)	1.9 (2.5)	3.1 (5.1)	0.1 (0.4)	0.3 (0.9)	0.1 (0.2)	0.1 (0.4)
Juan de Fuca	0.0 (0.1)	1.0 (1.6)	0.0 (0.1)	0.8 (1.6)	0.0 (0.2)	0.0 (0.1)	0.5 (0.9)	0.0 (0.1)	0.0 (0.1)
Coastal Wash	4.2 (2.2)	3.1 (1.9)	2.9 (2.1)	0.6 (1.2)	0.1 (1.0)	0.1 (0.3)	1.1 (2.1)	13.8 (4.2)	33.0 (6.6)
Low Col	0.0 (0.2)	0.0 (0.2)	0.0 (0.1)	6.7 (3.2)	7.7 (6.2)	2.6 (2.9)	0.6 (1.6)	3.6 (2.3)	0.0 (0.4)
Up Col-Sp	0.0 (0.1)	0.0 (0.1)	0.0 (0.1)	0.0 (0.1)	0.1 (0.7)	0.0 (0.1)	0.0 (0.2)	0.0 (0.2)	0.0 (0.1)
Up Col-Su/F	57.6 (6.5)	40.9 (5.0)	41.3 (5.7)	34.6 (5.4)	24.5 (9.3)	38.0 (5.9)	10.0 (4.4)	18.3 (5.3)	6.0 (4.0)
Snake-Sp/Su	1.0 (2.1)	0.3 (0.7)	0.2 (0.7)	0.1 (0.3)	0.2 (1.1)	0.1 (0.4)	7.3 (3.4)	0.3 (1.0)	0.1 (0.3)
Snake-F	1.8 (3.9)	0.0 (0.1)	1.5 (2.9)	0.1 (0.6)	0.1 (1.0)	13.8 (4.5)	2.1 (3.3)	6.0 (3.7)	1.0 (2.0)
North & Central O	8.3 (3.1)	8.8 (3.0)	8.6 (3.4)	11.4 (4.1)	2.7 (4.4)	16.3 (5.5)	14.0 (4.1)	13.9 (4.2)	41.4 (6.8)
South Oregon coas	0.0 (0.2)	0.0 (0.2)	0.6 (1.5)	0.5 (1.3)	4.3 (4.9)	3.8 (3.4)	0.0 (0.1)	0.0 (0.2)	3.3 (3.0)
Klamath/Trinity	0.0 (0.1)	0.5 (0.9)	0.0 (0.3)	0.1 (0.3)	0.1 (0.5)	0.0 (0.1)	0.0 (0.1)	0.0 (0.1)	0.0 (0.2)
Mid Col-Sp	0.0 (0.1)	0.0 (0.1)	0.0 (0.1)	0.1 (0.1)	2.1 (3.9)	0.0 (0.1)	0.0 (0.1)	0.0 (0.1)	0.0 (0.3)
Up Willamette	5.8 (2.8)	1.2 (1.2)	0.9 (1.3)	0.4 (1.4)	0.1 (0.6)	4.5 (2.5)	0.8 (1.5)	2.4 (2.1)	0.1 (0.5)
Cent Val-F	0.0 (0.2)	0.1 (0.3)	0.1 (0.2)	0.1 (0.3)	0.3 (1.2)	0.1 (0.2)	0.1 (0.3)	0.1 (0.3)	0.1 (0.3)
Cent Val-Sp	0.0 (0.1)	0.0 (0.1)	0.0 (0.1)	0.0 (0.1)	0.1 (0.6)	0.0 (0.2)	0.0 (0.1)	0.0 (0.1)	0.0 (0.1)

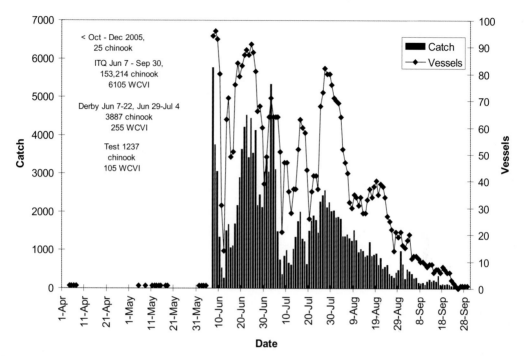

FIGURE 3. 2006 Chinook *Oncorhynchus tshawytscha* daily catch and effort in the northern British Columbia troll fishery.

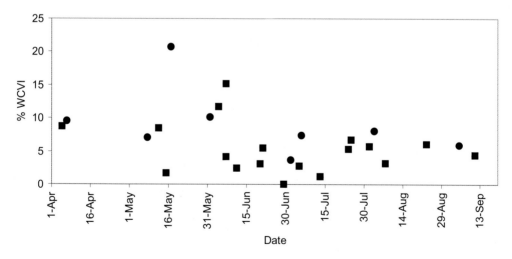

FIGURE 4. Proportion of west coast Vancouver Island (WCVI) Chinook salmon *Oncorhynchus tshawytscha* observed in the 2006 northern British Columbia troll fishery and test samples plotted against date sampled. ■ = Area 1; ● = Area 2W

TABLE 4. Chinook salmon *Oncorhynchus tshawytscha* catch in numbers of fish by stock from Area 1/101. Numbers were estimated by using salmon harvest numbers and percentage stock composition estimates (Table 2) from the 2006 test fishery and troll fishery harvest samples. Abbreviations are described in Appendix 1. Standard deviations appear in parentheses.

Area 1/101 Date Fishery	2006 Apr 4-6 Test	2006 May 11-14 Test	2006 May 15 Test	2006 Jun 3-4 Test	2006 Jun 7 Troll	2006 Jun 7 Troll	2006 Jun 7-19 Troll	2006 Jun 16-26 Troll	2006 Jun 17-26 Troll	2006 Jun 27-Jul 1 Troll
Catch	100	93	97	77	3,365	2,400	17,255	16,005	15,633	11,481
N	84	92	94	76	143	102	183	92	98	87
UPFR	0 (0)	0 (0)	1 (1)	1 (1)	120 (58)	69 (40)	288 (246)	25 (82)	405 (285)	12 (38)
MUFR	0 (0)	3 (2)	3 (2)	5 (2)	18 (36)	6 (16)	784 (367)	435 (404)	500 (353)	18 (62)
LWFR-F	0 (0)	0 (0)	0 (0)	1 (1)	3 (12)	1 (4)	2 (9)	4 (29)	3 (21)	2 (14)
NOTH	1 (1)	2 (2)	2 (5)	0 (0)	86 (57)	1 (5)	93 (120)	7 (35)	325 (289)	455 (253)
SOTH	12 (4)	30 (5)	30 (5)	26 (4)	1553 (142)	391 (87)	5714 (613)	7539 (863)	9025 (825)	5682 (632)
LWTH	0 (0)	1 (1)	0 (0)	0 (0)	1 (4)	23 (23)	120 (118)	6 (27)	7 (31)	5 (26)
ECVI	3 (2)	1 (1)	2 (1)	1 (1)	29 (28)	113 (54)	109 (107)	281 (247)	440 (321)	185 (176)
WCVI	9 (3)	8 (3)	2 (2)	9 (1)	142 (57)	365 (86)	424 (204)	887 (383)	493 (294)	13 (40)
SOMN	0 (0)	0 (0)	0 (1)	0 (0)	1 (4)	2 (9)	5 (25)	7 (35)	5 (24)	37 (92)
NOMN	9 (4)	2 (2)	2 (1)	1 (1)	182 (73)	42 (37)	914 (328)	1622 (535)	717 (386)	15 (49)
NASS	0 (0)	2 (2)	2 (1)	2 (2)	140 (64)	22 (27)	166 (161)	21 (80)	19 (73)	530 (270)
LWFR-Sp	0 (0)	0 (0)	0 (0)	0 (0)	0 (1)	0 (1)	35 (76)	3 (22)	4 (28)	2 (19)
LWFR-Su	0 (0)	0 (0)	0 (0)	0 (0)	0 (1)	0 (1)	1 (6)	1 (15)	1 (8)	1 (13)
QCI	0 (0)	0 (0)	0 (0)	0 (0)	0 (2)	0 (1)	1 (5)	170 (171)	1 (13)	1 (8)
Alaska	0 (0)	0 (0)	0 (0)	0 (0)	2 (10)	0 (2)	2 (15)	4 (27)	3 (20)	2 (16)
Taku	0 (0)	0 (1)	2 (2)	0 (1)	5 (18)	2 (8)	13 (50)	5 (28)	26 (96)	3 (18)
Stikine	0 (0)	0 (0)	1 (2)	0 (0)	2 (12)	61 (49)	8 (37)	9 (44)	118 (228)	5 (25)
Skeena	7 (5)	6 (4)	4 (4)	10 (3)	261 (155)	26 (36)	1405 (423)	975 (781)	279 (300)	381 (278)
Alsek	0 (0)	0 (0)	0 (0)	0 (0)	1 (5)	0 (3)	4 (22)	2 (14)	2 (14)	2 (14)
Puget Sound	0 (1)	0 (1)	0 (0)	0 (0)	44 (33)	64 (43)	106 (106)	7 (33)	155 (209)	102 (138)
Juan de Fuca	0 (0)	0 (0)	0 (0)	0 (0)	0 (1)	0 (1)	1 (6)	1 (8)	1 (7)	1 (6)
Coastal Wash	3 (2)	5 (3)	4 (2)	0 (1)	8 (18)	80 (65)	243 (178)	4 (26)	1096 (448)	38 (101)
Low Col	0 (0)	4 (2)	0 (0)	0 (0)	0 (3)	53 (43)	75 (158)	2 (14)	4 (31)	5 (36)
Up Col-Sp	0 (0)	0 (0)	0 (0)	0 (0)	1 (3)	2 (4)	2 (13)	4 (25)	3 (19)	3 (17)
Up Col-Su/F	27 (7)	11 (3)	16 (4)	11 (3)	414 (94)	532 (101)	3749 (546)	1292 (530)	1055 (447)	796 (329)
Snake-Sp/Su	0 (1)	0 (0)	0 (0)	0 (0)	2 (7)	2 (6)	8 (26)	11 (40)	12 (44)	8 (29)
Snake-F	5 (5)	0 (0)	0 (0)	0 (0)	56 (43)	2 (2)	1 (9)	689 (442)	1 (19)	1 (7)
North & Central O	15 (5)	16 (4)	28 (5)	8 (3)	230 (72)	517 (111)	1939 (475)	1783 (536)	894 (450)	2355 (508)
South Oregon coas	0 (1)	0 (0)	0 (0)	0 (0)	3 (14)	2 (9)	591 (311)	6 (35)	21 (79)	11 (51)
Klamath/Trinity	0 (0)	0 (0)	0 (0)	0 (0)	0 (3)	0 (2)	2 (13)	2 (17)	2 (18)	2 (19)
Mid Col-Sp	0 (2)	0 (0)	0 (0)	0 (0)	0 (3)	0 (2)	2 (11)	3 (22)	2 (16)	2 (14)
Up Willamette	6 (3)	1 (1)	1 (1)	1 (1)	60 (41)	23 (42)	441 (218)	186 (188)	3 (21)	796 (350)
Cent Val-F	0 (1)	1 (1)	0 (0)	0 (0)	1 (5)	1 (5)	6 (21)	9 (35)	7 (29)	6 (25)
Cent Val-Sp	0 (0)	0 (0)	0 (0)	0 (0)	0 (2)	0 (2)	2 (12)	2 (15)	2 (18)	2 (14)

TABLE 4. Continued.

Area 1/101 Date Fishery	2006 Jul 1-9 Troll		2006 Jul 6-20 Troll		2006 Jul 14-30 Troll		2006 Jul 15-30 Troll		2006 Aug 1-2 Troll & Test		2006 Aug 2-13 Troll		2006 Aug 16-Sep 1 Troll		2006 Aug 31-Sep 22 Troll	
Catch	19,287		8,424		13,022		12,349		9,381		12,702		11,288		4,610	
N	96		94		93		95		93		94		98		88	
UPFR	28	(85)	24	(58)	12	(38)	16	(48)	15	(46)	15	(46)	9	(27)	5	(15)
MUFR	916	(479)	264	(177)	17	(52)	70	(123)	460	(311)	18	(54)	10	(30)	5	(16)
LWFR-F	13	(72)	2	(15)	4	(30)	8	(42)	3	(20)	3	(25)	16	(60)	1	(6)
NOTH	613	(417)	235	(163)	457	(293)	524	(282)	6	(28)	33	(96)	4	(21)	2	(11)
SOTH	9563	(1043)	3357	(451)	5100	(688)	4249	(619)	3274	(516)	5449	(685)	1336	(369)	377	(142)
LWTH	8	(33)	3	(15)	7	(30)	6	(29)	6	(27)	5	(24)	4	(18)	2	(7)
ECVI	131	(259)	134	(127)	673	(328)	11	(41)	16	(50)	226	(200)	11	(36)	4	(14)
WCVI	546	(347)	108	(104)	696	(319)	837	(322)	542	(248)	415	(284)	689	(271)	208	(104)
SOMN	11	(54)	3	(13)	7	(31)	5	(24)	7	(36)	15	(70)	8	(34)	2	(10)
NOMN	917	(470)	440	(225)	183	(221)	57	(129)	14	(42)	14	(46)	15	(48)	7	(20)
NASS	45	(135)	9	(36)	261	(230)	76	(147)	5	(21)	18	(84)	6	(23)	3	(12)
LWFR-Sp	175	(194)	1	(10)	2	(17)	2	(15)	2	(15)	134	(133)	2	(16)	1	(4)
LWFR-Su	1	(11)	0	(6)	1	(8)	126	(128)	0	(5)	1	(8)	1	(6)	0	(2)
QCI	195	(195)	0	(4)	146	(147)	389	(219)	0	(5)	1	(12)	115	(115)	0	(2)
Alaska	3	(21)	1	(10)	2	(20)	2	(12)	1	(9)	2	(14)	1	(16)	1	(4)
Taku	8	(43)	53	(104)	3	(18)	5	(26)	3	(17)	3	(18)	3	(15)	1	(8)
Stikine	15	(65)	72	(119)	63	(146)	14	(60)	3	(16)	272	(198)	4	(20)	2	(7)
Skeena	139	(264)	535	(318)	225	(268)	255	(267)	7	(24)	11	(35)	9	(32)	4	(12)
Alsek	3	(25)	1	(9)	2	(14)	2	(13)	1	(10)	2	(17)	1	(8)	1	(4)
Puget Sound	217	(220)	38	(96)	17	(61)	14	(53)	133	(146)	16	(59)	5	(21)	1	(8)
Juan de Fuca	1	(11)	0	(5)	1	(13)	2	(18)	0	(4)	1	(8)	1	(8)	0	(2)
Coastal Wash	979	(557)	14	(62)	505	(283)	1287	(515)	914	(359)	70	(170)	2289	(535)	250	(127)
Low Col	254	(324)	3	(21)	636	(311)	29	(89)	10	(45)	597	(301)	316	(222)	2	(12)
Up Col-Sp	74	(178)	2	(12)	3	(17)	3	(18)	2	(13)	3	(17)	2	(14)	1	(6)
Up Col-Su/F	1188	(681)	1060	(303)	1641	(531)	1658	(499)	2599	(468)	2730	(666)	3149	(569)	711	(190)
Snake-Sp/Su	105	(226)	9	(40)	10	(39)	33	(82)	15	(54)	8	(30)	23	(76)	4	(13)
Snake-F	226	(505)	12	(49)	377	(400)	387	(319)	21	(109)	339	(371)	43	(155)	2	(11)
North & Central O	2416	(704)	1938	(378)	1687	(496)	1780	(514)	972	(359)	1093	(438)	3038	(600)	3005	(248)
South Oregon coas	12	(64)	3	(15)	9	(44)	20	(82)	305	(225)	299	(300)	161	(202)	4	(19)
Klamath/Trinity	3	(21)	1	(10)	2	(13)	2	(17)	2	(15)	2	(12)	1	(8)	1	(7)
Mid Col-Sp	5	(38)	1	(11)	2	(16)	2	(12)	2	(21)	2	(14)	2	(14)	1	(4)
Up Willamette	463	(319)	92	(113)	211	(236)	471	(268)	31	(87)	897	(374)	2	(12)	1	(5)
Cent Val-F	10	(44)	4	(17)	54	(110)	6	(26)	5	(22)	7	(29)	7	(26)	5	(19)
Cent Val-Sp	3	(20)	2	(17)	5	(35)	2	(16)	2	(11)	2	(17)	2	(18)	1	(4)

TABLE 5. Chinook salmon *Oncorhynchus tshawytscha* catch in numbers of fish by stock from Area 2W/142. Numbers were estimated by using salmon harvest numbers and percentage stock composition estimates (Table 3) from the 2006 test fishery and troll fishery harvest samples. Abbreviations are described in Appendix 1. Standard deviations appear in parentheses.

Area 2W/142 Date Fishery	2006 Apr 7 Test	2006 May 5-11 Test	2006 May 17-18 Test	2006 Jun 1-2 Test	2006 Jun 3 Test	2006 Jul 1-3 Test	2006 Jul 5-7 Test	2006 Aug 3-4 Test	2006 Sep 1-10 Test
Catch	100	100	100	80	20	100	100	100	70
N	96	96	95	79	20	96	85	85	68
UPFR	1.2 (1.1)	0.1 (0.4)	1.4 (1.3)	2.5 (1.8)	0.5 (0.8)	1.1 (1.1)	0.1 (0.4)	0.1 (0.4)	0.1 (0.3)
MUFR	0.1 (0.4)	0.2 (0.5)	0.2 (0.6)	0.5 (1.0)	0.8 (1.2)	0.1 (0.4)	2.8 (1.9)	4.9 (2.6)	0.1 (0.4)
LWFR-F	0.1 (0.6)	0.2 (0.6)	0.0 (0.1)	0.3 (0.8)	0.2 (0.5)	0.0 (0.1)	0.0 (0.2)	0.0 (0.2)	0.2 (0.7)
NOTH	0.0 (0.2)	0.0 (0.2)	0.6 (1.0)	0.1 (0.3)	0.0 (0.2)	0.0 (0.2)	3.1 (2.2)	0.2 (0.6)	0.0 (0.2)
SOTH	4.7 (2.2)	23.9 (4.4)	8.1 (3.0)	14.3 (3.6)	3.2 (1.6)	12.6 (3.5)	40.9 (5.7)	27.6 (5.1)	5.0 (2.3)
LWTH	0.0 (0.2)	0.0 (0.2)	0.0 (0.2)	0.0 (0.2)	0.1 (0.4)	0.0 (0.2)	0.0 (0.2)	0.1 (0.2)	0.0 (0.2)
ECVI	1.2 (1.3)	0.1 (0.5)	7.3 (2.8)	4.2 (2.0)	3.9 (1.7)	1.7 (2.3)	3.6 (2.3)	0.1 (0.3)	0.1 (0.4)
WCVI	9.6 (3.0)	7.0 (2.6)	20.7 (4.3)	8.1 (2.7)	0.0 (0.2)	3.6 (2.0)	7.4 (2.9)	8.0 (3.1)	4.1 (2.0)
SOMN	0.0 (0.2)	0.1 (0.4)	0.1 (0.2)	0.0 (0.2)	0.1 (0.3)	0.8 (1.7)	0.3 (0.8)	0.1 (0.3)	0.0 (0.2)
NOMN	3.4 (2.1)	5.3 (2.7)	0.7 (1.1)	0.2 (0.5)	1.9 (1.2)	0.1 (0.4)	0.1 (0.5)	0.2 (0.5)	0.1 (0.3)
NASS	0.1 (0.3)	0.1 (0.3)	2.5 (1.9)	0.1 (0.3)	0.0 (0.1)	0.1 (0.5)	0.1 (0.3)	0.1 (0.4)	0.1 (0.2)
LWFR-Sp	0.0 (0.1)	0.0 (0.1)	0.7 (1.0)	0.0 (0.1)	0.0 (0.1)	0.0 (0.1)	0.0 (0.1)	0.0 (0.2)	0.0 (0.2)
QCI	0.0 (0.1)	0.0 (0.1)	0.0 (0.1)	0.0 (0.1)	0.0 (0.1)	0.0 (0.1)	0.0 (0.1)	0.0 (0.1)	0.0 (0.0)
Alaska	0.0 (0.1)	0.0 (0.1)	0.0 (0.1)	0.0 (0.1)	0.0 (0.2)	0.0 (0.1)	0.0 (0.1)	0.0 (0.1)	0.0 (0.0)
Taku	0.0 (0.2)	0.0 (0.1)	0.0 (0.2)	0.0 (0.1)	0.0 (0.1)	0.0 (0.1)	0.0 (0.1)	0.0 (0.1)	0.0 (0.1)
Stikine	0.1 (0.4)	0.1 (0.5)	0.1 (0.6)	0.7 (1.5)	0.0 (0.2)	0.0 (0.2)	2.1 (2.5)	0.1 (0.2)	0.3 (0.7)
Skeena	0.2 (0.6)	0.1 (0.3)	0.1 (0.5)	0.1 (0.6)	0.1 (0.2)	0.2 (0.6)	1.7 (2.2)	0.1 (0.3)	0.0 (0.2)
Alsek	0.4 (0.8)	6.6 (3.4)	0.3 (0.9)	3.0 (2.6)	0.0 (0.1)	0.0 (0.1)	0.7 (1.4)	0.1 (0.3)	0.1 (0.4)
Puget Sound	0.0 (0.1)	0.0 (0.1)	0.4 (1.0)	0.0 (0.1)	0.6 (1.0)	0.1 (0.4)	0.1 (0.3)	0.0 (0.1)	0.0 (0.1)
Juan de Fuca	0.1 (0.3)	0.1 (0.4)	0.6 (1.1)	1.5 (2.0)	0.0 (1.0)	0.0 (0.1)	0.3 (0.9)	0.1 (0.2)	0.1 (0.3)
Coastal Wash	0.0 (0.1)	1.0 (1.6)	0.0 (0.1)	0.7 (1.3)	0.0 (0.0)	0.1 (0.3)	0.5 (0.9)	0.0 (0.1)	0.0 (0.1)
Low Col	4.2 (2.2)	3.1 (1.9)	2.9 (2.1)	0.5 (1.0)	1.5 (1.2)	2.6 (2.9)	1.1 (2.1)	13.8 (4.2)	23.1 (4.6)
Up Col-Sp	0.0 (0.2)	0.0 (0.2)	0.0 (0.1)	5.4 (2.5)	0.0 (0.1)	0.0 (0.1)	0.6 (1.6)	3.6 (2.3)	0.0 (0.3)
Up Col-Su/F	0.0 (0.1)	0.0 (0.1)	0.0 (0.1)	0.0 (0.1)	4.9 (1.9)	0.0 (0.2)	0.0 (0.2)	0.0 (0.2)	0.0 (0.1)
Snake-Sp/Su	57.6 (6.5)	40.9 (5.0)	41.3 (5.7)	27.7 (4.3)	0.0 (0.2)	38.0 (5.9)	10.0 (4.4)	18.3 (5.3)	4.2 (2.8)
Snake-F	1.0 (2.1)	0.3 (0.7)	0.2 (0.7)	0.1 (0.2)	0.0 (0.2)	0.1 (0.4)	7.3 (3.4)	0.3 (1.0)	0.1 (0.2)
Oregon coastal	1.8 (3.9)	0.0 (0.1)	1.5 (2.9)	0.1 (0.5)	0.5 (0.9)	13.8 (4.5)	2.1 (3.3)	6.0 (3.7)	0.7 (1.4)
S.Or./Cal coast	8.3 (3.1)	8.8 (3.0)	8.6 (3.4)	9.1 (3.3)	0.9 (1.0)	16.3 (5.5)	14.0 (4.1)	13.9 (4.2)	29.0 (4.8)
Up Klam/Trinity	0.0 (0.2)	0.0 (0.2)	0.6 (1.5)	0.4 (1.1)	0.0 (0.1)	3.8 (3.4)	0.0 (0.1)	0.0 (0.2)	2.3 (2.1)
Mid Col-Sp	0.0 (0.1)	0.5 (0.9)	0.0 (0.1)	0.0 (0.2)	0.0 (0.1)	0.0 (0.1)	0.0 (0.1)	0.0 (0.1)	0.0 (0.1)
Up Willamette	0.0 (0.1)	0.0 (0.1)	0.0 (0.1)	0.0 (0.1)	0.4 (0.8)	0.0 (0.1)	0.0 (0.1)	0.0 (0.1)	0.0 (0.2)
Cent Val-F	5.8 (2.8)	1.2 (1.2)	0.9 (1.3)	0.4 (1.1)	0.0 (0.1)	4.5 (2.5)	0.8 (1.5)	2.4 (2.1)	0.1 (0.3)
Cent Val-Sp	0.0 (0.2)	0.1 (0.3)	0.1 (0.2)	0.0 (0.2)	0.1 (0.2)	0.1 (0.2)	0.1 (0.3)	0.1 (0.3)	0.1 (0.2)

TABLE 6. Decision table describing the data delivered from the troll sampling program and how the test results contributed to the management of the troll fishery.

Area	Sample site description	Fishery	Dates fish were caught	Analysis Received	WCVI %	Comment	Management decision
101	LaPerouse Reef	Test	Apr 4-6	21-Apr	8.8		Fishery remains closed
2W/142	Buck Pt	Test	Apr 7	21-Apr	9.6		Fishery remains closed
2W/142	Buck Pt	Test	May 5-11	20-May	7.0		Fishery remains closed
Area101	LaPerouse Reef	Test	May 11-14	20-May	8.5		Fishery remains closed
Area101	LaPerouse Reef	Test	May 15	28-May	1.7		Open ITQ & derby fisheries June 7 north of Louis Pt.
2W/142	Buck Pt	Test	May 17-18	28-May	20.7		Keep remainder of Area 2W/142 closed.
2W/142	Buck Pt	Test	Jun 1-2	16-Jun	10.1		Keep remainder of Area 2W/142 closed.
2W/142	Tartu Inlet	Test	Jun 3	16-Jun	19.3	small sample size ($N = 20$)	Close derby fishery June 22. Data used in addition to the 7 June sample collected South of Frederick I.
101	LaPerouse Reef	Test	Jun 3-4	16-Jun	11.8	Test boat broken down June 4	
101	LaPerouse Reet	Troll	Jun 7	15-Jun	4.2	North of Frederick I.	Keep ITQ open until more fishery samples arrive.
101	Tian Head	Troll	Jun 7	15-Jun	15.2	South of Frederick I.	Close derby fishery June 22.
1/101		Troll	Jun 7-19	24-Jun	2.5	double sample ($N = 200$)	Re-open derby fishery June 29. Keep ITQ fishery open.
101		Troll	Jun 14-24			not submitted for analysis	
101	West of Langara	Troll	Jun 16-26	1-Jul	5.5		Fishery remains open
1/101	East of Langara	Troll	Jun 17-26	1-Jul	3.2		Fishery remains open
1/101		Troll	Jun 21 - Jul 3			not submitted for analysis	
101		Troll	Jun 27-Jul 1	18-Jul	0.1		Fishery remains open
2W/142	Tartu Inlet	Test	July1-3	18-Jul	3.6		Extend opening south to Hippa I.
1/101	Dixon & West Langara	Troll	Jul 1-9	18-Jul	2.8		Fishery remains open
2W/142	Buck Point	Test	Jul 5-7	18-Jul	7.4		Retain closure of southern areas.
1/101		Troll	Jul 2-14			not submitted for analysis	
1/101		Troll	Jul 6-20	30-Jul	1.3		Fishery remains open
1/101		Troll	Jul 14-30	18-Aug	5.3		Fishery remains open
1/101		Troll	Jul 15-30	24-Oct	6.8		This sample was above the trigger but was not submitted for analysis until after the fishery was closed.
Mixed	Langara to Tian	Troll	Jul 26 - Aug 5	18-Aug	5.8		Fishery remains open
101		Test	Aug 1-2	18-Aug	8.0		Retain closure of southern areas.
2W/142	Buck Pt	Test	Aug 3-4	20-Aug	3.3		Fishery remains open
1/101		Troll	Aug 2-13			not submitted for analysis	
Mixed		Troll	Jul 28 - Aug 14			not submitted for analysis	
101		Troll	Aug 16-Sep 1	20-Sep	6.1		No change. Above trigger but fishery effort was low and to close September 30.
1/101		Troll	Aug 12 - Sep 4			not submitted for analysis	
2W/142	Buck Pt, to Tian	Test	Sep 1-10	20-Sep	5.9		This sample was below the trigger but the area was not opened because of poor fishing and the late date.

The troll catch for the 2006 summer fishery of 158,338 Chinook salmon included 6,465 fish of WCVI origin. The catch of WCVI Chinook salmon was 102% of the preseason target. The total catch of Chinook salmon was 103% of the preseason target and 99.8% of the post season allowable catch (the Queen Charlotte Islands sport catch was lower than expected). The estimated postseason exploitation rate on WCVI Chinook salmon was 2.9% and the estimated harvest rate on the return of WCVI Chinook salmon to Canada was 3.3%.

The proportions of WCVI Chinook salmon in each sample were variable but tended to be highest in May and early June (Figure 4). When compared to samples collected in previous years, the tendency for high proportions of WCVI Chinook salmon to be in August samples was less in 2006 (Appendix 2).

Most of the Chinook salmon caught in the northern troll fishery were ocean type. The largest cohort was age 4_1 fish from the South Thompson stock group. Other large components included mixed age 4_1 and age 5_1 fish from the Upper Columbia Summer/Fall and the North and Central Oregon stock groups (Table 7). Few stream-type fish were represented in the samples, but there appeared to be problems with their identification. Taku, Stikine, Nass and Skeena stock groups are typically stream type fish, but the most of the samples assigned to these stock groups were aged as ocean type (Table 7).

Examination of the proportions of the large stock components by month show Fraser stock groups increasing from April to July and then decreasing to September; the Columbia component decreases from April to May, then remains relatively stable through August before decreasing in September; and the Oregon component remains relatively stable from April to August with a large increase in September (Figure 5). When the monthly stock proportions are separated by area (Figure 6) these patterns persist, though,

large differences existed between Area 1/101 and 2W/142 in the relative contributions by each stock group.

Discussion

The genetic sampling program of the 2006 northern British Columbia troll fishery supplied Chinook salmon harvest data by stock; this permitted the fishery to be successfully managed to reach the harvest level allocated within the Pacific Salmon Treaty, and to meet Canada's domestic conservation target for WCVI stocks. Trends in stock composition were used to regulate the time and area for 2006 troll fisheries. Commercial landings of troll-caught Chinook salmon were sampled, and stock-specific impacts were estimated with known precision using genetic data (Table 1). Stock-specific age structure was determined for the catch (Table 7).

A number of factors contributed to the success of the 2006 troll fishery and the sampling programs. The preseason forecast of the return of WCVI Chinook salmon to Canada was accurate, within 2% of the postseason estimate. Decision rules and management triggers were established in advance of the fishery. Sampling sites and protocols were previously tested and options were available for test fisheries and sampling of commercial landings. Past trends in the temporal and spatial patterns of large stock components were known and had been relatively stable for a few years. Some beneficial management actions like a boundary along the coastline to separate troll and sport fisheries were already established. Troll fishers were aggressive with respect to taking advantage of fishing opportunities.

Conditions in 2006 may not be representative of future fisheries. Test fishery observations and information from the sport fishery indicated changes in the distribution of Chinook salmon on the west side of Queen

TABLE 7. Chinook salmon *Oncorhynchus tshawytscha* age data by stock region for northern British Columbia troll fishery. Gilbert and Rich (1927) age designation system A_b where A = the age of the fish in years starting from the egg stage and b = the number of winters in fresh water starting from the egg stage. M = marine age only for those cases where the freshwater age could not be interpreted.

Stock Region	3_1	4_1	4_2	5_1	5_2	6_1	6_2	6_3	7_1	7_2	2M	3M	4M	5M	6M	Total aged
Taku		1		2	1							1				5
Stikine		1		2							1	1				5
QCI	4	1	1													6
NASS	2	3	2	1	4		2				1	1				16
Skeena		17	8	7	9		8			2	2	7	7			67
NOMN	3	18	2	13	7		1				2	9	2			57
WCVI	24	64		33		1					1	9	2			134
ECVI	11	12	1	7								4		1		36
UPFR		4	2		3						1	2				12
MUFR	1	8	7	3	18						4	5	1			47
NOTH	1	7	1	1	12	1					1	2				26
SOTH	15	413	7	135	5	3	3				4	54	22	2		663
LWTH													2			2
LWFR-Sp			1		2											3
LWFR-Su		1														1
LWFR-F												1				1
Puget Sound		4		3												7
Juan de Fuca	1	2														3
Coastal Wash	1	41	1	46	1	6					2	4	6	2	1	111
Up Col-Sp			1													1
Up Col-Su/F	17	158	6	205	6	14	12			2	8	13	24	4		469
Snake-Sp/Su		2		2									2			6
Snake-F	3	6		15	2						3		1			30
Mid Col-Sp		1				1										2
Up Willamette	4	14	3	11	4	1		1			1	6	4			49
Low Col	5	13		6		1	3					1	2	1		32
North & Central O	9	111	2	134	7	26	9		1	1	5	20	39	7		371
South Oregon coas	2	8	1	5		1				1						18

Winther and Beacham

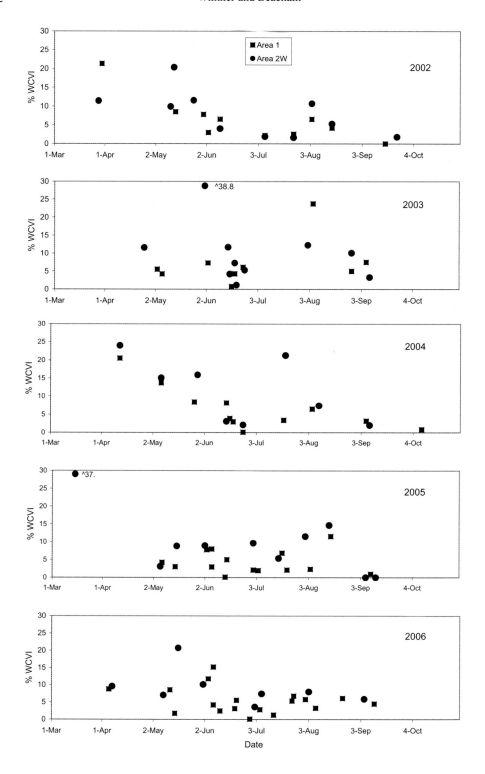

APPENDIX 2. Comparison of %WCVI component from Chinook salmon samples collected from 2002 to 2006. 2002 to 2005 data from Winther and Beacham (2006).

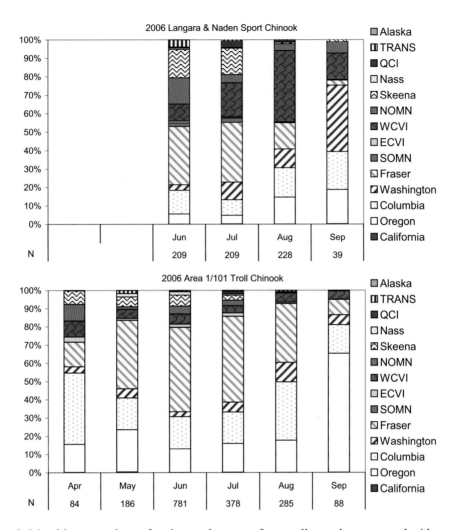

APPENDIX 3. Monthly proportions of major stock groups from troll samples compared with sport samples collected from Area 1/101 in 2006.

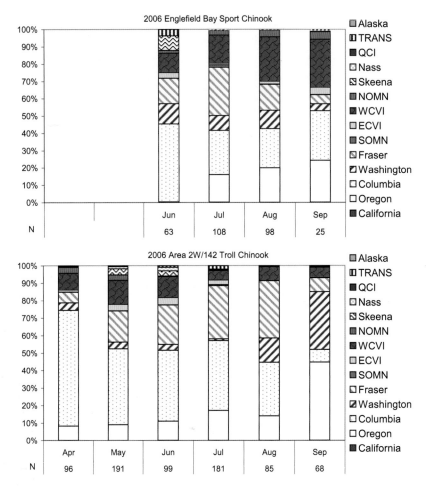

APPENDIX 4. Monthly proportions of major stock groups from troll samples compared with sport samples collected from Area 2W/142 in 2006.

American Fisheries Society Symposium 70:1005–1019, 2009

Failures to Incorporate Science into Fishery Management and Recovery Programs: Lessons from the Columbia River

JAMES A. LICHATOWICH[*]

Alder Fork Consulting
Columbia City, Oregon 97018, USA

RICHARD N. WILLIAMS

Center for Salmonids and Freshwater Species at Risk, University of Idaho
Hagerman, Idaho 83332, USA

Abstract.—The Pacific Northwest states of Oregon, Washington, California, and Idaho are engaged in a massive effort to restore depleted populations of Pacific salmon *Oncorhynchus* spp. The region's largest watershed, the Columbia Basin, is the focus of what has been called the world's largest attempt at ecosystem restoration. After 26 years of implementation, the failure of the program to achieve its modest recovery goal was the result, in part, of a failure to incorporate the latest science into the program. The fundamental assumptions and principles that guide the selection of recovery tasks and their implementation were not based on the latest scientific understanding of the salmon production system. Three impediments to the incorporation of science into management and recovery programs are identified: an inadequate conceptual foundation, fragmented institutional structures, and political interference. Each impediment is illustrated and discussed using case histories from the Columbia River.

Introduction

In 1980, the U.S. Congress enacted the Northwest Power Planning and Conservation Act (Power Act). One purpose of the act was to create greater parity between fish and electric power production in the management of the Columbia River. To implement the Power Act, Congress created the Northwest Power and Conservation Council (Council) made up of two representatives from the states of Oregon, Washington, Idaho, and Montana. Congress directed the Council to develop a fish and wildlife restoration program funded by the Bonneville Power Administration using power revenues (McConnaha et al. 2006). The first Fish and Wildlife Program (FWP) was adopted in 1982, and it has been amended periodically since then. The scope of the FWP and its cost constitutes what may be the largest attempt at ecosystem restoration in the world (Lee 1993).

Historical analysis conducted at the Council's direction estimated the annual pre-development salmon *Oncorhynchus* spp. runs at 10–16 million adult fish (Figure 1). By the early 1980s, the annual run (catch plus es-

[*]Corresponding author: jalich@comcast.net

capement) had declined to an average of 2.5 million fish (NPPC 1986). After estimating the losses attributable to the operation of the federal power system, the Council adopted a modest recovery goal of five million adults in the annual run, a doubling of the average run at the time the Power Act was enacted (Williams et al. 2006).

During the first twenty years of implementation (1982–2003), the Council spent 1.16 billion dollars in direct funding for fish recovery projects under the FWP. Adding in indirect costs, such as forgone power revenues when water is spilled at dams to facilitate downstream migration of juvenile salmon, brings the total cost of the FWP to $6.45 billion dollars (NPCC 2003). Since implementation of the Council's FWP, the estimated total number of salmon entering the Columbia River has fluctuated from 750 thousand to 3 million fish. During the late 1980s and the first few years

of 2000, salmon escapement to the river increased reaching a peak of about three million fish (Figure 1). This most recent increase was due, in part, to favorable ocean conditions. In 1999, several indicators suggested a return to a cool ocean regime favorable to salmon survival; however, this favorable change in ocean regime appears to have been short lived. Since 2002, the indicators suggest a return to less favorable ocean conditions (Bottom et al. 2006) and in the past few years, salmon escapement has declined.

Monitoring at the ecosystem level is inadequate to determine how the causes of higher salmon escapement in 2000–2003 might be separated into the effects of ocean conditions or the results of recovery actions taken by the FWP. In addition, the monitoring data (Figure 1) used for evaluation are escapement of salmon to the river, which includes harvest in the river but not ocean harvest. Total catch

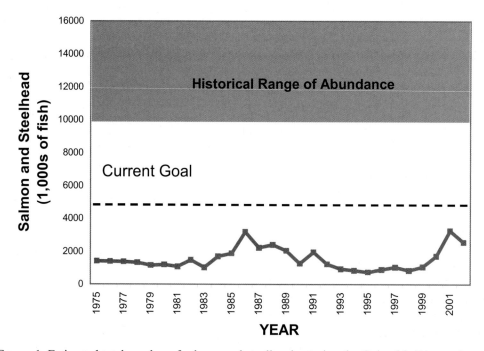

FIGURE 1. Estimated total number of salmon and steelhead entering the Columbia River prior to development (shaded area) from NPPC (1986). The estimated total number of salmon entering the Columbia River (1975–2002) from ODFW and WDFW (2006). The restoration goal for Pacific salmon in the Columbia River from Williams et al. (2006).

(all sources) and escapement to spawning data are not available and are needed to determine if the Council has achieved its goal of five million fish. However, after twenty years the program has not appeared to achieve its goal; the progress towards the recovery goal is muddled due to incomplete data.

In 1995, when total salmon escapement to the river reached a low of 750 thousand fish, the Council asked the Independent Science Group (ISG), a panel composed of eleven senior scientists and managers, to undertake a review of the scientific foundation of the FWP. A published summary of the ISG's subsequent report included the statement that follows:

"After reviewing the science behind salmon restoration and the persistent trends of declining abundance of Columbia River salmon, we concluded that the FWP's implied conceptual foundation did not reflect the latest scientific understanding of ecosystem science and salmonid restoration" (ISG 1999).

How could the Council's salmon recovery program, with its massive financial backing, fail to incorporate the latest science? The purpose of this paper is to address that question. In our approach, we draw a distinction between fishery science and fishery management, including restoration programs. Fisheries science includes the body of research conducted by academic and fish and wildlife management institutions, and others. Fisheries management includes the programs and policies intended to conserve and/or recover fish resources and their habitats. The separation between fishery science and fishery management means that the incorporation of the latest science into management and recovery programs is not automatic, but must be a consciously implemented process that should not be impeded. A brief historical sketch of the FWP and the findings of the ISG suggest that impediments exist to the incorporation of fishery science into the Columbia Basin's principal salmon recovery program. Three of those impediments are described here.

The paper is divided into three parts. First, three case histories are provided to illustrate delays or failures to incorporate science into management and recovery programs. Second, a description is provided of three impediments to the incorporation of science into fishery management and recovery programs. In the final section, the conclusions are presented.

Case Histories

Ecosystem Management

Fishery scientists have called for an ecosystem approach to salmon management (e.g., several papers in Stouder et al. 1997), which is consistent with the broader call for an ecosystem approach to the management of natural resources (Mangel et al. 1996). Recognizing this advance in resource management science, the Council emphasized an ecosystem approach to the recovery of Pacific salmon in its 1994 version of the FWP (NPPC 1994). The ecosystem approach was reflected in many of the measures in the FWP, especially in Section 7 (Salmon Production and Habitat). For example, under a subsection titled Ensure Biodiversity, the plan included nine measures, which encouraged work on the following topics:

1. Develop a Policy to protect wild spawning populations

2. Evaluate salmon survival in the rivers and estuary to understand the ecology and capacity of the basin.

3. Adjust hatchery releases to river carrying capacity.

4. Collect baseline data on population status and life history of wild populations.

5. Conserve genetic diversity.

6. Review procedures for conducting population vulnerability analyses.

7. Evaluate systemwide and cumulative impacts of existing and proposed artificial production projects.

8. Establish a biodiversity institute.

These project areas are basic elements in an ecosystem approach to salmon recovery in the basin. In revising the salmon recovery plan to emphasize an ecosystem approach, the Council recognized that biodiversity was an important aspect of that approach; however, the Council has limited control over which parts of the FWP are actually implemented. The salmon management agencies in the basin select the measures they will implement, prepare funding proposals, and then submit them to the Council.

Fish managers generally disregarded implementation of Section 7 of the FWP, and did not submit any proposals to implement the measures in the biodiversity subsection. The subsections under which the fish managers submitted the largest number of project proposals were those related to hatchery supplementation and new artificial propagation projects. In its review of the suite of projects submitted by the fishery managers, the Independent Scientific Review Panel (ISRP; for a description of the ISRP see Williams and Lichatowich 2009, this volume) noted that, "A noticeable discrepancy exists between the mix of projects actually funded and the ISRP's interpretation of the intent and priorities of the FWP. A somewhat greater discrepancy occurs between the mix of projects actually funded and the Fish and Wildlife Program, if the recommendations from recent scientific panels (report of the Snake River Recovery Team, Upstream, Return to the River, and National Fish Hatch-

ery Review Panel) are considered" (ISRP 1997).

The Council's attempt to incorporate an ecosystem approach to salmon recovery consistent with the latest science was thwarted by the implementation proposals submitted by salmon managers. However, this problem could have been overcome if the Council had released requests for proposals (RFP) targeted to the specific measures ignored by the managers. The RFPs released on an open competitive basis would have attracted interest from universities and consulting firms whose opportunities to participate in the Council's program were normally very limited. The Council did release a few targeted RFPs, but not enough to realign the program's implementation (Williams and Lichatowich 2009). Both the Council and the fish managers bear responsibility for the failure to implement the 1994 FWP consistent with the latest science.

The Stock Concept

Evidence that fish species were composed of reproductively isolated populations or stocks entered fishery science through studies conducted in Europe in the late 19th Century (Sinclair and Solemdal 1988). In the Pacific Northwest, as early as 1893, fish culturist and cannery owner, R. D. Hume, recognized differences in salmon populations from different streams and incorporated those observations into management recommendations (Hume 1893). However, it was not until 1939 that Willis Rich, after reviewing the results of salmon tagging experiments, described the importance of the stock concept for Pacific salmon (Rich 1939). At that time, some fish culturists recognized the implications of the stock concept to salmon management, i.e., the transfer of salmon between rivers (between stocks) was not a desirable management activity (Oregon Fish Commission 1933). Biologists constructed salmon management units to facilitate harvest regulation and these artificial constructs were sometimes referred to as stocks. The importance of biological stocks received little attention for the next several decades.

Interest in biological stocks surfaced again in the 1970s (Calaprice 1969), and in the 1980s and 1990s management agencies began inventorying biological salmon stocks (e.g., Howell et al. 1985; Nehlsen et al. 1991; Washington Department of Fisheries et al. 1993). Fifty-seven years after Rich identified stocks as the basic unit of management, Flagg et al. (1995) reported that one of the factors contributing to the decline of the lower Columbia River stocks of coho salmon *O. kisutch* was the continued stocking of universal donor coho stocks in the lower river tributaries, essentially ignoring the stock concept.

Although the importance of the biological stocks has been recognized for several decades, management practices such as harvest regulation are still, in some cases, based on management units that are aggregates of biological stocks. These artificial management units are constructed for bureaucratic efficiency often to the detriment of conservation objectives. For example, today, sixty-four years after Rich's paper, the harvest of salmon in the Columbia River is not based on escapement targets for biological stocks, but on mixed stock aggregates defined as fish passing convenient counting sites such as mainstem dams. This approach does not take into account the different productivities of the individual stocks or the variation in habitat quality of the different tributaries (Mundy 2006). The lack of stock and habitat specific escapement targets is not limited to the Columbia Basin (Knudsen 2000). Fisheries science has recognized the importance of the biological stock as the basis of sustainable management; however, that realization has not yet been incorporated into all appropriate management activities in the Columbia River basin.

Artificial Propagation

In 1903, thirty-one years after artificial propagation of Pacific salmon was initiated, some biologists recognized that they had little scientific basis for their hatchery programs. Recognizing the lack of a scientific basis for salmon propagation, Chamberlain (1903) declared:

"Until the salmon industry or the people choose to pay for several years {of} careful, expensive investigation, propagation must be taken on faith. Without this, even if our fisheries should increase, we could not be sure it was from the hatchery work…"

The success of hatcheries was taken on faith for another 20 years when two evaluations of artificial propagation were undertaken—a field study of artificial propagation carried out in British Columbia at the Cultus Lake Hatchery (Foerster 1936), and a statistical analysis of hatchery releases and adult returns in the Columbia Basin (Rich 1922). The Cultus Lake Hatchery study was a test of a key assumption in the use of artificial propagation, specifically that hatcheries produce adult salmon more effectively than natural propagation. The study showed that artificial propagation was no more effective than natural propagation. Following the publication of those results, hatcheries in British Columbia were closed. The statistical analysis of Columbia River hatchery releases and adult harvest did not find evidence that artificial propagation influenced the supply of salmon to the fishery; however, those findings had no effect on the operation of hatcheries in the Columbia Basin (Lichatowich 1999).

The 1930–1939 period was a critical decade for Pacific salmon in the Columbia Basin. The construction of the first three mainstem dams (Wells, Grand Coulee, and Bonneville dams) and development of the basin's hydroelectric system marked a new phase in the development of the river. Faced with the loss of habitat behind the impassable

Grand Coulee Dam and in the reservoirs behind Wells and Bonneville dams, managers used artificial propagation to mitigate for the expected loss of salmon production. Hatcheries were relied on to make up for lost habitat, even though fish culturists had not yet demonstrated the efficacy of artificial propagation (Lichatowich 1999). Biologists still took the success of hatcheries as a matter of faith, or "idolatrous faith" as one biologist described (Cobb 1930).

In the 1930s, the federal Secretary of the Interior recognized that mainstem dams in the Columbia Basin posed a serious threat to the sustained production of Pacific salmon. To ensure the mitigation plan had a high probability of success, the Secretary appointed a Board of Consultants to review the physical and biological feasibility of using hatcheries to mitigate the losses of natural production. The Board of Consultants recognized the uncertainty inherent in the decision to use artificial propagation as a mitigation tool, so they recommended an approach that in recent times would be called adaptive management. They recommended treating the plan to use artificial propagation as an experiment and cautioned the salmon mangers to accept the possibility of failure and, "…that the adoption of the plan for trial should not be understood as implying an indefinite commitment to its support, but only for so long as the results may reasonably appear to justify its continuance" (Board of Consultants 1939).

Sixty years after the Board of Consultants submitted its report, the Council undertook a review of artificial propagation in the Columbia Basin, which resulted in the adoption of ten policies to guide the use of hatcheries. Among those policies was this one: "Artificial propagation remains experimental. Adaptive management practices that evaluate benefits and address scientific uncertainties are critical" (NPPC 1999). When the Council rediscovered the need to treat the use of artificial propagation as an experiment,

it overlooked the fact that at a broad, basin level the experiment had already been carried out. Given the status of salmon in the Columbia Basin, it's clear that artificial propagation failed to achieve its early objectives of maintaining the supply of fish to the fishery and its later objectives of mitigating for lost habitat (Lichatowich et al. 2006).

Supplementation is the latest modification of the use of artificial propagation, and it is intended to rebuild depleted natural populations in marginal habitats. In its review of supplementation, the Independent Scientific Advisory Board (ISAB), which replaced the ISG in 1996, concluded that even though it was considered experimental, supplementation was being carried out in a way that will make comprehensive evaluation unlikely (ISAB 2003). Implementation of "experimental" uses of hatcheries without actually carrying out the experiment is a persistent problem. Without adequate monitoring and evaluation, learning by management agencies is impeded (Hilborn 1992), and institutional learning is an important part of the process of incorporating science into management programs.

The history of hatchery operations is a clear example of what Hilborn (1992) called "goal displacement," which occurs when a program's original objective and performance measure are replaced by another objective and performance measure. The original objective of artificial propagation was to increase or maintain the harvest of salmon, and the release of juveniles from hatcheries was one step in the process of achieving that goal. However, the original goal of artificial propagation has been displaced from adult returns to the release of juveniles. The new performance measure is the number of juveniles a hatchery releases rather than the contribution of the hatchery releases to the fishery or to escapement (Hilborn 1992).

Goal displacement was evident in a 1999 audit of the performance of 51 Oregon coastal and Willamette River hatchery programs. After a review of the audit, Oregon's Independent Multidisciplinary Science Team concluded that 41 of the 51 programs used smolt releases as a measure of performance and only 9 of the 51 programs used adult returns as the measure of performance (IMST 2000).

Goal displacement reduced hatchery evaluations to the number of juveniles released, and as a result, it focused research on those hatchery operations that lead directly to the release of juveniles. Consequently, the incorporation of science has been largely limited to the improvement of activities within the hatchery, such as animal husbandry, the formulation of nutritious feeds, disease identification and treatment, the genetics of breeding procedures, improvements in hatchery operation, and the design of better facilities (Williams et al. 2003). Did hatcheries meet their goal of maintaining the abundance of adult salmon? Science related to that question has been slow to develop. Goal displacement and the lack of adequate monitoring and evaluation have contributed to the failure of artificial propagation to achieve its goals. After more than a century of use, salmon management institutions have missed the opportunity to learn adaptively, and as a consequence, artificial propagation not only failed to meet its goals, but it has contributed to the depleted state of the salmon (NRC 1996).

The listing of Pacific salmon under the federal Endangered Species Act created a new reason to focus attention on artificially propagated fish outside the hatchery facility. The concern boils down to this question: Are artificially propagated fish equivalent to naturally propagated fish for the purposes of listing or delisting Pacific salmon? NOAA Fisheries recently released a draft hatchery policy which proscribes the conditions under which artificially propagated fish could be used to assess the status of an ESU (NOAA 2004). The policy was reviewed by the Salmon Re-covery Scientific Review Panel (SRSRP), a panel of independent scientists convened by NOAA Fisheries. The SRSRP found that the policy did not reflect the latest science (Myers et al. 2004). Even for this crucial problem, the development and incorporation of science regarding the consequences of artificial propagation beyond the hatchery fence has been impeded.

Impediments to the Incorporation of Science into Fishery Programs

In this section the discussion of the case histories is extended to examine three impediments to the incorporation of science into salmon management and recovery programs in the Columbia Basin. Those impediments are: inadequate conceptual foundation, fragmented institutional structure, and political interference.

Inadequate Conceptual Foundation

Several papers have called attention to the importance of the conceptual foundation used as an underlying presupposition in fisheries management and recovery programs (Rigler 1982; Bottom 1997; Frissell et al. 1997; Acheson and Steneck 1997; Williams et al. 1999; and Bottom et al. 2005). A conceptual foundation is the set of principles, assumptions, and beliefs about how an ecosystem and its fish production systems function. The conceptual foundation influences the development of management policies and programs, including fishery restoration programs. It determines what problems (e.g., limitations on fish production) are identified, what information is collected, and how it is interpreted, and as a result, establishes the range of appropriate solutions (Lichatowich et al. 1996). As a consequence, the conceptual foundation can determine the success or failure of management and recovery programs.

Conceptual foundations are buried so deep in the culture of management institutions that they can exert strong influence on policy and programs while rarely being subjected to critical review and evaluation (Botkin 1990; Evernden 1993).

In its review of the scientific basis of the Council's Fish and Wildlife Restoration Program in the Columbia River, the ISG concluded that the failure to achieve the program's modest goal was in part due to a conceptual foundation that was based on outdated or inadequate science (ISG 1999; Williams 2006). The ISG identified three global statements that characterized the conceptual foundation that has been used to guide the program:

• The number of adult salmon and steelhead *O. mykiss* recruited is primarily a positive response to the number of smolts produced. This assumes that human-induced losses of production capacity can be mitigated by actions to increase the number of smolts that reach the ocean; for example, through barging, the use of passage technology at dams, and hatchery production.

• Salmon and steelhead production can be maintained or increased by focusing management primarily on in-basin components of the Columbia River. Estuary and ocean conditions are ignored because they are largely uncontrollable.

• Salmon species can effectively be managed independently of one another. Management actions designed to protect or restore one species or population will not compromise environmental attributes that form the basis for production by another species or population (Williams et al. 1999)

This conceptual foundation, or a variation of it, has been in widespread use for most of the history of fishery management (Bottom 1997); however, that these assump-

tions would play such an important role in Columbia River salmon management was not inevitable. The pioneering work of some early fisheries biologists might have lead to a different conceptualization of fish production systems. For example, the holistic and ecological approach of biologists such as S. A. Forbes influenced fishery management in its early years (McIntosh 1985). In the Pacific Northwest, the work of Charles Gilbert, Willis Rich, and others stressed the importance of life history—habitat relationships and an ecological conceptualization of salmon production systems (Lichatowich 1999). At the same time, another approach to fisheries management, which led to a greatly simplified view of fish production systems, was gaining in importance. Managers shifted focus to the production of single species and management programs based on an agricultural view of watersheds and fisheries production systems (McIntosh 1985; Bottom 1997). Implicit in this approach was the belief that a simplified production system dependent on technology could maintain the abundance of salmon and other fisheries. Salmon management guided by that conceptual foundation led to a reliance on halfway technologies, i.e., management and restoration measures that treat symptoms without addressing their underlying cause (Meffe 1991). Halfway technologies are consistent with a "command and control" approach to management, which results in natural ecosystems becoming more brittle, less resilient, and less capable of long-term sustainability (Holling and Meffe 1995).

The reliance on halfway technology is clearly shown in the way funds have been allocated for salmon recovery in the Columbia Basin. Prior to 1980 and prior to the implementation of the Council's FWP, habitat restoration (a major cause of declining salmon abundance) received less than one percent of the funding for salmon recovery whereas hatcheries (treating the symptom of too few fish by making more) received forty-three percent of the funding. During the first ten years of the FWP, expenditures on habitat restoration improved slightly to about six percent of the salmon recovery budget; however, artificial propagation still received forty percent of the funds (Lichatowich et al. 2006). It is argued that an inadequate conceptual foundation impeded the use of new science and created several problems. Among those problems were the failure to implement any of the biodiversity measures in the 1994 version of the FWP; the lack of stock specific escapement targets; the reluctance to deal with the impacts of artificial propagation to the ecosystem beyond the hatchery; and the reliance on an approach to salmon recovery based on halfway technology and command and control management.

The simplified, techno-production system described in the conceptual foundation that formed the basis of salmon recovery in the Columbia River is not unique to that watershed or fishery. In an examination of the assessments of the northern cod stock prior to its collapse, Finlayson (1994) identified six assumptions (conceptual foundation) that described a "techno–utopian" approach to cod management. Three of those assumptions are:

• The universe is mechanistic and deterministic, and its workings are governed by a few fundamental and unvarying laws.

• These variables are knowable and their effects on the stocks are simple, continuous, and can be realistically modeled by an equation with a small number of parameters. Therefore, they are predictable.

• Science-based management can manipulate some of these variables (primarily fishing mortality). It can monitor the others to effectively control the system and produce (within certain broad limits) equilibrium states in general harmony with human needs and desires.

Strong parallels exist between this set of assumptions about the northern cod production system and the conceptual foundation that underlies salmon management and recovery programs in the Columbia Basin. A comparable conceptual management likely underlies some aspects of the fishery management of the Laurentian Great Lakes, especially Lake Michigan (e.g., Jones and Bence 2009, this volume).

To rectify the situation in the Columbia River, the ISG proposed an alternative conceptual foundation consisting of three assumptions.

• Restoration of Columbia River salmonids must address the entire ecosystem, which encompasses the continuum of freshwater, estuarine, and ocean habitats where salmonid fishes complete their life histories. This consideration includes human developments, as well as natural habitats.

• Sustained salmonid productivity requires a network of complex and interconnected habitats, which are created, altered, and maintained by natural physical processes in freshwater, the estuary, and ocean. These diverse and high-quality habitats, which have been extensively degraded by human activities, are crucial for salmonid spawning, rearing, migration, maintenance of food webs and predator avoidance, and for maintenance of biodiversity. Ocean conditions, which are variable, are important in determining the overall patterns of productivity of salmon populations.

• Genetic diversity, life history, and population diversity are ways that salmonids respond to their complex and connected habitats. These factors are the basis of salmonid productivity and contribute to the ability of salmonids to cope with environmental variation that is typical of freshwater and marine environments (Liss et al. 2006).

Fisheries science has largely adopted this conceptual foundation or some variation of it. Fisheries management has begun to slowly shift from a techno-agricultural to an ecological approach; however, progress has been slow and impeded by political agendas (Liss et al. 2006).

In 2000, the Council revised the FWP and, following the advice of the ISG, incorporated an explicit conceptual foundation into the plan. The revised plan called on the ISAB to review the scientific soundness and basin-wide applicability of the 2000 FWP. The ISAB concluded that the scientific principles making up the conceptual foundation were consistent with ecological theory. However, the ISAB also found that the linkage between the conceptual foundation and the plan's objectives was weak and the objectives were not especially consistent with the principles making up the conceptual foundation (ISAB 2001). The Council made an attempt to incorporate a scientifically sound conceptual foundation into its FWP, but fell short of translating the conceptual foundation's principles into the actual implementation mechanisms of the plan. It left the door open for a continuation of the status quo.

Fragmented Institutional Structure

The salmon's ecosystem extends from the headwaters down to the estuary and several hundred miles into the North Pacific Ocean. It is so large that humans have been unable to either conceive of or implement a coherent institutional structure capable of managing the salmon at the ecosystem level. In addition, the salmon's ecosystem is fragmented among several institutions, each making decisions that can affect the salmon directly or indirectly by altering the quality of the habitat. Some of those institutions have primary missions that can conflict with salmon conservation. For example, the mission of public and private power utilities that

operate hydroelectric dams can conflict with salmon conservation. In the Columbia Basin, a salmon smolt leaving the Lochsa River in Idaho will, in its migration to sea and back, pass through seventeen salmon management jurisdictions (Wilkinson and Conner 1983) and several other land and water management agencies whose decisions can affect salmon habitat.

The problems that fragmented institutional structures create for effective salmon management and restoration have been recognized for a long time. President Theodore Roosevelt mentioned one in his State of the Union Address for 1908. He was worried about the lack of effective harvest management in the lower Columbia River—the inability of the states of Oregon and Washington to agree on a unified set of regulations. Again in the late 1930s and early 1940s, the states of Oregon and Washington recognized the obstacles to effective salmon management that a fragmented institutional structure created (Lichatowich 1999). A special subcommittee of the Washington State Senate issued a report, which concluded that effective salmon management will be "… hopelessly defeated in obtaining any solution to the Columbia River fisheries unless we simplify our administration over the resource" (WSS 1943). The Oregon State Planning Board reached a similar conclusion (Lichatowich 1999). Following its review of the Pacific salmon crisis in 1996, the National Research Council concluded, "The current set of institutional arrangements is not appropriate to the bioregional requirements of salmon and their ecosystems," and that, "the current set of institutional arrangements contributes to the decline of salmon and cannot halt the decline" (NRC 1996).

The Snake River Salmon Recovery Team (SRSRT 1994) linked the fragmented institutional structure to the failure to incorporate the best science into salmon recovery programs in the Columbia Basin. In its final recommendations on recovery of salmon populations in the Snake River, the SRSRT characterized the situation as "… jurisdictional chaos, no one in charge, important decisions not based on science, and stifled science."

The current institutional structure stifles the incorporation of science into salmon management and recovery in two ways: 1) continued reliance on a flawed conceptual foundation, and 2) distribution of funds based on existing relationships rather than in accordance with science-based priorities. As discussed earlier, fisheries science has been advocating an ecosystem approach to management programs. Management of an ecosystem such as the Columbia Basin that is fragmented among several institutions, many of which have conflicting purposes, tends to favor activities constrained by narrowly defined agency missions. For fisheries, this favors a conceptual foundation based on simplifying assumptions about production processes and an emphasis on harvest management and artificial propagation. Those activities cause little conflict with the activities and jurisdictions of other institutions. In fact, mitigation hatcheries can help further economic development that conflicts with salmon conservation. Hatchery mitigation for the construction of hydroelectric dams is an example. The vision of a simplified salmon production system highly dependent on technology to circumvent ecological processes as embodied in the existing conceptual foundation has co-evolved with the fragmented institutional structure. Each reinforces the other, which means that any attempt to change the conceptual foundation will have to include institutional reform.

In the discussion of case histories, it is shown that in spite of the Council's adoption of an ecosystem approach to salmon recovery in the Columbia Basin, the management agencies largely "cherry picked" the measures out of the FWP that were consistent with the existing conceptual foundation,

i.e., they emphasized artificial propagation and the passage of juvenile salmonids at the mainstem hydroelectric projects. An ecosystem approach to salmon management requires cooperation among several agencies, institutions, and jurisdictions, which is difficult to obtain in a watershed the size of the Columbia River.

The second way that institutional fragmentation impedes the incorporation of science into management and recovery programs is more troubling. When huge sums of money were pumped into the Columbia Basin's highly fragmented institutional structure, it shifted some of the focus from the common goals of restoring salmon using the latest science to the division of funds among competing institutions. In his book, *Fishy Business*, Rik Scarce (2000) discusses this problem and the way it results in projects selected for funding based on a relationship network, rather than the scientific merits of individual proposals.

Political Interference

The authors recognize that salmon management and recovery policy must take into account not only science, but also economic, social, and political factors. In a basin the size of the Columbia, where the hydro-power system is a major driver in the region's economy, conflict and tradeoffs in the river's management is a fact of life. Such conflict, if properly managed, can be a source of learning (Lee 1993) and a means of ensuring the appropriate use of science in policy making. It can also have the opposite effect. We define political interference as the attempt to present a policy decision made for political or economic reasons as the outcome of scientific analysis when the science does not support the decision.

NOAA Fisheries' draft hatchery policy mentioned in the case histories above is an example of political interference. The SRSRP concluded that the policy did not reflect the published scientific research on the difference between hatchery and wild salmon and the implication of those differences for management and recovery programs. According to panel members interviewed by the Union for Concerned Scientists, they were told to take their recommendations out of the report or "see their report end up in a drawer." Some time later, the flawed policy was traced to a non-scientist political appointee (http://www. ucsusa.org/scientific_integrity/interference/ deleting-scientific-advice-on-endangered-salmon.html).

Important economic, social, or political reasons may exist that administrators at NOAA Fisheries took into account in drafting the hatchery policy. We do not dispute that they can and should take into account more than biological factors; however, when the scientists are asked to strip out their scientific findings to give cover to a salmon hatchery policy that runs counter to science, then the process has slipped into political interference. While many who have worked in salmon management and recovery during the last few decades know of examples of political interference, few have had the courage shown by the SRSRP to bring the problem to public attention and publish an account of it.

Conclusion

The depleted status of Pacific salmon in the Columbia Basin and the massive remedial efforts that are underway should have been a strong incentive to incorporate the latest scientific understanding of the salmon's biology and ecology into the management and recovery program. We described three impediments to the incorporation of science into management and recovery programs and, in spite of the massive funding for salmon recovery, those impediments receive little attention. We want to emphasize these are impediments and not total blocks.

Incorporating science into management and recovery programs requires successful institutional learning. Undoubtedly, salmon management institutions will continue to learn. What is not certain is whether the mode of learning will be adequate to overcome the crucial challenges to the salmon's persistence (Volkman and McConnaha 1993). Will learning be intentional and directed, or will the future be tied to outdated assumptions and beliefs? Will learning be encumbered by inadequate institutional structures, and subjected to political interference? All of these variables constrain the learning possibilities and impede the incorporation of science into management and recovery programs.

The Independent Scientific Advisory Board for the Columbia River salmon recovery program suggests that management is still tied to the past assumptions and beliefs to the detriment of salmon recovery (Williams 2006). The State of Washington's Independent Science Panel bluntly described this dependence on past assumptions and beliefs in its review of the state's salmon recovery program: "The proposed set of minor changes to existing programs and reliance on historically ineffective voluntary measures leaves the impression that tinkering with the failures of the past will restore the glories of the past" (ISP 2000). We believe this reliance on past approaches to salmon restoration indicates a program that is still tied to the old conceptual framework and its reliance on halfway technology. Yet a careful examination of those obstacles is always very difficult (Cronon 1995).

In his book on the integration of science and politics in the Columbia Basin, Lee (1993) offered an explanation for the reluctance of management agencies to critically examine the status quo. He discussed this problem in the context of single and double loop learning. Single loop learning takes place within the constraints of underlying theory or, to use our terminology, the conceptual foundation upon which the organization is based. Double loop learning breaks out of the constraints of single loop learning and includes a self examination of the conceptual foundation and its inadequacies in identifying and dealing with the problems facing the institution. Double loop learning—essential to adaptive management—is seldom undertaken (Botkin 1990; Evernden 1993; Lee 1993).

Overcoming the obstacles to institutional learning and the incorporation of science into management and recovery programs require one initial and fundamental step. The management agencies must put learning and incorporation of science on the agenda (Hilborn 1992), something which in our experience management agencies have been reluctant to do.

References

Acheson, J., and R. Steneck. 1997. Bust and then boom in the Maine lobster fishery: perspective of fishers and biologists. North American Journal of Fisheries Management 17:826–847.

Board of Consultants. 1939. Report of the Board of Consultants on the fish problems of the upper Columbia River: Section 1. Stanford University, Palo Alto, California.

Botkin, D. 1990. Discordant harmonies: a new ecology for the twenty-first century. Oxford University Press. New York.

Bottom, D., B. Riddell, and J. Lichatowich. 2006. The estuary, plume and marine environments. Pages 507–569 in R. Williams editor. Return to the river: restoring salmon to the Columbia River. Elsevier Academic Press, Burlington, Massachusetts.

Bottom. D. 1997. To till the water: a history of ideas in fisheries conservation. Pages 569–597 in D. Stouder, P. Bisson and R. Naiman, editors. Pacific salmon and their ecosystems: status and future options. Chapman and Hall, New York.

Bottom. D., C. Simenstad, J. Burke, A. Baptista, D. Jay, K. Jones, E. Casillas, and M. Schiewe. 2005. Salmon at river's end: the role of the estuary in the decline and recovery of Columbia River salmon. U.S. Department of Commerce, NOAA Technical Memorandum NMFS-NWFSC-69.

Calaprice, J. R. 1969. Production and genetic factors in managed salmonid populations. Pages 377–388 in T. G. Northcote, editor. Symposium on Salmon

and Trout in Stream. H. R. MacMillan Lectures in Fisheries, Institute of Fisheries, The University of British Columbia, Vancouver, British Columbia.

Chamberlain, F. M. 1903. Artificial propagation. Pacific Fisherman 1:(11)10.

Cobb, J. N. 1930. Pacific salmon fisheries. U.S. Bureau of Fisheries Document No. 1092, Washington, D.C.

Cronon, W. 1995. Forward: With the best intentions. Pages vii–ix in N. Langston, author. Forest dreams, forest nightmares: the paradox of old growth in the inland west. University of Washington Press, Seattle.

Evernden, N. 1993. The natural alien: humankind and environment. University of Toronto Press, Toronto, Ontario.

Finlayson, A. 1994. Fishing for truth: a sociological analysis of northern cod stock assessments from 1977–1990. Social and Economic Studies No. 52. Institute of Social and Economic Research. Memorial University of Newfoundland, St. Johns, Newfoundland and Labrador.

Flagg, T., F. Waknitz, D. Maynard, G. Milner, and C. Mahkhen. 1995. The effect of hatcheries on native coho salmon populations in the lower Columbia River. Pages 366–375 in H. L. Schramm, Jr. and R. G. Piper, editors. Uses and effects of cultured fishes in aquatic ecosystems. American Fisheries Society Symposium 15, Bethesda, Maryland.

Foerster, R. E. 1936. Sockeye salmon propagation in British Columbia. Biological Board of Canada, Bulletin No. 53, Ottawa.

Frissell, C., W. Liss, R. Gresswell, R. Nawa, and J. Ebersole. 1997. A resource crisis: changing the measure of salmon management. Pages 411–444 in Stouder, D., P. Bisson and R. Naiman, editors. Pacific salmon and their ecosystems: status and future options. Chapman and Hall, New York.

Hilborn, R. 1992. Can fisheries agencies learn from experience? Fisheries 17:4 6–14.

Holling, C., and G. Meffe. 1995. Command and control and the pathology of natural resource management. Conservation Biology 10:328–337.

Howell, P., K. Jones, D. Scarnecchia, L. Lavoy, W. Kendra, and D. Ortmann. 1985. Stock assessment of Columbia River anadromous salmonids. Volume I: Chinook, coho, chum and sockeye salmon stock summaries. Bonneville Power Administration, Portland, Oregon.

Hume, R. 1893. Salmon of the Pacific Coast. Schmidt Label & Lithographic Company, San Francisco.

Independent Multidisciplinary Science Team (IMST). 2000. Letter to Kay Brown, Oregon Department of Fish and Wildlife, Salem, Oregon. October 25, 2000.

Independent Science Group (ISG). 1999. Scientific issues in the restoration of salmonid fishes in the Columbia River. Fisheries 24:10–19.

Independent Science Panel (ISP). 2000. Review of statewide strategy to recover salmon: Extinction is not an option. ISP 2000–1. Governor's Salmon Recovery Office, Olympia, Washington.

Independent Scientific Advisory Board (ISAB). 2003. Review of salmon and steelhead supplementation. ISAB 2003–03. Northwest Power Planning Council, Portland, Oregon.

Independent Scientific Advisory Board (ISAB). 2001. Review of the biological objectives in the 2000 Fish and Wildlife Program. ISAB, 2001–6. Northwest Power and Conservation Council, Portland, Oregon.

Independent Scientific Review Panel (ISRP). 1997. Review of the Columbia Basin Fish and Wildlife Program as directed by the 1996 amendment to the Power Act. Annual Report, ISRP 97–1. Northwest Power Planning Council, Portland, Oregon.

Jones, M. L., and J. R. Bence. 2009. Uncertainty and fishery management in the North American Great Lakes: lessons from applications of decision analysis. Pages 1059–1081 in C. C. Krueger and C. E. Zimmerman, editors. Pacific salmon: ecology and management of western Alaska's populations. American Fisheries Society, Symposium 70, Bethesda, Maryland.

Knudsen, E. 2000. Managing Pacific Salmon escapements: the gap between theory and reality. Pages 237–272 in E. Knudsen, C. Steward, D. MacDonald, J. Williams, and D. Reiser, editors. Sustainable fisheries management: Pacific salmon. Lewis Publishers, Boca Raton, Florida.

Lee, K. 1993. Compass and gyroscope: integrating science and politics for the environment. Island Press, Washington, D.C.

Lichatowich, J. 1999. Salmon without rivers: a history of the Pacific salmon crisis. Island Press, Washington, D.C.

Lichatowich, J. A., L. E. Mobrand, R. J. Costello, and T. S. Vogel. 1996. A history of frameworks used in the management of Columbia River Chinook salmon. A report prepared for Bonneville Power Administration included in Report DOE/BP 33243–1, Portland, Oregon.

Lichatowich, J., M. Powell, and R. Williams. 2006. Artificial production and the effects of fish culture on native salmonids. Pages 417–463 in R. Williams, editor. Return to the river: restoring salmon to the Columbia River. Elsevier Academic Press, Burlington, Massachusetts.

Liss, W., J. Stanford, J. Lichatowich, R. Williams, C. Coutant, P. Mundy, and R. Whitney. 2006. Developing a new conceptual foundation for salmon conservation. Pages 51–98 in R. Williams, editor.

Return to the river: restoring salmon to the Columbia River. Elsevier Academic Press, Burlington, Massachusetts.

Mangel, M. and forty-one co-authors. 1996. Principles for the conservation of wild living resources. Ecological Applications 6: 338–372.

McConnaha, W., R. Williams, and J. Lichatowich. 2006. Introduction and background of the Columbia River salmon problem. Pages 1–28 in R. Williams, editor. Return to the river: restoring salmon to the Columbia River. Elsevier Academic Press, Burlington, Massachusetts.

McIntosh, R. 1985. The background of ecology: concept and theory. Cambridge University Press, New York.

Meffe, G. 1991. Techno-arrogance and halfway technologies: salmon hatcheries on the Pacific Coast of North America. Conservation Biology 6(3):350–354.

Mundy, P. 2006. Harvest management. Pages 465–505 in R. Williams, editor. Return to the river: restoring salmon to the Columbia River. Elsevier Academic Press, Burlington, Massachusetts.

Myers, R., S. Levin, R. Lande, F. James, W. Murdoch, and R. Paine. 2004. Hatcheries and endangered salmon. Science 303:1980.

National Oceanic and Atmospheric Administration (NOAA). 2004. Endangered and threatened species: proposed policy on the consideration of hatchery-origin fish in Endangered Species Act listing determinations for Pacific salmon and steelhead. Federal Register: 6931354–31359. Washington, D.C.

National Research Council (NRC). 1996. Upstream: salmon and society in the Pacific Northwest. Report of the Committee on Protection and Management of Pacific Northwest anadromous salmonids for the National Research Council of the National Academy of Sciences. National Academy Press, Washington, D.C.

Nehlsen, W., J. E. William, and J. A. Lichatowich. 1991. Pacific salmon at the crossroads: stocks at risk from California, Oregon, Idaho, and Washington. Fisheries 16:(2)4–21.

Northwest Power and Conservation Council (NPCC). 2003. Columbia River Basin Fish and Wildlife Program: twenty years of progress. Northwest Power and Conservation Council, Portland, Oregon.

Northwest Power Planning Council (NPPC). 1986. Council staff compilation of information on salmon and steelhead losses in the Columbia River basin. Columbia River Basin Fish and Wildlife Program, Portland, Oregon.

Northwest Power Planning Council (NPPC). 1994. Columbia River Basin Fish and Wildlife Program, Portland, Oregon.

Northwest Power Planning Council (NPPC). 1999. Artificial production review: report and recommendations of the Northwest Power Planning Council. NPPC 99–15 Portland, Oregon.

Oregon Department of Fish and Wildlife and Washington Department of Fish and Wildlife. 2006. Status Report: Columbia River fish runs and fisheries. Tables only. Oregon Department of Fish and Wildlife, Salem, Oregon.

Oregon Fish Commission. 1933. Biennial report of the Fish Commission of the State of Oregon to the Governor and the Thirty-seventh Legislative Assembly, 1933. State of Oregon, Salem, Oregon.

Rich, W. 1922. A statistical analysis of the results of artificial propagation of Chinook salmon. Manuscript Library, Northwest and Alaska Fisheries Science Center, NOAA Fisheries, Seattle, Washington.

Rich, W. 1939. Local populations and migration in relation to the conservation of Pacific salmon in the western states and Alaska. Department of Research, Fish Commission of the State of Oregon, Contribution No. 1. Salem, Oregon.

Rigler, E. 1982. The relationship between fisheries management and limnology. Transaction of American Fisheries Society 111:121–132.

Scarce, R. 2000. Fishy Business: Salmon, Biology and the Social Construction of Nature. Temple University Press, Philadelphia.

Sinclair, M., and P. Solemdal. 1988. The development of "population thinking" in fisheries biology between 1878 and 1930. Aquatic Living Resources 1:189–213.

Snake River Salmon Recovery Team. 1994. Final recommendations to the National Marine Fisheries Service. National Marine Fisheries Service, Seattle.

Stouder, D., P. Bisson, and R. Naiman, editors. 1997. Pacific salmon and their ecosystems: status and future options. Chapman and Hall, New York.

Volkman, J., and C. McConnaha. 1993. Through a glass darkly: Columbia River salmon, the Endangered Species Act, and adaptive management. Environmental Law 23:1249–1272.

Washington Department of Fisheries, Washington Department of Wildlife, and Western Washington Treaty Indian Tribes. 1993. Washington State salmon and steelhead stock inventory. Olympia, Washington.

Washington State Senate (WSS). 1943. Report on the problems affecting the fisheries of the Columbia River. Fisheries Interim Investigating Committee. Olympia, Washington.

Wilkinson, C., and D. Conner. 1983. The law of the Pacific salmon fishery: conservation and allocation of a transboundary common property resource. The University of Kansas Law Review 32:1.

Williams, R., P. Bisson, D. Bottom, L. Calvin, C. Coutant, M. Erho, C. Frissell, J. Lichatowich, W. Liss, W. McConnaha, P. Mundy, J. Stanford, and R. Whitney. 1999. Scientific issues in the restoration of salmonid fishers in the Columbia River. Fisheries 24:10–19.

Williams, R., and J. Lichatowich. 2009. Science and politics—an uncomfortable alliance: lessons learned from the Fish and Wildlife Program of the Northwest Power and Conservation Council. Pages 1021–1046 in C. C. Krueger and C. E. Zimmerman, editors. Pacific salmon: ecology and management of western Alaska's populations. American Fisheries Society, Symposium 70, Bethesda, Maryland.

Williams, R., J. Lichatowich, P. Mundy, and M. Powell. 2003. Integrating artificial production with salmonid life history, genetic and ecosystem diversity: A landscape perspective. Trout Unlimited, Portland, Oregon.

Williams, R., J. Stanford, J. Lichatowich, W. Liss, C. Coutant, P. Mundy, P. Bisson, and M. Madison. 2006. Return to the river: Strategies for salmon restoration in the Columbia River basin. Pages 629–666 in R. Williams editor. Return to the river: restoring salmon to the Columbia River. Elsevier Academic Press. Burlington.

Williams, R., editor. 2006. Return to the river: restoring salmon to the Columbia River. Elsevier Academic Press. Burlington.

American Fisheries Society Symposium 70:1021–1046, 2009
© 2009 by the American Fisheries Society

Science and Politics—an Uncomfortable Alliance: Lessons Learned from the Fish and Wildlife Program of the Northwest Power and Conservation Council

Richard N. Williams[*]

*Center for Salmonids and Freshwater Species at Risk, University of Idaho
3059 F National Fish Hatchery Road, Hagerman, Idaho 83332, USA*

James A. Lichatowich

*Alder Fork Consulting
P. O. Box 439, Columbia City, Oregon 97018, USA*

Abstract.—The Pacific Northwest states of Oregon, Washington, California, and Idaho are engaged in a massive effort to restore depleted populations of Pacific salmon *Oncorhynchus* spp. We examine here how science has been used by the Northwest Planning and Conservation Council (Council) in their Columbia River Basin Fish and Wildlife Program from 1997 to 2006, and how their decisions reflect a dynamic and uneasy interaction between science and politics, particularly with respect to artificial production. The Council directs approximately $125 million USD per year toward recovery actions that mitigate the Columbia River hydrosystem's (electricity, irrigation) impacts on fish and wildlife. The program does not have a clear and unambiguous goal, therefore, it is not clear how success is defined. In 1996, an amendment to the Northwest Power Act created a peer review process for projects funded through the Council's program. We use the record of that review process to examine how science has been used in the program. The scientific underpinnings of the Fish and Wildlife Program were strengthened in 1996, when the Independent Scientific Review Panel (ISRP) was formed to provide technical peer review of projects for the Council. Over the past decade, the Council has relied upon the ISRP's technical recommendations and the overall technical quality of projects has increased, as has project-level monitoring and evaluation. Recent versions of the Council's Fish and Wildlife Program (2000, 2004) used an explicit ecological and salmonid life-history-based conceptual foundation to direct program activities and funding decisions. The habitat portion of the fish and wildlife program is being directed by this conceptual foundation; however, many of the region's decisions about artificial production continue to rely on an outdated production-based conceptual foundation that is not ecologically sound. The region's reliance on large-scale artificial production programs to obtain recovery and rebuilding goals provides an example of the differences between the two conceptual foundations—they lead to different approaches and programs. Political interference, fragmented institutional structures, and an inadequate scientific (conceptual) foundation have reduced program effectiveness, hampered program evaluation, and hindered use of adaptive management approaches.

---

[*]Corresponding author: troutdna@cableone.net

Introduction

The year 2006 marked two milestone anniversaries in the Columbia River basin and the region's efforts to rebuild its once great salmon and steelhead runs—the 25th anniversary of the Northwest Power and Conservation Council (hereafter Council) and the 10th anniversary of an amendment to the Northwest Power Act that formalized scientific peer review in the region's fish and wildlife program and its individual projects. The Council was formed in 1981 after concern about the possible listing of Pacific salmon in the Columbia River Basin under the U.S. Endangered Species Act (ESA). The concern led to passage of the 1980 Pacific Northwest Electric Power Planning and Conservation Act by Congress (hereafter the Northwest Power Act). The Council, an interstate compact between Washington, Oregon, Idaho, and Montana, was charged to find a balance between providing the Pacific Northwest region with a reliable and efficient hydroelectric energy-producing system (Figure 1), and with developing an ambitious fish, wildlife, and habitat restoration program. Since 1981, fish and wildlife restoration efforts within the Columbia River basin have been directed by the Council's Fish and Wildlife Program, and, since the early 1990s, increasingly by the recovery needs of ESA-listed salmon and steelhead stocks (Williams 2006).

Restoration efforts in the Columbia River constitute a massive long-term experiment in fisheries and ecosystem restoration (Lee 1993). These efforts have been supported by roughly $3.7 billion USD that Bonneville Power Administration (BPA) spent on fish and wildlife restoration since the early 1980s through the Council's Fish and Wildlife Program (e.g., $148 million in 2005; General Accounting Office 1992; NPPC 2000; General Accounting Office 2002; NPCC 2005a; Williams 2006). Despite these expenditures, the abundance of wild salmon and steelhead

populations have not increased significantly since 1981; ten years after the Council came into existence, the first listing of Pacific salmon under the Endangered Species Act occurred. Since 1991, 13 Evolutionarily Significant Units (ESUs) of Columbia and Snake River salmon and steelhead stocks have been listed under the U.S. Endangered Species Act. Against this backdrop, several questions arise regarding the program: how has science been used to guide fish and wildlife restoration? Is the scale and complexity of the problem so large that we are unable to conduct meaningful recovery actions? Are recovery actions consistent with our scientific understanding of salmon and their ecosystem, or is science somehow being ignored or abrogated in recovery actions?

This paper examines how science has been used in the Columbia River Basin Fish and Wildlife Program over a ten-year period from 1997 to 2006, and how policy and management decisions within the program reflect a dynamic and uneasy interaction between science and politics. In 1996, an amendment to the Northwest Power Act created a formal peer review process for the restoration projects proposed and funded through the Council's Fish and Wildlife Program. The authors use the record of that review process to examine how science has been used in the Council's Fish and Wildlife Program. We do so through two different perspectives: first, through the interaction of the Council with its scientific advisory groups, and second through the suite of artificial production programs funded by BPA through the Council's program, a programmatic area that accounts for more than 40% of the annual fish and wildlife expenses (General Accounting Office 2002). In both of these arenas, the authors discuss the successes and failures, and describe how three impediments to the incorporation of science into the Fish and Wildlife Program have reduced program effectiveness, hampered program evaluation, and hindered adaptive management. The im-

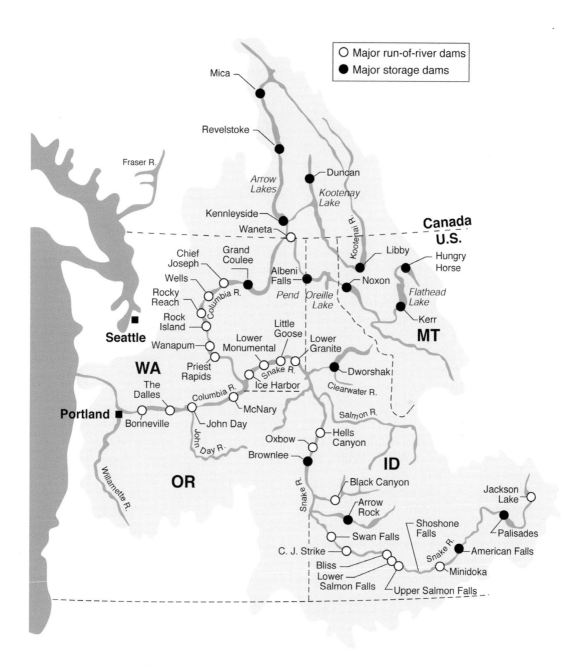

FIGURE 1. Map of the Columbia River basin, showing major rivers, lakes, run-of-the-river dams, and storage dams (from Williams 2006).

pediments are political interference, fragmented institutional structures, and an inadequate
scientific (conceptual) foundation.

Background on Columbia River Fisheries

Historical (i.e., predevelopment) annual
returns of anadromous salmon and steelhead
to the Columbia River Basin averaged about
15 million fish with substantial annual variation (Chapman 1986; NPPC 1986). Salmon
and steelhead abundance in the Columbia
River basin has held roughly steady from
1980 to the present, while the run composition has become increasingly dominated by
hatchery-origin fish. The Council had as its
original goal (NPPC 1984) a doubling of the
salmon and steelhead abundance observed in
the early 1980s from 2.5 million catch and
escapement to 5 million returning adults. So
far, little evidence of sustainable progress toward that goal exists. In 1994, the Council
modified its numerical goal and added the
constraint that increases in adult run strengths
should occur without adverse effects on biodiversity and the genetics of salmon and
steelhead stocks (NPPC 1994).

Obtaining catch and escapement data for
the basin has proven difficult (Lichatowich
and Williams 2009, this volume); however,
it is clear that in-river numbers of returning
adults have not increased in any significant
way since implementation of the Council's
Fish and Wildlife Program. Indeed, the increased returns and abundance observed from
2001–2003 appear to be more the result of a
fortuitous intersection of good environmental conditions for smolts combined with high
marine survival and adult returns than caused
by management and recovery actions (Bottom et al. 2006; Williams et al. 2006). Returns from 2002 to 2006 appear to be steadily
declining downward year by year (Figure 2).
Today, 25 years into the Council's rebuilding

effort, runs returning above Bonneville Dam
average about 1 million adults with most returning fish (~75%) being of hatchery origin.
Wild fish returns are about 1–2% of their historical levels (Williams 2006).

Scientific Review and Adaptive Management in the Columbia Basin Fish and Wildlife Program

The 1996 amendment to the Northwest
Power Act created a formal peer review process for projects seeking funding under the
Council's Fish and Wildlife Program. Currently, independent scientific review for the
Fish and Wildlife Program is implemented
by two groups: the Independent Scientific
Review Panel (ISRP) and Independent Scientific Advisory Board (ISAB). Each group
provides unique services to the program. The
ISRP reviews individual fish and wildlife
project proposals and makes recommendations on matters related to those projects and
their programmatic implications to the Council prior to their being funded by BPA. The
ISAB serves the Council, NOAA Fisheries,
and the Columbia Basin Indian Tribes in reviewing particular programmatic and scientific issues in the basin, either at the request of
those agencies, or as identified by the ISAB.

In 1996, following directions from the
power act amendment, the Council established an 11-member ISRP and the Scientific Peer Review Group (PRG), a pool of
scientists with appropriate expertise that assists the ISRP in its review responsibilities.
The ISRP and PRG includes scientists with
expertise in Columbia River anadromous
and resident fish ecology, statistics, wildlife
ecology, ocean and estuary ecology, fish husbandry, genetics, geomorphology, social and
economic sciences, and other relevant disciplines. Members are appointed by the Council from a pool of nominees recommended by
the National Research Council.

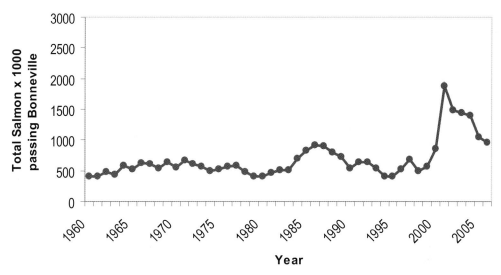

FIGURE 2. Total salmon passing Bonneville Dam (x 1000) from 1960–2006. Data from the Fish Passage Center (www.fpc.org).

The peer review of restoration projects requesting funding under the Council's Fish and Wildlife Program addresses several questions: are the projects based on sound science principles; do the projects have clearly defined objectives and outcomes with provisions for monitoring and evaluation of results; do the projects benefit fish and wildlife; and are the projects consistent with the Council's Fish and Wildlife Program? The reviews and recommendations from the ISRP include two feedback loops. First, the reviews are sent to the project's sponsors, so they have the opportunity to revise and resubmit their proposal for final review. Second, the ISRP develops final technical recommendations on the suite of proposals which are then sent to the Council. Based in part on the ISRP's reviews, the Council recommends a suite of projects to BPA for funding under the Fish and Wildlife Program. When the Council's recommendations differ from those of the ISRP, the Council is required to describe in writing (for Congress) the reasons for their recommendations. This procedure creates a transparent review and decision process.

Between 1997 and 2005, the ISRP evaluated and commented on over 1,800 fish and wildlife proposals, received and reviewed more than 600 responses to those evaluations, and released over 60 reports (ISRP 2005). Some 50 scientists from the United States and Canada participated in the various reviews. In addition, the ISRP led the review of subbasin management plans for 59 of the Columbia River Basin's 62 subbasins (ISRP and ISAB 2005b).

Over the ten-year history of the basin-wide peer-review process (1997–2006), the science groups' recommendations have resulted in a sustained dialogue between fisheries scientists (i.e., the review groups) and the Columbia Basin's fish and wildlife managers about what constitutes appropriate monitoring and evaluation at both project and programmatic levels (ISAB and ISRP 2004; ISRP 2005; ISRP and ISAB 2005c). This dialogue led to improved implementation and monitoring for individual projects, and the result is an example of adaptive management working at both project and institutional levels. The well-documented ISRP reviews, combined with the Council's formal feedback requirement to Congress, proved to be an excellent approach to the scientific review of management decisions; however, even that approach was not immune to political interference. For example, the gains achieved in monitoring and evaluation during the 1997–2006 period have recently been threatened by a shift in attitude from Council members and BPA that has signaled less political and financial support for monitoring activities. Because monitoring and evaluation are the fundamental keys needed to adaptively manage a program (Williams et al. 2006), a movement away from the decade-long commitment to monitoring and evaluation threatens the future of the entire fish and wildlife program. Recent efforts by the Council's Independent Scientific Review Panel may help balance the need for adequate monitoring and evaluation with the desire for greater fiscal accountability and cost-effectiveness. Several recent ISRP reports (ISRP 2007; 2008a; 2008b) have clarified the critical and necessary role of monitoring and evaluation for adaptive learning, while also identifying fruitful areas where consolidation and collaboration in data collecting and evaluation could lead to reductions in monitoring costs.

Peer Review, Science, Subbasin Planning and the Council's Fish and Wildlife Program

In this section, the authors summarize the evolution of an increasingly rigorous technical evaluation process for projects from 1997 through 2006—an example of adaptive management at an institutional and process level. This evolution occurred through increased interaction between reviewers and project proponents, and resulted in the improved technical quality of the proposals and projects. Nonetheless, measurable improvements in the status of fish and wildlife in the basin

have proven difficult to identify. An analysis of biological results has been attempted, in part, by requiring that all proposals to continue on-going work must document progress toward their stated objectives. However, the ISRP found that most project proposals did not report results at a level sufficient to document the overall program achievements (ISRP 2007). Instead, most projects reported completion of tasks, such as the number of miles of fencing installed in riparian projects or the number of juvenile fish released from hatcheries. Thus, working with the ISRP, the managers adaptively learned how to improve proposals, but adaptive learning was not generally evident in project implementation and monitoring for program effectiveness. The lack of meaningful documentation of progress towards Fish and Wildlife Program objectives is a serious deficiency in the region's continuing investment in salmon and steelhead restoration.

The Council and the region's agencies have taken substantial steps to address this deficiency in part through the implementation of a series of Intensively Monitored Watershed (IMW) projects, designed to understand the effects of habitat projects on salmonid populations and their habitats (Williams 2007). The Council's desire is to link habitat improvements and restoration activities to salmon and steelhead rebuilding goals and fiscal accountability—a laudable and appropriate goal. The Council's (and BPA's) efforts in this approach are linked to a larger network of intensively monitored watersheds, many along the Oregon and Washington coast. Projects supported under the Council's program occur in the Wenatchee, Tucannon, Yakima, John Day, and Lemhi Rivers. The IMW projects have brought a new level of coordination and collaboration to the region and are fostering efforts to develop standardized data collection, monitoring, and data sharing protocols (ISRP 2008a). For example, the Pacific Northwest Aquatic Partnership (PNAMP), in concert with the American Fisheries Society, compiled field protocols for monitoring and collecting fish population data that offer the potential for standardization of some methods. Another example is the Collaborative Systemwide Monitoring and Evaluation Project administered by the Columbia Basin Fish and Wildlife Authority that has made progress in developing a comprehensive regional monitoring and evaluation program, including development of a habitat monitoring pilot study in the Salmon River, Idaho (ISRP 2008b). Coordinated research, monitoring, and evaluation efforts such as these offer the best hope for the region to effectively link habitat actions to salmon restoration. Current discussions in this area focus on the cost of the IMW approach (high) and whether enough IMW projects occur in the eastern portion of the Columbia River basin so that information gained can be extrapolated to other salmon and habitat restoration needs in the basin's interior (Williams 2007).

Project solicitation in the Fish and Wildlife Program

Proposals submitted for funding through the Council's Fish and Wildlife Program respond to either open or targeted solicitations. Open solicitations broadly request projects intending to benefit fish and wildlife resources in the Columbia River Basin by mitigating impacts of the hydrosystem. Projects have ranged from research proposals such as testing the efficacy of new Passive Integrated Transponders (PIT tags) to proposals requesting funds for the fencing of riparian zones (grazing exclosures) or construction of new irrigation diversion structures that increase water savings and juvenile fish safety. Targeted solicitations have typically focused on a specific topic and requested sharply defined proposals.

Project proposals from the open solicitations have been addressed either through an annual review or a multi-year staged review of proposed and ongoing projects. Annual reviews occurred four times: in three sequential annual review cycles from 1997 to 1999 and again in 2006. A staged review process occurred from 2001 to 2003, when the ISRP sequentially reviewed projects and proposals from all subbasins throughout the Columbia River basin. Initially (in 1997), the ISRP found that the proposals varied so widely in information content and quality as to make meaningful review impossible. Subsequently, the ISRP (and Council) required that proposals have defined objectives and outcomes, demonstrable benefits to fish and wildlife, and adequate provisions for monitoring outcomes. During the 1998 and 1999 annual reviews, the ISRP initiated a written dialogue with project managers throughout the Columbia River basin that improved proposal content.

In 1999, the ISRP recommended to the Council that future review cycles should examine alternative review processes and multi-year funding for projects, as a need existed for a more considered and thorough review process than could be obtained through the annual review cycle. The Council responded by creating a multi-year review process where projects were grouped geographically by subbasins within eleven different large ecological provinces (Figure 3). This allowed the ISRP to systematically review sets of geographically related projects in a more thorough manner than the compressed timeframe of the annual review process (ISRP 2005).

The 2001–2003 review process gave the ISRP a better understanding of individual projects and their relationship to the Fish and Wildlife Program. Project sponsors were supportive of the process, as it gave them opportunities during the site visits and presentations to make certain that the ISRP accurately understood their concerns, projects, and written proposals. A consequence of this approach

FIGURE 3. Map of Columbia River Basin with Provinces shaded and Subbasins numbered.

was that project sponsors generally accepted the ISRP reviews, even when proposals did not fare particularly well. Considerable good will was generated throughout the basin via the new review process.

The ISRP also has been involved as the review body for a series of targeted solicitations, including reviews of Request for Proposals (RFPs) on specific topics, innovative (research and development) proposals, quick turnaround out-of-cycle emergency proposal requests, and reviews of specific artificial production programs.

Request for proposals

The ISRP, in its first annual review, recommended the use of targeted Requests for Proposals (RFPs) to address specific critical

uncertainties or information gaps not addressed by ongoing or continuing projects. In FY 1999, the Council and BPA, with assistance from the ISRP, developed two targeted RFPs that addressed critical uncertainties about the use of mainstem habitats by Chinook salmon *Oncorhynchus tshawytscha*, as well as their population, metapopulation, and genetic structure. The reports, analyses, and publications that resulted from these RFPs were extremely informative (Brannon et al. 2002; Dauble et al. 2003). The ISRP found this initial experience with the targeted RFP approach promising and has consistently recommended use of this approach to help resolve critical and controversial uncertainties not addressed by other projects. In spite of this advice, use of the targeted RFP process by the Council and BPA has been rare.

Innovative project solicitation

In 1997, the ISRP suggested that more emphasis should be placed on innovative ideas entering the Fish and Wildlife Program. Innovation often comes from outside the inner circles of salmon management institutions, such as the adaptation of transponder identification tags (PIT tags) used for marking racehorses and commodity shipments, to salmonid marking. Consequently, the ISRP recommended that the Council and BPA establish a special funding category to encourage innovative projects with the justification that a relatively small investment in a competitive solicitation for innovative projects could provide substantial improvement in the quality of research and recovery actions in the Columbia River Basin. Innovative projects should focus on "proof of concept," be pilot-scale, operate on modest to moderate budgets (<$200,000 USD), and be of relatively short duration (12–24 months).

In response, the Council established an innovative proposal competition allocated at just over 1% of the Fish and Wildlife Program's annual budget ($1–2 million USD). While the Innovative Funding Category has been used infrequently and inconsistently, results of this approach have been promising as several innovative projects have had important benefits to the region (ISRP 2005). For example, the retrospective review by ESSA Technologies (Innovative Project 34008; Marmorek et al. 2004) of past habitat improvement actions and their effect on salmon survival and abundance led directly to many recommendations on data needs and coordination among monitoring and evaluation projects that are currently underway.

For fiscal years 2001 and 2002, innovative proposals were allotted $2 million USD funding from the fish and wildlife program. For 2001, nine of the 66 innovative proposals reviewed by the ISRP were funded, while in 2002, the ISRP reviewed and ranked 37

proposals. The ISRP ranked the proposals on technical merit and their potential to benefit the fish and wildlife program, with the top three proposals tied in ranking. The Council recommended eight projects to BPA for funding; however, BPA funded only two of the recommended proposals, citing the BPA fiscal crisis as the reason. Project sponsors who received top ranking in the innovative competition and yet were not funded, likely lost faith in the Council's program and in the review and funding process. Will they submit proposals again?

Emergency and special-circumstance reviews

The ISRP was asked to conduct quick-turnaround out-of-cycle reviews on proposals (or sets of proposals) three times in response to perceived biological or political emergencies including the "High Priority" solicitation (2000; 96 proposals), the "Action Plan" solicitation (2001; 38 proposals), and the "Updated Proposed Action" (2005; 9 proposals). The High Priority and Action Plan projects offered actions ranging from replacing culverts to acquiring riparian habitat to testing selective fishing gear. Expedited reviews were requested. Almost half the Action Plan proposals failed the threshold criteria of the solicitation because they did not offer immediate actions that would result in "on-the-ground" benefits. Although BPA intended for the Action Plan projects to be short-term actions to help fish affected by the power system emergency in 2001, the subsequent contracts were not completed, nor work initiated, until 2002 (CBFWA 2004). The 2005 Updated Proposed Action proposals were a set of nine habitat projects developed by the Bureau of Reclamation in the Columbia Cascade Province intended to help achieve tributary habitat goals for Upper Columbia Spring Chinook and steelhead (ISRP 2005). None of the UPA projects were judged technically sound or recommended for funding by the ISRP.

The review process for all three reviews differed from the standard ISRP review process in several ways including the lack of site visits, oral presentations by project sponsors, or subbasin summaries that would have provided context or justification for the proposed action. In general, the quality of these emergency solicitation proposals fell well below those observed in the provincial and innovative reviews. Consequently, the ISRP recommended against further short-timeframe special-circumstance solicitations. Considering the low quality proposals generated, such solicitations could erode the improvements in accountability, transparency, fairness, and technical rigor that have been gained over the past ten years if made too frequently (ISRP 2005).

Artificial production and the Three-Step Review Process

In its initial report, the ISRP (1997) recommended that the Council permit funding for new individual artificial production projects only if project proponents could demonstrate they included risk analysis and ecosystem impacts in the project design. In response, the Council developed a process—the Three-Step Review Process—to review new artificial production initiatives. The Three-Step Review Process used three iterative review steps to ensure that new artificial production projects are scientifically and technically sound. Reviews occur at the conceptual design level (Step 1); the preliminary design and environmental (NEPA review) level (Step 2); and the final design and implementation level (Step 3).

From 1998 to 2006, the ISRP conducted over 20 Three-Step Reviews at the request of the Council, resulting in important changes for many projects, including the termination of several projects where ecological conditions likely precluded success. The Three-Step process is the most in-depth project-specific review conducted by the ISRP. The results of the process have improved some projects causing them to pursue strategies consistent with their specific taxa, habitats, and ecological conditions. The process also has often caused iterative interactions between the project sponsor, the Council, and the ISRP. This approach could be applied to other complex parts of the program.

Subbasin planning

The ISRP's early reviews of the Council's program and its projects (1998, 1999), repeatedly called for planning and assessments to occur at the subbasin scale. For example, reviews identified the need to coordinate habitat improvement projects at a subbasin scale to address habitat limiting factors in a prioritized defensible manner. In 2003, the Council, with a grant from BPA, provided funding to develop subbasin plans as a means to address this need.

The subbasin planning effort was a major step forward in development of a comprehensive strategy for recovery of salmon and steelhead within the major subbasins of the Columbia River. Watershed assessments, a core component of subbasin plans, called for an analysis of variables limiting fish and wildlife production and a prioritization of objectives and strategies to guide future recovery actions. In 2004, the jointly ISRP and ISAB reviewed subbasin plans for the 59 Columbia River subbasins and found that many plans had important deficiencies related to the assessment of tributary habitat and many did not reflect recent scientific knowledge pertaining to ecological restoration. Most plans had extensive habitat assessments for fish and wildlife limiting factors, but few translated those assessments into a prioritized set of limiting factors and strategies that could be used to guide future project selection and implementation within individual subbasins.

The ISRP noted that only approximately 25% of the subbasin plans were complete enough to guide fish and wildlife activities in a manner consistent with the Fish and Wildlife Program. A few subbasin plans were well done (e.g., the Flathead, Kootenai, Fifteenmile, Willamette, Hood, and Umatilla) and useful as models for subsequent revision of other subbasin plans (ISRP and ISAB 2005b). Most subbasin plans needed moderate or major revisions to become viable planning and guidance documents (ISRP and ISAB 2005b).

As a policy body, the Council operates by majority and its members serve at the pleasure of the governors of Idaho, Montana, Washington, and Oregon. To accept some subbasin plans into the Fish and Wildlife Program while rejecting others would have been politically unpalatable, even though the ISRP/ISAB joint technical review pointed out the widely varying quality and degree of completeness among the subbasin plans. This difficulty led the Council to accept all subbasin plans as guiding policy documents (NPCC 2005b); however, Council did so by dividing the subbasin plans into three groups based on the level of their completeness. The first group (23 of 59 plans) was accepted into the program largely without any technical revision in December 2004. The second group (29 plans) was accepted into the program in February 2005 after sponsors provided a supplement to their plans that included revisions recommended by Council. The seven remaining subbasin plans were accepted into the fish and wildlife program in the spring of 2005 after substantial revision at the direction of the Council. None of the revisions to subbasin plans in Groups 2 and 3 were vetted past the independent science groups for additional final review prior to acceptance into the program. From a scientific perspective, a final independent review of the revised subbasin plan would have been consistent with standard scientific peer review process. Such an approach would also have been consistent

with the Council's proposal review process where proposals that have been revised based on initial reviews from the ISRP were given a final review by the ISRP before any recommendations were passed on to Council.

An example of the difference between the ISRP/ISAB review findings and the Council policy actions for subbasin plans occurred with the Columbia Gorge, Salmon River, San Poil River, and Bruneau River Subbasin Plans. The ISRP/ISAB (2005) found all of these plans to be only partially complete and in need of substantial revision in the Assessment and Management Plan portions of their subbasin plans, yet the Council (NPCC 2005b) included all four in the first group of subbasin plans that were accepted into the fish and wildlife program in December 2004 without revision. Many of the subbasin plans did not adequately address linking production (natural and artificial) activities with habitat activities or with describing monitoring and evaluation to assess the biological benefits of management activities. The Council passed the additional work needed on these issues to ongoing regional planning efforts (NPCC 2005a) with the notion that these efforts would eventually feed back into subbasin plans when they were next revised.

Robust subbasin plans that identify limiting factors and prioritized actions should set the stage for future management actions and project proposals. The ISRP anticipates the need to review and judge future proposals in part by their conformity with existing subbasin plans. This requisite should make reviews by the ISRP more manageable and transparent, and reward efforts that tie projects to the plans. Unfortunately in the 2006 proposal review cycle that followed the subbasin planning exercise, the Council reverted back to the annual proposal review process where proposals were judged individually and not as part of a subbasin plan framework. Planning is currently underway for the next project solicitation cycle which is intended to be a staged review sequence similar to the 2001–2002 provincial review process. Hopefully, the Council will link the Subbasin Plans to project funding and selection in the next cycle.

Adaptive management and political interference

Over the past decade, the Northwest Power and Conservation Council has relied extensively upon the technical recommendations of their scientific advisory groups and as a consequence, the overall technical quality of proposals and projects increased, as did project-level monitoring and evaluation (ISRP 2005). The review process evolved starting with improvements in proposal format and content, increased attention to the reporting of biological results achieved (though serious deficiencies remain in this arena) and improvements in linking project objectives to project outcomes, and to designing monitoring and evaluation linkages to evaluate program effectiveness. Breakdowns in this process and in the science-policy relationship between the ISRP and Council occurred when political agendas or expediency subverted the evolving steps in the review protocol. Such breakdowns occurred more frequently in the small or off-cycle review efforts, such as the intermittent Innovative Project Review cycle or the three special-circumstance reviews (described above) than in the annual or provincial review processes (ISRP 2005). The large, more formal project review cycles appeared less vulnerable to political interference. This experience suggests caution in using one-time incident-driven review opportunities to address research or management needs in the fish and wildlife program. Given the long lag time between proposal review by the ISRP, funding recommendations by Council to BPA, and development of project contracts by BPA, as happened with the Action Plan project reviews in 2001, many of the proposed projects could have been submitted as proposals for funding under the next program-wide project solicitation and review process. If this had happened, greater thoroughness and fairness would have occurred through the review process.

Fragmented institutional structure

Another science-policy breakdown occurred at the funding and contracting level that undermined many of the positive aspects (e.g., thoroughness, fairness) of the provincial review process as perceived by the project sponsors. The Mainstem/Systemwide Province review occurred in 2002, near the conclusion of the two-year provincial review cycle. At that time, projects became much more aligned to the specific actions (e.g., Reasonable and Prudent Alternatives) in NOAA Fisheries' 2000 Biological Opinion than to the Council's Fish and Wildlife Program (ISRP 2005). In this instance, projects that had been reviewed favorably by the ISRP and subsequently recommended by Council to BPA for funding were overlooked in favor of less well-reviewed projects that were seen by BPA as dealing more directly with accountability issues related to its Endangered Species responsibilities and vulnerabilities. Projects that directly addressed Reasonable and Prudent Alternatives were given funding priority over other projects that had received stronger reviews. These decisions reflect the fragmented institutional and jurisdictional structure of salmon recovery in the Columbia Basin, where the Council is responsible for policy related to fish and wildlife mitigation for hydrosystem impacts (via the Fish and Wildlife Program); NOAA Fisheries is responsible for anadromous salmon and steelhead planning, management, and recovery under the Endangered Species Act; and BPA is responsible for funding projects through the Council's Fish and Wildlife Program and for funding projects associated with ESA mandates.

Inadequate conceptual foundation

Starting in 1994, the Council's Fish and Wildlife Program included a scientifically-sound conceptual foundation to direct program activities and funding decisions. The explicit scientific principles developed in the late 1990s consistent with this foundation were gradually moved from the program's main body into appendices and peripheral documents (NPPC 1997; NPPC 1998; NPPC 2000; NPCC 2005b). A retreat from the foundation and its principles was observed in the 2000 program and the 2005 amendment process. Even though the Council recognized the need to revise the conceptual foundation that underlies the Fish and Wildlife Program, it was unable to make the shift in priority from a strictly production paradigm (Bottom et al. 2005; i.e., the old conceptual foundation) to a conceptual foundation based on an integrated natural and artificial production system. At the management level, and occasionally at the policy level; however, decisions continue to arise from political interference (as described above) or from undeserved reliance on the traditional, but outdated production-based conceptual foundation that has driven much of the region's management and recovery actions for over a century. The region's continued reliance on large-scale artificial production programs to obtain the recovery and rebuilding goals is an example of the strong influence exerted by an inadequate but still influential conceptual foundation. This topic is the subject of the next section.

Artificial Production

Artificial production (stocking) programs—harvest augmentation, supplementation rebuilding programs, and captive brood-rescue programs—play a large part of the region's attempt to manage and re-cover salmon and steelhead populations. The Council's Fish and Wildlife Program is only one of several programs that provide support for artificial production programs within the Columbia River basin. Propagation programs funded outside of the Council's fish and wildlife program include the direct-funded (from BPA) Leavenworth hatchery, the lower Columbia River Mitchell Act production hatcheries, and the Lower Snake River Compensation mitigation hatcheries (ISRP 2005). Within the Council's program, support for artificial production consumes a substantial proportion (41%) of the multi-million dollar annual expenses (Figure 4; General Accounting Office 2002). Consequently, artificial production has received considerable focus and attention, scientifically and politically, as the basin's native salmonid communities have declined or have been significantly altered (ISRP 2005).

Large-scale reviews, such as *Upstream* (National Research Council (NRC) 1996) and *Return to the River* (Independent Scientific Group (ISG) 1996; Williams 2006), attributed the decline of native fish populations in the Pacific Northwest and the Columbia River Basin, in part, to large-scale, dis-integrated, and ineffective artificial production activities within the basin. These reports further concluded that a constellation of human activities (e.g., forestry, agriculture, grazing, hydropower, and development) played a major role in degrading and fragmenting viable habitat. Such degradation has, in turn, diminished the success of artificial production and supplementation activities and has been part of the reason they have failed to reverse declines of critically depressed salmon and steelhead populations. In addition, a suite of ecological and evolutionary risks has been recognized that need consideration, assessment, and amelioration in the Columbia Basin's large-scale artificial production program (Currens and Busack 2004; Myers et al. 2004; Nickum et. al 2004; RSRP (Salmon Recovery

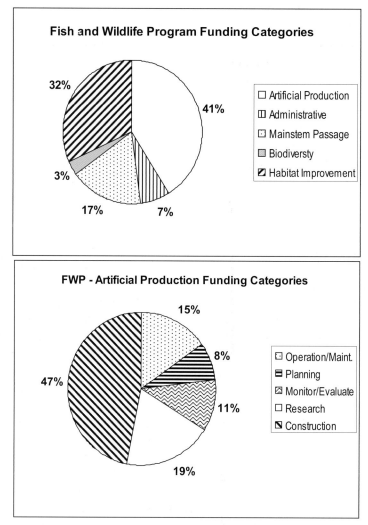

FIGURE 4. Distribution of funds in the Council's Fish and Wildlife Program (a) based on the FY1998 recommendations from CBFWA, including artificial production activities (b), which accounted for 41% of the proposed funding (from ISRP 1997).

Science Review Panel) 2004). Consequently, the region and basin are currently struggling to understand and balance artificial production's potential short-term demographic boost against the probable longer-term impacts it has to genetic structure and fitness of native fish populations (Goodman 2005; Araki et al. 2007a; 2007b). The struggle is presently playing itself out in a series of legal challenges and court decisions surrounding various new policies from NOAA-Fisheries that

attempt to define the role of hatcheries and hatchery fish in ESUs and in salmon recovery planning and implementation (HSRG 2009).

Over the past ten years, the ISRP has extensively reviewed artificial production programs. In 1997, the ISRP called for a complete moratorium on new artificial production initiatives until risk analysis and the potential for ecosystem impacts have been adequately addressed (ISRP 1997). Since that time, the ISRP has examined each BPA-funded artificial production project, often multiple times through various review processes, and extensively reviewed the large, complex artificial production programs in the basin, such as those in the Yakima, Hood, Klickitat, Grande Ronde, Clearwater, and Salmon River systems. Throughout these reviews, and consistent with *Upstream* (NRC 1996) and *Return to the River* (Williams 2006), the ISRP repeatedly concluded that the general approach to using artificial production in the Columbia River Basin is in need of major reform. Such a call for reform was recently raised again through the Council's Artificial Production Review and Evaluation (NPCC 2005a).

Several themes repeatedly emerged over the ISRP's review history of artificial production activities within the Columbia Basin. These themes include: the need to approach artificial production and supplementation as experiments that include defined treatments and appropriate experimental controls; rigorous monitoring and evaluation; technical peer review of design and analyses; a documented basis in defensible ecosystem management principles; and the use of specific appropriate performance metrics. The Council's Fish and Wildlife Program has placed a priority on native populations in native habitats, including calling for the establishment of reserves of core natural populations within a framework of healthy habitats. To implement this approach requires artificial production activities to be managed within a subbasin and habitat context, such as matching releases to subbasin (and estuary-marine) carrying capacities, periodic evaluation of program's progress toward achieving goals, and for overall subbasin production to either fully integrate or segregate artificial and natural production. To address these themes, the ISRP recommended that all future proposals for new or ongoing artificial production and supplementation projects be approved only when designed and treated as experiments within an adaptive management framework that included appropriate risk assessment and monitoring plans for periodic evaluation of benefits and contributions of artificial production toward natural reproduction.

Integrating natural and artificial production

The Council's 1994 and 1997 Fish and Wildlife Programs contained measures intended to increase production from natural and artificial sources by ensuring the successful integration of the natural and artificial production systems. In particular, the Council wanted to ensure that artificial propagation did not adversely affect natural production or biodiversity, and that harvest of artificially propagated salmon did not lead to coincident overharvest of naturally produced stocks. The 1994 and 1997 programs emphasized the need for planning, risk assessment, inventories of natural stocks, and estimates of biodiversity and carrying capacity prior to the implementation of artificial production programs. The ISRP was strongly supportive of this cautious approach to artificial production in the basin (ISRP 1997; 1998); however, review of the programs and project proposals for FY98 and FY99 revealed a pattern of funding and implementation of artificial production projects without first funding and implementing the requisite planning measures (Figure 5). Additionally, the ISRP concluded that inadequate evaluation had occurred of the effectiveness of existing artificial production programs. These issues led to the ISRP's call for a moratorium on construction and operation of new artificial propagation pending a more formal comprehensive examination of existing hatchery programs (ISRP 1997). Subsequently, the ISAB (2000a, 2000b) called for the development of risk assessment and risk management guidelines for hatchery production.

Interactions between the ISRP, project sponsors, and the Council from 1997 to

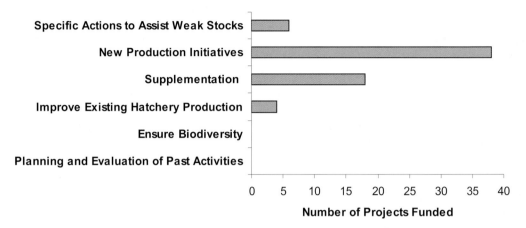

FIGURE 5. Distribution of projects funded by BPA from among the larger set of major artificial production measures in the 1994 Fish and Wildlife Program (from ISRP 1997). Each bar represents a set of projects or programs (i.e., measures) to be implemented in accord with the fish and wildlife program.

present (2008) have had a positive effect on the direction and scientific rigor of artificial production programs and projects within the Columbia Basin. The Council has initiated a number of specific measures or processes recommended by the ISRP, including a comprehensive review of artificial production throughout the basin (NPCC 2005a) and the in-depth Three-Step review process for new artificial production initiatives.

Below, the authors summarize major artificial production strategies used in the Columbia River Basin (supplementation, captive brood, and conservation hatcheries) followed by a description of critical uncertainties remaining in the use of artificial production. The section finishes with a description of how the region's use of artificial production as a rebuilding tool has been affected by fragmented institutional and management structure, political interference, and an inadequate scientific (conceptual) foundation.

Supplementation

Supplementation is the use of artificially-reared fish to enhance numbers of outmigrating juveniles to increase the numbers of natu-rally spawning adults in a target population. The approach has been a controversial option for rebuilding depressed salmon populations since its inception two decades ago (NRC 1996; Lichatowich et al. 2006). In spite of the controversy, supplementation has played, and continues to play, a central strategy intended to achieve the Council's Fish and Wildlife Program's goals. The Fish and Wildlife Program supports large-scale supplementation projects in the Hood, Yakima, Grande Ronde, Imnaha, Clearwater, and Salmon River basins.

The ISRP and ISAB, as well as their predecessor groups, the Scientific Review Group (SRG 1990) and Independent Scientific Group (ISG 1993; 1996), have consistently recommended caution in relying on supplementation programs to achieve Fish and Wildlife Program rebuilding goals. Other reviews of artificial production programs in the Columbia Basin and Pacific Northwest have been equally cautious and critical of supplementation (NRC 1996; Myers et al. 2004; RSRP 2004; Lichatowich et al. 2006). The ISAB (2003) and ISRP (2005) expressed the view that the uncertainty of both the benefits and the risks of supplementation are sufficient enough to put the merit of supplementation into question as a recovery strategy. Recent research has investigated the Hood River steelhead (anadromous rainbow trout) *O. mykiss* supplementation program and shown a 40% reduction in the natural-spawning fitness of hatchery-origin steelhead that had hatchery-origin parents compared to hatchery-origin steelhead that had wild parents (Araki et al. 2007a; 2007b). If the effect measured in Hood River steelhead is observed in other steelhead and Chinook salmon supplementation programs, it would demonstrate an important long-term genetic risk from supplementation (ISRP 2008).

The ISAB (2003) review of the use of supplementation in the Columbia River Basin challenged the pervasive perspective that the supplementation approach was contributing to recovery or maintenance of salmon and steelhead populations. The ISAB (2003) and ISRP (2005) have emphasized the need for rigorous evaluation of experimental design and results-to-date for existing supplementation programs. Consequently, both groups recommended that supplementation should: 1) be used sparingly and judiciously; 2) follow a protocol that uses natural-origin adults from the target population as parents; 3) be conducted with explicit experimental designs to reduce uncertainty; 4) include monitoring of performance standards for natural-origin and hatchery-origin adult abundance and per capita production rates; and 5) be coordinated across the Columbia River Basin so that the various supplementation efforts constitute a basin-wide adaptive management experiment.

In 2005, the ISRP and ISAB suggested approaches to monitoring supplementation that would allow a comprehensive evaluation of supplementation within the Columbia River Basin (ISRP and ISAB 2005d). Their recommendations included the need to establish: a uniform approach to evaluate the abundance, productivity, and capacity of target popula-

tions; more reference locations; and an evaluation of long-term fitness. Workshops in 2006 and 2007 brought together managers and biologists responsible for implementing many of the basin's supplementation projects (ISRP 2008a) and identified strong support among managers for an effort to coordinate monitoring and evaluation of supplementation across the Columbia River Basin. Efforts since the workshops have concentrated on two approaches: establishing monitoring protocols and analytical methods for long-term trend analysis for abundance and productivity in treated versus reference streams to evaluate demographic "boost" from supplementation; and intensive experimental studies to assess the long-term fitness effects of supplementation. A report outlining recommendations for evaluating both the demographic and long-term fitness effects of supplementation is expected in 2008.

Captive breeding

In captive brood programs, naturally produced eyed eggs from redds or out-migrating smolts are collected and reared in captivity to adulthood. These adults are then spawned in captivity and the subsequent progeny are released into the natural environment similar to standard supplementation programs. In some programs, mature adults are returned to the wild to spawn. Beginning in 1998, captive breeding and captive broodstock development for critically imperiled stocks became areas of increasing interest by fisheries managers throughout the region. Given the increasing vulnerability of the basin's stocks to stochastic demographic extinction, particularly upper river stocks, captive brood technology offered a tool with some promise for maintaining populations and genetic diversity as an interim measure while threats to survival were reduced or removed.

Captive breeding for recovery involves three major challenges: the selection of parents and their successful culture, successful reintroduction, and adequate survival of the second-generation progeny. Specifically, the use of captive brood technology (and the supplementation strategy) raised concerns about domestication, poor breeding success or survival, and increased disease sensitivity. The chance for success of this approach is uncertain given the factors that are causing fish stocks to be at low densities in the first place. The reliance on captive broodstock can be regarded as a short-term and temporary solution to the threat of extinction of these anadromous stocks.

In the 2000 Fish and Wildlife Program, the Council approved the use of captive breeding as a management tool to protect threatened endemic genotypes and (coupled with supplementation) to increase run-strengths. Within the Columbia River Basin, captive broodstock programs were established for Redfish Lake sockeye salmon *O. nerka*, and Salmon River (IDFG), Grande Ronde River (ODFW), Tucannon River spring-run Chinook salmon *O. tshawytscha* in the Snake River and the Wenatchee River spring-run Chinook salmon in the Columbia Cascade province. The Redfish Lake sockeye captive broodstock program was initiated in the early 1990s when less than ten adult sockeye salmon were returning to the Stanley basin annually. The remaining Snake River spring-run Chinook salmon captive broodstock programs operate in parallel with supplementation programs and were initiated because of the failure of existing supplementation programs to compensate for the rapid decline in salmon abundance.

While a basin-wide review of captive breeding strategy has yet to occur, in 2004 the ISRP reviewed captive propagation programs for sockeye salmon in Redfish Lake and for spring Chinook salmon in the Salmon and Grande Ronde Rivers (ISRP 2004). For the Redfish Lake and Salmon River programs, performance measures for juvenile

and adult salmon showed that the programs were rarely meeting their stated objectives. The Grande Ronde program, which has a better design than the one for Redfish Lake, has the potential to conclusively test whether or not captive propagation can achieve its rebuilding goals (ISRP 2004). Nevertheless, the ISRP concluded that, based on the scientific literature on captive propagation and on experiences within the Basin thus far, the outlook for using captive brood technology to achieve recovery of populations near extirpation or to reintroduce extirpated lineages is not encouraging.

Conservation hatcheries and NATUREs Rearing

Another important development in the use of artificial production technology as a tool for rebuilding declining salmon and steelhead populations has been the modifications of practices within the hatchery so that rearing conditions mimic natural conditions. This approach is based on the assumption that juvenile salmon and steelhead thus reared will be less affected by artificial selection and have increased survival after release from the hatchery when compared to juveniles reared under conventional hatchery practices.

Considerable resources have been invested to test and implement new approaches in artificial production, such as the evaluation of NATUREs (Natural Rearing Enhancement Systems) rearing on salmonid behavior, morphology, physiology, and post-release survival as well as their ecological interactions with wild fish (Flagg and Nash 1999; Flagg et al. 2000). The primary research for the NATUREs rearing effort has been conducted by NOAA Fisheries under the aegis of the Council's Fish and Wildlife Program. The NATUREs project had two major foci: to test the effects of NATUREs rearing-habitat using smolt-to-adult survival as a performance measure, and to investigate benefits of predator conditioning on juvenile migratory and adult survival. The research program required 8–10 years before meaningful results could be obtained; however, it has been implemented without a suitable hypothesis-driven and statistically rigorous monitoring program in several places (e.g., supplementation in the Yakima and Clearwater River systems).

Williams et al. (2003) criticized that the general approach to conservation hatcheries and the NATUREs approach were halfway technologies (Meffe 1992) that only tinkered with reforming the hatchery environment and would likely have little real survival benefit for returning adults. Instead, a more rigorous and strongly ecological-driven approach was proposed to conservation hatcheries, particularly for supplementation programs that were attempting to rebuild a demographically vulnerable stock. This approach, called a landscape hatchery approach, focused on rearing juveniles in near natural conditions (stream-like conditions, natural foods, natural temperature regimes, etc.) at low densities, and focusing monitoring on evaluating post-release survival of juveniles and returns of adults. In theory, such an approach should produce juveniles that retain much of the locally adapted gene complexes of their wild parents, and consequently have higher fitness than juveniles produced by conventional or NATUREs rearing hatchery practices; however, the concept has yet to be tested.

Hatchery production and smolt-to-adult survival rates

Hatchery production is effective at producing large numbers of smolts; however, the smolt-to-adult survival rates (SARs) of hatchery-reared fish have been disappointingly low and considerably lower than the smolt-to-adult survival rates of wild salmon or steelhead. Because of the low smolt-to-adult survival rates of hatchery fish, hatchery production has not succeeded quantitatively in compensating for lost production (Kostow et al. 2003; Kostow 2004; Lichatowich et al. 2006), nor has it produced fish cost-effectively (IEAB 2002a; 2002b).

These relationships are illustrated with an example from the Snake River Basin (Figure 6). The authors used a nonparametric trend analysis to determine whether significant differences occurred between the performance of wild fish as compared to hatchery fish based on SARs. In Figure 6, SARs for hatchery-origin summer steelhead were subtracted from wild fish SARs and the remainders plotted over time (years). If performance (i.e., SARs) is equal between the two groups, then the remainders for the 28 years of data should plot with roughly equal numbers above and below zero. If the majority of the values are positive, it indicates a better performance by wild fish than hatchery fish; whereas a majority of negative values indicates better performance by hatchery fish. Data for three years (1981, 1984, and 1991) were omitted, as wild and hatchery fish SARs were identical for those years. Chisquare analysis on the remaining 25 years of comparison showed a significantly higher performance by wild fish over hatchery fish. Only two annual values were negative, indicating that on 23 of 25 years wild Snake River steelhead showed significantly higher performance (SARs) than hatchery-reared steelhead ($\chi^2 = 17.64$, 1 = df, $p < 0.005$) (Williams et al. 2003).

Three critical uncertainties remain regarding the low smolt-to-adult survival rates: 1) Why are smolt-to-adult survival rates of both the wild and hatchery fish in the Columbia system generally low?; 2) Why do hatchery fish generally have lower smolt-to-adult survival rates than wild fish (PATH Scientific Review Panel 1998)?; and 3) Do hatchery fish have negative effects on the wild stocks with which they interact and interbreed? A great deal of scientific theory predicts decreased performance by hatchery fish compared to wild fish and negative interactions and effects between them; however, theory gives little insight into the magnitude or frequency of these occurrences (Goodman 2005).

Wild fish SARs were substantially higher than hatchery fish SARs in the first three years of the program, after which they remained higher, but showed a slightly downward oscillating pattern (Figure 6). This suggests an initial decrease in fitness by hatchery fish (as inferred from the SARs), followed by a period of adaptation and a decrease in the fitness differences between wild and hatchery origin fish. The diminishing of the difference in fitness between the two groups over time could be due to a number of factors that warrant investigation, such as the possibility of re-adaptation by hatchery fish or alternatively, explained by an overall lowering of the fitness of the two groups as interbreeding occurred between hatchery-origin and wild-origin steelhead. If the latter occurred, then homogenization of the two groups into one would be expected, resulting in less difference in fitness and performance measured by SARs between the two groups, but with a decrease in overall population level fitness.

Artificial production and subbasin planning

In 2005, the Council's Fish and Wildlife Program was amended to include Subbasin Plans for the basin's 59 subbasins. The subbasin plans describe visions, goals, objectives, limiting factors, and rebuilding strategies for fish and wildlife for each subbasin. The various Subbasin Plans provide the policy guidance for each subbasin within the Fish and Wildlife Program and for the fish and wildlife actions proposed and implemented in future solicitations.

In contrast to habitat and wildlife issues, where the Subbasin Plans often presented substantial analysis and planning, the subbasin planning effort and the subbasin plans were not adequate with respect to their consideration of artificial production. Almost without exception, the subbasin plans failed to adequately describe artificial and natural production elements within a subbasin and to provide a defensible overall production plan that integrated artificial and natural production with programs addressing the subbasin's limiting factors. The artificial and natural

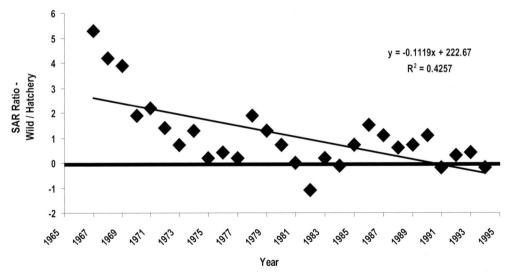

FIGURE 6. Plot of wild fish minus hatchery fish SARs (smolt-to-adult ratios) for summer steelhead from the Snake River Basin, 1967–1994. Data from Marmorek et al. 1998.

production components were either missing or were not linked to habitat limiting factors and proposed restoration activities. This deficiency was at odds with the Council's reliance upon supplementation as a key strategy for rebuilding depressed salmon and steelhead populations.

Consequently, the ISRP recommended to the Council that a defensible overall production plan be developed for each subbasin that integrates natural and artificial production elements and explicitly links them to prioritized habitat limiting factors and proposed habitat actions identified in the Subbasin Plan (ISRP 2005; 2006). This recommendation has not been implemented by the Council at the level of individual subbasins, but has been deferred to regional planning efforts such as the Artificial Production Review and Evaluation (APRE; NPCC 2005a). Results of this effort are to be integrated into subbasin plans when they are next revised and updated.

Looking into the future for natural and hatchery production

The Council has overseen several comprehensive reviews of artificial production that describe the need for reform and identify needed actions (NPPC 1999). Recently, the Council initiated an Artificial Production Review and Evaluation (APRE) process that will require hatchery programs to be consistent with basin-wide goals and priorities and to establish long-term management objectives for hatchery and wild stocks that describe measurable contributions to harvest and conservation (NPCC 2005a). Additionally, hatchery programs will be identified as either integrated with wild stocks or segregated from wild stocks and will describe how each program will contribute to long-term management objectives.

To achieve these objectives, methods are needed to assess the natural and artificial production in each subbasin and to evaluate the potential contributions of each to conservation and harvest. Several models exist, such as All H Analyzer (AHA; ISRP and ISAB 2005a) and Risk Assessment Modeling Project (RAMP; Busack et al. 2005) that can assist in evaluating risk and estimating carrying capacity for juvenile releases; however, the model outputs are driven by input parameters whose true values are unknown. At this juncture, the need is to encourage research and monitoring to obtain the empirical values for the missing parameters. Without studies that can lead to reliable data to populate the risk assessment models, it will be difficult to manage hatchery stocks and production adaptively to reduce impacts on wild stocks.

Conclusions about artificial production

Five major recommendations emerged from the ISRP's review history of artificial production activities within the Columbia Basin.

1. *Supplementation is an experiment.*—Require that all submissions for new or ongoing artificial production and supplementation projects be approved only when designed and treated as experiments within an adaptive management framework;

2. *Require technical design and risk assessment.*—Require appropriate ecological, disease, and genetic risk assessments be addressed as part of the design phase, before new projects are approved. Moreover, for ongoing projects, require retrospective risk assessments prior to additional funding.

3. *Require rigorous monitoring and evaluation.*—Require robust periodic evaluation of the benefits and contributions of artificial production toward natural reproduction. Such evaluations should occur at multiple levels (i.e., specific drainage, subbasin, province, and even basin). Evaluations should be

based on specific appropriate performance metrics.

4. *Use ecosystem management principles.—* Require artificial production programs to document how they are based on defensible ecosystem management principles. While the recent subbasin planning effort provided an entree into integration and coordination among programs and projects, require proposed projects to continue to enhance their tie-in with the fish and wildlife program with other artificial propagation projects basinwide.

5. *Require programmatic-level evaluation and reform.*—Programmatic-level evaluation and reform will require the region and the Council's program to undergo a paradigm shift in the uses of and expectations from artificial production.

In spite of the occasional success of artificial production programs at returning large numbers of salmon and steelhead to the Columbia River Basin, as happened from 2001 to 2003, a growing body of scientific literature exists that describes the limitations of hatchery-reared fish compared to wild fish, and the overall inability of artificial production programs to rebuild depressed salmon and steelhead stocks (Fleming and Petersson 2001; Chilcote 2003; Kostow 2004; Lichatowich et al. 2006; Araki et al. 2007a; 2007b).

Conclusions

We do not believe the current state of fisheries management for artificial production in the Columbia River Basin reflects the current state of fisheries science knowledge. Earlier, we identified three impediments to the incorporation of science into policy, and subsequently into management. The impediments are political interference, fragmented institutional structures, and an inadequate scientific (conceptual) foundation. Of these, we believe that an inadequate conceptual foundation lies at the heart of the failure of artificial production to rebuild salmon and steelhead runs in the Columbia River Basin.

Political interference

Political interference has played, and continues to play, a significant role in the failure of artificial production to rebuild declining salmon and steelhead runs in the Pacific Northwest. Many pivotal policy makers in the basin are making decisions assuming the perspective of an outdated inadequate conceptual foundation. This presupposition leads them to interfere with science when it points in a direction not consistent with their view of the salmon ecosystem. Recent examples of such interference include lawsuits about hatchery fish versus wild fish and about rainbow trout versus steelhead, where both suits could be traced to political activism and a desire to use hatchery fish or rainbow trout to boost counts of endangered or threatened populations (Lichatowich and Williams 2009, this volume). As another example, NOAA administrators attempted in 2004 to influence members of the Snake River Salmon Recovery Team (SRSRT) to alter the recommendations of their report that concluded that NOAA Fisheries' draft hatchery policy did not reflect the published scientific research on the difference between hatchery and wild salmon, and the implication of those differences for management and recovery programs (see report from the Union of Concerned Scientists at http://www.ucsusa.org/scientific_integrity/interference/deleting-scientific-advice-on-endangered-salmon.html). Fortunately, the Council's well-documented, formal, and transparent relationship with its independent scientific advisory groups generally serves as a guard against such egregious political interference in the fish and wildlife program.

Fragmented institutional structure

The multiple and fragmented jurisdictions within the Columbia River Basin also contributed to the failure of artificial production to recover salmon stocks. Projects were rarely coordinated at the large geographic scales of the subbasin, ecological province, or the entire Columbia River Basin, in spite of Fish and Wildlife Program policies that call for such coordination. Examples include the lack of coordination among the major supplementation projects in the basin to answer basic efficacy questions about the use of supplementation (ISAB 2003) and the lack of a common data currency for evaluating supplementation projects (ISAB 2003). Particularly telling is the lack of a Columbia River Basin Master Production Plan where overall goals and strategies for the integration of natural and artificial production are described. In a basin where more than 40% of an annual fish and wildlife budget of roughly $140 million is spent on artificial production, such an omission seems nothing short of astonishing.

Inadequate conceptual foundation

Finally, we believe the failure of artificial production to rebuild declining salmon and steelhead populations is directly tied to a more than century-old reliance on an inadequate and outdated production-based conceptual foundation—a belief system that still pervades much of the region's thinking on salmon production and recovery. This concept stands in contrast to habitat-based activities where the newer ecological-based conceptual foundation is generally used. Examples of actions related to an inadequate conceptual foundation with respect to artificial production include: the lack of integration of natural and artificial production in the majority of the subbasin plans adopted by the Council as part of the Fish and Wildlife Program in 2005; and

the lack of a Master Production plan as described above. Belief in a production-based conceptual foundation continues to support investment in large-scale artificial production facilities and programs.

Adoption of an ecologically-based conceptual foundation that focuses on salmon life history and habitat would facilitate the integration of natural and artificial production activities with habitat restoration activities within subbasin-level watersheds to match production (and hatchery releases) to the basin's carrying capacity and annual water and temperature cycles. Artificial production programs would likely become more precautionary and smaller scale in their operations. In addition, the region would invest in the level of monitoring and evaluation needed to track interactions among wild- and hatchery-origin fish with their habitat and with each other. Such an approach is long overdue. We hope that the recent efforts to establish a network of intensively monitored watersheds throughout the Columbia River Basin—coupled with the collaborative and coordinated approaches to standardized data collection, and analysis and the system-level evaluation of supplementation described above—are the first steps toward addressing the critical need to link salmon production with habitat in an integrated (natural and artificial) production model.

References

Araki, H., B. Cooper, and M. S. Blouin. 2007a. Genetic effects of captive breeding cause a rapid, cumulative fitness decline in the wild. Science 318:100–103.

Araki, H., W. R. Ardren, E. Olsen, B. Cooper, and M. S. Blouin. 2007b. Reproductive success of captive-bred steelhead trout in the wild: evaluation of three hatchery programs in the Hood River. Conservation Biology 21:181–190.

Bottom, D., B. Riddell, and J. Lichatowich. 2006. The estuary, plume and marine environments. Pages 507–569 in R. Williams, editor. Return to the river: restoring salmon to the Columbia River. Elsevier Academic Press, London, UK.

Bottom, D. L., C. A. Simenstad, J. Burke, A. M. Baptista, D. A. Jay, K. K. Jones, E. Casillas, and M. H. Schiewe. 2005. Salmon at river's end: the role of the estuary in the decline and recovery of Columbia River salmon. U.S. Department of Commerce, NOAA Tech. Memo. NMFS-NWFSC-68.

Brannon, E., M. Powell, T. Quinn, and A. Talbot. 2002. Population structure of Columbia River Basin Chinook salmon and steelhead trout. Report to Bonneville Power Administration, Portland, Oregon.

Busack, C. A., K. P. Currens, T. N. Pearsons, and L. Mobrand. 2005. Tools for evaluating ecological and genetic risks in hatchery programs. Bonneville Power Administration. Final Report, Project N. 2003–058-00. Portland, Oregon.

Chapman, D. W. 1986. Salmon and steelhead abundance in the Columbia River in the nineteenth century. Transactions of the American Fisheries Society 115:662–670.

Chilcote, M. 2003. Relationship between natural productivity and the frequency of wild fish in mixed spawning populations of wild and hatchery steelhead. Canadian Journal of Fisheries and Aquatic Sciences 60:1057–1067.

CBFWA (Columbia Basin Fish and Wildlife Authority). 2004. Columbia River Basin Fish and Wildlife Program: Rolling Provincial Review Implementation: 2001–2003. Portland, Oregon.

Currens, K. P., and C. A. Busack. 2004. Practical approaches for assessing risks of hatchery programs. Pages 277–290 in M. J. Nickum, P. M. Mazik, J. G. Nickum, and D. D. MacKinlay, editors. Propagated Fish in Resource Management. American Fisheries Society, Symposium 44, Bethesda, Maryland.

Dauble, D. D., T. P. Hanrahan, D. R. Geist, and M. J. Parsley. 2003. Impacts of the Columbia River hydroelectric system on main-stem habitats of fall Chinook salmon. North American Journal of Fisheries Management 23:641–659.

Flagg, T. A., B. A. Berejikian, J. E. Colt, W. W. Dickhoff, L. W. Harrell, D. J. Maynard, C. E. Nash, M. S. Strom, R. N. Iwamoto, and C. V. W. Mahnken. 2000. Ecological and behavioral impacts of artificial production strategies on the abundance of wild salmon populations. A review of practices in the Pacific Northwest. U.S. Department of Commerce. NOAA Technical Memo, NMFS-NWFSC-41.

Flagg, T. A., and C.E. Nash. editors. 1999. A conceptual framework for conservation hatchery strategies for Pacific salmonids. U.S. Department Commerce. NOAA Tech. Memo, NMFS-NWFSC-38.

Fleming, I. A., and E. Petersson. 2001. The ability of released hatchery salmonids to breed and contribute to the natural productivity of wild populations. Nordic Journal of Freshwater Research 75:71–98.

GAO (General Accounting Office). 1992. Endangered species: past actions taken to assist Columbia River salmon. General Accounting Office. Briefing Report to Congressional Requesters, GAO/RCED-92–173BR. Washington, D.C.

GAO (General Accounting Office). 2002. Columbia River Basin salmon and steelhead: Federal agencies' recovery responsibilities, expenditures and actions. U.S. General Accounting Office. Report to the U.S. Senate, GAO-02–612. Washington, D.C.

Goodman, D. 2005. Selection equilibrium for hatchery and wild spawning fitness in integrated breeding programs. Canadian Journal of Fisheries and Aquatic Sciences 62:374–389.

HSRG (Hatchery Scientific Review Group). 2009. Report to Congress on Columbia River Basin Hatchery Reform. Final Report. Long Live the Kings, Seattle, Washington.

IEAB (Independent Economic Advisory Board). 2002a. Artificial Production Review—Economic Analysis Phase 1. Northwest Power Planning Council. IEAB 2002–1, Part 1. Portland, Oregon.

IEAB (Independent Economic Advisory Board). 2002b. Artificial Production Review—Economic Analysis Phase 2. Northwest Power Planning Council. IEAB 2002–1, Part 2. Portland, Oregon.

ISAB (Independent Scientific Advisory Board). 2000a. Consistency of the Council's artificial production policies and implementation strategies with Multi-Species Framework Principles and Scientific Review Team Guidelines. Northwest Power Planning Council, National Marine Fisheries Service. ISAB 2000–3. Portland, Oregon.

ISAB (Independent Scientific Advisory Board). 2000b. Recommendations for the design of hatchery monitoring programs and the organization of data systems. Northwest Power Planning Council, National Marine Fisheries Service. ISAB 2000–4. Portland, Oregon.

ISAB (Independent Scientific Advisory Board). 2003. Review of salmon and steelhead supplementation. Northwest Power and Conservation Council. ISAB, 2003–3. Portland, Oregon.

ISAB (Independent Scientific Advisory Board) and ISRP (Independent Scientific Review Panel). 2004. Draft research, monitoring & evaluation plan for the NOAA-Fisheries 2000 Federal Columbia River Power System Biological Opinion. Northwest Power and Conservation Council. 2004–1. Portland, Oregon.

ISG (Independent Scientific Group). 1993. Critical uncertainties in the Columbia River Basin Fish and Wildlife Program. Bonneville Power Administration. Report to Policy Review Group, SRG 93–3. Portland, Oregon.

ISG (Independent Scientific Group). 1996. Return to the River: restoration of salmonid fishes in the Columbia River ecosystem (pre-publication version). Northwest Power Planning Council, Portland, Oregon.

ISRP (Independent Scientific Review Panel). 1997. Review of the Columbia River Basin Fish and Wildlife Program as directed by the 1996 amendment to the Power Act. Northwest Power Planning Council. Annual Report, ISRP 97–1. Portland, Oregon.

ISRP (Independent Scientific Review Panel). 1998. Review of the Columbia River Basin Fish and Wildlife Program as directed by the 1996 amendment to the Power Act. Northwest Power Planning Council. Annual Report, ISRP 98–1. Portland, Oregon.

ISRP (Independent Scientific Review Panel). 2004. Review of captive propagation program elements: Programmatic Issue 12 for the Mountain Snake and Blue Mountain Provinces. Northwest Power and Conservation Council. ISRP, 2004–14. Portland, Oregon.

ISRP (Independent Scientific Review Panel). 2005. Retrospective Report 1997–2005. Northwest Power and Conservation Council. 2005–14. Portland, Oregon.

ISRP (Independent Scientific Review Panel). 2006. Final review of proposals submitted for Fiscal Years 2007–2009 Funding through the Columbia River Basin Fish and Wildlife Program. Northwest Power and Conservation Council. ISRP, 2006–6. Portland, Oregon.

ISRP (Independent Scientific Review Panel). 2007. 2006 Retrospective Report. Northwest Power and Conservation Council. ISRP, 2007–1. Portland, Oregon.

ISRP (Independent Scientific Review Panel). 2008a. Retrospective Report 2007: adaptive management in the Columbia River Basin. Northwest Power and Conservation Council. ISRP, 2008–4. Portland, Oregon.

ISRP (Independent Scientific Review Panel). 2008b. Review of the Collaborative Systemwide Monitoring and Evaluation Project (CSMEP). Northwest Power and Conservation Council. ISRP, 2008–1. Portland, Oregon.

ISRP (Independent Scientific Review Panel) and ISAB (Independent Scientific Advisory Board). 2005a. Review of the All-H Analyzer (AHA). Northwest Power and Conservation Council. 2005–5. Portland, Oregon.

ISRP (Independent Scientific Review Panel) and ISAB (Independent Scientific Advisory Board). 2005b.

Scientific review of Subbasin Plans for the Columbia River Basin Fish and Wildlife Program. Northwest Power and Conservation Council. 2004–13. Portland, Oregon.

ISRP (Independent Scientific Review Panel) and ISAB (Independent Scientific Advisory Board). 2005c. Monitoring and evaluation of supplementation projects. Northwest Power and Conservation Council. 2005–15. Portland, Oregon.

ISRP (Independent Scientific Review Panel) and ISAB (Independent Scientific Advisory Board). 2005d. Monitoring and evaluation of supplementation projects. Northwest Power and Conservation Council. 2005–15. Portland, Oregon.

Kostow, K. E. 2004. Differences in juvenile phenotypes and survival between hatchery stocks and a natural population provide evidence for modified selection due to captive breeding. Canadian Journal of Fisheries and Aquatic Sciences 61:577–589.

Kostow, K. E., A. R. Marshall, and S. R. Phelps. 2003. Naturally spawning hatchery steelhead contribute to smolt production but experience low reproductive success. Transactions of the American Fisheries Society 132:780–790.

Lee, K. 1993. Compass and gyroscope: integrating science and politics for the environment. Island Press, Washington, D.C.

Lichatowich, J. A., M. S. Powell, and R. N. Williams. 2006. Artificial production and the effects of fish culture on native salmonids. Pages 417–466 in R. N. Williams, editor. Return to the river: restoring salmon to the Columbia River. Elsevier Academic Press, London, UK.

Lichatowich, J. A., and R. N. Williams. 2009. Failures to incorporate science into fishery management and recovery programs: Lessons from the Columbia River. Pages 1005–1019 in C. C. Krueger and C. E. Zimmerman, editors. Pacific salmon: ecology and management of western Alaska's populations. American Fisheries Society, Symposium 70, Bethesda, Maryland.

Marmorek, D. R., I. J. Parnell, M. Porter, C. Pinkham, C. A. D. Alexander, C. N. Peters, J. Hubble, C. M. Paulsen and T. R. Fisher. 2004. A Multiple Watershed Approach to Assessing the Effects of Habitat Restoration Actions on Anadromous and Resident Fish Populations. BPA Project 34008. Report to Bonneville Power Administration, Portland, Oregon.

Meffe, G. K. 1992. Techno-arrogance and halfway technologies: salmon hatcheries on the Pacific coast of North America. Conservation Biology 6:350–354.

Myers, R. A., S. A. Levin, R. Lande, F. C. James, W. W. Murdoch, and R. T. Paine. 2004. Hatcheries and endangered salmon. Science 303:1980.

NRC (National Research Council). 1996. Upstream: salmon and society in the Pacific Northwest. Report on the Committee on Protection and Management of Pacific Northwest Anadromous Salmonids for the National Research Council of the National Academy of Sciences. National Academy Press, Washington D. C.

Nickum, M. J., P. M. Mazik, J. G. Nickum, and D. D. MacKinlay editors. 2004. Propagated Fish in Resource Management. American Fisheries Society, Symposium 44, Bethesda, Maryland, Massachusetts.

NPCC (Northwest Power and Conservation Council). 2005a. Artificial Production Review and Evaluation: Report to Congress. Northwest Power and Conservation Council. 2005–11. Portland, Oregon.

NPCC (Northwest Power and Conservation Council). 2005b. Columbia River Basin Fish and Wildlife Program Subbasin Plan Amendments: findings and responses to comments. Northwest Power and Conservation Council. 2005–13. Portland, Oregon.

NPPC (Northwest Power Planning Council). 1984. Columbia River Basin Fish and Wildlife Program. A debt to the past.an investment in the future. Northwest Power Planning Council. Portland, Oregon.

NPPC (Northwest Power Planning Council). 1986. Council Staff Compilation of Information on Salmon and Steelhead Losses in the Columbia River Basin. Northwest Power Planning Council. Portland, Oregon.

NPPC (Northwest Power Planning Council). 1994. Columbia River Basin Fish and Wildlife Program. Northwest Power Planning Council. 94–55. Portland, Oregon.

NPPC (Northwest Power Planning Council). 1997. An integrated framework for fish and wildlife management in the Columbia River. Northwest Power Planning Council. NPPC 97–2. Portland, Oregon.

NPPC. 1998. A proposed scientific foundation for the restoration of fish and wildlife in the Columbia River. Northwest Power Planning Council. NPPC 98–16. Portland, Oregon.

NPPC (Northwest Power Planning Council). 1999. Artificial Production Review: Report and recommendations of the Northwest Power Planning Council. Northwest Power Planning Council. NPPC 99–15. Portland, Oregon.

NPPC (Northwest Power Planning Council). 2000. Columbia River Basin Fish and Wildlife Program: A Multi-species Approach for Decision Making. Northwest Power Planning Council. 2000–19. Portland, Oregon.

PATH Scientific Review Panel. 1998. Conclusions and recommendations from the PATH Weight of Evidence Workshop. ESSA Technologies. Formal Report, Vancouver.

RSRP (Salmon Recovery Science Review Panel). 2004. Report for the meeting held August 30–September 2, 2004. Northwest Fisheries Science Center, National Marine Fisheries Service, Seattle.

SRG (Scientific Review Group). 1990. Memorandum to Policy Review Group, July 25, 1990, Review of three supplementation proposals Portland, Oregon.

Williams, R. N., editor. 2006. Return to the river: restoring salmon to the Columbia River. Elsevier Academic Press, London, UK.

Williams, R. N. 2007. Summary of the Northwest Power and Conservation Council's science-policy exchange. Final Report to the Northwest Power and Conservation Council. Portland, Oregon.

Williams, R. N., J. A. Lichatowich, P. R. Mundy, and M. Powell. 2003. Integrating artificial production with salmonid life history, genetic, and ecosystem diversity: a landscape perspective. Issue Paper for Trout Unlimited, West Coast Conservation Office, Portland, Oregon.

Williams, R. N., J. A. Stanford, J. A. Lichatowich, W. J. Liss, C. C. Coutant, W. E. McConnaha, R. R. Whitney, P. R. Mundy, P. A. Bisson, and M. S. Powell. 2006. Conclusions and strategies for salmon restoration in the Columbia River. Pages 629–666 in R. N. Williams, editor. Return to the river: restoring salmon to the Columbia River. Elsevier Academic Press, London, UK.

American Fisheries Society Symposium 70:1047–1057, 2009

A Perspective on Coho Salmon Management in Oregon: Learning from Experience and Expecting Surprises

JIM MARTIN*

Berkley Conservation Institute
P.O. Box 1183, Mulino, Oregon 97042, USA

Abstract.—Described in this paper are my experiences with, and reflections on, managing salmon for 30 years with the Oregon Department of Fish and Wildlife. Specifically, I will focus on lessons learned from Oregon's struggle to effectively manage coho salmon *Oncorhynchus kisutch* in Oregon's coastal streams. In the 1980s–1990s, salmon managers discovered that the fishery management strategies were based on false assumptions regarding the capability of freshwater habitat to produce smolts, the constancy of ocean productivity, and the role of hatchery fish in coastal ecosystems. As managers, we misinterpreted spawning stock assessment data and stock-recruitment relationships, an error which, when combined with a pressing need to harvest returning hatchery fish, led to overly aggressive harvest strategies that drove the less productive stocks of Oregon's wild coastal coho salmon toward extinction. A progressive research program helped identify these errors and the new information generated through this research program helped fishery managers re-formulate management strategies to meet changing threats to coho salmon. As a result, federal listing of Oregon's coastal coho salmon stocks under the Endangered Species Act was avoided. The successful conservation and harvest of coho salmon stocks in the 1970s led to complacency among fishery managers, which then subtly shifted into arrogance over time. This shift caused managers to be slow to recognize the changes occurring in the ecosystem. Managers must not become complacent or arrogant in their abilities to manage; they must look for potential surprises and must be ready to respond to future challenges and threats to salmon. Three major lessons from were learned from the author's experiences with Oregon's coastal coho salmon. Lesson number one—be careful about the use of stock recruitment relationships in management. Meeting the minimum escapement goals does not mean that harvesting the rest of the population is a wise or sustainable practice. Lesson number two—carefully consider planting locations for hatchery fish, and how stocking locations and practices will change the distribution of fishing effort and affect fishing mortality of wild fish and confuse assessment indices. Lesson number three—challenge your assumptions under which you are managing. Conduct the research required to test your assumptions, and change management strategies when necessary. The two big future challenges facing coho salmon are the increasing size of human populations and predicted warming of the climate along Oregon's coast. The lessons learned over the past 30 years should be applied to future challenges to ensure the sustainability of salmon.

*Corresponding author: jtmartin@purefishing.com

Introduction

Pacific salmon are an important icon within the culture of the Pacific Northwest. Many are familiar with the story of the Columbia River, the effects of its dams, and the conflicts over its fisheries (Lichatowich 1999). The road to restoration of salmon in the Columbia River has been contentious and tumultuous, with few successes (Williams and Lichatowich 2009, this volume; Lichatowich and Williams 2009, this volume). The same troubles faced by Columbia River salmon have beset salmon elsewhere in the Pacific Northwest, including the coastline of Oregon.

This paper highlights the story of my experiences and reflections of managing salmon after 30 years with the Oregon Department of Fish and Wildlife. I began as a fishery biologist, eventually became chief of fisheries, and later became salmon advisor to the governor. These experiences provided me with wonderful opportunities to grapple with the science and politics of salmon and to integrate these two components of management for the benefit of the salmon. The story below focuses on Oregon's struggle to effectively manage the coho salmon *Oncorhynchus kisutch* in Oregon's coastal streams.

In the Beginning

The story of the Oregon coho salmon begins almost 40 years ago. After graduating from Oregon State University in 1969 with a B.S. degree, I was fortunate to begin work with the Oregon Department of Fish and Wildlife at the peak of the salmon heyday. It was like the Oklahoma Land Rush—the Gold Rush of Fish. What excitement! The fish biologists and managers were on a roll, evidenced by abundant fish and terrific fisheries. We were so full of ourselves and thought we knew everything about success-ful coho salmon management. In retrospect, we were experiencing 10 of the 15 best years of ocean survival in the last century. Of course, at the time we thought we really had the fishery and its production under our control. We believed production could be dialed up and down with our hatchery program and stocking. From our perspective, the sky was the limit for our fisheries. The ocean fisheries were going through the roof, so naturally, more salmon hatcheries were built. A fantastic new diet called the Oregon Moist Pellet was developed along with new disease treatments to improve the health of our stocked fish. The rapidly expanding, mixed stock ocean fishery was harvesting coho salmon to the tune of millions, a harvest which constituted 60–80% of the returning runs. In hindsight, flags should have been flying with danger signs, but they were not; our coho salmon fishery was driven primarily by the hatchery system, and we thought no end was in sight. With the rapid expansion of ocean commercial and recreational fisheries, and with charter boats in every port, the coast of Oregon was like one big boomtown.

Boom and Bust Salmon Fisheries

In 1976, the boom went through the roof for the offshore fisheries in northern California, southern Washington, and Oregon with a catch and escapement of over 4.5 million fish, combined hatchery and wild coho salmon. In 1977, the boom busted, and harvest dropped to less than a million, more than an 80% decline, and the "crap hit the political fan." We weren't getting fish into the fisheries. We weren't getting fish back to the hatcheries. The spawning index estimates in our assessments that had been showing spawning coho salmon at record high abundances through the 60s and early 70s now dropped through the bottom of the floor. We, the salmon managers, did not know what to say. We were speechless. What happened to cause this crash? Our hatchery production with our Oregon Moist Pellets was the same as before the crash. All of our disease treatments were administered just as before the crash. The hatcheries were pouring out smolts by the millions, just like they were before the crash. Our first management response was to use regulations to ratchet down fishery harvests. Reducing harvest might not seem radical now, but at that time, Oregon had never regulated the harvests of the ocean fisheries! The fishermen responded with, "What's the matter with you pointy-headed, bone-headed biologists? What are you thinking? You must have screwed up management somehow." We did not have any answers! You can't believe the beating we took when we started regulating harvests.

The First Coho Salmon Management Plan

The Oregon Department of Fish and Wildlife went back to the drawing boards in the late 70s and early 80s and developed the first coho salmon management plan. We wanted the new plan to be founded on solid science. One of the best statisticians in the entire department—a senior biologist with a lot of experience named Al McGie, was tasked with using stock-recruitment to build the foundation of the plan. We believed we had enough data to understand the big picture using this approach.

Al McGie started generating the stock-recruitment curve based on our spawning index counts from Oregon coastal streams (e.g., McGie 1980, 1981). Al first reconstructed the historical populations and documented how population abundance changed through each generation. He did this by using the density of spawning coho salmon (fish per mile in the standard index areas), and then expanding these numbers by the approximately 5,000 mi of coho habitat along the entire Oregon coast, and then apportioned the spawner abundance into the historical broods, taking into account the numbers of hatchery fish. He then went back and associated how many spawners had produced the broods—and boom, out came our very first stock-recruitment curve (Figure 1). We were so proud of it! We finally had the answer! We finally were beginning to manage Oregon coastal coho on a sound scientific footing.

The first Oregon coho salmon management plan founded on stock-recruitment resulted in great news about the future of the fishery (Oregon Department of Fish and Wildlife 1982). The news was super! If as few as 200,000 coho spawned, about 750,000 fish could be consistently produced in the next brood—sometimes even over a million could be produced. The population could sustain about a 67% annual harvest rate, and Oregon could still get access to the millions of hatchery fish that were stocked. Based on our stock–recruitment curve and our plan, the fishery would rebound and life would be good.

The plan was implemented, but the coho salmon numbers continued to decline. Even though we limited harvest rates to a conservative 50% of the estimated number of ocean fish, the number of coho salmon in the catch steadily declined. Finally, the bottom dropped out of even the spawning index numbers. We couldn't figure out what was wrong. We had a wonderful stock-recruitment curve and a terrific coho salmon management plan. The problem was the fish and the ecosystem didn't understand our plan and our projections. In response to this crisis, over the next decade, we initiated a focused research effort to dissect the assumptions of the plan and figure out what was going wrong (e.g., Solazzi et al. 1990). The bad news was that we spent a decade trying to nail down the problem, and during that decade, we allowed the fisheries

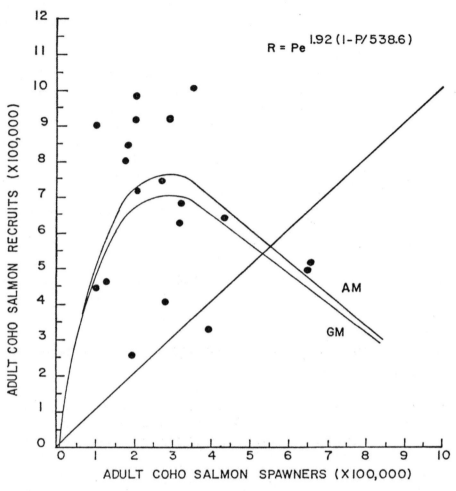

FIGURE 1. Recruitment curve for Oregon coastal coho salmon *Oncorhynchus kisutch* adults 1950–1968 (Oregon Department of Fish and Wildlife 1982).

to drive the coastal wild populations into the dirt. The good news was that we did identify our own mistakes, and tried to make things right.

Management Mistakes

The fundamental mistake made was that the spawning index numbers were not representative of Oregon coastal salmon streams. At that time, everyone who was originally involved with the creation of those spawning index numbers had retired. We assumed that the index numbers were representative of

numbers in all the coastal streams. Bad assumption! By conducting spawning surveys on a random set of streams, we found that the original spawning index streams represented the best of the best of coastal streams in terms of habitat quality and quantity, and their coho salmon populations represented the largest and most productive coho salmon runs— they were the cream of the crop. We speculated what must have been in the minds of the retirees who set up the index system. Where would one go to index abundance with the best precision? Likely, one would go to the locations with the largest aggregations of spawners. Unfortunately, no one had remembered the origin of the indices when we used them to develop the first stock-recruitment curve. The indices were originally intended to measure the relative abundance of salmon *in those particular streams* from time to time as management moved forward. The indices were never intended to provide a measure of adult spawning abundance that was representative of all Oregon coastal populations. The lesson learned here was the need to carefully document the methods used, the rationale and projected end use of the analysis, and the assumptions made in executing the analysis.

Mistake number two created no less of a problem than the first. The second mistake came in an effort to correct our estimated numbers of wild adult spawners based on the harvest rate. At the time, we did not actually know the true harvest rate on wild coho salmon. Only the harvest rate on hatchery fish was known because only the stocked fish carried any marks. Through research conducted in the 1980s, we discovered that hatchery fish were harvested at a much higher rate than wild salmon, so when we back-calculated while reconstructing the population abundance by mixing these two sources of numbers, we estimated that a 67% harvest rate was sustainable. This inflated miscalculation caused us to think that the wild fish were much more resilient to harvest than they actually were.

Mistake number three was paying too much attention to the actual predicted curve of the stock-recruitment curve and not considering the uncertainty around the curve. We paid too much attention to the line rather than remembering the scatter of the data points around it, essentially forgetting about the fog around the data points. Even with the uncertainty displayed by the data points, more existed because every one of those data points had a 20–30% measurement error or halo around it, which was further compounded by the fact that the data points were not a random sample of the spawning populations. A law should be enacted in fisheries biology making it illegal to present any stock-recruitment curve without displaying the data points. We made a huge mistake! We thought our calculations showed a productivity curve for Oregon coho salmon that would allow us to harvest at least half of the Oregon coast coho salmon in the ocean on a continual basis. We mistakenly thought the wild population was so big, so robust, and so resilient to harvest, that we could unleash fishing effort to catch all those extra hatchery fish we had in the system. Why was our extrapolation to sustainable harvest levels so important? If the fishery did not harvest those hatchery fish, and the hatchery fish all showed at the hatchery as surpluses, then the fishermen would riot against us the fishery managers. We were very, very sensitive to that possibility.

New Management Strategies

The management mistakes we had made drove the coho salmon using Oregon coastal streams to the point of listing under the Endangered Species Act. The crisis over the decline in population abundance and the controversy over potential listing became the genesis of the new coho salmon management strategy for the coast of Oregon. I hope the new management strategy will prove over time to be the solution. For the time being, the listing has been avoided.

The new management strategy was to manage hatchery and wild coho separately instead of together as we had done in the past. To facilitate that approach, mass marking of all the hatchery fish was instituted. All hatchery fish had marks, whereas the wild fish did not. Mass marking allowed separate management of the two types of coho salmon. The marked hatchery fish became fair game for the fisheries. At the same time, the wild fish, which were unmarked, could be released if caught in the fisheries. As a result of mass marking, the harvest and survival rates could be estimated for hatchery adults and the pressure could be taken off wild-origin spawning adults.

The mass marking approach allowed an accurate determination of the abundance of the wild coho salmon populations. The Oregon coastal wild populations were discovered to be so small in aggregate that it was no longer reasonable to harvest three-quarters of them, two-thirds of them, or one-third of them. There were simply not enough wild coho out there to harvest! The number of wild coho salmon adults was originally estimated to range from half a million to a million fish, but data from mass marking revised that estimate to 100,000–200,000 fish or possibly even less. All of a sudden, we realized that these wild fish clearly could not fuel our fisheries.

Recognition that wild fish could not be managed in the same way as hatchery fish was a revelation! Clearly, the management strategy needed to change. By mass marking all the hatchery coho salmon and promoting selective fisheries just for the hatchery fish, the fishing pressure could be taken off the wild coho populations. The selective fisheries approach was further enhanced by moving the stocking locations from the coastal streams in the south to the Columbia River in the north. This strategy resulted in a northerly shift in the fisheries to the mouth of the Columbia and permitted harvest of the hatchery fish in the ocean without incidentally catching the coastal wild fish further south. While the hatchery fish were accumulating off the mouth of the Columbia, the wild coastal fish could safely immigrate into the coastal streams for spawning without the harvest pressure generated by the hatchery fish. Thus, our new management strategy was to mass mark hatchery fish, create selective fisheries, and relocate the fisheries to the Columbia River. This management strategy is described in the Oregon Plan for Salmon and Watersheds (Oregon Coastal Salmon Restoration Initiative 1997).

At the end of my 30-year career for the Oregon Department of Fish & Wildlife, I worked as the salmon management advisor for Governor John Kitzhaber. My task was to unbury ourselves from this accumulated set of management mistakes and to successfully implement the new plan. A 10–15% harvest rate is now permitted on coastal wild fish and this rate currently seems sustainable. The hatchery fish now return to the Columbia River and support fisheries there (Figure 2). The great debate now focused on how to allow harvest of hatchery fish returning to the Columbia River and still protect the little vestigial upstream populations in the Columbia River which are listed under the Endangered Species Act. Maybe in another 20 years this debate will be solved.

Habitat Islands, Stock Recruitment, and Ocean Productivity

A key concept that helped our understanding of Oregon coastal coho salmon was that juvenile stream habitats were not uniformly the same across 5,000 mi of spawning area. The capability of these habitats to produce smolts to the ocean varied greatly along the Oregon coast. Recall that the historical spawning indices used in the 1980s were only recorded in the best spawning and juvenile rearing habitats. Smolt production at low abundance levels was concentrated in small clusters or islands of high productivity habitat surrounded by large haloes of medium to poor juvenile habitats. That variation in habitat quality among the streams was a critically important aspect that affected the ability of these fish to replace themselves. When ocean harvest rates were at 50%, combined with low ocean productivity, only the coho salmon in the highest quality habitat could replace themselves. Under

FIGURE 2. Sport fishery for hatchery coho salmon *Oncorhynchus kisutch* at Buoy 10, near the mouth of the Columbia River. This selective fishery uses fin clips to distinguish hatchery from wild coho salmon. Only hatchery coho salmon may be harvested by the anglers.

this scenario, the less abundant stocks in the low productivity habitat were in big trouble. We learned that managing based on the most abundant populations using the best spawning and juvenile rearing habitats will drive the less abundant stocks using less productive habitats to extinction.

In light of what we know now about Oregon coastal salmon, how should we have interpreted the stock-recruitment curve generated in the 1980s? Examination of the curve with the actual data reveals data points spread all around the fitted line. The best-fit curve is not based on a relationship of tightly clustered data points. We now know that what we were examining was not a single curve but was actually a series of curves—curves based on many stocks of salmon using many different stream habitats that each differed in juvenile productivity.

Not recognizing this distinction within the stock-recruitment curve caused us to manage for the average stocks, and our harvest management drove the weaker stocks towards extinction.

Last, managers must track annual changes in ocean productivity and adjust their management of salmon in response to these changes. Management errors can be absorbed when ocean survival is 15%, but disaster strikes when ocean survival decreases to 1.5% (like it did in 1977) and fisheries operate at the same high harvest rates. In Oregon, we found that if we maintained high harvest rates while during periods of low ocean productivity, the populations became smaller and fewer habitats were occupied. The populations just shrank in size and only used the streams with high productivity habitat islands. Unfortunately, these same islands were the sites at which our spawning indices were conducted. Thus, the indices were misleading, giving the false impression that more coho salmon productivity was not as variable from year to year as it is. In the low productivity habitats, populations were much more variable and their decline to extinction went undetected. When we started conducting spawning ground (live fish and carcass) counts randomly, no coho salmon occurred anywhere else except in those exceptional stream habitats—period!

Recommendations for Managing Salmon

Lesson number one—be careful about the use of stock-recruitment relationships in management. Meeting the minimum escapement goals does not mean that harvesting the rest of the population is a wise or sustainable practice. I suggest choosing more conservative harvest rates that will allow the natural ebb and flow of populations to occur without risking the sustainability of the population. In Oregon, when we removed the harvest pressure, even those populations in marginal habitats were able to replace themselves during periods of low ocean survival. When periods of high ocean survival came along, the remaining populations were able to re-colonize marginal and poor freshwater habitats. A distinct interaction exists among the harvest rate, the ocean productivity, and the freshwater production. We had to learn it the hard way. I hope you can learn from our mistakes.

Lesson number two—carefully consider stocking locations used for hatchery fish and how your stocking locations and practices will affect assessment indices, and the location of fishing pressure. Not until we started marking all the hatchery fish did we discovered that we were miscounting the salmon on the spawning grounds. We were under such extreme pressure caused by uncaught hatchery fish returning to the hatcheries that we decided to not release them at the hatchery. Instead we released them out in the coastal streams. Well, they came right back to their release location, our index spawning areas. Until we went to mass marking, we did not realize how much our spawning area index estimates were inflated by hatchery fish. In that period of 20 years, we suffered tremendously with the legacy of those bad decisions. Your stocking locations also will affect where fishing effort is expended. Herein lies a management opportunity to redistribute fishing effort away from wild stocks such as we did by moving our stocking locations north to the Columbia River mouth.

Lesson number three—challenge your assumptions. Conduct the research required to test your assumptions, and change management strategies when necessary. Don't become arrogant or complacent in your management approaches. In Oregon, we made a fundamental mistake by not challenging our analyses. We did not challenge the assumptions underlying the expansions of the spawning index numbers, nor did we check the assumptions underlying the reconstructed run size. Instead, we plowed forward and built a stock-recruitment relationship that did not represent our coastal coho salmon. We then used that relationship to manage our wild stocks into the ground. Initially, we were possibly a bit too proud to admit our mistakes. Be careful of stock-recruitment! Be careful of big high harvest rates that take off the back end of the run. Articulate and evaluate your assumptions. I'm very proud that we spent 15 years of concentrated research to figure out our mistakes (e.g., Emlen et al. 1990), and I'm even more proud that we used our new-found knowledge to change the management plan.

The Future Holds Even Bigger Challenges for Salmon Survival

For the Oregon coast, the challenges of the last century have been the proper use of harvest management and figuring out the proper and improper use of hatcheries. Some may think, "Well, we didn't list the Oregon coastal coho; we're out of the woods; we've taken all the harvest pressure off; we have relocated all those nonhatchery fish, we're in good shape." Not true! I am very, very worried about the next century because the challenges of the next century are going to be a lot more difficult to overcome. Increases in human populations and climate change are two examples.

What is happening on the Oregon coast in terms of human populations? Our population is exploding. Estimates suggest a quadrupling to a quintupling of our population in the Pacific Northwest over the next 100 years (Lackey et al. 2006). A lot of those people are going to relocate to the Oregon coast. A lot of them are going to convert agricultural land into residential land. This conversion with the attendant armoring of land surfaces with roofs, sidewalks, and streets combined with lawns, pesticides, and fertilizers will forever alter those low elevation valley-flow pucker-bush streams that are the salmon's home ground. The hydrology of the streams will change. Runoff will increase. The streams will become flashy. Wild coho salmon again will be in trouble. There's a big rock rolling right at them. It's called our population growth.

The coho salmon of Oregon are at the southern edge of their range. The reason it's the southern edge of the range is that it gets hot in southern Oregon. Why are there hardly any of coho left in northern California? Because it gets even hotter there. The second big rock rolling at coastal coho salmon is called the change in the climate. The predicted change in the climate approaching Oregon is a 500-mi shift in climate over the next 100 years. In oth-er words, the climate 500 mi south of us will move to Oregon. So 100 years from now the climate in Astoria and Portland is going to look like the climate they now have in San Francisco and Sacramento. Ask yourself, "How many coho are loitering around and using the small suburban coastal streams in San Francisco?" The answer is not many!

The potential effects of a changing climate should be sending up warning flags to salmon managers everywhere. The potential effects of climate change should be raising questions about future production. Will it go up or down? We should be challenging our assumptions. Stock-recruitment curves have, as a fundamental assumption, a constant environment. We should investigate multiple alternative hypotheses that we are investigating and discussing. How will climate change affect ocean currents and their productivity potential for salmon? Which will be the first habitats salmon can become extinct? Will coho salmon expand into any new habitats? What kind of surprises should we expect? What kind of warning system can managers build into the fishery management system to give us the best chance of detecting the first hint that surprises are starting to happen?

Application to Alaska Salmon Management

What would it mean to the residents of the Arctic-Yukon-Kuskokwim region if all of a sudden fishery managers announced, "We've got a little climate change, and we don't know what's going on, but we're going to have to shut these fisheries down?" In Oregon, when the ocean productivity changed and we reduced the harvest, the result was a tremendous political nightmare. For ocean commercial fishermen and charter boat owners and coastal businesses, the result was a traumatic pain. For Alaskans, the result would be nothing short of a cultural disaster. Alaska has big, powerful natural rivers that have not been altered by man's development, and this blessing could lull you into complacency—a complacency which could border on arrogance. If that happens, the wave of climate change will wash over you. The potential for de-coupling the rhythms of the river from the rhythms of the Bering Sea is high. If that de-coupling happens, a lot of populations will be in trouble. If complacency overcomes you, you are going to be facing a lot of rural people and others, and saying, "We don't know what happened, but something awful has happened." Don't let that happen to you.

Conclusion

Here's the moral of the story from my perspective—of the Oregon coho salmon story. Don't be slow on the uptake. Anticipate surprises. Build the flags into the management system. When that flag goes up, pay attention to it. Think about what might happen to the salmon in these wonderful systems of streams and oceans. Competence can easily morph into complacency, and then can subtly shift into arrogance. I recommend reading Jim Lichatowich's *Salmon Without Rivers* (1999). He describes the trap of thinking that we know so much about salmon we don't really need rivers anymore. Some of us in Oregon got caught in this trap. Remember, that the managers are people who care about the resource, but they must be looking for the surprises to come, and must be nimble and on their feet, ready to respond to the future challenges and threats to salmon.

Last, I will share a personal story. When I was a harvest manager, a research biologist working on coho salmon, and then later as chief of fisheries, I felt bad. I felt bad because we didn't know what was wrong and we had to face the fishermen. Our department had sold them the idea that a sky was the limit for the salmon fishery. We asked them, "How many

hatcheries do you want to build? That's how many fish you can have." That was the line we sold them. When the bottom fell out of the salmon fisheries, and we started to shut their fisheries down, I felt bad because we did not have answers. I felt bad when we came up with a stock-recruitment curve that was bogus. I felt bad when we had to admit our errors and had to change our management strategy. My son is a young fish biologist with the Oregon Department of Fish and Wildlife. He is one of those biologists out doing those randomized spawning surveys that I have described. One day, years ago, after being out in the pucker-bush crawling down the mountain to those streams and not finding any salmon, he walked up to me with his eyes on fire. I thought to myself, "Uh-oh, here it comes." You see, his eyes were on fire, and he looked at me and says, "Dad, you are the chief of fisheries. How could you let this happen?" I will never forget that feeling. I said to him, "I don't know, Art. We didn't mean to screw up, we just did, and I will spend the rest of my career digging out of it." That was when I felt the worst. That feeling I had of having him look me right square in the eyes and say, "How could you let this happen?" I don't wish that on any of you, and I will never forget that incident. Time has moved on since that day. We have a better understanding of salmon. Management has changed now. I hope that I will pass onto my son a legacy of Oregon coastal salmon populations that are abundant and healthy and robust and ready for the next challenge. A final bit of wisdom comes from Yogi Berra, who counseled, "It's not what you don't know that'll get you. It's what you're absolutely, positively sure of, that ain't so."

Acknowledgments

Charles Krueger and Allison Evans helped with translating my oral presentation into a paper for publication in the symposium proceedings.

References

Emlen, J. M., R. R. Reisenbichler, A. M. McGie, and T. E. Nickelson. 1990. Density-dependence at sea for coho salmon (*Oncorhynchus kistuch*). Canadian Journal of Fisheries and Aquatic Sciences 47:1765–1772.

Lackey, R. T., D. H. Lach, and S. L. Duncan, editors. 2006. Salmon 2100: the future of wild Pacific salmon. American Fisheries Society, Bethesda, Maryland.

Lichatowich, J. 1999. Salmon without rivers. Island Press. Washington, D.C.

McGie, A. M. 1980. Analysis of relationships between hatchery coho salmon transplants and adult escapements in Oregon coastal watersheds. Information Report Number 80–6. Oregon Department of Fish and Wildlife, Portland.

Lichatowich, J., and R. N. Williams. 2009. Failures to incorpoarate science into fishery management and recovery programs: lessons from the Columbia River. Pages 1005–1019 *in* C. C. Krueger and C. E. Zimmerman, editors. Pacific salmon: ecology and management of western Alaska's populations. American Fisheries Society, Symposium 70, Bethesda, Maryland.

McGie, A. M. 1981. Trends in escapement and production of fall chinook and coho salmon in Oregon. Information Report Number 81–7. Oregon Department of Fish and Wildlife, Portland.

Oregon Coastal Salmon Restoration Initiative. 1997. The Oregon plan: restoring an Oregon legacy through cooperative efforts. Coastal Salmon Restoration Initiative, Salem, Oregon. http://hdl.handle.net/1957/4985.

Oregon Department of Fish and Wildlife. 1982. Comprehensive plan for production and management or Oregon's anadromous salmon and trout. Part II: Coho salmon plan. Oregon Department of Fish and Wildlife.

Solazzi, M. F., T. E. Nickelson, and S. L. Johnson. 1990. An evaluation of the use of coho salmon presmolts to supplement wild production in Oregon coastal streams. Fishery Research Report 10. Oregon Department of Fish and Wildlife, Portland.

Williams, R., and J. Lichatowich. 2009. Science and politics—an uncomfortable alliance: lessons learned from the fish and wildlife program of the Northwest Power and Conservation Council. Pages 1021–1046 *in* C. C. Krueger and C. E. Zimmerman, editors. Pacific salmon: ecology and management of western Alaska's populations. American Fisheries Society, Symposium 70, Bethesda, Maryland.

American Fisheries Society Symposium 70:1059–1081, 2009

Uncertainty and Fishery Management in the North American Great Lakes: Lessons from Applications of Decision Analysis

Michael L. Jones* and James R. Bence

Quantitative Fisheries Center, Department of Fisheries and Wildlife
Michigan State University
13 Natural Resources Building, East Lansing, Michigan 48824, USA

Abstract.—Many fishery management decisions continue to be guided by science only through "best guess" interpretation of assessment information and deterministic models of fisheries and food webs; until very recently this was true of nearly all fishery management in the Great Lakes. However, fishery management decisions can be improved by formally considering uncertainty when evaluating management options; practical tools for doing this have become increasingly available. Accounting for uncertainty is important because acting as though the best guess is true may be substantially suboptimal if this leads to poor performance for other less likely, but still plausible, "states of the world." For a variety of critical Great Lakes fishery management issues, including determining appropriate investments in sea lamprey *Petromyzon marinus* control, setting suitable levels of salmonine stocking, and establishing percid harvest policies, are considered. In each case, the authors worked closely with fishery managers to conduct a decision analysis of management options they identified, using contemporary statistical methods to formally assess uncertainty about key fishery parameters and stochastic simulation to compare management options. These decision analyses were used by fishery managers to develop policies that more objectively account for uncertainty and to garner support from stakeholders and policy makers. The approach shows considerable promise for future fishery management in the Great Lakes, but may face substantial challenges as managers seek to more effectively involve stakeholders throughout the process, foster the requisite technical expertise within their agencies, and communicate the results of highly technical analyses to both stakeholders and decision makers. Three important aspects of salmon Arctic-Yukon-Kuskokwim region management for which a decision analysis approach would be particularly valuable are (1) the evaluation of different options for assessment sampling of returning adult salmon, used to determine whether escapement targets are being met; (2) strategies for in-season management of salmon harvest; and (3) setting annual escapement goals for individual stocks.

---

*Corresponding author: jonesm30@msu.edu

TABLE 1. The steps to a typical decision analysis (after Peterman and Anderson 1999).

Step	Task
1	Define management options
2	Define management objectives
3	Identify critical uncertainties (alternative states of nature)
4	Assign probabilities to alternative states of nature
5	Develop a model to forecast outcomes of management options, in terms of performance meeting management objectives
6	Rank management options in terms of their performance
7	Conduct a sensitivity analysis

tro-3-(trifluoromethyl) phenol, before they become parasites and migrate to the lakes to feed on large-bodied fishes, such as lake trout *Salvelinus namaycush*. This chemical control program reduced sea lamprey populations to 10% of precontrol levels (e.g., Heinrich et al. 2003; Lavis et al. 2003a). Other controls are being used to a lesser extent, including low-head barrier dams to prevent sea lamprey access to spawning habitats (Lavis et al. 2003b), traps to remove migrating adult sea lampreys as they enter rivers to spawn (Mullett et al. 2003), and the release of sterilized male sea lampreys into spawning habitats to compete with unsterilized males (Twohey et al. 2003). The GLFC has stated that they seek to increase the use of these alternative methods in the future, and thereby reduce reliance on chemical control (GLFC 2001).

The St. Marys River connects Lake Superior to Lake Huron (Figure 1), and unlike other Great Lakes streams that contain substantial larval sea lamprey populations, has too large a flow to treat with TFM at a reasonable cost. Increasing recruitment of sea lampreys from the St. Marys River led to a large increase in the abundance of sea lampreys in Lake Huron during the 1990s. Consequent-

ly, the GLFC sponsored the development of a strategy for integrated pest control of sea lampreys in this large river. In 1997, the strategy was adopted and included three tactics: use of an alternative chemical method (Bayluscide[1]) that enabled selective application of lampricide to 981 ha of larval sea lamprey habitat, deployment of traps to capture adult sea lampreys, and releases of chemically sterilized male sea lampreys into spawning areas (Schleen et al. 2003). Of these three tactics, the chemical control component was by far the most expensive.

The decision to adopt this three-pronged strategy was based on deterministic models presented to the GLFC that forecasted the effects of various management options on Lake Huron sea lamprey and lake trout populations along with a cost–benefit analysis of those management options (Schleen et al. 2003). However, the strategy was not designed as, nor was intended to be, a long-term strategy;

[1]Bayluscide is the commercial name for 2',5-dichloro-4'-nitrosalicylanilide, also known as niclosamide. Development of a granular formulation enabled the use of this lampricide for application to specific patches of larval habitat rather than to the entire river, as is required for conventional lampricide applications.

FIGURE 1. Map of the North American Great Lakes, showing the locations of the three case studies discussed in the paper: St. Marys River (sea lamprey control); Lake Michigan (salmonine stocking); and Lake Erie (walleye exploitation).

its objective was to substantially reduce the St. Marys River sea lamprey population in the short term. This control program was judged necessary in 1997 because of perceived large, but un-quantified, uncertainty about how effective the less costly control actions (trapping and sterile male releases) would be if implemented alone. However, an expensive long-term control strategy that relied heavily on chemical methods would re-direct limited funds from controlling other sea lamprey-producing rivers in the Great Lakes basin. Consequently, the GLFC was challenged with developing a feasible long-term strategy to maintain cost-effective control in the St. Marys River. Recognizing the need for a

long-term approach that better reflected uncertainty, the GLFC invited us to apply decision analysis. Our analysis began in 1999 and continued for three years. Punctuated by three workshops involving scientists, managers, and decision makers, the authors developed and evaluated the decision analysis, and then presented and discussed our findings with the GLFC on four occasions during 2001–2002.

At the initial workshop, levels of each of the three management tactics (trapping, sterile male release, and chemical control) that were to be considered were identified. The performance measures were to be the forecasted future abundance of parasitic sea lampreys in Lake Huron, the frequency of outcomes with parasitic sea lamprey abundance that exceeded a target level, and the net economic benefit of the option[2] (Table 2). The key uncertainties to be included were demographic processes (particularly recruitment dynamics) in the sea lamprey population, and implementation uncertainty for each control tactic (Table 2).

The first workshop was followed by a thorough investigation of these sources of uncertainty, and the development of a stochastic model to forecast future Lake Huron parasitic sea lamprey abundance, conditional on a particular set of management tactics being employed (Haeseker et al. 2007). The demographic analysis was completed using an inverse population modeling approach similar to statistical catch-at-age analysis (Fournier and Archibald 1982), which allowed us to quantify the uncertainty associated with sea lamprey population dynamics (Haeseker et al. 2003). Implementation uncertainty for trapping and releasing sterile male releases was quantified by examining empirical data on past inter-annual variation of each tactic's effectiveness. Implementation uncertainty for chemical control was quantified by examining inter-annual variation in the distribution of larval sea lampreys in the area targeted for chemical control (Haeseker et al. 2007), and assuming that future decisions about where to direct future chemical treatment would be based on historical larval distribution patterns derived from a single, exhaustive survey conducted during the mid-1990s;annual distributional surveys for larval sea lampreys in the St. Marys River would be prohibitively expensive.

At a second workshop attended primarily by technical experts, both the uncertainty analysis and the forecasting model were presented and criticized. The workshop led to further refinements of the model.

At the third workshop, and at several follow-on meetings with sea lamprey program staff, a specific set of management options was developed to be considered (Table 3), and used the forecasting model to compare their expected performance at achieving management objectives. The analysis revealed that the highest ranking management options included increased trapping and sterile male releases, and moderate amounts of chemical control (Table 3, Option 8). Rankings were similar for all three performance measures. A sensitivity analysis revealed that these rankings were also robust to two key assumptions, one about sources of sea lamprey to Lake Huron other than the St. Marys River, and a second about the economic benefit of reduced sea lamprey abundance. During winter 2002/2003, the GLFC adopted a control strategy similar to our highest ranking option; this strategy has continued since 2003.

Before our decision analysis, key GLFC commissioners and staff, as well as the lead author of this paper, were skeptical about the potential of trapping and sterile male releases as control options, believing that these methods would be rendered ineffective by large density-independent recruitment variation (Jones et al. 2003). By explicitly accounting for uncertainty, especially concerning sea lamprey demographics, the authors demonstrated that enhancing these methods had a high probability of contributing substantially to future suppression of sea lampreys in the St. Marys River. Without our modeling results, the GLFC likely would not have funded enhanced trapping and sterile male releases, principally because of a qualitative impression of the risks (i.e., likelihood of failure) associated with these methods.

In this decision analysis, accounting for uncertainty did not lead to a different conclusion. When the authors ran simulations with sea lamprey demographic uncertainty removed, i.e., using the maximum posterior density estimates of the demographic pa-

---

[2]Measured as the difference between the estimated benefit of reducing sea lamprey abundance (based on an implied value calculation; Lupi et al. 2003) and the annualized cost of the management option, discounted over a 27-year time horizon.

TABLE 2. Management options, management objectives and critical uncertainties selected for consideration by the participants in the St. Marys River sea lamprey control decision analysis.

Management options	Management objectives	Uncertainties
Trap adult sea lampreys—effectiveness levels of 40% and 70%	Minimizing the median forecasted abundance of parasitic sea lampreys in Lake Huron by 2012 (short term) and 2030 (long term)	Sea lamprey demographics: recruitment, larval survival rates, proportion metamorphosing-at-age
Release sterile male adult sea lamprey—sterile to fertile male ratios of 4:1 and 7:1	Maximizing the probability of achieving parasitic sea lamprey abundance below 114,000 in Lake Huron in 2012	Efficacy of Bayluscide applications, based on estimated uncertainty about future spatial distributions of sea lamprey larvae
Apply granular Bayluscide to high density areas—108, 216 and 812 ha	Maximizing the net economic benefit of the management option (see footnote to text)	Efficacy of trapping and sterile male releases, based on past variation in the efficacy of these methods

TABLE 3. Management options considered in the St. Marys River sea lamprey decision analysis, and their performance at achieving management objectives. Rates are expressed as proportions. Trapping rate is the proportion of the spawning run captured by traps; SMRT ratio is the ratio of sterile to fertile males in the spawning population. The target kill rate refers to the expected kill rate if the true larval population distribution was identical to that observed during the 1993–1996 survey, with the area of habitat treated in parentheses.

	Target rates			Sea lamprey abundance		Net benefit
Option	Trapping	SMRT	Kill (ha)	2030 Median	% < 114 000 in 2012	Median ($millions)
1	0	0	0 (0)	388,000	18.4	7.9
2	0.4	0	0 (0)	321,000	23.3	13.8
3	0.7	0	0 (0)	189,000	35.0	26.1
4	0.4	4	0 (0)	130,000	41.9	28.5
5	0.7	7	0 (0)	49,000	61.4	41.0
6	0	0	0.15 (108)	348,000	21.6	13.0
7	0.4	4	0.15 (108)	112,000	47.2	31.5
8	0.7	7	0.15 (108)	46,000	65.9	42.1
9	0.4	4	0.25 (260)	96,000	52.0	34.1
10	0.4	4	0.34 (812)	81,000	59.4	29.3

rameters and assuming zero process error in the stock–recruitment relationship, the rank order of management options did not change. Instead, the decision analysis gave decision makers more confidence in the merits of what they had previously judged to be a risky decision, despite the results of a deterministic analysis.

The GLFC also decided to support an ongoing larval assessment program in the St. Marys River using an efficient adaptive sampling strategy. This program would yield new data on sea lamprey recruitment dynamics that can be used to reduce uncertainty about the stock–recruitment relationship and thus potentially contribute to better-informed decisions in the future. With good spatial distribution information, implementation uncertainty can be reduced for future chemical treatments. Most importantly, it facilitates the use of a feedback control policy, wherein future chemical treatments are triggered by observations of sea lamprey densities that are sufficient to justify the expense. Our previous analyses assumed a fixed treatment schedule given the absence of such a monitoring program. Further decision analysis modeling will evaluate these feedback policies.

Case Study 2: Salmonine Stocking in Lake Michigan

Stocking of hatchery-reared salmonines is one of the primary fishery management tools available on Lake Michigan. Salmon and trout are annually stocked in large numbers to provide recreational fishing opportunities, restore native lake trout populations, and reduce the abundance of nonnative alewife *Alosa pseudoharengus*. High abundance of alewife is undesirable because this exotic species preys on larvae of native Lake Michigan fishes and at high densities experiences mass mortality (die-offs) which foul beaches that are of high recreational value.

Since the advent of major salmonine stocking programs in the mid-1960s, hundreds of millions of Chinook salmon *Oncorhynchus tschawytscha*, lake trout, rainbow trout *O. mykiss*, brown trout *Salmo trutta*, and coho salmon *O. kisutch* have been stocked into Lake Michigan (Kocik and Jones 1999; Hansen and Holey 2002). A tradeoff exists, however, between (a) stocking too few predator fish, allowing alewife abundance to rise to undesirable levels and foregoing potential harvest of predators; and (b) stocking too many predators, thereby exceeding the capacity of the alewife population to support the consequent predation pressure (Stewart et al. 1981). Indeed, a dramatic rise in Chinook salmon mortality rates (with commensurate loss of harvest) during the late 1980s in Lake Michigan is widely viewed as having resulted from too many stocked predators (Holey et al. 1998; Hansen and Holey 2002). Therefore, a critical question faced by Lake Michigan fishery managers was "how many salmon and trout should be stocked each year into Lake Michigan?" Again, we were invited by Lake Michigan fishery managers to apply decision analysis to this problem.

The decision analysis had four stages. First, the authors met with experts, managers and nongovernment stakeholders (recreational and commercial fishers) in March 2000 to discuss and agree upon management objectives, options, and critical uncertainties (Table 4). Second, historical data from Lake Michigan on salmonine harvests, diet, growth rates, and prey fish abundance were used to estimate parameters of a salmonine-prey fish population model and the uncertainty associated with the parameter estimates (Szalai 2003). Third, a decision model was developed to forecast the consequences—for alewife abundance, Chinook salmon growth, and Chinook salmon harvests—of alternative stocking strategies. Finally, the authors met again with experts, managers and stakeholders to demonstrate and discuss the model.

TABLE 4. Management options, management objectives and critical uncertainties selected for consideration by the participants in the Lake Michigan salmonine stocking decision analysis.

Management options

Category	Details
Adjust annual stocking rates of salmonines	Option 1 – Current stocking levels
	Option 2 – 50% reduction in Chinook stocking
	Option 3 – state-dependent policy[a]

Management objectives

Category	Performance measures
Maintain acceptable catch rates for salmonines	Median forecasted average annual Chinook harvest
	Proportion of outcomes with Chinook harvest < 100,000/yr
Minimize risks of elevated Chinook salmon mortality	Median forecasted age-3 Chinook salmon weight
	Proportion of outcomes with age-3 weight < 6 kg
Maintain predator-prey balance	Median forecasted alewife biomass
	Proportion of outcomes with alewife biomass < 500 kt

Critical uncertainties

Category	Rationale
Alewife recruitment dynamics	How much predation pressure can the alewife population support?
Chinook salmon feeding effectiveness	How successful are Chinook salmon at finding prey when the prey are relatively scarce?
Chinook salmon growth-survival linkages	How strongly coupled is Chinook salmon growth to natural mortality rates?

[a]Changes to stocking are triggered by forecasted changes in Chinook salmon weight at age 3 in the fall: stocking of all species is reduced 50% if fall weight falls below 7 kg and restored to current levels if fall weight increases above 8 kg.

The methods for quantifying uncertainties in the parameters of the forecasting model are described in detail in Szalai (2003). A brief estimation model was developed similar to statistical catch-at-age models to reconstruct the historical dynamics of Lake Michigan prey fish (alewife, bloater *Coregonus hoyi*, and rainbow smelt *Osmerus mordax*) populations, but including salmonine predators rather than fishing as additional mortality. By fitting the model to available data, prey fish abundance and recruitment were estimated from 1962–1999, as well as the effective search rate of Chinook salmon (i.e., success of Chinook salmon at feeding when prey fish became relatively scarce). This analysis used as inputs, estimates of the number of predator fish obtained from separate age-structured assessments, which played a role here similar to that of fishing effort in many traditional assessment models. These results were used to estimate the relationship between average recruitment and spawning stock size, as well as the variability about this relationship, for alewife, the key prey species in the system.

In addition, estimates of Chinook salmon mortality rates and size-at-age from 1985–1997 (from just prior to the sharp rise in mortality through the period of Chinook salmon recovery) were used to estimate a model of the dependence of Chinook salmon mortality on growth. It was hypothesized that reduced growth results in an increased probability of elevated mortality, potentially due to disease. It was also hypothesized that when elevated mortality occurs, it would persist for a period of time even after growth rates recover (i.e., there is a lag between improved growth rates and reduced mortality rates). This model is consistent with observations, but great uncertainty exists because evidence supporting this relationship comes from a single multi-year episode.

To evaluate stocking policy alternatives, we developed a stochastic model, based on the assessment models described above, that forecasted the alewife abundance and Chinook salmon abundance and size resulting from a specific policy. The model also included all other major stocked salmonine species as predators, and bloater and rainbow smelt as prey. All predators were modeled as dynamic and age-structured. Recruitment of predators in the model was treated as a known input because they derive from hatchery releases and measured production in the wild. For predators other than Chinook salmon, natural mortality was assumed constant and the effective search rate was set at a higher rate than for Chinook salmon. Growth rates of the other predators did not vary in the same manner as for Chinook salmon during the historical period, which suggests that their success at searching for prey was less affected by variations in alewife abundance, indicative of a higher search rate. For computational purposes, size at age for other predators was fixed rather than calculated based on modeled consumption. Prey species other than alewife were not modeled dynamically. Instead they were included as having a constant abundance at age. In this modeling effort, more effort was placed into incorporating details for the models of Chinook salmon and alewife both because of greater availability of information and because we believed that these two species play a dominant role in the system. Other predators were included in a dynamic fashion to retain the ability to evaluate policies, where the stocking of those species was changed. One of the two alternative prey species was benthic and the other was pelagic, and their inclusion should be viewed as an approach to incorporating alternative prey for salmonines when alewife became scarce.

Stocking policies were compared by looking for each performance indicator, at the distribution of outcomes, the median outcome, and the proportion of outcomes that exceeded or fell below a threshold value deemed to be undesirable. A wide range of outcomes were forecasted for each policy. For continued stocking at current levels, average annual Chinook salmon harvests were focused to be ranging from 6,500–360,000 fish per year (Figure 2). For this policy, forecasted average harvests of less than 100,000 fish per year were relatively common (29.7%, Table 5), with the most common result lying between 50,000 and 75,000 fish harvested per year (Figure 2, solid bars). Policies with fixed, but lower stocking rates resulted in poorer performance for harvest and alewife indicators, but better performance for Chinook weight (e.g., Table 5, "Reduce Chinook 50%"). In contrast, a state-dependent, or feedback policy in which stocking of all salmonines was reduced by 50% when age-3 Chinook weights measured in the fall declined below 7 kg (and restored to current levels when weight recovers to 8 kg), resulted in a substantially lower proportion of outcomes with harvests below 100,000 fish per year (15.7%, Table 5, "State

dependent"); although the range of possible future harvests was only slightly narrower (18,000–315,000 fish per year), and the alewife biomass performance indicators were worse than for other policies.

This policy analysis suggested two important consequences for decision makers seeking an appropriate policy for salmonine stocking. First, the results suggested that feedback policies, where stocking levels are dynamically adjusted in response to evidence of a deteriorating situation, substantially reduced the risk of poor outcomes with respect to Chinook salmon harvest and growth. Second, the uncertainties included in the forecasting model, particularly with respect to alewife recruitment, gave rise to a wide range of possible outcomes from a single policy, regardless of which policy was chosen. It was concluded that all feasible strategies still admitted a substantial possibility of undesirable

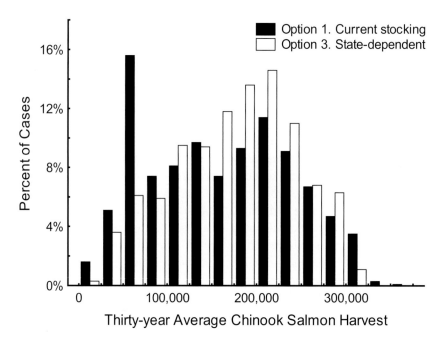

FIGURE 2. A comparison of the distribution of forecasted Chinook salmon *Oncorhynchus tshawytscha* harvests for two contrasting stocking policies. Shaded bars are for a policy representing continued stocking at current (2005) levels; Open bars represent a state-dependent policy with 50% reductions in stocking of all species when forecasted Chinook salmon age-3 weight falls below 7 kg, and increases in stocking to current levels if age-3 weight subsequently rises above 8 kg.

TABLE 5. Decision model outputs that summarize key performance measures for three Lake Michigan stocking policies.

Policy	Median Chinook harvest (numbers)	Proportion of harvests < 100,000	Median Chinook weight (kg)	Proportion of weights < 6 kg	Median alewife biomass (x10³ kg)	Proportion of biomasses > 500,000 MT
Current stocking	160,000	29.7	7.0	47.6	417,000	47.8
Reduce Chinook	126,000	35.4	9.9	41.2	667,000	53.6
State-dependent	182,000	15.7	11.6	33.9	870,000	59.5

consequences stemming from future Chinook salmon and alewife population trajectories. As a result, flexibility and careful monitoring will be essential to good management of this fishery.

During 2005, Lake Michigan fishery managers held public meetings with stakeholder groups around the lake to discuss options for future management of the stocking program. At these meetings, agency biologists presented data on recent trends in several indicators of the performance of the salmonine fishery (e.g., salmonine catch rates and growth rates, alewife abundance indices, prevalence of bacterial kidney disease in Chinook salmon). These data sets generally indicated moderately elevated stress levels in Chinook salmon, including recent declines in growth rates of Chinook salmon. These observations, together with the authors' decision analysis findings supporting a state-dependent stocking strategy (also presented at these meetings), enabled the Lake Michigan fishery managers to obtain public support for a reduction in Chinook salmon stocking rates. Stocking rates were reduced by 25% in 2006. Although the managers have not formally adopted a state-dependent stocking policy, it is expected that stocking rates will remain at this lower level until evidence is seen of good growth and abundant forage for Chinook salmon.

Case Study 3: Walleye Harvest Management in Lake Erie

Together with yellow perch *Perca flavescens*, walleye contribute to important commercial and recreational fisheries in Lake Erie. Walleye have the highest landed value (>CAN $10 million) of any Great Lakes commercial species in Canada, and are targeted by about five million angler-hours per year of recreational effort, primarily in Ohio and Michigan waters of Lake Erie. Before 2001, Lake Erie fishery managers used a fixed harvest rate ($F_{0.1}$ – Deriso 1987) policy to determine allowable harvests for walleye, based on the results of their stock assessments. However, even when this $F_{0.1}$ policy was in place fishing mortality (F) changed from year to year, reflecting changes in stock assessments and methods for determining $F_{0.1}$, and how uncertainty in stock assessment results was translated into the actual allowable harvest (LEWTG 2001). From the late 1970s to 2003, the Lake Erie walleye population experienced strong year classes only in 1984 and 1988. As a consequence, walleye yields declined steadily from 1995–2000 and Lake Erie fishery managers became concerned about risks of overfishing. In 2000, the $F_{0.1}$ policy was dropped and a fixed conservative harvest level was chosen that was projected to allow the stock to increase, while the issue of an appropriate long-term harvest policy was reviewed (LEWTG 2004). In 2002, the managers asked the authors to work with them to develop a decision analysis tool to inform future harvest policy for this fishery.

Beginning with a general workshop to explain decision analysis in fall 2002, we convened several meetings with fishery managers and biologists to guide development of a model to evaluate harvest policy options for Lake Erie walleye. Historically, the Lake Erie Committee—the multi-agency committee that collectively guides fishery management on Lake Erie—had used the results of an annual stock assessment to set total allowable harvests for both commercial and recreational fisheries. The stock assessments employed a statistical catch-at-age model to estimate stock size and recent harvest rates. The managers however, relied only on point estimates to determine harvest rates. The authors' decision analysis model was structurally similar to the retrospective stock assessment model, but with explicit consideration of uncertainty regarding walleye demographics. A range of policy options including both fixed and variable harvest rates were considered. The principal management objective identified by Lake Erie fishery managers was to maintain adult walleye abundance above a level that would provide for high quality commercial and recreational fisheries: 25 million fish that were age 2 and older. In addition to assessing average performance, managers also wished to evaluate policy performance based on the frequency of outcomes, wherein abundance failed to meet the 25 million fish target, and the duration of periods when abundance fell below the target level.

Early in the analysis, Lake Erie fishery managers and biologists agreed upon a set of critical uncertainties that the decision model should consider. First, they wished to determine how harvest policies were affected by uncertainty in the parameters of the statistical catch-at-age model, including initial population estimates, fishery catchability and age-specific vulnerability to the fishing gears, and natural mortality rates. Second, they wanted to include uncertainty in the stock–recruitment relationship for walleye in the decision model. Third, they were interested in uncertainty surrounding the relationship between walleye abundance and recreational fishing effort. Structural assumptions about both the stock–recruitment model (Ricker) and the recreational effort—abundance relationship (linear) were made, and uncertainty via the distribution of parameters for these relationships were evaluated. Existing statistical catch-at-age model was used to estimate parameters for each of these relationships. Monte Carlo Markov Chain methods were then employed to sample from the joint posterior probability distribution of the complete set of parameters, and thereby quantify the joint uncertainty in all the parameters that we explicitly considered.

The decision model forecasted future abundance of walleye conditional on a harvest policy for both commercial and recreational fisheries for a fifty-year time horizon. To account for parameter uncertainty, a single policy simulation was repeated 1,000 times, each time randomly selecting a set of parameters from the sample of the joint posterior distribution. Model outputs were then summarized as mean and median walleye abundances and harvests, proportions of simulation-years with abundance below 25 million age 2 and older fish, and a frequency distribution of durations of periods wherein abundance fell below 25 million fish.

In the final workshop managers defined a general state-dependent harvest policy to consider, wherein the commercial fishing mortality rate would be set at a constant low rate when population abundance was below 15 million fish (age-2 and older), and a constant high rate when population abundance exceeded 40 million fish, and increased with abundance in a piece-wise linear fashion for abundances between 15 and 40 million fish, with a change in slope at 20 million fish (Figure 3). The decision model was used to evaluate the performance of this policy, scaled upward and downward proportionally across all stock sizes (Figure 3), and compared its performance to a range of fixed harvest rate policies. Because recreational fishing effort has historically decreased when walleye abundance has been low, and jurisdictions where recreational fisheries dominated have generally not taken their full quota allocation, the policy adjustments to fishing mortality were only applied to the commercial fishery.

Comparisons between state-dependent and fixed fishing mortality rate policies are difficult, because the fishing mortality rates for the former, by definition, are not constant. For similar median fishing mortality rates over 1,000 simulations, the two types of policies produced similar median total harvests (Figure 4), while the risk of adult abundance falling below the 25 million fish target was slightly greater for the fixed fishing mortality rate policy. In view of these findings, and because of a desire to have a policy that lowered fishing rates when abundance was

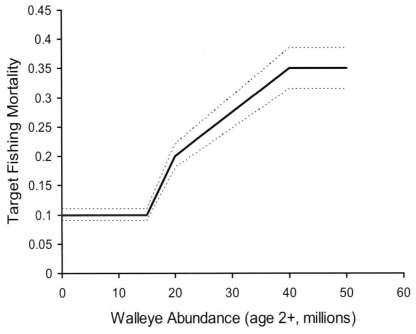

FIGURE 3. State-dependent harvest policies for the Lake Erie walleye *Sander vitreus* fishery. The solid line represents the policy adopted by Lake Erie fishery managers in 2005. Alternative state-dependent harvest policies increased or decreased fishing mortality rates by the same percentage at all population levels, and the dashed lines correspond to examples of 10% increases and decreases in the target fishing mortality rates from the adopted policy.

low, the Lake Erie fishery managers adopted a state-dependent harvest policy in 2005. They chose a policy that maintained fishing mortality rates below those that the authors' analysis suggested would result in the highest expected yields, because at high harvest rates the risk of periods of poor fishing due to low population sizes increased substantially.

The harvest policy implemented by Lake Erie fishery managers in 2005 resulted in commercial quotas in 2005 and 2006 that did not differ much from what would likely have been imposed based on their past procedures for setting harvest quotas. The 2003 year-class of walleye in Lake Erie was the largest on record since stock assessments began in 1978; this year-class recruited to the fishery in 2005, allowing substantially larger quotas than had been permitted for several prior years. It is likely that managers would

have increased quotas based on the observed strength of this year-class even in the absence of an explicit state-dependent harvest policy.

The decision analysis facilitated two important changes to the process for managing walleye exploitation in Lake Erie. First, the explicit consideration of risk in the decision model allowed managers to more objectively justify a policy perceived by the stakeholders as conservative. The analysis suggested that higher commercial fishing mortality rates would actually lead to higher sustained yields on average, but it also showed that large, unpredictable variation in walleye recruitment, well known to biologists and fishers alike, can frequently lead to declines in population size below levels associated with good fishing conditions, at these same higher fishing mortality rates. Second, the analysis motivated the development of a general rule for setting

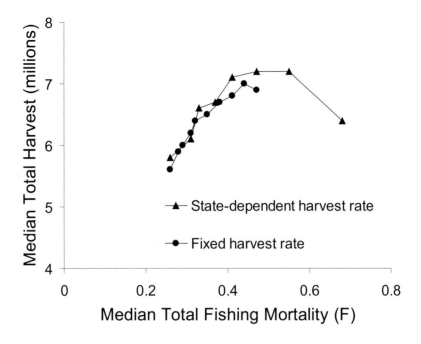

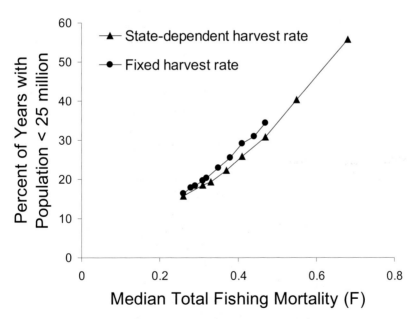

FIGURE 4. Top panel: Forecasted median walleye *Sander vitreus* harvests in the commercial and recreational fisheries, averaged over a 50-year simulation time horizon, for harvest policies with a range of fixed and state-dependent fishing mortality rates. Bottom panel: Forecasted percentages of simulation years wherein the adult walleye population fell below 25 million fish. The fishing mortality rate for each policy was calculated as the median value of *F* for commercial and recreational fisheries combined over 1,000 simulations of the policy.

commercial fishing mortality rates, eliminating the need to rationalize a new quota each year. Prior to 2001, this fishery was nominally managed by a constant fishing mortality rate policy; however, the reality was that managers responded in an ad hoc fashion to changes in walleye abundance in an attempt to avoid low populations. The policy adopted in 2005 was developed based on this same objective and can be applied to any future fishery state, at least until a decision is made to update the walleye population model used to evaluate this policy.

Discussion

Great Lakes fishery managers have begun to embrace formal consideration of uncertainty as an important part of their decision-making process. In each case study described above, managers were quite receptive to the use of decision analysis, and in the Lake Erie case, managers actually initiated the process. Decision analysis and other uncertainty-sensitive decision-making approaches are being used or actively discussed for several other Great Lakes fishery issues. These include development of harvest policies for yellow perch in Lake Michigan (Irwin et al. 2008), evaluation of alternative methods of larval sea lamprey assessment for determination of target streams for chemical control (Hansen and Jones 2008), and the use of real options analysis (Fenichel et al. 2008) to assist decisions about deliberately translocating fish species among the five Great Lakes.

Decision analysis is often advocated because explicitly accounting for uncertainty may suggest a different optimal decision than would result from a deterministic assessment of the choices available to managers. This outcome did not occur for any of the three case studies described herein. The same two options ranked highest for the St. Marys River decision analysis when a deterministic model was used. Stocking strategies for Lake Michigan were not explicitly evaluated using a deterministic model, but other lines of evidence from fishery assessments also had led managers to advocate a reduction in Chinook stocking rates until salmon growth rates stabilized or began to increase (James Dexter, Michigan Department of Natural Resources and Chair, Lake Michigan Committee, personal communication). In Lake Erie, fishery managers likely would have allowed higher fishing mortality due to the strength of the 2003 year-class, whether or not the decision analysis was conducted. In the case of sea lamprey management the analysis may have facilitated a decision that differed from that which would have occurred without the analysis, but only because of an overly pessimistic view of the uncertain potential of the nonchemical alternatives. In the other two cases, the decision analysis did not appear to significantly change the subsequent decisions.

What, then, has been the benefit to fishery managers of these decision analyses, and why is there a continued interest in the use of this approach? There may be three reasons as to why Great Lakes fishery managers consider decision analysis a useful tool. First, in each case the decision analysis provided a formal and transparent methodology for rationalizing and documenting the decisions that were ultimately made. Managers are frequently criticized for making decisions in an opaque fashion; stakeholders challenge the rationale for the decisions, and are left dissatisfied by the answers they get (e.g., "we feel we need to reduce stocking rates because the risks of an alewife population collapse are too great"). The decision analysis process can involve stakeholders directly, as in the Lake Michigan stocking decision analysis. Further, decision analysis requires clear, explicit statements of management objectives and options, and the process for evaluating management options involves a formal model wherein the performance of the different options can be deduced objectively from the set of assumptions and hypotheses that comprise the model. The model itself may be so complicated that understanding its behavior poses a large challenge, particularly to nontechnical stakeholder groups (and this remains a serious obstacle for the application of decision analysis to public policy), but it is nevertheless possible to document the basis for conclusions reached. A more transparent decision-making process builds trust between stakeholders and decision makers; the authors' impression is that a lack of trust is a primary reason why so many fishery management decisions are controversial, both in the Great Lakes region and elsewhere.

Second, in all three cases the decision analysis suggested that state-dependent policies, wherein changes to management are triggered by observations of changes in the state of the system, are likely to perform as well as, if not better than, nonfeedback policies. Numerous comparisons have been made of fixed-rate and feedback policies for exploited fisheries, and in many cases feedback policies have compared favorably to other alternatives, especially when the state of the system is observed with relatively low error (Deroba and Bence 2008). In the Great Lakes, however, feedback polices have generally not been used explicitly for harvest, stocking, or sea lamprey control (but see Krueger and Dehring 1986). Many, if not most, fisheries have experienced changes to management strategies as the system changes, but such changes tend to be reactions to system dynamics, not implementation of prescribed strategies according to a plan developed *a priori*. An example of this approach would be the Lake Erie walleye fishery prior to 2005.

Explicitly defined state-dependent policies are likely to be superior to more ad hoc reactive strategies for reasons beyond their performance in meeting the types of management objectives discussed above. The ability of management agencies to quickly implement ad hoc changes to management as a reaction to system changes, whether or not these occur as a consequence of prior management decisions, has decreased significantly in recent years, as stakeholder groups have become more influential. Managers now devote large amounts of time and effort to participatory processes intended to inform stakeholders and facilitate changes to management. Both managers and stakeholders with whom the authors have spoken during the past decade have frequently found these processes frustrating, stressful, and ineffective. A state-dependent policy that prescribes the management actions that should be taken across the range of plausible system states would avoid the need to "reinvent the wheel" every time the system changes. Admittedly, such a policy still requires a process to facilitate stakeholder buy-in, but the process could occur less often, and more importantly not at a time of crisis (e.g., very low stock abundances for an exploited fishery) when rapid decision-making is needed. Lake Erie fishery managers presented their state-dependent harvest policy to walleye fishermen in 2005 and remain optimistic that they have obtained buy-in for this approach. The real test, however, will come when walleye abundance falls to levels that call for a reduction in fishing mortality from recent levels.

Third, by incorporating process uncertainty into the models used to compare management options, particularly uncertainty about recruitment dynamics, each of the decision analyses exposed the limited extent to which decision makers can control the future states of these systems. This limitation was especially evident for Lake Michigan salmonine stocking. Both managers and stakeholders need to appreciate this extremely important reality. While management strategies that, on average, perform better than others through decision analysis can be identified, the long-term outcome of any strategy could be far worse (or better) than suggested by the expected, or average, outcome. For example the declining walleye yields in Lake Erie during the 1990s resulted primarily from a long period of years without high walleye recruitment, rather than from an overly liberal harvest strategy. This underscores the wisdom of the correct, if somewhat idealistic, view that decisions should be judged, not by their consequences, but by the quality of the thinking that went into making the decision in the first place. The highly uncertain future of each of the systems discussed here is undoubtedly typical of other fishery systems, and points to both the merits of policies that are state-dependent, and to the continuing need to learn about these systems and adapt management appropriately.

Finally, while each of the decision analyses discussed here involved highly technical analyses, it may be emphasized that the process of doing the decision analyses, more than the analysis itself, made these case studies effective. In each case the decision analysis involved active interactions with decision makers, fishery experts, and in the salmonine stocking case, nongovernment stakeholders. These interactions ensured that those using the results of the analysis retained a strong sense of ownership of the work throughout, even though their involvement in the actual uncertainty assessment or modeling may have been minimal. The skills necessary to conduct the technical work are not widespread in management agencies, so future applications of decision analysis will likely continue to require partnerships between decision makers and decision analysts. Such partnerships may actually be beneficial, because involvement of decision analysis experts that are not "within" the management agency may enhance the perception of neutrality of the analysis. Nevertheless, the more inclusive the process can be of experts, decision makers, and those stakeholders likely to be affected by the resulting decisions, the more likely the

analysis will lead to meaningful, beneficial changes to how fisheries are managed.

The authors' experience with decision analysis in the Great Lakes has obvious relevance to Pacific salmon management in the AYK region. Three important aspects of salmon management for which a decision analysis approach would be particularly valuable are (1) the evaluation of different options for assessment sampling of returning adult salmon, used to determine whether escapement targets are being met; (2) strategies for in-season management of salmon harvest; and (3) setting annual escapement goals for individual stocks.

These three options for an AYK salmon management decision analysis are hierarchically related. A powerful use of decision analysis is to assess the "value of information" for making decisions (Clemen and Reilly 2001, Chapter 12; de Bruin and Hunter 2003), wherein the management options are alternative assessment strategies rather than controls on fishing. AYK salmon fisheries use a variety of tools (weir counts, aerial spawning ground counts, tower observations) to assess adult salmon returns that yield escapement information of variable accuracy and precision (Menard et al. 2009, this volume). A formal assessment of these alternatives using decision analysis could help managers to allocate scarce monitoring resources. A decision analysis for in-season management could compare options for opening and closing fisheries based on these in-season assessment data and uncertainties about the population dynamics of salmon stocks. Finally managers could be aided by an even broader decision analysis that compared different escapement goals for salmon stocks while accounting for uncertainties about stock–recruitment relationships, long-term changes in stock productivity, and the quality of in-season and long-term data available to inform management.

From the experience in the Great Lakes, however, the authors would propose that the greatest benefit for AYK managers from adopting a decision analysis approach would result from the process, not the subject of the actual analysis. The transparency, objectivity, and inclusiveness of the decision analysis approaches described above can greatly aid decision makers to gain support for more defensible, flexible, and uncertainty-sensitive policies for the assessment and management of salmon fisheries.

Acknowledgments

The decision analysis projects discussed in the paper were supported by the Great Lakes Fishery Commission, Michigan Sea Grant College Program, and Michigan DNR Fisheries Division (Studies 230724, 230713, and 236102, with partial support from the USFWS Sport Fish Restoration Program). We thank the members of the Sea Lamprey Integration Committee, the Lake Michigan Committee, and the Lake Erie Committee for their guidance and support. Gavin Christie, James Dexter, and Roger Knight were especially helpful in facilitating our interactions with managers and stakeholders throughout the projects. This paper is contribution number 2008–09 of the Quantitative Fisheries Center at Michigan State University.

References

Butterworth, D. S., K. L. Cochrane, and J. A. A. de Oliveira. 1997. Management procedures: a better way to manage fisheries? The South African experience. Pages 83–90 in E. L. Pikitch, D. D. Huppert, and M. P. Sissenwine, editors. Global trends: fisheries management. American Fisheries Society, Symposium 20, Bethesda, Maryland.

Christie, G. C., and C. I. Goddard. 2003. Sea Lamprey International Symposium (SLIS II): Advances in the integrated management of sea lamprey in the Great Lakes. Journal of Great Lakes Research 29 (1):1–14.

Christie, G. C., J. V. Adams, T. B. Steeves, J. W. Slade, D. W. Cuddy, M. F. Fodale, R. J. Young, M. Kuc, and M. L. Jones. 2003. Selecting Great Lakes streams for lampricide treatment based on larval

sea lamprey surveys. Journal of Great Lakes Research 29 (1):152–160.

Clemen, R. T., and T. Reilly. 2001. Making hard decisions with DecisionTools. Duxbury. Pacific Grove, California.

de Bruin, S., and G. J. Hunter. 2003. Making the trade-off between decision quality and information cost. Photogrammetric Engineering & Remote Sensing 69:91–98.

Deriso, R.B. 1987. Optimal $F_{0.1}$ criteria and their relationship to maximum sustainable yield. Canadian Journal of Fisheries and Aquatic Sciences 44 (2): 339–348.

Deroba, J. J., and J. R. Bence. 2008. A review of harvest policies: understanding relative performance of control rules. Fisheries Research 96:210–223.

Fenichel, E. P., J. I. Tsao, M.L. Jones, and G. J. Hickling. 2008. Real options for precautionary fisheries management. Fish and Fisheries 9:1–17.

Fournier, D., and C. P. Archibald. 1982. A general theory for analyzing catch at age data. Canadian Journal of Fisheries and Aquatic Sciences 39:1195–1207.

GLFC (Great Lakes Fishery Commission). 2001. Strategic vision of the Great Lakes Fishery Commission for the first decade of the new millennium. Great Lakes Fishery Commission. Ann Arbor, Michigan.

Haeseker, S. L., M. L. Jones, and J. R. Bence. 2003. Estimating uncertainty in the stock-recruit relationship for St. Marys River sea lampreys. Journal of Great Lakes Research 29 (1):728–741.

Haeseker, S. L. , M. L. Jones, R. M. Peterman, J. R. Bence, W. Dai, and G. C. Christie. 2007. Explicit consideration of uncertainty in Great Lakes fishery management: decision analysis of sea lamprey control in the St. Marys River. Canadian Journal of Fisheries and Aquatic Sciences 64:1456–1468.

Hansen, M. J. and M. E. Holey. 2002. Ecological factors affecting sustainability of Chinook and coho salmon populations in the Great Lakes. Pages 155–179 in K. D. Lynch, M. L. Jones and W. W. Taylor, editors. Sustaining North American salmon: perspectives across regions and disciplines. American Fisheries Society, Bethesda, Maryland.

Hansen, G. J. A., and M. L. Jones. 2008. A rapid assessment approach to prioritizing streams for control of Great Lakes sea lampreys: a case study of adaptive management. Canadian Journal of Fisheries and Aquatic Sciences 65:2471–2484.

Healey, M. C. 1978. Dynamics of exploited lake trout populations and implications for management. Journal of Wildlife Management 42:307–328.

Heinrich, J. W., K. M. Mullett, M. J. Hansen, J. V. Adams, G. T. Klar, D. A. Johnson, G. C. Christie, and R. J. Young. 2003. Sea lamprey abundance and management in Lake Superior, 1957–1999. Journal of Great Lakes Research 29 (1): 566–583.

Holey, M. E., R. F. Elliot, S. V. Marcquenski, J. G. Hnath, and K. D. Smith. 1998. Chinook salmon epizootics in Lake Michigan: possible contributing factors and management implications. Journal of Aquatic Animal Health 10:201–210.

Irwin, B. J., M. J. Wilberg, J. R. Bence, and M. L. Jones. 2008. Evaluating alternative harvest policies for yellow perch in southern Lake Michigan. Fisheries Research 94:267–281.

Jones, M. L., J. F. Koonce, and R. O'Gorman. 1993. Sustainability of hatchery dependent salmonine fisheries in Lake Ontario: the conflict between predator demand and prey supply. Transactions of the American Fisheries Society 122:1002–1018.

Jones, M. L., R. A. Bergstedt, M. B. Twohey, M. F. Fodale, D. W. Cuddy, and J. W. Slade. 2003. Compensatory mechanisms in Great Lakes sea lamprey populations: implications for alternative control strategies. Journal of Great Lakes Research 29 (1):113–129.

Kocik, J. F., and M. L. Jones. 1999. Pacific salmonines in the Great Lakes basin. Pages 455–488 in W. W. Taylor, and C. P. Ferrari, editors. Great Lakes fisheries policy and management: a binational perspective. Michigan State University Press, East Lansing, Michigan.

Krueger, C. C., and T. R. Dehring. 1986. A procedure to allocate the annual stocking of salmonids in the Wisconsin waters of Lake Michigan. Fish Management Report 127. Wisconsin Department of Natural Resources, Madison, Wisconsin.

LEWTG (Lake Erie Walleye Task Group) 2001. Report for 2000 by the Lake Erie Walleye Task Group. Prepared for Lake Erie Committee, Great Lakes Fishery Commission. Ann Arbor, Michigan.

LEWTG (Lake Erie Walleye Task Group) 2004. Report for 2003 by the Lake Erie Walleye Task Group. Prepared for Lake Erie Committee, Great Lakes Fishery Commission. Ann Arbor, Michigan.

Lane, D. E., and R. L. Stephenson. 1998. A framework for risk analysis in fisheries decision-making. ICES Journal of Marine Science 55:1–13.

Lavis, D. S., M. P. Henson, D. A. Johnson, E. M. Koon, and D. J. Ollila. 2003a. A case history of sea lamprey control in Lake Michigan: 1979 to 1999. Journal of Great Lakes Research 29 (1):584–598.

Lavis, D. S., A. Hallett, E. M. Koon, and T. C. McAuley. 2003b. History of and advances in barriers as an alternative method to suppress sea lampreys in the Great Lakes. Journal of Great Lakes Research 29 (1):362–372.

Lupi, F, J. P. Hoehn, and G. C. Christie. 2003. Using an economic model of recreational fishing to evaluate the benefits of sea lamprey (Petromyzon marinus) control on the St. Marys River. Journal of Great Lakes Research 29 (1): 742–754.

Mullett, K. M., J. W. Heinrich, J. V. Adams, R. J. Young, M. P. Henson, R. B. McDonald, and M. F. Fodale. 2003. Estimating lake-wide abundance of spawning-phase sea lampreys (Petromyzon marinus) in the Great Lakes: extrapolating from sampled streams using regression models. Journal of Great Lakes Research 29 (1):240–252.

Peterman, R. M., and J. L. Anderson. 1999. Decision analysis: a method for taking uncertainties into account in risk-based decision making. Human and Ecological Risk Assessment 5:231–244.

Peterman, R. M., C. N. Peters, C. A. Robb, and S. W. Frederick. 1998. Bayesian decision analysis and uncertainty in fisheries management. Pages 387–398 in T. J. Pitcher, P. J. B. Hart, and D. Pauly, editors. Reinventing fisheries management. Kluwer Academic Publishers, Dordrecht, Netherlands.

Peters, C. N., and D. R. Marmorek. 2001. Application of decision analysis to evaluate recovery actions for threatened Snake River spring and summer Chinook salmon (Oncorhynchus tshawytscha). Canadian Journal of Fisheries and Aquatic Sciences 58:2431–2446.

Punt, A. E., A. D. M. Smith, and G. Cui. 2002. Evaluation of management tools for Australia's south east fishery. 3. Towards selecting appropriate harvest strategies. Marine and Freshwater Research 53:645–660.

Quinn, T. J., and R. B. Deriso. 1999. Quantitative fish dynamics. Oxford University Press, New York.

Sainsbury, K. J., R. A. Campbell, R. Lindholm, and A. W. Whitelaw. 1997. Experimental management of an Australian multispecies fishery: examining the possibility of trawl induced habitat modification. Pages 107–122 in E. K. Pikitch, D. D. Huppert, and M. P. Sissenwine, editors. Global trends: fisheries management. American Fisheries Society, Symposium 20. Bethesda, Maryland.

Schleen, L. P., G. C. Christie, J. W. Heinrich, R. A. Bergstedt, R. J. Young, T. J. Morse, D. S. Lavis, T. D. Bills, J. E. Johnson, and M. P. Ebener. 2003. Development and implementation of an integrated program for control of sea lampreys in the St. Marys River. Journal of Great Lakes Research. 29 (1):677–693.

Smith, B. R., and J. J. Tibbles. 1980. Sea lamprey (Petromyzon marinus) in Lakes Huron, Michigan, and Superior: history of invasion and control, 1936–1978. Canadian Journal of Fisheries and Aquatic Sciences 27:1780–1801.

Stern, P. C., and H. V. Fineburg, editors. 1996. Understanding risk: Informing decisions in a democratic society. National Academy Press, Washington, D.C.

Stewart, D. J., and M. Ibarra. 1991. Predation and production by salmonine fishes in Lake Michigan, 1978–88. Canadian Journal of Fisheries and Aquatic Sciences 48:909–922.

Stewart, D. J., J. F. Kitchell, and L. B. Crowder. 1981. Forage fish and their salmonid predators in Lake Michigan. Transactions of the American Fisheries Society 110:751–763.

Szalai, E. B. 2003. Uncertainty in the population dynamics of alewife (*Alosa pseudoharengus*) and bloater (*Coregonus hoyi*) and its effects on salmonine stocking strategies in Lake Michigan. Doctoral dissertation. Michigan State University, East Lansing, Michigan.

Twohey, M. B., J. W. Heinrich, J. G. Seelye, K. T. Fredricks, R. A. Bergstedt, C. A. Kaye, R. J. Schole-field, R. B. McDonald, and G. C. Christie, 2003. The sterile-male-release technique in Great Lakes sea lamprey management. Journal of Great Lakes Research. 29 (1):410–423.

TTWG (Tripartite Technical Working Group). 1984. Status of the fishery resource—1984. A report by the Tripartite Technical Working Group on the assessment of major fish stocks in the treaty-ceded waters of the upper Great Lakes: State of Michigan. Mimeo Report. Lansing, Michigan.

Walters, C. J. 1986. Adaptive management of renewable resources. Macmillan, New York.

Walters, C. J., and J. J. Maguire. 1996. Lessons for stock assessment from the northern cod collapse. Reviews in Fish Biology and Fisheries 6:125–137.

American Fisheries Society Symposium 70:1083–1101, 2009

Management Angels and Demons in the Conservation of the Atlantic Salmon in North America

Fred Whoriskey*

Atlantic Salmon Federation
St. Andrews, New Brunswick E5B 3S8, Canada

Abstract.—The Atlantic salmon *Salmo salar* in North America is much depleted. Present population abundance may be only about 4% of that at the time of European colonization, and almost all populations in the southern third of North America are at risk of biological extinction. Anthropogenic and natural factors have contributed to this situation. This paper reviews the biology of Atlantic salmon, documents current population status and management in North America, and identifies challenges to restoration. Atlantic salmon migrate from home rivers within the USA or Canada to ocean feeding areas in waters off the coast of Greenland where they mix with conspecifics from Europe. Exploitation during this migration and in interceptory fisheries in home waters posed a severe challenge to conservation of spawning populations. To address the impacts of the Greenland fishery, the North Atlantic Salmon Conservation Organization (NASCO), an international body with members from all Atlantic salmon producing countries, was established to set fishing quotas in the Atlantic Ocean and to pressure governments not respecting the quotas. In Canada, coastal commercial fisheries were also phased out to favor the more lucrative recreational angling industry. To provide incentives for reductions in commercial harvests, at least one wild salmon conservation organization initially supported salmon farming, which could provide commercial markets with a cheap source of fresh salmon. The phenomenal success of this industry helped shut down the interceptory commercial fisheries; however, its potential impacts on wild Atlantic salmon were not anticipated and some remain problematic. At present, adult salmon returns in North America remain near historic lows, and below conservation requirements. However, some rivers are producing surpluses, recreational fishing continues, and the key management goal is rebuilding North American returns. Live-release angling has been employed in many jurisdictions where harvest fisheries would pose conservation risks. While the practice has helped address the risks, a debate has been incited about the morality of angling should fish feel pain and show "awareness." With traditional fisheries management options failing to bring relief, rebounds in wild Atlantic salmon populations will depend on upturns in marine survival, ecosystem repairs, restoration of lost salmon production potential, and innovative interventions.

*Corresponding author: asfres@nb.aibn.com

Introduction

Anadromous salmonids historically were both abundant and widely distributed in the northern hemisphere (e.g., Scott and Crossman 1973; Groot and Margolis 1991). Their popularity as food and sport fishes, and their complex life cycles dependent on both fresh and salt water habitats made anadromous salmonids particularly susceptible to anthropogenic impacts (e.g., Lackey et al. 2006). The Atlantic salmon *Salmo salar* is a much studied, iconic sport fish. The species' population and management challenges are potentially shared by other anadromous salmonids; hence, the lessons learned in the conservation and management of Atlantic may provide insights to efforts with other species. It has been suggested before that salmon biologists from different regions would benefit from more frequent communication (North Pacific Anadromous Fish Commission 2002), if only because some comfort always derives from knowing that others in different places face similar challenges. This paper compares and contrasts the biology of Atlantic and Pacific salmon, then documents the present status of Atlantic salmon populations and the restoration challenges the species faces. This paper also traces the history of some of the remedial actions that have been attempted, and discusses how they led to new problems.

My perspective is that of a research scientist working for a nongovernmental organization (NGO) with a mandate to foster the conservation and wise use of the wild Atlantic salmon. I have tried to write in the spirit of the Salmon 2100 project (Lackey et al. 2006), which required a truthful assessment of how we got to where we are, before we attempt to determine a way forward. My focus is on the status of North American populations of the species, although the Atlantic salmon occurs widely in rivers draining to the northeast Atlantic Ocean as well. While as much as 19% of the wild Atlantic salmon production poten-tial in North America is in the USA, currently U.S. spawner returns are <1% of all returns to the continent (0.2% in 2006; ICES 2007). By necessity, most of this review is focused on Canada.

Biology and Distribution of Atlantic Salmon

The Atlantic salmon in some ways resembles Pacific salmonids, and in others it differs quite substantially. Atlantic salmon occurred naturally in more than 2,615 watersheds that drained to the north Atlantic Ocean (WWF 2001). In Europe, the natural range of the sea-run Atlantic salmon extended from Portugal north into the Baltic Sea, through Scandinavia and to Russia. The farthest east the species occurs is the Pechora River in Russia's Komi Republic (Martynov et al. 1994). On the North American continent, Atlantic salmon have historically been caught as far south as the Hudson River, but probably the southernmost major breeding population was in, or in close proximity, to the Connecticut River. The present distribution of the sea-run form extends into northern Quebec's Ungava region (Power 1981). Historically, Atlantic salmon may also have occurred in rivers draining to Canada's Hudson's Bay, and a single relict population with a limited "estuarine" migration still occurs there in the Nastapoka River (Morin 1991). A single river in Greenland (Kapisigdlit River [Godthåbsfjord]) has an Atlantic salmon population (Dunbar and Thomson 1979).

The Atlantic salmon is best known for its anadromous populations, but the species can complete its entire life cycle in freshwater. Landlocked populations, also known in Canada as "ouananiche," occur throughout the species range (Power 1958; Berg 1985) and though the two forms are genetically distinct (Verspoor and Cole 1989; Spidle et al. 2003), crosses between them produce viable offspring (Hutchings and Myers 1985; Sutterlin et al. 1987). Historically, the Atlantic salmon populations found in rivers draining to the North American Great Lakes probably migrated to these lakes rather than down the Saint Lawrence River to the Atlantic Ocean (Christie 1973; Webster 1982). Frequently the landlocked populations developed in places where a migration barrier occurred (e.g., postglacial land rebounding created a waterfall) but in many instances no such barriers exist (Power 1958). Exclusively freshwater populations of Chinook *Oncorhynchus tshawytscha* (Healey 1991), coho *O. kisutch* (Sandercock 1991), pink *O. gorbuscha* (Heard 1991) and sockeye (kokanee) *O. nerka* (Burgner 1991) salmon occur. None are known for the chum salmon *O. keta* although the species can be raised to maturity in freshwater hatcheries (Salo 1991).

The Atlantic salmon spawns in the autumn, with a trend toward earlier initiation of spawning in the north compared to the south. Eggs incubate in gravel redds over the winter, with emergence of fry in late spring or early summer. Juvenile Atlantic salmon, termed parr, will rear for about 2–3 years in freshwater in the south and up to five or more years in the north before migrating to the ocean as smolts (Marschall et al. 1998). In this respect, the Atlantic salmon resembles coho salmon (Sandercock 1991), steelhead (anadromous rainbow trout) *O. mykiss* (Quinn 2005), steam-type Chinook salmon (Healey 1991), and some sockeye salmon (Burgner 1991) populations that have extended periods of freshwater residence. However, no Atlantic salmon populations are known to have fry that migrate to the ocean soon after hatching as occurs for pink (Heard 1991) or chum (Salo 1991) salmon.

Atlantic salmon return with a high degree of fidelity to their birth rivers (Stasko et al. 1973). Those returning to spawn after a single year at sea are called grilse, and tend to be males. However, in Newfoundland male to female grilse ratios are about 1:1 (O'Connell et al. 2006). In Pacific salmon, fish returning after a single year at sea are called jacks, and occur in coho (Sandercock 1991), sockeye (Burgner 1991), and Chinook (Healey 1991) salmon. Most Atlantic salmon that spend more than one year at sea return to their natal rivers for their first spawning after two years. However, Atlantic salmon are known to spend up to five years at sea before returning for a first spawning (Hansen and Jacobsen 2000). Similar to anadromous Pacific salmonids, fish that spend more years at sea are larger upon return to the river than those that are at sea for fewer years (Scott and Crossman 1973).

At sea, grilse migrations in North America are believed to be relatively short and limited to ocean areas east of Newfoundland (Ritter 1989). By contrast, fish that mature after two or more years at sea cover a greater distance than early maturing fish (Ritter 1989; Reddin and Short 1991; Hansen and Jacobsen 2000). The oceanic feeding areas differ for North American and European populations of Atlantic salmon. The vast majority of two or more sea-year North American fish are believed to migrate to feeding grounds off the west coast of Greenland: although, some are found in feeding areas off the coast of the Faeroe Islands. By contrast, many southern European fish (from Scotland, south) will cross the Atlantic Ocean to join North American fish off Greenland (Reddin et al. 1988). The remaining southern European fish, and those from rivers north of Scotland, migrate to feeding areas off the Faeroe Islands (Ritter 1989; Hansen and Jacobsen 2000).

Unlike the Pacific salmon species (excepting steelhead), wild Atlantic salmon do not obligatorily die after spawning (e.g., Ducharme 1969). While many spawning Atlantics do not survive the fasting and other stresses of a spawning migration and the subsequent return to the sea, in some rivers a significant fraction of the spawning run is composed of repeat spawning fish. In the Miramichi River, at present 10–30% of first-time spawners may survive to reproduce a second time. On this river, fish ascending the river for a third and fourth spawning are regularly encountered, and a few fish returning for a seventh spawning have been detected in recent years (G. Chaput, DFO, personal communication).

The relatively small size of Atlantic salmon runs and the repeat spawning potential means that Atlantic salmon carcass are not, and may never have been, a major nutrient source for east coast streams and forests ecosystems as Pacific salmon carcasses are in the Pacific northwest (Stockner 2003). In small streams with depressed adult returns, Atlantic salmon smolts may actually take more nutrients away when they migrate than adults replace when they come back (Nislow et al. 2004).

North American Abundance of Atlantic Salmon

The abundance of wild Atlantic salmon in North America is severely depressed compared to what it was prior to European colonization (e.g., Dunfield 1985). Multiple stressors including habitat loss and degradation, construction of dams in rivers which blocked migration, and overfishing have contributed to these losses. By 1970 only about 32% of the species' original production capacity remained (Watt 1988, 1989). Since 1970, a precipitous decline in ocean survival has reduced the abundance of North American salmon off Greenland to about one eighth of their level in the early 1970s (Figure 1; ICES 2006). Thus, present numbers of North American wild salmon are somewhere around 4% of the species' historic abundance. Populations in many rivers south of Cape Breton, Nova Scotia are at risk of biological extinction (e.g., DFO 2000), and some of the populations within a subset of these rivers in both

Canada (Amiro 2003) and the USA (National Research Council 2004) have been designated as endangered under national legislation. However, north and west of Cape Breton populations remain relatively healthy.

North American Management Regimes

Jurisdiction for management of Atlantic salmon in North America is split between federal, and provincial or state authorities in Canada and the USA, respectively. In Canada, the federal government has the responsibility for management of the Atlantic salmon (DFO 1986). The Fisheries Act, and regulations made pursuant to the Act provide the legislative framework for management actions. Provincial governments and other federal agencies also have responsibilities that can affect Atlantic salmon (e.g., Provincial governments are the licensing authority for recreational fishing, and can lease water for fishing or issue permits for water use for other purposes). In Quebec, a 1922 memorandum of understanding between the Provincial and Federal governments delegated the administration and management of the Atlantic salmon to the government of Quebec. Within Canada, these shared responsibilities require that Federal and Provincial agencies cooperate to deliver effective management.

In Maine, until recently, the Maine Atlantic Salmon Commission (originally established in 1947 as the Atlantic Sea Run Salmon Commission) had the mandate to protect, conserve, restore, manage, and enhance Atlantic salmon habitat, populations, and sport fisheries within historical habitat in all (inland and tidal) waters of the State of Maine. The Commission had the sole authority to limit or prohibit the taking of Atlantic salmon in all state waters (see http://maine.gov/asc/). Regulations promulgated by the Commission were enforced by two other state

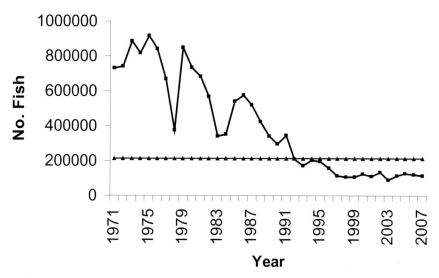

FIGURE 1. Estimated number of Atlantic salmon *Salmo salar* of North American origin off the coast of Greenland just prior to the commencement of the annual fishery. The flat horizontal line shows the estimated "North American reserve" (212,189 fish), which is the calculated number of salmon believed to be needed off Greenland to provide sufficient egg depositions to fully seed fresh water habitat in rivers in North America one year later. Factoring in natural mortality, these fish should provide the estimated 152,548 spawners needed to meet conservation egg depositions in North American rivers dependent upon 2-sea-winter spawners.

agencies, the Department of Inland Fisheries and Wildlife and the Department of Marine Resources, and these agencies could also emit additional regulations which helped promote salmon conservation. In July of 2007, a state government reorganization occurred in Maine. While the Maine Atlantic Salmon Commission still exists as a policy board for Atlantic salmon, most agency staff and their functions have been transferred a new unit in the Department of Marine Resources called the Bureau of Sea Run Fisheries and Habitat. In federal waters of the marine environment, jurisdiction for Atlantic salmon rests with the National Oceanic and Atmospheric Administration's National Marine Fisheries Service.

In the USA and Canada, the primary management objective is conservation of the species, with allocation of biological surpluses to First Nations and other fisheries contingent upon conservation first being ensured.

Biological reference points have been established to define "conservation," and

to guide Atlantic salmon management. The conservation goal is to ensure that sufficient egg depositions are realized each year to fully seed the freshwater habitats available for juvenile salmon rearing in individual rivers (Chaput et al. 1998; Caron et al. 1999). Annual egg depositions are calculated and compared to conservation thresholds from knowledge of the amount of habitat available within a river system, the number of spawners, the male-to-female ratio of the spawners, and female fecundity. This detailed information is available only from a few well-studied rivers; the results from these rivers are extrapolated to other less studied rivers when necessary. Biological reference points have been set using the best available data, and are subject to refinement as better information becomes available. Management of Atlantic salmon thus strives to be adaptive, and operate on a river-by-river basis.

For the Maritimes region and Newfoundland, the conservation threshold is an egg deposition rate of 2.4 eggs/m^2 of fluvial rearing habitat in a given river system. In addition, in insular Newfoundland where river channels flow through many lakes where juvenile salmon can rear, an additional egg deposition of 1.5 or 3.68 eggs/m^2 of lacustrine habitat, depending on latitude (CAFSAC 1991; Chaput et al. 1998) is factored into the calculation of a river system's conservation threshold.

The Province of Quebec has also established conservation reference levels in terms of egg deposition, using an analysis of available salmon stock/recruit relationships for Quebec rivers, and stream habitat quality rankings (ranks range from 0 in poor to 1 in the best habitats for juveniles). Based on these calculations, Quebec conservation egg depositions are 1.67 eggs per "salmon unit," where units are calculated as m^2 fluvial habitat times the applicable habitat-rank weighting factor.

Managers attempt to set harvest quotas at levels that leave adequate spawners to deposit sufficient fertilized eggs to meet or surpass the conservation threshold similar to Pacific salmon management in the Arctic-Yukon-Kuskokwim region (e.g., Menard et al. 2009, this volume). In all jurisdictions where harvests are permitted, mangers are encouraged to pick a quota that leaves a security space in case the harvest targets are overshot.

Homewater Fisheries

By comparison with Pacific salmon, the commercial landings of Atlantic salmon in North America are modest, especially after 1900. Scattered historical records indicated that this may not have always been the case. Humans, especially in the 19th and 20th centuries, have substantially altered Atlantic marine ecosystems and associated fisheries production (Saunders et al. 2006; Worm et al. 2006). For Atlantic salmon, historical records from the early 1800s show annual landings of perhaps as many as 70,000–100,000 Atlantic

salmon (about 860 metric tons from fisheries in the Baie des Chaleurs region alone; Dunfield 1985). These harvest numbers are similar to the current abundance of all multi-sea-winter Atlantic salmon believed to be at sea from all North American rivers (Figures 1 and 2), yet these Baie des Chaleurs landings probably came primarily from two river systems (Grand Cascapedia and Restigouche Rivers).

Current Atlantic salmon management regimes are focused on today's reality. The social benefits that flow from Atlantic salmon come primarily from sports fishing in freshwater. In Canada, the Atlantic salmon presently supports a recreational angling industry valued at >175$ million (CDN) per year (Whoriskey and Glebe 2002), and provides jobs in areas where alternative sources of revenues and employment are limited. Additional benefits could accrue, if salmon populations were healthier.

Canada's present homewater fishery policy for Atlantic salmon is focused first on meeting First Nation constitutionally guaranteed rights, then on sports angling. While commercial fishing at sea for Atlantic salmon occurred for centuries (Dunfield 1985), as the fish became scarce an economic and conservation driven rationalization occurred to favor the greater economic and social benefits that came from recreational angling. On the conservation side, coastal fisheries frequently intercepted fish from multiple river systems. It was and remains difficult to control the impacts of such interceptory fisheries upon individual river populations of Atlantic salmon (when a sea net catches a hundred fish, it could be 1 fish each from 100 rivers, or 100 fish from 1 river). Economically, by the mid-1980s commercial fisheries brought in only 7% of the total revenues from Atlantic salmon, versus 93% from recreational fisheries (Tuomi 1987). Decisions were made to favor the recreational fishery and phase out commercial fishing. Changes included the closure of most of the East Coast Atlantic salmon

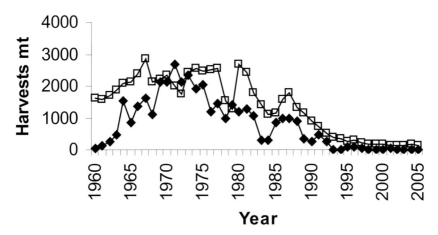

Figure 2. Landings of Atlantic salmon *Salmo salar* in Greenland (diamonds) and in Canadian homewater fisheries (open squares). Greenland totals are the combined West and East Greenland harvests. Canadian statistics are commercial, sport, and First Nations harvests combined. Data from ICES (2000, 2006). Values in metric tons.

hatchery system, excluding those that served as mitigation for environmental impacts or as live gene banks for endangered populations. The closures were made on the grounds that users should pay for private hatcheries if the stocking was for recreational purposes.

The phaseout of commercial fisheries in North America proceeded gradually, and to a certain degree in fits and starts. In Canada, the most concerted program was led by the Department of Fisheries and Oceans and retired more than 5,200 commercial salmon licenses throughout Atlantic Canada between 1972 and 1976 at a cost of $40 million (CDN) (Whoriskey and Glebe 2002). The total spent on the purchase of all commercial licenses during the phase-out exceeded $70 million (CDN).

The steps taken were: by 1960 commercial fishing for salmon around Anticosti Island was closed; by 1984 commercial fisheries of the Maritime Provinces (Nova Scotia, New Brunswick and Prince Edward Island) and along the south shore of the Gulf of St. Lawrence in Quebec were ended; in 1992 a Newfoundland inshore moratorium was instituted; and the final end came when the Province of

Quebec completed its gradual (1991–2000) phase-out by closing the remaining Quebec North Shore Gulf of St. Lawrence fisheries. Presently, recreational angling occurs in all Canadian Provinces that have Atlantic salmon rivers, and additional fisheries occur for First Nations or subsistence purposes. While initially these shutdowns of commercial fisheries temporarily bolstered adult returns to rivers, for unknown reasons sea survival continued to deteriorate and the abundance of Atlantic salmon returning to many North American rivers did not improve (Dempson et al. 2004; ICES 2006).

In the United States, commercial fishing for Atlantic salmon may have started as early as 1628, and continued until 1948, when severe declines in salmon abundance led to their closure (Baum 1997). Population declines continued post-1948 despite restoration efforts, and eventually resulted in a ban on all angling in the last remaining wild salmon rivers in Maine on 28 December 1999. This closure included the Penobscot River where the last remaining major (about 1,000 adults per year, but heavily supported with hatchery fish) run of Atlantic salmon in the USA occurs. In addition, eight Maine populations of salmon, not including the Penobscot, were listed as endangered under the Endangered Species Act on 13 November 2000, and no fishing will be permitted upon them until recovery occurs. A tightly controlled, short-duration, live-release fishery for Atlantic salmon was reinstituted in the Penobscot River in 2006, and may continue in future years as long as it does not endanger the conservation of the species (www.maine.gov/asc/).

Greenland

Fisheries off Greenland contain mixed populations of salmon from different continents, posing special difficulties for insuring conservation escapements to rivers of origin. Harvests of North American fish off Greenland have been of similar tonnages to those taken in homewaters (Figure 3). Greenland has a home-rule government, but is represented on the international scene by Denmark.

Dunbar and Thomson (1979) examined available fishery records from Greenland dating back to the late 1500s. The earliest documented captures of Atlantic salmon off Greenland date from the early 1600s. Dunbar and Thomson (1979) suggested that a cyclical trend occurred to the abundance of the species in these waters, with highs occurring around 1600, 1810, and the 1970s. Salmon were caught in Greenland's waters mostly for subsistence purposes until the present era.

Starting in 1960, a massive increase began in the harvest of salmon off Greenland (Figure 3). The fishery was (and is) typically prosecuted off the west coast in the autumn (mid-August to November), and the fish caught have been one (and occasionally more) year at sea, and would be one or more years away from returning to home rivers to spawn. A number of variables contributed to the rapid fishery expansion, including premium prices for Atlantic salmon in the marketplace, improved boats and fishing gear, improved preservation facilities, the importance

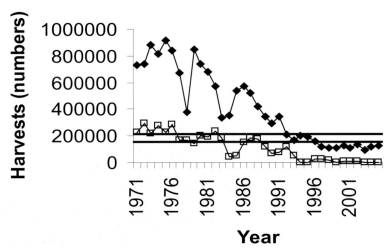

FIGURE 3. Annual number of fish of European and North American origin (diamonds) harvested at Greenland, calculated from average weights of fish captured off Greenland. Where data for particular years were missing, the previous five-year average was substituted. The numbers of North American fish are shown by the open squares. The upper horizontal flat line shows the number of North American fish off Greenland in the North American Reserve. The lower flat line gives the number of spawners needed to meet conservation egg depositions in all North American rivers.

of fisheries to the Greenland economy, and the ability to ship the product into markets (Paloheimo and Elson 1974a). Salmon harvesting peaked in 1971, when about 1,800 mt were taken.

The fishery was composed of both coastal and high seas vessels that used monofilament gill nets. In inshore areas, the nets tended to be fixed in place, whereas in the offshore areas nets were allowed to drift. Drift net lengths could extend up to 3.2 km (Kreiberg 1980).

These fisheries occurred within Greenland territorial waters and in the international waters outside territorial limits. The vessels prosecuting the fishery came principally from Greenland; however, vessels from Denmark, Norway, the Faeroes and Sweden also reported catches (ICES 2006).

The explosion in fishing pressure post-1960 off Greenland was met with great concern by salmon mangers in the countries where the fish spawned. Initially, no international mechanism existed to regulate this multi-nation, complex fishery, and it was feared it would cause a collapse in salmon returns, and ultimately the species (Paloheimo and Elson 1974a, 1974b). Persistent government and private pressure was brought on

Greenland to cap fishing effort. This resulted in the first quota in the Greenland fishery being established by the International Commission for Northwest Atlantic Fisheries (IC-NAF) in 1976, at 1,190 mt (Kreiberg 1980; Figure 4).

Nongovernmental organizations began lobbying for the creation of an international body that could specifically regulate Atlantic salmon interceptory fisheries at sea (e.g., the Greenland and Faeroe Island fisheries) in 1979. Efforts eventually resulted in the formation of the North Atlantic Salmon Conservation Organization (NASCO) in 1983 (Carter et al. 2003). Successes of the organization included ending fishing for salmon in the Norwegian Sea, and fostering reductions in salmon catches off Greenland and the Faeroe Islands (for a history of the start of the Faeroe fisheries, see Meister 1983). However, Carter et al. (2003) were concerned that NASCO meetings lacked "the urgency one might expect given the alarming reductions in Atlantic salmon." They suggested that the problem stemmed from NASCO's original terms of reference which perhaps confined the organization's mandate too narrowly to fisheries

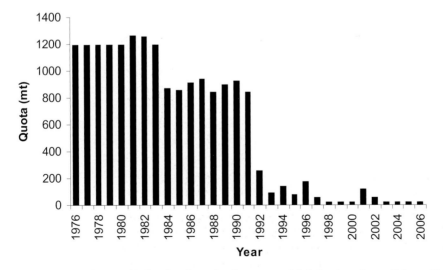

FIGURE 4. Quotas in metric tons (t) for the Greenland commercial Atlantic salmon fishery. Data from ICES 2006.

quota-setting, rather than more broadly to encompass other conservation imperatives. Carter et al. (2003) likened NASCO to a crustacean that needed to molt but could not, and has failed to grow into a needed new mandate.

The International Council for the Exploration of the Seas through its Working Group for North Atlantic Salmon provides independent scientific advice on quotas to NASCO (e.g., ICES 2006). The actual quotas adopted by NASCO for fisheries in the water adjacent to Greenland may exceed those recommended based on the scientific advice. This recognizes the fact that Greenland's right to fish in its territorial waters is guaranteed by the Law of the Sea Convention. In these circumstances, a NASCO negotiated quota could very well be more beneficial for salmon conservation than having no designated harvest cap at all. Barring political pressure or a will by member states to impose economic sanctions, NASCO has no way to enforce its quotas.

Some relief, from what was considered to be excessive fishing pressure, was provided by private sector interests that furnished funding to purchase Greenland annual quotas on a number of occasions. The fishery was suspended for a payment in 1993 and 1994 (ICES 2006), but fishing resumed thereafter until a new agreement was negotiated in 2002 with the Organization of Hunters and Fishermen in Greenland (KNAPK) to purchase the modest commercial quotas for a five-year period. This agreement has recently been renewed. A small (up to 20 mt) fishery for salmon is permitted under the agreement for subsistence purposes and local use (e.g., food for hospitals). Despite these efforts, the elimination of commercial fishing pressure off Greenland has not translated into significantly improved returns for wild Atlantic salmon in North America.

Salmon Farming

Given the difficulty in limiting commercial fisheries for wild Atlantic salmon, parallel thinking developed about how to address the problem. If the high prices paid for salmon were the driver of commercial fisheries, and if a way was found to reliably fill Atlantic salmon market needs at low prices, then market forces would act to decrease the wild harvests. Salmon farming, which had the potential of creating jobs using traditional skills, generating wealth in coastal areas, and potentially fostering the development of enhancement methods for wild fish, was a potential wild-fish conservation measure.

Sea cage farming of Atlantic salmon began in Norway in the 1970s, building on the previously developed knowledge of Atlantic salmon and hatchery methods that had already been established for enhancing wild populations. By 1980, Norwegian sea-cage salmon culture produced over 4,000 mt annually (ICES 2006). Other jurisdictions, including Canada and the USA were evaluating the industry for the potential economic and employment benefits that it offered.

The Atlantic Salmon Federation became one of the biggest promoters of the nascent aquaculture industry in North America (ASF 1977; Whoriskey 1998) in large part because of its perceived potential to replace salmon caught by interceptory fisheries. In 1973, ASF founded its Salmon Genetics Research Program, and by 1984 had focused it on screening Canadian East Coast wild Atlantic salmon lineages for their performance in culture and initiating domestication selection regimes to develop better performing aquaculture strains (Friars et al. 1997).

The phenomenal global growth of salmon farming was completely unanticipated. The species is now cultured within the native range of the Atlantic salmon and outside of its native range in the Pacific Ocean. In 2006, the most recent year for which statistics are available, over 1.26 million metric tons of Atlantic salmon are estimated to have been grown in sea cages (ICES 2007), and production is continuing to expand at a fast pace annually. Even Vietnam is now producing Atlantic salmon! This massive burst of farm production has affected the market price of salmon. In New Brunswick, the first farmed salmon that entered the market in competition with the wild-caught product sold for $7.70/kg (dressed) (CDN) in 1978. Farmed salmon prices peaked at $13.97/kg (CDN) in 1987, then dropped to a low of $4.40/kg (CDN) in 1996 when world production began to outstrip demand (Harvey and Milewski 2007). Present prices are above the 1996 minimum but still relatively low, and wild-caught Atlantic salmon could not now compete with them.

The potential for the industry to have unintended negative impacts upon wild Atlantic salmon populations was not anticipated at the industry's birth. These impacts forced the ASF to critically re-evaluate its positions (Whoriskey 2000a). ASF recognized that declines in North American wild Atlantic salmon populations antedated the inception of salmon farming. Thus, salmon farming was viewed as one of a number of potential contributors to the observed wild salmon population declines, and not the unique cause, although locally its impacts were considered significant. The organization transferred its broodstock program to the industry, and refocused on the interactions between farmed and wild fish. Within the native range of the Atlantic salmon, the primary concerns were with the genetic impacts of interbreeding between farmed strains of salmon and wild counterparts, and the potential for disease transmission among farmed and wild fish.

Unintended releases of farmed salmon have occurred in every region where the fish are cultured, and within the native range of Atlantic salmon, the farmed fish have entered wild salmon rivers and spawned. The fitness of the farm X farm and the wild X farm progeny in the wild is much reduced compared to that of wild X wild crosses (Fleming et al. 2000; McGinnity et al. 2003). In addition, the pure farm progeny could out-compete wild juveniles in streams, but fail to return after migration to sea. This problem depressed the number of wild juveniles migrating to sea as smolts, and failed to produce spawners to re-seed the rivers, pressuring the wild populations from two directions (McGinnity et al. 2003).

The east coast North American salmon farming industry is at present centered in the year-round, ice-free region across the USA-Canada border between Maine and New Brunswick. In this region, the Magaguadavic River system, which has a head-of-tide fish ladder that all salmon must use to migrate upstream, has been monitored since 1992 to document the status of local wild salmon populations and the numbers of escaped farmed salmon attempting to enter the rivers (Carr and Whoriskey 2004; Whoriskey et al. 2006). In 1994, the worst year for escaped farmed salmon, the farmed fish outnumbered wild salmon by a ratio of 10:1 (Figure 5). The escaped fish were entering wild salmon rivers where local run sizes were falling precipitously, for unknown reasons. However, better farm equipment and containment procedures, and a local reduction in production have contributed to a massive decrease in the numbers of escaped farmed salmon in rivers. For the first time since 1994, the wild fish outnumbered farmed fish in the Magaguadavic River in 2006 (Figure 5). While juvenile farmed Atlantic salmon are also escaping from freshwater hatchery facilities (Carr and Whoriskey 2006), containment procedures for these facilities should be easy and cost-effective to implement.

The second major concern about salmon farming is the potential for disease transmission to wild populations. Disease organisms

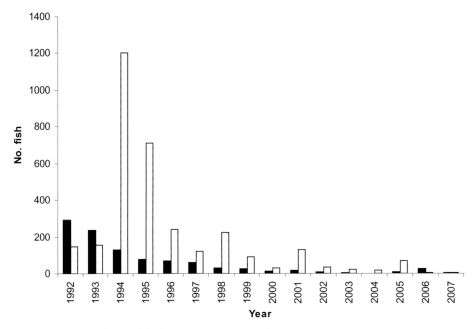

FIGURE 5. Numbers of wild (black bars) and escaped farm salmon (white bars) returning annually to the Magaguadavic River, New Brunswick.

are a part of the natural environment; however, aggregations of farm sites with large numbers of fish can favor the development of epidemics. The East Coast salmon farming industry was at one time the most concentrated salmon farming area in the world, with distances between farms as small as 600 m (Chang et al. 2005). With waterborne disease agents, an outbreak at one farm site has the potential to transmit the disease agent to adjacent farms, and to wild fish sharing the water mass.

The primary disease concerns for wild Atlantic salmon interests in North America are sea lice and infectious salmon anemia (ISA). A sea lice epidemic hit the East Coast industry relatively soon after it started, in the mid-to-late 1980s (Hogans 1995; MacKinnon 1997). Given the close proximity of the sites to each other, it was imperative for the industry's survival to bring this rapidly under control. Systematic monitoring of lice burdens of adult salmon and escaped farmed salmon returning

to the Magaguadavic River indicator site occurs (Carr and Whoriskey 2004). Over three years starting in 2001, the Department of Fisheries and Oceans sampled smolts in the Bay of Fundy region and screened them for sea lice (Lacroix and Knox 2005). Presumably due to the rigorous control measures implemented by the industry, no indication of a lice problem occurs in wild fish in this area.

Infectious salmon anemia (ISA), a viral infection, has proved very problematic. This disease and its virus were unknown to science until the first outbreak struck Norway in 1984. Subsequent to the first report, ISA has been detected in most major salmon farming areas (Whoriskey 2000b), and was present in the East Coast North American every year since its first detection in 1996 (Whoriskey 2000; Chang et al. 2005) until it was recently brought under control. No treatment is available, and infected farm cages with virulent ISA strains are destroyed. Wild fish, and escaped farmed fish entering the Magaguadavic River, have both tested positive for this virus (Carr and Whoriskey 2002). At present, it is not known what, if any, effect the virus is having on wild populations in the region.

When Traditional Management Measures Fail: "Lite" Fishing

Despite the increasingly stringent limitations imposed on harvests, the abundance of North American wild Atlantic salmon has remained stubbornly fixed at near historic low levels (Figure 1). The low abundance has led to an increase in live-release angling, which in theory leaves all the fun and societal benefits of angling intact with small-to-no salmon population consequences.

When practiced correctly (minimizing play times, not taking the fish from the water for extended periods for removal of hooks or photographs, fishing in cooler temperatures), it is clear that physiological impacts of the stress of angling are generally transitory (Tufts et al. 2000), and released fish will survive and spawn (Webb 1998; Whoriskey et al. 2000; Thorstad et al. 2003; but see Dempson et al. 2002). Some angled fish are recaptured a second or third time (Webb 1998; Whoriskey et al. 2000; Thorstad et al. 2003), with the shortest documented time interval between a first and second hook-up being a few minutes (Welles 1997).

While live-release angling is an effective conservation tool, its increased use has generated a new debate (Arlinghaus et al. 2007; Albertson 2009, this volume). Most humans accept the harvesting of fish for food as a morally justifiable activity; however, if the fish feel pain or have a sense of "awareness" then live-release angling could be considered to be cruel and morally unjustifiable. Evidence for and against whether fish feel pain, or are aware, has been published in the scientific literature. Rose (2002) reviewed the evidence that the neural system and brain of fish are not sufficiently developed to experi-

ence pain and awareness. This viewpoint has been challenged by experiments that generated results consistent with fish detecting and nonreflexively attempting to avoid noxious stimuli and pain (Sneddon 2003; Sneddon et al. 2003). It may be impossible to definitively answer with a scientific study whether or not fish are "aware." Regardless, animal-rights groups have taken up the cause, and the issue has been discussed in prestigious media outlets such as the New York Times (Cowell 2003). A great deal is at stake in the debate.

Moving Forward

With the exhaustion of traditional fishery management options, improvements to the numbers of Atlantic salmon returning to North America are going to have to be achieved either by nature improving salmon survival at sea, by clawing back lost production potential with recovery efforts, or finding innovative new management measures. No precise goals on a continental basis have been set for the restoration of the species by any known organization. Rather, organizations and individuals are independently attempting to identify opportunities where focused efforts can bring large, self-sustaining improvements in present salmon production. Some of these efforts are described below. It is clear that depending on hatcheries is not a viable long-term strategy to sustain or improve Atlantic salmon production. The biological risks of hatcheries are well known, and their costs make them vulnerable to closure when financial times become difficult.

Recovery activities are underway in both Canada and the USA for the rivers which have been designated as endangered. These activities are unlikely to provide immediate relief, but could result in improvements in the medium term. Canada's efforts for the inner Bay of Fundy populations have significant resource challenges. Endangered listings in Canada do not automatically result in the commitment of resources to support a recovery effort. In addition, the decline from relatively healthy to endangered status in the inner Bay of Fundy populations began in the early 1990s, and happened within less than 10 years (Amiro 2003). No significant changes in freshwater production potential occurred over this period, indicating that much of the problem results from unknown variables acting at sea. A recovery strategy is difficult to implement when the causes that need to be addressed are not known. In the interim, Canada has established a live gene bank capacity to maintain some of the inner Bay of Fundy river lineages, and continues limited monitoring activity.

By contrast, an extensive recovery program is underway for endangered populations in Maine, USA (e.g., National Research Council 2004; Fay et al. 2006). Potential freshwater threats including the introduction of exotic predators, dams barring migration, low pH and associated effects of toxic aluminum, water extractions, and others have been identified. Significant federal funding has been made available to support research and monitoring activities to identify and deal with threats, and collaborations have been forged among state, federal, and university scientists. River-specific live gene banking based out of the Green Lake hatchery has also been implemented for listed populations. While significant improvement in the status of Maine salmon have not yet occurred, the program has only been underway for about two salmon generations. It is unreasonable to expect in less than a decade to solve a problem that has been developing for 400 years.

Farther to the south in the USA, restoration efforts are underway in watersheds where Atlantic salmon have been extirpated, notably in the Connecticut River (Gephard et al. 2006). Researchers face a major challenge to develop a naturalized lineage of salmon from much more northerly donor populations.

Modest returns (214 salmon in 2006) are being achieved, but the absence of research into the variables affecting smolt-to-adult survival and adult recruitment to the spawning stock is hampering the program.

Other significant opportunities exist to restore lost salmon production potential in North America, although they may be very costly. The 65 rivers on the eastern shore of Nova Scotia, south of Cape Breton to the Bay of Fundy, have been heavily impacted by acid deposition. Their "normal" annual salmon production of about 45,000 adults was reduced by 50% by 1986 (DFO 2000). At present, it appears that the emission standards adopted by the USA and Canada are reducing acid depositions to the point that stream pH in this area should rebound. The problem is the time required for the rebound: it will take about 100 years for the limited buffering and cation exchange capacities of this region to re-establish themselves (Laudon et al. 2002; Clair and Hindar 2005).

Lime can be added to acid-impacted salmon streams to improve pH, with great socio-economic and conservation benefits for Atlantic salmon. Navrud (2001) reported that restoration of Atlantic salmon with liming had a benefit-to-cost ratio of 4.4 in selected salmon rivers in Norway. The Nova Scotia Salmon Association is presently spearheading a liming project using a lime doser to document the benefits to salmon in one of the impacted rivers in Nova Scotia (www.asf.ca). Dosers are costly, require regular maintenance, and are not a practical or economically feasible means to treat all of Nova Scotia's impacted streams. However, liming the surrounding forest, possibly from aircraft, could benefit both forest growth and salmon (Clair and Hindar 2005). Up front costs would be expensive, but once completed this technique could provide the needed 100 years of relief until natural processes are restored.

The restoration of depressed or lost ecosystem components, including salmon and other anadromous fishes, to rivers or river sections where they have been lost or depleted also holds great potential. Maine's Penobscot River is currently the focus of a major campaign to remove or substantially improve fish passage at four main-stem dams. The dams have caused fish mortality, or blocked access to freshwater habitat. This approximately $50 million (U.S.) fish passage project is designed as a win-win, with monies paid to remove or upgrade dams being used to retool remaining hydro facilities so that almost the same power output occurs as before. At the same time, access by anadromous fishes will be restored to 70–100% of their historic areas in the river.

The restoration of other anadromous fishes will also bring benefits. Populations of these fishes are currently depressed in many river systems (e.g., Saunders et al. 2006). Species like alewives *Alosa pseudoharengus* may have deposited significant quantities of marine derived nutrients into east coast rivers (Durbin et al. 1979; Garman and Macko 1998), fertilizing the streams to the benefit of the salmon. Alewife fry were probably food for young salmon in streams, and the arrival of the alewives moving upriver at the time that the salmon smolts were moving out to sea may have provided predator cover during a vulnerable life stage. The ecosystem contributions of species like alewives are underappreciated.

Despite everything, I remain optimistic about the future of Atlantic salmon, and I do not think I am insane. Healthy rivers in the salmon's range bring many benefits beyond the salmon, including clean drinking water that is essential for humans. Perhaps the greatest challenge is the formulation of integrated economic development models in these regions that foster economic activities dependent on river systems healthy enough for salmon. If this can be done, long-term protection will be in place for the salmon, and the salmon will put its own considerable powers to work in rebuilding itself to health.

Acknowledgments

I thank W. M. Carter and G. Chaput for sharing information with me. The text also benefited from the comments of three reviewers and the editors of the volume, for which I am grateful. This article ultimately expresses my personal interpretations and views of the available evidence. To the extent that there are errors of fact or interpretation, they are my own responsibility.

References

Albertson, L. 2009. Perspectives on angling for salmon on the Kuskokwim River: the catch and release sport fishing controversy. Pages 611–619 *in* C.C. Krueger and C.E. Zimmerman, editors. Pacific salmon: ecology and management of western Alaska's populations. American Fisheries Society, Symposium 70, Bethesda, Maryland.

Amiro, P. G. 2003. Population status of Inner Bay of Fundy Atlantic salmon (*Salmo salar*), to 1999. Canadian Technical Report of Fisheries and Aquatic Sciences No. 2488.

Arlinghaus, R., S. J. Cooke, J. Lyman, D. Policansky, A. Schwab, C. Suski, S. G. Sutton, and E. B. Thorstad. 2007. Understanding the complexity of catch-and-release in recreational fishing: an integrative synthesis of global knowledge from historical, ethical, social and biological perspectives. Reviews in Fisheries Science 15:75–167.

ASF (Atlantic Salmon Federation). 1977. Salmonid Aquaculture: Selected papers. International Atlantic Salmon Foundation Special Publication Series No. 7. St. Andrews, New Brunswick, Canada.

Baum, E. 1997. Maine Atlantic salmon: a national treasure. Atlantic Salmon Unlimited, Hermon, Maine.

Berg, O. K. 1985. The formation of non-anadromous populations of Atlantic salmon, *Salmo salar* L., in Europe. Journal of Fish Biology 27: 805–815.

Burgner, R. L. 1991. Life history of sockeye salmon (*Oncorhynchus nerka*). Pages 1–117 *in* C. Groot and L. Margolis, editors. Pacific salmon: life histories. The University of British Columbia Press, Vancouver.

CAFSAC. 1991. Definition of conservation for Atlantic salmon. Canadian Atlantic Fisheries Scientific Advisory Committee CAFSAC Advisory document 91/15. Ottawa.

Caron, F. P., M. Fontaine, and S. E. Picard. 1999. Seuil de conservation et cible de gestion pour les rivières à saumon (*Salmo salar*) du Québec. Faune et Parcs Québec, Direction de la faune et des habitats. Québec.

Carr, J., and F. Whoriskey. 2002. Assessment of Atlantic salmon in southwestern New Brunswick outer Bay of Fundy Rivers, with emphasis on the Magaguadavic River, 1992–2001. Report to the New Brunswick Environmental Trust Fund. Atlantic Salmon Federation, St. Andrews, New Brunswick, Canada.

Carr, J., and F. Whoriskey. 2004. Sea lice infestation rates on wild and escaped farmed Atlantic salmon (*Salmo salar* L.) entering the Magaguadavic River, New Brunswick. Aquaculture Research 35:723–729.

Carr, J. and F. Whoriskey. 2006. The escape of juvenile farmed Atlantics salmon from hatcheries into freshwater streams in New Brunswick, Canada. ICES Journal of Marine Science 63:1263–1268.

Carter, W., B. Kristiansen, C. Popuard, A. A. Rosenberg, and G. Porter. 2003. NASCO's future: a vision statement. Atlantic Salmon Federation, St. Andrews, NB and World Wildlife Fund, Washington, D.C. Available: www.asf.ca. (December 2008).

Chang, B. D., F. H. Page, R. J. Losier, D. A. Greenberg, J. D. Haffey, and E. P. McCurdy. 2005. Water circulation and management of infectious salmon anemia in the salmon aquaculture industry of Cobscook Bay, Maine and adjacent southwestern New Brunswick. Canadian Technical Report of Fisheries and Aquatic Sciences No. 2598.

Chaput, G., J. Allard, F. Caron, J. B. Dempson, C.C. Mullins, and M. F. O'Connell. 1998. River-specific target spawning requirements for Atlantic salmon (*Salmo salar*) based on a generalized smolt production model. Canadian Journal of Fisheries and Aquatic Sciences 55: 246–261.

Christie, W. J. 1973. A review of the changes in the fish species composition of Lake Ontario. Great Lakes Fishery Commission Technical Report No. 23, Ann Arbor, Michigan.

Clair, T., and A. Hindar. 2005. Liming for the mitigation for acid rain effects in freshwaters: a review of recent results. Environmental Research 13: 91–128.

Cowell, A. 2003. Hooked fish feel pain, British scientists say, roiling the waters. New York Times International Edition, 6 May 2003.

DFO (Department of Fisheries and Oceans). 1986. Strategies for the long-term management of Atlantic Salmon. Report of the Special Federal/Provincial Atlantic Salmon Working Group. Fisheries and Oceans Canada, Ottawa. Available: http://www.mar.dfo-mpo.gc.ca/science/diad/wasp/e/Policy-1986-e.html (December 2008).

DFO. 2000. The effects of acid rain on Atlantic salmon of the Southern Upland of Nova Scotia. DFO Maritimes Regional Habitat Status Report 2000/2E. Fisheries and Oceans Canada, Ottawa.

Dempson, B. D., G. Furey, and M. Bloom. 2002. Effects of catch and release angling on Atlantic salmon, *Salmo salar* L., of the Conne River, Newfoundland. Fisheries Management and Ecology 9:139–147.

Dempson, J. B., M. F. O'Connell, and C. J. Schwarz. 2004. Spatial and temporal trends in abundance of Atlantic salmon, *Salmo salar*, in Newfoundland with emphasis on impacts of the 1992 closure of the commercial fishery. Fisheries Management and Ecology 11: 387–402.

Ducharme, L. J. A. 1969. Atlantic salmon returning for their fifth and sixth consecutive spawning trips. Journal of the Fisheries Research Board of Canada 26:1661–1664.

Dunbar, M. J., and D. H. Thomson. 1979. West Greenland salmon and climactic change. Meddelelser om Grønland 202(4):1–19.

Dunfield, R. W. 1985. The Atlantic salmon in the history of North America. Canadian Special Publication of Fisheries and Aquatic Sciences No. 80.

Durbin, A. G., S. W. Nixon, and C. A. Oviatt. 1979. Effects of the spawning migration of the alewife, *Alosa pseudoharengus*, on freshwater ecosystems. Ecology 60: 8–17.

Fay, C., M. Barton, S. Craig, A. Hecht, J. Pruden, R. Saunders, T. Sheehan, and J. Trial. 2006. Status review for anadromous Atlantic salmon (*Salmo salar*) in the United States. Report to the National Marine Fisheries Service and U.S. Fish and Wildlife Service. Available: http://www.nmfs.noaa.gov/pr/species/statusreviews.htm (December 2008).

Fleming, I. A., K. Hindar, I. B. Mjølnerød, B. Jonsson, T. Balstad, and A. Lamberg. 2000. Lifetime success and interactions of farm salmon invading a native population. Proceedings of the Royal Society of London B, 267: 1517–1523.

Friars, G. W., J. K. Bailey, and F. M. O'Flynn. 1997. A review of gains from selection in Atlantic salmon (*Salmo salar*) in the Salmon Genetics Research Program. World Aquaculture 28(4): 68–71.

Garman, G. C., and S. A. Macko. 1998. Contribution of marine-derived organic matter to an Atlantic coast, freshwater, tidal stream by anadromous clupeid fishes. Journal of the North American Benthological Society 17: 277–385.

Gephard, S., T. Wildman, B. Williams, and D. Ellis. 2006. Diadromous fish enhancement and restoration 2006. State of Connecticut, Federal aid to sport fish restoration F50D27 Annual Performance Report.

Groot, C., and L. Margolis editors. 1991. Pacific salmon: life histories. UBC Press, Vancouver.

Hansen, L. P., and J. A. Jacobsen. 2000. Distribution and migration of Atlantic salmon, *Salmo salar*

L., in the sea. Pages 75–87 *in* D. Mills, editor. The ocean life of Atlantic salmon. Fishing News Books, Oxford, U.K.

Harvey, J., and I. Milewski. 2007. Salmon aquaculture in the Bay of Fundy: an unsustainable industry. Conservation Council of New Brunswick. Fredericton, New Brunswick.

Healey, M. C. 1991. Life history of Chinook salmon (*Oncorhynchus tshawytscha*). Pages 311–393. *in* C. Groot and L. Margolis, editors. Pacific salmon: life histories. The University of British Columbia Press, Vancouver.

Heard, W. R. 1991. Life history of pink salmon (*Oncorhynchus gorbuscha*). Pages 119–230 *in* C. Groot and L. Margolis, editors. Pacific salmon: life histories. The University of British Columbia Press, Vancouver.

Hogans, W. E. 1995. Infection dynamics of sea lice, *Lepeophtheirus salmonis* (Copepoda:Caligidae) parasitic on Atlantic salmon (*Salmo salar*) cultured in marine waters of the lower Bay of Fundy. Canadian Technical Report of Fisheries and Aquatic Sciences No. 2067.

Hutchings, J. A., and R. A. Myers. 1985. Mating between anadromous and nonanadromous Atlantic salmon (*Salmo salar*). Canadian Journal of Zoology 63: 2219–2221.

International Council for the Exploration of the Seas. 2006. Report of the Working Group on North Atlantic Salmon. International Council for the Exploration of the Seas CM 2006/ACFM:23. Copenhagen.

International Council for the Exploration of the Seas. 2007. Report of the Working Group on North Atlantic salmon (WGNAS). International Council for the Exploration of the Seas CM 2007/ACFM:13. Copenhagen.

Kreiberg, H. 1980. Report of the Greenland expedition. International Atlantic Salmon Foundation Special Publication Series No. 9, St. Andrews, New Brunswick.

Lackey, R. T., D. H. Lach, and S. L. Duncan, editors. 2006. Salmon 2100: the future of wild Pacific salmon. American Fisheries Society, Bethesda, Maryland.

Lacroix, G. L., and D. Knox. 2005. Distribution of Atlantic salmon (*Salmo salar*) postsmolts of different origins in the Bay of Fundy and Gulf of Maine, and evaluation of factors affecting migration, growth and survival. Canadian Journal of Fisheries and Aquatic Sciences 62:1363–1376.

Laudon, H., T. A. Clair, and H. F. Hemond. 2002. Long-term response in episodic acidification to declining SO_4^{2-} deposition in two steams in Nova Scotia. Hydrology and Earth System Sciences 6:773–781.

MacKinnon, B. 1997. Control of sea lice infections in salmonid aquaculture: alternatives to drugs. Aquaculture Association of Canada Special Publication No. 2: 61–64.

Marschall, E. A., T. P. Quinn, D. A. Roff, J. A. Hutchings, N. B. Metcalfe, T. A. Bakke, R. L. Saunders, and N. L. Poff. 1998. A framework for understanding Atlantic salmon (*Salmo salar*) life history. Canadian Journal of Fisheries and Aquatic Sciences 55 (Supplement 1):48–58.

Martynov, V., G. Chaput, J. Anderson, and F. Whoriskey. 1994. Fishes of the shallow rapids and riffles of the Pizhmia River, Pechora River basin, Russia. Canadian Technical Report of Fisheries and Aquatic Sciences No. 2000.

McGinnity, P., P. Prodöhl, P. A. Ferguson, R. Hynes, N. O'Maoiléidigh, N. Baker, D. Cotter, B. O'Hea, D. Cooke, G. Rogan, J. Taggart, and T. Cross. 2003. Fitness reduction and potential extinction of wild populations of Atlantic salmon, *Salmo salar*, as a result of interactions with escaped farm salmon. Proceedings of the Royal Society of London B 270:2443–2550.

Meister, A. L. 1983. The Faroese salmon fishing industry and its management. International Atlantic Salmon Foundation Special Publication Series, No. 11, St. Andrews, New Brunswick, Canada.

Menard, J., C. C. Krueger, and J. R. Hilsinger. 2009. Norton Sound salmon fisheries: history, stock abundance, and management. Pages 621–673 *in* C. C. Krueger and C. E. Zimmerman, editors. Pacific salmon: ecology and management of western Alaska's populations. American Fisheries Society, Symposium 70, Bethesda, Maryland.

Morin, R. 1991. Atlantic salmon (*Salmo salar*) in the lower Nastapoka River, Quebec: distribution and origin of salmon in eastern Hudson Bay. Canadian Journal of Zoology 69:1674–1681.

National Research Council. 2004. Atlantic salmon in Maine. The National Academies Press, Washington, D.C.

Navrud, S. 2001. Economic valuation of inland recreation fisheries: empirical studies and their policy use in Norway. Fisheries Management and Ecology 8:369–382.

Nislow, K., J. D. Armstrong, and S. McKelvey. 2004. Phosphorous flux due to Atlantic salmon (*Salmo salar*) in an oligotrophic upland stream: effects of management and demography. Canadian Journal of Fisheries and Aquatic Sciences 61: 2401–2410.

North Pacific Anadromous Fish Commission. 2002. Joint meeting on causes of marine mortality of salmon in the North Pacific and North Atlantic Oceans, and in the Baltic Sea. NPAFC Technical Report No. 4. Vancouver.

O'Connell, M. F., J. B. Dempson, and G. Chaput. 2006.

Aspects of the life history, biology and population dynamics of Atlantic salmon (*Salmo salar* L.) in Eastern Canada. Canadian Science Advisory Secretariat Research Document 2006/14.

Paloheimo, J. E., and P. F. Elson. 1974a. Effects of the Greenland fishery for Atlantic salmon on Canadian stocks. International Atlantic Salmon Foundation Special Publication Series, Volume 5, No. 1, St. Andrews, New Brunswick, Canada.

Paloheimo, J. E., and P. F. Elson. 1974b. Reduction of Atlantic salmon (*Salmo salar*) catches in Canada attributed to the Greenland fishery. Journal of the Fisheries Research Board of Canada 31:1467–1480.

Power, G. 1958. The evolution of the freshwater races of the Atlantic salmon (*Salmo salar* L.) in eastern North America. Arctic 11: 86–92.

Power, G. 1981. Stock characteristics and catches of Atlantic salmon (*Salmo salar*) in Quebec, and Newfoundland and Labrador in relation to environmental variables. Canadian Journal of Fisheries and Aquatic Sciences 38:1601–1611.

Quinn, T. P. 2005. The behavior and ecology of Pacific salmon and trout. American Fisheries Society in association with the University of Washington Press, Seattle.

Reddin, D. J., and P. B. Short. 1991. Post-smolt Atlantic salmon (*Salmo salar*) in the Labrador Sea. Canadian Journal of Fisheries and Aquatic Sciences 48: 2–6.

Reddin, D. J., D. E. Stansbury, and P. B. Short. 1988. Continent of origin of Atlantic salmon (*Salmo salar* L.) caught at west Greenland. Journal du conseil International pour l'Exploration de la Mer 44:180–188.

Ritter, J. M. 1989. Marine migration and natural mortality of North American Atlantic salmon (*Salmo salar* L.). Canadian Manuscript Report of Fisheries and Aquatic Sciences 2041, Halifax.

Rose, J. D. 2002. The neurobehavioral nature of fishes and the question of awareness and pain. Reviews in Fisheries Science 10: 1–38.

Salo, E. O. 1991. Life history of chum salmon (*Oncorhynchus keta*). Pages 231–309 in C. Groot and L. Margolis. Pacific salmon: life histories. The University of British Columbia Press, Vancouver.

Sandercock, F. K. 1991. Life history of coho salmon (*Oncorhynchus kisutch*). Pages 395–445 in C. Groot and L. Margolis, editors. Pacific salmon: life histories. The University of British Columbia Press, Vancouver.

Saunders, R. M., A. Hachey, and C. W. Fay. 2006. Maine's diadromous fish community: past, present and implications for Atlantic salmon recovery. Fisheries 31:537–547.

Scott, W. B., and E. J. Crossman. 1973. Freshwater Fishes of Canada. Fisheries Research Board of Canada, Bulletin 184, Ottawa.

Sneddon, L. U. 2003. The evidence for pain in fish: the use of morphine as an analgesic. Applied Animal Behaviour Science 83: 153–162.

Sneddon, L. U., V. A. Braithwaite, and M. J. Gentle. 2003. Novel object test: examining nociception and fear in the rainbow trout. Journal of Pain 4:431–440.

Spidle, A. P., S. T. Kalinowski, B. A. Lubinski, D. L. Perkins, K. F. Beland, J. F. Kocik, and T. L. King. 2003. Population structure of Atlantic salmon in Maine with reference to populations from Atlantic Canada. Transactions of the American Fisheries Society 132:196–209.

Stasko, A. B., A. M. Sutterlin, S. A. Rommell, Jr., and P. F. Elson. 1973. Migration-orientation of Atlantic salmon (*Salmo salar* L.). Pages 119–137 in M. W. Smith and W. M. Carter. Proceedings of the international symposium on the Atlantic salmon: management, biology and survival of the species. International Atlantic Salmon Foundation, St. Andrews, New Brunswick, Canada.

Stockner, J., editor. 2003. Nutrients in salmonid ecosystems: sustaining production and biodiversity. American Fisheries Society, Symposium 34, Bethesda, Maryland.

Sutterlin, A. M., J. Holder, and T. Benfey. 1987. Early survival rates and subsequent morphological abnormalities in landlocked, anadromous and hybrid (landlocked X anadromous) diploid and triploid Atlantic salmon. Aquaculture 64:157–164.

Thorstad, E. B., T. F. Næsje, P. Fiske, and B. Finstad. 2003. Effects of hook and release on Atlantic salmon in the River Alta, northern Norway. Fisheries Research 60: 293–307.

Tufts, B., K. Davidson, and A. T. Bielak. 2000. Biological implications of "catch-and-release" angling of Atlantic salmon. Pages 195–224 in F. G. Whoriskey and K. Whelan, editors. Managing Wild Atlantic salmon: new challenges-new techniques. Atlantic Salmon Federation, St. Andrews, New Brunswick.

Tuomi, A. I. 1987. Canada's Atlantic salmon recreational fisheries and their future: an economic overview. Atlantic Salmon Federation, Special Publication No. 14, St. Andrews, New Brunswick.

Verspoor, E., and L. J. Cole. 1989. Genetically distinct populations of resident and anadromous Atlantic salmon, *Salmo salar*. Canadian Journal of Zoology 67: 1453–1461.

Watt, W. D. 1988. Major causes and implications of Atlantic salmon habitat losses. Pages 101–111 in R. H. Stroud, editor. Present and future Atlantic salmon management. Atlantic Salmon Federation, Ipswich, Massachusetts.

Watt, W. D. 1989. The impact of habitat damage on Atlantic salmon (*Salmo salar*) catches. Pages

154–163 *in* C. D. Levings, L. B. Holtby, and M. A. Henderson, editors. Proceeding of the national workshop on the effect of habitat alterations on salmonid stocks. Canadian Special Publication of Fisheries and Aquatic Sciences No. 105.

Webb, J. H. 1998. Catch and release: the survival and behaviour of Atlantic salmon angled and returned to the Aberdeenshire Dee, in spring and early summer. Scottish Fisheries Research Report No. 62/1998.

Webster, D. A. 1982. Early history of the Atlantic salmon in New York. New York Fish and Game Journal 29(1):26–44.

Welles, D. 1997. Once hooked, twice shy. Atlantic Salmon Journal 46(4):15.

Whoriskey, F. 1998. The threat from aquaculture is the threat to aquaculture. Atlantic Salmon Journal 47(3):20–21.

Whoriskey, F. G. 2000a. The North American East Coast Atlantic salmon aquaculture industry: the challenges for wild salmon. Atlantic Salmon Federation, St. Andrews, New Brunswick, Canada.

Whoriskey, F. G. 2000b. Infectious Salmon Anemia (ISA): literature review and implications for wild salmon. International Council for the Exploration of the Seas Working Group for North Atlantic Salmon Working Paper 00/23.

Whoriskey, F. G., and J. Glebe. 2002. The Atlantic salmon recreational angling industry: economic benefits. Pages 77–91 *in* Lynch, K. D., M. L. Jones and W. W. Taylor, editors. Sustaining North American salmon: perspectives across regions and disciplines. American Fisheries Society, Bethesda, Maryland.

Whoriskey, F. G., S. Prusov, and S. Crabbe. 2000. Evaluation of the effects of catch-and-release angling on the Atlantic salmon (*Salmo salar*) of the Ponoi River, Kola Peninsula, Russian Federation. Ecology of Freshwater Fish 9: 118–125.

Whoriskey F., P. Brooking, G. Doucette, S. Tinker, and J. Carr. 2006. Movements and survival of sonically tagged farmed Atlantic salmon released in Cobscook Bay, Maine, USA. ICES Journal of Marine Science 63: 1218–1223.

Worm, B. L., E. B. Barbier, N. Beaumont, J. E. Duffy, C. Folke, B. S. Halpern, J. B. C. Jackson, H. K. Lotze, F. Micheli, S. R. Palumbi, E. Sala, K. A. Selkoe, J. J. Stachowicz, and R. Watson. 2006. Impacts of biodiversity loss on ocean ecosystem services. Science 414:787–790.

World Wildlife Fund. 2001 The status of wild Atlantic salmon: a river by river assessment. World Wildlife Fund, Washington, D.C.

American Fisheries Society Symposium 70:1103–1110, 2009

Sustaining Salmon: East, West, and North

DAVID POLICANSKY*

*Board on Environmental Studies and Toxicology, National Research Council
500 Fifth Street NW, Washington, D.C. 20001, USA*

Abstract.—Salmon (*Oncorhynchus* spp. and Atlantic Salmon *Salmo salar*) hold an unusual place among fishes due to their importance in cultures as food, sport fish, and as foci of political conflicts. They also are unusual in their anadromy, being important to freshwater, marine, and terrestrial ecosystems. This paper discusses five National Research Council studies of how to understand and sustain salmon in their various environments in Maine, the Pacific Northwest, and western Alaska. Lessons are formulated from a comparison of the studies that apply to all three regions as well as those that seem to apply only locally. The paper includes consideration of variations in life histories and abundance among the species as well as variations in physical environments and human societies in the places where salmon live.

Introduction

Salmon are remarkable for their anadromous life history; they start life in freshwater, migrate to sea, where they grow and mature, and finally return as adults to freshwater to spawn. The Pacific species all die after spawning; some Atlantic salmon survive to spawn again. Their anadromy has profound consequences. One is that because they return to and migrate up their natal stream to spawn, predators, including humans, can plan their activities around the seasonal bounty. In Alaska, coastal villages from the southeast to the west have traditionally depended on salmon for a substantial portion of their food (Glavin 2000), and many of them still do (Wolfe and Utermohle 2000). Salmon have been important in Alaska politics and controlling their management became a major factor in Alaska's drive to statehood (Policansky 2005; Cooley 1963).

Another profound consequence of anadromy is that salmon are exposed to environmental challenges in two very different environments, freshwater and marine; their populations, at least in theory, can be destroyed by sufficiently extreme conditions in either of the two environments. As a result of people's use of salmon and their vulnerability to environmental threats, salmon populations have been depleted in many areas where they once were abundant. Because salmon continue to be important to people for various reasons, including cultural ones, efforts to reverse the declines of salmon populations, and restore them in some cases, have been widespread throughout the northern hemisphere. Here, Briefly reviewed here are these restoration efforts, with a focus on studies by the National Research Council (NRC). Theconclusion is that it is far easier to prevent declines of salmon than to reverse them, especially when the declines are due to loss or degradation of habitat.

*Corresponding author: dpolican@nas.edu

has the greatest potential to make additional habitat available to salmon. In general, this means the dams closest to the sea and those that block the longest river reaches and the best potential salmon habitat.

• Address the problem of smolt mortality through research. One practical approach would be to add lime to streams experimentally, to either identify or rule out acidification as a problem.

• Continue to use hatcheries, at least in the short term, to supplement wild populations (river-specific stocking has been used exclusively in Maine since 1992) and as storehouses of fish from the various rivers. An urgent need exists to evaluate the effectiveness of stocking fry, parr, smolts, and even adults in terms of their success in producing returning adults.

The committee also recommended several longer-term actions, beginning with a comprehensive decision analysis that involves all the important stakeholders. No matter how technically feasible or effective a solution might be, the people who need to pay for the solution, either directly or indirectly by experiencing its consequences, must at least not oppose the solution, even if they do not support it, because the solution otherwise is unlikely to be successful. The committee provided some examples of such decision analyses, although they can be no more than examples until the stakeholders can provide inputs into the values of the various options.

The solutions proposed were potentially complex, expensive, and time-consuming. The decline of Maine's salmon occurred over more than 200 years, through a variety of assaults on them and their habitats, and reversing them cannot be expected to happen quickly or easily.

Salmon in the Pacific Northwest

As is true of Maine, the Pacific Northwest (northern California, Oregon, Washington, Idaho, and Montana) has experienced salmon declines and habitat changes over the past 150 years. In addition, the Pacific Northwest also has experienced a rapid growth in the human population; that growth is continuing in the first decade of the 21st century. Also, like Maine, the Pacific Northwest has relied extensively on hatcheries to mitigate the effects of dams by supplementing salmon populations.

The Columbia River basin occupies approximately half of the region, and it has been extensively dammed. Approximately 40% of the historical habitat of salmon in the Pacific Northwest is now unavailable to salmon because of dams that block upstream migration of adults and downstream migration of smolts (NRC 1996). Agriculture; forestry; and the development of human residential, commercial, and industrial activities have further changed the environments of salmon and the timing and availability of water in the basins. In addition, commercial, recreational, and traditional fishing for salmon in the Pacific Northwest is a far larger enterprise than it is, or ever was, in Maine.

The term "salmon" encompasses a much more complex biological reality in the Pacific Northwest than in Maine, where only one species occurs. In the Pacific Northwest, two major species occur today, Chinook and coho salmon. Both species are differentiated by run-timing (e.g., spring, summer, and fall Chinook salmon runs) as well as by adaptation to widely varying environments, ranging from small coastal streams to the mighty Columbia River. Pink salmon are rare in the region and never were abundant. Sockeye and chum salmon were once much more abundant than they are today. Only sockeye runs in the Columbia are significant now, exceeding 100,000 fish in some years (Fish Passage Center 2006).

The committee's report (NRC 1996) emphasized three viewpoints that were more novel in 1996 than they are today. The first was that local populations of salmon were organized in a *metapopulation* structure. That structure is one in which many locally adapted populations interact to maintain a cohesive whole through straying of salmon from their natal streams to other streams. As a result, a balance exists between gene exchange among local populations and local adaptation for each population. The committee concluded that the long-term survival of salmon required that urgent attention be paid to maintaining the genetic diversity that remained.

The second of the committee's viewpoints was a focus on human institutions. The committee concluded that human institutions had failed to protect salmon, largely because they do not operate in scales of time and space appropriate to the ecology of salmon. The committee recommended the development of an institutional structure that could function at a watershed scale, but with a coordinating function to ensure that larger perspectives also were taken into account.

The third relatively novel approach was a focus on ocean conditions and their influence on salmon productivity. The committee emphasized the importance of variations in ocean conditions that led to variations in the growth and survival of salmon during their time at sea. It concluded that although ocean conditions seemed to be unfavorable for salmon in the Pacific Northwest in the two decades before 1996 (when its report was published), those conditions would surely change and become more favorable, as they had been in the 1960s and early 1970s. The committee emphasized that when this occurred, the change should be viewed as an opportunity to make improvements in those aspects of salmons' environments that were amenable to human control, and not to mistakenly believe that somehow the problem had been solved.

The NC report also focused on other factors affecting salmon, such as the adverse effects of dams and hatcheries. It recommended that hatchery operations be altered to focus on helping the recovery of wild salmon populations rather than fisheries and to learn more about salmon. Hatchery management should not focus solely on the production of as many fish as possible. The report also urgently recommended studies of reach-specific survival of salmon in the Columbia basin and on finding ways to increase the survival of smolts migrating downriver past those dams. The report recommended that fishery managers focus on the escapements needed to protect salmon, rather than on maintaining fishery catches, and it recommended methods that recognized and prevented the adverse effects of mixed-population fisheries on less-productive populations.

The report concluded that despite the expenditure of large sums of money on salmon research, many important variables affecting salmon remained poorly known; it recommended the establishment of an independent science advisory board to recommend research priorities and assess restoration actions.

Finally, the report concluded that sustaining salmon would require a public valuation of salmon that would be sufficient to support the expensive, time-consuming, and sometimes disruptive actions needed to achieve this goal. As is the case in Maine, the decline of salmon in the Pacific Northwest has occurred over more than 100 years, and its arrest and reversal cannot be expected to happen quickly or inexpensively.

Salmon in the Klamath River

Although the Klamath River of northern California and southern Oregon is part of the Pacific Northwest, the NRC was asked to evaluate the scientific basis of documents concerning salmon in that river and two species of endangered suckers (family Catastomidae) in Upper Klamath Lake, and to recommend actions to sustain them (NRC 2004b). The report's conclusions about salmon are briefly summarized below.[1]

The Klamath Basin has been extensively modified in its upper regions by the U.S. Bureau of Reclamation's Klamath Project, begun in 1905, to support agriculture. Partly but not entirely in association with that project, six dams were constructed on the Klamath River downstream of Upper Klamath Lake. The numbers of salmon returning to the river, mainly coho and Chinook salmon, have declined substantially in the past 100 years. It is not clear whether, and if so how many, salmon ever ascended beyond Upper Klamath Lake. Klamath River coho salmon are listed as threatened under the Endangered Species Act. A hatchery that raises primarily Chinook salmon and steelhead is operated below Iron Gate Dam, the farthest downstream of all the dams.

The committee concluded that for restoration to be successful a broader focus than only on the Klamath Project was needed, and that the major tributaries of the Klamath River would have to be part of any successful plan to recover populations, especially coho salmon. Better coordination and organization throughout the basin of research and among many research institutions was needed. Removal or provision of fish passage at all small dams on tributaries should be accomplished within three years, and the removal of Iron Gate Dam on the Klamath River and Dwinnell Dam on one of its major tributaries (the Shasta River) should be seriously considered to improve passage and provide access to more habitat. Finally, hatchery operations should be changed as needed to benefit coho salmon, and such changes might include closure of hatcheries.

[1]Another NRC report on the Klamath basin was published in 2008 (NRC 2008). Its conclusions are consistent with those described here.

Salmon of western Alaska

The salmon of western Alaska's Arctic-Yukon-Kuskokwim (AYK) region and their habitats are different from those in Maine and in the Pacific Northwest, and the task of the committee examining them was different from the tasks of the other committees as well. Instead of being asked to advise on how to restore or sustain salmon in western Alaska, the committee was asked to advise the AYK Sustainable Salmon Initiative (SSI) on the development of a research and restoration plan for salmon. That report (NRC 2005) contained much information on salmon and on the region, but the report emphasized that before one could develop a restoration plan and program for AYK salmon, it was necessary to understand the causes of their declines, and even to know whether the declines in salmon run sizes that had been observed in the late 1990s and early 2000s reflected a long-term trend or instead a temporary fluctuation. The committee recommended that a framework or conceptual model of the ecosystem, including both its freshwater and marine components, be developed and that research topics be identified and prioritized based on that model or models. Three models were provided as examples, and the committee recommended research on such basic aspects of salmon biology as their numbers and distribution, and their genetic makeup as well as broader-scale understanding of the marine and freshwater processes affecting salmon. Factors should be partitioned between their freshwater and marine components that might be affecting salmon numbers. Finally, the committee concluded that better information was needed on the extent, nature, and distribution in space and time of human activities that affect salmon, and how much salmon are affected by those activities, which in the AYK region mainly consist of fishing. The AYK Sustainable Salmon Initiative took the NRC advice and produced in 2006 a research and restoration plan for the region to guide funding of projects (AYK SSI 2006).

The Lessons Learned

Studying salmon and how to sustain them in Maine and in the Pacific Northwest is discouraging at times, because of many adverse changes in their environments, hatchery stocking that has occurred forr more than 100 years, and the construction of many dams blocking the salmon passage. Both regions, but especially the Pacific Northwest, have undergone significant growth in human populations and in human activities, and as a result, enormous physical and societal infrastructures exist that make efforts to restore salmon, challenging at best. Because of the environmental changes and the physical and societal infrastructures, successful restoration will require large investments of money and human resources and significant institutional changes as well.

A striking aspect of salmon and their ecosystems in Alaska's vast AYK region, in contrast to Maine and the Pacific Northwest, is the small number of people who live there. The total population in 2000 was about 126,000 people, but nearly 83,000 of them lived in and around only one relatively small city, Fairbanks, located more than 1,500 km upriver from the sea. The only dam on the region's two major rivers, the Yukon and the Kuskokwim, is on the Yukon River at Whitehorse, Yukon Territory, more than 2,000 km upriver from the sea. Almost no roads exist except around settlements, and in and around Fairbanks. Travel between settlements in winter is mostly by air or snowmachine; in summer, it is by air or by boat.

As a result, the freshwater environments of AYK salmon are largely intact and undamaged, and the major biotic components of their ecosystems are present as well. Most of the original genetic diversity of the salmon populations seems to remain as well. In addition, most of the residents of the region have not moved there recently from elsewhere; they are people whose direct ancestors have lived with, and depended on, salmon for centuries, and salmon are extremely important to them (NRC 2005). Politically within Alaska, a great deal of support exists for protecting salmon.

Nevertheless, salmon in western Alaska do face problems. Some of the problems are amenable to human intervention on reasonably short time scales. For example, commercial fishing for pollock on the high seas intercepts salmon headed for AYK streams (Gisclair 2009, this volume; Stram and Ianelli 2009, this volume; Haflinger and Gruver 2009, this volume). Also, the release of billions of hatchery salmon smolts around the North Pacific (especially in Japan) has an unknown but potentially significant effect on AYK salmon through processes such as competition (e.g., Eggers 2009, this volume). Other problems, such as global climate change, will affect the AYK region and its salmon, although just how and in what direction those effects will be manifested is currently unknown, and no short-term interventions can affect climate change (e.g., Ruggerone 2009, this volume).

Nonetheless, the future for AYK salmon has the potential to be as bright as those of salmon anywhere on earth because the most difficult damage to reverse, habitat alteration, has been limited in the region so far (Policansky 2005). Although resisting development pressures and other human activities that degrade salmon habitats is a major challenge, and is required to sustain AYK salmon, the restoration of their habitats, a far greater challenge, is not required. It is far easier to prevent declines of salmon than to reverse them, especially when the declines are due to loss or degradation of habitat. Management of Alaskan AYK salmon fortunately can focus on conservation, in contrast to Maine and the Pacific Northwest, which have the more difficult task of restoration.

References

AYK SSI (Arctic-Yukon-Kuskokwim Sustainable Salmon Initiative). 2006. Salmon research and restoration plan. Bering Sea Fishermen's Association, Anchorage, Alaska.

Beland, K. F. 1984. Strategic plan for management of Atlantic salmon in the state of Maine. Atlantic Sea Run Salmon Commission, Bangor, Maine.

Cairns, D. K. 2001. An evaluation of the possible causes of decline in pre-fishery abundance of North American Atlantic salmon. Canadian Technical Report of Fisheries and Aquatic Sciences 2358. Department of Fisheries and Oceans, Science Branch. Charlottetown, Prince Edward Island.

Cooley, R.A. 1963. Politics and Conservation: The Decline of the Alaska Salmon. Harper & Row, New York.

Eggers, D. 2009. Historical biomass of pink, sockeye, and chum salmon in North Pacific Ocean. Pages 267–305 in C. C. Krueger and C. E. Zimmerman. Pacific salmon: ecology and management of western Alaska's populations. American Fisheries Society, Symposium 70, Bethesda, Maryland.

Fair, L. F. 2003. Critical elements of Kvichak River sockeye salmon management. Alaska Fishery Research Bulletin 10(2): 95–103.

Fish Passage Center. 2006. Adult returns for Columbia and Snake River dams. Available: http://www.fpc.org/adultsalmon/adultqueries/Adult_Table_Species_Graph.html (March 2007).

Gisclair, B. R. 2009. Salmon bycatch management in the Bering Sea walleye pollock fishery: threats and opportunities for western Alaska. Pages 799–816 in C. C. Krueger and C. E. Zimmerman. Pacific salmon: ecology and management of western Alaska's populations. American Fisheries Society, Symposium 70, Bethesda, Maryland.

Glavin, T. 2000. The last great sea: a voyage through the human and natural history of the North Pacific Ocean. Greystone Books, Vancouver, B.C.

Haflinger, K., and J. Gruver. 2009. Rolling hot spot closure areas in the Bering Sea walleye pollock fishery: estimated reduction of salmon bycatch during the 2006 season. Pages 817–826 in C. C. Krueger and C. E. Zimmerman. Pacific salmon: ecology and management of western Alaska's populations. American Fisheries Society, Symposium 70, Bethesda, Maryland.

Heard, W. R. 2005. Status of Alaska's salmon fisheries. Arctic Research of the United States 19:66–72.

Lynch, K. D., M. L. Jones, and W. W. Taylor, editors. 2002. Sustaining North American salmon: perspectives across regions and disciplines. American Fisheries Society, Bethesda, Maryland.

Maine Atlantic Salmon Task Force. 1997. Atlantic Salmon conservation plan for seven Maine rivers. March 1997. Maine Atlantic Salmon Commission, Augusta, Maine. Available: http://www.maine.gov/asc/ (March 2007).

NRC (National Research Council). 1995. Science and the Endangered Species Act. National Academy Press, Washington, D.C.

NRC (National Research Council). 1996. Upstream: salmon and society in the Pacific Northwest. National Academy Press, Washington, D.C.

NRC (National Research Council). 2002. Genetic status of Atlantic salmon in Maine. National Academy Press, Washington, D.C.

NRC (National Research Council). 2004a. Atlantic salmon in Maine. National Academies Press, Washington, D.C.

NRC (National Research Council). 2004b. Endangered and threatened fishes in the Klamath River basin. National Academies Press, Washington, D.C.

NRC (National Research Council). 2005. Developing a research and restoration plan for Arctic-Yukon-Kuskokwim (western Alaska) salmon. National Academies Press, Washington, D.C.

NRC (National Research Council). 2008. Hydrology, ecology, and fishes of the Klamath River basin. National Academies Press, Washington, D.C.

Policansky, D. 2005. Salmon and statehood. Pages 99–108 in T. Litwin, editor. The Harriman Expedition retraced: a century of change, 1899–2001. Rutgers University Press, New Brunswick, New Jersey.

Ruggerone, G. T., and J. L. Nielsen. 2009. A review of growth and survival of salmon at sea in response to competition and climate change. Pages 241–265 in C. C. Krueger and C. E. Zimmerman. Pacific salmon: ecology and management of western Alaska's populations. American Fisheries Society, Symposium 70, Bethesda, Maryland.

Stolte, L. 1981. The forgotten salmon of the Merrimack. U.S. Department of the Interior, Northeast Region, Washington, D.C.

Stouder, D. J., P. A. Bisson, and R. J. Naiman, editors. 1996. Pacific salmon and their ecosystems: status and future options. Chapman and Hall, New York.

Stram, D. L., and J. N. Ianelli. 2009. Eastern Bering Sea pollock trawl fisheries: variation in salmon bycatch over time and space. Pages 827–850 in C. C. Krueger and C. E. Zimmerman. Pacific salmon: ecology and management of western Alaska's populations. American Fisheries Society, Symposium 70, Bethesda, Maryland.

Williams, R. N. 2006. Return to the river: restoring salmon to the Columbia River. Elsevier Academic Press, Burlington, Massachusetts.

Wolfe, R. J., and C. U. Utermohle. 2000. Wild food consumption rate estimates for rural Alaskan populations. Technical Paper 261. Division of Subsistence, Alaska Department of Fish and Game, Juneau. Available: http://www.subsistence.adfg.state.ak.us/TechPap/tp261.pdf. (March 2007).

Section V

New Challenges, New Approaches

American Fisheries Society Symposium 70:1113–1114, 2009

Introduction to
New Challenges, New Approaches

CHARLES C. KRUEGER

Great Lakes Fishery Commission
2100 Commonwealth Boulevard, Suite 100, Ann Arbor, Michigan 48105, USA

CHRISTIAN E. ZIMMERMAN

U.S. Geological Survey Alaska Science Center
4210 University Drive, Anchorage, Alaska 99508, USA

This last section of the symposium volume represents a diverse set of perspectives representing a range of opinions from a broad group of authors (e.g., McPhee et al. 2009, this volume) to a single author's (e.g., Hanna 2009, this volume). Considerable effort was put forward during the last day of the symposium to interconnect participants in discussion groups focused on topics ranging from linkages between marine and freshwater systems (Moss et al. 2009, this volume) to management and research approaches (Cubitt et al. 2009, this volume; McPhee et al. 2009, this volume). Some papers in this section represent those discussions. This set of papers identifies a number of important issues that will need to continue to be addressed in future AYK management including the use of traditional ecological knowledge, potential effects of selective forces in fishing, climate variation, and the effects of ocean dynamics on salmon growth, survival, and movement.

Social issues were also discussed and are of equal importance to biophysical variables to consider in future salmon management of the AYK region. These issues include commercial versus recreational versus subsistence fishers; downstream versus upstream fishers; state versus federal management of subsistence fisheries; and data sharing among the scientific, management, and stakeholder communities. The conservation of salmon (*Oncorhynchus* spp.) is a shared value among all participants along with the belief that sustainable salmon yields will ensure sustainable rural communities in the region. This common value among all the participants provides a starting point for resolution of conflicts.

A call is made within several of the papers to consider a more holistic, ecosystem-based management of salmon stocks over their entire life history. All types of information should be connected or integrated over the salmon life cycle to be able to understand the influences of regional ocean and climate conditions. The first step to accomplishing this task is to provide opportunities to increase interaction between freshwater and ocean researchers and managers.

References

Cubitt, K. F., C. I. Goddard, and C. C. Krueger. 2009. Management strategies for sustainability of salmon in the Arctic-Yukon-Kuskokwim region. Pages 1217–1223 *in* C. C. Krueger and C. E. Zimmerman, editors. Pacific salmon: ecology and management of western Alaska's populations. American Fisheries Society, Symposium 70, Bethesda, Maryland.

Hanna, S. 2009. Sustaining salmon fisheries: the challenge of collaborative management. Pages 1199–1215 *in* C. C. Krueger and C. E. Zimmerman, editors. Pacific salmon: ecology and management of western Alaska's populations. American Fisheries Society, Symposium 70, Bethesda, Maryland.

McPhee, M. V., M. S. Zimmerman, T. D. Beacham, B. R. Beckman, J. B. Olsen, L. W. Seeb, and W. D. Templin. 2009. A hierarchical framework to identify influences on Pacific salmon population abundance and structure in the Arctic-Yukon-Kuskok-wim region. Pages 1177–1197 *in* C. C. Krueger and C. E. Zimmerman, editors. Pacific salmon: ecology and management of western Alaska's populations. American Fisheries Society, Symposium 70, Bethesda, Maryland.

Moss, J. H., N. Hillgruber, C. Lean, J. Mackenzie-Grieve, K. Mull, K. W. Myers, and T. C. Stark. 2009. Conservation of western Alaskan salmon stocks by identifying critical linkages between marine and freshwater life stages and long-term monitoring. Pages 1115–1125 *in* C. C. Krueger and C. E. Zimmerman, editors. Pacific salmon: ecology and management of western Alaska's populations. American Fisheries Society, Symposium 70, Bethesda, Maryland.

American Fisheries Society Symposium 70:1115–1125, 2009
© 2009 by the American Fisheries Society

Conservation of Western Alaskan Salmon Stocks by Identifying Critical Linkages between Marine and Freshwater Life Stages and Long-term Monitoring

JAMAL H. MOSS[*]

Auke Bay Laboratories, Alaska Fisheries Science Center
National Oceanic and Atmospheric Administration
17109 Point Lena Loop Road, Juneau, Alaska 99801, USA

NICOLA HILLGRUBER

University of Alaska Fairbanks, School of Fisheries and Oceans Sciences
17101 Point Lena Loop Road, Juneau, Alaska 99801, USA

CHARLES LEAN

Norton Sound Economic Development Corporation
P.O. Box 358, Nome, Alaska 99762, USA

JODY L. MACKENZIE-GRIEVE

Fisheries and Oceans Canada
100-419 Range Road, Whitehorse, Yukon Territory Y1A 3V1, Canada

KRISTIN E. MULL

Yukon River Drainage Fisheries Association
P.O. Box 750463, Fairbanks, Alaska 99775, USA

KATHERINE W. MYERS

University of Washington, School of Aquatic and Fisheries Sciences
P.O. Box 355020, Seattle, Washington 98195, USA

THOMAS C. STARK

Bering Sea Fishermen's Association
P.O. Box 80543, Fairbanks, Alaska 99708, USA

[*]Corresponding author: jamal.moss@noaa.gov

Abstract.—The interconnectedness of freshwater, estuarine, and marine domains, and the influence these dynamic habitats have on the health and proliferation of Arctic, Yukon, and Kuskokwim (AYK) region Pacific salmon *Oncorhynchus* spp. stocks are reviewed in this paper. Specific salmon life history and developmental stages reviewed are early freshwater residence, timing of ocean entry, early ocean residence (immature and maturing ocean stages), and mature stages. A comprehensive life-history approach that addresses hypotheses about the effects of climate forcing on matches and mismatches between salmon production, biological conditions, and the physical environment can be used to link freshwater and marine domains. We recommend that a long-term monitoring and ecosystem research program with a strong emphasis on teaching ecology, environmental biology, and salmon conservation be developed for the AYK region. Information provided by such a program would allow for an expanded understanding of the effect of climate as well as anthropogenic effects on western Alaskan salmon stocks.

Introduction

Pacific salmon *Oncorhynchus* spp. returns to the Arctic (Norton Sound), Yukon River, and Kuskokwim River (AYK) drainages increased dramatically in the late 1970s, then decreased to historic lows in the late 1990s, but have increased in recent years (e.g., Bue et al. 2009, this volume). The underlying causes for these interannual variations in survival are unknown, but changing freshwater environments, estuarine habitats, and ocean conditions are believed to be contributing factors. Recent investigations have shown that environmental conditions encountered by salmon during the first few months of life in the ocean are among the most critical (Beamish and Mahnkin 2001; Moss et al. 2005; Farley et al. 2007 ; Hillgruber and Zimmerman 2009, this volume). Commercial fishing contributes to interannual fluctuations in salmon returns despite large marine catches generally coinciding with increased salmon returns to the AYK region (Myers and Rogers 1988). Understanding how salmon use their habitat and the timing of their transition between freshwater, estuarine, and marine habitats is an important component to understanding the ecology of AYK salmon.

Recent efforts have been made to link freshwater and marine domains through a comprehensive life history approach that addresses hypotheses about the effects of climate forcing on the matches and mismatches between salmon migration and environmental conditions (AYK SSI 2006). Comprehensive modeling efforts have incorporated anthropogenic effects and fish-habitat relationships in conservation planning (Scheuerell et al. 2006), and the impacts of climate change, harvest policies, hatchery policies, and freshwater habitat capacity changes on salmon at the North Pacific scale (Mantua et al. 2007). However, the success of these and future efforts will be dependent on the amount and quality of available data, and a comprehensive and functional understanding of how salmon interact with their environment.

The objectives of this paper are to first explore the influence of freshwater, estuarine, and marine domains on AYK salmon stocks, and the influence these dynamic habitats have on salmon abundance, productivity, and health. The second objective is to make recommendations for developing a long-term monitoring program for studying western Alaskan salmon stocks. Existing long-term monitoring projects for Pacific salmon have demonstrated great success. Chum salmon *O. keta* scale growth patterns have been used to reconstruct marine growth to contrast size with oceanic and climatic conditions (Helle and Hoffman 1995). This program has been in operation for decades and strong linkages between climate, production, and salmon size have been identified. The Alaska Salmon Program (2008) has monitored Bristol Bay sockeye populations since 1946 (http://www.fish.washington.edu/research/alaska/), qualifying these populations as the most studied in Alaska.

Early Freshwater Residence

Limiting factors during the early life history of salmon such as fry emergence, smolt out-migration timing, predation, precipitation, temperature, and the quality of freshwater habitat can influence adult abundance and returns. Fry emergence and subsequent ocean entry timing can influence juvenile growth and ultimately marine survival of salmon, as adult salmon spawn at a time of year, resulting in the emergence of fry on a date that maximizes their potential for growth and survival (Quinn 2005). The eggs of all Pacific salmon species develop more rapidly when water temperature is elevated (Murray and McPhail 1988), and cooler temperatures will prolong emergence. However, other limiting factors such as decreased concentrations of dissolved oxygen can result in delayed hatching (Shumway et al. 1964). The movements of stream-rearing fry such as Chinook *O. tshawytscha*, coho *O. kisutch*, and sockeye *O. nerka* (stream and lake types) salmon are diverse, as these species may disperse to lakes downstream or upstream to small channel tributaries to rear before smolting (Quinn 2005). Fry and smolt out-migration timing has evolved in such a way to maximize growth and survival opportunities in both freshwater and marine environments. Pacific salmon migrate to sea earlier when spring conditions are mild (Burgner 1962; Roper and Scarnecchia 1999), and in-stream mortality during this life phase includes dis-

ease, stress from high water temperature, and predation. Salmon smolts are likely to reach the ocean earlier during years when river ice melts faster.

Climate change will likely alter patterns in egg deposition, alevin emergence, and smolt out-migration timing. Stream flow and temperature regimes have important effects on egg-to-fry survival and species-specific habitat use during the freshwater phase of the salmon life cycle (Everest and Chapman 1972; Murray and McPhail 1988; Dolloff and Reeves 1990). Altered temperature and flow regimes due to climatic change may have severe consequences for salmon egg development. Higher temperatures will increase the incidence of parasites and disease, such as *Ichthyophoniasis* in Chinook salmon (Kocan et al. 2004). Understanding the relationships between the causes of mortality and environmental conditions will be imperative.

Early Ocean Residence

The timing of ocean entry by juvenile salmon may determine the quality and quantity of habitat they encounter that will support growth and survival. Seasonal environmental variability such as estuary shape, river plume volume, flow direction, water clarity, salinity, and temperature may enhance or limit production (Hillgruber and Zimmerman 2009). Biological factors include prey density, composition of prey fields, and the density and spatial distribution of predators. Consequently, the timing of ocean entry will directly impact salmon smolt condition and growth, and may ultimately affect the survival of juvenile salmon during their first year at sea.

Chum salmon were the most abundant salmon smolt species in Kuskokwim Bay during June, indicating that fish could enter the bay as early as May (Hillgruber and Zimmerman 2009, this volume; Hillgruber et al. 2007). The timing of out-migration of

Kuskokwim chum salmon is similar to Yukon chum salmon stocks, for which peak outmigration occurs during late-June (Martin et al. 1986). Peak chum salmon smolt catches in Norton Sound occur during the middle of June, with a second peak occurring in mid-July (Nemeth et al. 2006). Coho smolts were not found during the course of this investigation, suggesting that they have an even earlier departure from the river and bay. Sea surface temperature (SST) experienced by different cohorts of outmigrating salmon in Western Alaska can vary dramatically with season; for example, SST can be 6–7°C in May, but may increase to >16°C within a one month residency in western Alaska estuaries.

For ectothermic animals such as fish, water temperature is one of the most pervasive environmental factors affecting metabolic rates and biochemical reactions. Within the range of tolerable temperatures, increases may lead to increased growth rates if energetic demands can be met with increased food supply. For example, results from laboratory experiments showed that maximum growth potential for juvenile sockeye salmon at 15°C could only be achieved with adequate food availability (Brett 1995). In addition to direct physiological affects, temperature may also have indirect effects. Salmon undergoing the smoltification process can experience additional stress due to elevated thermal experience, leading to various responses such as shifts in emigration timing and subsequently reduced marine survival, premature smolting, or lethality (Richter and Kolmes 2005).

Chum salmon juveniles have been shown to experience high size-selective mortality rates during their early marine life (Parker 1962; Bax 1983; Wertheimer and Thrower 2007). Juvenile salmon, particularly pink *O. gorbuscha* and chum salmon that enter the marine environment at comparatively smaller sizes, must grow quickly to avoid high mortality. Thus, estuarine and nearshore conditions favorable to rapid growth are likely to increase survival by effectively reducing the period during which the fish experience high predation pressure. Out-migration timing relative to the development of the zooplankton bloom and spatial distribution influences growth and survival. A better understanding of dietary needs, distributional patterns, and biological factors during the juvenile estuarine and nearshore marine residence is necessary to assess and compare growth and the probability of survival for different outmigrating cohorts of juvenile salmon inhabiting western Alaska estuaries (Farley et al. 2009, this volume).

Juvenile salmon not only undergo the physiologically stressful process of smoltification during out-migration, but they also need to learn how to capture a different suite of prey and avoid estuarine predators. In Kuskokwim Bay, chum salmon condition declined with fish size and season, indicating that juveniles were primarily allocating energy to maintenance and growth (Hillgruber, personal observation). However, juvenile salmon need to capture sufficient prey resources to prevent starvation and survive winter. Thus, the metabolism of the juvenile salmon will eventually shift from allocating the majority of energy from growth to energy storage.

Immature and Maturing Ocean Stages

There is currently no clear picture of where, when, and how immature and maturing AYK salmon die during the ocean phase of their life. The premise is that processes affecting AYK salmon in freshwater, estuarine, and marine ecosystems are interrelated; and anthropogenic impacts (e.g., fishing) contribute additional variability to ocean survival. In turn, variation in survival at immature and maturing ocean stages affects population structure of returning adult salmon to the AYK region. Annual variation in the timing of smolt outmigrations from freshwater might play a significant role in ocean distribution and migration routes of immature and maturing salmon. For example, information from high seas tagging experiments suggests that maturing Bristol Bay sockeye salmon from stocks with late-migrating smolts are more likely to be distributed in the Gulf of Alaska than stocks with early migrating smolts (Rogers 1986). If the timing of smolt outmigrations affects the ocean distribution of AYK salmon populations, then populations with early, middle, and late timing from the same watershed might experience vastly different environmental conditions and fishing mortality at immature and maturing stages.

A general understanding exists of ocean distribution and migration patterns of salmon, although stock-specific patterns may overlap broadly, particularly with those of other stocks originating from the same geographic region (Myers et al. 2007). Myers et al. (2009, this volume) reviewed recovery data from high seas tagging experiments, which provided limited information on where and when immature and maturing AYK salmon are distributed in the ocean. With some exceptions (e.g., early maturing males or jacks), immature and maturing AYK salmon occupy epipelagic habitats over deep ocean basins in spring and summer.

While productivity in deep-basin habitats is lower than that of shelf habitats, summer temperatures are cool (generally less than 15°C), which reduces bioenergetic demands for food. By moving to deep-basin habitats, immature and maturing AYK salmon can avoid high rates of predation, competition, and cannibalism that might occur in shelf habitats. Their seasonal migration routes, however, can include waters over the continental shelf (e.g., Aleutian Island passes), and older, larger AYK salmon may distribute in productive shelf habitats in the Bering Sea, Aleutian Islands, and Gulf of Alaska to feed on abundant prey resources.

Seasonal migrations of immature and maturing salmon in the ocean occur across broad fronts (Myers et al. 2009). Surface water temperatures cool, food supplies diminish in late fall, and immature AYK salmon move southward and eastward, reaching their southernmost extent in spring and early summer (Myers et al. 2009). This pattern is then reversed and distribution shifts northward and westward (Myers et al. 2009). The Subarctic Front, a narrow and meandering area of convergence, with relatively strong vertical mixing and high biological productivity, essentially marks the southern limit of AYK salmon distribution in the North Pacific Ocean during spring or early summer. Immature sockeye and chum salmon are often distributed well to the south of maturing fish during spring, and limited data from tagging indicates that maturing fish may be aggregated by size, age-group, or stock while they are still well offshore. Winter is likely the most critical survival period for immature and maturing salmon at sea, but there is little information on winter distribution of AYK salmon other than data collected by groundfish fishery observers in the eastern Bering Sea.

Climate-driven changes in open-ocean feeding areas and along the migratory routes of Asian and North American salmon in winter can result in predictable interannual changes in stock-specific distribution, migration patterns, and other biological characteristics (Myers et al. 2007). These shifts in ocean distribution can affect interception rates of immature and maturing salmon in marine fisheries, as well as timing of adult returns to their natal streams. At monthly time scales, Myers et al. (2009) could not distinguish differences between regional stocks of AYK salmon in the timing of their movements. The carrying capacity of immature and maturing salmon in the open ocean might be regulated primarily by decadal-scale changes in productivity. Decadal-scale cyclic fluctuations in abundance of salmon returning to different coastal regions are related to large-scale oceanographic and meteorological events (Francis and Hare 1994; Mantua et al. 1999). Changes in offshore distribution and migration patterns of AYK salmon after the well-established North Pacific regime shift of 1976–1977, however, are not known because there were few high seas salmon surveys after this period.

While immature and maturing salmon are widely dispersed in the open ocean (Quinn 2005), dense aggregations of immature and maturing salmon can occur in areas of sharp temperature gradient, strong vertical mixing, and high biological productivity. As in coastal areas, local changes in feeding conditions and distribution of prey have a strong effect on spatial and temporal variations in salmon distribution. Competition for food is most likely to occur between fish of the same species, stock, age, and maturity group, and is exhibited as density-dependent changes in ocean growth and survival (Ruggerone and Nielsen 2009, this volume). Given unlimited food resources, high growth rates in AYK salmon are most likely associated with relatively high (nonlethal) water temperatures in summer. A climate-induced change in distribution and abundance of their prey is likely a major cause of shifts in ocean distribution and migration routes of immature and maturing salmon.

Sea temperature is an important physical factor affecting growth, but bioenergetics models indicate that prey consumption is more important to ocean growth of immature and maturing salmon than temperature (Davis et al. 1998). Density-dependent prey limitation probably takes place in winter, when lipid stores are critical to salmon survival. Food-habit and bioenergetic studies provide evidence of feeding competition and density-dependent growth of immature and maturing salmon in summer. Behavior studies using data storage tags have provided significant new information on behavior of salmon with respect to ambient sea temperatures and depth (Walker et al. 2000, 2007). Summer data from tagged fish show considerable diurnal and shorter-term variation in ambient temperatures and swimming depth, indicating that nonlethal SSTs do not regulate the behavior of salmon on the high seas.

The time (start-of-return date) when maturing salmon begin to leave the open ocean might be a population-specific trait that is not affected by location at sea (Hodgson et al. 2006). On the other hand, empirical data suggest that sea temperatures in early spring trigger return migrations and determine migration rates, maturation schedules, and end-of-return dates when salmon enter their natal rivers (Myers et al. 2007).

Mature Stage

Although research continues on the high seas distribution and biology of AYK salmon (Myers et al. 2009), information on individual salmon movements of maturing adult salmon in the ocean immediately prior to their entry into freshwater is limited. The congregating of salmon at river mouths and deltas prior to initiating upstream migration is well documented, and it is at this time that maturing salmon undergo physiological changes in order to readjust to freshwater conditions. It is also unclear how conditions within this transitional environment affect the reproductive success of salmon.

Many stock-specific characteristics of Yukon River salmon are the result of natural selection influenced by local environmental conditions (e.g., thermal regime, discharge) in order to optimize fry emergence timing and maximize survival. Physiological changes during this transitional period, and how these changes lead to the observed characteristics and patterns is lacking in the AYK region. Studies from other regions suggest that timing of freshwater entry can be variable, and may depend on variables such as temperature and discharge (Quinn 2005). Ice coverage at the mouth of the Yukon River during spring could be a factor causing later than normal freshwater entry. However, spawning date may be relatively fixed and could shift in response to local environmental conditions (e.g., stream temperature). For example, the proportion of Chinook salmon destined for the upper Yukon River basin is higher early in the run, and, conversely, the proportion of Chinook salmon destined for lower river tributaries is higher later in the run (Eiler et al. 2004).

Yukon and Kuskokwim River chum salmon typically spawn at age-4, with older and larger individuals entering the river before younger, smaller fish (Molyneaux and DuBois 1998). The smaller Yukon River summer chum salmon, which are found in the lower reaches of the river, spawn in run-off streams, while larger fall chum salmon, which migrate to the upper river (and tributaries), spawn in groundwater or spring discharges (Molyneaux and DuBois 1998). Quinn (2005); this suggests several explanations for these observed patterns, which assume size-dependent tradeoffs, based on conditions at sea or on the spawning grounds. Spawning Yukon River Chinook salmon are usually 6 years of age (range: 3–8 years of age) when they initiate upstream migration, and recent findings suggest that the proportion of older (JTC 2006a), larger (Hyer and Schleusner 2005) fish is decreasing over time. In recent years, fishermen and biologists alike have documented an apparent decrease in the body size of Chinook salmon moving up the Yukon River (JTC 2006b; Evenson et al. 2009, this volume). Proposed causes for this apparent decrease in size include the potential for the influence of both environmental factors and fishery-induced selective pressures (JTC 2006b; Hard et al. 2009, this volume), and work continues to further assess the phenomenon. In addition to concern surrounding the economic implications of smaller salmon, reductions in salmon size could also lead to

reduced redd digging ability, fecundity, and genetic variability.

Mortality during upriver migration in the Yukon River system appears to be a result of fishing and predation rather than "prespawning" mortality (Quinn 2005). As the climate continues to warm, the effects of temperature on salmon energetics and survival could play an increasing role in prespawning mortality. For example, Fraser River salmon prespawning mortality was related to increased disease proliferation (Gilhousen 1990), and has been associated with increasing metabolic demands. Heard (1991) related prespawning mortality in pink salmon to intense crowding, high temperatures, and insufficient dissolved oxygen levels.

A high incidence of *Ichthyophonus* infection in Yukon River Chinook salmon has caused concern. Analyses completed by Kocan et al. (2004) suggested that the development, transmission, and pathogenicity of the *Ichthyophonus* organism within the host appeared to be positively correlated with water temperature, with warmer temperatures leading to higher mortality for Chinook infected with this parasite. Under generally warmer conditions, it is likely that increased prevalence of the organism and increased prespawning mortality of infected fish will result in a decrease in spawning success.

Warmer water temperatures in the Yukon River could also increase the incidence of prespawning mortality as a result of higher metabolic costs. Salmon store large amounts of fat to sustain them throughout the up-river migration to support reproductive costs (Quinn 2005), and the level of fat stored is positively related to the distance and elevation salmon must migrate to their spawning grounds (Quinn 2005). However, increased metabolic costs associated with migration in warmer conditions may lead to a mismatch between stored energy and energetic demands associated with migration and spawning. Linley (1993) and Kinnison et al. (2001)

reported that less energy was allocated to gonad development in females that undergo arduous migrations; however, the relationship
between energy allocation to gonad development, somatic tissues, and migration to timing is complicated under a climate warming
scenario.

Long-term Monitoring and Ecosystem Research Program

Kruse (1998) provided a timely review
of anomalous ocean conditions and ecosystem changes that may have been linked to
AYK salmon run failures in the late 1990s.
He concluded that the mechanisms causing the decline are not understood, and that
there is an urgent need for investigations of
plankton dynamics and marine life histories
of salmon in the North Pacific and Bering
Sea. The Bering Sea Task Force (Ulmer et al.
1999), formed in response to the salmon disaster, reviewed available scientific information and recommended that the North Pacific
Research Board (NPRB) be formed in order
to develop a comprehensive research plan for
improving our understanding of the Bering
Sea ecosystem. Specific goals were to improve forecasting, predict the marine ecosystem response to climate change, and facilitate
the management and protection of healthy,
sustainable fish and wildlife populations.
While salmon are not currently a major focus
of NPRB supported research, it is believed
that AYK SSI (Sustainable Salmon Initiative) can fill this gap and provide a significant
contribution over the next few years. In addition, the strong conceptual foundation of the
AYK Salmon Research and Restoration Plan
(AYK SSI 2006), which focuses on interactions between freshwater, estuarine, and marine processes and human activities that affect salmon survival, will lead to a synthesis
of knowledge that could not be obtained by a
singular focus on the Bering Sea ecosystem.

A long-term monitoring and ecosystem
research program with a strong emphasis on
outreach, teaching ecology, environmental
biology, and salmon conservation would be
an invaluable resource for the AYK region.
Such a program would rely heavily on a network of field research stations strategically
located on a river system where students,
faculty, agency biologists, and other user
groups could engage in short-term research
projects while contributing to the building
of a long-term dataset. This program should
focus on subsistence and commercially captured salmon stocks and be headquartered
at a university to facilitate collaborative research with faculty, and to develop a legacy
of graduate student projects and participation. Base funds for field research station
maintenance, equipment, and long-term data
collection should be administered through
the university. Governmental, residential,
and tribal entities would coordinate projects
and educational programs through the institute, and have access to living quarters and
laboratories. Ocean monitoring and ecosystem based research would be an integral part
of this program, and should be coordinated
and implemented through existing marine research and international treaty organizations
(e.g., NPRB, North Pacific Anadromous Fish
Commission, and North Pacific Marine Science Organization-PICES).

The proposed long-term monitoring program should focus on understanding the early
life history stages, specifically the early developmental period prior to leaving freshwater habitats, the estuarine environment, and
early marine residence. Therefore, a landbased operation will require the capability
to sample the lower reaches of big systems
such as the Yukon and Kuskokwim Rivers,
adjacent estuaries, and the nearshore marine
environment. Studies designed to identify
stock-specific sea emigration timing would
allow investigators to compare the residency
of juvenile salmon with the timing of events

in the physical environment, a fundamental link to understanding the differences in survival between stocks, their susceptibility to predation, and the importance of forage species.

Other research objectives would be to determine physical and biological factors influencing salmon production such as identifying carrying capacity of spawning and rearing habitats, understanding the importance of estuarine residence timing, and riparian ecology. The program should address a wide range of issues in ecology, such as the response of aquatic and marine environments to climate change, and the incorporation of local and traditional knowledge in western science. The infrastructure created by the field research stations will allow for sampling programs that are not directly related to fisheries management, such as long-term data sets built on climate change and catch statistics; while allowing for observation of fishery policy through population response to changes in fishing pressure and conservation measures in a cohesive manner. An endowment would be needed to ensure an indefinite continuation of the program.

Acknowledgments

We thank the Arctic Yukon and Kuskokwim Sustainable Salmon Initiative and three anonymous reviewers.

References

Alaska Salmon Program. Available: 2008. http://www.fish.washington.edu/research/alaska/ (March 2008).

AYK SSI (Arctic-Yukon-Kuskokwim Sustainable Salmon Initiative). 2006. Arctic-Yukon-Kuskokwim salmon research and restoration plan. Bering Sea Fishermen's Association, Anchorage, Alaska.

Bax, N. J. 1983. Early marine mortality of marked juvenile chum salmon (*Oncorhynchus keta*) released in the Hood Canal, Puget Sound, Washington, in 1980. Canadian Journal of Fisheries and Aquatic Sciences 40:426–435.

Beamish, R. J., and C. Mahnken. 2001. A critical size and period hypothesis to explain natural regulation of salmon abundance and the linkage to climate and climate change. Progress in Oceanography 49:423–437.

Brett, J. R. 1995. Energetics. Pages 1–68 *in* C. Groot, L. Margolis, and W. C. Clarke, editors. Physiological ecology of Pacific salmon. UBC Press, Vancouver, B.C.

Bue, F. J., B. M. Borba, R. Cannon, and C. C. Krueger. 2009. Yukon River fall chum salmon fisheries: management, harvest, and stock abundance. Pages 703–742 *in* C. C. Krueger and C. E. Zimmerman, editors. Pacific salmon: ecology and management of western Alaska's populations. American Fisheries Society, Symposium 70, Bethesda, Maryland.

Burgner, R. L. 1962. Studies of red salmon smolts from the Wood River lakes, Alaska. Pages 247–314 *in* T. S. Y. Koo editor. Studies of Alaska red salmon. University of Washington Press, Seattle.

Davis, N. D., K. W. Myers, and Y. Ishida. 1998. Caloric value of high-seas salmon prey organisms and simulated salmon ocean growth and prey consumption. North Pacific Anadromous Fish Commission Bulletin 1:99–109.

Dolloff, C. A., and G. H. Reeves. 1990. Microhabitat partitioning among stream-dwelling juvenile coho salmon, *Oncorhynchus kisutch*, and Dolly Varden, *Salvelinus malma*. Canadian Journal of Fisheries and Aquatic Sciences 47:2297–2306.

Eiler, J. H., T. R. Spencer, J. J. Pella, M. M. Masuda, and R. R. Holder. 2004. Distribution and movement patterns of Chinook salmon returning to the Yukon River basin in 2000–2002. U.S. NOAA Technical Memorandum NMFS-AFSC-148.

Evenson, D. F., S. J. Hayes, G. Sandone, and D. J. Bergstrom. 2009. Yukon River Chinook salmon: stock status, harvest, and management. Pages 675–701 *in* C. C. Krueger and C. E. Zimmerman, editors. Pacific salmon: ecology and management of western Alaska's populations. American Fisheries Society, Symposium 70, Bethesda, Maryland.

Everest, F. H., and D. W. Chapman. 1972. Habitat selection and spatial interaction by juvenile Chinook salmon and steelhead trout in two Idaho streams. Journal of the Fisheries Research Board of Canada 29:91–100.

Farley, E. V., Jr., J. M. Murphy, M. D. Adkison, L. B. Eisner, J. H. Helle, J. H. Moss, and J. L. Nielsen. 2007. Early marine growth in relation to marine stage survival rate for Alaska sockeye salmon (*Oncorhynchus nerka*). Fishery Bulletin 105(1):121–130.

Francis, R. C., and S. R. Hare. 1994. Decadal-scale regime shifts in the large marine ecosystems of the Northeast Pacific: a case for historical science. Fisheries Oceanography 3:279–291.

Gilhousen, P. 1990. Prespawning mortalities of sockeye salmon in the Fraser River system and possible causes. International Pacific Salmon Fisheries Commission Bulletin 26.

Hard, J. J., W. Eldridge, and K. Naish. 2009. Genetic consequences of size-selective fishing: implications for viability of Chinook salmon in the Arctic-Yukon-Kuskokwim region of Alaska. Pages 759–780 in C. C. Krueger and C. E. Zimmerman, editors. Pacific salmon: ecology and management of western Alaska's populations. American Fisheries Society, Symposium 70, Bethesda, Maryland.

Heard, W. R. 1991. Life history of pink salmon (*Oncorhynchus gorbuscha*). Pages 119–230 in C. Groot and L. Margolis, editors. Pacific salmon: life histories. UBC Press, Vancouver, B.C.

Helle, J. H. and M. S. Hoffman. 1995. Size decline and older age at maturity of two chum salmon (*Oncorhynchus keta*) stocks in western North America. *In* R. J. Beamish, editor. Climate change and northern fish populations. Canadian Special Publication of the Journal of Fisheries and Aquatic Sciences 121:245–260.

Hillgruber, N., C. E. Zimmerman. 2009. Estuarine ecology of juvenile salmon in western Alaska: a review. Pages 183–199 in C. C. Krueger and C. E. Zimmerman, editors. Pacific salmon: ecology and management of western Alaska's populations. American Fisheries Society, Symposium 70, Bethesda, Maryland.

Hillgruber, N., C. E. Zimmerman, S. E. Burril, and L. J. Haldorson. 2007. Early marine ecology of chum salmon (*Oncorhynchus keta*) in Kuskokwim Bay. North Pacific Research Board Final Report 327.

Hodgson, S., T. P. Quinn, R. Hilborn, R. C. Francis, and D. E. Rogers. 2006. Marine and freshwater climatic factors affecting interannual variation in the timing of return migration to freshwater of sockeye salmon (*Oncorhynchus nerka*). Fisheries Oceanography 15:1–24.

Hyer, K. E., and C. J. Schleusner. 2005. Chinook salmon age, sex and length analysis from selected escapement projects on the Yukon River. U.S. Fish and Wildlife Service, Alaska Fisheries Technical Report 87, Anchorage, AK.

Joint Technical Committee of the Yukon River U.S./ Canada Panel (JTC). 2006a. Yukon River salmon 2005 season summary and 2006 season outlook. Alaska Department of Fish and Game, Division of Commercial Fisheries, Regional Information Report No. 3A06–03, Anchorage, AK.

Joint Technical Committee of the Yukon River U.S./ Canada Panel (JTC). 2006b. Potential causes of size trends in Yukon River Chinook salmon populations. Alaska Department of Fish and Game, Division of Commercial Fisheries, Regional Information Report No. 3A-06–07, Anchorage.

Kinnison, M. T., T. J. Unwin, A. P. Hendry, and T. P. Quinn. 2001. Migratory costs and the evolution of egg size and number in introduced and indigenous salmon populations. Evolution 55:1656–1667.

Kocan, R., P. Hershberger, and J. Winton. 2004. Ichthyophoniasis: an emerging disease of Chinook salmon in the Yukon River. Journal of Aquatic Animal Health 16:58–72.

Kruse, G. H. 1998. Salmon run failures in 1997–1998: a link to anomalous ocean conditions? Alaska Fishery Research Bulletin 5:55–63.

Linley, T. J. 1993. Patterns of life history variation among sockeye salmon (*Oncorhynchus nerka*) in the Fraser River, British Columbia. Doctoral dissertation. University of Washington, Seattle.

Mantua, N. J., N. G. Taylor, G. T. Ruggerone, K. W. Myers, D. Preikshot, X. Augerot, N. D. Davis, B. Dorner, R. Hilborn, R. M. Peterman, P. Rand, D. Schindler, J. Stanford, R. V. Walker, and C. J. Walters. 2007. The salmon MALBEC project: a North Pacific-scale study to support salmon conservation planning. (NPAFC Doc. 1060) School of Aquatic and Fishery Sciences, University of Washington, Seattle. Available: http://www.npafc.org (March 2007).

Mantua, N. J., S. R. Hare, Y. Zhang, J. M. Wallace, and R. C. Francis. 1999. A Pacific interdecadal climate oscillation with impacts on salmon production. Bulletin of the American Meteorological Society 78:1069–1079.

Martin, D. J., D. R. Glass, C. J. Whitmus, C. A. Simenstad, D. A. Milward, E. C. Volk, M. L. Stevenson, P. Nunes, M. Savoie, and R. A. Grotenfendt. 1986. Distribution, seasonal abundance, and feeding dependencies of juvenile salmon and non-salmon fishes in the Yukon River Delta. NOAA OCSEAP Final Report, 55(1998):381–770.

Molyneaux, D. B., and L. DuBois. 1998. Salmon age, sex and length catalog for the Kuskokwim area, 1996–1997 progress report. Alaska Department of Fish and Game, Regional Information Report 3A-98–15, Anchorage.

Moss, J. H., D. A. Beauchamp, A. D. Cross, K. W. Myers, E. V. Farley, Jr., J. M. Murphy, and J. H. Helle. 2005. Higher marine survival associated with faster growth for pink salmon (*Oncorhynchus gorbuscha*). Transactions of the American Fisheries Society 134:1313–1322.

Murray, C. B., and J. D. McPhail. 1988. Effect of temperature on the development of five species of Pacific salmon (*Oncorhynchus*) embryos and alevins. Canadian Journal of Zoology 66:266–273.

Myers. K. W., N. Klovatch, O. F. Grisenko, S. Urawa, and T. C. Royer. 2007. Stock specific distributions of Asian and North American salmon in the open ocean, interannual changes, and oceanographic conditions. North Pacific Anadromous Fish Commission Bulletin 4:159–177.

Myers, K. W., and D. E. Rogers. 1988. Stock origins of Chinook salmon in incidental catches by groundfish fisheries in the eastern Bering Sea. North American Journal of Fisheries Management 8:162–171.

Myers, K. W., R. V. Walker, N. D. Davis, J. L. Armstrong, and M. Kaeriyama. 2009. High seas distribution, biology, and ecology of Arctic-Yukon-Kuskokwim salmon: direct information from high seas tagging experiments, 1954–2006. Pages 201–239 in C. C. Krueger and C. E. Zimmerman, editors. Pacific salmon: ecology and management of western Alaska's populations. American Fisheries Society, Symposium 70, Bethesda, Maryland.

Nemeth, M., B. Williams, B. Haley, and S. Kinneen. 2006. An ecological comparison of juvenile chum salmon from two watersheds in Norton Sound, Alaska: migration, diet estuarine habitat, and fish community assemblage. Final Report for 2003 and 2004. LGL Alaska Research Associates, Inc. and the Norton Sound Econoic Development Corporation.

Parker, R. R. 1962. Estimation ocean mortality rates for Pacific salmon (Oncorhynchus). Journal of the Fisheries Research Board of Canada 19:561–589.

Quinn, T. P. 2005. The behavior and ecology of Pacific salmon and trout. University of Washington Press, Seattle.

Richter, A., and S. A. Kolmes. 2005. Maximum temperature limits for Chinook, coho, and chum salmon, and steelhead trout in the Pacific Northwest. Reviews in Fisheries Science 13:23–49.

Rogers, D. E. 1986. Pacific salmon. Pages 461–476 in D. W. Hood and S. T. Zimmerman, editors. The Gulf of Alaska, physical environment and biological resources. U.S. Department of Commerce Ocean Assessments Division, National Oceanic and Atmospheric Administration, Washington D.C.

Roper, B. B., and D. L. Scarnecchia. 1999. Emigration

of age-0 Chinook salmon (Oncorhynchus tshawytscha) smolts from the upper South Umpqua River basin, Oregon, U.S.A. Canadian Journal of Fisheries and Aquatic Sciences 56:939–946.

Ruggerone, G., and J. Nielsen. 2009. A review of growth and survival of salmon at sea in response to competition and climate change. Pages 241–265 in C. C. Krueger and C. E. Zimmerman, editors. Pacific salmon: ecology and management of western Alaska's populations. American Fisheries Society, Symposium 70, Bethesda, Maryland.

Scheuerell, M. D., R. Hilborn, M. H. Ruckelshaus, K. K. Bartz, K. M. Langueux, A. D. Haas, and K. Rawson. 2006. The Shiraz model: a tool for incorporating anthropogenic effects and fish-habitat relationships in conservation planning. Canadian Journal of Aquatic and Fisheries Science 63:1596–1607.

Shumway, D. L., C. E. Warren, and P. Doudoroff. 1964. Influence of oxygen concentration and water movement on the growth of steelhead trout and coho salmon embryos. Transactions of the American Fisheries Society 93:342–356.

Ulmer, F., V. Alexander, S. Pennoyer, F. Rue, R. Samuelsen, A. Sturgulewski, H. Wilde, Sr., and J. Balsiger 1999. Bering Sea Task Force Report to Governor Tony Knowles. Available: http://www.eeo. state.ak.us/ltgov/bstf/finalbstf.html (March 2007).

Walker, R. V., K. W. Myers, N. D. Davis, K. Y. Aydin, K. D. Friedland, H. R. Carlson, G. W. Boehlert, S. Urawa, Y. Ueno, and G. Anma. 2000. Diurnal variation in thermal environment experienced by salmon in the North Pacific as indicated by data storage tags. Fisheries Oceanography 9:171–186.

Walker, R. V., V. V. Sviridov, S. Urawa, and T. Azumaya. 2007. Spatio-temporal variation in vertical distributions of Pacific salmon. North Pacific Anadromous Fish Commission Bulletin 4:193–201.

Wertheimer, A. C., and F. P. Thrower. 2007. Mortality rates of chum salmon during their early marine residency. Pages 233–247 in C. B. Grimes, R. D. Brodeur, L. J. Haldorson, and S. M. McKinnell, editors. The ecology of juvenile salmon in the northeast Pacific Ocean: regional comparisons. American Fisheries Society, Symposium 57, Bethesda, Maryland.

American Fisheries Society Symposium 70:1127–1142, 2009

Responses of Pacific Salmon Populations to Climate Variation in Freshwater Ecosystems

Daniel E. Schindler* and Lauren A. Rogers

School of Aquatic and Fishery Sciences, University of Washington
Box 355020, Seattle, Washington 98195, USA

Abstract.—The effects of changing climate on salmon populations depend on the species and life history of interest, local expressions of climate change, characteristics of habitat, and the adaptation of specific populations to geographic variation in habitat characteristics. Here we review some of the key changes in climatic conditions that have affected freshwater ecosystems used by Pacific salmon in the recent past and summarize how these will be further impacted by future changes in temperature and precipitation patterns. Recent climate change has affected some well-studied populations allowing for some generalization about climate impacts on specific populations. One recurrent response to warming in freshwaters is a positive growth response in juveniles and an acceleration of the freshwater component of life histories, although these responses are unlikely to occur at the southern range boundaries for salmon. In addition to substantial latitudinal variation in recent and expected climate impacts on salmon ecosystems, there is increasing evidence of regional variation among population responses to the same overriding regional changes in climate. Biocomplexity, defined as the variation in habitat characteristics and its associated suite of locally adapted populations, provides a portfolio effect to salmon stocks. A portfolio effect results from weakly correlated dynamics in the component populations of a salmon stock. A stock characterized by a high diversity of populations and their associated dynamics, is less sensitive to the variation in an individual population, compared to a stock with low diversity. This portfolio effect provides resilience to salmon fisheries in the face of ongoing climate change because fisheries integrate across the component diversity within stocks. While many of the future characteristics of freshwater habitats remain highly uncertain in the face of ongoing climate change, protection of diverse networks of viable habitat and the stock diversity that maps onto this landscape diversity, is one obvious strategy to ameliorate the effects of future climate change on salmon stocks.

Introduction

A hallmark of the ecology of Pacific salmon is their ability to colonize and thrive in a wide variety of habitat types in freshwater and marine ecosystems. This characteristic of salmon derives from the remarkable variation

in life history strategies expressed both among and within species (reviewed by Quinn 2005; Quinn 2009, this volume). Pacific salmon are currently distributed throughout the North Pacific basin north of about 35 degrees latitude. In North America, their range extends from central California into the Arctic Ocean. Across this geographic distribution, salmon

*Corresponding author: deschind@u.washington.edu

have adapted to a wide diversity of habitat conditions in a very diverse array of climate features. This diversity of geographic locations, habitat characteristics, and the life history adaptations to environmental variation makes understanding the effects of climate change on salmon complex and usually system specific. In this chapter, we provide an overview of some of the key aspects of climatic conditions affecting freshwater ecosystems, how these are currently changing as predicted by global climate system models, and how these might express themselves in salmon populations as climate continues to change in the future. We then summarize the basic life history variation observed among species of Pacific salmon, and discuss how species will be differentially sensitive to climate-induced variation in freshwater ecosystems as a result of these life history patterns. Finally, we discuss the idea of biocomplexity (*sensu* Hilborn et al. 2003) and how this conceptual framework emphasizing landscape heterogeneity and the biodiversity *within* species may provide strategies for managing salmon in light of ongoing climate change. This is not meant to be a thorough review of the effects of climate on salmon populations. Instead, we focus entirely on freshwater ecosystems, and highlight some key recent developments that we believe provide important perspectives about how to manage and conserve salmon in the context of ongoing global climate change.

Sources of Climate Variation and How it Translates into Freshwater Conditions

Climatic conditions have varied substantially throughout Pacific salmon ecosystems at a variety of temporal scales ranging from longer than inter-glacial periods to interannual variation. Observations of salmon population dynamics in the last century allow some inference about how we might expect salmon populations to respond to climate changes in the future. Although many salmon populations have responded to recent changes in climate regimes, it remains unclear which aspects of these population responses result from mechanisms that play out in marine versus freshwater habitats. Here we provide several examples of some of the changes in freshwater ecosystems that are responsive to recent climate change and may have important implications for salmon populations in the future.

Changes in winter snowpack

At high latitudes and in mountainous regions winter snowpack serves as an important storage pool of precipitation that provides aquatic ecosystems with melt-water during spring and summer. Recent analyses show that winter snowpacks are declining throughout the globe, despite increases in precipitation in some of these regions. For example, Mote et al. (2005) found that snowpack on April 1 declined as much as 29% between the 1950s to the 1990s in mountainous western North America, concurrent with modest changes in winter precipitation (–5% to + 2%). Most of this decline occurred at low to mid elevations where warming trends have had the biggest effect on snow accumulation. Snowpack at high elevation sites in the northwest U.S. showed little change during this time period, but might change with further warming. Similar trends have be observed in western Canada (Schindler and Donahue 2006) where winter snowpack conditions have declined significantly over the last century, with most of the declines occurring since the early 1970s. A notable exception for the 1950–2002 period was in central California where increasing winter precipitation led to increased April 1 snowpack. Thus, changes in the seasonality of precipitation, and whether it is stored as snow and ice will be critical to salmon habitat in ecosystems that rely on seasonal snowmelt as a water source (Barnett et al. 2005).

Changes in precipitation and water flow

One of the expected responses to a warmer climate is increased precipitation in north temperate coastal regions as the hydrologic cycle intensifies. In accordance with this prediction has been the observation that flows from the major rivers draining to the Arctic Ocean have increased significantly during the last 50 years (Peterson et al. 2006). Over this time period, northern river discharge has increased about 6% and appears largely a response to increased precipitation. There has been no comprehensive review of changes in total discharge of salmon rivers throughout the North Pacific but this result suggests that future climate warming may increase the water flows through many high latitude salmon ecosystems in the future (see below).

Although total freshwater flows will likely increase in many salmon ecosystems under warming climates, it is now evident that the seasonality of water flows is also responsive to changing climatic conditions. Between 1948 and 2000, most streams and rivers in western North America showed distinct changes towards earlier dates in the timing of the center of mass of annual flow and the timing of the spring snowmelt pulse. Most of these changes were on the order of 10–20 d (Stewart et al. 2004). Projections of future changes in flow timing of snowmelt dominated streams suggest that many salmon streams and rivers in western North America will pass the center of mass of annual flows over 30 d earlier than currently by the end of the 21st century (Stewart et al. 2004).

Changes in timing of spring ice break-up

The timing of spring ice breakup and freezeup on lakes and rivers represents an integrated response to changes in climatic conditions during late winter and spring seasons (breakup) and autumn cooling (freeze-up).

These variables have also been monitored extensively for scientific, economic, and other societal reasons over relatively long time periods. Freshwater ecosystems throughout the Northern Hemisphere have exhibited consistent trends towards later autumn freezing and earlier spring breakup during the last century (Magnuson et al. 2000), resulting in substantially longer ice-free seasons on lakes and rivers. In general, rates of change in the timing of spring breakup have been greater than the observed changes in fall freezeup.

Both long-term climate change and periodic modes of climate variability have had significant effects on spring ice breakup dates in the Northern Hemisphere. For example, Anderson et al. (1996) showed that El Niño Southern Oscillation (ENSO) variability had strong effects on the date of spring ice breakup in southern Wisconsin (USA), and Yoo and D'Odorico (2002) showed that the North Atlantic Oscillation (NAO) had strong effects on ice phenologies of lakes and rivers in Northern Europe. The Pacific Decadal Oscillation (PDO), a climate oscillation that has strong effects on climatological processes and production of Pacific salmon in western North America (Mantua and Hare 2002; Mantua et al. 1997; Mantua 2009, this volume) also appears to have strong effects on spring ice break-up dates on lakes in Alaska (e.g., Schindler et al. 2005). For example, on Lake Aleknagik of southwest Alaska, spring breakup date shifted about ten days earlier between the 1962 and 2002. About half of this trend was attributable to long-term climate warming and about half to the shift to the warm phase of the PDO that occurred in the mid 1970s (Schindler et al. 2005). Similarly, Sagarin and Micheli (2001) showed that spring ice breakup date on the Nenana River in interior Alaska showed a significant negative trend towards earlier breakup dates between 1920 and 2000, with most of the change occurring during the mid-1970s, approximately at the time of the PDO climatic shift.

Changes in lake thermal regimes and productivity

Lakes used as nursery systems by juvenile salmon are sensitive to changes in climatic conditions. At high latitudes, earlier spring ice break-up will extend the growing season for plankton and fish (Schindler et al. 2005). Lake warming will also change the timing of summer thermal stratification in lakes, thereby affecting the timing of seasonal phytoplankton blooms (Winder and Schindler 2004a) and how this primary production is transferred to zooplankton grazers (Winder and Schindler 2004b) and eventually to juvenile salmon (Hampton et al. 2006). Because different taxa and different trophic levels have the potential to respond differently to the same changes in thermal conditions in lakes, it is difficult to make general predictions about how energy flow to juvenile salmon will respond to future climate change. Climate warming will also increase the strength of thermal stratification in lakes, having important consequences for upwelling of nutrients from the hypolimnia of deep lakes. In salmon ecosystems at low latitudes (e.g., lower 48 states and southern BC) in particular, increased thermal stratification may reduce nutrient upwelling to the point that overall lake productivity may decline (Henderson et al. 1992).

Predicted latitudinal and seasonal trends in future climate

It is now certain that climatic conditions will continue to change in ways that have the potential to affect salmon populations throughout their range. Although there remains substantial variation among projections from global climate system models used to forecast future climate conditions, and individual model predictions also have high uncertainties associated with them, trends in model predictions are worth considering for the future of salmon populations. The Canadian Climate Impact Scenarios modeling website (http://www.cics.uvic.ca/scenarios/) was used to illustrate the direction and magnitude of annual temperature and precipitation changes expected at a coarse geographic scale along the west coast of North America by the middle of the 21st century (Figure 1). This tool provides spatially explicit climate scenarios based on a total of 32 different simulations produced by the leading climate models and future greenhouse gas emission scenarios. Between 35 and 70° N latitude, the average model output projects that annual temperatures will increase between about 2 and 4° C in the next 50 years, with the most pronounced increases occurring at high latitudes (Figure 1). Concurrent with these expected warming trends are distinct trends in expected future precipitation patterns. Salmon ecosystems near the southern edge of their range are expected, in general, to receive less annual precipitation while those above about 50° N are expected to receive increased annual precipitation. At 70° N, these increases are expected to be about 20% higher on average compared to simulated conditions in the 1961–1990 period (Figure 1).

Changes in the seasonality of thermal regimes and precipitation patterns will likely have greater effects on salmon populations than will changes in aggregate annual conditions. To illustrate the potential temporal heterogeneity in seasonal climatic conditions, the annual predictions were disaggregated from the model scenarios considered above to seasonal time frames (Figure 2). In general, most models predict that the most pronounced warming will occur during the summer at low latitudes (i.e., 40° N), while most warming is likely to occur during the winter and fall at the highest latitudes (i.e., 70° N). The transition between these two patterns is predicted to occur relatively smoothly with increasing latitude along the west coast of North America (Figure 2B).

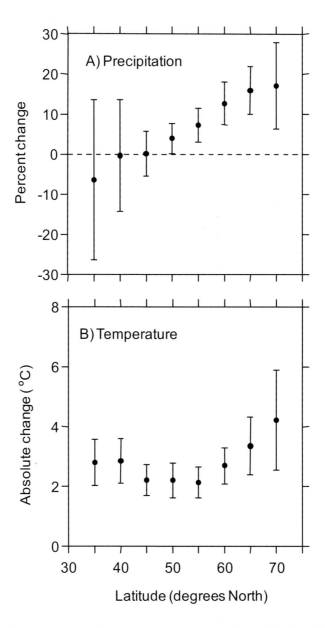

FIGURE 1. Climate change scenarios for changes in mean annual precipitation (a) and temperature (b) along the west coast of North America for the 2050s as a function of latitude. All changes are expressed relative to 1961–1990 climate baseline. Symbols represent the average forecast among global climate model scenarios (GCMs) and error bars represent standard deviations among model scenarios. Data were generated by the Canadian Climate Impact Scenarios website at http://www.cics.uvic.ca/scenarios/ that produces 32 different climate scenarios from 10 different GCMs and several different economic scenarios based on the IPCC 4th Assessment Report.

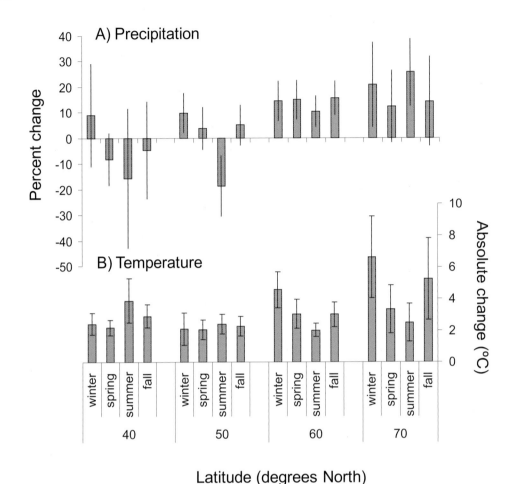

FIGURE 2. Comparison of projected changes in (a) precipitation and (b) temperature among seasons along the west coast of North America as a function of latitude. Data were generated and presented as in Figure 1.

The expression of global climate change on the seasonality of precipitation is also predicted to vary with latitude (Figure 2A). Near the southern range of salmon, models predict that the typical "Mediterranean" climate (i.e., dry summers, wet winters) will become even more pronounced in the near future. On average, climate models predict that precipitation in coastal regions at 40° N will increase about 10% during the winter relative to recent conditions, but that all other seasons will be drier (although there is high uncertainty in these predictions at this latitude). Summers are predicted to be on average about 17% drier than recent conditions.

By 50° N, models predict that summers will be about 20% drier than recent conditions but that more precipitation will fall during all other seasons of the year (Figure 3A). By 60° N, precipitation is predicted to increase during all seasons and this pattern extends as far north as 70° N where precipitation increases are expected to be most pronounced (~ 20% higher on average) during the winter and summer seasons.

In summary, coarse-scale climate scenarios for the 2050s generally suggest that con-

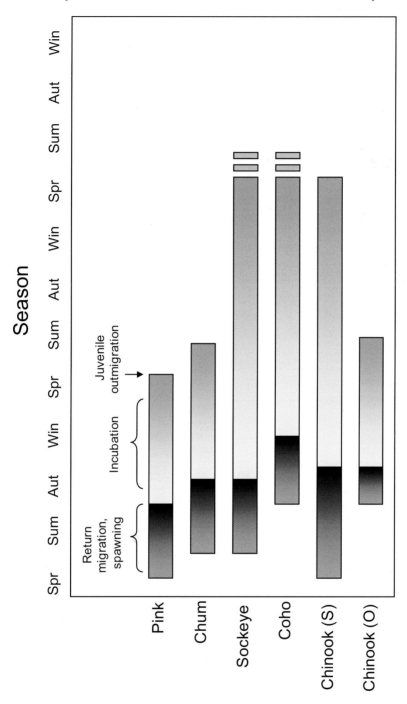

FIGURE 3. Generalized model of variation in the timing of key life history transitions in freshwater for five species of Pacific salmon *Oncorhynchus* spp. Chinook salmon *O. tshawytscha* have been split into the two dominant life history types (stream-type and ocean-type). Sockeye *O. nerka*, coho *O. kisutch*, and stream-type Chinook spend the most time as juveniles in freshwater habitats and may, therefore, be most sensitive to climate change impacts on freshwater ecosystems.

ditions for salmon at the southern end of their range will become increasingly inhospitable with both warmer and drier summers. By 60° N, however, future conditions might become more favorable for many salmon populations as both warmer winter conditions and more precipitation during all seasons may maintain and even enhance habitat suitability in many freshwater ecosystems for salmon across the northern extent of their range.

It is worth emphasizing that the regional climate signal experienced by any population is filtered by the geomorphology of the landscape inhabited by salmon. In turn, climate-driven changes in hydrologic flow regimes further modify geomorphic characteristics of salmon habitat through their effects on sediment transport and stream channel evolution (Dunne and Leopold 1978; Doyle et al. 2005). Thus, generating accurate forecast of site-specific environmental conditions experienced by salmon populations will require a better integration of geomorphology and climatology than is currently the norm.

Overview of Salmon Life Histories in Freshwater

Differences among the ecologies of Pacific salmon species (Figure 3) create variation in the types of climatic variation to which each species will be sensitive. Additional life history variation within species will further diversify the responses of populations to climatic conditions. Here the authors provide a broad overview of the life-histories represented by Pacific salmon species (see Groot and Margolis (1991) and Quinn (2005) for in-depth reviews), and speculate about species-specific sensitivity to climate-driven changes in freshwater ecosystems.

Of the five major species of Pacific salmon, pink salmon *Oncorhynchus gorbuscha* exhibit the simplest life history and spend the

least amount of time in freshwater. Adults return to freshwaters at 2 years of age to spawn in their natal habitats, typically coastal rivers and streams, although some populations may travel hundreds of kilometers upriver to spawn (Heard 1991). Spawning typically occurs in late summer and fall. Juvenile pink salmon emerge from the gravel in the spring and migrate directly to the coastal ocean, typically spending less time in freshwater than other species.

The use of freshwater environments by chum salmon *O. keta* is similar to pink salmon, and less prolonged than that of sockeye *O. nerka*, coho *O. kisutch*, or Chinook salmon *O. tshawytscha*. Like pink salmon, most chum salmon spawn in coastal rivers, sometimes traveling greater distances, as far as 2,000 km up the Yukon River (Salo 1991; Bue et al. 2009). In Alaska, Chum salmon return to spawn in summer or early autumn, with more southerly runs generally returning later in the season. After overwintering as embryos in the gravel, fry emerge and migrate downstream to estuaries in their first spring or summer of life, with earlier migrations at lower latitudes. More so than pink salmon, some chum salmon fry may spend days or weeks in freshwater (Quinn 2005), and typically make extensive use of estuaries (Salo 1991); however, juvenile use of the freshwater environment is still limited compared to most populations of sockeye, coho and Chinook salmon.

Sockeye salmon are unique in that they are the only species to make extensive use of lacustrine environments. Sockeye salmon spawn in rivers, tributary streams, and on beaches of lakes where there is sufficient upwelling to supply oxygen to embryos (Burgner et al. 1969). When fry emerge in early spring, in almost all cases they migrate downstream or short distances upstream to lakes, where they spend up to 3 years (most commonly 1 or 2) rearing before migrating to sea as smolts. This lake residency period is critical for juvenile growth and subsequent marine survival (Koenings et al. 1993). Seaward migration is generally concurrent with spring lake ice breakup, or lake warming, resulting in a latitudinal gradient in migration timing among populations, as well as interannual variability within populations (Burgner 1991).

While sockeye salmon spend a significant portion of their lives in lakes, coho salmon predominantly use streams as nursery systems before becoming smolts. Adults migrate to freshwater in late summer and fall and typically spawn in coastal streams and tributaries of major rivers between November and January (Sandercock 1991), later than other species on average. After a winter in the gravel, fry emerge and compete for food and territory in a dynamic stream environment, sometimes migrating between habitats with seasonal changes in stream flow (Quinn 2005). After 1 or 2 years in the stream environment, coho move seawards, generally around the time of peak spring flows or as streams warm in spring or summer.

Chinook salmon can be classified according to two major life history patterns. Stream-type fish generally spawn upstream, towards the headwaters of rivers, and upon emerging from gravel, juveniles may spend a year or more in streams and rivers before migrating to the ocean. This is the primary life history pattern among northern populations. Conversely, ocean-type Chinook salmon spend much less time in freshwaters, generally spawning closer to the ocean, and juveniles may migrate to sea after only a few weeks or months in freshwater. Ocean-type Chinook salmon are generally "fall-running" as well, meaning they make their return freshwater migration in the fall, spawning soon thereafter, whereas stream-type Chinook salmon often make the return migration as early as spring or summer, spending sometimes many months in freshwater before spawning in the fall (Healey 1991; Quinn 2005).

To summarize, pink, chum, and ocean-type Chinook salmon spend the least amount of time in freshwater habitat as juveniles, migrating to sea soon after emergence from spawning habitats. Sockeye salmon depend on lakes for rearing of juveniles, and coho and stream-type Chinook make extensive use of stream and river environments as juveniles. The additional time spent in the freshwater will make these latter species additionally sensitive to changes in freshwater conditions.

Based on generalized life histories (Figure 3) we can begin to identify climatic scenarios, which may differentially impact some species over others. The most obvious issue is changes in summer stream temperatures and flow, which we expect to have the smallest effects on pink, chum, sockeye, and ocean-type Chinook salmon, as juveniles of these species have typically already migrated to lakes (sockeye salmon) or out of freshwater environments completely by summer. Warm summer stream temperatures would mostly affect adults of these species during their spawning migrations. Juvenile coho salmon and stream-type Chinook salmon, however, reside in streams and rivers through their first summer. During their first summer, some populations of coho salmon fry have been shown to be sensitive to low flows, which reduce the stream area and thus the carrying capacity for juveniles, and increase vulnerability to predators (Smoker 1955; Seiler et al. 2002; Cederholm and Scarlett 1981). Low flows combined with warm air temperatures can result in water temperatures reaching lethally high levels for stream-dwelling salmonids, especially at southern latitudes (Salo 1991). Thus, future changes in summer flows or temperatures will differentially impact coho and stream-type Chinook salmon because their life history strategies place them at relatively high risk to warming summer conditions.

While the previous section, as well as Figure 3, emphasizes the differences between species in their use of freshwater environments, within a species, populations may vary drastically in their timing of return migration, date of spawning, emergence timing, number of seasons or years spent rearing in freshwater, preferred freshwater spawning and rearing habitat, and time of smolt out-migration. For instance, even within the same watershed, sockeye salmon spawn in habitats ranging from shallow tributary streams, to large rivers, to lake beaches (Burgner 1991), and in the Sacramento River, where historically, Chinook salmon spawned in every month of the year (Healey 1991). Intra-specific diversity is a defining feature of salmonid species, and often reflects population-specific adaptations to prevailing climatic conditions. The implications of this diversity will be revisited later.

Examples of Climate Effects on Salmon Populations

Unlike most species that interest ecologists, there is a relatively large amount of data collected over long time periods on salmon populations. Because salmon are commercially and culturally valuable species, substantial scientific research and monitoring of their populations have occurred over the last century. This accumulation of information has enabled some initial observations about how salmon populations have responded to variations in climate like those described above. Here, the authors provide a set of examples meant to highlight the types and magnitudes of responses that salmon populations have demonstrated in response to recent climatic variation.

The timing of spawning migrations of adult salmon to freshwaters shows wide variation across the watersheds of the North Pacific that appears to be responsive to localized thermal and hydrologic regimes of freshwater ecosystems (Hodgson and Quinn 2002). For example, migration timing of adult sockeye salmon is sensitive to freshwater temperatures greater than 19°C such that they either migrate earlier than expected in the summer to avoid midsummer temperature maxima or delay migration and move into freshwater systems after temperatures decline in the fall (Hodgson and Quinn 2002). In addition to geographic variation in timing of adult returns to freshwaters, interannual variation in migration timing within systems is sensitive to climatic factors and especially temperature regimes. For example, warming temperatures and lower flows during the summer in the Columbia River that have developed during the last few decades are associated with earlier migration dates for adult sockeye during their summer spawning runs (Quinn et al. 1997). Despite migration timing being partially cued by river temperatures, sockeye have experienced increasingly warmer water temperatures during their spawning migrations, and the changes in their migration timing have not kept pace with river warming trends. Travel rate during migration is also positively correlated with interannual differences in temperature (Quinn et al. 1997). Future effects of climate warming on the timing, rates, and success of adult spawning migrations will depend on interactions between river temperatures, river flow regimes, and body size and energy content upon initiation of migrations (Rand et al. 2006). In general, higher river temperatures, higher river flows, and smaller body sizes and energy contents will all increase mortality en route to spawning areas. Because body size and condition will largely be determined by marine processes, the ultimate effect on migrating salmon of climate driven changes in freshwater will partially depend on climate driven responses in the ocean.

A particularly compelling example of the effects of changes in the thermal environment on growth and life history strategies of salmon involves the responses of coho salmon to clear-cut logging in the Carnation Creek watershed of Vancouver Island, British Columbia (Holtby 1988). Logging of 40% of this watershed produced substantial stream warming due to the removal of the riparian canopy. Warming trends varied with season, ranging from about 0.7°C change in December to over 3°C warming in August. These changes in thermal regimes yielded several important responses in the juvenile coho salmon rearing in Carnation Creek. Warmer stream temperatures in winter were associated with earlier emergence of fry into the stream, resulting in an extension of the growth season by up to six weeks. This increase in growing season length was associated with substantially increased sizes of 1-year-old juveniles at the end of their first year of growth, which translated into higher rates of overwinter survival. There was also a switch in the dominant age of coho salmon smolts in the population. In cold (prelogging) years, the smolt run was composed of about 50% 1-year-old fish and 50% 2-year old fish. The warmer conditions due to logging caused a shift to a larger percentage of 1-year old smolts and relatively fewer 2-year old smolts. Further, warmer conditions during the spring were associated with earlier smolt migrations to the ocean, which may have reduced smolt-to-adult survival in the system because of temporal mismatches between coho entry to the ocean and availability of prey and densities of predators there. Across all life stages, warmer stream temperatures increased total coho salmon production by about 9% (Holtby 1988).

Warmer spring and summer temperatures, or shorter winter conditions, also translate into improved growth conditions for sockeye salmon in western Alaska. In Lake Aleknagik of the Wood River System of Bristol Bay, earlier spring ice break-up dates translated into increased summer water temperatures,

increased zooplankton densities, and increased rearing capacity for sockeye salmon fry in this system (Schindler et al. 2005). Similar warming trends in Lake Iliamna have also enhanced growth rates of juvenile sockeye salmon there (Rich et al.,2009). In addition to these enhanced growth rates of juvenile sockeye salmon has been a marked shift in the body condition of age-1 smolts and a distinct shift towards domination by age-1 smolts from the Iliamna Lake/Kvichak River system (Schindler et al., unpublished data) much like coho salmon in Carnation Creek, British Columbia. The increased growth rates of juvenile sockeye and coho in response to warmer water temperatures may be more general than appreciated as similar responses to warming stream conditions have been observed in Norwegian Atlantic salmon (*Salmo salar*, Jonsson et al. 2005).

Overall, there is convincing evidence that life history patterns of several populations of salmon are responsive to changing thermal conditions in freshwaters. In several cases, warmer environments actually improve growth conditions for juvenile salmon and speed up their life history strategies. In other cases, warm conditions have placed important constraints on migration of salmon through freshwaters as both adults and juveniles. The effects of changes in thermal conditions on salmon populations throughout their range will likely show substantial variation both among and within climatic regions, and among species, populations, and life history strategies.

Biocomplexity of Salmon

This study has shown that the growth and survival of salmon are sensitive to climate-driven changes in the freshwater environment. However, studies of the average response of populations to climate-induced change often ignore the variation among populations in terms of their responses to changing environmental conditions. Biocomplexity, defined as the combination of habitat diversity and the range of locally-adapted populations that maps onto this diversity, is gaining attention as an important feature of healthy, resilient salmon-producing ecosystems (Hilborn et al. 2003). The effects of this diversity are that each population's unique combination of spawning and rearing habitats, as well as the life history strategies evolved to those habitats, will result in different populations being sensitive to different aspects of climatic conditions. This diversity of responses among populations to regional climate forcing confers resilience to the stock-complex because population responses are often heterogeneous in time.

There is strong evidence of biocomplexity in salmon stocks, especially pristine stocks. In Bristol Bay, the aggregate sockeye salmon stock complex has supported a sustainable commercial fishery for over a century, but individual sockeye salmon stocks have varied considerably over time in their contributions to the overall commercial catch, which is a good proxy for total run size (Hilborn et al. 2003). The shifts in productivity observed in these stocks cannot be attributed to habitat degradation, hatchery effects, or trends in escapements. Instead, these shifts must indicate different responses by these stocks to over-riding environmental or climatic conditions. At this time, we do not know how much of this response diversity derives from differential survival rates in marine systems or in freshwater systems.

In general, Bristol Bay sockeye salmon stocks showed relatively low productivity in the 1950s to mid-1970s, a time period characterized by generally cool climatic conditions across the region. After 1976, sockeye salmon productivity increased substantially, coincident with warmer climatic conditions across the region (e.g., Baker 2009, this volume).

Differential responses of salmon populations to climate conditions over time have been demonstrated at a range of spatial scales. In one drainage within the Bristol Bay region, nine distinct stream-spawning populations of sockeye salmon within 40 km of one another showed only moderate correlation in their productivity over time, despite their close proximity, exposure to similar climatic conditions, and relatively similar spawning habitats (Rogers and Schindler, 2008). Similarly, 16 Fraser River sockeye salmon stocks were found to be only weakly coherent in their dynamics over time (mean correlation = 0.16) (Peterman et al. 1998). Even among more degraded stocks, ESUs (evolutionary significant units, Ruckelshaus et al. 2002) of Chinook salmon in the Columbia River and throughout the Pacific Northwest were found to respond differently to climate regime shifts (Levin 2003; Tolimieri and Levin 2004).

Such asynchronous dynamics could be due to a number of factors, including habitat- and population-specific responses to climate conditions. In the Kvichak River watershed of Bristol Bay, including Lake Iliamna, patterns of similarity in abundance among populations grouped by habitat, such that island beach spawners showed the highest covariation (Stewart et al. 2003). Beach spawners on islands typically spawn in shallow water and embryos buried there would be similarly affected by changes in lake level and ice cover (Stewart et al. 2003), whereas embryos in stream gravels may depend on different conditions. The strongest evidence for population- or habitat- specific responses to climate variation is given by Crozier and Zabel (2006) who demonstrate that juvenile Chinook salmon survival in the Salmon River basin (Idaho) is differentially affected by climate conditions depending on habitat characteristics, such as stream width and stream temperature.

Maintenance of life history diversity, as well as diverse spawning and rearing habitats, is important for maintaining resilience in salmon stocks during climatic change. Response diversity, defined as the range of species or population responses to environmental change, lends resilience to ecological systems by increasing the likelihood that some species or populations will thrive during times when others may not (Elmqvist et al. 2003). In the case of Pacific salmon, a diversity of responses may lead to the persistence of stock complexes and the stabilization of commercial fishery catches over time (Hilborn et al. 2003). In the Salmon River, Idaho, Chinook salmon populations have shown drastic declines over the past four decades, accompanied by a steady increase in the interannual co-variation in redd counts among tributary streams, suggesting a loss of resilience in this system (Isaak et al. 2003).

Degradation of salmon spawning and rearing habitat, loss of locally-adapted populations, and loss of certain salmon life-histories is threatening the biocomplexity and resilience of salmon stocks throughout their range, though primarily in the southern regions. In the Pacific Northwest, salmon are gone from nearly 40% of their original habitat, and habitat degradation and loss of connectivity has contributed to the threatened or endangered status of 26 ESUs (Ruckelshaus et al. 2002). In the Willamette and lower Columbia rivers, only 58% of the original habitat is still accessible to salmon due to anthropogenic barriers, with a disproportionately large impact on higher elevation, snowmelt-driven streams (Sheer and Steel 2006). Such patterns of habitat loss are likely responsible for the decrease in stream-type Chinook salmon populations in the Puget Sound region, which predominantly use snowmelt-driven streams (Beechie et al. 2006), and thus, habitat alteration can result in selective loss of certain life-histories.

Summary

Salmon have been extremely successful at colonizing and thriving in a variety of habitat types throughout the North Pacific basin. The physical conditions in these habitats have been variable over a variety of time-scales. The high diversity of life history strategies observed within and among Pacific salmon species (Quinn 2005) is reflective of their plasticity, adaptability, and abilities to succeed under a wide range of geomorphic, habitat, and climatic conditions. Future climate change is very likely to change the abundance and productivity of salmon throughout their current range and will likely enable them to expand their range northward into new habitats. In fact, populations found at high latitudes are probably going to benefit from changing climate before they suffer from it as has been observed in some Alaskan populations (Hilborn et al. 2003; Schindler et al. 2005).

It would be convenient for forecasting and monitoring salmon population responses to climate change if all populations in a region responded synchronously to changing environmental conditions. However, salmon stocks show considerable response diversity to regional climate changes (Peterman et al. 1998; Hilborn et al. 2003, Rogers and Schindler 2008). Although the observed intra-regional variation in population responses to climate could be treated as a nuisance to salmon management, this variation actually benefits commercial fisheries, which tend to integrate across the within-system variability in stock components (Hilborn et al. 2003). In fact, maintaining a diversity of populations that exhibit a range of response characteristics to changing climate is one way to build biological resilience in salmon fisheries. This strategy may not necessarily work for locally-based subsistence fisheries. Thus, to build insurance for salmon stocks and their associated commercial fisheries against future climate change, conservation and management strategies should protect heterogeneous landscapes of viable salmon habitat and attempt to maintain stock diversity by attempting to prevent overexploitation of unproductive stock components at any instance in time.

Acknowledgments

Our research is supported by the Gordon and Betty Moore Foundation, the National Science Foundation, the Alaska seafood processors, and the University of Washington School of Aquatic and Fishery Sciences. We thank Chris Boatright, Nate Mantua, and Chris Zimmerman for helpful reviews of an earlier version of this manuscript.

References

Anderson, W. L., D. M. Robertson, and J. J. Magnuson. 1996. Evidence of recent warming and El Niño-related variations in ice breakup of Wisconsin lakes. Limnology and Oceanography 41:815–821.

Baker, T. T., T. Sands, F. West, C. Westing, and C. Brazil. 2009. Management of the Nushagak District sockeye salmon fishery: how 50 years of data helps. Pages 963–976 in C. C. Krueger and C. E. Zimmerman, editors. Pacific salmon: ecology and management of western Alaska's populations. American Fisheries Society, Symposium 70, Bethesda, Maryland.

Barnett, T. P., J. C. Adam, and D. P. Lettenmaier. 2005. Potential impacts of warming climate on water availability in snow-dominated regions. Nature (London) 438:303–309.

Beechie, T., E. Buhle, M. Ruckelshaus, A. Fullerton, and L. Holsinger. 2006. Hydrologic regime and the conservation of salmon life history diversity. Biological Conservation 130:560–572.

Burgner, R. L., C. J. DiCostanzo, R. J. Ellis, G. Y. Harry, W. L. Hartman, O. E. Kerns, O. A. Mathisen, and W. F. Royce. 1969. Biological studies and estimates of optimum escapements of sockeye salmon in major river systems in southwestern Alaska. United States Fish and Wildlife Service Fishery Bulletin 67(2):405–459.

Bue, F. J., B. M. Borba, R. Cannon, and C. C. Krueger. 2009. Yukon River fall chum salmon fisheries: management, harvest, and stock abundance. Pages

703–742 in C. C. Krueger and C. E. Zimmerman, editors. Pacific salmon: ecology and management of western Alaska's populations. American Fisheries Society, Symposium 70, Bethesda, Maryland.

Burgner, R. L. 1991. Life history of sockeye salmon. Pages 1–117 in C. Groot and L. Margolis, editors. Pacific salmon: life histories. UBC Press, Vancouver.

Cederholm, C. J. and W. J. Scarlett. 1981. Seasonal immigrations of juvenile salmonids into four small tributaries of the Clearwater River, Washington, 1977–1981. Pages 98–110 in E. L. Brannon and E. O. Salo, editors. Proceedings of the Salmon and Trout Migratory Behavior Symposium. College of Fisheries, University of Washington, Seattle.

Crozier, L., and R. W. Zabel. 2006. Climate impacts at multiple scales: evidence for differential population responses in juvenile Chinook salmon. Journal of Animal Ecology 75:1100–1109.

Doyle, M. W., E. H. Stanley, D. L. Strayer, R. B. Jaconson, and J. C. Schmidt. 2005. Effective discharge analysis of ecological processes in streams. Water Resources Research 41:W11411.

Dunne, T., and L. B. Leopold. 1978. Water in environmental planning. Freeman, San Francisco, California.

Elmqvist, T., C. Folke, M. Nystrom, G. Peterson, J. Bengtsson, B. Walker, and J. Norberg. 2003. Response diversity, ecosystem change, and resilience. Frontiers in Ecology and the Environment 1:488–494.

Groot, C., and L. Margolis, editors. 1991. Pacific salmon: life histories. UBC Press, Vancouver.

Hampton, S. E., P. Romare, and D. E. Seiler. 2006. Environmentally controlled Daphnia spring increase with implications for sockeye salmon fry in Lake Washington, USA. Journal of Plankton Research 28:399–406.

Healey, M. C. 1991. Life history of Chinook salmon. Pages 311–393 in C. Groot and L. Margolis, editors. Pacific salmon: life histories. UBC Press, Vancouver.

Heard, W. R. 1991. Life history of pink salmon. Pages 119–230 in C. Groot and L. Margolis, editors. Pacific salmon: life histories. UBC Press, Vancouver.

Henderson, M. A., D. A. Levy, and J. G. Stockner. 1992. Probable consequences of climate change on freshwater production of Adams River sockeye salmon (Oncorhynchus nerka). GeoJournal 28:51–59.

Hilborn, R., T. P. Quinn, D. E. Schindler, and D. E. Rogers. 2003. Biocomplexity and fisheries sustainability. Proceedings of the National Academy of Sciences, USA 100:6564–6568.

Holtby, L. B. 1988. Effects of logging on stream temperatures in Carnation Creek, British Columbia, and associated impacts on the coho salmon (*Oncorhynchus kisutch*). Canadian Journal of Fisheries and Aquatic Sciences 45:502–515.

Hodgson, S., and T. P. Quinn. 2002. The timing of adult sockeye salmon migration into fresh water: adaptations by populations to prevailing thermal regimes. Canadian Journal of Zoology 80:542–555.

Isaak, D. J., R. F. Thurow, B. E. Rieman, and J. B. Dunham. 2003. Temporal variation in synchrony among Chinook salmon (*Oncorhynchus tshawytscha*) redd counts from a wilderness area in central Idaho. Canadian Journal of Fisheries and Aquatic Sciences 60:840–848.

Jonsson, N., B. Jonsson, and L. P. Hansen. 2005. Does climate during embryonic development influence parr growth and age of seaward migration in Atlantic salmon (*Salmon salar*)? Canadian Journal of Fisheries and Aquatic Sciences 62:2502–2508.

Koenings, J. P., H. J. Geiger, and J. J. Hasbrouck. 1993. Smolt-to-adult survival patterns of sockeye-salmon (*Oncorhynchus nerka*)—effects of smolt length and geographic latitude when entering the sea. Canadian Journal of Fisheries and Aquatic Sciences 50:600–611.

Levin, P. S. 2003. Regional differences in responses of Chinook salmon populations to large-scale climatic patterns. Journal of Biogeography 30(5):711–717.

Magnuson, J. J., D. M. Robertson, B. J. Benson, R. H. Wynne, D. M. Livingstone, T. Arai, R. A. Assel, R. G. Barry, V. Card, E. Kuusisto, N. G. Granin, T. D. Prowse, K. M. Stewart, and V. S. Vuglinski. 2000. Historical trends in lake and river ice cover in the Northern Hemisphere. Science 289:1743–1746.

Mantua, N. J. 2009. Patterns of change in climate and Pacific salmon production. Pages 1143–1157 *in* C. C. Krueger and C. E. Zimmerman, editors. Pacific salmon: ecology and management of western Alaska's populations. American Fisheries Society, Symposium 70, Bethesda, Maryland.

Mantua, N. J., S. R. Hare, Y. Zhang, J. M. Wallace, and R. C. Francis. 1997. A Pacific interdecadal climate oscillation with impacts on salmon production. Bulletin of the American Meteorological Society 78: 1069–1079.

Mantua, N. J., and S. R. Hare. 2002. The Pacific decadal oscillation. Journal of Oceanography 58:35–44.

Mote, P. W., A. F. Hamlet, M. P. Clark, and D. P. Lettenmaier. 2005. Declining mountain snowpack in western North America. Bulletin of the American Meteorological Society 86: 39–49.

Peterman, R. M., B. J. Pyper, M. F. Lapointe, M. D. Adkison, and C. J. Walters. 1998. Patterns of covariation in survival rates of British Columbian and Alaskan sockeye salmon (*Oncorhynchus nerka*) stocks. Canadian Journal of Fisheries and Aquatic Sciences 55:2503–2517.

Peterson, B. J., J. McClelland, R. Curry, R. M. Holmes, J. E. Walsh, K. Aagaard. 2006. Trajectory shifts in the Arctic and subarctic freshwater cycle. Science 313:1061–1066.

Quinn, T. P. 2005. The behavior and ecology of Pacific salmon and trout. University of Washington Press, Seattle.

Quinn, T. P. 2009. Pacific salmon population structure and dynamics: a perspective from Bristol Bay on life history variation across spatial and temporal scales. Pages 857–871 *in* C. C. Krueger and C. E. Zimmerman, editors. Pacific salmon: ecology and management of western Alaska's populations. American Fisheries Society, Symposium 70, Bethesda, Maryland.

Quinn, T. P., S. Hodgson, and C. Peven. 1997. Temperature, flow, and the migration of adult sockeye salmon (*Oncorhynchus nerka*) in the Columbia River. Canadian Journal of Fisheries and Aquatic Sciences 54:1349–1360.

Rand, P. S., S. G. Hinch, J. Morrison, M. G. G. Foreman, M. J. MacNutt, J. S. Macdonald, M. C. Healey, A. O. Farrell, and D. A. Higgs. 2006. Effects of river discharge, temperature, and future climates on energetics and mortality of adult migrating Fraser River sockeye salmon. Transactions of the American Fisheries Society 135:655–667.

Rich, H. B., T. P. Quinn, M. D. Scheuerell, and D. E. Schindler. 2009. Climate and intraspecific competition control the growth and life history of juvenile sockeye salmon (*Oncorhynchus nerka*) in Iliamna Lake, Alaska. Canadian Journal of Fisheries and Aquatic Sciences 66:238–246.

Rogers, L. A., and D. E. Schindler. 2008. Asynchrony in population dynamics of sockeye salmon in southwest Alaska. Oikos 117:1578–1586.

Ruckelshaus, M. H., P. Levin, J. B. Johnson, and P. M. Kareiva. 2002. The Pacific salmon wars: what science brings to the challenge of recovering species. Annual Review of Ecology and Systematics 33:665–706.

Sagarin, R., and F. Micheli. 2001. Climate change in nontraditional data sets. Science 294:811.

Salo, E. O. 1991. Life history of chum salmon. Pages 231–309 *in* C. Groot and L. Margolis, editors. Pacific salmon: life histories. UBC Press, Vancouver.

Sandercock, F.K. 1991. Life history of coho salmon. Pages 395–445 *in* C. Groot and L. Margolis, editors. Pacific salmon: life histories. UBC Press, Vancouver.

Schindler, D. E., D. E. Rogers, M. D. Scheuerell, and C. A. Abrey. 2005. Effects of changing climate on zooplankton and juvenile sockeye salmon growth in southwestern Alaska. Ecology 86:198–209.

Schindler, D. W., and Donahue, W. F. 2006. An impending water crisis in Canada's western prairie provinces. Proceedings of the National Academy of Sciences, USA 103:7210–7216.

Sheer, M. B., and E. A. Steel. 2006. Lost watersheds: barriers, aquatic habitat connectivity, and salmon persistence in the Willamette and Lower Columbia River basins. Transactions of the American Fisheries Society 135(6):1654–1669.

Seiler, D., G. Volkhardt, S. Neuhauser, P. Hanratty, and L. Kishimoto. 2002. 2002 wild coho forecasts for Puget Sound and Washington coastal systems. Washington Department Fish Wildlife, Olympia.

Smoker, W. A. 1955. Effects of streamflow on silver salmon production in western Washington. Doctoral dissertation. University of Washington, Seattle.

Stewart, I. T., D. R. Cayan, and M. D. Dettinger. 2004. Changes toward earlier streamflow timing across western North America. Journal of Climate 18:1136–1155.

Stewart, I. J., Hilborn, R., and T. P. Quinn. 2003. Coherence of observed adult sockeye salmon abundance within and among spawning habitats in the Kvichak River watershed. Alaska Fishery Research Bulletin 10:28–41.

Tolimieri, N., and P. Levin. 2004. Differences in responses of Chinook salmon to climate shifts: implications for conservation. Environmental Biology of Fishes 70(2):155–167.

Winder, M., and D. E. Schindler. 2004a. Climatic effects on the phenology of lake processes. Global Change Biology 10:1844–1856.

Winder, M., and D. E. Schindler. 2004b. Climate change uncouples trophic interactions in an aquatic ecosystem. Ecology 85:2100–2106.

Yoo, J. C., and P. D'Odorico. 2002. Trends and fluctuations in the dates of ice break-up of lakes and rivers in Northern Europe: the effect of the North Atlantic Oscillation. Journal of Hydrology 268:100–112.

American Fisheries Society Symposium 70:1143–1157, 2009

Patterns of Change in Climate and Pacific Salmon Production

Nathan J. Mantua*

*University of Washington, School of Aquatic and Fishery Sciences
Box 355020, Seattle, Washington 98195, USA*

Abstract.—For much of the 20th century a clear north-south inverse production pattern for Pacific salmon had a time dynamic that closely followed that of the Pacific Decadal Oscillation (PDO), which is the dominant pattern of North Pacific sea surface temperature variability. Total Alaska salmon production was high during warm regimes of the PDO and total Alaska salmon production was relatively low during cool regimes of the PDO. Leading hypotheses for the link between climate and Pacific salmon production have focused on changes in early ocean survival for juvenile salmon, but it is clear that climate also affects freshwater life stages and influences productivity. Over broad spatial scales, the PDO-related patterns in climate and Pacific salmon production were less prominent in the period 1990–2004 than in earlier decades of the 20th century, yet the regional associations between salmon production and temperatures were generally the same: warm periods coincided with high salmon production in Alaska, and cool periods off the west coast of the continental U.S. and British Columbia coincided with high salmon production in those regions. A case study of Norton Sound pink salmon provides one regional perspective on the links between changes in climate and salmon production. In the period 1962–1995, anomalously warm winter and spring climate in western Alaska and warm spring/summer temperatures in the eastern Bering Sea generally coincided with high pink salmon production. However, especially warm conditions for freshwater and early marine life stages for Norton Sound pink salmon coincided with both high and low levels of recruits per spawner for brood years 1996–2003, a period that experienced large inter-annual variations in Bering Sea, North Pacific, and tropical Pacific Ocean conditions.

Introduction

Previous studies report compelling evidence for variations in Pacific climate as primary causes for large-scale variations in Pacific salmon abundance during the 20th century (Beamish and Bouillon 1993; Hare and Francis 1995; Mantua et al. 1997). These studies and others have demonstrated that interannual to interdecadal variations in the Pacific Decadal Oscillation (PDO), the dominant pattern of sea surface temperature (SST) variations in the North Pacific, coincided with an inverse relationship in Pacific salmon production for most of the 20th century. When the PDO pattern is in its warm phase, the Aleutian Low atmospheric pressure cell is strong in winter and spring, bringing warm moist air into western North America and north into Alaska from the northwestern

*Corresponding author: nmantua@u.washington.edu

portion of the continental U.S. Under these atmospheric conditions, SSTs are typically warmer than average along the entire Pacific coast of western North America, including the Bering Sea and Gulf of Alaska, while at the same time being cooler than average in the eastern and central North Pacific between 30° and 50°N latitude (Mantua et al. 1997). Salmon production in Alaska was generally high during warm phases of the PDO from 1925–1946 and 1977–1998, while in these same periods salmon production for the west coast of the continental U.S. was generally low (Hare et al. 1999).

The regional salmon catch records showing the strongest correlation with the large-scale PDO index are those for western Alaska sockeye salmon *Oncorhynchus nerka* and pink salmon *O. gorbuscha*, where the time series of the PDO explains over 50% of the variability for 1925 to 1996 (Hare et al. 1999). In contrast, a series of studies provided evidence that much of the interannual coherence between different salmon stocks was manifest at spatial scales from a few hundred to perhaps a thousand km (Myers et al. 1997; Peterman et al. 1998; Pyper et al. 2001, 2002; 2005). Hilborn et al. (2003) showed that underlying what appears to be a broad regional coherence in western Alaska sockeye salmon population changes were complex patterns of productivity changes at the scale of the major fishing districts and watersheds in Bristol Bay, wherein watersheds that were once dominant producers for decades lost their importance, while formerly unproductive watersheds suddenly became sustained major producers for the region as a whole.

In this study, a brief review of large-scale and regional-scale perspectives on the patterns of linked climate and salmon production variations are offered from analyses that focus on spatial scales of coherence in salmon production ranging from 1000s to 100s of km. The analysis strategy adopted in this study is to use time series for salmon abundance and productivity to define years of interest, and then to conditionally sample the Pacific climate record to develop maps and time series indicating the space-time patterns of environmental covariations. Once the environmental patterns of interest are identified, the relative influences of the El Niño-Southern Oscillation (ENSO), Pacific Decadal Oscillation (PDO), and the global average temperature are assessed. Understanding the relative importance for these three large-scale patterns of climate variations is crucial for projecting the likely changes in North Pacific climate important for Pacific salmon in the next few decades and centuries. Beamish and Sweeting (2009, this volume) and Moss et al. (2009, this volume) argue that analyses of environmental variables in both freshwater and marine systems was needed to better understand what controls salmon productivity in the North Pacific and Arctic-Yukon-Kuskokwim region. Following this same perspective, indicators related to both freshwater and early marine environment are evaluated for evidence of robust relationships with salmon productivity.

Methods

The environmental data sets examined in this study were gridded sea and land surface temperatures and selected large-scale indices important for North Pacific climate. Monthly surface air temperature and precipitation for 1950–1999 were from the 0.5° latitude by 0.5° longitude gridded and interpolated fields from the University of Delaware (Willmott and Matsuura1995). Monthly sea surface temperatures for 1900–2006 were from Version 2 of NOAA's Extended Reconstructed 2° latitude by 2° longitude gridded fields of Smith and Reynolds (2004). Three large-scale climate indices examined here were the UK Met Office global surface air temperature record from 1900–2006, Mantua et al.'s

(1997) PDO index (JISAO 2009), and the Niño3.4 index from Kaplan et al. (1998). Sea surface temperature fields from the gridded data of Smith and Reynolds (2004) and observed monthly air temperatures from Nome archived by NOAA's Western Regional Climate Center (WRCC 2008) were used to provide regional perspectives for ocean and air temperatures for the eastern Bering Sea and Norton Sound region.

This study used annual salmon catch histories as indices of abundance, and stock-recruit indices as measures of annual levels of productivity. While total run-sizes or total biomass were preferable for tracking total salmon production, these data were not widely available. Catch series for Alaska salmon populations have been used extensively as indices of abundance in many previous studies (e.g., Beamish and Bouillon 1993; Hare and Francis 1995; Hare et al. 1999). Catch data were described by Hare et al. (1999) for the five major species of salmon for the period 1910–2004. Salmon productivity indices (SRi), developed as residuals from spawner-recruit relationships, were for pink salmon stocks from Norton Sound for brood years 1962–1995 (Pyper et al. 2001). An index of aggregate recruits-per-spawner for Norton Sound pink salmon based on harvest and escapement data for the Kwiniuk, Niukluk, Nome, Snake, North and El Dorado rivers was developed from the Banducci et al. (2007) annual catch and escapement estimates for 1995–2005. A record for the minimum annual returns to the Columbia River (lower river catch plus counts over Bonneville Dam) for spring Chinook salmon *O. tshawytscha* was obtained from the Oregon Department of Fish and Wildlife and the Northwest Power Council.

Sub-sample composites of environmental data, conditioned on periods of either high or low salmon abundance or productivity, were created to identify aspects of climate variations that were typically observed dur-

ing periods of high and low Alaska salmon productivity. The compositing approach used here included (1) ranking the values of the annual SRi according to their magnitude, (2) identifying the fry emergence and smolt migration year for the ten highest and lowest SRi values and grouping them into "high" and "low" productivity sub-samples, (3) creating new time series of the ten-member average monthly surface air temperatures in Nome for the 19-month period that begins in June of the brood year and ends in December of the fry emergence and smolt migration year for the high and low productivity sub-sample, and (4) creating ten-member average SST anomaly maps for May-August conditions representing the average SST anomalies experienced in the first summer for juvenile pink salmon in the high and low productivity groups.

Large-Scale Patterns of Climate and Salmon Variations

For much of the 20th century, an inverse north-south pattern of Pacific salmon production covaried with the interdecadal variations in the PDO pattern (Hare et al. 1999). Figure 1 shows five-year running averages for the observed catch history for all Alaska salmon from 1910 to 2004, and the observed catch plus escapement for Columbia River spring Chinook salmon from 1938 to 2002. For most of the 20th century, these regionally aggregated population groups were negatively correlated ($r = -0.57$ for three-year running averages over 1940–1999), wherein Alaska salmon landings were high from the mid-1920s through 1940s and from the late 1970s until 2004, while Columbia Basin spring Chinook salmon numbers tended to be low from the late 1930s through mid-1940s, high from the 1950s through mid-1970s, and then low from the late 1970s through mid-1990s.

Difference maps provided insights into the large-scale aspects of the relationships between surface temperature and Pacific salmon production changes. May through August averaging was chosen here to focus on a hypothesized "critical" early ocean period for many Pacific salmon stocks where variations in climate were thought to have especially large impacts on smolt-to-adult survival rates (Hare et al. 1999). A difference map showing May through August SST between 1977–1998 and 1950–1976 showed that SST changes corresponded with the large increases in Alaska salmon catches and the period of declining returns for Columbia Basin spring Chinook salmon (Figure 2). SST changes were positive throughout the subarctic regions of the North Pacific, including the Bering Sea, the Gulf of Alaska, and the northeast Pacific. At the same time, SSTs cooled across much of the North Pacific between about 30°N and 50°N latitude. Figure 3 shows seasonal averages for surface air temperature changes between the same periods. For Alaska and the rest of the Pacific Northwest the era of high Alaska salmon production from 1977–1998 was warmer than the era of low salmon production in 1950–1976. The largest air temperature differences between these two periods were found in the winter season (January–March), where surface temperatures in Alaska and western Canada were ~2–3°C warmer in the later period. The smallest temperature differences between these periods were found in summer (July–September), where surface temperatures in Alaska were ~0–1°C warmer in the later period. Temperature changes in spring and fall seasons were typically ~1–2°C warmer in the later period.

From a global perspective, the period since the 1970s was notable for the prominent and sustained rises in globally-averaged surface temperature, with especially large warming trends in the high-latitudes of the Northern Hemisphere (Figure 4; IPCC 2007). Wallace et al. (1995) showed that a substantial part of the late 1970s warming in the Northern Hemi-

sphere was related to interdecadal changes in atmospheric circulation, with the pattern of warming in western North America especially influenced by the persistently strong Aleutian Low pressure pattern that was part of the 1977 shift in Pacific climate. From a North Pacific perspective, the patterns of warming shown in Figures 2 and 3 bear a strong resemblance to the patterns of warming associated with the PDO-pattern of interdecadal variability (Mantua et al. 1997; Zhang et al. 1997).

From a North Pacific climate perspective, the period from 1997 through the early 2000s was notable for the rapid basin-scale changes that coincided with the extreme changes in the tropical ENSO. A visual analysis of the three climate indices (Figure 4) showed that ENSO, the PDO, and global average temperatures all underwent large interannual changes in the period since the mid-1990s. The Niño 3.4 index, which tracks ENSO variability, had extreme positive values indicating El Niño conditions from mid-1997 through the winter of 1998, and then rapidly changed to negative values (La Niña conditions) in the spring of 1998 that persisted into mid-2002. Similarly, the PDO index had large positive values from mid-1997 through spring 1998 indicating an extreme warm period for the Bering Sea, Gulf of Alaska, and northeast Pacific Ocean that were also followed by a rapid change to cooler conditions in these locations that persisted into 2002. Overland et al. (2001) showed that atmospheric teleconnections[1] initiated by the tropical ENSO likely altered wind and weather patterns in the North Pacific that resulted in the observed interannual shift in North Pacific SSTs (also see Peterson and Schwing 2003). Finally, global average surface temperatures spiked in association with the extreme 1997–1998 El Niño event, rising up to 0.2°C above the long-term warming trend for a period of about one year.

---

[1]Teleconnection in atmospheric science refers to climate anomalies being related to each other at large distances (typically thousands of kilometers).

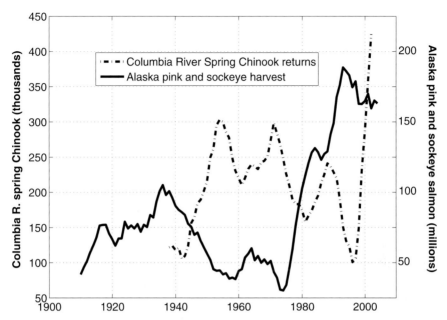

FIGURE 1. Historical salmon landings for Alaska from 1925–2004 and total Columbia River Spring Chinook returns from 1938–2002.

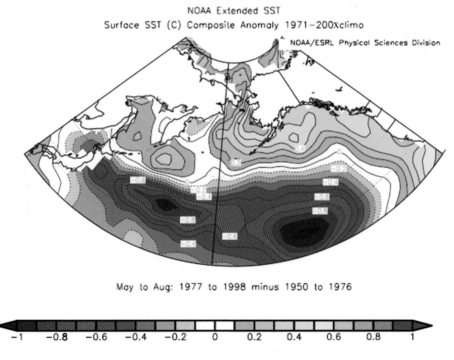

FIGURE 2. May-to-August SST anomalies (in °C) for 1977–1998 minus 1950–1976. Contour interval is 0.1 °C. Image provided by the NOAA/ESRL Physical Sciences Division, Boulder Colorado from their Web site: http://www.cdc.noaa.gov/.

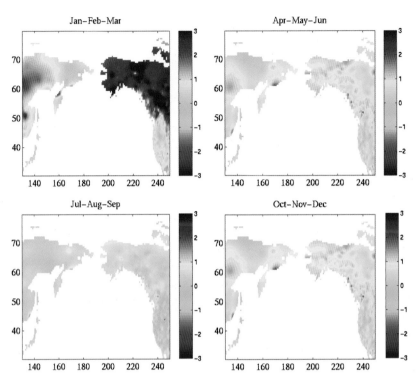

FIGURE 3. 1977–1998 minus 1950–1976 surface air temperatures (in °C) for (a) January-to-March, (b) April-to-June, (c) July-to-September, and (d) October-to-December.

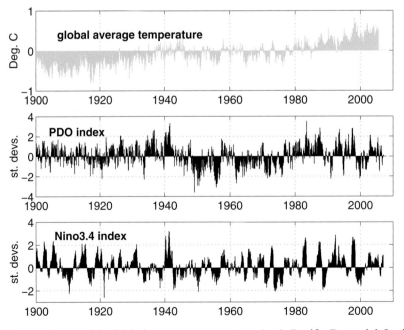

FIGURE 4. Time series monthly Global average temperature (top), Pacific Decaadal Oscillation (PDO) index (middle), and Niño3.4 index (bottom).

The combination of continued long-term global warming trends and large amplitude interannual climate changes associated with the change from tropical El Niño to La Niña conditions in 1998 contributed to North Pacific SST changes that were in part unlike the canonical PDO pattern (Figure 5). During the 1999–2002 period, important SST changes for Pacific salmon included a strong cooling of the northeast Pacific, especially west of Oregon, Washington, and British Columbia, and a moderation of the warm SSTs in the Gulf of Alaska and the Bering Sea. However, SSTs in the Bering Sea and Gulf of Alaska remained warmer than those in the cool PDO and the poor salmon production era of 1950–1976. More precisely, the cool-season (November–March) SST changes in the late 1990s projected strongly onto the second mode of North Pacific SST variations, and only weakly onto the PDO-pattern (Bond et al. 2003). Additionally, the average warm-season (May–August) PDO index value for 1999–2002 was similar to that for the 1950–1976 period. The switch to a coherent north-south salmon production pattern from the late 1990s through the early 2000s can be interpreted in part as a consequence of the breakdown in the PDO-related large-scale spatial coherence in the changing climate and ocean conditions of the northeast Pacific. The state of the climate system in seasons other than winter was likely to be important to the marine ecosystem and to salmon, and the nature of even large-scale climate variations important for salmon was richer than formerly appreciated.

Regional Patterns of Climate and Salmon Variations

To develop insights into the relationships between changes in salmon productivity and climate at regional spatial scales, we now shift our attention to a time series representing the composite annual fluctuations in Norton Sound pink salmon productivity. Pyper et al. (2001) developed the Norton Sound spawner-recruit index (SRi) for brood years 1962 to 1995 from the composite average for variations in spawner-to-recruit survival rates for pink salmon from four stocks or districts in Norton Sound (Nome, Golovin, Moses Point and Norton Bay, and Unalakleet) (Figure 6). This time series depicts a productivity history with large year-to-year and multiyear variations.

Differences between 19-month composite surface temperature time series that span the spawning, incubation, and seaward migration period observed during the ten highest and ten lowest brood years, in the 1962 to 1995 period, are shown in Figure 7. Temperature differences between the high and low productivity years were generally small and variable during the spawning period. In contrast, large and persistent differences were found for the incubation, fry emergence, and seaward migration months of January through May. All differences were positive for the months of January through November of the seaward migration year. A bivariate scatterplot of January through May average air temperature at Nome versus the Norton Sound RSi for the previous (brood) year showed a generally linear relationship between these indices, with a correlation coefficient $r = 0.52$ (Figure 8).

To develop insights into the characteristics of coastal ocean temperatures that typically covary with variations in the Norton Sound pink salmon RSi, composite maps for the early ocean period (May–August) for the ten highest and ten lowest brood years are shown in Figure 9. The high productivity composite has warm SST anomalies throughout the Bering Sea, with the largest anomalies found in the near-shore waters of the eastern Bering Sea. In contrast, the low productivity composite has cold SST anomalies throughout most of the Bering Sea, with the largest anomalies also found in the near-shore waters of the eastern Bering Sea.

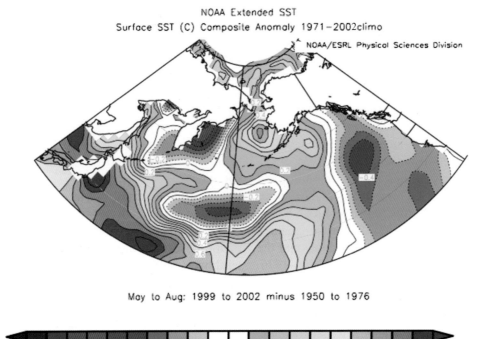

FIGURE 5. May-to-August SST differences (in °C) for 1999–2002 minus 1950–1976. Contour interval is 0.1 °C. Image provided by the NOAA/ESRL Physical Sciences Division, Boulder Colorado from their Web site at http://www.cdc.noaa.gov/.

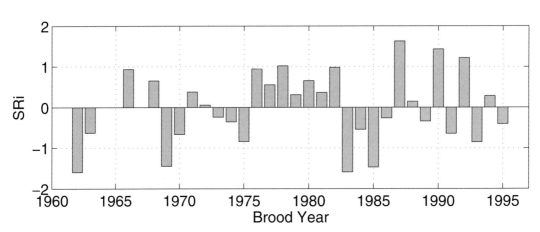

FIGURE 6. Annual Norton Sound pink salmon composite stock-recruit survival indices (SRi's) for brood years 1962–1995 (from Pyper et al. 2001).

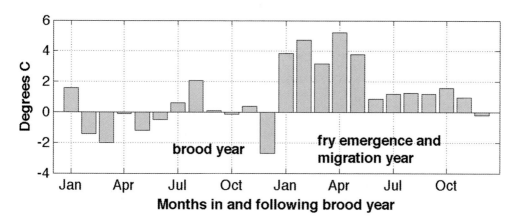

FIGURE 7. Differences between the monthly average surface air temperature in Nome, Alaska, for composites of the 10 highest and 10 lowest Norton Sound pink salmon SRi values for brood years 1962 to 1995.

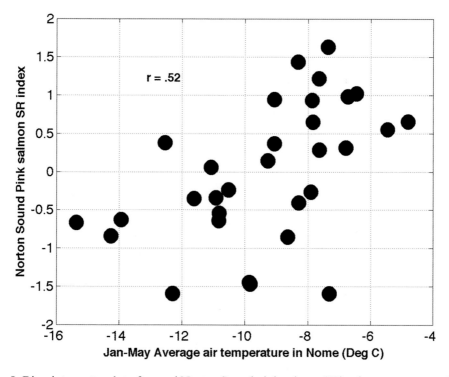

FIGURE 8. Bivariate scatterplot of annual Norton Sound pink salmon SRi values versus annual January-to-May averaged Nome, Alaska, air temperatures in the following year. These two series are correlated at a level of $r = +0.52$.

(a)

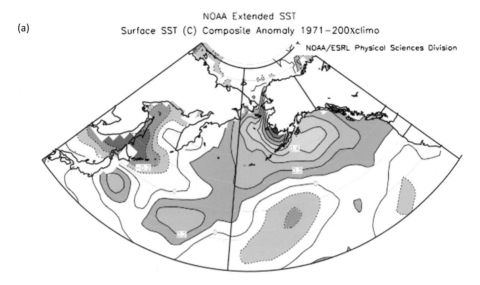

NOAA Extended SST
Surface SST (C) Composite Anomaly 1971-200Xclimo

NOAA/ESRL Physical Sciences Division

May to Aug: 1978,1969,1981,1967,1977,1983,1979,1993,1991,1988

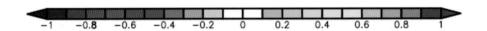

(b)

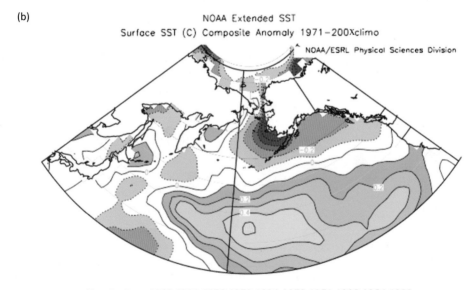

NOAA Extended SST
Surface SST (C) Composite Anomaly 1971-200Xclimo

NOAA/ESRL Physical Sciences Division

May to Aug: 1963,1984,1986,1970,1994,1976,1971,1992,1964,1985

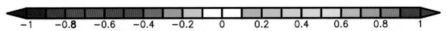

FIGURE 9. Composite May-to-August SST anomalies for years showing (a) the averages for the 10 highest and (b) 10 lowest SRi values for Norton Sound pink salmon productivity in the period 1962–1995. Anomalies are computed with respect to the 1971–2000 May-to-August climatology. Contour interval is 0.1 °C. Image provided by the NOAA/ESRL Physical Sciences Division, Boulder Colorado from their Web site at http://www.cdc.noaa.gov/.

An aggregate recruits-per-spawner index developed from the Banducci et al. (2007) annual catch and escapement estimates for the Kwiniuk, Niukluk, Nome, Snake, North and El Dorado rivers for 1995–2005 is shown in Figure 10a (see also Menard et al. 2009; this volume). In this period, productivity exceeded two recruits-per-spawner for brood years 1995, 2001, 2002, and 2003, while productivity was less than one recruit-per-spawner for brood years 1997 and 1998. Note that no attempt was made to fit a stock-recruit curve to these data because of the short length of this time series, so no attempt was made to remove possible impacts of density dependent processes.

Figure 10b shows a bivariate scatterplot between January–May average surface air temperatures in Nome (corresponding to the fry emergence and ocean migration year) and the recruits-per-spawner index. A notable feature of these data were that especially warm conditions for freshwater and early marine life stages for Norton Sound pink salmon coincided with both high and low levels of recruits-per-spawner for brood years 1996–2003. May–August SSTs in the eastern Bering Sea were warmer than average in 1997 and 1998, especially cold in 1999, near average in 2000, and slightly cooler than average in 2001, yet less than two recruits-per-spawner occured for each of these broods. For these years, little evidence existed for a coherent relationship between productivity and winter-spring air temperatures or spring-summer near-shore ocean temperatures. Ocean entry years 2002, 2003, and 2004 did, however, have warm conditions in winter, spring, and summer, and greater than two recruits-per-spawner for each year.

Discussion

Co-varying patterns of climate and salmon production variations depend upon the spatial scale of interest. Aggregating catch data across large regions like the state of Alaska leads to the identification of climate patterns with comparable scales of coherence, namely across the entire North Pacific Ocean and western North America. At this scale, Alaska salmon abundance for all five commercially harvested species covaries among regional populations through time, and the PDO index accounts for nearly 50% of the interannual to interdecadal variance in Alaska salmon abundance (Hare et al. 1999). A regional perspective based on the ten highest and ten lowest years of Norton Sound pink salmon productivity identifies regional patterns of climate variation that were nearly mirror images in character between the high and low productivity subsamples. A key finding in this analysis was that the high productivity years in the 1962–1995 period were associated with warmer than average winter-spring air temperatures and summertime SST, while the low productivity years were more strongly associated with cold periods in winter-spring air temperatures and summer SST. However, especially warm conditions for freshwater and early marine life stages for Norton Sound pink salmon coincided with both high and low levels of recruits-per-spawner for brood years 1996–2003, a period that experienced large interannual variations in Bering Sea, North Pacific, and tropical Pacific ocean conditions.

The north-south inverse production pattern for North Pacific salmon, along with the PDO pattern of North Pacific climate variability, was prominent in the period from 1925 through the mid-1990s, but less prominent in the period from the late 1990s to early 2000s. This latter period was marked by sustained warming trends at the global scale, throughout the Arctic, and over Alaska. Statewide Alaska salmon production remained near historic highs, although some large population groups (like Yukon River Chinook and chum salmon, and Norton Sound pink salmon)

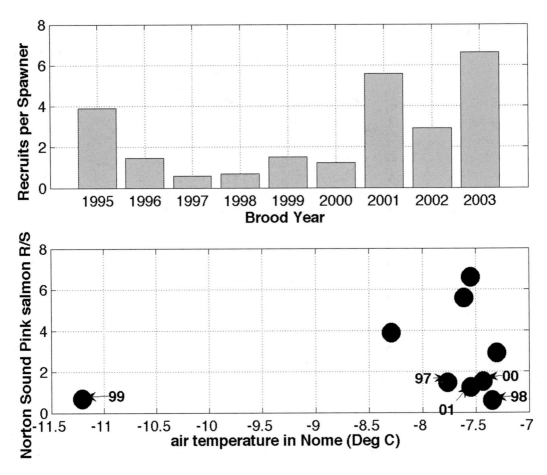

FIGURE 10. (a) Aggregate recruits-per-spawner index developed from Banducci et al.'s (2007) annual catch and escapement estimates for the Kwiniuk, Niukluk, Nome, Snake, North and El Dorado rivers for 1995–2005. (b) Bivariate scatterplot of Norton Sound pink salmon recruits-per-spawner values versus annual January-to-May averaged Nome, Alaska, air temperatures corresponding to the fry emergence and ocean migration period.

experienced periods of very low abundance and productivity in some years. As shown by Hilborn et al. (2003) and discussed by Schindler and Rogers (2009, this volume), the same regional-scale climate forcing can contribute to a wide diversity of productivity responses in the same species but across different population groups. This diversity of sensitivity at the stock and watershed level poses a substantial challenge for those interested in predicting future changes in salmon productivity in response to a changing climate.

Leading hypotheses for the link between climate variations and Pacific salmon production have focused on changes in early ocean survival for juvenile salmon, but it is clear that climate also affects freshwater life stages and influences productivity. For example, warm winter and spring temperatures extend the ice-free period in Alaska's lakes and streams, and can contribute to increased productivity in freshwater environments that lead to more rapid growth rates for rearing juvenile salmon (Schindler and Rogers 2009).

Warming winter and springtime surface temperatures in the 1948–2000 period have been linked with advanced runoff timing in many snowmelt watersheds in western North America (Stewart et al. 2004). Changes in hydrologic regimes can be important for the reproductive success of salmon in freshwater. For example, Battin et al. (2007) found that for Washington State's Snohomish River basin, future climate favors a transition to more winter precipitation falling as rain and less as snow, which in turn increases peak winter flows while eggs are incubating; these projected hydrologic changes caused large decreases in the simulated reproductive success for Chinook salmon in that watershed. A finding here shows, in recent decades, anomalously warm temperatures in both the freshwater and marine regions that juvenile Alaska salmon use while rearing was associated with periods of high abundance for Alaska salmon as a whole. At the scale of Norton Sound, this pattern was evident for brood years 1962–1995, but less clear for brood years 1996–2000 when highly variable environmental conditions coincided with sustained low productivity.

Monitoring of both physical and ecological changes in freshwater and marine environments is a necessary step for better understanding of the relative importance of climate on freshwater and marine productivity for salmon, yet this kind of monitoring is relatively rare around the Pacific Rim. An improved understanding for climate on salmon also begs for new studies integrating research efforts around the full lifecycle of salmon, because it is lifecycle survival and productivity that contributes to their population dynamics (AYK SSI 2006).

A strong scientific consensus has emerged that global average temperatures will continue to rise in the coming century because of human-caused increases in atmospheric greenhouse gas concentrations (IPCC 2007). Based on climate model projections, global average temperatures are expected to rise from 1–6°C by 2100, and western Alaska's surface temperatures are expected to rise at substantially greater rates (IPCC 2007; Schindler and Rogers 2009).

For Alaska salmon populations that currently occupy habitats that are far from thermal stress levels in freshwater and marine environments, additional warming may serve to benefit productivity for some years into the future. Based on recent periods of anomalously warm ocean temperatures in the subarctic North Pacific and Bering Sea, and periods of warm winter and spring surface air temperatures over Alaska, relatively small amounts of warming in the future will likely continue to favor high productivity for Alaska salmon. However, more extreme ocean warming like that observed in 1997 and 1998 may push North Pacific and Bering Sea ecosystems into states that no longer favor high productivity for Alaska salmon.

Acknowledgments

I thank Steven Hare for providing west coast salmon catch records, the NOAA/ESRL Physical Sciences Division for providing online access to climate data and plotting software, Randall Peterman for providing the Norton Sound pink salmon SR indices, and three anonymous reviewers for their helpful comments. This publication was partially funded by the Joint Institute for the Study of the Atmosphere and Ocean (JISAO) under NOAA Cooperative Agreement No. NA17RJ1232, Contribution # 1414.

References

Banducci, A., T. Kohler, J. Soong, and J. Menard. 2007. 2005 Annual Management Report, Norton Sound, Port Clarence, and Kotzebue. Alaska Department of Fish and Game, Fishery Management Report No. 07–32, Anchorage.

Battin, J., M. W. Wiley, M. H. Ruckelshaus, R. N. Palmer, K. K. Bartz, H. Imaki, and E. Korb.

2007. Projected impacts of climate change on salmon habitat restoration. Proceedings of the National Academy of Sciences, USA 104:6720–6725.

Beamish, R. J., and D. R. Bouillon. 1993. Pacific salmon production trends in relation to climate. Canadian Journal of Fisheries and Aquatic Sciences 50:1002–1016.

Beamish, R. J., and R. M. Sweeting. 2009. The history of surprises associated with Pacific salmon returns signals that critical information is missing from our understanding of their population dynamics. Pages 1159–1168 in C. C. Krueger and C. E. Zimmerman, editors. Pacific salmon: ecology and management of western Alaska's populations. American Fisheries Society, Symposium 70, Bethesda, Maryland.

Bond, N. A., J. E. Overland, M. Spillane, and P. Stabeno. 2003. Recent shifts in the state of the North Pacific. Geophysical Research Letters 30:2183–2187.

Hare, S. R., and R. C. Francis. 1995. Climate change and salmon production in the Northeast Pacific Ocean. Canadian Special Publication of Fisheries and Aquatic Sciences 121:357–372.

Hare, S. R., N. J. Mantua, and R. C. Francis. 1999. Inverse production regimes: Alaskan and West Coast salmon. Fisheries 24:6–14.

Hilborn, R., T. P. Quinn, D. E. Schindler, and D. E. Rogers. 2003. Biocomplexity and fisheries sustainability. Proceedings of the National Academy of Sciences, USA 100:6564–6568.

IPCC (Intergovernmental Panel on Climate Control). 2007. Summary for Policymakers: Contribution of Working Group I to the Fourth Assessment Report of the Intergovernmental Panel on Climate Change. Geneva, Switzerland.

Kaplan, A., M. Cane, Y. Kushnir, A. Clement, M. Blumenthal, and B. Rajagopalan. 1998. Analyses of global sea surface temperature 1856–1991. Journal of Geophysical Research 103:18,567–18,589.

Mantua, N. J., S. R. Hare, Y. Zhang, J. M. Wallace, and R. C. Francis. 1997. A Pacific interdecadal climate oscillation with impacts on salmon production. Bulletin of the American Meteorological Society 78:1069–1079.

Menard, J., C. C. Krueger, and J. R. Hilsinger. 2009. Norton Sound salmon fisheries: history, stock abundance, and management. Pages 621–673 in C. C. Krueger and C. E. Zimmerman, editors. Pacific salmon: ecology and management of western Alaska's populations. American Fisheries Society, Symposium 70, Bethesda, Maryland.

Moss, J. H., N. Hillgruber, C. Lean, J. Mackenzie-Grieve, K. Mull, K. Myers, and T. C. Stark. 2009.

Conservation of western Alaskan salmon stocks by identifying critical linkages between marine and freshwater life stages and long-term monitoring. Pages 1115–1125 in C. C. Krueger and C. E. Zimmerman, editors. Pacific salmon: ecology and management of western Alaska's populations. American Fisheries Society, Symposium 70, Bethesda, Maryland.

Myers, R. A., G. Mertz, and J. Bridson. 1997. Spatial scales of interannual recruitment variations of marine, anadromous, and freshwater fish. Canadian Journal of Fisheries and Aquatic Sciences 54:1400–1407.

Overland, J. E., N. A. Bond, and J. M. Adams. 2001. North Pacific atmospheric and SST anomalies in 1997: Links to ENSO? Fisheries Oceanography 10:69–80.

Peterman, R. M., B. J. Pyper, M. F. Lapointe, M. D. Adkison, and C. J. Walters. 1998. Patterns of covariation in survival rates of British Columbian and Alaskan sockeye salmon (Oncorhynchus nerka) stocks. Canadian Journal of Fisheries and Aquatic Sciences 55:2503–2517.

Peterson, W. T., and F. B. Schwing. 2003. A new climate regime in northeast Pacific ecosystems. Geophysical Research Letters 30(17):1896.

Pyper, B. J., F. J. Mueter, and R. M. Peterman. 2005. Across species comparisons of spatial scales of environmental effects on survival rates of Northeast Pacific salmon. Transactions of the American Fisheries Society 134:86–104.

Pyper, B. J., F. J. Mueter, R. M. Peterman, D. J. Blackbourn, and C. C. Wood. 2001. Spatial covariation in survival rates of Northeast Pacific pink salmon (Oncorhynchus gorbuscha). Canadian Journal of Fisheries and Aquatic Sciences 58:1501–1515.

Pyper, B. J., F. J. Mueter, R. M. Peterman, D. J. Blackbourn, and C. C. Wood. 2002. Spatial covariation in survival rates of Northeast Pacific chum salmon. Transactions of the American Fisheries Society 131:343–363.

Schindler, D. E., and L. A. Rogers. 2009. Responses of Pacific salmon populations to climate variation in freshwater ecosystems. Pages 1127–1142 in C. C. Krueger and C. E. Zimmerman, editors. Pacific salmon: ecology and management of western Alaska's populations. American Fisheries Society, Symposium 70, Bethesda, Maryland.

Smith, T. M., and R. W. Reynolds. 2004. Improved extended reconstruction of SST (1854–1997). Journal of Climate 17:2466–2477.

Stewart, I. T., D. R. Cayan, and M. D. Dettinger. 2004. Changes toward earlier streamflow timing across western North America. Journal of Climate 18:1136–1155.

Wallace, J. M., Y. Zhang, and J. A. Renwick. 1995. Dynamic contribution to hemispheric mean temperature trends. Science 270:780–783.

Willmott, C. J., and K. Matsuura. 1995. Smart interpolation of annually averaged air temperature in the United States. Journal of Applied Meteorology 34:2577–2586.

WRCC (Western Regional Climate Center). 2008. Alaska regional climate summaries. Available: http://www.wrcc.dri.edu/summary/climsmak.html (March 2008).

Zhang, Y., J. M. Wallace, and D. S. Battisti. 1997. ENSO-like interdecadal variability: 1900–93. Journal of Climate 10:1004–1020.

(Figure 1). The Canadian catch in 2008 was around 10,000 t, less than one sixth of the historic average and only 1% of the total Pacific salmon catch by all countries (Figure 2). No one would question the abilities and contributions of these two visionary scientists and a number of their colleagues. However, the unexpected effects of climate have changed our thinking about the population ecology of Pacific salmon and it is time for the young Turks to think differently.

Pacific Salmon Fisheries by All Countries

The fishery for Pacific salmon, by anyone's account, has to be considered to be remarkable. The authors think it is the world's most important fishery because of the commercial and cultural importance of the half dozen key species and because these species dominate the daytime biomass of fishes in the surface waters of the subarctic Pacific. They suspect that supporters of cod, herring, hake, sardines and anchovies might have other rankings of importance. However, in addition to the cultural and commercial importance, Pacific salmon are fairly well managed. Start with the record of the North Pacific Anadromous Fish Commission (NPAFC), remembering that it originated as the International North Pacific Fisheries Commission (INPFC) in 1952. NPAFC now has five member countries: Canada, Japan, Korea, Russia and the United States and all have agreed not to fish Pacific salmon on the high seas. Coordinated enforcement within the NPAFC has virtually eliminated the high seas fishing of Pacific salmon as any vessel trying to fish illegally most likely will get caught.

Look at the total Pacific salmon catch in the past 20 years (Figure 2). The highest total catch occurred in 2007, the second highest in 1995, and third highest in 2005. In fact, the catch of Pacific salmon has been at historic high levels for the past 15 years.

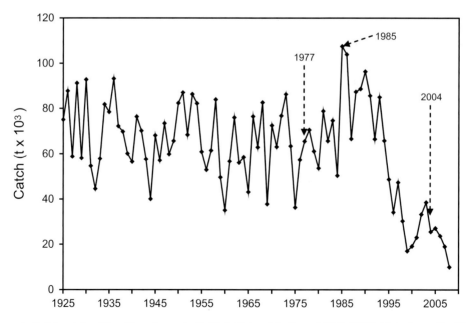

FIGURE 1. Total catch of Pacific salmon in British Columbia from 1925–2008 (data from the North Pacific Anadromous Fish Commission statistical yearbook 2002, see http://www.npafc.org/new/publications/Statistical%20Yearbook/index.htm).

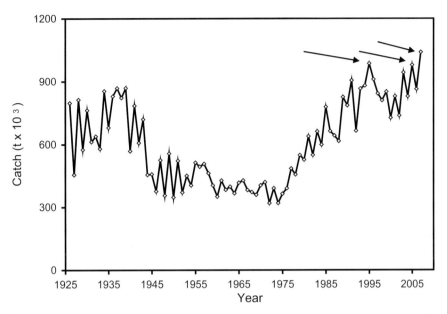

FIGURE 2. Total catch of Pacific salmon by all countries from 1925–2005, arrows indicate the largest catches (data from the North Pacific Anadromous Fish Commission statistical yearbook 2002, see http://www.npafc.org/new/publications/Statistical%20Yearbook/index.htm).

There is variability, as expected, but there is no disputing the trend. It is fair to conclude that Pacific salmon are well managed internationally and currently are at historic high levels of abundance. However, it is equally fair to conclude that we do not understand why the abundances are so large or what to expect over the next 50 years as global warming impacts the ecology of Pacific salmon life cycles in fresh water and in the ocean.

The general public are puzzled that scientists are unable to explain why Pacific salmon in general are doing so well and why it is so difficult to forecast returns. Biologists studying Pacific salmon, however, have learned to expect the unexpected. There are some who believe that it is not possible to forecast Pacific salmon returns reliably. The authors do not share this belief because scientists now have the technology and the international cooperation to understand how recruitment of Pacific salmon is regulated in the ocean. Accurate forecasting requires studies of the whole life

cycle of salmon. If our modern salmon science dates from Dr. Ricker's paper on stock and recruitment in 1954, then it would appear that continuing to do the same things scientists did in the past 50 years probably will get us more or less where we are now in 2059.

Most scientists agree that the current high catches of Pacific salmon are a result of favorable ocean and climate conditions. Combining information on Pacific salmon production in freshwater or from hatcheries with an understanding of how ocean conditions regulate the marine survival will explain how recruitment is determined. The understanding of these processes will provide regional fisheries managers with new models that will more accurately link climate and physical processes to recruitment, abundance and distribution. There is a great need to act now because Pacific salmon are generally abundant and the next 50 years is a dangerous period for the management of Pacific salmon because of climate change.

The importance of carrying out "whole life cycle studies" of Pacific salmon can be shown from the history of managing coho salmon *Oncorhynchus kisutch* in the Strait of Georgia. The coho salmon story in the Strait of Georgia could start in the 1950s when reliable data became available, but 1977 is a good beginning as it was the official start of the Salmon Enhancement Program (Fisheries and Environment Canada 1978). Scientists studying Pacific salmon in the early 1970s believed that there was *a lot of headroom for the expansion of salmon populations before the rearing areas of the ocean became a limiting factor*. The Salmonid Enhancement Program was based on the assumption that there was unused rearing capacity in the ocean. All major species of Pacific salmon were enhanced in this program with the objective of doubling the annual catch of Canada's Pacific salmon, from about 25 million fish in the early 1970s to 50 million fish per year by 2003 (60,000 t to 120,000 t). It was believed that the biological potential to increase the

production of coho salmon still remained in fresh water and salt water, but losses through environmental damage and overfishing had greatly reduced production. Artificial rearing of coho salmon in hatcheries would increase the egg to fry or egg to smolt survival, resulting in large increases in the number of juvenile coho salmon entering the ocean. Climate and ocean conditions were recognized to affect marine survival, but the effects were believed to be random. Although it was not explicitly written, the assumption was that average marine survival would not change greatly as the ocean had the capacity to produce greater abundances of coho salmon.

Coho salmon in the Strait of Georgia traditionally supported an important commercial and sport fishery (Figure 3). However, beginning about the late 1980s, there were declines in the escapements of wild coho salmon as well as declines in the marine survival of coho salmon produced in hatcheries (DFO 1990,1992; Irvine et al. 1992). These declines in abundance occurred despite the

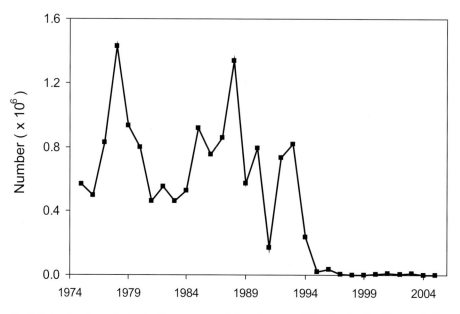

FIGURE 3. Catch of coho salmon in the commercial and sports fisheries in the Strait of Georgia from 1975–2005 (see http://www.pac.dfo-mpo.gc.ca/species/salmon/salmon_fisheries/catchstats_e.htm).

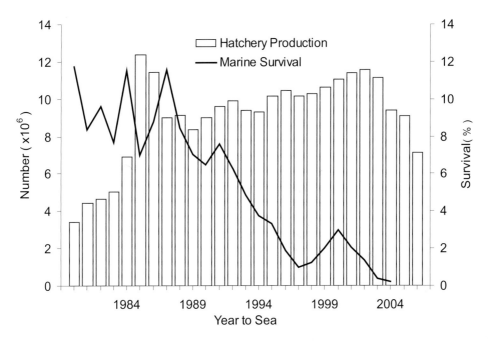

FIGURE 4. Hatchery production and marine survival of coho salmon in the Strait of Georgia from 1980–2006. Marine survival is shown as the year smolts enter the ocean. Brood year survival would be two years earlier, i.e., marine survival for 2004 is for coho salmon that spawned in 2002 and returned as adults in 2005 (Beamish et al. 2008).

attempts of hatcheries to rebuild and restore abundances (Figure 4). Overfishing and fresh-water habitat loss were believed to be responsible for the decline in wild coho salmon as evidenced by the consensus reached in the final report of the Coho Steering Committee (DFO 1992) on how to restore abundances of coho salmon. This two-year study published in 1992 determined that the declines resulted primarily from overfishing and habitat loss although it was acknowledged that in the longer term, "studies of the carrying capacity of estuarine and marine survival and growth in the Strait of Georgia should be conducted to evaluate whether the marine carrying capacity is being taxed." Participants in the study concluded that because the catch of enhanced coho (not wild coho) salmon had risen rapidly as a result of the hatchery program, it was tempting to simply produce more coho salmon in hatcheries and solve the problem.

The authors of the coho salmon report wrote that, "It can be argued that coho stocks could be rebuilt simply by expanding this enhancement effort several fold." The authors also cautioned that this approach would be expensive and there was accumulating evidence of detrimental effects of hatchery-reared coho salmon on wild stocks. The major recommendation of the Coho Steering Committee was to reduce the exploitation rate from about 75–80% to 65–70%. The benefits of a 10% reduction in fishing and an expanded vigilance in protecting freshwater habitat was calculated to produce 300,000–800,000 more coho salmon in six to twelve years. In fact, in six years (1998) the coho salmon fishery had virtually collapsed (Figure 3).

In 1997 the authors started a study of the marine phase of the life cycle of coho salmon in the Strait of Georgia (Beamish et al. 1999, 2000a; Sweeting et al. 2003). The abundances of juvenile coho salmon was determined each July, using the catches from a large trawl net and the volume of water fished (Beamish et al. 2000b). From 1998–2006, about 75% of all coho salmon released from hatcheries had their adipose fin removed. The number of these fin-clipped coho salmon in our catch were used to estimate the percentage of hatchery and wild coho in the Strait of Georgia (Figure 5A). We used this percentage and the known number of coho salmon smolts produced in hatcheries (Figure 4) to estimate the total number of wild and hatchery coho smolts that entered the Strait of Georgia (Figure 5B). We estimated the early marine survival up to about mid July by dividing the abundance estimates from the survey (Figure 5C) by the total number of smolts entering the strait (Figure 5B). This estimate of early marine survival (Figure 5D) was then compared with the final brood year marine survival (Figure 4). Brood year survival was determined using coded-wire tag recoveries from fisheries and from the coho salmon returning to the eight largest hatcheries (Beamish et al. 2008).

The variability in early marine survival up to July among years ranged from about 3% to 20%. It was observed that the average length of coho salmon in July was positively related to brood year marine survival (Figure 6). The lowest early marine survival occurred when the coho salmon in July were smaller. In years when the early marine survival was higher (1998–2001) there was still a substantial mortality that occurred later in the year, as evidenced by the corresponding brood year survival. The authors propose that this later-in-the-year mortality was related to the smaller fish not surviving the winter (Beamish et al. 2004). They also propose that the variability in marine survival is strongly related to very early marine growth. In years when coho salmon growth is very rapid, prior to the July surveys marine survival and abundance was higher. However, the brood year

survival in recent years was substantially less than those observed in the late 1970s and early 1980s (Figure 4). Thus, it was concluded that the capacity for the Strait of Georgia to produce coho salmon is much reduced today compared to 30 years ago, probably because prey abundance is reduced by the time most coho salmon enter the Strait of Georgia. The authors are of the opinion that carrying capacity relates to the capacity for coho salmon to grow quickly once they enter the Strait of Georgia. The very high marine survival in the past would result from very good early marine growth. The large abundances in the past resulted from the high marine survival and not only the number of individuals that entered the ocean. The authors' study of the marine phase of the coho salmon life cycle shows that accurate forecasting of coho salmon returns requires more information than the number of spawning individuals or even the number of smolts entering the ocean.

Three examples are provided that show that technology and international cooperation exist to carry out the research to define how recruitment of Pacific salmon is regulated and to improve forecasting. Urawa (2004) and Urawa et al. (2005) used genetic stock identification to identify the seasonal migration of chum salmon *O. keta* of Japanese origin (Figure 7). The study showed that chum salmon of Japanese origin spend their second and third winter in the Gulf of Alaska. Urawa et al. (2005) speculated that chum salmon of Japanese origin carried out extensive migrations into the Gulf of Alaska in the winter because their preferred temperature range in the winter may be more widely available in the eastern North Pacific. Whatever the reason turns out to be, it is important to understand that winter conditions in the Gulf of Alaska affect the production of chum salmon produced in hatcheries in Japan. The study shows that migration models for all chum salmon stocks are possible because of the ability to identify the country of origin of chum salmon and the

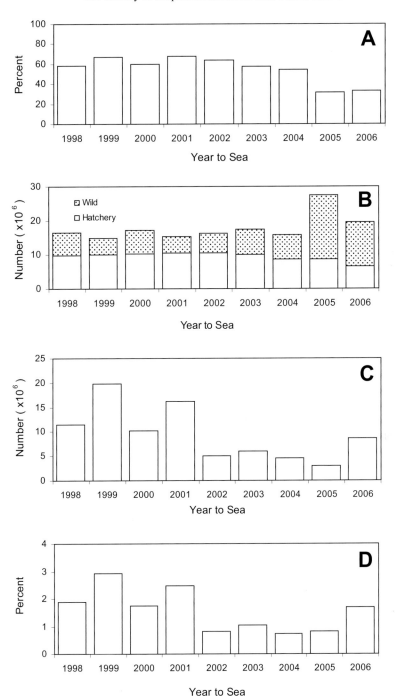

FIGURE 5. A) Percentage of hatchery fish in the coho salmon catches in the Strait of Georgia in July 1998–2006. B) Total numbers of wild and hatchery coho salmon smolts in the Strait of Georgia from 1998–2006, calculated using hatchery and wild percentages and hatchery production. C) July abundances of coho salmon for the Strait of Georgia from 1998–2006, excluding all U.S. fish. D) Early marine survival (ocean entry to mid-July) of coho salmon in the Strait of Georgia from 1998–2006 (Beamish et al. 2008).

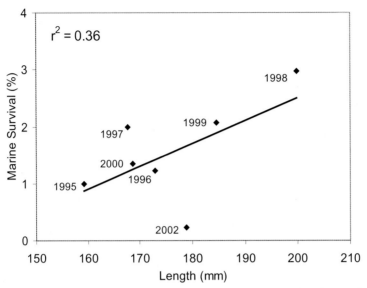

FIGURE 6. Average length of coho salmon in the July surveys compared to the marine survival for the brood year shown. The catch year is two years later than the brood year (Beamish et al. 2008).

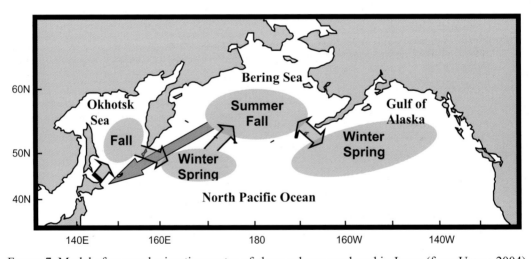

FIGURE 7. Model of seasonal migration routes of chum salmon produced in Japan (from Urawa 2004).

willingness of scientists to share samples. Surveys conducted in the major ocean feeding areas of chum salmon that monitor the abundance and condition can be associated with climate and ocean conditions to improve the accuracy of forecasting models of chum salmon returns.

Stock proportions and country of origin of immature sockeye salmon *O. nerka* sampled throughout the Bering Sea in 2002 and 2003 were identified in the Annual Report of the Bering-Aleutian Salmon International Survey (BASIS) 2004 (NPAFC, 2005) and in Habicht et al. (2005). Samples of immature sockeye salmon were collected throughout the Bering Sea in 2002 and 2003 through a cooperative research effort among Japan, Russia and the United States (Habicht et al. 2005; Helle et al. 2005). DNA analysis was used to show the location of immature sockeye salmon of Russian and United States origin. Studies such as these for immature sockeye salmon can be linked to climate and ocean data to determine how stocks that rear in different areas of the North Pacific are affected by regional variability in ocean habitat. This kind of study was also carried out by Kaga et al. (2006) for chum and pink salmon *O. gorbuscha*. They showed that the total lipid content of chum and pink salmon caught in the Gulf of Alaska in the winter of 2006 was significantly lower than in the western North Pacific. The low lipid content of pink salmon in the Gulf of Alaska may be related to the coast-wide poor marine survival that was observed in 2006. The three studies emphasize the importance of monitoring immature Pacific salmon in their ocean habitats and associating the growth and condition of these fish with regional climate and ocean conditions (see also Mantua 2009, this volume).

Fran Ulmer, former lieutenant governor of Alaska and U.S. representative to the North Pacific Anadromous Fish Commission (NPAFC), was mainly responsible for the Bering-Aleutian Salmon International Survey (BASIS) that started in 2001. BASIS was a concept that gave authority to work already in progress. BASIS created a team of researchers who worked as a family. Everyone was willing to help their colleagues and share data. As a result, millions of dollars of ship time and scientific information was shared annually among investigators in all Pacific salmon producing countries. Researchers were capable of determining where Pacific salmon were in the ocean, where they came from and their condition. Thus, BASIS and NPAFC helped to create an international team of researchers, determined to identify the processes that regulate Pacific salmon abundances in the ocean.

Conclusion

The authors propose that it is time to establish an international effort to carry out the research needed to improve forecasting. Philanthropic organizations and governments need to cooperate to provide adequate funds to support teams that will carry out this research. This may be difficult at first as it requires that organizations with different mandates cooperate to fund a common objective of conducting whole life cycle studies. This means that researchers looking at freshwater issues must work together with the researchers studying ocean impacts. Equally difficult is the need for commitments of five to ten years by the researchers and by managers and patrons of Pacific salmon research.

Scientists from all Pacific salmon producing countries have shown an ability to work in harmony to resolve the long-standing mysteries of Pacific salmon production. This cooperation and advances in genetic stock identification make it possible to understand the physical and biological processes that regulate recruitment. This understanding will complete our knowledge of the life history strategy of the various species of Pacific salmon and provide fisheries managers with new models that more accurately link climate and physical processes to recruitment, abundance and distribution. It is this understanding that will incrementally improve our ability to forecast until it becomes what Bill Ricker called the "Watson effect" (a reference to Sherlock Holmes). According to Watson effect, everything becomes simple once it is discovered. It is time to focus our funding on whole life cycle studies of Pacific salmon so that forecasting eventually becomes "elementary."

Acknowledgment

We appreciate the assistance that Lana Fitzpatrick provided with the preparation of the manuscript and figures.

References

Beamish, R. J., G. A. McFarlane, and R. E. Thomson. 1999. Recent declines in the recreational catch of coho salmon (*Oncorhynchus kisutch*) in the Strait of Georgia are related to climate. Canadian Journal of Fisheries and Aquatic Sciences 56:506–515.

Beamish, R. J., D. J. Noakes, G. A. McFarlane, W. Pinnix, R. M. Sweeting, and J. R. King. 2000a. Trends in coho marine survival in relation to the regime concept. Fisheries Oceanography 9:114–119.

Beamish, R. J., D. McCaughran, J. R. King, R. M. Sweeting, and G. A. McFarlane. 2000b. Estimating the abundance of juvenile coho salmon in the Strait of Georgia by means of surface trawls. North American Journal of Fisheries Management 20:369–375.

Beamish, R. J., C. Mahnken, and C. M. Neville. 2004. Evidence that reduced early marine growth is associated with lower marine survival of coho salmon. Transactions of the American Fisheries Society 133:26–33.

Beamish, R. J., R. M. Sweeting, K. L. Lange, and C. M. Neville. 2008. Changing trends in the population ecology of hatchery and wild coho salmon in the Strait of Georgia. Transactions of American Fisheries Society 137:503–520.

Department of Fisheries and Oceans Canada (DFO) 1990. Coho resource status and management planning process. September 1990. Available from the D.F.O. Library, Pacific Biological Station, Nanaimo, BC, Canada.

Department of Fisheries and Oceans Canada (DFO). 1992. Strait of Georgia coho planning process and recommendations: South Coast coho initiative final report. Coho Steering Committee Final Report. March 1992.

Fisheries and Environment Canada. 1978. The salmonid enhancement program. A public discussion paper. Information Branch, Fisheries and Marine Science, Vancouver.

Habicht, C., N. V. Varnavskaya, T. Azumaya, S. Urawa, R. L. Wilmot, C. M. Guthrie III, and J. E. Seeb. 2005. Migration patterns of sockeye salmon in the Bering Sea discerned from stock composition estimates of fish captured during BASIS studies. North Pacific Anadromous Fish Commission Technical Report No 6:41–43.

Helle, J. H., K. W. Myers, and J. E. Seeb. 2005. National overview of BASIS research for the United States. North Pacific Anadromous Fish Commission Technical Report No. 6:13–15.

Irvine, J. R., A. D. Anderson, V. Haist, B. M. Leaman, S. M. McKinnell, R. D. Stanley, and G. Thomas. 1992. Pacific Stock Assessment Review Committee (PSARC) annual report for 1991. Canadian Manuscript Report of Fisheries and Aquatic Sciences 2159.

Kaga, T., S. Sato, M. Fukuwaka, S. Takahashi, T. Nomura, and S. Urawa. 2006. Total lipid contents of winter chum and pink salmon in the western North Pacific Ocean and Gulf of Alaska. North Pacific Anadromous Fish Commission. Document 962. National Salmon Resources Center, Fisheries Research Agency, 2–2, Nakanoshima, Toyohira-ku, Sapporo 062–0922, Japan.

Mantua, N. 2009. Patterns of change in climate and Pacific salmon production. Pages 1143–1157 *in* C. C. Krueger and C. E. Zimmerman, editors. Pacific salmon: ecology and management of western Alaska's populations. American Fisheries Society, Symposium 70, Bethesda, Maryland.

North Pacific Anadromous Fish Commission (NPAFC). 2005. Annual Report of the Bering-Aleutian Salmon International Survey (BASIS) 2004. NPAFC Document 857. BASIS Working Group Committee on Scientific Research and Statistics, NPAFC, Vancouver, BC, Canada.

Ricker, W. E. 1973. Two mechanisms that make it impossible to maintain peak-period yields from stocks of Pacific salmon and other fishes. Journal of the Fisheries Research Board of Canada 30:1275–1286.

Sweeting, R. M., R. J. Beamish, D. J. Noakes, and C. M. Neville. 2003. Replacement of wild coho salmon by hatchery-reared coho salmon in the Strait of Georgia over the past three decades. North American Journal of Fisheries Management 23:492–502.

Urawa, S. 2004. Stock identification studies of high seas salmon in Japan: a review and future plan. North Pacific Anadromous Fish Commission Technical Report No 5:9–10.

Urawa, S., T. Azumaya, P.A. Crane, and L. W. Seeb. 2005. Origins and distribution of chum salmon in the Central Bering Sea. North Pacific Anadromous Fish Commission Technical Report No 6:67–69.

American Fisheries Society Symposium 70:1169–1176, 2009
© 2009 by the American Fisheries Society

An Integrated Conceptual Model in Salmon Ecology

MICHAEL WEBSTER*

Wild Salmon Ecosystems Initiative, Gordon and Betty Moore Foundation
1661 Page Mill Road, Palo Alto, California 94304, USA

Abstract.—In recent years, salmon ecologists have conducted a series of studies that revised longstanding concepts and added new kinds of information to the collective understanding of how salmon ecosystems function. The implications of these studies have been far-ranging and may lay the groundwork for a new emerging conceptual model of salmon ecology, management, and conservation. This paper argues that this model integrates the interrelated concepts of scale, connectivity, and biocomplexity, which underlie ecosystem function and have direct implications for management decisions and the scales at which effective management must operate. Provided that these concepts continue to stand up to scientific and applied rigor, they will formalize an integrated model of how salmon ecosystems operate that incorporates and broadens decades of system-specific studies. While many of these ideas are already informing management decisions, integrating or connecting these concepts will change the context for future decisions. As we enter a time of accelerating global change, the context in which management decisions are made will have an overwhelming influence on the future health of ecosystems and the livelihoods of those who depend on them.

Introduction

Most conservation and management decisions regarding Pacific salmon *Oncorhynchus* spp. are based to some degree on scientific information. However, the enormous number of scientific studies that have been conducted on salmon ecology makes it difficult to identify what data and information are most relevant to consider for any particular decision. To cope with an overabundance of highly specific information, it is argued here that most practitioners rely on a set of general concepts that are based on highly influential studies and accumulated weight of evidence on the importance of specific ecological processes. Together, this set of concepts sets the context or conceptual model for management

and conservation decisions. Such a conceptual model of salmon ecology has the potential to guide sound decision making, provided that the underlying concepts are sound.

The purpose of this manuscript is twofold. First, it describes how the Gordon and Betty Moore Foundation approaches funding scientific research aimed at accelerating the acquisition of conservation- and management-relevant information. Second, it argues that the field is currently in a state of rapid evolution that is leading to a new conceptual model, which may lead to improved conservation and management decision making. To illustrate this evolution, it describes significant scientific contributions of recent decades, as well as some exciting projects that are currently underway.

*Corresponding author: michael.webster@moore.org

Moore Foundation's Salmon Initiative

The objective of the Wild Salmon Ecosystems Initiative (WSEI) of the Moore Foundation is to maintain a healthy salmon ecosystem at the scale of the North Pacific. WSEI invests in a host of projects in three countries: Russia, Canada, and the United States. The bulk of the investments focus on watershed conservation and management because of the belief that intact spawning and rearing habitat is the foundation of healthy salmon ecosystems. WSEI also makes investments aimed at minimizing potential threats to wild salmon associated with fisheries, hatcheries, and net pen salmon aquaculture.

All WSEI projects proposed for funding are evaluated within a conceptual model of how salmon ecosystems function, drawing heavily from scientific research. While past research is critical in informing investment decisions, WSEI also invests in new research. Determining what topic areas to invest in has required a critical evaluation of the past field of research results to identify promising areas.

This chapter describes some of the most exciting areas of research in recent years and how some of the projects WSEI has supported through the year 2007 may contribute to the advancement of some emerging concepts in salmon science.

An Integrated Conceptual Model

In recent years, salmon ecologists have conducted a series of studies that are revising longstanding concepts and adding new kinds of information to the collective understanding of how salmon ecosystems function. The implications of these studies are far-ranging and may be laying the groundwork for an emerging conceptual model of salmon ecology, management, and conservation. This new model integrates the interrelated concepts of scale, connectivity, and biocomplexity, which underlie ecosystem function and have direct implications for management decisions and the scales at which effective management must operate. Critical aspects of these concepts are illustrated by four important areas of research that have developed over the last decade. The studies focus on:

1. The effect of changing climate regimes on temporal and spatial differences in salmon production,

2. The observation of high-seas interactions among stocks that have historically been viewed as independent,

3. Paleolimnological studies of long-term change in salmon populations, and

4. The demonstration of the role of biocomplexity in maintaining long-term production.

Climate regimes

Salmon populations have been studied primarily at the scale of individual watersheds. Management at this scale is appealing for a host of reasons, including: many fisheries operate at this scale, land use planning and restoration usually occur at this scale or smaller, and most fish return to their natal watershed. However, the observation that climate cycles might be driving the relative productivity of salmon along the entire west coast of North America (Hare et al. 1999; Mantua et al. 1997; Mantua 2009, this volume; Beamish and Sweeting 2009, this volume) fundamentally calls into question the notion of purely watershed-based management. While watersheds may continue to be the most appropriate scale for many management decisions, changing ocean regimes demonstrate that local productivity is influenced by larger-scale processes that are not uniform across the range of Pacific salmon, nor are they static across time (Myers et al. 2009, this volume).

Ocean interaction

A longstanding paradigm and the rationale for salmon production hatcheries is that an excess productive capacity exists in salmon ecosystems, especially in the Pacific Ocean such that an increase in smolt production will lead to a net increase in system-wide productivity. However, two recent examples demonstrate that this assumption may not always be the case. In Japan, chum hatchery operators have observed diminishing returns at high levels of hatchery smolt production, implying that the carrying capacity of wide-ranging chum salmon had been reached (Kaeriyama 1999). In another example, the production of Bristol Bay sockeye was reduced in the presence of highly-abundant Russian pink salmon (Ruggerone et al. 2003, 2005; Ruggerone and Nielsen 2009, this volume). Taken together, these examples demonstrate that, at certain times and places, the levels of salmon production seen today approach the maximum potential.

Paleolimnology

Long-term observations of salmon population dynamics are typically collected as part of fishery management activities. Therefore, whenever large declines in populations occur, it is impossible to rule out the possibility of fishery over-harvest. The problem boils down to a lack of experimental controls on the long-term effects of harvest. However, recent studies of stable isotopes trapped in the sediments of sockeye salmon *O. nerka* lakes has afforded a first-ever look at how salmon populations change over the course of centuries and millennia prior to the advent of modern commercial fisheries (Finney et al. 2000, 2002). Over the long term, populations did not simply bounce around a con-

stant mean; instead, they remained at multiple stable states for periods of decades or centuries and they rapidly shifted to alternate states. The longstanding expectation of stable local production over the long term is unwarranted because processes operate at multiple timescales that can cause fundamental shifts in local productivity.

Biocomplexity

Many of the principles of salmon management during the last century have tended to homogenize and simplify salmon populations: fishing seasons and escapement goals can truncate the duration of runs (i.e., higher exploitation rates on the tails), mixed stock fisheries tend to overharvest the least productive stocks, hatcheries favor a subset of wild stock traits chosen for particular run timing, spawning location, or some other attribute. However, a recent study outlines the perils of this approach by demonstrating the essential role of population and watershed diversity in long-term productivity. The relative productivity of alternate watersheds in Bristol Bay, Alaska has changed dramatically over the last century, with previously small populations now dominating much of the production, while formally dominant watersheds are now producing relatively few fish (Hilborn et al. 2003). At the same time, the overall production of the region has stayed relatively stable, which demonstrates that stock diversity spread across watersheds can buffer systems from individual watershed trends. The same processes may be occurring at smaller scales as well, arguing that biocomplexity begets ecological resilience, even in intensively managed systems (Quinn 2009, this volume).

Together these studies and many others are outlining an integrated conceptual model for salmon ecology, management, and conservation. Key scientific components to this model include:

1. Salmon ecosystems are subject to hierarchically-scaled processes in space and time and, specifically, local ecosystems respond to long-term, large-scale processes.

2. Spatially segregated watersheds are ecologically connected by shifts in climate and ocean interactions.

3. Biocomplexity drives ecosystem resilience and long-term productivity.

These results have two critical implications for effective management and conservation. First, local decisions must anticipate and understand processes operating on larger temporal and spatial scales (see McPhee et al. 2009, this volume). Second, protecting biocomplexity is essential for ecosystem resilience and sustaining salmon production over broad spatial scales.

The research described above points towards fruitful avenues for future research including:

1. Scale: How have large-scale processes driven salmon productivity in the past? How might they affect productivity in the future?

2. Connectivity: When and where do direct ecological linkages affect salmon populations? How might indirect linkages related to climate play out as global climate change advances?

3. Biocomplexity: How is biocomplexity quantified? When and where does biocomplexity exist? How does it affect ecosystem processes?

Projects Underway

By partnering with different research groups, WSEI has supported a number of projects to pursue some of these questions.

Each of these studies is predicated on foundational studies such as those described above, with the ultimate aim of informing management and conservation decisions. Current projects are described below.

POST

The Pacific Ocean Shelf Tracking (POST) project was developed to give a first-ever look at the complexity, diversity, and consequences of early ocean survival and migration of juvenile salmon. POST uses surgically implanted tags that are detected by curtains of receivers along the continental shelf. The result is a novel opportunity to track where and when salmon are traveling and dying along the coast. The emerging picture is every bit as complex as freshwater ecology, with substantial variability in mortality and migration among and within watersheds.

SaRON

The Salmonid Rivers Observatory Network conducts standardized studies of salmon biocomplexity and hydrologic function in pristine watersheds spanning British Columbia, Alaska, and Kamchatka. By probing the function of pristine systems, SaRON aims to understand how biocomplexity affects watershed productivity and inform management decisions to protect or restore natural biocomplexity. As part of this work, investigators are also exploring how hydrological processes form available habitat. Next steps will include the development of general mathematical models that combine information on how biological and physical processes interact to determine productivity at the watershed scale.

Bristol Bay biocomplexity

This research study was responsible for the key studies of salmon biocomplexity described above. The next steps are focused on understanding how biocomplexity relates to productivity and resilience at multiple scales. Initial analyses indicate that the same kinds of patterns that were observed among the watersheds of Bristol Bay are observed at smaller scales within watersheds as well. In addition, this project is exploring how an understanding of biocomplexity can be used to refine escapement targets and harvest strategies.

Salmon MALBEC

The Salmon Model for Assessing Links Between ECosystems (MALBEC) is a new tool that knits together existing information on salmon stocks around the Pacific Rim to explore possible interactions and future scenarios. The model tracks salmon populations throughout their life cycle for all major stocks of sockeye, pink *O. gorbuscha*, and chum *O. keta* salmon, creating an opportunity to explore multi-stock interactions at the scale of the North Pacific Basin. Specific scenarios can then be incorporated to generate hypotheses about the consequences of changes in stock productivity, hatchery production, climate change, and fisheries practices.

Paleoecology synthesis

Expanding on key research described above, this project is collecting cores from sockeye salmon lakes around the Pacific Rim with the aim of developing a synthetic picture of sockeye salmon populations change over the past centuries and millennia. While previous work has shown how single populations have varied in the past, this work will identify whether or not populations were synchronized in their dynamics across a suite of spatial scales up to the entire Pacific Rim.

Climate synthesis

Anecdotal evidence that climate change is affecting salmon is on the rise and in-

cludes shifting run times, emerging diseases, and the expansion of salmon populations to Arctic Ocean rivers. The goal of this project is to identify and address some of the most pressing open questions about the effects of climate change on salmon ecosystems. This project uses a synthesis approach that draws on existing data and information to explore possible future scenarios.

Advancing an Integrated Conceptual Model

How do these projects fit together and how do they advance salmon science? While the activities and conclusions from each of these studies will touch on many different scientific questions, they all contribute to a formalization of an integrated conceptual model.

Scale

First, consider the overarching questions related to scale, and particularly how large-scale processes can set the context for local and regional decision-making. A first step is simply identifying the relevant scales and processes. While the foundational work on varying climate regimes brought these issues to the forefront, the hypothesized linkage between Alaskan and Pacific Northwest productivity has only been observed for less than two full cycles, and recent observations may be hinting at a third state (N. Mantua, University of Washington, personal communication). Currently, only one highly promising avenue exists for getting past the problem of no long-term productivity baseline: accessing information locked in lake cores. If successful, the Paleoecological Synthesis project will serve as the foundation to a historical understanding of the temporal and spatial organization of salmon production at a basin-wide scale over ecologically relevant time scales.

Anticipating and adapting to large-scale change will not only benefit from a better understanding of what happened in the past, it must also consider what the future might hold. Both the MALBEC and Climate Synthesis projects aim to do exactly this at the North Pacific scale. MALBEC will use ecosystem and climate modeling to predict possible future scenarios, and the Climate Synthesis project will synthesize diverse information to draw conclusions about possible climate effects. While these broad, Pacific-Rim-Scale analyses may offer insight across large areas, they may prove less appropriate for watershed-scale predictions. The SaRON project aims to fill this gap by explicitly modeling changes in biological and physical processes at the watershed scale.

Connectivity

A growing body of evidence suggests that salmon populations are directly interconnected at a variety of scales, including populations arising on either side of the Pacific. The MALBEC project will systematically examine when and where direct interactions between populations might occur in the ocean and explore the possible net effects at the Pacific-Rim Scale. Widespread populations may also respond similarly to large-scale changes in environmental conditions and productivity. The MALBEC model will examine how different populations might fare under a host of different environmental factors and management practices. The Paleoecological Synthesis study will look at past changes in widely-spaced sockeye salmon populations to examine whether and at what scales of space and time synchrony has occurred.

Biocomplexity

New research on biocomplexity focuses on how aspects of biological and physical diversity drive ecosystem processes at lo-cal to regional scales. The SaRON project is discovering new aspects of biocomplexity in pristine rivers throughout the North Pacific that drive watershed productivity. The Bristol Bay Biocomplexity project is examining similar questions at multiple scales, ranging from all of Bristol Bay to the interactions between adjacent creek- and lake-spawning sockeye. This project also aims to apply this information directly to management practices by developing new fisheries models that explicitly consider different aspects of biocomplexity. The POST project has opened up the study of biocomplexity to the coastal ocean. The picture that is emerging from these studies is that, in relatively pristine systems, biocomplexity exists everywhere and it underpins ecosystem resilience and productivity.

Management and Conservation under an Integrated Conceptual Model

All of these studies are in a phase of rapid discovery and are generating information that will inform management and conservation decisions to come. Fully incorporating these ideas into management decisions will require translating general ecological principles into practical management applications. The fundamental principle that is emerging is that management and conservation decisions should explicitly protect biocomplexity while anticipating the influence of larger-scale processes. Effective application may require changes in management practices, especially regarding harvest and watershed habitat management.

In the case of harvest, biocomplexity may be preserved by developing increasingly sophisticated fisheries practices that account for mixtures of relatively weak and strong stocks. Specific actions might include refining stock identification and monitoring, changing overall harvest, moving fisheries farther into watersheds where individual stocks can be separately managed, and using ecologically-defensible escapement goals (note that increasingly sophisticated stock differentiation in fisheries and/or a move towards terminal fisheries, could allow increases in harvest on the strongest stocks). However, refining stock specificity and escapement targets may not be sufficient for long-term biological or economic sustainability if they are based on the expectation of long-term stability in production. In anticipation of changing productivity, managers could develop specific thresholds for alternative fisheries models. For example, if run size drops below or rises above a certain level, fisheries might include an explicit plan to move to the location of fisheries effort or change escapement targets. To be clear, these activities do occur today, but most often they are *post hoc* responses to crises. Given our ever-increasing ability to anticipate the kinds of changes that might be on the horizon, this exercise can move from the realm of *post hoc* reaction to proactive anticipation.

In the case of watershed habitat management, maintaining local productivity may require protecting interconnected habitats that are used by different species, populations, life history strategies, and ontogenetic stages. Under this model, watersheds would not be viewed as a series of independent components to be managed separately, but rather a network whose interconnections must be preserved to maintain function and resilience. While this idea by itself is not new, a growing body of research is uncovering the details of how watershed components interact, creating a new opportunity to make explicit predictions about the consequences of alternative activities to biocomplexity, productivity, and resilience. At larger spatial scales, watersheds or major tributaries might also be viewed as part of interacting networks that maintain direct linkages through straying, but that also protect biocomplexity among watersheds to enhance system-wide resilience in the face of environmental change.

Conclusions

The concepts articulated as part of an integrated model have long existed within the collective wisdom of salmon experts. What is new is a growing weight of evidence that is elevating their status within the scientific, management, and conservation communities. Provided that these concepts continue to stand up to scientific and applied rigor, they will formalize an integrated model of how salmon ecosystems operate that incorporates and broadens decades of system-specific studies. While many of these ideas are already informing management decisions, integrating these concepts will change the context for decisions to come. As we enter a time of accelerating global change, the context in which management decisions are made may have an overwhelming influence on the health of ecosystems and the livelihoods of those who depend on them.

Acknowledgments

I thank Daniel Schindler, Jack Stanford, Aileen Lee, Charles Conn, and Pic Walker who provided comments and constructive discussion that improved the content of this manuscript. I also thank the AYK SSI symposium organizers for inviting me to participate in this symposium and proceedings. The views expressed above are my own and do not necessarily represent the policy of the Gordon and Betty Moore Foundation.

References

Beamish, R. J., and R. M. Sweeting. 2009. The history of surprises associated with Pacific salmon returns signals that critical information is missing from our understanding of their population dynamics. Pages 1159–1168 *in* C. C. Krueger and C. E. Zimmerman, editors. Pacific salmon: ecology and management of western Alaska's populations. American Fisheries Society, Symposium 70, Bethesda, Maryland.

Hare, S. R., N. J. Mantua, and R. C. Francis. 1999. Inverse production regimes: Alaskan and West Coast salmon. Fisheries 24:6–14.

Finney, B. P., I. Gregory-Eaves, J. Sweetman, M. S. V. Douglas, and J. P. Smol. 2000. Impacts of climatic change and fishing on Pacific salmon abundance over the past 300 years. Science 290:795–799.

Finney, B. P., I. Gregory-Eaves, M. S. V. Douglas, and J. P. Smol. 2002. Fisheries productivity in the northeastern Pacific Ocean over the past 2,200 years. Nature (London) 416:729–733.

Hilborn, R., T. P. Quinn, D. E. Schindler, and D. E. Rogers. 2003. Biocomplexity and fisheries sustainability. Proceedings of the National Academy of Sciences, USA 100:6564–6568.

Kaeriyama, M. 1999. Hatchery programmes and stock management of salmonid populations in Japan. Pages 153–167 in B. R. Howell, E. Moksness, and T. Svasand editors. Stock enhancement and sea ranching. Blackwell Scientific Publications, Oxford, U.K.

Mantua, N. 2009. Patterns of change in climate and Pacific salmon production. Pages 1143–1157 in C. C. Krueger and C. E. Zimmerman, editors. Pacific salmon: ecology and management of western Alaska's populations. American Fisheries Society, Symposium 70, Bethesda, Maryland.

Mantua, N. J., S. R. Hare, Y. Zhang, J. M. Wallace, and R. C. Francis. 1997. A Pacific interdecadal climate oscillation with impacts on salmon production. Bulletin of the American Meteorological Society 78:1069–1079.

McPhee, M. V., M. S. Zimmerman, T. D. Beacham, B. R. Beckman, J. B. Olsen, L. W. Seeb, and W. D. Templin. 2009. A hierarchical framework to identify influences on Pacific salmon population abundance and structure in the Arctic-Yukon-Kuskokwim Region. Pages 1177–1198 in C. C. Krueger and C. E. Zimmerman, editors. Pacific salmon:

ecology and management of western Alaska's populations. American Fisheries Society, Symposium 70, Bethesda, Maryland.

Myers, K. W., R. V. Walker, N. D. Davis, J. L. Armstrong, and M. Kaeriyama. 2009. High seas distribution, biology, and ecology of Arctic-Yukon-Kuskokwim salmon: direct information from high seas tagging experiments, 1954–2006. Pages 201–239 in C. C. Krueger and C. E. Zimmerman, editors. Pacific salmon: ecology and management of western Alaska's populations. American Fisheries Society, Symposium 70, Bethesda, Maryland.

Quinn, T. P. 2009. Pacific salmon population structure and dynamics: a perspective from Bristol Bay on life history variation across spatial and temporal scales. Pages 857–871 in C. C. Krueger and C. E. Zimmerman, editors. Pacific salmon: ecology and management of western Alaska's populations. American Fisheries Society, Symposium 70, Bethesda, Maryland.

Ruggerone, G. T., E. Farley, J. Nielsen., and P. Hagen. 2005. Seasonal marine growth of Bristol Bay sockeye salmon (*Oncorhynchus nerka*) in relation to competition with Asian pink salmon (*O. gorbuscha*) and the 1977 ocean regime shift. Fishery Bulletin 103: 355–370.

Ruggerone, G. T., and J. Nielsen. 2009. A review of growth and survival of salmon at sea in response to competition and climate change. Pages 241–265 in C. C. Krueger and C. E. Zimmerman, editors. Pacific salmon: ecology and management of western Alaska's populations. American Fisheries Society, Symposium 70, Bethesda, Maryland.

Ruggerone, G. T., M. Zimmermann, K. W. Myers, J. L. Nielsen, and D. E. Rogers. 2003. Competition between Asian pink salmon (*Oncorhynchus gorbuscha*) and Alaskan sockeye salmon (*O. nerka*) in the North Pacific Ocean. Fisheries Oceanography 12:209–219.

American Fisheries Society Symposium 70:1177–1198, 2009
© 2009 by the American Fisheries Society

A Hierarchical Framework to Identify Influences on Pacific Salmon Population Abundance and Structure in the Arctic-Yukon-Kuskokwim Region

Megan V. McPhee[*]

Flathead Lake Biological Station, The University of Montana
32125 Bio Station Lane, Polson, Montana 59860, USA

Mara S. Zimmerman[1]

Department of Fisheries and Wildlife
Michigan State University, Lansing, Michigan 48824, USA

Terry D. Beacham

Department of Fisheries and Oceans
Pacific Biological Station, Nanaimo, British Columbia V9T 6N7, Canada

Brian R. Beckman

Northwest Fisheries Science Center, NOAA Fisheries Service
2725 Montlake Boulevard East, Seattle, Washington 98112, USA

Jeffrey B. Olsen

Conservation Genetics Laboratory, U.S. Fish and Wildlife Service
1011 East Tudor Road, Anchorage, Alaska 99503, USA

Lisa W. Seeb[2] **and William D. Templin**

Alaska Department of Fish and Game, Gene Conservation Laboratory
333 Raspberry Road, Anchorage, Alaska 99518, USA

Abstract.—The causes of spatial and temporal variation in Pacific salmon abundance are poorly understood. An additional challenge in the Arctic-Yukon-Kuskokwim (AYK) region is the expansive and remote nature of salmon habitat. In this paper, the authors discuss a hierarchical framework that may prove helpful in identifying key variables regulating Pacific salmon abundance. The hierarchical framework considers processes that act at multiple scales of space and time, identifies generalizations across scales, and considers interactions among variables operating at different scales. This framework is used to address three overarching questions for the AYK region:

[*]Corresponding author: megan.mcphee@flbs.umt.edu
[1]Current address: Washington Department of Fish and Wildlife, 1111 Washington Street SE, Olympia, WA 98501, USA
[2]Current address: School of Aquatic and Fishery Sciences, Box 355020, Seattle, WA 98195, USA

1) What are the important units of focus for conservation and management? 2) What are the factors that control abundance and connectivity of these units? 3) How can these two questions be integrated to better understand and manage Pacific salmon? Genetic and ecotypic units are organized hierarchically in space and time. Genetic units of AYK salmon have been identified at a local level among tributaries in the Yukon and Kuskokwim drainages, the Norton Sound, and at a regional level where all species share similar genetic discontinuities. Ecotypic units are habitat-organismal trait associations characteristic of Pacific salmon, but are not well documented for AYK stocks. The processes controlling abundance and connectivity among these units also occur at multiple hierarchical levels with respect to life history, space, and time. Identifying the scale at which processes or interaction among processes have the largest relative impact on salmon recruitment will be critical to effectively managing Pacific salmon. Four feasible lines of study proposed for gathering informative data from the expansive and remote AYK region include: (1) a spatial comparison between habitat and spawning populations, (2) a comparison of mortality as related to life history diversity, (3) compilation of existing migration data to explain patterns in migration timing, and (4) coordination of genetic data to test hypotheses regarding population structure. Use of existing long-term data and coordination of ongoing research efforts should be of high importance for AYK biologists and managers.

Introduction

Salmon fisheries are highly complex systems, due to the involvement of multiple species, habitat domains, stakeholders, regulatory agencies, markets, and cultures (Peterson 2000). *Biocomplexity*, which focuses on the biological aspects of this complexity, is beginning to enter the lexicon of fisheries science (Hilborn et al. 2003; Naiman and Latterell 2005; Achord et al. 2007) A key concept in the application of biocomplexity to fisheries management is that a diversity of components in a complex system may enhance resilience, as exemplified by the stability of overall numbers of sockeye salmon in the Bristol Bay region, despite large annual fluctuations in individual stock size (Hilborn et al. 2003). This result leads to the perception that biocomplexity is a desirable quality of an ecosystem. However, complexity could also cause paralysis in taking management actions when humans are forced to manage ecosystems with little data or understanding of interactions between populations and environment. This problem is particularly severe in remote regions where biological sampling is difficult and expensive. Therefore, new ways of approaching the study, management, and conservation of salmon ecosystems are needed, and the organizing principle of biocomplexity could be valuable to this endeavor.

Biocomplexity is more than the acknowledgment that biological systems are complicated. It stems from the growing recognition that ecological systems are the result of biological and physical processes acting at multiple scales of time and space, and complexity arises when processes acting at different scales interact and/or override each other (Cadenasso et al. 2006). Implicit in this concept is the idea that understanding processes at one spatial and temporal scale may not allow us to predict how systems will behave at a different scale. For example, biologists may be able to quantify all of the variables that influence the number of smolts produced from a single tributary, but this does not mean that they can then predict the number of adult salmon that will return to that region in a given year. Fortunately, spatial and temporal scales can be conceptualized hierarchically, with biological units existing at small spatial/temporal scales being nested within larger scales (Figure 1). This hierarchical approach involves identifying the appropriate spatial and temporal scales at which to study a given process (e.g., the number of smolts produced from a tributary). By using results from small-scale studies to predict patterns at large scales, one can determine the scale at which local studies (e.g., adult salmon returns) cannot sufficiently explain large patterns, thus indicating where additional research needs to be focused.

Salmon populations lend themselves well to a hierarchical view of their spatial and temporal organization (Figure 1). Salmon populations are structured hierarchically, with fine-scale subdivision occurring at the level of the local breeding population (*deme*) and a regional *metapopulation* (a population of populations; see Glossary) emerging as a result of connectivity between breeding populations (Policansky and Magnuson 1998). The entire species' range is then composed of regional metapopulations. Recognition of this hierarchical pattern of population structure is central to identifying management and conservation units (Waples 1995; Waples et al. 2001; Gustafson et al. 2007).

Ecological processes affecting salmon populations are also organized hierarchically. For example, the suitability and productivity of both juvenile and adult salmon habitat is a function of processes acting at multiple spatial scales. Climate and underlying geology

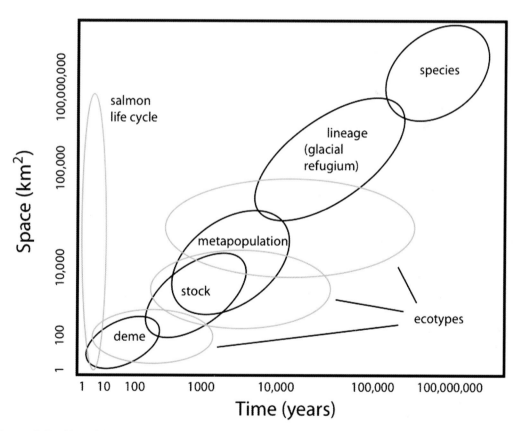

FIGURE 1. Pacific salmon (genus *Oncorhynchus*) can be organized into units occurring over hierarchical scales in space and time (after Holling 1992). Ecotypic variation can span multiple spatial and temporal scales, depending on species and genetic architecture (degree of phenotypic plasticity). Population complexity arises in part because the salmon life cycle encompasses disparate spatial scales.

affect habitat at the regional scale, while processes such as upwelling and coarse woody debris affect habitat at local scales which then contributes to variation in individual growth and survival (Frissell et al. 1986). Recognition of different ecological processes acting at different hierarchical scales is central to furthering our understanding of mechanisms that affect salmon abundance.

In this paper, the authors discuss how a hierarchical approach to studying salmon populations can guide future research in regions where management information needs are acute but baseline data are scarce. The authors focus on the Arctic-Yukon-Kuskokwim (AYK) salmon populations and associated fisheries of northwestern Alaska. Between 1997–2002, disastrously low returns of various AYK stocks, in combination with a depressed market for wild salmon, led to economic hardship in the region and resulted in the call for research efforts focused on understanding the causes of variation in salmon abundance over space and time (AYK SSI 2006). The Arctic-Yukon-Kuskokwim Salmon Research and Restoration Plan is based on a conceptual model that includes biological, physical, and human processes interacting with the salmon life cycle to produce variation in salmon abundance (AYK SSI 2006). These processes interact across multiple spatial and temporal scales and thus have the potential to confound each other's effects. An important goal of the AYK Sustainable Salmon Initiative (SSI) is to prioritize research to maximize information gained towards managing sustainable salmon fisheries. To meet this goal, a framework is needed to organize processes included in the conceptual model. Here, it is suggested that a hierarchical framework will help to focus ecological and genetic approaches to investigating variation in salmon abundances.

The hierarchical framework described here emerged from the 'Genetics, Ecology, and Management' break-out session convened at the 2007 AYK SSI symposium. To this end, the authors review what is known

about AYK populations and discuss strategies for research that will be most fruitful in improving the understanding of the dynamics of AYK salmon populations. The focus is on three overarching questions: 1) What are the important units of focus for conservation and management actions in the AYK region? 2) What are the factors that control abundance and connectivity of these units in the AYK region? and 3) How can the first two questions be integrated to better our understanding and management of AYK salmon?

Units of AYK Salmon Conservation and Management

The *stock* is the fundamental unit of salmon management, yet "stock" can be defined many ways, ranging from strictly biological considerations (Ricker 1972) to definitions that take into account fisheries management structure as well (Mundy and Mathiesen 1981). For the purposes of the AYK SSI, a stock is defined as "aggregations of demes characterized by sites from which their individual escapement counts are obtained" (AYK SSI 2006). This definition of stock exists at an intermediate scale of hierarchical salmon population organization; it is more finely resolved than the regional scale, yet further subdivision to the deme is possible. Identification of AYK stocks is a logical first step in cataloging salmonid diversity in the region. However, the resolution afforded by genetic stock identification methods may not be fine enough to delineate the degree of *ecotypic* (locally suitable morphological and life history) differentiation at the local spawning population level, which is a fundamental unit of salmon population dynamics and resilience (Healey and Prince 1995; Quinn 2009, this volume). Thus, identification of units of *ecotypic variation* is another essential component of pattern in AYK salmon.

Genetic variation and stock identification

Stock identification is a key part of managing fisheries. If stock composition data are used to guide fishery managers in decisions on fishery openings and closures, the estimated stock compositions in harvest and escapement need to provide the level of resolution necessary for management, they need to be timely in their availability, and they need to be accurate. Identification of Pacific salmon to local origin is crucial to the understanding of their population-specific responses to recent climatic regime shifts in the north Pacific Ocean (Welch et al. 2000; Mueter et al. 2002). Identification of biological and physical factors responsible for the shifting fortunes of salmon populations requires identification of fish sampled in freshwater or on the high seas to region or population of origin. Should mixed-stock fisheries intercept stocks of conservation concern, then with the aid of high-resolution stock composition estimates, it might be possible to structure a fishery in order to harvest abundant stocks while providing protection to stocks of conservation concern (ADFG 2003; Templin et al. 2004; Winther and Beacham 2009, this volume; Beacham et al. 2009, this volume). Finally, because genetic diversity provides the basis by which salmon are able to adapt to changing environmental conditions, conservation of genetic diversity is important for ensuring salmon viability in a region (Waples et al. 2001; Gustafson et al. 2007; Waples 2009, this volume). Therefore, comprehensive surveys of salmonid genetic variation for populations spawning in the Arctic-Yukon-Kuskokwim region are necessary for effective resource management decisions.

The key requirement for applying any stock identification technique is accurately estimating stock composition to the smallest tractable unit, which in some cases can be to the local area, but in many cases requires identification to the river or lake of origin. This is accomplished by identifying stocks based on unique patterns of variation at *genetic markers*, which include allozymes (protein variations), microsatellites (short repeated units of DNA), and SNPs (single nucleotide polymorphisms, or differences in a single 'letter' of the genetic code). Genetic data from many individuals per stock make up the *baseline*, which describes the pattern in genetic variation across stocks. Individual fish (such as those taken in a mixed-stock fishery) can then be assigned back to one stock or another by comparing its *genotype* to the baseline.

The five Pacific salmon species of interest in the AYK region (Chinook *Oncorhynchus tshawytscha*, chum *O. keta*, pink *O. gorbuscha*, coho *O. kisutch*, and sockeye *O. nerka*) differ in their degree of genetic differentiation over space, with Chinook, coho, and sockeye salmon showing the greatest degree of differentiation (e.g., Crane et al. 2004; Beacham et al. 2006; Templin et al. 2006, Habicht et al. 2007), and chum and pink salmon showing the lowest (although regional estimates of stock composition are still possible; ADFG 2003; Seeb et al. 2004; Chen et al. 2005). In all cases the key component of the analysis is the baseline of genetic information. For the estimated stock compositions to be accurate, the baseline needs to be comprehensive, accurately representing all stocks in the fishery samples, and there must be sufficient genetic differentiation among stocks or populations. Although temporal stability of genetic variation relative to population differentiation over space is a key characteristic of both allozyme (Grant et al. 1980; Gharrett et al. 1987) and DNA-level variation (Beacham and Wood 1999; Tessier and Bernatchez 1999; Miller et al. 2001), some level of monitoring of key baseline populations over time should be conducted to ensure that the baseline remains an accurate reflection of stocks' genetic variation.

The first step in conserving genetic diversity and applying genetic variation to mixed-stock fishery management decisions is to conduct comprehensive surveys of genetic variation within the geographic regions of concern. Early genetic work in the AYK region was conducted on chum and Chinook salmon using allozyme markers. These studies found differentiation between summer-run and fall-run chum salmon within drainages in the Yukon River (Wilmot et al. 1994; Crane et al. 2001) but little geographic differentiation among summer-run chum salmon populations over most of western Alaska (Seeb and Crane 1999). Yukon River Chinook salmon showed considerably greater genetic differentiation between stocks based on locality (Gharrett et al. 1987; Beacham et al. 1989), and this variation could be applied to stock identification (Wilmot et al. 1992; Templin et al. 2005). However, the coarse level of population discrimination available from allozymes, coupled with allozyme requirements of lethal sampling and cryopreservation, was not sufficient for applications requiring high resolution among regions or populations in the Yukon River drainage. The need for increased stock identification resolution has led to the development of DNA-based stock identification techniques for Yukon River Chinook and chum salmon (SNPs, Smith et al. 2005; microsatellites, Scribner et al. 1998; Beacham et al. 2006; Flannery et al. 2006; Templin et al. 2006; Beacham et al. 2009; amplified fragment length polymorphisms, Flannery et al. 2007), and for chum and Chinook salmon in the Kuskokwim River (SNPs, Gilk et al. 2009, this volume; microsatellites, Templin et al. 2004). Utter et al. (2009, this volume) provide a more detailed review of genetic studies of AYK stocks to date.

Ecotypic variation

A basic premise of salmon biology is that local populations adapt to local conditions over evolutionary time so that individual *fitness* (survival and reproduction) is maximized relative to environmental conditions and variability (Quinn 1985; Quinn 2009; Waples 2009). Thus, the *phenotypes* (organismal traits, such as body shape or life history) found in a population tend to be related to the environmental attributes of the habitat. These specific phenotypes, when they are related to specific environmental conditions, are termed *ecotypes* (Turesson 1922). As an example, the migration and spawning times of Chinook and sockeye salmon populations are correlated with natal habitat temperatures. Chinook and sockeye salmon that spawn in the cold waters of high-elevation headwater streams migrate and spawn earlier than those spawning in warm, low elevation habitats (Brannon 1987; Beechie et al. 2006). Important environmental factors shaping salmon ecotypes included freshwater thermal regime, elevation, groundwater flow, presence of lakes, hydrographic (flow) regime, river size, distance of spawning habitat from the ocean, and physical attributes of spawning habitat (e.g., Keeley et al. 2005). Together, the environment shapes both the timing of key life history events (ocean versus riverine gonadal maturation, adult freshwater migration, spawning, duration of embryonic and larval periods, emergence, duration of freshwater rearing, and smolting) as well as the morphological characteristics of different life history stages (Groot and Margolis 1991; Quinn 2005). Presently, little is known about the ecotypic diversity within and between various stocks of AYK species, with the exception of chum salmon, where morphological and genetic distinction between summer- and fall-run stocks has been measured (Beacham et al. 1988a; Gilk et al. 2009), and sockeye salmon, where both riverine and lake-type forms have been found in the Kuskokwim drainage (Molyneaux and Brannian 2006).

Ecotypic diversity may or may not parallel patterns in genetic diversity. Genetic units reflect colonization history, and therefore are often organized hierarchically within a drainage or region. In contrast, ecotypes reflect local habitat conditions that represent a spatial mosaic more than a strict hierarchical structure. One of the most common methods currently used to catalog salmon diversity is to document genetic divergence among *selectively neutral* genetic markers that do not contribute to fitness. This approach discriminates populations that have been genetically isolated (limited exchange of individuals between breeding populations) over enough generations to develop differences at these neutral genetic markers. If populations are isolated through time they also have the opportunity to diverge phenotypically (through *selection*, or enhanced reproduction of individuals that possess beneficial genetic traits) and become adapted to their local habitat. Thus, under some conditions, genetic differentiation may reflect levels of phenotypic differentiation. However, it must be emphasized that genetically neutral markers are, by definition, independent of genetic traits underlying phenotypically important attributes (Hard 1995; Wang et al. 2002). Thus, cases exist where neutral genotypes differ due to genetic isolation but phenotypes are similar due to similar environments, and where neutral genotypes are similar but phenotypes differ due to different environments (Beacham et al. 1988b; Taylor et al. 1996; Waples et al. 2004). Additionally, if selection has resulted in rapid or recent genetic changes at specific traits, this will not be reflected in divergence at neutral genetic markers (McKay and Latta 2002).

Although a substantial part of a population's response to environmental variation is likely *local adaptation* (mediated by genetic change across generations), salmon also have the ability to respond to environmental variability over short time scales (e.g., the life span of one individual) by displaying *phenotypic plasticity*. Phenotypic plasticity can be defined as the ability of a single individual to develop alternate phenotypes in response to different environmental cues and is thought to be adaptive in many cases (West-Eberhard 1989). Although plasticity refers to environmentally induced traits, the capacity to produce induced responses has a genetic basis (e.g., Hutchings et al. 2007). However, little is currently understood about the genetic basis for plasticity in salmonids (Thorpe et al. 1998; Hutchings 2003).

Traits that show phenotypic plasticity in salmon might include age and size at maturity, and size and seasonal timing of smolting. For example, a juvenile salmon might smolt at age-1 or age-2, depending on the environmental conditions it experiences early in life. Different phenotypic responses to different environmental cues can result in a better match of phenotype to environment than might be achieved by selection on a genetically-determined single expression of a trait, which would reflect a long-term average of environmental conditions. Selection for plasticity in expression would be especially advantageous when environmental conditions frequently fluctuate. The Pacific Rim region occupied by Pacific salmon is characterized by environmental variability that ranges from geological (glacial) to climatic (Pacific Decadal Oscillation; PDO) to seasonal (El Niño) time scales. Salmon appear able to exploit this environment in the face of these multiple scales of environmental variation (Montgomery 2000; Jacobs et al. 2004), partly due to phenotypic plasticity. Given the current variability of the AYK region and predicted increase in environmental variation due to global climate change, the degree to which beneficial traits are genetically "hard-wired" is crucial to knowing the spatial scale at which ecotypic variation must be conserved. Thus, relevant research questions would be as follows. What is the relationship between genetic diversity and ecotypic diversity in salmon? What kinds of environments promote ecotypic diversity and phenotypic plasticity in salmon populations?

Mechanisms of Abundance and Connectivity of Salmon Populations

Mechanisms behind variation in salmon abundance

Spawner abundance is often the first variable considered by managers when predicting future salmon returns, and is based on the hypothesis that density-dependence is the primary process driving salmon recruitment (Ricker 1954; Ricker 1975). However, stocks do not always respond as predicted by density-dependent processes (Hutchings and Reynolds 2004), and predictions based on spawner-recruit correlations can be uninformative in fluctuating environments (Bradford et al. 2009, this volume). For example, Oregon coast coho stocks, managed based on spawner abundances, crashed to unexpectedly low levels in the 1990s (Martin 2009, this volume). Similarly, returns of chum salmon to Japanese hatcheries have fluctuated sharply over two decades despite similar releases over time (S. Urawa, North Pacific Anadromous Fish Commission, personal communication). Predictions on salmon recruitment are only as accurate as the state of understanding on how different variables influence salmon abundance. Furthermore, considering how environmental inputs influence salmon recruitment from spawning stocks will be critical given the long-term environmental changes projected for the AYK region (Mantua 2009, this volume).

A logical way to approach salmon abundance is to examine variables that control abundance along each step of the salmon life cycle (Thompson 1959; Mobrand et al. 1997). The abundance of returning AYK salmon has the potential to be limited by different environmental variables at each life history stage. These variables are correlated to varying degrees (e.g., stream and air temperatures) and operate at different hierarchical scales (e.g.,

local inter-gravel water temperatures versus regional air temperatures). Furthermore, the relative importance of these variables changes across the stages of salmon life history. For example, egg survival and development is influenced by water temperature (Murray and McPhail 1988) and spawner densities (Burgner 1991). Parr mortality is influenced by winter stream flows (Bradford et al. 2001; Lawson et al. 2004), annual air temperatures (Lawson et al. 2004), and juvenile densities (Bradford et al. 2009). Juvenile abundance in the first year of ocean residency are influenced by predation (Brodeur et al. 2003), competition (Ruggerone and Goetz 2004; Ruggerone et al. 2005), upwelling timing (Fisher and Pearcy 1988), sea surface temperatures (Farley et al. 2009, this volume), and overwinter mortality (Beamish and Mahnken 2001; Moss et al. 2005). The survival of migrating spawners is influenced by fishery harvests, predation (Burgner 1991; Quinn and Buck 2001), stream flows (Heard 1991), migration lengths (Beauchamp 2009, this volume), and latitude (Nemeth et al. 2009, this volume). Most of the information on these variables has come from lower latitudes, and studies are needed to examine their effects within the context of the AYK system. Furthermore, abundance at an earlier life history stage may better predict salmon recruitment than spawner density, particularly if a certain stage is subject to strong density-independent regulation or if background conditions affect the shape of density-dependent curves. Much is to be gained by examining the spawner-recruit relationship across life history to stages to determine if, and at what stage, the spawner-recruit relationship can break down.

The relative influence of different environments is a key question which may help narrow focus on potential variables limiting salmon abundance and the scales at which they operate (Figure 2). The relative influence of riverine versus marine environments is still not well understood and may differ by species and life history. For example, fry residency in freshwater environments varies from a few weeks to three years, and body size at ocean entry varies nearly sevenfold (Groot and Margolis 1991). Therefore, variables like stream temperatures, flooding events, and marine-derived nutrients are more likely to affect species, such as sockeye, Chinook and coho salmon, that spend substantial rearing time in freshwater than those species that rapidly migrate to the marine environment such as pink salmon (Finney et al. 2000; Bradford et al. 2001; Wipfli et al. 2003; Beauchamp

2009). Species with extended freshwater residencies subsequently undergo a second bottleneck upon ocean entry which is largely attributed to upwelling patterns and predation (Brodeur et al. 2003; Beamish et al. 2004). In comparison, early life history mortality of pink and chum salmon fry, which spend little time in freshwater habitat, would be influenced sooner by sea surface salinities, sea surface temperatures (SST), and ocean productivity. In support of this hypothesis, a study from southeastern Alaska (Mueter et al. 2005) observed that the mortalities of pink

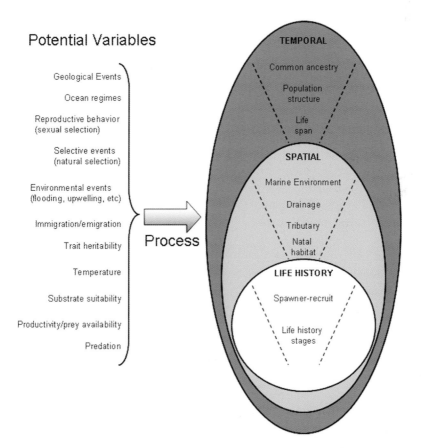

FIGURE 2. Hierarchical framework for explaining variation in Pacific salmon abundance in the Arctic-Yukon-Kuskokwim region. Salmon are organized into hierarchical units, or patterns, with respect to life history, space, and time. Life history, spatial, and temporal units are presented in order of increasing specificity; more general units encompass more specific units. Processes link potential variables with salmon abundance at each spatial and temporal scale. Variables may influence abundance at any level of organization. The relative importance of different variables, as well as interactions among variables, will likely be based on the unit studied and/or managed.

and chum salmon fry were most closely correlated with SST at the time of ocean entry; however, the mortality of sockeye salmon juveniles in the same region was most closely correlated with SST prior to their ocean entry (Mueter et al. 2005). As ocean and air temperatures are generally correlated, the sockeye salmon results may reflect an increased importance of freshwater habitat on mortality rates of this species as compared to pink and chum salmon (Mueter et al. 2005).

The marine life history stage is a critical period for establishing abundance, but has proven difficult to study. Genetic stock identification approaches (discussed above) are particularly well suited to investigate patterns of salmon marine migration routes and the variation due to population-level factors, temporal effects, and interactions with changing climatic conditions. As available data become increasingly more accurate and precise in describing the existing genetic characteristics of salmon populations, the identification of migrating salmon stocks throughout their various life history stages in the marine environment will become an achievable goal. For example, variation in migration routes among populations of Japanese chum salmon from year to year was investigated using protein markers. These populations globally shifted their marine distribution between the Bering Sea and the Gulf of Alaska depending on life stage and season (S. Urawa, North Pacific Anadromous Fish Commission, personal communication). Combining stock composition information derived from genetic data with juvenile abundance information, such as that being collected through Bering-Aleutian Salmon International Survey (BASIS) research (Farley et al. 2009), will likely be a particularly fruitful approach, especially as studies span multiple years and climatic conditions.

Another important source of variation in abundance is fishing mortality (bycatch interception fisheries, targeted commercial, sport, and subsistence fisheries). Whether fisher-ies exert differential fishing mortality among stocks within a drainage system is important to know, so that overfishing of weak stocks can be prevented. Monitoring fisheries that intercept AYK stocks using genetic stock identification has been undertaken in the Yukon River for Chinook salmon (Templin et al. 2005) and chum salmon (Scribner et al. 1998; Crane et al. 2001), but interception rates for AYK stocks are largely unknown for a number of other major fisheries such as those conducted in Bristol Bay, the Alaska Peninsula, and Bering Sea.

Salmon survival rates in the Bering Sea are affected by incidental harvest or bycatch from trawl fisheries for walleye pollock *Theragra chalcogramma* (Gisclair 2009, this volume; Haflinger and Gruver 2009, this volume; Stram and Ianelli 2009, this volume). Western Alaska stocks of Chinook salmon are estimated to contribute more than 50% of this incidental harvest based on high seas tagging experiments (external tags, coded-wire tags, data storage tags) (Myers et al. 2009, this volume). More detailed information is needed to evaluate the effects of the bycatch, which has reached historic levels in recent years, and genetic methods can provide more spatially and temporally stratified coverage at a level of accuracy and precision beyond that provided from tagging studies. Stock-specific bycatch information can be used to evaluate the efficacy of management actions such as salmon savings areas, rolling "hot spot" closures, or a bycatch cap. The potential also exists to combine ecological and genetic stock identification information to provide a tool to forecast future run strengths.

Processes contributing to salmon abundance are hierarchical in time, ranging from single lifespan events to long term glacial and tectonic processes. Thus, prior events have the potential to influence the outcome of more immediate, short term events. For example, salmon mortalities due to flooding may be buffered by immigration from neighboring streams. Flooding is a short-term event whereas stream networks that promote connectivity are generated by long-term processes. Additionally, survival and growth of Pacific salmon are often correlated across life history stages, thus linking the effects of freshwater and marine environments. Growth in freshwater may indirectly influence marine survival (Ruggerone and Nielsen 2009, this volume), as well as age structure of the spawning population (Vollestad et al. 2004). For example, the 2002 rebound of Kuskokwim River Chinook salmon was associated with increased growth in freshwater habitats (Ruggerone and Nielsen 2009). Within the marine environment, early growth contributes to first winter survival (Beamish and Mahnken 2001; Beamish et al. 2004). Links between one life history stage and the next might be overlooked in a correlational study but would be apparent if one considered the process of salmon recruitment from a life history perspective. If marine growth and survival is influenced by previous freshwater growth, the influence of freshwater environments on salmon abundance may be underestimated especially in species with longer freshwater residencies.

Understanding the causes and consequences of population connectivity

The term *population connectivity* refers to the relationship between habitat and the extent and pattern of migration and gene flow (movement of genes from one population to another) linking spatially and/or temporally distinct populations. Papers in this symposium and other venues describe population connectivity as a necessary feature of healthy and resilient Pacific salmon populations (Cooper and Mangel 1999). Although evidence for the importance of population connectivity of salmon has come mainly from intensively studied regions suffering extensive human-mediated habitat loss (e.g., the Pacific Northwest; Waples et al. 2001;

Gustafson et al. 2007), conclusions from these studies have implications for the current and long-term health of salmon occupying the relatively pristine AYK region. Without immigration a number of variables could adversely impact the long-term heath of these populations including the annual volatility in run size, the harsh sub-arctic environment, and habitat impacts of climate change, fisheries, and habitat degradation due to mining and other factors. Understanding how these populations are connected through immigration and how habitat features and life history influence these connections will provide important insight into how the populations will respond to natural as well as human-caused environmental changes.

Evaluating population connectivity in salmon is challenging because direct estimates of the rate and pattern of immigration are difficult to acquire. For this reason genetic data are a valuable tool because it reveals patterns of population relatedness that can be used to infer patterns of population connectivity and factors influencing immigration. Although a detailed examination of population connectivity has not been done for salmon species in the AYK region, the general patterns of population relatedness described in the genetic papers presented at this symposium provide a good starting point for more detailed studies to follow. For example, a common theme of these papers is that the level of population relatedness, while varying across species, exhibits some spatial and temporal (inter-annual) coherence (e.g., Beacham et al. 2009; Gilk et al. 2009). In addition, the spatial population structure is generally organized hierarchically. The similarity among species (e.g., Chinook, chum, coho) in the geographic location of significant genetic discontinuities suggest similar historical events have affected each species and may be influencing contemporary immigration patterns similarly. Likewise, the concordance in hierarchical patterns suggests that landscape features may have similar influences on population connectivity among species. However, inter-specific variation in the degree of population relatedness, as well as species-specific differences in population relatedness associated with life history variation (e.g., summer versus fall run chum salmon), indicate that important differences exist among species with respect to immigration and patterns of population connectivity. These similarities and differences require more detailed examination to understand the causes and consequences of population connectivity in each species and to be able to anticipate how, and at what spatial scale, changes in the environment will influence each species.

Toward a More Holistic Understanding of Salmon Variation in Space and Time

The authors have proposed a hierarchical approach useful for understanding the variables contributing to variability in Pacific salmon abundances in the AYK region (summarized in Figure 2). Salmon population organization is defined in terms of genetic and ecotypic/life history units which are hierarchical in space (e.g., local habitat, river reaches, watersheds, geographic region) and time (e.g., contemporary migrations, evolutionary history). The processes leading to genetic and ecotypic units and their abundance are also hierarchical in space (local interactions to ecosystem processes) and time (within a single lifespan to geologic history). The salmon life history itself is hierarchical, with adults having been influenced by events acting over various spatial scales at each life stage prior to reaching the spawning grounds.

Research programs framed within the context of spatial and temporal scales and mindful of processes that operate or emerge across scales are most likely to contribute to an understanding of trend and causes of vari-

ation in AYK salmon abundance. The most effective research questions will be asked at the appropriate level of hierarchical organization (Frost et al. 1988). To identify this level, researchers must consider the potential processes operating from local to regional scales and justify their initial focus at one of these levels. For example, landscape-level studies will provide insight into population connectivity, hotspots in productivity (freshwater and marine), and associations between phenotype and habitat. The availability of technology such as *remote sensing* (e.g., Whited et al. 2007) offers promising potential for landscape level studies of the AYK region. In comparison, local case studies provide insight into the evolution of ecotypic variation (genetically-mediated local adaptation versus phenotypic plasticity), interactions influencing abundance, indirect effects of marine derived nutrients, and seasonal and life history related movements across habitats. Studies that identify links between local processes and landscape features would be particularly informative. Pacific salmon are widely recognized for their potential to undergo rapid evolutionary change at local levels (Swain et al. 1991; Hendry et al. 2000; Unwin et al. 2003). However, local adaptations may represent a level of biocomplexity that is impractical to manage; certainly, management of stocks at the fine spatial scales characteristic of sockeye salmon populations (e.g., Ramstad et al. 2004; Habicht et al. 2007) seems to be intractable in systems as large as the Kuskokwim or Yukon river drainages. Understanding the processes that lead to such fine-scale variation will guide management toward protecting the mechanisms that maintain diversity rather than trying to manage each component of diversity in isolation.

A hierarchical approach involves focusing in and out across scales to identify patterns and processes and to determine how processes interact with each other across scales (Pickett et al. 2005). The use of this approach will be particularly helpful for AYK salmon management if the variables with the most influence on salmon abundance lay toward the extremes of the spatial or temporal scale. For example, growth in the early ocean environment may be a critical determinant of recruitment at a regional level (Beamish et al. 2004; Farley et al. 2009), but will only be understood if juveniles are identified as a key life history stage and near-shore marine habitats identified as key habitats. Alternately, processes that contribute to effective population size (Olsen et al. 2009, this volume) may be key determinants of recruitment at a local level, especially in stocks with limited immigration. Difficulties in predicting recruitment are likely to come from biocomplexity at intermediate levels where the number of potential variables influencing salmon abundance is high. More variables increase the potential for interactions among variables and the possibilities for delayed responses from indirect effects. Linking small-scale studies to large-scale patterns remains an important challenge, but a first step would be determining the scale (deme, stock, drainage) at which salmon populations must be quantified and understood in order to obtain reasonable predictability for the regional fishery.

Practical Applications for AYK Salmon

A major challenge to salmon biology in the AYK region is the practical aspect of designing a study and gathering data from this expansive and remote area. Four feasible lines of study include (1) a spatial comparison between habitat and spawning units, (2) a comparison of mortality as related to life history diversity, (3) compilation of existing migration data to explain patterns in migration timing, and (4) coordination of genetic data to test hypotheses regarding population structure.

Habitat and spawning units

If habitat availability is a major contributor to salmon production, the relationship between habitat and spawning units (both genetic and ecotypic) will be critical to understanding salmon abundances. In addition to the traditional abundance estimators such as weir/tower counts and aerial surveys, novel methods for studying salmon abundance should be considered. For example, redds are a variable that have the potential to inform researchers on the population size (number of redds), population structure (aggregations and spatial organization of redds), and ecotype (seasonal timing, redd location relative to other environmental variables). Quantifying redds is most feasible in areas with high water clarity. For example, one could count redds in visual surveys on foot or from the air. One might even be able to use satellite photographs to discern and count redds in clear-running rivers. In turbid waters caused by glacial silt, different satellite sensing systems (RADAR, LIDAR) might be able to detect the depressions that spawning females make in the substrate. Coupling redd observations with habitat characterizations, such as stream geomorphology, substrate size, temperature, and flow, will allow identification of key habitat for salmon. Developing relationships between crucial habitat variables and characteristics that can be remotely sensed (e.g., channel complexity) would facilitate telescoping on-the-ground studies outward to a region as vast as AYK. Finally, characterizing the variability of these factors in a dynamic landscape will help us to understand and predict variability in salmon abundance.

Life history diversity and mortality

The diversity of life histories among Pacific salmon provides an opportunity for comparative studies that examine the variables contributing to salmon mortality and recruitment variation. How do environmental variables affect stage-specific mortality for species or stocks with different life histories? How is reproductive investment (number and size of eggs) affected by environmental variables, and how does this translate to recruitment for fishes with different life histories? Comparisons among species could be done at a regional level and ecotypic comparisons at a local level. Does the relative effect of the marine conditions differ based on the proportion of life history spent in the marine environment? Does migration distance influence recruitment success in years of low marine productivity? What variables influence early life history mortality of species or ecotypes with lacustrine versus riverine nursery habitats? Studies taking this approach should help to predict different temporal trends in the abundances of species, stocks, and ecotypes in the dynamic AYK region.

Migration timing

Temporal differences in the timing of adult migrations may also influence salmon recruitment as the timing of spawning events is often tightly coupled to characteristics of the local spawning habitat (Burgner 1991). Use of existing local knowledge may be an effective way to gather information on the timing of adult migrations as fishermen are already well acquainted with stocks and run timing. Knowledge held by residents of subsistence fishing communities located within in the AYK watersheds could be compiled and correlated with observed environmental variables associated with each drainage (spatial comparison across stocks) and year (temporal comparison within stocks). The combination of run times and mixed-stock analysis of each run may provide preliminary understanding of the diversity of ecotypes present in a region.

Coordination of genetic studies

Genetic approaches are well suited to the study of migratory pathways during the marine life stage. This knowledge will contribute to the investigation of physical and biotic interactions between AYK salmon and the marine environment during this important life history stage. In addition, genetic tools can provide accurate and precise information on the extent of fishing mortality (bycatch interception fisheries, targeted commercial, sport, and subsistence fisheries) on different AYK stocks, and lead to the development of methods to mitigate the effects of this incidental harvest. The generation of large amounts of genetic data are becoming more rapid and cost-effective, which should facilitate the development of stock-specific migration models and stock-specific estimates of interception rates throughout the migratory corridor. Stock-specific information may also prove to be highly informative in understanding marine mortality and forecasting future run strengths.

Genetic samples of salmon from remote sites in the AYK region are valuable for researchers working on stock identification of mixed stock fisheries or testing hypotheses about the structure and connectivity among AYK stocks. Although genetic stock identification can be the responsibility of the agency managing the fishery, in practice it often is a more collaborative effort. Due to the high cost and difficulty of sampling the AYK region, DNA samples, in the form of noninvasive fin clips preserved in 95% ethanol, should be collected whenever researchers are handling salmon in remote locations and made readily available to genetics researchers. Genetic samples of adults from the spawning grounds are particularly valuable, as they provide the most information about stock structure at the local breeding population scale. These tissue collections will add to the baseline dataset and to on-going studies of the geographical distribution of genetic diversity in the AYK region. While specific research questions often require unique genetic tools, genetic baselines for stock identification purposes should be standardized in order to reduce redundancies and maximize limited research funds. The approach has been pursued by the Chinook Technical Committee of the Pacific Salmon Commission that has funded and encouraged development of standardized DNA databases for Chinook salmon (Seeb et al. 2007). To this end, existing genetic data on AYK salmon stocks should be broadly available to researchers.

Conclusion

In conclusion, spatial and temporal variation of Pacific salmon abundance is characteristic of, but not unique to, the AYK region. Spatial variation has been observed in other productive fisheries (Hilborn et al. 2003), and single stocks are known to fluctuate across decades and centuries (Finney et al. 2002; Hilborn et al. 2003). Although salmon have been well researched in other watersheds, we caution against assuming that data from more southern populations will predict sources of variation in salmon abundance in the AYK region. Indeed, the transfer of processes regulating salmon abundance across latitudes is an important question remaining to be answered. In this essay we have proposed a hierarchical approach to understanding the AYK salmon system. While identifying the critical scale(s) in space and time at which salmon abundance is regulated will be the greatest challenge for researchers, it is also most likely to return fruitful management decisions. The biocomplexity framework argues against managing only the most productive stocks and offers a long-term perspective that may conflict at times with the immediate management requirement of ensuring adequate harvests for subsistence communities.

Anthropogenic contributions to salmon mortality in the AYK region must be understood within the context of ecological and genetic processes discussed in this paper and elsewhere (e.g., Hard et al. 2009, this volume). In the absence of anthropogenic inputs, salmon abundances are still observed to vary considerably (Finney et al. 2002; Hilborn et al. 2003). Indeed, fish abundances in general are predicted to vary based on endogenous, self-regulatory mechanisms (Ricker 1954), and Pacific salmon abundances fluctuate based on large-scale environmental variables such as ocean regimes (Beamish et al. 1999) that are outside the realm of managerial manipulation. By recognizing the processes generating these fluctuations, anthropogenic sources of salmon mortality can be better characterized and better managed.

Acknowledgments

We thank the following participants in the "Genetics, Ecology and Management" break-out session of the 2007 AYK symposium for their contributions: G. Garvin , J. Hard, M. Smith, S. Urawa, and J. Wenburg. J. Hard and three anonymous reviewers also provided comments that substantially improved this manuscript.

References

Achord, S., R. W. Zabel, and B. P. Sandford. 2007. Migration timing, growth, and estimated parr-to-smolt survival rates of wild Snake River spring-summer Chinook salmon from the Salmon River basin, Idaho, to the Lower Snake River. Transactions of the American Fisheries Society 136:142–154.

ADFG (Alaska Department of Fish and Game). 2003. Yukon River Salmon Negotiation Studies, Completion Report July 1, 2000–June 30, 2003. Regional Information Report No. 3A03–24, Alaska Department of Fish and Game, Division of Commercial Fisheries, AYK Region, Anchorage, Alaska.

AYK SSI (Arctic-Yukon-Kuskokwim Sustainable Salmon Initiative). 2006. Arctic-Yukon-Kuskok-

wim Salmon Research and Restoration Plan.
Bering Sea Fisherman's Association, Anchorage,
Alaska.

Beacham, T. D., and C. C. Wood. 1999. Application of
microsatellite DNA variation to estimation of stock
composition and escapement of Nass River sockeye
salmon (*Oncorhynchus nerka*). Canadian Journal of
Fisheries and Aquatic Sciences 56:297–310.

Beacham, T. D., C. B. Murray, and R. E. Withler.
1988a. Age, morphology, developmental biology, and biochemical genetic stock identification
of Yukon River fall chum salmon (*Oncorhynchus
keta*). Fishery Bulletin 86:663–674.

Beacham, T. D., R. E. Withler, C. B. Murray, and L. W.
Barner. 1988b. Variation in body size, morphology, egg size, and biochemical genetics of pink
salmon in British Columbia. Transactions of the
American Fisheries Society 117:109–126.

Beacham, T. D., C. B. Murray, and R. E. Withler. 1989.
Age, morphology, and biochemical genetic variation of Yukon River Chinook salmon. Transactions
of the American Fisheries Society 118:46–63.

Beacham, T. D., J. R. Candy, K. L. Jonsen, J. Supernault, M. Wetklo, L. Deng, K. M. Miller, R. E.
Withler, and N. Varnavskaya. 2006. Estimation of
stock composition and individual identification of
Chinook salmon across the Pacific Rim by use of
microsatellite variation. Transactions of the American Fisheries Society 135:861–888.

Beacham, T. D., I. Winther, K. L. Jonsen, M. Wetklo,
L. Deng, and J. R. Candy. 2008. The application
of rapid microsatellite-based stock identification
to management of a Chinook salmon troll fishery
off the Queen Charlotte Islands, British Columbia.
North American Journal of Fisheries Management
28:849–855.

Beacham, T. D., K. D. Le, M. Wetklo, B. McIntosh,
T. Ming, and K. M. Miller. 2009. Population
structure and stock identification of chum salmon
from western Alaska determined with microsatellite DNA and major histocompatibility complex
variation. Pages 141–160 in C. C. Krueger and
C. E. Zimmerman, editors. Pacific salmon: ecology and management of western Alaska's populations. American Fisheries Society, Symposium 70,
Bethesda, Maryland.

Beamish, R. J., and C. Mahnken. 2001. A critical size
and period hypothesis to explain natural regulation of salmon abundance and the linkage to climate and climate change. Progress in Oceanography 49:423–437.

Beamish, R. J., D. J. Noakes, G. A. McFarlane, L.
Klyashtorin, V. V. Ivanov, and V. Kurashov. 1999.
The regime concept and natural trends in the pro-
duction of Pacific salmon. Canadian Journal of
Fisheries and Aquatic Sciences 56:516–526.

Beamish, R. J., C. Mahnken, and C. M. Neville. 2004.
Evidence that reduced early marine growth is
associated with lower marine survival of coho
salmon. Transactions of the American Fisheries
Society 133:26–33.

Beauchamp, D. A. 2009. Bioenergetic ontogeny: linking climate and mass-specific feeding and life-cycle growth and survival of salmon. Pages 53–71 in
C. C. Krueger and C. E. Zimmerman, editors. Pacific salmon: ecology and management of western
Alaska's populations. American Fisheries Society,
Symposium 70, Bethesda, Maryland.

Beechie, T., Buhle, E., Ruckelshaus, M., Fullerton, A.,
and Holsinger, L. 2006. Hydrologic regime and
the conservation of salmon life history diversity.
Biological Conservation 130:560–572.

Bradford, M. J., J. A. Grout, and S. Moodie. 2001. Ecology of juvenile Chinook salmon in a small non-natal stream of the Yukon River drainage and the role
of ice conditions on their distribution and survival.
Canadian Journal of Zoology 79:2043–2054.

Bradford, M., A. vonFinster, and P. Milligan. 2009.
Freshwater life history, habitat, and the production
of Chinook salmon from the upper Yukon basin.
Pages 19–38 in C. C. Krueger and C. E. Zimmerman, editors. Pacific salmon: ecology and management of western Alaska's populations. American Fisheries Society, Symposium 70, Bethesda,
Maryland.

Brannon, E. L. 1987. Mechanisms stabilizing salmonid
fry emergence timing. Canadian Special Publications of Fisheries and Aquatic Sciences 96:120–
124.

Brodeur, R. D., K. W. Myers, and J. H. Helle. 2003.
Research conducted by the United States on the
early ocean life history of Pacific salmon. North
Pacific Anadromous Fish Commission Bulletin
3:89–131.

Burgner, R. L. 1991. Life history of sockeye salmon
(*Oncorhynchus nerka*). Pages 1–118 in C. Groot,
and L. Margolis, editors. Pacific salmon life histories. UBC Press, Vancouver, B.C.

Cadenasso, M. L., S. T. A. Pickett, and J. M. Grove.
2006. Dimensions of ecosystem complexity: heterogeneity, connectivity, and history. Ecological
Complexity 3:1–12.

Chen, J.-P., D.-J. Sun, C.-Z. Dong, B. Liang, W.-H. Wu
and S.-Y. Zhang. 2005. Genetic analysis of four
wild chum salmon *Oncorhynchus keta* populations in China based on microsatellite markers.
Environmental Biology of Fishes 73:181–188.

Cooper, A. B., and M. Mangel. 1999. The dangers of ignoring metapopulation structure for the conservation of salmonids. Fishery Bulletin 97:213–226.

Crane, P. A., W. J. Spearman, and L. W. Seeb. 2001.
Yukon River Chum Salmon: Report for Genetic

Stock Identification Studies, 1992–1997, Regional Information Report No. 5J01–08 Alaska Department of Fish and Game, Anchorage, Alaska.

Crane P., D. Molyneaux, S. Miller, K. Harper, and J. K. Wenburg. 2004. Genetic variation among coho salmon populations from the Kuskokwim River region and application to stock-specific harvest estimation. Final Report for Study 03–041, Fisheries Resource Monitoring Program, Office of Subsistence Management, U.S. Fish and Wildlife Service, Anchorage, Alaska.

Farley, E. V., J. Murphy, J. Moss, A. Feldman, and L. Eisner. 2009. Marine ecology of western Alaska juvenile salmon. Pages 307–329 in C. C. Krueger and C. E. Zimmerman, editors. Pacific salmon: ecology and management of western Alaska's populations. American Fisheries Society, Symposium 70, Bethesda, Maryland.

Finney, B. P., I. Gregory-Eaves, J. Sweetman, M. S. V. Douglas, and J. P. Smol. 2000. Impacts of climatic change and fishing on Pacific salmon abundance over the past 300 years. Science 290:795–799.

Finney, B. P., I. Gregory-Eaves, M. S. V. Douglas, and J. P. Smol. 2002. Fisheries productivity in the northeastern Pacific Ocean over the past 2,200 years. Nature (London) 416:729–733.

Fisher, J. P., and W. G. Pearcy. 1988. Growth of juvenile coho salmon (Oncorhynchus kisutch) off Oregon and Washington, USA, in years of differing coastal upwelling. Canadian Journal of Fisheries and Aquatic Sciences 45:1036–1044.

Flannery, B., T. Beacham, M. Wetklo, C. Smith, W. Templin, A. Antonovich, L. Seeb, S. Miller, O. Schlei, and J. Wenburg. 2006. Run timing, migratory patterns, and harvest information of Chinook salmon stocks within the Yukon River. United States Fish and Wildlife Service, Alaska Fisheries Technical Report Number 92.

Flannery, B. G., J. K. Wenburg, and A. J. Gharrett. 2007. Variation of amplified fragment length polymorphisms in Yukon River chum salmon: population structure and application to mixed-stock analysis. Transactions of the American Fisheries Society 136:911–925.

Frissell, C. A., W. J. Liss, C. E. Warren, and M. D. Hurley. 1986. A hierarchical framework for stream habitat classification: viewing streams in a watershed context. Environmental Management 10:199–214.

Frost, T. M., D. L. DeAngelis, S. M. Bartell, D. J. Hall, S. H. Hurlbert. 1988. Scale in the design and interpretation of aquatic community research. Pages 229–258 in S. R. Carpenter, editor. Complex interactions in lake communities. Springer-Verlag, New York.

Gharrett, A. J., S. M. Shirley, and G. R. Tromble. 1987.

Genetic relationships among populations of Alaskan Chinook salmon (Oncorhynchus tshawytscha). Canadian Journal of Fisheries and Aquatic Sciences 44:765–774.

Gilk, S., D. Molyneaux, T. Hamazaki, J. A. Pawluk, and W. D. Templin. 2009. Biological and genetic characteristics of fall and summer chum salmon in the Kuskokwim River, Alaska. Pages 161–179 in C. C. Krueger and C. E. Zimmerman, editors. Pacific salmon: ecology and management of western Alaska's populations. American Fisheries Society, Symposium 70, Bethesda, Maryland.

Gisclair, B. R. 2009. Salmon bycatch management in the Bering Sea walleye pollock fishery: threats and opportunities for western Alaska. Pages 799–816 in C. C. Krueger and C. E. Zimmerman, editors. Pacific salmon: ecology and management of western Alaska's populations. American Fisheries Society, Symposium 70, Bethesda, Maryland.

Grant, W. S., G. B. Milner, P. Krasnowski, and F. M. Utter. 1980. Use of biochemical genetic variants for identification of sockeye salmon (Oncorhynchus nerka) stocks in Cook Inlet, Alaska. Canadian Journal of Fisheries and Aquatic Sciences 37:1236–1247.

Groot, C., and L. Margolis, editors. 1991. Pacific salmon life histories. UBC Press, Vancouver, B.C.

Gustafson, R. G., R. S. Waples, J. M. Myers, L. A. Weitkamp, G. J. Bryant, O. W. Johnson, and J. J. Hard. 2007. Pacific salmon extinctions: quantifying lost and remaining diversity. Conservation Biology 21:1009–1020.

Habicht, C., L. W. Seeb, and J. E. Seeb. 2007. Genetic and ecological divergence defines population structure of sockeye salmon populations returning to Bristol Bay, Alaska, and provides a tool for admixture analysis. Transactions of the American Fisheries Society 136:82–94.

Haflinger, K., and J. Gruver. 2009. Rolling hot spot closure areas in the Bering Sea walleye pollock fishery: estimated reduction of salmon bycatch during the 2006 season. Pages 817–826 in C. C. Krueger and C. E. Zimmerman, editors. Pacific salmon: ecology and management of western Alaska's populations. American Fisheries Society, Symposium 70, Bethesda, Maryland.

Hard, J. J. 1995. A quantitative genetic perspective on the conservation of intraspecific diversity. Pages 304–326 in J. Nielsen, editor. Evolution and the aquatic ecosystem: defining unique units in population conservation. American Fisheries Society, Symposium 17, Bethesda, Maryland.

Hard, J. J., W. Eldridge, and K. Naish. 2009. Genetic consequences of size-selective fishing: implications for viability of Chinook salmon in the Arctic-Yukon-Kuskokwim region of Alaska. Pages

759–780 *in* C. C. Krueger and C. E. Zimmerman, editors. Pacific salmon: ecology and management of western Alaska's populations. American Fisheries Society, Symposium 70, Bethesda, Maryland.

Healey, M. C., and A. Prince. 1995. Scales of variation in life history tactics of Pacific salmon and the conservation of phenotype and genotype. Pages 176–184 *in* J. Nielsen, editor. Evolution and the aquatic ecosystem: defining unique units in population conservation. American Fisheries Society, Symposium 17, Bethesda, Maryland.

Heard, W. R. 1991. Life history of pink salmon (*Oncorhynchus gorbuscha*). Pages 119–230 *in* C. Groot, and L. Margolis, editors. Pacific salmon life histories. UBC Press, Vancouver, BC.

Hendry, A. P., J. K. Wenburg, P. Bentzen, E. C. Volk, and T. P. Quinn. 2000. Rapid evolution of reproductive isolation in the wild: evidence from introduced salmon. Science (Washington D.C.) 290:516–518.

Hilborn, R., T. P. Quinn, D. E. Schindler, and D. E. Rogers. 2003. Biocomplexity and fisheries sustainability. Proceedings of the National Academy of Sciences USA 100:6564–6568.

Holling, C. S. 1992. Cross-scale morphology, geometry, and dynamics of ecosystems. Ecological Monographs 62:447–502.

Hutchings, J. A. 2003. Norms of reaction and phenotypic plasticity in salmonid life histories. Pages 154–174 *in* S. C. Stearns and A. P. Hendry. Evolution illuminated: salmon and their relatives. Oxford University Press, New York.

Hutchings, J. A., and J. D. Reynolds. 2004. Marine fish population crashes: consequences for recovery and extinction risk. Bioscience 54:297–309.

Hutchings, J. A., D. P. Swain, S. Rowe, J. D. Eddington, V. Puvanendran, and J. A. Brown. 2007. Genetic variation in life-history reaction norms in a marine fish. Proceedings of the Royal Society of London, Series B 274:1693–1699.

Jacobs D. K, T. A. Haney, and K. D. Louie. 2004. Genes, diversity, and geologic process on the Pacific coast. Annual Review of Earth and Planetary Sciences 32:601–652.

Keeley, E. R., E. A. Parkinson, and E. B. Taylor. 2005. Ecotypic differentiation of native rainbow trout (*Oncorhynchus mykiss*) populations from British Columbia. Canadian Journal of Fisheries and Aquatic Sciences 62:1523–1539.

Lawson, P. W., E. A. Logerwell, N. J. Mantua, R. C. Francis, and V. N. Agostini. 2004. Environmental factors influencing freshwater survival and smolt production in the Pacific Northwest coho (*Oncorhynchus kisutch*). Canadian Journal of Fisheries and Aquatic Sciences 61:360–373.

Mantua, N. 2009. Patterns of change in climate and Pacific salmon production. Pages 1143–1157 *in* C. C. Krueger and C. E. Zimmerman, editors. Pacific salmon: ecology and management of western Alaska's populations. American Fisheries Society, Symposium 70, Bethesda, Maryland.

Martin, J. 2009. A perspective on coho salmon management in Oregon: learning from experience and expecting surprises. Pages 1047–1057 *in* C. C. Krueger and C. E. Zimmerman, editors. Pacific salmon: ecology and management of western Alaska's populations. American Fisheries Society, Symposium 70, Bethesda, Maryland.

McKay, J. K., and R. G. Latta. 2002. Adaptive population divergence: markers, QTL and traits. Trends in Ecology and Evolution 17:285–291.

Miller, K. M., K. H. Kaukinen, T. D. Beacham, and R. E. Withler. 2001. Geographic heterogeneity in natural selection of an MHC locus in sockeye salmon. Genetica 111:237–251.

Mobrand, L. E., J. A. Lichatowich, L. C. Lestelle, and T. S. Vogel. 1997. An approach to describing ecosystem performance "through the eyes of salmon." Canadian Journal of Fisheries and Aquatic Sciences 54:2964–2973.

Molyneaux, D. B., and L. K. Brannian. 2006. Review of escapement and abundance information for Kuskokwim area salmon stocks. Alaska Department of Fish and Game, Fishery Manuscript No. 06–08, Anchorage.

Montgomery, D. R. 2000. Coevolution of the Pacific salmon and Pacific Rim topography. Geology 28:1107–1110.

Moss, J. H., D. A. Beauchamp, A. D. Cross, K. W. Myers, E. V. Farley, J. M. Murphy, and J. H. Helle. 2005. Evidence for size-selective mortality after the first summer of ocean growth by pink salmon. Transactions of the American Fisheries Society 134:1313–1322.

Mueter, F. J., R. M. Peterman, and B. J. Pyper. 2002. Opposite effects of ocean temperature on survival rates of 120 stocks of Pacific salmon (*Oncorhynchus* spp.) in northern and southern areas. Canadian Journal of Fisheries and Aquatic Sciences 59:456–463.

Mueter, F. J., B. J. Pyper, and R. M. Peterman. 2005. Relationships between coastal ocean conditions and survival rates of northeast Pacific salmon at multiple lags. Transactions of the American Fisheries Society 134:105–119.

Mundy, P. R., and O. A. Mathiesen. 1981. Abundance estimation in a feedback control system applied to the management of a commercial salmon fishery. Pages 81–98 in K. B. Haley, editor. Applied operations research in fishing. Plenum, New York.

Murray, C. B., and J. D. McPhail. 1988. Effect of incubation temperature on the development of 5 species of Pacific salmon (*Oncorhynchus*) embryos and alevins. Canadian Journal of Zoology 66:266–273.

Myers, K. W., R. V. Walker, N. D. Davis, J. L. Armstrong, and M. Kaeriyama, 2009. High seas distribution, biology, and ecology of Arctic-Yukon-Kuskokwim salmon: direct information from high seas tagging experiments, 1954–2006. Pages 201–239 *in* C. C. Krueger and C. E. Zimmerman, editors. Pacific salmon: ecology and management of western Alaska's populations. American Fisheries Society, Symposium 70, Bethesda, Maryland.

Naiman, R. J., and J. J. Latterell. 2005. Principles for linking fish habitat to fisheries management and conservation. Journal of Fish Biology 67B:166–185.

Nemeth, M., B. Williams, R. C. Bocking, and S. N. Kinneen. 2009. Freshwater habitat quantity and coho salmon production in two rivers: an initial study to support the development of habitat-based escapement goals in Norton Sound, Alaska. Pages 73–96 *in* C. C. Krueger and C. E. Zimmerman, editors. Pacific salmon: ecology and management of western Alaska's populations. American Fisheries Society, Symposium 70, Bethesda, Maryland.

Olsen, J. B., S. J. Miller, K. Harper, and J. K. Wenburg. 2009. Genetic health and variables influencing the effective number of breeders in western Alaska Chinook salmon. Pages 781–795 *in* C. C. Krueger and C. E. Zimmerman, editors. Pacific salmon: ecology and management of western Alaska's populations. American Fisheries Society, Symposium 70, Bethesda, Maryland.

Peterson, G. 2000. Political ecology and ecological resilience: an integration of human and ecological dynamics. Ecological Economics 35:323–336.

Pickett, S. T. A., M. L. Cadenasso, and J. M. Grove. 2005. Biocomplexity in coupled natural-human systems: a multidimensional framework. Ecosystems 8:225–232.

Policansky, D., and J. J. Magnuson. 1998. Genetics, metapopulations, and ecosystem management of fisheries. Ecological Applications 8:S119–S123.

Quinn, T. P. 1985. Homing and the evolution of sockeye salmon, *Oncorhynchus nerka*. *In* M.A. Rankin, editor. Migrations: mechanisms and adaptive significance. Contributions in Marine Science, Supplement to volume 27:353–366.

Quinn, T. P. 2005. The behavior and ecology of Pacific Salmon and Trout. University of Washington Press, Seattle, Washington.

Quinn, T. P. 2009. Pacific salmon population structure and dynamics: a perspective from Bristol Bay on life history variation across spatial and temporal scales. Pages 857–871 *in* C. C. Krueger and

C. E. Zimmerman, editors. Pacific salmon: ecology and management of western Alaska's populations. American Fisheries Society, Symposium 70, Bethesda, Maryland.

Quinn, T. P., and G. B. Buck. 2001. Size- and sex-selective mortality of adult sockeye salmon: Bears, gulls, and fish out of water. Transactions of the American Fisheries Society 130:995–1005.

Ramstad, K. R., C. A. Woody, G. K. Sage, and F. W. Allendorf. 2004. Founding events influence genetic population structure of sockeye salmon (*Oncorhynchus nerka*) in Lake Clark, Alaska. Molecular Ecology 13:277–290.

Ricker, W. E. 1954. Stock and recruitment. Journal of the Fisheries Research Board of Canada 11:559–623.

Ricker, W. E. 1972. Hereditary and environmental factors affecting certain salmonid populations. Pages 27–160 *in* R. C. Simon and P. A. Larkin, editors. The stock concept in Pacific salmon. H. R. MacMillan Lecture Series in Fisheries. University of British Columbia, Vancouver B.C.

Ricker, W. E. 1975. Computation and interpretation of biological statistics of fish populations. Fisheries Research Board of Canada Bulletin 191.

Ruggerone, G. T., and F. A. Goetz. 2004. Survival of Puget Sound Chinook salmon (*Oncorhynchus tshawytscha*) in response to climate-induced competition with pink salmon (*Oncorhynchus gorbuscha*). Canadian Journal of Fisheries and Aquatic Sciences 61:1756–1770.

Ruggerone, G. T., E. Farley, J. Nielsen, and P. Hagen. 2005. Seasonal marine growth of Bristol Bay sockeye salmon (*Oncorhynchus nerka*) in relation to competition with Asian pink salmon (*O. gorbuscha*) and the 1977 ocean regime shift. Fishery Bulletin 103:355–370.

Ruggerone, G. T., and J. L. Nielsen. 2009. A review of growth and survival of salmon at sea in response to competition and climate change. Pages 241–265 *in* C. C. Krueger and C. E. Zimmerman, editors. Pacific salmon: ecology and management of western Alaska's populations. American Fisheries Society, Symposium 70, Bethesda, Maryland.

Scribner, K. T., P. A. Crane, W. J. Spearman, and L. W. Seeb. 1998. DNA and allozyme markers provide concordant estimates of population differentiation: analyses of US and Canadian populations of Yukon River fall-run chum salmon (*Oncorhynchus keta*). Canadian Journal of Fisheries and Aquatic Sciences 55:1748–1758.

Seeb, L. W., and P. A. Crane. 1999. High genetic heterogeneity in chum salmon in Western Alaska, the contact zone between northern and southern lineages. Transactions of the American Fisheries Society 128:58–87.

Seeb, L. W., P. A. Crane, C. M. Kondzela, R. L. Wilmot, S. Urawa, N. V. Varnavskaya, and J. E. Seeb. 2004. Migration of Pacific Rim chum salmon on the high seas: Insights from genetic data. Environmental Biology of Fishes 69:21–36.

Seeb, L. W., A. Antonovich, M. A. Banks, T. D. Beacham, M. R. Bellinger, S. M. Blankenship, M. Campbell, N. A. Decovish, J. C. Garza, C .M. Guthrie, III, T. A. Lundrigan, P. Moran, S. R. Narum, J. J. Stephenson, K. J. Supernault, D. J. Teel, W. D. Templin, J. K. Wenburg, S. F. Young, and C. T. Smith. 2007. Development of a standardized DNA database for Chinook salmon. Fisheries 32:540–542.

Smith, C. T., W. D. Templin, J. E. Seeb, and L. W. Seeb. 2005. Single nucleotide polymorphisms provide rapid and accurate estimates of the proportions of U.S. and Canadian Chinook salmon caught in Yukon River fisheries. North American Journal of Fisheries Management 25:944–953.

Stram, D. L., and J. N. Ianelli. 2009. Eastern Bering Sea pollock trawl fisheries: variation in salmon bycatch over time and space. Pages 827–850 in C. C. Krueger and C. E. Zimmerman, editors. Pacific salmon: ecology and management of western Alaska's populations. American Fisheries Society, Symposium 70, Bethesda, Maryland.

Swain, D. P., B. E. Riddell, and C. B. Murray. 1991. Morphological differences between hatchery and wild populations of coho salmon (*Oncorhynchus kisutch*)—environmental versus genetic origin. Canadian Journal of Fisheries and Aquatic Sciences 48:1783–1791.

Taylor, E. B., Foote, C. J., and Wood, C. C. 1996. Molecular genetic evidence for parallel life-history evolution within a Pacific salmon (sockeye salmon and kokanee, *Oncorhynchus nerka*). Evolution 50:401–416.

Templin, W., C. Smith, D. Molyneaux, and L. Seeb. 2004. Genetic diversity of Chinook salmon from the Kuskokwim River. Final Report for Study 01–70, Office of Subsistence Management, U. S. Fish and Wildlife Service.

Templin W. D., R. L. Wilmot, C. M. Guthrie III, and L.W. Seeb. 2005. United States and Canadian Chinook salmon stocks in the Yukon River can be segregated based on genetic characteristics. Alaska Fishery Research Bulletin 11:44–60.

Templin, W. D., N. A. Decovich, and L. W. Seeb. 2006. Yukon River Chinook salmon genetic baseline: Survey of Pacific salmon commission loci for U.S. populations. Alaska Department of Fish and Game, Fishery Data Series No. 06–46, Anchorage.

Tessier, N., and L. Bernatchez. 1999. Stability of population structure and genetic diversity across generations assessed by microsatellites among sympatric populations of landlocked Atlantic salmon (*Salmo salar* L.). Molecular Ecology 8:169–179.

Thompson, W. F. 1959. An approach to population dynamics of the Pacific red salmon. Transactions of the American Fisheries Society 88:206–209.

Thorpe, J. E., M. Mangel, N. B. Metcalfe, and F. A. Huntingford. 1998. Modelling the proximate basis of salmonid life-history variation, with application to Atlantic salmon, *Salmo salar* L. Evolutionary Ecology 12:581–599.

Turesson, G. 1922. The species and the variety as ecological units. Hereditas 3:100–113.

Unwin, M. J., M. T. Kinnison, N. C. Boustead, and T. P. Quinn. 2003. Genetic control over survival in Pacific salmon (*Oncorhynchus* spp.): experimental evidence between and within populations of New Zealand Chinook salmon (*O. tshawytscha*) Canadian Journal of Fisheries and Aquatic Sciences 60:1–11.

Utter, F. M., M. V. McPhee, and F. W. Allendorf. 2009. Population genetics and the management of Arctic-Yukon-Kuskokwim salmon populations. Pages 97–123 in C. C. Krueger and C. E. Zimmerman, editors. Pacific salmon: ecology and management of western Alaska's populations. American Fisheries Society, Symposium 70, Bethesda, Maryland.

Vollestad, L. A., J. Peterson, and T. P. Quinn. 2004. Effects of freshwater and marine growth rates on early maturity in male coho and Chinook salmon. Transactions of the American Fisheries Society 133:495–503.

Wang, S., J. J. Hard, and F. Utter. 2002. Genetic variation and fitness in salmonids. Conservation Genetics 3:321–333.

Waples, R. S. 1995. Evolutionarily significant units and the conservation of biological diversity under the Endangered Species Act. Pages 8–27 in J. Nielsen, editor. Evolution and the aquatic ecosystem: defining unique units in population conservation. American Fisheries Society, Symposium 17, Bethesda, Maryland.

Waples, R. S., R. G. Gustafson, L. A. Weitkamp, J. M. Myers, O. W. Johnson, P. J. Busby, J. J. Hard, G. J. Bryant, F. W. Waknitz, K. Neely, D. Teel, W. S. Grant, G. A. Winans, S. Phelps, A. Marshall, and B. M. Baker. 2001. Characterizing diversity in salmon from the Pacific Northwest. Journal of Fish Biology 59A:1–41.

Waples, R. S. 2009. Conserving the evolutionary legacy of Arctic-Yukon-Kuskokwim salmon. Pages 125–139 in C. C. Krueger and C. E. Zimmerman, editors. Pacific salmon: ecology and management of western Alaska's populations. American Fisheries Society, Symposium 70, Bethesda, Maryland.

Waples, R. S., D. J. Teel, J. M. Myers, and A. R. Marshall. 2004. Life-history divergence in Chinook salmon: historic contingency and parallel evolution. Evolution 58:386–403.

Welch, D. W., B. R. Ward, B. D. Smith, and J. P. Eveson. 2000. Temporal and spatial responses of British Columbia steelhead (*Oncorhynchus mykiss*) populations to ocean climate shifts. Fisheries Oceanography 9:17–32.

West-Eberhard, M. J. 1989. Phenotypic plasticity and the origins of diversity. Annual Review of Ecology and Systematics 20:249–278.

Whited, D. C., M. S. Lorang, M. J. Harner, F. R. Hauer, J. S. Kimball, and J. A. Stanford. 2007. Climate, hydrologic disturbance, and succession: drivers of floodplain pattern. Ecology 88:940–953.

Wilmot, R. L., R. E. Everett, W. J. Spearman, and R. Baccus. 1992. Genetic stock identification of Yukon River chum and Chinook salmon 1987 to 1990. Progress Report to the U.S. Fish and Wildlife Service, Anchorage, Alaska.

Wilmot, R. L., R. J. Everett, W. J. Spearman, R. Baccus, N. V. Varnavskaya, and S. V. Putivkin. 1994. Genetic stock structure of Western Alaska chum salmon and a comparison with Russian Far East stocks. Canadian Journal of Fisheries and Aquatic Sciences 51(Supplement 1):84–94.

Winther, I., and T. D. Beacham. 2009. Application of Chinook salmon stock composition data for management of the northern British Columbia troll fishery, 2006. Pages 977–1004 *in* C. C. Krueger and C. E. Zimmerman, editors. Pacific salmon: ecology and management of western Alaska's populations. American Fisheries Society, Symposium 70, Bethesda, Maryland.

Wipfli, M. S., J. P. Hudson, J. P. Caouette, and D. T. Chaloner. 2003. Marine subsidies in freshwater ecosystems: Salmon carcasses increase the growth rates of stream-resident salmonids. Transactions of the American Fisheries Society 132:371–381.

baseline – database describing the genetic variation that exists among and between stocks; used to assign individual fish back to specific stocks based on their genotypes.

biocomplexity – a conceptual model for understanding biological complexity as the sum of hierarchical biological units and the physical/biological processes that affect these units. Biocomplexity arises when processes act at different scales in space and time and interact across these scales, such that understanding at one scale does not ensure predictability at another scale.

deme – the smallest genetic unit of a population; the local breeding group.

ecotype, ecotypic variation – organismal characteristics among members of a population or species that are associated with increased survival and/or reproduction in certain environments. The degree to which these traits are genetically determined varies.

fitness – the probability that an individual will survive to reproductive age combined with its rate of successful reproduction

genetic baseline – see *baseline*

genetic marker – a variable characteristic of an organism's DNA (such as a DNA sequence or a protein variant) that can be classified or quantified, allowing analysis of genetic variation within and between populations

genotype – description of an individual's characteristics at a particular genetic marker or suite of markers

local adaptation – the existence of phenotypes that increase survival and/or reproduction in the specific environment a population inhabits, due to population changes in genetic variation that affects relevant traits

metapopulation – a collection of populations that interact with each other demographically and genetically by exchanging migrants; a "population of populations"

phenotype – an observable characteristic of an organism, such as body shape or age at maturity. Can be determined by genetic or environmental factors, usually by a combination of these.

phenotypic plasticity – the ability of a single genotype to produce different phenotypes, as mediated by environmental factors

population connectivity – the degree to which populations interact with each other through exchange of migrants; it is often influenced by landscape structure which either facilitates or inhibits migration between populations

remote sensing – collecting physical data from a site without having to be on the ground at that site; methods include satellite or aerial imagery, RADAR

selection – changes in frequency of a phenotype in a population as a result of increased or decreased survival and/or reproduction of individuals possessing that phenotype

selectively neutral – a trait (or more commonly, a genetic marker) that is not associated with differences in survival and/or reproduction

stock – a level of biological organization that serves as the fundamental unit for fisheries enumeration and management; in this paper we use the definition adopted by AYK SSI: "aggregations of demes characterized by sites from which their individual escapement counts are obtained," (AYK SSI 2006, p. 77)

American Fisheries Society Symposium 70:1199–1215, 2009
© 2009 by the American Fisheries Society

Sustaining Salmon Fisheries:
The Challenge of Collaborative Management

SUSAN HANNA[*]

Oregon State University
229 Ballard Extension Hall, Corvallis, Oregon 07331, USA

Abstract.—The Arctic-Yukon-Kuskokwim (AYK) Salmon Research and Restoration Program explicitly recognizes the integration of human dimensions with salmon ecosystems. This paper addresses the collaborative management approach to integration by summarizing how collaborative processes work and how they influence management performance. Collaborative fishery management includes stakeholders in a number of management functions such as data collection, research, planning, design, decision-making, monitoring, evaluation, and enforcement. This approach is included in the general category of "co-management," which refers to the sharing of authority and responsibility among government and stakeholders. Co-management is a process, rather than a tool, of management. The direct involvement of stakeholders in the planning and control of their fisheries offers the potential of improving the performance of fishery management in promoting sustainability. Realizing the potential depends on the extent to which key co-management principles are addressed. These principles relate to three management components: background conditions in the fishery, management structure, and management operations. Background conditions that affect the performance of co-management include uncertainty, history, and context. Elements of fishery structure relating to co-management performance include boundaries, scale, representation, and participation. Fishery management operations influence co-management performance through stability and flexibility, cost effectiveness, and equity. The principles underlie co-management performance through the effect they have on transaction costs and incentives. Columbia River salmon recovery provides a good example of the influence of transaction costs and uncertainty on collaborative management and resource recovery. The complexity of Columbia River Basin co-management includes scale, fragmentation, scientific uncertainty, and legacy. These variables lead to co-management research suggestions for the AYK Salmon Research and Restoration Program.

Introduction

The goal of the Arctic-Yukon-Kuskokwim (AYK) SSI Research and Restoration Program is to improve salmon management and promote its restoration through a collaborative and inclusive process (AYK SSI 2006). The program is based on the fundamental concept that the sustainability of communities and the sustainability of salmon in the AYK region go hand in hand. However, the vastness of the AYK region, the degree of ecosystem variability, the dispersion of human populations, and the context of resource dependence all present challenges to collabor-

[*]Corresponding author: susan.hanna@oregonstate.edu

ative management and restoration (Hilsinger et al. 2009, this volume). The diversity of the human context adds further complexity; the region has 118 tribes, 13 Native languages, high numbers of households in poverty, and an economy based on both subsistence and commercial use of resources (Pete 2007).

The goal of the AYK SSI Research and Restoration Program is also the basic task and great challenge of fishery management: to promote healthy interactions among people, fish, and ecosystems. To do this, management must reflect social, ecological, and economic goals for the ecosystem, and it must integrate commercial, subsistence and recreational interests, and reflect the patterns of resource use over space and time. Management must be flexible enough to adapt to change, and it must fully represent the many interacting components of the context in which it operates (Hanna 2002).

Collaborative fishery management is intended to achieve better integration of people and ecosystems by making management more inclusive, flexible, and adaptive. The intent of this approach is to make management more informed and effective by broadening the scope of decision makers and the information included in decision-making. This approach views salmon ecosystems through the human lens, reflecting a meaning of sustainability that includes the role of people in accomplishing it.

This paper addresses the question of integrating people with salmon ecosystems through collaborative management. It summarizes some key understandings of how collaborative processes work and how they influence management performance. Recent recommendations related to human dimensions of salmon management in the AYK region are summarized and then considered in light of what is known about collaborative management and key principles for success. Two important components of collaborative processes are highlighted–transaction costs

and incentives. Finally, some lessons are summarized that were learned from a large-scale salmon research and restoration effort in the Columbia River Basin, and conclusions are offered by summarizing key complexities and identifying research questions related to building effective collaborative management in the AYK region.

Recommendations Related to Human Dimensions of AYK Salmon Ecosystems

In making recommendations for the development of an AYK SSI Research and Restoration Plan, the National Research Council (NRC) Committee on Review of Arctic-Yukon-Kuskokwim (Western Alaska) Research and Restoration Plan for Salmon used three system "frameworks" within which to structure research questions: 1. life cycles of salmon and their environments; 2. sustainable salmon, emphasizing human social, economic, and political linkages; 3. resilience of the AYK salmon-human system, highlighting the dynamic nature of the human and biophysical systems over multiple generations. The NRC committee noted that although some of the questions that arise are common to all the frameworks, using three frameworks allows each to provide different insights and can lead to different questions (NRC 2004).

Two themes pervade the research questions developed under the three frameworks (NRC 2004). The first theme concerns the populations, numbers, and distribution of salmon. "We need to have a much better accounting system for AYK salmon: we need to know how many there are, we need to know where they spend their time during all phases of their life history, and we need to understand how populations of salmon within each of the species are differentiated" (NRC 2004).

The second theme concerns human behavior and motivation. "We need to understand much better what people in the region are doing with respect to salmon and why they are doing those things. To some degree, that applies also to people outside the region. We need to know how many people are fishing, when they fish, how many fish they take, and what factors affect those behaviors. Better information is needed on the numbers and kinds of fish taken by human activities in the region and in other areas, where AYK salmon can be caught during their oceanic migrations. We need to understand what factors influence the development, promulgation, and enforcement of fishing regulations, including how federal and state laws concerning conservation of biological diversity and protection of subsistence rights are translated into management regulations. We also need to understand what factors influence people's compliance with those regulations" (NRC 2004).

Both the NRC recommendations and the subsequent AKY Salmon Research and Restoration Plan (AYK SSI 2006) challenge the entrenched perspective that ecosystem-based fishery management is solely a biological concern. The view of fishery management as biology is a legacy of a management approach that sets simple conservation rules and leaves the human system to take care of itself. This management approach has been accompanied by a tendency to think of management as needing to meet objectives designed around biological reference points—for example, maximum sustainable yield—rather than an integration of biological, ecological, economic and social reference points. As a result, human dimensions of management are often dismissed as "politics" that undermine the "real" objectives of management. This perspective has been both the cause and the consequence of chronically low levels of investment in human dimensions research. A similar lack of investment has occurred in building the skills and capacities that comprise the human capital of management (Hanna 1995b). Taking a contrasting view,

the AYK plan provides operational detail to the truism that fishery management is managing people, not fish (AYK SSI 2006).

What is Collaborative Management?

Collaboration includes teamwork, partnership, group effort, alliance, and cooperation. Collaborative fishery management implements these efforts by involving stakeholders in a number of management functions such as data collection, research, planning, design, decision-making, monitoring, evaluation, and enforcement. The collaborative approach is included in the general category of "co-management," and this term is used in this paper to represent the broad suite of activities under collaborative management.

Fishery co-management refers to the sharing of authority and responsibility among government and stakeholders. Co-management is fundamentally a de-centralized approach to information gathering: it is decision-making and implementation that involves a wide range of stakeholders as consultants, advisors or co-equal partners. Sen and Nielsen (1996) detail five types of co-management that represent different collaborative combinations of user groups and government:

1. Instructive: government as the decision maker exchanges information with user groups;

2. Consultative: government as the decision maker consults with user groups but may not take their advice;

3. Cooperative: government and user groups are partners in decision-making;

4. Advisory: government as the decision maker takes user group advice;

5. Informative: user groups as the decision makers inform government of decisions.

Over time, fishery management has moved increasingly toward greater integration with stakeholders, as managers have found that management often works better with stakeholder involvement. "Working better" in the fishery management context means that management is more likely to meet its objectives, be perceived as fair, and reduce the cost of conflict. Stakeholder participation is important to a number of management outcomes. Interaction among stakeholders can often overcome special interests and contribute to common goals (Hanna 1995a). Participation can contribute and interpret local ecological knowledge for the information base used for decisions, thereby making management adaptable and enforceable (Pinkerton 1989; Ostrom 1990). Participation also may increase the reliability of monitoring and enforcement, and contribute to the resolution of the inevitable conflict between interest groups. However, as Jentoft and McCay (1995) note, structuring stakeholder participation is not a simple matter. Some management tasks lend themselves to decentralized control while others do not. For example, decisions about tributary habitat restoration or the conduct of a terminal salmon fishery may be well suited to a decentralized approach, while estimating biomass or deciding on system-wide escapement levels is not. The question of suitability for decentralization often depends on the context of the fishery and the characteristics of stakeholders.

Co-management is a process used in fisheries worldwide. It carries particular appeal in small-scale fisheries where stakeholders have a tradition of interacting with one another and a desire for control over local resources. Small-scale fisheries are usually conducted in near-shore areas where the behavior of fishery participants can be locally monitored and rules can be locally enforced. Also because of their proximity to shore, small-scale fisheries are often most in need of effective management. Near-shore areas absorb the spillover effects of activities in other sectors, making small-scale fisheries vulnerable to pollution, habitat destruction, and competing uses of water space. They also experience spillover effects of problems in offshore fisheries, including displaced fishing effort, gear conflicts, and localized depletions. Perhaps most importantly, small-scale fisheries are good candidates for co-management because they often have local or regional importance disproportional to their size as the basis of economic activity, food security, and social networks (Pinkerton 1989; Hanna 1994; Pomeroy and Williams 1994; Jentoft and McCay 1995; Wilson et al. 2003). However, observed conditions under which co-management has traditionally taken place are not necessarily the conditions necessary for co-management today. Contemporary mapping, positioning, and communication technologies may make it possible to expand the geographic scale of co-managed fisheries and coordinate across more diverse groups than was previously the case.

For all of these reasons, the direct involvement of stakeholders in the planning and control of their fisheries offers the potential for improving the performance of fishery management in promoting sustainability. The idea behind co-management is that people vested in planning and decision-making are more likely to engage in long-term thinking than those who are not, so they will act accordingly. As with any form of management, costs and benefits exist to active stakeholder participation and for co-management to achieve its full potential, it must be carefully designed and implemented (Hanna 1995b).

Co-management is a management process rather than a management tool. Within co-management, any of the full range of management tools—for example gear controls, effort controls, territorial use rights, or individual quotas—may be employed.

Principles of Co-Management: What Do We Know About Making It Work?

At the broadest level, fishery management of any type must bring individual behavior into line with social objectives. Management must solve the collective action problem, which exists when actions that are rational from the individual point of view are not rational from a collective point of view (Sandler 1992). The "tragedy of the commons" parable of open access resources is a prime example of a collective action problem (Hardin 1968). Without a resolution of this problem, management is unable to generate a resilient integration of people and ecosystems.

To solve the collective action problem, management must meet two key conditions. The first condition is to provide the right incentives to coordinate subsistence, commercial and recreational uses, to control levels of use, enforce rules, and to adapt to change. The second condition is to contain transaction costs. Transaction costs are the costs of doing the business of fishery management, such as: gather information, design regulations, organize participants, participate in meetings, monitor conditions, and enforce regulations. They are both monetary and nonmonetary in nature.

To be most effective in promoting long-term sustainability, management must also perform several functions. Management must coordinate multiple objectives and organizational tasks. It must generate information and develop legitimate and flexible decision processes. Management must also take a long-term perspective to accommodate intergenerational claims to resource services (Hanna 1998). Management's task is to fulfill these functions within a set of specific legal, economic, and social objectives. Fishery co-management has the same task. The economic question facing any process of management,

including co-management, is whether it achieves its objectives and performs its functions in a cost-effective way (Hanna 2003a).

Experience with co-management in fisheries worldwide (see, for example, Wilson et al. 2003) has generated valuable understanding of some key co-management principles. These pertain to background conditions in the fishery, fishery management structure, and fishery management operations.

Background conditions in the fishery

Three important background conditions affect the performance of fishery management. These are uncertainty, history, and context. Uncertainty is always present: ecosystems vary, climate changes, markets expand and contract, and government policies evolve. Uncertainty shapes expectations and behavior because it influences the degree of assurance people have over present knowledge and future conditions. History also plays an important role, because past actions create a path that shapes the set of available or imaginable alternatives in the present. Context is key, because the ecological, economic, sociocultural, and regulatory setting of the fishery influences how the general principles of fishery management are specifically applied.

Fishery management structure

Principles of co-management relate to important aspects of fishery structure, including boundaries, scale, representation, and participation. Management depends on clearly defined and consistent boundaries, whether political, geographic, or jurisdictional. Boundaries must also be accepted as legitimate. The number of boundaries or scales over which fishery co-management is coordinated, for example community, state, and regional, directly affects the difficulty of management. It is somewhat rare in practice that political and ecosystem boundaries are fully aligned, and scale mismatch between the two is common (Ostrom 1990, 1995).

The scale of management affects the degree of coordination required, because local or regional co-management is nested within larger institutional jurisdictions requiring coordination of objectives at different levels (Jentoft 1989; Ostrom 1995; Young 1996). The scale issue is also related to incentives of management participants, which for consistency purposes should be compatible across scales. In the ideal, co-management would reflect the larger societal goals for fisheries as well as local objectives. However, instead of the ideal, there is the real situation of national governments, states, regions, and local entities placing different weights on management objectives such as efficiency, equity, or ecological diversity. The different objectives arise from the diverse contexts and traditions at various scales, resulting in difficulties in both "scaling up" small-scale system properties to large-scale systems and "scaling down" national policies to community levels (Young 1996).

Representation and participation lie at the heart of co-management. If representation is fully consistent with the functional groups of interest that exist in the fishery, such as gear groups or target fisheries, decisions are more likely to reflect the full array of interests and vest stakeholders in the process (Jentoft and McCay 1995; Ostrom and Schlager 1996). Full representation also diminishes the possibility of "free riding" where some stakeholders receive the benefits of co-management without contributing to its cost (Hanna 2003a). Stakeholder characteristics, such as traditions of participation in fishery management or other political arenas, sources of knowledge, levels of education, geographic dispersion, levels of financial resources, and the existence of organized interest groups all affect the level of participation (Pinkerton 1989; Hanna 1995b; McCay 1996; Sen and Nielsen 1996).

Fishery management operations

Principles of co-management related to fishery management operations address stability and flexibility, cost effectiveness, and equity. The procedures of fishery management are typically rather sluggish or rigid in response to changing fishery conditions. Procedural rules may be cumbersome because they are constructed to emphasize predictability, transparency, and inclusion (Hanna 2002). However, responsiveness and adaptability often require a flexibility that can work in opposition to stabilizing objectives of fishery management, such as reducing uncertainty. Abrupt changes may completely undermine co-management if they require adjustments in coordination, representation, or implementation. Finding a careful balance between stability and flexibility within a particular fishery context is a challenge to co-management. Pinkerton provides an in-depth analysis of the conditions necessary for this balance in her description of "complete co-management" (Pinkerton 2003).

The operation of fishery management entails many costs. The costs of management are both monetary (for example expenditures for travel, information acquisition, monitoring) and nonmonetary (time spent at meetings and negotiations). The cost-effectiveness of management operations—achieving objectives at the lowest cost—matters because both money and time have alternative uses. Management that fits well with a fishery context will be most likely cost-effective in generating information, coordinating stakeholders, developing regulations, and responding to change. It is for this reason that co-management is easier within homogeneous groups: shared values and culture make it easier to craft common goals and workable processes and therefore reduce the costs of coordination or negotiation. In contrast, irreconcilable values differences among stakeholders or power imbalances that preclude compromise can create burdensome management costs.

Management decisions create winners and losers, and affect the distribution of benefits and costs among stakeholders. If stakeholders view a management decision as unfair, they have an incentive to undermine it. If they view the underlying structure of the management decision as fair, they have an incentive to participate even if they lose in a particular decision. For this reason, maintaining equity is a basic requirement of sustainability. In many cases, co-management has a natural equity advantage over other processes, because it is built on stakeholder representation, legitimacy, and empowerment (Jentoft 1989; 2005). Failure to reach legitimate agreements may create incentives for sabotage among co-management participants. Conflicts of interest may also prevent effective enforcement of regulations (Hanna 1994). However, co-management may also counter the tendency to corrupt established rules, because the participation of knowledgeable stakeholders who participate in the design of sanctions against violators lowers the probability that regulations will be easily circumvented (Ostrom 1990).

Transaction costs and incentives of management

The principles described above are important to co-management performance through the effect they have on transaction costs and incentives. As noted, the many transactions required to coordinate people and information create costs. Transaction costs are an inevitable part of management, but their magnitude and distribution is influenced by the way the management is organized (Eggertsson 1990). The co-management principles are key determinants of the type, magnitude, and distribution of transaction costs that are generated by co-management processes. Underlying these costs are properties of the ecosystem—its complexity or level of resource scarcity, the properties of people—the traditions and skills

they bring to management, and properties of management—how responsibilities are distributed, how conflicts are resolved, and how management tasks are funded.

The principles are also key determinants of the incentives facing people engaged in management. Co-management is challenged to ensure that stakeholders and the government have the appropriate incentives to take social costs and benefits into account, to make the appropriate tradeoffs among costs and benefits, and to promote stewardship (Hanna 1998). One of the central dilemmas of fishery co-management is how to resolve the collective action problem. Autonomous behavior promotes individual well-being without regard to the collective good, but in turn, the collective good may subsume many different individual objectives. Fishery sustainability requires the development of incentives that promote the collective good, and the dependence of people on the outcomes of collective group actions is one of the important incentives for participating in co-management.

The incentive problems that are created by centralized management processes have generated interest in finding alternative institutional forms, particularly those such as co-management, to broaden participation and shift authority away from the center. Co-management approaches can also create incentives incompatible with long-term sustainability if care is not taken in their design. The design task for co-management is to contain transaction costs and to promote incentive structures that are less vulnerable to short-term interests.

Co-Managing for Recovery: the Columbia River Basin Example

Columbia River Basin salmon are a good example of the complexity of collaborative management and resource recovery. The institutional environment of salmon recovery is extremely complex because of the involvement of many private, local, regional, state, tribal, federal, foreign, and international entities. These entities each have their own jurisdictions, but often also have overlapping authorities and responsibilities for a range of functions, including harvest management, regulation, habitat protection, permitting, enforcement, and research (ISAB 2005).

The context

The Columbia River is 1,240 mi long, draining a basin area of 260,000 square miles of Canada and the USA (Anon. 2000), a scale that, like the AYK region, embodies significant complexities in the laws, organizations, and procedures for salmon biodiversity restoration. The Columbia River basin supports a suite of anadromous salmonid populations that are similar to the AYK region and that also provide a migrating connection to the North Pacific ecosystem. Unlike the AYK region, the Columbia River Basin is experiencing rapid population growth.

The Columbia River Basin comprises a large number of interests and authorities. The Northwest Power and Conservation Council was created by the 1980 Northwest Power and Conservation Act to be a regional forum and point of influence for decisions about energy production and fish and wildlife recovery in the Columbia Basin. The Columbia River Basin Fish and Wildlife Program, developed with public input, represents the long-range regional plan for fish and wildlife protection through changes in river operations, habitat, population productivity, and harvest (Lichotowich and Williams 2009, this volume; Williams and Lichatowich 2009, this volume). The program is intended to protect, mitigate, and enhance fish and wildlife affected by the hydrosystem, a vast network that includes 150 hydroelectric projects, 18 mainstem dams, and 250 reservoirs (North-

west Power and Conservation Council 1994; Northwest Power and Conservation Council 2000b; Northwest Power and Conservation Council 2000c).

The Fish and Wildlife Program integrates the Endangered Species Act (ESA), the Northwest Power Act, and the fish and wildlife programs of the states and tribes. The program is implemented at three geographic levels: the Columbia River Basin, 11 ecological provinces of similar climate and geology, and 52 watershed-based sub-basins. Its objective is to maximize coordination by avoiding duplication of sub-basin assessments and by resolving conflicting sub-basin plans (Columbia Basin Fish and Wildlife Authority 1999).

The salmon problem

Once supporting the world's largest runs of Chinook salmon *Oncorhynchus tshawytscha* and large runs of coho salmon *O. kisutch*, sockeye salmon *O.nerka,* and steelhead *O. mykiss* (Williams 2006), the Columbia River Basin now contains 13 salmon runs listed for protection under the Endangered Species Act (ESA) (NOAA Fisheries Northwest Region 2008). The operation of the federal Columbia River power system (FCRPS) is under continuing litigation for compliance with the ESA. Many other competing interests depend on the use of the river—irrigation, transportation, recreation—or the fish—tribal subsistence and commercial, recreational and lower river commercial gillnet fisheries. All complicate the salmon recovery problem.

The number of entities involved in the management of Pacific salmon fisheries and the number of overarching legal mandates require a high degree of coordination and cooperation among parties to control harvest impacts across jurisdictions. This coordination is evidenced in an extensive and detailed system of scientific advice and management decision-making. Both formal and informal coordination of advisory and decision-making functions occur (Hanna 2000; ISAB 2005).

The coordination system has evolved in response to changing biological, oceanic, terrestrial, legal, social, and economic environments. Over time, the physical effect of river and coastal uses on salmon, estuaries and the coastal zone, and laws enacted to protect salmon from extinction have increased connectivity among a number of fishery interests through increasingly complex consultations and coordination. These connections represent an adaptation to formal requirements, physical and natural environments, and human dynamics. They are regional institutional adaptations to ecosystem-level requirements.

Still, attainment of salmon recovery is problematic. Large-scale variability and the scientific uncertainty created by variability are significant limiting factors in the attainment of management objectives and the monitoring of progress. Species listed under the ESA must have a recovery plan containing "objective, measurable criteria" for de-listing that include both salmon populations and ESUs (evolutionarily significant unit—a collection of one or more salmon populations that share similar genetic, ecological, and life history traits). Population criteria include population abundance, productivity, spatial distribution, and genetic diversity. ESU criteria provide a framework for deciding how many and which populations to recover to what levels of health. Recovery must address not only population criteria, but also the threats that caused the species to become listed, such as habitat degradation, harvest, disease and predation, and regulatory mechanisms (NOAA Fisheries Northwest Region 2008).

Legal mandates for co-management

Columbia River Basin co-management encompasses entities such the Columbia River Intertribal Fish Commission, the North-west Power and Conservation Council, the Columbia Basin Fish and Wildlife Authority, and watershed councils. The primary basis for Columbia River Basin co-management is a set of two key legal agreements.

Indian Treaty Fishing Rights.— Through treaties with the United States signed in 1855, Indian tribes reserved the right to take fish at their usual and accustomed places. After a lengthy period of litigation, the Federal District Courts determined in two separate decisions in 1968 and 1974 that treaties entitle tribes to 50% of the harvestable surplus of fish originating in or passing through their usual and accustomed fishing places (the "Belloni" and "Boldt" decisions, extensively described in Blumm 2002). Non-Indian governments are not authorized to regulate Indian fishing except when necessary for resource conservation (Singleton 1998).

Columbia River Compact.— Congressionally mandated, the Oregon-Washington coordination was instructed to manage, in coordination with Treaty Indian tribes, the commercial fisheries in the Columbia River. The Compact must consider the effect of commercial fishing for salmon, steelhead, and sturgeon in the Columbia River on escapement, treaty rights, and sport fisheries, as well as the impact on species listed under the Endangered Species Act (ESA). Although the Compact has no authority to adopt sport fishing seasons or rules, it indirectly regulates these fisheries by making commercial-recreational allocation of allowable impacts on protected stocks (WDFW/ODFW 2005).

Supporting these formal mandates for co-management are the explicit coordination mechanisms established under the Northwest Power Act and the Endangered Species Act. Actions for salmonid management and recovery taken under these legal authorities are by necessity coordinated among state, tribal, and federal entities.

Complexities of management and recovery

Despite the comprehensive scope of the Fish and Wildlife Program and other coordinating mechanisms of the Columbia River Basin, a number of problems remain. Principal among them are disparities in the causes of problems and their remediation points, external costs and benefits, competing interests, fragmented jurisdictions, and scientific uncertainty. These have been outlined comprehensively in Lichatowich (1997, 1999), Lichatowich and Williams (2009), Singleton (1998), ISAB (2005), Williams (2006), and Williams and Lichatowich (2009).

The causes and remediation points of salmon decline are not necessarily the same, but are often diffuse across a number of points in space. For example, pollution that degrades stream quality is usually from non-point sources. Forest practices upstream, or land development practices in the larger region, may take place outside the boundaries of a watershed but have effects realized within the boundaries of a watershed. Remediation actions taken only within the boundaries of the watershed will then fail to address the incentives at work at the larger scale.

Decision-making is more effective when those who pay and those who benefit from payment are the same—when the costs and benefits of decisions are "internalized" to those who make them. But in salmon recovery, those who pay for improvements in salmon conditions are not necessarily those who will benefit, and costs are external to the decision. If people who improve habitat are assured of realizing the benefits of those improvements, the incentives to invest in habitat restoration are strongest. Instead, the costs and benefits of rehabilitating salmon habitat are unevenly distributed. Costs and benefits do not necessarily accrue at the same time and space scales; for example, restoration actions involve investment costs for those in proximity to the habitat area, but may result in benefits realized over much larger areas. Similarly, the costs of restricting fish harvests to protect wild stocks are borne by particular groups of fishermen, but the benefits of wild stock protection accrue to the population at large.

Restoration actions embody tradeoffs among diverse and competing interests. It is tempting, but unrealistic, to imagine that objectives for salmon rehabilitation have the same level of priority for all Columbia River interests, or that even the existence of recovery objectives reflects consensus. In practice, the number of interests in the Columbia River system and the intensity of river use means ensuring the existence of competing interests, high-valued tradeoffs, and gains for some requiring reductions for others. Further complicating decisions about which recovery actions to take is the amount of scientific uncertainty about the outcome of rehabilitation strategies and the appropriate scale for their application. This uncertainty creates confusion about the incentives appropriate to promote recovery actions.

An additional complicating factor is that the jurisdictions of agencies and organizations charged with making resource decisions are complex and fragmented. Decisions about in-river harvests, power sales, dam operations, irrigation withdrawals, fish passage, hatchery production, and habitat protection are the responsibility of entities with overlapping boundaries, competing objectives, and incomplete authorities to accommodate the full scale of causes or effects. The decision landscape is balkanized across two national governments, fourteen tribes, nine federal agencies, and five states, as well as, many municipal entities. A directory of organizations with an interest in Columbia River salmon posted on the Northwest Power and Conservation Council website is 83 pages long. No overarching coordination mechanism exists. Land is owned in federal, state, tribal, and private form. A northern Idaho Chinook salmon passes through 17 separate management jurisdictions—international, federal, state and tribal—during the course of its life migrations (Wilkinson 1992).

Institutional problems related to fragmentation of Columbia River salmon management and the need for improved coordination have been recognized for some time, as noted in several historical accounts (Cone and Ridlington 1996; Lichatowich 1999; Taylor 1999.) Theodore Roosevelt highlighted problems of interstate fishery management and the need for coordination in his 1908 State of the Union message, proposing that Pacific fisheries be federalized. In the 1930s, the beginning of mainstem dam construction required interstate coordination for salmon protection, leading to the formation of the Interstate Fish Conservation Committee. By the 1940s, the Columbia River Interim Investigative Committee, concerned with depleted salmon stocks, pointed to the problem of fragmentation as a factor preventing restoration.

Coordination and co-management

Separate actions have been taken to lessen the problem of jurisdictional fragmentation. In 1977, the four Columbia River Treaty Tribes—the Yakama, Umatilla, Warm Springs, and Nez Perce—formed the Columbia River Intertribal Fish Commission (CRITFC). In that same year state and federal management of ocean salmon harvests were coordinated under the Pacific Fishery Management Council, established by the Fishery Conservation and Management Act. The Northwest Power Planning and Conservation Act of 1980 (Power Act), while not directly addressing the question of fragmented authority over salmon, led to actions to coordinate the interests of Oregon, Washington, Idaho, Montana, and the Treaty Tribes by establishing the Northwest Power and Conservation Council.

Under the Power Act, the states, federal government, and tribes are organized as the

Columbia Basin Fish and Wildlife Authority (CBFWA) to coordinate research planning and funding of the Fish and Wildlife Program. International coordination has been enhanced by the 1985 United Sates-Canada Salmon Interception Treaty (Wilkinson 1992). The latest institutional attempt to improve coordination is the Columbia River Basin Forum, created through a 1999 Memorandum of Agreement among federal, state and tribal governments which have management responsibilities for Columbia River Basin fish and wildlife.

In the 1994 report by the Snake River Recovery team, the lack of a unified coordinated salmon restoration plan was identified as one cause of salmon decline (Bevan et al. 1994). Shortly thereafter, the National Research Council recommended addressing the fragmentation issue through bio-regional cooperative management and the integration of management authority (National Research Council 1996). The 1996 amendments to the Northwest Power Act added requirements to use scientific advice on consistency and coordination before funding research under the Fish and Wildlife Program. In 1999, the development of the conceptual plan "Conservation of Columbia Basin Fish" by the nine-agency Federal Caucus was an attempt to achieve better regional coordination and a unified regional direction for salmon recovery (Federal Caucus 1999). Most recently the Independent Science Advisory Board, in its compendium *Return to the River* (Williams 2006), recommended that salmon mitigation measures be coordinated in their planning and implementation.

These regional recommendations, while reflecting the need for coordination and integration to reduce fragmentation, also reflect a strong interest in maintaining traditional authorities. The institutional structure is now decentralized, with an emphasis on developing consensus "co-management" types of solutions. The National Research Council report *Upstream* (1996) supported this type of structure and recommended experimentation with co-management approaches to salmon management problems.

Lessons Learned

The Columbia River Basin salmon recovery experience offers a number of lessons related to transaction costs and incentives.

Large–scale ecological variability and the accompanying scientific uncertainty are endemic to salmon ecosystems of the Columbia River Basin. They require that recovery and other management actions be monitored and evaluated for effectiveness, and so are significant sources of transaction costs. The scale of the basin creates challenges for monitoring and evaluation. However, combining the coarse-scale knowledge from basin-wide monitoring with the fine-scale knowledge of particular areas from local monitoring would provide complementarity in the information base that could reduce the transaction costs of information gathering.

The Basin has a fragmented jurisdictional landscape, but in combination with the Columbia River Compact and Indian treaty fishing rights, the ESA has served as a powerful "hammer" or incentive to enforce consultation and coordination among jurisdictions. However, the ESA also introduces vulnerabilities to ecosystem management by placing the focus of attention and resources on the subset of protected species to the possible detriment of other ecosystem components. Incentives to focus on long-term goals for salmon recovery are provided, but sometimes at the expense of taking an ecosystem-level perspective. Nevertheless, the overarching benefit of a forcing mechanism remains the reconciliation of fragmented jurisdictions through consultation processes. Consultation will be beneficial to the extent that a formal structure for coordination among co-management participants is made explicit and provides an incentive to participate.

Significant levels of scientific uncertainty continue to affect decisions about salmonid management and recovery, including uncertainty about the appropriate scale for action that is exacerbated by the failure to do comprehensive monitoring and evaluation. Uncertainty is also created by information distortion done for strategic advantage. The continuance of competition among traditional authorities maintains these externalities and generates transaction costs of coordination and negotiation. The universal problem of externalities, when the costs and benefits of an action do not accrue to those taking the action, also provides a disincentive to take a long-term approach to sustainability, and generates transaction costs as attempts are made to internalize them.

Co-Management Research for AYK Salmon Management and Recovery

The experience of salmon co-management in the Columbia River Basin is informative to many of the challenges faced by AYK salmon management and recovery, and to the research needed to implement effective co-management. Similarities exist between the Columbia River and AYK salmon recovery issues, such as the need for management that adapts to rapidly changing conditions. Some important differences also exist, most notably the wide dispersion of human populations in the AYK region and the importance of AYK salmon for subsistence as well as income. Developing co-management processes in the AYK region faces the daunting problem of building new institutional processes while recovering depleted resources. The overview of co-management provided in this paper combined with the example of the Columbia River Basin offer some suggested directions for co-management research that will assist in meeting this dual challenge.

Guidance is available for co-management design in several publications based on experience with co-management implementation (cf. Pomeroy and Williams 1994; Pinkerton and Weinstein 1995; Halls et al. 2005a; 2005b; Pomeroy and Rivera-Guieb 2006 ; Gottesfeld et al. 2009, this volume; Pinkerton 2009, this volume). Tending to the design requirements of effective fishery co-management in the small scale, while at the same time remaining adaptive to developments in fishery management in the large scale, poses a set of challenges to developing and implementing co-management. However, this challenge also presents great opportunities, for example the gains to be realized from combining complementary local ecological knowledge with system-level scientific knowledge.

The tendency to address many fishery management problems on large scales has led to a reliance on aggregated scientific information that is difficult to relate to the more location-specific information on which co-management decisions are likely to be based. The more restrictive regulations and precautionary limits necessary for salmon recovery require finer-scale understanding of salmon subpopulations and their ecosystems. The problem of addressing management problems at a large scale to the detriment of local-scale knowledge suggests that management decisions need to be supported not only by aggregate coarse-grain information, but also by localized fine-grain information. This combined approach is a need that co-management would be well-positioned to address in the AYK region, through the active involvement of a widely dispersed human population in biological monitoring. The associated research questions are about the design of knowledge production systems that provide the right incentives for stakeholders to participate, and the integration of diverse sources of knowledge at cost-effective levels. Research could usefully address how to reconcile different information-gathering approaches of scientists and community members in a combined small-scale/large-scale monitoring program.

As the example of the Columbia River basin has shown, fragmentation of authorities can prevent management from achieving consistency at a regional scale. This problem is addressed partially in the Columbia River basin through the forcing mechanism of the ESA and other agreements, complemented by the recognition that the problem of salmon recovery is a collective one, requiring participation and collaboration. Research addressing co-management's potential to resolve the problem of fragmentation could evaluate the incentives required to construct a forcing mechanism for collaboration. It could also analyze the transaction costs associated with decentralized processes of decision-making that strengthen institutions at community levels. Research could assess mechanisms to contain coordination costs and incentives for coordination across community, regional, national, and international scales. Such research would also enhance understanding of the divergent views of social equity that may complicate the development of management objectives.

As with any new management process, the introduction of co-management will not be on a clean slate. Instead, co-management will be layered over the history of previous management approaches, which will carry a large legacy. This legacy creates a path-dependence that constrains the number or type of actions that can be taken in the present. Research could be directed at how, against the backdrop of the AYK management legacy, co-management could cost-effectively expand the information base to accommodate tradition and local knowledge, and to build active management participation across a widely dispersed population.

Complicating the legacy problem, and in a manner similar to the Columbia River Basin, significant levels of scientific uncertainty continue to affect decisions about salmonid management and recovery. Uncertainty has implications for the scale of scientific information acquisition, as discussed above. In addition, uncertainty places a premium on incentives for social learning as well as on institutional flexibility and adaptation, the design attributes of which can be addressed through directed social science research. Research can also address the design questions associated with how to develop representation and participation on a scale that is administratively cost-effective while also ecologically functional.

Finally, but importantly, is co-management's potential to build management legitimacy. Research could beneficially highlight the importance of management structure and processes in building co-management legitimacy. Such research would include questions of how to build trust, develop management capacity, and maintain management commitment across diverse participants in an environment of uncertainty and change. Research could assess how to balance accountability and independence, as well as how to minimize opportunities to undermine or circumvent management decisions. Legitimacy research would also look at the incentives necessary to develop conflict resolution processes that accommodate heterogeneous participants.

Conclusion

Co-management offers great promise for the integration of human and ecological systems in ways that promote fishery sustainability. However, as the Columbia River Basin example illustrates, the path to integration in large-scale ecosystems is neither clear nor simple. One of the most basic problems is a definitional one: the use of the term "co-management" to cover a wide variety of arrangements, including the most cursory interaction with user groups, weakens co-management's meaning. More importantly, it also weak-

ens the understanding of co-management's principles and functions and their application within a specific fishery context. An all-encompassing definition of co-management tends to divert attention from the issues of incentives and transaction costs so fundamental to management performance.

Sometimes a tendency exists to romanticize co-management as a natural and intuitive approach to management. However, looking at the range of problems faced by co-management, or indeed any type of management, it is argued that pragmatism, rather than romance, is needed. Co-management processes introduced into the AYK region will require a significant investment in practical actions such as information collection, capacity development among participants, and procedural design.

A pragmatic perspective on co-management is present in the AYK Salmon Research and Restoration Plan (AYK SSI 2006). The Plan notes that the steering committee's 2004 vision statement includes as a core component the goal of developing and implementing "a capacity building program which enables rural residents of the AYK region to effectively participate in co-management of AYK salmon resources" (AYK SSI 2006). This statement conveys a commitment to providing co-management participants with the tools needed to engage in a management partnership with state and federal authorities. Research support for this capacity-building objective could include assessments of educational approaches best suited to the diversity of languages and tribal cultures throughout the region. Research could also address how participation could best be structured—for example, are there definitions of "community" that would go beyond the standard spatial basis of that term to include other types of alignments, such as people who use the same gear type but do not live in the same place.

In a climate of government reluctance to further invest in fishery management, the challenge exists to obtain the operational support for co-management research and implementation. The challenge as well as the opportunity for the AYK SSI Program is to invest in research surrounding the major issues of co-management—scale, fragmentation, legacy, uncertainty, and legitimacy—in a way that will help promote the restoration and sustainable management of salmon in the AYK region.

Acknowledgments

This research was supported by the Coastal Oregon Marine Experiment Station (COMES) at Oregon State University. I thank four anonymous reviewers for helpful suggestions.

References

Anonymous. 2000. "Columbia River, North America," Microsoft ® Encarta ® Online Encyclopedia 2000. http://encarta.msn.com © 1997–2000 Microsoft Corporation. All rights reserved.

AYK SSI (Arctic-Yukon-Kuskokwim (AYK) Sustainable Salmon Initiative). 2006. Arctic-Yukon-Kuskokwim salmon research and restoration plan. Bering Sea Fishermen's Association, Anchorage, Alaska.

Bevan, D., J. Harville, P. Bergman, T. Bjorn, J. Crutchfield, P. Klingeman and J. Litchfield. 1994. Snake River recovery team: final recommendations to the National Marine Fisheries Service. National Marine Fisheries Service, Portland, Oregon.

Blumm, M. 2002. Sacrificing the salmon: a legal and policy history of the decline of Columbia River Basin salmon. Book World Publications, Den Bosch, Netherlands.

Columbia Basin Fish and Wildlife Authority. 1999. FY 2000 draft annual implementation work plan. Northwest Power and Conservation Council, Portland, Oregon.

Cone, J., and S. Ridlington, editors. 1996. The Northwest salmon crisis: a documentary history. Oregon State University Press, Corvallis, Oregon.

Eggertsson, T. 1990. Economic behavior and institutions. Cambridge University Press, Cambridge, U.K.

Federal Caucus. 1999. Conservation of Columbia Basin fish: building a conceptual recovery plan. Draft manuscript, December 1999, Spokane, Washington. Available: http://www.salmonrecovery.gov (December 2008).

Gottesfeld, A., C. Barnes, and C. Soto. 2009. Case history of the Skeena Fisheries Commission: developing aboriginal fishery management capacity in northern British Columbia. Pages 921–939 in C. C. Krueger and C. E. Zimmerman, editors. Pacific salmon: ecology and management of western Alaska's populations. American Fisheries Society, Symposium 70, Bethesda, Maryland.

Halls, A. S.,R. I. Arthur, D. Bartley, M. Felsing, R. Grainger, W. Hartmann, D. Lambert, J. Purvis, P. Sultana, P. Thompson, and S. Walmsley. 2005a. Guidelines for designing data collection and sharing systems for co-managed fisheries. Part 1: Practical guide. FAO fisheries technical paper No. 494/1. FAO, Rome.

Halls, A. S.,R. I. Arthur, D. Bartley, M. Felsing, R. Grainger, W. Hartmann, D. Lambert, J. Purvis, P. Sultana, P. Thompson, and S. Walmsley. 2005b. Guidelines for designing data collection and sharing systems for co-managed fisheries. Part 2: Technical guidelines. FAO fisheries technical paper No. 494/2. FAO, Rome.

Hanna, S. 1994. Co-management. In K. L. Gimbel, editor. Limiting access to marine fisheries: keeping the focus on conservation. Center for Marine Conservation and World Wildlife Fund, Washington, D.C.

Hanna, S. 1995a. User participation and fishery management performance within the Pacific Fishery Management Council. Ocean and Coastal Management 28(1–3):23–44.

Hanna, S. 1995b. Efficiencies of user participation in natural resource management. Pages 59–68 in S. Hanna and M. Munasinghe, editors. Property rights and the environment: social and ecological issues. World Bank, Washington, DC.

Hanna, S. 1998. Institutions for marine ecosystems: economic incentives and fishery management. Ecological Applications 8(1) Supplement:170–174.

Hanna, S. 2000. Designing institutions for Columbia River Salmon: identifying the key uncertainties. Pages 77–90 in P. Koss and M. Katz, editors. What we don't know about Pacific Northwest fish runs: an inquiry into decision-making under uncertainty. Proceedings of the Portland State University Salmon Symposium, July 78, 2000, Portland, Oregon.

Hanna, S. 2002. Managing the human-ecological interface: marine resources as example and laboratory. Ecosystems 4(8):736–741.

Hanna, S. 2003a. Economics of co-management. Pages 51–60 in D. Wilson, J. R. Nielsen and P. Degnbol, editors. The fisheries co-management experience: accomplishments, challenges and prospects. Kluwer Academic Publishers, Dordrecht, Netherlands.

Hanna, S. 2003b. Conclusion: the future of fisheries co-management. Pages 304–314 in D. Wilson, J. R. Nielsen and P. Degnbol, editors. The fisheries co-management experience: accomplishments, challenges and prospects. Kluwer Academic Publishers, Dordrecht, Netherlands.

Hardin, G. 1968. The tragedy of the commons. Science 162:1243–1248.

Hilsinger, H., E. Volk, G. Sandone, and R. Cannon. 2009. Salmon management in the Arctic-Yukon-Kuskokwim region of Alaska: past, present and future. Pages 495–519 in C.C. Krueger and C.E. Zimmerman, editors. Pacific salmon: ecology and management of western Alaska's populations. American Fisheries Society, Symposium 70, Bethesda, Maryland.

Independent Science Advisory Board (ISAB). 2005. Report on harvest management of Columbia Basin salmon and steelhead. ISAB 2005–04, Northwest Power and Conservation Council (2005). Available: http://www.nwcouncil.org. (December 2008).

Jentoft, S. 1989. Fisheries co-management: delegating responsibility to fishermen's organizations. Marine Policy 13(2):137–154.

Jentoft, S. 2005. Fisheries co-management as empowerment. Marine Policy 29(1):1–7.

Jentoft, S., and B. McCay. 1995. User participation in fisheries management: lessons drawn from international experience. Marine Policy 19(3):227–246.

Lichatowich, J. 1997. Evaluating salmon management institutions: the importance of performance measures, temporal scales and production cycles. Pages 69–87 in D. J. Stouder, P. A. Bisson, R. J. Naiman, editors. Pacific salmon and their ecosystems: status and future options. Chapman and Hall, New York.

Lichatowich, J. 1999. Salmon without rivers: a history of the Pacific salmon crisis. Island Press, Washington, D.C.

Lichatowich, J. A. and R. N. Williams. 2009. Failures to incorporate science into fishery management and recovery programs: Lessons from the Columbia River. Pages 1005–1019 in C. C. Krueger and C. E. Zimmerman, editors. Pacific salmon: ecology and management of western Alaska's populations. American Fisheries Society, Symposium 70, Bethesda, Maryland.

McCay, B. J. 1996. Common and private concerns. Pages 111–126 in S. Hanna, C. Folke, and K.-G. Mäler, editors. Rights to nature: ecological, economic, cultural and political principles of institutions for the environment. Island Press, Washington, D.C.

National Research Council (NRC). 1996. Upstream: salmon and society in the Pacific Northwest. National Academy Press, Washington, D.C.

National Research Council (NRC). 2004. Developing a research and restoration plan for Arctic-Yukon-Kuskokwim (Western Alaska) salmon. National Academy Press, Washington, DC.

NOAA Fisheries Northwest Region. 2008. Salmon recovery website. Available: http://www.nwr.noaa.gov/Salmon-Recovery-Planning/Salmon-Recovery-FAQ.cfm (December 2008).

Northwest Power and Conservation Council. 1994. Columbia River Basin fish and wildlife program. Council document 94–55. Portland, Oregon.

Northwest Power and Conservation Council. 2000a. Human effects analysis of the multi-species framework alternatives. Phase II Final Report. Council document 2000–5. Portland, Oregon.

Northwest Power and Conservation Council. 2000b. Congressional update. February 8. Portland, Oregon.

Northwest Power and Conservation Council. 2000c. Congressional update. January 14. Portland, Oregon.

Ostrom, E. 1990. Governing the commons. Cambridge University Press, Cambridge, UK.

Ostrom, E. 1995. Designing complexity to govern complexity. Pages 33–46 in S. Hanna and M. Munasinghe, editors. Property rights and the environment: social and ecological issues. World Bank, Washington, D.C.

Ostrom, E., and E. Schlager. 1996. The formation of property rights. Pages 127–156 in S. Hanna, C. Folke, and K.-G. Mäler, editors. Rights to nature: ecological, economic, cultural and political principles of institutions for the environment. Island Press, Washington, D.C.

Pete, M. 2007. Resilience of social systems in the face of ecological and regulatory change and fisheries declines. Presented at the Sustainability of the Arctic-Yukon-Kuskokwim Salmon Fisheries: what do we know about salmon ecology, management and fisheries? February 6–9, 2007, Anchorage, Alaska.

Pinkerton, E., editor. 1989. Cooperative management of local fisheries: new directions for improved management and community development. University of British Columbia Press, Vancouver.

Pinkerton, E. 2003. Toward specificity in complexity: understanding co-management from a social science perspective. Pages 61–77 in D. Wilson, J. R. Nielsen, and P. Degnbol, editors. The fisheries comanagement experience: accomplishments, challenges and prospects. Kluwer Academic Publishers, Dordrecht, Netherlands.

Pinkerton, E. 2009. The Skeena watershed partnership:

learning from success and failure in salmon management. Pages 903–919 *in* C. C. Krueger and C. E. Zimmerman, editors. Pacific salmon: ecology and management of western Alaska's populations. American Fisheries Society, Symposium 70, Bethesda, Maryland.

Pinkerton, E., and M. Weinstein. 1995. Fisheries that work: sustainability through community-based management. The David Suzuki Foundation, Vancouver, British Columbia.

Pomeroy, R. S., and M. Williams. 1994. Fisheries co-management and small-scale fisheries: a policy brief. International Center for Living Aquatic Resources Management, Manila, Philippines.

Pomeroy, R.S., and R. Rivera-Guieb. 2006. Fishery co-management: a practical handbook. CABI Publishing and International Development Research Centre Cambridge, Massachusetts.

Sandler, T. 1992. Collective action: theory and applications. University of Michigan Press, Ann Arbor.

Sen, S., and J. R. Nielsen. 1996. Fisheries co-management: a comparative analysis. Marine Policy 20(5):405–418.

Singleton, S. 1998. Constructing cooperation: the evolution of institutions of co-management. The University of Michigan Press, Ann Arbor.

Taylor, J. E. III. 1999. Making salmon: an environmental history of the Northwest fisheries crisis. University of Washington Press, Seattle.

Washington Department of Fish and Wildlife and Oregon Department of Fish and Wildlife (WDFW/ODFW). 2005. Joint state management of Columbia River salmon and sturgeon non-Indian harvest allocations. Olympia, Washington.

Wilkinson, C.F. 1992. Crossing the next meridian: land, water and the future of the West. Island Press, Washington, D.C.

Williams, R. N., editor. 2006. Return to the river: restoring salmon to the Columbia River. Elsevier Academic Press, Burlington, Massachusetts.

Williams, R., and J. Lichatowich. 2009. Science and politics—an uncomfortable alliance: lessons learned from the Fish and Wildlife Program of the Northwest Power and Conservation Council. Pages 1021–1046 *in* C. C. Krueger and C. E. Zimmerman, editors. Pacific salmon: ecology and management of western Alaska's populations. American Fisheries Society, Symposium 70, Bethesda, Maryland.

Wilson, D. C., J. R. Nielsen, and P. Degnbol, editors. 2003. The fisheries co-management experience: accomplishments, challenges and prospects. Kluwer Academic Publishers, Dordrecht, Netherlands.

Young, O. R. 1996. Rights rules and resources in international society. Pages 245–264 *in* S. Hanna, C. Folke, and K.-G. Mäler, editors. Rights to nature: ecological, economic, cultural and political principles of institutions for the environment. Island Press, Washington, D.C.

Introduction

The purpose of this paper is to provide a perspective on the fisheries management strategies used for ensuring the sustainability of salmon *Oncorhynchus* spp. in the Arctic-Yukon-Kuskokwim (AYK) region. The paper is based upon discussions that were held among a broad group of commercial and subsistence fishers, management biologists, senior resource managers, and academicians at the symposium entitled, "*Sustainability of the Arctic-Yukon-Kuskokwim Salmon Fisheries*" (this volume). The group focused on evaluating the effectiveness of the past and current management of the salmon fisheries and developing recommendations for improved management. This paper provides a synopsis of the topics and nature of the discussions; however, our own emphasis and interpretation have been interjected.

Sustainability: a Shared Value

Salmon management in the AYK region focuses on the goal of long-term sustainability of populations and their fisheries through management of adult escapement to spawning streams. The goal of the long-term sustainability of salmon populations and fisheries capable of providing benefits to future generations is a shared value among all involved in salmon management, including: subsistence and commercial fishers, fishery managers, and academicians. The belief exists that a sustainable yield of salmon will ensure sustainable rural communities in the AYK region. Explicit recognition of these shared values might be viewed as obvious, but this shared value could provide a point of common agreement with which to initiate or begin difficult decisions. Explicit recognition through discussion of shared values should be used to begin difficult negotiations. This approach would be useful whether the dis-

cussions are within management agencies, between management agencies, or between fishery stakeholders and management agencies. Knowing that a common value exists can help participants focus on solving the problems of the fisheries and not on attacking each other (Fisher and Ury 1991).

Escapement Goal Management

Uniform endorsement existed for a shift in salmon management to one based on escapement goals; however, concerns were expressed if the goals were determined solely based on maximum sustained yield (MSY) concepts. Escapement goals are defined as the number of adult spawners allowed into spawning streams but not caught by fisheries. Although escapement-based management of salmon in the region has been successful (Hilsinger et al. 2009, this volume), to ensure sustainability of salmon populations and fisheries, escapement goals must be set below the biological escapement goals (BEGs) currently used for salmon management in the region. BEGs are defined as the escapement of a specific number of adult salmon that provide the greatest potential for maximum sustained yield (Alaska Department of Fish and Game 2001). These goals are based on the concepts associated with maximum sustainable yield or MSY by state statute (5 ACC 39.222), but have a number of potential problems regarding the sustainability of all stocks. For example, this type of management will tend to over-fish weak or less productive stocks (Larkin 1977). MSY management also requires the assumption of a constant environment within which to calculate stock–recruitment relationships. Recent changes in ocean productivity in the Bering Sea have been well documented (e.g., Grebmeier et al. 2006), and these make MSY-focused management especially challenging. Therefore, because of the uncertainties associated with the calculation of BEGs, a precautionary management approach may be to establish escapement goals above the current BEG levels to allow for more escapement of salmon and to ensure sustainability of salmon stocks under both constant and changing conditions.

Management Decision Making

Fishery stakeholders and managers believed that decisions have been timely, made at the correct scale (single stock), and generally based on a mixture of traditional ecological knowledge (TEK) and conventional science. In-season salmon management of the Yukon and Kuskokwim rivers has benefited greatly from weekly conference calls between the management working groups and the users as a means to gather real-time information (Bue et al. 2009, this volume; Linderman and Bergstrom 2009, this volume). During teleconferences, fishers share their current experiences and perceptions about the strength of on-going salmon runs, and this information is compared to assessment data gathered by the management agencies. Information has been shared openly in both directions during these conference calls and has fostered trust, increased the quality and quantity of information, and improved in-season decision-making. The teleconferences have improved the capacity of stakeholders to use fishery information, and thus caused a change in the type of information desired by the stakeholders. Fishery participants now request more detailed information than in the past about salmon populations and are asking more complex questions of managers. This process should be encouraged to continue.

Conventional Science and Traditional Ecological Knowledge

Wise salmon management decisions result from the integration of all types of knowl-edge, including conventional science and TEK (Brelsford 2009, this volume). Within the constraints of this paper, TEK refers to the knowledge of local indigenous people. A need exists to investigate TEK to know if, how, and when TEK should be used in management decision making. For example, TEK in some localities suggests that the size of the Arctic lamprey *Lampetra camtschatica* runs in the winter can be used to indicate the magnitude of future salmon spawning runs. Additionally, the smoothness of the ice is believed to indicate the strength of salmon runs that will occur in the summer. Jagged ice, which impedes the movement dog sleds and snow machines, indicates abundant salmon, whereas, smooth ice indicates low runs. Native aboriginal people look for indicators throughout the winter in the snow and ice that will help predict the abundance of the coming summer's salmon runs. The use of traditional ecological knowledge could provide additional management information and improve management decision-making.

Among managers and fishery stakeholders, this blending of knowledge occurs adequately, for the most part, in the management of AYK salmon fisheries. However, in certain segments of the AYK salmon fisheries, the inclusion of all types of knowledge could be improved. For example, management of salmon in the Yukon River between U.S. and Canada could be enhanced by increased incorporation of TEK in fishery management decisions by the bilateral Yukon River Panel and by the Joint Technical Committee, which advises the panel.

Information Needs for Salmon Management

The process of salmon management must be adaptive and continually evolving because management occurs in a dynamic and complex system including oceans and rivers, and serves subsistence, commercial, and sport fisheries. Much of the management of salmon focuses solely on the regulation of harvest in, or adjacent to, rivers during the spawning runs. Requisite management information will always be incomplete because the dynamic nature of the ecosystem renders some components of historic information irrelevant. Developing management strategies that encourage learning and adaptation may help address this conundrum. With such large areas to manage within the AYK region and the effects of dynamic ocean environments in combination with the large differences between upriver and downriver harvest needs, it is a reality that there are "pieces that will fall through the cracks" in salmon management. Fishery stakeholders need to comprehend the difficult challenges of making decisions with insufficient information that face fishery managers.

Effective in-season management of single stocks of salmon in the Yukon and Kuskokwim rivers requires the collection of assessment data to describe the run-strength of stocks and the extent of the on-going, stock-specific harvest. Currently, the amount of data collected inhibits the ability of agencies to manage more intensively to protect weak stocks. Better descriptions of population stock structure (e.g., Beacham 2009, this volume) and estimates of subsistence and commercial harvest are key information needs for management. Funds need to be found and then protected so that they can be used for the maintenance of all the data sets. Furthermore, all data sets should be accessible to stakeholders. The Alaska Department of Fish and Game (ADFG) is working diligently to achieve this objective.

The nonrandom harvest of salmon from the runs, in terms of size, life history, and sex could pose a threat to the sustainability of AYK salmon. Some individual fishers can and do target specific sizes of salmon for harvest, and these large salmon (typically multi-ocean year females) are harvested in numbers disproportionate to their occurrence in the run. The genetic and ecological effects that such a harvest will have on the long-term sustainability of salmon populations are unknown. Therefore, exploration of the effects of selection on the sustainability of populations should be a priority for research (e.g., Hard 2009, this volume). Specific topics include the nature and extent of selective harvest and its potential effects on population genetics and dynamics, and what potential management strategies could be used to accommodate such harvests and still ensure fishery sustainability.

Knowledge and understanding about AYK salmon runs appears to progress much faster and further when the spawning runs are small in comparison to when the runs are large. Times of adversity create an urgent need to rationalize, to understand, and to learn about salmon and the fisheries they support. Knowledge of salmon runs has advanced considerably in the most recent downturn in abundance in the late 1990s and early 2000s (Utter et al. 2009, this volume). For example, when a stock appears to arrive later than normal in a spawning season, a late run—previously viewed as a run, simply late in arriving—could be either strong or weak in terms of abundance. However, in recent years strong late runs have become increasingly rare. Runs now termed "late" are more likely to actually be poor runs. This observation gave rise to the description that the run had "run out of late." Times of salmon scarcity have also revealed tensions among manager-stakeholder relationships. Effective communications are easier when there are many fish, but when fish are scarce, time can be wasted on assigning blame.

Management Strategies

In times of salmon scarcity, management decisions have a potentially greater and further reaching effect than when runs are abundant. Managers and fishery participants were in general agreement that the subsistence fisheries should not be closed, if at all possible, during periods of low abundance. Rather, management of subsistence harvest should recognize and prioritize the different uses within the subsistence harvest. For example, when salmon runs are low and a concern exists over their long-term sustainability, the State of Alaska can adopt a harvest permitting approach known as Tier II. The Tier II permitting system should be modified to establish priorities based on types of subsistence use. For example, the highest or first priority for subsistence use should be given to fisheries for human food. The second priority should be afforded to fisheries where the salmon are used as food for dogs. A third priority in subsistence in harvest allocation should be to "customary trade" where salmon are used in noncommercial exchange for minimal monetary exchange (Alaska Statute 6.05.940(8)). Implementation of this would require studies to gain an understanding of the proportions of subsistence harvests allocated for human food, for dog food, and for customary trade. "Fairness" in the choice of who is allowed to participate in the subsistence fishery is also a concern among some fishery participants. In typical subsistence fisheries (non-Tier II), no distinction exists between those who routinely and historically have fished for subsistence (in some cases for several generations of descendents) and a 'newcomer' or new resident who may wish to do so.

Salmon fishing during years with low spawning runs are regulated within subsistence and commercial fisheries to occur within specific time "windows" during the week (e.g., fishing permitted three days per week; Hamazaki 2008). The effective application of window regulation of subsistence harvests by managers is a challenging proposition. The aim of windows regulations in subsistence fishing is to provide an opportunity to catch

fish while allowing a portion of the run to escape each week. The advantage is that windows are flexible in their application and are only used if needed. However, window time frames may not correspond with weather that is suitable for drying salmon, therefore constraining subsistence activities further than intended. Window harvest regulations can be confusing and therefore require clear communication to stakeholders.

Little effective interaction occurs between the fishery managers of the AYK region and the managers of the ocean fisheries. Fisheries management decisions occur in-season and at a fine geographic scale within the Yukon and Kuskokwim rivers. Nevertheless, the effects of these decisions on the overall status and sustainability of salmon stocks is likely dwarfed by the effects of changes in the oceans. Much greater effects than in-river management may be occurring through the ocean bycatch of salmon stocks (e.g., Gisclair 2009, this volume), stocking of Asian-origin chum salmon, and changing ocean conditions (e.g., Downton and Miller 1998; Mueter et al. 2002; Beamish 2009, this volume; Mantua, 2009, this volume). Opportunities should be explored to enhance effective interaction among all managers to achieve more holistic, ecosystem-based management of salmon stocks in the ocean and the rivers (Rearden, 2009, this volume). Although, the North Pacific Management Council includes a position for an AYK fishery manager, little information or communication actually flows from the AYK region to the council. Strategies need to be developed and implemented to improve communication and interaction with the North Pacific Management Council.

Tensions in AYK Fisheries

Several tensions exist with the salmon fisheries community including: commercial versus recreational versus subsistence fishers; downstream versus upstream fishers; and state versus federal management of subsistence fisheries (Stein and Krueger 2009, this volume). Some of these tensions have long histories, substantially add to the social complexity of management, and will likely persist into the future. However, the belief existed that the long-standing tensions between the downstream and upstream fishers have decreased in the Yukon and Kuskokwim rivers because of the increased and open communication that has occurred during the weekly conference calls. The overlap between federal and state management of subsistence fisheries wastes not only energy, but also funds. Therefore, efforts to reduce this overlap and tension would improve relationships and provide for better use of the limited funds available for management of the fisheries.

Conclusions

Drawing on past experiences and looking to the future, more effective management strategies will be developed and tensions will be reduced when all fishery participants are fairly represented within the management decision-making process. The end result of this evolution will be the continued sustainability of AYK salmon and the fisheries these salmon support. Trust and credibility between parties are important components in this process and must continue to be earned and improved. Compromise among parties on management decisions is a requirement if management is to move ahead to make and implement decisions. Decisions should be accepted when they can "be lived with" even though they were not exactly what was desired. Such consensus, however, should be viewed and accepted as success, even though the decision made may not perfectly satisfy all concerned.

Management of salmon fisheries in the AYK region is a challenging proposition con-

sidering the size of the region, diversity of species and stocks, and complexity of human systems of villages and governance. Fishery management is focused on the intersection between fish and humans. More needs to be known about both segments—fish, in terms of stock structure and prediction of run sizes and yields—and humans, in terms of subsistence and commercial harvest needs, the nature of selective fishing, and strategies to improve communication. Connections also need to be forged between the managers of the freshwater phases of salmon and the managers of the oceans. With improved information, communication, and cooperation, successful management of AYK salmon will be possible, and will help ensure their sustainability and opportunity for use by future human generations.

Acknowledgments

The authors thank the following working group participants for their enthusiastic and candid participation: Fred Bue, John Burr, James Charles, Orville Huntington, Weaver Ivanoff, Gene Sandone, Tim Sands, Carl Sidney, Roy Stein, Doug Sweat.

References

Alaska Department of Fish and Game. 2001. Sustainable salmon fisheries policy for the state of Alaska. Available: Juneau. http://www.adfg.state.ak.us/special/susalpol.pdf (January 2009)

Beacham, T. D., K. D. Le, M. Wetklo, B. McIntosh, T. Ming, and K. M. Miller. 2009. Population structure and stock identification of chum salmon from western Alaska determined with microsatellite DNA and major histocompatiability complex variation. Pages 141–160 in C. C. Krueger and C. E. Zimmerman, editors. Pacific salmon: ecology and management of western Alaska's populations. American Fisheries Society, Symposium 70, Bethesda, Maryland.

Beamish, R. J., and R. M. Sweeting. 2009. The history of surprises associated with Pacific salmon returns signals that critical information is missing from our understanding of their population dynamics. Pages 1159–1168 *in* C. C. Krueger and C. E. Zimmerman, editors. Pacific salmon: ecology and management of western Alaska's populations. American Fisheries Society, Symposium 70, Bethesda, Maryland.

Brelsford, T. 2009. "We have to learn to work together:" current perspectives on incorporating local and traditional/indigenous knowledge into Alaskan fishery management. Pages 381–394 *in* C. C. Krueger and C. E. Zimmerman, editors. Pacific salmon: ecology and management of western Alaska's populations. American Fisheries Society, Symposium 70, Bethesda, Maryland.

Bue, F. J., B. M. Borba, R. Cannon, and C. C. Krueger. 2009. Yukon River fall chum salmon fisheries: management, harvest, and stock abundance. Pages 703–742 *in* C. C. Krueger and C. E. Zimmerman, editors. Pacific salmon: ecology and management of western Alaska's populations. American Fisheries Society, Symposium 70, Bethesda, Maryland.

Downton, M. W., and K. A. Miller. 1998. Relationships between Alaskan salmon catch and North Pacific climate on interannual and interdecadal time scales. Canadian Journal of Fisheries and Aquatic Sciences 55:2255–2265.

Fisher, R., and W. Ury. 1991. Getting to yes—negotiating agreement without giving in, 2nd edition. Penguin Books, New York.

Gisclair, B. R. 2009. Salmon bycatch management in the Bering Sea pollock fishery: threats and opportunities for western Alaska. Pages 799–816 *in* C. C. Krueger and C. E. Zimmerman, editors. Pacific salmon: ecology and management of western Alaska's populations. American Fisheries Society, Symposium 70, Bethesda, Maryland.

Grebmeier, J. M., Overland, J. E., Moore, S. E., Farley, E. V., Carmack, E. C., Cooper, L. W., Frey, K. E., Helle, J. H., McLaughlin, F. A., and S. L. McNutt. 2006. A major ecosystem shift in the northern Bering Sea. Science 311:1461–1464.

Hamazaki, T. 2008. Fishery closure "windows" scheduling as a means of changing the Chinook salmon subsistence fishery pattern: is it an effective management tool? Fisheries 33:495–501.

Hard, J. J., W. H. Eldridge, and K. A. Naish. 2009. Genetic consequences of size-selective fishing: implications for viability of Chinook salmon in the Arctic-Yukon-Kuskokwim region of Alaska. Pages 759–780 *in* C. C. Krueger and C. E. Zimmerman, editors. Pacific salmon: ecology and management of western Alaska's populations. American Fisheries Society, Symposium 70, Bethesda, Maryland.

Hilsinger, J. R., G. Sandone, R. Cannon, and E. Volk. 2009. Salmon management in the Arctic-Yukon-Kuskokwim Region of Alaska: past, present, and future. Pages 495–519 *in* C. C. Krueger and C. E. Zimmerman, editors. Pacific salmon: ecology and management of western Alaska's populations. American Fisheries Society, Symposium 70, Bethesda, Maryland.

Larkin, P. A. 1977. An epitaph for the concept of maximum sustained yield. Transactions of the American Fisheries Society 106:1–11.

Linderman, J. C., Jr., and D. J. Bergstrom. 2009. Kuskokwim management area: salmon escapement, harvest, and management. Pages 541–599 *in* C. C. Krueger and C. E. Zimmerman, editors. Pacific salmon: ecology and management of western Alaska's populations. American Fisheries Society, Symposium 70, Bethesda, Maryland.

Mantua, N. 2009. Patterns of climate change and Pacific salmon production. Pages 1143–1157 *in* C. C. Krueger and C. E. Zimmerman, editors. Pacific salmon: ecology and management of western Alaska's populations. American Fisheries Society, Symposium 70, Bethesda, Maryland.

Mueter, F. J., D. M. Ware, and R. M. Peterman. 2002. Spatial correlation patterns in coastal environmental variables and survival rates of salmon in the north-east Pacific Ocean. Fisheries Oceanography 11:205–218.

Rearden, M., and D. Gillikin. 2009. A perspective on ecosystem-based fishery management of the Kuskokwim River: a 2015 vision of the future. Pages 601–609 *in* C. C. Krueger and C. E. Zimmerman, editors. Pacific salmon: ecology and management of western Alaska's populations. American Fisheries Society, Symposium 70, Bethesda, Maryland.

Stein, R. A., and C. C. Krueger. 2009. Salmon fishery management within the Arctic-Yukon-Kuskokwim region: emergent issues and unspoken themes. Pages 1225–1231 *in* C. C. Krueger and C. E. Zimmerman, editors. Pacific salmon: ecology and management of western Alaska's populations. American Fisheries Society, Symposium 70, Bethesda, Maryland.

Utter, F. M., M. V. McPhee, and F. W. Allendorf. 2009. Population genetics and the management of Arctic-Yukon-Kuskokwim salmon populations. Pages 97–123 *in* C. C. Krueger and C. E. Zimmerman, editors. Pacific salmon: ecology and management of western Alaska's populations. American Fisheries Society, Symposium 70, Bethesda, Maryland.

American Fisheries Society Symposium 70:1225–1231, 2009
© 2009 by the American Fisheries Society

Salmon Fishery Management within the Arctic-Yukon-Kuskokwim Region: Emergent Issues and Unspoken Themes

ROY A. STEIN*

*Aquatic Ecology Laboratory, Department of Evolution, Ecology, and Organismal Biology
The Ohio State University, 1314 Kinnear Road, Columbus, Ohio 43212, USA*

CHARLES C. KRUEGER

*Great Lakes Fishery Commission
2100 Commonwealth Boulevard, Suite 100, Ann Arbor, Michigan 48105, USA*

Abstract.—As part of the Sustainability of the Arctic-Yukon-Kuskokwim (AYK) Salmon Fisheries Symposium held in Anchorage, Alaska during February 5–9, 2007, we identify and discuss the issues that connect the symposium's presentations and papers (this volume), especially those focusing on AYK stock status and management. We also describe themes that, based on our experience, we know exist but were not explicitly discussed by symposium participants. Issues emerging from the symposium included: different mechanisms affecting stock abundance, cooperation between industry and management, the challenges of stock-recruit curves, effects of broad-scale environmental instability, biocomplexity and stock-specific management, management power-sharing, and conflicts among fisheries. Two unspoken themes were (1) the management tensions between up-river and down-river fishers on the Yukon and Kuskokwim rivers and between state and federal management authorities, and (2) data sharing among the scientific, management, and stakeholder communities. Understanding how escapement goals were set, and identifying where shared values exist among stakeholder groups and managers were themes that should have gained attention and discussion. Each of the themes could provide a focus for future discussion, research, and resolution, thus leading to alternative ways to manage salmon in the region.

Introduction

In response to recent, rather dramatic variation in salmon abundance in the Arctic-Yukon-Kuskokwim (AYK) region of Alaska, the AYK Sustainable Salmon Initiative (SSI) was established through congressional funding in 2002. As part of the AYK SSI and in an effort to assess the current state of knowledge about AYK salmon stocks, a symposium was organized and held February 5–9, 2007 in Anchorage, Alaska. Within the context of the symposium presentations, we sought to identify emerging themes within the Arctic-Yukon-Kuskokwim (AYK) salmon management. Of 28 papers presented, some have been published herein (Krueger and Zimmerman 2009, this volume). In addition, our

*Corresponding author: stein.4@osu.edu

thoughts have been informed by the formal discussions that occurred after each session and by informal conversations after-hours. Because we believe that summarizing these presentations and associated discussions was impractical, we provide what we consider quite a personal view on emergent issues and unspoken themes that underpinned the conference. We bring to this summary, not only the experience of hearing the session papers, but also our collective experiences working within the National Research Council during 2003–2005 and the AYK-Sustainable Salmon Initiative since its inception. Each of us have had the opportunity to visit villages, listen to elders, and consider the management and science that was done.

Below, we begin by offering a brief synopsis of our perspective on the status and management of the AYK salmon stocks, based on the symposium. In addition, we identify common threads or concepts, that is, emergent themes that connected the symposium presentations. We also offer our own identification of a few themes we know exist but were unspoken.

Status of Salmon Stocks

The status of salmon stocks across the three regions of the AYK were summarized by several presentations, given mostly by Alaska Department of Fish and Game (ADF&G) managers and researchers. In short, Pacific salmon abundance by species has varied across the AYK region among rivers and through time.

Norton Sound

Within the Norton Sound Region Watershed, Nome chum salmon *Oncorhynchus keta*, identified as a "stock of concern" (and remains so) by the ADF&G in 2000, have increased since 2003 relative to the late 90s,

but chum salmon harvests remain low, owing to poor markets (Menard et al. 2009, this volume; Magdanz et al. 2009, this volume). Whereas pink salmon *O. gorbuscha*, sockeye salmon *O. nerka*, and coho salmon *O. kisutch* harvests have increased, Chinook salmon *O. tshawytscha* is the one species that has shown no signs of recovery.

Yukon River

Based on reconstructed run sizes within the Yukon River watershed, chum salmon have increased dramatically since the late 1990s; subsistence and commercial harvest have mimicked these increases (Bue et al. 2009, this volume). These stocks are no longer designated stocks of concern by ADF&G. Subsistence and commercial harvest have increased for coho salmon since 2003 as compared to the late 1990s. Whereas subsistence harvest of Chinook salmon has remained stable, commercial harvests have declined by 60% (Bradford et al. 2009, this volume; Evenson et al. 2009, this volume). Chinook salmon remain a stock of concern for ADF&G.

Kuskokwim River

Within the Kuskokwim watershed, chum salmon were designated as a "yield concern" by the ADF&G in 2001, but runs during 2002 through 2006 were either above average or well above average (Linderman and Bergstrom 2009, this volume; Gilk et al. 2009, this volume). Escapement indices from 13 index streams for Chinook salmon have revealed that returns of this species have increased during the late 1990s, with run sizes ranging from average to highest on record. Though catches vary by sub-district, subsistence harvest has been down only slightly since the late 1990s while commercial catches have been quite low. Low levels of commercial exploitation for chum, Chinook, and sockeye salmon have occurred owing to poor market conditions.

Fishery Management

Salmon fisheries in the AYK region are managed via stock recruit curves to attain escapement goals and achieve sustainable fisheries (Clark et al. 2009, this volume). Actual management goals vary among rivers and depend on available information for their definition (Hilsinger et al. 2009, this volume). The goal types include: 1) Biological Escapement Goals (BEG's), which require the most information and must be biologically and scientifically defensible, 2) Sustainable Escapement Goals (SEG's), which require less information, 3) Optimal Escapement Goals (OEG's), which take into account allocation and biological factors, and 4) Sustainable Escapement Threshold (SET's), below which a stock cannot maintain itself (Clark et al. 2006). All goals have been defined and determined by ADF&G, with the acknowledgment that, in many systems, precisely how these stock/recruit curves are drawn through the data can be as much art as science. As in-season goals are set, ADF&G uses advice from advisory groups, such as the Kuskokwim Salmon Working Group, the weekly conference calls arranged by the Yukon River Drainage Fisherman's Association, and others. With this background to the salmon stock status and fishery management that occurs within the AYK Region, the authors offer the following emergent themes that connected presentations at the symposium.

Emergent Themes

Different mechanisms affect stock abundance

Abundance of the five salmon species returning to rivers to spawn varied across the three regions through time, suggesting that different mechanisms (biotic, abiotic, or human-induced, freshwater or marine) influence their relative abundance. No one mechanism or variable (e.g., spawning stock size or ocean bycatch) explained the variation reported over the region. During some years, local or regional synchrony in run sizes occurred, but asynchrony occurred during other years (e.g., Anvik River; Burr 2009, this volume). These mechanisms affected salmon runs at different geographic scales—such as the synchronous regional declines across the AYK region during the late 1990s and early 2000s. In this case, likely one common variable such as ocean conditions (e.g., sea temperatures) may have influenced the relative abundance of all salmon stocks. Asynchronous differences in declines and recovery of individual stocks by river also occurred. These differences might be explained for each individual stock by unique combinations of variables affecting the entire life history of the salmon species.

Cooperation between industry and management

As evidenced by the interaction between the walleye pollock *Theragra chalcogramma* fishery and salmon managers, industry and fishery organizations can come together, as they have done in the Bering Sea, to work cooperatively to solve substantive problems associated with salmon bycatch (Haflinger and Gruver 2009, this volume; Gisclair 2009, this volume; Stram and Ianelli 2009, this volume). Salmon bycatch by the pollock fishery in the Bering Sea and the Aleutian Islands has increased dramatically in recent years. In 2006 alone, an estimated 80,000 Chinook salmon and 700,000 chum salmon were harvested as bycatch, of which 25–33% of these fish originated from the AYK region.

Most of the concern expressed by salmon managers and fishers has centered on the fact that salmon bycatch has been increasing since about 2000. Increasing bycatch could result from either 1) more salmon in the Bering Sea or 2) better capture techniques by the pollock fishery resulting in more salmon caught. The consensus seemed to be that more salmon in the Bering Sea has caused the salmon bycatch to increase.

The industry, by recognizing what was happening, responded with a new approach— avoiding salmon hot spots (i.e., moving out of areas in which the salmon catch is high). This new approach remains to be refined, even though initial results seem encouraging. In turn, work is underway to develop salmon excluder devices for pollock trawls that intend to exploit behavioral differences between pollock and salmon. This new technology, coupled with avoiding high-density salmon areas, has served to increase the optimism that salmon bycatch by the pollock fishery will decline in the future.

The challenges of stock-recruit curves

Stock-recruit curves for each individual salmon stock require lots of data! Gathered at a rate of only a single point per stock per year, collecting these data is daunting, demanding both patience and hard work. With advances in technology (e.g., hydroacoustics), more and better data may be collected through time. Adding variables beyond stock size (e.g., sea temperatures) may improve recruitment prediction and reduce the size of the residuals between actual observations and the predicted curve.

Broad-scale environmental instability

The validity of classical stock–recruitment relationships require the assumption of environmental stability. Changing ocean conditions (most definitely) and perhaps variability in freshwater conditions challenge this assumption (Mantua 2009, this volume; Schindler and Rogers 2009, this volume). Some elements of stochasticity as well as other variables (mentioned above) should be included in these relationships with the explicit perspective that harvest policies must be conservative if they are to be based on stock–recruitment relationships.

Biocomplexity and stock-specific management

Stock-recruit curves apply, by definition, to a single stock; hence, if stock management is employed, then stock identification techniques, whether by microsatellites, otolith microchemistry, or other means, need to be substantially expanded. Stock-specific management is required if one desires to preserve the biocomplexity of stocks that support and help stabilize regional run sizes and harvest (Hilborn et al. 2003; Quinn 2009, this volume). Fishing multiple stocks at a single Maximum Sustained Yield (MSY) will take its greatest toll on the least productive stocks, reducing overall genetic and ecological heterogeneity (Larkin 1977).

Management power sharing

ADF&G, while listening to stakeholders, still holds nearly all of the management power in terms of decision-making within the AYK Region. Power sharing would allow the decision-making to be shared. Many of the stakeholders in the region advocate, sometimes vociferously, this approach to management. However, if power sharing is to occur then a sharing of responsibility and accountability for decisions also must occur. In any co-management arrangement, the responsibility for management successes and failures must be shared.

Sport fisheries conflicts

Sport fisheries in the AYK region do not harvest large numbers of salmon and thus do not threaten stock viability. However, sport fisheries can be a source of friction between anglers and rural communities (Albertson 2009, this volume; Burr 2009, this volume). Anglers from outside the region, fish for the same fish important to local community subsistence and commercial fisheries. Sometimes these anglers provide little or no return benefits to the region. Interestingly, some local residents are now successfully providing guide services to sport anglers (Albertson 2009, this volume), and the potential for such benefits are starting to be recognized. Realizing economic benefits to local residents and their associated communities from sport fisheries seem to be in its infancy; however, with increasing benefits will likely come a reduction in conflicts.

Unspoken Themes

Rearden and Gillikin (2009, this volume) provided a perspective on salmon management where optimism and future-looking held the day. From our perspective, and in the spirit of their study, we offer a set of themes that we believe exist and wished would have emerged during the formal presentations and associated discussions. In our view, addressing these themes will further promote success of salmon management in the AYK region.

Management tensions

Several tensions exist within the management arena, but these tensions went unidentified in the presentations and papers. They are listed here to acknowledge their presence and their continuing influence on the process of fishery management in the AYK Region: 1) Upriver versus downriver fishers within the Kuskokwim and Yukon river systems, 2) state versus federal jurisdiction in the area of subsistence issues (Buklis 2002), and 3) data sharing within the scientific, management, and stakeholder communities. The au-

thors' take on these tensions is that they have been, for whatever reason, muted within the symposium, possibly for the sake of keeping peace. In our view, the recognition of these tensions and their full discussion will make for better management. We therefore encourage both managers and stakeholders to expressly acknowledge and directly deal with these tensions wherever and whenever they occur. In particular, we encourage ADF&G and the relevant federal management agencies to recognize the value of sharing information. Each should come together to make available a user-friendly, web-accessible, database of all monitoring data relevant to stock-recruit analyses and the subsequent development of escapement goals in the AYK Region. Easily accessible information contributes to power sharing and accountability for all participants.

Transparency of escapement goal decision-making

Management authorities should make the process of, and theory behind, the setting of escapement goals for stocks easily understandable and transparent to the fishing community, to the scientific community, and to the public. A better understanding by all participants of the process of escapement goal-setting should foster more constructive and positive interactions with the management agencies than in the past.

Identification of shared values

All participants in the fishery and its management should commit to identifying their shared or common values for the salmon resource. In our view, symposium participation demonstrated that such a set of common values exists. The recognition that shared values exist provides a context for all to work together for the conservation of AYK salmon. A serious commitment should be made by all participating parties to respect different roles and the identities of those within the management-stakeholder community. We urge that this spirit of cooperation and information-sharing continue beyond the confines of this symposium.

Conclusion

AYK salmon management is remarkable in its focus on specific stocks, metapopulations (e.g., Canadian-born fall chum salmon), and inclusion of local knowledge (e.g., Yukon River in-season teleconferences). Management is being conducted in a data-poor environment over an amazingly complex array of stocks, species, and drainage systems spread over a geographically vast landscape. Future challenges include improving stock-specific data as well as understanding variables that regionally affect salmon stocks in common. Easy access to information and open decision-making will reduce political-social tensions and promote cooperation among management agencies and stakeholders. All of the themes identified within this paper provide a focus for future discussion, research, and resolution, which may lead to alternative ways to manage salmon and help sustain the region's fisheries.

References

Albertson, L. E. 2009. Perspectives on angling for salmon on the Kuskokwim River: the catch and release sport fishing controversy. Pages 611–619 *in* C. C. Krueger and C. E. Zimmerman, editors. Pacific salmon: ecology and management of western Alaska's populations. American Fisheries Society, Symposium 70, Bethesda, Maryland.

Bradford, M., A. von Finster, and P. A. Milligan. 2009. Freshwater life history, habitat and the production of Chinook salmon from the upper Yukon Basin. Pages 19–38 *in* C. C. Krueger and C. E. Zimmerman, editors. Pacific salmon: ecology and management of western Alaska's populations. American Fisheries Society, Symposium 70, Bethesda, Maryland.

Bue, F. J., B. M. Borba, R. Cannon, and C. C. Krueger. 2009. Yukon River fall chum salmon fisheries: management, harvest, and stock abundance. Pages 703–742 *in* C. C. Krueger and C. E. Zimmerman, editors. Pacific salmon: ecology and management of western Alaska's populations. American Fisheries Society, Symposium 70, Bethesda, Maryland.

Burr, J. M. 2009. Management of recreational fisheries in the Arctic-Yukon-Kuskokwim region of Alaska. Pages 521–539 *in* C. C. Krueger and C. E. Zimmerman, editors. Pacific salmon: ecology and management of western Alaska's populations. American Fisheries Society, Symposium 70, Bethesda, Maryland.

Buklis, L. S. 2002. Subsistence fisheries management on federal public lands in Alaska. Fisheries 27(7):10–18.

Clark, J. H., A. McGregor, R. D. Mecum, P. Krasnowski, and A. M. Carroll. 2006. The commercial salmon fishery in Alaska. Alaska Fishery Research Bulletin 12:1–146.

Clark, R. A., D. R. Bernard, and S. J. Fleischman. 2009. Stock-recruitment analysis for escapement goal development: a case study of Pacific salmon in Alaska. Pages 743–757 *in* C. C. Krueger and C. E. Zimmerman, editors. Pacific salmon: ecology and management of western Alaska's populations. American Fisheries Society, Symposium 70, Bethesda, Maryland.

Evenson, D. F., S. J. Hayes, G. Sandone, and D. J. Bergstrom. 2009. Yukon River Chinook salmon: stock status, harvest, and management. Pages 675–701 *in* C. C. Krueger and C. E. Zimmerman, editors. Pacific salmon: ecology and management of western Alaska's populations. American Fisheries Society, Symposium 70, Bethesda, Maryland.

Gilk, S., T. Hamazaki, D. Molyneaux, J. Pawluk, and W. Templin. 2009. Biological and genetic characteristics of fall chum salmon in the Kuskokwim River, Alaska. Pages 161–179 *in* C. C. Krueger and C. E. Zimmerman, editors. Pacific salmon: ecology and management of western Alaska's populations. American Fisheries Society, Symposium 70, Bethesda, Maryland.

Gisclair, R. 2009. Salmon bycatch management in the Bering Sea walleye pollock fishery: threats and opportunities for western Alaska. Pages 799–816 *in* C. C. Krueger and C. E. Zimmerman, editors. Pacific salmon: ecology and management of western Alaska's populations. American Fisheries Society, Symposium 70, Bethesda, Maryland.

Haflinger, J., and J. Gruver. 2009. Rolling hot spot closure areas in the Bering Sea walleye pollock fishery: estimated reduction of salmon bycatch during the 2006 season. Pages 817–826 *in* C. C. Krueger and C. E. Zimmerman, editors. Pacific salmon:

ecology and management of western Alaska's populations. American Fisheries Society, Symposium 70, Bethesda, Maryland.

Hilborn, R., T. P. Quinn, D. E. Schindler, and D. E. Rogers. 2003. Biocomplexity and fisheries sustainability. Proceedings of the National Academy of Science, USA 100:6564–6568.

Hilsinger, J. R., E. Volk, G. Sandone, and R. Cannon. 2009. Salmon management in the Arctic-Yukon-Kuskokwim Region of Alaska: past, present, and future. Pages 495–519 *in* C. C. Krueger and C. E. Zimmerman, editors. Pacific salmon: ecology and management of western Alaska's populations. American Fisheries Society, Symposium 70, Bethesda, Maryland.

Krueger, C. C. and C. E. Zimmerman, editors. 2009. Pacific salmon: ecology and management of western Alaska's populations. American Fisheries Society, Symposium 70, Bethesda, Maryland.

Larkin, P. A. 1977. An epitaph for the concept of maximum sustained yield. Transactions of the American Fisheries Society 106:1–11.

Linderman, J., and D. J. Bergstrom. 2009. Kuskokwim management area: salmon escapement, harvest, and management. Pages 541–599 *in* C. C. Krueger and C. E. Zimmerman, editors. Pacific salmon: ecology and management of western Alaska's populations. American Fisheries Society, Symposium 70, Bethesda, Maryland.

Magdanz, J. S., E. Trigg, A. Ahmasuk, E. Trigg, P. Nanouk, D. Koster, and K. Kamletz. 2009. Patterns and trends in subsistence salmon harvests: Norton Sound–Port Clarence area, Alaska 1994–2003. Pages 395–431 *in* C. C. Krueger and C. E. Zimmerman, editors. Pacific salmon: ecology and management of western Alaska's populations. American Fisheries Society, Symposium 70, Bethesda, Maryland.

Mantua, N. J. 2009. Patterns of change in climate and Pacific salmon production. Pages 1143–1157 *in* C. C. Krueger and C. E. Zimmerman, editors. Pacific salmon: ecology and management of western Alaska's populations. American Fisheries Society, Symposium 70, Bethesda, Maryland.

Menard, J., C. C. Krueger, and J. Hilsinger. 2009. Norton Sound salmon fisheries: history, stock abundance, and management. Pages 621–673 *in* C. C. Krueger and C. E. Zimmerman, editors. Pacific salmon: ecology and management of western Alaska's populations. American Fisheries Society, Symposium 70, Bethesda, Maryland.

Rearden, M., and D. Gillikin. 2009. A perspective on ecosystem-based fishery management of the Kuskokwim River: a 2015 vision of the future. Pages 601–609 *in* C. C. Krueger and C. E. Zimmerman, editors. Pacific salmon: ecology and management of western Alaska's populations. American Fisheries Society, Symposium 70, Bethesda, Maryland.

Schindler, D. E., and L. A. Rogers. 2009. Responses of Pacific salmon populations to climate variation in freshwater ecosystems. Pages 1127–1142 *in* C. C. Krueger and C. E. Zimmerman, editors. Pacific salmon: ecology and management of western Alaska's populations. American Fisheries Society, Symposium 70, Bethesda, Maryland.

Stram, D., and J. N. Ianelli. 2009. Eastern Bering Sea pollock trawl fisheries: variation in salmon bycatch over time and space. Pages 827–850 *in* C. C. Krueger and C. E. Zimmerman, editors. Pacific salmon: ecology and management of western Alaska's populations. American Fisheries Society, Symposium 70, Bethesda, Maryland.

Section VI

Peer Reviewer Acknowledgments

Peer Reviewer Acknowledgments

The editors thank the many peer reviewers of this volume. Their careful reviews of manuscripts yielded many helpful suggestions that improved the volume immensely. Thanks for the time and effort taken out of your busy schedules.

Jean Adams
Jeff Adams
Milo Adkison
Robert Al-Chokhachy
David Anderson
Chris Arp
Elizabeth Benolkin
Craig Blackie
Nicholas Bond
Robert Bosworth
Mike Bradford
Taylor Brelsford
Caroline Brown
Mason Bryant
Phaedra Budy
Brian Bue
Carl Burger
Sean Burril
Kelly Burnett
Lance Campbell
Richard Cannon
Stephanie Carlson
Theodore Castro-Santos
Mike Cofffing
Steve Coghlan
Penny Crane
Keith Criddle
Beatrice Crona
Fiona Cubitt
Elisabeth Duffy
Walt Duffy
Jason Dunham
Joseph Ebersole
Mark Ebener
Gregg Erickson
Lowell Fair
James Finn
Stephen Fried

Mark Fritsch
Masa-aki Fukuwaka
Marc Gaden
Harold Geiger
Susan Georgette
Anthony Gharrett
Sara Gilk
Becca Gisclair
Christopher Goddard
Stewart Grant
Correigh Greene
Richard Gustafson
Susan Hanna
Kyle Hartman
Steve Hewett
Nicola Hillgruber
Anne Hollowed
Lance Howe
Tom Iverson
Orlay Johnson
Gary Kofinas
Jeff Koppelman
Charles Lean
Jim Magdanz
Nate Mantua
Bernie May
Megan McPhee
Chanda Meek
Julie Meka
Hal Michael
Scott Miehls
Steve Miller
Jessica Miller
Jeff Miner
Douglas Molyneaux
Kelly Moore
Jamal Moss
Katherine Myers

Barbara Neis
Matt Nemeth
Tammy Newcomb
Kurt Newman
Jeffrey Olsen
James Overland
Holly Patrick
George Pess
David Policansky
Jonathon Pyatskowit
Pete Rand
Greg Ruggerone
Daniel Schindler
Robin Schrock
Marianne See
Brian Shuter
Charles Simenstad
William Smoker
Chris Stark
Todd Steeves
Roy Stein
Diana Stram
Joan Trial
Marc Trudel
Tevis Underwood
Eric Volk
Vanessa von Biela
Robert Walker
Mathew Walsh
Jia Wang
Robin Waples
Thomas Weingartner
Amy Welsh
John Wenburg
Alex Wertheimer
Fred Whoriskey
Richard Wilmot

Index

Bolded words are main subjects
Italicized *f* and *t* refer to figures and tables

G

N